The Best of SO-BAD-387

LOS ANGELES
&
SOUTHERN CALIFORNIA

4th Edition

Editor-in-Chief
André Gayot

Editor
Catherine Jordan

Contributing Editors
Colleen Dunn Bates (L.A. Restaurants Editor), Jeff Book,
Mark Ehrman, Liz Gardner, Anne Gregor, Allan Halcrow,
Jeffrey Hirsch, Max Jacobson, Norman Kolpas, Larry Lipson,
Kitty Morgan, David Nelson, Angela Rinaldi, Dennis Schaefer,
David Shaw, Merrill Shindler, Debbie Sroloff, Sherrie Strausfogel,
Kim Svetich, William Tomicki, Linda Zimmerman

Publisher
Alain Gayot

GaultMillau

Paris ■ Los Angeles ■ New York ■ London ■ Munich ■ San Francisco ■ Vienna

ANDRÉ GAYOT PUBLICATIONS

Bring You

The Best of Chicago	The Best of New England
The Best of Florida	The Best of New Orleans
The Best of France	The Best of New York
The Best of Germany	The Best of Paris
The Best of Hawaii	The Best of San Franciso
The Best of Hong Kong	The Best of Thailand
The Best of Italy	The Best of Toronto
The Best of London	The Best of Washington, D.C.
The Best of Los Angeles	The Best Wines of America

The Food Paper - Los Angeles
The Food Paper - San Francisco
Tastes Newsletter

Copyright © 1984, 1988, 1990, 1993 by Gault Millau, Inc.

Published by Gault Millau, Inc.
5900 Wilshire Blvd., 29th Floor
Los Angeles, CA 90036

Please address all advertising queries to:
Precision Marketing International
9016 Wilshire Blvd., #366
Beverly Hills, CA 90211

Please address all comments regarding
The Best of Los Angeles to:
Gault Millau, Inc.
P.O. Box 361144
Los Angeles, CA 90036

Library of Congress Cataloging-in-Publication Data
The Best of Los Angeles & Southern California / editor-in-chief, André
Gayot; editor, Catherine Jordan; contributing editors, Colleen Dunn
Bates . . . [et al.]. — 4th ed.
    p.   cm.
Rev. ed. of: The Best of Los Angeles. Rev. ed. © 1990.
Includes indexes.
ISBN 1-881066-01-0 : $18.00
1. Los Angeles (Calif.) — Guidebooks. I. Gayot, André.
II. Jordan, Catherine. III. Gault Millau (Firm) IV. Best of Los Angeles.
V. Title: Best of Los Angeles and Southern California.
F869.L83B47   1993
917.94'940453—dc20
                                                            92–40137
                                                               CIP

Printed in the United States of America

CONTENTS

A Map of Southern California

The map below is an easy-to-use guide to Southern California's varied regions. Each numbered area corresponds to a chapter in this book, in the order that the chapters appear. All the outlying areas are easily reachable by car for a day or weekend trip: the farthest major city from L.A. is San Diego, at 132 miles (*see* below for more distances).

See MAPS section in the back of the book for more detailed maps.

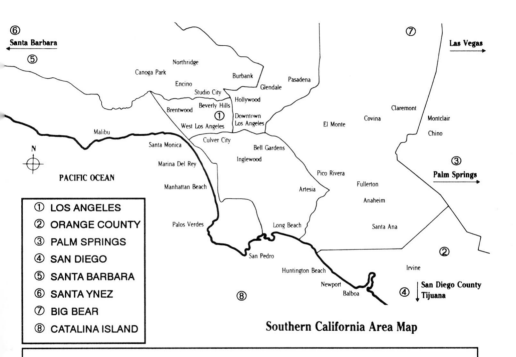

① LOS ANGELES
② ORANGE COUNTY
③ PALM SPRINGS
④ SAN DIEGO
⑤ SANTA BARBARA
⑥ SANTA YNEZ
⑦ BIG BEAR
⑧ CATALINA ISLAND

Southern California Area Map

DISTANCES (in miles)

Within L.A.:

LAX to Downtown, 14
LAX to Santa Monica, 10
LAX to Beverly Hills, 13
Beverly Hills (B.H.) to Santa Monica, 12
B.H. to Malibu, 27
B.H. to Long Beach, 24
B.H. to S.F. Valley (Sherman Oaks), 16
B.H. to S.G. Valley (Pasadena), 17

From L.A. to*:

Orange County (Newport), 43
Palm Springs, 109
San Diego, 132
Santa Barbara, 95
Santa Ynez, 142
Big Bear, 105
Catalina, 26 (from Long Beach Harbor)

* *Distances calculated from civic center to civic center.*

1

The Continuing L.A. Drama

I t was not without warning that things began to change. Nevertheless, there was a collective feeling of disbelief—combined with great sadness and shock—when, one morning in the spring of 1992, furor and clamor filled the streets of Los Angeles. The media worldwide promptly concluded that the California dream had come to an end. And since the May days of civil unrest, all manner of magazine and newspaper has scrutinized the ailing patient, noting with concern that, among other worrying concerns, the once-golden state's population has soared 25 percent in just the last decade. The frighteningly apocalyptic results: overflowing freeways, shrinking public services, skyrocketing housing costs and a Babel-like linguistic cacophony which now can be heard even in the city's elementary schools, where children from fifty countries speak as many as thirty different languages. It's no wonder that businesses and industries in ever greater numbers seem to be fleeing the congestion of Los Angeles in search of greener, more peaceful, pastures.

True enough. But we hardly have to perpetuate the cliché of carefree Southern California with its procession of impossibly healthy blonde surfers, bikini-clad beauties and stylish couples in luxury convertibles in order to see that there remains much here to lend credence to the old myth. Smog still hovers over the basin, but pollution has been reduced by fully 50 percent in the last ten years and today the entire world is studying the California model for environmental protection. Big industry may be closing up shop and moving away but thousands of small businesses are flourishing. Researchers continue to break new ground in laboratories all over L.A.; the boom in biotechnology was born here and will grow with the region into the next century.

California's patchwork ethnic populace, with its multiplicity of tongues, provides a unique opportunity by widely and welcomingly opening the state to many of the world's most important emerging cultures. It may take still more heated change to forge the complete fusion of this remarkable melting pot society but, after all, cosmopolitan cities everywhere in the world are struggling for a renewed sense of identity in the post-nuclear era.

Already, at any rate, the coalition of peoples and cultures that makes up contemporary Los Angeles works well in the kitchen. Dining here has become a more and more exciting adventure every passing year as, building on the long-rooted heritage of Italian, Mexican, and indigenous American cuisines, a new Franco-California alliance of ingredients, recipes and techniques was formed over twenty years ago. This joint venture, of course, was only a prelude to the "nouvelle" episode of the '80s. Tastes continued to grow more sophisticated as chefs from the Pacific Rim countries added their invaluable knowledge to the mix: Franco-Japanese-California style became hip. And the integration of international cuisines is still moving forward here faster than almost anywhere else in the world. Today you can dine in a few LA.. places that offer surprisingly well-balanced Italo-Sino-Franco-Japanese-California specialties.

If we can achieve such satisfying rapprochement in the kitchen, why shouldn't we hold out hope for finding solutions to our problems elsewhere? Since our last edition, Southern California has changed in many profound ways. And it's certain to continue changing. Though the California dream is still very much alive. It no longer can be viewed only in black and white. Today it's a brilliantly diverse, Technicolor epic with a multicultural cast of millions. We hope this book reflects the enthralling drama which is currently playing in neighborhoods everywhere in Los Angeles.

André Gayot

ABOUT THE RESTAURANTS

Much News is Good News

As we sink into the '90s, Los Angeles is reeling from the devastating double whammy of the recession and the riots. The restaurant business has been particularly hard hit: restaurants, from chic hot spots such as Citrus and Valentino to countless little neighborhood cafés, have found themselves with a distressing number of empty tables in the last couple of years. In 1991, we saw the passing of L'Ermitage, arguably L.A.'s most important restaurant of the modern age. Michael's has filed for Chapter 11, Seventh Street Bistro and Trumps have closed their doors, and La Toque still struggles valiantly to survive. (A lucky few have been spared; ordinary proles still can't get an 8 p.m. Spago reservation, and Friday night still finds several dozen people milling around outside El Coyote, waiting for a table.)

There are myriad reasons for the drop in restaurant business. The recession has tightened many purse strings. Even before the riots, some prosperous people, even those unaffected by the recession, have been troubled at the thought of spending $28 for a veal chop when so many are going hungry. The baby boomers, those notoriously self-indulgent folk who made goat-cheese pizza and tiramisu household words in the '80s, are more likely to stay home and eat spaghetti with the kids than to drop $200 for a dinner out.

But let's not start a post-mortem for L.A.'s dynamic restaurant scene yet. For plenty of us are still going out to eat, and plenty of us still appreciate cooking as an art and the restaurant as an invaluable community center, a place for renewing social and familial ties and establishing new ones, as well as a place to quiet rumbling stomachs. When we break bread together (speaking biblically now), we enjoy a treasured bit of time away from responsibilities and the rat race, a chance to let good food and wine soothe our savage souls.

In fact, though we hate to see our restaurant friends suffering through hard times, we must admit that the recession is certainly good news for the average L.A. diner—for these restaurants are having to work harder to win your patronage. There's a little less attitude being displayed at the scene spots, a little more attention being paid to seating people at the time they've actually reserved, a little more care being displayed in such telling details as the bread basket and the wine-by-the-glass selection. There's less deification of the chef, which means the average 23-year-old chef no longer thinks he or she is the best thing since sliced foie gras. So these chefs are more likely to cook you a decent meal than spend all their time hustling up more lucrative jobs. And there's been a strong move toward controlling—sometimes even lowering—prices.

Though the recession and the neo-'50s aspects of recent times have led to an increase in comforting, plain-food joints (typified by the Daily Grills), creative cooking has hardly vanished from this free-wheeling city. L.A. is still on the cutting edge, and just as people are likely to wear it here first and drive it here first, they're likely to eat it here first. In Pasadena, Yujean Kang's is re-inventing Chinese food in a way that would surprise the best-fed citizen of the People's Republic. On La Cienega, Nobu Matsuhisa is cooking Japanese-influenced seafood dishes that are breathtaking in both their flavors and their inventiveness. At City, Mary Sue Milliken and Susan Feniger boldly throw together the cuisines of India, Thailand, Italy and Korea into an exciting melting pot. At Patina, Joachim Splichal continues to work miracles with potatoes and seafood. At Citrus, Michel Richard manages to take a chicken salad or a piece of grilled sea bass into a celestial realm.

L.A. has also snatched up the baton first held by Chez Panisse and its Bay Area peers in the quest for first-rate produce. We're thrilled to see a marked increase in the number of restaurants that offer as much organically grown produce as possible, along with fresh herbs, range-fed, hormone-free chicken, mother-raised veal, first-

3

press olive oils and vine-ripened tomatoes and fruits. (Chefs are no doubt realizing that they have much less work to do in the kitchen if they start out with great ingredients.) And the dramatic increase in meat-free dishes coming from the city's finest kitchens is proof that restaurants now recognize that vegetarians have moved beyond bean sprouts—and that many carnivores are giving up the red stuff several nights a week.

Not only is Los Angeles one of the world's more inventive restaurant cities, it's simply one of the very best. And we don't mean "best" exclusively in the fancy-French sense, though we've had recent meals at Patina, Citrus, L'Orangerie, Valentino and Santa Barbara's Citronelle that rivaled almost any meal we've had in France or Italy (and some individual dishes at Campanile, Chinois, La Toque, Fennel and Remi ranked up there, too). Of course, the marked difference between the L.A. versus the European experiences was that in L.A., restaurants tend to be much more relaxed. This has its down side, evidenced primarily by inept, disinterested service—but the up side is that atmospheres tend to be less stuffy and pretentious, dress is more casual, and (compared to most of Europe) prices are lower.

Los Angeles has what few other great cities have: a staggeringly polyglot population. We have the largest number of people of Mexican descent outside Mexico. The largest Filipino population outside the Philippines. More Salvadorans than in any city in the world except San Salvador. More Koreans than in any city in the world except Seoul. The largest concentration of Asian-Pacific people in the United States. The second-largest Jewish population in the world. Consequently, L.A. is a veritable Garden of Eden for the food lover, ripe with nearly every fruit the world has to offer. No matter how well one knows the city and its environs, there's always a surprise to be found—perhaps an elegant Burmese restaurant in Whittier, a great rib joint in Altadena, a sublime sushi bar in Burbank, a chic Vietnamese restaurant on La Brea, a dazzling Chinese seafood house in San Gabriel, a tasty Salvadoran café in Hollywood or a colorful Peruvian restaurant in Van Nuys. In these restaurants you're likely to find fruits and vegetables you've never tasted before, fish you've never heard of, dishes made from animal parts you'd never have dreamed of eating—and so often these flavors are terrific.

Clearly, a good many of our restaurants are well worth your hard-earned dollars (we've taken pains in the pages that follow to steer you away

from those that aren't). Whether you're a visitor or a resident, get out there and eat. Just do it carefully and thoughtfully. Choose a restaurant for its food, service and setting, not its celebrities; choose restaurants that respect the environment and offer fresh, healthy (as opposed to health) foods; choose restaurants that offer a fair value, whether it serves foie gras or meatloaf; and balance your restaurant spending with support of your community's food banks, shelters and soup kitchens. When you find a great restaurant whose cooking, atmosphere and price range suit you, patronize it regularly instead of continually dashing off to the latest spot that Madonna was reputed to visit. Regular patronage is the best way to get a good table, good service and extra effort from the chef, and supporting the restaurants you like is one way to help ensure that it'll still be there the next time you call for a reservation. And be as adventurous as the city and its chefs—for if it's true that we are what we eat, we might as well forgot being safe, reliable or ordinary, and opt for being exciting, progressive and exotic.

Using Our Rating System

What decides the rating of a restaurant? What is on the plate is by far the most important factor. The **quality of produce** is among the most telling signs of a restaurant's culinary status. It requires a great deal of commitment and money to stock the finest grades and cuts of meat and the finest quality of fish. There is tuna, for example, and there's *tuna*. Ask any sushi chef. One extra-virgin olive oil is not the same, by far, as the next. Ditto for chocolates, pastas, spices and one thousand other ingredients. Quality restaurants also attune themselves to seasonal produce, whether it be local berries or truffles from Italy.

Freshness is all-important, too, and a telling indication of quality. This means not only using fresh rather than frozen fish, for example, but also preparing everything from scratch at the last possible moment, from appetizers through desserts.

What else do we look for? **Details** are telling: if sauces are homogeneous, you know that the kitchen is taking shortcuts. The bread on the table is always a tip-off; similarly, the house wine can speak volumes about the culinary attitude and level of an establishment. Wine is food, and wine lists and offerings can be revelatory. A list doesn't have to be long or expensive to show a commitment to quality.

Finally, among the very finest restaurants, **creativity** and **influence** can be determining factors. These qualities, however, are relatively unimportant for simply good restaurants, where the quality and consistency of what appears on the plates is the central factor. A restaurant that serves grilled chicken well is to be admired more than a restaurant that attempts some failed marriage of chicken and exotic produce, or some complicated chicken preparation that requires a larger and more talented kitchen brigade than is on hand. Don't be taken in by attempted fireworks that are really feeble sideshows.

Our rating system works as follows: restaurants are ranked in the same manner that French students are graded, on a scale of one to twenty. The rankings reflect *only* our opinion of the food; the decor, service, wine list and atmosphere are commented upon within each review. Restaurants that are ranked 13/20 and above are distinguished with toques (chef's hats) according to the table below. For a complete index of every restaurant in the book by rating, please see the "Toque Tally" on the following pages.

Exceptional 🎩 4 toques, 19/20 and 19.5/20

Excellent 🎩 3 toques, 17/20 and 18/20

Very good 🎩 2 toques, 15/20 and 16/20

Good 🎩 1 toque, 13/20 and 14/20

Keep in mind that we are comparing L.A.'s restaurants to the very best in the world. Also, these ranks are *relative*. A 13/20 (one toque) may not be a superlative ranking for a highly reputed (and very expensive) restaurant, but it is quite complimentary for a small place without much culinary pretension.

Unless otherwise noted, the prices given are for a complete dinner for one, including an appetizer, main course and dessert per person, along with tax and tip. This estimate *does not* include wine or other drinks, which are nearly impossible to guess. Those who like to eat lightly, sharing appetizers and desserts, will spend less. Though the recession has helped reign in tabs, some prices continue to creep up, so forgive us if a restaurant has become more expensive by the time you visit it. Credit cards are abbreviated as follows: **AE**: American Express and/or Optima, **D**: Discover Card, **DC**: Diners Club and/or Carte Blanche, **MC**: MasterCard, **V**: VISA.

Advice & Comments:

- *On dressing*: L.A. doesn't usually dress up to go out, but it does dress in one or another version of its costume-party style. In a handful of the more conservative places, men still wear ties, and jackets are almost de rigueur. But in the trendy spots, anything goes—fur coats to leather pants, cowboy boots to Reebok's. One wouldn't want to overdress for Spago or Cicada or underdress for L'Orangerie or Rex.

- *On chefs*: When you make reservations in a place with a famous chef, check to be sure he or she will be there, not traveling across the country demonstrating Californian cuisine. Also, all chefs have good days and bad, so don't be too put off if your experience is less stellar than was ours; with luck it will be better.

- *On valets*: Most restaurants in this car-dominated culture have parking valets. Be prepared to tip the valet $2 to $5—more if you want your Ferrari handled with TLC.

PLEASE EXCUSE US . . . (AND THE CHEFS)

In many L.A. restaurants, chefs stay barely long enough to collect their first paycheck. This can—and frequently does—wreak havoc on a restaurant, which can go from good to bad overnight when the chef leaves. Menus are also subject to the winds of change, and the dishes we've described may no longer be available when you visit. We ask your forgiveness if a restaurant is somewhat different when you visit it. We've done everything we can to keep up with the always-changing L.A. dining scene. Smaller areas such as Santa Barbara are far more stable, but if change is slower to take place, it's still inevitable.

■ *On smoking (or not)*: Certain L.A. communities, particularly Beverly Hills, have been slugging it out over whether or not to ban smoking in restaurants. At this writing, smoking is still allowed, though most restaurants have distinct no-smoking areas. Be sure to specify the appropriate area when you reserve a table.

■ *On outdoor dining*: There are very few outdoor cafés in this city, which would be so conducive to the pleasures of basking in the sun and watching the city roll by. The few that do have a patio, a terrace or a sidewalk tables are indexed in the back of the book, under the heading "Outdoor Dining."

■ *On seafood*: Oddly, it's hard to find superbly fresh Pacific seafood (although the salmon is good) or seafood from any part of the world, except in the city's best sushi restaurants. Thankfully, there are some newcomers who are striving to secure the best seafood, a trend we hope to see furthered.

■ *On tipping*: Only a small handful of restaurants handle tipping European-style, by adding 15 percent to your bill. Aside from those few, a gratuity is automatically added only for large groups (which tend to undertip). Otherwise, keep in mind that 15 percent of your pretax bill (including drinks) is customary.

Toque Tally

18/20

Citrus
Patina

17/20

Chinois on Main
Citronelle at Santa Barbara
  Inn (*S.B.*)
L'Orangerie
Valentino

16/20

Antoine at Le Meridien
  (*O.C.*)
Azzura Point at Loews
  Coronado Bay (*S.D.*)
Bikini
Campanile
Champagne Bis
La Chaumiere
Downey's (*S.B.*)
Marius at Le Meridien (*S.D.*)
Mille Fleurs (*S.D.*)
Pascal (*O.C.*)
Rex Il Ristorante

Ritz-Carlton Dining Room,
  Laguna Niguel (*O.C.*)
Sai Sai at Biltmore Hotel
La Toque
The Wine Cask (*S.B.*)
Winesellar & Brasserie (*S.D.*)
Yujean Kang's Gourmet
  Chinese Cuisine

15/20

City Restaurant
Four Oaks
George's at the Cove (*S.D.*)
Georgian Room at
  Ritz-Carlton/Huntington
Granita
Hotel Bel-Air Dining Room
Joss
Locanda Veneta
The Mandarin
Matsuhisa
Michael's
Opus
Pavilion at Four Seasons
  Hotel (*O.C.*)
Pazzia
Primi
Regent Beverly Wilshire
  Dining Room
Robata
Röckenwagner
Shiro
Spago

14/20

Allegro
Angeli Mare
The Belgian Lion (*S.D.*)
La Brasserie at Bel Age Hotel
Ca'Brea
C'est Fan Fan
Le Chardonnay
Chaya Brasserie
Cindy Black's (*S.D.*)
David Slay's La Veranda
Diaghilev at Bel Age Hotel
Le Dôme
Drago
Empress Pavilion
Fennel
Fino
Fleur de Vin
Ginza Sushi-Ko
Golden Truffle (*O.C.*)
Grant Grill at U.S. Grant
  Hotel (*S.D.*)
Gustaf Anders (*O.C.*)
Hal's Bar & Grill
Harold & Belle's
Hy's
Jitlada
Joe's
Katsu
Kitayama (*O.C.*)
Koutoubia
Lake Spring Cuisine
Lunaria

La Marina at Four Seasons
  Biltmore Hotel (*S.B.*)
Pacifica del Mar (*S.D.*)
Parkway Grill
Picnic
Pinot Bistro
Remi
Ritz-Carlton Dining Room,
  Marina del Rey
Ritz-Carlton Dining Room,
  Rancho Mirage (*P.S.*)
Ruth's Chris Steak House
Seafood City
La Serenata de Garibaldi
The Towers at Surf & Sand
  Hotel (*O.C.*)
Trastevere (*S.D.*)
Tryst
Tulipe
Vim

13/20

Akbar
Angeli Caffè
Antonio Orlando
Astrid's Bistro (*S.B.*)
Aunt Kizzy's Back Porch
Authentic Café
Bamboo Inn
Barsac Brasserie
Bellablue
Belvedere at Peninsula Hotel
Bernadette's (*S.B.*)
Bice
Bistango (*O.C.*)
Bistro 45
The Bistro
The Bistro Garden, Beverly
  Hills
The Bistro Garden,
  Coldwater Canyon
Bombay Café
Border Grill Santa Monica
Brigitte's (*S.B.*)
Broadway Deli
Brother's Sushi
Café Katsu
California Cuisine (*S.D.*)
Carrots
Castel Bistro
Celestino
Cha Cha Cha
Chaya Venice

Chef Tien
Chez Hélène
Chez Mélange
Chianti Cucina
Chianti Ristorante
China Sea
Cuistot (*P.S.*)
Depot
Dobson's (*S.D.*)
Dolly Cunard's (*P.S.*)
Dragon Regency
East India Grill
El Emperador Maya
Five Feet (*O.C.*)
Five Feet Too (*O.C.*)
Fragrant Vegetable
Gardens at Four Seasons
  Hotel
Gaylord
Il Giardino
Gilliland's
Giorgio
Golden Truffle (*O.C.*)
Harbor Village
Harry's Bar and American
  Grill
Hugo's
Hu's Szechwan Restaurant
Indigo
The Ivy
J'Adore
Jitlada (*S.F. Valley*)
JW's at Anaheim Marriott
  (*O.C.*)
Katsu 3rd
La Loggia
Louie's (*S.B.*)
Louis XIV
Madeo
Ma Maison at Hotel Sofitel
Mandalay
Marouch
Mary's Lamb
Michael's Waterside
  Inn/Waterside Bistro (*S.B.*)
Morton's
Natraj Cuisine of India
  (*O.C.*)
Oaks on the Plaza at
  Doubletree Pasadena Hotel
Ocean Avenue Seafood
Ocean Seafood
Off Vine
The Original Sonora Café
Osteria Nonni
Otani—A Garden Restaurant
  (*P.S.*)

Oyster's (*S.B.*)
The Palace Café (*S.B.*)
The Palm
Pane e Vino (*L.A.*)
La Parrilla
Posto
Prego (*L.A. & O.C.*)
Rainwater's (*S.D.*)
Rancho Valencia Resort
  Dining Room (*S.D.*)
Riva at Loews Santa Monica
  Beach Hotel
R23
Ruth's Chris Steak House
  (*P.S.*)
Saddle Peak Lodge
Sante (*S.D.*)
Shenandoah Café
Sirocco at Stouffer
  Esmerelda Resort (*P.S.*)
Sofi Estiatorion
Splashes at Surf & Sand
  Hotel (*O.C.*)
A Thousand Cranes at New
  Otani Hotel
Tommy Tang's
Top of the Cove (*S.D.*)
Toscana
Trattoria Angeli
Trattoria Farfalla
Vines (*B.B.*)
Water Grill
Yang Chow

12/20

Al Amir
Antonello (*O.C.*)
Atlas Bar & Grill
Araz
Armstrong's Fish Market &
  Seafood Restaurant (*C.I.*)
Babette's
Banzai Cantina (*S.D.*)
Barnabey's
Bayou Bar & Grill (*S.D.*)
Beau Rivage
Bistro 201 (*O.C.*)
El Bizcocho at Rancho
  Bernardo Inn (*S.D.*)
Brophy Bros. Clam Bar &
  Restaurant (*S.B.*)
Café Bravo (*S.D.*)
Café Delfini
Café Pierre
Café Vallarta (*S.B.*)

Camille's
Capri
Carroll O'Connor's Place
Cha Cha Cha
Chalet de France
Chan Dara
Chao Praya (*S.F. Valley*)
Chartreuse
Chasen's
El Chavo
La Chêne
Chez Jay
El Cholo
Cicada
Il Cielo
The Clay Pit
Coley's Place
Cold Spring Tavern (*S.B.*)
Crocodile Cantina
I Cugini
Cynthia's
Daily Grill (*all 3 branches in L.A. & O.C.*)
Dan Tana's
Da Pasquale
Dominick's
Duplex
Emilio's
El Encanto Dining Room (*S.B.*)
Engine Co. No. 28
Fama
Farfalla La Brea
Fio's (*S.D.*)
Five Crowns (*O.C.*)
La Fonda Roberto's (*S.D.*)
Il Fornaio (*O.C. &S.D.*)
Il Forno
Gardel's
Gardens of Taxco
George Petrelli's Steak House
George & Sigi's Knusperhäuschen (*B.B.*)
The Grill on the Alley
Habash Café
Harvest Inn
The Hitching Post (*S.Y.*)
Hollywood Canteen
Hortobagy
Houston's
Hungarian Budapest
Hymie's Fish Market
Iroha Sushi
The Ivy at the Shore
Jake's Grill
JB's Little Bali

Jimmy's
Kachina (*O.C.*)
Kachina Grill (*L.A.*)
Kaktus
Lawry's The Prime Rib
La Xiang
Lincoln Bay Cafe
Locanda del Lago
Ma Bé
Mandarette
Maple Drive
Marcello Ristorante
Mario's Peruvian Seafood
Matty's on Melrose
Mexica
Mezzaluna (*L.A. & O.C.*)
Mi Piace
Mi Ranchito
Misto
Mistral Brasserie
Mon Kee
Montana's (*S.D.*)
Montecito Café (*S.B.*)
Muse
Neptune's Net
North Beach Bar & Grill
Olí Olá
L'Opera
Orleans
Pane Caldo Bistrot
Pane e Vino (*S.B.*)
Paoli's Pizzeria & Pasta House (*P.S.*)
Papadakis Taverna
Papagallo's (*S.B.*)
Pappagallo
Paradise Café (*S.B.*)
La Pergola
Piatti (*S.B.*)
Pine Avenue Fish House
La Plancha
Plum Tree Inn
Rangoon Racquet Club
Rebecca's
Restaurante del Bol Corona (*S.D.*)
Rincon Chileno
Ritz (*O.C.*)
Rondo
Roxxi
Sabor!
Sanamluang Café
Scott's Seafood Grill and Bar (*O.C.*)
Sfuzzi (*S.D.*)
Shahrzad
Shame on the Moon (*P.S.*)

Shibucho
Shihoya
Siamese Garden
Siamese Princess
Sushi Nozawa
Talesai
Tête-à-Tête (*O.C.*)
Thee White House (*O.C.*)
Trilussa
Trinity
Tropical Garden
Tuttobene
Tutto Mare (*O.C.*)
Valley Seafood Garden
La Vie en Rose (*O.C.*)
Wallaby Darned
Warszawa
West Beach Café
Val's
Zuni Grill (*O.C.*)

11/20

Adriano's
Aldo's (*S.B.*)
Amelia's (*O.C.*)
Los Arrieros
Babalu
The Blue Whale Lakeside (*B.B.*)
Café La Bohème
Café Maurice
Café Piemonte (*O.C.*)
Café Prego (*C.I.*)
Café del Rey
Carmelo's (*O.C.*)
Las Casuelas (*P.S.*)
Catavinos
Chad's (*S.B.*)
Chao Praya (*L.A.*)
Chin Chin
Chopstix
The Chronicle
Columbia Bar & Grill
DC3
Delacey's Club 41
La Famiglia

> *Gault Millau's ratings are based solely on the restaurants' cuisine. We do not take into account the atmosphere, decor, service and so on; these are commented upon in the reviews.*

8

11/20 *(cont.)*

La Finestra
The Fish Market (*S.D.*)
La Frite Café
Genghis Cohen
Gourmet 88
The Grand House
Hola Madrid
Horikawa
The Iron Squirrel (*B.B.*)
John Dominis (*O.C.*)
Kabob House Restaurant
  (*O.C.*)
Kate Mantilini
Kiyosaku (*P.S.*)
Knoll's Black Forest Inn
L.A. Farm
Legends
Lew Mitchell's Orient
  Express
Marix Tex Mex
Marix Tex Mex Norte
Maryland Crab House
Matteo's
Maurice's Snack 'n' Chat
McCormick & Schmick's
  (*O.C.*)
Il Mito
Moonlight Tango Café
Moustache Café
The Nest (*P.S.*)
Nicky Blair's
Noodles
Pacific Dining Car (*both L.A.
  branches*)
Piazza Rodeo
The Ranch House (*S.B.*)
Red Lion Tavern
Ristorante Mamma Gina
  (*P.S.*)
Ristorante Villa Portofino
  (*C.I.*)
Rive Gauche Café
Rosalind's
17th Street Café
72 Market Street
Siam Corner Café
Siam Mania
Simon & Seafort's
Stepps on the Court
Teru Sushi
Thai House
Tivoli Cafe
Topanga Fresh Fish Market
Trader Vic's
Tra Fiori

Tusk
Typhoon
Vivo Trattoria
The Whale & Ale
Yankee Tavern (*O.C.*)
Zipangu

10/20

The Athenian (*O.C.*)
Ballard Store & Wine Bar
  (*S.Υ.*)
Barbacoa (*O.C.*)
Borrelli's
Brentwood Bar & Grill
Las Brisas (*O.C.*)
Café Athens
Café Montana
Café Zoolu (*O.C.*)
Caioti
Las Casuelas Nuevas (*P.S.*)
El Circo Barcelona (*S.D.*)
Dar Maghreb (*P.S.*)
Delmonico's
La Dolce Vita
Dynasty Room at Westwood
  Marquis Hotel
Epicentre
Fab's Italian Kitchen
The Great Greek
Hamlet Gardens
El Mariachi (*O.C.*)
Far Niente
Lula
Marrakesh (*O.C.*)
Mattei's Tavern (*S.Υ.*)
Matteo's: A Little Taste of
  Hoboken
Metro
Musso & Frank's Grill
Orso
Osteria Panevino (*S.D.*)
The Palms (*S.D.*)
Paradise
Pavarotti and Stein
Prado
Prezzo
Roxbury
Salute!
Salvatore's (*S.D.*)
Shane on the Glen
Spaghettini
Stoney's
The Tower
Tribeca
Tse Yang

Le Vallauris (*P.S.*)
Wally's Desert Turtle (*P.S.*)
Zio & Co.

9/20

The Bottle Inn
Channel House (*C.I.*)
La Scala Boutique
La Scala Malibu
La Scala Presto

8/20

Charlie Brown's World
  Famous Malibu Sea Lion
Gladstone's 4 Fish

7/20

Cabo Cabo Cabo
El Coyote
Fung Lum

No Rating

*(Those restaurants we were unable
to rate at press time because of a
sudden change of chef or ownership)*

Checkers Hotel Dining
  Room
La Gran Tapa (*S.D.*)
Stonehouse at San Ysidro
  Ranch (*S.B.*)
Xiomara

HOW TO CHOOSE?

In order to help you sift through the more than 500 restaurant reviews in this book, we've included listings in the back of the book, of restaurants By Area, By Price and By Cuisine, and by specific features such as Breakfast, Brunch, Bar Scene, Kid-Friendly, Late-Night, Light Eating, Vegetarian and more. *See* the INDEXES section on page 404.

ABOUT THE HOTELS

Choosing a Hotel

To help you easily find the hotel (or inn, or resort) that best matches your budget, establishments in this book are listed in sections by price, from most expensive to least expensive: **Top of the Line, Luxury, Moderate** and **Practical.** The symbol that accompanies each review indicates in which price category the hotel belongs, and for the purposes of this book, we have defined the categories based on the average starting price of a single or double room:

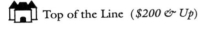 Top of the Line (*$200 & Up*)

Luxury (*$150 & Up*)

Moderate (*$100 & Up*)

Practical (*Under $100*)

Our opinion of each lodging is expressed in the text, where we describe and comment upon the decor, service, atmosphere, rooms, amenities, location and so on. Read the reviews carefully to select the hotel (within the appropriate price category) that best suits your needs and your tastes.

Credit cards are abbreviated as follows: **AE**: American Express and/or Optima, **D**: Discover Card, **DC**: Diners Club and/or Carte Blanche, **MC**: MasterCard, **V**: VISA. "All major cards" indicates that the hotel accepts all of the above cards. Information is also given as to whether or not breakfast is included in the room rate, and if

the hotel has a "No Smoking" policy throughout.

For a complete index of all hotels in this book By Area & Price, please see the INDEXES at the back of the book.

Advice & Comments

- Our reviews give the prices of accommodations at high season. During off season, rates can be as much as 30 percent to 50 percent lower than their peak-season highs. If you're on a tight budget, it might be wise to schedule your trip directly before or directly following high season.

- Be sure to call ahead to inquire about special packages (such as Friday-to-Sunday or, at resorts, packages that include meals, spa treatments or sports activities) and discounts offered at certain times of the year.

- In the hotel world, there is almost no such thing as an absolute rate. Room charges fluctuate by season, availability, quality of view, proximity to the ocean (at beachfront resorts) and so on. Don't be afraid to negotiate a lower rate at any time, and don't take "no" for an answer until you're sure you can't negotiate any further.

- Don't assume that hotels falling under the "Top of the Line" or "Luxury" headings are truly luxurious: the place may position and price itself that way, but that doesn't mean it delivers the goods. Conversely, "Practical" doesn't necessarily indicate that the lodging offers no more than bare-bones accommodations; some truly charming and comfortable inns, bed-and-breakfasts and even motels can be found in this category.

LOS ANGELES

RESTAURANTS

Contents

The symbols that accompany each review indicate the rating on a scale of one to twenty. The rankings reflect *only* our opinion of the food; the decor, service, wine list and atmosphere are explicitly commented upon within each review. Restaurants that are ranked 13/20 and above are distinguished with toques (chef's hats): For further explanation, as well as an index of restaurants by rating, please see "About the Restaurants" in the INTRODUCTION.

For comprehensive listings of restaurants By Area, By Price and By Cuisine, and by specific features such as Breakfast, Bar Scene, Kid-Friendly, Late-Night, Light Eating and more, see the INDEXES section at the back of the book.

L.A. Area

Encompasses L.A. proper and all of the Westside, including Downtown, Hollywood, West Hollywood, Bel Air, Beverly Hills, Brentwood, Westwood, West L.A., Century City, Culver City, Venice, Marina del Rey, Santa Monica, Pacific Palisades and Malibu.

11/20 Adriano's
2930 Beverly Glen Circle, Bel Air 90077; (310) 475-9807
Italian. Lunch Tues.-Fri., Dinner Tues.-Sun. All major cards.

If you mention to the average westsider that you're having dinner at Adriano's, reactions will vary. Food enthusiasts will tell you that it is old-fashioned and lacks innovation. Others will rhapsodize about how much they love the place,

precisely because it *is* old-fashioned. Clearly there are lots of the latter out there, because Adriano's remains open year after year, while so many others close their doors. Owner Adriano Rebora used to work on a cruise ship, and he has transferred some of that formality to his pretty dining room filled with prosperous, well-dressed diners. The food should be better than it is given the stiff prices, but it can be happily nostalgic to order such retro-Italian standards as veal cutlets, spaghetti carbonara and tartuffo ice cream. For many, this is the only kind of Italian food. A dinner costs about $40.

Akbar
590 Washington St., Marina del Rey 90292; (310) 822-4116
Indian. Lunch Sun.-Fri., Dinner nightly, Brunch Sun. All major cards.

Outside, the sunny Marina teams with athletic life. Inside, all is cool, dark and soothing, with sparkling crystal on the tables, white napery and wonderful, overpowering fragrances. "Feel the grandeur of a Moghul," says the menu, a little hyperbolic in these politically correct times perhaps, but not so far flung in here. Anyone familiar with Indian food will know these dishes are prepared with care. For a good cross-section of appetizers, try the hors d'oeuvres combination, chicken tikka smoked in the tandoor, samosa pancakes filled with peas and potatoes, sheekh kebab and the intriguing papadum, spiced wafers made from lentil flour. Tandoori dishes are sheer perfection, though the mild vindaloos concede too much to the American palate. As a nod to ancient Moghuls, gulab jaman, a golden ball of sweetened milk, is decorated with a piece of silver leaf. Dinner costs about $20 per person.

12/20 Al Amir
5750 Wilshire Blvd., Wilshire District (L.A.) 90036; (213) 931-8740
Middle Eastern. Lunch Mon.-Fri., Dinner Mon.-Sat. All major cards.

Al Amir ("The Prince") sits in the midst of Wilshire Courtyard, in a grandly opulent, futuristic setting. Inside, things are a mix of classic Middle Eastern and moderne. The tables are full of business-suited diners, and conversations are hushed. Al Amir doesn't offer traditional meze combinations these restaurants are famous for, but rather individual ones in small portions. To us, $3.25 seems high for a bowl of pickled vegetables, though not as high as $11.50 for a small plate of grilled prawns. Therer are many dishes we've never encountered: bazenjan makdous, a pair of Japanese eggplants filled with ground nuts and moistened with olive oil, salads made with lamb brains or tongue and four raw-lamb dishes. At $10 or so, many of the main courses (lamb cutlets, grilled chicken in garlic sauce) are better bargains than the appetizers. Service is generally respectful, though often confused. It feels odd having to dress up to dine here, given the informality of other restaurants of this genre. We're not suggesting belly dancers; just the usual appointments to help a prince relax. Dinner costs about $35 per person.

Angeli Caffè
7274 Melrose Ave., W. Hollywood 90046; (213) 936-9086
Italian. Lunch Mon.-Sat., Dinner nightly. AE, MC, V.

When it first opened, Angeli was so small you had to step outside to change your mind. Da dum. It was expanded a couple of years back, but it is still no mean feat choosing from the marvelous little dishes prepared by chef Evan Kleiman. Angeli is the antithesis of the old-style, red leatherette Italian-American restaurant. Lighting is bright and decor is minimalist. Waiters look interchangeable with customers. As is often the case at restaurants specializing in grazing, this place can be noisy. Star dish here is pizza from the wood-burning oven, topped with true Italian ingredients: pesto, onions, pine nuts, ricotta, mozzarella, Parmesan, prosciutto or sometimes simply olive oil and garlic. They are all terrific. Suppli are toothsome, simple rice croquettes filled with melted cheese. In croquettes di patate, potato replaces the cheese. Nosh on any of the perfect little antipasti plates, bread scraped with garlic, various frittatas, smoked meats and lots of olives. Angeli's winning formula has led to two Angeli spinoffs, but this is the original, and we'll always love it. Dinner is about $45 per person.

Angeli Mare
Marina Marketplace, 13455 Maxella Ave., Marina del Rey 90292; (310) 822-1984
Italian. Lunch Mon.-Fri., Dinner nightly. All major cards.

This is the third (and newest) in the growing family of Angeli restaurants, and in this case,

three is obviously the charm. Owner/chef Evan Kleiman hits the mark square at this seaside haven. Warm lighting adds sparkle to rich marble tables, and curved polished beams recall sitting in an overturned boat—or a particularly classy whale. Unlike the other two restaurants, there is a full bar to augment a small but appealing wine list. Furthermore, both service and food are absolutely first-rate here. Marvelous thin-crust pizzas, salads like Caesar, caprese and a delicious panzanella made with thick toasted bread, tomato chunks, capers and bell peppers and a classic roast chicken are mainstays. Daily specials favor seafood. We can't predict what you'll be offered, but we can tell you that dishes we've tried have been spectacular; a robust Tuscan fish soup with assorted shellfish and a thick slab of toasted bread; a juicy salmon topped with smooth pesto. Finish with a heaping bowl of vanilla gelato topped with a crumble of homemade brownies. Buonissimo. A meal costs $25 to $35 per person.

11/20 Los Arrieros
2619 W. Sunset Blvd., Echo Park 90026; (213) 483-0074
Columbian. Lunch & Dinner Wed.-Mon. MC, V.

Columbia is a temperate land of tropical fruits, corn, potatoes and beans, ingredients which work their way into most Columbian recipes. Seafood and meats are big on Columbian tables as well, especially beef (although Columbian beef dishes tend to be tough, despite slow cooking). Los Arrieros, whose name pays homage to donkey-riding cowboys, is easily one of the most attractive South American restaurants in town, with dark-tiled floors, polished wood tables and hanging wrought-iron lamps. The menu is big, 26 entrées, (many of which are convenient combination plates like bandeja especial, steak, a fried egg, pork skin, rice, plantains and a corn cake.) Fritanga is pork ribs, tiny chunks of stewed beef, pork skin, fried liver and small pieces of veal tripe. Ask for your grill items undercooked, because all too often they're overcooked. Best dishes here are stews, particularly the seafood concoction called concha Cartegenera, a conch shell overflowing with shrimp, squid, fish and a slightly ponderous cheese sauce. A dinner costs $10.

12/20 Atlas Bar & Grill
3760 Wilshire Blvd., Mid-Wilshire District (L.A.) 90010; (213) 380-8400
Californian/International. Lunch Mon.-Fri., Dinner Mon.-Sat. All major cards.

Mario Tamayo is a fellow unfazed by odd parts of town. His first restaurant was Cha Cha Cha, on a bad block in Silverlake. He followed that with Café Mambo, on an odd block in East Hollywood. His third and boldest restaurant sits in the restored Wiltern Theatre building, on the trendless corner of Wilshire Boulevard and Western Avenue. It's as close as we come these days to the great nightclubs of the '30s, a large, handsome, gilded space, in which women who sound and look like Billie Holiday sing, while waiters swirl through the room carrying plates of serviceable, if unexciting, California chow: pizza, pasta and lots of grilled stuff. The food is mostly well prepared, though it's only peripherally the point of coming here. To experience the true flavor of Atlas, go late and dress for the occasion—tuxedos and gowns are not out of line. Chanel looks good, too. And by the way, Tamayo is easy to identify—he's got the most Mephistophelean moustache and beard this side of Hades. About $35 apiece for dinner.

Aunt Kizzy's Back Porch

Villa Marina Shopping Center, 4371 Glencoe Ave., Marina del Rey 90292; (310) 578-1005
Soul Food. Lunch & Dinner daily., Late Supper Fri.-Sat. No cards.

Villa Marina Shopping Center has a multiplex theater, major markets and assorted restaurants, making parking on weekends a serious challenge. Once you've overcome that, you'll encounter some down-home southern cooking, as good as it gets in L.A. The recipes that make up this menu hail from Texas and Oklahoma, the home states of owners Adolph and Mary Dulan. Try the superb catfish and hush puppies, the ultra-crunchy fried chicken, the perfect beef short ribs, and succulent smothered pork chops—all served with monster-sized quantities of red beans and rice, black-eyed peas, okra, corn, collard greens or candied yams. Fresh-squeezed lemonade is served in a mason jar; for dessert, feast on sloppy, sweet peach cobblers, pineapple-coconut cake and sweet-potato pie. A dinner costs around $15.

Authentic Café

7605 Beverly Blvd., Melrose-Fairfax District (L.A.) 90036; (213) 939-4626
American/Southwestern. Lunch & Dinner daily. No cards.

It would be easy to miss the Authentic Café—a small storefront on a street where no one does much walking—except for the large crowd *always* waiting in front. The still-small interior has recently expanded to include a tortilla station and cappuccino bar, but seating, at high tables and counter stools, is limited. Chef/owner Roger

Hayot, formerly of Wave and the Cheesecake Factory, wears a great number of hats here. He cooks, answers the phone and mans the cash register in his eclectic café, best described as New Mexicanish. Much of the menu runs to nachos, tamales, and other southwestern fare, but there are also curious pizzas (topped with chicken sausage and such), oddball pastas (including one made with chicken, corn and chipotle chile) and good Chinese dishes, including great Szechuan dumplings. Is the Authentic Café authentic? We're not sure, but we're happy to eat here every day. One caveat: the café has never had a liquor license, and now you are not allowed even to bring your own beer or wine. Expect to pay about $12 per person for dinner.

11/20 Babalu

1001 Montana Ave., Santa Monica 90403; (310) 395-2500
Caribbean/International. Breakfast, Lunch & Dinner Tues.-Sun. MC, V.

Babalu is as much fun as its name implies, and the cuisine just as jumbled—part Caribbean, part Mexican, part Italian, part Southwestern, part Asian and probably all Californian, today's great culinary catch-all term. The tone is set by its nutty decor—it looks like something a bunch of talented sixth graders might have done as a class project. The place is small, service is a little zany, and the food is just good enough so that we'd go back without much prompting: there are crabcakes, chicken "satay" with a coconut-lime-curry sauce, chicken-and-chile sausage with avocado relish. The dessert menu returns safely to America, offering homemade-fruit pies (peach, mixed berry, apple-blueberry crumble), dynamite Key-lime pie, raspberry mousse cake. Dinner runs about $20 per person.

12/20 Babette's

3100 Washington Blvd., Marina del Rey 90291; (310) 822-2020
French. Lunch Tues.-Fri., Dinner Tues.-Sat. AE, MC, V.

In a city where the lusty cooking of Italy has become dominant, Babette's is one of the few French spots that reminds us just how casual, easygoing and fun bistro food can be. It's a pleasant little café, with dreams of being something a bit more than that, on a busy stretch of Washington Boulevard not far from the sea. There's a cozy outdoor patio and a lot of dishes that might best be described as old-school Californian-French, which means the menu yields neither a cassoulet nor an excess of kiwi fruit. Instead, Caesar salad is paired with smoked salmon, sea bass with tapenade, and tournedos of salmon with angel-hair pasta and sun-dried tomatoes. At heart, this is a good neighborhood restaurant, a modernized version of such old French hangouts as La Grange and Alouette. It's worth stopping in if you live nearby. A dinner costs about $25.

12/20 Beau Rivage
26025 Pacific Coast Hwy., Malibu 90265;
(310) 456-5733
French/Continental. Lunch Mon.-Fri. & Sun.,
Dinner nightly. All major cards.

This exceedingly romantic Mediterranean country cottage across Coast Highway from the beach is reminiscent of a French or Italian villa, well-aged and very pleasant. It's lovely to sit on the patio full of wrought-iron furniture and bougainvillea, and catch the occasional salty ocean breeze from across the street. The menu includes many traditional tastes, with its wide assortment of Continental favorites, from veal chops in puff pastry to stuffed veal, from fettuccine in a sauce of wild mushrooms and Madeira to angel hair with garlic and feta. Besides an impressive wine list, which includes some fine Champagnes and Champagne rosés, cheered us up, and for those who can pay, the owner stocks vintage Cognacs and Armagnacs. The setting is more charming than most, the service is from the old school, and the owners are always there, always asking how things are. Dinner can easily cost $60 per person, choosing carefully, you can spend $40.

The Belvedere at Peninsula Hotel
9882 Little Santa Monica Blvd., Beverly Hills 90212; (310) 273-4888
French. Breakfast & Lunch daily, Dinner nightly, Brunch Sun. All major cards.

If you can afford it, you'll love The Belvedere in the new ultraposh Peninsula hotel. From the large tables set with fine silver and crystal to the proper sommelier, it's a last bastion of conservative chic; everybody looks like they couldn't decide whether to invite Ron and Nancy or Ted and Jane to dinner. Running the kitchen is Peter Davis, who most recently cooked in a swanky Hong Kong dining room; the guest chef (there'll be a new one each year), Akira Hirose, prepares just four specials each night: perhaps superb sautéed langoustines with zucchini and a potato-spinach purée or sautéed red snapper in a miso-garlic sauce with a vivid ratatouille. Memorable "regular" dishes have included rosemary-scented rack of lamb with smoked garlic, and marvelously subtle poached oysters in Champagne. A few

dishes, like the grilled veal steak with wild mushrooms and creamed onion, displayed the sort of agreeable blandness common to hotel dining rooms. But given the obvious ability in the kitchen, we're confident that the cuisine will continue to improve. In fact, we won't be a bit surprised if the rating goes up in the next edition of this book. Let's just hope the prices don't also go up: dinner runs upwards of $60 per person.

Bice
301 N. Canon Dr., Beverly Hills 90210;
(213) 272-2423
Italian. Lunch Mon.-Sat., Dinner nightly. All major cards.

The food is finally living up to the considerable hype that accompanied Bice's arrival in L.A. At press time, Giovanni Pinato, who had been a chef alongside Bice's Patrick Clark for a year already, was taking over as the solo chef, and planned to switch to the theme of northern Tuscan and Milanese dishes. Past dishes have included gnocchi that were as light as we always hoped they'd be and risotto besotted with white truffles—the sort of preparation that makes the uninitiated understand what the fuss over this priceless fungus is all about. There are grilled dishes, too, and pastas that have been truly exquisite. Desserts are worth saving room for, especially the flaky, fragrant hot apple tart (order it early, since it takes twenty minutes to bake) and the gelati. The staff is thoroughly professional and blissfully anticipatory (our waiter thoughtfully moved us midway through a meal when he noticed that the Apache dancers next to us were fumigating us with cigarette smoke). It's rare to see a restaurant begin as such a disaster and become so accomplished. It just goes to show what a virtuoso new chef, astute management—-and very deep pockets—can do. Dinner costs about $45 per person.

Bikini
1413 5th St., Santa Monica 90401;
(310) 395-8611
Eclectic. Lunch Mon.-Fri., Dinner Mon.-Sun., Brunch Sun. AE, MC, V.

In brief introductory remarks on his menu, John Sedlar pays homage to his native Southwestern cuisine, as well as to the food of France, Italy and Japan. For some chefs, such a tribute would seem either presumptuous or disingenuous. Not Sedlar. This, after all, is a man who trained with the patron saint of Los Angeles French chefs—Jean Bertranou—and who went on to become the pioneer padre of modern

Southwestern cuisine at the now-defunct St. Estèphe. And this is a man who now manages, on a single menu, to offer souvlaki, ravioli, nacatamal, kaiseki, chop suey and choucroute. Since Sedlar still feels most comfortable when inspired by his Southwestern roots, you might want to try the Mayan enchilada (made with grilled shrimp and a mole sauce) or the Pacific prawns poached in vanilla and served with a salad of jicama and lime.

We prefer some of the dishes with an Asian influence. Sedlar's menu descriptions, like his stunning plate presentations, make dining here a true delight for all the senses; ever playful, he offers an appetizer called "egg foo yong double happiness": two duck eggs, scrambled with gingered duck confit and bits of water chestnut, mushroom, bamboo shoots and scallions and put back in their shells. It's marvelous. So is the saddle of lamb, grilled with Indian spices and served with two spicy sauces, one of curry the other of peanut. But Sedlar has a sure hand with almost any cuisine, and his souvlaki—three strips of lamb on skewers, served with a tapenade of Kalamata olives and chunks of feta cheese—would make Zorba dance. Unfortunately, except for the fresh fruit with infusions of passion fruit juice, the desserts are less than stunning, especially the sweet tamale. We hope that, with the opening of his new tamale bar as we went to press, Sedlar improves upon this disappointment. Bikini is one of the most striking restaurants in town, a soaring room with clean, contemporary lines, a brilliant use of lighting and a single wall of undulating rosewood. A dinner is about $44.

The Bistro
246 N. Cañon Dr., Beverly Hills 90210; (310) 273-5633
Continental. Dinner Mon.-Sat. All major cards.

The actual bistroness of The Bistro often gets obscured by its celebrity status: the Hollywood faces who show up at this reasonably authentic re-creation of a Parisian boîte distract most diners from the good solid food that makes its way out of the kitchen. But beyond the formidable presence of owner Kurt Niklas (former head waiter at the legendary Romanoff's) at the door, and the preferential seating, this is actually one of the few restaurants in town producing the sort of bistro cuisine that's so antithetical to a celebrity following. And now that the recession and Hollywood's fickleness have taken their toll (business is off and lunch is no longer served), it's a bit easier for regular rich folks, as opposed to famous rich folks, to enjoy a solid bistro dinner here. The onion soup is thick with the sweetness

of long-cooked onions and the stretch of too much cheese. The oxtail soup is first-rate, and best on cold days. The steak tartare is nearly perfect, mixed to order at your table, along with a bestiary of dishes right out of the comfort-food hall of fame—veal cutlet Parmigiana, Hungarian goulash with Spätzle, roast duck à l'orange, tournedos Rossini, frogs' legs Provençal and the tarte Tatin of our dreams. As we went to press, restaurant replaced the old crimson carpeting with a handsome, gleaming wood floor, and the chef announced plans to add a few lighter dishes to the classic menu. Thankfully, even with freshening, The Bistro will always be The Bistro. Dinner runs about $45 apiece.

The Bistro Garden
176 N. Cañon Dr., Beverly Hills 90210; (310) 550-3900
Continental. Lunch Mon.-Sat., Dinner Mon.-Sat. All major cards.

Trendy restaurants come and go in this town, but the Bistro Garden is forever. The Ladies Who Lunch gather here daily or weekly, and at night their husbands and select friends join the crowd of moguls and Hollywood heavyweights for dinner in the glowing, French-style dining room, with its chandeliers and lavish flower bouquets.

Owner Kurt Niklas and son Christopher have steadfastly kept the food simple and classic: you can begin with salmon tartare, caviar or perhaps French onion soup au gratin, then move along to veal Milanese, grilled lamb loin with black pepper in mint sauce or sautéed halibut. A satisfying plateful of Swiss bratwurst with warm potato salad is one of the few authentic German offerings on the menu, probably introduced by Kurt himself, who hails from Munich. Of course, the Ladies Who Lunch stick to greens; Bibb lettuce, spinach, endive-and-watercress salad, a veritable forest's worth. The unrecognized are sent off to a dark corner of the restaurant to eat the specialties du jour. The chocolate soufflé, rich in texture and and marvelous in flavor, has aquired fame of its own. Dinner is $50 per person; lunch is about $25.

Bombay Café
12113 Santa Monica Blvd., W.L.A. 90025; (310) 820-2070
Indian. Lunch Tues.-Fri., Dinner Tues.-Sun. MC, V.

A visit to this bright, ambitious little spot is an encounter with one of the tastiest, least expected new cuisines of the '90s: Californian-Indian food. The cheerful room, located on the second floor of a mini-mall, appears to be even larger than it is, thanks to an abundance of mirrors. The four owners (Meeta, David, Neela and Bill) have an open kitchen and a menu so enticing we've often been tempted to throw up our hands and say "Bring one of everything!" Start with sev puri, a quintessential bit of Indian street food consisting of little crisps (like gourmet tortilla chips) topped with chopped onions, potatoes, cilantro and a trio of piquant chutneys. Or the plump, tasty, burrito-like frankies, stuffed with chicken, lamb or cauliflower. We've never tasted anything quite like the crispy shrimp dish called haldi jhinga; the eggplant and yogurt purée called smoked bharta; the tandoori-chicken sausages called reshmi kebabs; or the tandoori-chicken salad, heavy with scallions and cilantro. Dishes change from day to day, and even the fascinating roster of chutneys changes with manic regularity. Dinner runs $15 to $22 per person.

 ## Border Grill Santa Monica
1445 4th St., Santa Monica 90401; (310) 451-1655
Mexican. Lunch Mon.-Sat., Dinner nightly, Late Supper Fri.-Sat. AE, MC, V.

Susan Feniger and Mary Sue Milliken have a knack for presaging restaurant trends—or perhaps just starting them. In the early '80s, their miniature City Café helped spawn the revitalization of Melrose, while introducing Californian cuisine to Angelenos who couldn't afford Michael's. A little later, their City Restaurant became a classic '80s spot, a barren warehouse showcasing a pricey, wildly eclectic assortment of international dishes. And then, as the new decade dawned, they kicked off the downscaled '90s by opening this raucous, intensely colorful Mexican joint. It's hardly cheap—margaritas are a whopping $6—but if you order right you can eat very well for a fair price. Start with the warm tortilla chips served with a trio of zingy salsas, then skip the costly entrées in favor of several smaller dishes, all of which are delicious: three little tubs of vibrant ceviche; platano empanadas, banana-flavored turnovers stuffed with black beans; sweet, smooth tiny green corn tamales tied in neat little bundles; marvelous cold Yucatán tacos topped with seafood (lobster, shrimp, crab, salmon or sea bass), lettuce, salsa and guacamole. Share a coconut flan for dessert and you'll want for nothing, except perhaps a pair of earplugs to shut out the din. A dinner-size sampler of small dishes runs about $20 per person.

> *Prices are based on a complete dinner for one, including an appetizer, entrée, dessert, tax and tip—but excluding wine or any other beverage.*

 ## La Brasserie at Bel Age Hotel
1020 N. San Vicente Blvd., W. Hollywood 90069; (310) 854-1111
Continental. Breakfast, Lunch, Dinner & Late Supper daily; Brunch Sun. All major cards.

They are just a touch modest here. It's much more than a brasserie—with its gorgeous view of the lights of Hollywood, its elegant and subdued decor, its elbow space and its swift service, it could easily position itself as a top-notch restaurant. Thank God you only pay brasserie prices. They do pizzas, pastas and sandwiches, and they do them well. Traditional brasserie fare is also served, but with personal touches: broiled Norwegian salmon comes on a bed of spinach, fresh pasta is garnished simply with tomatoes and basil leaves, osso buco with a risotto of pancetta, Parmesan and mushrooms. But the star attraction is Mr. Michel Montignac. Not the man himself—the one who has revolutionized France's eating habits with his acclaimed "The More You Eat Well, The More You Lose Weight" theory. But as part of a move into the United States, he personally designed a menu for La Brasserie, based on the idea that eating well means carefully selecting natural ingredients and avoiding those that cause an overproduction of sugar in the body. Good foie gras, non-pasteurized Brie, organic bread and pasta, and even chocolate are perfectly respectable, dietetically correct foods, according to Montignac.

He worked with chef Jean Claude Seruga to produce this titillating "dietetic" menu. We happily had voluptuous foie gras, accompanied by mushrooms and green beans, knowing we were shedding a few bothersome ounces. Authentic and natural Chaource and Brie cheeses with a slice of Montignac bread and a glass of Caymus Cabernet Sauvignon helped us gleefully eliminate some more of that unwanted weight. Even the flourless chocolate cake—a bit hefty—contributed to the success of this healthy program and to our enjoyment. Believe it or not, the Montignac diet works—we have many witnesses who swear by it. If this marvelous stuff is dietetic, we volunteer to be Montignac's guinea pig and subscribe permanently to La Brasserie's fitness plan. Dinner costs $25 per person.

10/20 Brentwood Bar & Grill
11647 San Vicente Blvd., Brentwood 90049; (310) 820-2121
Californian. Lunch Mon.-Fri., Dinner Mon.-Sat. All major cards.

Judging from the name, and from the fact that the Brentwood Bar & Grill was opened by the people who run Bob Burns in Santa Monica, you would be reasonable to expect this place to be a traditional bar and grill with straightforward American food. Instead, it's a most elegant restaurant with flatteringly subdued lighting, black-leather banquettes and prices as high as the real estate in these parts. It's a serious room that highlights the serious activity in the kitchen, which can be seen through three large glass panels. Rising to the challenge of a wildly Californian menu, we ordered the sweet-potato ravioli stuffed with Gorgonzola, sitting in a walnut pesto and topped with shoestring sweet-potato fries; the ahi tuna with fennel and a Kalamata olive sauce; and an unusual amaretto cookie flan. Entrées prepared with such a jumble of incompatible ingredients usually don't succeed, and these were no exception—flavors were muddled and disjointed. What was more interesting was the bar in the front, handsomely fitted with leather banquettes and serving a less expensive traditional bar menu. You'll spend at least $35 apiece in the dining room, probably more.

Broadway Deli
1457 3rd St., Santa Monica 90401; (310) 451-0616
American/French. Breakfast, Lunch & Dinner daily. AE, MC, V.

Ever since California Pizza Kitchen proved that chain restaurants could appeal to yuppies who wouldn't be caught dead in a Velvet Turtle, we've seen an explosion in stylish, affordable chains, from the Daily Grill to Chopstix. And now Michel Richard (Citrus, Citronelle), Bruce Marder (Rebecca's, West Beach) and Marvin Zeidler are out to conquer the world with the Broadway Deli.

Anchoring one end of the Third Street Promenade, the cavernous, high-tech space is filled with roomy booths, a long, open kitchen fronted by a dining counter, and a continual crush of people waiting upward of an hour. The Jewish-deli standards that the name evokes are available, but the best dishes are those you'd find in a French bistro or an American mom's kitchen: wonderful macaroni and cheese, a meaty, savory lamb shank on a bed of garlicky white beans, salty but satisfying French onion soup, a good Caesar salad and crisp, salty fries. Things get more contemporary with Richard's extraordinary crab coleslaw and the faddish charred turkey steak. The breads are great, the bagels divine, and the desserts almost as good as Citrus's. Keep an eye out: before long, there'll probably be a Broadway Deli in your neighborhood. Let's hope so. Dinner ranges from $15 to $25 per person.

7/20 Cabo Cabo Cabo
Century City Shopping Center, 10250 Santa Monica Blvd., Century City 90067; (310) 552-2226
Mexican. Lunch & Dinner daily. All major cards.

There aren't many restaurants around that actually make us long for Taco Bell. But this shopping-mall member of the RJ's/Gladstone's family makes Taco Bell seem absolutely exquisite by comparison. The Mexican dishes taste no better than if they had been freshly defrosted freezer meals, the salsa bar looks like it's cleaned on a whim every once in a while, and the attitude clearly says customers are such a bother. The restaurant recently remodeled, moving the entrance from one side to another, which was the restaurant equivalent of trying to keep the Titanic afloat by rearranging the furniture. At least it's cheap—but not cheap enough. About $10 per person for dinner.

Ca'Brea
346 S. La Brea Ave., Melrose-La Brea District (L.A.) 90036; (213) 938-2863
Italian. Lunch Mon.-Fri., Dinner Mon.-Sat., Late Supper Fri.-Sat. AE, MC, V.

The idea behind Ca'Brea was partially to catch the overflow from this duo's other restaurant, Locanda Veneta, which has always been far smaller than its considerable group of fans would like it to be. The result is an attractive restaurant that is, perhaps, even more popular than Locanda Veneta. It's three times the size, and rarely has an empty table. When you visit, you find out why: here is one of the most appealing menus in town.

Outside of some of the better restaurants in Tuscany and Venice, where have you encountered dishes like formaggio di capra alla pancetta e spinaci, in which sweetly musky goat cheese is wrapped with salty pancetta, baked and served on a bed of garlicked spinach? There's fagioli conzi alla salvia con costicine, which brings a fabulous plate of sundry and assorted beans, flavored with lick-them-clean baby-back ribs and a kick of sage. There's risotto with a ragoût of porcini mushrooms, and always a tasty risotto special. There's seafood bigoletti, which is home-made Venetian spaghetti with lobster, clams, scallops, shrimp and porcini in a light tomato sauce. Finish with caramel cream, topped with a intensely fudgy sauce, or the old-fashioned apple tart, served warm with a sweet "balsamic" sauce. The problem with Ca'Brea is not that the eating becomes boring but that it becomes addictive: you want to come back, week after week. And so does everyone else. Dinner costs about $32 per person.

10/20 Café Athens

1000 Wilshire Blvd., Santa Monica 90403;
(310) 395-1000
Greek. Lunch Tues.-Fri., Dinner Tues.-Sun.,
Late Supper Fri.-Sat. All major cards.

Birthday-party planners need look no further—at this offshoot of the Valley's Great Greek, the wine flows freely, noisy groups eat too much rich, garlicky Greek food, and the waiters sing "Happy Birthday" in Greek as often as they dance to the balalaika music. To make the most of your evening, you should a) submit willingly when a waiter pulls you up to join a line of dancers; and b) order the "family-style deluxe dinner" ($21.95 per person), a feeding frenzy for the whole table. There's a tangy Greek salad, vibrant tabouli, garlicky burned-butter pasta sprinkled with sharp kasseri cheese, and various spread-like starters paired with superb pita bread, from straightforward hummus to a fabulous melanzanasalata (eggplant purée). There's a long-roasted baby lamb and standard-issue stuffed grape leaves. On the down side, much of the food might disappoint those who lust for the genuine Greek thing. For our most recent dinner, the calamari was dry and the spiced meatballs were soured with too much lemon. But who cares? This is good-time food, just the thing to eat while you drink retsina and clap along to the music. Dinner is about $26 per person.

11/20 Café La Bohème

8400 Santa Monica Blvd., W. Hollywood
90069; (213) 848-2360
Japanese-Italian. Lunch & Dinner daily, Late
Supper Fri.-Sat., Brunch Sat.- Sun. All major
cards.

Café La Bohème is, first and foremost, a breathtaking bit of design. It's an immense barn of a room, dressed up like a lush post-modernist opera house, with heavy draperies on the walls, a roaring fireplace in one corner, an interior pond, and a statue of an Earth mother with a globe on her head. Running around the border is a mezzanine, from which spectators can observe (*sans* opera glasses) the doings down below. The first American branch of a Japanese restaurant chain that includes a number of restaurants in Tokyo and Yokohama, the restaurant cost the owners a princely sum to pull off. Oddly, the service is actually highly attentive and warm, not the norm in places of this ilk—the waiters wear name tags and inquire endlessly as to the state of the meal. The food is . . . weird. The owners describe the cuisine as, "California with the flavors of Italy, France, the Middle East and Mexico." Which translates as a decent pizza topped with "drunken" chicken flavored with a mix of Middle Eastern spices, on pizza bread shot with herbs and pinenuts. The spaghettini topped with caviar and seaweed includes a generous portion of baby clams and shimeji mushrooms. The simpler dishes are the most successful: pork kakuni is a mound of slow-cooked, shredded pork, tender and sweet; the pasta carbonara is a good, classic rendition. The place is a ton of fun. You don't need to spend a fortune, either—the most expensive item on the menu is rack of lamb at $18.50. Dinner costs about $40 per person.

12/20 Café Delfini

147 W. Channel Rd., Santa Monica 90402;
(310) 459-8823
Italian. Dinner nightly. MC, V.

This tasty bit of Italy by the blue Pacific is casual, tiny and always mobbed—don't even think of stopping in without a reservation. The kitchen makes a nice salad that's simple and yet great, just a toss of sliced tomatoes and onions topped with anchovies and olive oil. It's been a long time since we've had a steaming bowl of zuppe di pasta e fagioli, that classic bean and pasta soup, and this version made us regret avoiding it for so long; it was rich, earthy, sensuous and lots of fun, reminiscent of the pleasures that used to be found in necking to Johnny Mathis albums, back in a simpler age. The penne Siciliana, with its stew of bell peppers, eggplant and tomatoes, and the rigatoni Gorgonzola, with its thick layer of potent cheese, were perfect pastas; they tasted even better the next day, when the flavors had had time to meld in our refrigerator. And there's more to choose from, from grilled chicken breast to veal piccata in the sort of lemon sauce that makes licking the plate clean mandatory. Dinner costs about $20 per person.

11/20 Café del Rey

4451 Admiralty Way, Marina del Rey 90292;
(310) 823-6395
Californian. Lunch & Dinner daily, Brunch
Sun. AE, MC, V.

The view of the Marina: terrific. The parking: convenient. The design: open, bright and airy. The wine: there are plenty of nice choices by the glass. Service: fine. Prices: very fair. After this, things get a little more complicated. Dining at Café del Rey is sort of like wandering around a multi-cultural baazar, in which among the overwhelming choices, there is something for everyone. Chef Katsuo Nagasawa makes an ambitious stab at a Californian/Mediterranean mélange with touches of Caribbean, Japanese and straight American. The results can be very good—and they can also be a might overconceived. An adventurous version of niçoise salad features smoked salmon and "wild" bacon in place of the usual tuna, and the whole is drizzled with Champagne vinaigrette; the Caesar salad includes—surprise!—prosciutto and smoked chicken. A Cuban black-bean soup is given a luxurious dollop of crème fraîche; a tasty quesadilla, stuffed with Cheddar, wild mushrooms and grilled veggies, features pita bread instead of a tortilla; osso buco is accompanied by coconut rice studded with raisins. Among the many salads, sandwiches, pastas, pizzas and entrées, the hesitant diner can find a good, solid burger (with Vermont Cheddar), a Mozzarella/tomato/basil pizza and an Angus rib-eye steak with crushed peppercorns. Dinner runs about $30 per person.

 ## Café Katsu

2117 Sawtelle Blvd., W.L.A. 90025; (310) 477-3359
French-Japanese. Lunch Mon.-Sat., Dinner nightly. All major cards.

Café Katsu is minimalist in the Japanese extreme, and save for a few pieces of oft-changed abstract art mounted on the otherwise bare walls, a ringer for a sensory deprivation chamber. Food, on the other hand, is quite down-to-earth and even rather stable, albeit unquestionably exotic. The Japaneseness of the cooking is less pronounced here than at Katsu on Hillhurst, the restaurant which spawned this one, with a slant distinctly toward France. The delicacy of these entrées are unquestioned, from a menu that changes as liberally as the art on these walls. Most of them lean toward seafood: roasted lotte fish with artichokes in a lobster sauce, striped bass pole (sautéed, then grilled) with calamari and morels, grilled swordfish in a saffron sauce, sautéed scallops with lobster ravioli. This may be a shopping mall restaurant, but it is arguably the best shopping mall restaurant in all of Los Angeles. Dinner runs about $25 per person.

11/20 Café Maurice

747 N. La Cienega Blvd., W. Hollywood 90069; (310) 652-1609
French. Dinner & Late Supper nightly. MC, V.

Café Maurice is one of the most-difficult-to-get-into restaurants in L.A. This we'll add to the category of all the world's unexplainable phenomenae. Here's one of the most unpretentious spots in town, a dark roomful of booths and wood tables, given slapdash touches of old-world bistro glamour with etched-glass mirrors, wine bottles clustered around, Toulouse Lautrec–era prints stuffed into old frames. Here's a menu of some of the most traditional, rustic bistro fare in town. Here are the owners themselves, doing all the cooking, tending the bar, waiting on tables. And L.A. loves Café Maurice—mostly because it's the rare restaurant that doesn't try to be anything beyond what it is: a gathering place for food and drink. In addition to assorted Europeans and neighborhood folk, French chefs (we've spied some of the city's best) and trendy nightclub-goers come to soak up the unadulterated bistro ambience and wash down some simple food with inexpensive wine. Getting a patio table in good weather can be even more of a challenge than getting one inside—once you do, try the poulet normande (chicken breast in a creamy white-wine sauce with sautéed mushrooms), the fresh, generous niçoise salad, the côte d'agneau (lamb ribs, roasted Provençale-style with ample rosemary and thyme). Everything is reliably good, except for the rather bland pastas and the erratic, non-English-speaking service. The sound system belts out everything from Edith Piaf to the Gipsy Kings, and you can order food until 1 a.m. every night of the week. Dinner costs no more than $10 to $20 per person.

10/20 Café Montana

1534 Montana Ave., Santa Monica 90402; (310) 829-3990
Californian. Breakfast, Lunch & Dinner Tues.-Sun., Brunch Sun. AE, D, MC, V.

With its plate-glass walls facing the street, Café Montana puts you right in the middle of the Montana shopping district, which is bustling by day. But at night, unfortunately, there is nary a soul on the street. The menu bounces wildly from potstickers to a grilled-vegetable quesadilla to koldunai (Lithuanian meat dumplings). We tried the skewered chicken with a Thai-style peanut sauce, and wished we hadn't; the chicken was cooked to death, and the peanut sauce was much greasier than it needed to be. The Chinese chicken salad was equally unfortunate: deflavorized, rather gristly chicken, watery black mushrooms, baby corn and pea pods over too much lettuce. We must say, however, that many adore this place, returning again and again for such simple dishes as the roast chicken and the mixed grill. And we like the place at breakfast, when the contemporary interior is bright and cheerful and the food seems more competent. Lunch costs $12 per person, dinner $20.

10/20 Caioti

2100 Laurel Canyon Blvd., Hollywood 90046; (213) 650-2988
Italian/Californian. Lunch & Dinner daily. AE, MC, V.

There is much debate as to whether Ed LaDou actually invented the California pizza, or whether—as it was with the radio—he was one of many who contributed to its birth. In any case, he was there in the early days, coming up with madcap pizzas for Wolfgang Puck at Spago, and later for the California Pizza Kitchen chain. At his own restaurant, deep in the wooded glen of Laurel Canyon, LaDou continues to create some of the oddest pizzas in town, served in a setting right out of the Addams Family: a dark, ramshackle place underneath the venerable Laurel Canyon General Store. But there's a fine madness in LaDou's cooking: in the pizzas topped with marinated pork, black beans, chorizo, jalapeños and smoked Gouda; with prosciutto, cantaloupe, Gorgonzola, pine nuts and parsley; with chicken meatballs and green-peppercorn curry sauce. The man's imagination knows no limits—he's the Leonardo Da Vinci of pizza. And even when his combinations don't quite work, his crust always does: it's unfailingly crisp and crunchy. In the way that New Yorkers journey to John's Pizzeria for a taste of the real thing, Angelenos go to Caioti to eat at the source. Dinner runs about $15 per person.

Campanile
624 S. La Brea Ave., Melrose-La Brea District (L.A.) 90036; (213) 938-1447
Italian/Mediterranean. Breakfast daily, Dinner Mon.-Sat. AE, MC, V.

There is nothing dazzling about the food at Campanile—no gastronomic pyrotechnics of the sort that astonish the palate, the mind and, often, the eye at Citrus or Patina. But Campanile does have simple, hearty, rustic (choose your adjective) food that is consistently excellent and constantly improving. "Consistency" may be the key word for chef Mark Peel now. You can confidently pick almost anything; in fact, the most difficult aspect of dining here these days is deciding which of the many temptations to succumb to. How do you choose an appetizer, for example, among grilled sardines with a fennel salad; grilled quail salad with shoestring potatoes; scallop ceviche served in the shell; warm poached mozzarella with pesto; and the dozen or so other starters? Our two favorites, from a recent dinner: a spectacular soup made with roast turnips and scallion oil; and a risotto flavored with truffles and basil and topped with three perfectly cooked, tender-but-firm spot prawns. The grilled prime rib may still be the best single dish on the menu, but it now has a great deal of company—and competition—from a changing variety of fish dishes and from the grilled quail, the rosemary-charred baby lamb, the veal liver (especially when it's sliced thick and cooked rare) with a potato-

and-onion galette and the venison sautéed with a sauce of huckleberries and juniper berries.

More than at any other restaurant in Southern California, Campanile is the place where you should be required by law to save room for dessert. Nancy Silverton is Peel's wife, Campanile's co-owner and, more important to the dining public, a baker and pastry chef extraordinaire. Every night, she creates a half dozen or so remarkable desserts. Her lemon tart is properly tart, accompanied by sour cherries (great idea!). Her ginger shortcakes with huckleberries and crème fraîche ice cream is the current standout, but that could change tomorrow . . . and the day after that and the day after that, as she comes up with each new creation. If this were a just world, for example, her sourdough "doughnuts" (served with ricotta fritters, preserved boysenberries and nouya ice cream) would put Winchell's out of business in 30 seconds. The wine list includes a wide range of unusual Italian whites and young reds that properly complement Peel's food. If you like grappa, be sure to end the meal with grappa di Sassicaia, or one of the other 75 on the list. Dinner is $40 per person.

12/20 Capri
1616 Abbot Kinney Blvd., Venice 90291; (310) 392-8777
Italian. Dinner nightly. AE, MC, V.

Despite barren white walls and concrete floors, this place has lots of warmth, thanks to the remarkably hospitable (and handsome) staff. And despite a skimpy menu, the cooking is terrific, thanks to the skill of chef Fabio Flagiello. An eclectic crowd of locals (rather conservative-looking middle-aged couples mixed in with high-style, 30ish men and women in black) have already claimed this unpretentious place as their own, and it's no wonder. Tortina di polenta is a layering of fried polenta, prosciutto, artichoke hearts and wild mushrooms. Cornetto di pesce spada is a foccacia "bowl" filled with chunks of grilled swordfish and sweet red peppers. Quadradi in concasse consists of large pasta squares spilling out of two baked tomatoes. The flavors are fresh and pure, and the creativity provides a welcome change from the standard angel hair with tomato and basil. Who needs art on the walls? This place has it on the plates. About $25 per person for dinner.

For comprehensive listings of restaurants By Area, By Price and By Cuisine, and by specific features such as Breakfast, Kid-Friendly, Late-Night and more, see the INDEXES at the back of the book.

12/20 Carroll O'Connor's Place

369 N. Bedford Dr., Beverly Hills 90210;
(310) 273-7585
*American/Continental. Lunch & Dinner
Mon.-Sat., Late Supper Fri.-Sat. Brunch Sun.
All major cards.*

It was about time someone called a spade a spade—this has always been Carroll O'Connor's place. In the 1970s, when it was a clubby, New York–style grill called The Ginger Man, a coterie of prosperous men in suits and ties would gather to knock back a scotch or two, swap talk and sing along with the piano. As the proprietor (and the well-known actor), O'Connor's characteristic geniality kept his clients coming back.

It's still the same sort of civilized, comfortable place today, where patrons immediately lose five years in the glow created by Victorian-style chandeliers, gleaming brass and rich woods. The difference is that Carroll's place is no longer chiefly a bar where you order a steak to go with your scotch. Since renaming the restaurant in 1989, O'Connor has gradually brought it into the present with a full menu of American dishes: in addition to the grill fare (free-range chicken, blackened prime rib, lamb or veal chop), there are fresh-fish offerings and easy pastas. Nothing jars the senses: there are standard appetizers such as calamari and crabcakes, and desserts are homemade and (a little too) solid. We sat on the sidewalk terrace, a rare treat in L.A., and we chose a very good bottle of Shafer Merlot from the mostly Californian wine list. This is also a big spot for entertainment-industry Sunday brunch meetings. Dinner costs $25 to $35 per person.

Carrots

2834 Santa Monica Blvd., Santa Monica 90404; (310) 453-6505
Pacific Rim. Dinner Mon.-Sat. MC, V.

First things first: Carrots is called Carrots not because the restaurant has introduced a new, carrot-intensive cuisine, but because chef Fred Iwasaki and his wife were born in the Year of the Rabbit. Restaurants have been named for stranger reasons than that. There is not, in fact, a single carrot on the menu at Carrots. The chef, an alumnus of Wolfgang Puck's homage to Franco-Chinoiserie, does an admirable job with this unusual genre. The mini-mall dining room serves as an understated backdrop for dishes such as a marvelous salad of rock shrimp, crab and salmon. As befits the Cal-Asian style, the cooking is generally light, though not necessarily lite—portions are generous and flavors stand at attention. Sautéed seafood cakes arrive with a port-wine sauce. You'll do well if you order the grilled salmon with a red-onion butter, the thinly

sliced, perfectly grilled New York steak with a snappy onion sauce or the grilled marinated lamb with a garlic-butter sauce. Dessert is limited to one or two varieties of sorbet and ice cream. Dinner costs about $15 per person.

Castel Bistro

12100 Wilshire Blvd., W.L.A. 90025;
(310) 207-4273
French. Lunch Tues.-Fri., Dinner Tues.-Sat. All major cards.

Here is where talented chef Jean-Pierre Bosc has established his new headquarters. Bosc's most outstanding credit to date is Fennel restaurant, which he turned into a first-rate sophisticated French bistro. He continues the theme here, with a cuisine based on fish and the robust flavors of southern France and Italy. Unfortunately, Castel's decor and ambience are as bistro-like as the Sheraton hotel group is a chain of bed-and-breakfasts. Instead of a cozy, noisy room, you get an enormous, high-ceilinged space with a lot of massive paintings of what appear to be clowns in compromising positions.

We have gone here continually expecting great things from chef Bosc—and though we've eaten well, we've left each time with a feeling of vague dissatisfaction that what we ate was not quite up to Bosc standards. House-smoked salmon is served atop an onion cream astride a crispy, crunchy tart; the same smoked salmon reappears in a sort of inside-out salad, in which warm lentils in a shallot dressing are folded within a wrapper of fish. A terrine of goat cheese, grilled eggplant, Anaheim chiles and olives makes another satisfying starter. There are pastas (try the squid-filled ravioli in a saffron-and-pumpkin sauce), as well as main courses of lamb osso buco served with a small cassoulet, classic rôtisserie chicken (a tad overdone and a bit fatty—but still good) and a house bouillabaise for all of $16.50. Other soup choices have been a bit salty. The wine list, though brief, is a well-chosen range of mostly French and Californian picks, with twelve wines by the glass. Service is extremely solicitous. If only the the space is given a dose of *joie de vivre*, and Bosc can give the food a does of his usual inspiration, we'll be among the first to make it a regular stop. About $35 per person for dinner.

Celestino

236 S. Beverly Dr., Beverly Hills 90212;
(310) 859-8601
Italian. Lunch Mon.-Fri., Dinner nightly. AE, MC, V.

Several years ago, Celestino Drago, a young chef newly arrived from Italy, quickly distinguished himself in the kitchens of Il Giardino and

Chianti Cucina, becoming one of L.A.'s leaders in the authentic-Italian movement and in the process developing an intensely loyal clientele. Naturally, he opened his own restaurant—the eponymous Celestino—and naturally (given the typical nature of the relationship between L.A. chefs and business partners), he later decided to leave, still owning a percentage and his name still on the door. Now he's used the rest of his name and opened Drago in Santa Monica, while Celestino's chef, Eligio Foseca, carries on the work of the master. Foseca prepares everything with Celestino's skill, especially the lobster risotto, the shellfish steeped in a tomato broth (which had us dunking prodigal amounts of bread in it) and the signature spaghetti with seafood in a parchment bag. Foseca has also mastered the dishes from Celestino's beloved Sicily, which are scarce in L.A., despite its several billion Italian restaurants. And desserts, arranged on a rustic pine table in the middle of the dining room, are considerably better than the Italian norm. Service remains gracious in the country-Italian storefront, with its tile floors and white-washed walls hung with modern art. Dinner runs about $40 per person.

 C'est Fan Fan
3360 W. 1st St., Silverlake 90004;
(213) 487-7330
French-Chinese. Lunch Tues.-Fri., Dinner Tues.-Sun. AE, MC, V.

This sublime little gem sits on the site of the late, legendary Lyon and the later, legendary Chabuya, a converted sushi bar with a counter facing a tiny kitchen. Chef Hajime Kaki is Japanese, but he blends French and Chinese in almost equal measures. He's a veteran of both Wolfgang Puck's Chinois on Main and New York's acclaimed China Grill, and the man is a gifted maverick. Kaki is the whole show here—no prep or sous-chefs, and he's quite a showoff. Nothing is prepared in advance; when you order Kaki's revisionist chicken salad, he butchers a whole chicken, complete with head, right in front of you. What a spectacle. Actually, many of his creations are exquisite. Crabmeat crêpes are smooth and sly, with the unexpected addition of cheese, earthy slivers of mushroom and dabs of papaya and raspberry purées. Another favorite here is the simply named Chinese bread, an impossibly puffy pancake filled with chopped meat, mushrooms, vegies, a light touch of hoisin and lots of ginger. Don't miss entrées like Peking duck, infused with garlic and plum sauce, but turn your head, if you're squeamish, during the preparation of the wonderful lobster, drawn and quartered live, a

Japanese tradition called iki-zukuri. Desserts are limited to ice cream, but they are always home-made and superb. A creamy, chunky peach ice cream comes enhanced with cubes of fresh fruit and a squeeze of lime. A great value, especially considering the free cooking lessons. Dinner runs about $25.

12/20 Cha Cha Cha
656 N. Virgil Ave., Silverlake 90004;
(213) 664-7723
Caribbean. Lunch & Dinner daily, Brunch Sun. All major cards.

The black-clad hordes that once posed here have long moved on to such la mode places as Picnic and Opus, and we couldn't be happier about it. Nowadays, this color-washed café on the seedy border of Hollywood and Silverlake is nothing more than a cheerfully exotic Caribbean joint with a relaxed atmosphere, infectious island music on the stereo, and good eats. We quite like the flaky empanadas, the savory chicken-and-black-bean-filled sopes (like tiny tostada cups), the camarones al caribe (shrimp sautéed in butter, garlic and Caribbean spices) and the creamy house flan. The cooking is lively and robustly flavored, and it makes for an interesting change of pace. Dinner will run about $30 per person.

 Champagne Bis
10506 Little Santa Monica Blvd., Century City 90025; (310) 474-6619
French/Californian. Lunch Tues.-Fri., Dinner Tues.-Sun. All major cards.

Champagne was once the province of chef Patrick Healy, long one of our favorite chefs in Los Angeles. His *cuisine du soleil* ("cuisine of the sun") brought Los Angeles self-named "rustic" dishes that we returned to eat again and again.

These days, the restaurant is under his wife Sophie's directorship, who had been running the front of the house with charm. She has kept everything intact, with nary a change in the menu or the space. The chef, a 26-year-old New Yorker named Vaughn York, has been in Champagne's kitchen for two years, and did much of the cooking during Healy's time. He continues to prepare the same menu, divided into four distinct sections: "contemporary California," "spa," "rustic" and "gastronomic," a six-course dinner that changes nightly. The rustic French menu features such specialties as cassoulet, braised veal shank and pan-fried rib-eye steak; the California menu includes fresh, piquant salads and such inventive seafood creations as a layered "cake" of crayfish, eggplant, black olives, onions and bell peppers. We have yet to determine whether Champagne Bis will follow in the dazzling footsteps of its predecessor. Reports so far have been shining, so we'll remain confident that York will uphold the high rating of 16/20 that Champagne acquired in its early days. Dinner for one costs $55 to $75.

12/20 Chan Dara
1511 N. Cahuenga Blvd., Hollywood 90038; (213) 464-8585
11940 W. Pico Blvd., W.L.A. 90066; (310) 479-4461
Thai. Lunch Mon.-Fri., Dinner nightly. AE, MC, V.

These days L.A. hot spots last about as long as it takes to say "*Franco-Japonaise,*" so it is quite remarkable that Chan Dara is still one of the best and most popular Thai restaurants in town. The two small, airy, casual dining rooms are jammed day and night with lively young regulars and more than the occasional celebrity. (Despite its handsome decor, the Larchmont branch is a little less popular and not quite as good as the original.) Typical dishes are done extremely well—a good, crunchy, not-too-sweet mee krob with fresh cilantro; chewy pad Thai noodles; a spicy beef pa nang; and commendable satays. The barbecued chicken is a mainstay, and in recent years the restaurant has added good grilled fresh water shrimp and catfish. The two-starred (for hotness) Thai barbecued sausage could stand some improvement in the taste and texture departments, but it is served salad style with lettuce and cucumber and is dressed in a wonderful ginger-lime concoction. Go for the provocative crab and shrimp curry as well as spicy fried rice with fresh mint and chili. Beer, wine, Thai iced tea and coffee and refreshing Thai lemonade are served. A third branch is in the tiny village of Larchmont (310 N. Larchmont Blvd., 213-467-1052). About $15 to $20 with a beer.

11/20 Chao Praya
6307 Yucca St., Hollywood 90038; (213) 466-6704
Thai. Lunch, Dinner & Late Supper (until 1:30 a.m. Fri.-Sat.) daily. All major cards.

At its worst, the food can be overly greasy and the service impossible. But Chao Praya, one of L.A.'s oldest and most established Thai restaurants, is rarely at its worst. It does most of the Thai standbys quite well—satays, yum yai salad, Napa cabbage soup, Thai fried noodles, mint and chili with shrimp, chicken or pork—and leaves creativity to its newer rivals. The best dish is probably the addictive barbecued chicken, sweet, crunchy and spicy. Fried whole fish with toppings like mushroom, chili sauce, curry sauce, garlic sauce and ginger are sure bets here, and a rather extensive selection of soups are always satisfying.

The once-shabby Hollywood restaurant has been handsomely and dramatically remodeled. It is rumored that the Valley location, in Sherman Oaks, is even better than the original. About $15 per person for dinner.

Le Chardonnay
8284 Melrose Ave., W. Hollywood 90048; (213) 655-8880
French. Lunch Mon.-Fri., Dinner Mon.-Sat. All major cards.

For a while now, Angelenos have seen Le Chardonnay as the bistro of L.A.'s dreams. This one has all the right elements—it's a gorgeous replica of the venerable Vagenende on Paris's boulevard Saint-Germain, an art-nouveau vision of gleaming woodwork and sparkling mirrors; it offers a casual menu rich with words like "kidneys," "garlic" and "lamb" (though many of them are given lighter, Californian interpretations); the waiters wear traditional bistro garb.

It's almost impossible not feel warmth radiating from within—the place smacks of a relaxed evening spent eating highly reliable comfort foods. In one corner, chickens and ducks slowly turn on a tall rotisserie, dripping juices into the pan below. In the rich, amber glow of the lighting, diners look particularly handsome and happy. The regularly changing menu itself is less traditional: most of the dishes have a French base, but regional American or Californian ornamentations. Louisiana crabcakes come with a lemon–mustard seed sauce; salmon is grilled with basil, olive oil and roasted garlic cloves; and roast medallions of venison in an Armagnac sauce are garnished with black peppercorns and accompanied by most unusual pineapple fritters. For the traditionalist, there's always the spit-roasted chicken with pommes frites or the charbroiled New York steak. You'll spend about $50 apiece for dinner.

8/20 Charley Brown's World Famous Malibu Sea Lion
21150 Pacific Coast Hwy., Malibu 90265; (310) 456-2810
American. Lunch & Dinner daily, Brunch Sun. All major cards.

Sunday brunch at the Sea Lion is a many-stationed circus. Tourists, fresh-scrubbed families and second-date couples wander in a calorie-induced daze between the at least ten food stations, making enormous salads; serving themselves yogurt; wideloading their plates with oysters, clams, mussels, lox, raw tuna and herring; asking the cooks-in-waiting to make an omelet, fajitas or pasta; loading up their second plates with barbecued chicken and ribs; and, finally, choosing from trays of leaden desserts and flavored coffees. The appeal is that there's an ocean view from almost every table, and unlimited quantities of food, making up for the mediocre quality. An extra fillip is the choice of mimosas, sparkling wine or orange juice with the fixed-price brunch ($18.99). Recently sold to the Charley Brown's chain by restaurateur-to-the-masses Bob Morris, the Sea Lion serves the exact same chain-chow found at the rest of the Charley Brown's. Why, oh why can't L.A. get its fair share of affordable ocean-view restaurants that bother to serve good cooking? Dinner starts at $25 per person.

12/20 Chartreuse
1909 Wilshire Blvd., Santa Monica 90404; (310) 453-3333
Swiss/Continental. Lunch Mon.-Fri., Dinner Mon.-Sat. AE, MC, V.

Chartreuse might have been named for the oddly medicinal French liqueur, or perhaps simply for a small country house, but it's a charmer no matter how you look at it. Part of a mini restaurant row in Santa Monica, it continues to be one of the best (and only) Swiss eateries in town. Chef Bruno Moeckli loves to showcase his Alpine roots in such dishes as the delicious Roquefort soufflé, crispy potato Rösti topped (parsimoniously) with sour cream and two caviars and salad served with fried Camembert. Beyond that, the menu dashes from lamb curry to roast duck with gooseberries, from risotto with mushrooms and shrimp to a classic entrecôte with a café de Paris sauce. Portions are large and food is filling. Depending on the owner's mood, you may even get a complimentary glass of Chartreuse, an acquired but interesting taste. Dinner is about $30 per person.

12/20 Chasen's
9039 Beverly Blvd., W. Hollywood 90048; (310) 271-2168
Continental. Lunch Tues.-Fri., Dinner Tues.-Sun. All major cards.

Late in 1991, this most venerable of Old Hollywood watering holes decided to open, for the first time, for lunch. And in the process, Chasen's—beloved of the Reagans and the Sinatras—was virtually born again. While the nighttime clientele and staff remain ancient, wrapped in the gossamer threads of Old Money, the daytime Chasen's is a far younger creature, with a suboctogenarian group of servers who actually talk to you about the food. With light streaming into the rear room and patio, it actually turns out to be a pretty restaurant, in a Golden Age of Hollywood way, where the good cooking

of Musso & Frank's and the Pacific Dining Car is given a more sedate setting. There are plenty of modest salads, uncluttered with duck breasts and Maytag blue cheese—in this world, salads are simple affairs with greens and bits of bacon. The chile still isn't on the menu, and it's still surprisingly good. The main courses tend to be larger for lunch than for dinner, served with pilaf and potatoes and such. Come the evening, the Grand Dames and Grand Dudes descend from Bel Air and Brentwood for their carpetbagger steaks and Old Fashioneds. But during the day, there's a spring in the step of those lunching at Chasen's. Even the bartender is a bit friendlier, if begrudgingly so. And yes, it now takes credit cards—a sure sign that the times, they are a-changin'. About $40 per person for dinner.

La Chaumiere
Century Plaza & Towers, 2055 Ave. of the Stars, Century City 90067; (310) 551-3360
French. Lunch Mon.-Fri., Dinner nightly. All major cards.

Is this L.A.'s best-kept dining secret? If so, we're elated to have discovered it, and we still wonder why the Century Plaza veiled this most elegant and distinguished restaurant behind a comfy, modest little name like La Chaumiere ("the thatched cottage"). The rather rural appellation doesn't reflect the majesty and serenity of this semi-rotunda, where it's easy to imagine that you're joining Czar Nicholas for a bite in his private dining room at St. Petersburg's Rose Palace. Alder-wood paneling sets off the abundant crystal, silver and flower arrangements, all in a handsome display of good taste.

With such decor, did the hotel really need to bother with a good chef? Thankfully, the property's general managers, Bernard Agache and Jacque Villeneuve, decided that it was necessary. To maintain the mystery to the end, they called in the most French of the Japanese chefs from Montreal, Canada: Tadashi Katoh. Although he doesn't (yet) appear weekly on "Good Morning America" to reveal the secrets of his Belgian waffles, you should remember his name, for he is one of the most talented chefs we have met lately. His eyes are as sharp as his sharpest knife, and not only does he speak four languages fluently, he also has taught his cuisine to speak pristine French. Can you imagine a Japanese chef doing foie gras in sweet port as perfectly as they do in Périgord? The short, balanced menu is pure enchantment, in ways both small and grand: an ethereal tomato coulis with a touch of basil reminded us, after many a red-sauce disaster, that tomatoes can become a delicacy in expert hands.

We tried the grilled prawns, succulent and crisp and not the slightest bit dehydrated, and chalked them up as one of Katoh's Franco-Japonaise secrets. We were taken to the summits with his lemon-butter sauce accompanying beautifully cooked Mediterranean turbot, even more than with the truffle sauce that surrounded the paupiette of Dover sole. Everything that passes through Katoh's hands is extremely carefully executed (down to the baby vegetables, which are usually more pretty than tasty)—it's nothing astoundingly new, just perfectly done. Katoh has certainly been to the good schools in Japan, but if he had a chance now to rub shoulders with the Bocuses and other French luminaries, he would achieve yet another level of perfection.

The desserts leave some room for improvement. As beautiful as they are to look at, they don't quite measure up to the rest of the show. Once this is taken care of, an evening at La Chaumiere will be superb to the last bite, when the city's high rises and Westwood's Mormon Temple light up and bring the evening to a glorious finish. Dinner costs about $50 per person.

12/20 El Chavo

4441 W. Sunset Blvd., Silverlake 90027;
(213) 664-0871
Mexican. Lunch & Dinner daily. No cards.

Lovely guitar music envelopes you as you grope your way to your table at El Chavo, a commendable, but dark Mexican restaurant with a passionately devoted following. There's barely enough light to read the menu, full of worthwhile dishes from enchiladas to more imaginative creations. Our favorite is the terrific mole sauce, available with tongue or chicken. The poached Sonora chicken, perhaps El Chavo's most popular dish, can be dry, but its saving grace is a delicious, well-balanced sauce of tomato, bacon, onion, olives and chiles. Pork dishes are tender and succulent, but watch out for the fiery pork chile verde. The classics—tostadas, enchiladas, chiles rellenos—are all terrific. The tasty margaritas are automatically poured as doubles. Dinner runs $15 per person.

Chaya Brasserie

8741 Alden Dr., W. Hollywood 90048;
(310) 859-8833
International. Lunch Mon.-Fri., Dinner nightly. AE, MC, V.

This terminally chic place attracts as hip a crowd as it did years ago. Asian waiters sport black-and-white ensembles in a lively but discreet bistro atmosphere; fashionable rock plays on the stereo; walls are hung with pine-framed mirrors at rakish angles; a lush grove of bamboo trees soars to the ceiling in the center of the restaurant. But don't let the L.A. style fool you into thinking that you won't eat well here; quite the opposite is true. Its spiritual ancestor, La Petite Chaya, was one of the first restaurants to combine French and Japanese cuisines, and Chaya Brasserie takes a page from that book, opting for a blissful marriage of Mediterranean and French with mild Asian overtones. Chef Shigefumi Tachibe has a light touch and a talent for exotic combinations that come off as pure and unaffected. Starters include plump pan-fried oysters over Rösti potatoes, succulent and delicate Halibut sashimi bathed in a ginger dressing, spicy shrimp on a bed of savory couscous and escargots cocotte (snails slowly braised in a mini-casserole with chopped mushrooms, swimming in a garlic-parsley butter). Grilled Hawaiian tuna is given a sensuous bite with anchovy butter; veal chop comes with sun-dried blueberries in a red-wine sauce; lobster ravioli is dressed in a light pesto cream sauce. This is a hot late-night spot because of its short but choice supper menu, which, incidentally, includes some of the best fries in town. Brasserie prices, mais non!—a dinner will run at least $50.

Chaya Venice

110 Navy St., Venice 90291;
(310) 396-1179
New American/Mediterranean. Lunch Mon.-Fri., Dinner nightly, Late Supper Mon.-Sat., Brunch Sun. All major cards.

Chaya Venice is a hypermoderne teahouse perched at the very edge of America (on the ground floor of a condo/restaurant/retail complex just south of Main Street's main drag). Seated at a table in this loud, bustling, stylized bistro, especially in one of the booths in the back, you have a sense that you're someplace that's both very L.A. and very otherworldly at once; we'll call it the Spaceship Chaya. If Chaya Brasserie was the natural evolution of the now-defunct Franco-Japonaise pioneer La Petite Chaya, then Chaya Venice (in its first incarnation, at least) moved things along one generation further. In its latest incarnation, though, it has de-evolved—the cuisine has gone from a zen simplification of La Petite Chaya's complexities to a new American/Mediterranean menu that lacks snap. Gone are the elaborate sauces and reductions; they've been replaced with lamb osso buco with white beans, veal osso buco with saffron rice, fried jalapeño fritters, grilled Hawaiian shrimp and so forth. Gone as well are many of the Asian dishes: the sea bass sashimi with a ginger-mustard sauce, the broiled sea eel, the Hawaiian tuna spring rolls. Instead, you can order minestrone, sautéed sea bass or angel hair with tomato and basil. If truth be told, we preferred Chaya Venice when the menu was filled with oddities and eccentricities. Now it's just . . . another good restaurant. About $40 per person for dinner.

Checkers Hotel Dining Room
Checkers Hotel, 535 S. Grand Ave., Downtown 90071; (213) 624-0000
American. Breakfast & Lunch Mon.-Sat., Dinner nightly, Brunch Sun. All major cards.

When chef Thomas Keller was cooking for Checkers Hotel's dining room, he earned quite a following with his dazzling presentations and fine food. New chef William Valentine has since taken the helm, coming from a position as executive sous-chef at Windsor Court in New Orleans, which is quite simply one of the best hotels, with one of the best restaurants, in that city. The cuisine at Checkers is bound to change gradually as Valentine settles in, but when we went to press, we hadn't had enough time to observe the chef in his new post. We'll just say that the menu offered dishes similar to those we had enjoyed before: soft-shell crab roll with spiced cucumber vinaigrette; sauté of foie gras with seared blackberries; an entrée of grilled swordfish with vegetables from Provence (most notably niçoise olives). For main courses, there was a roasted rack of lamb with poppy-seed vinaigrette and garlic couscous, and pan-roasted striped bass with crawfish tails and basmati rice. There are a number of fruit and ice cream desserts, as well as an opera cake and chocolate marquise, but the star is the apple-cranberry strudel with caramel ice cream. The dining room, all muted colors and luxurious fabrics, is as subdued and conservatively elegant as the businesslike diners. Dinner is about $57 per person.

 ## Chez Hélène
267 S. Beverly Dr., Beverly Hills 90212; (310) 276-1558
French. Lunch Mon.-Sat., Dinner nightly. All major cards.

Chez Hélène survived a dicey Venice location for several years, but when owner Micheline Hebert moved her funny little auberge to Beverly Hills, the restaurant deservedly began to thrive. What's intriguing is how utterly old-fashioned this place is. It's reminiscent of the small French bistros we remember from the late '50s, the type of place we lingered in for hours over a good cup of steaming cappuccino. Outside, there's a lot of brick and greenery. Inside, there's polished wood—and a nicely subdued air. Dishes are made for casual dining—simple food perfect for a get-together with old friends. The small menu offers a good cream of tomato soup, a garden-variety French onion soup, escargots de Bourgogne and a trio of quiches: Lorraine, spinach and seafood. The lamb stew is hardy, pungent, musky and solid, the sort of dish found at provincial restaurants across France. Equally filling is the cassoulet, one of the best in Los Angeles. Good desserts, too; a fine bread pudding, a rich chocolate tarte and, naturellement, poires (pears) belle Hélène. Dinner per person, from $25 to $35.

12/20 Chez Jay
1657 Ocean Ave., Santa Monica 90401; (310) 395-1741
American. Lunch Mon.-Fri, Dinner nightly. All major cards.

This legendary refuge for beach bums, writers and artists, now in its venerable 35th year of existence, is like a high-class dive. Sawdust, mirth, mayhem and good food are all orchestrated by an affable adventurer named Jay Fiondella, who keeps the mood going full tilt. Potatoes baked with bananas—Spock's favorite dish in the official Star Trek cookbook—flow out of the kitchen like wine and, despite a rough-and-ready ambience, this is a fine place for thick steak au poivre, shrimp curry and even lobster thermidor. For those in the know there's a secret back room, accessed through a door in the rear of a closet in the restaurant's office. Dinner costs about $30 per person.

 ## Chianti Cucina
7383 Melrose Ave., W. Hollywood 90046; (213) 653-8333
Italian. Lunch Mon.-Sat., Dinner nightly. AE, MC, V.

Cucina began as the baby brother of Chianti, and quickly became a formidable little restaurant with its own loyal following. The visuals are great—as you watch dishes for both restaurants being prepared and hustled off to tables. Most of the right side is the kitchen itself, where chefs perform with a minimum of self-consciousness. The result: a marvelous weekly changing menu on which you'll find lovely small portions of marinated, grilled baby chicken; or beef filets with green peppers; as well as several satisfying pastas and risotti. As befits the best Italian food, simple dishes such as thinly seared tuna, spinach tagliolini and luscious veal chops are offered. A complete dinner costs about $40 per person; a simpler meal of salad, pasta and a glass of wine will run about $20.

Chianti Ristorante
7383 Melrose Ave., W. Hollywood 90046;
(213) 653-8333
Italian. Dinner nightly. AE, MC, V.

Despite the throngs of trendy Melrose mini restaurants, Chianti thankfully has retained a romantic, reserved, old-world atmosphere. Among its best dishes are shrimp and clams in a robust, aromatic tomato-garlic broth, black and white pasta with bay scallops and cream, wild boar chops with grilled porcini and a number of homemade pastas. There are the solid spit-roasted meats and veal dishes that can be difficult to find in these days of carpaccio and arugula, and that feeling of comfort pervades the entire restaurant, from the attentive service to the dark and discreet booth seating. The wine list offers many excellent Italian bottles. Prices are reasonable, considering the timeless elegance: about $50 for a dinner.

China Sea
2130 S. Sawtelle Blvd., Ste. 200, W.L.A.
90025; (310) 473-8948
Chinese. Lunch & Dinner daily. All major cards.

From the street, the second floor China Sea appears to be a clean, generic, well-lit place, the sort of spot you'd imagine to be, well, ordinary. Think again. This is a truly exceptional Chinese restaurant, capable of minor miracles. Witness the wonderful sticky chicken wings, neither too sweet nor too sour, a delightful shrimp confetti salad, tossed jubilantly with bean sprouts, julienned carrots, snow peas, bay shrimp and black sesame seeds, divine barbecued chicken and spareribs. The sybaritic joys of shrimp with honey-glazed walnuts (is there a better combination under Heaven?) are equally unforgettable, and the dish's cousins, double-sauced yin yang shrimp, Szechuan shrimp and salty crispy shrimp, the stuff dreams are made of. We only had the chance to dream about lemon scallops, spicy fried calamari, crispy pepper-skin chicken. But we'll be back. How fine it is, incidentally, to find a place where customers count—and where the food is excellent to boot! Dinner costs about $18.

11/20 Chin Chin
8618 Sunset Blvd., W. Hollywood 90069;
(310) 652-1818
11740 San Vicente Blvd., Brentwood 90049;
(310) 826-2525
Chinese. Lunch & Dinner daily, Late Supper Fri.-Sat. AE, MC, V.

Yuppie dim-sum mania in L.A. started on Sunset Boulevard, at a tiny, noisy, always-jammed sidewalk café called Chin Chin. (If you're claustrophobic, visit the Brentwood branch instead, which is more spacious and less crowded, with a pleasant outdoor patio.) This is Americanized dim sum, and though the quality can be inconsistent and the menu could be more inventive, the food can still be delicious—very fresh Max's noodle soup, good shredded chicken salad, plump potstickers with an addictive cilantro dipping sauce, comforting bao buns, crisp spring rolls and succulent soy-ginger duck. You can have an agreeable light meal for less than $10.

Chinois on Main
2709 Main St., Santa Monica 90405;
(310) 392-9025
Chinese/Eclectic. Lunch Wed.-Fri., Dinner nightly. All major cards.

The chairs are uncomfortable. The tables are too small and jammed together. The noise level is nearly deafening. The prices (appetizers average $16) are among the highest in town. The novelty of the cuisine—Chinese, via Japan, Austria, France and California—begins to feel like déjà vu. Reservations during prime dining hours are as hard to come by as candor on the political campaign trail. But Chinois remains the best of Wolfgang Puck's restaurants. To begin with, it's the one Puck restaurant in which the decor, striking as it is, seems in keeping with the food. More important, the food itself—if no longer quite as dazzling as it once was—remains among the best and most unusual in the city. The menu is wisely divided into two parts: "Chinois classics" (whole sizzling catfish with ginger and ponzu sauce, grilled Mongolian lamb chops, Shanghai lobster risotto with ginger and green onions) and newer dishes (stir-fried lamb with Maui onion rings on a bed of radicchio, lobster tempura in a sweet mustard sauce, charred pork chop with an apple-fennel chutney). Our favorite appetizer on one recent visit featured spicy duck sausage, flecked with chunks of pistachio and coated with a sweet-plum glaze that nicely complemented the tart bite of the sausage. Our favorite main course was a crisp quail, cut into pieces and set in a circle around the plate, the legs, thighs and breast parts alternating with sections of orange and grapefruit, all in a sweet-and-sour star-anise sauce. The clams and mussels with peppered linguine and a garlic–black bean sauce, a blend of several of our favorite tastes—didn't work as well. Neither have

For all the city's newest and best restaurant addresses, look for The Food Paper *(published quarterly by André Gayot/Gault Millau) on newsstands everywhere. Or, call (800) LE BEST 1 for a subscription.*

28

ABSOLUT L.A.

On a turnout along the Coast Highway

just north of Laguna Beach

there's a place where the talk is usually about water.

They call it the Shake Shack.

Perrier. Part of the local color.

the other pastas the kitchen occasionally tries. The wine list, heavy on California selections, is good and varied, the desserts less so. Dinner is about $60 per person.

12/20 El Cholo

1121 S. Western Ave., Mid-Wilshire District (L.A.) 90006; (213) 734-2773
Mexican. Lunch & Dinner daily. AE, MC, V.

El Cholo has been around even longer than El Coyote—since 1927—and is still great fun. The menu is more ambitious than in the days when combination plates were the only real choices, and the food seems better—and homier than ever. Those lively young people are mostly USC students, who love El Cholo for its incredible margaritas and festive atmosphere. But the food is good too: the taco tray, a make-your-own meal of tortillas, chicken, beef, sauces and beans; chicken breasts in flour tortillas with guacamole and zucchini; salsa verde crab enchiladas; and the famous homemade green-corn tamales (from June to September). El Cholo's chicken enchiladas may be the best in town—the sort of dish that native Angelenos yearn for. Dinner, with one of the restaurant's perfect Cuervo Gold margaritas, is about $16 per person.

11/20 Chopstix

7229 Melrose Ave., W. Hollywood 90046; (213) 937-1111
Chinese. Lunch & Dinner daily. D, MC, V.

Chopstix takes the concept of high-tech dim sum and turns it into "win sum dim sum"—complete with "new-wave noodles" and "radical rice." When it opened, it was one of the freshest restaurant concepts in town, and though still good, it's no longer as fresh nor as consistent in quality. The menu begins with a section called Salads for the South Pacific, which includes a very good chicken salad, a Thai shrimp-papaya salad, a lemon-shrimp concoction and peanut-ginger sesame noodles, all of which are good warm-ups for the dim sum to follow. These are not the dim sum you eat with tea in Chinatown, though they're clearly relations. The Southern California potstickers seem familiar until you notice they're filled with chicken and spinach and glazed in orange sauce. Sea bass surprise is loaded with sea bass and mushrooms. The menu flows along in that sort of fashion, from mu shu and stir-fries through noodles, spareribs and Oriental burritos. Chin Chin and Mandarette were the next generation of dim sum when they opened; Chopstix moves things yet further along. It really is dim sum and then sum. And then sum more. Dinner costs about $15.

12/20 Cicada

8478 Melrose Ave., W. Hollywood 90046; (213) 655-5559
French. Lunch Mon.-Fri., Dinner Mon.-Sat. AE, MC, V.

If Cicada is any indication, the '90s will be the decade of the politically correct restaurant. Organic fertilizer is used to grow the organic produce used in the dishes, and the menu describes the "country dishes, heavy sturdy tableware, salad bowls made from the limbs of olive trees" and the "recycled paper/cards and environmentally pure cleansers." All this is illustrative of Cicada's lofty ambition: to be the ultimate '90s restaurant, offering healthful comfort food, moderate prices, no attitude, a pseudo-rustic, vaguely Tuscan decor and intelligent but informal service. And it achieves that in every respect, except, perhaps, with the food.

Chef Jean-François Meteigner, who spent ten years producing haute cuisine at L'Orangerie, doesn't seem as skilled at cooking bistro fare as fancy stuff. The lamb osso buco with oregano and sage turned out to be a dark, dank hunk o' meat that tasted overwhelmingly of allspice. The crispy lobster and leek ravioli was, in fact, mushy on the inside and soggy on the outside. The chocolate flourless cake tasted dusty. We've been more fortunate at lunch, with a lovely salad of jumbo prawns and scallops, given a subtle spark with a bit of cayenne; and a seductive crab-and-lobster bisque (which has been inconsistent at dinner). Even when the food fails, Cicada is a fun place to be, friendly and full of good-looking people, including a respectable number of famous faces drawn by owners Bernie Taupin (Elton John's lyricist) and Stephanie Haymes, who runs the front room with the same perky professionalism that won her such a following at Le Dôme. Dinner costs about $35 per person.

12/20 Il Cielo

9018 Burton Way, Beverly Hills 90211; (310) 276-9990
Italian. Lunch Mon.-Sat., Dinner Mon.-Sat. All major cards.

Il Cielo means "the sky," which is exactly what you see (smog and fog willing) when you look heavenward from the lovely outdoor patio that surrounds this place. It's an oddity of a restaurant, basically a sweet little house plonked down on a wide, immaculately groomed street lined with posh condominiums. Out on the lovely stone patio, water trickles from the mouth of a stone lion; plants run riot through the rear garden; and lovers draw close together. The food is good, in the style of such local favorites as Pane

Caldo, Tuttobene and Chianti Cucina. While sitting under the stars (and usually next to a few), you can eat carpaccio with bits of white truffle and shavings of Parmesan, smoked scamorza cheese with baked eggplant, baby frogs' legs grilled with shallots and garlic, plump shrimp cavorting in risotto blackened with squid ink, lobster grilled with garlic and lemon, and filet mignon with some mouthwateringly savory spinach. In other words, good, honest Italian cooking, served in a setting that's perfect for people who either are in love or would like to be in love by evening's end. About $35 apiece for dinner.

Citrus
6703 Melrose Ave., Melrose-La Brea District (L.A.) 90038; (213) 857-0034
French. Lunch Mon.-Fri., Dinner Mon.-Sat. All major cards.

To know the true Citrus is to know that it's actually two restaurants in one. One is calm and comfortable inside, the other is a noisy and frenzied scene outside on the large covered patio, where you have a view of the kitchen and where you can see and be seen by the other people who want to see and be seen. And in a deeper sense, the kitchen actually serves two restaurants, too—one merely very, very good, and one truly divine—but you can order from either no matter where you sit. You can either order straight off the menu, or you can skip the menu and simply ask chef Michel Richard (or his talented chef de cuisine, Alain Giraud) to make whatever they feel like making. Given a free hand, they will dazzle you. After more than five years of success, in which time chef Richard has gained enormous celebrity and committed himself to numerous other projects (among them the Santa Barbara restaurant, Citronelle, and a growing number of Broadway Delis), Citrus still serves some of the best, most creative food in all of Los Angeles.

The merely very, very good Citrus offers a seasonally changing menu. From a recent winter menu, for example, you could have ordered a hearty corn chowder or a delicate salmon terrine, followed by properly undercooked swordfish with lentils vinaigrette, or duck breast with couscous and figs, or venison with a red wine–celery sauce. Then, for dessert (and remember that Richard began his career as a pastry chef) you could have ordered the world's best crème brûlée. Or a chocolate cup with orange semolina mousse. Or a lemon tart. Or a carmelized apple tart with cheesecake ice cream.

But Richard and Giraud grow weary of cooking the same dishes all the time—even the restaurant's marvelous signature dish, the

sautéed scallops with deep-fried Maui onion rings. Which brings us to the "second" Citrus: the "off-the-menu" Citrus. Citrus has a separate "gourmet menu" every day for anyone who wants it, but better still, just tell your waiter to leave your meal in the hands of the chef. If Richard is off tending to one of his other enterprises (which he's doing fairly often these days), don't hesitate to ask Alain Giraud. His cooking isn't quite the epiphany that Richard's is, but he has absorbed a great deal of the master's skill, and you will eat very well indeed at his table.

A recent lunch ordered in this fashion began with a single strip of pepper-cured gravlax and a single, perfect oyster in a cucumber gelée. Then, lobster cannelloni, a wide band of black-and-white striped pasta wrapped around chunks of lobster, served in a simple but spectacular sauce of olive oil, chives and bits of crab, all slightly flavored and colored to a faint roseate hue with, of all things, beet juice. Next came one of the best foie gras preparations we've ever had, served on a bed of creamy polenta, a perfect backdrop for the rich, velvety foie gras. The "main course"—an oxtail gratin, the meat surrounded not by potatoes but by macaroni—was robust and tasty. We had barely recovered when a remarkable dessert arrived: an apple napoleon in which, instead of flaky pastry, paper-thin slices of apple were the "leaves" layered between the filling. The leaves were sweet and crisp to the point of being brittle, layered with a softer filling of apple chunks and whipped cream. Those six courses cost $65. The wine list at Citrus has improved considerably in recent years, but as with most restaurants these days, it has few older vintages; only eight of the almost 200 selections are dated before 1980. But there's an intelligent collection of young California Chardonnays and Cabernets, two dozen French Bordeaux and a few Italian bottles. Dinner (not including wine), if you order from the menu, can cost a very reasonable $50 or a well-spent $70.

City Restaurant
180 S. La Brea Ave., Melrose-La Brea District (L.A.) 90036; (213) 938-2155
International/Eclectic. Lunch Mon.-Sat., Dinner nightly, Brunch Sat.-Sun., Late Supper Fri.-Sat. All major cards.

It would be fair to say that the Restaurant Row–ification of La Brea began half a decade ago with City Restaurant. Opened by Susan Feniger and Mary Sue Milliken (who also run the Border Grill), City was, and is, one of the first restaurants to explore the Pan-Pacific boundaries of what's sometimes referred to as Cal-Asian cooking. In this massive, gray-concrete postmodernist (or prefuturist, or whatever the heck it is) warehouse, you can watch the cooks at work in the kitchen via a TV monitor in the bar. In the dining room, you'll find red-pepper flakes and cumin seeds as seasonings on every table, along with a menu so eclectic the cuisine can only be described as City Cuisine (the name of the house cookbook), for any other attempt to describe it would fall ludicrously short.

Even the simplest of dishes can be sublime. Consider the small appetizer of grapefruit and avocado slices with a honey, lime and sour cream dressing; you've never tasted better grapefruit and avocado. The potato pancakes are nothing short of awe-inspiring: shredded white and sweet potatoes are griddled and served with chunky applesauce and crème fraîche—they're so crisp on the outside that biting into one is like breaking the top of a crème brûlée. There's Parmesan-cream gnocchi, grilled tofu with soba noodles, Thai red curry duck, roast salmon in salsa verde and a grilled lamb chops with a warm ratatouille. At Saturday brunch you can order what may be the best eggs Benedict in town, served on a puffy brioche with roast pork and an orange-flavored hollandaise. The smoked fish (smoked in-house) with cream cheese, black bread and a potato-onion salad puts your average bagel with a schmear to shame. And the desserts are deservedly legendary. About $45 per person for dinner.

12/20 The Clay Pit
Chapman Market, 3465 W. 6th St.,
Mid-Wilshire District (L.A.) 90005;
(213) 382-6300
Indian. Lunch & Dinner daily. All major cards.
We were delighted to discover this friendly Indian indoor-outdoor café tucked away in a restored 1920s marketplace among mid-Wilshire's office buildings. On a warm summer evening, it's quite fine to sit on this lovely brick courtyard, listening to the splashing fountains and exploring the cuisine of India. The standards are given their due respect: garlic naan, irresistible kulcha bread stuffed with onion and herbs, pakoras (thick slices of fried mild homemade cheese sandwiching a spicy chile-herb blend), staggeringly rich spinach-and-cheese sag paneer and all sorts of mesquite-broiled tandoori dishes (succulent baby rack of lamb, tuna with curry sauce, chicken finished in a fiery fresh tomato sauce). Purists can finish with one of the cloyingly sweet milk-based desserts, but we prefer to sip our Indian beer and savor the night air. About $15 per person.

12/20 Coley's Place
5035 W. Slauson Ave., Ladera Heights
90056; (213) 291-7474
Jamaican. Lunch & Dinner Mon.-Sat. AE, MC, V.
Mysteriously, there aren't many restaurants with cloth napkins and good service in Ladera Heights, the upscale, predominately black neighborhood northeast of LAX. But now Coley's has come to fill the void with an admirable Creole-tinged Jamaican cuisine. Though located in a sterile mini-mall, the place exudes warmth and personality, from Veda Coley's gracious greeting to the softly lit interior. In his crisp chef's whites, Don Coley makes regular rounds, making sure his prosperous clients are happy. They are. Seafood is a strong suit, notably the extraordinary shrimp St. James: lots of tender shrimp and okra swimming in a subtly spicy, barely sweet coconut-cream sauce. Conch fritters are as crisp and light as tempura, and just as addictive. Delicious Jamaican patties are stuffed with beef and shrimp. The chicken Lockerton, a huge, deep-fried, banana-stuffed chicken breast, is the antithesis of nouvelle cuisine, but it tastes great. And the peach cobbler is pure nostalgia, sweet and delicious. Dinner runs $25 to $30 per person.

11/20 Columbia Bar & Grill
1448 N. Gower St., Hollywood 90028;
(213) 461-8800
American. Lunch Mon.-Fri., Dinner Mon.-Sat. AE, MC, V.
Not long ago this Hollywood hangout attracted press attention and lots of giggles when a hot-headed manager sent out a letter to prominent Paramount TV producers, accusing their staffs of stealing furniture and carelessly strewing mints about the bar. This typifies the Columbia Bar & Grill—it wants so badly to be the Musso & Frank's of our age but can't get it quite right. Owner Wayne Rogers (of "MASH" fame) built a handsome American spot in a restaurant-poor area near Paramount, complete with a booth-lined bar, brick patio and a user-friendly menu stocked with Caesar salads and crabcakes. Its comfort, convenience and fairly consistent food made it a popular spot for B-grade lunch meetings, TV-show wrap parties and after-work kibbutzing. But the Columbia is never as good as everyone wishes it were—the pastas, grilled fish, steaks and such are only average, and the atmosphere lacks that indescribable aura that all great hangouts have. Although some of the offended Paramount workers still stop in after work, it's doubtful they'll ever turn this place into a Hollywood legend. About $15 per person for lunch and $35 for dinner.

7/20   El Coyote

7313 Beverly Blvd., Melrose-La Brea District
(L.A.) 90036; (213) 939-2255
Mexican. Lunch & Dinner daily. MC, V.

Some Mexican restaurants are home to interesting regional cooking and home cooking. Others, such as El Coyote, churn out countless gallons of refried beans and rice laden with glutinous orange cheese. El Coyote is hugely successful at its business: some 1,000 people a day pass through these worn doors, bent on having a good time and a very cheap dinner, and they get both. But those bent on finding good food are well advised to pass by El Coyote's overflowing combination plates, and its tostadas piled with mountains of canned peas and carrots. The decor combines the fake-peeling-plaster look with kitschy Mexican folk art. So many people have a fondness for this thoroughly unpretentious landmark, including fraternities, sororities, Hollywood rockers, out-of-towners and cheap dates, that it will always do a roaring business. A huge dinner will set you back $5 to $10 apiece.

12/20   I Cugini

1501 Ocean Ave., Santa Monica 90401;
(310) 451-4595
*Italian. Lunch & Dinner daily, Late Supper
Fri.-Sat. All major cards.*

I Cugini is a creation of the same people who brought us Ocean Avenue Seafood, The Water Grill and Long Beach's 555 East and the Pine Avenue Grill. And like their other restaurants, this is first and foremost one hot-looking joint. It sits on a major piece of prime Santa Monica real estate. Outside is a fine patio that offers a view (past the homeless people in the park across the street) of the ocean behind a squall of palm trees. Inside is an extraordinary dining room rife with detail, from the walls painted with picaresque scenes of city life to the wooden chairs painted with *faux* cracks. A good deal of deep frying goes on in the kitchen, in dishes like the fried zucchini flowers filled with fontina cheese and the fritto misto di pesce, a fry of calamari, cod and smelt. The thin, crisp pizzas may be the best dishes here—try the Napoletana model, with marinated tuna and anchovies. Take note of the house obsession with things smoked: smoked mozzarella, smoked prosciutto and so forth. Bowtie pasta with smoked prosciutto, for instance, was also supposed to include porcini mushrooms. We could see the porcini, but we couldn't taste even a hint of them, so overwhelming was the smoked flavor. Still, this hearty Tuscan food will satisfy more often than not. Dinner costs about $30 per person.

For a complete guide to our restaurant ranking system, plus a Toque Tally listing restaurants by rating from highest to lowest, see "About the Restaurants" in the Introduction chapter.

12/20   Cynthia's

8370 W. 3rd St., W. Hollywood 90048;
(213) 658-7851
American/Californian. Lunch Mon.-Fri., Dinner nightly, Brunch Sun. AE, MC, V.

The quintessential neighborhood bistro, Cynthia's is an offshoot of Cynthia Hirsch's adjacent catering company, which keeps many a film crew well fed. Her movie-catering business explains the menu's eclectism: figure-conscious actors and producers can nibble on the niçoise salad with seared ahi tuna, while hard-working grips and stuntmen can refuel with a homey slab of meatloaf. The tiny storefront is given a bit of elegance with candlelight and impressive art-for-sale, but you come here for the tasty, copiously served food, fair prices and Hirsch's gregarious good cheer. Try the thick, peppery corn chower, the crisp fried chicken, the lighter-than-it-looks slab of pesto lasagne and the seriously caloric chocolate-mousse cake; the applesauce accompanying the roast pork is the apple-pie filling of our dreams. A few dishes have more heft than taste, but for the most part this is great home cooking for the '90s at '70s prices. You'd best share the appetizer or dessert course, or both; if you do, you'll spend less than $20 per person.

12/20   Daily Grill

11677 San Vicente Blvd., Brentwood 90049;
(310) 442-0044
Beverly Connection, 100 N. La Cienega
Blvd., W. Hollywood 90048; (310) 659-3100
*American. Lunch & Dinner daily, Late Supper
Fri.-Sat., Brunch Sat.-Sun. AE, MC, V.*

The Daily Grill, now a major chain, sprung full-blown from The Grill in Beverly Hills. Here you can find some of the city's finest steaks and chops, and though prices can be very high for what you get, they're dramatically lower than those charged at the Daily Grill's cousin in Beverly Hills. The only trade-off is in the style, which here is casual, noisy and hectic. The menu is a virtual Smithsonian of Great American Dishes: linguine and clams, mushroom-barley soup, shrimp Louie, Joe's Special, chicken pot pie, calf's liver with bacon and onions, steamed spinach, potatoes Lyonnaise, potatoes O'Brien, tapioca pie. An order of the fine Caesar salad followed by the broiled garlic half chicken is comforting enough to make you forget that deal you've just blown. A dinner costs less than $20.

12/20 Dan Tana's

9071 Santa Monica Blvd., W. Hollywood
90069; (310) 275-9444
Italian. Dinner & Late Supper nightly. AE, D, MC, V.

Clubbiness has always been considered a high virtue in restaurants, especially the dark, intimate, male sort of clubiness that allows celebrities to conduct their affairs with discretion. This is exactly what makes Dan Tana's tick. It also happens to be one of the better New York–style Italian restaurants in town, and has been for about twenty years. Most of the celebs come for tried-and-true dishes like spaghetti with meatballs, mostaccioli, ravioli with meat sauce, veal saltimbocca, veal piccata, shrimp fra diavolo, chicken cacciatore, and to chew the fat with Dan Tana himself, from the Slavic side of the Adriatic, it's true, but still the undisputed master of old-style Hollywood schmoozing. Dinner costs around $40 per person.

12/20 Da Pasquale

9749 Little Santa Monica Blvd., Beverly Hills
90210; (310) 859-3884
Italian. Lunch & Dinner Mon.-Sat. AE, MC, V.

At one time, Pasquale was the pizza chef at Angeli. Then he set up his parents in Atwater at a wonderful little pizza-and-pasta café called Osteria Nonni. His third venture in the very heart of Beverly Hills began as a tiny storefront, then doubled in size when the storefront next door became available. It's still small, and it's still continually packed. Service is pokey—the staff spends a lot of time chatting with customers and with each other. In the classic trattoria tradition, this is not a restaurant to go to if you're in a big rush. But it is a fine place to go for some of the happiest Italian food in town. The menu is simple: there's a pizzaesque focaccia-of-the-day and a half dozen calzones, filled variously with mozzarella, ricotta, artichokes, eggplant, sausage, goat cheese, spinach, prosciutto, Parmesan, olives and so forth. There are a handful of salads and a bunch of good pastas; don't miss the linguine with fresh tomatoes, dried ricotta (which tastes amazingly like feta), sun-dried tomatoes, radicchio, basil and lots of garlic. About $20 apiece for a casual but delicious dinner.

David Slay's La Veranda

225 S. Beverly Dr., Beverly Hills 90212;
(310) 274-7246
Californian/Italian. Lunch Mon.-Fri., Dinner nightly. All major cards.

When someone leaves behind successful restaurants in St. Louis and comes to Beverly Hills to show us Angelenos a thing or two about California cuisine—well, lunacy is certainly too tame a word. But if David Slay is a lunatic, we'll commit ourselves to his asylum any day. For this Missourian has brought café-lined South Beverly Drive one of its best restaurants, an extremely enjoyable American bistro for the '90s that only seems to get better. It's not an inexpensive place, but given the appeal of the surroundings, the quality of the cooking and the warmth and intelligence of the waiters, it's an excellent value.

Slay, who was raised in the restaurant business in St. Louis, studied with Gérard Vié at Les Trois Marches in Versailles and came home to open and run a succession of restaurants. Then, in 1991, Slay and his wife, Gale, who runs the front room, set off for Beverly Hills. Their place is comtemporary but not harsh, with cream-colored walls, simple black chairs, effective lighting and tasteful modern art (including a great Garbo portrait). The culinary style is Californian/Italian—fashionable, perhaps, but not shallow and crowd-following. For starters, don't neglect to order the feathery deep-fried spinach tossed with lemon and Parmesan. Entrées bring such good things as flawless calf's liver with caramelized onions, prosciutto and mushrooms, or baked chicken with whole garlic, herbs and an oregano vinaigrette, which is surely the Sunday chicken dinner served in heaven. And for once, the chocolate-walnut tart with caramel sauce isn't an overly sugary dressed-up candy bar. Plan on spending $30 per person for dinner.

11/20 DC3

2800 Donald Douglas Loop North, Santa Monica Airport, Santa Monica 90405;
(310) 399-2323
American. Lunch Tues.-Fri., Dinner Tues.-Sat., Brunch Sun. All major cards.

Take a unique setting (the runway of an airport), have major contemporary American artist Charles Arnoldi act as designer, have a finger on the Zeitgeist of a fickle, concerned-with-appearances showbiz town, add one savvy restaurateur and *voila!* You should be ready for take-off, right? Well, not quite. True, DC3's location is dramatic, and the bold architecture and interiors are breathtaking. The food, however, just seems too darn expensive for what it is: simple American fare such as grilled steaks and fish, oysters, salads and so on. Added to that, the restaurant started to charge admission to the bar on the weekends, putting off even the crowd of ponytailed guys and tiny-black-skirted gals. However, well-known owner Bruce Marder (who also masterminded West Beach Café and Rebecca's and who has a hand in the Broadway Deli) should be given credit for being one of the progenitors of the hip, slick L.A. eatery. Dinner runs about $45 per person.

10/20 Delmonico's Seafood Grille
9320 W. Pico Blvd., W.L.A. 90035;
(310) 550-7737
Seafood. Lunch Mon.-Fri., Dinner nightly. All major cards.

Named for the legendary robber-baron watering hole in turn-of-the-century New York, Delmonico's is a California incarnation of its namesake, serving as a good, functional seafood restaurant in a city conspicuously lacking in good seafood. The enormous space is made more intimate with dividers and banquettes. The menu is, in truth, more Italianate grill than seafood house—one section deals with pastas, another concentrates on steaks and chops, and a third lists such specialties as osso buco, paillard de veau (grilled veal scallop) and grilled quail. We have long wanted to come here and order such venerable seafood classics as Maryland she-crab soup or Florida stone-crab claws, but they are not, unfortunately, offered at Delmonico's. Meantime, what *is* offered suffices: Boston clam chowder, various grilled fish and pan-sautés and a fine rainbow trout with oyster stuffing. Two-pound Maine lobster, nicely broiled is reasonably priced here, and there is a good wine list. Dinner should range from $25 to $35 per person.

Diaghilev at Bel Age Hotel
Bel Age Hotel, 1020 N. San Vicente Blvd., W. Hollywood 90069; (310) 854-1111
French/Russian. Dinner Tues.-Sat. All major cards.

Sergey Diaghilev, a Russian ballet impresario known for discovering new artistic talents in the early twentieth century, spent many years in Paris persuading eminent painters and composers to work for the Ballet Russe. This explains Diaghilev's menu, which combines traditional Russian dishes with French influences. Shaslik Caucasian, traditionally made with lamb, is here prepared with venison. Chicken Kiev has a non-traditional (but undeniably delicious) truffle sauce. Borscht is served hot with red beets and cold with yellow beets and chives; both are successful interpretations of the classic. As befits an elegant Franco-Russian restaurant, there is an extensive caviar menu (ranging in price from $40 to $100 for a serving), to be paired with one of the chilled flavored vodkas, brought to the table in decanters. In addition to its culinary excellence, Diaghilev is host to Emanuil Sheynkman, considered the foremost balalaika player in the

western world, and his wife, who accompanies him on the piano. Diaghilev would have approved of this dramatically elegant room—mirrors, flowers, enveloping banquettes, paintings from some of Diaghilev's peers—and the opulent desserts, particularly the chocolate confections. A memorable spot for a special occasion. Dinner starts at $45 per person.

10/20 La Dolce Vita
9785 Santa Monica Blvd., Beverly Hills 90210; (310) 278-1845
Italian. Dinner Mon.-Sat. All major cards.

No one really goes to old-fashioned restaurants like this just for the food. Rather, Beverly Hills matrons and yesterday's celebrities show up here to be coddled and cared for. Therefore, service is delightfully unctuous, in a room thick with curved leather banquettes. But everyone feels comfortable here—this is home cooking for people who don't have to cook, and at prices that can be staggering. There are no surprises on this menu, which is exactly how the crowd here likes it—stuffed mushrooms, baked clams, minestrone, veal piccata, veal marsala, spaghetti carbonara, linguine with clams. Steak Sinatra, made with green peppers, pretty much defines the heavy-handed style. A dinner costs about $45.

Le Dôme
8720 Sunset Blvd., W. Hollywood 90069; (310) 659-6919
French. Lunch Mon.-Fri., Dinner & Late Supper Mon.-Sat. All major cards.

Despite the fickleness of the movers and shakers in this town, Le Dôme—practically considered an eminence grise because of having survived for almost ten years—has maintained its star-studded clientele and sterling reputation. The rooms have been redecorated to advantage, the lighting is more flattering than ever, and service is both professional and fair, though celebs are hardly ignored. The crowd is pretty, polished and powerful, and surprise (!), the kitchen turns out remarkably good bistro fare. Stars and lunching ladies opt for the luxurious warm-duck salad on lightly dressed curly endive, or the mix of toss of Belgian endive, mâche and beets in a lemon-mustard dressing. Steamed pink snapper, sautéed rabbit and grilled free-range chicken, as well as more substantial dishes such as grilled calf's liver, roast leg of Sonoma lamb and nigh-unto-perfect osso buco are solid examples of gourmandise. One joy of Le Dôme is that your great uncle can get a hefty order of steamed pig's knuckle with sauerkraut and you can nibble on Hawaiian tuna sashimi or a spinach salad with smoked salmon and trout—and you'll both have trouble finding fault with your meal. Desserts are still wickedly good, particularly the creamy, puckery lemon tart and the devour-every-crumb, warm caramelized apple tart. One added plus here is the people-watching—if you pay close enough attention, you're sure to pick up some really juicy gossip. Lunch costs about $20; dinner runs $35 or more per person.

12/20 Dominick's
8715 Beverly Blvd., W. Hollywood 90048; (310) 657-8314
American. Dinner Mon.-Sat. All major cards.

For decades, this discreet joint didn't need mentions in *Daily Variety* to keep its handful of tables full; the intensely loyal clientele loved the smoky atmosphere and no-frills fare. But a while back a foolish prettying-up job was undertaken, and the old customers recoiled in horror. Now they're being welcomed back by new owner Lynne Giler, a devoted longtime customer who put it back the way it was. It's still tiny, but there's plenty of privacy in the roomy leather booths to trade Mike Ovitz gossip. The bar's a proper bar—all you'll notice is your solid martini, not some conspicuous design statement. And the jukebox is an old one, stocked with the Andrews Sisters and Duke Ellington. Dominick's is so comfortable, so full of the ghosts of old L.A., that it soothes spirits sorely tried by scene dining. The menu soothes, too: sharp Caesar salad, a hilariously dated house salad with cubes of cheese and salami, steaks, tasty lamb chops with mint jelly, homey mashed potatoes, tasteless creamed spinach and a few well-prepared, more contemporary seafood specials. Far less soothing are the prices: about $45 each for dinner.

Drago
2628 Wilshire Blvd., Santa Monica 90403; (310) 828-1585
Italian. Lunch Mon.-Fri., Dinner nightly. All major cards.

We aren't sure what Celestino Drago's middle name is, but we hope it's a colorful one so that he can use it for his next restaurant. His first, Beverly Hills's Celestino, still bears his Christian name, and now this new Santa Monican honors the family name. Though he reportedly still owns a piece of Celestino (which continues serving this accomplished Italian chef's original dishes), Drago is now devoting himself lock, stock and sauté pan to his new place. Drago's menu embraces the earthy joys of Italian cooking, combining the rustic, rarely seen dishes of his beloved Sicily with some of the elegant creations from his

last place (like the seafood and spaghetti baked in parchment). You'll find lots of very similar dishes: cannellini beans with tuna, several kinds of carpaccio, various pastas, risotto with seafood or with leeks, grilled salmon or veal chops, roasted baby lamb or quail. Surprisingly, some dishes were better at Celestino in his absence; at Drago, a bit of blandness was evident in the beef-and-lobster carpaccio with a mâche salad and the swordfish with caponata. Less country-style than Celestino, Drago's large dining room is sophisticated: chairs shrouded in white fabric, an elegant wine cellar whose glass walls reveal the contents of a good wine list, and a small bar in front. Celestino regularly emerges from the kitchen to sit with old friends full of congratulations. These congratulations are deserved, but comparisons to his former restaurant will continue to be made until Celestino introduces some new dishes that reflect the innovative spirit that first brought him acclaim. Dinner costs about $40 per person.

12/20 Duplex
1930 Hillhurst Ave., Los Feliz 90027; (213) 663-2430
Californian. Lunch Tues.-Fri., Dinner Tues.-Sun. All major cards.

In L.A.'s pantheon of restaurants, there are seven major types: High Showbiz (i.e., Spago), Low Showbiz (Barsac Brasserie), Gourmet (Patina), Old Standby (Lawry's), Young Hipster (Authentic Café), Neighborhood (Trattoria Farfalla) and Ethnic (Jitlada). Duplex is none of the above, which might explain its struggle to survive these last four years. It's too far east to be Showbiz, too unpretentious to be Gourmet, too ambitious to be Neighborhood, too subdued to be Young Hipster. It calls itself an Urban Roadhouse, which translates as a contemporary American restaurant in quietly stylish Los Feliz.

The outside is painted a homely pale green, and the soaring, austere lines of the interior (built to house La Petite Chaya) have been softened a little with candlelight and old wooden furniture. The chef is one Mark Carter, formerly the pastry chef at Bernard's at the Biltmore during its glory days, which implies that he knows a tart from a parfait. And indeed he does—the desserts are all worth their calories. The rest of the food has its ups and downs; our last few meals were mostly up. We've never been let down by the soup; we still love the crafty appetizer of tea-smoked chicken with a spiced-noodle pancake and the very tender veal steak with lots of thyme. Don't miss one of the many unusual iced teas. Dinner runs about $20 apiece.

10/20 Dynasty Room at Westwood Marquis Hotel

930 Hilgard Ave., Westwood 90024;
(310) 208-8765
Continental. Dinner nightly. All major cards.

Given the wealth of other options, Angelenos rarely eat in hotel dining rooms. And there's good reason for that—few have distinguished themselves from the pack. The Dynasty Room is part of that undistinguished pack. Tucked into the elegant Westwood Marquis near UCLA, it serves as a refuge for well-to-do tourists and single businesspeople who are uneasy venturing out into the L.A. night. It also acts as a safe house for nearby residents entertaining visiting relatives. Quiet and subtly attractive, the Dynasty Room serves expensive old standards brought up-to-date with Asian noodles here or a sprig of rosemary there. We haven't tried anything that sent us reeling with joy, but it's always been very pleasant, aided by the most cordial of staffs. Dinner costs $40 or so per person.

East India Grill

345 N. La Brea Ave., Melrose-La Brea District (L.A.) 90046; (213) 936-8844
Indian. Lunch & Dinner daily. MC, V.

The East India Grill is the creation of Sumant Pardal, who (along with the folks at the Bombay Café) is reshaping L.A.'s perception of Indian food. Outside the high-tech café is a small, pleasant patio, where you can wait for a table while nibbling on aloo papri chat, a sort of Indian potato salad served atop small crackers; it's as good as any potato salad we've ever tasted. The cuisine is largely built around small dishes—no meal would be complete without orders of potato-filled samosas, curried mussels, superbly crisp calamari or the pizzalike kulchas (oven-baked naan) topped with garlic and tomatoes, or tamarind and ginger, or mango and spinach. Pardal gets adventurous with the lobster johl, in which a broiled lobster tail is annointed with a balm of garlic, cilantro and chili, and the lamb (or chicken) kebab cooked in a fascinating yogurt and cashew marinade. The daily buffet lunch ($6.95 on weekdays and $9.95 on weekends) is a real treat, a series of bowls and warming trays filled with all sorts of wonderful things. Expect to spend $15 per person for dinner.

12/20 Emilio's

6602 Melrose Ave., Melrose-La Brea District (L.A.) 90038; (213) 935-4922
Italian. Lunch Mon.-Fri., Dinner nightly, Brunch Sun. All major cards.

Rome has Alfredo's, New York has Mama Leone's and L.A. has Emilio's, a monument to high camp where the food is actually edible. Ambience is another story. If the people who built the Madonna Inn turned their attention to constructing Italian restaurants, the finished product would probably look very much like Emilio's. The place, which sits on the eastern edge of the hyper-trendy section of Melrose, is pure Fellini, with fountains gurgling colored waters, garish oils of rustic scenes lining the walls and wrought iron punctuating the whole affair. At the heart of it all is Emilio himself, an effusive *paesano* who used to run Jack Warner's private dining room at Warner Bros. He is apt to appear in a white suit and a fire-engine-red shirt. The man even plays the concertina. As expected, this menu is encyclopedic and, apparently, overwhelming to the kitchen. You want it, you got it: osso buco, roast suckling pig, veal pappagallo, and it may even be good. Sundays, there is a gargantuan buffet dinner. Dinner costs about $35 per person.

Empress Pavilion

988 N. Hill St., Chinatown (L.A.) 90012;
(213) 617-9898
Chinese. Dim Sum, Lunch & Dinner daily. All major cards.

The exceedingly ornate and exceptionally fine Empress Pavilion would seem more at home on Hong Kong's Nathan Road; it's about the most solid performer Los Angeles' Chinatown has. Like most Hong Kong–style restaurants, this place is awesomely large, with an assortment of sliding walls that open to easily accommodate a total of 500 diners. Half the restaurant is reserved for open seating, making it one of the biggest Chinese restaurants in town. Despite the volume of business here, the food can be miraculous and thanks to a complex network of runners and servers, dishes come zooming across the room sizzling and steaming.

In traditional Hong Kong style, there are 175 regular dishes to choose from, some of the best of which are listed as "Gourmet Selections" and "Mandarin Szechuan Specialties." No meal here should be without the fabulous sautéed prawns with honey-glazed walnuts, not just for the walnuts, which are a delightful little dessert tossed into the middle of the meal, but for the prawns, which are both plump and perfectly cooked—tender but solid, without a hint of rubberiness. Fried prawns in lemon sauce—perfect prawns with an understated lemon sauce—are another hit. Then there is the well-traveled shrimp and chicken with black-bean sauce, at the Empress, an oeuvre to be remembered. We wholeheartedly suggest you order the Maine lobster or the Dungeness crab (both cooked however you wish), served in heaping portions, more than you'd ever expect and expertly chopped. Among the unusual desserts, consider honeydew melon in tapioca cream or the walnut purée, a souplike delight. A superb dinner can be had for $20.

12/20 Engine Co. No. 28

644 S. Figueroa St., Downtown (L.A.)
90017; (213) 624-6996
American. Lunch Mon.-Fri., Dinner Mon.-Sat. All major cards.

Saturday night in downtown L.A., and all signs of life have vanished. We drive the Metrorail-mangled streets, lit by the wan glow of empty office-building lobbies. Maybe there's no hope down here. But then we walk into Engine Co. No. 28, a humble brick building among the downtown's charmless mass of glass-and-granite towers. Shades of old San Francisco. From the soaring, ornate tin ceiling to a string of cubbyhole booths with burnished wood and handsome upholstery, we've actually unearthed, well, a landmark. The music in here is landmark, too—Billie Holiday, Frank Sinatra—and every booth is stocked with well-dressed business types, speaking in controlled whispers. It took years to restore this 1912-vintage firehouse (the last one built to handle horse-drawn trucks), and the care and planning is evident. Decor is well-mannered, the wine list superb and the service thoughtful. Food may not be the best in town, but much of it is delicious: chewy grilled garlic bread, thin, perfect French fries, fat, juicy cheeseburgers on thinly sliced sourdough bread, first-rate pan-fried crabcakes and more. The whisky-fennel sausages, juicy and mildly seasoned, come with some of the best red cabbage ever. Pass on the bitter Firehouse chile, humdrum smoked salmon, massive, too-dry grilled pork chop or gloppy rice pudding. But that's okay—a dessert like the exquisite chocolate layer cake will keep us coming back until Blade Runner becomes a reality. Dinner runs $25 to $35.

10/20 Epicentre

200 S. Hill St., Downtown (L.A.) 90012;
(213) 625-0000
Californian. Breakfast & Lunch Mon.-Fri., Dinner Mon.-Sat., Brunch Sun. All major cards.

For those unfamiliar with the language of earthquake country, an epicenter is the point on the earth's surface that sits directly above the center of an earthquake. The Japanese, not unfamiliar with earthquakes, apparently figured that any culture that invented Disneyland is a sucker for themes, and opened this restaurant in the newly built Kawada Hotel. Tempting fate (and jokes), the decor tries to simulate post-quake

chasms in concrete panels, and the menu contains dishes that use earthquake buzzwords. "Epitizers" include "San Andreas Soup" and "Epi Salad." The "Curry on the Richter Scale" entrée allows you to choose chicken or shrimp and the desired degree of hotness by picking a number on the scale measuring a quake's magnitude. Most of the desserts on the "Aftershock" menu are pretty good, but stay away from "Psychedelic Ice Cream," a mess of ice cream and puddles of syrup. If you can get past the silly name and sillier theme, Epicentre is a respectable, much-needed addition to the skimpy collection of restaurants in this neighborhood. A pretheater menu is served from 5 p.m. to 6:30 p.m., and there's valet parking. Dinner costs about $25 per person, lunch about $15.

 ## L'Escoffier at Beverly Hilton

9876 Wilshire Blvd., Beverly Hills 90210;
(310) 274-7777
French. Dinner Tues.-Sat. All major cards.

Michel Blanchet, one of the pioneers who introduced L.A. to traditional French cuisine at the eponymous L'Ermitage restaurant, is now in command at this almost-landmark restaurant atop the Beverly Hilton hotel. Over the years, the space has seen many a wedding and other social fête; and its elegant, even solemn, character was in obvious need of a dose of ginseng to experience its second youth. At night, the lights of Beverly Hills would animate the night outside; discreetly played music would entice handsome couples to dare to step onto the dance floor—it was a beautiful scene, but gastronomy lurked quietly, almost unnoticed, in the background.

These days, the robust Michel Blanchet displays his experience and his classical technique to turn out dishes such as filet of John Dory on a bed of spinach, accompanied by artichokes and diced tomatoes; or lamb chops surrounded by Chanterelles and endives, which illustrate perfectly his seriousness and his consistency. For a recent dinner, a perfectly traditional thin apple pie, enhanced by a stunning wine such as Clos Vougeot, concludes a dinner whose overture consisted of an equally traditional quiche.

We don't anticipate any major overhaul nor revolution in the kitchens of L'Escoffier, but with

See the "And Also . . ." section on page 89 for additional brief listings of L.A. restaurants, many of them chains, old standbys or places to go for a quick, no-frills meal.

a professional like Blanchet running things, we are assured that the job will be seriously—if not very imaginatively—well done. For such good and lasting services, Michel well deserves to don his a toque once again.

12/20 Fama

1416 4th St., Santa Monica 90401;
(310) 451-8633
Californian/Italian. Lunch Mon.-Fri., Dinner nightly. AE, MC, V.

Fama has been around since 1989, cooking perfectly decent Californian-Italian food. And yet it just can't get the respect it deserves. We even received a letter from owner Mary Fama Röckenwagner complaining about how everyone flocks to her husband, Hans's, first place (Röckenwagner), while their other place (named for Mary) gets short shrift. And her complaint isn't without merit—while Röckenwagner's Californian-French cooking is often praised, Fama's simpler cuisine is too often dismissed as just neighborhood food. It's a curiosity of a neighborhood restaurant: it has a very modern design, it's noisy, and the menu runs from the mundane to the nutty. The best things to eat are the simple salads, pizzas and the German-style onion-and-bacon tart; pastas can be good, and pastas can be not so good. Fama is like the child that consistently scores B-pluses while its sibling is a straight-A student. Attention should be paid to both. Dinner costs about $20 per person.

11/20 La Famiglia

453 N. Canon Dr., Beverly Hills 90210;
(310) 276-6208
Italian. Lunch Mon.-Fri., Dinner Mon.-Sat. All major cards.

The red-leatherette decor at La Famiglia has several Beverly Hills touches: paisley linens, delicate crystal, mirrored paneling, and Tiffany lamps hanging from cozy, low ceilings. Furthermore, owner Joe Patti is forever in attendance, greeting his customers, preparing spinach and beet pastas tableside and proudly sending out free samples of his homemade gelati. Veal and chicken dishes are prepared with competence, if not with brilliance. What makes the restaurant memorable is Patti's *nuova cucina* spa-cuisine: a spate of low-calorie dishes designed to please a figure-conscious clientele. A delicate whitefish and lemon sole are poached quickly in white wine, calamari is cooked in a spicy tomato broth and served in a tiny kettle, pastas are lightly sauced. The wine list has a good number of reasonably priced Italian vintages. Dinner costs about $40 per person.

12/20 Farfalla La Brea

143 N. La Brea Ave., Melrose-La Brea District (L.A.) 90036; (213) 938-2504
Italian. Lunch Mon.-Sat., Dinner nightly, Late supper Fri.-Sat. All major cards.

It boasts one of L.A.'s trendiest addresses, and with that come all the attendant pros and cons. The crowd is a study in L.A. cool, awash in ponytails and black minis. The service, by a team of young, fun-loving Italian men, is wildly uneven—sometimes friendly and prompt, sometimes goofy or lackadaisical. That said, we must admit that we love this lively, friendly place. Behind the bar is the ground-floor dining area, flanked by a bustling open kitchen and a brick wall, and featuring a (genuine!) fireplace that's kept blazing in the wintertime. Upstairs is a cozier room with wood floors and another bar. And though the food isn't always as good as at is at the original, smaller Farfalla in Los Feliz, many of the dishes measure up: the roast chicken, scattered with wild mushrooms and surrounded with roasted vegetables and potatoes, is equally succulent. The pizzas are equally crisp-crusted and delicious. The fat gnocchi with smoked chicken and sun-dried tomatoes is just as opulent; the rigatoni e tre funghi, a creamy bowlful of pasta with porcini, champignon and shiitake mushrooms, melts in the mouth the same way. There are a few worthy new dishes, and there are some ordinary dishes. A dinner costs $25 to $30.

Fennel

755 N. La Cienega Blvd., W. Hollywood 90069; (310) 657-8787
French. Lunch Tues.-Sat., Dinner Tues.-Sun. All major cards.

This new, relocated Fennel is a bird of an entirely different feather than the original Fennel Restaurant in Santa Monica. These days, it's a simple place serving the kind of homey bistro fare we dream of but so rarely find in Southern California. Italian food guru Mauro Vincenti, Fennel's co-owner and the owner of Rex and Pazzia, is still involved, as is Michel Rostang, one of the four French greats behind Fennel's original "rotating chefs" concept. But otherwise nothing's the same. The new chef is Laurent Grangien, Rostang's partner in Paris's acclaimed Bistro d'à Côté. The location has moved from Ocean Avenue to a small space adjoining Pazzia, a friendly room with blackboard menus, bistro chairs and bistro-style posters. The honest cooking combines robust flavors with careful, intelligent preparations. And the prices are a far sight less than at the previous Fennel. The duck confit is the kind you get in France, rich and flavorful beyond description. In fact, everything we've tried brought back happy memories of great meals in Paris's bistros, from the warming, saffron-flavored Provençal-style mussel-fish soup, to the salad of warm Lyon sausage on a bed of lentils, to the delicious mesclun salad with roasted goat cheese, potatoes, and pine nuts, to the thick slab of potent half-smoked salmon with green lentils, to the classic rôtisserie chicken with and a potato gratin that'll make you swoon. The inexpensive, tasty house wines are a good match for this substantial food, and you can end your meal on a perfect note by sharing a three-dessert sampler—perhaps a pot chocolat, pear tart and lemon tart. Dinner costs $25 to $30 per person.

12/20 Il Forno

2901 Ocean Park Blvd., Santa Monica 90405; (310) 450-1241
Italian. Lunch Mon.-Fri., Dinner Mon.-Sat. AE, MC, V.

Il Forno is an unpretentious trattoria and a big neighborhood favorite, a lively, friendly place featuring authentic regional Italian cooking at reasonable prices. Il Forno is as bustling a scene as the nearby DC3, but one always feels welcome in here. The antipasto bar is a terrific experience: you make your selections and they're dished out to you. Arancini di riso are little rice croquettes with porcini mushrooms and a melt of cheese in the center, positively irresistible. A northern Italian rendition of carpaccio comes bathed in a fragrant olive oil with capers on a bed of shredded radicchio. Pizzas, particularly the rustica with sun-dried tomatoes, smoked cheese, basil and olive oil, are a dream, with thin, crisp crusts. Pastas are perfectly al dente. Il Forno also features a spa menu, and the healthy items on it sacrifice nothing when it comes to taste. In fact, if you order from it, you may feel virtuous enough to eat dessert; try the other-worldly tiramisu loaded with Strega liqueur. Dinner won't cost more than $20 per person.

Four Oaks

2181 N. Beverly Glen Blvd., Bel Air 90077; (310) 470-2265
French. Lunch Tues.-Sat., Dinner nightly, Brunch Sun. MC, V.

Despite a flurry of managerial changes early in 1992, what may be L.A.'s prettiest country-style French restaurant remains just that—a lovely cottage nestled in Beverly Glen canyon, with a fine outdoor dining area and some often remarkably good food by young chef Peter Roelant. Roelant learned his skills at Girardet and L'Orangerie. And Four Oaks has given him a setting where he's been able to lighten up his sauces and his

soups, creating a sort of Cuisine of the Glen: mixed baby greens with candied lemon skins, baby Maine lobster with fresh peaches in a Champagne sauce, lamb filet with a sweet-garlic pancake and so forth. Despite the fact that Four Oaks is just moments off Sunset Boulevard, and no distance at all from Beverly Hills, it remains secluded, even a bit of a secret. It's the kind of place every city should have. About $55 per person for dinner.

Fragrant Vegetable

11859 Wilshire Blvd., W.L.A. 90025; (310) 312-1442
Chinese/Vegetarian. Lunch & Dinner daily. AE, MC, V.

In the beginning, Fragrant Vegetable was called the Vegi Food Kitchen, an unfortunate name that brings to mind brown rice and alfalfa sprouts. Luckily the name was changed, because these surprisingly stylish restaurants, located in West L.A. and a Monterey Park shopping center (see "Restaurants – *San Gabriel Valley*"), are far more Fragrant Vegetables than Vegi Food Kitchens. The menu features quite a few different Chinese fungi: tree ears, black moss and so forth. All the "pork," "beef," "chicken" and "shark's-fin" dishes on the menu are actually made with bean curd and presented on the plate trompe l'oeil, which is surprisingly successful. The chicken, made with bean-curd skins, is similar to white-meat chicken. The bean-curd pork has the same red coloring as char siu pork. All told, there are 86 items on the menu, bean curd and mushrooms being the most popular ingredients. The mushrooms tend to be quite musky and earthy, especially the stewed black mushrooms topped with black moss, a dish called Buddha's Cushions. This is vegetarian cooking that is full enough of flavor to make the most devout carnivore happy. Dinner runs about $15 apiece.

12/20 Fritto Misto

601 Colorado Ave., Santa Monica 90401; (310) 458-2829
Italian. Lunch Mon.-Sat., Dinner nightly. MC, V.

Fritto Misto's menu proclaims that it's a "neighborhood café," and by gosh, that's exactly what it is: a storefront with a simple, casual menu. Inside a hum of activity, as effusive owner Chaz Gaddie bustles about the room, suggesting a pasta or insisting that you taste the empanadas. And they are good—exotic little pastries filled with shrimp and pancetta in a garlic cream sauce, or chicken with creamed spinach, or vegetables in a marinara sauce. You can make quite a satisfying meal out of appetizers: the namesake dish of deep-fried shrimp, calamari, artichoke hearts and whatever vegetables chef David Williams feels like cooking; garlic shrimp on a bed of black and white pasta; sausage and roasted peppers over linguine; wonderfully crisp calamari. You'll be tempted to try them all, particularly since the prices are so low, but be warned that they're very generously served. Pastas are of the mix-and-match variety: start with spaghettini, linguine, fettuccine, fusilli, ravioli or "pillows," then add marinara sauce, oil and garlic, butter and garlic, garlic cream, pesto or four-cheese sauce, and toss in anything from shrimp to sun-dried tomatoes. End with the satsifying crème brûlée. Bring your own wine; plan on $15 per person for dinner.

12/20 Gardel's

7963 Melrose Ave., Melrose-Fairfax District (L.A.) 90046; (213) 655-0891
Argentinian/Italian. Lunch Tues.-Fri., Dinner Mon.-Sat. AE, MC, V.

In the early '80s, Argentinian cuisine seemed on the verge of becoming the Next Big Thing. Purveyors of this hearty peasant cooking, with its innate love of beef, proliferated; in fact, Western Avenue began to be called Little Buenos Aires. And then, as quickly as they had appeared, most of them disappeared. All that really remains is the Gaucho Grill chain and Gardel's. By far the most elegant Argentinian L.A. has ever had, Gardel's is named for Carlos Gardel, a legendary tango musician who died in 1935. His mildly decadent rhythms fill the air as customers consume remarkably large dishes of matambre (literally "hunger killer"), the Argentinian cognate of Germany's rouladen, a flank steak rolled around a fantasy of pickles, pimientos, hard-cooked eggs and herbs. No visit to Gardel's is complete without a plate of ajo al horno: a head of baked garlic, the interior of which you squeeze onto thick slices of bread. The best way to taste a lot of the menu is with the parrillada, a mixed grill of skirt steak, sweetbreads, sausages and short ribs. Pastas abound, most made with lots of garlic. This is not cooking for the weak of heart, or of spirit. Dinner runs about $28 per person.

 ### Gardens at Four Seasons Hotel

300 S. Doheny Dr., Beverly Hills 90048; (310) 273-2222
American. Breakfast, Lunch & Dinner daily, Brunch Sun. All major cards.

When a hotel dining room really hits the mark, it can be a most soothing and elegant retreat from a frenzied, cellular-phone-filled world. Gardens is just such a place, combining the Four Seasons's

trademark good looks with elegant food that successfully treads that fine line between innovation and comfort. It's an ideal place for doing business, thanks to its large, well-spaced tables appointed with thick linens and heavy silver. It's also a good place for romance, thanks to its warm colors, flattering lighting and profusion of glorious flower arrangements.

The menu is contemporary American, which means a little of this and a little of that: a rich gratin of macaroni and mascarpone, fabulous stir-fried Maine lobster with fragrant jasmine rice, a Mediterranean antipasto with eggplant, artichoke, zucchini and truffle pesto, perfectly cooked New York steaks and free-range veal chops, chic salads and refined desserts that usually taste as good as they look. As one would expect of one of Los Angeles's very best hotels, a single-dish lunch can easily cost $25 per person, and a three-course dinner runs about $60.

12/20 Gardens of Taxco

1113 N. Harper Ave., W. Hollywood 90046; (213) 654-1746
Mexican. Dinner Tues.-Sun. All major cards.

Unless you have friends in Mexico City, Gardens of Taxco may be the closest you'll ever come to experiencing a home-style dinner with a Mexican family. This dark, cozy spot glows with folksy decor, featuring tacky red table candles, colored lights, garish oil paintings and a strolling guitar player. There is no menu; instead, one of the family members comes to your table and graciously recites the formula to you: you choose either pork, chicken, beef or shrimp, and the four dishes in that category are described in detail (complete with heartfelt recommendations such as "the chicken, it seems as if it were born in the sauce".) Then, you order a couple of the marvelously refreshing wine margaritas and sit back as a parade of savory dishes arrives at your table: chips, hot salsa and pickled vegetables; steaming albóndigas soup (broth with small, spicy meatballs); miniature tostadas; an entrée such as grilled shrimp in cilantro-cream sauce or chicken mole. Dinner comes to a rich finish with chocolatey cream sherry and banana-cream custard. Dinner costs no more than $17 per person ($22 with margaritas).

Gault Millau's ratings are based solely on the restaurants' cuisine. We do not take into account the atmosphere, decor, service and so on; these are commented upon within the reviews.

Gaylord
50 N. La Cienega Blvd., W. Hollywood
90211; (310) 652-3838
*Indian. Lunch & Dinner daily, Brunch Sun. All
major cards.*

The Gaylord restaurant chain traces its genealogy back to 1941, when the first Gaylord opened in New Delhi. Since then, branches have spread to Asia and Europe—and all the way to L.A. Chefs at each branch are said to have been trained at the original Gaylord in New Delhi, but even if this is so much hype, expect sophisticated Indian cooking, among the best in town. The restaurant is plainly elegant, thick with mauves, pinks, grays and mirrored walls. This Gaylord is hidden away in a La Cienega office building and may lack visual drama, but the food more than compensates. The menu meanders through terra cognita—mulligatawny soup, fine tandoori dishes, reliable kebabs—good dishes that have, over the years, become old friends. We only wish things were less predictable, even if the prediction says delicious. Dinner costs about $35 per person.

11/20 Genghis Cohen
740 N. Fairfax Ave., Melrose-Fairfax District
(L.A.) 90036; (213) 653-0640
*Chinese. Lunch Tues.-Fri., Dinner Tues.-Sun.
AE, MC, V.*

Genghis Cohen, in the heart of L.A.'s Jewish community, attempts to offer creative Chinese cooking in a sophisticated ambience. The results are mixed, but the concept is noble. The restaurant is sleek and contemporary, with comfortable banquettes and good recorded jazz. This consciously hip setting is somewhat offset by the hokey menu gags: cocktails called Lounge Lizard and Ori-Yentl; an appetizer assortment called Shanghai Schwartz's #1 Nosh; poultry dishes entitled Our Fowlest. Cooking actually skirts several Chinese provinces, Szechuan being the favorite. Crispy fried chicken wings come with every dinner, along with respectable hot-and-sour soup. Pan-fried dumplings are meaty and juicy, alongside a delicious chili sauce. Kung pao chicken is fine, and three-flavor mu shu, filled with shrimp, chicken and pork, is marvelous, each flavor distinct. About $20 for a dinner.

12/20 George Petrelli's Steak House
5614 Sepulveda Blvd., Culver City 90230;
(310) 397-1438
*Steakhouse. Lunch Mon.-Fri., Dinner nightly.
All major cards.*

They've been doing what they do at Petrelli's since 1931, when it was Joe Petrelli's and there was no such thing as the San Diego Freeway. These days, the place is run by Joe's son George, who does a great job of carrying on the family tradition of serving good, properly cooked, generously portioned steaks at very low prices. It looks like the quintessential California roadhouse, with a big bar, country-western entertainment, smart waitresses and a kitchen that churns out hundreds of meals a day, each in a matter of moments. Just like in the old days, you get a full meal for your $15 (or so): beef noodle soup, tossed green salad, a choice of potatoes and vegetables, bread and coffee. The most expensive item on the menu is the extra-large porterhouse at $20.95; most of the steak dinners are under $15. The beef is dressed in the back of the restaurant—ask George and he'll show you. You can also order such golden oldies as eggplant parmigiana and breaded veal cutlets; kids can order from a big children's menu. The steaks may not be quite as good as Ruth's Chris's or The Palm's, but dinner here is a great deal for the money. Dinner costs about $20 per person.

Il Giardino
9235 W. 3rd St., Beverly Hills 90210;
(310) 275-5444
*Italian. Lunch Mon.-Sat., Dinner nightly. All
major cards.*

When Il Giardino first opened, it was a new and welcome kind of Italian restaurant—a rustic, simple sort place in the flats of Beverly Hills. The '80s decade was the era of the Italian restaurant in Los Angeles, with new and better Italian restaurants opening all over the city by the week. Perhaps because standards have risen steadily, we just aren't that impressed by Il Giardino any longer. Things have slipped seriously since the 1980s, and old-time customers can go away disappointed. But a newcomer to the restaurant will be suitably impressed with the cuisine, and a spate of new dishes is offered: tempting specials have included veal scaloppine with asparagus in a red-wine sauce, ravioli with artichoke, spaghetti with lobster. The waitstaff is friendly and helpful. Dinner runs about $55.

Gilliland's
2424 Main St., Santa Monica 90405;
(310) 392-3901
*International. Lunch Mon.-Fri., Dinner
nightly. Brunch Sun. AE, MC, V.*

Gilliland's is a real melting pot, at once Mediterranean, Indian, Irish and American. Restaurants of this nature are often in love with themselves, but this one is absolutely devoid of pretension. Owner Gerri Gilliland is a real pop-

41

ulist; she's added a glass front and a cheerful awning to make the place more homey, and lowered lunch prices to the point of being laughable. Nibbles such as light cubes of cornmeal polenta and the marvelous blarney-cheese-and-onion tart make ideal starters. Steadfast entrées on her ever-changing menu include chicken stuffed with goat cheese in rosemary butter; a thick leg of lamb flavored with mint, garlic and rosemary and grilled with red onions and eggplant; an audacious duck confit with jalapeño peppers and garlic fettuccine. The shamelessly traditional Irish beef stew is served with a chopped potato-and-onion concoction called champ. A dinner costs $25.

Ginza Sushi-Ko

3959 Wilshire Blvd., Mid-Wilshire District (L.A.) 90010; (213) 487-2251
Sushi. Lunch Mon.-Fri., Dinner Mon.-Sat. All major cards.

Ginza Sushi-Ko is almost certainly L.A.'s most unusual sushi bar. It's also almost certainly L.A.'s most expensive restaurant, and its most exclusive. Like at Tokyo's private restaurants, the ones hidden away on the upper stories of office buildings, privacy is its cachet, which is what attracts major celebrities such as Madonna. What attracts the top-level Japanese businessmen you'll see here is the perfection of the sushi—there may well be none better in town. Unfortunately, neither privacy nor perfection are inexpensive commodities; a meal at Ginza Sushi-Ko, if you somehow manage to get in, will cost you a samurai's ransom. Tucked in a Wilshire Boulevard pod mall, Sushi-Ko is understatement incarnate, bearing only a simple sign over the door. The setting is aesthetically pure: just a sushi counter and a few tatami rooms, with polished wood serving as the only design element.

The fish, as a rule, is shipped in daily from Tokyo's Tsukiji Market, the greatest fish market in the world. Much of it is fish we have never heard of. And since there's no menu (you're simply served until you cry "uncle"), it was hard to tell exactly what we were eating. What we do know was that every slice of fish, every dot of roe, every grain of rice was presented as artfully and masterfully as could be. Fish we had never seen were served beneath condiments we had never see. We felt like someone who had learned to like $5 bottles of Mountain Red and was suddenly confronted with a 1961 Château Margaux. It was wonderful sushi. For a dozen orders of sushi, the bill was more than $300 for two. To paraphrase the American Express ads, we had discovered the high—the very high—price of privilege. Dinner runs at least $150 per person.

Giorgio

114 W. Channel Rd., Santa Monica 90402; (310) 459-8988
Italian. Dinner nightly. DC, MC, V.

Giorgio may not have an ocean view (precious few L.A. restaurants do), but there's no doubting you're at the beach here. Tucked in Santa Monica Canyon just around the corner from Pacific Coast Highway, it's a casual, cheerful spot that would fit right into an Italian or Greek beach town: white walls hung with a few blue-and-gray silkscreens, white wooden chairs, closely packed tables draped with white linens, an earth-colored tile floor, a no-frills open kitchen and, to complete the effect, a few impossibly handsome Italian beach-boy waiters, who can sometimes be more charming than efficient. Owner/chef Giorgio Baldi hails from the Tuscan beach resort town of Forte dei Marmi, so it's not surprising that his seafaring dishes are as superb as they are. Caciucco is a heady, generously served soup-stew of calamari, shrimp, salmon and swordfish in a zesty herb-tomato broth. Huge grilled prawns, smoky and sweet, sit atop a bed of creamy saffron risotto. Every night brings a different grigliata mista, a bounteous assortment of grilled fresh fish. If you aren't feeling fishy, try Giorgio's take on the ubiquitous spaghetti with tomato sauce and basil—the tomatoes are cooked down to an unspeakably creamy richness with butter—or sink into the comfort of the lamb shank with long-roasted potatoes and garlicky spinach. Desserts include snappy fresh-fruit tarts and creamy tiramisu, which may be a cliché these days, but is still a joy to eat when it's good. A pasta dinner runs about $22 apiece, a seafood dinner about $35.

8/20   Gladstone's 4 Fish

17300 W. Pacific Coast Hwy., Pacific Palisades 90272; (310) GL-4-FISH
Seafood. Breakfast, Lunch & Dinner daily. All major cards.

We always take out-of-town visitors to Gladstone's, to show off the sweeping Palos Verdes-to-Malibu coastline view. The outdoor deck here allows free public access, making it a great spot to enjoy a beer and eat handfuls of terrific roasted-in-the-shell peanuts. This fact has not escaped half the population of Los Angeles, which congregates here every weekend to ogle each other and the view. As for the food, well, it's passable: there's a decent chowder, served with a hot sourdough loaf, fresh fish that's often mesquite-grilled (but it may as well be frozen given its distinct lack of flavor). Little else here is worth trying. That goes double for foot-high foam-rubbery slabs of chocolate cake. People wait up to two hours for tables, thanks to the great beachfront location. Dinner costs about $20 per person.

 ## Granita
23725 W. Malibu Rd., Malibu 90265;
(310) 456-0488
Californian. Lunch Wed.-Sun., Dinner nightly, Brunch Sun. All major cards.

With the opening of Granita, the fearless Wolfgang Puck gave L.A. it's best reason to venture north of Santa Monica for dinner. Granita's name (inspired, of course, by the Italian ice), might also have been something like Wolfworld by the Sea, for Puck's wife and exuberant designer, Barbara Lazaroff, has created a characteristically zany atmosphere. You feel as if you were sitting in the midst of a Disney animation strip, surrounded by lots of blue color and wavelike shapes. Of the previous Puck creations (among them L.A.'s Spago, Chinois on Main and the now-defunct Eureka) this one reminds us most of Spago, with its open kitchen, creative pastas, pizzas cooked in a wood-burning oven and wonderful appetizers that can be combined to create a fine meal. The menu reflects Granita's location by the sea: sizzling scorpion fish on baby cress with a soy-ginger glaze, seared scallops with vegetable ravioli. The rest of the menu is Puck at his best, both recognizable and exotic at the same time, and decidedly Cal-Asian. Bluefin-tuna carpaccio comes with ginger rice and a delicate soy vinaigrette. A Chinese duck is sweetened with peach chutney. Chatham clams are served with Chinese black-bean sauce and sweet peppers.

The place to sit is outside, where you can watch the sun setting over the Malibu hills while nibbling on one of the best Caesar salads in town. Dinner runs about $50 or more per person.

12/20 The Grill on the Alley
9560 Dayton Way, Beverly Hills 90210;
(310) 276-0615
American. Lunch & Dinner Mon.-Sat. All major cards.

We were instantly set at ease in the Grill, a quintessentially American place unspoiled by culinary fads. Settling into our spacious, comfortable booth, surrounded by the likes of Elliot Gould, Marsha Mason and prosperous-looking local stockbrokers, we were pleased to discover a large menu altogether devoid of fashion. Fashion can be wonderful, but sometimes one gets a hankering for basics, and that's what you'll find at The Grill—honest, simple cooking emphasizing high-quality ingredients. Imagine perfectly fresh clams and oysters on the half shell, excellent

steaks and lamb chops, an aromatic and flavorful grilled garlic chicken, steamed vegetables that are, amazingly, fresh and not overcooked, a near-perfect hamburger and a delicious pecan pie. Salads can be disappointing, but you'll be quick to forgive by the end of the meal. The handsome men's-club decor, the friendly, unobtrusive service and a sophisticated clientele conspire to lure us back again and again. Prices reflect the neighborhood and the quality; the limited wine list is overpriced. This is the original grill that spawned Southern California's growing Daily Grill chain. Dinner will cost about $35 per person.

 ## Hal's Bar & Grill
1349 Abbot Kinney Blvd., Venice 90291;
(310) 396-3105
American. Breakfast Sat.-Sun., Lunch & Dinner daily, Late Supper (until 1 a.m.) Fri.-Sat., Brunch Sat.-Sun. AE, MC, V.

Hal's is yet another hip, arty restaurant serving simple American/international dishes, except this one is less pretentious than most of its neighbors, not to mention being more capable and less expensive. A long, roomy bar and an interesting local clientele make this a great place to unwind and listen to soft jazz, and the dinner menu, which changes weekly, is refreshingly short and simple. Entrées come with soup of the day or a delicious Caesar salad, so appetizers aren't strictly necessary. But many are irresistible: one week might bring a terrific steamed-salmon "purse" filled with a mousse of scallops and yellow peppers, another a robust risotto with tomatoes, basil and black olives. Excellent entrées range from duck breast risotto with wild mushrooms, thyme and asparagus to a simple New York steak with shallot and rosemary mayonnaise and good fries. This is not fancy food, but chef Greg Gevurtz and staff cook it with the same care and precision found in the most elegant French fare. That standard carries through to desserts, neither too heavy nor too petite: an exceptionally smooth crème caramel; an individual apple brown-butter tart and best of all, Hal's sundae—seriously chewy chocolate ice cream, a scoop of vanilla-bean ice cream, dollops of fudge, intense caramel sauce and a dusting of ground nuts. Good, low priced wines, too. About $25 per person.

10/20 Hamlet Gardens
1139 Westwood Blvd., Westwood 90024;
(310) 824-1818
American. Lunch & Dinner daily. AE, MC, V.

Here is a showroom of every Californian outdoors-indoors design cliché of the '80s—ficuses arching to the skylights, terra-cotta floors, weathered brick walls. The room is pleasant, pretty and airy, all the more lamentable that this food is generic fare that puts fish, chicken and veal through the motions. Hamlet Gardens tries embarassingly hard to be an upscale version of Hamburger Hamlet. A pianist serenades dinner guests while eager young waiters make guacamole from a tableside cart. But this is Westwood, after all, and with few decent places nearby, Hamlet Gardens is, if nothing else, a safe choice. Dinners and cocktails are generous, service is pleasant, and there are even a few good things to eat; a delicious pizza with pesto, prawns and sliced red onions; gooey desserts. Try bread pudding with caramelized apples on crème Anglaise. Dinner can cost as much as $40 per person.

Harold & Belle's
2920 W. Jefferson Blvd., South-Central (L.A.) 90018; (213) 735-9023
Soul Food. Lunch & Dinner Wed.-Mon. AE, MC, V.

Outsized portions are frequently a sign of slipshod cooking, but at Harold & Belle's, L.A.'s best (and most elegant) soul food restaurant, the quality is as impressive as the gargantuan quantity. Therefore, this place is always full, and you'd better make reservations far in advance. This is no down-home dive, either, so trot out your Sunday best. Food here is a spicy taste of heaven. Appetizers can be are bigger than main courses in more moderate restaurants; main courses are suitable for groups of four. A heaping and wonderful plate of Louisiana-style hot links sparkles with fire, thanks to a four-alarm dipping sauce. Clam chowder is really a massive bowl of thick, moderately spicy soup-stew, heavy with clams and potatoes. Main courses rarely fail to evoke laughter and gasps of incredulity: piles of corn on the cob, fine potato salad and entrées such as fish Suzette, a changing special of three massive filets of pan-fried breaded fish topped with a cream-laden crayfish sauce. There's much to choose from: fried catfish, soft-shell crabs, breaded Louisiana oysters, shrimp Creole, shrimp Ryan (with mushrooms and scallions in a brown sauce), even hyperbolic po' boy sandwiches. Desserts are also monsters. A dinner costs $25 to $35.

Harry's Bar and American Grill
ABC Entertainment Center, 2020 Ave. of the Stars, Century City 90067; (310) 277-2333
Italian. Lunch Mon.-Fri., Dinner nightly. All major cards.

Unless you work in Century City, it's easy to let Harry's slip from your consciousness. One even forgets just how good it is. Clubby and warm, this restaurant transcends the sterility of Century City, while maintaining a civilized singles scene and a skilled kitchen. What separates Harry's from most power-lunch boîtes is the quality of the food. Bread and breadsticks make a fresh, satisfying start. Appetizers and salads are delicious, from a simple insalata caprese to a lovely, roseate carpaccio in a good olive oil. The much-abused vitello tonnato here is about as good as the dish gets, and the air-dried, wafer-thin bresaola (dried, salted beef filet) is tender and flavorful. Harry's does a fine job with grilled meats, too, especially the steaks and chops. Desserts such as the exceptional cappuccino soufflé are a must. Perfect for after movie or theater dining, but a fine place to eat anytime. Dinner costs about $35 per person.

12/20 Hollywood Canteen
1006 Seward St., Hollywood 90028; (213) 465-0961
American. Lunch Mon.-Fri., Dinner Mon.-Sat. AE, MC, V.

The Hollywood Canteen improves on the Daily Grill's neo-'40s formula by adding a heavy dose of hip, a clubby back room and some modern twists on the bar-and-grill-chow basics. The formula works—this is a way cool place to read scripts over a lunchtime salad or meet friends for dinner in one of the roomy burgundy booths. Located in Hollywood's hard-working warehouse district, the building is one of those classic little stucco jobs from the '30s, and the interior evokes the days of *The Big Sleep*. But the '90s are evident in the kitchen's use of organic foodstuffs. This is the kind of place where you find a few dishes you like and stick with them. We're quite fond of the thick clam chowder, the crisp potato pancakes with velvety smoked salmon, the rare glazed salmon, the baseball steak and the lemon meringue pie. Less impressive were the plain grilled swordfish and the bland Caesar salad. But we love the place, faults and all. And we sincerely hope that it'll be open again for breakfast by the time you read this. About $20 per person for dinner.

11/20 Horikawa
111 S. San Pedro St., Little Tokyo (L.A.) 90012; (213) 680-9355
Japanese. Lunch Mon.-Fri., Dinner nightly. All major cards.

Horikawa is a fantasyland of bamboo screens and gently burbling fountains. One side is a busy sushi bar; across the lobby is an attractive, soothing lounge ideal for trysts. Most *gaijin* head for the teppan room, where groups of diners gather around a grill for the Benihana-style dishes. Surprise! In this case, the dishes really taste Japanese. The chef arrives tossing handfuls of shrimp into the air. They grill up instantly. Onions are chopped, mushrooms and zucchini sliced, bean sprouts herded about. After that comes the heavy artillery: steaks (New York, filet mignon or rib eye), chicken, lobster tails and scallops. It's a group experience, with the chef as unwitting guru. At the end of the meal, he receives a brisk ovation. For a splurge, try the deluxe ryotei dinner, $110 per person. Otherwise expect to pay about $30 to $50.

Hotel Bel-Air Dining Room
701 Stone Canyon Rd., Bel Air 90077;
(310) 472-1211
American/French. Breakfast, Lunch & Dinner daily. All major cards.
Going to the Bel-Air for lunch, brunch or dinner involves a certain amount of planning. Reservations must be made sufficiently far in advance for whatever special occasion you've chosen to celebrate, and the proper attire must be chosen, along with the proper companion. This is not the sort of experience that should be wasted on the uninterested or unobservant—it may be the single most romantic dining experience in town.

You get to the Bel-Air by threading your way past some of L.A.'s grandest estates. You give your car to one of the obsessively polite parking attendants, and then meander across small stone bridges, over ponds crowded with swans, to the main dining room, which, like everything here, is easy to miss. The dining room is as elegant as they get, with bowers of flowers flowing out of vases the size of Geo Storms, and a fireplace crackling in the corner (even if the temperature outside is in the 90s). Chef George Mahaffey left just as we went to press, and new chef Gary Clauson, previously with the St. James's Club, planned to continue serving the same formal-but-not-fussy cuisine Mahaffey created for the restaurant. It's what you might call born-again American, with a California-Oriental lilt. House-smoked salmon with toast sits next to tempuraed quail served with a salad of truffle-flavored potato crisps, smoked corn, roast shallots and a sun-dried cherry vinaigrette. And grilled Petaluma chicken breast with rosemary-scented mashed potatoes is just down the menu from smoked-chanterelle-and-rabbit ravioli served with glazed cipolline onions. The menu changes with the seasons. The cost is serious, but then so is the meal, so is the setting and so is the content-

ment felt as you drive back down the hill into the real world. Dinner runs about $55 a person.

12/20 Houston's
Century City Marketplace, 10250 Santa Monica Blvd., Century City 90067;
(310) 557-1285
American. Lunch & Dinner daily. AE, MC, V.
This Southern-based chain has created one of the best concepts in mass-market dining we've seen: a good-looking, upscale-steakhouse setting is paired with food that is surprisingly affordable and exceptionally good. A popular premeal nosh is the Chicago-style spinach-and-artichoke dip, a shockingly caloric bowl of creamed spinach and artichoke hearts topped with melted cheese, accompanied by sour cream, salsa and tortilla chips. The huge, oval-shape pizzas are deliciously odd, made out of what tastes like crisped pita bread; try the Thai chicken, New Orleans–style shrimp or caponata versions. Other good dishes include the fine hickory burger, the intriguing chile-topped Texas burger (served only on Saturdays), the sundry salads and the barbecued ribs with a mildly hot and sweet sauce. The meat absolutely drops off the bones. Less than $20 per person for dinner.

Hugo's
8401 Santa Monica Blvd., W. Hollywood 90069; (213) 654-4088
Italian. Breakfast, Lunch, Dinner & Late Supper daily, Brunch Sun. AE, MC, V.
Hugo's started life as one of L.A.'s best butcher shops. Today it is more of an entertainment-industry hangout, with both exotic and traditional antipasti, salads, pastas and veal dishes. We love the sandwich with hot sausages and sweet roast peppers, and the pasta vercelli, with tomato, capers, basil and anchovies. Various chicken and veal entrées include classic and dishes with a twist (chicken marsala with piquant sun-dried tomatoes). Breakfast at Hugo's is exemplary, with a range of garlicky pastas and egg dishes designed for large appetites. Among favorites are the eggs carbonara (scrambled with prosciutto, bacon and scallions) and the signature pasta Mama (a hearty jumble of fresh pasta and scrambled eggs with parsley and Parmesan). The terrific coffee is frequently replenished. The setting isn't elegant—it looks like a chic butcher shop—but there is no denying the cheer and good comfort. Despite a Hollywood-heavyweight clientele, tables are relatively easy to come by. About $15 for a pasta lunch, and anywhere from $25 to $40 per person for dinner.

45

12/20 Hungarian Budapest

7986 Sunset Blvd., Hollywood 90046;
(213) 654-3744
*Hungarian. Lunch Mon.-Fri., Dinner nightly.
AE, MC, V.*

Unlike in New York and Chicago, Eastern European restaurants in L.A. are as rare as waiters without scripts in their back pockets. This spot is located in (what else?) a mini-mall on Sunset, a dumpling's throw from the Director's Guild, and it's worth any trip you have to make. This food is so authentic that those who have only dabbled in Hungarian cuisine may even find it a bit off-putting. The goulash, for instance, which in America is usually a beef stew flavored with paprika, is wholly genuine—a hot pot of stewed cabbage and mixed smoked meats that tastes nothing like Dinty Moore. As an appetizer, the Hungarian cold-cut plate is big enough to satisfy a table of four. If you also try the consommé with enormous liver dumplings, you'll have difficulty tucking into the main courses: big plates of veal paprikash with dumplings, paprika chicken with dumplings, remarkable stuffed cabbage and so forth. The desserts are mostly crêpe-like creations. An attempt has been made to dress up the standard cramped pod-mall space with such niceties as white tablecloths and flowers, and the service is friendly, if a bit harried. Expect to pay about $20 per person for a huge dinner.

Hu's Szechwan Restaurant

10450 National Blvd., Palms 90034;
(310) 837-0252
Chinese. Lunch Mon.-Sat., Dinner nightly. CB, DC, MC, V.

You don't have to venture to Monterey Park or Chinatown for wonderful Chinese food—when you find can find it in Palms, of all places. There's almost always a wait for a table in Hu's bare-bones dining room, because this Szechuan food has stayed terrific: fiery Szechuan dumplings, tender kung pao chicken, aromatic curried chicken, rich and pungent shrimp with a Szechuan tomato sauce, savory dried-fried string beans with ground pork, and a Mandarin chicken salad that is a perfect foil to all the spicy dishes. How much chili is used depends on the chef's whim; don't be shy to ask if you like the heat. Plan on spending a very reasonable $12.

12/20 Hymie's Fish Market

9228 W. Pico Blvd., Wilshire District (L.A.)
90035; (310) 550-0377
Seafood. Lunch Mon.-Fri, Dinner nightly. AE, MC, V.

Fish market by day, seafood restaurant by night, Hymie's still packs them in, despite hefty prices. One reason is the homey, unpretentious atmosphere: a cozy dining room with wood trim, marlin trophies and an aquarium filled with curious fish. Another is the warm service. But the most important reason is the fresh seafood, simple and well prepared. Fish are either broiled or sautéed (absolutely no frying, salt or frills), and embellished with garlic butter or Dijon mustard—swordfish, John Dory, trout, red snapper, salmon or delicious sand dabs, all of which are well-suited to bare-bones preparation. Try oysters to start, and choose the salad over the overly floury chowder. Dinner runs $35 per person.

Hy's

10131 Constellation Ave., Century City
90067; (310) 553-6000
American/Steakhouse. Lunch Mon.-Fri., Dinner Mon.-Sat. All major cards.

When you first walk into Hy's, especially on a weekend evening, you are assaulted by music so loud that you seek the source of the throbbing, pulsating beat—and the source is, of course, the bar, home to what appears to be a frenzied singles scene. But when you walk a few more steps into the restaurant proper, you are suddenly in another world entirely: a quiet, civilized world, almost too civilized for a steakhouse. But who's complaining? Not us. Especially not when we order Hy's steak. Oh sure, the menu has chicken and veal and pasta and a half dozen fish and shellfish preparations, but—trust us—you want the steak, preferably the 16-ounce New York strip or the 25-ounce T-bone. All steaks also come in smaller sizes—and, if you've just completed a triathalon, in larger sizes as well. One longtime customer—a thin woman in her 60s, known to the staff as "Mrs. Steak"—always orders a two-pounder and eats every bite. Her steak costs $50. If you eat a more modestly sized steak, you'll pay only about that for your entire dinner.

Indigo

8222 W. 3rd St., W. Hollywood 90048;
(213) 653-0140
New American. Lunch Mon.-Fri., Dinner nightly. All major cards.

Every once in a while, a restaurant pops up that really gets it right. Indigo is a notable example. Heading up the kitchen is Tony DiLembo, once Barbra Streisand's private chef. His menu is a tough one in terms of making choices, but only because everything sounds so good. Chinese crisp-fried baby squid with spicy chili sauce, virtually greaseless, is one dish you just can't stop eating. Chicken-and-spinach potstickers, ribboned with cilantro and scallions, embodies sweet, sour, tart and salty, all rolled into one. Pizzas sound weird but work. Imagine one with sautéed escarole, Provolone, Kalamata olives, capers, pine nuts and white raisins. Whew. We couldn't get enough chicken satay with peanut sauce—the tender white meat was perfectly grilled, and the smooth, hot peanut sauce really sneaks up on you. Fabulous chicken chile comes in a huge ceramic bowl—a thick, musky version clogged with cubes of chicken and blue-corn tortilla chips. Charred flank steak is infused with garlic and served with a red-onion-and-thyme relish and a side of excellent fried potatoes. And just to show DiLembo's range, Thai shrimp and papaya salad comes with grilled shiitake mushrooms, pine nuts and onions in a lime-ginger vinaigrette. For dessert, cobblers are the best bet, and there is a slightly coarse-textured crème brûlée. In short, Indigo won't leave you blue. Dinner can be had for a very fair $25 per person, though depending on what you eat, it can run upward of $35.

The Ivy

113 N. Robertson Blvd., W. Hollywood
90048; (310) 274-8303
*American. Lunch & Dinner daily, Brunch Sun.
All major cards.*

Don't let its homey, tumbly-rambly English cottage/garden look fool you—The Ivy is one of L.A.'s most intense power-meal boîtes. The most coveted tables are those on the utterly charming patio; only Tinseltown's most potent and beautiful can command those seats. It's one of the prettiest restaurants in town. Co-owner Lynn von Kersting is a supremely talented designer (she also owns and curates the Indigo Seas shop next door). From the smallest planter overgrown with fragrant flowers to the hand-painted dishes on which the food is served, no detail has gone unnoticed. Huge roses bloom everywhere, and the chintz upholstery is soft and strategically worn; every time we eat here, we wish we could just move in.

Oh yes, the food. It can be quite wonderful—in fact, it's a whole lot better than it needs to be. From the hot, peasanty molasses bread to the best tarte Tatin in town (The Ivy began life as L.A. Desserts, which quickly became the only place for Hollywood trendies to purchase their sweets), you'll rarely encounter a culinary misstep. The food is basic California-ized Americana—no ruffles and flourishes, just well-made, no-nonsense dishes served in unchic hefty portions: one of L.A.'s best Caesar salads, a divine crab salad, perfect crabcakes (crisp on the outside, fat and juicy on the inside), great meatloaf

and prime rib yand even a bang-up burger at lunchtime. And the desserts are divine: delicious chocolate-chip cookies, homemade ice creams and fresh berry pies. All this rusticity doesn't come cheap—expect to spend about $50 apiece, perhaps more—but you're not likely to be disappointed, and the people watching is pretty fascinating.

12/20 The Ivy at the Shore

1541 Ocean Ave., Santa Monica 90405;
(310) 393-3113
*American. Lunch & Dinner daily, Brunch Sun.
All major cards.*

Ivy at the Shore is packed to the rafters every night with celebrities and those who have been coming here for years. Decor is what you might get if you crossed Miss Sadie Thompson with avant-garde architect Brian Murphy—a sort of sophisticated bamboo shack, with vintage Hawaiian shirts hanging on the walls next to some Very Important Art. The lounge area is quite comfortable, with bamboo-and-tropical-print sofas and chairs; it's a good place for serious people-watching. As for the restaurant itself, the optimum place to sit is the semi-enclosed outdoor patio. Owners Lynn von Kersting and Richard Irving haven't strayed too far from the original Ivy's menu: Why mess with a good thing? Salads, particularly the Caesar, are generous and delicious, and the crabcakes are the best in town even their minuscule size. Cajun pizza, fresh-fish dishes, prime rib and meatloaf—they're are all just fine, as are sides of crackling Maui-onion rings and crispy french fries. Desserts are delicious (especially the tarte Tatin), and the tropical drinks are properly strong and sweet. There's Sunday brunch, too: light, puffy pancakes, fluffy omelets and a good selection of salads. Dinner costs about $40 per person.

12/20 Jake's Grill

1622 Ocean Park Blvd., Santa Monica
90405; (310) 399-2036
*American. Lunch & Dinner Tues.-Sun., Brunch
Sun. MC, V.*

Unlike its parent, the Seventeenth Street Café on fashionable Montana Avenue, Jake's sits on a Sunset Park block notable for its aggressive ordinariness. And yet this jolly place is worth driving a distance to get to, as long as you can handle eating dinner surrounded by lots of energy molecules disguised as children. It's a family restaurant in the best sense of the word, where noise and chaos are happily tolerated and where families sick of Chuck E. Cheese can have proper food. Of course, there's lots of the fried, starchy stuff that kids adore: lightly spiced red-onion rings, big platters of crunchy french fries and sweet-potato fries, real mashed potatoes, good garlic bread. You can graze till you drop on delicious Chinese chicken salad, Cajun meatloaf, Korean kalbi ribs, a tasty blue-corn chicken quesadilla and a wonderful BLT with three cheeses. There isn't an item on the menu over $8.95. About $12 per person (less for little ones).

12/20 Jimmy's

201 S. Moreno Dr., Beverly Hills 90212;
(213) 879-2394
Continental. Lunch Mon.-Fri., Dinner & Late Supper Mon.-Sat. All major cards.

If you want to witness the eternal theater of Beverly Hills in one glance, you must come here. The Chinoise decor is charming, touched with that subtle bit of kitsch that gives chic restaurants their warmth and gaiety. If you have the chance to get a table under one of the large white parasols in the garden courtyard, you will be so happy you won't even notice that 30 minutes have passed before your first dish arrives. When the food does come, you'll tuck happily into your lobster salad; thick, fresh peppered salmon; or rack of lamb. You'll likely take more note of the celebrities around you then what you're eating. Jimmy's isn't merely a restaurant, but also a club for beautiful people who only eat because it's time to. Fortunately, the food is more than just perfunctory. The immensely successful owner, Jimmy Murphy, was maître d' at The Bistro, and has spared no expense with this namesake venture. He should, however, advise his captains that a little more warmth and attentiveness would encourage his less famous customers to return more often. About $35 per person for lunch, $60 per person for dinner.

Jitlada

5233 W. Sunset Blvd., Hollywood 90027;
(213) 667-9809
Thai. Lunch & Dinner Tues.-Sun. MC, V.

Los Angeles' best Thai restaurant is snuggled into a tacky mini-mall in the heart of multiethnic Hollywood. Thais from all around flock to eat in it. It's a warm, cozy place, but not nearly as nice as its sister restaurant in the Valley. The food here is better: appetizers include perfect spring rolls, moist and peppery barbecued chicken, deep-fried fresh squid, and minced pork marinated in lemon juice, ginger and shallots. Soups are excellent, particularly the poh-taek, a hot-and-sour broth spiked with lemon grass and loaded with various fish and shellfish. Outstanding curry dishes include beef pa nang, a beef tamarind with

potatoes and onions, and fried catfish with green curry and bamboo shoots. Dish number 43, simply called "Shrimp Specialties," is momentarily shocking (and thereafter delicious) when it arrives on the table—three massive crustaceans served in the shell, each nearly the size of a baby lobster. There is a Thai language menu on the back page. But beware: these dishes are hot enough to set your mouth blazing for weeks to come. Per person, dinner costs $15 to $20.

Joe's

1023 Abbot Kinney Blvd., Venice 90291;
(310) 399-5811
New American. Lunch Tues.-Fri., Dinner Tues.-Sun., Brunch Sun. AE, MC, V.

"Happiness," sang Ethel Waters in the movie *Cabin in the Sky*, "is a thing named Joe." Happiness is also a restaurant named Joe, which sits in the tiny, oddly shaped space that used to house Röckenwagner. After years of serving as a chef at Café Katsu and Brentwood Bar & Grill, chef Joe Miller finally got a space where he can be himself. And a very impressive self he turns out to be.

The storefront is quite comfortable and easy to be in, with food to match—call it nouvelle American with Mediterranean and Asian touches, at pleasantly low prices. The elegant tuna tartare, served with a small cucumber salad, is a variation on the spiced chopped tuna found in sushi bars, only far more subtle. The arugula salad, flavored with basil-scented oil and tossed with those small mozzarella tips called ovoline, has a little surprise in its middle: a gently sautéed slice of eggplant. The osso buco of lotte is one of those culinary jokes chefs amuse themselves with: a filet of firm, lobsterish lotte in a circle shape that resembles a veal knuckle. But the best dishes are the simplest. Our favorite is the broiled crispy chicken with herbs and garlic slipped beneath the skin. On the side is a baked potato topped with a Parmesan gratin. The roast beef comes with wonderful mashed potatoes. The salmon comes with asparagus and wild rice. No tricks, no exhibitionism: it's no surprise that the desserts include a fine tarte Tatin and a forthright vanilla yogurt with strawberry sauce. Expect to spend about $35 per person for dinner.

Joss

9255 Sunset Blvd., W. Hollywood 90069;
(310) 276-1886
Chinese. Lunch Mon.-Fri., Dinner nightly. All major cards.

Joss has been around for close to a decade. And in that time, it's never really gotten the respect it deserves. In fact, it is the L.A. equivalent of the legendary Lai Ching Heen in Hong Kong's Regent Hotel, serving Chinese food that's at once traditional and brilliantly creative.

Joss represents a singular vision, in this case the vision of Cecile Tang Shu Shuen, a woman with deep roots in the Hong Kong film business. Her segue to Hollywood was a natural one. And Joss has, indeed, accumulated quite a show-business clientele, particularly among executives and producers, who appreciate the quiet sophistication of the setting and the excellent wine list as much as the cooking. One of the things that they all inevitably order is one or more of the highly creative dumplings, like the deep-fried dumplings filled with Peking duck. They're slightly crisp yet sensually tender, a successful melding of Peking duck and potstickers. There are a multitude of other great dumplings filled with lamb and leeks, with spinach and pork, with chicken and Napa cabbage, with shrimp and bamboo shoots. No meal here is complete without an order of the cheerfully named Street Vendor's Aubergine, an eggplant-and-seafood pâté with a voluptuously soft inside and an outside that crunches and crackles. Where the scallion pancakes found in most Chinese restaurants are unfortunate tributes to grease and oil, these are wondrous and light, and topped with Louisiana crab. Notable dishes include the crab won tons with a biting Szechuan chili-garlic sauce; the fabulous Hunan ham in a cherry-blossom honey sauce; the spare ribs marinated in lichee liqueur. A complete meal at Joss calls for an order of such dishes as the clay pot rice sprinkled generously with chunks of lap cheung sausage (a cardiologist's nightmare incarnate); Szechuan yu-shiang eggplant with a full-flavored, almost overwhelmingly strong brown sauce; and some of the best kung pao chicken in town. This often-brilliant cooking is perfectly balanced yin and yang—for about $40 to $50 per person.

12/20 Kachina Grill

Wells Fargo Center, 333 S. Hope St., Downtown 90071; (213) 625-0956
Southwestern/Mexican. Lunch Mon.-Sat., Happy Hour Mon.-Fri., Dinner Mon.-Sat. All major cards.

The Southwestern stampede of the last decade has left us pretty cold, so we were surprised by how much we enjoyed downtown's new Kachina Grill, on the second floor of the Wells Fargo Center. For the most part, the food is beautifully presented, generously served and, most importantly, tasty. The margaritas are a perfect balance of tangy and sweet, with a good jolt of tequila. The huge outdoor patio, surrounded by granite-and-glass towers, is a pleasant place to wait while you munch of the great chips.

Owned by David Wilhelm (the chef/restaurateur behind Laguna's Kachina and Irvine's Bistro 201) and the sharp Samaha brothers (also behind Roxbury, the fashionable West Hollywood nightclub/restaurant), this rambling, noisy place is mobbed at lunch, convivial at happy hour and dead on weekends (the common curse of downtown restaurants). The most memorable dishes are the chile relleno with a crispy blue-cornmeal coating and papaya and red-onion salsa, a cliché, no doubt, but a tasty one; the moist, richly flavorful grilled salmon tucked into a corn husk, the whole served with a subtle green-chile pesto; tiny lamb chops with an earthy ranchera sauce and roasted potatoes; and the addictive sweet-corn pudding, a cross between cornbread and polenta. Good lunchtime choices include the ubiquitous tostada (dressed up and very tasty here) and the grilled chicken sandwich with mild green chiles and grilled onions. If a sweet tooth must be attended to, try the rich pecan-chocolate pie and the slightly less rich chocolate bread-and-butter pudding. Lunch runs about $12 a person, dinner from $20 to $30.

12/20 Kaktus

400 N. Canon Dr., Beverly Hills 90210; (310) 271-1856
Mexican/Southwestern. Lunch Mon.-Sat., Dinner nightly. All major cards.

The cooking rises above mere trendiness—it's actually quite tasty and sometimes even authentic. This is a good place to liberate outdated habits that dictate eating an entrée at every meal—instead, just order appetizers. Recommended are the tamalitos, corn husks filled with creamy corn, or the empanadas, small, half-moon shaped pies filled with savory meat or chicken. On a return visit you can sample such main courses as del dia quesadillas—sirloin strips with poblano chiles wrapped in a toasted tortilla—or the more familiar tacos, tostadas and enchiladas. The desserts are great, especially the flans and the crème brûlée, and the margaritas are first class. Dinner ranges from $20 to $30 apiece, depending on what you order.

11/20 Kate Mantilini

9101 Wilshire Blvd., Beverly Hills 90210; (310) 278-3699
American. Breakfast, Lunch, Dinner & Late Supper daily, Brunch Sun. AE, MC, V.

Kate Mantilini is Hamburger Hamlet's jump onto the all-American bandwagon, a solid steak house, named in homage to a hard-boiled female fight promoter. It offers a large, straightforward,

49

menu of dressed-up truckstop food, circa 1947 with white-aproned waiters to match, and a dramatically stark interior from those architectural hipsters, Morphosis. Food is decent without being brilliant, but the restaurant has a few key things going for it. For one, it's open until 2 a.m., making it one of L.A.'s select late-night spots. For another, it's conveniently located on the corner of Wilshire and Doheny. And, lastly, it serves just the kind of treats you crave for a late-night supper: oysters; juicy, tasty roast chicken; baked potatoes with all the fattening trimmings; huge bowls of steaming cappuccino (actually caffè latte, with a good dose of milk). Expect generous breakfasts and, for lunch and dinner, grilled steaks, liver and onions, retro salads, deep-dish apple pie and good basic burgers. Friendly waiters and busboys are more than attentive. Tabs vary considerably, depending on what is ordered: anywhere from $15 to $30 per person.

Katsu

1972 Hillhurst Ave., Los Feliz 90027;
(213) 665-1891
Sushi. Lunch Mon.-Fri, Dinner Mon.-Sat. AE, MC, V.

For a long time, this was considered the best sushi bar in Los Angeles. And to many, it still is, though there is more and more remarkable competition these days. The fish is still fine at this minimalist Los Feliz destination. After a decade, the rigidly austere black-and-white decor is still ahead of its time, though the world has done a lot to catch up. The entry is a curious room filled with nothing but design elements, which change every few months; it's like entering through an art gallery. And there's art on every table as well: plates that are still remarkable today as fancy presentations become more and more common. Katsu's sushi is utterly above reproach: perfect slices of richly flavored yellowtail (hamachi), silky sea bass (shiromi), blood-dark tuna (both maguro and the highly prized fat-marbled toro), exquisitely oily mackerel (saba), crunchy jumbo clam (mirugai) and sea urchin (uni) that's like a mouthful of the sea itself. A sushi dinner runs about $35 apiece.

Katsu 3rd

8636 W. 3rd St., W. Hollywood 90048;
(310) 273-3605
Japanese/Sushi. Lunch Mon.-Fri., Dinner Mon.-Sat. AE, MC, V.

Katsu 3rd's pun of a name refers to its location, on Third Street, and its position as the third restaurant opened by chef/designer Katsu (look for the guy with the exceedingly short crewcut,

a 'do he sported long before Sinead O'Connor came along). True to Katsu's minimalist aesthetic, there's no real sign in front, just a funny, flapping banner and a chalkboard on which "Katsu 3rd" is written when the restaurant is open. It's every bit as underplayed inside—it's like sitting inside a gigantic whitewashed bento box, almost shocking in its simplicity. The menu is country Japanese, with occasional subtle influences from China, Thailand, France or Italy. This is surely the only Japanese restaurant in town that serves the regional Japanese dish resembling beef brisket. And it's about as good as brisket gets, a small clump of remarkably tender meat cooked in a Madeira sauce (which tastes surprisingly like miso) with carrots, potatoes and turnips. It's every bit as distinctive as the piquant, perfectly balanced salad of broiled salmon marinated in a citrus dressing (or any of the six perfect salads), the starter of succulent but oh-so-fragile sake-marinated butterfish, or the poached tai fish in a pear-brandy sauce, served on a bed of shiitake, enoki and shimeji mushrooms—Katsu cuisine, served in a very Katsu setting. The sushi is very good, and very reasonably priced: some orders are only $2. Dinner costs about $25 or more per person.

11/20 Knoll's Black Forest Inn

2454 Wilshire Blvd., Santa Monica 90403;
(310) 395-2212
German. Lunch Tues.-Fri., Dinner Tues.-Sun. All major cards.

The enduring popularity of Knoll's Black Forest Inn proves that there's more to Los Angeles than the stereotypes repeated ad nauseum in the media. Given the population's reputed desire to eat nothing but arugula salads and thin-crusted pizzas, it's interesting to note that this substantial restaurant continues to draw regulars and attract newcomers hungering for the richness of German food. The front of the restaurant mimics a tavern in the Black Forest, with beer steins and waiters and waitresses in native costume, but when you step into the back dining room you could be anywhere. There is no mistaking the authenticity of menu, however. Main courses tend toward meat, potatoes and red cabbage, and all are prepared with skill. Best bets are the bratwurst, knackwurst and schnitzels, particularly when paired with one of the good German Reislings. If by some miracle you don't feel full after your entrée, move on to the hazelnut torte or chocolate truffle cake for dessert. Dinner starts at $25 per person.

Koutoubia

2116 Westwood Blvd., Westwood 90024;
(310) 475-0729
Moroccan. Dinner Tues.-Sun. AE, MC, V.

There are dinners, and then there are dining adventures. Koutoubia offers the latter: the effusive owner/chef, Michel Ohayon greets his guests in an authentic *djellaba*, or floor-length Moroccan costume, and guides them to soft-cushioned seats arranged around circular brass tables. The waiter comes by before the first course to pour warm water over everyone's hands, since your digits serve as the only utensils here. Walls have been draped with fabric to project the illusion of a Moroccan tent, and the effect lends charm and mystery. Our favorite dish here is b'stilla, a light, flaky pie filled with chicken (traditionally, squab) and almonds topped with spiced powdered sugar. It's served extremely hot, so resist the temptation to plunge right in. Spicy merguez sausage with couscous is another marvel, and we also like the lamb, lemon chicken, brains and assorted Moroccan salads—beets, marinated carrots, a mixture of eggplant, olive oil, tomatoes and peppers and another of chopped onion, cucumber and tomatoes. Your best bet here is to ask for recommendations. Ohayon aims to please. Ask him to recommend a wine, too. He has a few older Burgundies that go particularly well with lamb dishes. Probably about $30, but more if you order a multi-course feast.

11/20 L.A. Farm

3000 W. Olympic Blvd., Santa Monica
90404; (310) 829-0600
Californian. Lunch Mon.-Fri., Dinner Mon.-Sat. All major cards.

There is no farm at L.A. Farm: no cows, no pigs, no chickens, no ducks—except, of course, for the cooked ones found on your plate, and the artistic representations of live ones found in these several rooms. Owner/chef Jean-Pierre Peiny, ex of La Serre, was clearly bored cooking stuffy meals in the Valley. Now, in this very comfortable setting, he has filled his menu with oddities drawn from the cuisines of Asia, the Mediterranean and downhome America. You can dash about the culinary world, stopping in the East for Thai shrimp or Cantonese-style duck, in the south of France for chicory salad with duck, in the interior of France for coq au vin, then in New York for a steak or braised corned beef. If only the cooking lived up to the promise of the menu and the setting. An order of raw beef and cured duck turned out to be a plate of very fatty duck "prosciutto" and a mound of steak tartare studded with sesame seeds, a misguided taste combination. The crispy duck in the chicory salad was more fatty than crispy. Our french fries never arrived. The waiter proudly announced that the ice cream was Häagen-Dazs. We'd rather buy Häagen-Dazs at the market. Dinner runs about $40 apiece.

12/20 Lawry's The Prime Rib

55 N. La Cienega Blvd., W. Hollywood
90069; (310) 652-2827
American. Dinner nightly. AE, MC, V.

For many, Lawry's is the ultimate dining experience—huge slabs of savory prime rib cut tableside to order, simple, crowd-pleasing accompaniments and reasonable prices. Never mind that you feel as if you're eating in a factory—you're getting your money's worth. Carvers serve from silver carts wheeled around the huge, brightly lit room, a royal chamber dominated by a fresco of Versailles and giant eighteenth-century portraits. Owner Lawrence Frank has built a small empire by doing the simple things, and his prime rib is truly outstanding, marvelously tender and rich in taste and aroma. Other dishes, save the good creamed spinach, are forgettable: huge baked potatoes, a tasteless Yorkshire pudding, ho-hum salads. Service is friendly but often slow. About $30 per person.

11/20 Legends

1311 Third Street Promenade, Santa Monica
90401; (310) 451-2332
American. Lunch & Dinner daily, Late Supper Fri.-Sat. AE, D, MC, V.

The second sports bar opened by former Los Angeles Ram Dennis Harrah and rugby player John Morris, Legends is either a dream come true or a nightmare, depending on your level of devotion to sports. Four satellite dishes feed sixteen screens; from any given vantage point, chances are you're looking directly at a half dozen different games but hearing the action from only one of them. The amazing thing about Legends is the food, which is much better than you'd expect of a sports bar. Friendly waitpersons in sports drag deliver a tasty array of fattening stuff: deep-fried chicken "fingers" with a thick honey-mustard sauce (basically chicken-flavored candy); deep-fried artichoke hearts sprinkled with Parmesan; deep-fried shrimp; deep-fried zucchini with ranch dressing; deep-fried french fries smothered in chili and cheese (sense a theme here?). The beef ribs are especially good: big, sloppy things dripping a sweet, smoky sauce. This is food that allows you to eat without taking your eyes off the game—that it's good is a bonus. About $15 per person for dinner.

11/20 Lew Mitchell's Orient Express

5400 Wilshire Blvd., Wilshire District (L.A.)
90036; (213) 935-6000
Chinese. Lunch Mon.-Fri., Dinner Mon.-Sat. All major cards.

In a town where only 50 percent of restaurant ventures last a year, and then only a small percentage of those last a second year, Lew Mitchell has achieved an Olympian feat by staying in business since the '60s. His is simply a handsome Chinese restaurant serving a roster of all the Mandarin and Szechuan dishes that have become familiar to Western palates. Most are done well: pork with glass noodles; a "sizzling" trio of chicken, shrimp and beef (stir-fried in piping-hot oil, with a mildly peppery savory sauce); orange-peel chicken; shrimp with black mushrooms; lobster with black-bean sauce; black mushrooms with Chinese cabbage; beef with zucchini; Peking duck. At night the dining room is transformed into a grand-style restaurant/lounge with subdued lighting and a piano player. Dinner costs about $25 to $35 per person.

12/20 Lincoln Bay Café

1928 Lincoln Blvd., Santa Monica 90405;
(310) 396-4039
American/Italian. Lunch Tues.-Fri., Dinner Tues.-Sun. AE, MC, V.

Location is not the key to this place, stuck as it is amid the urban clutter of Lincoln Blvd., home to gas stations, auto repair shops and bus fumes. But that makes this extremely friendly storefront even more welcome of an oasis. Lincoln Bay is the perfect neighborhood restaurant: friendly, comfortable and easy on the eye, absent of all pretension and attitude, yet not without style. Chef Eddie Herbert once manned the stoves at the former Ritz Café, which explains the cuisine's Southern bent. Big Al's gumbo is the same marvelous stuff the Ritz used to serve. Savory pork chops share a plate with delicious (but intensely sweet) pecan-studded yams. Herbert strays beyond Dixie with a host of other good dishes, from the excellent whole artichoke on a bed of finely diced roasted peppers in vinaigrette to the superb, melt-in-your-mouth osso buco. One disappointment was the rigatoni with house-smoked turkey, arugula and pine nuts—the blazing-hot sauce overwhelmed the flavors of the primary ingredients. Dessert also brought a disappointment—doughy, tasteless profiteroles—but at other dinners, we've found plenty of winners, most notably the pecan diamonds, tiny pecan pies that are probably 500 calories per bite, and worth every one. The prices are as friendly as the staff: $20 to $25 apiece for dinner.

12/20 Locanda del Lago

231 Arizona Ave., Santa Monica 90401;
(310) 451-3525
Italian. Lunch & Dinner Tues.-Sun. AE, MC, V.

From your table in this *locanda*, you get a great view of the human drama enfolding on the Third Street Promenade—it's just like being in a real city. The interior matches the muted colors of ancient Tuscan villas; it's like sitting inside an earth-toned Lego building with big windows. The menu pairs the really unfamiliar dishes of Lombardy with the Italian food we've become so accustomed to. One of the most notable regional dishes is the pesce di lago in carpione, an appetizer of lake trout marinated in wine and balsamic vinegar and topped with a julienne of vegetables. Small regional twists abound: bresaola is served with grapefruit wedges; salmon carpaccio is marinated in orange and thyme; crespelle (crêpes) are filled with fontina from the Valle d'Aosta, where fontina was born. A good meal can be made out of the appetizers and pastas, which are better than the entrées. Dinner for one costs about $40.

Locanda Veneta

8638 W. 3rd St., W. Hollywood 90048;
(310) 274-1893
Italian. Lunch Mon.-Fri., Dinner Mon.-Sat. All major cards.

Seated elbow-to-elbow in this clean-lined, trattoria, it's hard not to be struck by an overwhelming sense that you're in Venice. It's not just because of the name, and not just because of the food—it's also because of the ineffable feeling of being suspended in time. On a warm summer's night, you can feel the evening's breeze flowing in through the windows, you can smell the green olive oil being poured over the carpaccio, you can hear the sizzle of roast lamb (served in a mustard-walnut sauce). Close your eyes (or, alternately, drink enough Pinot Grigio) and you'll surely hear the songs of the gondoliers and the slap of the waters hitting the shores of the great lagoon. The menu is both simple and select, yet it bulges with dishes you must order. By all means, if it's in season, order the frittura di bianchetti: panfried whitebait (tiny fish) served with a fine pile of vinegared onions cooked to a mush. By all means order the trittico di mozzarelle, which is nothing more or less wonderful than a trio of freshly made mozzarellas with tomatoes (which truly taste like tomatoes), basil and extra-virgin olive oil. By all means order the huge grilled langoustines, sweet and smoky and juicy. In Venice, you can eat this well at Il Corte Sconta. But Venice is far away. If only we had the Piazza San Marco to stroll through afterwards, instead of the Beverly Center. . . . You'll spend about $35 per person for dinner.

 ## Louis XIV
606 N. La Brea Ave., Melrose-La Brea District (L.A.) 90036; (213) 934-5102
French. Dinner Mon.-Sat. MC, V.

After nearly five years of booming business, Louis XIV (referred to by the French and Francophiles as "Louis Quatorze" and by others as "Louis the Fourteenth") has just finished a renovation of its space. The high-ceilinged, barnlike space has retained its rough romance, with its cozy loft areas for dining, sponge-painted walls and heavy wooden tables bearing statuesque candles—and it's still one of the hippest, loudest restaurants in L.A. While you wait (which might be for a long time), a crush of Europeans and leather-clad clubgoers circulate among the tables, sharing kisses and bottles of Côtes-du-Rhone. The menu has some new offerings, but there are still plenty of old favorites. Appetizers include mixed greens and chèvre in an olive-oil vinaigrette, a simple tomato salad with fresh basil leaves, roasted red peppers in a garlic-and-anchovy sauce, grilled oyster mushrooms with breaded lamb in mint sauce. There's a no-nonsense style to all the food here: steak pommes frites, steak au poivre (with green peppercorns), filet mignon Bordelaise, grilled salmon with fried baby onions. Dinner is $20 to $30 per person.

10/20 Lula
2720 Main St., Santa Monica 90405; (310) 392-5711
Mexican. Lunch & Dinner daily, Brunch Sat.-Sun. MC, V.

Gerri Gilliland's other restaurant, Gilliland's, has long comforted souls with its reliably good American and Irish cooking. This neuvo-Mexican restaurant (several blocks away from the other) couldn't serve a more different cuisine, though it can be similarly warm and comforting. Lula (named for Gilliland's Mexican mentor, master chef Lula Betran) offers reasonable prices (you can make a fine meal of appetizers alone, running mostly from $3 to $5), a contained noise level and an unpretentious atmosphere. In Lula's bright, convivial setting, indulging a margarita or two seems just the thing to do. Which is what most people do, as the margaritas are fresh, tangy, balanced—superb. As accompaniments, there are fine, crispy chips with tasty salsas, chunky guacamole, squash blossoms stuffed with cheese, good green-corn tamales, a sweet corn pudding, and a fiercely hot mini chile relleno made with a

stuffed jalapeño pepper instead of the usual poblano. Beware of the minuscule appetizer *platos*, which, at $9 or so, are not Lula's best deal. Neither are the larger *platillos Mexicanos*, which are decent but unexciting, and tend to be heavy. The fresh *pescado* (fish) of the day is a good bet. Dinner runs about $15 per person.

 ## Lunaria
10351 Santa Monica Blvd., Century City 90067; (310) 282-8870
French. Lunch Tues.-Fri., Dinner Tues.-Sun. All major cards.

Although it may seem that there's one hip restaurant per BMW on the westside, there are still a few areas that are surprisingly lacking in good spots, particularly Century City. Which makes Lunaria as welcome to the neighborhood as a martini is to Nick Charles. And Nick Charles would feel right at home here. For one thing, he could get a proper drink at the proper bar. For another, he'd appreciate the relaxed elegance of the interior, with its roomy armchairs, lovely watercolor paintings, skillful lighting and glass-walled kitchen. And he'd be relieved to find a grown-up, intelligent refuge from L.A.'s self-consciously hip little-black-dress crowd. He might even like the suave live jazz in the adjacent lounge. Owner Bernard Jacoupy is one of the area's great hosts, the man who made his namesake Bernard's so extraordinary in the early '80s, who later made Irvine's Antoine so wonderful. To this restaurant, he brought Dominique Chavanon, Antoine's talented former chef, who's now cooking more casual and contemporary bistro food. Our favorites? A little tart topped with deeply caramelized onions and chunks of savory smoked duck, followed by a richly flavorful lamb T-bone on a bed of cassoulet beans. Or, if that's too heavy, the crisp crab and vegetable "pancake" with a mango vinaigrette and the monkfish in a spicy glaze with a vegetable paella. The desserts are dreamy, particularly the gorgeous caramelized banana-pecan linzertorte topped with Tahitian vanilla ice cream. Expect to spend $35 to $40 apiece for dinner.

12/20 Ma Bé
8722 W. 3rd St., W. Hollywood 90048; (310) 276-6223
Californian/Mediterranean. Lunch & Dinner Tues.-Sun., Brunch Sun. All major cards.

The exceptionally inviting setting—an ivy-covered facade, a flower-lined, European-style terrace, blond woods balanced by warm colors in the upholstery and carpeting, a fireplace warming the upstairs dining room, romantic Frank Sinatra tapes playing at the handsome bar—makes it pretty easy to overlook the fact that Ma Bé has lost the culinary sparkle it had in its early days, when chef Claude Segal created a pseudo-Mediterranean cuisine as seductive as the interior design. Segal has long since departed, and while the food is similar in style, its execution is only average. Grilled whitefish and marinated chicken entrées were humdrum. One of our old favorites, grilled bacon-wrapped prawns on a bed of greens, was dry. Recently, the veal ravioli and the red-pepper gazpacho were fine but weren't any better than similar dishes elsewhere in town. Though the chocolate cake was delicious, the crème brûlée tasted like a burnt marshmallow. We still love lunching on the terrace, but we don't expect too much of the food. Service is cordial. You'll spend from $30 to $40 apiece for dinner.

Madeo

8897 Beverly Blvd., W. Hollywood 90048;
(310) 859-4903
Italian. Lunch Mon.-Sat., Dinner nightly. All major cards.

L.A. has its Famous Celebrity Restaurants and its Secret Celebrity Restaurants. Madeo is one of the latter. At lunchtime, it's a working person's standby—but instead of lunch pails and racing forms, these working stiffs carry cellular phones and copies of *Daily Variety*. That's because Madeo is located in the building that houses International Creative Management (ICM). So the roomy booths and tables are sprinkled liberally with agents and their clients, the latter whom are dressed down and low-key (like Michelle Pfeiffer, who was sitting next to us at a recent meal). This is the kind of Italian food agents and movie stars (and we) can eat daily: a first-rate carpaccio, sliced (apparently) with a microtome and topped with bits of artichoke, thick slices of Reggiano Parmesan and a drizzle of greenish olive oil; pizzas that feature excellent crusts and such toppings as Gorgonzola and porcini; an extraordinary thick Tuscan soup called ribollita, made with bread and cabbage; and good ravioli filled with branzino (Italian sea bass). A superb lunchtime choice is the antipasti misti, which you select from a heavily laden table near the front door. There are about a dozen dishes to choose from: fine, dry bresaola (paper-thin strips of cured beef), steamed clams and mussels, creamy

> *Some establishments change their closing times without warning. It is always wise to check in advance.*

buffalo mozzarella, excellent risotto and so on. A simple lunch is about $16 apiece, a full dinner about $40.

Ma Maison at Hotel Sofitel

8555 Beverly Blvd., W. Hollywood 90048;
(310) 278-5444
French. Lunch & Dinner Tues.-Sat. All major cards.

Ma Maison (which translates as My House), in the Sofitel hotel, looks more like "Mon Jardin" (My Garden). Under the restaurant's signature white umbrellas and the brown wood beams, you'll find a bucolic atmosphere, the kind you'd expect to find in a country house on a late spring evening. Considering its location in this busy section of the city (wedged between Beverly Hills and West Hollywood, across from the Beverly Center), the ambience is a tour de force, to the credit of the decorator and the maître d', Maurice Ferrer, who has sprinkled the room with interesting paintings. Floral upholstery adds to the country feeling—you expect at any moment to see the chef, Markus Schaedler, pop in with an armful of lettuces, string beans and tomatoes that he's just picked in the back yard.

Fittingly, Schaedler prepares a "California Sunshine" salad of tomatoes in a sherry vinaigrette—crisp and simple, as it's done in the country. Lightness is the motif here, the dishes eschewing the richness of cream and butter. Broiled ahi tuna with spinach and lightly blackened swordfish on a bed of tomatoes and mushrooms benefit from this approach. Pastas and pizzas are offered, too, dressed up with toppings such as Brie cheese or smoked salmon. But the real fun of this elegant and soothing place is its new prix-fixe bistro menu—a prix-fixe composed of courses like jambon forestière (ham garnished with sautéed mushrooms), boudin pommes purée (blood sausage with mashed potatoes), and braised beef with onions, which can be had, along with a glass of red or white wine, for a mere $20! At that price, your own *maison* might have difficulty competing with Ma Maison. About $25 to $35 per person.

Mandalay

611 N. La Brea Ave., Melrose-La Brea District (L.A.) 90036; (213) 933-0717
Vietnamese. Lunch Thurs.-Fri., Dinner Tues.-Sun. All major cards.

If you can't bear the thought of another insalata mista and bowl of pasta, stop in this cool, stylish La Brea spot and discover (or rediscover) the joys of Vietnamese cooking. We used to have to look hard in L.A. to find Vietnamese-French fare, the hybrid cuisine that resulted from

France's almost 100-year occupation of Saigon, but Mandalay has helped to rectifiy the situation. The spareness of the high-ceilinged storefront is softened by white table linens and a small jungle of potted palm and rubber trees. Service is provided by suave Asian women who can be trusted for menu advice. The occasional dish can be justly accused of blandness, but in general the food is quite good, redolent with garlic, lemon grass, ginger, curry and that all-important Asian ingredient, fish sauce (here it's less pungent than usual). Try the goiga salade, an addictively tangy chop of cabbage, chicken and shrimp, and the chao tom, an incredibly savory shrimp "pâté" wrapped around sugarcane sticks and grilled. You pull off a piece of the pâté, wrap it in a gossamer-thin sheets of rice paper, add accompanying bean sprouts and shredded carrot, top it with a dollop of hoisin sauce, and voila!—a Vietnamese burrito. Other good choices include the little brochettes of chicken with a delicate apricot-plum dipping sauce, the grilled catfish fillet and, to conclude, the smooth flan and the delicious fried bananas tucked inside crisp pastry wrappings. About $27 per person for dinner.

12/20 Mandarette

8386 Beverly Blvd., W. Hollywood 90048; (213) 655-6115
Chinese. Lunch Mon.-Fri., Dinner nightly. MC, V.

Not just a dim sum place, Mandarette was among the first L.A. restaurants exclusively dedicated to grazing—an unfortunate term that denotes herds of yuppies stampeding trendy eateries to nibble on bite-sized dishes. Phillip Chiang, son of the Mandarin's Cecilia Chiang, wisely spotted this developing trend toward eating a variety of small tastes instead of one large entrée. And, fortunately, most of the tastes served in this contemporary, comfortable room are agreeable: juicy steamed pork dumplings, good onion pancakes, earthy cold eggplant in a garlic-soy sauce, classic bao buns filled with tasty barbecued pork, and so on. That's not to say these dishes are exceptional, just good. Sticking to the smaller dishes, you can eat for about $12.

The Mandarin

430 N. Camden Dr., Beverly Hills 90210; (213) 272-0267
Chinese. Lunch Mon.-Fri., Dinner nightly. All major cards.

Among aficionados of things culinary, Chinese food can be a thing of worship. The search for the quintessential Chinese restaurant can become tantamount to a nomadic search for the Holy Grail. This is part of the reason why we looked forward to revisiting the revamped Mandarin in Beverly Hills. A venerable force in Chinese cuisine since 1975, when Madame Cecilia Chiang opened this branch of her San Francisco restaurant, The Mandarin was one of the first Chinese restaurants to elevate L.A.'s chow mein–dulled taste buds to another realm. But by the time it was ravaged by fire a few years back, it had lost some of its éclat. Chiang handed the restaurant's reins over to her most charming and creative son, Phillip, who wisely kept The Mandarin's good bones intact and gave both the decor and the food a flattering face-lift. It's still lovely: less fussy and more inviting.

As for the menu, many of the items are available in "small tastes", allowing you to sample a number of delights (though they are expensive). Don't miss the minced chicken in a lettuce cup, a perfect summer dish. The shrimp in a puffy batter are wonderfully fresh and nongreasy—a textbook example of how batter-fried foods should be prepared. The spicy boiled wonton sprinkled with chopped scallions and vegetable preserves is light and piquant, but for us the paramount Mandarin appetizer is a marvelous dish of glazed walnuts served cold on a bed of fried spinach leaves. This dish is an amazement. The fried spinach is as dry and transparent as parchment, the walnuts nestled on this rustling bed are honeyed and crisp. The Chinese chicken salad is what Chinese chicken salad should be; the dumplings and breads, such as the steamed, threaded biscuit sprinkled with sweet-smoky Virginia ham, are delicious. The Mandarin also does one of the best Peking ducks in town; just remember to order it at least two hours in advance. You'll spend about $35 apiece for dinner.

12/20 Maple Drive

345 N. Maple Dr., Beverly Hills 90210; (310) 274-9800
American. Lunch Mon.-Fri., Dinner nightly. All major cards.

Spago is closed for lunch. So, for that matter, is Morton's. But the movers and shakers who run the entertainment industry must eat someplace. The place of choice for many is producer Tony Bill's backstreet alternative: Maple Drive. The large, multileveled space includes a variety of patios and, in the rear, a number of carefully secluded booths. These are accessible by a second, more discreet entrance, through which patrons such as Barbra Streisand, Elton John and Arnold Schwarzenegger usually enter. It's a restaurant attuned to details, from the bird's-eye maple bar to the custom-designed furnishings. But basically, in the style of Tony Bill's other restaurant,

72 Market Street in Venice, this is a Hollywood canteen, a good spot to go for American dishes, with elements drawn from Asia and the Mediterranean. In fact, Leonard Schwartz, former executive chef at 72 Market Street, is now running the kitchens here. In much the same way that 72 Market is best known for its meatloaf, Maple Drive is renowned for its chicken soup, a dish that soothes the stomach of many a middle-level movie executive. The studio moguls who often throw parties here know how to order well: take their lead and try the foie gras sautéed with apples and turnip greens, the quail with string beans, the lamb with assorted olives. About $50 per person for dinner.

12/20 Mario's Peruvian Seafood

5786 Melrose Ave., Hollywood 90004;
(213) 466-4181
Peruvian. Lunch & Dinner daily. MC, V.

When Francisco Pizarro landed in Peru in the sixteenth century, he expected to find gold and emeralds on the ground. Instead he found potatoes, which were the most important staple of the gentle Incas. Which is why you'll find such wonderful potato dishes in this plain, brightly lit room charged with the sounds of South American music. The best of the preparations is papas á la huancaina, a sort of egg-and-potato salad that's one of the great joys of Peruvian cooking. But Mario's is really about seafood. The cold squid salad with onion, tomatoes, celery and olives puts most Italian calamari dishes to shame. Choros á la criolla (steamed mussels buried beneath a mass of pickled onions) isn't subtle, but it's awfully good. Everyone seems to order the platters of saltado de mariscos, a stir-fry of shrimp, squid, octopus, onions and tomatoes, with french fries on the side (the French may have invented pommes frites, but the Peruvians have got them down pat). Tallarin de mariscos tosses in some spaghetti as well. A mere $10 per person for dinner.

11/20 Marix Tex Mex Playa

118 Entrada Dr., Pacific Palisades 90402;
(310) 459-8596
Mexican. Lunch & Dinner daily, Late Supper Fri.-Sat., Brunch Sat.-Sun. MC, V.

Like its West Hollywood counterpart, this '80s-style cantina is always packed to the gills. The reasons for this are plentiful: a great location (just off Pacific Coast Highway north of Sunset), low prices (entrées for about $7), tasty, trendy Mexican food (fajitas, Mexican pizzas, blue-corn tortilla casseroles) and free-flowing drinks (good margaritas, Mexican beer). It all adds up to a cheerful party atmosphere: pitchers of margaritas

are passed around, fresh tortilla chips are devoured, conversation is lively, and the noise level is loud. Food is satisfying if messy to eat, which suits the hang-loose ambience. You won't go wrong with the fajitas, a sizzling platter of grilled vegetables, beans and chicken, beef or shrimp. Limited reservations are taken, so expect a long wait by the bar—it may turn out to be the best part of the evening. Dinner with a margarita runs about $12 to $18.

11/20 Marix Tex Mex Café

1108 N. Flores Dr., W. Hollywood 90069;
(213) 656-8800
Mexican. Lunch Mon.-Fri., Brunch Sat.-Sun., Dinner nightly, Late Supper Fri.-Sat. MC, V.

When Victoria Shemaria and Mary Sweeney turned this formerly failing French restaurant into a thriving Tex-Mex eatery, they made a major contribution to the culinary culture of Los Angeles. They also proved that Mexican restaurants can be fun, hip and even good for the weight-conscious. Not only has this particular brand of Tex-Mex succeeded beyond all expectations, it has become all the rage. Count on a party atmosphere, a chic, mostly gay clientele and a long wait for a table. Food is informal and tasty: good fajitas, made with either beef, chicken or shrimp, and perfect with grilled vegetables and beans; heavy chalupas and chimichangas from New Mexico; passable margaritas; salsas both mild and fiery. Mostly, Marix is great fun, no matter the occasional imperfection. And the price is right: around $12 per person.

Marouch

4905 Santa Monica Blvd., Hollywood 90029; (213) 662-9325
Middle Eastern. Lunch & Dinner Tues.-Sun. AE, MC, V.

Marouch offers one of the largest Middle Eastern menus in the city: in all, 130 items. Hugely satisfying appetizer assortments, served for parties of two or more, are staggeringly complex. The meze (appetizer assortment) for six comprises twenty dishes, most of them large enough to serve as main courses. The spread for two includes eight dishes and covers most of your table. The Marouch experience is built around grazing and a multitude of flavors. Consider the marvelous baked kibbeh, a meatloaf cake of ground veal, beef, bulghur wheat and pine nuts—you simply get can't enough of it. Moughrabiye is a stew of couscous topped with the most tender chicken and beef imaginable, and mehshi kousa is an assortment of squash, eggplant, grape leaves and bell peppers filled with rice and ground beef. Farroug, barbecued chicken served with a garlic sauce, is a marvel; a whole chicken costs all of $8.50 ($6 to go). Marouch is astonishing, probably the best Lebanese/Armenian/Middle Eastern restaurant in Los Angeles. Dinner costs about $20.

11/20 Maryland Crab House
2424 W. Pico Blvd., Santa Monica 90405; (310) 450-5555
Seafood. Lunch & Dinner Tues.-Sun. CB, DC, MC, V.

A thoroughly agreeable, family-run seafood house that is, to the best of our knowledge, the only place in L.A. to get hot spiced hard-shell crabs from Eastern waters. Order them by the dozen and have at them with a mallet, or be lazy and opt for backfin crabcakes, deviled crab, broiled fresh fish or a garlicky Norfolk style preparation of shrimp, crab or scallops instead. This is strictly casual eating; tables sport paper mats and cloth napkins, and bibs are practically required. Homemade rum buns, dill pickles and a choice of baked, fried or mashed (with sour cream and chives) potato comes with main courses, as well as your choice of crunchy homemade coleslaw, fresh vegetables or a pint-sized salad bar. If you must, there are hamburgers, steaks and chicken. Dinner costs $25 per person.

Matsuhisa

129 N. La Cienega Blvd., W. Hollywood 90048; (310) 659-9639
Japanese/Sushi. Lunch Mon.-Fri., Dinner nightly. All major cards.

L.A. is the gateway to the Pacific Rim and, most enjoyably, to the cuisine of the Pacific Rim. Since 1990, Matsuhisa has doubled in size, taking over the restaurant next door. Added to the space are a few more tables and a tempura bar, where chef Nobu Matsuhisa makes the freshest, most delicious, most interesting tempura in town. For those who think tempura is nothing but shrimp and vegetables in a jacket of flannel-flavored batter, Matsuhisa's tempura is a revelation—major religions have been based on things less awe-inspiring than the tempuraed sea urchin wrapped in a shiso leaf. The rest of the menu is equally awe-inspiring, for to dine at Matsuhisa is to rediscover the joys of adventurous eating all over again. Though the sushi can be as good as any in town, the dishes of choice are the house specialties, unusual creations reflecting Nobu's experience in Japan, Peru and Los Angeles. Try the salmon in pepper sauce, the squid "pasta" (paper-thin shavings of buttery squid) with garlic sauce, the mussels in garlic sauce, the halibut

cheek with pepper sauce, the baked black cod, the tiger shrimp in pepper sauce. Leave yourself in the chef's hands, and pray for sea scallops filled with black truffles and topped with caviar. At Matsuhisa, you're paying for the food, not the setting. And if you lose control, you may be paying quite a bit: as much as $70 per person. A more controlled dinner costs about $50.

11/20 Matteo's
2321 Westwood Blvd., Westwood 90064; (310) 475-4521
Italian. Dinner Tues.-Sun. AE, MC, V.

The night to show up at this affable, old-fashioned Italian restaurant is Sunday, when the stars descend in droves. Looking around the restaurant—which feels almost like a private club—you see enough famous faces to last you for weeks. Working the room and schmoozing with your dear friends Frank Sinatra and Don Rickles is really the best reason to visit. Dishes are representative of the Italian food of the '50s, named for the many regulars: pork chops pizzaiola Steve Allen; cauliflower mostacciole Walter Matthau; manicotti Dolly Parton; spaghetti bolognese Ernest Borgnine. But no one pays much attention to the food; they're too busy blowing kisses. Dinner costs around $35.

10/20 Matteo's: A Little Taste of Hoboken
2323 Westwood Blvd., Westwood 90064; (310) 474-1109
Italian. Lunch & Dinner Mon.-Sat. AE, MC, V.

Few who have eaten in the Italian restaurants of Hoboken would deny that there's a special something called Hoboken Style. Find it at this small, casual diner, a snappy, inexpensive version of the palazzo next door. Where there are tablecloths at Matteo's, you eat off Formica in Hoboken. Where the lights are dim in Matteo's, you can perform brain surgery in Hoboken. Where service is fairly proper at Matteo's, it's more comical in Hoboken. This is Italian soul food: the style is mostly southern Italian and Sicilian—one does not find carpaccio here. Red sauce abounds, as do massive portions. Mangia, mangia. The superb broccoli salad is nothing more than steamed broccoli in garlic dressing, but it is big enough to gorge you on. Heavily breaded stuffed artichoke, scungilli (conch) salad and fried calamari are among the best in town. Continue, if you dare, through the thick, unutterably rich lasagne, manicotti, baked rigatoni or baked eggplant. Conclude with spumone or cannoli. A dinner runs $20 or so.

12/20 Matty's on Melrose

7728 Melrose Ave., Melrose-Fairfax District
(L.A.) 90046; (213) 937-2801
Italian. Lunch Mon.-Fri., Dinner nightly. AE, MC, V.

Matty Danza, brother of Tony Danza (of "Who's the Boss" fame), is easy to identify—he's the guy in the suit who's working every table as if his life depended on it. He seems to know everyone; in fact, he probably does know everyone, since a lot of his brother's friends drop by for a drink and a plate of pasta after rehearsals and tapings. Occupying a Melrose space that's been the grave of many a restaurant, Matty's is a California version of a New York Italian restaurant, complete with all the noise, energy and good food. The really good news here is that the food is abundant and satisfying, starting with crisp "Mulberry Street Specials" such as fried calamari, fried shrimp and fried scungilli. The seafood orgy can easily feed two—a whole Maine lobster, shrimp, scallops, clams, mussels, squid and a great tomato sauce are heaped over a bed of linguine. Matty's may be the only true New York–style Italian eatery in L.A. Dinner will cost you $25 or so apiece.

11/20 Maurice's Snack 'n' Chat

5549 W. Pico Blvd., Wilshire District (L.A.) 90019; (213) 930-1795/931-3877
Soul Food. Breakfast, Lunch & Dinner daily. No cards.

We aren't the biggest fans of Maurice's—service is eccentric, the decor is tacky and some of the dishes could be improved. But that's not to say we don't like the place, because we do. It's fun and completely unpretentious, and there are plenty of good things to eat: heavy but tasty fried chicken, messy short ribs, wonderful yams, honest liver and onions and such comforting desserts as coconut cake and cobbler. Accompanying vegetables are mostly forgettable but, as with any restaurant of this genre, it's impossible to leave hungry. Maurice's enjoys a loyal following, so make reservations if you plan to visit on a weekend. About $12 per person.

10/20 Metro

7302 Melrose Ave., Melrose-La Brea District
(L.A.) 90046; (213) 935-1678
Italian. Lunch & Dinner daily. All major cards.

This high-tech Melrose Italian eatery is notable for a number of reasons, none of which involve food. Some of the world's most bizarre chandeliers dangle from its ceiling—industrial-age oddities that could be classified as punk-rock tech. Then there's the bar scene, which on a recent Saturday night featured lots of "Beverly

Hills 90210" wannabes leaning against whatever it is the bar is made out of. As for the food—well, the risotto was laughably underdone (it was actually crunchy), the pizza was adequate but undistinguished; the grilled chicken was too dry; and the pastas hesitated between being underdone or overdone. About $28 per person for dinner.

12/20 Mexica

7313 Beverly Blvd., Melrose-La Brea District
(L.A.) 90036; (213) 933-7385
Mexican. Lunch Mon.-Fri., Dinner nightly. AE, MC, V.

Every neighborhood needs a good Mexican restaurant, and Mexica (pronounced "me-SHEE-ka") has assumed the mantle hereabouts. A few retro touches will remind you that this used to be the Chinese Kitchen, a '30s-style Chinese diner. The ceiling is high, the wall clock is neon, the booths are roomy, and '30s and '40s music plays on the stereo. But the tilework, masks and vivid wall murals put you in the mood for a Bohemia and some chips and salsa (which, by the way, are excellent). Despite the touches of trendiness in the decor, the food is authentic, occasionally a bit too much so—the carne asada was as dry as most Mexican beef dishes are. But everything else we've tried has been great, from the sweet green-corn tamales to the impeccably creamy flan. Best bets are the marvelous little empanada-like quesadillas, filled with such things as zucchini flowers or potato and chorizo; any of the shrimp dishes, such as the simple grilled skewer of juicy marinated shrimp, peppers and onion; and anything with the dark, deeply flavorful mole sauce. Dinner shouldn't cost more than $20 per person.

12/20 Mezzaluna

9428 Brighton Way, Beverly Hills 90210;
(310) 275-6703
11750 San Vicente Blvd., Brentwood 90049;
(310) 447-8667;
Italian. Lunch Mon.-Sat., Dinner nightly. AE, MC, V.

This franchise of the chic Aspen/New York restaurant is as bright, friendly and hip as a Beverly Hills restaurant gets. If you don't mind a bit of soot on your pizza, the sidewalk tables are delightful. Inside are moon-faced tiles, a fine antique bar and waiters who seem happy to be there, even though they'd rather be starring in soap operas. At the bar, stylish women, often in a certain mode of clingy dress, sip wine with men who are wearing their loosest Armani suits, without a tie. Mezzaluna is quite proud of its pizzas—made by a fellow from Brooklyn, they have a crackerlike crust unlike any we've tasted in Canarsie or Bensonhurst. They're very good, and sparingly topped with such things as pesto or porcini. Even more interesting are the many carpaccios, paired, for instance, with avocado and hearts of palm, or sautéed olives and tomatoes. The rest of the menu is both familiar and creative, from the wonderful mixed grilled vegetables to the pappardelle with musky porcini to the grilled swordfish with an eggplant confit. For dessert, try the vanilla ice cream plopped into hot espresso. Dinner will run you about $40.

 ## Michael's
1147 3rd St., Santa Monica 90403; (310) 451-0843
Californian/American. Lunch Tues.-Fri., Dinner Tues.-Sun., Brunch Sat.-Sun. All major cards.

From its foundations on up, Michael's is a paean to everything Californian. Sitting on the patio, a glass of sparkling wine in hand, you are cooled by Pacific breezes, lit by the stars and bathed in the scent of flowers. When plates of delicate, subtle finger foods—perhaps some foie gras, or a nibble of gravlax—arrive, you want to give yourself over completely to the chamber-of-commerce-style idea of California as Garden of Eden. The creator of this earthly paradise is one Michael McCarty, a culinary innovator—not to mention a remarkably self-assured entrepreneur who made his restaurant a synonym for California dining before he hit the age of 30. In the riotously successful '80s, he had lots of customers who didn't blink at spending $100 apiece for dinner. But those days are gone. He is still quick to perceive and react to culinary trends and changes in the tastes of his clients. And thus far he has managed to stay in business, lowering prices long before it became fashionable and continuing to be the gregarious, glad-handing, consummate California restaurateur.

Michael's serves elegant food that's reasonably innovative—meaning not too outlandish—to a well-groomed westside crowd. The combination of just enough ginger with lime and cilantro in a seafood cassoulet gives the dish great finesse; the lobster in the seafood salad almost achieves perfection. Delicately moist, the East Coast scallops melt in the mouth, their accompanying thin cuts of bacon discreetly underlining the flavor of the dish rather than adding, as is often the case, an overpowering note. (Complexity can be expressed simply; it's a matter of measure and talent.) A well-balanced Cognac sauce lends a savory richness to the foie gras from New York and the Carpinterias squab. Desserts, from the caramel-custard torte with layers of caramel and

chocolate to the five sorbets and eight different cookies, won't send you into the same heavenly orbit—but since we're already in paradise at Michael's, we'll behave like angels and forget this slight disappointment. It could take you the duration of your dinner to wade through the huge, well-chosen wine list, which begins with $15 bottles and continues up into the stratosphere. Expect to pay $65 per person.

12/20 Mi Ranchito
8694 W. Washington Blvd., Culver City 90232; (310) 837-1461
Mexican. Lunch & Dinner daily. MC, V.

Since 1972, the Telona family has been introducing Angelenos to the seafood-intensive cuisine of Veracruz. They use vegetable oil rather than the customary lard, which compromises flavors just a little. It's a small price to pay for potentially lowering your cholesterol level by double digits. In a fairly zany, kitsch-filled room (complete with a remarkable jukebox stocked with about 100 Spanish-language CDs), you can sample a large and uniformly terrific collection of Veracruzan dishes, all served with a fine fish soup, tortillas, rice, beans and other sides: camarones al mojo de ajo, plump, juicy shrimp, cooked in garlic until they reek in the most delightful way; shrimp Veracruzana, in a sauce of tomatoes, peppers and olives; huachinango (red snapper) either stuffed, grilled, fried, garlicked or Veracruzed; and various caldos, huge bouillabaisse-like stews thick with fish and shellfish. And yes, they do make combinations of enchiladas and tacos, tamales and burritos—but you'll surely abandon them after tasting the cocido (a beef stew that's to Mexico what chicken soup is to Eastern Europe) and the pozole (pork and hominy soup). For dessert, there's a flan of awesome richness. Dinner runs about $12 apiece.

12/20 Mon Kee
679 N. Spring St., Chinatown (L.A.) 90012; (213) 628-6717
Chinese Seafood. Lunch & Dinner daily. All major cards.

Mon Kee always seems to have a line out the door, probably because the food has remained good down through the years. The restaurant earned a place in local history by introducing countless Westerners to the joys of Chinese seafood, and by pioneering the way for similar establishments in Monterey Park and Alhambra. This food is uniformly tasty: juicy shrimp coated with rock salt, delicious stir-fried rock cod in a sweet-and-sour sauce, scallops with chicken and snow peas and, best of all, the generous, messy crab in either black-bean or ginger sauce. This will be enough to help you overlook the lino-leum-and-vinyl design scheme. Expect a long wait for a table. About $15 or $20 per person.

Morton's

8800 Melrose Ave., W. Hollywood 90069; (310) 276-5205
American. Dinner Mon.-Sat. All major cards.

Peter Morton created the Hard Rock Café, and was one of the first restaurateurs to recognize that culinary Americana means good eats. This place is perhaps the quintessential power hangout for the entertainment industry, the place where the term A-table is defined in this town. The menu changes with regularity, but you might run into starter fare like a finely muscled black-eyed pea soup; a plateful of cold East Coast oysters; or mâche and radicchio tossed with goat cheese and slices of fresh pear. Morton's main courses are simple but exceptional: Chesapeake Bay crabcakes kept company by a Dijon-mustard mayonnaise, marvelous grilled lamb chops mari-nated in cracked pepper, olive and thyme, grilled lime chicken (free range, of course) and a won-derful plate of grilled, roasted or steamed vege-tables combining red, green and yellow peppers, eggplant, mushrooms, fennel, tomatoes and more—it's one of the best in town. On weeknights, particularly Monday, Morton's is a veritable commissary for Hollywood's heaviest of hitters, including all the major studio chefs, agents, and more than a few stars. Great Califor-nia red wines, too, with names that read like a Pantheon, and an impressive (if expensive) list of red Bordeaux. Dinner costs about $35.

11/20 Moustache Café

8155 Melrose Ave., Melrose-Fairfax District (L.A.) 90069; (213) 651-2111
American. Lunch Mon.-Fri., Dinner & Late Supper nightly (until 2 a.m. Fri.-Sat.). AE, MC, V.

As displayed by the ever-present row of customers' Rolls-Royces and Mercedeses lined up along its front, The Moustache is hardly suf-fering from a lack of business. We, however, won't be rushing back. True, the trellis- and plant-lined enclosed patio is a charming spot to lunch, though the tables are crammed uncom-fortably close together. Some of the dishes are competent, such as the seafood salad and the Swiss-cheese-and-tomato crêpe. But others don't quite make it: the more elaborate entrées are best left unordered and the much-acclaimed chocolate soufflé is uneven. Service is notoriously slow. But this hasn't stopped throngs of Holly-wood starlets and minor moguls from making the Moustache a resounding success. Lunch, if you

stick to one of the omelets or crêpes, should cost under $20, dinner closer to $30. Another, less glamorous, branch in Westwood serves the same menu (1071 Glendon Ave.; 310-208-6633).

12/20 Muse

7360 Beverly Blvd., Melrose-La Brea District (L.A.) 90036; (213) 934-4400
Californian. Lunch Tues.-Sat., Dinner Mon.-Sat., Late Supper Fri.-Sat. All major cards.

After more than a decade, this place remains one of L.A.'s best-kept secrets—virtually sign-less, with a blank concrete exterior on one of the busiest streets in town. There is method to this seeming madness, for the diners who go to Muse want to do their musing with a modicum of privacy—we've seen folks ranging from Bruce Springsteen to G. Gordy Liddy there, making it a sort of sub-Spago. Interestingly, the early-'80s minimalist design has managed to remain fresh and vibrant, and the aura of ultramodernism comforts more than it alienates. With the depar-ture of chef Vaughan Allen, the food has been in a bit of a state of flux, though the overall style seems intact: California cuisine with a modest Asian touch, along with some curious little Mex-ican fillips. A good example are the lettuce-leaf "tacos" filled with minced chicken moistened with a peanut vinaigrette, and the steamed salmon topped with a trio of caviars. Throughout the comings and goings of chefs over the last decade, the desserts have remained exemplary. Dinner runs about $40 per person.

10/20 Musso & Frank's Grill

6667 Hollywood Blvd., Hollywood 90028; (213) 467-7788
American. Lunch & Dinner Tues.-Sat. All major cards.

This clubbish Hollywood landmark continues to be hugely popular, and even we are not com-pletely immune to Musso's charms. The bar is great—loaded with lore—the ambience has you dreaming of Hollywood of the '40s, and some (not all) of the myriad dishes are more than sat-isfying. Most notable are the grilled steaks and chops. The rest of the menu celebrates the food of yore: sauerbraten, chicken pot pie, short ribs, filet mignon, sautéed scallops in a white-wine sauce and on and on. Vegetables and salads are no better than what you'd expect from a diner, but do come for a drink—you haven't been to Hollywood if you haven't been to Musso's. A breakfast menu, offered at all times, includes sat-isfying omelets and "flannel cakes," which are thin, delicate pancakes served with a special but-ter sauce. Dinner will be about $15 per person.

A GRAND ACHIEVEMENT.

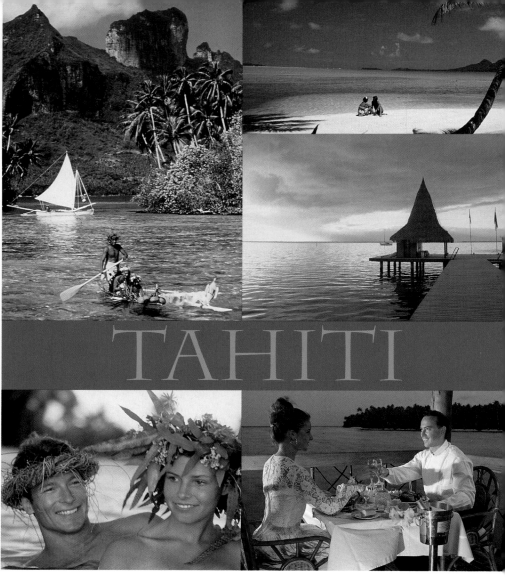

Step back in time, experience the magic of Tahiti.
It's almost like a dream; white sand beaches, crystal waters beyond
blue, surrounding the most beautiful islands in the world.

Call 1 (800) 828-6877 for your free 52 page Tahiti color brochure.

Islands in the Sun
Travel specialist since 1965

12/20 Neptune's Net

42505 Pacific Coast Hwy., Malibu 90265;
(310) 457-3095
Seafood. Breakfast, Lunch & Dinner daily. MC, V.

This quintessential California beachfront restaurant is found a short distance away from the Ventura County Line; its overgrown shack just across the highway from Leo Carrillo State Beach. Inside, you find an ample supply of surfers drinking beer, eating fries and digging happily into mounds of seafood, corn on the cob and some of the best clam chowder this side of the Saint Lawrence Seaway. This is a rough-and-ready sort of restaurant, where you do everything yourself and don't mind it one bit. The routine is simple: you head for the tank room, where you order shrimp (large, jumbo or colossal), lobster (both Eastern and Western), crab (rock and king), clams and oysters, all by the pound. Corn is sold by the ear; chowder by the pint. You then head for the general store next door, where you order drinks or baskets of deep-fried fish. When your number is called, you dig in with your plastic utensils at one of the long, gnarly wooden tables on the deck. Expect a broad cross-section of customers, from Porsche drivers to rednecks. Ah! If only all California seafood restaurants could be like this one. Dinner costs about $15.

12/20 Nicky Blair's

8730 Sunset Blvd., W. Hollywood 90069;
(310) 659-0929
Continental. Dinner Mon.-Sat., Late Supper Mon.-Sat. All major cards.

The original Nicky Blair's was a mainstay of the celebrity dining circuit from 1971 through 1975, the year it burned to the ground. The revived Nicky Blair's is one of those Hollywood restaurants where you're either part of the scene or you're not. Just standing at the bar, you could fill a sociologist's textbook. Listen in on these conversations, chatter loaded with industry buzzwords: points, grosses, the package, high concept. The spirits of Giorgio, Bijan and Georgette Klinger hover over this room. And the food? It's mostly Italian/Continental cuisine in the style of the old Perino's, and it's all perfectly fine. Count on standards like calamari fritti, mozarella marinara and prosciutto with melon for starters. There's a generous list of pastas, most of them swathed in cream sauce or marinara sauce, and many chicken breast preparations. Classic veal dishes and fresh grilled fish will satisfy you, but they won't distract you unduly from the fascinating crowd. The vast wine list covers most of California, France and Italy. Dinner costs about $45.

12/20 North Beach Bar & Grill

111 Rose Ave., Venice 90291;
(310) 399-3900
American/Steakhouse. Lunch Mon.-Fri., Dinner nightly, Brunch Sun. AE, MC, V.

Jonathan Borofsky's ominous 30-foot-high ballerina-clown sculpture looming over North Beach's entrance leads one to expect an outlandish decor and food of the charred-sea-snake-with-wasabe-pineapple-chutney variety—but, in fact, the place is soothing and handsome, populated with normal-looking people eating steaks and onion rings. Roomy wicker armchairs fill the bar, solid wooden chairs fill the dining room, and your basic Bauerware crockery is displayed as objets d'art. Even if you don't dine here, hang awhile in the bar and sample the crisp Caesar salad; thick, sweet grilled corn-clam chowder; unspeakably light beer-batter onion rings; or the fiendishly rich North Beach bread, thick toasted sourdough topped with cheese and sweet onion. Entrées, from a standard New York steak with herb butter to a pleasant, but not crisp-skinned, roast garlic chicken (the sort any of us might make at home on Sunday), do a workmanlike but unmemorable job. Desserts run to such upscale-American standards as flourless chocolate cake and ice-cream sundaes. A steak dinner runs about $40 per person; a smaller meal can easily run $20.

Ocean Avenue Seafood

1401 Ocean Ave., Santa Monica 90401;
(310) 394-5669
Seafood. Lunch & Dinner daily, Brunch Sun. All major cards.

This bustling, upscale seafood restaurant/oyster bar has a bright new look, more room and textured, sponged walls. it has to be classed among the better seafood restaurants in town, like its sibling, downtown's Water Grill. Service is smooth, the atmosphere is cheery, and the kitchen turns out an impressive daily-changing seafood feast: New England clam chowder, crisp crabcakes and a fine blackened catfish filet.

This may not be a grand-style seafood house—but give it twenty years or so, and it just might rank up there. In the meantime, it's a fine place for a seafood dinner, with a prime, seaside location to boot. Dinner runs about $30 per person.

> *Because of the mercurial nature of L.A.'s restaurant scene, it's always wise to call ahead to make sure a particular establishment is still open.*

Ocean Seafood

747 N. Broadway, Chinatown (L.A.) 90012;
(213) 687-3088
Chinese Seafood. Dim Sum, Lunch & Dinner daily. MC, V.

What used to be the rather down-at-the-heels Miriwa, a Chinese restaurant from a former era, has turned into one of old Chinatown's best Cantonese seafood houses. It's now a rambling, mildly glitzy second-story Hong Kong–style eatery famed for some of the best dim sum in town (rivalled only by nearby Empress Pavilion and Harbor Village in Monterey Park), not to mention flawlessly fresh seafood. Much of the fish and shellfish comes from giant tanks filled with lobsters, crabs, all sorts of finned fish and, most wonderfully, live shrimp, which are served five different ways, and which taste infinitely better fresh from the tank than fresh from the freezer. As is true at most Chinese restaurants, the best way to eat here is with a large group; preorder a banquet featuring such house specialties as deep-fried live shrimp on bamboo sticks, braised whole abalone, pan-fried lobster with ginger and green onions, baked crab with black-bean and chili sauce and deep-fried whole fish. What Mon Kee was to Chinese seafood in the early '80s, Ocean Seafood is in the '90s—a revelation and a joy. About $30 per person (much less for dim sum).

Off Vine

6263 Leland Way, Hollywood 90028;
(213) 962-1900
Californian. Lunch Mon.-Fri., Dinner nightly. AE, MC, V.

In concept, we love this small, out-of-the-way café—it's a neighborhood restaurant in a restored bungalow on a quiet side street. The atmosphere is comfortable and casually chic, with white-washed walls, a fireplace, Herb Ritts photos (in a nod to contemporary L.A. style), and Adirondack chairs dotting the front lawn. In practice, too, we have had some very good meals here; we have memories of one of the best Caesar salads in town and calamari as crisp as pretzels. Among the starters we've come back for are cheese-stuffed chiles rellenos in a puddle of tomatillo sauce, topped with chile-pepper purée, and waferlike potato pancakes crowned with sour cream, caviar and herbs. A short, sweet list of entrées tends towards the simple and solid: grilled New York strip steak, veal tenderloin in a peach-green-peppercorn sauce, pastas, daily fresh fish. Desserts are homemade—we flip over the fragrant blueberry-crumble pie. It's a real treasure to find such a slice of gentility in this land of lunacy. Dinner costs about $25 per person.

12/20 Olí Olá

15200 Sunset Blvd., Pacific Palisades 90272;
(310) 459-9214
Italian. Lunch Mon.-Fri., Dinner nightly. All major cards.

The spirit of *abbondanza* reigns here. Olí Olá occupies the space that used to house Lido, a handsome second-story room in the midst of the mysteriously restaurant-poor Palisades. Under the direction of chef Agostino Sciandri, the food sparkles. His kitchen crew makes fine versions of all the usual modern Italian dishes—carpaccio, bocconcini con basilico, bruschetta, scampi—but he's come up with many intriguing twists as well. Like the bouquet of fresh vegetables that sits on every table as a pre-appetizer appetizer. Or such appetizers as trippa con fagioli (tripe with white beans) and tonno marinato (tuna marinated in balsamic vinegar). Risotti abound—with fresh asparagus tips, with squid and sweet chard, with quail, with veal sauce. The kitchen makes a wonderful roasted veal shank and a great liver and onions. Dinner costs $30 or more per person.

Opus

2425 W. Olympic Blvd., Santa Monica 90404; (310) 829-2112
Seafood/French. Lunch Mon.-Fri., Dinner Mon.-Sat. AE, MC, V.

We like to think of this magnificent creation as Opus One. As is customary in pieces of classical music, we've numbered it as the first restaurant that chef Eberhard Müller can call his own. With his partner, Charles Almond, and his executive chef, Ian Winslade, Müller has created a seafood symphony on the order of New York's legendary Le Bernardin, where he Winslade last teamed up. The seafood-only concept represents a true challenge for a chef, as the quality of the day's catch can't be anything less than first rate. There may be a subtle potato or a modest bit of spinach tucked away under the crab salad or hiding under the John Dory respectively, but essentially, the fish is the main act, the star attraction. Opus hides itself in a gleaming new office-building complex a mile from the Pacific Ocean. The curvaceous wood paneling and muted colors are cooly sensual, as pure and unadorned as those fish dishes.

Müller opens his menu with a seductive list of "raw temptations": diced tuna in citrus sauce, marinated monkfish salad, salmon tartare (no beef here, remember!). You can also choose from a selection of seared, poached and grilled appetizers, such as oysters (seared) with truffle and leeks, or halibut slices (poached) in celery jus. There's nary a flaw in any of these creations, nor in the entrées, which range from a succulent cut of halibut poached in a warm vinaigrette sauce, to crisped black bass with marinated white beans, to roasted monkfish with lentils braised in red wine. If you want a broader sampling of sea creatures, and a marvelous display of the chefs' talents, opt for the $55 prix-fixe menu. The wine list is composed of some pricey offerings. In the the Champagne category, the average price hovers around $98; as for wines, the Montrachet Dom Ramonet (a French Chardonnay) goes for $425, and it's still not the most expensive bottle available. Never mind this, and order the Pouilly-Fumé from P. Figeat—at $28, it's one of the best wine values we've found in town, and it will do justice to just about anything Eberhard composes. There's no mistaking this symphony's crescendo in the desserts, including a stunningly rich hazelnut-chocolate cake and an apple tart that would astound even a French grandmother. It's a grand experience, at price: lunch costs about $30; dinner, $55 to $70 per person.

 L'Orangerie

903 N. La Cienega Blvd., W. Hollywood 90069; (310) 652-9770
French. Dinner nightly. All major cards.

Our first meal under new chef Jean-Claude Parachini's reign was one of the best we've had in California. We could not say the same of the "old" L'Orangerie—under its previous kitchen regime, the food was elegant and well prepared, but not always worth the investment. We still tremble at the thought of paying such a sum for an evening of transitory pleasure, but Parachini's food makes it seem almost conscionable. The high romance of the setting hasn't changed a bit. This petite Versailles is divided into three rooms, each with high ceilings, stately French windows and larger-than-life flower displays. Our favorite room is the center *faux* patio, with its iron armchairs, large, private tables and galaxy of tiny white lights. Service is provided by suave young Frenchmen. The wine steward with the winning smile will help you choose an admirable French bottle in your price range, if that is at least $40, preferably $60 or more.

Though only 31, Parachini has been perfecting his craft since the age of 14 at some of the world's best restaurants, from Le Vivarois and L'Ambroisie in Paris to La Grenouille in New York. His is an opulent, celebratory cuisine, full of refinement but hardly prissy. The feuillantine of langoustines and sesame seeds with a curry sauce, for instance, sent us reeling. The spices gave the dish an intoxicating aroma, but their flavor was masterfully subtle, just the thing to complement the sweetness of the small langoustines and the richness of the crisp pastry. A very different appetizer, the stew of young vegetables with fresh mint and coriander, could inspire a diehard carnivore to become a vegetarian. Every dish is worthy of a long eulogy, but we'll summarize by saying that each one—from the crusty grilled prime rib with marrow bones and a lush, tarragon-infused béarnaise, to the spectacular, almost Vietnamese-tasting roasted duck with spices, apple, quince and saffron, to the best crème brûlée on the planet to the powerful trilogy of chocolate desserts—boasts a distinct personality and deft balance of flavors. Some even acheive greatness.

Under chef Parachini—and the continuing skillful management of Gerard Ferry—L'Orangerie is a superb place for those who appreciate seriously fine cooking to hold a seriously fine celebration. (We're already planning celebrations for the Vernal Equinox, April Fool's Day and perhaps even Secretary's Day.) You'll spend $75 to $90 per person for a three-course dinner.

 The Original Sonora Café

445 S. Figueroa St., Downtown (L.A.) 90071; (213) 624-1800
Mexican/Southwestern. Lunch Mon.-Fri., Dinner nightly. All major cards.

Probably no trend came and went more rapidly than Southwestern cuisine; oceans of blue-corn tortillas and dishes made with obscure chiles sporting hefty price tags. No wonder the trend quickly fell flat. The Original Sonora Café, a cousin of the El Cholo chain, is one of the survivors. The management knows exactly what it is doing at this cool, downtown bank-building restaurant, which is highlighted by a high-concept, stylized Santa Fe decor. The menu is filled with all the right dishes: duck tamales, tequila-marinated fish, blue-cornbread madeleines, spectacular carnitas with earthy black beans—all delicious. The only bad news is daytime parking. It could bankrupt you. Go at night instead, when parking is free. Dinner costs about $25.

 Orleans

11705 National Blvd., W.L.A. 90064; (310) 479-4187
Cajun/Creole. Lunch Mon.-Fri., Dinner nightly. AE, MC, V.

Orleans remains one of the few survivors of the Great Cajun/Creole Panic of the early '80s, when everyone and his brother was doing blackened something or other. And it remains a survivor for good reason—it was, and is, one of the few Cajun/Creole establishments that had a clue

63

about what it was doing. Thanks to the occasional fine-tuning of its menu by master chef Paul Prudhomme (the king of Cajun cuisine), Orleans has stayed as good as ever, even though the culinary style is no longer new. Aside from Farmer's Market's wonderful Gumbo Pot, this is our favorite place in town for jambalaya, gumbo, crayfish etouffée and Cajun popcorn—dishes that make up in fiery excitement what they lack in subtlety. Stick with the beloved standards—some of the newer dishes are fairly ghastly, especially a thing called "turducken" that's a combination of, yes, turkey, duck and chicken. Expect to spend about $35 per person for dinner.

10/20 Orso
8706 W. 3rd St., W. Hollywood 90048; (310) 274-7144
Italian. Lunch, Dinner & Late Supper daily. MC, V.

Though there are plenty of us who miss the old Joe Allen (and plenty of us who think the last thing L.A. needs is another radicchio-and-carpaccio emporium), this branch of a popular Broadway after-theater Italian hangout has developed quite a following, especially among middle-level celebrities who want to be seen but don't want to be noticed. The room, with lots of warm wood and soft angles, is noisy, busy, crowded. This is a hot spot that has very little self-consciousness to get in the way of a good time and a decent meal. Orso is a fine place to drop by late-ish (it's open until around midnight every night) for pizza made with a hard, crackly crust, as well as very good pastas, fair veal and passable chicken. The bottom line is that if a dish is simple, the kitchen will probably do it well. Subtlety is not the strong suit at Orso—being there is the point. And on a warm summer's night, the secluded patio is a lovely spot to escape the world. Dinner costs you about $35.

Osteria Nonni
3219 Glendale Blvd., Atwater 90039; (213) 666-7133
Italian. Lunch Tues.-Fri., Dinner nightly. MC, V.

Atwater is a friendly, melting-pot community populated by working-class Latinos, Anglos and a recent influx of Asians, a place where Chevy sedans, not Saabs, are the norm. But wait—isn't this little storefront filled with men in ponytails and assorted cool types in requisite shades of black? There's a reason why, of course. The founding chef at this little charmer was once the pizza chef at Angeli, and he brought his incomparable recipes with him. Knockout pizza dough is the core of the menu, going into the ten or so

pizzas, most of the lunchtime panini (sandwiches) and that basket of warm bread on your table. The rest of the menu runs to simple starters, including an excellent antipasto assortment and a sharp, tangy green salad; a half dozen modest and sometimes dull pastas (spaghetti marinara, spaghetti with butter and Parmesan), grilled dishes like whole baby chicken and, of course, tiramisu, generic but completely satisfying. The wine selection is sensibly priced and appealing, the caffè lattes appropriately frothy and the prices a steal: dinner runs under $15.

11/20 Pacific Dining Car
1310 W. 6th St., Downtown (L.A.) 90017; (213) 483-6000
2700 Wilshire Blvd., Santa Monica 90403; (310) 453-4000.
American/Steakhouse. Open daily 24 hours (Brunch menu Sun.) MC, V.

Pacific Dining Car has built up a loyal and sizable following through sheer longevity—and to many this steak and chop house is indeed beyond criticism. It's undeniably a fun place to visit: the front room looks like a railway car from the halcyon days of the Union Pacific, with a warm and rather clubby ambience. Breakfasts and appetizers are always good here, and so, for that matter, is the service. The chile is exceptional, spareribs are wonderfully smoky and French-fried zucchini is positively addictive. But if you go expecting a sublime steak, you may leave disappointed—they're good, not exceptional. Dinner can run from $40 to $60 per person.

The Palm
9001 Santa Monica Blvd., W. Hollywood 90069; (310) 550-8811
American/Steakhouse. Lunch Mon.-Fri., Dinner nightly. All major cards.

One explanation for The Palm's enormous popularity is that the noise and chaotic service in this New York–style steakhouse is not as offensive as it would be in an elegant French or Italian restaurant. Another reason is that it's fun; another is that the steaks, while not the pinnacle, perhaps, are consistently high class. Besides, The Palm serves the best accompaniment to a steak that you can find this side of a great bottle of red Burgundy—thick, crispy, addictive cottage fries. This duo, along with a piece of The Palm's splendid, straight-from–New York cheesecake is one of the best simple dinners in Southern California. The Palm serves far more than steak, though. They now have Maryland crab on the menu, along with chicken, fish and lobsters so large you'll think they're special effects. Come before 7 p.m. or after 9:30, to avoid the inevitable evening cacophony. Regardless, bring money. Dinner will top $60 per person, and $100 isn't out of the question.

12/20 Pane Caldo Bistrot

8840 Beverly Blvd., W. Hollywood 90048; (310) 274-0916
Italian. Lunch Mon.-Sat., Dinner nightly, Brunch Sun. AE, MC, V.

A recent change of management seems to be emphasizing a more casual atmosphere for this second-story Italian favorite, one of the first real trattorias to open in Los Angeles. Which is a bit odd, for Pane Caldo already seemed pretty casual to us, a place you'd look rather silly all dressed up. Situated over a quirky antique mall (don't miss the shop that specializes in turn-of-the-century posters, Pane Caldo continues to be a major destination for local talent agents out for a lunch that's just a lunch, not a scene. The larger menu now offers 25 antipasti (try the grilled eggplant with mascarpone), soups (including a real minestrone) and salads, along with an even dozen pizzas (we're quite fond of the one topped with grilled vegetables). You can segue from there into any of the fifteen pastas (if you can't make up your mind, try the sampler of any three). Call it a bistro, call it a trattoria—whatever it is, it offers good portions at low prices, in a relaxed setting where Italian is spoken as much as English. Dinner runs $25 per person.

Pane e Vino

8265 Beverly Blvd., W. Hollywood 90048; (213) 651-4600
Italian. Lunch Mon.-Sat., Dinner nightly. AE, MC, V.

We still think back to that sparkling day in Santa Barbara, capped off with a magical dinner at Montecito's Pane e Vino (literally, Bread and Wine). The Chianti, the fragrant bread soup, the sublime risotto, the grilled shrimp . . . it was one of those perfect simple Italian meals that inspires one to sell the house and flee to Tuscany. So when we saw the late, unlamented Baci transmogrify into a southern outpost of Pane e Vino, we scurried over, our appetites at the ready. After all, the co-founder of both branches, Claudio Marchesan, is one of the fathers of the Italian trattoria in California.

This place is even better looking than its parent, all warm, earthen tones and Tuscan-ish details. Grills sizzle in the open kitchen, patrons laugh and chat. The outside patio, with walls covered in flowers and climbing vines, inspires the fantasy that we're entertaining in our villa somewhere in the Mediterranean. There are fresh, simple salads and some very good appetiz-

ers (try the grilled shrimp with feta cheese and mint leaves, served in a small pool of olive oil, or the fine prosciutto wrapped around a fat breadstick); the sausages and peppers with polenta make a good, hearty meal and several of the pastas, including the arrabiatta and the puttanesca, are spicy and full of flavor. We've also had a gooey, rather bland risotto, and the clay-roasted chicken was succulent and lemony one time. Less than $20 for a pasta dinner, $25 with meat or seafood.

La Parrilla

2126 Brooklyn Ave., E.L.A. 90033; (213) 262-3434
Mexican. Breakfast, Lunch, Dinner & Late Supper daily. AE, MC, V.

Very little English is spoken at La Parrilla (which means "The Grill"), an authentic Mexican restaurant located in the heart of the Mexican barrio. La Parrilla is much prettier than most of its neighbors, thanks to earthenware bowls hanging from the walls and a large collection of decorative tiles. It's also just plain better—in fact, it's one of the best Mexican restaurants in town. The menu is in Spanish, but the staff is eager to please, and will do their best to translate. Signs tout the wonders of the house menudo (a traditional hangover cure made from tripe), pozole and tamales, all made fresh on weekends. Handmade tortillas are served with lunch, and salsa is fresh and strong, perfumed with crisp onions and cilantro. Mexican seafood is outstanding here; a massive, deep-fried red snapper topped with a light tomato-and-olive sauce, wonderful camarones al mojo de ajo and a seafood parrillada for two. Dinner runs about $15 per person.

Patina

5955 Melrose Ave., Hollywood 90038; (213) 467-1108
French. Lunch Tues.-Fri., Dinner nightly. All major cards.

Simply stated, Patina offers what is probably the most completely satisfying fine dining experience in Los Angeles. On any given day, it's difficult to say who is the best chef in town, Joachim Splichal at Patina or Michel Richard at Citrus; sometimes we even disagree among ourselves on this point. But there is no doubt that this elegantly minimalist place is the more attractive and comfortable of the two, with finer place settings and appointments, more consistently attentive service and a much better wine list. Perhaps this is because Patina is a more formal (almost reserved) restaurant—it's hard to imagine Splichal saying he'd like diners to think of

Patina as "Jack's Place" the way Richard says he'd like diners to think of Citrus as "Mike's Place." But whatever the reason, Patina is more likely to remind one of a superb restaurant in the French countryside than any other restaurant in Los Angeles. Indeed, Splichal's charming wife, Christine, welcomes guests at the front of the house and sets the tone for the entire operation, much as the chef/proprietor's wife so often does in the French countryside.

Patina may be at its absolute best in the fall and winter, when game is in season; at various times last year, we had a marvelous woodcock, a delightfully gamey grouse, wild duck with figs and caramelized pearl onions and one of the best venison dishes in memory: venison medallions with celery-root chips served in a sauce of foie gras and pepper. Splichal also works wonders with items rarely found on menus in Los Angeles—or anywhere else in the United States, for that matter. Under "Odd Things" are listed cock's comb with curly cabbage and pearl onions in a Pinot Noir sauce; a meltingly delicate calf's brain with baby leeks and crushed capers in a simple brown-butter sauce; sweetbreads in phyllo dough with foie gras, cabbage and a sauce made with dry Riesling from Splichal's native Germany; and sautéed rabbits' kidneys—thirteen of them, each a single, chewy bite. But Splichal paints just as impressive a gastronomic picture when less extraordinary ingredients are on his palette. His signature dish is a corn blini topped with crème fraîche and smoked salmon. The humble, ordinary potato achieves undreamed-of dimensions in his hands. His Santa Barbara shrimp with mashed potatoes and potato-truffle chips may be the only dish other than the corn blini that has remained on the menu from day one, and deservedly so. But we can also recommend the potato lasagne with wild mushrooms and Italian parsley sauce and the cold potato soup with smoked eel—among many other dishes.

Comme plat principal? Well, if you're a meat-and-potatoes sort, how about a gratin of lamb with mashed potatoes and garlic? You prefer fowl? Choose from among chicken, duck and squab, the latter done with duck liver and the world's best homemade potato chips. Fish? Take your pick: salmon, whitefish, tuna, striped bass and so on. The salmon is steamed and served with an artichoke vinaigrette; the whitefish is wrapped in leeks and served with polenta and chanterelles; the tuna is peppered, cooked rare and served with Chinese vegetables and ponzu sauce; the striped bass (our favorite) is paired with fennel and plum tomatoes. Patina also has three cheese courses,

each made with a different cheese and one bringing a surprise: a potato layer cake with goat cheese and fresh thyme. There are a baker's dozen desserts; our favorites include the soufflé of bitter chocolate with coriander sauce and raspberries, and the phyllo squares with caramelized pears and an Armagnac-prune ice cream. Splichal has assembled his 23-page wine list carefully, and while many bottles are great wines, if you choose as intelligently as he did, you can find a few reasonable ones, from France and California alike. But only a few. This is an expensive list; for example, only about 20 of the 300 or so red Burgundy and Bordeaux are less than $40. Dinner costs $50 or more per person.

 Pazzia

755 N. La Cienega Blvd., W. Hollywood 90069; (310) 657-9271
Italian. Lunch Tues.-Fri., Dinner Tues.-Sun. All major cards.

Pazzia—Italian for "craziness" or "madness"—is a relaxed place, with a high-ceilinged, hard-surfaced, contemporary decor; the customers dress casually and the waiters wander around like relatives at a family reunion. But what ultimately matters is what's on the plate, and you'll find that the simple, even rustic, Italian food here can be very good. Take, for instance, the gnocchi with pesto and tomato, the essence of simplicity: we're not sure we've ever tasted a better gnocchi. Pasta is also uniformly excellent. Spaghetti with shrimp, clams and squid ink is our favorite, but we can also be tempted by the pappardelle with a pigeon ragoût and the pumpkin-squash ravioli. Like the gnocchi, the ravioli are surprisngly light: goose-down pillows as opposed to the leather footstools that both these dishes resemble in less skillful hands. The risotto (which changes daily) is among the best in town. Pazzia's version of pappa al pomodoro, a seventeenth-century Tuscan porridge of tomatoes, bread and olive oil, is as comforting as a call from your best friend—although another soup on the menu, zuppa di fagioli e pesce, made with beans, mussels, clams and leeks, can be as overbearing as a call from your mother-in-law. The gelati are so rich and creamy and satisfying that if you try one—the hazelnut in particular—your tongue will be eternally grateful. Main courses tend to be the least successful dishes, though the grilled salmon with a purée of black olives, garlic and capers is very successful indeed—a surprisingly happy marriage of strong, potentially conflicting flavors. Dinner runs about $38 per person; a five-course tasting menu is about $56.

11/20 Piazza Rodeo

208 Via Rodeo, Beverly Hills 90210;
(310) 275-2428
*Italian. Breakfast, Lunch & Dinner daily,
Brunch Sun. DC, MC, V.*

Piazza Rodeo, on Via Rodeo, sits at the top of the Beverly Hills equivalent of Rome's Spanish Steps. With its impressive assortment of ultra high-ticket shops, this is the sort of street that's supposed to exist in jet-set locales like Milan, Monte Carlo, Forte di Marmi, Palm Beach and the like. At one of Piazza Rodeo's charming café tables, you can nibble on surprisingly good, if predictable, café food, at true café prices. It's a cozy spot for a perfectly decent Caesar salad, heavy on the garlic; toasted rosemary bread with tomatoes and basil; a clever chicken salad made with sun-dried tomatoes and pancetta; sandwiches of grilled vegetables on rosemary bread with a tomato olive spread, and tuna with fennel and scallions; bowtie pasta with fresh sugar snap peas (a wonderful combination); and linguine with clams in a cream sauce. In the evening, there are a few more serious dishes, like sautéed chicken breast and a New York steak; for breakfast, there are fritatas—Italian open-faced omelets made with porcini, sausage and pesto. As is the custom in Europe, 15 percent is automatically added to the check. Per person, lunch is around $12 per person, dinner less than $20.

 ## Picnic

8771 W. Pico Blvd., W.L.A. 90035;
(310) 273-1166
*French. Lunch Mon.-Fri., Dinner Mon.-Sat. All
major cards.*

What's a chef to do once he's cooked for various heads of state, headed the kitchens of such acclaimed restaurants as L'Archestrate and La Ciboulette in Paris and manned the burners at some of Los Angeles' most fashionable restaurants (including Café Four Oaks, Bistango and Ma Maison)? If his name is Claude Segal, he opens an unpretentious neighborhood bistro where he offers his own version of Californian-French food flavored with plenty of fresh herbs and olive oil and just enough butter and cream. He keeps the portions generous and the prices reasonable. Welcome to Picnic.

The restaurant's warm, inviting atmosphere makes quite an impression in this otherwise grungy neighborhood around Pico and Robertson boulevards. From the plush green booths and banquettes to the lush murals painted in the style of Manet to the little complimentary bowls brimming over with pistachios, Picnic just feels good. And it tastes good, too. Almost any entrée

here makes a wonderful, soul-satisfying meal. Braised veal shank unexpectedly arrives off the bone in its own tender juices, with sweetly caramelized onions and carrots; a special of thinly sliced rare duck breast finds a good home on top of a bed of sautéed pears with a reduction of raspberry–red wine sauce; half of a well-charred marinated chicken is served over the kind of paper-thin buttery potatoes and onions known to abruptly end most diets.

The only low point on the menu is the salads. The ones we tasted were filled with interesting ingredients, such as smoked duck breast and frizzled sweet potatoes, but suffered from blandness. Order a bowl of berries and cream or some of the wondrously smooth mango sorbet (one of the sexiest desserts in town), and you'll quickly get over the disappointment. Lunch costs about $20 per person, dinner about $35.

 ## Pierre's Los Feliz Inn

2138 Hillhurst Ave., Los Feliz 90027;
(213) 663-8001
*French/Continental. Lunch Mon.-Fri., Dinner
nightly. All major cards.*

Pierre came to L.A. and opened this little restaurant even before Walt Disney built his famous amusement park in Anaheim. That was in 1955, and native Frenchman Pierre Pellech has been serving his roast duck and cassoulet here since 1951. At the time, this sort of *cuisine du terroir*, or "cuisine of the earth," was a rarity: the sort of solid cooking you'd find at an inn in the French countryside, but not in the hills of Los Angeles. More than four decades later, several dozen new cuisines have emerged, thousands of restaurants have opened and closed, and Pierre's is still a rare jewel, still offering roughly the same menu.

Pierre was hired to come to the United States as the personal chef of the wealthy Huntington Hartford, and he never went back. Several jobs and a few ventures later, he opened Pierre's and began to serve Angelenos such regional country dishes as roast pork with Calvados-cream sauce and cassoulet (a hearty casserole featuring white beans and sausage)—some of which are still on the menu today. A crock of rich, country-style foie gras comes to the table gratis (as much as you can indulge in) with freshly baked bread. Though he no longer cooks, Pierre oversees every detail (he continues to cure his own olives and preserve his own cherries). Desserts, such as apple tart and crème brûlée, are faultless classics delivered by old-school waiters. Dinner costs about $35 per person.

12/20 La Plancha

2818 W. 9th St., Downtown (L.A.) 90006;
(213) 383-1449
6207 York Blvd., Highland Park (L.A.)
90042; (213) 255-1416
*Nicaraguan. Lunch & Dinner Tues.-Sun. MC,
V.*

Two reasons to eat at Downtown's La Plancha
are fine Nicaraguan food at rock-bottom prices
and owner Milton Molina, an ebullient fellow
who promotes this cuisine like Barnum promoted his circus. Order the empanada and the
nacatamal and Milton will push more on you:
"What, you don't want the fried cheese? It comes
special in 40-pound blocks, all the way from San
Francisco." Milton is right, of course. The cheese
is remarkable. Nacatamals are like grown-up tamales filled with anything and everything:
chicken, pork, whole chiles, carrots, tomatoes
and even prunes (complete with pits). Among
the many meat dishes, choose chopped or shredded ones over the often-tough grills. All the
entrées come with rice, a small salad of chopped
cabbage and tomatoes, and sides of both soft and
crisp fried plantains. The decor is dreary, but
Milton's personality could brighten a crypt.
Newly opened as we went to press: La Plancha
Grill in Highland Park. Dinner runs about $14.

12/20 Plum Tree Inn

937 N. Hill St., Chinatown (L.A.) 90012;
(213) 613-1819
Chinese. Lunch & Dinner daily. AE, MC, V.

The garish but well-appointed Plum Tree is
almost elegant by Chinatown standards. It's a
humbler version of the better-known Panda
Inns, but the food is actually superior. Among
the compelling choices here are a classic Peking
duck, a deliciously spicy Hunan-style lamb, admirable kung pao chicken, perfectly balanced
pungent shrimp and a subtly sauced mixed vegetable plate. Pass on the overly spicy hot-and-
sour soup and the bland sizzling chicken;
whatever else you eat should be consistently satisfying. The service, while not effusive, is pleasant. Dinner will run $20.

10/20 Prado

244 N. Larchmont Blvd., Hancock Park
(L.A.) 90020; (213) 467-3871
*Caribbean. Lunch Mon.-Sat., Dinner nightly.
All major cards.*

If it's new and it's not Italian or Pacific Rim,
it must be Caribbean, one of the hot cuisines of
the '90s. We're still not sure about this Caribbean
business—granted, it's fun, but is the food any
good? At Prado, the answer is yes and no. There's
no question about the decor, however. It's as
sweet as can be: a teeny room with mismatched

chairs, graceful chandeliers and an extra-high
ceiling painted with clouds, angels and *putti.*
"Charm" is an overused word, but Prado has
loads of it. It also has pedigree, being a venture
of Toribio Prado (the chef who, along with Mario
Tamayo, brought us Cha Cha Cha), and his
brother, Javier, who cooked at Le Restaurant and
The Ivy. We'll accentuate the positive first: a Caesar salad; sweet, moist corn tamales with sour
cream, golden caviar and a tomatillo sauce; flam-
ing papaya shrimp, the just-hot-enough sauce
tempered with papaya and tangy-sweet pineapple; and the deeply caramelized tarte tatin. As for
the bad news, the menu is short and limited in
appeal—too many of the dishes are spicy one-
notes. Such is the case with the camarones negros
and the pollo negro, both overwhelmed by fiery
sauces; why use good shrimp or chicken when
you can hardly taste it? About $24 apiece for
dinner.

Prego

362 N. Camden Dr., Beverly Hills 90210;
(310) 277-7346
*Italian. Lunch Mon.-Sat., Dinner nightly, Late
Supper Fri.-Sat. All major cards.*

We have a couple of knee-jerk reactions that
make us want to bypass Prego. First of all, it's
part of a chain, secondly, the chain is owned by
a large restaurant conglomerate. So how do we
explain the fact that Prego is one of our favorite
Italian restaurants? Perhaps because it is a relatively genuine trattoria, with reasonable prices,
very good food and an ambience that is loads of
fun. Or perhaps because talented chef Andrea
Rogantini, returned from a stint in Orange
County, is back behind the range. When you
enter Prego, the first thing you see is the wood-
burning pizza oven, spewing fire and smoke and
disgorging excellent pizzas. The atmosphere is
intensely relaxed, with chummy service and
dishes that need no introduction: lovely carpaccio, reasonably light gnocchi, pappardelle
(flat noodles) in a tomato-and-rabbit ragoût, and
wonderful grilled meats. Dinner runs $20 to $30
per person.

Primi

10543 W. Pico Blvd., W.L.A. 90064;
(310) 475-9235
*Italian. Lunch Mon.-Fri., Dinner Mon.-Sat. All
major cards.*

Primi began as an experiment—a restaurant
without main courses (hence the name, as in
"primi piatti," or "first courses.") But this was in
1985, when "grazing" was a perfectly acceptable
substitute for the word "eating." Thankfully,

times and tastes change, and people have come to realize that cows graze; people eat. This handsome, contemporary space now holds a more conventional restaurant, complete with main courses. The hearty ones are the best: crispy chicken, osso buco, chicken sausages, roast rabbit with sweet peppers. The grilled Norwegian salmon with a lentil purée is the most interesting of the fish dishes. But, as in most Italian restaurants, Primi's first courses (appetizers) and second courses (pastas) are still the standouts. The Caesar salad is one of the best in town, and the soups—minestrone and pasta e fagioli (with a touch of olive oil)—are wonderful on a winter evening. We're even fonder of the duckling crespella (crêpe) and the grilled eggplant with black olives from owner Piero Selvaggio's native Sicily. Like the crespella, the lobster cannelloni is surprisingly light, and the garganelli with shrimp may be the best of the "everyday" pastas. While some of the dishes are inconsistent, the risotto is almost invariably excellent, whether it's paired with seafood, asparagus, porcini and Parmigiano or lamb and a Barolo sauce. The wine list isn't as encyclopedic as the list at Selvaggio's flagship restaurant, Valentino, but the selections—especially the Chiantis and other Tuscan offerings—nicely complement the cuisine, and it's not hard to find a good bottle at a reasonable price. Service, under the direction of Donato, the maître d', is attentive without being intrusive. Dinner is about $40 per person.

12/20 Rangoon Racquet Club

9474 Santa Monica Blvd., Beverly Hills 90210; (310) 274-8926
English/American. Lunch Mon.-Fri., Dinner Mon.-Sat. All major cards.

We were among the many disappointed patrons when longtime owner Manny Zwarf closed this Beverly Hills landmark. But the good news is that it reopened at press time as a grill-style restaurant. Rumor has it that the teak bar looks better than ever, and that chef John Guattery (late of The Heritage in Santa Monica) is knocking them dead with dishes like aged rib steak, grilled peppered tuna and swordfish with a sweet Indonesian soy sauce. Dinner can run from $30 to $45 apiece.

12/20 Rebecca's

2025 Pacific Ave., Venice 90291; (310) 306-6266
Mexican. Dinner nightly. All major cards.

Restaurateur Bruce Marder's foray into high-end Mexican cooking remains very much alive and well. As at his other successful ventures, the nearby West Beach Café and DC3, Rebecca's

draws one of the trendiest crowds in town. In fact, the bar scene is largely unequalled in Los Angeles—nowhere else do so many beautiful young women in miniaturized black dresses gather in one spot to drink so many tequilas. Once you get past the bar (and the general condescending attitude), the food is surprisingly good—what little of it is served to you. The shrimp empanadas, tasty little things, are no bigger than afterthoughts. The lobster enchilada is a pleasant bite. The sea scallop ceviche is a reminder that the high cost of sea scallops has to be passed on somehow—like in a tiny portion. We've enjoyed very good charred tuna in a cilantro salsa, charred Pacific swordfish and charred New York steak (they like to char things here). Rebecca's works best when you're in the mood for it—which is to say, a night when time doesn't matter and someone else is driving, so you can down more than your fair share of tequila anejo. Don't expect Mexican-restaurant prices: you'll spend about $40 a pop for dinner.

11/20 Red Lion Tavern

2366 Glendale Blvd., Silverlake 90039; (213) 662-5337
German. Lunch & Dinner daily. MC, V.

German is the preferred language in this convivial neighborhood tavern, where German expatriates, students and hard-drinking locals come for hearty, inexpensive dinners. The small downstairs room has a dozen tables and an eight-seat bar, with a simple Bavarian decor; upstairs is a second dining room and another tiny bar, which is populated strictly by regulars. The charming, costumed waitresses (mostly German) keep busy delivering plates loaded with goulash, Wiener Schnitzel, sauerkraut, sausages, smoked pork, red cabbage and hearty sandwiches. There's a complete lack of pretension both in atmosphere and cuisine—this is simple, honest cooking that is both well prepared and tasty. Excellent beers are on tap, like Ritter Brau and Munich Weissbeer; there is also a small selection of German wines. Plan on $11 per person.

Regent Beverly Wilshire Dining Room

9500 Wilshire Blvd., Beverly Hills 90212; (310) 274-8179
American/Continental. Breakfast, Lunch & Dinner daily, Brunch Sun. All major cards.

The Dining Room not only bears no resemblance to anything in this hotel's past, it looks like no other hotel dining room in L.A. It's a beautiful but odd space, as if Louis XIV journeyed to the end of the twentieth century to design a restaurant. The room is at once highly classical and stringently modern; trompe l'oeil murals of the countryside and glowing woods blend with a massive glassed-in kitchen that dominates the room. It's a formal room but also an amazingly comfortable one. The menu, which varies from day to day, is a lot less formal, and a lot less expensive, than you might expect. What used to be a French menu is now basically American, lightly influenced by French, Italian and Japanese cuisines. You can have a marvelous meal that's as American as at your average diner—only infinitely better: the clam chowder, Cobb salad, veal chops with garlicked mashed potatoes, cheesecake—a hard combination to beat. You can also luxuriate in an utterly decadent Maine lobster salad with apples and sweet corn; sautéed whitefish with pink-grapefruit butter; or crisply roasted chicken with a parsnip-rosemary purée. The cuisine is venerable yet modern, just like the room—and it is just as skillfully executed as the decor. The hotel's trademark style has long been to innundate the customer with service, surrounding you with staff who anticipate your needs before you do. Just as you're thinking that another basket of cheese bread would be a fine idea, it shows up.

The same is true of the Lobby Lounge—a large room filled with the sort of handsome overstuffed furnishings seen in *New Yorker* cartoons of men's clubs during the age of the Raj. The fine, heavy bar against one wall is buttressed by painted pastoral scenes. The menu is decidedly unique: on the same bill of fare are a smoked-chicken salad in a ginger-lime dressing, an egg-white omelet and a platter consisting of a tiny hot dog, a diminutive hamburger and a minute Reuben sandwich. Desserts include children's dreams such as chocolate-marshmallow-honey ice cream topped with coffee sauce. Dinner in the dining room costs about $45 to $50 per person; the lounge runs about $20.

 ## Remi
1451 Third Street Promenade, Santa Monica 90401; (310) 393-6545
Italian. Lunch & Dinner daily. All major cards.

Every time we eat at this handsome branch of the New york restaurant, no matter what we order, we keep returning to one particular dish of polenta. It's a very large appetizer, a creamy, rich bed on which lie pieces of squid in a pool of squid ink. The squid is slightly chewy, the ink faintly briny, the polenta smooth as velvet and almost sweet. The combination plays a symphony on your palate; it is one of the best dishes in town. But, yes, of course, there are other dishes on the menu. The best of the pastas is probably the linguine with mussels, scallops, shrimp and chopped fresh tomato. The best of the main courses is either the grilled quail (wrapped in bacon and served with lentils) or the simple rack of lamb, grilled with garlic. For those who like to experiment, the smoked goose prosciutto is worth trying. For the traditionalist, the carpaccio or the mozzarella and tomatoes are nice starters. Risotto is not as good as at several other Italian restaurants in the area, and the ravioli with tuna, ginger and tomato sauce may be the most ill-advised marriage since Elizabeth Taylor and Eddie Fisher, but most of the other pastas are eminently edible. And there's more than food to recommend Remi: service is professional and unfailingly friendly, the decor—sort of Ralph Lauren goes Venetian, with crisp navy-and-white-upholstered banquettes and highly polished ship-quality woodwork—is extremely good looking, and the passing parade of Third Street Promenaders is amusing to watch. Dinner averages $40 to $45 per person.

 ## Rex Il Ristorante
617 S. Olive St., Downtown (L.A.) 90014; (213) 627-2300
Italian. Lunch Thurs.-Fri., Dinner Mon.-Sat. All major cards.

Rex's owner, Mauro Vincenti, imports some of the finest raw products—the best prosciutto, the best Parmigiana—for the food here, and he's always trying to find just the right chef to work magic with these ingredients. Most recently, the magic is being done by a very talented woman chef named Odette Fada.

Fada creates wondrous, satisfying dishes such as hearty soup of spelt, prosciutto and spinach. The spelt (a grain) is blended with vegetable stock to produce a porridge-like soup that provides the perfect backdrop for the slightly salty, slighty chewy strips of prosciutto. Pastas have always been the stars at Vincenti's restaurants (dating back to his first place, Mauro's, in Glendale) and Rex is no exception. Try the fettuccine with pesto Trapanese, the pappardelle with rabbit, the pasta corta (short pasta) with sausage and Pecorino, the . . . well, just take one of the two-foot long breadsticks, close your eyes and point to virtually any pasta on the menu. You won't be disappointed. Main courses are less successful, but for an unusual treat, try the chicken cacciatora; any resemblance between this and what, in red-checked-tablecloth establishments, we've come to think of as chicken cacciatora, is purely coincidental. Small slices of moist, tender chicken breast are fanned out in a sauce of rosemary, anchovies, vinegar and garlic, and accompanied by strands of red pepper and slivers of artichoke heart. Each bite is an epiphany—and, at $18, it's the least expensive main course on the menu. Desserts, alas, are largely uninspired. But the wine list is 48 pages long and features most of the big names of Italy; try a 1978 Barolo from Ceretto. And the setting is magical, a re-creation, inside the glorious Oviatt Building, of a gleaming 1930s art-deco ship's dining room. It may well be the most beautiful restaurant in town. It's surely one of the most expensive: $60 or more per person for dinner.

12/20 Rincon Chileno

4352 Melrose Ave., Hollywood 90046; (213) 666-6075
Chilean. Lunch & Dinner Tues.-Sun. All major cards.

The cooking of Chile, a long, coastal string bean of a country, is populated by seafood. Don't be surprised to find this tiny, nondescript restaurant by Chilean expats, who come for the small selection of dishes rarely found north of Valparaiso. Very little English is spoken here, but with only eight tables, the place exudes warmth and conviviality. Dishes are uncompromisingly cooked to Chilean tastes. Abalone served cold with papas mayonesa or salsa verde is chewy, the style preferred in Chile. The salsa verde, freshly made and thick with coriander, is magnificent, worth a visit all by itself. Congrio is fish (not eel) to a Chilean, flaky, nearly tasteless and filled with hundreds of tiny bones. Paella de mariscos Rincon Chileno, the Chilean version of bouillabaisse, is the best dish in the house—a spicy white broth filled with clams, crab, shrimp and fish. Wash these goodies down with Argentinian Santa Fe beer in eighteen-ounce bottles. About $15 per person.

The Ritz-Carlton Dining Room, Marina del Rey

4375 Admiralty Way, Marina del Rey 90292; (310) 823-1700
Californian/French. Dinner Tues.-Sat. All major cards.

It's solemn but not pompous, formal but not rigid. Intimacy is the language softly spoken by the Oriental rugs and the Queen-Anne bureauso and tables, which warm up the dark-wood-paneled Ritz-Carlton's clubbish atmosphere. The dining room is infused with the marina life outside: white sails blossom on the ocean and gulls streak through the blue sky. Eighteenth-century paintings of magnificent ships bring the sea right into the room.

We are on board with Louis Chalus, who studied deep in the heart of traditional French cooking at Paris's Le Grand Véfour. Because he is so well-versed technically, this chef can do everything and consistently do it well. Chalus takes full advantage of the vast array of exotic products available locally, and of an educated clientele who are hungry for new flavors and innovative combinations of international cuisines. East meets west in the juxtaposition of soft-shell crab tempura and daikon sprouts; quenelles combine Dungeness crab with avocado, and are sprinkled with a vinaigrette of caviar; fresh figs accompany duck-breast prosciutto with basil and olive oil.

The entrées invite you to navigate from the crispiness of Peking duck to the solidity of German Spätzle. There is also tender and savory Colorado lamb, unexpectedly surrounded by couscous (the chef is fond of couscous), and "Pacific style" bouillabaisse, in which lobster from the Atlantic, salmon from the North Sea and mahimahi from the Pacific swim together in a lemongrass broth. These dishes display a fertile creativity, titillating our tastebuds and carrying us along on waves of flavor far from the usual banality of luxury-hotel dining. This is why we like this restaurant: in his search for new dishes, the chef never drops anchor for long. As for the desserts, we'll be patient and allow the kitchen some time to add a few more (and sexier) treats to the modest array of well-done homemade sorbets and ice creams, the feuilleté of caramelized apple and the chocolate-raspberry napoleon tarte. Dinner costs about $60 per person.

Riva at Loews Santa Monica Beach Hotel

1700 Ocean Ave., Santa Monica 90401; (310) 458-6700
Californian/Italian. Dinner Mon.-Sat., Brunch Sun. (Coast Café: Breakfast, Lunch & Dinner daily). All major cards.

This is probably the best ocean-view restaurant in town. Riva offers perfectly fine food, and affords a glorious view of the Pacific Ocean. A seat on the spacious open patio, either at sunset or for Sunday brunch, is one of the most coveted view spots in town. Mediterranean food is the forte of the place, and you'll do best to stick to the simpler dishes: fried calamari, bufala mozzarella, penne with a homemade sausage sauce, grilled tuna with sun-dried tomatoes. Duck, a house specialty, is nicely roasted and decently degreased.

The Sunday brunch buffet is the way to experience Riva at its best: a seafood station is piled with jumbo shrimp, ceviche, oysters, smoked salmon and so on; breakfast items run from eggs

Benedict to various omelets to waffles with strawberries and cream; another table holds a number of unimaginative but good hot entrées; there are heaps of cheeses and fresh fruits and unlimited Champagne. At $31, it's not a steal, but it's certainly a good deal, and the setting is a sure winner with any guest from out of town. Dinner costs about $35 to $45 per person.

Robata
250 N. Robertson Blvd., Beverly Hills 90211; (310) 274-5533
Japanese/Sushi. Lunch Mon.-Fri., Dinner nightly. All major cards.

Robata ("paddle" in Japanese) is not a robata-yaki restaurant at all (where a paddle is used to hand pick morsels for grilling from a giant mound of mixed foods) but a transcendent sushi bar and kaiseki restaurant, serving the Japanese equivalent of a formal banquet. In Kyoto, where the kaiseki dinner was born, it's not unusual to spend as much as $1,000 a person for one of these feasts, served on lacquerware 300 or 400 years old and enjoyed at great leisure. In L.A., a number of restaurants serve an Americanized take on this ritual; Robata has been one of the leading exponents over the last several years. Following a change of ownership and a corresponding period of thin business in 1991, the restaurant changed hands once again in early 1992. The new proprietor, Toshio Kato is committed to maintaining the high standards that earned Robata a 15/20 rating in 1990.

Food served here comes close to perfection. Each dish draws a gasp. There are three kaisekis available—one with ten courses, another with eleven and a third with twelve—each progressing slowly from soup and sashimi to grilled, fried and stewed dishes. The exquisite arc of the meal, further defined by a selection of expensive sakes (preferably served cold), is inexorable, undeniably awesome. That a meal here, with sake, could easily cost well over $100 per person (making this among the most expensive restaurants in town) is definitely sobering. The best rationalization: it would cost a good deal more in Kyoto.

Röckenwagner
2435 Main St., Santa Monica 90405; (310) 399-6504
French/Californian. Breakfast, Lunch & Dinner daily. AE, MC, V.

For years, the stereotypical French restaurant was a grand place where maître d's wielded oversize menus, while sommeliers intimidated the more naïve diners into spending a fortune for a wine whose name they couldn't pronounce. Then came sleek restaurants serving bastardized versions of *la nouvelle cuisine*, where the food was treated as high art (with corresponding high prices), and the ordinary diner still felt intimidated. But then there have always been a few modest and friendly places, devoted more to fine, pure flavors than pretension and profit. In the '80s, Röckenwagner was such a place—a closet-sized Venice storefront run by the empassioned young Röckenwagner couple. What the place lacked in size, elegance and attitude it made up for in creativity, enthusiasm and terrific cooking.

Now Röckenwagner has hit the big time, moving into a soaring space in the Frank Gehry-designed Edgemar complex. The interior, an ultra-stylized interpretation of a town square, is visually exciting yet comfortable. We love sitting under the gracefully bowed wooden trusses, preferably in one of the handsome upholstered booths. The short menu hews to the modern French style: unfussy yet elegant, lighter than traditional French food but hardly following the California-spa credo that eschews all flavor-enhancing fats. Oh, sure, there's light fare, from Sally Fama's garden salad, a colorful jumble of leaf lettuces, tomato, jicama, green onion, avocado and basil, to the oven-roasted cod with zucchini spaghetti and an "essence of vegetable" sauce. But those who think the key to the French Paradox is to consume more meat and butter will adore the barbecued pork and garlic millefeuille, a stack of crisp, thin pastry leaves sandwiching saucy-sweet bits of pork—not to mention the juicy medallions of pork tenderloin topped with slabs of goat cheese and surrounding a mountain of chubby Spätzle. Among the other creations worth trying: delicate dumplings stuffed with minced vegetables and lots of sweet crayfish; an amusing "short stack" of smoked wild Scottish salmon, potato chips, crème fraîche and caviar; the "salmon trio," in which smoked salmon, juicy grilled salmon and salmon-studded mashed potatoes combine to form a divine trinity of fish.

The wine list, though on the pricey side, offers plenty of good wines. The glow of dinner continues when dessert arrives, whether you choose the crisp warm-apple "pizza," the silken warm chocolate tart with a scoop of hazelnut parfait, or one of the many other selections. We often subscribe to the "less is more" theory—but in Röckenwager's case, more is so much more. About $43 per person for a memorable dinner.

Prices are based on a complete dinner for one, including an appetizer, entrée, dessert, tax and tip—but excluding wine or any other beverage.

12/20 Rondo
7966 Melrose Ave., W. Hollywood 90046;
(213) 655-8158
Italian. Lunch Mon.-Fri., Dinner Tues.-Sat. All major cards.

Rondo has more than doubled in size since opening, so you can understand how popular this Italian storefront has become. One feels inspired to graze here, and tends to ignore more substantial dishes such as lamb chops, an assortment of veal dishes and grilled salmon—all good. Inveterate grazers will gravitate toward smaller dishes: one of the best calzones in town, exceedingly crisp pizzas, crunchy crostini, chubby gamberi in a cream sauce, scampi paired with white beans. There are fine risottos fashioned with artichokes or porcini, and toothsome lobster ravioli. Many little dishes, incidentally, can add up to a big ticket. Dinner costs close to $35.

11/20 Rosalind's
1044 S. Fairfax Ave., Wilshire District (L.A.) 90019; (213) 936-2486
African. Lunch & Dinner daily. MC, V.

Famed for its ground-nut stew and Nigerian goat, this spot serves the rarely found cuisine of Africa. Rosalind's is one of a multi-ethnic cluster of Fairfax eateries: a deli, a Chinese restaurant, an Italian restaurant and an Indian restaurant. No wonder that we love L.A.! Rosalind's menu moves from exotic West African dishes like Ghanan yam balls to Central African pilli pilli sauce to Liberian pepper chicken. Also offered is the other-worldly cuisine of Ethiopia: highly spiced stews eaten with a type of millet pancake called injera. Despite the forbidding appearance of these dishes, there are few ingredients you won't recognize. You may not be familiar the way they're put together, but you'll probably love the taste. Service is friendly, if slow. Dinner costs about $15.

10/20 Roxbury
8225 Sunset Blvd., W. Hollywood 90069;
(213) 656-1750
American. Dinner Tues.-Sat. All major cards.

Roxbury began life as Preston Sturges' Player's Club in the '40s and later became the Imperial Gardens. Now it's a dance and supper club that's become a favorite for entertainment-industry parties; it's the right place at the right time in the right part of town. Chef Walter Hungerford's food is probably the best of all the local dance clubs'. The culinary style is best described as contemporary regional-American: cream of acorn-squash soup, barbecued ribs with garlic slaw, crabcakes, sweet-corn tamales, Southern fried chicken with mashed spuds, Maine lob-

ster with seafood-saffron rice, homemade cornbread stuffing. About $35 to $40 apiece for dinner.

 ## R23
923 E. 3rd St., Downtown (L.A.) 90013;
(213) 687-7178
Japanese. Lunch Mon.-Fri., Dinner Mon.-Sat. MC, V.

Opened by several chefs from Katsu (one of L.A.'s highbrow sushi institutions), R23 sits towards the back of a graphic arts complex at 923 East Third Street. The place is not easy to find. It's actually less a conventional-looking restaurant than simply a space in which food is served. The floor is polished wood, bare brick covers the walls, and the chairs are basically cardboard packing crates with cushions. There are several widely spaced tables that are very busy during lunch and almost empty at night, which can be a little alienating. But any sense of deprivation you feel will be forgotten when the food arrives. It's wonderful, some of the purest sushi in town. During a recent visit, there was toro, the fatty-belly cut of tuna that's prized above all others. It was elegantly understated, the color of faded roses, and a fine opening to a lavish sushi feast. The traditional dishes are all here—yellowtail, mackerel, jumbo clam, sea urchin, sea eel—and all are perfectly prepared. California roll is about as orchidaceous as things get—don't expect to find anything called rock-and-roll on this minimalist menu. There's a handful of other dishes, but sushi is the point of the place. Dinner will cost $25 to $30 per person, lunch about $10 to $12.

 ## Ruth's Chris Steak House
224 S. Beverly Dr., Beverly Hills 90212;
(310) 859-8744
American/Steakhouse. Dinner nightly. AE, MC, V.

Fire damage closed Ruth's Chris for much of 1991, and when it reopened late in the year—completely remodeled, looking much more upscale and much less like a steakhouse—there were those who worried that it might have lost its character. Not to worry. The quintessential character of Ruth's Chris is what's on the plate, and what's on the plate may be the best steak in town, still perfectly cooked and still served sizzling hot, with melted butter oozing across the top (unless your cardiologist has advised you that while you can survive a sixteen-ounce New York steak, your arteries look like the Santa Monica Freeway at rush hour, and one extra pat of butter is likely to send you into instant tachycardia). You could order veal, lamb, chicken or fish, but then, why

73

come here? Stick with the steak and choose from among seven preparation of potatoes. (Our favorite is the crisp, extra-thin shoestrings.) Our favorite dessert is the bread pudding with whiskey sauce. Dinner ranges from $44 to $50 apiece.

12/20 Sabor!
2538 Hyperion Ave., Silverlake 90039; (213) 660-0886
American/Latin. Lunch Tues.-Fri., Dinner nightly, Brunch Sun. AE, MC, V.

It may sound silly to combine the flavors of the American South (fried chicken, crabcakes, popcorn-style crayfish) with the flavors of Latin America (pupusas, quesadillas filled with cheeses and epazote, roasted pasilla chile relleno), but these two soul foods coexist happily in this cheerful little Silverlake restaurant. Also coexisting happily is a typically Silverlake clientele: straight, gay and lesbian, white, Latino and black, young trendies and sixtysomething professorial types. They all crowd into this tiny, rough-plaster-walled storefront room, which is warmed by soft lighting and tropical plants. Best bets are the soups (try the Yucatán chicken-lime soup), the crabcakes, the crisp, juicy fried chicken and the hearty Creole pasta: angel hair with sweet rock shrimp, spicy Creole sausauge, tomatoes, chipotle chiles and a garlic cream sauce. Smooth, rich flan ends the meal on an appropriately soothing note. Service is exceptionally solicitous (perhaps a bit too much so at times), and the margaritas are tasty. Dinner costs $20 to $30 per person.

Sai Sai at Biltmore Hotel
The Biltmore, 501 S. Olive St., Downtown (L.A.) 90014; (213) 624-1100
Japanese/Sushi. Lunch Mon.-Fri., Dinner nightly. All major cards.

SaiSai is a restaurant that could well have been plucked straight from the extremely fashionable Rappongi District in Tokyo and transplanted, untouched, in downtown Los Angeles. Every detail is truly Japanese, from the remarkable food to the striking, contemporary setting to the exceptionally gracious and efficient service. SaiSai also could be L.A.'s most exquisite dining secret, hidden away as it is in the basement of downtown's Biltmore Hotel. The room is dramatically illuminated and contains a great deal of opaque glass, effectively placed to separate the many private dining areas from the main room. As is often the case with fine Japanese food, much of the appeal lies in the minutest of touches. Order one of the six varieties of sake and it comes perfectly chilled, the way it's served at better

places in Japan. You are also given a choice of a dozen lovely Japanese glass and ceramic cups from which to sip it. Order the sashimi (seven pieces, including the highly prized fatty cut of tuna called toro, for $18), and you'll find your fish virtually floating on an elegant, flower-shaped glass tray.

The menu's terse descriptions ("deep-fried shrimp ball," "cold beef," "clear soup with special ingredients") don't begin to tell the story. There's a delicate tangle of velvety fresh-squid shavings that resembles pasta; there's a marvelous shabu shabu, sliced prime beef floating in a dark, savory broth. SaiSai's most outstanding offering, however, is its kaiseki dinners. These are, of course, expensive propositions—but they cost about half what the same grand meal would cost in Tokyo, and are surely one of the most authentic renditions of kaiseki in this country. The kaiseki is a fluid procession of dishes, perfectly coordinated to balance one another, and reflecting the season in both ingredients and presentation. One such dinner began with a series of lavish starters, then moved on to a perfect plate of sashimi, then to the sakuramushi ("cherry blossom"), which was a plate of illuminated shrimp, sprinkled with bits of 24-karat gold, and a filet of whitefish resting on a preserved cherry leaf. The ecstasy continued until the last course, an orange-peel cup filled with fresh strawberries, kiwi, melon and so on.

Perfection has its price, though, so prepare yourself for the $22 plate of sushi, the $45 shabu shabu and sukiyaki dinners, and the $50 to $60 kaiseki courses. Dinner costs a minimum of $45 per person and as much as $80 or more for a kaiseki.

12/20 Sanamluang Café
5176 Hollywood Blvd., Hollywood 90027; (213) 660-8006
Thai. Lunch, Dinner & Late Supper (until 4 a.m.) daily. No cards.

See review in "Restaurants – *San Fernando Valley.*"

9/20 La Scala Boutique
410 N. Cañon Dr., Beverly Hills 90210; (310) 550-8288
Italian. Lunch & Dinner Mon.-Sat. All major cards.

The tables here are always filled with Hollywood agents and seasoned members of the Beverly Hills social set, coiffed and toting the proper accoutrements. Owner Jean Leon, who has been creating and running restaurants for this crowd since the 1970s, certainly has his formula for success down. And he sure keeps his crowd satisfied, because these people come back again and again, and they have the means to eat anywhere they choose. You can be sure they're not coming for the transcendent dining experience. The famous Leon chopped salad, a Ladies Who Lunch mainstay for many years, isn't bad. The rest of the menu reads like a Top 40 list of Italian dishes popular over the decades. Regulars happily order "the usual": mozzarella marinara, spaghetti bolognese, breaded veal cutlets and the like. Dinner runs $35 per person.

9/20 La Scala Malibu
3835 Cross Creek Rd., Malibu 90265;
(310) 456-1979
Italian. Lunch Tues.-Fri., Dinner Tues.-Sun. AE, MC, V.

In Malibu, where residents have well-padded incomes and a flair for good living, people frequent La Scala. That would be difficult to explain if it weren't for the fact that this restaurant is convenient to the beach-bound crowd and that it's far prettier than its Beverly Hills progenitor (especially the rooms that have been added). A sweet patio area helps you forget that you're sitting in the middle of a shopping mall. Food is best described as a historic overview of Italian cuisine: mozzarella marinara, ratatouille niçoise, lasagne al forno and spaghetti carbonara rule the roost. A special reserve wine list is made available to privileged parties. Dinner costs at least $40 per person.

9/20 La Scala Presto
11740 San Vicente Blvd., Brentwood 90048;
(310) 826-6100.
Italian. Lunch & Dinner Mon.-Sat. All major cards.

New branches of La Scala keep popping up like wild mushrooms. Most everything that hails from the kitchens here—salads, pastas and pizzas—lacks zest, to put it gently. Given the formidable number of satisfying (even superb) Italian restaurants in the city, it's difficult to rave about the salads, pasta dishes, veal and chicken here. To be fair, portions are quite ample and prices are fairly low, so of course all branches do a land-office business. We must congratulate the owners for their phenomenal success in mass-marketing their formula. Look for a La Scala to sprout soon in your neighborhood. Dinner runs about $20 per person.

La Serenata de Garibaldi

1842 E. 1st St., E.L.A. 90033;
(213) 265-2887
Mexican. Breakfast, Lunch & Dinner Tues.-Sun., Brunch Sun. MC, V.

More than one person has threatened us with bodily harm if we go public with our adoration for La Serenata—it's hard enough as it is to score a table, and the regulars certainly don't want the place overrun. But journalistic duty compels us to tell you about the culinary joys to be found in this friendly East L.A. seafood restaurant. Those in the know park in the back parking lot (accessed by an alley) and enter through a kitchen hallway, where wicker baskets heaped with fresh produce attest to the cuisine's serious intent. The dining room is modest but not without sophistication; bold, contemporary art-for-sale lines the walls, and vivid Mexican cloths cover the tables. Meals start with a complimentary plate of homemade tortilla chips, wedges of cheese quesadillas and a bowl of first-rate hot sauce. At lunchtime (when workers from the L.A. Times and City Hall compete for tables), most diners opt for one of the reasonably priced lunch specials, particularly the superb gorditas: masa "pockets" (like miniature, corn-flavored pitas) stuffed with chicken, pork or fat shrimp, along with fresh tomatoes, red onions, lettuce, cilantro and a dash of hot sauce. Dinnertime finds the loyal regulars splurging on one of the many fresh-seafood specials, from whole grilled snapper with a variety of sauces to about a dozen camarones (shrimp) preparations, including one with the incomparable mojo de ajo, the mother of all garlic sauces. Meals start with divine fresh soups (lentil, vegetable and such) and are paired with buttery rice and either black beans or savory pinto beans. Lunch runs about $10 per person; a superb seafood dinner $25 or $30.

11/20 17th Street Café
1610 Montana Ave., Santa Monica 90403;
(310) 453-2771
American. Breakfast, Lunch & Dinner daily. MC, V.

All manner of Montana Avenue cafés vie for the considerable disposal income of the locals, but perhaps none deserve patronage as much as this unpretentious spot. Formerly the home of Café Montana (now in slicker quarters a block away), this simple room, with its hardwood floors, modern art and good-looking regulars tries to be all things to all neighbors, and pretty much succeeds. Whether you're craving a sausage-and-eggs breakfast, a chopped-salad lunch or a seafood-pizza dinner, you'll find it here, and you'll probably like it, too. The classic Chinese chicken salad will make you forget all those bad interpretations you've suffered through. The angel hair with tomato and basil will make you realize why this simple dish has become the macaroni-and-cheese of the '90s. The grilled chicken breast sandwich is given interest with smoked mozzarella and red-leaf lettuce. The grilled salmon is infused with a pesto marinade. This is a neighborhood restaurant in the best sense of the word, one you might visit daily if you lived hereabouts. A simple lunch runs about $10, dinner $20 to $27.

11/20 72 Market Street

72 Market St., Venice 90291; (310) 392-8720
American. Lunch Mon.-Fri., Dinner nightly, Brunch Sun. All major cards.

We're sad to say that 72 Market Street, heretofore one of our favorite restaurants in town, has slipped a couple of notches. Its troubles may have something to do with the departure of both executive chef Leonard Schwartz and longtime general manager Julie Stone, and the arrival of new chef Dean Kahn. Schwartz now cooks at Tony Bill's other highly successful restaurant, Maple Drive. Whatever the reason, even the old standbys just ain't what they used to be—that is, if they're even available. On our last lunchtime visit, the kitchen was out of its signature meatloaf—at 1 p.m. Now, meatloaf isn't a dish of rare, esoteric ingredients, nor is it made to order. It's only the most popular dish (along with the "kick-ass"chili—which left our posteriors firmly planted on their seats this time around) on the menu. Other tongue-cluckers were the previously wonderful Caesar salad, which was overdressed and oversalted. The grilled salmon was soggy and flavorless, and the pasta of the day was so salty we had to order another bottle of mineral water. We genuinely like 72 Market Street: the space is terrific and the fun crowd is star- and artist-studded. But what's happening in the kitchen? About $40 per person.

12/20 Shahrzad

1422 Westwood Blvd., Westwood 90025; (310) 470-3242
Middle Eastern. Lunch & Dinner daily. CB, DC, MC, V.

The various branches of this minichain (there's another in Sherman Oaks and a cousin restaurant two doors away called Flame) maintains standards far beyond those of the typical neighborhood ethnic joint. They are professionally run

restaurants that offer consistently good Persian-style food at quite reasonable prices. In addition to juicy, tender kebabs, the lamb (or chicken) tahchin is a special treat—a superb polo (rice mixture) with saffron-infused, yogurt-marinated lamb layered atop tah dig (a crispy yogurt, egg and rice base). Well worth trying are the traditional beef, chicken and veal stews: fesenjan covers the meat and rice in a rich, slightly sweet walnut-and-pomegranate paste; gormeh sabzi combines it with red beans, vegetables and dried limes. Don't pass up the mast o'khiar, a yogurt-and-cucumber dipping sauce studded with crushed herbs, walnuts and raisins. Dinner costs about $15 per person.

10/20 Shane on the Glen

2932 Beverly Glen Circle, Bel Air 90077; (310) 470-6223
Californian/Southwestern. Lunch Mon.-Fri., Dinner nightly. All major cards.

At Shane, the table you're assigned is key: if you sit downstairs, you'll find yourself being poked by your neighbors, for there isn't enough room between the tables for a gerbil to pass comfortably. The best seats are on the edge of the balcony, overlooking the restaurant below. And they're always occupied. The Barbara Lazaroff–designed setting, colorful and noisy, can get on one's nerves. The food is a passable mix of 1980s fare: Spagoesque pizzas, topped with lamb sausage, sage and red chili; chicken and tomatillo salsa; pancetta and shiitake mushrooms. Crunchy calamari fritti come with a saffron-garlic sauce; duck tostadas and beef quesadillas are pretty good; and the many pastas range from the ordinary to the orchidaceous—try the saffron farfalle with Louisiana shrimp. The grilled chicken with rosemary and lime, paired with skinny, crispy fries, is one of the best in town. A dinner costs $30 to $40.

12/20 Shibucho

3114 Beverly Blvd., Silverlake 90057; (213) 387-8498
Little Tokyo Square, 333 S. Alameda St., Little Tokyo (L.A.) 90013; (213) 626-1184
Japanese/Sushi. Little Tokyo: Lunch & Dinner daily. Silverlake: Dinner nightly. AE, MC, V.

Sushi bars are no longer quite as crowded as they used to be in greater Los Angeles, but the two Shibuchos continue to function exactly as they always have, filled with Japanese hungry for real, Tokyo-style sushi. These are not the sort of restaurants where you can tell the chef to bring you fifteen pieces of sushi at once. Sushi is served at a polite pace, one piece at a time, at a rate the chef feels is appropriate. Try to get pushy and you'll find your meal slows down considerably. The offerings are fresh and quite fine, particularly the belly cut of tuna called toro (in season). There's an elegance to eating at Shibucho that's uniquely Japanese, particularly at the branch in Little Tokyo Square. Ask for omakase, "chef's choice," and you'll be rewarded with the best morsels the chef has on hand. Dinner ranges from $30 to $50 per person.

11/20 Siam Corner Café

10438 National Blvd., Palms 90066;
(310) 559-1357
Thai. Lunch & Dinner daily. MC, V.

Siam Corner Café does, indeed, sit on a corner—a remarkably ethnic corner. Within a dumpling's throw are Indian, Chinese, Italian and French restaurants, along with a burrito shop and the indefinable Menagerie. This little place looks like any number of other Thai places in town. But the food is much better than the norm. Mee krob is crisp and sweet, without being sugary and bland. The larb (ground beef or chicken with mint, lime and chili) fills the mouth with a gentle fire that builds with each bite. The peanut sauce is delicate and spicy without being overly oily. And the house specialties are well worth tasting: finger-lickin'-good barbecued chicken; an awesome sauté of shrimp, scallops, squid, crab, clams and fish mixed with chili, onions, mint and green beans; a fascinating pan-fried noodle dish with seafood called pad khi mow talay; and something called Siam Corner scampi, which isn't really scampi—but it's a fine dish anyway. About $12 per person for dinner.

12/20 Siamese Garden

301 Washington Blvd., Marina del Rey 90292; (310) 821-0098
Thai. Lunch & Dinner daily. AE, MC, V.

Hidden away behind a wall of lush greenery, directly on Venice's Grand Canal and next door to the rowdy Baja Cantina (its absolute antithesis), is a converted bungalow housing this most enchanting Thai restaurant. Once you've made your way down the brick pathway and stooped through the tiny doorway into the candlelit dining room, you feel as if you've just been let in on a wonderful secret. The ambience is warm and intimate, with a cluster of tables and a few very private booths romantically concealed behind gauzy curtains. Everything on the menu is good, but there are several star attractions. Try the pla goong, an appetizer of lightly grilled shrimp served cold over a bed of shredded onions moistened by lime juice and spiced with fresh mint. The whole fried catfish is wondrous, a crispy,

sweet-hot skin concealing tender flesh; the noodle dishes range from good to excellent, with the house special usually triumphing over the phad Thai; satays are commendable. Service is gracious and courteous. About $15 per person.

12/20 Siamese Princess

8048 W. 3rd St., W. Hollywood 90048;
(213) 653-2643
Thai. Lunch Mon.-Fri., Dinner nightly. AE, MC, V.

As the name implies, the Siamese Princess exudes a certain aura of royalty. The walls are hung with countless framed pictures of the Thai royal family and various other royalty from around the world. The ambience smacks of faded elegance. The service is courtly, though the waiters sometimes need flagging down. And the menu is certainly an impressive one, filled with dishes found nowhere else in Los Angeles: lamb satay, chicken with walnuts, pork tossed with crisply fried noodles, duck dumplings (filled with duck and escargots) and so forth. The food can be very good, but it's rarely quite as good as it should (or could) be. Despite its regal edge, and the international reputation of chef Victor Sodsook, we're not among the more zealous clientele who regard the place as the heighth of Thai cooking. We do know that we like our mee krob crisper and with more shrimp than the mee krob we last tasted here; and we weren't entirely taken with the oiliness of the peanut sauce.Otherwise, unluckily, we keep ordering nothing but decently ordinary fare. Dinner runs about $30 per person.

11/20 Siam Mania

7450 Beverly Blvd., Melrose-Fairfax District (L.A.) 90036; (213) 939-2466
Thai. Lunch Mon.-Fri., Dinner nightly. All major cards.

As Thai restaurants go, this one is predictably sleek and high-tech and has predictably good food. A point in its favor is that it's soothing and quiet: you can actually talk in here. Satay is presented with one saucer of unctuous peanut sauce, and another filled with chopped cucumbers and four toast points. Stuffed chicken wings have been boned and filled with well-seasoned noodles and vegetables. Shrimp in red curry sauce, served in a pineapple shell, has a sweet coconut taste balancing its hotness. Most nights the specials are seafood dishes. The restaurant is often

See the "And Also . . ." section on page 89 for additional brief listings of L.A. restaurants, many of them chains, old standbys or places to go for a quick, no-frills meal.

markedly empty and a little less than warm, but the food makes great take-out. A dinner runs $15 to $20.

Sofi Estiatorion
8030 W. 3rd St., W. Hollywood 90048; (213) 651-0346
Greek. Lunch Mon.-Sat., Dinner nightly. MC, V.

Sofi is Sofi Konstantinidis, a Greek-born M.D. who took up cooking when she moved to America with her architect husband Konstantin. Her recipes are adaptations of the dishes made by her grandmother, who was once, according to legend, the best Greek cook in Istanbul. This food has real soul, so much so that it is hard to believe you aren't eating in a small taverna in Athens. Too many of L.A.'s Greek restaurants are inauthentic, but Sofi is completely genuine and just plain good. Open your meal with pikilia, which are mixed appetizers including feta cheese doused with olive oil and scattered with crumbled oregano; keftedes, the definitive meatball; dolmadas, veal, lamb and rice in tiny grape leaves; and chtapodi, octopus vinaigrette. You can also begin your meal with a combination of Greek salads, mixing and matching tzatziki (yogurt and cucumbers), patzari (yogurt and beets), melitzana (eggplant and peppers), tarama (red caviar dip) and more. There's a sublime moussaka, an eggplant and ground meat casserole that is probably the best in town; plump, elegant shrimp wrapped in bacon; and a plethora of finger foods made with phyllo: kolokithopita (zucchini, feta, cottage cheese, eggs, dill), kreatopita (lamb, mushrooms, onions, pine nuts, lemon juice) and more. The pungent Retsina, Greece's traditional white wine, does wonders when it comes to cutting through this divine heaviness. A dinner costs about $25.

Spago
1114 Horn Ave., W. Hollywood 90069; (310) 652-4025
Californian. Dinner nightly. All major cards.

From the day it opened, Spago has been the single most important restaurant in Los Angeles, the restaurant that, more than any other, made L.A. one of the most influential, innovative restaurant cities in the world. Spago has served as the spawning ground for a whole generation of chefs, trained by Wolfgang Puck and versed in the art of creating food that's at once serious and casual, formal and down-home. It's the restaurant that every tourist wants to visit—without fail, they clamor about "Spago's," mispronounced with a long "a" and a possessive "s."

Hovering a half block above the Sunset Strip, Puck's first-born is a mishmash of curious modern art, oversized glass windows (off which noise bounces like so many auditory rubber balls) and an open kitchen centered around a wood-burning brick pizza oven. For us, the oven is the raison d'être of Spago, for from it come the pizzas that redefined upscale eating in Los Angeles. Suddenly, a great restaurant didn't have to serve foie gras and truffles to be taken seriously. The pies are topped with all the ingredients that have become the touchstones of California cuisine: freshly made duck sausage; Santa Barbara shrimp; artichokes, leeks and pancetta; garlic, prosciutto, goat cheese and red onions; and various combinations of fresh basil, cheeses and peppers both red and yellow. A calzone also comes from this oven, filled with three cheeses, prosciutto, eggplant, garlic and more. Year after year, the pizzas and calzones remain perfect, and Puck does a fine job of training his people. His present executive chef, François Kwaku-Dongo, worked his way from a line-cook position under Wolfgang's wing, and now he seems fully capable of flying on his own.

All this said, however, we do have a concern: Puck just may be spreading himself too thin, with Chinois on Main, Granita, Postrio (in San Francisco), a branch of Spago opening in Las Vegas, a handful of books, enough charitable events for a dozen chefs, various TV appearances, the blessing of the fishing fleet and the numerous other celebrity events he presides over. With so many balls in the air, will Puck be able to maintain the high standards that have made him such a success?

That remains to be seen. Meanwhile, the celebrities still pack the place night after night—where else would you see Ahmet Ertegun dining with Phil Spector, or Tom Cruise breaking bread with Rob Reiner? California cuisine is defined here . . . even if, like California, it occasionally gets a bit shaky. You can spend $30 for a simple salad and pizza; a full dinner runs $50 or more.

11/20 Stepps on the Court
Wells Fargo Center, 350 S. Hope St., Downtown (L.A.) 90071; (213) 626-0900
Californian. Lunch Mon.-Fri., Dinner nightly. All major cards.

What is not surprising about Stepps is its popularity with downtown's young urban professionals: the decor, the menu and the service all were clearly designed by clever corporate minds who took great pains to create the right kind of place. What is surprising is the quality of the food.

The menu is sizable and well-conceived, offering a sampling of almost everything this demographic loves. Pastas, of course, are mainstays, such as spinach tortellini in a light tomato-basil sauce, as are interesting salads and daily fish specials (grilled over mesquite charcoal). Desserts include a fine lemon mousse and a smooth chocolate-espresso pot de crème. The attractive, open, split-level dining area is packed at lunch, making reservations a must, and even dinnertime can be lively, a rarity downtown. Free parking. About $15 per person for lunch, $30 for dinner.

10/20 Stoney's
11604 San Vicente Blvd., Brentwood 90049; (310) 447-6488
Californian. Lunch Mon.-Fri., Dinner Mon.-Sat. MC, V.

Sensing the promise of a comfortable neighborhood restaurant, we forgave and forgot the glitches we suffered through during Stoney's opening week and returned several times to watch its progress—and thankfully it did make progress, though there's still plenty of room for improvement. Stoney, the chef, can be seen peeking anxiously from the kitchen window into the restaurant while her partner, Jane, cordially welcomes diners into this modern, gray-walled restaurant. The partners emigrated from London two years ago, which explains the appealing British-style eclecticism of the menu: spring rolls, Sumatran shrimp linguine, Chinese noodles (Stoney makes the noodles herself), Tuscan rosemary chicken, pastas and nontraditional hamburgers. A worthy special one night was Black Angus steak in black-bean sauce nestled in a basket molded out of french-fried potatoes. The desserts have improved along with the rest of the cuisine, notably the excellent chocolate roulade filled with mocha cream and the creamy cheesecake. At press time, the place still hadn't gotten it's liquor license. Dinner starts at about $25 per person.

12/20 Talesai
9043 Sunset Blvd., W. Hollywood 90069; (310) 275-9724
Thai. Lunch Mon.-Fri., Dinner Mon.-Sat. All major cards.

There are some cuisines for which elegance is unsuited. Though there are upscale Mexican restaurants, for instance, chicken in mole sauce served on fine china is a good example of what might be called gilding the lily. In much the same way, the kind of Thai food we have in L.A. seems to work best in a casual, down-home setting, where you can eat immense plates of noodles and shrimp without having to worry about what it's going to cost you (a royal Thai banquet in Bangkok will change your view forever, but so far in L.A., Thai dining covers only the casual end of the spectrum). Talesai is the only truly upscale Thai restaurant in town, a contemporary space in which service is solicitous and dishware is attention-getting. Prices are far higher than the norm (though still not very high; even at the top of the scale, Thai food isn't very expensive), and portions are smaller. This is haute Thai, much like the food at the legendary Oriental Hotel in Bangkok. On paper, we approve of this sort of thing. But in practice, Talesai's food is just a bit disappointing. Thai cooking is best when it's abundant, but here "abundance" is not a watchword. The mee krob is daintily served and a bit too sweet, without nearly enough shrimp and pork. Thai salads are usually awash with shrimp and pork but the yum yai here is closer to just, well, a salad (albeit an exotic one). The good news is that there is a bit of a celebrity crowd, and that the noodle dishes, though smallish, are delicious. After dinner you can venture east on Sunset Boulevard and take in the colorful heavy-metal nightlife on the Strip. Dinner costs about $35 apiece.

11/20 Thai House
8657 W. Pico Blvd., W.L.A. 90035; (310) 274-5492
1049 Gayley Ave., Westwood 90024; (310) 208-2676
Thai. Lunch Mon.-Fri., Dinner nightly. MC, V.

Thai House is bare, minimalist, postmodern, neo-nouvelle, 21st-century retro . . . choose your buzzword and run with it. This is truly the land of grey-on-grey concrete. It is, we assume, supposed to be a blank frame surrounding bright, colorful dishes. But a certain minimalism has crept into the menu; though there are 70 items, it's still small by Thai standards. But there are a few unique house specialties. Consider the dish called Ugly Duckling, a half duck stewed with a wide assortment of Asian spices. Or the fabulous hor mok, a very nice, very hot seafood stew with red curry, coconut milk and Thai basil. Otherwise, this is basically a fine place to go when you want to dress in black and strike a pose while nibbling on delicious chicken satay, stuffed chicken wings, well-chilied squid salad or spicy-and-sour seafood soup. The naked shrimp is actually one of the best-dressed dishes in town. About $15 per person for dinner.

A Thousand Cranes at New Otani Hotel

120 S. Los Angeles St., Downtown (L.A.)
90012; (213) 629-1200
Japanese. Breakfast, Lunch & Dinner daily. All major cards.

In many ways, Japanese cooking embraces the fine art of trompe l'oeil—and therefore is often as satisfying visually as it is on the palate. A Thousand Cranes embodies this most Japanese aesthetic; its decor further expresses this ideal with subdued lighting, blond wood walls and traditionally garbed waitresses. Sparely furnished tatami rooms look out on a neatly sculpted Japanese garden, where rocks and stones are arranged harmoniously, water trickles gently into a waiting pool and delicate shrubs blend into one another like cloud banks. Yet just beyond the garden lies the mottled gray skyline of Los Angeles, hidden here, just as a Tokyo restaurant would conceal adjacent, starkly designed skyscrapers. A Thousand Cranes has a sushi bar, a tempura bar (quite rare in America) and a row of tables at which various stews are cooked over small tabletop heating elements. Japanese brunch, an unusual affair where East and West collide, is served on Sundays. The best bets here are sushi or tempura. Dinner ranges from $35 to $100 per person, and spending even more is not impossible.

11/20 Tivoli Café

153056 Sunset Blvd., Pacific Palisades
90272; (310) 459-7685
Italian. Lunch & Dinner daily. MC, V.

The oddest thing about this Palisades Village sister of Il Forno and La Vecchia is how very . . . *quiet* it is. Where its siblings are the essence of modern Italian-restaurant chaos, with noise levels approaching your average airport runway, Tivoli is a modest neighborhood eatery, in which families feed their kids pizza and pastas and old friends get together for an inexpensive meal. Despite the coffee-shop look of the place, the food is actually pretty interesting stuff: a starter of roasted peppers and goat cheese topped with sun-dried tomatoes; a salad of spinach, endive, sautéed scallops and goat cheese; sandwiches filled with roast leg of lamb or with eggplant and radicchio; pizzas topped with shiitake mushrooms or with goat cheese. There's a pizza called pizza magica, one half of which is topped with shiitakes and the other with shrimp: an unexpected dish served in an unexpected setting. About $20 per person for dinner.

Tommy Tang's

7473 Melrose Ave., Melrose-La Brea District
(L.A.) 90036; (213) 651-1810
Thai/Sushi. Lunch Mon.-Fri., Dinner nightly. All major cards.

As terminally trendy Melrose continues to evolve and devolve, certain restaurants have emerged as long-term survivors. A decade from now, we won't be the least bit surprised to find the small-black-dress-and-motorcycle-jacket crowd still waiting for a table at Tommy Tang's; this restaurant certainly draws the hottest crowd of any Thai eatery in town. And with a popular branch in the Tribeca section of New York, this is also the only bicoastal Thai restaurant in town. And as at the Hard Rock Café, the food here is better than it needs to be.

Do as the regular crowd does, and get a table up on the large, Spanish-tiled patio, climbing with ivy and filled with potted trees and flowering plants. Order the signature "original Tommy duck" which, though pricey, is the highlight of the menu. With it, try the chicken satay served with one of L.A.'s best peanut sauces; the shrimp in a hot-and-sour lemon grass broth; the Malaysian clams; or the spicy mint noodles. There's a sushi bar adjacent to the restaurant, called Tommy Sushi, where you can nibble on good sashimi and sip on one of the many wines offered by the glass, while waiting for a table inside. The enterprising Tang, who grows all his own herbs for the kitchen here, has built a mini-empire around his restaurants: he produces a line of Tommy Tang seasonings, curry pastes and sauces, and is the author of a successful book and video. Dinner costs about $30 apiece.

11/20 Topanga Fresh Fish Market

522 S. Topanga Canyon Blvd., Malibu
90290; (310) 455-1728
Seafood. Dinner nightly. MC, V.

On many an evening, we'd rather be relaxing at the Topanga Fresh Fish Market over plain broiled fish than sitting stuffed into an evening outfit and staring down at something drowning in a fancy cream sauce. This ramshackle fish market serves some of the best seafood in Southern California. Yes, this is Shack Cuisine at its best: order your meal at one window, pay for it at another, and then eat it off of paper plates. A blackboard lists the choices, most of them exceptional and all of them served with killer spuds and coleslaw crunchy enough to make your jaw sore. By all means order the fish chowder, which positively defines the genre. As an appetizer, try splitting a seafood quesadilla, which may spoil your appetite for anything that follows. Then choose from creatures like mahi mahi, shark, snapper, salmon, halibut, swordfish, scallops (in a buttery broth), scrumptious shrimp and delicious lobster. Anarchy seems to reign here, but somebody must be in charge. The food's just too damned good. Dinner costs about $15.

 ## La Toque
8171 Sunset Blvd., W. Hollywood 90069; (213) 656-7515
French. Lunch Mon.-Fri., Dinner Mon.-Sat. All major cards.

Among restaurant cognoscenti, Ken Frank is one of the best-known chefs in Los Angeles. There are many reasons for this: his years working in seventeen different restaurants before opening La Toque; his considerable talent and his thirteen years of hard work at La Toque. These last two have won him much critical acclaim. And yet his fame has never spread beyond the limited bounds of the foodie world. Though his restaurant is popular with movie-industry lunchers, it has never caught on with the fickle public at dinner time. That it hasn't is a shame. Even though the cuisine has remained at a plateau in recent years (after a stunning ascent), La Toque is still one of the best French restaurants in town. And it has plenty of charm; outside is all the action of the Sunset Strip, but inside this little blue cottage is all the warmth French country inn.

Frank's tightly operation keeps him enslaved to his ovens and deprives him of the opportunity most top chefs have to visit other leading restaurants here and abroad to observe and absorb what other talented chefs are doing. No wonder he seems less inspired than he once did. But he remains a master saucier, particularly skillful when composing sauces for fish, which provide a perfect canvas for his deft touch. The salmon with blood-orange sauce is one of the best fish presentations in town, the tartness of the blood oranges somehow accentuating the flavor of the salmon. Also remarkable is his swordfish with a sauce made from Kalamata olives. This is one of the few restaurants we know where the main courses are consistently better than the appetizers, but if you want a potato pancake like no Jewish grandmother ever made, try the Rösti potatoes topped with sour cream and golden caviar. One disappointment is the Caesar salad, which is abundant with garlic and weak in every other way. Definitely save room for desserts. On one recent visit, we were positively transported by the praline

cheesecake: layers of cheesecake and praline mousse that was so light we almost forgot that it probably doubled our cholesterol overnight. About $45 per person for dinner; a special six-course extravaganza is $65.

 ## Toscana
11663 San Vicente Blvd., Brentwood 90049; (310) 820-2448
Italian. Lunch Mon.-Sat., Dinner nightly. All major cards.

As much as we love Toscana, we must admit that it isn't always easy to dine here. You have to make reservations at least a week in advance, and you have to have plenty of patience. When you arrive at your reserved time, you probably won't be seated for awhile, especially on a Saturday night. But getting angry and stalking out would be a big mistake—because when you finally get to your table, the festive air will cheer you, as will the authoritative waiters and the marvelous Tuscan flavors. From your table you can watch the chefs maintain an easy pace as they cook aromatic steaks seasoned with olive oil, along with thin-crusted pizzas, sizzling veal chops and irresistible foccacia, all in the cavernous wood-burning oven. The pastas are many, and an admirable risotto can be ordered with white truffles and porcini when available. In October, Toscana flies in from Italy fresh, fragrant porcini mushrooms, which are grilled with olive oil and garlic or prepared in a special pasta. Because game is popular in Tuscany, the kitchen offers tasty venison and boar dishes when they can find good meat locally. Desserts are good, particularly the ricotta cheesecake. Though pricey, the wine list is varied, including several of the currently popular "super Tuscan" reds. The full menu is served at the counter. Dinner for one starts at $30.

10/20 The Tower
1150 S. Olive St., Downtown (L.A.) 90015; (213) 746-1554
American. Lunch Mon.-Fri., Dinner Mon.-Sat. All major cards.

Atop the Transamerica Building, 32 floors above L.A.'s sprawl, sits The Tower, probably the most spectacular view restaurant in town. Only the view says "Los Angeles," though—the interior looks like an expensive corporate dining room, which is basically what the place is. Well-dressed senior executives enjoy formal, accommodating service (dishes are covered with silver domes, which the maître d' whisks away with a flourish) and reasonably well-prepared American food. No newfangled black-bean sauces or angel hair with sun-dried tomatoes here; lunch runs to simple, healthful fish and seafood dishes, and dinner gets a bit more ambitious, with duck, quail, oxtail and pheasant. Desserts aren't worth the calories. The beautiful vistas, especially at lunch or at sunset sipping a cocktail, make The Tower hard to dismiss, but the check is as grand as the panorama: lunch for one can easily cost $40 per person, and dinner is higher. On the other hand, there is complimentary valet parking.

12/20 Trader Vic's at Beverly Hilton

9876 Wilshire Blvd., Beverly Hills 90210;
(310) 274-7777
Polynesian. Dinner nightly. All major cards.

In a city where change and progress is the prevailing motif, Trader Vic's, after all these years, remains the same: a bar with a restaurant attached. Which is why its loyal crowd of Beverly Hills couples in their 50s and 60s don nice evening attire and come here for any and every occasion. The point is as much to soak up the nostalgic ambience of an era lost as it is to eat the Polynesian fare, which runs to "pupu" platters and "coco" shrimp. The other attraction is exotic tropical drinks, which all have that authentically strong, sweet character. Trader Vic's is a truly colorful slice of history. Dinner costs about $50 a head.

 ## Trattoria Angeli

11651 Santa Monica Blvd., W.L.A. 90025;
(310) 478-1191
Italian. Lunch Mon.-Fri., Dinner nightly. All major cards.

Despite its metal catwalk and postmodern design, this is a true trattoria. It was the second of the three, highly successful Angeli restaurants in L.A., and like the others, it's a trendy, lively place for sharing bottles of Chianti and plates of authentic, unfussy Italian food. Pizza alla checca with fresh tomatoes is great, and pizza Angeli, with smoked mozzarella, garlic and a tomato-basil sauce, will make you swear off of those strangely topped California pizzas forever. Terrific spaghetti alla carbonara (egg, cheeses, pancetta, onion and fresh basil) is a best bet among the pastas. Other winners include a tasty potato-onion pie with mushrooms; verdure alla griglia, an antipasto assortment of grilled vegetables; and the perfect pollo arrosto, a crisp-skinned, garlicky roast half chicken. Trattoria Angeli breaks with authenticity to offer a few lovely cakes and fruit tarts, desserts not strictly Italian. A bowl of fresh-brewed espresso topped with flan is well-nigh perfect. A heavenly lemon

tart has a chewy crust and a sublime sweet-tart filling. The menu and wine list are more extensive than those at the original Angeli Caffè on Melrose Avenue. Expect to spend anywhere from $25 to $35.

 ## Trattoria Farfalla

1978 Hillhurst Ave., Los Feliz 90027;
(213) 661-7365
Italian. Lunch Mon.-Fri., Dinner nightly. All major cards.

Now that sprawling Farfalla La Brea has taken Hollywood by storm, it's actually possible to get a table in this chic little brick-walled trattoria—you only have to wait ten minutes these days. Whatever the wait, though, these simple dishes are mostly marvy. Insalata Farfalla, for instance, is a crisp Caesar-style salad atop a round of crackling pizza bread, an inspired twist. Tagliolini is prepared with lots of sweet shrimp, garlic and just the right amount of olive oil. Roasted chicken is simple perfection. All the pizzas are terrific, and the creamy tiramisu goes down beautifully with a cup of house espresso. Dinner runs from $20 to $28 or so per person.

10/20 Tribeca

242 N. Beverly Dr., Beverly Hills 90210;
(310) 271-1595
American. Lunch Mon.-Fri., Dinner nightly, Late Supper Mon.-Sat. All major cards.

Tribeca is, in its own way, the right restaurant in the right spot at the right time—a good enough place to eat and a decent spot to drink, a surviving bastion of '80s-style yuppiedom in the midst of Beverly Hills. Named for one of the Big Apple's hottest alternative neighborhoods, Tribeca is the creation of a team of New York restaurateurs who have put together a high-concept establishment that is, at its worst, a New York poseur among the palm trees. The bar downstairs is noisy and busy, filled with people in Italian suits downing the currently correct drink. There's a smaller bar upstairs that's more private and intimate, populated with young women who don't want to battle the vicious downstairs singles scene. The restaurant that surrounds the upstairs bar is filled with wood and leather, easy lighting and a subdued air that's convivial without being noisy. And the menu is rich with all the right buzz words: free-range chicken, tuna carpaccio, Maryland crabcakes, cranberry-jalapeño relish, fig-and-mint relish, fried leeks, tiramisu. As far as the food goes, the jalapeños rellenos are really stuffed with crab. The crabcakes could be crisper. The Caesar salad is workmanlike. In New York, they'd probably call this a California restaurant; in California, we say it's New York. About $35 per person for dinner.

12/20 Trilussa

9601 Brighton Way, Beverly Hills 90210; (310) 859-0067
Italian. Lunch Mon.-Sat., Dinner nightly. All major cards.

Trilussa is a perfectly delightful little Roman café, and not just because of its terrific, inexpensive food. It's the Los Angeles branch of a two-café chain in Rome, which means that beyond being just another L.A. Italian restaurant, Trilussa provides a Roman experience transferred, virtually untouched, to America. On most nights, the doors and windows are all open, allowing you to feel that you're outside. Close your eyes and listen carefully to the animated chatter: the waiters are yelling at the kitchen in Italian; the customers are yelling at the waiters in Italian; the maitre d' is yelling at whoever comes by in Italian. It's just like Italy.

The menu starts with five different bruschettas, slices of toasted Tuscan bread topped with everything from prosciutto to tuna with arugula. Then, there are sandwiches made on soft, herbaceous focaccia bread, flavored with nothing more than oregano, rosemary and oil, or nothing less than dry-cured bresaola. Making up the bulk of the menu are 25 pizzas: thin, cracker-crust creations topped simply with tomato and mozzarella on the one hand, with truffles and mozzarella on the other, and with such items as hard-cooked eggs, gorgonzola, corn and whole black olives sprinkled somewhere in between. There's more serious food, too: a good penne carbonara and angel hair with four cheeses. Service can be a bit bizarre. When in a Roman restaurant, however, do as the Romans do—yell at the waiter in Italian, pour yourself another glass of Pinot Grigio, and sit back and enjoy. Trilussa is also perfect for lunch, with its sunny interior, light menu and amusing people-watching. Dinner costs about $20 apiece, lunch about $15.

12/20 Trinity

6810 Melrose Ave., Melrose-La Brea District (L.A.) 90036; (213) 857-1417
American. Dinner & Late Supper Mon.-Sat. AE, MC, V.

Filling the small space that once held Fellini's, Trinity a venture of the two nightclub impresarios behind the once-hot disco Bar One, which explains the clubby ambience: a beefy dude outside checks your name on the reservations list, sleek little bits of Spandex pass as the waitresses' outfits, celebrities can be seen at every

other table, and the pool table in the back room lends an appropriate pseudo-blue-collar air. And how pseudo it is—the same Tanqueray and tonic that sells for $2.75 at the Formosa and $4.50 at Musso & Frank's is $6 here. So naturally we expected to find silly food-as-sculpture and the finest in service-with-a-sneer. Instead, we were surprised to discover a decent nouvelle-Americana menu and service that is often charming (once you get a reservation and then have it honored). If you steer clear of the bone-dry chicken pot pie, you're likely to have a most enjoyable meal: salmon yam cake, a weird but good twist on the crabcake; a salad of seriously spicy arugula ringed with lean duck breast; entrées of the hearty-homey variety (roast chicken, rack of lamb); and chocolate-brownie or banana-cream pies that will put you into a sugar-fat daze. Dinner runs $25 to $30 per person.

12/20 Tropical Garden

637 S. Fairfax Ave., Wilshire District (L.A.) 90036; (213) 933-5231
Caribbean. Lunch & Dinner daily, Late Supper Fri.-Sat. AE, MC, V.

Boy, that Prado family gets around. This Caribbean spot is, not surprisingly, owned by a Prado—specifically, Alberto. His first cousin, Toribio, was (along with Mario Tamayo) the flamboyant force behind the two Cha Cha Cha restaurants, Prado restaurant and the now-defunct Café Mambo. But this is Alberto's first restaurant of his own, and he and partner/chef Mario Guerrero have learned their business well.

The garish pink-and-lavender building that holds the Tropical Garden sits on a run-down strip near Fairfax and Wilshire. When you step inside, however, all thoughts about the dirt and grit of the city fall away. Chock full of vibrant Latin American oil paintings and enormous tropical plants, this place is a tribute to the Carmen Miranda camp-and-kitsch school of decor. Service (often by Alberto himself) is chatty and affable. The Caribbean menu will be hauntingly familiar to anyone who has eaten at Cha Cha Cha. A good meal can be constructed of nothing but appetizers—a couple of sweet corn tamales topped with sour cream, tomatillo salsa and golden caviar; thick, star-shaped corn tortillas filled with tender chicken and grilled vegetables. Entrées are less ebullient but are well executed—and all are served with black beans, yuca fries and plantains. We would gladly forgo the listed entrées, however, for either of the seafood specials: a very serious seafood paella, tasty and teeming with sea creatures; and camarones negros, grilled jumbo shrimp swathed in a spicy, earthy sauce that we wanted to spoon up and eat by itself. Dinner costs about $17 per person (about $25 if you choose one of the seafood specials), lunch about $10.

Tryst
401 N. La Cienega Blvd., W. Hollywood 90048; (310) 289-1600
Eclectic. Lunch Mon.-Fri., Dinner nightly, Late Supper Thurs.-Sat. AE, MC, V.

The day it opened, Tryst instantly turned into the hottest place in town, something that restaurants of this ilk have a tendency to do. Tryst's exceedingly outré decor, compliments of designer Ron Meyers, is an extravagant fantasy setting, replete with lush paintings of nymphs and lavish copper detailing. The habitués are every bit as important to the look as the sconces and the chairs. They are well aware of this, and dress with appropriate drama.

Chef Ralf Marhencke makes a bold go at Pacific Rim/Californian cuisine, a style of cooking he did well during his brief glory days at Noa Noa restaurant. In addition to appetizers, he offers "hot bites," and "cold bites," almost all of which make either a substantial appetizer or a light main course. It's a most quirky menu: halibut sashimi is listed alongside barbecued baby-back pork ribs in a smoked-tomato sauce. Almost every table has an order or two of those ribs, which come with a tangle of crispy shoestring fries; our ribs were tasty, but we wish they had come from a plumper pig. Even better is the honey-glazed chicken salad. No L.A. menu would be complete without pizza, and Tryst's passable version is a cracker-like creation with cheese welded to the surface, dotted with delicacies like shrimp and Moroccan sausage. If it's a light, on-the-run meal you're wanting, while trying to look as if you've just taken a meeting with a Hollywood studio head, pizza is an excellent choice. Entrées come in surprisingly generous portions, and are also very fairly priced for such a cutting-edge eatery. The catfish is a big critter, hanging off the ends of its plate, fairly crisp outside, and fairly sweet inside. The sesame-crusted tuna, on the other hand, suffers from bitterness. Our favorite entrée is the roasted half chicken, flavored with lemon and herbs, with a mountain range of heavily

---

Don't be afraid to call a restaurant to inquire about anything you need to know: the wine list, the night's specials (you can often reserve a dish in advance), how busy it is that night . . . the information is yours for the asking!

---

whipped mashed potatoes on one side. That chicken is one reason we love Tryst; the other is that it is open every day of the week until 2 a.m., which for Los Angeles is positively radical. Dinner runs about $30 to $40 per person, lunch about $17.

10/20 Tse Yang
151 S. Doheny Blvd., Beverly Hills 90210; (310) 278-8886
Chinese. Lunch & Dinner daily. All major cards.

Tse Yang was actually born in Paris, which explains why the menu is written in both English and French. This also explains the French accent found in a few of the dishes here—after all, how many Chinese restaurants offer grenouilles (frogs) or poulet au citron vert (lightly breaded chicken in a lime sauce). The interior of this place must have cost a Mandarin's ransom. Everywhere you look there are highly polished brass accents, elegant woods, exotic silks. Even the ceilings are a treasure, a Sistine chapel of carvings, ornate filigree and polished highlights. So it's all the more of a letdown when one discovers that the food ranges from decent to quite disappointing. This is Chinese food filtered through the more conservative cooking style of old Europe—and it somehow misses the mark. Best bets are appetizers, particularly "les délices de Pekin à la vapeur" (or, to us Americans, steamed dumplings). Precious few are served for a high price, but what you do get are good. Les hors d'oeuvres arc en ciel (rainbow appetizers) translates as a trio of cold dishes: smoked beef, chicken and tofu. Tse Yang smoked salmon is wonderful, too, the first salmon we've encountered in a Chinese restaurant. The best approach to dining here is to order a range of the more successful starters. We rather like one dessert, a fruit cup with ice cream, so we'll overlook the fact that the fruit came drowned in Triple Sec. Service is formal, French and fine. Dinner will set you back around $45.

Tulipe
8360 Melrose Ave., W. Hollywood 90048; (213) 655-7400
French. Lunch Mon.-Fri. Dinner nightly. AE, MC, V.

Some restaurants get all the breaks: frequent mentions in *Daily Variety*, gaggles of Rolls-Royces in the parking lot and patronage by the sort of people who order Château Pétrus as easily as others order Miller Lite. Tulipe could easily have become such a place, with its fashionable location (on the site of the original Ma Maison), its skilled chefs from formerly fashionable restaurants (Roland Gibert, ex of Bernard's, and Maurice Peguet, ex of L'Escoffier), its comfortable, stylishly minimalist interior and its very good contemporary French bistro food. The prices are even reasonable, by nice-French-restaurant standards. But for some mysterious reason Tulipe has struggled a little. No mobs of smug studio v.p.s here, no phalanxes of black-mini-clad young ladies—fortunately for us, since we can easily get a table and enjoy our meal in peace. At $20, the weeknight prix-fixe—soup or salad, your choice of a meat or fish course, a dessert—is a fabulous buy. The regular menu is a bargain, too, with many entrées in the $14 to $15 range. At these prices, you don't expect—and you don't get—the brilliance of the city's very best French restaurants, but you do get good, creative food. The daube de canard—duck braised in Corbière wine, baked in clay, chilled and served with baby carrots, onions and its own juices—is a lovely, hearty appetizer. The Fourme d'Ambert blue cheese and pears tucked in warm feuilleté pastry is equally delicious, and Gibert's memorable pig's trotters (stuffed with savory California snails) from Bernard's days has been born again here. For main courses, the fish and seafood are for the most part good, particuly the striped sea bass with a potato crust and the sea scallops on a bed of Maui onions; good meat choices include the terrific osso buco with a macaroni "cake" and the roasted baby chicken with fries. Less successful is the grilled muscovy duck breast with five spices and orange honey, an intensely flavored dish whose flavors don't marry well. Desserts are guaranteed to bring a smile to your dentist's face as well as your own: chocolate puff pastry with bitter-chocolate cream and pistachio sauce, hazelnut praline with espresso sauce, apple tart with Calvados sauce. The wine list is intelligently chosen and for the most part fairly priced, and there's an excellent roster of eight French and Californian wines available by the half-carafe, full carafe or bottle. Dinner runs $25 to $40 per person.

11/20 Tusk

10925 W. Pico Blvd., W.L.A. 90064; (310) 470-7570
Thai. Lunch Mon.-Sat., Dinner nightly. AE, MC, V.

"Tusk" is apparently an acronym for "The Ultimate Siamese Kitchen." (To us, this as silly as the restaurant called Thai, which stands for "Think Hungry and Indulge.") Name aside, Tusk is a handsome setting, complete with fine linens and controlled service. According to the menu, when the Roongfangarm family moved from Lampang in the north to Bangkok, "It was our young Uncle Chote who introduced us to

the best foods." Uncle Chote's quest for the best dishes in Bangkok were legendary in the family, and Pat and Boon Roongfangarm have gone to considerable effort to recreate those dishes here. If you taste carefully, you'll notice that the larb has mint, basil and a hint of roasted rice powder. The wonderful fish cakes with string beans are served with a delicate sweet-and-sour cucumber sauce. There's a delicious salad called Speedy Papaya Tuk Tuk, made of grated papaya and carrots, grilled shrimp, tomatoes, cabbage and a honey-tamarind dressing. There's a terrific crispy duck salad. And there are lots of other specialties, from roast pork with onions, garlic and pineapple sauce to a dish called the Voyage of the Killer Shrimp, which must be ordered just for the name. Dinner costs about $15 per person.

12/20 Tuttobene

945 N. Fairfax Ave., W. Hollywood 90046; (213) 655-7051
Italian. Lunch Mon.-Fri., Dinner nightly. All major cards.

After a half decade, Tuttobene remains the definitive Silvio di Mori creation, a casually elegant Italian bistro that has been home to some of the most authentic, and best, trattoria cooking in town. Silvio is easy to find—when he's in the restaurant, the chances are good that he'll be in the kitchen, attired in a beautiful Brioni suit, stained with sauces that he's busily cooking and tasting. (The man can't leave his food alone.) Few chefs in town make a better plate of grilled vegetables flavored with balsamic vinegar. Nowhere is the vitello tonnato more piquant. We recently had a plate of smoked Norwegian salmon and marinated fresh chanterelles in truffle oil that made us wonder why we bother going to Italy to eat. It was followed by beet pasta with a half lobster in a Pinot Grigio sauce. The osso buco served with polenta and spinach is just the near side of sublime. We were sorely disappointed by a couple of recent meals; we can only hope this is a temporary lapse and not the sign of a downhill slide. Dinner runs about $30 or $40 apiece.

11/20 Typhoon

3221 Donald Douglas Loop South, Santa Monica 90405; (310) 390-6565
Pacific Rim. Lunch Tues.-Fri., Dinner Tues.-Sun., Brunch Sun. AE, MC, V.

If Pacific Rim cooking is The Next Big Thing, we often ask ourselves, then why are three out of four new restuarants Italian? But every now and then, an Asian-blendo restaurant comes along—a Chaya Brasserie, a Chinois on Main, a Shiro, a Matsuhisa—that becomes a significant ingredient in L.A.'s ever-improving restaurant stew. Typhoon is not as serious as its predecessors—as evidenced by its cocktail menu, where you'll find such brain-whompers as the Sucker Hole—but it's no less welcome. Located on the south side of Santa Monica Airport's runways, Typhoon is an enchanting spot at twilight. You can gaze out the Cinemascope windows at the vintage prop planes, small-scale airport buildings and deeppurple Santa Monica Mountains. The kitchen crew is an Asian United Nations and China, Japan, Thailand, Korea, the Philippines, India, Vietnam and Burma are each represented with at least one dish on the menu. We've been failed by a bowl of gelatinous tofu egg-drop soup and some off-tasting Vietnamese beef, but we won't soon forget the Japanese eggplant with garlic rice. When you combine the buttery eggplant (bathed in a dark, slightly spicy sauce) with the nutty, garlic-bombed rice, you have a creation that'll make vegetarians weep for joy. Everything else we've tried, from the pungent kim chee, to the savory shui mai dumplings, to the crisp shrimp tempura, to the warming udon soup, was as enjoyable as it was affordable. About $16 to $23 apiece for dinner.

Valentino

3115 Pico Blvd., Santa Monica 90405;
(310) 829-4313
Italian. Lunch Fri., Dinner Mon.-Sat. All major cards.

Going to Valentino for dinner is like going to your best friend's house for Christmas. You know you're going to be well taken care of. You know you'll have a lot to eat. You know you'll have a good time. Of course, unless your best friend is Milan's renowned Giuliano Bugialli, you're not likely to eat like you will at Valentino. Even in an era when Italian restaurants seem to be opening quicker than you can say "tiramisu," Valentino remains one of the two or three best Italians in Southern California. Its three dining rooms are attractive and skillfully lighted, with decibel levels that allow you to take in the food without undue distraction. The service is attentive. The wine list is still the best in the West. And the food is exquisite.

But the food is the most difficult part of the dining experience to discuss with any specificity. Oh sure, there's the menu. You could start with Tuscan bean soup with barley and prosciutto or the sausage and lentils. Then you could have cacio e pepe (whole wheat spaghetti with sharp cheeses and black pepper) or risotto with seafood. There's also a whole range of traditional main courses: osso buco, veal chop, sweetbreads,

eggplant parmigiana. But to order from the menu is to miss the unique pleasure of dining at Valentino. This is a restaurant with 10, 20, 30 specials that change every night. Owner/host Piero Selvaggio, a consummate restaurateur, will be delighted to recite them all for you. So will his waiters and captains. Listen carefully. Take notes. Ask questions. Discuss the various options among yourselves. Then order. Since the kitchen occasionally (and mistakenly) leans toward Frenchified versions of Italian food, you should lean toward the most Italian-sounding of the dishes. Or just put yourself in Selvaggio's hands. Tell him what you like and what you don't like. He'll take care of the rest. Yes, we know him personally, so he knows our tastes—and attends to our needs—better than most. And, yes, we have heard sporadic reports of unhappiness from diners new to the restaurant. But these complaints are uncommon; even strangers generally report ecstatically on their experience at Valentino.

Of course, wine may contribute to their ecstasy. Valentino has a truly remarkable wine list— 66 pages, almost evenly divided among Italians, Californians and French—and it's reasonably priced compared to other top-of-the-line restaurants. We counted more than 200 selections under $30 in the first 30 pages alone. You can comfortably put yourself in Selvaggio's hands for wine selection, too; we'll just say that the list has five pages of Barolo, more than 50 of them for less than $50 each. You won't find such a wide, decently priced selection of this magnificent wine anywhere else. Dinner from the menu costs $45 or more per person—considerably more if you order one of the more exotic specials (watch out for the risotto with truffles!) or if you have four courses.

12/20 Versailles

10319 Venice Blvd., Culver City 90034;
(310) 558-3168
Cuban. Lunch & Dinner daily. AE, MC, V.
1415 S. La Cienega Blvd., L.A. 90035;
(310) 289-0392
Cuban. Lunch Mon.-Fri., Dinner nightly. AE, MC, V.

A palace this isn't. The original Versailles in Culver City is, however, a lively, noisy, crowded Cuban restaurant, filled with a cross-section of Cubans, hipsters and industry lions from nearby MGM. Well, no wonder. Who doesn't love a bargain? Prices are low and food is fresh. Oh, some complain about it being greasy, but that's because they've ordered roast pork or deep-fried whole Florida pompano instead of Versailles's roast chicken, which is, simply, the best roast chicken in town. Crisp-skinned, this giant half chicken tastes of a wonderful lime-vinegar marinade laced with raw garlic, and is served with slices of sweet raw onion, fried plantains and a plate of white rice and black beans. The beans may be on the dry side, but at $25 for two, tip included, who cares. Refresh yourself with the iced orange juice, a mango shake or a cup of marvelously strong espresso. The much smaller La Cienega branch doesn't quite have the Cuban-fiesta ambience of the original, but the roast chicken is still an epiphany.

Vim
831 S. Vermont Ave., Mid-Wilshire District (L.A.) 90005; (213) 480-8159
Thai. Lunch & Dinner daily. No cards.

Because the food at Vim is so remarkably inexpensive, there's a tendency to order every dish that sounds good. This is dangerous, because it's all so wonderful that you're likely to eat everything you ordered. Which can make you very large. A better strategy would be to begin with the single most expensive dish on the menu, the spicy-hot seafood soup (all of $6.50, and it feeds four easily): a volcano of a hot pot, with a small ocean of fish and shelled creatures basking in a broth that could raise the dead and heal the sick. It's probably the best spicy-hot seafood soup in town. There are some seventeen soups to choose from, making at least seventeen trips here imperative. After the soup, it's wise to cool down with the hot-and-sour shrimp salad, a forest of greens populated by a double handful of perfectly cooked shrimp. Because the grungy (though centrally located) neighborhood is far from high-rent, and because no money has been wasted on decor (straight ahead Formica and fluorescent lighting), what you pay for is on your plate: tender-as-butter beef with green chilis and onions; crispy sliced catfish with spicy-hot sauce; joyous oysters with an awesome ginger and oyster sauce; the best phad Thai noodles we've ever tasted; and a dish not on the menu called pineapple rice, a must-order for all old Vim hands. The cost is usually less than $10 per person, including Singha Beer.

11/20 Vivo Trattoria
5750 Melrose Ave., Melrose-La Brea District (L.A.) 90038; (213) 463-3115
Japanese-Italian. Lunch Mon.-Fri., Dinner Mon.-Sat. MC, V.

Years ago we discovered how happily the cuisines of Japan and France can be wed. At Vivo Trattoria, Osaka-born restaurateur Yuko Yoshimura has shown us yet a newer alliance, this one between Japan and—gasp—Italy. As principal of a catering business that was highly popular with the entertainment industry, Yoshimura worked with chef Tetsuya Kurokawa to develop a menu that played to Angeleno's long-running love affair with Italian food but, at the same time, reflected a decided Japanese influence. The use of uncompromisingly fresh ingredients (including organic produce and free-range chicken) and a cunning balance of robust flavors and more subtle tastes are Kurokawa's twin signatures. At what other trattoria in town can you order the daily "soba della casa" and be served a bowl of hearty buckwheat noodles—cooked to a perfect al dente—and sauced with a cross-cultural mix of onions, enoki mushrooms, sausage and green peppers? On another visit we found the same skinny noodles buried beneath a jumble of bonito tuna, kaiware (radish sprouts) and seaweed. There are two good, classic Italian lasagnes on the lunch menu, and an intriguing spaghetti dish "alla Mentaiko," employing spicy cod eggs, kaiware and calamari, among the dinner entrées. Kurokawa is skilled at preparing fish: try the posted specials or order black cod from the menu. Vivo Trattoria is set in a reconfigured 1930s house, a good bit to the east of Melrose's trendiest strip. The decor is spare but comfortable; the whitewashed walls form a minimalist backdrop for a number of decorative ethnic accent pieces. Service is unhurried and thoughtful (bottled spring water is served gratis); a modest wine list offers several outstanding values. Lunch includes salad and soup and is less than $8; dinner runs from $25 to $30.

12/20 Warszawa
1414 Lincoln Blvd., Santa Monica 90401; (310) 393-8831
Polish. Dinner nightly. All major cards.

Warszawa may be located on the westside, but it's like no other L.A. restaurant. You leave your reservation on an answering machine, and no one calls you to confirm. It doesn't advertise. It doesn't attract the typical ethnic-restaurant foodies or baby moguls wearing their baseball caps backwards. No, Warszawa is a serene, civilized restaurant, an excellent place to pay homage to the end of the Eastern Bloc and the dawning of a new Poland. The series of small, softly lit dining rooms once comprised a private home; period posters reflecting Polish culture cover the walls, and lace curtains cover the windows. Start with one of the potato-based vodkas, which will set your appetite on edge for a fine bowl of borscht or hearty potato pancakes. Then continue with one of the delicious, generously served Polish classics, from roast duck and hunter's stew to veal paprikash and stuffed cabbage. If you can manage to put away any more rich food (which is doubtful), the cheesecake and chocolate-cream walnut cake are the two best desserts. You can't order a double decaf cappuccino here, but that's not what Warszawa is all about. Dinner costs $25 per person.

Water Grill
544 S. Grand Ave., Downtown (L.A.)
90013; (213) 891-0900
Seafood. Lunch Mon.-Fri., Dinner nightly; AE, MC, V.

If downtown Los Angeles ever rises, like Lazarus, from the dead, places like the Water Grill will be among the reasons why. It looks like an ocean of money went into the decor: there's a brilliant collision here between the streamlined art deco of the Golden Age of Hollywood, and the dark, intense wood-and-brass look of clubby fish spots like New York's Grand Central Oyster Bar. In perfect L.A. style, this is a restaurant that was born looking as if it had a past, and a shady one at that. At the center of the room is an elegantly curved bar, one part of which is dedicated to beverages (including a good number of micro-brewed beers), the other end of which belongs to an oyster bar, which is the pride and joy of the place. Five types of oysters are on the menu seasonally: Malpeques (from Prince Edward Island), Fanny Bays (British Columbia), Kumamotos (Oregon), Chiloés (Chile) and Coromandels and Rock oysters (both from New Zealand). We didn't stop there, but moved on to some Alaskan side-stripe shrimp ($10 a half pound), Santa Barbara spot prawns ($11 a half pound) and Puget Sound pink scallops ($8 a half pound). They're damned good—but the mortgage payment can quickly be squandered here. Beyond the oyster bar, there's a big menu to explore, a large part of which proudly brags about what's fresh that day—Copper River salmon, Arctic char, Hawaiian albacore—and another large part of which deals with Pacific Northwest seafood. These offerings are not as successful as those at the bar: the sturgeon is grilled with hackleback, petrale sole is sautéed with hazelnuts, char is roasted and served with wilted greens. These dishes are good, but not

consistent in quality and not stunning enough for the prices. You can't go wrong, however, with the clam chowder, so rich it's the seafood equivalent of mom's chicken soup. Dinner costs $40 or more per person.

12/20 West Beach Café
60 N. Venice Blvd., Venice 90291;
(310) 823-5396
Californian. Lunch Tues.-Fri., Dinner nightly, Late Supper Thurs.-Sat., Brunch Sat.-Sun. All major cards.

The West Beach was Bruce Marder's first restaurant, and it remains his best. It's still nothing more than an art filled shoebox with a crowded bar and tables huddled together like intimate friends, a beachside café where service is performed by a team of aspiring actors obviously waiting patiently for that big break. The upside is the wondrous jolt of energy you get here, plenty of culinary enthusiasm and lots of fine, creative food. Salads tend toward the exotic, pastas toward the unusual; both are prepared with a variety of rare ingredients (Manchego cheese, fedelini). Entrées can be equally outré—pumpkin tortellini in lamb sauce, grilled trout with a mignonette of eggplant and porcini mushrooms, roast rack of lamb with sage in a gratin of eggplant, zucchini and tomatoes glazed with Locatelli Romano cheese. Dishes may not always work, but one is rarely bored. The check, incidentally, can be an adventure in itself: this place only looks like a small beachside café; the prices are pure haute. Dinner costs a good $55.

Yang Chow
379 N. Broadway, Chinatown (L.A.) 90012;
(213) 625-0811
Chinese. Lunch & Dinner daily. AE, MC, V.

Yang Chow's happy diners obviously aren't here for the decor, which is as functional and brightly lit as many other Chinese restaurants. It's the food: Szechuan wontons in a tasty, aromatic broth; juicy pan-fried dumplings, among the best in town; shrimp in a fabulous tomato-garlic sauce; a fine kung pao chicken; Yang Chow lamb, slices of lamb and broccoli stems in a rich brown sauce; Szechuan beef, a heavenly combination of chewy, hot and sweet; and pan-fried noodles with mixed ingredients, a delicious tangle of hearty noodles, shrimp, chicken, beef and vegetables. Even that old war horse, cashew chicken, passes muster here, and the many Szechuan dishes are spiced with a restrained hand, so the chilies don't overwhelm the other flavors. Dinner will be about $15.

For more ideas on money-saving meals, see the listing of restaurants under the "$15 & Under" heading, in INDEXES at the back of the book.

11/20 **Zipangu**
802 Broadway, Santa Monica 90401; (310) 395-3082
Italian-Japanese/Sushi. Lunch Tues.-Fri., Dinner Tues.-Sun. AE, MC, V.

Zipangu means "Italian" in Japanese, signifying yet another cross-cultural L.A. restaurant. If an Italian-Japanese restaurant sounds a little contrived, it is. There's something so fundamentally different about the cuisines—one based in such things as olive oil, tomatoes and cheese, the other in soy sauce, ginger and raw fish—that combining them seems little more than an exercise in cleverness. The Japanese influence is evident in the near-invisible outside signage, the ultraminimal decor, notable primarily for a sushi bar and smooth, hard surfaces, and the pleasant waiters, many of whom barely speak English. Most of the food is well prepared, but none of it is better than at any number of Japanese or Italian restaurants in town: an attractive sushi combination; a salad combining radicchio and crisp-baked salmon skin with a ponzu dressing; a tangle of spaghetti with seafood, tomatoes, olive oil, garlic and parsley; a more-French-than-Italian rack of lamb with a tasty sauce of garlic, green peppercorns and mustard. Though the food is just fine, Zipangu must be careful that it doesn't end up diluting two of the world's great cuisines instead of creating an exciting new one. Anywhere from $20 to $35 per person for dinner.

And Also . . .

Asuka, 1266 Westwood Blvd., Westwood 90024; (310) 474-7412. *Japanese. Lunch Mon.-Fri., Dinner nightly. All major cards.* A casual sushi spot offering all the standards (try the raw quail egg sushi), as well as reasonably priced full dinners: teppanyaki (grilled), tempura (deep-fried in batter) and sukiyaki (flash-cooked in a savory-sweet broth). Dinner, about $15 per person.

Benihana of Tokyo, 38 N. La Cienega Blvd., W. Hollywood 90211; (213) 655-7311. *Japanese. Lunch Mon.-Fri., Dinner nightly. All major cards.* This high-concept Japanese chain restaurant continues to be as popular as ever with young date-nighters and tourists; the food is fresh, simple and fairly tasty. Four other locations. Dinner, $25 per person.

Benvenuto Café, 8512 Santa Monica Blvd., W. Hollywood 90069; (310) 659-8635. *Italian. Lunch Mon.-Fri., Dinner nightly. AE, MC, V.* A small room and an outdoor patio set back from the street make this the ideal casual setting for munching herbed focaccia dipped in olive oil, fairly classic pizzas, panini and pastas. On the patio at night, with a rush of traffic going by, you can close your eyes and pretend for a moment that you're in New York. Dinner, $10 to $18 per person.

The Black Whale, 3016 Washington Blvd., Marina del Rey 90292; (310) 823-9898. *Steakhouse. Lunch & Dinner daily. AE, MC, V.* A venerable he-man-style tavern serving agreeable seafood and steak dishes to the Marina crowd. Dinner, $30 to $50 per person.

Broadway Bar & Grill, 1436 3rd St., Santa Monica 90401; (310) 393-4211. *American. Lunch & Dinner daily. All major cards.* One of the city's best burgers, topped with Irish bacon, is served in this comfortable, San Francisco–style bar and grill. Good Caesar salad and great desserts. Dinner, $20 per person.

Café Gale, 8400 Wilshire Blvd., Beverly Hills 90211; (213) 655-2494. *Lunch Mon.-Fri., Dinner nightly, Brunch Sun. All major cards.* A bright little café located on a restaurant-poor stretch of Wilshire Boulevard, Café Gale merits a visit for someone wanting a quick lunch in the area. No culinary thrills—just decent French-Asian food in a shiny, lively (loud) setting. Appetizers and Asian fare, such as the potstickers, are better than entrées. Lunch, $15 per person.

Casa Carnitas, 4067 Beverly Blvd., Hollywood 90004; (213) 667-9953. *Mexican. Lunch & Dinner daily. MC, V.* A reliable neighborhood Mexican restaurant serving dirt-cheap Yucatecan dishes to a primarily Latino crowd. You'll spend $10 or less per person.

Casablanca, 220 Lincoln Blvd., Venice 90291; (310) 392-5751. *Mexican/Moroccan. Lunch & Dinner daily. MC, V.* Not everything here is worthy, but the calamari steak is very good, and the atmosphere is festive. Dinner, $20 per person.

Chart House, 18412 Pacific Coast Hwy., Malibu 90265, (310) 454-9321. *American. Dinner nightly. All major cards.* What makes the Malibu branch of this resort-area chain notable is its fabulous ocean-view setting. On the menu, you'll find the same fresh, predictable salad bar, steaks and grilled fish as at every Chart House. Expect a long wait, and expect to spend about $25 per person.

Cheesecake Factory, 362 N. Beverly Dr., Beverly Hills 90210; (310) 278-7270. *American. Lunch & Dinner daily. All major cards.* "Factory" is the operative word at these always-mobbed restaurants, where commercial kitchens churn out thousands of hearty salads, pastas, entrées and dense pieces of cheesecake. Other locations in Marina del Rey, Woodland Hills and Redondo Beach. Dinner, $18 per person.

El Colmao, 2328 W. Pico Blvd., Downtown (L.A.) 90006; (213) 386-6131. *Cuban. Lunch & Dinner Wed.-Mon. No cards.* This Cuban diner makes up for its scruffy neighborhood with marvelous food at bargain prices. Try the roast chicken or shrimp with yellow rice. Dinner, $9 per person.

Dale's Bistro, 361 N. La Cienega Blvd., W. Hollywood 90048; (310) 659-3996. *French. Lunch Mon.-Fri., Dinner Tues.-Sat. MC, V.* On a street that has metamorphosed in recent years into Bistro Row, Dale's Bistro was one of the first. A charming and civilized little room sets the stage for decently done classics (boeuf Bourguignon) and not-so-classics (escargot wontons).

89

And Also . . . (cont.)

Dar Maghreb, 7651 W. Sunset Blvd., Hollywood 90048; (213) 876-7651. *Moroccan. Dinner nightly. MC, V.* The belly dancers may be more interesting than the food, but the b'stilla is delicious and the setting is perfect for rowdy birthday-party groups. You can feast for $30 per person.

Flame, 1442 Westwood Blvd., Westwood 90025; (310) 470-9131. *Persian. Lunch & Dinner daily. CB, DC, MC, V.* Just two doors away from Shahrzad, this Persian restaurant is under the same ownership, and is a slightly more casual version of its cousin, with basically the same menu. *See* review of Shahrzad in this section.

La Grange, 2005 Westwood Blvd., W.L.A. 90025; (310) 279-1060. *French. Lunch Mon.-Fri., Dinner Mon.-Sat. All major cards.* Practically a relic for its 24-year history on the westside, this old-world French spot is dependable for the classics: noisette of lamb, duck à l'orange, poulet jurassienne, entrecôte and quite a few fish dishes. Prix-fixe menus can be had for $10 or $15; à la carte dinner costs about $28 per person.

Inagiku, Bonaventure Hotel, 404 S. Figueroa St., Downtown (L.A.) 90071; (213) 614-0820. *Japanese. Breakfast & Lunch Mon.-Fri., Dinner Sat.-Sun. All major cards.* Located on the sixth floor (not easy to find) of the enormous Bonaventure hotel, this is a reliable Japanese restaurant noted for its excellent tempura bar. Dinner, $32 per person.

Kippan, 260 N. Beverly Dr., Beverly Hills 90210; (310) 858-0535. *Japanese. Lunch Mon.-Fri., Dinner nightly. All major cards.* Newly opened as we went to press, this narrow storefront in central Beverly Hills is as casual as a sushi bar gets. The sushi is star, making a better impression than contemporary Japanese surprises such as soft-shell crab in a cream-pepper sauce with garlic bread. Many of L.A.'s servers could take a lesson from the extremely gracious hosts. Dinner, $25 to $35 per person.

L.A. Trattoria, 8022 3rd St., Melrose-La Brea District (L.A.) 90069; (213) 658-7607. *Italian. Lunch Tues.-Fri., Dinner Tues.-Sun. All major cards.* Envision a casual, affordable, storefront offering unremarkable pizzas, pastas, risotti, roasted meats and tiramisu—and you have this eatery pegged. The food is passable, the good wine list has some tasty, inexpensive Italian Cabs, and the location is convenient to the Beverly Center. Dinner, $20 or more per person.

Louise's Trattoria, 9 branches include 1008 Montana Ave., Santa Monica 90403, (310) 394-8888; 342 N. Beverly Dr., Beverly Hills 90212, (310) 274-4271; 7505 Melrose Ave., Hollywood 90046, (213) 651-3880. *Italian. Most branches: Lunch & Dinner daily, Brunch Sun. AE, MC, V.* This fast-growing chain has a branch in every port. The predictable pastas and pizzas make a good quick lunch, at $10 or less per person. Other branches in Brentwood, West L.A., Larchmont Village, Glendale, Hungtington Beach and Redondo Beach.

Lucy's Café El Adobe, 5536 Melrose Ave., Hollywood 90038; (213) 462-9421. *Mexican. Lunch & Dinner Mon.-Sat. MC, V.* Back when Melrose was nothing but a strip of print shops, Lucy's was a regular stop-in for some big names: Hubert Humphrey, John Denver, Brenda Vaccaro, Alan Cranston. Today it remains dark as a cave, with ersatz brick walls and plastic shrubbery. The food is, shall we say, edible Mexican. The margaritas (frothy and delicious) and the ambience (comfortable and conspiratorial) may explain Lucy's success. Dinner with margaritas, $15 per person.

Malibu Adobe, 23410 Cross Creek Rd., Malibu 90265; (310) 456-2021. *Southwestern. Lunch & Dinner daily. All major cards.* We think of this terrific-looking place, designed by Ali McGraw, as Santa-Fe-by-the-Sea. It's a great spot for new-age jazz, high-style get-togethers and slushy margaritas. The food is simply not the point. Dinner costs about $30 per person.

The Marquis West, 3110 Santa Monica Blvd., Santa Monica 90404; (310) 828-4567. *Continental. Lunch Mon.-Fri., Dinner nightly. All major cards.* Substantial and safe, with crests on the walls, dark booths and a clientele that looks like they might be friends of the Reagans (if a bit less chic), this place serves copious portions of well-prepared Continental food. Dinner, $44 per person.

Menagerie, 3347 Motor Ave., W.L.A. 90034; (310) 202-8808. *Eclectic. Lunch & Dinner daily. AE, MC, V.* If we had an "eccentric" category, this would be it. In a modern, neon-lit space in an otherwise deserted West L.A. neighborhood, wacky owner/chef Robert Blaisch (also a scientist and inventor) creates a goulash of American/Italian/Japanese cuisine, with touches from all around the globe: there are yucca "hash browns" with pineapple-peppercorn chutney, tempura mushrooms stuffed with shrimp mousse, ribs and steaks in a teriyaki–black cherry marinade. Many dishes shine, some confuse. Dinner, from $25 to $30 per person.

Moody's, The Sheraton Grande Hotel, 333 S. Figueroa St., Downtown (L.A.) 90071; (213) 617-1133. *American. Lunch & Dinner daily. All major cards.* A polished-wood, San Francisco–style pub inside a major downtown hotel. It's a comfortable, reasonably priced spot for a Caesar salad and a steak sandwich, for $13 to $25 per person.

Oriental Seafood Inn, 4016 Lincoln Blvd., Marina del Rey 90292; (310) 306-9088. *Chinese. Lunch & Dinner daily. AE, MC, V.* Yuppies who don't want to venture as far as Chinatown, let alone Monterey Park, come here for a fix of Hong Kong-style Chinese seafood and Cantonese standards. Dinner, $15 to $20 per person.

Osteria Romana Orsini, 9575 W. Pico Blvd., W.L.A. 90035, (310) 277-6050. *Italian. Lunch Mon.-Fri., Dinner Mon.-Sat. All major cards.* This upscale Italian near Century City is at its best at lunchtime, when businesspeople fill their plates from the excellent antipasti buffet. Dinner, $32 per person.

Packard Grille, 4301 Figueroa St., Highland Park 90065, (213) 223-1200. *American. Lunch & Dinner daily, Brunch Sat.-Sun. AE, MC, V.* This welcome café in restaurant-poor Highland Park is lodged in a former Packard dealership that has been restored with taste and verve. It's a fine, inexpensive neighborhood spot for fried calamari, roast chicken, crisp fries and chocolate-bourbon cake. Dinner, $15 to $20 per person.

Panda Inn, Westside Pavilion, 10800 W. Pico Blvd., W.L.A. 90064; (310) 470-7790. *Chinese. Lunch & Dinner daily. AE, MC, V.* A stylish minichain serving up reasonably authentic, if sometimes bland, Chinese food. Dinner, with beer, runs $15 per person.

Il Piccolino, 641 N. Highland Ave., Wilshire District (L.A.) 90036; (213) 936-2996. *Italian. Lunch Tues.-Fri., Dinner Tues.-Sun. AE, MC, V.* This casual, affordable offshoot of Emilio's restaurant serves tasty salads, pastas and pizzas, along with marvelous french fries. Dinner, $20 per person.

Ritza, 5468 Wilshire Blvd., Wilshire District (L.A.) 90036; (213) 934-2215. *Russian. Lunch & Dinner Tues.-Sun. MC, V.* The hearty, lamb-based cuisine of the newly re-established country of Georgia is featured at this ornate restaurant, where a live band plays on weekends and the vodka always flows freely. Dinner, $18 per person.

Santo Pietro, 2954 Beverly Glen Circle, Beverly Hills 90077; (310) 474-4349. 12001 Ventura Pl., Studio City 91604; (818) 508-1177. 1000 Gayley Ave., Westwood 90024; (310) 208-5688. *Italian. Lunch & Dinner daily. AE, MC, V.* This casual spot caters to a loud and convivial crowd, serving pizzas, pasta and salads, as well as marvelously addictive little garlic rolls. The Westwood branch is filled with rowdy UCLA students most nights of the week. Dinner, $15 per person.

St. Mark's, 23 Windward Ave., Venice 90291; (310) 452-2222. *Seafood/Californian. Dinner Tues.-Sun. All major cards.* A hyper-trendy jazz supper club with a celebrity-studded crowd, mostly good music and mostly good Californian fare (including abundant fresh-seafood dishes). Dinner, about $45 per person.

Tamayo, 5300 E. Olympic Blvd., E.L.A. 90022; (213) 260-4700. *Mexican. Lunch & Dinner daily. All major cards.* Good, standard-issue Mexican dishes are served in a gorgeous 1928 Spanish mission-style building. The setting alone is worth a visit. Dinner, $15 per person.

The Tam O'Shanter, 2980 Los Feliz Blvd., Atwater 90027; (213) 664-0228. *American. Lunch Mon.-Fri., Dinner nightly, Brunch Sun. All major cards.* An appealing pseudo-Scottish tavern run by the Lawry's folks, serving well-prepared roasts and chops and good sandwiches in the bar. Lunch, $10; dinner $15 to $25 per person.

Toledo, 11613 Santa Monica Blvd., W.L.A. 90025; (310) 477-2400. *Spanish. Lunch Tues.-Fri., Dinner Tues.-Sun. AE, MC, V.* A quaint two-room *casa* with Spanish food that is more dependable than inspired. Dinner will run about $25 per person.

El Torito Grill, 9595 Wilshire Blvd., Beverly Hills 90210; (310) 550-1599. *Mexican/Southwestern. Lunch & Dinner daily. AE, MC, V.* This upscale cousin of the national chain transcends its relatives. Though it's mass-market food, it's anything but dull. Try the quesadilla with oven-smoked chicken, the blue-corn nachos with black beans and cheese or the crisp red-

corn taquitos stuffed with chicken or beef. In fact, skip the entrées entirely and order a collection of appetizers. You'll get out the door for $15.

Uzen, 11951 Santa Monica Blvd., W.L.A. 90025; (310) 477-1390. *Japanese/Sushi. Lunch Mon.-Fri., Dinner nightly. AE, MC, V.* The former Ike-Ichi is now in the hands of Uzen International Corporation, and it has metamorphosed into a white-tableclothed dining room/sushi bar serving the usual counter fare plus kappo—little treats intended to be consumed with a jumbo Japanese beer. Dinner, under $20 per person.

Whitney's, 1518 Montana Blvd., Santa Monica 90403; (310) 458-4114. *New American. Lunch, Tea & Dinner Mon.-Sat., Brunch Sun. AE, MC, V.*

This small, friendly restaurant on Montana Avenue serves simple egg dishes, salads, pastas and other specialties made with regional ingredients. Half orders of pastas and salads can be had for half the price. Dinner, $20 per person.

Zumaya's, 5722 Melrose Ave., Hollywood 90038; (213) 464-0624. *Mexican. Lunch & Dinner daily. All major cards.* Fairly classy Mexican chow at fairly reasonable prices is served in this charming little spot near Paramount Studios and Hancock Park. Dinner, $14 per person.

San Fernando Valley

Encompasses Sherman Oaks, Studio City, North Hollywood, Toluca Lake, Universal City, Burbank, Encino, Van Nuys, Tarzana, Woodland Hills, Calabasas, Granada Hills and Canoga Park, as well as Thousand Oaks and Saugus.

 ## Akbar

17049 Ventura Blvd., Encino 91316; (818) 905-5129
Indian. Lunch Sun.-Fri., Dinner nightly. All major cards.

This branch of Marina del Rey's Akbar is even more popular than the original. It serves some of the best Indian food in Southern California. Everything is well prepared: crisp samosas, fragrant breads (like onion kulcha), cool raitha, piquant chutneys and tandoori dishes, most notably chicken tikka, first smoked and then broiled in a blazing hot clay oven. The cooking is imaginative and skilled here, the ambience is pleasant and the service is good. Even the wine list impressed us, something we don't expect of an Indian restaurant. About $12 per person.

91

12/20 Araz
11717 Moorpark Ave., Studio City 91604;
(818) 766-1336
Armenian/Lebanese. Lunch & Dinner Tues.-Sun. AE, MC, V.

We have the unfortunate violence in Beirut to thank for this Middle Eastern storefront gem—the Syrian-Armenian owner/chef fled the Lebanese capital with his family to the relative safety of Studio City. He cooks assertive food, liberally employing fresh and dried herbs. His plates are attractive and more than amply portioned. And best of all, the prices here are about as low as you'll find for such enjoyable fare. In addition to the usual kebabs, here prepared faultlessly, we've been charmed by a sensational-looking salad called fettouch, topped with chopped mint and the sharp-flavored berry called sumak; a spicy Syrian dipping sauce called mouhammara; a superb appetizer plate of garlicky lamb's tongue; juicy, marinated quails; and grilled Armenian sausages known as soujouk. A meal runs about $14 a person.

Bamboo Inn
14010 Ventura Blvd., Sherman Oaks 91423;
(818) 788-0202
Chinese. Lunch & Dinner daily. AE, D, MC, V.

All is friendly at the Bamboo Inn, the interior of the restaurant is full of bright pastels and fish tanks teeming with life. The smart diner would be well advised to begin with an order of spiced Chinese cabbage, one of those perfect dishes you can nibble on throughout the meal. And what follows is potentially quite a bit. Certain appetizers are mandatory: plump fried dumplings with crispy nut-brown skin; aromatic beef and smoked fish, both so rich with flavor that you find yourself gasping as they float over your taste buds; even an exceptional lightly dressed barbecued chicken salad. In fact, the kitchen has a skilled hand with chicken in general, producing one of the best kung pao chickens in the city, along with many a tasty variation on the theme: sliced chicken in garlic sauce, chicken with cashew nuts, diced chicken in tangerine sauce, jade chicken (smothered in greens). Several remarkable lamb dishes are drawn from the Szechuan and Hunan areas, and there are subtly prepared vegetables galore. (Don't miss the dry-sautéed string beans and the meatless—for a change—hot spicy eggplant.) Though the seafood dishes are the menu's most expensive, some are worth the splurge, particularly the hot braised shrimp, scallops in garlic sauce, filet of fish in black-bean sauce and sweet-and-pungent shrimp. Dinner runs about $16 per person.

Barsac Brasserie
4212 Lankershim Blvd., N. Hollywood 91602; (818) 760-7081
French. Lunch Mon.-Fri., Dinner Mon.-Sat. All major cards.

From the people who brought us La Loggia, here's Barsac. Catering to the same movie studio crowd, this handsome, contemporary designed bistro offers a mélange of French and Italian fare. Barsac didn't have a bottle of Barsac (a sweet French wine) in the house when it first opened, but after an initial flurry of criticism, it now makes sure there's always one handy. Crammed with people from The Biz at lunchtime, Barsac is nearly forgotten at night; a leisurely dinner here can be a very gratifying experience. Chef Didier Poirier prepares worthy warm-duck and warm-scallop salads, along with a fine rabbit pâté, well-prepared brains with capers, pasta shells with a snail ragu, and a comforting plate of roasted veal sausages with sauerkraut. Prepare to spend about $26 per person.

Bellablue
12321 Ventura Blvd., Studio City 91604; (818) 508-6444
Italian. Lunch Mon.-Fri., Dinner nightly. All major cards.

The nearby studio crowd has adopted this zingy, diminutive, blue-toned dining room, especially for its lunchtime buffet spread prepared by ex-Il Giardino chef Gabriele Tani. Evenings draw a fashionable throng, many of them pals of snow-maned co-owner/maître d' Livio Betti, who they got to know during his days as the G.M. of the once spiffy private club, Tramps. Lots of good polenta and crostini dishes are turned out by Tani, along with impeccable pastas and an immensely gratifying plate of roast veal, sliced to order from a large, gleaming carving cart. Although the personable Betti sometimes cajoles customers into trying too many dishes, Bellablue provides one of the more memorable dining experiences in the Valley. Dinner costs about $27 per person.

The Bistro Garden at Coldwater
12950 Ventura Blvd., Sherman Oaks 91604; (818) 501-0202
Continental. Lunch Mon.-Fri., Dinner nightly. All major cards.

The Bistro Garden at Coldwater sure makes an impression. It's a large, opulent, European-style winter garden setting, with a beautiful tiled floor and a scattered grove of light-strung trees. German-born Kurt Niklas, owner of the Bistro Garden in Beverly Hills (an institution for as long

ABSOLUT APPEAL.

MAISON LOUIS JADOT

Impeccable Burgundies
Since 1859

as we can remember), has brought much of his time-tested menu to the Valley. Grilled pesto shrimp and salmon tartare (a finely minced version heavy on the capers) are good starters, though the anchovy-poor Caesar salad doesn't quite measure up to the standards in the Beverly Hills restaurant. You won't go wrong with dishes like lamb in rosemary sauce or grilled swordfish with herb butter, and the kitchen does good work with steaks and chops. Dinner runs about $40 per person.

Brother's Sushi

21418 Ventura Blvd., Canoga Park 91364; (818) 992-1284
Japanese/Sushi. Lunch Tues.-Fri., Dinner Tues.-Sun. AE, MC, V.

There may be a dearth of great Continental and Chinese restaurants in the Valley, but when it comes to sushi, the area is mightily stocked. In the beginning (the late 70s) there was Teru Sushi, and then came the fine Iroha Sushi. Brother's Sushi originally opened in Reseda, but moved to Canoga Park a while back; it has retained an attractive look and a supply of very good fish. Few people sit anywhere but at the sushi bar, where most of the customers are Japanese. The bar is the province of a sushi chef named Goro, who's been a master for more than twenty years, and much of his handiwork is superb—grilled bonito, ever-so-slightly cooked along one edge; miso asari, the prized soy-bean soup prepared with a pair of perfectly steamed cherrystone clams. Deep-fried soft-shell crabs are among the best in town, and a luxuriant lobster hand roll overflowing with chunked meat, is pure ecstasy. Dinner will cost between $20 and $25 per person.

12/20 Camille's

13573 Ventura Blvd., Sherman Oaks 91423; (818) 995-1660
French. Lunch Tues.-Fri., Dinner Tues.-Sat. AE, MC, V.

Camille's is dressed in the colors and finery of an aging grande dame: rose and emerald abound, pictures hang in gilded frames, well-aged vases are carefully placed. Stepping through the door from busy Ventura Boulevard is a mild shock, because Camille's seems so far removed from the world outside. Chef Peter Schwalder specializes in very good French dishes done with modern touches—nouvelle in tone if not in spirit. A chilled tomato soup comes flavored with spinach and cucumbers. In one dish a filet of sole is given a counterpoint of smoked salmon. In another veal contrasts with beef marrow and morel mushrooms. Scallops are done perfectly in an elegant saffron butter. The wine list offers a fine selection

of California wines. This is one of the Valley's great secrets. Dinner can be a bit stiff, about $40 per person.

Cha Cha Cha

17499 Ventura Blvd., Encino 91316; (818) 789-3600
Caribbean. Lunch & Dinner daily, Brunch Sun. All major cards.

A Valley offshoot of East Hollywood's Cha Cha Cha, this restaurant is a hit all around. Executive chef and co-owner Toribio Prado has managed to make this place look cheery and festive; his take on Caribbean/Cuban food is larger than life and twice as colorful, like what the meals in a restaurant in *The Little Mermaid* would look like. Served on oversize pineapple-emblazoned plates are such dishes as crispy jerk pork served with three salsas; fresh, meaty crabcakes with a zingy sauce; spicy camarones negros (fat, juicy shrimp sautéed in a sexy, hot black-pepper sauce and served over a bed of coconut rice); and a free-range veal chop prepared with a calypso twist. At this writing, the desserts needed a little work—odd, since the flans and tarte Tatin at Prado's other eateries are so great (he learned most of his dessert tricks during a stint at The Ivy). But that's a relatively small quibble. Cha Cha Cha fills a long-empty niche in the Valley: a slightly wacky ethnic restaurant that's user-friendly, moderately priced and home to terrific food. Dinner costs about $30 per person.

12/20 Chao Praya

13456 Ventura Blvd., Sherman Oaks 91423; (818) 789-3575
Thai. Lunch & Dinner daily. All major cards.
See review in "Restaurants – *L.A. Area.*"

Chef Tien

17823 Chatsworth St., Granada Hills 91344; (818) 360-3997
Chinese. Lunch Mon.-Sat., Dinner nightly. AE, MC, V.

The acclaimed veteran chef who opened the China Palace in Culver City has resurfaced here in the outer reaches of the Valley, much to the surprise and good fortune of nearby residents. In a redecorated former Mongolian-barbecue storefront, Tien delivers superb platters of full-flavored cold and hot appetizers and Szechuan-fiery soup and stew pots filled with tender meats and/or seafood. From more than 25 soup selections, we usually opt for the clay pot of whole catfish swimming in a spicy, steaming broth. You won't find a better chicken in black-bean sauce anywhere. And garlic fanciers will shiver with delight with every bite of Chef Tien's sliced pork in garlic sauce. It's relatively cheap, too—less than $15 a person for dinner.

12/20 La Chêne

12625 Sierra Hwy., Saugus 91350;
(805) 251-4315
French. Dinner daily, Brunch Sun. All major cards.

Some would say La Chêne sits in the middle of nowhere, with its remote, back roads Canyon Country location. But there's great warmth under this roof, and it's one of the only real *relais* in all of Southern California. The exterior design is river rock held together with stucco, a venerable look that feels strangely modern. There's rock on the inside, too, most notably in the fireplace set into a corner of the dining room. Beyond that, it's pretty plain in here: paper placemats and utilitarian banquet-hall chairs—like a gussied-up Elks Club. The menu is printed on a blackboard, and listings run the gamut of country French. Just name it—escargots, tongue vinaigrette, shrimp Escoffier, veal forestière, frogs' legs Provençale, duck à l'orange, roast quail Veronique—and you'll find it on this encyclopedic menu. Classics like the onion soup and filet mignon au poivre are especially good here, and beef tongue with capers melts in the mouth. Dinner should cost no more than $30.

11/20 Chin Chin

12215 Ventura Blvd., Studio City 91604;
(818) 985-9090
Cuisine. Lunch & Dinner daily, Late Supper Fri.-Sat. All major cards.

See review in "Restaurants – *L.A. Area.*"

12/20 Daily Grill

16101 Ventura Blvd., Encino 91316;
(818) 986-4111
American. Breakfast Sat.-Sun., Lunch & Dinner daily, Late Supper Fri.-Sat. All major cards.

See review in "Restaurants – *L.A. Area.*"

10/20 Fab's Italian Kitchen

4336 Van Nuys Blvd., Sherman Oaks 91423;
(818) 995-2933
Italian. Lunch & Dinner daily. MC, V.

At first Fab's appeal is a mystery, but once you get a whiff of the aromas coming out of the kitchen, and glance at the menu, you understand. Look for old-fashioned standards at low prices, and expect them to be pretty good, if unsophisticated. Generous pizzas; an enormous chopped salad; pasta Bolognese; and such comfort entrées as veal marsala, eggplant Parmigiana and whitefish pizzaiola are the mainstays here. Try the respectable calamari fritto and the deliciously cheesy veal saltimbocca as well. Entrées come with a side of good spaghetti and there are a couple of decent Chiantis on an otherwise limited wine list. A newly built side room provides a breath of fresh air, and additional seating for the inevitable crowds. Less than $20 per person.

11/20 La Finestra

19647 Ventura Blvd., Tarzana 91356;
(818) 342-2824
Italian. Lunch Tues.-Fri., Dinner Tues.-Sun. AE, MC, V.

Alumnae from Adriano's in Beverly Glen can be found all over town running their own restaurants. At this cheerful-looking, casual Valley trattoria are two more: Mario Tidu, who worked both in Adriano's kitchen and in the dining room and Fabrizio Amati, a partner and the maître d' here. Sardinian-born Tidu, influenced by his mother's cooking and that of Adriano's chef Ueli Huegli, makes airy gnocchetti in a fresh tomato sauce, a thin-crust pizza and traditional chicken Sardu, a lovely, down-home dish combining moist chicken with Kalamata olives, capers, fresh rosemary and tomatoes. Tidu and Amati, both personable chaps, regularly tour the tables and paisley-upholstered banquettes in their small dining room, chatting with regulars and newcomers alike. And they've kept tabs down: dinner usually runs less than $18 per person.

11/20 La Frite Café

15013 Ventura Blvd., Sherman Oaks 91403;
(818) 990-1791
French. Lunch & Dinner daily, Late Supper Fri.-Sat., Brunch Sun. AE, MC, V.

These days, charming cafés and bistros are popping up like mushrooms after a rain. Amidst the growing throng, this stands out as a delightful little café. The sweet, homey setting is the main draw, and the simple bistro fare (with the occasional Italian or Californian dish added) usually sends us home contented and full. For starters, escargots come, as tradition dictates, by the half dozen or dozen; steamed artichoke comes with a vinaigrette for dipping; onion soup comes with the requisite cheese crust. You'll hardly suffer for lack of choice: there are ten green salads, ten crêpes, several quiches, a number of pizzas, and main dishes from rack of lamb to poached salmon to Italian sausages with a tangle of ratatouille. If you're looking for a pleasant spot for a simple meal or for dessert and espresso, you could do far worse. About $15 for lunch, $25 for dinner. Also 22616 Ventura Boulevard, Woodland Hills, (818) 347-6711.

7/20 Fung Lum
222 Universal Terrace Pkwy., Universal City 91608; (818) 763-7888
Chinese. Lunch & Dinner daily, Brunch Sun. AE, MC, V.

To visit Fung Lum (*maple grove* in Cantonese) is to believe the boast of its having cost millions to construct. The restaurant is a splendid, painstaking re-creation of an historic building. (The owners, the Pang family, also have Fung Lums in Hong Kong, Tapei and in Campbell, California.) When you approach this palace in the moonlight, the experience borders on the divine. Entering, you encounter ornamental tiles, sculptured carpets, hand-carved woodwork, celadon porcelains and extravagant flower arrangements. The food, however, is another story. Of the 130 dishes on the menu, we have had a few good ones: Chinese kale with oyster sauce, minced squab (an appetizer), tender greens with black mushrooms and fresh bamboo shoots and steamed catfish. But the list ends there. Steamed rice is mushy; pan-fried dumplings are barely recognizable; special lemon chicken is smothered in a cloying batter—and on and on. Spurn any dishes that are not purely Cantonese; avoid the duck dishes completely. The years roll by, tourists come and go (Fung Lum is adjacent to Universal Studios), and the less than satisfying food continues to be ladled up en masse. About $25 per person.

10/20 The Great Greek
13362 Ventura Blvd., Sherman Oaks 91423; (818) 905-5250
Greek. Lunch & Dinner daily. AE, DC, MC, V.

Zorba would feel right at home here, a taverna where ouzo and retsina flow like water, great bouzouki music resounds and a line of frenzied dancers snakes across the room with gusto. Appetizers are the kitchen's main strength, particularly the Greek salad, the spanakopita and the delicious, very garlicky tzatziki. Entrées include all the usuals—moussaka, shish kebabs and so on—but they've been denatured. To get the most out of this Greek experience, we recommend concentrating on the retsina, the appetizers and the dancing—in which case the bill will come to about $20. A larger meal will set you back about $30.

11/20 Hola Madrid
15910 Ventura Blvd., Encino 91436; (818) 783-8765
Spanish. Lunch Tues.-Fri., Dinner Tues.-Sat. D, MC, V.

Judging from L.A.'s successive love affairs with the cuisines of France and then Italy, and contin-uing south, Spanish food should be next. It's certainly worth every food-lover's while to get acquainted with this salt-of-the-earth cuisine, which is liberal in its use of garlic. Hola Madrid is one of the only truly Spanish places in L.A. The menu, the wines, the owners and the chefs here are Spanish—and so is a good part of the clientele. Begin with sangria, the speciality of the house, delivered in a large beer pitcher. Continue with very good tapas, such as chorizo (Spanish sausage) in red wine; Galician-style octopus; roasted peppers and eggplant; steamed mussels. The vast array of paellas and main dishes is equally fine. If you're planning on a romantic evening, be sure to arrive early since traditional Spanish music is played very loudly from 9:30 on. Dinner costs $20 to $30 per person. Afterwards you may want to visit Hola! the nightclub next door, where a live orchestra keeps things lively.

12/20 Hortobagy
11138 Ventura Blvd., Studio City 91604; (818) 980-2273
Hungarian. Lunch Tues.-Sun., Dinner nightly. MC, V.

Eastern European restaurants are rarely design-conscious, so Hortobagy comes across as almost handsome—simple but warm, with comfortable booths. Visit this restaurant with a serious carnivore, and Hortobagy's Wooden Platter becomes a must: a groaning board for two piled high with spicy pork sausages, breaded slabs of veal and liver, vinegared potato salad, marinated red cabbage and a small hillock of rice. A smaller version called the Farmer's Plate gives you more sausages but no veal or liver; the goulash here, thick, hearty and honest, is topped with a dollop of sour cream. This is one of the only restaurants in L.A. still cooking with lard, a Hungarian tradition. For dessert, have the magnificent palacsinta: crêpes rolled with jam, cheese, and walnuts or poppy seeds. A dinner runs about $10.

12/20 Iroha Sushi
12953 Ventura Blvd., Studio City 91604; (818) 990-9559
Japanese/Sushi. Lunch Mon.-Fri., Dinner nightly. MC, V.

Iroha Sushi is partially hidden on a pathway behind the Garendo Gallery, but once you've figured out access, you'll have found one of the Valley's best sushi shops. Many say the single best item here is the spiced tuna: tender chopped tuna mixed with wasabe and shichimi—literally seven spices. The result is a spiced tuna salad perfect as sashimi or in a hand roll. They've mastered the art of the hand roll at Iroha; there is a superlative salmon-skin roll (very crisp), and a first-rate California roll—a dish that traditionalists consider to be Americanized but that's surprisingly popular with visiting Japanese. Dinner costs about $20.

Jitlada
11622 Ventura Blvd., Studio City 91604; (818) 506-9355
Thai. Lunch Mon.-Fri., Dinner daily. MC, V.

With its large windows and pleasant pastel decor, Jitlada may be the best-looking Thai restaurant in town. But it isn't the decor that really matters here, because this food is some of the best Thai food in the San Fernando Valley. Tasting mee krob here is a revelation; instead of a cloying mass of sugary noodles you discover a most subtle dish, strongly flavored with coriander. The squid appetizer has a deliciously crunchy batter. Barbecued chicken is so seductively spiced that one has to resist the temptation to eat the bones. Super salads, especially the pungent Thai sausage salad and the complex yum yai (cucumbers, carrots, onions, tomatoes, shrimp and chicken) rarely fail to please. And we can't get enough of the crispy Bangkok duck, the intensely spiced, very garlicky pompano or the stir-fried asparagus with bacon and cashews. This restaurant lacks the authentic repertoire of its Hollywood counterpart. Dinner is a bargain at $15 to $20 per person.

La Loggia
11814 Ventura Blvd., Studio City 91604; (818) 985-9222
Italian. Lunch Mon.-Fri., Dinner nightly. AE, MC, V.

Sometimes the Valley's hill people feel like dressing up and heading over the hill to Spago or The Ivy. Other times they feel like putting on khakis and getting a good plate of pasta in the neighborhood. When the mood is casual, folks are likely to head for this terrific Italian spot. Crowded day and night with locals (including some famous faces) and studio toilers, La Loggia combines intimacy and casual good cheer with straightforward Italian food. As is usually the case in such trattorias, you're best off forgoing the entrées and desserts in favor of the delicious salads, antipasti, pastas and pizzas. Try the grilled

> *Gault Millau's ratings are based solely on the restaurants' cuisine. We do not take into account the atmosphere, decor, service and so on; these are commented upon within the reviews.*

seafood-sausage starter, duck-stuffed tortolloni in a porcini sauce, pizza with tasso ham, wild mushrooms and black olives, and lasagne stuffed with pumpkin, zucchini, spinach and ricotta. Every neighborhood should have a place like La Loggia. A pasta dinner costs about $20 per person.

12/20 Marcello Ristorante
140 W. Hillcrest Dr., Thousand Oaks 91360; (805) 371-4367
Italian. Lunch Mon.-Fri., Dinner nightly. AE, MC, V.

Alums from Adriano's (others can be found at Gennaro's, Gaetano's, La Finestra and Far Niente) are at work in this neat shopping-center café, a popular place with a few outdoor tables and low prices: most appetizers, soups and pastas are less than $10, and generously portioned entrées are under $15. Worthy dishes include the rich risotto with either mushrooms or leeks and peas, the hearty appetizer of grilled sausages and polenta, the osso buco with Barolo sauce and the locally made creamy mozzarella. Marcello has become such a hit that the owners have opened a second restaurant (Bel Paese) in Arcadia. You'd have to try hard to spend more than $20 a person.

11/20 Marix Tex Mex Norte
16240 Ventura Blvd., Encino 91316; (818) 789-5400
Mexican. Lunch Mon.-Fri., Dinner nightly, Late Supper Fri.-Sat. AE, MC, V.

Marix Tex Mex Norte is the third and grandest branch of the Marix group, and one of the first Mexican restaurants in the Valley to rise above the boredom level. It's a massive restaurant, with a semi-open kitchen and a glassed-in tortilla counter, from which flows a constant supply of fresh hot flatbreads. The large terra-cotta-tiled bar makes a good, strong margarita and attracts a sizable cross-section of Valleyites, especially young swingers: this may be one of the world's greatest conglomerations of acid-washed denims under one roof. Order Marix's trademark fajitas, a sizzling platters of chicken, beef, shrimp or vegetables steaming like locomotives on a trestle, and served with grilled onions, tortillas, guacamole and salsa. Toss in queso fundido (melted cheese topped with chorizo) and a Mexican pizza, and you'll find your denims just got too tight. This food is both fun and good; nobody says it's good for you. Dinner costs about $17 per person.

Mary's Lamb
10820 Ventura Blvd., Studio City 91604;
(818) 505-6120
American. Breakfast & Lunch Mon.-Fri., Dinner nightly, Brunch Sat.-Sun. AE, D, MC, V.

Pretty, doe-eyed television actress Mary Cadorette serves her lamb three ways—roasted, grilled or as an appetizer with a mint pesto—in this charming, tree-shaded residence-turned-restaurant. Here muffins are baked daily and fresh house-baked biscuits are paired with gravy and Mary's own sausage. It's a quaint, kitchen-cupboard sort of place, with a kitchen that's capable of doing a first-rate job on just about anything: a tasty, herbal meatloaf, a juicy steak in a Cabernet sauce, skillfully made crab turnovers, crabcakes, smoked turkey wrapped in tortillas and a mustard-glazed, herb-crusted roasted rack of—you guessed it—lamb. You should be able to have a lovely dinner for $25 or less per person.

12/20 Mistral Brasserie
13422 Ventura Blvd., Sherman Oaks 91423;
(818) 981-6650
French. Lunch Mon.-Fri., Dinner nightly. AE, MC, V.

Mistral Brasserie (really more a bistro than a brasserie) sits in the midst of one of the more interesting restaurant rows in Los Angeles. Within a quick walk is Casa Vega (Mexican), the Great Greek, Jean's Blue Room (old-style French), Maria's Kitchen (Italian), the Bistro Garden, Marrakesh and a wide assortment of Thai places and sushi bars. What Mistral offers is a casual alternative to the Continental formality found at the Bistro Garden; this is a fine, handsome neighborhood place to go for the well olive-oiled cooking of Provence, from the traditional pizza called pissaladière (choux-pastry crust topped with caramelized onions, olives, herbs and anchovies) through classic versions of steak tartare, pommes frites, grilled entrecôte and stewed chicken. People dress down for this place, as if they were Provençals dropping into their village bistro for a bite. All that's missing is a larger assortment of anis and pastis, and a bottle of absinthe hidden in the back for special customers. Dinner runs about $25 per person.

11/20 Il Mito
11801 Ventura Blvd., Studio City 91604;
(818) 762-1818
Italian. Lunch Mon.-Fri., Dinner nightly, Brunch Sun. AE, MC, V.

This relative newcomer is in the vanguard of bringing the Valley the kind of good, contemporary Italian food that the westside has been enjoying for a few years. The chef/owner, a ponytailed Iranian chap named Michael Fekr, learned his chops during a stint at Locanda Veneta under master Antonio Tommasi, and if Fekr's food doesn't exactly have the clear, fine edge of his tutor's, the student nevertheless acquits himself quite nicely. Il Mito ("the myth") quickly became a hangout for the hip, showbizzy types who populate the nearby studios, as well as a welcome destination for neighborhood folks. The restaurant has the requisite designer touches, and such dishes as bruschetta, risotto with porcini and lentils, roasted chicken and various pastas and grilled fish are just fine. Given the quality of the food, prices are reasonable: $25 or less for a dinner.

11/20 Moonlight Tango Café
13730 Ventura Blvd., Sherman Oaks 91423;
(818) 788-2000
New American. Dinner nightly. All major cards.

Moonlight Tango Café is a born-again deco nightclub, circa 1920—the sort of place always featured in Marx Brothers and Bette Davis movies. Frosted-glass and brass fixtures and photographs of Parisian café society by Brassaï adorn the walls. A band attired in white tuxedos performs period songs. But if you're expecting bistro cooking from a half century back, forget it. The creation of one Ernie Criezis, also the inspiration behind The Great Greek in Sherman Oaks and a dozen other restaurants in varied locations, this place offers such ultra-modern fare as good crabcakes with a biting red salsa; a whipped avocado-caviar purée reminiscent of a Greek taramo; Cajun sausage and braised greens; angel-hair pasta with Sicilian sausage; and grilled chicken breast stuffed with goat cheese. Welcome to L.A.! The bottom line here is fun. Where else can you encounter a real live conga line, singing waiters who can really sing and "Hernando's Hideaway," played as a birthday song? Dinner runs about $25.

12/20 La Pergola
15005 Ventura Blvd., Sherman Oaks 91403;
(818) 905-8402
Italian. Lunch Mon.-Fri., Dinner nightly. AE, MC, V.

The charm of al fresco Southern Italian–style dining is undeniable, especially when it's set thousands of miles from Naples in the middle of the San Fernando Valley. Many Valley denizens, including a number of heavyweights from the areas movie-industry population, make La Pergola a regular stop. They're invariably welcomed with open arms by owner/chef Tindaro ("Tino") Pettignano. The best dishes here are those that employ fresh vegetables, herbs and spices from Pettignano's six-thousand-square-foot garden in back: he chops up eggplant or mildly sweet chunks of butternut squash and tosses them together with rigatoni; for a plate of capelli d'angelo primavera (angel-hair pasta), he'll use the best fresh vegetables of the day, usually zucchini and their blossoms, cauliflower, tomatoes and peas. Garden tomatoes appear atop bruschetta and several pizzas; artichoke hearts accompany a chicken breast swathed in a marsala-butter sauce; fresh Romaine and arugula show up in simple green insalatas. Filling out the menu is a sizable list of classic pasta preparations and such regional dishes as grilled swordfish and veal scaloppine. Ask for a bowl of garden figs for dessert (when in season), and don't be surprised if, as you leave, Pettignano sends you off with a three-pound eggplant. Dinner costs between $20 and $30 per person.

Pinot Bistro

12969 Ventura Blvd., Studio City 91604; (818) 990-0500
French. Lunch Mon.-Fri., Dinner nightly. All major cards.

These days, many a successful restaurateur parlays his or her talents into a second (third, fourth, fifth) venture; the most ambitious among them create chains or entire restaurant families. Perhaps it was inevitable, then, that chef Joachim Splichal come up with Pinot Bistro, designed to be the more casual, younger sibling of his brilliant but pricey Patina restaurant on Melrose Avenue. Pinot's doors opened just before we went to press, and our inaugural meals here comprised exactly what we expected: beautifully done country–style French food.

Executive chef Octavio Becerra (formerly executive chef at Patina) is actually cooking a less formal, countrified version of the food at Patina, what Splichal calls "bistro fare with a twist." A galette is made with a socca (a chickpea-flour crêpe from Provence) and topped with shredded chicken and grilled onions; a "beignet" of goat cheese comes with chilled ratatouille. Straight-up classic bistro dishes include escargots with parsley, butter and garlic, and a salad of escarole with poached eggs, bacon and croutons. True to its name—which refers to the Pinot family of grapes that are responsible for all the great red Burgundies—this restaurant's wine list offers a good selection of those, as well as Californian Pinot varietals. The stylized setting recalls a warm and handsome old-world bistro; the dark-wood paneling and château doors are genuine French-bistro relics unearthed by Splichal in France. Dinner costs $25 to $30 per person.

Posto

14928 Ventura Blvd., Sherman Oaks 91423; (818) 784-4400
Italian. Lunch Mon.-Fri., Dinner nightly. AE, MC, V.

The menu at Piero Selvaggio's (he of Valentino and Primi) newest restaurant proclaims it to be "A Restaurant of Simplicity and Good Things." Actually, the interior design is a bit on the elaborate side, with a multitude of interesting details. But the food is possessed of the sort of simplicity that is nearly impossible to achieve at home (it's easier to make a successful soufflé than a really good roast chicken with mashed potatoes). Your meal kicks off with the addictive amusement called frico: thick slices of very good Parmesan, fried until almost crunchy. You absolutely can't stop eating the accursed things. It's important to try the motherly soup of barley, porcini and chicken meatballs; and if it's cold outside try the long-braised beef stew flavored with Barolo and enriched with polenta croutons. There's a wonderful kebab of snails and pancetta—crisp texture alternating with soft—served with polenta and garlicky spinach. Have a plate of best-quality prosciutto with roasted peppers and the tiny mozzarella called ovoline. And there's the fabulous shrimp and lobster polpette (seafood cakes) on a bed of warm leeks with balsamic vinegar. And Selvaggio still makes the best tiramisu in town, bar none. Dinner runs about $40 per person.

10/20 Prezzo

13625 Ventura Blvd., Sherman Oaks 91423; (818) 905-8400
Italian. Lunch Mon.-Fri., Dinner nightly, Late Supper Tues.-Sat. AE, MC, V.

At first glance, Prezzo looks like any of a dozen other Valley singles bars, the bar area filled with platoons of dressed-to-kill young women and men. But, surprisingly, the food here is actually decent. In fact, beneath the din of pounding rock music, the kitchen does a more than serviceable job. The carpaccio Cipriani, though a bit over-chilled, is good—paper-thin slices of beef scattered with arugula and fresh Parmesan. The pastas are good, too, and pizza is of the Spago/California Pizza Kitchen school. Grilled dishes—pette di pollo (marinated chicken) and such fish as salmon and swordfish—are particularly reliable. They've completely remodeled recently; the front patio is now covered. Plan on spending $25 per person.

11/20 Rive Gauche Café

14106 Ventura Blvd., Sherman Oaks 91423;
(818) 990-3573
French. Lunch & Dinner daily, Brunch Sun. All major cards.

If this pleasant Valley café is the Left Bank, the Right Bank (across the street) features a Ralphs supermarket. Sort out this and other imponderables while enjoying a glass of wine at this small French-style café, popular among a clientele Stephen Sondheim once referred to as "The Ladies Who Lunch." Food is simple café-French: quiches and crêpes of good quality, appetizers such as coquilles St-Jacques, brunch items like eggs St-George—an eggs Benedict variation in which the Canadian bacon is replaced by crab— and a spate of salads. Come for dinner when the cooking becomes more upscale: bouillabaisse, raspberry duck and other dishes of that ilk. Rive Gauche is a bright, well-lit place and a haven for chatty, sometimes ribald suburban conversation. A light lunch will run about $12 per person; dinner about $20.

Saddle Peak Lodge

419 Cold Canyon Rd., Calabasas 91302;
(818) 222-3888
American. Dinner Wed.-Sun., Brunch Sat.-Sun. AE, MC, V.

The only thing that prevents Saddle Peak Lodge from achieving superstardom is its far flung location—in the middle of the Santa Monica Mountains, halfway between Malibu and Calabasas. This skillfully refurbished 50-year-old lodge (said to have once been a former bordello) boasts several handsome, rustic dining rooms, some with fireplaces; it feels like a country retreat. Sit in the small room on the top floor, and view the surrounding mountain peaks through French doors. Ah, Wilderness! Game—venison, pheasant, brook trout—is the specialty of the house, and the opinionated waiters here will let you know it post haste. Such good alternatives as vodka-cured salmon, hunter-style rack of lamb, sweetbreads and Lake Superior whitefish round out the versatile menu. Start with the perfect salad of endive, watercress, goat cheese and walnuts, progress to the discreet juniper-berry sauced roast venison and leave room for the excellent side dishes. Ingredients tend to be of exceptional quality,and the marvelous atmosphere diverts you from any lapses that might occur in the kitchen. The desserts, such as cheesecake, come in mountain-man portions. This place is especially lovely for weekend brunch. None of this comes cheaply, as few good things do— count on spending $50 or more per person.

10/20 Salute!

21300 Victory Blvd., Woodland Hills 91367; (818) 702-9638
Italian. Lunch Mon.-Fri., Dinner nightly. AE, MC, V.

Silvio Di Mori is an evangelist of authentic Italian cooking; here he preaches the gospel of pasta to suburbanites. This restaurant is in an office building in the ghastly Warner Center, and there's not much Italian- looking about is. For lunch, Salute! serves chicken-teriyaki sandwiches and cashew chicken salad, along with decent pizzas and a bunch of pastas. At dinner the choices are a bit more Italianate. About $25 per person for dinner.

12/20 Sanamluang Café

12980 Sherman Way, N. Hollywood 91605; (818) 764-1180
Thai. Lunch, Dinner & Late Supper (until 4 a.m.) daily. No cards.

Sanamluang's business card proclaims this the home of "Best Noodles in Town". Whether they're the very best is uncertain, but this place is certainly in contention for the biggest variety: a few dozen noodle dishes lurk on this menu, along with countless other creations. Instead of mee krob, you'll find such rarely encountered dishes as koo chai, puffy rice biscuits filled with chopped Chinese vegetables and served with a darkly viscous sweet-and-spicy sauce, or rahd nah, an immense heap of rice noodles with Chinese broccoli, baby corn, chicken, pork, pork stomach, squid and shrimp, topped with a fried egg. Many of the dishes have so many ingredients that you'll get dizzy trying to figure out what's what. For instance, floating in the yen ta fo, a hot-and-sour noodle soup that's as good as it gets, are squid, shrimp, jellyfish, fish cakes, fish balls, spinach and won tons. This cuisine is also rich in salads and rice dishes (does anything sound better than fried garlic and pepper over rice, with either shrimp, pork, beef or chicken?). Virtually nothing costs more than $5. In exchange, amenities are simple: the flourescent lighting is strong, you eat on Formica, service is instantaneous and only cash is accepted. But for those late, late nights when nothing else will do but some duck-feet stew, Sanamluang is open until four in the morning. Dinner is about $10 per person.

9/20 La Scala Presto

3821 Riverside Dr., Toluca Lake 91505; (818) 846-6800
Italian. Lunch Mon.-Fri., Dinner Mon.-Sat. All major cards.

See review in "Restaurants – *L.A. Area*."

12/20 Shahrzad

13615 Ventura Blvd., Sherman Oaks 91403;
(818) 905-6363
17547 Ventura Blvd., Encino 91316;
(818) 906-1616
Persian. Lunch & Dinner daily. CB, DC, MC, V.

See review in "Restaurants – *L.A. Area.*"

12/20 Shihoya

15489 Ventura Blvd., Sherman Oaks; (818) 986-4461
Japanese/Sushi. Lunch Mon. & Wed.-Fri., Dinner Wed.-Mon. AE, MC, V.

Shihoya is a temple of Japanese discipline where you must do exactly as you are told. Upon arrival, the hostess asks if you have eaten here before. If you haven't, prepare for a long lesson in sushi-bar etiquette. You are told why sushi must be consumed in a particular sequence, from lighter textured fish to heavier, as listed on the menu. Once you progress to heavy, you cannot go back—until your next visit. If you do not abide by the rules at this sushi bar, you risk being banished to the dining room. Annoying as this may seem, it's a worthwhile cultural encounter—and the sushi served here justifies your perserverance. Elegantly arranged sashimi appetizers include a marvelous landscape of deep-fried sculpin and sharply spiced fuguzukui halibut, shaped like small rose petals. Lighter textured fish may include jumbo clams, abalone, bream, salmon, or crab. Heavier varieties run to oyster, barracuda, Spanish mackerel, sea urchin, fish roe and the illustrious toro (fatty belly of tuna). Dinner can be superlative, but don't fret if you are not awarded a gold star for your good conduct. You may spend $30 for sushi, $60 for a lavish, multi-course kaiseki.

12/20 Sushi Nozawa

11288 Ventura Blvd. #C, Studio City 91604; (818) 508-7017
Japanese/Sushi. Lunch Mon.-Fri., Dinner Mon.-Sat. All major cards.

Sushi Nozawa is located in one of those accursed pod malls, but after eating many a fine meal in many an accursed pod mall over the past few years, we've learned not to judge prematurely. SPECIAL TODAY—TRUST ME! reads the sign over the sushi counter, and you'll do well to heed it. Ask chef Nozawa for omakase (chef's choice), and put up a hand when you've had enough. Proud yet self-effacing, Nozawa makes bites that live up to his bark. He uses only the best fish, refusing to serve any below his incredibly high standards. Nozawa walks you through a meal here: dip this, don't dip that; mussels are better on Thursdays; eat this one in a single bite,

please. But rather than offending, Nozawa effectively educates his customers: his attention helps render a dinner here a truly sensual experience. Nozawa also instructs his guests regarding the provenance of his bounty: fat, firm shrimp come from Santa Barbara; briny, freshly harvested mussels are New Zealand imports; the list stretches on. Roseate salmon is layered with glassy seaweed noodles, divine mussels are bathed in a rice-vinegar broth, complex hand rolls are bound in crispy, toasted sheets of seaweed. Some flavors are subtly concealed, and like the proverbial Chinese puzzle box, appear magically as others vanish, awakening your taste buds to Nozawa's handiwork. A sushi dinner costs about $25.

11/20 Teru Sushi

11940 Ventura Blvd., Studio City 91604; (818) 763-6201
Japanese/Sushi. Lunch Mon.-Fri., Dinner nightly. All major cards.

Many credit (or blame) Teru Sushi with launching the sushi craze in Los Angeles. There was sushi before Teru, of course, but mainly in places frequented by Japanese businessmen. Teru was the first sushi bar to cater to American tastes, and it's been packed to the proverbial gills ever since it opened. It's quite theatrical in here: a chorus line of samurais who scream on cue every time a customer comes through the door. Without enough sake running through your veins, all the hubbub could give you quite a headache; with enough sake, you'll probably go native yourself. Despite the increased local competition, the crowds here haven't abated a whit, and Teru Sushi is still great fun. Plan on a weekend's wait for dishes like tiger's eye (salmon stuffed in squid, then baked and sliced), sea flowers (halibut or red snapper shaped into flower petals) and ludicrous combination rolls apparently invented to appeal to the taste of sake-drenched yuppies. Dinner will run $30 per person.

12/20 Valley Seafood Garden

21318 Saticoy St., Canoga Park 91304; (818) 710-8081
Chinese/Seafood. Lunch & Dinner daily. MC, V.

Stick to the Hong Kong–style seafood at this unlikely winner on auto-repair row in Canoga Park and you'll revel in the food's tastiness, its quantity and its moderate prices. The oysters (for as little as $6 a half dozen) are irresistible—large, fat bivalves, sometimes still in the shell—steamed and served in a lilting black-bean sauce or braised in port wine with ginger and scallions. We also adore the giant scallops, which often weigh in at four ounces each and which are best when simply pan fried. At lunchtime, the small steamed whole fish in a light soy broth is a bargain for less than $5. Reckon on spending $12 to $15 for dinner for one.

12/20 Val's

10130 Riverside Dr., Toluca Lake 91523; (818) 508-6644
Continental. Lunch Mon.-Fri., Dinner Mon.-Sat. All major cards.

Like the people who laughed at the fellow who sat down at the piano (and stopped laughing when he started to play), we must admit that we chuckled when we first stood in front of Val's. Someone has clearly poured a lot of money into creating what looks like a branch of L'Orangerie. Yet they've given it a name as inelegant as Val's. And they've come up with a menu that is best described as haute Continental, not the trendiest of culinary styles at the moment. Cards on the tables call Val's "The World's Most Beautiful Restaurant," and it certainly is a fabulous space, with some spectacular art (the huge renderings of ancient bowls are amazing) and a great assortment of flowers cascading out of Volkswagen-size vases. Power seems to ooze from the customers seated in the main dining room. The food ranges from the classic to the surprisingly innovative, from snails in mushroom caps and petite marmite (a clear consommé served from the earthenware marmite in which it is cooked) to saffroned mushroom soup and broiled shrimp wrapped in a scallop mousse and phyllo dough. These dishes have their moments: the chicken breast stuffed with shrimp and spinach in a red-pepper coulis is fine in concept and lovely to behold, but when we tried it the chicken was a bit dry, the sauce a tad underflavored and the accompanying vegetables overcooked and tough. But there's lots of promise here, and lots of style. Dinner runs $40 or more per person.

10/20 Zio & Co.

5242 Van Nuys Blvd., Van Nuys 91401; (818) 784-8051
Italian. Lunch Tues.-Fri., Dinner Tues.-Sun. MC, V.

Zio sits somewhere between a funky fun place like Maria's Kitchen and a serious temple of gastronomy such as La Loggia. It's a combination trattoria/deli with a design scheme based on oversized papier-mâché characters—a room filled with waves of whimsy. Food is cheerful and simple: some of the best pizza in the Valley, good calzone and in a huge refrigerator case an unparalleled selection of antipasti. You can find better Italian in the Valley, but for good neighborhood

fare at Van Nuys prices, the gold strike is right here. Dinner costs about $15 per person.

And Also . . .

Caffè Giuseppe, 18515 Roscoe Blvd., Northridge 91324; (818) 349-9090. *Italian. Lunch Mon.-Fri., Dinner nightly. MC, V.* An ultra-spiffy deep-Valley caffè serving a good variety of pastas and a tasty thin-crust pizza. Dinner, about $20 per person.

L'Express, 3575 Cahuenga Blvd. West, Studio City 90068, (213) 876-3778; 14910 Ventura Blvd., Sherman Oaks 91403, (818) 990-8683. *California-nian/French. Breakfast, Lunch, Dinner & Late Supper daily. MC, V.* A typical California-French brasserie, more handsome than some but no better than others, with a reliable array of salads, omelets and sandwiches. The croissants are dreamy. A meal will run anywhere from $12 to $32.

Luna Rossa, 4627 Van Nuys Blvd., Sherman Oaks 91423; (818) 981-9380. *Italian. Lunch & Dinner daily. AE, MC, V.* The classic neighborhood Italian joint: small, cozy and worlds away from pretention—and rare in this city of hip trattorias. Home-style dishes are largely of the lasagne/manicotti variety. Don't miss the pretty patio in back. Dinner, $15 or so per person.

Santo Pietro Bar & Grill, 12001 Ventura Pl., Studio City 91604; (818) 508-1177. *Italian. Lunch Mon.-Fri., Dinner nightly. MC, V.* This cheerful California-Italian trattoria serves families and local studio types an uneven collection of pastas, seafood dishes and pizzas. Dinner runs about $20; lunch or a simple pizza dinner will cost much less.

Shain's, 14016 Ventura Blvd., Sherman Oaks 91423; (818) 986-5510. *Continental. Lunch Mon.-Sat., Dinner nightly, Brunch Sun. All major cards.* Thirteen years in business hasn't changed this quiet Tudor-house restaurant much: ye olde menu still offers tuna melts and shrimp cocktails for lunch; and filet of sole Veronique, New York steak Diane and filet mignon Rossini for dinner. Dinner, $25 to $35 per person.

Stratton's Parkside Grill, 16925 Ventura Blvd., Encino 91316; (818) 986-2400. *American. Lunch & Dinner daily. All major cards.* American grill food is the order of the day for the crowd here; the locals don't expect (and don't get) any more than reasonably priced, predictable burgers, steaks and salads. Dinner, $20 or so.

The Wine Bistro, 11915 Ventura Blvd., Studio City 91604; (818) 766-6233. *Californian. Lunch Mon.-Fri., Dinner Mon.-Sat. AE, MC, V.* The convenience and comfort of this studio-close bistro make it a popular lunch spot with show-biz honchos, though the food is lackluster. A dinner costs about $35.

Because of the mercurial nature of L.A.'s restaurant business, it's wise to call and verify that a particular establishment is still open.

San Gabriel Valley

Encompasses Pasadena, Glendale, San Gabriel, Rosemead and Monterey Park.

Antonio Orlando

One W. California Blvd., Pasadena 91105;
(818) 356-0086
*Italian. Lunch Mon.-Fri., Dinner Mon.-Sat.
AE, DC, MC, V.*

Chef Antonio Orlando has lived a charmed life in Los Angeles. Born in Salerno, Italy, he came to maturity as the executive chef at Valentino, and later as chef/owner at Fresco, easily two of the best Italian restaurants in all of Los Angeles. In the case of his third restaurant, success may be a bit less immediate. For although Orlando's food continues to be very good, it must become even better to overcome its current setting. Antonio Orlando sits in a warehouse-like structure with an outdoor patio that offers a view of the parking lot, a private dining room that looks as if the decor was taken from a do-it-yourself design magazine, and a dreary main dining room in which, on our last visit, a moribund group of pictures was hung crookedly on the walls. To avoid these mistakes, and ask for one of the bar-area booths, which seem to be the most desirable tables in the house.

When the food finally arrives, it's often good enough to divert your attention solely to your plate. Start with the pizza-esque bread, which comes rubbed with garlic, olive oil and salt. And don't miss Antonio's risotto with porcini, creamy and elegant, and served in a very generous portion—for a modest $10. The entire menu is fairly simple and reasonably priced; none of the pastas is priced over $10. This place could be a success with a little redecoration. Dinner costs $20 or so per person.

Bistro 45

45 S. Mentor Ave., Pasadena 91106;
(818) 795-2478
French. Lunch Tues.-Fri., Dinner Tues.-Sun. All major cards.

Bistro 45, with its retro-moderne, art deco–influenced look, to be far more romantic, especially if you come with the right companion. The creation of Robert Simon, one of the founders of the late, lamented Café Jacoulet, this is a bistro that isn't a bistro, a casual California restaurant with a patina of French formality. You'll eat well in this good-looking room if you order with care—and you'll probably eat well even if you don't. If we have one small complaint, it's that the kitchen is reticent with its herbs and spices, resulting in food that is sometimes a bit underflavored. If the dishes were human, many would suffer from extreme shyness. One of the best things we tried was the duck salad, which wasn't the least bit shy. At its heart was a marvelous confit of Muscovy duck, which was probably so high in cholesterol that our life insurance agent would have doubled our premium if he had seen us eating it. The same Muscovy duck appears as an entrée, paired with a tasty raspberry sauce; the kitchen here does good work with duck. Not quite as richly flavored are the sweetbreads (which were a bit overcooked) with a raspberry vinaigrette. And the tuna tartare needed a bit of zip—more coriander, more lemon, more lime. Boldly, the kitchen tries its hand at a cassoulet, and though the beans are a bit dry, there's plenty of duck, sausage and rabbit; it's a good cassoulet, but not a definitive one. Dinner costs about $45 per person.

11/20 Catavinos

119 W. Green St., Pasadena 91105;
(818) 578-1764
Southwestern. Lunch & Dinner daily. MC, V.

Hidden in a little warren of turn-of-the-century buildings around the corner from Colorado Boulevard in Old Town lies this convivial Southwestern café. The cool space is handsomely outfitted with thick plaster walls, solid Southwestern furniture and objets d'art beaming with primary colors. About half the dishes here are straight-ahead Mexican (carne asada tacos, chicken mole, pork adobada, taquitos with guacamole), and the other half reflect a California sensibility. Take the tasty black-bean pancakes paired with a "spicy" (*not!*) orange sauce, for instance, an homage to the currently trendy potato pancake and crabcake. Or the roasted half chicken with a jalapeño-orange sauce, which doesn't speak a word of Spanish. Some of the creations are more colorful than flavorful; best bets are the tender calamari steaks sautéed with lemon, garlic and cilantro, and, for those pining for Baja, the mahi mahi tacos dressed with a tomatillo sauce and pico de gallo. Sadly, there's no tequila to add an air of Mexican madness, so you'll have to make do with a Bohemia or a wine margarita. Dinner ranges from $12 to $25 per person.

11/20 Chopstix

46 W. Colorado Blvd., Pasadena 91101;
(818) 405-1111
Chinese. Lunch & Dinner daily. D, MC, V.
See review in "Restaurants – *L.A. Area.*"

11/20 The Chronicle

897 Granite Dr., Pasadena 91101;
(818) 792-1179
*Continental. Lunch Mon.-Sat., Dinner nightly.
All major cards.*

What you may remember most about The Chronicle—even is you never eat— is the reasonably priced, 74-page wine list. The restaurant itself is simple and charming in the style of a '20s men's hunting lodge. One room recalls with nostalgia old Pasadena; the other has the cozy feel of a living-room. Food here is something of a metaphor for Pasadena; pleasant and reliable, but rarely dazzling. Starters like fresh oysters and clams, lovely cold poached salmon, creamy oysters Rockefeller and a perfect Caesar salad are straightforward enough. Uncomplicated entrées neither disappoint or nor impress; best are the broiled swordfish, tender sand dabs, a by-the-book snapper meunière. Desserts, too, are traditional. About $20 for lunch, $40 for dinner.

12/20 Crocodile Cantina

626 N. Central Ave., Glendale 91203;
(818) 241-1114
Mexican. Lunch & Dinner daily, Late Supper Fri.-Sat. AE, MC, V.

We love Pasadena's Parkway Grill and Crocodile Café (the creations of restaurateurs Bob and Gregg Smith and chef Hugo Molina), and we expect great things of their new Crocodile Cantina, the first in what they hope will be a booming chain. Our first visits to this lively, colorful cantina were disappointing, but the kitchen now seems to have smoothed out the kinks. This place has settled into being a fun, affordable spot with good margaritas and reliably tasty, if not necessarily mind-blowing, food. The cooking is a pastiche of regional Mexican (tangy, juicy ceviche tostadas; totopas, tiny crisp tortillas topped with smoked duck, a sweet sauce, black beans, pickled red cabbage, crema mexicana and ranchero cheese—a great blend of sweet, tangy, savory and sharp) and trendy Southwestern (blue-corn and smoked-chicken taquitos; delicious coconut cheesecake). The fabulous cappuccinos can serve as dessert: bowl-size cups capped with perfectly steamed milk and served with a tray of cinnamon sticks and coffee-flavored M&Ms. We can think of worse things than a Crocodile Cantina in every neighborhood. About $15 per person for dinner.

11/20 Delacey's Club 41

41 S. Delacey St., Pasadena 91105;
(818) 795-4141
American. Lunch & Dinner daily. All major cards.

Had enough gnocchi with porcini lately? Overdosed on salmon in puff pastry? Then head to this reassuring bar and grill for a proper American Scotch-and-steak repast. A throwback to the manly restaurants in the cigar-smoking, whisky-swilling days of yore, Delacey's is rife with nostalgia: high-backed wooden booths, mosaic tile floors, thick white tablecloths, burnished dark wood, hanging schoolhouse light fixtures. The menu brings to mind L.A.'s venerable Musso & Frank's, and contains all the chophouse standards, from Cobb salads to onion rings to cheesecake, with a few more contemporary touches (garlic mashed potatoes, good wine-by-the-glass) thrown in to draw the yuppies. If you keep your expectations modest and steer clear of dishes that are clearly inappropriate to such a place (like the confused pasta alla checca with—of all things—mussels), you're likely to put away a most enjoyable meal. We've been pleased with the powerful Caesar salad, the cheesy onion soup, the substantial burger and the crisp fries. Dinner runs about $22 per person, more if you order steak or chops.

Dragon Regency

120 S. Atlantic Blvd., Monterey Park 91754;
(818) 282-1089
Chinese/Seafood. Lunch & Dinner daily. MC, V.

We never thought we would taste Chinese seafood better prepared than that at served at Mon Kee in Chinatown. And, indeed, Mon Kee's food remains near and dear to our taste buds. But where Mon Kee is merely great, Dragon Regency is ethereal. The chef, Chun Wong, used to cook at Imperial Dynasty in Chevy Chase, Maryland, a wealthy Washington suburb—and Washington's loss is definitely L.A.'s gain. Dragon Regency is on the edge of one of the many shopping centers that make up Monterey Park's burgeoning Chinatown. The large dining room is attractive, as Chinese restaurants go. The menu is divided into such categories as beef, pork, shrimp, lobster, fish snout, eel and frog. As is usually the case with this kind of restaurant, there's too much to choose from. Good selections include braised whole abalone with oyster sauce; double-pleasure fresh Eastern sole (cooked twice, so the skin and bones are as edible as potato chips); pan-fried crab with garlic and black-bean sauce; pan-fried shrimp with special salt; and the most marvelous frog in a powerful garlic sauce. By all means, do try the snake soup if it's in season. Everything is good: flavors are brilliantly intense but delicate enough to allow the taste of the seafood to come through. You'll spend about $15 apiece for dinner, more if you splurge on lobster or abalone.

El Emperador Maya
1823 S. San Gabriel Blvd., San Gabriel 91776; (818) 288-7265
Mexican. Lunch & Dinner Tues.-Sun. AE, MC, V.

El Emperador Maya ("the Mayan Emperor") is a small street-corner restaurant specializing in the cooking of the Yucatán, the Mexican land mass jutting out into the Caribbean. Yucatecan food is like a distant and dreamlike cousin of the more standardized cuisine found throughout most of Mexico. Consider, for instance, panuchos—tiny tortillas stuffed with black beans and marinated turkey with pickled red onions; a better dish than this is difficult to imagine. Taste cochinita pibil (the definitive Yucatecan dish), a stew of marinated pork flavored with achiote (annatto seed) and steamed in a Mayan pot called a pibil, and you will wonder how pork could possibly be this tender. Poc chuc Don Belos is a pork chop coated with an assortment of herbs and spices so aromatic you'll want to lick it like an ice cream cone. In fact, every single dish at El Emperador Maya is utterly tempting—from the enchilada in mole sauce to the nearly perfect guacamole, from the thick crunchy chips to the chicken with onions, peppers, tomatoes, olives, garlic and rice. You'll also find L.A.'s best flans here (one banana, the other cheese). We do not know of better Mexican food than this. Dinner shouldn't exceed $10.

10/20 Far Niente
204 1/2 N. Brand Blvd., Glendale 91203; (818) 242-3835
Italian. Lunch Mon.-Fri., Dinner nightly. All major cards.

A puffy, balloonlike, individual loaf of bread, shiny-slick from its olive oil coating and fragrant with the seductive smell of rosemary, is served to you within moments of your being seated. This tasty starter, replenished without your even asking, can be followed by generous portions of mostly well-turned pastas (try the triple pasta option for two) and an excellent grilled veal chop with a balsamic vinegar–sweet onion sauce. While the battuta profumata (thin-sliced, peppered beef with rosemary and garlic) was disappointing one night, a wine-and-sage-flavored

chicken breast with artichoke hearts another night more than compensated for the earlier disappointment. Note that the quality of your dining experience here depends on which waiter you get—some are deft and attentive, others are not. The cheerful dining room is rather romantic at night, when candles flicker on the cozy tables. Around $25 to $30 per person.

Fleur de Vin
70 S. Raymond Ave., Pasadena 91105; (818) 795-0085
French. Lunch Tues.-Fri., Dinner & Late Supper Tues.-Sun., Brunch Sun. AE, MC, V.

This place suits Old Town Pasadena to a "T": comfortable and conservative enough to please the old-money, Brooks Brothers–clad crowd, but just challenging enough to attract baby boomers who demand more than Continental standards. Handsome and cozily elegant, the corner storefront space is warmed by burnished wood beams, white table linens, a piano and a small, friendly wine bar, where an admirable rotating selection of French and Californian selections are poured each night. The traditional food manages to be comforting yet not stodgy; it's prepared with care and a restrained hand. Salads include an excellent blend of rich duck confit, pine nuts and watercress and a variation on the beloved frisée lardon: mesclun with little chunks of warm, smoky bacon. You can also start with fine gravlax or delicious lobster ravioli in a lobster-tarragon sauce. Steak lovers must not pass up the tender Roquefort-topped filet in a port wine sauce. Pasta with a seafood fricassee has a rich saffron taste and lots of good shellfish. End your meal with the classic lemon tart or the flourless chocolate cake with vodka-lime ice cream. About $37 per person for dinner.

Fragrant Vegetable
108 N. Garfield Ave., Monterey Park 91754; (818) 280-4215
Chinese/Vegetarian. Lunch & Dinner daily. AE, MC, V.

See review in "Restaurants – *L.A. Area.*"

Georgian Room at Ritz-Carlton/Huntington, Pasadena
Ritz-Carlton/Huntington Hotel, Oak Knoll Ave., Pasadena 91106; (818) 568-3900
French. Dinner Wed.-Sun. All major cards.

We know the '80s are over, and we're all supposed to be wearing functional khakis and making our own macaroni and cheese. But once in a while it sure is grand to spend a few hours in a grand dining room. And this restored dining room in the stately old Huntington Hotel is as grand as they come, all gilt and silver and crystal, with a stunning barrel-vaulted ceiling and a swarm of tuxedoed waiters overseen by a maître d' in white tie and tails. The clientele reflects the old-money Pasadena neighborhood: lots of soberly dressed men and their handsome wives. Like many Ritz-Carlton chefs, Bernard Bordaries was wooed away from France, where he had his own Toulouse-area restaurant. Bordaries is skilled in classic technique, yet his cuisine reflects contemporary and regional influences, from the olive coulis served with the rack of lamb to the aromatic fresh herb crust on the sweet and moist John Dory filet. That's not to say that he is an acolyte of California cuisine—no cherimoya chutneys or blue-corn polentas corrupt this food. The cold appetizer of Maine lobster, sweetbreads and snow peas drizzled with truffle juice is elegance incarnate, the sort of dish one imagines Prince Albert of Monaco having for lunch. Ditto the leek and fennel galette sprinkled with beluga caviar. Heartier, more substantial dishes include a flavorful veal chop with fat gnocchi pillows, and a savory rack of lamb stuffed with chanterelles, zucchini and an olive coulis. Desserts range from a seductive classic layering of roasted pear, warm chocolate and pistachios to chic sorbets such as passion fruit and mascarpone. Naturally, dinner costs $55 or more per person.

11/20 Gourmet 88

315 S. Brand Blvd., Glendale 91204; (818) 547-9488
Chinese. Lunch & Dinner daily. AE, MC, V.

The Chinese consider 88 a lucky number, hence this restaurant's name. If we could list 88 reasons to dine here, we would, but unfortunately space doesn't permit. But here are eight good reasons: an order of pan-fried dumplings, which comprises an octet of the lightest, fluffiest, plumpest potstickers ever. After enjoying these delights, along with some equally delicious shu mai, you can settle into a luxurious combination platter of moist lobster, chicken and pork with firm, flavorful vegetables. Or on the lighter side, try the refreshing cold duckling salad. Braised, sliced rock cod is another skillfully handled entrée. Occasionally, the adept serving staff in this revamped pastel coffee shop moves meals along a little too fast for comfort. Prices are a bit high by Chinese-restaurant standards, though dinner doesn't usually top $20 a person.

Harbor Village

111 N. Atlantic Blvd., Monterey Park 91754; (818) 300-8833
Chinese. Lunch & Dinner daily. All major cards.

We've never had a really great dinner at this branch of the acclaimed Hong Kong (and Northern Californian) restaurant chain. But we've eaten arguably the best dim sum in Southern California here. The roast-pork filling in the steamed char siu bao is rich with flavor, sweet yet quite subtle. The har gow (filled with shrimp) and shu mai (little pastry flowers stuffed with a variety of meats) are nigh-on perfect, presented still hot in little steamers. The roast pork slices are so good you'll want to make an entire meal of them. They are, oddly, served with the same cooked soybeans that come with the roast duck (which could do with a bit more crispness). The adventurous dim sum-mer would be well advised to grab plates of the marinated octopus and the intensely crisp ribs. And if you see a sort of rolled char siu bao going by, nab it—it's unique and completely unforgettable. We still look forward to a first-rate dinner at Harbor Village, and we'll try again. Lunch runs about $15 per person.

12/20 Harvest Inn

550 N. Brand Blvd., Glendale 91203; (818) 956-8268
Chinese. Lunch Mon.-Sat., Dinner nightly. All major cards.

Once we got over the surprise of the terrific baked oysters in a garlicky, Gallic-style butter sauce spiked with cilantro, we continued to fly high with the "Vegetable Goose" appetizer, an artistic tofu-skin-wrapped all-vegie dish named for its birdlike shape. All this in a Chinese restaurant set in a Glendale office building? Yes, but pass on the allegedly spicy (actually bland) Szechuan bean curd and Chinese cabbage dishes; instead order the sizzling catfish or sweet-and-pungent chicken. Or play a game of culinary heads or tails: flip a coin to decide which of the traditional Chinese dishes to try—fish head in casserole or fish tail in brown sauce. It's several notches above the usual neighborhood Chinese joint, both in terms of cooking and decor. But you'll pay for the quality: figure at least $25 per person for dinner.

Lake Spring Cuisine

219 E. Garvey Ave., Monterey Park 91754; (818) 280-3571
Chinese. Lunch & Dinner daily. MC, V.

Lake Spring is one of the few Shanghai-style restaurants this side of Hong Kong; here the heavy, rich cooking of Shanghai stands in direct contrast to the light style of most Cantonese cuisine. One of the great delights of Shanghaiese cuisine is the hairy crab that shows up on the menu every autumn; filled with roe and steamed with ginger tea and vinegar sauce, it's a true delicacy. Shanghai cooking involves many sauces, especially a pungent red sauce and an intense brown sauce; a lot of soy sauce and sesame oil is also used. The meat of choice, visible on virtually every table, is pork, particularly the large rump roast that the menu describes as "noisette pork pump." This dish, in which the pork is cooked long and slow in a sauce of soy and rock sugar could easily feed four. It's a wonderful creation, though it tends to hinder your ability to eat anything else. Much of the menu is pork related: pemmican-like ching chiang cured pork; shrimp and shredded pork with bean-curd soup; salted pork with bamboo-shoot casserole; pepper-seasoned pork chops; vermicelli and ground pork; spicy eggplant and shredded pork. This is, to point out the obvious, hog heaven . . . though not especially for the hog. Save room to sample some of the remarkable seafood dishes too. Jade shrimp is a brilliant creation—lovely, melt-in-your-mouth baby shrimp tossed in a perfect sauce of puréed spinach and herbs. Scallops in garlic sauce are fat and sweet. You might notice that the menu also includes a number of "neutralize" dishes—neutralize duck, neutralize ham, neutralize pan-fried noodles. The term refers to the bean curd the dishes are made with, trompe l'oeil replicas of meat. Dinner runs $20 per person.

12/20 La Xaing
117 E. Broadway, Glendale 91205; (818) 243-8686
Modern Chinese. Lunch Mon.-Sat., Dinner nightly. All major cards.

Modern Chinese cuisine can be described thus: it has its roots in authentic chinese cooking, but follows no rules other than those made up as the chef goes along. This is where La Xaing fits in: Modern Chinese cuisine is here filtered through a Japanese screen. Call it Sino-Japonais if you wish, or Japanese-Chinois—the bottom line is food that is an appealing puzzlement. So, for that matter, is the room, which proudly wears the money that was poured into it. Contrary to everything around it in the oversized Glendale Exchange shopping complex, there's a postmodernist elegance to La Xaing (roughly, "Midnight Jasmine"), with its decorative columns that rise to support nothing, and its remarkable tilework.

The menu was built by a Japanese chef named Peter Nagashima, who trained in Hong Kong

and then set off for the U.S. to cook dishes unlike anyone else's. This he has accomplished, though with some dishes more successfully than others: the chicken salad comes close to the standard issue Chinese. There's a marvelous dish called shrimp Mandarin, with an extraordinarily light red-wine sauce, served on a delicate bed of vermicelli. There's hardly a dish on the menu that doesn't borrow from several cuisines, from the chef's reinterpretation of beggar's chicken (which he's turned into a sort of chicken Wellington), to his perfectly fried Louisiana catfish. The bird's-nest delight is delightful and they serve the most grease-free eggplant with garlic sauce in town. Sadly, the restaurant doesn't seem to be doing the business it should; Glendale may still be too timid for this sort of bold cuisine. It's a shame, for the cooking at La Xaing is fascinating. Dinner costs about $30 per person.

12/20 Mi Piace
25 E. Colorado Blvd., Pasadena 91103; (818) 795-3131
Italian. Lunch Mon.-Fri., Dinner nightly, Late Supper Fri.-Sat. (until 1:30 a.m.) AE, MC, V.

Unlike most of the current crop of trendy trattorias, Mi Piace has one foot firmly planted in the present and the other just as firmly planted in the past. The present is evident in the high-tech interior, and the past is evident in the food—though it's not full-out retro, it leans pleasantly in that direction. Nowhere on the menu do such dishes-of-the-moment as "risotto" and "carpaccio" appear; instead, you come here for very good mozzarella marinara, steamed broccoli and green beans in a lemon-garlic sauce, crunchy calamari fritti, linguine with a well-spiced meat sauce, and eggplant parmigiana. Crisp-crusted New York–style pizzas are topped with familiar stuff like pepperoni and mushrooms. The only real concession to the moment are the California-style pizzas, with goat cheese or barbecued chicken. And the big, gooey, clasic American-style desserts are more than satisfactory. Enough with tiramisu—bring on the cheesecake! About $20 per person for dinner.

11/20 Noodles
215 N. Central Ave., Glendale 91203; (818) 500-8783
Californian. Lunch & Dinner daily. MC, V.

Noodles is a compendium of all the chic L.A.-restaurant motifs—baseball-capped cooks in an open kitchen, a mesquite-stoked pizza oven, deconstructivist protruding ducts—but something about this place still smacks of mass-market restauraturing. Nevertheless, Noodles has given Glendale a big lift foodwise, and has no doubt already spawned its own imitators. Food is exactly as good as it needs to be: doughy herb-and-olive-oil-brushed rolls, tasty pizzas, crisp Caesar salad and pastas topped with duck sausage or pesto concoctions. The best dish here is a thick grilled-tuna sandwich served with addictive waffle fries—perfect for lunch. A dinner is $15 to $20.

Oaks on the Plaza at Doubletree Hotel
191 N. Los Robles Ave., Pasadena 91101;
(818) 792-2727
Californian. Lunch Mon.-Sat., Dinner nightly, Brunch Sun. All major cards.

The contemporary Californian food, commendable service, and splendid Mediterranean-like setting inside the pristine new Doubletree Hotel established new standards for Pasadena when it opened in 1989. (It even predated Fleur de Vin and the Ritz-Carlton's Georgian Room, today's shining stars.) All these restaurants arrived at a time when Pasadena is finally blossoming as a destination in its own right, and as a result, visitors and locals alike are today being better fed than ever before. What they're fed here by the Swiss-born chef, Jacob Stark, is a Californian/Italian/Pacific Rim medley of techniques, ingredients and tastes.

For starters, he might offer breaded risotto cakes in a sauce of wild mushrooms, or mesquite-seared Hawaiian tuna with fennel and plum sauce. There's always a pick of rich little brioche pizzas with toppings that vary daily. For the main course, in addition to some tasty pastas and salads, there are quite a few good mesquite-grilled offerings. We've also enjoyed a rack of lamb roasted with an herbed peanut crust; and a plateful of Santa Barbara shrimp spiced with Thai peppers and served with a cooling pineapple-mint sauce. Keep an open mind when ordering here, and most of the time, you won't be disappointed. Dinner costs about $32 per person.

12/20 Pappagallo
42 S. Pasadena Ave., Pasadena 91105;
(818) 578-0224
Italian. Lunch Tues.-Sat., Dinner Tues.-Sun. All major cards.

If you're hungry for Italian food in L.A., you have about 300 dining options. In Pasadena, where the choices are fewer, this friendly little place is worthy of note—it's a fine candidate in the Cal-Italian category. Upon entering through a gorgeous leaded glass door, you'll be ushered into a brick-walled, glass-ceilinged dining-room or outside to a fairytale tree-lined courtyard.

What comes from the kitchen is fresh, simple and very tasty: mussels in garlic butter and melted Parmesan, roasted eggplant rolled around a trio of provolone, prosciutto and red bell pepper. The "Cal" in the cuisine description refers to occasional Californian twists and interpretations: a garbanzo salad includes black beans and goat cheese; lasagne is layered alternately with spinach pasta and tender duck meat. If you want no-frills northern Italian, try a veal dish (there are five), or one of the fresh-fish offerings. Dinner runs about $25 per person.

Parkway Grill
510 S. Arroyo Pkwy., Pasadena 91105;
(818) 795-1001
Californian/American. Lunch Mon.-Fri., Dinner nightly, Brunch Sun. All major cards.

The Parkway Grill has had a packed house since its opening in the 1980s. The fans aren't here solely for the food; they also love the snappy service and the handsome decor, a blend of the old (worn brick walls, polished woodwork, carved wooden bar) and the new (open kitchen, modern art). While chef Hugo Molina's kitchen isn't as seminal as Alice Waters's or Wolfgang Puck's, it's no slouch in the California-cuisine department. In recent years Molina has acknowledged his—not to mention California's—Latino heritage in dishes like the robust black-bean soup with smoked pork and lime cream. To this influence he adds tributes to Italy (linguine with sea food, tomatoes, garlic and basil), Asia (whole fried catfish with ginger, scallions and a lime-soy sauce), California (pizza with duck and radicchio) and heartland America (grilled New York steak with homemade mustard and grilled onions). A sure bet is the spectacular lobster-stuffed cocoa crêpe in a saffron-infused lobster-bisque sauce swirled with a sun-dried-tomato cream. Desserts—apple-currant bread pudding, s'mores, cheesecakes, cobblers—hew to the American style of being substantial and sweet. The wine list is a Californian "Who's Who," full of worthy, if expensive, bottles. Dinner runs $30 or so per person; about $40 if you have a meat or fish entrée.

12/20 Roxxi
1065 E. Green St., Pasadena 91106;
(818) 449-4519
Californian/Eclectic. Lunch Mon.-Fri., Dinner nightly. AE, MC, V.

The eccentric menu at Roxxi will be familiar to anyone who has eaten at Shane, the Spago–inspired restuarant in Beverly Glen. Roxxi was designed by its original chef, Norman Cheng, and relects a mixed heritage—with roots in Italy, California, the Southwest and Asia—in keeping with Cheng's experience at both Shane and Spago. Cheng has departed, but these days new chef Jim Harringer is continuing to serve up the same late-twentieth-century chow: vegetable ravioli soup with tomato salsa, pomegranate risotto (standard risotto given a sweet-tart bite and ruby color with a reduction of pomegranate juice), a duck tamale with chile sauce and sour cream. Despite its bizarre makeup, the food is far more accessible than it sounds. Main courses run from grilled rack of lamb with rosemary-smoked garlic sauce and ranch beans to roast duck with zinfandel-plum sauce, fried yam chips and baby bok choy. The all-California wine list offers 28 Chardonnays and a decent selection of reds. Dinner costs about $32 per person.

Seafood City
7540 E. Garvey Ave., Rosemead 91770; (818) 571-5454
Chinese. Dim Sum, Lunch & Dinner daily. AE, MC, V.

When we first entered this room, all rich crimson and gold and lined with lobster- and eel-filled tanks, we were transported to Kowloon. Not only does this place look like the real Hong Kong thing, what is served tastes like the real thing, too. Start with the cold platter of musky, slightly dry (which is good) barbecued pork and soy sauce chicken. Unless you're a fan of texture over taste, pass on the dishes made with jellyfish, shark's fin, bamboo fungus and sea cucumber. Instead, delve into the shrimp and prawn dishes: pan-fried prawns with chili and black-bean sauce, or with spicy salt, or with sweet-and-sour sauce (a quantum leap beyond the sugary goop we grew up eating). Consider the sautéed fresh flounder filet with ham and mushrooms, the deep-fried rock cod with corn sauce, the wonderful clams in a spicy satay sauce, the exceedingly odd stuffed dried scallops with melon slices, the squab, the duck, the hot pots . . . the menu goes on and on. Dinner runs about $20 per person.

Shiro
1505 Mission St., South Pasadena 91030; (818) 799-4774
French-Japanese. Dinner Tues.-Sun. MC, V.

L.A.'s restaurants are known for lots of good things—creativity, adventurousness, informality and allowing us to sit next to Robert de Niro or Michelle Pfeiffer—but consistency is not one of them. Which makes Shiro such a rare jewel. Night after night for these last half-dozen or so years, owner/chef Hideo Yamashiro (who goes by the nickname Shiro) has created dishes from

a short, seafood-intensive menu, and we've yet to see him falter. For his considerable talent, reliability and fair prices, he has been rewarded with a devoted following; even in the depths of the recession, the place was booked every night.

Chef Shiro combines a Japanese eye for high-quality, ultra-fresh fish with the technical facility of a superb French saucier; the resulting dishes are always delicious. The menu here changes nightly, but a handful of Shiro's classics are usually offered—like the large Chinese-style ravioli stuffed with a perfectly seasoned shrimp and salmon mousse, paired with a rich but subtle smoked salmon sauce or a vibrant tomato-basil sauce, or the whole sizzling catfish with ponzu (a soy-based sauce). There's usually a first-rate salmon dish, perhaps moist Pacific king salmon with one of several herb sauces. We were delighted at recent meal by fat, sweet Canadian scallops in a gloriously fragrant saffron sauce. The rest of the details here are carefully thought out too: good desserts (the crème brûlée with raspberries is definitive), waiters who are there when you need them but disappear when you don't, and several tasty wines for under $20. Shiro has the trappings of many bistros which are successful these days—an open kitchen, exposed ceilings, white walls—but the noise level is within reason. And the tab is more than fair: about $32 per person for an elegant seafood dinner, the likes of which could cost $50 on the Westside.

11/20 Tra Fiori
91 N. Raymond Ave., Pasadena 91103; (818) 796-2233
Italian. Lunch Tues.-Sat., Dinner Tues.-Sun. AE, MC, V.

The space that once held Café Jacoulet now holds Tra Fiori. Jacoulet's umbrellas and laid-back atmosphere have been replaced by Japonica with formality . . . the sort of *faux* formality that inspired our waiter to recite the specials at great length, in a florid, nearly Shakespearean accent. We only wish he was as good at getting bread and San Pellegrino to the table. Although the interior is certainly chic, we couldn't help but wish we were someplace with more sense of *la dolce vita*. The food isn't bad either, it just isn't sufficiently inspired for the money. An appetizer of shiitake, oyster and wild mushrooms topped with hollandaise and Parmesan tasted slightly bitter, and the sauce was overly complicated. The kitchen here has a penchant, in fact, for putting too much stuff in the dishes; you wind up with a sort of fussy French reinterpretation of Italian cuisine. The New York steak "al crudo," for instance, could be fine—just a very rare steak on a bed of arugula.

But by the time it's been topped with a hard-cooked egg, baby artichoke, Parmesan and an olive oil–shallot dressing, it's way out of control. You're better off with the simpler pan-roasted breast of chicken on a bed of Tuscan beans. About $40 per person for dinner.

Xiomara

69 N. Raymond Ave., Pasadena 91103;
(818) 796-2520
Californian/French. Lunch Mon.-Fri., Dinner nightly. AE, MC, V.

After brief relationships with three talented chefs (Robert Gadsby, Christopher Cavallero and, as we went to press, Patrick Healy, ex of Champagne restaurant), Xiomara is still struggling to establish consistency. Xiomara is the name of both the restaurant and its petite proprietor, a Cuban chef whose enthusiasm matches her strong ideas. Because it is impossible to rank the restaurant before we published, we'll just say that it has promise, and will probably be worthy of a visit regardless of what develops. Service is fine, and so is the location, on Raymond Avenue's developing restaurant row in the heart of Old Town Pasadena. Xiomara offsets the old-fashioned charm of its 100-year-old building with a contemporary (but not hard-edged) decor. Black lacquer and granite are softened by richly hued blond and cherry woods, resulting in a handsome, subtly elegant environment that's as quiet as its neighborhood. Dinner is about $43 per person.

 ## Yujean Kang's Gourmet Chinese Cuisine

67 N. Raymond Ave., Pasadena 91103;
(818) 585-0855
Modern Chinese. Lunch & Dinner daily. All major cards.

It surprised us to learn that one of the top-rated Chinese restaurants in the city is a quirky spot in suburban Pasadena called Yujean's. Even more surprising was our discovery (along with the rest of L.A.'s food cognoscenti) that this new place is also one of the most expensive Chinese eateries in town, with one of the best wine lists we've seen in ages. After some shakiness in the kitchen in the early days, the food here is now nothing short of awesome, spectacular, breathtaking. Kang makes fascinating food, many of his dishes are so odd as to defy description. Consider "Picture in the Snow," a brown-stock soup filled with a julienne of chicken, ham and black and enoki mushrooms, topped with a layer of meringue decorated with a village scene constructed

out of vegetable slivers. Many of the dishes sound as if they could be gimmicky disasters: catfish sautéed with kumquats, lobster sautéed with fava beans, Chinese polenta with minced ham and leeks. Each and every one, however, is a wondrous creation, incorporating remarkable interplays of taste and texture that we've never witnessed even in China or Hong Kong. This restaurant alone lures so many people from L.A. to Pasadena each night, the city should give Kang an award for his contribution to local culture—and commerce. Dinner costs about $30 or more per person.

And Also . . .

Ciao Yie, 54 W. Colorado Blvd., Pasadena 91102; (818) 578-7501. *Chinese-Mediterranean. Lunch & Dinner daily. D, DC, MC, V.* This café in the heart of Old Town is uneven but interesting; the kung-pao pizza is surprisingly tasty.

Crown City Brewery, 300 S. Raymond St., Pasadena 91102; (818) 577-5548. *American. Breakfast Sun., Lunch & Dinner daily. AE, MC, V.* A convivial, unpretentious brewpub with tasty, inexpensive sandwiches, ribs and home-brewed beer.

Panda Inn, 111 E. Wilson Ave., Glendale 91206; (818) 502-1234; 3472 E. Foothill Blvd., Pasadena, (818) 793-7300. *Chinese. Lunch & Dinner daily. AE, MC, V.* This stylish minichain has done a pretty good job of introducing unadventurous suburbanites to reasonably authentic, if sometimes bland, Chinese food. Dinner for one, with beer, runs $15 or so.

The Raymond, 1250 S. Fair Oaks Ave., Pasadena 91105; (818) 441-3136. *Californian. Lunch Tues.-Fri., Dinner Tues.-Sun., Brunch Sun. All major cards.* This cozy thirteen-year-old Pasadena restaurant is all that's left of the now-defunct historical Raymond Hotel. The homespun food is as charming as all the handcrafted wood inside and the beautiful outdoor gardens. Lunch tends toward big salads and pastas, and there's a generous sirloin-tip sandwich. For dinner, you can count on good fish, veal, chicken, and rack of lamb. Dinner, $30 to $40 per person.

Stoney Point, 1460 W. Colorado Blvd., Pasadena 91105; (818) 792-6115. *Continental. Lunch Mon.-Fri., Dinner Mon.-Sat. MC, V.* The kind of comfortable Continental restaurant that is nearly extinct, Stoney Point does a surprisingly good job with such dishes as sweetbreads or steak with bordelaise sauce. Dinner for one, with wine, costs about $45.

For all the city's newest and best restaurant addresses, look for The Food Paper *(published quarterly by André Gayot/Gault Millau) on newsstands everywhere. Or, call (800) LE BEST 1 for a subscription.*

South Bay

Encompasses Manhattan Beach, Redondo Beach, Hermosa Beach, Torrance, Palos Verdes Estates and Rolling Hills Estates, as well as Gardena, Inglewood, Long Beach, San Pedro and Seal Beach.

12/20 Barnabey's Hotel Dining Room

3501 N. Sepulveda Blvd., Manhattan Beach 90266; (310) 545-5693
Austrian. Breakfast, Lunch & Dinner daily. All major cards.

Chef Stephen Lloyd has replaced Austrian Andreas Kisler, but this restaurant's Middle European cooking has remained. Klare rindsuppe (clear beef soup) and plenty of excellent salads make up the starters. A light Wiener Schnitzel, poached salmon with leek sauce and an updated game platter of quail, venison and rabbit with black-currant sauce are some of the stellar entrées. For those who think that modernization has its limits, try old-world fare like paprika hendl mit Spätzle (a Viennese pasta dish) and, for dessert, mohr im hemd (Moor in a Shirt), warm chocolate cake with chocolate sauce. The Victorian setting could be mistaken for Biedermeier. The wine list includes a number of award-winning bottles, all priced around $16. Dinner runs $35 per person.

10/20 Borrelli's

672 Silver Spur Rd., Rolling Hills Estates 90274; (310) 541-2632
Italian. Lunch Mon.-Fri., Dinner nightly. All major cards.

Clearly, there's still a taste for the old-fashioned Italian food that flourished in the heyday of the straw-clad Chianti bottle. Borrelli's is proof positive of this theorem. It's an affable enough place; the kitchen prepares some decent seafood and is particularly adept at calamari and scallops. One of the best dishes here is shrimp Capri, a whimsically named concoction of plump shrimp wrapped in prosciutto, served with sautéed peas and mushrooms in a cream sauce. Pastas can be unorthodox, as in fettuccine Michelangelo, which is enlivened by sautéed chicken. Dinner costs about $30 per person.

If you need to cancel a dinner reservation, please—be courteous to the restaurant and call well in advance.

9/20 The Bottle Inn

26 22nd St., Hermosa Beach 90254; (310) 376-9595
Italian. Dinner nightly. All major cards.

Summing up the Bottle Inn requires only a description of its decor, which is built around a collection of miniature liquor bottles (the kind served on airplanes); hundreds of them decorate the walls. The place looks like a cave, nary a window opens to the world outside. Service is pleasant enough. Edible dishes include the calamari al filetto or one of the veal preparations, especially saltimbocca alla Romana, pounded veal stuffed with sage, prosciutto and Fontina cheese. Dinner costs around $25.

12/20 Café Pierre

317 Manhattan Beach Blvd., Manhattan Beach 90266; (310) 545-5252
Mediterranean/International. Lunch Mon.-Fri., Dinner nightly. AE, MC, V.

Jumping from the south of France to the south of California, the highly eclectic, multipaged menu here offers a good number of Mediterranean creations. The place is jammed nightly with upscale beach people happy to have found such a cheerful, noisy room in which to browse through a remarkably encyclopedic wine list and order some of the best bouillabaisse and grilled fish in the area. Café Pierre (there is no Pierre, by the way; the chef is Guy Gabrielle) serves something—in fact, many things—for everyone, from traditional steak au poivre to chicken and duck-sausage cassoulet; from polenta with Gorgonzola to lamb links with jalapeño. And the beach is just down the street. About $30 per person for dinner.

12/20 Chalet de France

23254 Roberts Rd., Torrance 90505; (310) 540-4646
French. Lunch Mon.-Fri., Dinner nightly. All major cards.

Chalet de France prepares classical French cuisine with no surprises. The interior has a forgettable quasi-chalet decor with passé leather banquettes, but the restaurant is comfortable and quiet and has a pleasant outdoor terrace. The chef could be called a clever technician; he cooks by the rules and makes few mistakes. Starters, such as an excellent house pâté, seafood crêpes, scampi au diable and a lovely smoked salmon, do not disappoint. Entrées are predictable but good: sweetbreads financière, quail with raspberry sauce, salmon béarnaise, veal Normande. The flame-thrower act (flambéed steaks, cherries jubilee, crêpes Suzette) is big here and the clientele obviously enjoys it. Among desserts, there's an excellent napoléon and an even better cheesecake with raspberry purée. Personable, professional service. Dinner will run $35 per person.

Chez Mélange
Palos Verdes Inn, 1716 Pacific Coast Hwy., Redondo Beach 90277; (310) 540-1222
Californian/Eclectic. Breakfast, Lunch & Dinner daily, Brunch Sun. All major cards.

South Bay restaurateurs Michael Franks and Robert Bell have gone on to open Fino, Misto and Depot, each of which is a good deal more modern and trendy than their original restaurant, Chez Mélange. With age, the place (it's in the lobby of an upscale motel) has come to seem a bit stodgy. But it remains an impressive touchstone for tracking the development of good eating in the South Bay. Franks and Bell offer a wildly eclectic menu, with dishes ranging from the Middle East and the Orient to the Pacific Northwest and New Orleans. There's a Champagne and vodka bar and a caviar and oyster bar. When visiting chefs come to town, this comfortable venue at the foot of the Palos Verdes Penisula is often where they come to cooking. Chez Mélange may no longer be the most daring restaurant in town, but it remains one of the most reliable. And where else can you find restaurateurs who make their own sausages and some of the best sushi in the South Bay—without collapsing beneath the weight of culture shock? Dinner costs about $30 per person.

Depot
1250 Cabrillo Ave., Torrance 90501; (310) 787-7501
Calfornian/Eclectic. Lunch Mon.-Fri., Dinner Tues.-Sun. AE, MC, V.

The duo responsible for Depot—Michael Franks and Robert Bell—have the single best culinary track record in the South Bay. Indeed, it could be said that the South Bay is, ahem, their oyster. They began with Chez Mélange in Manhattan Beach, moved on to Misto and Fino, and now we have their fourth, largest restaurant, for which they've remodeled a dilapidated Red Car Line terminal. The restaurant is handsome and easy to settle into. There are whitewashed beams up above, opulent wooden pillars that support nothing scattered here and there, and a well-secluded bank of booths against one wall. It's a post-modernist setting that's just right for the post-modernist cuisine of Chef Michael Shafer, an imposing bear of a man who often emerges from the kitchen to cast a watchful eye about the room. Shafer's cooking is multi-ethnic: in it you can find evidence of Mexico, Japan, traditional American, England, Thailand, China, Italy, France and the Southwest. In other words, your basic California culinary experience. The appetizers are the most intriguing items on the menu: rock shrimp and garlic sausage, mashed potato pancakes topped with corn and oysters (a big fat oyster riding atop each cake), crabcake flautas with avocado salsa. This is the sort of multi-cultural restaurant where a grilled-duck-and-fennel cassoulet sits comfortably next to "Thai-dyed" chicken served with black-bean "twists." Dinner runs $30 or more per person.

Fino
Hillside Village, 24530 Hawthorne Blvd., Torrance 90505; (310) 373-1952
Mediterranean. Dinner nightly. AE, MC, V.

Chef Robert Bell is clearly smitten with the sunny food of Spain, France and Italy. Here he serves up some of the tastiest dishes in Southern California: osso buco in a chile-infused broth, fritto misto with assorted crispy seafood and Caesar dressing and a toothsome grilled seafood napoleon. There are pastas, of course, but (in an act of culinary heresy) no pizzas. Chow down instead on the house bread dipped in fruity olive oil, some salty olives and a glass of fino (a pale, light sherry). We love this stuff. The wine prices here are fair; the desserts rich. Despite Fino's wild popularity, Bell and his partner, Michael Franks (also the talented duo behind South Bay eateries Chez Mélange, Misto and Depot), have adopted a limited reservation policy to reward walk-in business. Allow about $35 per person for a full dinner.

11/20 The Grand House
809 S. Grand Ave., San Pedro 90731; (310) 548-1240
Continental. Lunch Tues.-Fri. & Sun., Dinner nightly. AE, MC, V.

As we went to press, The Grand House was closed for summer maintenance. When it reopens, this place should deliver the same it's delivered in recent years: predictable Continental chow. The setting remains lovely, particularly the pretty backyard with its massive, towering stone pine. The menu is more safe than interesting—baked Camembert, cheese triangles, calamari steak, Pacific red snapper, veal medallions, entrées flavored with pink peppercorns, that sort of cooking. Dinner costs about $28 per person.

12/20 Habash Café

233 Pacific Coast Hwy., Hermosa Beach
90260; (310) 376-6620
Middle Eastern. Lunch & Dinner Mon.-Sat. AE, MC, V.

Some restaurants offer ambience, others innovation. Then there are the places with character. Welcome to the Habash Café, a Hermosa Beach landmark. For more than twenty years Mama Habash has been dishing up Middle Eastern specialities including a definitive falafel, wonderful mjedara (lentil and rice salad) and ethereal lentil soup—in short, Levantine home cooking. Besides these treats, the faithful keep coming back for the hummus, the meltingly tender stewed squash and the sweet, sticky pastries. This is a pleasant, unpretentious place, rather like a coffee shop, except that this coffee is thick, sweet and redolent of cardamom. Prices here are family-friendly: you can be fairly certain of getting out the door for less than $10 per person.

12/20 Houston's

1550-A Rosecrans Ave., Manhattan Beach
90266; (310) 643-7211
American. Lunch & Dinner daily. AE, MC, V.
See review in "Restaurants – *L.A. Area.*"

J'Adore

742 Yarmouth Ave., Palos Verdes Estates
90274; (310) 541-3316
French. Dinner Tues.-Sat. All major cards.

J'Adore is one of the South Bay's hidden treasures—and given its location, it's likely to remain hidden. It's located off Palos Verdes Drive West, and the journey, from anywhere other than the immediate South Bay area, is a real expedition. The room itself is romantic in an utterly simple way, and the charming owner/chef, José Dahan, encourages couples to take a stroll outside between courses. Dahan, a native of Toulouse, has created a seven-course, $39 prix-fixe menu that ranks as one of the Southland's better values. Dahan's enthusiasm for cooking is infectious. ("Try our fabulous rack of venison from New Zealand with grilled eggplant. It's outrageous!") We were most impressed by the ahi with a spicy orange sauce and the soft-shell crabs with couscous. The prix-fixe menu permits choices, such as between an authentic bouillabaisse, or a rabbit in cream sauce with crêpes. As a midmeal break, apple sorbet comes, tasting as tart as a new pippin. Desserts like cold lemon soufflé and exotic seijoa sorbet (a New Zealand fruit) hold up their end of the meal, and the wine list, though small, provides some apt selections. Dinner costs $45 to $55 per person.

12/20 JB's Little Bali

217 E. Nutwood St., Inglewood 90301;
(310) 674-9835
Indonesian. Dinner Thurs.-Sun. MC, V.

We think this is the best Indonesian cooking in town. There's only one meal served at JB's—a rijstaffel, Dutch for "rice table," referred to on the placemat menu as "The Works." In an atmosphere that smacks of latter-day Somerset Maugham, Diane and Hans Oei start you off with gado gado (cold vegetables moistened with an exotic peanut sauce) and then build a huge spread around steamed white rice. Dishes arrive at a frantic pace—satay sapi (a chili-flavored shish kebab), pangsit goreng (sweet ginger-sauced meatballs), daging bumbu rujak (coconut-milk-flavored beef), sambal goreng kentang (sweet shoestring potatoes) and more, much more. The dishes mix and match tastes and are unified by the binding force of the rice. For dessert, there's a milky brown gelatin that tastes of brown sugar. Dinner is around $20 per person.

12/20 Misto

24558 Hawthorne Blvd., Torrance 90505;
(310) 375-3608
New American/International. Lunch Tues.-Sat., Dinner nightly. AE, MC, V.

In this friendly, noisy, nondescript trio of rooms, the tables are packed so closely together that you can't help but wonder what your neighbors are eating—and if they wouldn't mind giving you a taste. Misto serves the most soothing sort of comfort chow, the kind of food that will do more to relax an unsettled spirit than a year on an analyst's couch. The menu is American/Italian/Cajun/Mexican/French/Japanese/Chinese/Californian—in other words, there's something for everyone. Highly seasoned shrimp spiedini are as plump and perfect as you please. They do ribs here as well as the better soul food houses in town, crisp on the outside and meaty within, and served with a sauce that'll warm your blood on the foggiest Torrance night. Traditionalists are catered to by the French onion soup and the first-rate Caesar salad. And we love Misto for bringing back the concept of the sandwich as a dinner entrée, thanks to a definitive Sloppy Joe and an even sloppier muffalettas. The chefs even make the good old BLT into a main course, by transforming it into an extraordinary pizza topped with a cardiologist's nightmare of cheese, bacon and mayonnaise. But who wants to live forever anyway? About $20 per person for dinner.

12/20 L'Opera
101 Pine Ave., Long Beach 90802;
(310) 491-0066
Italian. Lunch Mon.-Fri., Dinner nightly, Late Supper Fri.-Sat. All major cards.

High-style Italian restaurants are old news in L.A., but, believe it or not, they haven't yet arrived in every Southern California burg. But it won't be long before every town and suburb big enough to have a K-Mart has its own chic spot serving tuna carpaccio. Now Long Beach has its own such place: L'Opera, an extraordinarily handsome Northern Italian restaurant in a grand old former bank building downtown.

The columns, high ceilings, ornate moldings and rich woodwork evoke the Belle Epoque, but new touches, notably clusters of halogen ceiling fixtures and a glass-walled kitchen, keep the overall feeling crisp and clean-lined. The wine list illustrates the restaurant's fashionable ambitions, with fine Italians, socially correct Californians (Cakebreads, Grgichs, Stag's Leaps), and collection of grappas, ports and Cognacs. The service is personable and efficient without being pretentious; neither is the food at all pretentious. Intensely flavorful goose prosciutto is paired with good mozzarella and drizzled with olive oil infused with sun-dried tomatoes. Fried calamari and whitebait are tender and tasty. Salads are perfectly dressed with balsamic vinaigrettes. The lobster-and-ricotta-stuffed mezzaluna pasta has loads of lobster flavor. Only a couple of entrées disappointed, most notably the too dry roast free-range chicken. The dessert collection is heavy on special-occasion sweets, like the "Vulcano," described as "an eruption of chocolates flowing with whipped cream, fresh berries and berry sauce." Dinner costs around $30 per person.

12/20 Papadakis Taverna
301 W. 6th St., San Pedro 90731;
(310) 548-1186
Greek. Dinner nightly. MC, V.

This is a warm, family place alive with old-fashioned values and traditions. Macho-man waiters dance and sing, and Papadakis himself leads ladies by the hand to their tables and bestows ceremonial kisses. Everyone comes here to have fun which entails enormous Greek dinners, plenty of wine and a parade of dancers snaking their way through the dining room at all times. Starter choices are legion: anginares (artichoke hearts in phyllo), kalamaria Alexandra (stuffed squid), Greek cheeses and olives, stuffed grape leaves and a handful of phyllo pastry triangles. Careful pac-

ing is essential if you plan on making it to dessert—dinners come with salad and the traditional avgolemono (a delicious lemon-rice soup); entrées are generous. Indulge in the arni ala Papadakis (tender, flavorful lamb in pastry), psari ala Papadakis (sea bass in phyllo) or pastistio (pasta with meat and béchamel). And by all means try the heavenly baklava and spice cake—if there's room. There's a suprisingly good wine list containing several boutique favorites. Dinner costs about $35 per person.

10/20 Paradise
889 W. 190th St., Gardena 90248;
(310) 324-4800
Californian. Lunch Mon.-Sat., Dinner nightly, Brunch Sun. AE, MC, V.

Getting lost is part of the experience of going to Paradise (is this an uncanny metaphor for life?), for although the place sits at the intersection of two of the busiest freeways in Los Angeles, there's no easy way to get to it. The postmodernist setting, with its multitude of indescribable angles, odd colors and quirky decor (pink plastic flamingos and various forms of sea life), is a little . . . much. The food remains serviceable (and occasionally better), with the usual assortment of dishes that mix a bit of Mexico with a bit of Thailand with a bit of China with a bit of Italy. The kitchen makes good pizzas and grills a decent chicken, and the salads aren't bad. If you don't work or live around here, the food doesn't offer much reason to risk getting lost. Dinner costs about $20 per person.

10/20 Pavarotti and Stein
762 Pacific Ave., Long Beach 90813;
(310) 437-3324
Italian/Jewish. Lunch Mon.-Fri., Dinner Tues.-Sat. AE, D, MC, V.

The proprietors of this engaging place—Mr. and Mrs. Boresztein—are from Buenos Aires, Argentina. Their home town has large Italian and Jewish communities, and it's obvious that these folks know their way around both cuisines. The restaurant is in a converted fire station full of tiny rooms; we like to sit in the flower-filled, brick-lined courtyard and listen to the clang of the trolley cars outside. What the Boreszteins have cooked up here sounds like it could be a gallery of Italo-Judaic culinary Frankensteins like gefilte-fish lasagne and matzoh carbonara. Fear not. This is simply an Italian restaurant where you can also get a few Jewish dishes. It's a real kick to dip a slice of the good housemade challah in your basil-infused olive oil, but that's about as close to an actual melding of these two cuisines as it gets.

There are plenty of pastas, from eastern European–potato varenikes and cheese kreplach to credible linguine al pesto and tagliatelle with two cheeses. The best entrées are on the order of the osso buco, a fairly classic version of the marrow filled veal shank in a rich, grainy tomato-based sauce. And do save room for lush desserts like ice cream glass "Stein," a bowlful of frothy zabaglione, chunks of baked meringue, fresh strawberries, vanilla ice cream and thick hand-whipped cream. Dinner should run about $26 per person, lunch around $10.

12/20 Pine Avenue Fish House
100 W. Broadway, Long Beach 90802;
(310) 432-7463
Seafood. Lunch & Dinner daily. All major cards.

One of two southern outposts run by the same company responsible for Ocean Avenue Seafood, the Water Grill and I Cugini (their other Long Beach restaurant is 555 East), this place looks more than anything like an old-style chophouse, with its tile floors and wooden booths. In fact, it's a good place to go for some fine deep-fried calamari, a good selection of fresh oysters and clams, plenty of seafood dishes served over pasta and a remarkable selection of American wines and microbrewery beers. There's an easiness to Pine Avenue which makes it a great place to drop by on an evening when you're just not sure what you're in the mood for. The kitchen also makes fish sandwiches. If the alder-smoked salmon sandwich is on the menu when you're there, go for it—it's a far, far cry from the salmon burgers so many of us suffered through in school all those years ago. You'll spend $30 per person for dinner.

Shenandoah Café
4722 E. 2nd St., Long Beach 90803;
(310) 434-3469
American. Dinner nightly. AE, MC, V.

Fans of true American cuisine will want to rally 'round the flag after a meal at this unpretentious, authentic and reasonably priced café. The cheery dining areas are done up like New Orleans drawing rooms, with gingham-clad waitresses serving dishes like beer-batter shrimp, beef brisket in barbecue sauce and wonderful country sausages. As you might expect of a good American place, the meat and the fish dishes are the best. Two in particular are worth a drive here: riverwalk steak, a thinly sliced flank steak in a mustard-caper sauce, and the very juicy blackened swordfish. Starters are unnecessary; dinners come with incredible warm apple fritters, a fine salad and homemade rolls. About $25 per person for dinner.

11/20 Simon & Seafort's
Catalina Landing, 340 Golden Shore, Long Beach 90802; (310) 435-2333
Seafood. Lunch & Dinner daily. All major cards.

The bar here draws a raucous, fun-loving crowd, which you'll probably be pulled into as you wait for a table. The bar appetizers are better overlooked; save your appetite for some of the good main dishes: fine New England clam chowder cleverly thickened with crushed crackers and clam chunks; Copper River salmon that is about as good as salmon gets; a perfectly decent red snapper in a ginger-cream sauce and some nicely turned Chilean swordfish in a vermouth-garlic butter. A dinner costs about $25 per person.

10/20 Spaghettini
3003 Old Ranch Pkwy., Seal Beach 90740; (310) 596-2199
Italian. Lunch Mon.-Fri., Dinner nightly All major cards.

Seal Beach is a bucolic bedroom community with its fair share of chain restaurant; Spaghettini has attempted (without roaring success) to put it on the culinary map. It's a hypertrophic Tuscan palace (Orange County–style), with wings and rooms that never seem to end—and on weekend evenings, every one of them appears to be filled. Not surprisingly, there are quite a few pastas on this menu: tomato-basil pasta, grilled sausage pasta, various seafood pastas. These are lightweight dishes, true, but when combined with, say, the restaurant's perfectly decent mini cioppino, the result is a pleasant meal for $11 or $12. Everything has a certain enthusiasm, especially the fine selection of crunchy, California-style pizzas topped variously with jumbo shrimps, artichokes, salami and other goodies. These make fine preludes to hearty entrées like chicken marsala, grilled lamb chops and sautéed shrimp. The bottom line here is fun and filling fare, as the buoyant owners bring the gospel of good bread and olive oil to Seal Beach. Dinner should run about $20 per person.

For comprehensive listings of restaurants By Area, By Price and By Cuisine, and by specific features such as Breakfast, Bar Scene, Late-Night, Light Eating and more, see the INDEXES section at the back of the book.

12/20 Wallaby Darned

617 S. Centre St., San Pedro 90731;
(310) 833-3629
Australian. Breakfast Sat.-Sun., Lunch & Dinner daily. MC, V.

Remember the jokes about the world's thinnest books? How about the one titled *Great Australian Dishes*. Well believe it or not, there's an agreeable version of an Ozzie tucker in this simple San Pedro café with a memorable name. Standout curries are made in the creamy Western style, but have lots of bite. They'll even throw a shrimp or two on the barbie if you insist. Proprietor John Lindfield knows his way around a kitchen, and so his pavlova—the obligatory antipodean dessert—is rather like a classic vacherin, crisp of meringue and studded with fruit. Along with the thin book, a rather thick tome, *Great Australian Wines* is almost ready for publication. The wine list here is replete with deserving unknowns like Krondorf, Coonawarra and Taltarni: wonderful, complex reds from booming south Australia. There's plenty of beer, too, and even the Aussie national food supplement Vegemite, a pungent soy spread only a native could love. Dinner runs about $15 per person.

11/20 The Whale & Ale

327 W. 7th St., San Pedro 90731;
(310) 832-0363
English. Only open for private parties of 30 or more. AE, MC, V.

This simulacrum of a British pub took three years to bring to fruition; the time was spent mostly in working out the complexities of rehabilitating a handsome old San Pedro building. Food rates as pleasant rather than wonderful, due in part to an undersized kitchen. Best dishes include duck in a sharp bigarade sauce, chicken with roast potatoes and steak-and-kidney pie. Beer flows freely here and there is a modest wine list. Prices (which like the menu are set by prior arrangement) should run to about $25 per person.

And Also . . .

Pancho's, 3615 Highland Ave., Manhattan Beach 90266; (310) 545-6670. *Mexican. Lunch & Dinner Mon.-Sat. MC, V.* An attractive two-tiered hacienda beloved of beachy locals; the combo-plate Mexican food is generic but satisfying, and the bar is always hopping. Dinner, less than $20 per person. ◆

BARGAIN BITES

Contents

The Simple Pleasures

Los Angeles has no shortage of both elegant temples of fine cuisine and big-name restaurants with star-studded clientele. But you'll be missing out on some of the city's finest if you limit your eating to such places, because L.A. also has some of the country's best fun food—incomparable taco and burrito stands, sizzling Cuban, Russian or Mongolian dives, great burger joints, charming breakfast spots. The adventurous nosher can find cafés of every breed, dim sum spreads that rival those in Hong Kong, and inspired pizzas with just about any topping a chef can dream up. And it's difficult to beat the bargains you can find at these places. After all, at what L.A. restaurant can you dine for $5 to $15? Here is where you'll find people who appreciate good food anywhere, anytime, whether it's elegantly arranged and served on fine china, or hurled over a Formica counter.

There are literally thousands of places in the L.A. area to grab a bite and save a buck, and we've sought out only the best. Forgive us if we've inadvertently left out your favorite. For now, at least, your secret is safe!

Barbecue

Benny's Barbecue
4077 Lincoln Blvd., Marina del Rey 90292;
(310) 821-6939
*Summer: Open Mon.-Sat. 11 a.m.-10 p.m., Sun. 2 p.m.-
10 p.m. Winter: open Mon.-Sat. 11 a.m.-10 p.m., Sun.
4 p.m.-10 p.m. No cards.*

The way to identify good barbecue is to follow your nose. And you can smell the food cooking at Benny's from at least two blocks away. Though there are a few tables, this is really take-out food—from the superb ribs bathed in a fiery sauce to what may be the best hot links in town, more like meatloaf in a skin, with lots of peppercorns and plenty of bite. One of their generous dinner specials and a soft drink will set you back less than $10.

Carl's Bar-B-Q
5953 W. Pico Blvd., Fairfax District (L.A.) 90035;
(213) 934-0637
*Open Mon.-Thurs. noon-10 p.m., Fri.-Sat. noon-11 p.m.,
Sun. 2 p.m.-9 p.m. No cards.*

Carl's is one of L.A.'s best barbecue joints— out of its huge brick barbecue emerge messy, wonderful hickory-smoked ribs and chicken, superb hot links and tender roast beef and pork, all awash in a barbecue sauce that is sweet, vinegary and spicy at the same time. It comes medium (which is bold) and hot (which will take your breath away). The decor consists of stacks of hickory logs concealed by a battered big-screen TV that elicits a running stream of commentary from Houston-native Carl himself. A heap of barbecue can cost from $7 to $14, but the best lunch bargain is the succulent chopped pork sandwich for just $1.50.

Dr. Hogly Wogly's Tyler, Texas Barbecue
8136 N. Sepulveda Blvd., Van Nuys 91402;
(818) 780-6701
Open daily 11:30 a.m.-10 p.m. MC, V.

The fame of this unpretentious restaurant has spread so much that there's usually a crowd lining the walls. Named for original owner Johnny Greene, who got his nickname in 1932 when he was a chubby delivery boy for a Piggly Wiggly market in Texas, the joint is decorated in Early American vinyl and Formica. Dig into good Texas hot links, fantastic spareribs, tender chicken and delicious beef brisket. All the meat is smoked on the premises. You'll be so full it'll be hard to succumb to the tempting pecan and sweet-potato pies. Dinner will run about $15.

Mom's Bar-B-Q House
14062 Vanowen St., Van Nuys 91405;
(818) 786-1373
*Open Mon.-Thurs. 11 a.m.-9:30 p.m., Fri. 11 a.m.-10
p.m., Sat. noon-10 p.m. No cards.*

Deep in the heart of Van Nuys lies an unprepossessing mini-mall that houses this treasure. Mom's dishes up some of the city's best barbecue. The decor is strictly rec-room, but the beef and pork ribs, chicken, hot links, fried chicken, fried chicken livers and rib tips will render you blind to your surroundings. While the meats aren't quite as tender as those at Dr. Hogly Wogly's, they're delicious and authentically smoky. The sides are terrific, too, especially the macaroni and cheese and the long-cooked baked beans. Even after the mammoth portions, don't eschew the pineapple-coconut cake: the perfect antidote to the heat of Mom's sauce. Dinner runs under $10.

Mr. Jim's Pit Bar-B-Que
5403 S. Vermont Ave., South-Central L.A. 90037;
(213) 778-6070
10303 Avalon Blvd., Watts 90003; (213) 757-0221
Open daily 11 a.m.-10 p.m. No cards.

That inimitable hickory barbecue smell hits you about a block before you reach this little take-out. The incredible pork spareribs are the reason to come here; the beef ribs are tasty but a little tough. Order your ribs medium, and you'll get a smoky, rather sweet sauce; a hot order is true to its word. Rib dinners are served with the typical bland white bread, good, thick baked beans and potato salad. If you can possibly save room for one of the delicious little sweet-potato tarts, it will be worth it. Mr. Jim's is not for the meek of heart—both neighborhoods can be intimidating. Under $10 for a barbecue orgy.

Warren's BBQ
4916 1/2 W. Slauson Ave., Ladera Heights 90056;
(213) 294-2272
*Open Mon.-Thurs. 11 a.m.-9 p.m., Fri.-Sat. 11 a.m.-9:30
p.m., Sun. 2 p.m.-7 p.m. AE, MC, V.*

Located in an upscale black neighborhood, Warren's is a spic-and-span barbecue haven in an area that has no lack of good barbecue. You can eat in or take out, and owner Warren Gray is a knowledgeable guide through the world of wood-smoked meats. The hot links are spicy and grainy; the ribs and chicken are falling-off-the-bone tender. Warren also serves Cleveland-style pork sandwiches and heavenly barbecued boudin blanc sausage. The beans are smoky, the slaw is tart, and the sweet-potato pie is so good that you won't mind if its sweetness makes your fillings ache. A robust combo dinner followed by dessert will run about $12.

Cafés

L.A. Area

Encompasses L.A. proper and all of the Westside, including Downtown, Hollywood, West Hollywood, Bel Air, Beverly Hills, Brentwood, Westwood, Century City, Santa Monica, Venice, Marina Del Rey, Pacific Palisades and Malibu.

Axe

510 Santa Monica Blvd., Santa Monica 90401;
(310) 458-4414
Breakfast, Lunch & Dinner Mon.-Sat., Brunch Sun. No cards.

We never went to Cal Berkeley, and we've only been to the town itself for dinner at Chez Panisse. But we feel as if we've been there every time we stop by Axe (pronounced, incidentally, "Ah-SHAY"). Comfortably warm wooden tables, chairs and stools, lots of plants, high ceilings, and a tiny loft all conspire to make you feel as if the radical-chic sixties never ended. The food, however, is up-to-the-minute nineties: an excellent vegetable salad with organic greens, eggplant, potatoes, carrot, walnuts and optional grilled chicken; grilled spinach and goat cheese sandwiches; good pastas; wholesome soups; and outstanding cookies, brownies, cakes and pies—all baked on the premises. You'll shell out $10 to $15 for a satisfying lunch or dinner.

Babalu

1002 Montana Ave., Santa Monica 90403;
(310) 395-2500
Breakfast, Lunch & Dinner daily. DC.

Babalu is a terrific addition to the generally mediocre Montana Avenue restaurant scene. The decor is in a colorfully wacky Caribbean mode, and while the food isn't exactly gourmet fare, it's imaginative and tasty, served by friendly waitresses and waiters. While Caribbean is the prevalent culinary influence here, the menu jumps all over the map: pastas, burgers, chicken satay with coconut-lime sauce, homemade sausages. The desserts are a treat, from the Key-lime pie to the coconut flan and various cakes and tarts. Lunch will only set you back about $12.

Brentwood Country Mart

225 26th St., Brentwood 90402;
(310) 394-5818/394-4705; Office (310) 395-6714
Open Mon.-Sat. 9 a.m.-6 p.m. No cards.

Like a miniature, non-touristy version of L.A.'s Farmer's Market, the Brentwood Country Mart—implausibly plopped in the midst of one

of the Westside's most chichi neighborhoods—attracts a devoted crowd of locals who gather at the outdoor redwood tables. The few stalls surrounding this meeting spot—where you're likely to recognize a celebrity or two—include an excellent newsstand and bookstore called The Book Nook, the Le Buffet burger stand and Mart Coffee & Juice Bar, which serves fruit juices, ice creams, yogurt shakes and coffees. Just inside, next to the supermarket, is Marjan's, a barebones coffee shop that offers serviceable deli sandwiches, all-American salads and platters of meat loaf, knockwurst, brisket and sliced turkey. We wouldn't go out of the way to eat at any of these places; but if you're in the vicinity, it's a relaxing and enjoyable place to stop. Lunch, around $10.

Café des Artistes

1534 N. McCadden Pl., Hollywood 90028;
(213) 461-6889
Lunch Tues.-Fri. & Sun., Dinner Tues.-Sun. All major cards.

Don't let the grimness of the block deter you from venturing past the row of hedges that fronts this beautiful little converted bungalow. On the bright patio or in the serene dining room, you can lunch, dine or brunch on salads, pastas and simple entrées. We have been least pleased with lunch; but we could not have been more pleased with the lovely (and immensely popular) Sunday brunch, when a classical trio plays, and an impeccable array of fruit, juices, sparkling and still wines, breads, salads, meats and desserts are laid out and fluffy omelets are made to order. It's one of our favorite brunches in town. Be sure to try the marvelous crème caramel. Brunch runs about $20.

Café Beverly Wilshire

The Regent Beverly Wilshire, 100 S. Rodeo Dr., Beverly Hills 90212; (310) 275-5200
Breakfast, Lunch, Dinner & Late Supper daily, Brunch Sun. All major cards.

When the Regent hotel folks redid the tired, old Beverly Wilshire, a gorgeous phoenix rose from the ashes. Yet the powers that be wisely left one little corner intact, with the same, good old American breakfast menu virtually unchanged (except that the quality of the ingredients and cooking is far better). For dinner and lunch, habitués can still order the famed McCarthy salad (iceberg lettuce, beets, Swiss and cheddar cheeses, egg yolk, egg white, diced tomato, bacon and turkey—a mouthful), a most delicious chili and an adorable platter that consists of a miniature hot dog, hamburger and Reuben sandwich. The french fries are faultless. Save room for goodies from the fountain, especially the decadent sundae of chocolate-marshmallow and honey ice creams washed in a rich coffee sauce and garnished with biscuit leaves. Lunch or dinner runs about $25.

Café Figaro
9010 Melrose Ave., W. Hollywood 90069; (310) 274-7664
Lunch Mon.-Sat., Dinner & Late Supper nightly. AE, MC, V.

For years Café Figaro has been immensely popular with L.A.'s under-30 set. Much of this popularity was due to L.A.'s former lack of simple French and Italian cafés, though now places much better than Café Fig, as it's called, are abundant. But these big, rather shabby rooms still fill up fast on the weekends; we attribute this to the low prices, good location, relatively late hours and comfortable, casual atmosphere—where else in L.A. can you read the eponymous Parisian newspaper plastered to a wall? Certainly the food isn't the draw—the hamburgers, sandwiches, omelets, simple entrées and generous desserts are fair to mediocre. Wine and beer are served. About $15 for dinner.

Café SFA
Saks Fifth Ave., 9600 Wilshire Blvd., Beverly Hills 90212; (310) 275-4211
Lunch Mon.-Wed. & Fri.-Sun., Dinner Thurs. (until 7:30 p.m.). All major cards.

If you aren't bored to death with quiche and spinach salad, you'll enjoy the simple light-lunch fare served in this little café lurking behind Saks's gourmet kitchen department. It's a very pretty, feminine-looking place, in shades of rose and terra cotta, with satisfying food that will help you recover from a tiring shopping spree. About $18 for a light lunch with dessert and an invigorating cappuccino.

Caffè Latte
6254 Wilshire Blvd., Wilshire District (L.A.) 90048; (213) 936-5213
Breakfast Mon.-Sat., Lunch daily, Dinner Tues.-Sat. MC, V.

Caffè Latte is run by young, affable Tom Kaplan, whose family owns Hugo's in West Hollywood, and this café is as big a hit as papa's place. Yet another gem in a mini-mall, it is popular not only with neighborhood residents but with designers, writers and other creative sorts. The decor is sweet, and what's on the menu is solid and enticing: egg dishes, pastas and pancakes for breakfast, sandwiches (including a first-rate BLT), pastas and grilled items for lunch and dinner. Caffè Latte also serves Jody Maroni's supernal, exotic sausages (such as chicken with fig and duck with orange and cumin) and excellent coffee roasted right on the premises, sold in bulk as well as by the cup. Breakfast and lunch run under $10, dinner under $20.

Caffè Luna
7463 Melrose Ave., Melrose-Fairfax District (L.A.) 90046; (213) 655-8647
Breakfast, Lunch, Dinner & Late Supper (until 3 a.m. Sun.-Thurs., until 5 a.m. Fri.-Sat.) daily.

A magnet for Europeans and urban types who live the late-night café life, Caffè Luna has crowds lining up along its sponge-painted walls and crowding its small wooden tables day and night. They come to sip the generous lattès and Italian wines by the glass, smoke cigarettes, and trade gossip and philosophies with the other hip people who frequent the café (Mickey Rourke and Kiefer Sutherland are among the regulars). The food could be a good deal better, but where else can you munch on crusty panini and pizzas, *insalata* and pasta salads at 3 a.m.? It's a cozy place to read the paper over breakfast, too. Service can be seriously lackadaisical, so count on lingering for awhile. A large breakfast costs about $10, dinner $14 or so.

Caffè Roma
350 N. Cañon Dr., Beverly Hills 90210; (310) 274-7834
Lunch Mon.-Sat., Dinner & Late Supper nightly. All major cards.

Caffè Roma is yet another chic meeting spot for the Beverly Hills crowd—a crowd tending toward men draped in gold chains and women in nightclub attire. In spite of a deafening noise level and high prices it continues to be a highly popular meeting place. The little pizzas are good, and the lunch buffet is acceptable, but the antipasti, pastas and Italian standards are much better elsewhere. If you must, stop in here at midnight and sip an espresso in the courtyard. You'll spend $30 per person for lunch, $45 for dinner.

For all the city's newest and best eateries, look for The Food Paper *(published quarterly by André Gayot/Gault Millau) on newsstands everywhere. Or, call (800) LE BEST 1 for a subscription.*

Cutters

Colorado Place, 2425 Colorado Ave., Santa Monica
90404; (310) 453-3588
Lunch Mon.-Fri., Dinner nightly. AE, MC, V.

Junior executives zip over here in their junior
BMWs, perhaps after a quick stop at the health
club, to have a few drinks and nibble on generic
California cuisine (meaning hip dishes from everywhere but California)—Cajun pastas, Italian
pastas, salads with Chinese, Japanese and Thai
influences and grilled fish from Hawaii and the
Pacific Northwest. Making the scene and making
new friends is more the point than the food,
which is all done better elsewhere. Unless you
enjoy a loud, yuppie-bar ambience, Cutters is
most pleasant for an early lunch, when it's relatively peaceful. Under $15 for lunch and $30 for
dinner.

Figtree's Café

429 Ocean Front Walk, Venice 90291;
(310) 392-4937
Breakfast, Lunch & Dinner daily. All major cards.

Though Figtree's has only been open since
1978, we feel as if the sixties and the eighties
collide here—with the only taste of the nineties
being a few Southwestern/Pacific Rim touches
in the food. The ambience inside is casual, welcoming Venice coffeehouse; but we've sometimes encountered haughty upscale
attitude—shades of the Reagan era—from the
waiters. Tofu, seafood and chicken are the pro-
teins of choice on the menu, and such dishes as
burritos, tostadas, pastas, stir-fries and fresh fish
are tasty and filling. The bakery counter offers an
imaginative range of baked goods—predominantly whole-wheat and sweetened with honey.
Around $15 for a light lunch, $25 for a seafood
dinner.

Flora Kitchen

460 S. La Brea Ave., Melrose-La Brea District (L.A.)
90036; (213) 931-9900
*Breakfast, Lunch, Dinner & Late Supper daily. AE,
MC, V.*

Rita Azar, who set a new standard for hip
flower shops with Rita Flora, cannily grabbed
hold of the adjoining shop, knocked a doorway
through, and opened Flora Kitchen—one of the
most appealing little self-service cafés we know.
Queue up at the counter to order a plate of one,
two or three imaginative salad selections from an
ever-changing Mediterranean-ish roster (grilled
chicken with baby artichokes, citrus roasted peppers with goat's cheese), or a generous sandwich
(we're fond of the seared ahi tuna with arugula

and yellow tomato salsa on La Brea Bakery's olive
bread). Flora also offers house-baked treats, including huge cranberry muffins, rustic pies and
tarts, and ginger scones the size and shape of
giant cookies. It's better to eat quickly here,
though—it's a bit of a chore to try and relax on
those high, teetery stools. Under $12 for lunch
with a good cup of cappuccino.

Il Fornaio

301 N. Beverly Dr., Beverly Hills 90210;
(310) 550-8330
Breakfast, Lunch & Dinner daily. MC, V.

This successful import from Italy is both a
good café and a wonderful bakery, where you can
find all manner of delicious and very authentic
Italian breads, tortes and cookies. Closed for remodeling when we went to press, it should be
open again by January 1993 (call first).
Businesspeople, sightseers and professional
Rodeo Drive shoppers fill the café at lunchtime,
nibbling on one of six daily pastas, Italian sandwiches, pizzas (genuine Italian, not California),
calzone and pastries. Prices aren't bad: about $17
for a pasta, pastry and cappuccino lunch.

Il Fornaio Caffè e Kiosko

633 W. 5th St., Downtown (L.A.) 90071;
(213) 623-8400
Breakfast (open 6:30 a.m.) & Lunch Mon.-Sat. MC, V.

Excuse us if this sounds a bit crazy, but we've
fallen in love with a stairway. The romantic steps
in question are the new open-air flight on the
western side of the First Interstate World Center
tower. And with a glorious view of the Central
Library, as well as the waterfall that cascades
down their median, these Bunker Hill Steps give
downtown its own answer to Rome's Spanish
Steps. How appropriate, then, that their second-
floor landing includes an indoor/outdoor
branch of Il Fornaio, serving that elite chain's
outstanding own-baked pastries, pizzas and
breads, along with generous sandwiches, salads
and soups. There's even an adjoining newsstand—how continental! Under $5 for a light
breakfast, around $7 for lunch.

Gianfranco

11363 Santa Monica Blvd., W.L.A. 90025;
(310) 477-7777
Breakfast Mon.-Sat., Lunch & Dinner daily. MC, V.

One of the city's earlier casual pasta cafés,
Gianfranco is a lively, charming eat-in/take-out
Italian deli. The bright, modern room is dominated by huge deli cases stocked with beautiful
antipasti, salads, pastries, hot and cold pastas,

cheeses and meats. Most of the homemade pastas are quite nice (try the fettuccine al pesto), and the salads and antipasti are always tasty. The pastries and the veal and chicken dishes, however, are disappointing. But there are plenty of good, inexpensive Italian wines, delicious gelati and rich cappuccinos. Lunch or a light dinner for under $20.

Gorky's Café
536 E. 8th St., Downtown (L.A.) 90014; (213) 627-4060
Breakfast (open 6:30 a.m.) & Lunch daily, Dinner & Late Supper Tues.-Sun. All major cards.

The Hollywood branch has closed now, but the original Gorky's remains on the fringe of the garment district, where the homeless congregate en masse. That world is left behind once you step into the high-ceilinged room filled with an amusing mishmash of executives, artists, eccentrics and those who are simply slumming. The menu aptly describes Gorky's as a "Russian avant-garde café with working people's prices." Pick up a plastic cafeteria tray and pile on such simple, generous peasant fare as piroshki, Polish sausage with sauerkraut, and blintzes—then sit down at one of the long Formica tables or in one of the rustic booths, and enjoy. There are also some fine salads and sandwiches, good omelets and a couple of hearty daily specials. Also note that they've recently added a brew pub that's become all the rage in the evening. Here, $12 will fill even a starving Cossack.

Grand Avenue Bar
Biltmore Hotel, 515 S. Grand Ave., Downtown (L.A.) 90071; (213) 624-1011
Lunch & Dinner Mon.-Fri. All major cards.

A little Siberia, but a very chic Siberia, with high ceilings, marble tables, Mies van der Rohe chairs and a big screen TV, in front of which sit solid executive sorts who line up at the elegant, daily-changing buffet. Though relatively costly, for what you get it's the best lunch value downtown—$17.95 lets you dine to your heart's content on such good things as seafood or vegetable terrines, duck pâté, a ballotine of turkey, cold pastas, delicate salads, thin-sliced prime rib and beautiful desserts. After 5 p.m. the local offices empty out and the bar fills up with a crowd of businesspeople.

The Gumbo Pot
Farmer's Market, 6333 W. 3rd St., Melrose-Fairfax District (L.A.) 90036; (213) 933-0358
Breakfast & Lunch daily. No cards.

No need to spend $20 to $40 a head at a Cajun restaurant—not when you can come to the Gumbo Pot in touristy Farmer's Market and get great Cajun/Creole food for a fraction of that price. The best things here are the incredible muffelata sandwiches; the flavorful gumbo yaya with chicken, shrimp and andouille sausage; and the moist cornbread studded with whole corn, sweet roasted chiles and cheese. Also good are the sinful beignets, the not-too-hot Cajun meatloaf and the sweet-potato salad with apples, pecans and raisins. Everything is available to go. Get a soda from a neighboring stand and plan to spend about $6 to $8 per person for lunch.

Hard Rock Café
Beverly Center, Beverly & La Cienega Blvds., W. Hollywood 90048; (310) 276-7605
Lunch, Dinner & Late Supper daily. AE, MC, V.

We're amazed at how often we find ourselves joining the throngs at the Hard Rock for lunch, or after work for a beer or two. This hyperbolic restaurant and bar is famous the world around as a tourist mecca, and even worse, it's practically the nucleus of the city's after-dark teen scene. So what are we doing here, being jostled by Japanese schoolgirls dressed in Hard Rock T-shirts? We're having great fun—checking out the sea-foam–green Cadillac plunging through the roof, the loud, energetic rock-and-roll, the fantastic collection of movie-and-music memorabilia, the hopping bar, the white-uniformed waitresses. Surprisingly, the food is pretty good, especially the succulent, lime-grilled chicken, burgers, chili and apple pie à la mode. A must-visit for out-of-towners, and a refreshingly casual stop-in for Angelenos. About $12 for chicken, fries and a beer.

Hot Wings Café
7011 Melrose Ave., Melrose-La Brea District (L.A.) 90038; (213) 930-1233
Lunch Mon.-Sat., Dinner & Late Supper nightly. No cards.
314 N. Brand Blvd., Glendale 91203; (818) 247-4445
Lunch & Dinner daily, Late Supper Fri.-Sat. No cards.

A great place to know about, if only because its Westside branch is one of the cheapest places to eat on ever-upscale Melrose (and because it's open late). Hot Wings serves up a collegiate atmosphere and good, simple food: juicy Reuben sandwiches, good burgers and French dips, classic New York cheesecake, and honest cappuccinos. The specialties are all imports from the East Coast, from tasty buffalo chicken wings with fiery dipping sauces to Philly steak sandwiches. About $9 for a sandwich and an imported beer.

These small eateries may change their closing times without warning. It's always wise to check in advance.

I. Magnin Wilshire Tea Room

3050 Wilshire Blvd., Mid-Wilshire District (L.A.)
90010; (213) 382-6161
Lunch Mon.-Sat. AE, MC, V.

We're relieved to report that I. Magnin's acquisition of Bullock's Wilshire, one of L.A.'s most gorgeous art-deco landmarks, has not affected the haven that its fifth-floor Tea Room has always been. If you want to step back into a genteel and proper era, the Tea Room offers a welcome retro respite from a world gone bonkers. Chances are that if your hair isn't a certain shade of blue and you're not clad in Chanel, you'll be considered slightly suspect. But that's okay—the service is still charming and the food is comforting and much better than you may expect. Salads and sandwiches are fresh and tasty, the breads and muffins in a basket on the table are homemade, and the afternoon tea is a quiet riot of finger sandwiches, scones and pots of jams and Devonshire cream. Lunch will run about $12, tea around $11.

Killer Shrimp

523 Washington Blvd., Marina del Rey 90292;
(310) 578-2293
Lunch & Dinner daily. No cards.

It's not really a café, not really a restaurant—there's actually nothing in L.A. quite like this eatery. In its minuscule mini-mall space with its minuscule outdoor patio, Killer Shrimp serves one thing only: huge, plump Gulf shrimp, cooked to your order in a rich, Cajun-spiced broth that they've simmered for ten hours. The best dish (and the best deal) is their generous peel-and-eat pile, which comes with a basketful of warm, fresh cubes of French bread for dunking in the sauce. Skip the other two items on the menu—already-peeled shrimp served over pasta or rice—which are fairly bland-tasting and not nearly as fun to eat. A shrimp-and-bread dinner for one costs $10.95.

Kings Road Café

8361 Beverly Blvd., W. Hollywood 90048;
(213) 655-9044
Breakfast, Lunch & Dinner daily; Late Supper Wed.-Sat. No cards.

Though the name may suggest a taste of swinging London, in fact it comes from the side street upon whose corner this casual little charmer is located. The menu reminds us of some of our favorite little trattorias in Italy: gutsy, crusty breads; fresh antipasti dressed with olive oil; crisp pizzas. Breakfast may well be the best time to visit, though, for the eggs baked with goat cheese in olive oil and served with toasted olive bread, or the unusual sweet risotto with

dried figs. We love to go solo, buy a paper or magazine at the newsstand just outside, and read as we sip a cup of excellent espresso. Under $8 for breakfast, $15 at lunch.

Kokomo

Farmer's Market, 6333 W. 3rd St., Melrose-Fairfax District (L.A.) 90036; (213) 933-0773
Breakfast & Lunch daily. No cards.

The times certainly are a-changin'—who'd ever expect to find a neohip café like Kokomo ensconced in that Valhalla for tourists, Farmer's Market? It's just an orange pit's throw away from the Gumbo Pot, the owners of which are also responsible for Kokomo. The fare is sort of gourmet-coffee shop, including a superb BLT made with organically grown tomatoes, thick-sliced bacon and pesticide-free lettuce. Kokomo also does mean burgers and chicken sandwiches and habit-forming sweet-potato fries, as well as hearty morning fare. In fact, Kokomo has become a major power breakfast and lunch scene for music and show-biz folk; among the patrons are David Byrne and Axl Rose. To handle the crush, Kokomo's has opened a separate take-out counter, one stall down. About $10 for lunch.

Mario's Cooking for Friends

7475 Beverly Blvd., Melrose-Fairfax District (L.A.) 90036; (213) 931-6342
Deli: Lunch & Dinner Mon.-Sat. Dining room: Lunch & Dinner Mon.-Sat. (until 11 p.m.) All major cards.

The food at this neighborhood Italian deli/café/catering company is every bit as appealing as the clean-lined design of the deli and the sponge-painted, frescoed, marble-countered dining room. Glass deli cases hold gorgeous salads, trays of savory rôtisserie-roasted chicken, every kind of prepared meat and an array of cheeses. The kitchen also prepares thick sandwiches made with the dense, flavorful house bread (many are less than $5 and are accompanied by a green salad) and a few simple entrées. The dining room features many of these items at slightly higher prices, along with good fresh pastas and veal, chicken and fish cooked to order. Lunch runs about $15, dinner $18 to $25.

Marmalade

710 Montana Ave., Santa Monica 90403;
(310) 395-9196
Breakfast (open 6:30 a.m. Mon.-Fri.), Lunch & Dinner daily. AE, MC, V.

This bright, charming neighborhood café is packed to the skylights with fresh scones, muffins, pastries and desserts baked on the premises. You can join the throngs for a large, steaming cup of coffee or a bite here (tables open up frequently)—or take home a roasted chicken, a loaf of bread or any of a number of warm and cold salads and pasta dishes. They also carry a fine selection of specialty cheeses, jams and condiments.

Michel Richard
310 S. Robertson Blvd., Beverly Hills 90211;
(310) 275-5707
Breakfast & Lunch daily, Dinner Mon.-Sat. AE, MC, V.
The twinkly Richard hasn't had anything to do with this place for a decade or so. We wonder: is it the association with his famous name, or the simple charm of this modest shop that keeps it constantly packed? After tasting the croissants, strawberry tarts, "mado" with hazelnuts, "fleur d'automne" and "auteuil" of chocolate and the "opéra" (a Lenôtre creation that is famous worldwide), we tend to think the place draws the crowd on its own merit. However, we find the regular menu overpriced and rather inconsistent: for $10 to $14, there are several different quiches, salads, omelets and such daily specials as the sauté of lamb with rosemary. Stick to the sweets and the espresso drinks, and you can pass a lovely hour or two for about $7.

MOCA Café
Museum of Contemporary Art, 250 S. Grand Ave.,
Downtown (L.A.) 90012; (213) 617-1844
Lunch Tues.-Sun. MC, V.
Though its name has changed from Il Panini, MOCA Café is still a terrific lunch spot for museum visitors and local denizens. Sandwiches are terrific: try the smoked salmon with bacon and sweet-hot mustard. Pasta salads are fine, and there are wines by the glass to accompany lunch and espressos to end it. If the weather is hot, try to sit inside—the outdoor tables are shaded by umbrellas, but the sun heats the marble underfoot and bakes diners. Lunch for around $8.

Mongolian Bar-B-Q
5401 Hollywood Blvd., Hollywood 90027;
(213) 464-6888
Lunch Tues.-Fri., Dinner Tues.-Sun. No cards.
A good find for those on a budget. At dinner, $6.95 gets you a small bowl of soup (usually pretty bad), a bowl of rice, plenty of addictive sesame rolls and two high-as-you-can-pile-'em bowls of tasty Mongolian barbecue. You work your way around the buffet, heaping your bowl with beef, lamb, pork, turkey and/or all kinds of vegetables: bean sprouts, carrots, celery, cabbage and so on. You then give this bowl to one of the proprietors, who douses it with sauce, as hot (or mild) as you want. The whole mess is quick-cooked on the large, open Mongolian barbecue grill, and best eaten stuffed inside the aforementioned hollow sesame rolls. There's no atmo-

sphere and no frills, just a lot of good food for the money. Westsiders can go to its former cousin restaurant (now under different ownership), Mongol's (1064 Gayley Ave., Westwood 90024; 310-824-3377).

Netty's
1700 Silverlake Blvd., Silverlake 90026;
(213) 662-8655
Lunch & Dinner Mon.-Sat. DC, MC, V.
The prisonlike chain-link fence surrounding Netty's is as offputting as a first impression can get. Fight the urge to run away, and venture into this little neighborhood joint. What you'll find is terrific, right-on-target food. Netty and her husband (both formerly chefs) have put together an eclectic menu that spans the map from Italy to Salvador. The pasta dishes are delicious, the cold case is always filled with fresh, flavorful salads, the entrées and pastas come with good pesto bread and the tamales are a real treat. The menu is a repertory of about 100 dishes, and while most of the business is take-out and catering, you can dine on the outdoor patio—the place has a certain charm. If you want beer or wine, bring your own, and dine sumptuously for under $16.

Odeon
625-A Montana Ave., Santa Monica 90403;
(310) 451-9096
Breakfast (open 6:30 a.m. Mon.-Sat.) & Lunch daily, Dinner Tues.-Fri. No cards.
There's never been a time of day when we haven't found a crowd at Odeon—which, apart from its many other charms, resides on ever-more-chic Montana. It has the ambience of a stylish French neighborhood café—with a marble floor, a few little wooden tables and chairs, and a glass counter/display case where you can order anything from fresh, generous salads and pastas to slices of pizza to sandwiches on their own-baked, hand-sliced breads. Weekend brunch features outstanding omelets (the Greek with feta, olives, spinach and tomato is a standout). And at any time of day, Odeon is worth a stop for their pastries and coffees. Around $10 for lunch or brunch.

Le Petit Four
8654 W. Sunset Blvd., W. Hollywood 90069;
(310) 652-3863
Breakfast & Lunch daily, Dinner Mon.-Sat. (until 11 p.m.). All major cards.
This charming sidewalk café doubles as a pâtisserie and gourmet-food shop, featuring Fauchon products. Inside, colorful Delacroix posters line the walls and out on the coveted sidewalk tables, interesting streetlife teems by and patrons laugh and toast one another. The

THE BOMBAY SAPPHIRE MARTINI. AS ENVISIONED BY MICHAEL GRAVES.

POUR SOMETHING PRICELESS.

Bombay® Sapphire™ Gin. 47% alc/vol (94 Proof). 100% grain neutral spirits. ©1992 Carillon Importers, Ltd., Teaneck, N.J. ©1992 Michael Graves.

Taste
America's
Finest

Mendocino Mineral Water

Mendocino Beverages International 1-800-669-9973

terrines, croquettes, Caesar salads and quiches are a cut above those at most other cafés in town, and the pizzas are surprisingly good—with paper-thin, slightly sweet crusts. The house-made pastries are outstanding; many of the better restaurants in town pass off Le Petit Four's pastries as their own. Service is friendly. With a good espresso or a glass of wine, lunch costs about $21.

La Poubelle

5907 Franklin Ave., Hollywood 90028;
(213) 465-0807
Dinner nightly, Late Supper Fri.-Sat. AE, MC, V.

La Poubelle is a genuine French neighborhood café, which no doubt explains the numbers of French among the clientele. The food, like the somewhat shabby decor, is basic, comforting and unexceptional—the omelets, crêpes, onion soup, salads and simple entrées are tasty and reasonably priced, though not worth a trip from another part of town. If you do stop in, however, don't neglect to order the dessert crêpe filled with vanilla ice cream, bananas and hot fudge sauce. The friendly French owner, Mme. Koster, often serves you personally. Supper costs about $20.

The Rose Café

220 Rose Ave., Venice 90292; (310) 399-0711
Breakfast & Lunch daily, Dinner Mon.-Sat. MC, V.

One of Venice's premier hangouts, the Rose Café is a unique hybrid: all at once it's a bohemian coffeehouse, a beachy self-service café and a charming brunch spot. The building itself is an enormous warehouselike space, airy enough to accommodate the inevitable weekend swarms. If you sit inside, you can linger over your cappuccino and croissant for as long as you wish—and most of the patrons, who seem to have no end of time on their hands, take full advantage of this. If you prefer service, there's a sunny side patio with a full menu. The salads, quiches and pastries are unfortunately secondary to the beachy-bohemian atmosphere, but in this case, that's more than all right. About $12 for lunch.

Rösti

908 S. Barrington Ave., Brentwood 90049;
(310) 447-8695
Lunch daily. AE, MC, V.

The owners of nearby Toscana restaurant opened this rôtisserie/take-out in late 1990. The main protein is terrific rosemary-scented, flattened and grilled chicken—some of the juiciest, most flavorful poultry we've tasted. The traditional sides are crusty roasted potatoes fragrant with olive oil, and al dente fresh vegetables. Rösti also offers a good range of cold antipasti (we like the white beans with Italian tuna) along with

fresh pastas of the day, pizzas and sandwiches. While there are a few little tables and some window counter stools, we've come to think of this as just the thing to take home and eat while watching a really good video. About $15 per person.

The Sidewalk Café

1401 Ocean Front Walk, Venice 90291;
(310) 399-5547
Breakfast, Lunch & Dinner daily, Late Supper Fri.-Sat. All major cards.

Probably the only café in town where roller skates are the preferred footwear. This crowded outdoor patio abuts the Venice Beach boardwalk, making a visit here immensely entertaining, especially on a summer weekend, when the passing parade of humanity turns into a virtual freak show. Unfortunately, to enjoy this you'll have to put up with humdrum food, a utilitarian patio, and a truly dingy interior. Keep your choice as simple as possible—a no-frills omelet or burger. About $10.

The Source

8301 W. Sunset Blvd., W. Hollywood 90069;
(213) 656-6388
Breakfast, Lunch, Dinner & Late Supper daily. All major cards.

The white-robed spiritualists are long gone from this L.A. health-food institution, which Woody Allen poked fun at years ago in *Annie Hall*. But it hasn't changed *too* much—you can still get loads of sprouts, healthy salads, brown-rice vegetarian burgers, juices, sandwiches and vegetable concoctions—and no alcohol. The food is quite good, the prices reasonable, breakfast a delight, and the clientele an interesting mix of locals and vegetarian devotees. Request a patio table for a good view of Sunset Boulevard's passing parade. About $12 for lunch.

Sweet Lady Jane

8360 Melrose Ave., W. Hollywood 90069;
(213) 653-7145
Breakfast, Lunch & Dinner (until 11 p.m.) Mon.-Sat. No cards.

One of L.A.'s few sit-down dessert cafés, Sweet Lady Jane has all the charm of a cozy London tea room. It also serves divine home-made desserts: the cheesecakes are perfection (they come in a bouquet of varieties), the lemon tart is heaven and the cookies are big and soft. The coffee is served French-filter–style, and there's also an assortment of teas and other coffee drinks. On weekend evenings after nine or so, there may be a wait to get in, but it's well worth it. Service is quite friendly, and you can indulge in a dessert and beverage for under $8.

Tavern on Main

2907 Main St., Santa Monica 90405;
(310) 392-2772
Lunch, Dinner & Late Supper daily. MC, V.

Santa Monica's busy Main Street suffers from no lack of nosheries and cafés, but one of the better contenders is Tavern on Main, a fine-looking boîte serving up revisionist Americana food in pleasant surroundings. The '30s-era grill decor features a long bar, tiled floors and lots of dark wood. There's also a charming outdoor patio, especially nice for brunch and lunch. The food is unexpectedly fresh and well prepared: generous sandwiches on French rolls, meatloaf, chili. The waffle-cut french fries are excellent, and there's a good selection of salads and lighter fare. Prices are low, about $12 per person for lunch.

Vienna Café

7356 Melrose Ave., Melrose-La Brea District (L.A.) 90046; (213) 651-3822
Breakfast, Lunch, Dinner & Late Supper daily. MC,V.

If you want to know what's hot in Vienna, Austria these days, pay a visit to this little jewel of a café. Attired in the rich golds and greens of celebrated Viennese artist Gustav Klimt's work, the café is yet another eatery spawned by a successful wholesale bakery. This one serves a full menu of Mediterranean café fare (no wiener dogs): we love the crusty sandwich piled with roasted red peppers, eggplant and zucchini. A light lunch with a cappuccino costs $10.

Who's on Third

8369 W. 3rd St., W. Hollywood 90048;
(213) 651-2928
Breakfast & Lunch (until 5 p.m. Mon.-Fri.) daily. MC, V.

Welcome to the postmodern coffee shop. Who's has grafted all the menu trappings of an old-fashioned, small-town luncheonette—from pancakes to French toast, tuna melts to BLTs—and crammed them, along with a few tables and a counter and stools, into a hole-in-the-wall space close by the Beverly Center. The food is good and generous, with some contemporary twists like pesto pasta salads and breakfast linguine; the ambience is unremittingly hip, complete with graffiti-like paintings. You'll have a wait ahead of you at peak breakfast and lunch hours. Breakfast or lunch, about $8; brunch under $10.

For a full listing of cafés and other Bargain Bites open late at night, see "Late-Night Bites" in the INDEXES section at the back of the book.

Zabie's

3003 Ocean Park Blvd., Santa Monica 90405;
(310) 399-1150
Breakfast & Lunch Mon.-Sat., Dinner Mon.-Fri. No cards (checks accepted).

Ocean Park Boulevard has become a hotbed of good dining—not least for this fine little storefront café—actually a minuscule take-out joint with just a few tables and a counter. It is, however, charmingly decorated—and the food can't be faulted. The regularly changing menu includes a spicy vegetarian black-bean chili, tangy sesame noodles, hot Szechuan green beans and a first-class Caesar salad. There are sandwiches, hot and cold pastas and various prepared salads. The pastry chef here turns out beautiful Shaker lemon pies, fruit turnovers wrapped in cream-cheese crusts, buttery shortbread cookies studded with pine nuts, and rich, fudgy brownies. This place packs quite a punch in its tiny space. Lunch is about $12.

San Fernando Valley

Gee, I Can't Believe It's Fish!

14066 Vanowen St., Van Nuys 91405;
(818) 988-3474
Lunch & Dinner Mon.-Sat. No cards.

To paraphrase the old adage, you can't judge a restaurant by its name. Located in the same mini-mall that houses the excellent Mom's Bar-B-Q House, Gee (as we'll call it from here on out) is little more than a kitchen, a counter and a few tables. The Cajun craze may be moribund, but don't tell these folks; the owners are straight from bayou country, and they crank out fried clams, hush puppies, gumbo, jambalaya and catfish to beat the band. You'll get a copious amount of food for around $10.

Maria's Italian Kitchen

13353 Ventura Blvd., Sherman Oaks 91432;
(818) 906-0783
Lunch Mon.-Sat., Dinner daily (until 11 p.m. Mon.-Sat.). D, MC, V.

16608 Ventura Blvd., Encino 91436;
(818) 783-2920
Lunch Mon.-Fri., Dinner daily (until 11 p.m. Fri.-Sat.) D, MC, V.

There's always a wait to get into these little Italian delis and cafés. Their popularity can be attributed to two things: the low prices and the down-home, retro Italian food. This is the kind of simple Italian food that everyone loves, from Italian-style pizza to linguine with pesto to meaty lasagne. If you can't stand the crowds, you can get food to go. A very reasonable $15 per person.

Mogo's

4454 Van Nuys Blvd., Sherman Oaks 91403;
(818) 783-6646
Lunch Mon.-Sat., Dinner nightly. All major cards.

Hidden away in a corner mall, Mogo's is an upscale version of Hollywood's Mongolian Bar-B-Q. There's a buffet stocked with meats and vegetables, an open barbecue, a pile-it-as-high-as-you-can attitude. But Mogo's has spacious, comfortable tables, a soothing decor, relaxed service and meats that seem fresher. The only thing it lacks is Mongolian Bar-B-Q's delicious sesame rolls. But this place offers a great meal in a bowl, an all-you-can-eat, create-your-own mix of beef, pork, turkey, lamb, vegetables and savory or spicy sauces. You pay a little more for the atmosphere: about $12 for a dinner.

Stanley's

13817 Ventura Blvd., Sherman Oaks 91423;
(818) 986-4623
20969 Ventura Blvd., Woodland Hills 91316;
(818) 346-4050
Lunch & Dinner daily (until 11 p.m.; bar until 2 a.m.). AE, MC, V.

If you're looking for love *and* a good hamburger, salad or piece of grilled fish, head for Stanley's, a Valley hot spot. The bar scene hustles and bustles, to say the least; playing second fiddle to the nightly action is the café, which serves better California-style bar-and-grill fare than you might expect. Ingredients are fresh, the cooking is consistent, if uninspired, and the prices aren't bad: about $15 for a light dinner.

San Gabriel Valley

Birdie's

17 S. Raymond Ave., Pasadena 91105;
(818) 449-5884
Breakfast & Lunch daily, Dinner Mon.-Sat., Brunch Sun. V.

Muffins are the specialty of the house at Birdie's, a friendly, '70s-style café with a small outdoor patio. The muffins are huge, fresh and uniformly delicious, from the healthy bran to the decadent chocolate chip. Breakfast is the best meal here—fresh juice, good omelets and egg dishes and, of course, muffins—but we also like Birdie's for lunch and dessert. The baked goods are also available to go from the bakery counter by the door. Under $8 for breakfast.

Burger Continental

535 S. Lake St., Pasadena 91101; (818) 792-6634
Breakfast, Lunch & Dinner (until 10:30 p.m.) daily. MC, V.

Despite its name, there's a lot more to Burger Continental than beef patties. Much of the food is Greek and Armenian (huge plates of lamb kebabs and rice pilaf, moussaka, hummus with pita bread), some of it is American (charbroiled fish and prime rib) and some of it is Italianish (garlicky scampi). While you stand in line at the counter, one of the gregarious brothers who own this place will come by to take your order, which will include a simple salad bar and heaps of rice and vegetables. You eat all this in the brick outdoor patio, which is kept warm with heaters at night. It's popular with local college students, who put away pitchers of beer and platefuls of food. We love Burger Continental much more for its chaotic nuttiness than for the food—but you won't be disappointed with either. About $14 for a large meal for one.

Café Habana

46 E. Colorado Blvd., Pasadena 91101;
(818) 793-2233
Lunch daily, Dinner & Late Supper Tues.-Sun. AE, MC, V.

One of the better of the Cubans that have popping up around town in the past couple of years, Café Habana recently moved across town from Melrose to much bigger, high-ceilinged digs in Pasadena's Old Town. They're still serving the usual Cuban specialties—garlicky shrimp, roast pork—and, while the roast chicken here isn't nearly the epiphany that Versailles's is, Café Habana's version manages to acquit itself nicely. The Cuban sandwich is the real deal—a veritable Dagwood piled with roast pork, ham, pickles and Swiss cheese on a loaf of Cuban bread (typically bone-dry) slathered with mayonnaise, butter and mustard. On a hot summer day, a pitcherful of the sangría here will refresh your spirits. About $18 for dinner; lunch runs about $10.

Crocodile Café

140 S. Lake Ave., Pasadena 91101; (818) 449-9900
Lunch & Dinner daily, Late Supper Tues.-Sat. All major cards.

Gregg and Bob Smith are two very smart businessmen. After importing Californian cuisine to Pasadena via their extremely popular Parkway Grill, they then brought Melrose Avenue's café craze to Pasadena via the Crocodile Café, which has also been packed since the doors opened. Is the food worth the wait during peak dinner hours? Probably not. But if you come at an off-time—a late lunch, an early dinner—you'll enjoy the tasty, inexpensive salads, pastas, pizzas and chic sandwiches. Weather permitting, skip the bright, bustling interior (replete with open kitchen, naturally) and sit on the quieter patio tucked a couple of steps below Lake Avenue. Under $15 for a simple meal.

Julienne
2649 Mission St., San Marino 91108;
(818) 441-2299
*Breakfast (open 7 a.m. Mon.-Fri.) & Lunch Mon.-Sat.
MC, V.*

You can tell the food at Julienne will be great just from the decor—a loving re-creation of a tiny small-town French bistro. Sue Campoy opened this take-out shop and café as an adjunct to her deservedly successful catering business, and now her fame has spread beyond the protected San Gabriel Valley. Fresh rosemary, the house herb, shows up in several wonderful dishes, chief among them the amazing rosemary-raisin bread and the lovely chicken Normandy. There are always several delicious salads, a different quiche each day, a seasonal soup or two, a handful of tempting entrées (roasted lemon-herb chicken, for one) and fabulous, unfussy desserts, from brownies to lemon bars. Lunch, with dessert, will run about $15.

Old Town Bakery
166 W. Colorado Blvd., Pasadena 91105;
(818) 792-7943
*Breakfast, Lunch, Dinner & Late Supper daily. No cards
(checks accepted).*

Southern California's bakery renaissance continues apace, and these days, Old Town Bakery has a good deal of impressive competition. Better than the bread (which comes in about a dozen varieties, including olive, rosemary and even tomato–oat bran) are owner/pastry chef Amy Pressman's cakes and pies. They look like cartoon-size confections, but they taste seriously divine. We love the gooey Milky Way cake, the sophisticated chocolate terrine, complete with edible gold leaf, the fresh-fruit shortcakes and the pies made from fruits in season. There's an outdoor patio as well as the tables inside. You can snack guiltily for about $7.

Robin's
395 N. Rosemead Blvd., Pasadena 91107;
(818) 351-8885
*Breakfast (open 7 a.m.), Lunch, Dinner & Late Supper
daily. AE, MC, V.*

If you fear places that are bright, cheerful and cater to children, skip this one. But if you're looking for a family restaurant that not only tolerates kids but actually encourages their visits, you're in the right place. You and the kids can get basic coffee-shop fare as well as more ambitious items (omelets filled with goat cheese, French garlic sausages), all done very well and with some imagination. The kids have their own menu, starring an excellent french toast encrusted with corn flakes and raisin-nut cereal. There are also french toast specials for hungry adults, made with bananas and walnuts one day, fresh berries and whipped cream the next. Breakfast runs under $7.

Chicken

California Chicken Café
6805 Melrose Ave., Melrose-La Brea District (L.A.)
90038; (213) 935-5877
Lunch & Dinner Mon.-Sat. No cards.

Taking its cue from the many Mexican chicken spots that have sprung up over the past decade, this popular new bare-bones place has them lining up at the counter to buy succulent, marinated, rotisserie-cooked chicken to eat in or take home. Sold in quarters, halves, whole, or chunked and rolled up with vegetables to make one of their burrito-like "chicken wraps," the birds come with commendable side orders—especially the rice pilaf with red peppers, and the red potatoes sauteed with onions and garlic. You can eat well here for under $7.

Kokekokko
360 E. 2nd St., Little Tokyo (L.A.) 90012;
(213) 687-0690
Dinner & Late Supper Mon.-Sat. MC, V.

Kokekokko is what a Japanese rooster crows at the crack of dawn. This terrific Little Tokyo spot is devoted to chicken yakitori—which has far more scope than one might predict. Since the menu isn't in English, ask your waiter to simply bring you his favorite choices, and you'll get a parade of delights: skewers full of chicken livers, grilled chicken, gizzards, chicken skin, wings, chicken meatballs, and chicken kebabs with okra and squash, all traditionally followed by chicken soup and chopped chicken and rice. Each dish is so different, you don't feel as if you're getting "chickened" to death. The crowd is young and exclusively Japanese, and the staff is enthusiastic and helpful. Dinner under $20.

Koo Koo Roo
3450 W. 6th St., Mid-Wilshire District (L.A.)
90020; (213) 383-6414
Lunch & Dinner Mon.-Sat. No cards.
8393 Beverly Blvd., W. Hollywood 90048;
(213) 655-9045
Lunch & Dinner (until 11 p.m.) daily. No cards.

We still haven't figured out in which language *koo koo roo* translates as *cock-a-doodle-do*, but it must be from a language of a people who are very health-conscious. Both branches—the first two of nine to have opened in the area as we go to press—are bright, better-than-average fast-food joints. The chicken is skinless, and it's grilled simply over an open flame after being marinated in a blend of vegetable juices. It's served with a crispy lavoshlike bread, with Middle Eastern-inspired side orders of a cucumber-and-onion salad, tomato and onion salad, bulgur wheat, mixed-bean salad or terrific warm eggplant salad. This food is very tasty, very fresh and very healthy, and for a paltry $5, it's yours for the taking.

Pollo Dorado
4830 Hollywood Blvd., Hollywood 90027;
(213) 663-3628
Lunch & Dinner daily. No cards.

We couldn't possibly cover all the Mexican grilled-chicken places—the El Pollo Locos, Pollo Thises and Pollo Thats—because there are far too many of them. They're all similar, they're all cheap and most all of them are as good as this place. Here $6.99 will get you a whole chicken, marinated and barbecued on a huge open grill, along with ten corn tortillas and your choice of salsas from the salsa bar. The chicken is salty, tender and quite tasty—and it's much healthier than fried chicken. You can eat at the fast-food-style tables or, better yet, take it home.

Roscoe's House of Chicken 'n' Waffles
1514 N. Gower St., Hollywood 90028;
(213) 466-7453/466-9329
Breakfast, Lunch, Dinner & Late Supper (until 3:30 a.m. Fri.-Sat.) daily. AE, MC, V.

5006 W. Pico Blvd., Wilshire District (L.A.) 90019;
(213) 934-4405/936-3730
Breakfast, Lunch, Dinner & Late Supper (until 2 a.m. Fri.-Sat.) daily. AE, MC, V.

106 W. Manchester Ave., South-Central L.A. 90003;
(213) 752-6211/752-7053
Breakfast, Lunch, Dinner & Late Supper (until 1 a.m. Fri.-Sat.) daily. AE, MC, V.

The combination may sound like the kind of offbeat joint *New Yorker* cartoonist Roz Chast might have invented. But we assure you that this down-home combination really works, with bites of sweet, lightly cinnamon-flavored waffle perfectly complementing juicy, crisply coated fried chicken. Try some of the peppery, oniony stewed greens on the side; but steer clear of the mild gravy, which quickly turned to paste as it cooled on our plates. The three locations are crowded at all hours with regulars filling up on Southern comfort food for under $12.

Zankou Chicken
5065 Sunset Blvd., Hollywood 90027;
(213) 665-7842
Lunch, Dinner and Late Supper daily. No cards.

This little joint is fast food at its best. Zankou serves Armenian/Middle Eastern food that is

unbelievably good and astoundingly cheap. The real draw here is, obviously, chicken: big, fat birds roasted on a rotisserie until they're crisp and crackling. Infused with garlic, they're served with a thick, scrumptious dipping sauce, and with side dishes of tabouli and hummus dip, all of which can be tucked into pita bread. Zankou also serves excellent stuffed grape leaves, shwarma, shish kebab and falafel, and while there are tables, we think it's best taken home. A meal costs $7.

Coffeehouses

L.A. for the past few years has been in the throes of a coffeehouse craze. Each of the seemingly hundreds of new joints offers its own free-wheeling mix of good (often sophisticated) coffees and espresso drinks. Some offer pastries and desserts too; others have a light menu of salads and soups. Many coffeehouses are fascinating hybrids, supplementing their drinks with anything from books, art shows or poetry readings to pool tables, films or live music. The evolution of the casual java joint has brought the coffeehouse to significant heights as part of L.A.s night scene, so we've listed some of the city's best coffeehouses along with the bars and clubs. *See* "LOS ANGELES Nightlife."

Coffee Shops & Diners

Barron's Café
4130 W. Burbank Blvd., Burbank 91505;
(818) 846-0043
Open Mon.-Fri. 7 a.m.-7:30 p.m., Sat. 8 a.m.-1 p.m. No cards.

Let Ed Debevic's play all-American make-believe—this Burbank institution is the real thing, as American as they come. The neighborhood is bare-bones Burbank, the interior is cozy, cluttered, kitschy Americana, the waitresses are friendly pros, and the food is good, hearty and cheap. Breakfast is the main event: rich french toast, good pancakes, crisp bacon and simple eggs, along with plenty of good coffee. You'll dine among the blessedly unpretentious—men wearing Cat caps and work boots, women tending to small children. A really good breakfast can be had for $7.

Beverly Hills Breakfast Club
9671 Wilshire Blvd., Beverly Hills 90210;
(310) 271-8903
Open Mon.-Sat. 7 a.m.-6 p.m., Sun. 8 a.m.-3 p.m. AE, MC, V.

Okay, so this place is a little too self-conscious and the food is a little uneven. But it's hard to fault a fun, attractive restaurant that's located in the heart of ultra-rich Beverly Hills and costs only $7 a head for breakfast or lunch. You won't go wrong with the eggs, the delicious french toast, the respectable tuna-salad sandwich or some of the simpler salads. It's well located for a break from a Neiman's-Saks-Magnin's shopping spree. Under $5 for breakfast, $8 for lunch.

Café '50s
838 Lincoln Blvd., Venice 90292; (310) 399-1955
Open Sun.-Thurs. 7 a.m.-11 p.m., Fri.-Sat. 7 a.m.-midnight. No cards.

4609 Van Nuys Blvd., Sherman Oaks 91403;
(818) 906-1955
Open Sun.-Thurs. 8 a.m.-midnight, Fri.-Sat. 8 a.m.-1 a.m. MC, V.

One of the early contenders in the neodiner movement, Café '50s is great fun. Fifties posters line the walls of these cheery but authentically dingy diners, which are full night and day. Perky waitresses and busboys sing in full voice with the great (but loud) jukebox oldies; patrons also sing along sometimes, when they aren't busy eating the simple fare named for Patsy Cline, Fats Domino, Ritchie Valens and *Leave It to Beaver.* The burgers are good, the salads passable and the prices low—under $8.

Chili John's
2018 W. Burbank Blvd., Burbank 91506;
(818) 846-3611
Open Tues.-Fri. 11 a.m.-7 p.m., Sat. 11 a.m.-4 p.m. No cards.

Chili John's, an old-fashioned, brightly lit lunch counter that reminds us of something Edward Hopper might have painted, has been an institution on sleepy Burbank Blvd. for 50-odd years. John Isaac perfected his chili recipe back in Wisconsin: a rich, headily aromatic mixture based on ground steak, generously seasoned with chili powder and other spices and simmered for twenty hours. You can get it mild, medium or authentically hot—ladled straight into a bowl, over your choice of red beans (excellent) or spaghetti (flaccid and boring). There's also—shades of the present day—a good version made from freshly ground chicken. Finish with a slab of their own lemon- or pineapple-cream pie—a great refresher for the tastebuds. About $16 for a big bowl of chili, pie and a beverage.

Dinah's
6521 S. Sepulveda Blvd., Westchester 90045;
(310) 645-0456
Open daily 6 a.m.-10 p.m. All major cards.

Dinah's is that sprawling, tacky-looking coffee shop that you always pass on the way to LAX, the one with with signs announcing its all-you-can-eat meals for under $6. Next time, don't just pass it by—stop in and enjoy some pretty darned good plain ol' food. Breakfast is the unsung treat here. The pancakes are the size of Frisbees, and the huge, puffy, skillet-baked German apple pancake dusted with powdered sugar is one of our favorite morning treats in town. The tasty omelets and other egg dishes are also of grand proportions—all for less than $8.

Duke's
8909 W. Sunset Blvd., W. Hollywood 90069;
(310) 652-9411
Open Mon.-Fri. 7:30 a.m.-9 p.m., Sat.-Sun. 7:30 a.m.-4 p.m. No cards.

Duke's has survived its move to Sunset Boulevard and a more contemporary, fashionable decor, though we miss the charm of the old place in the worn Tropicana Motel on Santa Monica Boulevard. Duke's is legendary in L.A., sort of a Polo Lounge for the hip and happening who line up on the sidewalk every weekend morning. Breakfast is the meal to have here, and for good reason—it's simple, generous and very good. Nothing fancy, just the eggs-bacon-omelet-pancake basics. About $7 for breakfast.

DuPar's Coffee Shop
12036 Ventura Blvd., Studio City 91604;
(818) 766-4437
Open Sun.-Thurs. 6 a.m.-1 a.m., Fri.-Sat. 6 a.m.-4 a.m. AE, MC, V.

There are branches of DuPar's all around Los Angeles, but this one is by far the best. The food is no different than what you'll find at the other locations, but the clientele makes this one of the hippest Valley early-morning/late-night hangouts. Studio executives, trendy teenagers, actors and Sherman Oaks suburbanites all frequent DuPar's, drinking the good coffee and eating excellent french toast, pancakes, egg dishes and pies (the rest of the food is decent but mediocre). About $7 for breakfast.

For more money-saving meal ideas, see "Cheap Eats" in the INDEXES section at the back of the book, which lists full-fledged restaurants where you can eat for $15 or less.

Ed Debevic's

134 N. La Cienega Blvd., Beverly Hills 90048;
(310) 659-1952
Open Sun.-Thurs. 11:30 a.m.-11 p.m., Fri.-Sat. 11:30 a.m.-1 a.m. MC, V.

The owner of Ed Debevic's brought the blueprint for his Chicago retro-diner to L.A. five years ago, cloned it on La Cienega Boulevard and was an instant success. This huge, slick diner is campy and theatrical, but what it lacks in authenticity it makes up for in zany fun. Outlandish, gum-cracking waitresses serve up decent but lifeless diner standards (meatloaf, burgers, chili, french fries) while busboys clown and sing along with blaring rock oldies. People can't get enough of it—Debevic's is packed night and day. The chaos and mediocre food give us a headache, but we can't be too critical: you can make the red-hot scene, get fed and get out for less than $10 for lunch or dinner.

Jan's

8424 Beverly Blvd., Melrose-Fairfax District (L.A.) 90048; (213) 651-2866
Open daily 6 a.m.-1 a.m. D, MC, V.

Jan's is the quintessential '50s coffee shop, complete with Googie-style architecture, acres of Formica and Naugahyde—and homey, down-to-earth food that's as good as coffee-shop fare gets. An eclectic crowd converges here, from seniors to punkers to nerds. They all dine happily on generous portions of meatloaf and mashed potatoes, burgers, salads, blue-plate specials, homemade pies and puddings, all of it fresh and properly cooked. Breakfasts are huge and satisfying, and if you're a root-beer-float fan, Jan's whips up one of L.A.'s best. Dinner is about $8.

John O'Groats

10516 W. Pico Blvd., W.L.A. 90064;
(310) 204-0692
Open Mon.-Fri. 7 a.m.-3 p.m., Sat.-Sun 7 a.m.-2 p.m. MC, V.

We hate to publicize this wonderful place—part of its charm lies in its relative obscurity, and we would love to continue to be seated quickly here. The owners, Robert and Angelica Jacoby will tell you how they visited the tiny Scottish town of John O'Groats, and were so impressed that they named their restaurant for it. The Jacobys will feed you well, with housemade crisp, nongreasy fish and chips; omelets stuffed with spinach or homemade salsa; marvelous biscuits; home-fried potatoes; and tasty soups. Since the kitchen is tiny and the staff is small, expect a lag time between ordering and eating—but it's worth the wait. Under $7 for breakfast or lunch.

Larry Parker's Beverly Hills Diner

206 S. Beverly Dr., Beverly Hills 90212;
(310) 274-5655
Open daily 24 hours. All major cards.

Were diners ever this hip in the '50s? TV screens flash music videos, an impressive sound system belts out the hot dance music of the minute, zany waitresses chat up the patrons and the gargantuan menu covers it all: burgers, endless sandwiches and omelets, pancakes, pastas, vegie plates, Mexican, Chinese . . . you name a dish, they'll make it happen. The merely okay food isn't the draw: high-school students and lawyers alike crowd into the fire engine–red booths and the sidewalk tables to grab a bite and have a great time. Don't miss the huge, creamy-rich Häagen-Dazs shakes. A meal costs $10 to $15.

Millie's Country Kitchen

10318 Sepulveda Blvd., Mission Hills 91345;
(818) 365-7597
Open Sun.-Thurs. 6 a.m.-11 p.m., Fri.-Sat. 6 a.m.-midnight. All major cards.

This upscale chain coffee shop is as perky and bright as a calico apron, and it serves immense portions of good-ol'-boy food that's more than a cut above all the chain competitors'. When you've got a hankering for chicken-fried steak, fried chicken with mashed potatoes, biscuits and gravy, pot roast and deep-dish pies, you could do a lot worse than Millie's. It's a great place for kids and seniors—kind of a campy bit of ex–urban America, at pre-inflation prices. You'll let a couple of notches out of your belt for around $10.

Millie's Inc.

3524 W. Sunset Blvd., Silverlake 90026;
(213) 661-5292
Open Mon.-Fri. 7 a.m.-midnight, Sat. 8 a.m.-4 a.m., Sun. 8 a.m.-10 p.m. No cards.

Millie's is a real insider's place, where musicians, artists and assorted neighborhood folk hang out, trading jokes and insults with owner Magenta and her wacky crew. The food is hearty, homemade, cheap and good. Heavy biscuits and gravy are the thing to get here, along with eggs and seriously spicy home-fried potatoes. The decor is bare-bones retro diner, and the countertop jukebox music is always great. Under $8 for breakfast or lunch.

Norms

1601 Lincoln Blvd., Santa Monica 90404 (Branches everywhere); (310) 540-0074
Open daily 24 hours. No cards.

Owned and operated by Norman Royback (that's Norm) and his family since 1949, Norms, with its slew of branches all over Southern California, steadfastly preserves the heyday of the

131

fifties moderne coffee shop. Frankly, we find them a little bit depressing, like entering a time machine that whisks us back to the Eisenhower era. But, when we're short on cash, we can't argue with the value of their generous $8 steak dinner, a great deal with several side dishes.

Original Pantry Café/Bake Shoppe

877 S. Figueroa St., Downtown (L.A.) 90017; (213) 627-6879
Café: open daily 24 hours. Bake Shoppe: open Mon.-Fri. 6 a.m.-3 p.m., Sat.-Sun. 6 a.m.-9 p.m. No cards.

This little gem hasn't been a "bake shoppe" for a few years; it's actually a full-fledged café and diner. The main café is a poor man's Palm: plain food (and plenty of it) cooked well, and a team of veteran, no-nonsense waiters. Prominent L.A. attorney and businessman Richard Riordan is the owner, and he and his circle of L.A.-business elite are often in residence. But all manner of other regulars come for the delicious charbroiled steaks, the oversized pork and lamb chops and daily specials like macaroni and cheese. Breakfasts are legendary; enormous omelets, very good bacon and pan-fried potatoes and thick sliced breads. If you crave frills, ambience, chatty service or privacy, this place ain't for you. But where else can you feed a family of four for $30—and still need doggie bags?

The bake shop next door is tiny—just a handful of tables and a counter. The breakfasts are the same gut-busting feasts, and the bakery makes guilty pleasures such as sticky buns, cinnamon rolls and brownies. Lunch runs about $8 or less.

Rae's

2901 Pico Blvd., Santa Monica 90405; (310) 828-7937
Open daily 5:30 a.m.-10:30 p.m. No cards.

This small, turquoise-blue joint is a classic '50s diner—the real thing, not a re-creation. As at most of L.A.'s good breakfast spots, patrons line up outside on weekends, waiting patiently for a chance to be served good pancakes, french toast, omelets and biscuits with gravy by frenetic uniformed waitresses. Hardly elegant, but good, home-style breakfasts at thoroughly reasonable prices: about $6.

Rose City Diner

45 S. Fair Oaks Ave., Pasadena 91105; (818) 793-8282
Open daily 6:30 a.m.-2 a.m. No cards.

Rose City is evidence enough that this pseudodiner business has gone far enough. In a glistening, neo-'50s setting that reeks of phoniness, dolled-up waitresses serve dismal diner fare to a happy crowd that seems to thrive on the retro look and inexpensive food. Personally, we'd rather have a simple tuna sandwich at home, or eat at an honest, all-American coffee shop where we feel perfectly comfortable stuffing ourselves. About $8 for a burger and a shake.

Vickman's

1228 E. 8th St., Downtown (L.A.) 90021; (213) 622-3852
Open Mon.-Fri. 3 a.m.-3 p.m., Sat. 3 a.m.-1 p.m., Sun 7 a.m.-1 p.m. No cards.

Another L.A. institution. The two vast, barebones rooms that make up Vickman's are reminiscent of an Eastern European mess hall. Fittingly, it fills up at opening (3 a.m. except Sundays) with hard-working folk from the nearby flower and produce markets, who come to fill up on eggs and pancakes before the long day begins. Lunches offer deli sandwiches, basic salads and a few daily specials (chicken schnitzel, barbecued spare ribs) priced at around $6. Vickman's is a bakery more than anything else, and its sweet rolls, coffee cakes, pies and cakes are absolutely delicious, if a bit on the heavy side. Breakfast is less than $5.

Village Coffee Shop

2695 N. Beachwood Dr., Hollywood 90068; (213) 467-5398
Open Mon.-Fri. 8 a.m.-6:30 p.m., Sat. 8 a.m.-5 p.m. No cards.

Known as the Beachwood Café to its many regulars, this simple coffee shop in the Hollywood Hills is a favorite of the many actors who live in the neighborhood. The menu lists classic coffee-shop fare, from pancakes and various omelets to juicy french dips and hamburgers. The food is plain and good, and the atmosphere is friendly and unhurried (except on Saturdays, when a crowd gathers to while away the morning hours, reading the papers filling up on honest food). About $14 for breakfast or lunch for two.

Zucky's

431 Wilshire Blvd., Santa Monica 90401; (310) 393-0551
Open daily 24 hours. All major cards.

For those cruising the desolate streets of Santa Monica at 3 a.m., desperately seeking sustenance, here's where to go for everything from omelets to hot sandwiches to cheesecake.

We're always interested to hear about your discoveries, and to receive your comments on ours. Please feel free to write to us, and do state clearly exactly what you liked or disliked.

Delis

Art's Deli

12224 Ventura Blvd., Studio City 91604;
(818) 762-1221
Open daily 7:30 a.m.-9:30 p.m. All major cards.

Art's is certainly one of the best delis in town, though it's also among the most expensive. Addicts come from all over to be crowded into this big room, done in gold tones of vinyl and Formica, and served by the usual abrupt, unsmiling waitresses. You'll quickly forgive the place when you bite into the outstanding lean corned beef sandwich, very fresh lox, first-rate smoked-fish platter, fresh-baked bagels or one of the monstrous combination sandwiches. Giant color photos of these creations line the walls, along with signs proclaiming, EVERY SANDWICH IS A WORK OF ART. We can forgive the smiling, rotund patron, Art Ginsberg, though—anyone who prepares deli so consistently well can make all the bad puns he wants. Under $15.

Canter's

419 N. Fairfax Ave., Melrose-Fairfax District (L.A.)
90036; (213) 651-2030
Open daily 24 hours. MC, V.

Located in the heart of L.A.'s Jewish community, Canter's is certainly the best-known deli in town. Unfortunately, its reputation is undeserved, unless you're a native and have a sentimental, Proustian attachment to the place (as we do). The serving staff has almost no patience and even less charm, and the bland chicken soup would be hard pressed to cure even the sniffles. The rest of the deli fare is decent but not much more, and in good deli tradition, the desserts are awful. But Canter's deserves praise for staying open 24 hours a day. And, it's the only deli in L.A. proper that feels authentic. About $12.

Carnegie Deli

300 N. Beverly Dr., Beverly Hills 90210;
(310) 275-3354
Open Sun.-Thurs. 7:30 a.m.-10 p.m., Fri.-Sat. 7:30 a.m.-midnight. AE, MC, V.

The king of the New York delis is thriving in L.A., thanks to the largesse of large billionaire Marvin Davis. This version, with its dark wooden booths and panoramic views of bustling Beverly Drive, is far spiffier than the comfortably run-down New York original. But, for the most part, the food hasn't lost anything in the translation, except that the rye bread in Manhattan is better. You'll get quintessential deli fare: great corned beef and pastrami, tender brisket (ask for it with

the authentically lumpy mashed potatoes), the best smoked fish outside of Barney Greengrass in New York, state-of-the-art potato pancakes and blintzes, a soul-satisfying mushroom-and-barley soup and the best cheesecake in the known world. The portions are beyond gargantuan, so keep in mind when you initially blanch at the prices that just about anything you order can be shared. Dinner is about $15.

Greenblatt's Delicatessen

8017 W. Sunset Blvd., Hollywood 90046;
(213) 656-0606
Open daily 9 a.m.-2 a.m. AE, MC, V.

Deli-lovers accustomed to the standard lack of any decor will be pleasantly surprised at Greenblatt's. Its small upstairs dining room is handsome and comfortable, a place where you can sit and schmooze for hours over a hot pastrami and coffee without being rushed. While not great deli, the food is perfectly fine, if a little expensive. Don't miss the great cheesecake, but pass on the pecan pie. The place doubles as a wine shop (*see* "LOS ANGELES Shops"). About $14 for a sandwich dinner.

Junior's

2379 Westwood Blvd., W.L.A. 90064;
(310) 475-5771
Open Mon.-Thurs. 6:30 a.m.-11 p.m., Fri. 6:30 a.m.-12:30 a.m., Sat. 7 a.m.-12:30 a.m., Sun. 7 a.m-11 p.m. MC, V.

The erstwhile "Cadillac of delis" has acquired a streamlined new look of late. Its sleekly remodeled interior, all blond wood and natty upholstery, is so California-contemporary you may forget you're there for pastrami and lox. The sliced meats and smoked fishes are, to our taste, as good as any we've tried in other local establishements, even in New York. Sandwiches are generous and the chicken soup—a fine-tasting, nongreasy elixir—comes packed with generous chunks of meat and vegetables, as well as a mini-loaf of rye bread. We're partial to the dinner specials, particularly the roasted half-chicken. Lunch runs about $10; dinner about $14.

Langer's

704 S. Alvarado St., Downtown (L.A.) 90057;
(213) 483-8050
Open daily 6:30 a.m.-9 p.m. MC, V.

A sign in the window reworks an old adage: "When in doubt, eat hot pastrami." Wise advice, especially if you eat Langer's legendary pastrami, which is lean, delicious and copiously served. We counted at least 27 pastrami dishes on the extensive menu, the rest of which lists all the deli classics: blintzes, lox, chopped liver, gefilte fish and so on. The corned beef is terrific, the various soups are tasty, and the rye bread is the best in town. Despite the bad neighborhood and the dismal atmosphere, Langer's is one of our favorite delis in L.A. Go figure. About $11 for lunch.

Mort's Malibu Deli
3894 Cross Creek Rd., Malibu 90265;
(310) 456-2444
Open Mon.-Thurs. 8 a.m.-9 p.m., Fri.-Sat. 8 a.m.-10 p.m., Sun. 8 a.m.-8 p.m. AE, MC, V.

A good deli in Malibu? Who would believe it? Well, it's true—and it's not just good for Malibu; it could easily hold its own in Los Angeles proper. The room itself is bright and tastefully decorated. The Nova Scotia lox and other smoked fish are absolutely fresh and delicious, the pastrami is lean and peppery, the corned beef tasty and rich, and the chopped liver as good as grandma's. You may well see a few stars, making the inevitable wait for a table easier to endure. Lunch for under $10.

Nate 'n' Al's Delicatessen
414 N. Beverly Dr., Beverly Hills 90210;
(310) 274-0101
Open daily 7:30 a.m.-9 p.m. AE, MC, V.

Who would think that a small, unadorned coffeeshop would become on of the most established industry hangouts in Beverly Hills (the industry being Hollywood, of course)? A strange assortment of slick studio executives, well-to-do Beverly Hills matrons, TV actors and cigar-chomping men gather here regularly. The huge menu presents the full range of moderately priced deli fare, which has a tendency to be dull—just-average lox, tasteless corned beef sandwiches and soups that are sometimes bland. But the cheese blintzes are terrific, the pickles great and most of the sandwiches respectable. Deli aficionados run the risk of being disappointed, but stargazers will love the schmoozfest. About $10 for lunch.

Pico Kosher Deli
8826 W. Pico Blvd., Rancho Park 90035;
(310) 273-9381
Open Sun.-Thurs. 9 a.m.-7:30 p.m., Fri. 9 a.m.-2:30 p.m. No cards.

One of the few genuine kosher (not "kosher-style," a euphemism for "nonkosher") delis in town, Pico Kosher is a nondescript-looking room filled with people chewing on superb corned beef and pastrami sandwiches. The food here is good enough for any Jewish mother to approve. About $20 for lunch for two.

Stage Deli
Century City Mall, 10250 Santa Monica Blvd., Century City 90067; (310) 553-3354
Open Mon.-Thurs. 7:30 a.m.-11 p.m., Fri.-Sat. 7:30 a.m.-midnight, Sun. 7:30 a.m.-10 p.m. AE, MC, V.

The legendary Stage Deli in New York would be a little embarrassed by its wimpy relative in L.A. On the up side, it's a good-looking place, cavernous and decorated with old movie posters, and the food is generally quite good, as long as you stick to the sandwiches, salads and such standards as potato pancakes, blintzes and stuffed cabbage. But on the down side, the soups taste bland and packaged—a deli that serves a poor chicken soup should be ashamed of itself—and the desserts often seem tired. Service varies wildly from professional and attentive to sloppy and indifferent. We are, however, still supporters of the Stage—especially since it's a great spot for pre- or post-movie and theater dining in Century City. We just wish they would pay a little more attention to detail. Dinner is about $15.

Dim Sum

Although L.A.'s Chinese community has been going out for tea lunches—otherwise known as dim sum—as long as Chinatown has been around, the rest of the city has only recently discovered the many joys of this fine tradition. "Dim sum" loosely translates as "delights of the heart," which is exactly what they are—delicious, savory (and sometimes sweet) small dishes, from buns and dumplings to spring rolls and spareribs.

You'll find dim sum served in two ways. The first and most authentic is found at Chinese restaurants in Chinatown or the Monterey Park/Alhambra area. Chinese women navigate stainless-steel carts through the large dining rooms, showing off the carts' contents for anyone interested. If their English is no better than your Chinese, you can just point to the dishes that intrigue you. They usually run from $1.25 to $2 each; your tab is figured by counting the number of empty plates on the table or the number of rubber-stamp marks on your check.

The other is at one of the growing crop of trendy, anglicized dim sum cafés, foremost among them Chin Chin and Chopstix (*see* listings in "LOS ANGELES Restaurants"). The offerings in those places can be quite good, the scene is bright and lively and you can get out easily for under $20 per person.

ABC Seafood
205 Ott St., Chinatown (L.A.) 90012;
(213) 680-2887
Dim sum daily 8 a.m.-2:30 p.m. MC, V.

ABC is a well-respected, better-than-average Chinese seafood restaurant that serves very good dim sum every day. Young women who can sometimes be less than friendly work the large, open room, hawking their wares: open-faced meat dumplings called shu mai, shrimp hidden in thick rice noodles, barbecued pork, baked and steamed bao buns and all manner of other exotic dishes. The selection is broader than at most Chinatown dim sums, and the quality is much better than average. Less than $8 per person.

Bao Wow

17209 Ventura Blvd., Encino 91316;
(818) 789-9010
Dim sum, Lunch & Dinner daily. MC, V.

One of the new breed of dim sum restaurants, Bao Wow has combined a hip, high-tech decor and a square Encino mini-mall location with surprisingly decent dim sum. While tables of teenage Valley girls giggle around you, you can sample delicious "dancing shrimp," crisp pan-fried shrimp dumplings; "dumplings on fire," which have quite wonderful flavors but little fire; good shu mai and pan-fried wontons; and fine lo mein noodles. The house specialty, bao buns, can be very good if they are fresh, and not so good if they've been sitting in the steamer for a few hours. They also offer other Chinese stir-fry dishes, priced higher than the dim sum. About $10 for a dim sum meal.

Chin Chin

8618 Sunset Blvd., W. Hollywood 90069;
(310) 652-1818
11740 San Vicente Blvd., Brentwood 90049;
(310) 826-2525
See review in "LOS ANGELES Restaurants."

Chopstix

7229 Melrose Ave., W. Hollywood 90046;
(213) 937-1111
46 W. Colorado Blvd., Pasadena 91101;
(818) 405-1111
See review in "LOS ANGELES Restaurants."

Empress Pavilion

988 N. Hill St., Chinatown (L.A.) 90012;
(213) 617-9898
Dim sum daily 9 a.m.-3 p.m. MC, V.

Chinatown's most promising restaurant in eons is also one of the city's finest dim sum houses. The setting is grand in the Hong Kong style, with a series of sliding walls that can make the restaurant either huge or intimate. For dim sum, it's authentically huge, though not quite as chaotic as it can get elsewhere. Waitresses who are a tad friendlier than most (though they're still not about to chat you up) wheel by the usual carts laden with the usual range of dim sum delights, but the freshness and flavor of each is much better than usual. Our only complaint is that the selection seems fairly ordinary. Under $10 per person.

Mandarin Deli

Chinese Food Center, 727 N. Broadway, Chinatown (L.A.) 90012; (213) 623-6054
Dim sum daily 11 a.m.-9 p.m. No cards.
356 E. 2nd St., Little Tokyo (L.A.) 90012;
(213) 617-0231
Dim sum Sun.-Thurs. 11 a.m.-9:30 p.m., Fri.-Sat. 11 a.m.-10 p.m. All major cards.

The sign over the original Mandarin Deli says NOODLES AND DUMPLINGS, and if you look in the window you'll see the chefs making those very dishes. The flawless pan-fried dumplings come to your table still steaming and are best eaten flavored with a bit of hot chili oil and a splash of white vinegar. There are also boiled-fish and pork dumplings. The savory, heart-warming noodle soups work especially well if coupled with the Mandarin-style cold noodles, which are bathed in a richly spiced sesame sauce. Atmosphere is nonexistent at the Chinatown branch, but the Little Tokyo branch boasts comfortable booths and an attempt at a decor. Under $10 for a huge meal.

New World Restaurant

2000 W. Main St., Alhambra 91801;
(818) 282-8833
Dim sum daily 8 a.m.-3 p.m. MC, V.

Here is one of the best dim sums in town. New World—which used to be called Casa de Oriente—is a large, opulent, handsome place, with much better than average service and uniformly good food. All the dim sum are great—bao buns, potstickers, rice noodles and much, much more—but the real winners are the sweets, from sesame balls with red bean paste to incredible coconut snowballs filled with a sweet peanut purée. Try to restrain your orders—there's always sure to be an enticing dish on the next cart that's wheeled by. Dim sum costs under $15.

Ocean Seafood

747 N. Broadway, Chinatown (L.A.) 90012;
(213) 687-3088
Dim sum daily 9 a.m.-3 p.m. MC, V.

When this place was called Miriwa, it was one of our favorite dim sum palaces in town. Now, under new ownership, we've been delighted to discover that it's even better. The owners have smartened up the premises, and service is smarter, too: The women pushing carts piled high with steamer baskets now seem downright eager to please customers who might not speak Chinese. And they offer a more imaginative and higher-quality selection of dim sum than just about anyplace in town, ranging from standards like shu mai and har gow to almost nouvelle seafood creations like deep-fried seaweed-wrapped shrimp rolls and translucent rice paper wrappers filled with scallops and cilantro. One word of caution: Westerners tend to be automatically offered the most mainstream selections, and we've discovered some of our favorite new dim sum by pressing the servers to show us everything they have on their carts. Plan to spend about $10 for a veritable feast.

Hamburgers & Sandwiches

The Apple Pan

10801 W. Pico Blvd., W.L.A. 90064;
(310) 475-3585
Open Tues. & Sun. 11 a.m.-midnight, Fri.-Sat. 11 a.m.-1 a.m. No cards.

The acclaimed Apple Pan is a godsend for the absolutely starving—your order will be hurled at you in about 45 seconds. The cooks/waiters race around inside the horseshoe-shaped counter (no tables—service would take too long), spewing forth hamburgers (try the hickory burger), Virginia ham sandwiches and apple pie à la mode, all of which are delicious and quite satisfying. Those waiting for seats will stare ravenously at you, making sure you devour your food as quickly as it was thrown at you. About $9 for a burger, Coke and pie.

Barney's Beanery

8447 Santa Monica Blvd., W. Hollywood 90069;
(213) 654-2287
Open daily 10 a.m.-2 a.m. AE, MC, V.

Not for the indecisive—Barney's offers some 150 hamburgers, 20 hot dogs, 50 sandwiches 90 omelets, 25 scrambled egg dishes and 65 variations of chili. Needless to say, with a menu this monstrous you can't expect the finest cuisine. It's all edible, but you don't come to Barney's for the food—you come for the appealingly scruffy atmosphere and the fantastic beer selection: more than 200 labels from around the world. The place is a maze of pool tables, coffee shop–like booths, video games and a long, dark bar. The city of West Hollywood has thankfully forced Barney's to take down the NO FAGGOTS ALLOWED sign that was over the bar, but the clientele is still conspicuously straighter than the neighborhood. Under $12 for a chiliburger with fries and an excellent beer.

The Burger That Ate L.A.

7624 Melrose Ave., Melrose-Fairfax District (L.A.) 90046; (213) 653-2647
Open Sun.-Thurs. 11:30 a.m.-10 p.m., Fri.-Sat. 11:30 a.m.-10:30 p.m. No cards.

Like a special effect run amok from a 1950s horror flick, T.B.T.A.L.A.'s eye-catching architecture portrays a gargantuan burger on a sesame bun, chomping down on City Hall. It's garish fun, perfectly in tune with Melrose's visual cacophony. While there's plenty of patio seating, we prefer to cower beneath the giant tomato slice that hovers over the indoor counter—the better to view the chefs preparing large, thick, juicy burgers, as well as crisp, thin fries. We suggest, though, ordering your burger without the radioactive-green relish they tend to slather on here. About $7 should vanquish a rampaging appetite.

Cassell's Hamburgers

3266 W. 6th St., Mid-Wilshire District (L.A.) 90020; (213) 480-8668
Open Mon.-Sat. 10:30 a.m.-4 p.m. No cards.

Hard-core fans of the classic burger swear by Cassell's, considered by many to serve the best hamburger in town. You won't be able to get sprouts, avocado, caviar or other such trendy nonsense on your burger here. Instead, you'll get a simple, large hamburger made with freshly ground beef, huge buns, homemade mayonnaise and fresh lettuce, tomatoes and pickles. The spicy homemade potato salad is as good as its reputation warrants. At lunchtime you'll have to stand in line with the local pinstripe-suit set at the order counter; no attempt at decor, comfort or ambience has been made. Under $7 for a cheeseburger, fries and fresh lemonade.

Hampton's

1342 N. Highland Ave., Hollywood 90028;
(213) 469-1090
Open Mon. 7 a.m.-3 p.m., Tues.-Thurs. 7 a.m.-10 p.m., Fri. 7 a.m.-11 p.m., Sat.-Sun. 5 p.m.-10 p.m.
4301 Riverside Dr., Burbank 91505; (818) 845-3009
Open Mon.-Fri. 7 a.m.-10 p.m., Sat. 7 a.m.-11 p.m., Sun. 10 a.m.-11 p.m. AE, MC, V.

Not for the burger purist, Hampton's lets all the stops out—here you can find burgers topped with everything imaginable, from bacon, avocado and chili to caviar and grape jelly. Stick to the simpler combinations, which can be very good. For the health-conscious, there's a delicious turkey burger; for the splurger, there's a wonderful cheesecake. The Burbank branch (in the neighborhood of Toluca Lake) is great for star-spotting, because of its proximity to the Valley movie studios. Both branches of Hampton's are handsome in a '70s sort of way, with lots of wood and greenery—which means these burgers will cost more than those at its rival, Cassell's. About $10 per person for a hamburger lunch or dinner—more if you add a slice of the oustanding "fudge pie."

Johnny Rocket's
7507 Melrose Ave., Melrose-Fairfax District (L.A.) 90046; (213) 651-3361
474 N. Beverly Dr., Beverly Hills 90210; (310) 271-2222
14561 Ventura Blvd., Sherman Oaks 91403; (818) 501-1000
Open Sun.-Thurs. 11 a.m.-midnight, Fri.-Sat. 11 a.m.-2 a.m. No cards.

Imagine a slick neodiner, throw in a mob of Melrose Avenue scenesters and the most hyperactively cheerful staff imaginable, and you get Johnny Rocket's. Check your local pod mall today, you may well find that one of these bright burger spots has just sprung up. The fare is limited to burgers, fries, fountain drinks and pies, and it's all pretty good, especially the juicy, smallish burger (the meat of which has been seasoned) and the generous shakes. There's always a crowd, and there's no order to the wait—arguments over who gets seated sometimes flare up among the hungry people lining the wall. You can also sit at an outside table. The other branches are popular with parents and kids. About $9 for a burger, chili fries and Coke.

Mo Better Meatty Meat Burger
5855 W. Pico Blvd., Wilshire District (L.A.) 90019; (213) 938-6558
Open Mon.-Thurs. 11 a.m.-8 p.m., Fri.-Sat. 11 a.m.-10 p.m.

Those of us who have been fans for many years still call it Meatty Meat Burger, even though the shop—which consists of a take-out window and outdoor tables—got a "mo better," spiffy new green building, complete with neon detailing. The burgers here are, indeed, big, juicy, perfectly seasoned and—well, "meatty." We like ours with a generous helping of grilled onions, and over time we tend to avoid the lackluster chili—more like a slightly spicy Bolognese sauce. The freshly cut fries are terrific—as big as Lincoln Logs. If only they could do something about the slow service: we've waited up to twenty minutes for an order. About $6.

Philippe's Original Sandwich Shop
1001 N. Alameda St., Downtown (L.A.) 90012; (213) 628-3781
Open daily 6 a.m.-10 p.m. No cards.

Philippe's is an L.A. classic. Since 1908, businesspeople, tourists, truck drivers and the unemployed have been lining up at the huge counter to order wonderful beef, pork or lamb french-dip sandwiches. The decor of this cavernous landmark is early fast food: sawdust on the floors and high stools along shared tables. The signature French dip sandwich at Philippe's goes for $3.40, which is hard to beat. Round out your sandwich with a decent potato salad and one of the many imported beers, or try Philippe's coffee, still Depression-priced at ten cents a cup. It isn't the greatest coffee in town, but it's a dime well spent.

Pie 'n' Burger
913 E. California Blvd., Pasadena 91106; (818) 795-1123
Open Mon.-Fri. 6 a.m.-10 p.m., Sat. 7 a.m.-10 p.m., Sun. 7 a.m.-8 p.m. (winter) & 7 a.m.-9 p.m. (summer). No cards.

A no-frills place with a no-frills name that says it all. The pecan pie is to die for, all the other pies are very good, and the simple, all-American hamburger is fresh and tasty. Otherwise, except for good fries and soft drinks, forget it. The decor and prices are coffee-shop classic; the service ditzy and perfunctory. Under $10 for a burger, fries, pie and a beverage.

Russell's
5656 E. 2nd St., Long Beach 90803; (310) 434-0226
Open Mon.-Thurs. 7 a.m.-10 p.m., Fri.-Sat. 7 a.m.-11 p.m., Sun. 7 a.m.-9 p.m. MC, V.

Without a doubt one of the very best burger spots in Southern California. Burgers are juicy, messy and completely delicious, especially when topped with the great homemade chili. The other winners in this cheery café are the crisp hash browns and the astonishingly tall and light meringue cream pies. You will not be disappointed by the pies, from the sour cream to the banana to the peanut-butter version, or the panoply of shakes, sundaes and malts. Service is friendly, and the atmosphere is lively with local gossip. Under $8 per person for lunch.

Tommy's
2575 W. Beverly Blvd., Rampart 90057; (213) 389-9060
Open daily 24 hours. No cards.

Tommy's has earned an amazing reputation for a tiny, greasy neighborhood burger joint in a seedy area. We don't dare criticize Tommy's, or an army of its incredibly devoted fans will surely burn every book in print. So we'll say this: the burgers themselves aren't much, but the topping is—a glob of messy, spicy, intensely aromatic, impressively tasty chili that seems to have some magical addictive powers. No matter what hour, you'll find a crowd (primarily of students from nearby U.S.C.) eating chiliburgers along the makeshift counter lining the parking lot. There are a couple of other Tommy's, but to purists, this is the one and only. You can stuff yourself on a burger and a soft drink for under $4.

Wolfe Burgers
46 N. Lake St., Pasadena 91101; (818) 792-7292
Open daily 6:30 a.m.-midnight. No cards.

Hamburger heaven: these delicious charbroiled burgers range from a kid-size one-sixth of a pound to a hulking two-thirds of a pound. Dress your burger the way you like it at the condiment bar, and by all means accompany it with an order of the fantastic onion rings, among the best in town. Everything's fresh and delicious, from the hot chili to the creamy, light flan for dessert. Our only complaint is that the burgers are sometimes overcooked. Wolfe's recently added breakfast to its repertoire. There are two plant-filled rooms in which you can enjoy this most American of foods, with a bottle of Corona or a root beer float, all for about $6.

Hot Dogs

Jody Maroni's Sausage Kingdom
2011 Ocean Front Walk, Venice 90292;
(310) 306-1995
Open Mon.-Fri. 10 a.m.-5 p.m., Sat.-Sun. 9 a.m.-6 p.m. No cards.

Even if Jody Maroni's little stand wasn't located right on zany Venice beach it would be worth driving to—from any part of town. Jody makes his own sausages, selling them as hot dogs to the beach people and in quantity to L.A. restaurants and home kitchens. He usually has about a dozen varieties available to eat at the stand, from old favorites (knackwurst, Italian sausage) to his own fanciful inventions (Mexican jalapeño sausage, Indian sausage). They are all wonderful beyond belief—once you try one, you'll want to try them all. About $6 for lunch.

Law Dogs
14114 Sherman Way, Van Nuys 91405;
(818) 989-2220
Open Sun.-Thurs. 10 a.m.-10 p.m., Fri.-Sat. 10 a.m.-midnight. No cards.

Started by a bored lawyer, Law Dogs is a no-frills stand with two main choices: the smaller Jury Dog or the larger (quarter-pound) Law Dog, plus the usual mustard-relish trimmings (cheese is extra). You'll eat your good (but not

exceptional) hot dog at the stand-up counter in this heart-of-the-Valley neighborhood. You'll get a dog, a bag of potato chips and a soft drink for less than $4.

Pink's Hot Dogs
711 N. La Brea Ave., Melrose-La Brea District (L.A.) 90038; (213) 931-4223
Open daily 7 a.m.-2:30 a.m. No cards.

Much ado has been made about Pink's chili dogs, which are indeed very tasty—so tasty, indeed, that throngs of customers put up with dirty tables, an unsavory Hollywood neighborhood and often-lukewarm sodas. Still, the delicious all-beef hot dogs (served with lots of messy all-beef chili on request) make Pink's worth a visit. A bargain at around $4.

Rubin's Red Hots
15322 Ventura Blvd., Sherman Oaks 91403;
(818) 905-6515
Open Sun.-Thurs. 8 a.m.-7 p.m., Fri.-Sat. 8 a.m.-9 p.m. No cards.

Rubin's main distinction is that it unequivocally has the nuttiest architecture of any hot dog stand we've ever seen. It looks like a combination car wash/jungle gym, and there's even a little Parisian-style kiosk selling magazines and flowers—go figure. Though tasty, these Chicago-style dogs just don't crackle and spit the way they should. The relish seems to be a bizarre product of modern chemistry—it's an otherwordly shade of green that practically glows in the dark. Rubin's also serves veal bratwurst, steakburgers, chicken-breast and swordfish sandwiches. The chili is first-rate, as are the french fries. Lunch runs about $6.

Tail of the Pup
329 N. San Vicente Blvd., W. Hollywood 90048;
(310) 652-4517
Open Mon.-Sat. 6 a.m.-6 p.m., Sun. 9 a.m.-4:30 p.m. No cards.

One of the few remaining examples of L.A.'s roadside-pop architecture of the twenties (and consequently a favorite subject of photographers who have tried to capture the essence of the city), the landmark Tail of the Pup is hidden away on San Vicente Boulevard. The stand is little more than a huge stucco hot dog, and it's worth a visit just for a look at this rare gem of programmatic design. While you're studying the architecture, try one of the good hot dogs or hamburgers. Lunch for under $5.

The Wiener Factory
14917 Ventura Blvd., Sherman Oaks 91403; (818) 789-2676
Open daily 11 a.m.-9 p.m. No cards.

Quite simply, some of L.A.'s best hot dogs can be had at The Wiener Factory. It's an amusing little dive with an outdoor take-out counter and a rustic indoor area with tables. The basic dog is great, but our unsurpassed favorite is the thick, juicy, spicy Polish dog, which is quite addictive. This is worth going out of your way for. And, complete with a drink and some potato salad, you'll leave no more than $5 poorer.

Ice Cream & Frozen Yogurt

Baskin-Robbins
10916 Kinross Ave., Westwood 90024 (Branches everywhere); (310) 208-8048
Sun.-Thurs. 10 a.m.-midnight, Fri.-Sat. 11 a.m.-1 p.m. No cards.

It may be fashionable to look down our noses at the pink-and-brown shops and the cutesy flavor names at dear old 31 Flavors. Taste buds acclimated to so-called gourmet ice creams may find many of the selections overly sweet and lacking in dimension. But let's be honest. These are the places where we all first learned how good and exciting ice cream could really be. Plus, they're a sight more widespread and easier to find than any upstart competitors. They now offer surprisingly good soft-serve frozen yogurt, as well as a selection of light flavors. And the good ol' rocky road, burgundy cherry, and the vanilla and mint versions of chocolate chip (actually flakes of good bittersweet chocolate) set a standard that's still hard to beat.

C.C. Brown's
7007 Hollywood Blvd., Hollywood 90028; (213) 464-9726
Open Mon. & Wed. 1 p.m.-10:30 p.m., Tues. & Thurs. 1:30 p.m.-10:30 p.m., Fri.-Sat. 1 p.m.-midnight. No cards.

According to local legend, C.C. Brown, Jr., invented the hot fudge sundae, taking twenty years to perfect his sauce recipe. It may be true—you can't dispute the stunning simplicity and impeccable quality of the dessert as it is served here. A single scoop of their own rich, creamy vanilla fills an iced stainless-steel dish. On top go roasted almonds and a snowcap of real whipped cream. A generous little pitcher on the side holds the fudge. Other sundaes are also served, along with sandwiches and salads—but ice cream perfection can be had for less than $6.

Double Rainbow
7376 Melrose Ave., Melrose-Fairfax District (L.A.) 90046; (213) 655-1986
Open Sun.-Thurs. 10 a.m.-midnight, Fri.-Sat. 10 a.m.-1 a.m. No cards.
1898 Westwood Blvd., Westwood 90025; (310) 470-6232
Open Mon.-Thurs. 8 a.m.-11 p.m., Fri. 8 a.m.-midnight, Sat. 8 a.m.-midnight, Sun. noon-11 p.m. No cards.

Clean, spare, brightly lit and adorned with changing displays of original art, these parlors have the look and feel of an upscale Baskin-Robbins. The flavors, however, taste far richer and more complex than those of America's favorite chain—witness the white pistachio, coffee bean and Heath Bar crunch as outstanding examples. There's also a rotating roster of excellent nonfat yogurt flavors, along with decent espresso drinks and decadent cheesecakes. Two generous scoops cost $2.95.

Fair Oaks Pharmacy and Soda Fountain
1526 Mission St., S. Pasadena 91030; (818) 799-1414
Open Mon.-Sat. 9 a.m.-9 p.m., Sun. noon-7 p.m. No cards.

Since 1915, the Fair Oaks Pharmacy has served its South Pasadena Community as a traditional corner soda fountain. Recently, owner Michael Miller bought and installed the turn-of-the-century fixtures from a pharmacy in Joplin, Missouri, turning his shop into a gloriously authentic slice of Americana. We feel like wide-eyed youngsters here, bellying up to the marble counter with its chrome stools and stained-glass cabinetry. The ice cream they use in their traditional sundaes, shakes and sodas is, to our tastes, only so-so; but the ambience—and the friendly service from clean-cut local kids—makes this an experience worth seeking out. And there's also a welcome contemporary touch: an espresso machine. Around $7 for a sundae and a cappuccino.

Häagen-Dazs
Century City Mall, 10250 Santa Monica Blvd., Century City 90067 (Branches everywhere); (310) 552-0417
Open Sun. 11 a.m.-10 p.m., Mon.-Thurs. 10 a.m.-10 p.m., Fri.-Sat. 10 a.m.-11 p.m. No cards.

We remember a time, about a decade ago, when the name Häagen-Dazs was on everyone's lips, and its rich, beguilingly flavorful ice cream in everybody's mouth. Shops were fairly scarce, and you always had to join a queue to get a scoop. Now its array of ice creams seems almost as wide as Baskin-Robbins', the shops as widespread, the competition from other gourmet brands fiercer. Has familiarity bred contempt? Naw! We still love the ice cream; we're just not as inclined to go out of our way for it—especially if we can buy a carton of that good vanilla or coffee in our local supermarket. If you visit a shop, do try the excellent frozen yogurt. Single scoops start at $1.65.

Humphrey Yogart

Brentwood Gardens, 11677 San Vicente Blvd., Brentwood 90049; (310) 207-2206
Open Sun.-Thurs. 10 a.m.-10:30 p.m., Fri.-Sat. 10 a.m.-midnight. No cards.

Beverly Connection, 100 N. La Cienega Blvd., W. Hollywood 90048; (310) 652-1941
Open Sun.-Thurs. 11 a.m.-11 p.m., Fri.-Sat. 11 a.m.-midnight. No cards.

4574 Van Nuys Blvd., Sherman Oaks 91493; (818) 906-2490
Open Mon.-Fri. 10 a.m.-11:30 p.m., Sat. 10 a.m.-midnight, Sun. 11 a.m.-11:30 p.m. No Cards.

Stroll unawares into a Humphrey Yogart and you'll think you've walked into either a very hip, young private party or a casting call for California's beautiful people. Miles of shiny hair, expanses of perfect teeth, Hollywood types in leather jackets emblazoned with the title of their latest movie. What's the attraction? Why, the best frozen yogurt in Los Angeles, that's what. Humphrey's serves about a zillion different varieties. The yogurt is scooped straight from hardpack containers into grinders that soften and blend it with the added ingredients, ingredients such as espresso grounds, blueberries, cream cheese, peanut butter, Heath Bars . . . and on! It also serves pretty good sandwiches and salads. Yogurt and a cappuccino comes to about $5.

The Lion & The Bear

12219 Santa Monica Blvd., W.L.A. 90025; (310) 820-7550
Open daily noon-11 p.m. No cards.

201 S. Beverly Dr., Beverly Hills 90212; (310) 274-8732
Open Sun.-Thurs. noon-10 p.m., Fri.-Sat. noon-11 p.m. No cards.

If ice cream were furniture, the good stuff they dish up fresh at The Lion & the Bear would be Swedish modern—a clean, spare and utterly elegant Scandinavian take on Italian gelati. These first two U.S. branches of Sweden's most successful gourmet chain offer an impressive array of color-categorized treats: Bear ice cream, an egg-free low-calorie concoction; Lion ice cream, made with eggs; Lion sorbet, free of milk, eggs

and fat; and low-fat yogurt. Flavors across the board are innovative and eye-openingly good: Cognac-orange, Jack Daniels chocolate, mango and lingonberry are just a few highlights. With such specials as gazpacho sorbet, they're generous with their little tasting spoons. Maybe now that they've changed their name from the tongue-tangling Swedish—Lejonet & Bjornen—the popularity they deserve will follow. Two big scoops for just $2.75.

Penguin's Place

8474 W. 3rd. St., W. Hollywood 90048 (Branches everywhere); (213) 653-8895
Open daily 11 a.m.-10 p.m. No cards.

Penguin's it was that awakened us to the possibility that frozen yogurt could actually taste better than just good. With their rotating roster of soft-serve flavors—mocha, cappuccino and the various cheesecakes are still among our favorites—they're responsible, at least in this region and in our eyes, for the fact that no self-respecting full-size or mini mall today is without its iced lactobacillus outlet. Kudos to them for that—and the yogurt is still a tasty bargain at $1.40 or more.

Robin Rose

215 Rose Ave., Venice 90291; (310) 399-1774
Open Sun.-Thurs. 11 a.m.-11 p.m., Fri.-Sat. 11 a.m.-midnight. No cards.

Wells Fargo Center, 333 S. Grand Ave., Downtown (L.A.) 90071; (213) 687-8815
Open Mon.-Fri. 10 a.m.-5:30 p.m. No cards.

6735 1/2 Fallbrook Ave., West Hills 91307; (818) 999-9299
Open Sun.-Thurs. 11 a.m.-10 p.m., Fri.-Sat. 11 a.m.-midnight. No cards.

Credit Robin Rose with enlightening our palates to the decadent delight of gourmet ice cream flavored with liqueurs. Every taste of its sinful array of flavors—Bailey's Irish Cream, Chambord Raspberry, Kahlua Almond Truffle and on and on—is a delightful revelation. Her Raspberry Chocolate Truffle, combining black raspberries and Chambord liqueur has been copied by legions of competitors. Teetotallers and weightwatchers can find a number of equally delicious selections free of alcohol and high levels of butterfat. The parlors are remarkably casual and welcoming. Single scoops are priced between $1.50 and $1.85.

Some establishments change their closing times without warning. It is always wise to check in advance.

Japanese Noodles

Asahi Ramen
2027 Sawtelle Blvd, W.L.A. 90025; (310) 479-2231
Lunch & Dinner Mon.-Wed. & Fri.-Sun. 11:30 a.m.-8:30 p.m. No cards.

Very popular with locals in the Westside's Little Tokyo along Sawtelle, this small, bright shop always seems to have a few customers waiting at the door. Their fresh noodles—a generous portion—are cooked appealingly al dente and served with a variety of toppings in a light but flavorful meat broth. The gyoza—little, crescent-shaped potstickers with a finely textured, gingery pork filling—are excellent. About $8 will fill you up.

Mishima
11301 Olympic Blvd., #210, W.L.A. 90064; (310) 473-5297
Lunch & Dinner Tues.-Sun. MC, V.

Frankly, we wonder why this new noodle shop in a swank mini-mall has local critics raving and customers lining up outside. Yes, the wheat or buckwheat noodles are made fresh here. But those we've sampled seemed bland, the broth they floated in was thin, and portions—as noodle houses go—were small. Could it be that the oversized celebrity autographs—Dennis Hopper prominent among them—on the wall give Mishima a cachet its competitors lack? For us, that does't merit the $9 or so you'll spend—slightly more than most other establishments.

Umemura
11301 Olympic Blvd, #101, W.L.A. 90064; (310) 479-5400
123 S. Onizuka St., #303, Little Tokyo (L.A.) 90012; (213) 620-9023
1724 W. Redondo Beach Blvd., Gardena 90247; (310) 217-0970
Lunch & Dinner daily. No cards.

We keep returning to Umemura. There's no pretension at all in its plain white walls and wooden tables and chairs. The service is swift and absolutely charming. And the selection of ramen bowls is astoundingly good. We've enjoyed their tender, subtly flavored, freshly made noodles with clear meat broth, soy-doused broth and robust miso broth, topped with anything from stir-fried vegetables to boiled pork wontons, barbecued pork to spicy Korean-style pickled cabbage. Portions are as big as a kitchen mixing bowl—at the excellent value of about $8 per person.

Yokohama Ramen
11660 Gateway Blvd., W.L.A. 90064; (310) 479-2321
Lunch & Dinner Mon. & Wed.-Sun. 11:30 a.m.-9 p.m. MC, V.

The noodles at this small, efficient-looking café in (of course) a mini-mall have people lining up to get in. You can choose between noodles with soup; noodles stir-fried with a variety of ingredients, such as barbecued pork and vegetables; pan-fried soft noodles; and delicious cold noodles. Yokohama also serves good pan-fried dumplings, as well as a terrific version of Chinese chicken salad. You can dine like a glutton for about $8.

Mexican

Burrito King
2109 W. Sunset Blvd., Echo Park 90026; (213) 413-9444
Open daily 7 a.m.-midnight. No cards.

Once the king of the burrito stand, Echo Park's Burrito King is now up against some pretty tough competition, from Yuca in Los Feliz to such chains as La Salsa on the westside. Its quality also seems to have slipped a bit—the carnitas burritos, soft tacos and large tostadas can still be very good, but not consistently so. Its late hours make it a worthwhile place to keep listed in your little black book. And the prices, at well under $5, are still excellent.

El Conchinito
3508 W. Sunset Blvd., Silverlake 90026; (213) 668-0737
Open daily 11 a.m.-9 p.m. MC, V.

The owner of this plain little diner is from Montuleño in the Yucatán, and this is the place to find the very appealing cuisine of his homeland. It's Mexican-style food with a West Indies influence: less spicy and more delicate than typical Mexican fare (though the dark-red chile sauce on the table is rich and hot). Try the salbute, a puffy corn tortilla topped with lettuce, onion and turkey, beef or pork; the pollo Montuleño, a small, marinated half chicken sandwiched between two tortillas and topped with tomato salsa and grated cheese. And by all means try one of the licuados, those marvelous Mexican shakes made with fruit, milk and ice. About $8.

Lucy's

1922 Olympic Blvd., Santa Monica 90404;
(310) 828-5003
Open daily 9 a.m.-8 p.m. MC, V.

Many for whom Lucy's is a standby treat it only as a take-out stand, hardly noticing the small, bare-bones dining room. Maybe the basic tacos, enchiladas, rellenos and burritos taste better eaten out of their paper wrappers; we find them no better or worse than those at the hundreds, of other Mexican dives throughout greater L.A. One highlight of dining in, though, is the terrific chicken-and-vegetable soup that starts a meal—it's full of meat and rice, and fragrant with cilantro. Under $10 for a combo plate and a beverage.

Mrs. Garcia's

11106 W. Olympic Blvd., W.L.A. 90064;
(310) 473-6322
8510 W. 3rd St., W. Hollywood 90048;
(310) 657-1002
Open daily 8:30 a.m.-10 p.m. No cards.

These little mini-mall taco shops, now spreading all over town, were an immediate success—and for good reason. The tacos al carbón are authentic and good—two small, soft corn tortillas, topped with grilled steak or chicken, marinated pork or beans, cheese and guacamole; you then add your own dose of several salsas, ranging from very mild to fiery. The steak (carne asada) is done better elsewhere, but it's still good; the chicken and pork are delicious. You can also get hearty burritos, tostadas and enchiladas. About $6.

El Nopal

10426 National Blvd., W.L.A. 90034;
(310) 559-4732
Open Mon.-Thurs. 11 a.m.-9 p.m., Fri.-Sat. 11 a.m.-10 p.m., Sun. 11 a.m.-9 p.m. D, MC, V.

Billed as "The Home of the Pregnant Burrito," El Nopal is a fine neighborhood place that serves good, fresh Mexican food for very low prices. The famed pregnant burrito, a giant mass of chicken, avocado, green peppers, onions, beans and cheese, is definitely enough for two. The nachos, quesadillas, enchiladas, tacos and taquitos are also good bets, and service is quick and friendly. Dinner runs under $10.

Poquito Más

3701 Cahuenga Blvd. West, Studio City 90068;
(818) 505-0068
Open Sun.-Thurs. 10 a.m.-midnight, Fri.-Sat. 10 a.m.-1 a.m. No cards.

Poquito Más vies with Yuca's as our favorite taco/burrito place in town. In a sort of no-man's-land on Cahuenga Boulevard (across from Universal Studios), Poquito Más makes incomparable carnitas, which go into generous, delicious burritos and soft tacos. Tasty fish tacos are usually on offer, and the tostadas are perfection. You can eat inside in a tiny room, or outside on a makeshift patio. There's always a crowd, but the friendly crew keeps the food coming. Count on spending about $7 for a meal.

La Salsa

11075 W. Pico Blvd., W.L.A. 90064;
(310) 479-0919
Open daily 8 a.m.-10 p.m. No cards.
11901 Santa Monica Blvd., W.L.A. 90025;
(310) 473-7880
Open daily 11 a.m.-10:30 p.m. No cards.

Probably the most popular taco al carbón chain in town, with outlets now to be found in such tony locations as Malibu, Beverly Hills and Brentwood. Great soft tacos and burritos are filled with succulent meats (including grilled chicken); you then douse your taco or burrito with a variety of salsas from a well-stocked salsa bar. One plus here for those who burn for the real thing: the salsas marked "hot" really are. You'll spend about $8 for a satisfying meal.

El Tepayac Café

812 N. Evergreen Ave., E.L.A. 90033;
(213) 268-1960
Open Sun.-Mon. & Wed.-Thurs. 6 a.m.-9:45 p.m., Fri.-Sat. 6 a.m.-11 p.m. No cards.

Burrito lovers from all over the city make regular pilgrimages to East L.A.'s El Tepayac. You'll probably have to wait in line before you get a seat in the garish little dining room, but you're sure to make friends with some of the many El Tepayac fanatics in line with you. The menu lists lots of Mexican standards, most of which are good, but burritos are the thing to get. They're huge beyond belief, chock-full of all kinds of delicious things: machaca, chile verde, beans, rice, guacamole and more. Watch out for the seriously hot salsa. About $5 for lunch.

Yuca's Hut

2056 N. Hillhurst Ave., Los Feliz 90027;
(213) 662-1214
Open Mon.-Sat. 11 a.m.-6 p.m. No cards.

We know New Yorkers who land at LAX and head straight for Yuca's. As well they should—this is the quintessential L.A. taco stand. It sits in

---

Looking for the best Mexican chow? These are the places to grab a bite, but if you're looking for a nicer place to dine, see the Mexican heading under the "By Cuisine" INDEXES at the back of the book.

the parking lot between a liquor store and a real estate office, and there's always a line at lunch, when Dora and her family dispense some of the best carnitas and carne asada tacos and burritos we've ever had the honor to taste. Get a Dos Equis from the liquor store, grab one of the rickety tables in the sunshine, order a couple of tacos, and enjoy one of L.A.'s great small pleasures. Dinner will cost about $6.

Pizza

California Pizza Kitchen
207 S. Beverly Dr., Beverly Hills 90210;
(213) 275-1101
330 S. Hope St., Downtown (L.A.) 90017;
(310) 626-2616
Lunch, Dinner & Late Supper daily. All major cards.

This burgeoning empire just keeps on growing. There are now branches throughout Southern California, as well as in Atlanta, Chicago and Hawaii and rumors of more to come in Europe. The smart owners have brought Spago-style cuisine to the masses, and the masses love it. In a bright, high-tech setting, you can get simple individual-size designer pizzas, such as fresh tomato, garlic and basil; duck sausage, fresh spinach, sun-dried tomatoes and roasted garlic. The cutesy numbers aren't for everyone: the "BLT" is topped with bacon, tomato, lettuce and mayonnaise; the "Thai-style" with chicken, bean sprouts and peanuts. The salads, calzones and pastas are generous and good. Also, eight other branches in greater L.A., including the Beverly Center (310-854-6555), Brentwood Gardens (310-826-3573) and the Glendale City Center (818-585-9020). About $18 per person.

Casa Bianca
1650 Colorado Blvd., Eagle Rock 90041;
(213) 256-9617
Dinner & Late Supper (until 1 a.m. Fri.-Sat.) nightly. No cards.

Casa Bianca is a no-nonsense, old-fashioned (it's been around since 1955) pizza place, where everyone seems to know one another, and the room is decorated with Chianti bottles and posters of Naples. The pizza is excellent, with a crisp, thin crust, hearty tomato sauce and the perfect amount of cheese. The spaghetti and meat balls and the linguine with clam sauce are the kind you dream about, and the lasagne is about as comforting and homey as food can get. Definitely worth a detour. A pizza and pasta feast costs about $12.

Damiano Mr. Pizza
412 N. Fairfax Ave., Wilshire District (L.A.) 90036;
(213) 658-7611
Lunch, Dinner & Late Supper (until 5 a.m. Sun.-Thurs., 6 a.m. Fri.-Sat.) All major cards.

We know homesick New Yorkers who swear by this little joint on Fairfax. So does half of Hollywood, and so, for that matter, do we. It's a disaster of a place except for one thing: the pizza. The thing to do is jam yourself into the minuscule entrance, plonk down $4 for one of the many imported lagers or ales while you wait (which can be forever), shout to your companions above the cacophony of the kitchen and the scratchy sound system, and when you finally get seated in one of the grungy, dimly lit booths, tuck joyfully into one of the thin-crusted, abundantly topped and well-seasoned pizzas. Special toppings are the jumbo scampi, fresh clams, eggplant, spinach, and just plain garlic—lots of it. There's a large menu of Italian standbys, too. A spanking-new, contemporary space has been grafted on next door to accommodate the crowds, but it has not a shred of the character of the original space. You can escape well-fed for $10. Another branch is at 1511 S. Robertson Blvd., (310) 556-3100.

Jacopo's
490 N. Beverly Dr., Beverly Hills 90210;
(310) 858-6446
15415 Sunset Blvd., Pacific Palisades 90272;
(310) 454-8494
11676 W. Olympic Blvd., W.L.A. 90064;
(310) 477-2111
8166 Sunset Blvd., W. Hollywood 90069;
(213) 650-8128
Lunch & Dinner (until midnight) daily. AE, MC, V.

The brick-floored and -walled Beverly Hills Jacopo's is cozy to some and cramped and uncomfortable to others, and the other branches are rather cold and prefab looking. The service can be shaky, too, so we prefer to get take-out. Despite this, Jacopo's is extremely popular with the designer-sweatsuit crowd, who seem to love the very cheesy pizza. Two people sharing a pizza and beverages will spend about $13 each.

Lamonica's N.Y. Pizza
1066 Gayley Ave., Westwood 90024;
(310) 208-8671
Lunch & Dinner daily, Late Supper Fri.-Sat. No cards.

Lamonica's sells good New York–style pizza, whole or by the slice, to the hordes of Westwood pedestrians. The crust is thin and light, the sauce and cheese delicious, and the toppings simple. You can eat inside, but it can get crowded and stuffy. We like to do it New York style: outdoors, people-watching along Village sidewalks. And if you don't want to face the bustle of the Village,

Lamonica's delivers to westside locations. Dinner will cost you about $6.

Little Toni's
4745 Lankershim Blvd., N. Hollywood 91602;
(818) 763-0131
Dinner & Late Supper nightly (until 2 a.m.). All major cards.

Little Toni's is the kind of nondescript neighborhood Italian restaurant one would visit only upon a recommendation. So here it is: Little Toni's makes an excellent pizza. Get the thin crust—it's delicious and evenly crisp—with several of the generous and fresh toppings (we like bacon, onion, green pepper and sausage). This is a cheese-lover's pizza, favoring mozzarella over sauce. Wash it down with a pitcher of imported beer, and you'll escape for about $10 per person.

Mario's
1001 Broxton Ave., Westwood 90024;
(310) 208-7077
Lunch, Dinner & Late Supper (until 12:30 a.m. Sat.) daily. All major cards.

One of the few restaurants worth going to in the Westwood morass, Mario's is a cartoon version of an Italian restaurant, with checkered tablecloths and Chianti bottles hanging from the ceiling. The pizza is better than good, and the pizza topped with pesto and bacon, however bad for you, is a marvel. Other Italian standards can be underwhelming. About $12 for a pizza meal.

Palermo
1858 N. Vermont Ave., Los Feliz 90027;
(213) 663-1430
Lunch & Dinner Mon. & Wed.-Sun. MC, V.

The years have gone by and the location has changed, but Palermo remains as popular as ever. Locals and fans from across the city don't mind the long wait, as long as the house keeps the free industrial-strength wine flowing. The big draw here is the thick-crusted, Sicilian style pizza, marvelously spicy and flavorful, and loaded with toppings. True, it's too heavy for more refined palates (nothing here, save Mama's cannoli, can be described as delicate), but what a taste! The heavy pastas are also good in a rustic way, but by all means avoid anything even slightly fancy, particularly the scampi and the veal. Under $9 for a pizza meal.

Silvio's Pizza
10251 Santa Monica Blvd., Century City 90067;
(310) 277-9911/ 286-1797
Lunch & Dinner (until 7 p.m.) Mon.-Sat. No cards.

This sweet little place occupies a space across the street from the Century City Shopping Center. It's a great premovie stop, and it's well worth the detour to the other side of the road. The pizzas and pastas are old-fashioned and delicious, and the owners are as sweet as can be, constantly refilling sodas gratis and making sure that everything is okay. Silvio's is a mom-and-pop restaurant that deserves a lot of support, and we hope it makes its way among the corporate pizza Goliaths. If we have anything to do with it, though, they'll keep selling pizzas for a long time to come. Dinner for two, with beverages, is about $20.

Vittorio!
16646 Marquez Ave., Pacific Palisades 90272;
(310) 459-3755
Dinner Tues.-Sun. No cards.

The best-kept secret in the Palisades, Vittorio!'s pocket-size pizza-and-pasta shop hidden off Sunset Boulevard serves terrific food in an ambience of utter Italian chaos. Not only will your waiter be an aspiring actor, he'll probably sing to you as he sprinkles Parmesan on your spaghetti. The pizza is classic and very good. Shared pizza costs about $7 per person. ◆

HOTELS

Contents

World-Class Bungalows

L os Angeles has never been famous for its luxury hotels. In fact, there traditionally has been an almost reverse snob appeal regarding luxury; secluded and often rustic bungalows were sought after by both the seasoned traveler and the nouveau riche. But the last few years have seen a dramatic change. While seclusion and discretion are still desired by many of L.A.'s hotel guests, most are now also demanding the level of accommodations they've come to expect in the world's great cities, from New York to London to Hong Kong. And Los Angeles hoteliers have been meeting the challenge by upgrading their properties and service, and by opening some impressive new places.

The two hotels most beloved by the entertainment industry, the Beverly Hills Hotel and the Château Marmont, spent too long resting on

their respective laurels. But the Sultan of Brunei has finally bought up the properties surrounding the Pink Lady (locals' fond nickname for the Beverly Hills Hotel), and it will soon be closed down for a couple of years while he spends a chunk of his fortune turning it into a lavish resort. And the luster is being restored to the historic Château, which has been undergoing a seemingly endless renovation; we just hope the bungalows aren't made *too* posh.

L.A.'s newest crop of hotels, from the ultra-discreet, ultra-moneyed Peninsula, to the sleek, stylish Hotel Nikko, to the gloriously restored Ritz-Carlton Huntington, is proof enough that Los Angeles has become one of the best hotel cities in the country, if not the world. Now if it can just get more of those small, charming, under-$100 inns so common in San Francisco, it might become *the* best hotel city in the world.

A word regarding price: We've quoted each hotel's full, regular rate. Keep in mind that most offer corporate discounts and/or bargain package deals; most also offer weekend rates, which can be substantially less. Also, rates fluctuate from season to season, so call ahead to inquire about the best rate offered during the time period you'll be traveling.

How to use this chapter: The symbol that accompanies each review indicates in which price category the hotel belongs. Categories are Top of the Line ($200 & Up), Luxury ($150 & Up), Moderate ($100 & Up) and Practical (Under $100), and for the purposes of this book, we have defined the categories based on the regular starting price of a single or double room. *See also* the INTRODUCTION chapter, under "About the Hotels."

L.A. Area

Encompasses L.A. proper and all of the Westside, including Downtown, Hollywood, West Hollywood, Bel Air, Beverly Hills, Brentwood, Westwood, Century City, Santa Monica, Venice, Marina Del Rey, Pacific Palisades and Malibu.

Top of the Line ($200 & Up)

Bel Age
1020 N. San Vicente Blvd., W. Hollywood 90069; (310) 854-1111, Fax (310) 854-0926
Suites $195-$500. All major cards.

The luxurious Bel Age is designed in a French Provençal style, cleverly disguised as an nondescript apartment building on a quiet street, like so many of the Ashkenazy brothers' hotels. The handsome lobby is done in blond-wood paneling and marble, with hand-carved wood chandeliers; pieces from the Ashkenazys' extensive fine-art collection adorn the walls, and classical music plays in the background. Like its cousins, Bel Age is composed entirely of suites, which feature rosewood and pecan furniture, wet bars, private balconies and myriad amenities, from bathrobes to multi-line phones. The south-facing suites on the upper floors have expansive city views. Extras include a rooftop pool and spa, limousine service and a new business center, and talent agents will appreciate the poolside paging. By all means have a Franco-Russian dinner at the elegant Diaghilev dining room, and by all means enjoy the sumptuous Sunday brunch.

The Beverly Hills Hotel
9641 Sunset Blvd., Beverly Hills 90210; (310) 276-2251, Fax (310) 271-0319
Rates subject to change. All major cards.

The Pink Lady, as this hotel is affectionately called by its patrons, is scheduled to close her doors for a makeover—and not just a little nip-and-tuck, either. For the duration of 1993, and probably 1994 as well, the hotel's owner, the Sultan of Brunei, will part with lots of his untold millions on a massive renovation and reorganization that he hopes will make this famous landmark one of the world's finest urban resorts. This is fabulous news, because the hotel was long due for a sprucing up. The forthcoming new Beverly Hills Hotel will no doubt be lavish and luxurious (we've heard tell of a lake, waterfalls, fireplaces in the bathrooms and other such extravagances);

we'll have to wait and see whether the renovation can bring back the enormous cachet the bungalows, the poolside patio and the Polo Lounge enjoyed for so many years.

The Beverly Hilton Hotel
9876 Wilshire Blvd., Beverly Hills 90210; (310) 274-7777, Fax (310) 285-1313
Singles $200-$240, Doubles $225-$265, Suites $400-$900. All major cards.

When Merv "singer/actor/talk-show host/game-show mogul" Griffin bought this old dinosaur and gussied her up, she slowly began to transform into the star she once was. Designer-to-the-stars Waldo Fernandez completely refashioned the lobby, landscaping and rooms. The result is a vast improvement over the original; the large rooms, most with terraces and city views, are quite lovely. Even its old, dearly loved Polynesian restaurant, Trader Vic's, was remodeled, though deep down it has remained basically the same—actually rather a comfort in this fast-changing city. The elegant and formal dining room, L'Escoffier, changed and updated as we went to press, hiring talented chef Michel Blanchet (ex of L.A.'s renowned L'Ermitage) to prepare a classic French menu. Perched on the edge of Beverly Hills, the hotel is also just a short drive from Westwood or West Hollywood.

L'Ermitage
9291 Burton Way, Beverly Hills 90210; (310) 278-3344, Fax (310) 278-8247
1-Bedroom Suites $285-$475, 2-Bedroom Suites $485-$625, Penthouse Suite $1,500. AE, MC, V.

Artur Rubinstein stayed here. If Beethoven had visited Los Angeles, he would have stayed here, too. It's that select and elegant. The proprietors are the legendary Ashkenazy brothers, who obviously know how to make (and, more lately, also lose) a fortune. L'Ermitage is in a class of its own; not the least of its distinctions is its unique small size in a city of huge hotels. Located on a street lined with chic condos, it looks more like a genteel European apartment house than a hotel. The 112 suites, most of which were recently renovated, are beautifully appointed, with fireplaces, proper wet bars, richly upholstered furniture and fabulous marble bathrooms. Guests receive a score of amenities and faultless service; there's more than one employee per customer. The walls display an astonishing collection of original nineteenth-century art. A rooftop pool and restaurant allow guests to remain sequestered on the property.

And only in Los Angeles: The next-door annex, Le Petit Ermitage, offers sixteen luxurious suites that cater to—what else?—guests recovering from cosmetic surgery! Amenities at this new offshoot include nursing care, meals, transporation to and from the doctor's office and a physician on 24-hour call.

 ## Four Seasons Hotel
300 S. Doheny Dr., Beverly Hills 90211;
(310) 273-2222, Fax (310) 274-4121
Singles $270-$290, Doubles $295-$315, Suites $355-$2,000. All major cards.

Canada's Four Seasons chain creates human-scale hotels in the best of taste, catering to a prosperous clientele that likes the convenience of a modern hotel without too much ostentatiousness. This one is among L.A.'s very best hotels, perched on the cusp between fashionable Beverly Hills and trendy West Hollywood. With 285 rooms, it is small by modern hotel standards, ensuring a good level of service and a serene lobby. Each large, handsome room is equipped with a private balcony, two two-line phones, a fully stocked minibar, a remote-control TV in the bedroom and a black-and-white TV in the bathroom, a built-in hair dryer and terry robes; most of the rooms have swell views. All the expected amenities are supplied—from the fourth-floor pool, spa and sundeck to the 24-hour concierge service—and the common areas are rife with marble and glorious flower arrangements. The dining room, Gardens (*see* "LOS ANGELES Restaurants"), and its smaller cousin, The Café, are successfully pairing first-rate California cuisine with polished service; they're among the best spots in town for an elegant business meal.

 ## Hotel Bel-Air
701 Stone Canyon Rd., Bel Air 90077;
(310) 472-1211, Fax (310) 476-5890
Singles $225-$395, Doubles $265-$435, Suites $480-$2,000. All major cards.

If Sleeping Beauty were to wake up in Southern California, no doubt she'd find herself in the enchanted gardens of the Hotel Bel-Air. The grounds here are so beautiful and fairy-tale perfect, it's hard to believe they're real. You will be charmed by the swans, the trees, the eleven acres of private park, the welcoming reception with its crackling fire and the quasi-country-château architecture. No two rooms are alike; the better ones have terraces and wood-burning fireplaces. If staying or dining here is beyond your means, be sure to come for a drink on the patio just before twilight—it's one of the most magical, peaceful spots in all of Los Angeles. Now owned by a Japanese investment group (which paid more than $110 million—nearly $1.2 million per room), the Bel-Air is still as stunning and luxurious as ever. The restaurant's superb fare brings together the best features of American, Mediterranean and Californian cuisines. Whether you're looking for a safe haven on a business trip, pampering yourself for a weekend or spending your wedding night, you won't regret splurging on a room here. And the Sunday brunch is still the loveliest in town.

 ## Hotel Nikko at Beverly Hills
465 S. La Cienega Blvd., Beverly Hills 90048; (310) 247-0400, Fax (310) 247-0315
Singles $220-$285, Doubles $245-$310, Suites $325-$1,200. All major cards.

Don't let the ordinary-looking stucco-and-glass exterior of this spanking-new hotel fool you: the inside is something else again. Rarely have we seen a hotel so successfully combine high-tech wizardry with creature comforts and personal charm. It's a soothing, sophisticated retreat that's sure to win the hearts of many a business traveler, particularly those from the worlds of advertising, design, entertainment and fashion. From the extremely personable employees to the first-rate business center, the Nikko meets exacting standards. Even the basic rooms are spacious, with a clever two-person desk, state-of-the-art phones, sliding shoji screens, comfortable seating, Japanese steeping tubs, a complete entertainment system (TV, VCR, CD player, with access to a 200-CD library), coffeemakers and a mind-blowing bedside command center, which lets you turn on lights, play a disc, check the time in Paris and even consult movie schedules with the touch of a finger. Extras include a pool, a lavish health club, meeting rooms galore, free parking and free limousines.

Matrixx, the hotel's main dining room, takes you further into high-tech territory. With your own matrix of ingredients, you can compose a personalized dinner combining any of seven pastas with any of nine different sauces, and the waitress will modem your order to the kitchen. If you're in the private dining room, you can perform your own magic Matrixx trick: simply pushing a button will transform a glass wall into an opaque barrier. A Californian dinner will cost about $25 per person. You can also dine at the acclaimed Morton's of Chicago steakhouse, just adjacent.

JW Marriott Hotel
2151 Ave. of the Stars, Century City 90067;
(310) 277-2777, Fax (310) 785-9240
*Singles & Doubles $209-$269, Suites $375-
$2,500. No-smoking floors. All major cards.*

From the street, and particularly at night, this
relatively new 375-room Marriott looks spectacular, an artfully lit stepped building with handsome landscaping. Popular for banquets and with
business groups, it has a welcoming and personal
setting rare for a hotel this size. We love the huge
bathrooms and the comfort of the rooms. Amenities abound, from complimentary limousine service to a complete fitness center, indoor and
outdoor swimming pools, a business center and
an afternoon tea where you may unwind after all
that activity. It's a short walk to the ABC Entertainment Center (home of the Shubert Theatre,
Harry's Bar and movie theaters) and the Century
City Marketplace. The restaurant, JW's, offers a
terrific, affordable pretheater dinner; on weekdays, the hushed atmosphere is ideal for doing
business.

Other Marriott hotels in L.A. are in Woodland
Hills and near LAX airport (*see* this chapter for
reviews), as well as Marina del Rey and Torrance.

The Peninsula Beverly Hills
9882 Santa Monica Blvd., Beverly Hills
90212; (310) 273-4888,
Fax (310) 858-6663
*Singles & Doubles $265-$320, Suites $390-
$2,500. All major cards.*

This new luxury hotel is so discreet that many
Angelenos don't even know it's there—in fact,
countless commuters who drive by every day
never even noticed it being constructed. That's
just the way the seriously moneyed clientele likes
it; these people wouldn't be caught dead being
paged poolside at the Beverly Hills Hotel, and
they certainly aren't interested in rushing off to
the latest impossible-to-get-into nightclub. No,
they're here because they adore the Peninsula in
Hong Kong, long considered one of the world's
best; because the interior decor is opulent in a
quiet, homey way (if one's home is in Monaco);
because the 200 rooms are deeply comfortable,
equipped with such necessities as down comforters, VCRs and voice mail; because the Belvedere
serves an elegant Asian-tinged French cuisine in
a hushed, formal setting; and because the service
is personal and professional. The capacious suites
and villas come complete with fireplaces, spas and
private terraces. After a dip in the rooftop lap
pool, you can lounge in a private cabana; if you
need a lift to Tiffany, one of the house Rollses
will drop you off; and if duty calls, you can manage your affairs through the business center.

The Regent Beverly Wilshire
9500 Wilshire Blvd., Beverly Hills 90212;
(310) 275-5200, Fax (310) 274-2851
*Singles & Doubles $255-$395, Suites $550-
$4,000. All major cards.*

This beauty is absolutely unrecognizable to
those who knew her in her original incarnation,
before the Hong Kong–based Regent Group
bought her a few years back. The lobby is a trove
of gorgeous antiques, woods, marbles and glass,
outfitted like a Regency/Directoire–era dream.
Under management by the ever-expanding Four
Seasons chain since mid-1992, the Beverly Wilshire hasn't missed a beat; its crackerjack white-
gloved service continues on every level.

Rooms are positively luxurious, with gigantic
marble bathrooms, silky bed linens, period furniture and double-glazed windows to obviate any
street noise. The sumptuous dining room also
happens to serve some of the best hotel food in
the city (*see* "LOS ANGELES Restaurants").
There's also a café that replaced the former Pink
Turtle (a popular spot for breakfast and elegant
late-night nibbles), and nibbling and sipping afternoon tea in the Lobby Lounge is too sophisticated for words. A first-rate health spa on
premises offers up-to-the-minute exercise equipment and pampering services (*see also* review,
page 197). Unequivocally one of the best hotels
in the city.

St. James's Club
8358 Sunset Blvd., W. Hollywood 90069;
(213) 654-7100, Fax (213) 654-9287
*Singles & Doubles $190, Suites $260-$650. All
major cards.*

The St. James's Club tries to be all things to
all people: a tony, private club; a chic, members-
only hostelry and restaurant; and a hotel. You
don't have to be a club member to stay here; a
temporary membership fee of $8 per night will
be tacked onto your bill. To us, the real attraction
of the club is the building itself, a dazzling deco
beacon that began life as the swank Sunset Towers in 1931, home to luminaries like Jean
Harlowe, Clark Gable and Marilyn Monroe. The
St. James's folks took over in 1985, pumped $40
million into its restoration. While the exterior is
absolutely gorgeous, the interiors are a bit *de
trop*—a bit more deco than anything in that period ever was. But for those who like to feel
important and like—dare we say—members of
the club, this could be just the ticket.

The smallish rooms have two-line telephones,
and for recreation there's a beautiful swimming
pool, an outdoor lounging area that really does
feel like something out of a much grander era,

and a fully equipped health spa. You can also take advantage of the business center, meeting rooms, extensive film and book library and secretarial services. The restaurant (once private but now open to the public, as of fall 1992) is wonderful—the food is fresh and well-prepared and the atmosphere is right out of an Astaire-Rogers movie. The Club Lounge and Bar is an elegant spot to unwind. The hanging collection of Hollywood portraits by photographers George Hurrell and Clarence Sinclair Bull are worthy of a museum and, last but certainly not least, the panoramic city views are spectacular.

 ## Sunset Marquis
1200 N. Alta Loma Rd., W. Hollywood 90069; (310) 657-1333, Fax (310) 652-5300 *Suites $215-$490, Villas $450-$1,000. All major cards.*

Back in the good ol' days of rock 'n' roll, when drug-crazed musicians hurled TV sets out windows, the Sunset Marquis was one of the Strip's premier party pads. But these days the place is as docile as the times and the neighborhood; the kind of stars who stay here today, are more likely to be up nights feeding babies than partying. On a quiet street just off the Sunset Strip, the apartment-style hotel and adjacent villas (converted homes) cater to a low-key crowd of music- and entertainment-industry types. The main building displays some of that '60s-modern L.A. style found throughout Hollywood, which only adds to the charm of the place. The junior suites are rather dated and dark, but the larger suites are airy and comfortably furnished, with good bathrooms, and the villas have lots of Spanish-style charm. A few dozen bunnies (of the Thumper, not the Hefner, variety) populate the surprisingly pretty grounds, which include a couple of pools, a waterfall, a sauna and a private outdoor café.

 ## Westwood Marquis
930 Hilgard Ave., Westwood 90024; (310) 208-8765, Fax (310) 824-0355 *1-Bedroom Suites $220-$325, 2-Bedroom Suites $250-$650. All major cards.*

An attentive reception, elegance and warmth come as a surprise from behind the severe, stark lines of the raw concrete exterior, and these surprises explain the good reputation of this all-suite hotel. The excellent Westwood Village location (near UCLA and a short drive to Beverly Hills) is another plus. Only the condo-style construction is a disappointment. The decor in the suites varies from clean, contemporary lines to updated French-country charm. Penthouse suites include a butler, complimentary breakfast and evening

hors d'oeuvres. Regardless of which suite you choose, you can make good use of the complete health spa and the two pools, one of which is set in a lovely garden and features casual poolside dining. High tea is served from 3 p.m. to 5 p.m. in the Marquis bar, and the lavish Sunday buffet brunch is among the town's most elegant, popular and expensive.

Luxury ($150 & Up)

 ## The Beverly Pavilion
9360 Wilshire Blvd., Beverly Hills 90212; (310) 273-1400, Fax (310) 859-8551 *Singles $150-$175, Doubles $170-$195, Suites $265-$415. All major cards.*

This newish hotel has several things going for it: a superb location within walking distance of Beverly Hills shopping; a rooftop pool and a sundeck with a 320-degree view of the city; excellent, personable service; and a good Californian/Continental restaurant, Colette. The lobby is a little cramped, though it's nicely appointed, and the 110 small but upscale rooms and suites are quiet and attractive. Try to get a west-facing room on one of the top floors—you'll be rewarded with a lovely sunset view. A good value given the extremely high-rent neighborhood.

 ## Biltmore Hotel
515 S. Olive St., Downtown (L.A.) 90013; (213) 624-1011, Fax (213) 655-5311 *Singles $175-$245, Doubles $205-$245, Suites $275-$1,900. No-smoking floors. All major cards.*

A few years ago, this grande dame was given yet another face-lift, and the interior is once again aglow. The former lobby was transformed into a lovely bar, complete with mellow live jazz, a tiled fountain, lush plants and beautiful beamed and painted ceilings. A handsome new lobby was created out of one of the old meeting rooms, and the Crystal Ballroom is as glorious as ever. Most of the rooms are colorful, modern and rather small, but there are some lovely old-fashioned suites with large living rooms and fireplace mantels. The restored 1920s art-deco pool (featured in the movie *Bugsy*) is a ravishing place to take a dip. The Club floor caters to business travelers, who are tended to by a valet and who enjoy complimentary breakfast, cocktails and hors d'oeuvres. This is the ideal choice for businesspeople who need to stay downtown but dislike the sterility of the big chain hotels.

Hidden in the basement of the Biltmore Hotel is the restaurant Sai Sai. Built to entertain the high standards of the hotel's sizable Japanese clientele, Sai Sai is relatively unknown by most of the populace of Los Angeles, yet is probably the most exquisite and certainly the most authentic Japanese restaurant in the city (*see* "LOS ANGELES Restaurants"), with prices to match.

 ## The Bonaventure
5th & Figueroa Sts., Downtown (L.A.)
90071; (213) 624-1000, Fax (213) 612-4800
Singles $150-$190, Doubles $175-$215, Suites $325-$2,010. All major cards.

On the outside, this self-contained minicity looks like a mirrored espresso machine. The interior, designed for conventions, has no fewer than 1,474 rooms, 28 meeting rooms and a honeycomb of boutiques, discos, bars and restaurants. You'll need a safari guide to find your way around, especially if you're trying to reach one of the upper-floor restaurants. When you make it successfully to the top, don't miss the dramatic nighttime views from the 34th-floor revolving bar. The hotel's finest quarters are the five-bedroom Huntington Suite, stocked with Chinese antiques and dazzling crystal chandeliers. Reserve one of the rooms on the upper floors, which have terrific views.

 ## Century Plaza & Towers
2025 Ave. of the Stars, Century City 90067;
(310) 551-3300, Fax (310) 551-3355
Singles $175-$275, Doubles $220-$305, Suites $300-$3,000. All major cards.

In the heart of Century City, on what was once the back lot of 20th-Century Fox studios, this immense curvilinear monument to Cinemascope is a super-production in itself. On this big screen and behind it, in the multi-mirrored sunken lobby and the 1,072 rooms, runs a great deal of action. Many an important social event takes place here, making it one of the city's most active hotels. For one of the most elegant hotel experiences in L.A., especially if your taste runs more to seclusion and less to a convention vibe, the newer, 30-story Towers next door will do beautifully. The rooms are quiet, the atmosphere throughout is subdued, and the view, stretching from the mountains to the Pacific, is superb. It's like being in an entirely different hotel—which, in fact it is, with a separate entrance and its own fine restaurant, La Chaumiere (*See* "LOS ANGELES Restaurants").

The hotel's proximity to Beverly Hills's shopping and dining and Century City's cinemas and live theater is a real plus. There are tennis courts,

a pool, a coffee shop and a piano bar. Because of its grandeur and its great array of facilities, the Century Plaza Towers has been a favorite of several recent United States presidents.

 ## Château Marmont
8221 W. Sunset Blvd., W. Hollywood
90069; (213) 656-1010, Fax (213) 655-5311
Singles & Doubles $145-$190, Suites $210-$550, Bungalows $395-$450. All major cards.

This romantic, solid-as-a-rock castle (built in 1927) attracts celebrities of a certain type—the low-key, earthier ones, from Sam Shepard to Joni Mitchell. Musicians, writers and actors often hole up for months at a time, to finish a script, compose an album or simply chill out for awhile. The hotel has been in a constant state of renovation since the 1970s, and today, under new owners André Balazs and Campion Platt, most of the 62 rooms and bungalows are in pretty good shape, combining old-world charm with ample creature comforts. The poolside Cape Cod bungalows provide sanctuary from the glitter and tinsel of Hollywood, and these highly coveted accommodations come with fully equipped kitchenettes for those who aren't keen on having their photos snapped at Spago. Château Marmont also has an impressive wine cellar and a romantic view of L.A. at night, when the real stars come out.

 ## Checkers Hotel Kempinski
555 S. Grand Ave., Downtown (L.A.)
90071; (213) 624-0000, Fax (213) 626-9906
Singles & Doubles $185-$235, Suites $400-$850. All major cards.

Located between the Biltmore and Library Square, this small (190-room) Kempinski hotel has all the earmarks of success: beautiful, muted furnishings (no expense has been spared here; there's quite a cache of antiques scattered about), a business communications center, on-site laundry and dry cleaning services, 24-hour room service, a rooftop lap pool and spa with tanning, Jacuzzi and massage facilities, as well as saunas, a steam room and an exercise studio. While the rooms aren't exactly spacious, they are luxurious, and each has phones with call-waiting and phone-mail systems. There's also a cozy library and four meeting rooms. Much like its sibling, San Francisco's lovely Campton Place, Checkers is exactly the kind of discreet, first-class hotel downtown so desperately needed. And the handsome restaurant, as at Campton, is of the first order, serving fine contemporary American cuisine (*see* "LOS ANGELES Restaurants").

Doubletree Marina del Rey

4100 Admiralty Way, Marina del Rey 90292;
(310) 301-3000, Fax (310) 301-6890
*Singles & Doubles $170-$190, Suites $260-
$1,280. All major cards.*

Recently taken over by the Doubletree group,
the former Marina Beach Hotel is a textbook
example of that thoroughly tasteful muted-Cali-
fornia-pastel look so prevalent these days. During
the week, business travelers keep its 200-plus
rooms filled; on the weekends, when rates drop
considerably, you'll find a lot more fun-seekers.
They come for a weekend of poolside lounging,
tan-improving, sailing and strolling boutique-
and-restaurant-lined Main Street in nearby Venice. The rooms are soothing in design and
perfectly comfortable. On the top floor, a terrific
window-lined lounge makes an ideal rest stop
around sunset.

Le Dufy

1000 Westmount Dr., W. Hollywood
90069; (310) 657-7400, Fax (310) 854-6744
Suites $145-$225. All major cards.

One of the Ashkenazy brothers' best hotels,
Le Dufy combines comfort, exceptional service,
reasonable prices and a great West Hollywood
location. Like L'Ermitage and Le Parc, this all-
suite hotel looks and feels more like an apartment
building; the atmosphere is quiet, sophisticated
and most discreet. The 120 compact suites are
attractively decorated with colorful contemporary furnishings; most have sunken living rooms,
gas-powered fireplaces and small balconies, and
the larger suites have full kitchens, making them
ideal for extended stays. Weary travelers can relax
by the pool or in the rooftop Jacuzzi, from which
there is a dazzling panoramic view on a clear day.

Hotel Inter-Continental

California Plaza, 250 S. Olive St.,
Downtown (L.A.) 90012; (213) 617-3300
*Singles $165-$225, Doubles $195-$255. All
major cards.*

As we went to press, L.A. was expecting a
much-desired Christmas present to its downtown area, in the form of this $100 million
branch of the international chain. Judging from
the standards at Inter-Continental's one-hun-
dred hotels worldwide (which include San
Francisco's Mark Hopkins and the majestic Wil-
lard in Washington, D.C.), this hotel should impress both the world-weary traveler with high
standards and the businessperson looking for
both opulence and convenience. Part of the California Plaza (one of the largest urban revitaliza-

tion projects in North America, in an area that
seriously needs the boost), the hotel has the Museum of Contemporary Art as a neighbor, and
reflects MOCA's avant-garde lines with a sleek,
modernist design. There are 20,000 feet of meeting and banquet space; large rooms with floor-
to-ceiling glass windows; a health club; and quick
access to the city's Civic Center, Convention
Center and Music Center. The Inter-Continental
provides perhaps the final proof for skeptics that
L.A. has become a world-class hotel city.

Hyatt Regency Los Angeles

711 S. Hope St., Downtown (L.A.) 90017;
(213) 683-1234, Fax (213) 629-3230
*Singles $149-$189, Doubles $169-$209, Suites
$225-$550. All major cards.*

Blending into its downtown setting with a
sleek, neutral glass exterior, this high-rise business hotel was recently given a tasteful overhaul.
The below-ground-level lobby blends the contemporary with the traditional to good effect,
with soaring ceilings, blond woods, white marble, potted palms and plush carpets. A vast
amount of meeting space makes this a popular
convention hotel; solo business travelers make
use of the comfortable lounges on the executive-
class concierge floors. Done in soft browns and
beiges, the rooms are comfortable, quiet and
very pleasant, if rather generic. The trademark
Regency Club floors offer VIP treatment and
lounges for informal meetings.

Loews Santa Monica Beach Hotel

1700 Ocean Ave., Santa Monica 90401;
(310) 458-6700, Fax (310) 458-6761
*Singles $175-$275, Doubles $195-$295, Suites
$300-$2,000. All major cards.*

Santa Monica's byzantine zoning laws, the
Coastal Commission and various and sundry political machinations have sadly kept L.A.'s
beachfront-hotel population close to zero. However, inroads are being made, and there has been
much talk of opening oceanfront hotels in Santa
Monica, Venice and Malibu. The first entry to
open this sandy sweepstakes in 1991 was this
large (350 rooms and 35 suites) resort. The design motif has all the right colors and textures of
the moment, and the handsome, clubby-looking
interiors take their design cues from Britain. The
magnet here is location: right on the beach,
across the street from the chichi Ivy at the Shore
and just a skip away from Main Street and nutty
Venice Boardwalk. Amenities include an in-

door/outdoor swimming pool that overlooks the beach, a fitness center complete with personal trainers, a business center and gobs of meeting space. Riva, the hotel's seafood restaurant, has a lavish Sunday brunch and some of the best views in the city (see "LOS ANGELES Restaurants").

 Los Angeles Hilton and Towers
930 Wilshire Blvd., Downtown (L.A.)
90017; (213) 629-4321, Fax (213) 488-9869
Singles $150-$201, Doubles $170-$221, Suites $375-$575. All major cards.

After several years of ongoing renovation, this well-located Hilton has finally been completed. The lobby is now quite attractive, abuzz with tourists and Asian businessmen. The several restaurants include the elegant Cardini, which serves regional Italian cuisine in a series of intimate dining rooms. The rooms are just what you would expect of a big-city, business-oriented Hilton: comfortable and functional; those located in the Towers boast fabulous views. The hotel is within walking distance of the fine Seventh Street Marketplace. Other Hiltons in L.A.: Universal City (*see* review this chapter), Baldwin Hills and on Figueroa Street downtown.

 Ma Maison Sofitel
8555 Beverly Blvd., W. Hollywood 90048;
(310) 278-5444, Fax (310) 657-2816
Singles & Doubles $180-$220, Suites $250-$400. All major cards.

A cross between a French château and a contemporary glass building, this unique hybrid commands attention even from a distance. The rooms are nicely appointed and decorated in a sort of California-ized French-country scheme; also appreciated are the terrific location—across from the Beverly Center, on the edge of West Hollywood and smack in between Santa Monica and downtown—and the lovely views from the upper floors. The illustrious Ma Maison restaurant serves contemporary French fare; popular with hotel guests is the more casual café, La Cajole, which serves good French bistro–like cuisine. Amenities include a heated outdoor pool, sauna, fitness center, massage facilities and many meeting rooms. The hotel also has an arrangement with nearby golf courses and tennis courts.

 Le Mondrian
8440 Sunset Blvd., W. Hollywood 90069;
(213) 650-8999, Fax (213) 650-5215
Suites $165-$365. All major cards.

This hotel that once belonged to the Ashkenazy brothers is a highly visible, boldly painted Sunset Strip landmark. As of this writing, the

hotel had gone into receivership and been turned over to a hotel-management company. However, the company plans to maintain the standards set by the Ashkenazy brothers, and the contemporary suites are as attractive and comfortable as ever, many with spectacular views that stretch to the ocean. Other amenities include a 24-hour health spa, a large pool and whirlpool, and pleasant patios for sunning or lunching.

 The New Otani
120 S. Los Angeles St., Downtown (L.A.)
90012; (213) 629-1200, Fax (213) 622-0980
Singles $135-$170, Doubles $160-$195, Suites $340-$750. All major cards.

If you're homesick for Tokyo and its consummate hospitality, don't fret. You can spend a night at The New Otani in a tatami suite, with futon beds, ofuro baths and first-class service. East meets West in this modern hotel, where the Garden in the Sky presents a serene half-acre Shinto garden to ease the pains of a harrying business day. There are Western-style rooms, which also have a soothing appeal in their less-is-more design. The Otani is more than a hotel—it offers cultural introductions to Zen archery, shiatsu massage, flower arranging and a host of Japanese arts for fine (but simple) living. The multilingual staff is as gracious and courteous as can be.

 Le Parc
733 Westknoll Dr., W. Hollywood 90069;
(310) 855-8888, Fax (310) 659-7812
Suites $165-$250. All major cards.

The Ashkenazy brothers have done it again with this intimate, genteel hotel in a quiet residential area. The upwardly mobile clientele appreciates Le Parc's proximity to West Hollywood's countless galleries, restaurants and design showrooms. Some of the signature art collection of these entrepreneurial businessmen is scattered throughout the 152 compact suites, each of which features a sunken living room, fireplace, wet bar, kitchenette, bedroom and bathroom. The roof is a veritable miniresort, sporting a gym, tennis court, pool, spa and sun deck, designed to keep the music and advertising industry guests in good shape. There's also a fine little restaurant, Café Le Parc.

 Ritz-Carlton, Marina del Rey
4375 Admiralty Way, Marina del Rey 90292;
(310) 823-1700, Fax (310) 823-2403
Singles & Doubles $185-$295, Suites $385-$1,750. All major cards.

It's no surprise that savvy travelers are driving the short distance from LAX to stay at this elegant new hotel. The Ritz-Carlton imposes its own brand of hushed elegance on the Marina's casual, beachy atmosphere, and there's no denying the luxury and comfort of this 336-room waterfront hotel. The rooms are furnished in classic good taste; many have French doors leading to balconies overlooking the bobbing boats. Like all upscale hotels these days, there's a concierge floor offering special services to people who pay a few bucks more; this is a particularly good one, offering enough complimentary food to live on for a week. The sophisticated new dining room has given guests a good reason to stay in for dinner (*see* "LOS ANGELES Restaurants"). Although the hotel has become popular for chic meetings and conferences, fun is not neglected: amusements include tennis courts, a lovely pool and a fitness center.

The Sheraton Grande Hotel

333 S. Figueroa St., Downtown (L.A.) 90071; (213) 617-1133, Fax (213) 613-0291
Singles $175-$225, Doubles $195-$245, Suites $450-$900. All major cards.

Of downtown's chain hotels, this quiet highrise is probably your best bet. Its collection of 469 guest rooms, augmented by restaurants, bars, meeting spaces, banquet rooms and movie theaters, was carefully designed to create some feeling of intimacy in a large-scale hotel. The large guest rooms are stocked with all the necessities, from two-line phones to complimentary morning coffee and newspapers. The World Trade Center is right across the street; most of downtown's highrises are a walk away. The adjacent Laemmle fourplex is L.A.'s best-kept movie-theater secret: even on opening night of a touted blockbuster, there's never a crowd. Moody's, a polished-wood, San Francisco–style pub, is a comfortable, reasonably priced spot for a Caesar salad and a steak sandwich.

Other Sheratons in L.A. area: Santa Monica, Universal City and LAX (*see* reviews this chapter); Long Beach, Redondo Beach and Anaheim.

Moderate ($100 & Up)

Beverly Rodeo Hotel

360 N. Rodeo Dr., Beverly Hills 90210; (310) 273-0300, Fax (310) 859-8730
Singles $140-$160, Doubles $160-$180, Suites $250-$390. All major cards.

If you want to be the first one on the block to get inside Giorgio and avoid the touristy throngs, or if you have an early-morning appointment at Bijan to pick up your $5,000 suit, then the Beverly Rodeo is the perfect place to stay. Other than

its location, though, there is little to recommend it. The rooms are small and ordinary, featuring a standard-American-motel design. But most people don't spend too much time indoors when they have all that fabulous shopping ready at their fingertips. The quasi-sidewalk-café makes for good people-watching. Drop in for drinks rather than for the food.

Carlyle Inn

1119 S. Robertson Blvd., W.L.A. 90035; (310) 275-4445, Fax (310) 859-0496
Singles $105-$120, Doubles $125-$140, Suites $140. All major cards.

The Carlyle favorably compares itself to a small European inn, which is at odds with the stark exterior—you'd never confuse this concrete bunker with a country château. But this new hotel not without its charms: there are just 32 compact, comfortable, well-equipped rooms; service is personal and very attentive, whether you need a memo typed or theater tickets arranged; and instead of the roll-and-coffee offered at most "affordable" hotels, guests are presented with a fairly lavish (and free) breakfast buffet, not to mention a complete afternoon tea. This stretch of Robertson isn't exactly elegant, but neither is it unsavory, and it's quite convenient to Century City, Beverly Hills and Westwood. A good westside choice for the business traveler on a budget.

Century City Inn

10330 W. Olympic Blvd., Century City 90064; (310) 553-1000, Fax (310) 277-1633
Singles & Doubles $104-$129, Suites $144. All major cards.

This small, industrial-looking *faux* château is decently appointed and inexpensive. Rooms have VCRs, refrigerators and microwaves, and the business center has computers, fax machines and copiers. It's a perfectly acceptable place to stay for those on a brief business trip or on a budget—and you can't beat its westside location. Service is perky.

Chesterfield Hotel Deluxe

10320 W. Olympic Blvd., Century City 90015; (310) 556-2777, Fax (310) 203-0563
Singles & Doubles $125-$175. All major cards.

A little glitzier than its neighbor, the Century City Inn, the Chesterfield offers relatively moderate rates for its decent rooms. For grown-ups, there's a cocktail lounge and a Jacuzzi; the kids can watch movies on cable or closed-circuit TV after they've exhausted themselves exploring the city with their parents. The location is great for those doing business on the westside or those who want to be near the shops, theaters and fun in Century City and Beverly Hills. A number of business-entertainment packages and student rates are available. Parking is free.

Guest Quarters Suite Hotel

1707 4th St., Santa Monica 90401;
(310) 395-3332, Fax (310) 452-7399
Single Suites $145-$165, Double Suites $165-$185. All major cards.

Perched unromantically next to the Santa Monica Freeway and across the street from the Santa Monica Civic Center, this new, no-nonsense hotel pursues the harried business traveler with larger-than-normal all-suite accommodations, at prices compatible with most expense accounts. There's no doubting the value and comfort of the suites, which come complete with bedroom, living area (with sleeper sofa), dining area and wet bar. Amusements include a pool, spa and simple fitness center; for fun you can also explore the shops and restaurants on nearby Main Street, or walk several blocks to the beach.

Holiday Inn Westwood Plaza

10740 Wilshire Blvd., Westwood 90024;
(310) 475-8711, Fax (310) 475-5220
Singles $120, Doubles $130, Suites $225. All major cards.

This Holiday Inn is posher than you might expect, with attractive furnishings and decor. You may be surprised to be greeted by a doorman, welcomed to the attractive lobby and housed in a tastefully decorated room. This nineteen-story branch is a find, for its great location (near UCLA, Westwood and Beverly Hills), its understated elegance, better-than-average service, free parking, pool/spa area and reasonable prices.

Hyatt on Sunset

8401 W. Sunset Blvd., W. Hollywood 90069; (213) 656-4101, Fax (213) 650-7024
Singles $135-$155, Doubles $155-$175, Suites $350-$550. All major cards.

In rock 'n' roll's wild 'n' woolly era, the late '60s through the late '70s, this hotel was better known as the Riot House. Today, however, things have calmed down a bit, and nostalgia buffs will enjoy the art-deco lobby. Popular with movie and record types, the Hyatt has standard decor. It does, however, offer a superb location, perfect for travelers who want to walk to Spago or Tower Records or to stroll along fashionable Sunset Plaza, where some of the best-looking people in the world congregate. A small, comfortable, modest place.

Malibu Beach Inn

22878 Pacific Coast Hwy., Malibu 90265;
(310) 456-6444, Fax (310) 456-1499
Singles & Doubles $125-$250. AE, MC, V.

At last, Malibu has a decent hotel. And the Malibu Beach Inn suits its setting as perfectly as would a red convertible. The low-slung, three-story inn is a lovely, a muted-pink-stucco Mediterranean hacienda with a red-tile roof, fountains in the courtyard entry and small lobby, rough-hewn beams, tilework galore and glorious ocean views. The rooms have Mexican-tiled fireplaces, plantation shutters, berber carpeting, VCRs and terraces overlooking the ocean; top-floor rooms have high tongue-and-groove wood ceilings. A few steps down from the lobby is the beach, lined with $3 million shacks belonging to the famous and the just plain rich. The inn is skimpy on amenities—curiously, there's neither a pool nor a spa, and there's no restaurant—but the friendly staff can arrange for all sorts of sporting activities, from tennis to windsurfing. A free Continental breakfast is served on a sea-swept terrace.

Miramar Sheraton

101 Wilshire Blvd., Santa Monica 90401;
(310) 394-3731, Fax (310) 458-7912
Singles $125-$165, Doubles $145-$185, Suites & Bungalows $200-$400. All major cards.

This Sheraton is so steeped in history that a house historian keeps track of all the gossip. Its original sixteen bungalows, which were recently torn down and replaced with fancy new ones, were havens for Greta Garbo, Humphrey Bogart and Howard Hughes. Betty Grable used to sing here. And the Pacific is still a seashell's throw away, though not easily accessible. As we went to press, the Miramar was undergoing a massive renovation to give it a much-needed new lobby, pool area, and general refurbishment. The 305 rooms are divided between the older (and more charming) brick Palisades building, the contemporary Ocean Tower and the bungalows; many of the upper rooms have superb ocean views. Since the hotel had not yet re-opened at press time, we'll just say its future looks promising. The approach to this historic monument is perhaps the most impressive: wrought-iron gates open to an awesome 100-year-old Moreton Bay fig tree.

Radisson Bel Air Summit

11461 W. Sunset Blvd., Bel Air 90049;
(310) 476-6571, Fax (310) 471-6310
Singles $109-$169, Doubles $119-$189, Suites $199-$209. All major cards.

Formerly the Bel Air Sands, this unobtrusive hideaway is now a member of the Radisson chain. It's located near the San Diego Freeway, making it conveniently central for those who have business on the westside. It's popular with a movie-colony clientele, as well as for local executives who use it as a convenient meeting place and watering hole. The interior now has an ultra-moderne decor, very cool and sleek, yet comfortable. The 181 rooms are spacious and attractive, and each comes complete with a VCR (there's a video library as well); the meeting and banquet rooms can handle up to 300 people. Active sorts can use the swimming pool and tennis courts. Echo, the airy restaurant, has an interesting international menu and a most pleasant bar—both of which appeal to the many local couples who come here for quiet weekend retreats.

Ramada Hotel Beverly Hills
1150 S. Beverly Dr., Beverly Hills 90212;
(310) 553-6561, Fax (310) 277-4469
Singles $120, Doubles $130, Suites $200. All major cards.

If you're bargain hunting in Beverly Hills, this place is a good find. The price is right for the tony location, and the hotel is pleasant, efficient and modest. For media junkies, each room is equipped with a VCR. Suites are comfortable and have spectacular views of Century City and Beverly Hills. It's friendly around the Ramada; you'll appreciate the professional staff, the pool and the free shuttle to local points of interest and shopping. Guests are offered complimentary use of the nearby Family Fitness Center.

Le Rêve
8822 Cynthia St., W. Hollywood 90069;
(310) 854-1114, Fax (310) 657-2623
Suites $100-$160. All major cards.

A discreet apartment building acts as the facade for this small hotel. Le Rêve, one of the prolific Ashkenazy brothers' many creations, is very well located—adjacent to Beverly Hills, close to the galleries and shops, yet isolated enough for the privacy-minded (and since so few locals have even heard of it, you'll have privacy in spades). There are 80 small suites in all, each tastefully decorated in a French-country prints-and-pine mode. Most have fireplaces, some have kitchenettes and balconies, and all offer multiline telephones so you don't have to worry about missing that big call from your agent. There's a rooftop garden with a heated pool and Jacuzzi, and though there's no restaurant, room service is available from the on-premises kitchen from 7 a.m. to 10:30 p.m. Le Rêve offers lots of location and comfort for the price.

Shangri-la Hotel
1301 Ocean Ave., Santa Monica 90401;
(310) 394-2791, Fax (310) 451-3351
Studios $99, Singles & Doubles $130-$142, Suites $190-$210, Penthouse $365. All major cards.

This marvelously located art-deco hotel should have been the setting for a Raymond Chandler detective story; as things stand, it's an offbeat lodging choice for such luminaries as Diane Keaton and Robert De Niro. The Shangri-la's suites have been restored to their original '30s decor—in most cases, quite successfully. Shell lamps illuminate the pink-and-mauve color scheme, frosted mirrors adorn the walls, and deco-style furniture graces the rooms. Some of the smaller rooms are *too* small, but because of the Shangri-la's open design, all 50 rooms are cross-ventilated and have beautiful ocean views. Among its droll charms are suites with Murphy beds in the kitchens. The area is wonderful for people-watching, especially on Wednesday, when the streets are cordoned off and transformed into a festive outdoor farmer's market. The Shangri-la isn't for everybody—but if you're a fan of the charming and eccentric, this place is for you.

Practical (Under $100)

Bay View Plaza
530 Pico Blvd., Santa Monica 90405;
(310) 399-9344, Fax (310) 399-2504
Singles & Doubles $80-$119, Suites $225-$250. All major cards.

The Bay View Plaza is actually Holiday Inn's version of a luxury hotel, a little glossier and plusher than the average Holiday Inn. The place looks fine enough, it's only five blocks from the beach and the prices will leave you enough cash to enjoy nearby Main Street's shopping and good dining. Extras include two swimming pools, a health club and Jacuzzis in some of the suites.

Beverly Crest Hotel
125 S. Spalding Dr., Beverly Hills 90212;
(310) 274-6801, Fax (310) 273-6614
Singles $80-$90, Doubles $90-$100. All major cards.

This nondescript 54-room budget hotel is easy to pass by, though its loyal clientele swears by its service and convenient location. Its most compelling feature is its proximity to the shops along Wilshire Boulevard. The compact rooms lack character and style, but they are clean and neat. The Astroturfed pool area and the coffee shop are havens for tired shoppers who have just returned from sorties on Rodeo Drive.

Beverly Hillcrest Hotel
1224 S. Beverwil Dr., Beverly Hills 90212;
(310) 277-2800, Fax (310) 203-9537
Singles $85, Doubles $100, Suites $140-$200. All major cards.

High atop a knoll, with a commanding view of Beverly Hills, this monument to the '60s can make you pine for Frank Sinatra tunes and long cars with fins. The Beverly Hillcrest's loyal following is attributable to the experienced staff, some of whom have been with the hotel since it opened in 1965; the Miami-moderne decor has also been with the hotel since 1965, and things are looking a tad worn these days. Nonetheless, the rooms are sizable and have a private balcony or lanai patio, and the prices are low for the neighborhood. The rooftop restaurant affords a spectacular view of the sparkling city.

Beverly House Hotel
140 S. Lasky Dr., Beverly Hills 90212;
(310) 271-2145, Fax (310) 276-8431
Singles $78-$98, Doubles $88-$98 (incl. breakfast). All major cards.

This cute Colonial-style hotel on a quiet residential street may be just around the corner from The Peninsula and The Beverly Hilton, but it's miles away in terms of price and amenities. It bills itself as a "small, charming European hotel," but it's really more of a small, clean, American motel, the smell of air perfume pervading the hallways. Rooms are small and bathrooms are smaller, but the place is clean, friendly, air conditioned and a great value for the neighborhood. Extras include free parking and a modest Continental breakfast.

Channel Road Inn
219 W. Channel Rd., Santa Monica 90402;
(310) 459-1920, No fax
Doubles $95-$165, Suites $155-$195. No smoking. AE, MC, V.

Los Angeles suffers from a dearth of bed-and-breakfasts, especially on the westside and, more particularly, near the beach. Of the few, the most charming is the Channel Road Inn. A fine specimen of shingle-clad Colonial-revival architecture, this former residence was built in Santa Monica in 1910, moved to its present location in the early '60s, then bought and lovingly restored by the current owners in 1988. The fourteen rooms and suites all have private baths; most have ocean views. Home-baked breads and muffins are served as part of the Continental breakfast each morning; refreshments are offered in the afternoons. Secretarial services are available, there's a hillside spa overlooking the Santa Monica Bay, and you can rent bicycles and order a picnic lunch. There are also nearby horseback-ri-

ding and tennis facilities—and, best of all, you're within walking distance of the beach (just a block away). The tariff is very fair since the location alone could command far more.

The Comstock
10300 Wilshire Blvd., Westwood 90024;
(310) 275-5575, Fax (310) 278-3325
Suites $95-$290. All major cards.

If you're looking for a westside home-away-from-home, this may be the place. It's a converted apartment building, and it still looks like one, the tiny white lights decorating the entryway notwithstanding. Each of the 73 suites has a living room (except for the few studio suites), and all are tastefully decorated, featuring Chippendale-style furniture and a comfortable ambience. The inner courtyard (with a pool and spa) makes for relaxed California living at its best. There's a charming little bistro, Le Petit Café.

Del Capri Hotel
10587 Wilshire Blvd., Westwood 90024;
(310) 474-3511, Fax (310) 824-0594
Singles $85, Doubles $95-$105, Suites $110-$140. All major cards.

Half hidden by high-rise luxury condos, the Del Capri boasts simple charms that remain undiminished by time or real-estate developers. Once a favorite haven for stars such as the late Ingrid Bergman, this intimate hotel combines privacy with all the comforts of home at a very reasonable price. Most of the 80 suites have full kitchenettes, cable TVs and whirlpool tubs. While not luxurious, the Del Capri is neat, clean and hospitable, and the veteran staff is efficient and friendly. Half of the suites overlook the free-form swimming pool and serene flower garden. Extras include free parking, free Continental breakfast served in your room, and shuttle service to nearby UCLA and the shopping/entertainment areas in Beverly Hills, Century City and Westwood. An excellent value for the trendy westside.

Hilgard House
927 Hilgard Ave., Westwood 90024;
(310) 208-3945, Fax (310) 208-1972
Singles $99, Doubles $109-$129 (incl. breakfast). AE, MC, V.

An affordable alternative to the elegant Westwood Marquis across the street, this quiet little hotel next to UCLA caters to visiting professors and parents, businesspeople headed for Westwood's high-rises, visitors to UCLA Medical Center and just plain tourists. Above the tiny, wood-paneled bookish lobby are 55 clean, pleasant rooms with window seats, refrigerators, Co-

Taste the World

GLENMORANGIE SINGLE MALT SCOTCHES

Produced only for the single-malt drinker. Bottled at ten years, its first peak. And 18 years, sherry-finished.

GENTLEMAN JACK

The first new whiskey from Jack Daniels in this century. Charcoal mellowed before and after aging.

SEMPÉ ARMAGNAC

Distilled from St. Emilion grapes, aged in Limousin oak; Sempé exemplifies the finest brandy France has to offer.

BUSHMILLS BLACK BUSH

Bushmills~triple distilled in County Antrim since 1608. Black Bush~Sherry-aged, malt-finished, with a touch of grain whiskey.

Brown Forman Beverage Company, Louisville, KY © 1992. 40% and 43% alcohol by volume (80 and 86 Proof)

Jordan Sparkling Wine Company, P.O. Box 1919, Hillsburg, CA 95448

lonial-style furniture and small, plain bathrooms. There's no restaurant, but Westwood Village, with its countless cafés, bars, restaurants, theaters and shops, is just around the corner. The low room rates also include parking.

Holiday Inn Hollywood
1755 N. Highland Ave., Hollywood 90028; (213) 462-7181, Fax (213) 466-9072
Singles $95-$115, Doubles $110-$125, Suites $145. All major cards.

Hollywood's sidewalk scene—with its motor-cycle-gang members, head-bangers, bewildered tourists, record producers, stray ladies of the evening and sundry other characters—provides the less-than-orthodox backdrop for this pleasant place. The 468 rooms are cozy, comfortable and of the predictable Holiday Inn design school; many have good views. The location is great for visiting the Hollywood Bowl and local tourist sights, and the revolving restaurant on the 23rd floor provides a wonderful view.

The Hollywood Roosevelt
7000 Hollywood Blvd., Hollywood 90028; (213) 466-7000, Fax (213) 462-8056
Singles $95, Doubles $115, Suites $160-$1,500. All major cards.

One of the linchpins of Hollywood's much-ballyhooed (but not yet fully realized) redevelopment, this 1920s beauty was restored to its original loveliness several years ago. The spacious lobby is a wonderful place in which to linger, with its tilework, painted ceilings, baby grand piano and photos of Gable and Lombard. Overhead you'll see the balconied mezzanine, which is a minimuseum of Hollywood history and lore. Film, TV and record executives have rediscovered the Roosevelt (so named for Teddy); they like to confab in the wonderful old meeting rooms. The hotel is home to a terrific '40s-style jazz supper club, the Cinegrill. Although some of the rooms can be small, they all combine period charm with modern comforts. If you sign that big deal, celebrate in the two-story Celebrity Suite, worth every penny of its $1,500-a-night tag.

Jamaica Bay Inn
4175 Admiralty Way, Marina del Rey 90292; (310) 823-5333, Fax (310) 823-1325
Singles & Doubles $90-$140. AE, MC, V.

Tucked among the high-rise glitz of the Marina's condos and luxury hotels, this modest little Best Western motel is an anomaly—it's better suited to a funky beach town in the Florida Keys. It's the only on-the-beach hotel in the Marina; out in the salt air, you can enjoy a no-frills

bar, pool and spa, and pleasant beachfront café. The bathrooms are minuscule, but otherwise the rooms are quite large and very clean, decorated with a little more taste than your average motel (though that air-perfume smell can linger in the hallways). All the rooms have lovely views of the Marina through swaying palm trees, and most have lanais or terraces. An excellent value.

Kawada Hotel
200 S. Hill St., Downtown (L.A.) 90012; (213) 621-4455, (800) 752-9232, Fax (213) 687-4455.
Singles $58-$75, Doubles $62-$80, Suites $135. All major cards.

A hotel that positions itself as the stopover for "upscale travelers on a budget," the Kawada is a welcome addition to downtown—giving business travelers one of the most affordable options in L.A. It's extraordinarily inexpensive, especially for what you get: each of the clean, serviceable rooms gives you a refrigerator, a TV, a VCR and two phones (one in the bathroom). Just a few minutes' walk takes you to Chinatown and Little Tokyo, the Music Center or MOCA. The restaurant, Epicentre, serves Californian fare in an earthquake-themed (!) setting.

The Mayfair Hotel
1256 W. 7th St., Downtown (L.A.) 90017; (213) 484-9789, Fax (213) 484-2769
Singles $75-$115, Doubles $85-$130, Suites $130-$350. All major cards.

Located on the western fringe of downtown, on a rather scruffy but not scary block, this Best Western hotel is a good spot for the budget-conscious business traveler who needs to be downtown. We wish that the 1984 renovation would have preserved the 1920s charm of the rooms, but except for the columned, skylit lobby (very popular for location filming), the hotel is pretty generic. Still, it offers comfortable, clean rooms and free parking. Extras include a pleasant restaurant, a bar and nonsmoking rooms; the "sundeck" is really just a grim tar roof.

Ramada West Hollywood
8585 Santa Monica Blvd., W. Hollywood 90069; (310) 652-6400, Fax (310) 652-2135
Singles & Doubles $99-$109, Suites $120-$130. All major cards.

West Hollywood is certainly an exceptional city, which is perhaps why this Ramada is quite an exceptional Ramada. From the outside, with its beyond-weird lampposts, sculptures and mobiles (much of it designed by artisan Peter Shire) it looks a bit like a postmodern art museum. The lobby is one you might encounter on Mars, with its odd, brightly colored overstuffed furniture. Take note that the Ramada is located on the site of the beloved old Tropicana Motel, once home to the likes of Tom Waits and Rickie Lee Jones. The rooms and suites are nicely decorated in a moderne mode, and amenities include a swimming pool and the use of the Sports Connection fitness club across the street.

Royal Palace
1052 Tiverton Ave., Westwood 90024;
(310) 208-6677, Fax (310) 824-3732
Singles & Doubles $60, Suites $90-$100.
All major cards.

Neither royal nor palatial, this small, economical 36-room hotel does have an excellent Westwood location, close to the entertaining street life, shops and UCLA student scene, and the price can't be beat. The rooms are spartan but come with kitchens, which are appreciated by the many visiting professors who make this their temporary shelter. Service is friendly. Parking is free, which is cause enough for celebration.

The Sovereign
205 Washington Ave., Santa Monica 90403;
(310) 395-9921, Fax (310) 458-3085
Singles $69-$79, Doubles $79-$89, Suites $99-$199. AE, MC, V.

Okay, so the paint's peeling and the shower's mildewing. The Sovereign compensates for its faded funkiness with loads of 1920s Mediterranean charm and a superb location—one block from Ocean Avenue and Palisades Park, on a quiet residential street between Wilshire and trendy Montana. The small rooms are pretty grim; better to spend a little more on a large suite with a kitchen. Many of the rooms in this former apartment building have ocean views through French doors or windows, and some have tiny Juliet balconies. The Sovereign has a number of full-time residents of all ages.

The Venice Beach House
15 30th Ave., Venice 90291;
(310) 823-1966, No fax
Doubles $80-$110, Suites $125-$150. No smoking. AE, MC, V.

On one of Venice's "walk streets" (tiny, tree-lined walkways that were once canals) sits this blue stucco Craftsman-era bed-and-breakfast. As L.A. residents know, Venice's funky charm sometimes borders on the undesirable, but all is idyllic and peaceful on this street. Inside, the unadorned dark woodwork typical of a Craftsman house has been lightened with the judicious use of pale pink paint and floral fabrics. Accommodations range from simple, homey, shared-bath rooms over-

looking the garden to the ocean-view Pier Suite, with a sitting room, fireplace and private bath. Venice Pier, Washington Street's tourist shops and cafés, and the wide, sandy beach are all about a two-minute walk away; you can borrow the inn's bikes for more adventurous outings. A delightful, affordable alternative.

San Fernando Valley

Encompasses Sherman Oaks, Studio City, North Hollywood, Toluca Lake, Universal City, Burbank, Encino, Van Nuys, Tarzana, Woodland Hills, Calabasas, Granada Hills and Canoga Park, as well as Thousand Oaks and Saugus.

Moderate ($100 & Up)

Sheraton Universal Hotel
333 Universal Terrace Pkwy., Universal City 91608; (818) 980-1212, Fax (818) 985-4980
Singles $125-$180, Doubles $145-$205, Suites $375-$700. All major cards.

A modern, 458-room hotel located right on the Universal Studios lot, this is a mighty popular destination for tourists whose major goal is a studio tour. It's also conveniently near the Universal Amphitheatre, The Burbank Studios and the Hollywood Bowl. Some of the upper rooms have great views; all are comfortable and done in pastels. A pool, spa and small but well-equipped workout room provide respite from the rigors of sightseeing.

Universal City Hilton and Towers
555 Universal Terrace Pkwy., Universal City 91608; (818) 506-2500, Fax (818) 509-2058
Singles & Doubles $129-$184, Suites $250-$1,200. All major cards.

Just when we're starting to remember the name of this upscale hotel, it changes again. A few years back, it was the Sheraton Premiere, then it became the Registry, and now it's a Hilton. Clearly the big chains have had a problem making a go of this property, but Hilton seems game for the challenge. While the next-door Sheraton Universal attracts tourists headed for Universal Studios, this glitzier high-rise goes after business and creative types visiting the nearby movie studios (when we last stopped by, the Kentucky Headhunters and entourage were checking in). The gleaming 24-story tower encases an attractive plant-filled lobby, some decent restaurants and ordinary but spacious rooms. Ask for a room on an upper floor, and you'll get a fabulous nighttime view of the Valley.

Warner Center Marriott
21850 Oxnard St., Woodland Hills 91367;
(818) 887-4800, Fax (818) 340-5843
Singles $128, Doubles $148, Suites $350-$1,500. All major cards.

The area of Woodland Hills known as Warner Center has mushroomed at the hands of bullish developers: office buildings, department stores, chain restaurants and tract housing, and it's still growing like mad. Even Angelenos are astounded at this enormous growth in the hinterlands. The newish Warner Center Marriott was created to serve this bustling community. It's a huge place with an emphasis on meeting and convention facilities; there are meeting rooms of every conceivable size, and a full kosher kitchen that can serve 60 to 600. Predictably, this Marriott immediately became a popular west Valley wedding spot. Rooms are comfortable and pleasant in that cookie-cutter, chain-hotel way.

Practical (Under $100)

La Maida House
11159 La Maida St., N. Hollywood 91601;
(818) 769-3857, No fax
Doubles $80-$145, Suites $155-$210. No smoking. MC, V.

Scattered throughout the Valley's countless tract houses are the occasional mansions, reminders of an era gone by, the days when the Valley was populated by wealthy ranchers. La Maida House is one such mansion, and, happily, it has been converted to a luxurious bed-and-breakfast for hotel-weary travelers.

The 7,000-square-foot Mediterranean villa, built in the 1920s, is nestled among grounds lush with magnolia trees, orchids and hundreds of roses. Owner Megan Timothy has decorated its seven spacious rooms and suites in good taste, with polished floors, wicker furniture, ceiling fans, pretty fabrics and tiled bathrooms. The atmosphere is refined and relaxed, the rooms are comfortable, and the breakfast (featuring eggs freshly hatched by La Maida's chickens) is lovely. Timothy prides herself on her cooking; with advance notice she prepares gourmet dinners for guests.

Sportsmen's Lodge
12825 Ventura Blvd., Studio City 91604;
(818) 769-4700, Fax (818) 877-3898
Singles $94-$155, Doubles $104-$160, Suites $180-$300. All major cards.

We hadn't been to Sportsmen's Lodge in many, many years, and frankly, we never thought we'd set foot there again, not after all those dreary chicken banquets we had to endure in our formative years. So it was quite a surprise to walk into this beloved Valley motel and discover its comfortable charm. Rooms are cheerfully decorated in country-pine furniture and shades of dusty rose, green and blue. The large pool is centered in a protected courtyard. The bright coffee shop is a proper coffee shop, not a "café" serving $10 pancakes like at so many other hotels in town. There's a tiny, cozy pub and a modest exercise room. In short, there's a lot for the money, in a convenient, smack-in-the-middle-of-the-Valley location. And the adjacent restaurant is still feeding Rotary and Kiwanis clubs from miles around. Don't forget to ask for the AAA and AARP discounts.

> *Room prices are based on regular rates during the high season. Most hotels offer discounted rates and special packages in the off-season and during certain times of the year. Be sure to inquire.*

San Gabriel Valley

Encompasses Pasadena, Glendale, San Gabriel, Rosemead and Monterey Park.

Luxury ($150 & Up)

Ritz-Carlton/Huntington, Pasadena
1401 S. Oak Knoll Ave., Pasadena 91106;
(818) 568-3900, Fax (818) 568-3159
Singles & Doubles $145-$240, Suites $350-$2,500. All major cards.

They don't make 'em like this anymore. Its future jeopardized by earthquake damage, its size scaring off most developers and hoteliers, the once-glorious Huntington Hotel sat empty for several years. But Prince Charming, in the form of the Ritz-Carlton, came along to make this 83-year-old beauty glow again. And glow she does, from the 23 acres of gorgeous rolling grounds to the stunning barrel-vaulted ceiling of The Georgian Room, where chef Bernard Bordaries shows off some pretty impressive French fare (*see* "LOS ANGELES Restaurants.") Within minutes of opening, rhe Ritz became *the* socially correct place for Pasadenans to have tea, debut their daughters, celebrate weddings and entertain clients; the extensive conference and meetings rooms are also attracting image-conscious corporations. The 383 amply proportioned rooms are suitably luxe, with marble bathrooms, thick robes, honor bars and multiple phones. On the grounds are tennis courts, an Olympic-size pool, a fitness center, a spa and gardens in which to wander. And by westside standards, the room rates are a bargain, though the restaurants aren't cheap. Proximity to downtown makes this a fine choice for the business traveler with a car.

Moderate ($100 & Up)

Doubletree Pasadena
191 N. Los Robles Ave., Pasadena 91101; (818) 792-2727, Fax (818) 795-7669
Singles & Doubles $119-$139, Suites $250-$950. All major cards.

Pasadena is increasingly becoming a destination city in its own right, with its revitalized Old Town, its famed museums and its historic houses, not to mention the Rose Bowl and a certain parade. This pristine new hotel makes an excellent base in the Rose City. Located midway between Old Town and the Lake Street business district, it's a most handsome 360-room hotel with a clean-lined Mediterranean feel. Even the more modest standard rooms are large and tastefully appointed, with plantation shutters, window-seat sofas, artful sketches and lovely indirect lighting. The Oaks on the Plaza restaurant does a better-than-average job with contemporary Californian cuisine, which you can work off later in the fitness center. The Doubletree anchors the north end of the fountain-filled Plaza Las Fuen-

For a comprehensive listing of all hotels in this book By Area & Price, see the INDEXES section at the back of the book.

tes, a chic business-and-retail center. An excellent and affordable base for those who want to be based on the east side (downtown L.A. is ten minutes by car).

South Bay & Airport

In addition to the following hotels, those in Marina del Rey (the Doubletree, Jamaica Bay Inn and Ritz-Carlton Marina del Rey) and Venice (the Venice Beach Inn) are also convenient to the airport. See "Hotels – *L.A. Area*" for these listings.

Luxury ($150 & Up)

Marriott Los Angeles
5855 W. Century Blvd., Westchester 90045; (310) 641-5700, Fax (310) 337-5358
Singles $144-$149, Doubles $154-$159, Suites $200-$1,000. All major cards.

Once the flagship of the chain, this ten-story highrise has been renovated and redecorated in a typical upscale-chain-hotel style. The expansive sunken lobby bar employs a harpist at cocktail hour to soothe business travelers and tourists who stumble back to the hotel after a taxing day in L.A. You'll notice an attention to detail for which the Marriott chain is famous, and the rooms are spacious and comfortable, if not fancy. The three restaurants range from coffee-shop basic to hotel-Continental elegant; other amusements include a disco and a pool area with a lush tropical garden and outdoor bar. This hotel is ideal for corporate travelers who want to conduct business in a resortlike setting just minutes from the airport.

Moderate ($100 & Up)

Barnabey's
3501 N. Sepulveda Blvd., Manhattan Beach 90266; (310) 545-8466, Fax (310) 545-8466
Singles & Doubles $129-$159, Suites $149-$450. All major cards.

There is something rather bizarre about having a piece of Victorian England sequestered in a community more renowned for its surfer mentality than its cultural heritage. Nonetheless,

Barnabey's has an ersatz old-world charm that some find wonderful, and others find out of place in this environment. The rooms are filled with antiques, deep carpets and lots of bronze, oak and carved marble. The rather claustrophobic Victorian dining room serves very good Continental cuisine (the chef is Viennese), along with high tea presented by servers in Victorian dress. Despite the old-fashioned atmosphere, however, all the modern conveniences are provided, making a stay here comfortable.

 ## Hyatt Regency Long Beach
200 S. Pine Ave., Long Beach 90802;
(310) 491-1234, Fax (310) 432-1972
Singles $139, Doubles $159. All major cards.

This sleek spot could be called a business resort, geared in every way for business but situated on a lush slice of land with well-groomed gardens and a miniature lagoon. Right next door to the Long Beach Convention Center, the hotel also offers its own enormous convention facilities, including two ballrooms and a 12,000-seat sports arena. Business travelers can use a computer, get a document typed or rent a cellular phone from the fully equipped business center. The more than 500 rooms are comfortable and ultra-efficient: a "Robobar" dispenses drinks and snacks, a make-up mirror and hair dryer allow you to spruce up in a pinch.

 ## Portofino Inn
260 Portofino Way, Redondo Beach 90277;
(310) 379-8481, Fax (310) 372-7329
*Singles & Doubles $140-$200, Suites $245-$275.
All major cards.*

For a taste of the sort of South Bay living that Beach Boys legends are made of, check into this cheerful waterfront hotel. Rooms, done in peachy florals, are full of comfy overstuffed furniture in California '80s pastels, and most have a view of either the Pacific Ocean or King's Harbor. The vibe is young and active: you can use the hotel's bikes to explore the 25-mile beachfront path, work out in the fitness center, rent a boat for a sail, sign up for one of Redondo Sports Fishing's day trips, explore the shops and restaurants at Fisherman's Wharf, swim in the pool or just catch some rays on your balcony. A few miles south of LAX (complimentary shuttles daily), the Portofino is a superior alternative to the airport hotels. It's a lovely little spot for a beachy weekend escape at an affordable weekend price.

 ## Radisson Plaza Hotel
1400 Parkview Ave., Manhattan Beach
90266; (310) 546-7511, Fax (310) 546-7520
*Singles $130-$140, Doubles $150-$160, Suites
$225-$340. All major cards.*

This newish, large (400 rooms) West Coast flagship of the Radisson chain does a pretty spectacular business for a mass-market chain hotel— and you do get quite a bit for your money. The grounds are lovely, with lots of fountains and waterfalls; indoors, in the atrium lobby, are acres of glitzy marble, terrazzo, etched glass and woods. One of the main draws here is the golf course (complete with pro shop); additional recreational facilities include a fully equipped health spa, a swimming pool and bicycle rentals. The Plaza Club Level provides laundry and pressing service, twice-daily maid service and a lounge. The rooms are good-sized and attractive in that fancy-corporate-hotel mode, and there are a business center and voluminous meeting facilities. The restaurant, Califia, serves surprisingly tasty California cuisine; so does the more casual indoor/outdoor Terrace Bistro.

 ## Ramada Renaissance Hotel
111 E. Ocean Blvd., Long Beach 90802;
(310) 437-5900, (800) 228-9898,
Fax (310) 499-2512
*Doubles $125-$160, Suites $150-$190, Deluxe
& Renaissance Suites $400-$900. All major
cards.*

In the heart of Long Beach's business district, just a hop, skip and a jump from the Long Beach Convention Center and Civic Center, this twelve-story Ramada is a well-appointed, plush haven for the business traveler. The "Renaissance Club" on the hotel's two top floors has a private lounge and four luxurious suites. Teleconferencing facilities and in-house audio-visual facilities are available, and stressed-out guests can avail themselves of the Universal-equipped workout room, sauna, spa and pool, or rent bikes to ride along the oceanfront. The French dining room, Floreale, serves classic American/Continental fare in a subdued and elegant atmosphere.

 ## Sheraton Los Angeles Airport Hotel
6101 W. Century Blvd., Westchester 90045;
(310) 642-1111, Fax (310) 410-1267
*Singles $115-$155, Doubles $135-$175, Suites
$180-$200. All major cards.*

If you need to stay near the airport, the Sheraton is as good a choice as any. The lobby does little more than provide a walkway to the elevators. The staff, however, offers some warmth to the conventioneering clientele that keeps this place active. The compact rooms feature a minimalist decor with little style, but the suites are spacious and comfortable. If you're satisfied with efficiency and a predictable atmosphere, this Sheraton will do.

Practical (Under $100)

Hotel Queen Mary
Pier J (end of Long Beach Fwy.), Long Beach 90802; (310) 432-6964, Fax (310) 437-4531
Singles & Doubles $85-$185, Suites $240-$900. All major cards.

If you're looking not only to get away from it all but to get away in the style of the Carnegies, Gettys and Vanderbilts, stay at the Hotel Queen Mary, resplendent in its authentic deco decor.

Wood paneling, marvelous overstuffed vintage furniture and ship-style bathrooms reflect the golden age. And it's a far cry from the oil rigs in Long Beach Harbor, and from the casual California feeling of so many other local lodgings. Some of the rooms have been remodeled, and the luxury-ship feeling has been well preserved. There are more than 380 rooms on three decks, in shapes accommodating the ship's hull. It's wise to request an outside room, as the inside chambers, although less expensive, have no cheery portholes. If you enjoy the elegance of an era gone by, treat yourself to a more decadent visit to the past in one of the first-class suites, complete with two parlors, two bedrooms, two baths and *two* maid's rooms. There are a few concessions to the present; each room has a telephone and the ubiquitous TV set. Nostalgia fans can be married by the ship's captain and honeymoon in splendor. ◆

NIGHTLIFE

Contents

Doing the Suburbs

Y ou don't "do the town" in Los Angeles; L.A.'s "townness" has dissolved into its mighty suburbs. Therefore, you'll spend the evening driving through these 'burbs, looking for signs of vitality and action. Still, there's a lot going on across this vast metropolis. Whether you're a fast-track single looking for new friends, a jazz buff, a club aficionado or a fan of the classic neighborhood bar, you'll find what you're after somewhere in L.A. We must tell you, however, that the city's nightlife scene is extremely fickle and fractured. The hottest clubs tend to be moveable feasts, invading a venue for one or two nights a week and then, in a few months, moving on. Of course, we keep our information as current as possible, but for more up-to-the-minute listings, check the *L.A. Weekly*, the *Reader*, the *Los Angeles Times*'s "Calendar" section or *Los Angeles* magazine. Cover charges and hours change frequently, so check first. And remember

that a 2 a.m. closing time usually means that the last call for drinks is at 1:30 a.m.

Unfortunately, the L.A. club-hopper is dependent on the automobile. Keep in mind California's tough drunk-driving laws; if you're going to be celebrating, hire a taxi or have one of your group be the evening's nondrinking "designated driver." Or, join the throngs of Angelenos that have opted to party à la mineral water or espresso drinks instead of alcohol.

Bars

Atlas Bar & Grill

3760 Wilshire Blvd., Wilshire District (L.A.) 90010; (213) 380-8400
Open Mon.-Thurs. 11:30 a.m.-1 a.m., Sat.-Sun. 11:30 a.m.-2 a.m. All major cards.

A throwback to the L.A. elegance of the '30s. Gigantic lightning bolts and beautiful starbursts adorn this high-ceilinged room adjacent to the Wiltern Theater. When you're finished oohing and ahhing at the decor, take a gander at the smartly-dressed sophisticates eddying around you. Finally, of course, you'll want to direct your gaze stageward, where an eclectic booking policy insures that something delightfully out of the ordinary (jazz or cabaret) is taking place.

Baja Cantina

311 E. Washington St., Marina del Rey 90291; (310) 821-2252
Open Mon.-Sat. 11:30 a.m.-1 a.m., Sun. 10:30 a.m.-1 a.m. AE, MC, V.

This cluttered but comfortable bar hosts the same mating frenzies found at almost every Marina bar. Its clientele pulls up and hops out of jeeps or BMWs, sporting that same buffed, tanned, beach-chic look that dominates so many beach spots. But this place is nicer for a relaxed drink and conversation in its cozy, plant-filled Mexican-style setting. Don't pass up the appetizers—they're made with the fresh tortillas prepared to order on a grill in the middle of the room.

163

Barney's Beanery
8447 Santa Monica Blvd., W. Hollywood 90069;
(213) 654-2287
Open daily 10 a.m.-2 a.m. AE, MC, V.

The small, always-full bar at Barney's offers an unbeatable selection of beers from around the world (over 200) and a friendly, somewhat gritty atmosphere featuring well-used pool tables, lots of rather worn dark wood and a display of international license plates. The regulars aren't exactly chic or clean-cut, but we like the refreshing honesty of the place—and Bono, of the rock band U2, has been known to shoot a game of pool here.

Boardner's
1652 N. Cherokee Ave., Hollywood 90028;
(213) 462-9621
Open daily 10 a.m.-2 a.m. No cards.

If you've been to Boardner's in the distant past, come on back, because you'll hardly recognize it today. The main room is still a grungy space with a distinctive hook-shaped bar. Out in back, though, the patio's been refurbished to include a small bar and a beautiful Mediterranean-tiled fountain. And look, there's a next door, too! And it's elegant. Dubbed "The Casablanca Room," it features brass lamps, a video monitor that plays Bogey movies and other films of that period and framed vintage movie posters on the walls. But even with all that extra space—and this is new, too—there's usually a line outside of Hollywood citizenry clad in their official uniform of black denim jeans, black leather jacket and hair dyed the official shade of black.

The Burgundy Room
1621 1/2 N. Cahuenga Blvd., Hollywood 90028;
(213) 465-7530
Open nightly 8 p.m.-2 a.m. No cards.

A place with this many Harleys parked out in front can't be all bad. Once inside, you'll find the narrow bar packed with a throng of young scenesters, especially of the film and music industry variety. If you can make your way to the back, you'll find an excellent jukebox with a more idiosyncratic selection than you find at the standard-issue models all over town. The bar itself has quite an interesting history. Almost a century and a half old, it has made the trek from the Midwest to San Francisco, where it survived the great quake before it was deemed sturdy enough to withstand the daily Hollywood mayhem it endures in its present location.

Bob Burns
202 Wilshire Blvd., Santa Monica 90404;
(310) 393-6777
Open Sun.-Thurs. 11:30 a.m.-midnight, Fri.-Sat. 11:30 a.m.-1 a.m. All major cards.

Call us square. See if we care. We *like* Bob Burns. That's right, the tartan rug, the paintings depicting English horse-racing scenes, the fireplace and the gas-burning lanterns: it all makes us feel cozy. But it's the act here that keeps us coming back. Piano-bar singer Howlett Smith and his sidekick, known simply as Brina, deliver their mix of oldies and originals with a spry theatricality—conveying the meaning as well as music in every lyric. They perform Saturday through Tuesday, 9 p.m. to 1 a.m. When you've finished your fling with ear-splitting rock-and-roll—or you've got your parents with you—this is the place to go.

Carlos 'n' Charlie's
8240 Sunset Blvd., W. Hollywood 90046;
(213) 656-8830
Open Mon.-Fri. 11 a.m.-2 a.m., Sat.-Sun. 5 p.m.-2 a.m. All major cards.

Mix a successful chain of Mexican restaurants with an easygoing California attitude and you get Carlos 'n' Charlie's. This import works as well as the originals, which are found in various cities in Mexico. The bar is generally crowded, active and glittery, and the kitchen maintains its good reputation. It's a comfortable spot for an evening or an after-theater drink, the kind of convivial place that would make a good setting for an upscale beer commercial. The upstairs cabaret provides more action, hosting a variety of entertainment and dancing (the cover ranges from $7 to $10). The club gets some name talent, and it's hard not to have a good time. The marquee outside announces a Joan Rivers workshop for would-be comedians, and La Joan herself performs once in a while.

Carroll O'Connor's Place
369 N. Bedford Dr., Beverly Hills 90210;
(310) 273-7585
Open Mon.-Sat. 11:30 a.m.-1 a.m. AE, MC, V.

A New York bar, complete with an Upper East Side decor and an appropriately prosperous, professional clientele. This lively, handsome pub, formerly known as The Ginger Man, now eponymously renamed, is a fun spot to meet old friends, make new ones or have a restorative and a decent meal after a Beverly Hills shopping spree.

Casey's Bar and Grill
613 S. Grand Ave., Downtown (L.A.) 90017;
(213) 629-2353
Open Mon.-Fri. 11 a.m.-10:30 p.m. AE, MC, V.

The house is full weeknights during happy hour, when downtown's business sorts come to Casey's to wind down or gear up for the night. Amid a handsome, comfortable Irish-pub decor they talk shop and sports with co-workers and exchange small talk with new-found friends. Though it's convivial and lively at 6 p.m., by 9 p.m. most everyone has headed elsewhere. Wednesday nights, there's live musical entertainment.

Cassidy's Pub
500 S. Sepulveda Blvd., Manhattan Beach 90266;
(310) 372-7666
Open Tues.-Fri. 5 p.m.-2 a.m., Sat. 8 p.m.-2 a.m. AE, MC, V.

A young crowd hits Cassidy's to dance on the tiny dance floor and let the deejay put them through their paces. A well-known singles place in the beach area, Cassidy's is worth a visit for its lovely outdoor terrace, where you can sit with a friend before an open fire and enjoy a drink under the stars.

Cat and Fiddle Pub
6530 Sunset Blvd., Hollywood 90028;
(213) 468-3800
Open daily 11:30 a.m.-1:30 a.m. AE, MC, V.

The Cat and Fiddle's Hollywood neighborhood is full of clubs and ethnic restaurants, and the people who venture there like that kind of life. The place attracts a young, good-looking Hollywood crowd as well as a healthy dose of Britons, most of whom are remarkably unpretentious. Everyone seems to have a good time, whether inside shouting over the noise and the terrific jukebox, or outside in the stunning Spanish-style courtyard quietly nursing a pint of British ale. There's live jazz on Sundays, and a full menu for those who don't want to drink their dinner.

Chez Jay
1657 Ocean Ave., Santa Monica 90401;
(310) 395-1741
Open daily 11 a.m.-1:30 a.m. AE, MC, V.

After a hard day in the California sun, it's sometimes good to get away from it all. Chez Jay is a beach bar, more popular in the summer than in the winter, but with a year-round philosophy of "Live now, pay later." It's something of a hangout for writers and artists, a quiet place with sawdust on the floor and good American food

served at cozy, red-vinyl booths. The eclectic jukebox plays tunes from the 1930s and '40s, along with such classics as Lou Reed's urban hit, "Take a Walk on the Wild Side." Owner Jay's friendliness is reflected in the ambience.

The Circle
2926 Main St., Santa Monica 90405;
(310) 399-9948
Open Mon.-Wed. 2:30 p.m.-2 a.m., Thurs. noon-2 a.m., Fri.-Sun. 10 a.m.-2 a.m. No cards.

The Circle is where the real people of Santa Monica go to drink. It's a refreshing break from the sterile yuppie bars that plague Main Street. There's nothing here but affordable drinks, a large 360-degree bar, pinball, pool, a great jukebox and plenty of friendly, laid-back folks.

Cutters
Colorado Place, 2425 Colorado Ave., Santa Monica 90405; (310) 453-3588
Open Mon.-Thurs. 11:30 a.m.-10:30 p.m., Fri. 11 a.m.-11:30 p.m., Sat. 5 p.m.-10:30 p.m., Sun. 5 p.m.-9:30 p.m. AE, MC, V.

The warehouses in this neighborhood are dark by the time Cutters lights up each night, and this place does light up. The kitchen has a good reputation and the well-stocked and brightly lit bar area—the shelving of which reaches up the wall to the height of two basketball players—is a sight to behold. Cutters attracts a young, well-to-do, professional group of men and women who worry about car payments and corporate buyouts and who don't smoke cigarettes. About the only creativity here is on the walls, but Cutters is a clean, comfortable place with a graceful, art-deco elegance to it. Located in a low-rise office and shopping complex called Colorado Place, the bar supplies validated underground parking, so the elements won't ruin the paint on all the BMWs.

The Dresden Room
1760 N. Vermont Ave., Los Feliz 90027;
(213) 665-4294
Mon.-Sat. 10 a.m.-2 p.m., Sun. 3 p.m.-1 a.m. AE, DC, MC.

Once, the gold lamé-clad husband and wife duo of Marty and Elayne Roberts were singing "Embraceable You" in near-obscurity. Now, they are considered the vanguard of the lounge-music revival, and they dish out their hot mix of jazz, standards and an occasional contemporary tune to a house packed with young scenesters. Their national reputation has been steadily enhanced by visits from such Hollywood bigwigs as David Lynch, Michelle Pfeiffer and Kiefer Sutherland. The adjacent restaurant serves decent, if pricey, food, but we prefer the lounge—where all the entertainment is—particularly the seats at the piano bar. Marty and Elayne perform Tuesday through Saturday, 9 p.m. to 1 a.m. Tuesday is also open-mike night, when anything can happen and usually does.

Engine Co. No. 28

644 S. Figueroa St., Downtown (L.A.) 90017; (213) 624-6996
Open Mon.-Fri. 11 a.m.-10 p.m., Sat. 5 p.m.-10 p.m. All major cards.

On the day it opened, the Engine Company immediately became downtown's best bar. Granted, that's a pretty easy accomplishment, given downtown's pathetic lack of good watering holes, but this place would make the grade even in New York or San Francisco. It's a manly sort of place, full of polished dark wood, conservatively upholstered booths and lots of properly suited professional types. We prefer to visit a little later, when the considerable after-work crowd has thinned a bit and we can better hear the swell old standards on the stereo. The bartenders are as friendly as the drinks they pour.

Formosa Café

7156 Santa Monica Blvd., W. Hollywood 90038; (213) 850-9050
Open Mon.-Sat. 11 a.m.-1:30 a.m. AE, MC, V.

Saved from the wrecking ball by a massive public outcry, the Formosa lives on as a landmark of L.A. culture clash. This far-out Far East restaurant and bar is built railroad car-style, and inside, mixed in with all the Chinese lamps are pictures of any Hollywood celebrity you'd care to name. Elvis, in particular, is given much space and there's practically a shrine to him in the front room. Also, the food's not bad, the drinks are cheap and the thick leatherette booths are as comfy as we like them to be.

Grand Avenue Bar

The Biltmore, 506 S. Grand Ave., Downtown (L.A.) 90071; (213) 624-1011
Open Mon.-Fri. 5 p.m.-9 p.m. All major cards.

This very civilized bar, located in a very civilized hotel, plays host to the downtown deal-making, happy-hour set that prefers a more sedate atmosphere than Casey's or Itchey Foot. It's tastefully done in browns that complement the tiled walls and marble tables, and live jazz brightens the mood and the dull business talk. The lovely buffet lunch is so popular that there's rarely room left over for nondining bar patrons, but it becomes a full-fledged bar at 4 p.m., when upscale hors d'oeuvres are served and vintage wine is poured by the glass. Like downtown itself, the bar is generally deserted after 9 p.m. The Biltmore now has another entirely worthy bar, an

attractive piano lounge located in the former lobby.

Harry's Bar and American Grill

ABC Entertainment Center, 2020 Ave. of the Stars, Century City 90067; (310) 277-2333
Open Mon.-Fri. 11:30 a.m.-midnight, Sat.-Sun. 5 p.m.-midnight. All major cards.

Sometimes, after we've been in Harry's awhile, we forget where we are. This replica of Harry's Bar in Florence is as charming as its cousins sprinkled throughout the world: there's the ubiquitous wood paneling, the handsome brass detailing and the attractive clientele that appears to be successful, well groomed and well fed. This is practically the only spot for a nightcap after a show at the Shubert or a movie at one of the several plush theaters here. Harry's also serves a fine Italian meal. All in all, a clean, well-lighted place.

Hollywood Athletic Club

6525 Sunset Blvd., Hollywood 90028; (310) 962-6600
Open daily 11 a.m.-2 a.m. Cost: $8 per hour for first person, $2 per hour each additional person Sun.-Wed.; $10 per hour for first person, $2 per hour each additional person Thurs.-Sat. ($3 per hour, per person daily until 6 p.m.). All major cards.

They've spared no expense in creating the Hollywood Athletic Club, so you shouldn't expect to either. This is the height of elegance for Hollywood: Pocket billiards is, after all, a gentleman's game. The old, refurbished 1920s building rises up out of the grungy neighborhood with its big windows, plenty of gleaming wood, beautifully upholstered luxurious couches and touches of art deco. You'll find two cavernous pool-table-filled rooms which pulsate to thumping, CD-clear music. The tables are filled to capacity most nights with moneyed rocker types in stylishly ripped jeans, cigarettes dangling from their lips at rakish angles. If you're forking over the big bucks for an evening's round of eight-ball, have one of the blonde Hollywoodette barmaids deliver the expensive drinks to your table. Otherwise, hang out in the postmodern bar. If you're feeling like a bite, there's an espresso and food bar serving up fine, fresh sandwiches, pastas and finger foods.

Jingo

7321 Santa Monica Blvd., W. Hollywood 90046; (213) 850-1488
Open nightly 7 p.m.-2 a.m. All major cards.

One of the hippest spots around, Jingo comprises three differently-themed interconnected rooms, so the potential for an evening-affirming discovery seems—literally—just around the corner. Enjoy the dim, but not too dark bar, where a deejay spins the latest synthpop. Things rock in the pool-table-equipped art-deco room, where piped-in music greets the ear. Finally there's the "Plush Room," where you can cuddle up with your longtime mate or newfound friend on the thick burgundy sofas under the fine oil portrait.

J. Sloane's
8623 Melrose Ave., W. Hollywood 90069;
(310) 659-0250
Open daily 11:30 a.m.-2 a.m. MC, V.

This is an honest-to-god, sawdust-on-the-floor, help-yourself-to-a-bag-of-popcorn kind of place. More suited to Eugene, Oregon, than West Hollywood, the clientele at Sloane's is straight, young and often dressed in plaid flannel. The decor is as frantic as the crowd, with model ships, airplanes, movie posters and assorted oddities hanging from the ceiling. There's a small, much-used dance floor with a deejay providing good music, while upstairs a frantic foosball game is generally in progress. The management has thoughtfully installed a siren that wails every few minutes to keep the crowd energized.

Kelbo's
11434 W. Pico Blvd., W.L.A. 90064;
(310) 473-8128
Open daily 11 a.m.-1:30 p.m. All major cards.

This sprawling Polynesian Tiki fantasy isn't exactly *House & Garden* material. But we love it. Weeknights in the bar, you can sip high-octane umbrella drinks, while everyone carries on, karaoke-style. The results have been known to vary from the surprisingly OK to the truly hideous. There's also dancing under a gargantuan coconut in the Cocobowl Lounge (cover most nights). If you've been waiting for a chance to wear all your Hawaiian shirts somewhere, your prayers have just been answered.

Molly Malone's Irish Pub
575 S. Fairfax Ave., Wilshire District (L.A.) 90036;
(213) 935-1577
Open daily 11:30 a.m.-2 a.m. MC, V.

For years this plain, dark neighborhood pub has attracted L.A.'s Irish Americans, who love the nondescript but very Irish decor, the good Irish music, the darts competitions, the Guinness on tap and the straightforward approach to drinking. There's no pretension and no hustling here—just a relaxed, folksy atmosphere with a clientele to match.

L.A.'s nightspots—particularly the hottest, trendiest ones—have been known to close or change their format within weeks or months of opening. It's always wise to call in advance.

The Polo Lounge
Beverly Hills Hotel, 9641 Sunset Blvd., Beverly Hills 90210; (310) 276-2251
Open daily 7:30 a.m.-1:30 a.m. All major cards.

They're all here: old stars, dolled-up young women, producers and a crowd of voyeurs on hand to watch. The action at this Hollywood mecca is created and perpetuated by the sheer number of people who are eagerly waiting for some action, particularly it seems, at precisely 6 p.m., when The Polo Lounge is the most eclectic center in town. Breakfast is a must for deal makers, and lunch on the outdoor patio is an event. This is the place to come to watch the small dramas of the grand life.

Port's
7205 Santa Monica Blvd., W. Hollywood 90046;
(213) 874-6294
Open Sat.-Thurs. 6 p.m.-2 a.m., Fri. 5 p.m.-2 a.m. AE, MC, V.

One of the original industry "hangs," Ports still proves to be quite a draw. The black-walled, black-ceilinged, black-floored rooms are almost always teeming with young, well-heeled Hollywood types, with more than a few celebrities poking their heads in, their smiles glowing phosphorescent under the black lighting that illuminates even the restaurant area. Most of the action is at the bar, though, where, a spherical fish tank hangs from the ceiling. More cozy is the salon-like back room, and there are even more intimate alcoves where you can have drinks while you pitch someone your script, or dine in a darkly romantic way.

Rebecca's
2025 Pacific Ave., Venice 90291;
(310) 306-6266
Open Sun.-Thurs. 6 p.m.-midnight, Fri.-Sat. 6 p.m.-2 a.m. All major cards.

Rebecca's—sister to the West Beach Café across the street and DC3 over at the Santa Monica Airport—is still one of the hottest bars (and restaurants) in town. The Frank Gehry–designed interior is as wild as the ambience: huge papier-mâché crocodiles and an octopus float overhead, and the marble and metal surfaces serve as great conductors for the considerable noise level. You will fit in here especially well if you're: 1) a 30ish executive man wearing Armani or Ralph Lauren and driving a BMW, Saab or Porsche; 2) a 30ish creative-type man (artist, designer) sporting a ponytail and an oversized black outfit; or 3) an attractive, gainfully employed 20ish-to-30ish woman with carefully moussed hair and designer leathers. Nebbish computer programmers and mild-mannered, bookish types need not apply.

167

Regent Beverly Wilshire Bar

9500 Wilshire Blvd., Beverly Hills 90212;
(310) 275-5200
*Open Sun.-Thurs. 11 a.m.-midnight, Fri.-Sat. 11 a.m.-2
a.m. All major cards.*

Tired of the scenes, the smooth operators, the
pickup places? Then head to this civilized oasis
and lose yourself in one of the monstrous martinis (mixed to perfection, we might add). This
spiffy new watering hole in the newly spruced-up
Beverly Wilshire is the perfect hotel bar: elegant
but not ostentatious, relaxed but not boring,
lively but not irritatingly loud. Terrific appetizers
are served during the after-work hours, and a
skilled pianist plays all evening long. Dress up a
bit, and by all means head across the lobby before
or after your bar visit for an excellent meal in the
dining room.

Residuals

11042 Ventura Blvd., Studio City 91604;
(818) 761-8301
Open daily noon-2 a.m. AE, MC, V.

Sure, there are plenty of places to hang out
where you'll spot bona-fide celebrities, but nowhere else do you find such a concentration of
faces seen in sitcoms and commercials. Located
in a mini-mall in Studio City, the bar (actually
with the logo "Re$iduals") will give you a free
drink in exchange for a residual check of under
$1. There's also a tote board where you can see
what films/TV shows/commercials/equity-
waiver-plays the bar's regulars are currently
working on. The drinks are cheap (the wine is
especially good) and folks here are friendly. It's
kind of like Cheers for everyone who hopes to
someday actually be on Cheers.

Revolver

8851 Santa Monica Blvd., W. Hollywood 90069;
(310) 550-8851
*Open Mon.-Thurs. 4 p.m.-2 a.m., Fri.-Sat. 4 p.m.-4 a.m.
Sun. 2 p.m.-2 a.m. No cards.*

You get the feeling that this mostly male neighborhood crowd was weaned on TV—they stand
around mesmerized by the video shows on monitors throughout the club. It's always packed,
more with chic, clean-cut young men than older,
more sophisticated types.

Smalls

5574 Melrose Ave., Hollywood 90038;
(213) 469-8258
*Open Mon.-Fri. 4 p.m.-2 a.m., Sat. 5 p.m.-2 a.m., Sun.
8 p.m.-2 a.m. MC, V.*

On the vanguard of the L.A. bar renaissance,
this not-so-little hole-in-the-wall may be called
Smalls, but the crowds here are anything but.
You have rockers, film-industry types and just
plain folks mixing it up in this smoky bar, decorated to look like something of a gothic dungeon.
Get here by around 9:30 and you'll avoid the
long lines of helmet-clutching hipsters that invariably form.

The Snake Pit

7529 Melrose Ave., W. Hollywood 90046;
(213) 852-9390
*Open Mon.-Fri. 4:30 p.m.-2 a.m., Sat.-Sun. 11:30 a.m.-2
a.m. MC, V.*

The last thing you'd expect to find on the
Melrose strip is a fun, happening and relatively
unpretentious bar like this one. Easy on the
sports and heavy on the bar, the Snake Pit throbs
with revelers even on weeknights, owing to its
strict adherence to such sound policies as a more-
than-ample selection of on-tap beers (many unavailable anywhere else), tasty and reasonably
priced bar food and an eclectic jukebox. So check
your 'tude at the door, and come on in.

Stanley's

13817 Ventura Blvd., Sherman Oaks 91403;
(818) 986-4623
Open daily 11:30 a.m.-2 a.m. AE, MC, V.

If the girl of your dreams has hair out to there,
a leather miniskirt and serious fingernails, by all
means rush right over to Stanley's, where you'll
find the pickings fat. The handsome but neutral
decor—white walls and blond wood—makes for
a good people-watching backdrop. The adjacent
restaurant serves the expected California-casual
food.

Stepps on the Court

Wells Fargo Court, 330 S. Hope St., Downtown
(L.A.) 90017; (213) 626-0900
*Open Tues.-Sat. 11 a.m.-11 p.m., Sun. 4 p.m.-9 p.m.,
Mon. 5 p.m.-9 p.m. AE, MC, V.*

If you're single, under 40, wear a Brooks
Brothers uniform and work downtown, then
you'll certainly want to check out the bar at
Stepps after work. Both the restaurant and the
bar were carefully designed to attract just such a
crowd, and they have succeeded famously.
There's a big-screen TV for the game of the
moment, decent wines by the glass, a fabulous
collection of single-malt scotches, the required
high-noise level and plenty of good-looking professionals of both sexes. The restaurant serves
moderately priced, trendy dishes that are decent
if not inspired.

---

*For the best spots to nosh at midnight, see the
indexes of Late-Night Restaurants and Bites in
INDEXES at the back of the book.*

Stratton's Grill

1037 Broxton Ave., Westwood 90024;
(310) 208-0488
Open Mon.-Fri. 11:30 a.m.-2 a.m., Sat.-Sun. 11 a.m.-2 a.m. All major cards.

Stratton's Grill is a well-lit, coolly decorated place with a long bar as the featured centerpiece of the house. Handsome young men pour drinks, and attractive young women wait on a mix of dressed-up UCLA students and fashionable young professionals from the area's banks and office towers. The happy hour (weekdays from 5 p.m. to 7 p.m.) is one of Westwood's best, but there are no specials on drinks.There is also a reasonably priced menu that lists creative bar food.

The Tam O'Shanter

2980 Los Feliz Blvd., Atwater 90039;
(213) 664-0228
Open Mon.-Sat. 11 a.m.-1 a.m. All major cards.

Kind of a cross between an Irish Pub and Snow White's chalet, The Tam O'Shanter came into being as an adjunct to the old Disney studios. But don't let these ersatz origins scare you. This is a fun place, with a fine beer and beverage selection and top notch entertainment. We especially recommend seeing Bobby "Fats" Mizzel, who performs foot-stompin' country-western and rockabilly here every Tuesday through Thursday. In between sets, be sure to get up and walk around. You won't believe how many rooms there are, each one with a decor that offers its own delightful bit of blarney.

Tequila Willie's

3290 N. Sepulveda Blvd., Manhattan Beach 90266;
(310) 545-4569
Open daily 11 a.m.-2 a.m. All major cards.

Located in a Manhattan Beach mall, this frantically decorated bar is one of the hot spots for the young beach residents who cram into the place every evening. The clientele ranges from young office workers still dressed for work to ultra-cool dudes in T-shirts and jams. As interesting as the clientele are the cluttered decor and the backgammon games. You can have a tolerable, inexpensive Mexican dinner here (it's part of the El Torito chain).

T.G.I. Friday's

13470 Maxella Ave., Marina del Rey 90291;
(310) 822-9052
Mon.-Thurs. 11 a.m.-2 a.m., Fri. 11 a.m.-11 p.m., Sat. 11 a.m.-2 a.m., Sun. 10 a.m.-2 a.m. All major cards.

This noisy, hectic, crowded place would fascinate anthropologists studying the tribal rites of the California singles scene. Pretty, healthy-looking people play the overnight mating game with other pretty, healthy-looking people—all ages, all sizes, all types. In all, it's an amusing and entertaining marketplace. Although food isn't the issue here, you'll find a 23-page menu, complete with an index, listing over 165 dishes, many of which are deep-fried. The decor is a lively clutter of Americana.

Tiki-Ti

4427 Sunset Blvd., Silverlake 90027; (213) 669-9381
Open Wed.-Sun. 6 p.m.-2 a.m. No cards.

If Timothy Leary were Polynesian, his house would look something like the Tiki-Ti. This tiny, cluttered bar juxtaposes funky tropical motifs (primitive face masks) with '60s tackola (lava lamps and wave machines). And the drinks! No humdrum beer or wine here. No, Mike the barman, usually dressed in a garish Hawaiian shirt, serves up delicious and powerful tropical concoctions—the sort of drinks usually served with an umbrella. Go ahead, try a Ray's Mistake, "151" Rum Sizzle or Vicious Virgin. Be aware that in typical tropical fashion, the Tiki-Ti seems to have a cavalier relationship with its posted hours. As a matter of fact, the locals refer to it as "that place that only opens when they feel like it." A one-of-a-kind bar that's definitely worth a visit.

Tom Bergin's

840 S. Fairfax Ave., Fairfax District (L.A.) 90036;
(213) 936-7151
Open Mon.-Fri. 11 a.m.-1 a.m., Sat. 4 p.m.-2 a.m., Sun. 4 p.m.-10 p.m. All major cards.

Bergin's is a cozy, dark-as-night pub whose button-down clientele is a mix of L.A.'s Irish Americans, local businesspeople and preppy college students. The substantial local Irish community has made Bergin's and nearby Molly Malone's its home away from home for years. Bergin's highly touted Irish coffee is worthy of all the praise, and the dining room behind the bar serves decent pub fare. It gets particularly rowdy here when USC wins a football game. If you need a spot for a very private conversation (romance or espionage) steal into one of these dark booths with someone at about 5 p.m. and no one will ever be the wiser.

West Beach Café

60 N. Venice Blvd., Venice 90291; (310) 823-5396
Open Mon. 6 p.m.-1:30 a.m., Tues.-Fri. 11:30 a.m.-1:30 a.m., Sat.-Sun. 10 a.m.-1:30 a.m. All major cards.

You'll find a fabulous collection of beers, Cognacs, wines by the glass, pretty women and handsome men affiliated in one way or another with the art world, and a scene that will seduce you into returning as often as possible. It's civilized but fun, and you're sure to meet someone interesting-looking and quite possibly worth

169

talking to. But dress up a bit: this is casual chic at its best. The later it gets, the better it looks.

Ye Olde King's Head
116 Santa Monica Blvd., Santa Monica 90401;
(310) 451-1402
Open daily 11 a.m.-2 a.m. No cards.

For a minute we thought we took a wrong turn and went across the Channel instead of across town. British accents abound in this authentic English pub; also in abundance are pale-complexioned Watney's drinkers and darts (and, ahem, draughts) fanatics. Owners Phillip and Ruth Elwell have worked hard to make this a real neighborhood pub. They sponsor darts competitions, along with local cricket, rugby and soccer teams. It's predominantly male, with a good number of scruffy beach people during the week. In the bar, you can order Guinness, John Courage, Watney's and Bass on tap (and English rock on the jukebox); in the adjoining restaurant, you can munch on great fish and chips. The crowd gets thick on weekends, when a line usually forms outside after 9 p.m.

Cabarets

Café Largo
432 N. Fairfax Ave., Fairfax District (L.A.) 90036;
(213) 852-1073
Open Tues.-Sat. 7 p.m.-2 a.m., Sun. 6 p.m.-midnight. Cover varies (2-drink minimum). AE, MC, V.

Former Lhasa Club impresario Jean Pierre Boccara took Lhasa's artsy and experimental booking policy and gave it a decidedly uptown twist. His new Largo presents an eclectic mix of folk, rock 'n' roll, poetry and performance art. While dyed-in-the-wool hipsters are put off by its spanking-clean, hushed-tone fine dining ambience, the thirtysomething clientele with a yen for off-the-beaten-path entertainment feels right at home. The food, although a bit on the expensive side, is quite good (if nouvelle in portion), and there's a full bar to assist you in the fulfillment of the two-drink minimum.

El Cid
4212 W. Sunset Blvd., Silverlake 90029;
(213) 668-0318
Open Wed.-Sun. 6:30 p.m.-2 p.m. Shows Wed. 8:30 p.m., Thurs. & Sun. 8 p.m. & 10 p.m., Fri.-Sat. 8 p.m., 10 p.m. & midnight. Reservation suggested. Cover $7 (or no cover with dinner). All major cards.

Descend the stairs off this bleak stretch of Sunset Boulevard and enter a completely different time and place. This former movie studio

(D.W. Griffith shot *Birth of a Nation* here) was taken over 30 years ago and turned into an authentic replica of a sixteenth-century Spanish tavern. Dine on hearty, garlicky Spanish cuisine while you watch world-class Flamenco dancers clack catchy rhythms out of their castanets and toe taps as part of a full-length production. The food's pricey, but quite good. And besides, the experience is well worth it.

La Cage L.A.
643 N. La Cienega Blvd., W. Hollywood 90069;
(310) 657-1091
Open Sun.-Thurs. 7 p.m.-2 a.m., Fri.-Sat. 6 p.m.-2 a.m. Shows Sun.-Thurs. 9:15 p.m., Fri.-Sat. 8 p.m. & 11 p.m. Cover $7.50 with dinner, $12 with drinks (2-drink minimum). DC, MC, V.

Female impersonators entertain a straight, touristy crowd. The costumes rival those in Vegas, if the entertainment doesn't. The sound system overwhelms the starlets, but apparently the glitter makes audiences forget such technicalities. The best fun is the rambling mistress of ceremonies, who manages to approach the clever bitchiness immortalized in the film for which this place was named. The waiter/waitresses are great—it's all one big costume party featuring men who are as entertaining as the tinsel onstage.

Carlos 'n' Charlie's
See "Bars" in this chapter.

Gardenia
7066 Santa Monica Blvd., Hollywood 90038;
(213) 467-7444
Open Mon.-Sat. 7 p.m.-midnight (dinner until 10:30 p.m.). Shows Mon.-Sat. 9 p.m. Cover varies. AE, MC, V.

This supper club is beautiful to look at: subdued lighting, mirrors, gray-and-salmon coloring and white trees with tiny lights framing the stage area. After dinner, Gardenia turns into a watering hole for the smart set, with reasonably good jazz and cabaret entertainment. The food is nothing special, but you'll enjoy sharing dessert, drinks and music in an elegant setting that makes singles bars seem terribly adolescent.

The Queen Mary
12449 Ventura Blvd., Studio City 91604;
(818) 506-5619
Open Tues.-Sun. 11 a.m.-2 a.m. Showtimes vary. Cover $5. No cards.

Since the room was engulfed in darkness when we entered, we could not be certain that it was the queen of England who was sliding a five-dollar bill into the tiny, silver-spangled G-string of a handsome young dancer. In case it wasn't really she, we can only urge her to come with her family to celebrate her next birthday at this respectable establishment bearing her ancestor's name. She would surely adore these people, who wear dresses and hats that are little different from her own, and who remove them with great elegance. They show nothing so personal as would shock the queen, and their movements at the boldest consist of bestowing kisses on women who are bewitched by the beauty of their bodies. Wednesday through Sunday evenings, the stage is reserved for female-impersonator shows. It can get rather complicated—in this specialized world, where one changes one's sex as readily as a woman changes her dress, nothing is for sure, not even a name. Reservations are suggested.

The Rose Tattoo
665 N. Robertson Blvd., W. Hollywood 90069; (310) 854-4455
Cabaret: open Sun. & Tues.-Thurs. 7:30 p.m.-midnight; Fri.-Sat. 7:30 p.m.-2 a.m.; Restaurant: open Tues.-Sat. 6:30 p.m.-11 p.m., Sun. 11 a.m.-3 p.m. & 6:30 p.m.-11 p.m. Shows continuous from 8 p.m. Cover varies. All major cards.

The Rose Tattoo is one of the most decent, charming places in the world. Well-bred, beautiful gay men who adore the company of ladies gather here to meet one another and drink scotch at the small, closely spaced tables. In this room you will never see a vulgar gesture; at The Rose Tattoo, even the most flamboyant queens are straight. If you go to The Rose Tattoo only once in your life, go on Halloween evening. There, in the tent with crystal chandeliers and the stage (converted from the parking lot), you'll experience an unforgettable show. The men wear extravagant dresses, and we bet that Escoffier would have died instantly had he seen, as we did, some celebrated chefs in tutus and net stockings.

Coffeehouses

Bourgeois Pig
5931 Franklin Ave., Hollywood 90026; (213) 962-6366
Open Sun.-Thurs. noon-2 a.m., Fri.-Sat. noon-4 a.m. No cards.
1029 Abbot Kinney Blvd., Venice 90291; (310) 396-9255
Open Tues.-Sun. 11 a.m.-2 p.m. No cards.

Easily the most bar-like cafe around, the Pig offers its customers, heavy on industry-types with a healthy dose of Scientologists coming in from the Celebrity Center across the street, black walls, muted lighting, a gothic motif and—an innovation for its time—a red felt pool table. Music blares, people mix and the drinks, though priced

for Bourgeois pocketbooks, are at least hefty. No entertainment.

Cinema Café
7160 Melrose Ave., W. Hollywood 90046; (213) 939-CAFE
Open Tues.-Sun. 3 p.m.-1 a.m. Closed Monday. MC, V. (Movies free with $3 minimum purchase.)

There hasn't been a place this fun on Melrose Avenue for years. Amid all the thrift store furniture and bric-a-brac, are, natch, a few directors chairs, movie posters and other Tinsel touches. The Cinema Cafe also has the greatest collection of board games – Sorry, Monopoly, Battleship, etc.—of any coffeehouse in town. Of course, as its name implies, there are also movies shown in the back roomtheater (actually a video monitor). Offering itself up as avenue for the independant filmmaker, Cinema shows non-Hollywood feature films, shorts, documentaries and other off-the-beaten-celluloid-track material. Students are also encouraged to bring and screen their films.

Congo Square
1238 Third Street Promenade, Santa Monica 90401; (310) 395-5606
Open Sun.-Thurs. 8 a.m.-2 a.m., Fri.-Sat. 8 a.m.-3 a.m. No cards.

This worldbeat-themed, upmarket cafe on the newly revamped Santa Monica promenade is named after the famous New Orleans square where black slaves were allowed to gather and perform. This Congo square keeps the faith by booking jazz, blues, Carribean and African bands every Friday and Saturday night (occasionally Thursday, too) and playing the canned variety over the P.A. the rest of the time. As expected, the crowd here—as it is everywhere along the new Promenade—is young and well-dressed.

The Espresso Bar
34 S. Raymond Ave., Pasadena 91105; (818) 356-9095
Open Mon.-Thurs. noon-1 a.m., Fri.-Sat. noon-2 a.m., Sunday noon-midnight. No cards.

The oldest extant coffeehouse in Los Angeles, the hard-to-find Espresso Bar is approached through an alley off Raymond Avenue in the heart of old Pasadena. Lots of brick and a crackling fireplace give the joint a nice, cozy feel. Assorted intellectuals, artists, hip teenagers and neighborhood shoppers sip espresso drinks or all-American coffee around small tables in this high-ceilinged, wood-floored old room, complete with an old upright piano. The entertainment schedule here varies, but Tuesday is open-mike night, with all the usual inherent hazards; ditto for Wednesday and its spoken-word performances.

Highland Grounds
742 N. Highland Ave., Hollywood 90038;
(213) 466-1507
Open Mon.-Thurs. 8 a.m.-1 a.m., Fri. 8 a.m.-2 a.m.,
Sat. 10 a.m.-3 a.m., Sun. 2:30 p.m.-1 a.m. MC, V. Cover
$2-$3 for entertainment.

Why do we like Highland Grounds? First of all, they serve what has to be the best coffee in town. They're the only café that roasts their own beans, with the exception of Caffè Latte, which is also owned by Tom Kaplan. The food, a short menu of such healthful goodies as a grilled-eggplant sandwich or vegetable-studded rice, is excellent, if not cheap. It's spacious and comfortable here with a fine outdoor patio court and eye-pleasing SoHo decor within. And finally, as if all this wasn't enough, there's always high-caliber entertainment here for not too heavy of a cover charge.

Iguana Café
10943 Camarillo St., N. Hollywood 91602;
(818) 763-7735
Open Sun & Tues.-Thurs. 3 p.m.-1 a.m., Fri.-Sat. 3
p.m.-4 a.m. Cover varies for entertainment. No cards.

We thought we had inadvertantly entered one of the last surviving head shops in Southern California, but no, it's just that Iguana is not your ordinary café. Tarot cards, handscreened T-shirts, handmade jewelry, used books and records and other oddities are for sale here, along with potato chips and other packaged snacks and bottled beverages. The emphasis here is on the entertainment and big names like John Doe, Exene Cervenka, Dave Alvin and John Densmuir have played acoustic or spoken word sets here. Oh, and here's a twist—the coffee's free. It sits in a pot in the corner. Help yourself.

In Arty's
36 E. Holly St., Pasadena 91103; (818) 793-3723
Open Mon.-Wed. 5:30 p.m.-12:30 a.m., Thurs. 11:30
a.m.-12:30 a.m., Fri. 11:30 a.m.-1:30 a.m., Sat. 5:30
p.m.-1:30 a.m. No cards.

The coffeehouse reaches new heights at In Arty's, a stylish Old Town Pasadena spot that combines the hang-loose informality of a coffeehouse with the comfort and atmosphere of an upscale lounge. For the price of a cup o' java, you can settle in at a comfortable table or booth, chit-chat to your heart's content and listen to amiable live jazz. Unlike at L.A.'s other coffeehouses, wine, Champagne and beer are also served; the food offerings run to desserts and simple appetizers and snacks. In Arty's is at its best at Thursday and Friday lunches and on weekend nights.

Insomnia
7286 Beverly Blvd., Hollywood 90036;
(213) 931-4943
Open Sun.-Thurs. 9 a.m.-2 a.m., Fri.-Sat. 9 a.m-3 a.m.
MC, V.

The quintessential yupscale coffeehouse, this place was called Java until late 1992, when it changed ownership and was reborn as an elegant Bohemian-Victorian parlor (any mélange is possible these days). High-gloss yellow, *faux*-marble walls and a jumble of beautiful old furniture exude warmth and drama at the same time—perhaps you're meant to fantasize that you're having a quiet get-together at your own mansion, as you nosh on the fine, simple food and good espresso drinks and teas with the rest of the young-and-going-places clientele.

Joe Café
12232 1/2 Ventura Blvd., Studio City 91604;
(818) 760-7563
Open Sun.-Thurs. 9 a.m.-1 a.m., Fri.-Sat. 9 a.m.-2 a.m.
MC, V.

You won't find any poets or musicians performing here in the Valley's first espresso bar. They just supply an elegant environment of *faux* aged walls, comfortable seating and unobtrusive art to accompany your sandwich, caffè latte and conversation.

Jabberjaw
3711 W. Pico Blvd., Pico-Crenshaw District (L.A.)
90006; (213) 732-3463
Hours vary. Occasional cover. No cards.

Serious pierced and tattooed demi-mondes down their java at Jabberjaw, a dark hard-to-find hole-in-the-wall on a nondescript section of Pico Boulevard. You'll probably hear it before you see it, because on most weekend nights and even occasionally during the week, L.A.'s most raucous and cutting edge bands let loose here, rocking the caffeine-charged house. If you need an extra dose of energy to handle the heavy underground music, order up a bowl of Lucky Charms or a couple of Pop Tarts from their extremely weird menu.

The Living Room
110 S. La Brea Ave, Los Angeles 90036;
(213) 933-2933
Open Sun.-Thurs. 8:30 p.m.-2 a.m., Fri.-Sat. 8:30 a.m.-4
a.m. No cards.

You want trendy? Let's just say that we heard that the Material Girl herself prefers this opulent café that replicates a Viennese tea room, L.A.-style. The plush purple sofas and brass chandeliers glow, almost making up for the $5 ficettes.

And even when Madonna's not here, the place still brims with the young, happening, good-looking and well-to-do who set the tone for L.A.'s nightlife. So sit, sip, and soak up .

The Novel Café

212 Pier Ave., Santa Monica 90405;
(310) 396-8566
Open Sun.-Thurs. 8 a.m.-midnight, Fri.-Sat. 8 a.m.-2 a.m. AE, MC, V.

This place is sooooo civilized. You're surrounded by lots of wood and old tomes like in some tenth-century English salon. They let you read most of the books (some of the new ones are for sale only) and many people do. They sit in one of the cushiony chairs, sipping the way-above-par coffee, engrossed in some finely bound classic. Also, a cozy place for quiet conversation.

Onyx/Sequel Gallery

1804 N. Vermont Ave., Los Feliz 90027;
(213) 660-5820
Open daily 9 a.m-3 a.m. No cards.

Poets scribbling blank verse on coffee-stained napkins share tables—and colored formica tables, at that—with gung-ho screenwriters plugging out hope-to-be blockbusters on laptops. One of the oldest of the L.A. java joints, the Onyx is low on attitude—the caffeinated equivalent of a neighborhood bar. The specialties here are the homemade soups and very good, reasonably priced Sunday brunches. On most Sundays, a band performs in the gallery next door (often jazz or experimental) and Wednesdays are set aside for spoken word.

The Pikme-up

5437 W. 6th St., Wilshire District (L.A.) 90036;
(213) 896-9348
Open Sun.-Thurs. noon-1 a.m., Fri.-Sat. noon-3 a.m. (sometimes later). No cards.

The primarily young, club-hopping crowd that packs the Pikme-up most evenings must like a couple of spoonfuls of kitsch in their coffee. The atmosphere here is colorful and variegated, with plenty of outrageous art and wacky posters to delight the eye. The bathroom—covered in arty drawings and interesting witticisms—has to be one of the most interesting in town. The menu offers a few treats like iced frappés, and peanut-butter-and-jelly sandwiches, and bagels and Brie, and there's an irregular schedule of performances—generally acoustic music and spoken word for your evening's entertainment.

Troy Café

418 E. 1st St., Downtown (L.A.) 90012;
(213) 617-0790
Open Sun.-Thurs. 11 a.m.-1 a.m., Fri.-Sat. 11 a.m.-3 a.m. Cover varies. No cards.

Downtown's first—and so far only—java joint makes for a perfect charge-up before or after an evening of clubhopping. The coffee here is excellent, served up behind a long bar with an array of fine baked treats. On Thursday through Saturday nights, Troy can even be your primary evening's destination, since there's usually some kind of entertainment—fine jazz, folk or spoken word.

Van Go's Ear

9 Westminster Ave., Venice 90291; (310) 399-6870
Open daily 24 hours. No cards.

This is a place that practices what its caffeine preaches and, therefore, never closes. It sports an unpretentious and haphazard motif, drawing tourists from the local youth hostel as well as serving as the last bastion of scruffy, ungentrified Venetians. There will more than likely be some kind of Grateful Dead–inspired jam session going on when you get there, but really, that only adds to the place's unique charm.

Young Moguls, Inc.

1650 N. Hudson Ave., Hollywood 90028;
(213) 461-1833
Open Sun.-Wed. 7 p.m.-2 a.m., Thurs.-Sat. 7 p.m.-4 a.m. Cover $2 nightly (incl. $1 credit toward purchase). AE, MC, V.

This is a coffeehouse à la *Blade Runner.* The huge space is filled with all sorts of futuristic art, a few pool tables, a school bus, hovercraft and plenty of other wacky, futuristic stuff. In keeping with its one-step-beyond theme, "smart drinks" (unusual juice concoctions reputed to increase your brain power) are served in addition to the usual beverages. There's occasional entertainment here, but the activity of choice seems to be just wandering around—smart drinks notwithstanding—in a wowed stupor.

This section lists cafés and coffeehouses of a particular genre: most are late-night hangouts with minimal menus. For reviews of more than 50 full-fledged cafés, see "LOS ANGELES Bargain Bites."

Comedy & Magic

Comedy and Magic Club

1018 Hermosa Ave., Hermosa Beach 90254;
(310) 372-1193
Open nightly. Hours & showtimes vary. Cover $7-$15 (2-drink minimum). AE, MC, V.

This club keeps beach residents entertained with generally first-rate acts, including such big names as Jay Leno and Harry Anderson. The place is roomy, and you can get decent snack foods or a full-fledged dinner before the show. It's a popular, reasonably priced club whose weekend shows usually sell out (reservations are required). One of the best selling points here is higher-class comedy that doesn't reduce itself to the cheap, often vulgar thrills presented in many L.A. clubs. As a matter of fact, on Friday and Saturday afternoons the Comedy and Magic Club offers comedy for kids (call for times). It celebrates its own New Year's Eve in July, and it's a party not to be missed!

The Comedy Store

8433 W. Sunset Blvd., W. Hollywood 90069;
(213) 656-6225
Open nightly 7:30 p.m.-2 a.m. Showtimes vary. Cover $6-$14 (2-drink minimum). AE, MC, V.

The dreary interior is brightened by the hopeful talent seeking fame and fortune. Comic relief comes from a changing-nightly cast of stand-up performers, some of whom have already hit the big time and return to try outnew material. The humor is usually topical, often with direct sexual overtones. Drinks are expensive.

Groundlings Theatre

7307 Melrose Ave., W. Hollywood 90046;
(213) 934-9700
Shows Thurs. 8 p.m., Fri.-Sat. 8 p.m. & 10 p.m., Sun. 7:30 p.m. Ticket prices $10-$17.50. AE, MC, V.

The Groundlings is probably the best place in town for comedy. No tired, stand-up shtick here—this is a cozy professional little theater showcasing a talented troupe of performers. Many Groundlings have gone on to the big time, most notably Paul Rubens, a.k.a. Pee-Wee Herman. The main show on Friday and Saturday, which changes every few months, is generally a collection of funny set pieces with the occasional improv thrown in. The Sunday show features a different cast and different skits, but it's still funny; the late shows are more experimental. No

liquor is served; the lobby snack bar sells junk food and sodas.

The Ice House

24 N. Mentor Ave., Pasadena 91106;
(818) 577-1894
Shows Mon.-Thurs. 8:30 p.m.; Fri. 8:30 p.m. & 10:30 p.m.; Sat. 7:30 p.m., 9:30 p.m. & 11:30 p.m.; Sun. 9 p.m. Cover varies (2-drink minimum). MC, V.

A New York–style comedy club with exposed brick walls and a cozy, earthy ambience. The Ice House was a real ice warehouse in the 1920s. By the early '70s it had become an acclaimed comedy house featuring the likes of Steve Martin and Lily Tomlin. After some slow years it shut down; now it's back on the scene, showcasing fair-to-good stand-up comics and improv shows, with the likes of Roseanne Arnold and Bobcat Goldthwaite as occasional surprise guests. The 7 p.m. Sunday show is amateur night, and performances can be painful. Fried snack foods are offered, and the two-drink minimum is loosely enforced.

Igby's

11637 W. Pico Blvd., W.L.A. 90064;
(310) 477-3553
Hours vary. Cover $6.50-$10 (2-drink minimum). All major cards.

A bit more casual (and therefore having a welcome looser spirit) than the long-established Improv and Comedy Store, Igby's is a fine place to hear hot young stand-up comics. The setting is intimate, the drink prices fair, and the talent almost always worth a listen.

The Improvisation

8162 Melrose Ave., W. Hollywood 90069;
(213) 651-2583
Open daily noon-2 a.m. Shows Tues.-Thurs. 8 p.m. & 10:45 p.m.; Fri.-Sat. 7:30 p.m., 9:45 p.m. & 10:45 p.m.; Sun. 8 p.m. & 10:45 p.m. Cover $8-$11 (2-drink minimum). AE, MC, V.

321 Santa Monica Blvd. Santa Monica 90401;
(310) 394-8664
Open nightly 7 p.m.-2 a.m. Shows Sun.-Thurs. at 8 p.m., Fri.-Sat. at 8 p.m. & 10:30 p.m. Cover varies (2-drink minimum). AE, MC, V.

Budd Friedman first found fame and fortune with his Improv Club in New York; once that took off, he moved to L.A. to open this place, a spacious brick-walled club that bears a strong resemblance to its New York brother. Friedman, obviously a frustrated stand-up comic himself, occasionally emcees the generally good shows that feature top local comics; many of today's top comedy superstars came out of one or both Improvs, and some of them stop by now and then for impromptu performances. Weekends get crowded with a touristy/date crowd. The later shows are usually better—more spontaneous.

Drinks are quite expensive. Simple dinners are served in the adjacent café.

L.A. Cabaret

17271 Ventura Blvd., Encino 91316;
(818) 501-3737
Open Sun.-Thurs. 6 p.m.-midnight, Fri.-Sat. 6 p.m.-2 a.m. Shows Sun.-Thurs. 8:30 p.m.; Fri. 8:30 p.m. & 10:30 p.m.; Sat. 7:30 p.m., 9:30 p.m. & 11:30 p.m. Cover $6-$12 (2-drink minimum). AE, MC, V.

This small cabaret, formerly the Laff Stop, is primarily a comedy club, though a few nights are reserved for musical entertainment. A string of stand-up comedians takes the stage nearly every night, and though the greats don't usually drop by to try out new acts, as at the Comedy Store or The Improv, the level of entertainment is nearly as high. The room is comfortable, and the drinks are good, if a tad expensive. On the down side, the audience has to endure a few too many bad comedians and MCs.

Los Angeles Theatresports

Theatre/Theatre, 1713 N.Cahuenga Blvd., Hollywood 90028; (213) 469-9689
Shows Mon. 8 p.m., Sat. 8 p.m. & 10:30 p.m. Tickets $6 Mon., $10 Sat. No cards.

It's improv with a twist. Teams compete in various improv games while audience members are picked as judges. The judging, of course, becomes part of the fun, so even when the scenework withers, the entertainment value remains high.

The Magic Castle

7001 Franklin Ave., Hollywood 90028;
(213) 851-3314
Open nightly 5 p.m.-2 a.m. Shows continuous. Members only; cover $7.50 with guest card. All major cards.

The Magic Castle has achieved quite a reputation. It's a weird and wonderful idea: and a great place to spend an entire evening trying to figure out how the professional magicians perform their sleight-of-hand tricks. The labyrinth of rooms in this fantastic converted mansion are all filled with experts plying their trades; the big room has a full-blown show. Watch out if you sit in the front row—you'll wind up onstage as part of the act. People dress up to come here, and many have dinner first. Don't. Our last dinner here was so poor we found ourselves wishing a magician would pop in and make it disappear. It's a members-only club, but it isn't too difficult to find someone who can get you a guest card.

> *Some establishments change their closing times without warning. It is always wise to check in advance.*

Dance Clubs

No matter where you are in Los Angeles, you're probably no more than a few minutes away from a hopping, throbbing dance club. However, at the city's cutting edge, the clubs don't seem to stay at one address for more than a month or two. It is, therefore, wise to check the listings in the *L.A. Weekly* for these clubs-of-the-moment.

Below are the more stable venues, which we can promise (more or less) will be pumping out dance music for crowded floors for quite some time to come. Also, please note that the distinction between music clubs and dance clubs tends to blur—some of the following venues feature live music, and many music clubs listed later in this chapter boast great dance floors. Check those listings as well before planning your evening.

Blak:Bloo

7574 Sunset Blvd., W. Hollywood 90046;
(213) 876-1120
Open nightly. Hours & cover vary.

Blak:Bloo (pronounced "Black and Blue" by those in the know) one of those club space time-share deals, where each night is really it's own separate club. But no matter what theme has invaded these gothic digs the night you arrive—industrial, funk/groove, house—you'll find the joint hopping with the hip and smartly dressed. Even though the club is not that immense, the dance floor is so well insulated from the dining area, that two independent musical experiences, say, canned Europop and live rhythm-and-blues, can and do go on simultaneously.

Club Lux

2800 Donald Douglas Loop, Santa Monica 90405;
(310) 399-1577
Open Thurs.-Sat. 10 p.m.-2 a.m. Cover $10. All major cards.

You can imagine the Jetsons getting down in a place like this. This is futurism as it was conceived of in the '60s, with atomic motifs and space-age wallpaper. Of course the Jetsons don't guzzle Dom Perignon and scarf down haute cuisine like they do here. No, the crowd in this newest of ultra-chic dancespots is hip, well-to-do and on the make. Who knows, if you're lucky, maybe during the following week, somebody you met here will actually pick up their car phone and call you. They're also confident enough to shake it on a dance floor that's raised up high like a big undulating pedestal. Those who don't have struttable stuff are weeded out by the attitude-heavy doormen who stand sentry outside. Fore-warned is foredressed.

Crush Bar

The Continental Club, 1743 N. Cahuenga Blvd., Hollywood 90028; (213) 461-9017
Open Thurs.-Sat. 9 p.m.-2 a.m. Cover $5 Thurs., $7 Fri.-Sat. No cards.

Papa's got a brand-new bag in these nostalgic '90s, and the '60s Motown soul of the Crush sends out a freewheeling message: do what you want to do. A variety of deejays spin those golden oldies for a new generation of boppers. Frequented by a younger crowd, most of whom were watching cartoons when the music played here was originally recorded, the Crush maintains a feverish dance pace that rapidly turns it into a house of sweat. After an evening here, you'll have to rev up the little Pontiac GTO and take that miniskirt or those pleated trousers to the cleaners.

Denim & Diamonds

3200 Ocean Park Blvd., Santa Monica 90405; (310) 452-3446
Open nightly. Hours & cover vary. All major cards.

Throw those suits and gowns in the closet and put your jeans back on, pardner, because this hot new club plays Country. Yep, that's right, this spacious club serves up three dance floors where urban cowboys can shake it to live bands or the latest country, country-rock and rockabilly tracks. Folks here is friendly and not too concerned with bein' part of some damn-fool-city-slicker scene, so it's your two-step and not your tailoring that you need to worry about. If you're feeling a little unsure, though, there are free dance lessons every night from 7 to 7:30 and 8 to 8:30.

Florentine Gardens

5951 Hollywood Blvd., Hollywood 90028; (213) 464-0706
Open Fri.-Sat. 8 p.m.-4 a.m. Cover varies. No cards.

This immense barn of a dance club is located in a typically bizarre Hollywood spot: it sits on garish Hollywood Boulevard between a triple-X-rated movie theater and a Salvation Army tabernacle. The sizable crowd is young (18 and over), dressed up and enthusiastic about the loud and trendy music.

Kingston 12

814 Broadway, Santa Monica 90401; (310) 451-4423
Hours & cover vary. All major cards.

This is *the* place to go in L.A. when you're feeling *i-rae*. The crowd here is a mixed bag of hipsters, funksters, rastas and plain old westsiders. A fun-loving crowd, they come here to shake it on Kingston's enclosed dance floor to the deejay-spinned, steady stream of island music or to the solid roster of local and international reggae bands. For the quintessential Jah-loving Kingston 12 experience, it's best to come on the weekend.

Mayan

1038 S. Hill St., Downtown (L.A.) 90015; (213) 746-4287
Open Fri.-Sat. 9 p.m.-4 a.m. Cover $8-$12 Fri., $10-$15 Sat. AE, MC, V.

We don't know anybody who gives you more bang for your megabuck than Mayan. Once a vaudeville theater, then a porno venue, Mayan was saved from the wrecking ball and turned into an opulent club. Its magnificent pre-Columbian decor has been painstakingly restored and some wacked-out lunarscapes and art installations added. The people here are not the elite group that patronized the place in its exclusive heyday, but they've all come here to dance and have fun, and frankly, we're glad to be here with them.

The Palace

1735 N. Vine St., Hollywood 90028; (213) 462-3000
Open most nights. Hours vary; concerts usually start at 8 p.m.; dancing 10:30 p.m.-4 a.m. Cover $10-$15 for dancing; cover for concerts varies. AE, MC, V.

Star Wars meets the twenties. The people who run this place look like they're hooked up with NASA; earphones (probably to muffle the deafening sound), laser machines and monitoring screens are the tools of this dancing trade. The Palace does double-duty as both a concert hall and dance club. On concert nights, dancers move in after the concertgoers move out; Saturday nights are frequently reserved for dancing only, with the music beginning about 8 p.m. It's a great-looking place, a refurbished architectural gem modernized with a pretty good sound system and mind-boggling lights. The crowd tends to be 18-and-over sophisticates with carefully moussed hair and the latest fashions. One of the more fun clubs in town.

Shark Club

1024 S. Grand Ave., Downtown (L.A.) 90015; (213) 747-0999
Open Thurs.-Sat. 9 p.m.-2 a.m. Cover $15. AE, MC, V.

Fog machines, a 21st-century light show, megasound system and oodles of shark motifery make this place a totally over-the-top disco experience. Add to the mix plenty of young trendies in their Melrose Avenue finest, getting down to the latest sounds. And, as if that isn't appetizing enough, you get to make one free pass at the buffet. Try to pile up as much of the pasta, salad and the many other tasty tidbits as you can. You'll need the energy on the dance floor.

Spice
7070 Hollywood Blvd., Hollywood 90028; (213) 460-7070
Open Tues.-Sun. Hours & cover vary. AE, DC, MC, V.

This spacious multi-entertainment complex features a differently themed club each night. You'll usually find dancing in the main room, while bands, comedians and even soft-core strippers (nothing too shocking) entertain in the adjacent lounge. The crowd here seems to be comprised mostly of movie-studio receptionists and agent wannabes who while away the evening shuttling between rooms, ogling the go-go dancers or looking for the evening's big score.

The Strand
1700 S. Pacific Coast Hwy., Redondo Beach 90017; (310) 316-1700
Open nightly 4 p.m.-2 a.m. Cover varies. AE, MC, V.

Formerly Annabelle's, The Strand has a reputation for attracting performers of the highest caliber—from Todd Rundgren to Hunter S. Thompson to Johnny Cash. The crowd is attractive, and there are often some great dancers. There are three bars, three dance floors and plenty of people to whoop it up with. The kitchen serves pretty good Californian cuisine.

Jazz

At My Place
1026 Wilshire Blvd., Santa Monica 90401; (310) 451-8596
Open nightly 7 p.m.-2 a.m. Showtimes & cover vary (1-drink minimum). MC, V.

This cavernous nightclub is dark and packed with serious and appreciative listeners. The murky atmosphere must be intended to further highlight the well-lit stage, where good music is presented nightly. Jazz and rhythm-and-blues are the headliners. There are several shows each evening, so call ahead for information.

The Baked Potato
3787 Cahuenga Blvd., Studio City 91604; (818) 980-1615
Open nightly 7 p.m.-2 a.m. Shows nightly 9:30 p.m. & 11:30 p.m. Cover $10. AE, MC, V.

In this small, plain room, it's clear that more attention has been paid to the music than the decor. A casually dressed and unusually mixed crowd, of every color, arrives late to hear good local jazz and fusion bands. Dinner of a sort is served—huge baked potatoes, stuffed with ev-

erything from cheese and spinach to steak with pizzaiola sauce—and it's fun, inexpensive and quite tasty.

Birdland West
105 W. Broadway Ave., Long Beach 90802; (310) 436-9341
Hours, showtimes & cover vary. (2-drink minimum). AE, MC, V.

A fine club with excellent sound and a welcoming vibe, Birdland West is well worth the drive to Long Beach. It draws such first-rate talents as Les McCann and Eddie Harris, and the clientele treats the music with respect. Owner Al Williams is a respected drummer whose quintet comprises the house band. A full dinner menu is served, along with the usual cocktails, beer and wine.

Le Café
14633 Ventura Blvd., Sherman Oaks 91403; (818) 986-2662
Shows Sun.-Thurs. 8 p.m. & 10 p.m., Fri.-Sat. 9 p.m. & 11 p.m. All major cards.

This small, intimate room upstairs from the restaurant attracts a dedicated jazz crowd who enjoy listening to the music up close. The accent here is on the spicy Latin and South American jazz, and some of the performers who play here you'll not catch anywhere else. The food—which runs the gamut from Continental to Cajun—is tasty and pricey, as are the beverages. It's advisable to come early for big-name acts, since the place fills up very quickly.

Catalina Bar and Grill
1640 N. Cahuenga Blvd., Hollywood 90028; (213) 466-2210
Open nightly 7 p.m.-2 a.m. Shows nightly 9 p.m. & 11 p.m. Cover varies (2-drink minimum). All major cards.

The neighborhood may look pretty grungy, but once you've stepped inside, all that disappears. This is a class joint. You'll find yourself bathed in soft, rose-colored light, while being served delicious, moderately priced Continental cuisine. Catalina offers a full bar, validated parking and, of course, its real attraction, some of the biggest names in jazz onstage.

The Cinegrill
Hollywood Roosevelt Hotel, 7000 Hollywood Blvd., Hollywood 90028; (213) 466-7000
Shows Tues.-Thurs. 9 p.m., Fri.-Sat. 8:30 p.m. & 10:30 p.m. Cover $10-$20 (2-drink minimum). All major cards.

Take a step back to the time when stepping out for the evening was in order. Grab your top hat and your cane, put on the ritz, and enter the glittery world of old-time Hollywood. Like the once-seedy Roosevelt itself, The Cinegrill has been restored to the glory of its Hollywood heyday, and the remodeling reeks of subdued charm. The Cinegrill recalls the era when first-class hotels offered the best talent in town; it headlines performers fresh from New York in shows that generally last about an hour. Hollywood Boulevard, however, is not the beauty queen it was back when there were people around who had voted for Teddy Roosevelt, for whom the hotel is named. The noted Walk of Fame is now home to a more seamy clientele, though local officials are trying to clean up the area. Any stepping out should therefore be done inside the attractive hotel, which also has a nice, expensive restaurant called Theodore's.

J.P.'s Money Tree
10149 Riverside Dr., Toluca Lake 91602; (818) 769-8800
Open daily 10 a.m.-2 a.m. Shows Mon.-Sat. 9 p.m.-1:30 a.m., Sun. 8 p.m.-12:30 a.m. No cover. MC, V.

The Money Tree has a devoted band of followers in and around Toluca Lake, but its reputation is beginning to spread beyond the neighborhood. Writers, camera operators, character actors and technicians from the many nearby studios come to this small, friendly (albeit too gloomy) bar/restaurant to hear good to very good jazz singers perform. Happily, there's no cover charge—something of which the management is quite proud—so for the price of a drink or a steak dinner, you can relax for a few hours and listen to fine, old-fashioned jazz.

Lunaria
10351 Santa Monica Blvd., W.L.A. 90025; (310) 282-8870
Open Tues.-Sun. 8:30 p.m.-1 a.m. AE, MC, V.

This lovely, grown-up spot is a nice refuge from the trendy throngs—its relaxed elegance and warm lighting lull you into the civilized mood necessary to appreciate sophisticated jazz. These acts are usually good. The only choice you have to make is whether you'd like to sit up close by the bar and order single-match scotches to fulfill the drink minimum, or head for the dining room, where they have graciously installed a removeable partition so you can see the band while you dine on the good French fare.

Nucleus Nuance
7267 Melrose Ave., W. Hollywood 90046; (213) 939-8666
Open nightly 7 p.m.-2 a.m. Shows nightly 9:30 p.m., 11 p.m. & 12:30 a.m. Cover $5 for tables in front room. AE, MC, V.

There's a positive beat at Nucleus Nuance that says it's all right to drop what you're doing, put on those natty clothes and go listen to the jazz or blues band featured that night. It has an open,

sophisticated atmosphere, the kind of place where the saxophone and the wine flow freely. A long hallway leading to the main room is lined with photos of old-time Hollywood stars. A young to middle-age professional crowd hangs out here, and it can get intimate on weekends. Come here for romance, dessert and liqueurs.

Vine Street Bar & Grill
1610 N. Vine St., Hollywood 90028; (213) 463-4375
Open Tues.-Sat. 5 p.m.-midnight. Shows Tues.-Sat. 9:15 p.m. & 11:15 p.m. Cover varies (2-drink minimum). DC, MC, V.

This elegant, costly club consistently offers the best in headline entertainment, with a crowd of aficionados. It's priceless to be able to hear popular entertainers like Nina Simone in such a small club. It's like stumbling into a Chicago blues dive and coming across B.B. King playing. Vine Street also serves Italian food that's better than the standard supper-club fare, but it's expensive, and you have to pay admission even if you're dining. But you won't mind when you get a chance to listen to the likes of Joe Williams, Eartha Kitt and George Shearing working on new and old material in the intimate setting.

Music Clubs

Los Angeles has traditionally been a great place to hear live rock 'n' roll. There are dozens of venues, of every size, showcasing major stars and next year's stars. In this section, we've listed some of the better music nightclubs in town, but we haven't included the theaters and concert arenas, where you'll find the higher-end performers. One of our favorites is the **Wiltern Theatre** (box office, 213-380-5005; ticket reservations, 213-480-3232), both a physically and acoustically beautiful hall that tends to attract more jazz, soul and progressive music than rock; of the outdoor arenas, the best are the **Greek Theater** (213-665-1927), a delightful outdoor amphitheater, and the **Universal Amphitheater** (recorded information, 818-980-9421; box office 818-777-3931), a huge venue which offers every comfort.

Al's Bar
305 S. Hewitt St., Downtown (L.A.) 90013; (213) 625-9703
Open Mon.-Fri. 6 p.m.-2 a.m., Sat.-Sun. 2 p.m.-2 a.m. Cover $3-$7. No cards.

The downtown loft scene is the closest thing L.A. has to New York's SoHo, and Al's Bar sits smack in the middle of it all. Though it's been revamped, it has maintained some of its rough edges; Al's is usually crowded, smoky, raw and loud. It is not for the faint of heart. Dress is casual to downright seen-better-days, and the bar serves beer and wine. Friday through Monday Al's presents live music, and it has a good reputation for attracting some first-class bands. Tuesday and Wednesday are theater nights, featuring a way-out mix of dramatic goings-on. Thursday is "no talent night," with a variety of off-the-wall acts. Weekends bring quite good bands.

Club Lingerie

6507 W. Sunset Blvd., Hollywood 90028;
(213) 466-8557
Open Mon.-Sat. 9 p.m.-2 a.m. Cover varies. No cards.

While other clubs have come and gone, Lingerie has managed to chart a course that has kept it on the hot-spot list for a number of years. The bare-bones brick decor transcends the cartoony motifs that have relegated otherclubs to the has-been bin. It also allows you to see the stage from just about anywhere in the club. Lingerie has always maintained a loyal group of yuppie Hollywood rockers, while its heads-up booking policy, featuring the most happening bands in town, helps hook in the errant hipsters who would otherwise be out seeking newer thrills at newer venues. We always enjoy the costume-party ambience; most of the clientele seem as intrigued with what everyone else is wearing as with what the latest rock, reggae or rhythm-and-blues bands have to play.

Coconut Teaszer

8117 Sunset Blvd., W. Hollywood 90046;
(213) 654-4773
Hours & cover vary. MC, V.

Don't let the Hotel California, salmon-and-green motif fool you. This place is a cauldron of high-decibel grungeosity. The new and improved Teaszer books the cream of L.A.'s rock scene and draws a young, dedicated and energetic crowd; Sunday nights are rock marathons featuring band after band in short, sharp succession. Black rocker gear seems to be de rigueur, with nary a primary color to be seen. There's outdoor seating to cool off from the breakneck slamming, and large drinks for the same purpose.

FM Station

11700 Victory Blvd., N. Hollywood 91606;
(818) 769-2220
Open Sun.-Thurs. 8:30 p.m.-2 a.m., Fri.-Sat. 8:30 p.m.-4 a.m. Cover varies. MC, V.

It's hard to figure this place out. FM Station (named acronymically for Filthy McNasty, the proprietor of this unique establishment) is the spandex capital of the Valley. You'll see band after

band of young men with long moussed hair cranking out the kind of ear-splitting music that everybody's parents hate. But then, in between sets, a kind of latter-day Saturday Night Fever takes hold, with deejays spinning the most danceable tunes imaginable. The place is full of bars and tables, and couches where you can rest, drink or order munchies. There's a great dance floor and a room in back where you can rest your ears and shoot a little pool.

Genghis Cantina

Genghis Cohen, 740 N. Fairfax Blvd., Fairfax District (L.A.) 90046; (213) 653-0640
Showtimes & cover vary. All major cards.

This small performance venue attracts some big talent who come by to do a few acoustic rounds here. Big entertainment-industry execs come in, too, to listen and chow down on the great nouvelle Chinese food they serve at the restaurant. You won't find hipsters here—either onstage or in the crowd—but after a long week putting together production deals, who needs ripped jeans and screaming guitar solos?

King King

467 S. La Brea Ave., Wilshire District (L.A.) 90036;
(213) 934-5418
Open Tues.-Sat. 11 a.m.-2 a.m., Sun.-Mon. 9 p.m.-2 a.m. Shows nightly 10:30 p.m. & 12:30 a.m. No cards.

At King King, it's all about the music. Whether they're offering rockabilly, blues, Cajun or reggae, the performers tend to be perennials—accomplished musicians with a dedicated local following—as opposed to the hot bands *du jour*. Occasionally, when one of their big jam sessions erupts, someone like Dave Alvin or Tom Waits will get onstage and join the fray. It's like one big party, and as is usually true when the draw is the music and not the scene, the emphasis here is on getting down, not getting ahead.

McCabe's Guitar Store

3101 Pico Blvd., Santa Monica 90405;
(310) 828-4497
Shows Fri.-Sat. 8 p.m. & 10:30 p.m. Cover $12.50-$20. All major cards.

A throwback to the early '60s, McCabe's is a place for all musical seasons: guitar/mandolin/banjo shop by day, folk music school by night, concert hall on Friday and Saturday. It is the only place of its type, and it showcases lesser-known artists from the Southern world of bluegrass, folk, blues and gospel—with the occasional big-name rock band thrown in. The small auditorium holds only 150, so all the seats are good, and the sound system is top-notch. No liquor license, but no one here seems to have any trouble whooping it up on tea and cookies.

179

The Palace

1735 N. Vine St., Hollywood 90028;
(213) 462-3000
Open most nights. Hours, showtimes & cover vary. AE, MC, V.

The Palace attracts a higher level of performer than most clubs—usually upbeat rockers like the Stray Cats, Oingo Boingo, Nirvana and Concrete Blonde. The handsomely renovated twenties theater has decent acoustics, but it's clearly a place more appropriate for partying than for serious listening. The few seats usually go to those who eat in the restaurant prior to the show, so most guests have to stand. After the shows, the concert hall turns into a dance hall for a fashionable college-age crowd.

The Palomino

6907 Lankershim Blvd., N. Hollywood 91606;
(818) 764-4010
Open Mon.-Sat. 11 a.m.-2 a.m., Sun. 4 p.m.-midnight. Showtimes & cover vary. AE, MC, V.

This country-western institution is struggling against the tide of all the newer, nicer, up-and-coming spots. The Palomino clings to its faded glory and continues to attract top country and rockabilly names, along with some lively rock bands. And so, in turn, the raucous fans keep coming back for more. Thus, the legend lives on. Monday night is "talent" night, which has to be seen to be believed.

Raji's

6160 Hollywood Blvd., Hollywood 90028;
(213) 469-4552
Open nightly 9 p.m.-2 a.m. Cover $5-$7. No cards.

A favorite with L.A.'s hipsters, Raji's is the quintessential rock dive. Upstairs, you'll find a long bar serving beer and wine and a crowd jamming to one of the best jukeboxes in town. The action doesn't really heat up, though, until you go underground. At the foot of the stairs there's a window through which Indian dishes are sold. Hang a right and enter the cavernous performance area. Raji's is known for hosting some of the best rock bands in town. Expect high-decibel, high-energy fare—everything an up-and-coming rock band should be.

The Roxy

9009 W. Sunset Blvd., W. Hollywood 90069;
(310) 276-2222
Open most nights. Shows most nights 8 p.m. Cover varies. DC, MC, V (except for shows).

More than a few years back now, The Roxy was probably the best pop nightclub in town; it hosted everyone from Bruce Springsteen to Jackson Browne to the Blasters. Then, it became home to a couple of long-running plays and stopped booking music. Now it's back in the music world, although thus far its bookings have been more or less limited to lesser-known local bands. We can only hope that this comfortable, well-designed club will start booking the quality names it used to.

Shamrock

4600 Hollywood Blvd., Silverlake 90027;
(213) 666-5240
Open nightly 10 p.m.-2 a.m. Cover varies. No cards.

This one-time drinker's bar got itself a booking agent and now L.A.'s hottest underground bands churn out the power chords on the Shamrock's ample stage. You can get up close where it's nice and loud or take refuge on the flip-side of the two-sided bar where it's slightly less raucous. There are a few pool tables for in-between set relaxation.

The Troubadour

9081 Santa Monica Blvd., W. Hollywood 90069;
(310) 276-6168
Hours & showtimes vary. Cover $5-$10. No cards.

National fame was once The Troubadour's, back in the early '70s, when it was one of the premier spawning grounds for the burgeoning folk-rock movement; musicians The Troubadour helped launch include Elton John, Jackson Browne and Linda Ronstadt. Now this concert club is rather run-down, playing host to dozens of heavy metal and garage-band rock groups. Much of the crowd sports black-leather jackets, long, feathered hair (both sexes), tattoos and other such head-banger trappings. These days it's more for tough-talking rockers who like ear-splitting, 30-minute guitar solos. The exception is the Tuesday "Sanctuary," an innovative forum for acoustic-guitar bands, heavy-metal bands who go acoustic for the night, and other atypical acts.

Whisky a Go-Go

8901 Sunset Blvd., W. Hollywood 90069;
(310) 652-4205
Open most nights. Hours & cover vary. No cards.

In the Sunset Strip's heyday, The Doors' Jim Morrison stripped down to his love beads and the band got banned from the Whisky. In those days it was one of L.A.'s most popular venues and the launching ground for many new bands. The Whisky boarded up its own doors a few years ago, but now the owners of the neighboring Roxy have breathed new life into the progressive club. Since there's no age limit, the crowd is young—and black leather and silver studs rule the night. The bands as well as the crowd are primarily New York Dolls–style glam rockers, so differentiating the sexes can get tricky. ◆

SHOPS

Contents

Shopping L.A.'s Sprawl

From Santa Monica to Pasadena, Angelenos shop their share of independent stores and offbeat boutiques. But when time or need necessitates serious nonstop shopping, they park their cars in the immense parking lots of the immense shopping centers sprinkled all over the Southern California landscape and make their purchases at one of countless clone stores: Ann Taylor, Williams-Sonoma, The Limited, Laura Ashley, The Gap and Banana Republic, to name just a few of the better ones. This is by no means a purely American phenomenon—witness the incredible worldwide success of Italy's Benetton—but it seems to thrive especially well in our car culture.

Thankfully, you don't have to be a slave to the malls to shop in L.A. The city is also home to some stellar street shopping not enclosed by shopping-center walls. If you feel an urge to do that most un-L.A. thing—walk outdoors—park your car and stroll: on Beverly Hills's ultra-posh **Rodeo Drive**; in Hollywood's vibrant **Sunset Plaza** on the Sunset Strip; along the burgeoning and hip **La Brea Avenue**; in young, clean-cut **Westwood Village**; on Pasadena's charming **Lake Street** or Old Town Pasadena's **Colorado Boulevard**; on Hancock Park's tiny, quaint **Larchmont Boulevard**, on Santa Monica's café-lined **Montana Avenue**; or on beachy-chic **Main Street** in Venice. You'll enjoy the fresh air, an unhurried view of L.A., and you'll find some terrific little independent shops that you'd never find in a mall. These are the kinds of places we've

outlined in the pages that follow, without ne-
glecting the better chain stores, which have become almost essential to modern life.

Also, note that this chapter includes a number
of services, from L.A.'s most talked-about luxuries to the bare necessities. Health spas, sports
clubs and beauty salons can be found under
"Beauty & Health," and an extensive listing of
the city's best caterers, gourmet take-out and
wine shops can be found under "Food." Check
the "Rentals" and "Services" sections to find
anything from a computer to a watch repairer to
a babysitter.

Antiques & Collectibles

American Country

Avenue Antiques
5641 Melrose Ave., Larchmont Village 90038;
(213) 856-4245
Open Tues.-Fri. noon-6:30 p.m., Sat. 11 a.m.-5 p.m.

This is one of few places in L.A. which carries
new vintage stock, such as area rugs and linoleum
from the '40s. Other pieces of classic Americana
include nineteenth century furniture with original painted surfaces, pre-war ceramics, architectural elements, hooked rugs, birdhouses, shard
pottery and whimsical folk art. The emphasis is
on the handmade, while the assortment is eclectic, unusual and always changing.

Country Pine & Design
1318 Montana Ave., Santa Monica 90403;
(310) 451-0317
Open Mon.-Sat. 10 a.m.-6 p.m., Sun. noon-4 p.m.

A Montana Avenue mainstay, Country Pine &
Design carries furniture and folk art dating from
the early 1800s through the 1940s, but is best
known for its painted pine furniture from Penn-
sylvania. Interspersed between quaint collector
pine pieces are iron tables, sea grass wickerwork,
turn-of-the-century botanical prints, needle-
point pillows, Tramp Art boxes, Majolica pottery
and a glittering array of Miriam Haskell vintage
jewelry.

Indigo Seas
123 N. Robertson Blvd., Beverly Hills 90048;
(310) 550-8758
Open Mon.-Sat. 10 a.m.-6 p.m.

This retail partner to the romantic Ivy restaurant surrounds you with a sense of history,
whether it be the deep South, glamorous old
Hollywood or the colonial Caribbean. On our
last visit, we found dark green folding "regatta"
chairs, Victorian iron doorstops in dog or sweet-
heart bouquet shapes, antique watering cans and
colorful vintage tablecloths to complement overstuffed, floral chintz-covered chairs. Also available here is the rustic, handpainted pottery in a
rose and ivy pattern made especially for The Ivy
by a factory in Peru.

Art Deco & Art Nouveau

Dazzles
13805 Ventura Blvd., Sherman Oaks 91423;
(818) 990-5488
Open Tues.-Sat. noon-6 p.m.

A sparkling, attractive little place done with
care and attention to detail. It has one of the
largest selections of campy celluloid jewelry in
the city; each colorful trifle is temptingly displayed in long neat rows. There's also a good
assortment of picture frames, tubular chrome
and lacquer tables, lighting fixtures and a few
upholstered chairs. Everything is in mint condition, the prices are fair, and the service is first-
rate.

Harvey's
7367 Melrose Ave., W. Hollywood 90046;
(213) 852-1271
Open Mon.-Thurs. 10:30 a.m.-6 p.m., Fri. 10:30 a.m.-8 p.m., Sat. 10:30 a.m.-6 p.m., Sun. noon-5 p.m.

Decomania practically oozes out the front
door of this friendly, funky art-deco department
store, stocked with oodles of lamps, desk accessories, cigarette lighters, pictures, mirrors and
furniture—including a bounty of rattan sofas,
tables and chairs that were particularly popular in
the '40s. Expect to pay Melrose prices. Some of
the accessories may be in less-than-perfect condition, so perfectionists may choose to shop elsewhere.

Mid-Melrose Antiques
5651 Melrose Ave., Hollywood 90038;
(213) 463-3096
Open Mon.-Sat. noon-6 p.m.

Specializing in art nouveau, Mid-Melrose puts
its accent on the theatrical. On our last visit, we
just missed seeing the eight-foot-tall male angel

and the life-sized painting of an enraged gorilla. Whether you love it or hate it, this shop caters to Hollywood's taste for the dramatic and the magical, buffered by some serious eighteenth-century antiques.

Papillon Gallery
8816 Melrose Ave., W. Hollywood 90046; (310) 246-1107
Open Mon.-Fri. 10 a.m.-6 p.m., Sat. 11 a.m.-5 p.m.

Originally located in a velvet-carpeted Sherman Oaks showroom, this shop now displays more precious things in less space. It's still one of the most glamorous, alluring shops of its kind, specializing in decorative and fine arts from 1860 to 1960, with an emphasis on sculpture and paintings. Other must-see items include glass and ceramic objets d'art, period light fixtures and some furniture, deco silver coffee services, tiny enameled picture frames, crystal perfume bottles and—surprise—a wonderful collection of '40s-era gold jewelry.

Piccolo Pete's
13814 Ventura Blvd., Sherman Oaks 91423; (818) 990-5421
Open Tues.-Sat. 11 a.m.-6 p.m., Sun. noon-5 p.m.

There's some art nouveau here, but the bulk of the merchandise is either art deco or in the art deco mode. The shop stocks plenty of furniture and light fixtures, including figural lamps. Upstairs you'll find goods from the '40s and '50s and colorful paintings and posters. The rear of the shop houses a substantial selection of California pottery. All the wares are in good condition.

Shapes Gallery
8444B Melrose Ave., W. Hollywood 90069; (213) 653-0855
Open Mon.-Fri. 10:30 a.m.-5 p.m., Sat. by appt. only.

One of the last bastions for French furniture from 1925 to the late 1940s. Each extravagantly crafted console, desk, dining table, chair and daybed has been restored to its original luster. There are also some finely selected lamps, vases, art glass, architectural pieces and posters.

Thanks for the Memories
8319 Melrose Ave., W. Hollywood 90069; (213) 852-9407
Open Mon.-Wed. & Fri.-Sat. 1:30 p.m.-6 p.m.

Requisite gray walls enhance a substantial array of restored black-and-chrome art deco furniture: a good assortment of upholstered chairs; a small but lovely array of Lalique; glass and crystal perfume bottles from the 1920s and 1930s; and a large collection of jewelry, including '20s vintage pieces, Mexican silver from the '40s and men's watches, cuff links and belt buckles.

China & Pottery

Buddy's
7208 Melrose Ave., Melrose-La Brea District (L.A.) 90046; (213) 939-2419
Open Tues.-Sat. 11 a.m.-6 p.m.

Buddy's was the first store in L.A. to call attention to Bauer, the highly collectible pottery from California kitchens of the '30s. But Bauer is just the beginning of owner Buddy Wilson's brilliantly displayed colored-pottery collection; other familiar names are Fiesta, Catalina, Harlequin and Franciscan. He also carries stunning American art pottery (primarily vases by Rookwood, Roseville, Teco, Fulper) and corresponding Craftsman furniture, produced between 1900 and 1918 (Gustav Stickley, Limberts and Roycroft). One of Melrose Avenue's oldest gems.

Foster-Ingersoll
805 N. La Cienega Blvd., W. Hollywood 90069; (310) 652-7677
Open Mon.-Fri. 10 a.m.-4:45 p.m.

This small, well-staffed shop attracts those who want to create table settings with an eclectic, mismatched look. The focus is on new goods, but there's an ample selection of exquisite old china to augment current tableware. On several occasions we've spotted beautiful sets of hand-painted service and dessert plates, all of which sell quickly.

Clocks

California Clockmakers Guild
7971 Melrose Ave., Melrose-Fairfax District (L.A.) 90046; (213) 653-1081
Open Mon.-Fri. 11 a.m.-4:30 p.m.

A pleasing assortment of primarily nineteenth-century wall clocks fashioned from wood, as well as a smaller selection of floor and mantel timepieces that are professionally installed if purchased here. The owners have been in business nearly 40 years, and all clocks come with a written one-year guarantee. The service is friendly and personalized, the atmosphere comfortable and relaxed.

Jacobsohn's
8304 W. 3rd St., W. Hollywood 90048; (213) 655-6105
Open Tues.-Fri. 10 a.m.-5 p.m., Sat. 10 a.m.-4 p.m.

Jacobsohn's has the largest selection of antique clocks in the Southland—all sorts of sizes and shapes from England, France, Germany and America. Most of the clocks are fashioned from wood and brass, but you'll see crystal, marble and nearly every other conceivable material used as well. About 100 timepieces are on hand, and 80 percent are ticking and chiming. Try visiting on the hour for an unusual midmorning or afternoon concert.

Furniture

The Antique Guild
8800 Venice Blvd., Culver City 90034;
(310) 838-3131
Mon.-Fri. 10 a.m.-7 p.m., Sat. 10 a.m.-6 p.m., Sun. 11 a.m.-6 p.m.

Once upon a time, this was *the* place to go for inexpensive antiques. Now about two-thirds of the antiques have been replaced by reproductions, including the company's own line of furniture, Guild Hall. Nonetheless, there is still plenty of old furniture at low to moderate prices, from pine trunks and armoires to oak dining-room sets. The many other branches around town stock mostly reproductions.

The Antique Mart
809 N. La Cienega Blvd., W. Hollywood 90069;
(310) 652-1282
Open Mon.-Fri. 10 a.m.-noon & 1 p.m.-4 p.m., or by appt.

The Antique Mart overflows with confused clutter. Tiny trifles are crammed into curio cabinets, and antique American and English furniture and paintings spill from nooks and crannies. Owner Alice Braunfeld has been in the business for more than 40 years. She guarantees everything she sells, and the prices are realistic.

Baldacchino
919 N. La Cienega Blvd., W. Hollywood 90069;
(310) 657-6810
Open Mon.-Fri. 9 a.m.-5 p.m.

The small, elegant collection of eighteenth- and nineteenth-century French and Continental furniture—everything from period side chairs to dining tables—is a feast for the eyes. Antique crystal chandeliers twinkle from a sixteen-foot ceiling, an abundance of Oriental porcelain is on hand, and you'll also find one of the best selections of reproduction bouillotte lamps in the city.

Bruce Graney & Company
Cal-Fair Plaza, Ste. 512, One W. California Blvd.,
Pasadena 91105; (818) 449-9547, (213) 681-7008
Open Mon.-Sat. 10 a.m.-5 p.m.

Graney is known for its eighteenth- and nineteenth-century English furniture, and just about the most sophisticated carved-pine bookcases in town. A native of Pasadena, Graney stocks only furniture that is in superb condition, and considering the quality of the goods, the prices seem fair. Dining tables and chairs are usually in fine

supply, and there's always a good assortment of bookcases, armoires and small tables.

Charles Pollock Antiques
8478 Melrose Pl., W. Hollywood 90069;
(213) 651-5852
Open Mon.-Fri. 9 a.m.-5 p.m.

In addition to the good selection of country English antiques and Scandinavian Biedermeier empire pieces, there's a smattering of Oriental furniture and porcelains. Large-scale pieces are usually featured.

Connoisseur Antiques
8468 Melrose Pl., W. Hollywood 90069;
(213) 658-8432
Open Mon.-Fri. 9 a.m.-5 p.m.

This is the hall of mirrors—opulent, glittery and Hollywood-style. One of the largest collections of nineteenth-century crystal chandeliers in the country drips from the high ceiling; these in turn are reflected in a staggering assortment of Venetian mirrors. If you can tear your eyes away from this splendor in the glass, you'll find a good deal of eighteenth-century French furniture sitting amid signed terra-cotta statues from Italy and other accessories. If you're still not satiated, ask about the other shop in the Pacific Design Center. Not for everyone, but certainly worthwhile if you're aiming for a drop-dead interior.

Equator Antiques
160 N. La Brea Ave., Melrose-La Brea District
(L.A.) 90036; (213) 933-6535
Open Mon.-Sat. 10 a.m.-6 p.m.

Equator Antiques imports primitive furniture from Brazil, home of a little-known cache of Portuguese-influenced pieces from the early nineteenth century. Huge farmhouse tables are humbled only by massive armoires, many still clad in clinging chips of old paint, handcarved and caned benches and Spanish altars.

J.F. Chen Antiques
8414 Melrose Ave., W. Hollywood 90069;
(213) 655-6310
Open Mon.-Fri. 10 a.m.-5 p.m.

The prices of J.F. Chen's colorful and substantial array of Oriental porcelains, from cachepots to garden stools, won't give you heart failure. So what if some of the goods aren't museum quality? Just drape a strand of ivy over a nick, and no one will be the wiser. There's also a fine selection of Oriental and Continental furniture and many neoclassical pieces, which the accommodating staff can help you locate.

John J. Nelson Antiques
8472 Melrose Pl. & 8461 Melrose Pl.,
W. Hollywood 90069; (310) 652-2103
Open Mon.-Fri. 9 a.m.-5 p.m., Sat. by appt.

Each time we've visited, there's been a warm greeting and a helpful attitude from the sales staff at both of the shops. A good selection of eighteenth- and nineteenth-century French provincial furniture fills several rooms—lots of tables, buffets and armoires. The wares have a well-worn, old-money quality, both of which might be mandatory if you choose to shop here, since the prices reflect the quality of the merchandise.

Licorne
8432 Melrose Pl., W. Hollywood 90069;
(213) 852-4765
Open Mon.-Fri. 9 a.m.-6 p.m., Sat. 10:30 a.m.-5 p.m.

A large, austere showroom with good-quality French provincial furniture from the eighteenth and nineteenth centuries. Primarily big pieces, with stately designs and a sense of opulence.

La Maison Française
8420 Melrose Pl., W. Hollywood 90069;
(213) 653-6534
Open Mon.-Fri. 9 a.m.-5 p.m., Sat. noon-4 p.m.

This sumptuous shop features château-quality European antiques, from Gothic and Renaissance tapestries to chandeliers and Baccarat crystal. Sometimes the owner's indifference can be annoying—perhaps decorators receive better treatment. If you're game, try the store's other outlet (8435 Melrose Ave., 213-653-6540) for architectural elements, period mantles, fireplaces and flooring.

Paul Ferrante
8464 Melrose Pl., W. Hollywood 90069;
(213) 653-4142
Open Mon.-Fri. 9 a.m.-5 p.m.

Known for its lighting fixtures, Paul Ferrante is always busy and bustling. The place brims with antique chandeliers, Chinese porcelains and French and English furniture. Well-heeled locals are dismayed if they can't find it here. Custom work is a specialty.

The Pine Mine
7974 Melrose Ave., Melrose-Fairfax District (L.A.)
90046; (213) 653-9726
Open Mon.-Sat. 10 a.m.-5:30 p.m.

An extraordinary amount of English and Irish country pine comes from this cozy shop. The majority of goods are plain, but the selection and variety are ample and include pieces with more decorative moldings. Everything is pine—from dressers to side tables, crocks to cupboards, boxes to benches—and the prices are reasonable.

Quatrain
700 N. La Cienega Blvd., W. Hollywood 90069;
(310) 652-0243
Open Mon.-Fri. 9 a.m.-5 p.m., Sat. 10 a.m.-5 p.m.

Fifteen pounds of potpourri are scattered in various antique porcelain and crystal bowls throughout the shop. If you think the scent of the stuff is bold, wait until you see the containers in which it's kept: a superb gathering of faintly exotic yet tasteful seventeenth- and eighteenth-century antiques, from Continental to Oriental, plus some of the most beautiful mirrors in town, which, like everything, are in mint condition. Manager Phillip M. Jelly Jr. sums up the owners' philosophy: "We like things a little unusual. You won't find boring British mahogany here."

Ralf's Antiques
807 N. La Cienega Blvd., W. Hollywood 90069;
(310) 659-1966
Open Mon.-Fri. 10 a.m.-5 p.m., Sat. 11 a.m.-3 p.m.

A sensible emporium, Ralf's has hardly any cute little curios to distract the eye from the good assortment of seventeenth- through nineteenth-century French and English provincial furniture. This isn't the shop for those with grand houses or ideas, since most of the pieces are moderately sized and could easily fit in with most decors. There are usually lots of lowboys, Windsor chairs, sideboards, cricket tables and armoires, as well as some antique silver and paintings. Fair prices and a helpful staff.

Richard Gould Antiques
216 26th St., Santa Monica 90402; (310) 395-0724
Open Mon.-Fri. 10 a.m.-4 p.m., Sat. by appt.

Far from mighty Melrose Place is a two-room shop chock-full of English furniture and accessories that date from the late seventeenth through nineteenth centuries. The Gould family has been in the antiques business for more than 30 years, and their reputation is as solid as the many oak tables they feature. Chinese export porcelain is also in good supply, as is an assortment of early metalware. Good quality and realistic prices.

Robert Yeakel
1099 S. Coast Hwy., Laguna Beach 92651;
(714) 494-5526
Open Tues.-Sat. 9:30 a.m.-5 p.m.

See "ORANGE COUNTY Shops."

Therien & Co.
716 N. La Cienega Blvd., W. Hollywood 90069;
(310) 657-4615
Open Mon.-Fri. 9 a.m.-5:30 p.m., Sat. 9 a.m.-4 p.m.

Across a brick-paved courtyard studded with olive trees is the entrance to Therien & Co., an antique gallery that reveals itself, one room at a time, until finally opening up to a showroom of palatial proportions. Much like its well established San Francisco twin, Therien & Co. specializes in seventeenth to early nineteenth century European antiques of extraordinary quality. Commodes and chandeliers, consoles, cabinets, chairs, *objet d'arts* and other glorious links with the past are arranged as they would be in a lavish yet lived-in home. There is a large showing of highly collectible Swedish neoclassic furniture and some remarkable pillows, such as a beaded eighteenth- century Russian design. Therien Studio next door features reproduction furniture.

West World Imports
171 E. California Blvd., Pasadena 91105;
(818) 449-8565
Open Mon.-Fri. 9 a.m.-5 p.m., Sat. 10 a.m.-5 p.m.

The brick-covered courtyard entrance brimming with nineteenth-century charrettes (carts)—is a prelude of things to come. Inside this spacious shop, there's a bountiful assortment of eighteenth- and nineteenth-century English and French provincial furniture spread throughout eight rooms. Proprietors Betty and Jim Wade keep an apartment in France, and Jim heads to Europe about every six weeks to round up the goods. The abundant stock is continually replenished, and there's always a roomful of antiques on sale.

Williams Antiques
1714 Euclid St., Santa Monica 90404;
(310) 450-2550
Open Mon.-Sat. 9 a.m.-5 p.m.

Williams is one of our favorite haunts for pine furniture, since the offerings are plentiful, the prices fair, the service caring, and the wares attractively displayed. The pine-only stock is primarily from the eighteenth and nineteenth centuries and is a refined lot. Cupboards and armoires seem to be emphasized, and any item purchased can later be traded in to finance future shopping sprees in this charming shop.

Jewelry

David Orgell
320 N. Rodeo Dr., Beverly Hills 90210;
(213) 272-3355, (310) 273-6660
Open Mon.-Sat. 10 a.m.-6 p.m., Sun. noon-5 p.m.

The glittering selection of antique and estate jewels, located toward the rear of the shop, includes expensive, exquisite pieces—among them fine examples by Cartier, Tiffany and Fabergé. These are definitely top-drawer goods—the type you'll want to store in a safe.

Frances Klein
310 N. Rodeo Dr., Beverly Hills 90210;
(310) 273-0155
Open Mon.-Sat. 10:30 a.m.-5:30 p.m.

If your taste in jewelry tends toward the art nouveau and art deco periods, you'll have a field day with Klein's collection of estate and antique jewels—they're valuable finds for the collector and simply for the lover of fine things. Her pieces are rare and beautiful, and many have been designed by such famous jewelers as Bulgari and Cartier.

Kazanjian Jewels
9808 Wilshire Blvd., Ste. 300, Beverly Hills 90212;
(310) 278-0811
Open by appt. only.

Known for purchasing estate jewelry, Kazanjian Jewels is geared toward the wholesale trade, but serves a retail clientele as well. Call first and make an appointment; at that time, discuss your jewelry needs with a salesperson, and, with luck, a good selection of baubles will be on hand for you to survey.

Matinee
10 E. Holly St., Pasadena 91103; (818) 578-1288
Open Wed.-Sat. 11:30 a.m.-5 p.m., Sun. 1 p.m.-5 p.m.

This veritable treasure trove of vintage designer costume jewelry includes such names as Miriam Haskell, Schiaparelli, Eisenberg and Joseff of Hollywood (a designer to matinee idols of the '30s and '40s), plus a superb collection of Bakelite and celluloid pieces and some old hats with a new twist. All of it works wonderfully with today's clothing. A dazzling selection at reasonable prices, considering the quality. Don't miss the goods in the window.

Morgan & Co.
1131 Glendon Ave., Westwood 90024;
(310) 208-3377
Open Mon.-Sat. 10 a.m.-5 p.m.

A fine-jewelry manufacturer, Morgan & Co. showcases a choice selection of antique and estate jewelry in its Westwood shop. You'll also find plenty of restored watches from 1915 to 1950.

Regency Jewelry
8129 W. 3rd St., Melrose-Fairfax District (L.A.) 90048; (213) 655-2573
Open Tues.-Sat. 10 a.m.-4 p.m.

Hardly la crème de la crème, but there is a great deal of old jewelry (costume and fine) at fair prices. A friendly staff, a good jewelry-repair service and a certified appraiser are on the premises.

Slightly Crazed

7412 Melrose Ave., Melrose-Fairfax District (L.A.)
90046; (213) 653-2165
Open Mon.-Sat. 11 a.m.-6 p.m.

The specialty here is vintage watches and jewelry, including pieces by Joseff, Eisenberg, Weiss, Bakelite and semiprecious enamels by Vega. But we couldn't overlook the wide array of collectible art and California pottery, vintage appliances (blenders, toasters) and Bakelite flatware. Watch repair on the premises.

Le Vieux Paris

342 N. Rodeo Dr., Ste. 202, Beverly Hills 90210;
(213) 272-1884
9606 Santa Monica Blvd., Beverly Hills 90210;
(310) 276-9558
Open Mon.-Fri. 10 a.m.-5 p.m.

You can always count on this small shop on Rodeo Drive to carry a good assortment of antique and estate jewelry, as well as a few objets d'art; that's why it has such a loyal clientele.

Wanna Buy a Watch?

7410 Melrose Ave., Melrose-Fairfax District (L.A.)
90046; (213) 653-0467
Open Mon.-Sat. 11 a.m.-6 p.m.

This place is headquarters for stylized vintage timepieces from World War II to 1960—everything from more affordable gold-filled models by Rolex and Cartier to rare exotics by Patek Phillipe and Vacheron Constantin. Add to that Hamilton's new line of classic '40s look-alikes, and you'll begin to understand why this is where serious collectors and celebrities like to spend time and money.

Markets

Antiquarius

8840 Beverly Blvd., W. Hollywood 90048;
(310) 854-6381
Ground floor open Tues.-Sat. 11 a.m.-6 p.m.; 2nd floor open Tues.-Sat. 11 a.m.-10:30 p.m.

Collectively, the 40 like-minded merchants at Antiquarius are reminiscent of the Paris bookstalls that line the banks of the Seine. Over the years, the building has turned into a talked-about source for authentic, high-quality collectibles, particularly antique jewelry. There's a vast array of attractively priced jewels for everyday use, as well as some selected multidigit dazzlers. Along the way are unusual finds in contemporary jewelry, paintings, Victorian silver, Persian rugs, bronzes, crystal and kaleidoscopes. While all the shops deserve a brief visit, several are noteworthy. Excaliber: antique and estate jewelry and restored vintage alligator handbags. Frances Frazen: silver-handled makeup brushes and

French art glass, circa 1900. Neil Lane: estate jewelry from the '20s to '40s with an emphasis on workmanship and beauty, as well as a number of signed pieces, including Cartier and Tiffany. Peskin's Jewelers: antique and period jewelry, gem lab and certified appraiser. Russian Antiques: art objects, icons and hand-painted miniature boxes. Second Time Around: vintage and contemporary watches, both new and used.

Santa Monica Antique Market

1607 Lincoln Blvd., Santa Monica 90404;
(310) 314-4899
Open Mon.-Sat. 10 a.m.-6 p.m., Sun. noon-5 p.m.

With complimentary valet parking and a warehouse-sized space full of antiques and collectibles, this is the premiere antique market on the westside. Quality is paramount, and goods are priced accordingly. In addition to fine vintage linens, purses, iron beds, garden accessories, classical lighting and costume jewelry, there are many dealers who specialize in a certain period or collectible: religious icons, British Colonial imports, American Indian artifacts, Arts and Crafts, Victorian and American and European Country. Selection ranges from the late Renaissance through the 1950s and includes the expected English, French, German, Italian, Austrian and Belgian pieces. Add to that a quilt specialist, a clock specialist and an expert in refurbishing vintage telephones.

Westchester Faire

8655 S. Sepulveda Blvd., Westchester 90045;
(310) 670-4000
Open Mon.-Sat. 10 a.m.-6 p.m., Sun. noon-5 p.m.

You'll enter via the mall's upper level, where fifteen contemporary gift shops keep company with several fast-food outlets. The mall, located on the lower level (take the escalator), houses 52 stalls and a dizzying assortment of all sorts of collectibles, ranging from Depression-era glass, old toys and advertising and military memorabilia, to crystal, china and jewelry. A sharp eye may spy some true antique treasures, but for the most part the offerings are not geared for those who haunt Sotheby's. Nonetheless, this is a fine place—and you never know what might turn up next week.

Quilts

Ludy Strauss/The Quilt Gallery

1015 Montana Ave., Santa Monica 90403;
(310) 393-1148
Open Mon.-Sat. 11 a.m.-5 p.m., or by appt.

Strauss specializes in antique and Amish quilts, hooked rugs (one of the most impressive selections on the West Coast), American folk art and painting. Everything is geared from an artistic viewpoint, with graphic patterns and bold colors. All are in fine condition and available in a broad price range. In the folk art area, there are unusual weather vanes and carved wooden pieces that, as Strauss puts it, "say something about the culture or individuality of the maker."

The Margaret Cavigga Quilt Collection

8648 Melrose Ave., W. Hollywood 90069;
(310) 659-3020
Open Mon.-Sat. 10 a.m.-5 p.m.

Somewhat of a legend on Melrose, chatty Margaret Cavigga stocks more than 400 quilts, old and new, crib to king-size, circa 1805 through the present. She also writes and sells books on American antique quilts. Some of the older quilts are exquisite; new ones are attractive but not always of the highest quality. Prices can be pretty astonishing.

Peace and Plenty

7320 Melrose Ave., Melrose-La Brea District (L.A.) 90046; (213) 937-3339
Open Mon.-Sat. 11 a.m.-6 p.m., Sun. noon-5 p.m.

This homey shop has a serene atmosphere, good lighting and a highly selective cache of pre-1940 quilts, coverlets and folk art. Merchandise is displayed in gallery fashion, with most of the quilts—all of which are in excellent condition—suspended from white walls. Among the other goodies: contemporary jewelry, folksy European pottery, picture frames, an eclectic assortment of paper items and cat-oriented gifts for feline lovers.

Silver

David Orgell

320 N. Rodeo Dr., Beverly Hills 90210;
(213) 272-3355, (310) 273-6660
Open Mon.-Sat. 10 a.m.-6 p.m., Sun. noon-5 p.m.

David Orgell once said that nothing announces status more quickly than Georgian silver dispersed throughout a home. If you share his philosophy, rush to the phone and make an appointment to visit the Georgian Room. Here you're apt to find sets of service plates by Paul Storr, along with a bounty of exquisite hand-crafted items. Of course, you'll need more than status to pay for the privilege of owning such treasures. Less costly silver collectibles located near the store's entrance include dazzling antique biscuit boxes, fish services, serving pieces, trays, tea sets and more.

Twentieth Century/ Modern

Antennae

13059 Ventura Blvd., Studio City; (818) 907-1810
Open Mon.-Fri. 10 a.m.-5 p.m., Sat. 10 a.m.-4 p.m.

Antennae stocks an array of "as is" furnishings and decorative objects, many neo-classical in nature. Though inventory changes constantly, one can almost always find old gilded mirrors, wonderfully beat-up leather luggage and a variety of wooden boxes. There is an outstanding selection of lamps in all price ranges, from a crystal candlestick bedside fixture from the '40s to a pair of Empire-style columns with gilded gold capitals. Especially popular are old fishing baskets for the Ralph Lauren look and Victorian shell art—boxes, planters and picture frames hand-decorated with findings from the sea.

Blagg's Antiques & Decorative Art

2901 Rowena Ave., Silverlake 90039;
(213) 661-9011
Open Thurs.-Sat. 1 p.m.-9 p.m. and by appt.

Larry Blagg's shop carries an appealing mix of deco and arts and crafts, primitive and Baroque styles. In this setting, a large shard garden pot from the twenties doesn't look out of place next to a tall iron plant stand shaped like a crown or an overstuffed club chair covered in a salt-and-pepper weave. Blagg's theory, "good design is good design" carries through in a fine collection of blue-chip art pottery, revamped furniture, artwork by listed Californian artists, textiles and tile and iron work, all rotated on a weekly basis.

Circa Antiques

3608 Edenhurst Ave., Atwater Village 90039;
(213) 662-6600
Open Tues.-Sat. noon-8 p.m., Sun. noon-5 p.m.

Owner Tom Kiefer's collection of cast-iron beds recalls the gentle grace of a Mid-Western home at the turn-of-the-century. The beds, most of them in a splendid state of "romantic decay," range from simple farmer's styles to upper-crust Victorian, with ornate castings in the shapes of flowers, ram's heads, pineapples or fleurs-de-lis. Beyond beds, this is also the place to find immigrant trunks, weather-beaten Adirondack chairs, quilts, interesting lamps and outdoor lighting fixtures, as well as a good selection of American country and primitive-style furniture and decorative accents.

188

Elizabeth's Place
4360 Tujunga Ave., Studio City 91604;
(818) 762-2060
*Open Tues.-Sat. 11 a.m.-5 p.m., Wed. noon-5 p.m., Sun.
by appt.*

This converted 1940s house filled with "age-enhanced" treasures—and its charming sister store, Elizabeth's Too next door—are filled with reasonably priced, old English country furniture, hooked rugs and hand-picked vintage linens. Scavenger's Paradise is a backyard full of plumbing hardware, antique stonework, wrought iron, lighting fixtures, old doors, garden ornaments, pedestal sinks, porch swings and other architectural gems for homeowners who relish the hunt.

Fat Chance
162 N. La Brea Ave., Melrose-La Brea District
(L.A.) 90036; (213) 930-1960
Open daily 11 a.m.-6 p.m.

Important designer furniture and accessories from the '50s and '60s, including that of Charles Eames, Herman Miller and George Nelson. After over fifteen years in business, Fat Chance is itself a fixture.

House of Style
6907 1/2 Melrose Ave., Melrose-La Brea District
(L.A.) 90038; (213) 935-4430
Open Tues.-Sat. noon-6 p.m.

Modern American furniture by famous names is the house specialty here. Big-ticket production pieces by such notables as George Nelson or Gilbert Rohde for Herman Miller, Paul Frankl, Norman Cherner and Harry Bertoia share the floor with many well-priced options in both furniture and accessories. We spied a freeform '50s coffee table with glass top in original condition, a Charles Eames bent plywood lounge chair and a black lacquer bar shaped like a movie camera. On a smaller scale, there are Swedish ceramic vases from the '40s and '50s in wild shapes, odd vintage photographs by unknown names and well-worn wooden transportation toys from the '30s and '40s.

Modernica
7386 Beverly Blvd., Fairfax District (L.A.) 90036;
(213) 933-0383
Open Mon.-Fri. 11 a.m.-6 p.m., Sat.-Sun. noon-6 p.m.

Many of owner Jay Novak's twentieth century design finds are not only unusual and well-crafted but extremely stylish. Here you can pick up a Heywood-Wakefield end table, a set of Thonet bentwood chairs or an authentic Craftsmen-style rocking chair. Modernica also offers restyled pieces, such as cast aluminum chairs from the '40s, each with a different jelly bean-colored seat and back of Knoll fabric. Attractively priced re-

productions include Charles Eames' classic Erector Set-like storage units, selling for a fraction of the going auction price for originals. Don't miss the matte green pottery from the Mid-West, perfect with modern or blond wood furniture or the spinning assortment of globes, from illuminated models to rare and intriguing military forms.

Off the Wall
7325 Melrose Ave., Melrose-La Brea District (L.A.)
90046; (213) 931-1185
Open Mon.-Sat. 11 a.m.-6 p.m.

The name says it all. Off the Wall sells weird but fantastic stuff, most of which happens to be vintage 1930 to 1950, according to co-owner Dennis Boses. In this carnival of kitsch, it's not uncommon to see a life-sized cow on display, next to restored jukeboxes, neon miscellanea, chrome pieces, mechanical memorabilia, fantasy furniture, trains, planes and automobiles. As Boses says, everything here is "bigger than it should be, smaller than it should be or moves when you think it won't."

Ohio
1409 Abbot Kinney Blvd., Venice 90291;
(310) 450-4664
Open Tues.-Sun. noon-5 p.m. & by appt.

If you're looking for sleek retro design, this roomful of American furniture and *objets* from the twentieth century is your bag. You'll find 50s-style upholstered living-room furniture, art-deco vanities, unusual ceramics, pop-art ashtrays and more. Ask owner Carol Hillman to help you—she does all the buying herself, and she has the enthusiasm to match her know-how.

Pom-Pom
7315 Santa Monica Blvd., W. Hollywood 90046;
(213) 876-4846
Open daily 11 a.m.-8 p.m.

It may appear unremarkable from the outside, but this comfortable, high-ceilinged storefront shop is a well-considered collection of treasures, from antique pine chests and rocking chairs to hand-wrought iron wine racks to used Levis. There's nary a silly item in the store; owners Hilde and Phillipe Leiaghat (who once owned the now-defunct restaurant, Chapo) choose everything with an eye for quality. Prices are fair and the service charming.

Skank World
7205 Beverly Blvd., Fairfax District (L.A.) 90036;
(213) 939-7858
Open Tues.-Sat. 2 p.m.-6 p.m. & Mon. by appt.

Long before the current flea market craze, Linda Gershon was assembling furniture designed to catch a collector's eye in her small

Skank World shop. Inventory varies but often includes a cache of office furniture from the late '50s and early '60s. On our last visit, we spotted chrome-framed sofas and white marble tables in original and restored condition.

Villa America
1958 Hillhurst Ave., Los Feliz 90027;
(213) 953-1920
Open Tues.-Sat. 10 a.m.-6 p.m., Fri. 10 a.m.-9 p.m., Sun. noon-5 p.m.

This shop takes a "crumbling villa" approach to decorating, specializing in classical fixtures and furnishings that are either left in their original, faded state or modified for extra flair. Upholstered pieces range from glamorous (a tufted, bronze-colored Victorian fainting couch) to elegant and whimsical (dining chairs that sport gilded wings). Panels of vintage hand-blocked linen and yards of damask are available to contribute to the "lived-in" feeling. Accessories and accents include original American paintings by listed and unknown artists, tapestry and lambskin pillows with down fillings and an array of wrought iron.

Western Americana

Cadillac Jack
6911 Melrose Ave., Melrose-La Brea District (L.A.) 90038; (213) 931-8864
Open Mon.-Sat. 10 a.m.-7 p.m.

Walking into Cadillac Jack is like visiting a Midwestern relative's home that's been frozen in post–World War II days. Owners Penny and Don Kolclough are devoted to twentieth-century American design; their collection includes cowboy furniture and accessories, wagon-wheel furniture, pistol- or horse-motif clocks, boot-motif lamps and Wallace rodeo-pattern restaurant china. One entire room displays Heywood Wakefield solid-birch furniture of the 1930s through the 1950s. Everything here is in mint condition; for furniture and lighting in original condition (with prices to match), visit Cadillac Jack's 7,000 square foot warehouse at 1123 Lillian Way (about ten minutes away).

Federico
1522 Montana Ave., Santa Monica 90403;
(310) 458-4134
Open Mon.-Sat. 11 a.m.-6 p.m.

Hailing from Oaxaca, Mexico, owner Federico is an authority on American Indian and Mexican folk art, and he stocks his shop accordingly. There's a substantial collection of pre-Columbian, Colonial and contemporary Mexican textiles, Navajo textiles, beadwork, baskets and furniture. The store is also known for antique and contemporary jewelry by such masters of Mexican silver as William Spratling, Frederick Davis and Margot of Tasco.

Hemisphere
1426 Montana Ave., Santa Monica 90403;
(310) 458-6853
Open Mon.-Sat. 10:30 a.m.-6 p.m.

If rustic elegance is your goal, Hemisphere can help you dress the part. This store showcases a rich mélange of home furnishings, art objects and collectible fashion from the American Southwest, Mexico, South America—all around the western world. Here authentic Navajo crushed-velvet "broomstick" skirts, Guatemalan shirts, hand-tooled belts, old trade beads, silver jewelry, boots and moccasins are right at home with Early California Monterey furniture, Afghan dhurries, Navajo rugs, pottery and a library of related books.

Jack Moore American Arts and Crafts
59 E. Colorado Blvd., Pasadena 91105;
(818) 577-7746
Open Wed.-Sat. 1 p.m.-5 p.m.

Jack Moore devotes his store to two design styles near and dear to California's past: mission oak (also known as Craftsman), furniture found in many local bungalows from the years 1900 to 1920; and the hacienda style of 1920 to 1940, ranging from Spanish to Monterey to the newly collectible "motel cowboy" style. Add to that a smattering of paintings, tile-topped tables, California and art pottery, vintage Mexican serapes, a few late-nineteenth-century ranch artifacts and old Southern Californian books, maps and magazines.

Beauty & Health

Beauty Boutiques

Aveda Esthetique
Beverly Center, Beverly & La Cienega Blvds., W. Hollywood 90048; (310) 288-4510
Open Mon.-Fri. 10 a.m.-9 p.m., Sat.-Sun. 10 a.m.-8 p.m.

Mention aromatherapy and Aveda comes to mind. This first West Coast concept store for the Aveda Corporation offers hair, skin, body and home cleaning products made with distilled, organic flower and plant essences. But it's what's *not* in Aveda products that counts: they're developed without petroleum-based or animal-tested ingredients. The salon-like store also offers minifacials, stress-relieving scalp massages and hair and makeup services.

Bath & Body Works

Beverly Center, Beverly & La Cienega Blvds., W. Hollywood 90048; (310) 659-1248
Open Mon.-Sat. 10 a.m.-9 p.m., Sun. 11 a.m.-6 p.m.

With its latest foray into personal care, The Limited Corporation offers well-priced, natural beauty products displayed as they would be in a country market in America's heartland. Everything from aromatherapy products to toiletries and men's skin care are presented, produce-stand style, to entice the senses. Homeopathic soaps are made with essences of eucalyptus, ginger and chamomile, shower gels scented with freesia flowers and bathing herbs and massage oils formulated to calm, energize and soothe. Also find loofahs, sponges and a library of books with topics ranging from healthy cooking to fitness and massage.

Body Scents

13826 Ventura Blvd., Sherman Oaks 91423; (818) 905-6744
Open Mon.-Fri. 11 a.m.-6 p.m., Sat. 10 a.m.-5 p.m., Sun. noon-4 p.m.

Body Scents offers its own line of skincare using kitchen ingredients packaged in refillable bottles. A mild foaming facial cleanser is formulated with oat flour and lemon oil; Aloe Vera and nourishing sea algae go into a light, super-moisturizing lotion. The store also blends fragrant natural oils of your choosing into unscented creams and lotions. Products range from scented glycerin soaps to shaving gel with aloe, and can be shipped.

Crabtree & Evelyn

Beverly Center, Beverly & La Cienega Blvds., W. Hollywood 90048; (310) 657-1152
Open Mon.-Fri. 10 a.m.-9 p.m., Sat. 10 a.m.-6 p.m., Sun. 11 a.m.-6 p.m.

We come here for English products in an old-London atmosphere: assorted soaps, shampoos, scented bath oils, fine boar-bristle hairbrushes, china bathroom accessories and shaving supplies (as well as such edible goodies as cookies, preserves and exotic mustards). Any of the merchandise can be packed into an attractive gift basket. Crabtree & Evelyn products are also sold at The Soap Plant, Fred Segal Santa Monica and many other stores (including Century City Shoping Center, Westside Pavilion, The Galleria at South

Bay, Sherman Oaks Galleria, Glendale Galleria and South Coast Plaza.

Fred Segal Essentials/ Fred Segal Scentiments

Fred Segal Santa Monica, 500 Broadway, Santa Monica 90401; (310) 458-3766
Open Mon.-Sat. 10 a.m.-7 p.m., Sun. noon-6 p.m.

Fred Segal is synonymous with the latest and the best, at prices to match. Essentials carries natural skin, hair-care and bathing products, including the entire line of hard-to-find Kiehls products, Alba Botanica, Dr. Hauschka and Dr. Geometti's seaweed products from Rome. We checked off our entire gift list upon discovering exotic toothbrushes and twenty-plus different toothpaste flavors from all over the world.

Neighboring Scentiments specializes in fragrance-related products for the home and body. Here you can have a fragrance named after yourself, blended to order and kept on file for future reference. Or choose from up to 150 unusual and imported perfumes. There are scented and aromatherapy candles from Rigaud and Manuel Canovas, soaps in whimsical shapes (fruits, hearts and cupids), potpourri, cosmetic and bath accessories and vintage hatboxes. Don't miss the showcase of antique-silver perfume bottles and men's grooming accessories. Custom gift baskets are available.

Homebody

8500 Melrose Ave., W. Hollywood 90069; (310) 659-2917
Open Mon.-Sat. 10 a.m.-6 p.m., Sun. noon-5 p.m.

Homebody may look out of place, tucked away in this pink-and-black, postmodern-gone-mad building, but it always enchants with its fragrant gift ideas. Owner Susan Fonarow is an aromatherapist who will custom-scent a full line of lotions and gels with your choice of essence.

H20 Plus

Beverly Center, Beverly & La Cienega Blvds., W. Hollywood 90048; (310) 659-4788
Open Mon.-Fri. 10 a.m.-9 p.m., Sat. 10 a.m.-8 p.m., Sun. 11 a.m.-6 p.m.

A high-style retail chain with its own head-to-toe product line for men, women, children and babies. Moisturizing beauty benefits aside, these products sound, look and smell terrific. Some of nature's most intriguing aromas—casaba melon, mango, calla lily and lotus—are captured in intensely colorful gels and lotions, packaged with splashy labels and displayed on waves of glass. Also in Sherman Oaks Fashion Square and South Bay Galleria.

M.A.C. Cosmetics
8700 Santa Monica Blvd., W. Hollywood 90069;
(310) 854-0860
Open Tues.-Sat. noon-7 p.m., Sun. noon-5 p.m.

In the beauty biz, everyone from models to movie stars is talking about M.A.C., the Toronto, Canada-based cosmetics line developed by a professional makeup artist. Besides being politically correct (nothing is tested on animals), M.A.C. cosmetics come in an awesome range of matte formula colors at reasonable prices.

Shu Uemura Beauty Boutique
Century City Shopping Center, 10250 Santa Monica Blvd., Century City 90067; (310) 284-8214
Open Mon.-Fri. 10 a.m.-9 p.m., Sat. 10 a.m.-6 p.m., Sun. 11 a.m.-6 p.m.

This Japanese specialty chain carries its own skincare line based on plant extracts and organically derived ingredients. The cleansing oil contains over nine different natural emollients, including safflower, corn, avocado and camellia oils. This is our first choice for beautifully designed, first-quality makeup brushes and professional cosmetic cases.

The Soap Plant
7400 Melrose Ave., Melrose-La Brea District (L.A.) 90046; (213) 651-5587
Open Mon.-Wed. 10:30 a.m.-11 p.m., Thurs.-Sat. 10:30 a.m.-midnight, Sun. 11 a.m.-8 p.m.

Where else but on Melrose would you find a psychedelic-colored new-wave soap shop? Actually, it's the gift items that are ultra-trendy (cactus-shape salt and pepper shakers, artsy books, Keith Haring T-shirts, wacky cigarette lighters, milk cow and Mexican ceramics); the soaps, perfumes and oils are by such trusted traditionalists as Caswell-Massey, Crabtree & Evelyn and Pears. La Luz de Jesus art gallery (upstairs), Zulu ethnic clothing and jewelry (next door) and Wacko cards (a few doors west) are all part of The Soap Plant's miniempire. This is eccentric L.A. at its best.

Tottenham Court
12206 Ventura Blvd., Studio City 91604;
(818) 761-6560
Open Mon.-Sat. 10 a.m.-6 p.m., Sun. noon-4 p.m.

Designed to resemble an Edwardian chemist's shop, this store is brimming with luxurious soaps, colognes, shaving accessories and bath sundries—stocking primarily European merchandise, including Bronnley, Woods of Windsor, Trumper (perfumer to Her Majesty), Caswell-Massey and Crabtree & Evelyn. Gift baskets can include any of the shop's sterling-silver trifles and be shipped or delivered anywhere. Phone orders are welcome.

Hair Salons

Allen Edwards Salon
345 N. Camden Dr., Beverly Hills 90210;
(310) 274-8575
17460 Ventura Blvd., Encino 91413;
(818) 981-7711
20037 Ventura Blvd., Woodland Hills 91364;
(818) 887-7330
Open Mon.-Wed. & Fri.-Sat. 8:30 a.m.-5 p.m., Thurs. 8:30 a.m.-7 p.m.

Award-winning stylist Allen Edwards has spent twenty years designing images for a demanding clientele: Mary Hart, Donna Mills, Cathy Lee Crosby and Dustin Hoffman among them. In this studiolike atmosphere (filtered lighting, polished concrete floors), you can stop in for a simple cut or be pampered from a long list of hair, makeup and manicure services, with special attention given to professional women at the Beverly Hills branch. Other branches in Long Beach (310-493-6466), Newport Beach (714-721-1666) and Irvine (714-251-6315).

Blades
801 N. Larrabee St. #10, W. Hollywood 90069;
(310) 659-6693
Open Tues., Wed. & Fri. 10 a.m.-6 p.m., Thurs. 11 a.m.-7:30 p.m., Sat. 9:30 a.m.-6 p.m.

One of West Hollywood's more stable institutions (over a decade old), Blades still leads the pack when it comes to short and chic haircuts at reasonable prices for men and women. The upscale salon boasts lots of natural lighting ("perfect for color application") and a panoramic view of the Pacific Design Center and Santa Monica Boulevard.

Bruno & Soonie
404 N. Cañon Dr., Beverly Hills 90210;
(310) 275-8152
Open Tues.-Sat. 8 a.m.-6 p.m.

This shop is best known for its celebrity client roster. Years ago, Bruno and Soonie were two of the top stylists at Jon Peters. When they opened their own shop, it was an overnight success—and still ranks among L.A.'s top salons. Stylists at this remarkably relaxed salon have a knack for creating cosmopolitan yet individualized cuts.

Burton Way Salon
9020 Burton Way, Beverly Hills 90211;
(310) 274-5411
Open Tues.-Sat. 8:30 a.m.-5:30 p.m.

Despite its Beverly Hills address, this salon ranks high in personal service and feels more like it's located in the Italian countryside than amid the urban sprawl. Known for their creativity in haircuts, expert color by Londoner Jane Paddon and health-oriented manicures by Marni Alba, the staff all use top-notch products. Best of all, the back windows look out over the garden of the adjoining Il Cielo restaurant.

Christophe
348 N. Beverly Dr., Beverly Hills 90210; (310) 274-0851
Open Mon. 10 a.m.-5 p.m., Tues.-Wed. & Fri.-Sat. 8:15 a.m.-6:30 p.m., Thurs. 8:15 a.m.-9 p.m.

One of Beverly Hills's most sought-after appointments is a date with Christophe, the Belgian hairdresser that opened this sleek salon in 1985. He and his 45 hairdressers have cut and coiffed the hair of an endless roster of stars that includes Julio Iglesias, Dustin Hoffman, Steven Spielberg, Christina Ferrare, Maria Shriver . . . and on and on. There's no haughty attitude—the salon is warm and friendly, with an espresso bar in the front where you can rejuvenate, have a bite to eat and chat. Some excellent French products are used and sold here; the salon also offers manicures, pedicures and body and scalp treatments.

Doyle-Wilson
8006 Melrose Ave., Melrose-Fairfax District (L.A.) 90046; (213) 658-6987
Open Tues. 9 a.m.-5 p.m., Wed.-Sat. 9 a.m.-7 p.m.

Low-key and coolly modern, Doyle-Wilson is the antithesis of a Beverly Hills salon. Haircuts here are on the leading edge—they look more natural and less overly "finished."

José Eber
224 N. Rodeo Dr., Beverly Hills 90210; (310) 278-7646
Open Mon. 9 a.m.-6 p.m., Tues.-Fri. 8:30 a.m.-8 p.m., Sat. 8:30 a.m.-6 p.m., Sun. noon-5 p.m.
Beverly Center, Beverly & La Cienega Blvds., W. Hollywood 90048; (310) 855-1410
Open Mon.-Fri. 10 a.m.-9 p.m., Sat. 10 a.m.-6 p.m.

José "Shake your head, darling" Eber is the stylist to the stars, and unless your face has been on the cover of *People*, he won't even consider taking you. What he will do is conduct a "hair consultation," updating you on color, texture and style. After that, one of his fleet of accomplished stylists in these two impossibly trendy salons will give you a skillful, chic cut (for an additional fee).

Joseph Martin
Rodeo Collection, 421 N. Rodeo Dr., Beverly Hills 90210; (310) 274-0109
Open Mon.-Sat. 8 a.m.-6 p.m., Thurs. 8 a.m.-8 p.m.

A marble-floored, ivory-and-black enclave in the Rodeo Collection, Joseph Martin has an impressive number of English-trained stylists on staff—35 at last count. Each is highly specialized in a different area of hair styling. In addition, there are such professional salon services as fa-

cials, electrolysis, makeup and manicures. An exclusive product line is formulated to Martin's specifications and sold at the counter. Valet parking.

Ménage à Trois
8822 Burton Way, Beverly Hills 90211; (310) 278-4430
Open Tues.-Sat. 7 a.m.-6 p.m.

This spacious beige-and-chrome salon is highly recommended for mature women who want a cut that's stylish but not too trendy. The able staff includes manicurists, who also provide pedicures and sculptured-nails services.

Micheal Villella
Sunset Plaza, 8616-A Sunset Blvd., W. Hollywood 90069; (310) 657-4756
Open Tues.-Sat. 9 a.m.-8 p.m.

Hair stylist/actor Micheal Villella's salon is practically a one-man show, tucked away in chic Sunset Plaza. Art-covered walls and jazz music contribute to the deco-moderne, gallerylike atmosphere. A choice spot for a soothing haircutting experience, color or perm.

Umberto
416 N. Canon Dr., Beverly Hills 90210; (310) 274-6395
Open Tues.-Sat. 9 a.m.-6 p.m., Thurs. 9 a.m.-7 p.m.

The quintessential Beverly Hills salon, Umberto is a high-profile favorite among models, celebrities and ordinary folk smitten with the Beverly Hills mystique. Large and bustling with 65 stylists, several of whom are celebs in their own right, Umberto offers all the usual services—hair cuts, color, perms, hair extensions, waxing, facials, manicures, makeup applications and scalp treatments—plus a lot of extras. There are specialized makeup and skincare products by M.A.C., Gerda Spillman and Phyto, loads of hair accessories and a mini-shop stocked with Umberto brand hair dryers (longer cords, stronger motors), rollers, irons, wavers, heating caps and hair brushes in all shapes and price ranges. This is the only hair salon we know of that features a professional hair photo studio for perfectly styled and coiffed family portraits.

Umberto Men
452 N. Camden Dr., Beverly Hills 90210; (310) 274-0393
Open Tues.-Sat. 9 a.m.-6 p.m., Thurs. 9 a.m.-7 p.m.

Umberto Men is a toned-down version of the main salon (*see* review above), with a few less frills.

Fitness Clubs

Jackson Sousa Training Facility

24955 Pacific Coast Hwy., Malibu 90265;
(310) 456-7800
*Open Mon.-Fri. 6 a.m.-9 p.m., Sat. 8 a.m.-5 p.m., Sun.
8 a.m.-2 p.m.*
Loews Santa Monica Beach Hotel, 1700 Ocean Ave.,
Santa Monica 90401; (310) 458-6700
Open daily 6 a.m.-9 p.m.

Beyond a career spent helping the rich and famous get in shape, fitness trainer Jackson Sousa has logged an impressive track record working with cancer patients. His original Malibu training facility, with its serene design and spectacular ocean view, sports premium cardiovascular/weight equipment (Cybex, Polaris, Precor, Gravitron), private one-on-one training, physical therapy and orthopedic sports rehabilitation, nutritional counseling, a massage therapist and private classes in yoga, tai-chi, kung-fu, aerobics, dance, gymnastics and women's self-defense. The Loews Santa Monica Beach Hotel facility, complimentary to hotel guests, features air-powered Kaiser and Cybex weight equipment, private sessions with a Sousa staff member and classes in aerobic workouts, yoga and circuit training.

The Sports Club

1835 S. Sepulveda Blvd., W.L.A. 90025;
(310) 473-1447
1980 Main St., Irvine 92714; (714) 975-8400
Mon.-Fri. 5:30 a.m.-11 p.m., Sat.-Sun. 8 a.m.-7:30 p.m.

More than an athletic club, this $27 million dollar, multi-purpose sports complex tackles the business of keeping fit in typical L.A. fashion, attracting the hippest of the hip with the utmost in recreational facilities and resort amenities. In addition to 12,000 square feet of fully equipped gyms with private trainers, there is a Sports Medicine/Fitness Evaluation Clinic, full court basketball and volleyball, a banked and surfaced indoor running track, racquetball, squash and outdoor paddle tennis. The indoor-outdoor pool opens onto a spacious split-level sundeck overlooking the city, while the locker rooms boast oak lockers, grooming aids and relaxation lounges. Need we mention the hair and nail salon, tanning facility, pro shop, restaurant, valet parking, shoe shine, massage, child care and believe it or not, car washing and detailing? Selected hotels, such as The Four Seasons and the Beverly Hills Hotel, provide Sports Club/L.A. passes to guests.

The Sports Connection

2929 31st St., Santa Monica 90405; (310) 450-4464
8612 Santa Monica Blvd., W. Hollywood 90069;
(310) 652-7440
21345 Hawthorne Blvd., Torrance 90503;
(310) 316-0173
*Mon.-Thurs. 6 a.m.-11 p.m., Fri. 6 a.m.-10 p.m., Sat.-
Sun. 7 a.m.-7 p.m. (Call first, branch hours vary).*

This was one of the first clubs to capitalize on L.A.'s fitness-obsessed lifestyle. Its concept of the "country club atmosphere" hardly compares to its big brother, The Sports Club. Still, the facilities continue to attract the sleek of physique—it's one of the most profitable health club chains (per club) in America. There are two well-used aerobics classrooms, a swimming pool, racquetball (not at all the branches), cardiovascular center with top-notch fitness machines, co-ed and private women's weight-training gyms, spa facilities, a juice bar and pro shop.

Voight Fitness and Dance Center

980 N. La Cienega Blvd., W. Hollywood 90069;
(310) 854-0741
*Mon.-Thurs. 8:30 a.m.-12:30 p.m., 3:30 p.m.-8 p.m.,
Fri. 8:30 a.m.-7 p.m., Sat. 8 a.m.-7:30 p.m., Sun. 8
a.m.-6:30 p.m.*

Voight has always offered a wide variety of energy-intense classes taught by champion instructors, such as step classes, high- (and we mean high) and low-impact aerobics, body-sculpting and circuit-training. But lately, Voight is funk-aerobics headquarters for the city's nightclub set. Two of the classes receiving the most raves: "City Jam," featuring the latest hip/hop moves as seen on MTV and "Jamm 'N Funk," combining aerobics with funk, jazz and dance moves.

Skincare Salons

Aida Grey

9549 Wilshire Blvd., Beverly Hills 90212;
(310) 276-2376
Open Mon.-Sat. 9 a.m.-5 p.m.

One of the gurus of skin care, Aida Grey now sells her own line of cosmetics and creams at her full-service salon. There are many devotees of her facials, but she also offers hair styling, makeup applications, manicures, pedicures, waxing, acupressure massage, lash tints, paraffin and scalp treatments and electrolysis. Services can be purchased individually, or you can indulge in the comprehensive "Day of Beauty" package.

Aida Thibiant Skin and Body Care Salon
449 N. Cañon Dr., Beverly Hills 90210;
(310) 278-7565
Open Mon.-Sat. 9 a.m.-5:30 p.m., Thurs. 9 a.m.-10 p.m.

Thibiant's French techniques and treatments are developed in her own laboratory. All her products are free of lanolin, waxes and mineral oils and are perfect for people with problem, sensitive or allergic skin. In addition to facials, the salon offers body massages, a cellulite treatment, waxing, makeup application and the panthermal bath, which supposedly aids in weight loss and improves circulation. Add to the list the new "Trichology Clinic," a service that analyzes the hair and scalp and prescribes an appropriate treatment.

The Face Place
8701 Santa Monica Blvd., W. Hollywood 90069;
(310) 855-1150
Open Mon.-Sat. 8 a.m.-5 p.m., Wed.-Thurs. 8 a.m.-7 p.m.

Treatments at this well-established salon are based on modern, medically proven techniques rather than cosmetic methods. Instead of masks, massages or creams, clients here (half of whom are professional men) follow clinical programs designed for long-range results. A 75-minute facial uses The Face Place's exclusive product line; other services, such as lash and brow tinting, waxing, manicures and pedicures, are available at an additional charge.

Georgette Klinger
312 N. Rodeo Dr., Beverly Hills 90210;
(310) 274-6347
Open Mon.-Tues. 9 a.m.-4:30 p.m., Wed. 10 a.m.-7 p.m., Thurs.-Fri. 9 a.m.-6 p.m., Sat. 8 a.m.-5 p.m.

With spa boutiques cropping up all over the country, this salon is devoted to retarding the aging process. After a two-hour workover and workout, you will emerge with the benefit of the well-trained staff's specialties, such as facials, scalp treatments, massages and so on. Services range from a vegetable peeling mask for men and women to a full hedonistic day of beauty care.

Nance Mitchell Company
330 N. Lapeer Dr., Beverly Hills 90211;
(310) 276-2722
By appt. only.

Author/lecturer/skin-care specialist Nance Mitchell concentrates on antiaging education and treatment using two exclusive products for women and men: a nonabrasive enzyme exfoliator and a "Youth Lift" tightening mask. You can

experience both by asking for the "Star Treatment." An authority on preventive and corrective skin care, Mitchell offers up-to-the-minute consultations on corporate image, nutrition, cosmetic surgery and total grooming. Geared to the international set, her products are designed to adapt to different climates.

Ole Henriksen of Demark Skin Care Center
Sunset Plaza, 8601 W. Sunset Blvd., W. Hollywood 90069; (310) 854-7700
Open Tues.-Sat. 8 a.m.-5:30 p.m.

Using products and techniques developed in Denmark, this salon takes an almost holistic approach to skin care. The all-natural product line is based on botanical extracts. Ole Henriksen provides light acid peels for comprehensive rejuvenation, as well as full body waxing, lash and brow tinting, makeup, manicures and pedicures. His celebrity-heavy following keeps the salon packed; be prepared to make your appointment weeks in advance.

The Skin Spa
17487 Ventura Blvd., Encino 91316;
(818) 995-6999
Open Tues.-Thurs. 9 a.m.-9 p.m., Fri.-Sat. 9 a.m.-6 p.m.

The menu at The Skin Spa lists several innovative whole-body treatments designed to "cushion the shocks of daily life." One of our favorites, called "Ocean Spa," uses the therapeutic powers of blue seaweed, which is harvested off the coast of France and farmed inland, resulting in a pleasant floral fragrance. After an invigorating salt glow rub-down, the body is cocooned in the revitalizing blue seaweed, then given a gentle, contouring massage using long, liquid strokes. Complete with ocean sounds, the 90-minute ritual has all the calming, restorative effects of a sea cruise.

Vera's Retreats
2980 Beverly Glen Circle, Ste. 100, Bel Air 90077; (310) 470-6362
Open Mon. & Sat. 9 a.m.-5 p.m., Tues. & Fri. 9 a.m.-6 p.m., Wed.-Thurs. 9 a.m.-8:30 p.m.
18670 Ventura Blvd., Tarzana 91356;
(818) 881-7707
Open Tues. & Fri. 9 a.m.-6 p.m., Wed.-Thurs. 9 a.m.-8:30 p.m., Sat. 9 a.m.-5 p.m.

Vera Brown's pastel-hued salons provide a pleasant dose of pampering at a reasonable cost. Here a half day or full day of services may include superb massages, waxing, electrolysis, makeup lessons, brow and lash tinting and some of the finest facials around, incorporating all-natural, aloe vera–based products. Vera's latest wonder is called "facial contouring," which involves an amazing machine that seems to actually "iron" fine lines away, at least temporarily.

Spas

See also "PALM SPRINGS Hotels" for hotels and resorts that offer spa treatments.

The Ashram
2025 McKain Rd. (mailing address: P.O. Box 8009), Calabasas 91302; (818) 222-6900

Located in the hills of Calabasas, not far from Malibu, The Ashram (meaning "spiritual retreat") is not for the fainthearted. It's probably the toughest spa in the country. Director Anne-Marie Bennstrom has put together a Spartan regime that results in serious benefits. A typical day includes yoga, a two-hour hike straight up a mountain, an hour of weight-lifting exercises, an hour of pool sports, calisthenics, an evening walk and more yoga. The only real luxury is the daily one-hour massage. This absorbing mind-body adventure will be unlike anything you've ever experienced. Since there are only about eleven guests per week, a familylike relationship develops among guests and staff. All you need to bring is a bathing suit, undergarments and shoes; all other spa attire is provided. Since it costs a healthy sum per person per week, most of the guests (male and female) are fairly affluent superachievers. Book at least three months in advance.

Beverly Hot Springs
308 N. Oxford Ave., Wilshire District (L.A.) 90004; (213) 734-7000

All it takes is a soak in the effervescent, sodium bicarbonate-laced pools of Beverly Hot Springs to remind us that one of L.A.'s greatest natural resources is within urban reach. Discovered by drillers at the turn of the century, the pure alkaline mineral waters gush from a natural artesian well two thousand feet below the city. The muscle-melting bath (included in the entrance fee) can be accompanied by a 45-minute Shiatsu massage or a soothing body treatment with a mixture of milk, honey and cucumber. Finish up in the black-lacquer cafe, serving a savory tonic of ginseng-chicken soup.

Burke Williams Day Spa and Massage Centre
11645 Wilshire Blvd., W.L.A. 90025; (310) 479-6500

A variety of mood-enhancing amenities contribute to the well-being of mind and body at Burke Williams. One option might begin by slipping into a thick terry robe and enjoying a nerve-restoring blend of herbal tea. From the essential oil bar in the steam room, spray on the aromatherapy mist of your choice: a calming blend of cedar wood and marjoram, a tonic mixture of peppermint and birch or a resperatory aid of eucalyptus and pine. After a cool shower and a few minutes of solace, an individual chamomile whirlpool bath readies you for the "Pure Relaxation Massage." Using a botanically based body cream, two massage therapists work simultaneously to flush out toxins and relieve tension. Inquire about the many other treatments offered. As we went to press, the spa was relocating to larger quarters in Santa Monica (1460 4th St., Ste. 100), so call before visiting.

Cal-a-Vie
2249 Kilbirnie Dr. (mailing address: 2249 Somerset Rd.), Vista 92084; (619) 945-2055

Husband and wife William and Marlene Power spent five years researching the spas of Europe before founding Cal-a-Vie, a secluded 126-acre retreat that combines American fitness techniques with fabled European treatments. This three-year-old spa now ranks among the country's best. Following morning exercise, afternoons are devoted to relaxation and rejuvenation through such blissful treatments as a cocoon-style "sea wrap" to detoxify and restore the body's mineral balance, soothing hydrotherapy or a gentle aromatherapy massage. The cuisine is low in sodium, rich in carbohydrates and incorporates many fresh herbs. A favorite with the fiftysomething crowd, but also popular with young professionals, the spa hosts men's weeks, mother-daughter weeks and other special programs. The inclusive fee is as extravagant as the facilities.

La Costa Resort & Spa
2100 Costa del Mar Rd., Carlsbad 92009 (619) 438-9111

A very country club–like atmosphere pervades La Costa, which is a luxury resort as well as a health spa. There are actually two spas here—one for men and one for women—but both are equally lavish. The grounds are gorgeous, and the spa building houses Roman pools, Swiss showers, steam rooms, massage and facial cubicles and a large beauty salon. The program begins with a medical evaluation and a meeting with your spa counselor to discuss your goals for the visit. A typical day begins at 7:30 a.m. with breakfast in your room, followed by a half-hour walk and a stretch class. What you do after this can be anything from aerobics to yoga to golf.

You can schedule beauty treatments and massages for any time during the day. The meals are delicious and appetizing yet a typical day's calorie intake is a mere 800. Sophisticated, affluent couples frequent this spa, most of whom wouldn't last a day at a rigorous place like The Ashram. Four-day minimum stay.

The Golden Door

777 Deer Springs Rd., San Marcos 92069 (mailing address: P.O. Box 463077, Escondido 92046); (619) 744-5777

Forty miles northeast of San Diego lies a peaceful replica of a Japanese country inn. The Golden Door, with its superb reputation for the perfect balance of exercise, diet, beauty treatments and serenity, is considered one of the country's best spas, if not *the* best (and *the* most expensive). Credit is due to Deborah Szekely, who has been involved with health resorts for over 40 years. Don't fear that this place is a snobbish haven for the ultra-rich; all 39 guests are put into matching spa-supplied exercise garb, sans jewelry, makeup or fancy hairdos, so no one really knows (or cares) if the next woman is an heiress or a waitress who has saved all her tips to come here.

The day begins at 6 a.m. with a hike. Once back, you'll find a breakfast tray and the day's schedule, which might include a stretch class, aerobics, an herbal wrap, water ballet, pool volleyball, a steam bath or sauna, a massage in your room, a choice of sports activities, yoga or a Japanese whirlpool bath. The newest treat is a body scrub with rose-scented clay and silicone beads, administered with silk mitts. The low-calorie, low-sodium, low-cholesterol gourmet menus are delicious. Diet or not, we would happily dine again on the rosemary grilled chicken, summer asparagus with red-beet vinaigrette and wonderfully light pastries. All you need to bring is a swimsuit, leotard and shoes—everything else is provided. There are men's and couples' weeks a few times a year, but most of the week-long sessions are for women only.

The Oaks at Ojai

122 E. Ojai Ave., Ojai 93023; (805) 646-5573

Owned by fitness enthusiast Sheila Cluff (who also owns The Palms), The Oaks is extremely popular among Southern Californians who want to experience a week at a spa without having to spend a fortune. Located in downtown Ojai (an absolutely charming town), The Oaks caters to mature men and women, as well as to younger people who aren't on a strict exercise-and-diet regime but would like to begin one. The facilities are hardly luxurious, and the food is pretty dismal, but there's a warm, friendly atmosphere and a well-trained staff. The day begins with a walk through scenic Ojai, followed by a breakfast of fresh fruit and a minuscule bran muffin. For the rest of the day, it's up to the individual guests to decide how much exercise they want. A variety of classes run all day; they include stretch, aerobics, yoga and aqua aerobics. When we visited we noticed that the slimmer guests participated in almost all of the classes, while the plumper ones chose to gossip by the pool. Guests can follow a 750-calorie-per-day diet or tailor meals to their personal needs. We were amused to learn from the owner of a local drugstore how many candy bars he sells to Oaks guests who jog over for a quick fix. A two-night minimum stay is required at all times.

Rancho La Puerta

Tecate, Baja California, Mexico (mailing address: P.O. Box 463057, Escondido 92046) ; (619) 744-4222, (800) 443-7565

Founder Deborah Szekely, who also started The Golden Door, opened "The Ranch" with her husband, Edward, in 1940. But this coed natural health resort is not at all like its super-elegant sister spa. The facilities themselves are modest, though there are six tennis courts, three swimming pools, a hot whirlpool, indoor and outdoor gyms and a Swedish massage center. It's up to each guest to decide how much exercise and how much pampering to include in his or her daily schedule. But unlike those at other unstructured spas, most of the guests are serious fitness enthusiasts who are here to push their fitness limits. The selection of exercise classes and sports activities is grand, and there are also beauty treatments, for a modest extra charge. The lacto-ovo-vegetarian diet is basically what it sounds like: 1,000 calories per day, including a nice variety of milk products, nuts, grains, fish and eggs. There's also a virtuous liquid diet that features almond milk and gazpacho. The seven-day plans are very popular with young singles. Complimentary transportation to and from San Diego Airport on Saturdays.

Regent Beverly Wilshire

9500 Wilshire Blvd., Beverly Hills 90212; (310) 275-5200

This million-dollar health spa in the heart of Beverly Hills's Regent hotel (now managed by Four Seasons) is hard to beat for convenience and classic luxury. Two dual-temperature hot tubs, modeled after Sophia Loren's in Italy, are part of a newly landscaped pool area replete with creeping figs, bougainvillea and Cypress trees. The fitness center, complimentary to hotel guests, features computerized exercise equipment, including Lifecycle, Liferower and Stairmaster, daily classes in aerobics, circuit training, muscle conditioning and stretching, professional instructors for one-on-one training and Swedish or Shiatsu massage. The "Day of Rejuvenation" package includes a spa manicure with paraffin treatment, therapeutic cleansing facial and a health-conscious lunch. Salon beauty treatments are available to non-guests.

Books, Newsstands & Stationery

New Books

The independent book store is considered by many to be the last bastion of free thought in America. We've outlined below the best of the independents and those chains with deep and broad selections.

The small stores can't beat the larger chains, however, for convenience. These often carry a solid collection of the latest fiction, nonfiction and best-sellers just around the corner. When it comes to prices, the last word is **Crown Books**. This chain store has locations literally all over the city, and the savings are so pronounced, many Angelenos won't go anywhere else to buy new books. With the introduction of **SuperCrown Books** (four in L.A.), locals can pick from a selection that's twice as large, and special order, too. **B. Dalton Booksellers** and **Waldenbooks** are small, well-organized chains that stock all the latest fiction and nonfiction. Waldenbooks also carries some art books, gift items and a noteworthy assortment of videos and books on tape. It also does more special ordering and mail order than most other chains.

Amok
1764 N. Vermont Ave., Downtown (L.A.) 90027; (213) 665-0956
Open Mon.-Sat. 11 a.m.-9 p.m., Sun. 11 a.m.-7 p.m.

If you haven't already guessed by its name, this gash-in-the-wall bookshop specializes in subversive, fringe literature—from thought-provoking to the just-plain frightening (*How to Kill, Vols. 1–7*). While the number of books found on the

shelves here is limited, their 376-page catalog of more than 2,500 obscure titles (of which a few we're sure are banned in some states) is available at the shop or by sending $11.95 to The Amok Data Institute, P.O. Box 777, Oakland 94504.

Big and Tall Books/Café
7311 Beverly Blvd., Melrose-Fairfax District (L.A.) 90036; (213) 939-5022
Open daily 9 a.m.-2 a.m.

Finally, L.A. has the kind of combination bookstore-and-café that it has long lacked. Not only palate-pleasing food (pastas and sandwiches), but also soul-satisfying food for thought: Up-to-the-minute continental philosophy, fiction overlooked by mass-market booksellers, even unavailable European-art-gallery catalogues. A browser's delight.

Bodhi Tree Bookstore
8585 Melrose Ave., W. Hollywood 90069-5199; (310) 659-1733
Open daily 11 a.m.-11 p.m.

Organic, holistic, New Age: All these terms apply to Bodhi Tree, a bookstore filled with good reads on holistic healing, meditation, psychology and the like. You will also find gifts along the same lines, as well as greeting cards, crystals, incense and a good selection of environmental-music and meditation records. Those in search of self-enlightenment will find their mecca here.

Book Soup
8818 W. Sunset Blvd., W. Hollywood 90069; (310) 659-3110
Open daily 9 a.m.-midnight.

A haven for art- and literature-loving bibliophiles, and for expatriates of other countries looking for home papers. The shop carries a particularly good collection of books on film and entertainment, music and cooking, as well as a fine selection of new and classic fiction and periodicals. It's not difficult to drop in unexpectedly on a first-time or a famous author holding a book-signing here (Helmut Newton, Dominick Dunne, Ann Beattie and David Byrne have been among recent signings). Quiet by day and crowded by night, Book Soup is one of the better browsing bookstores in the city.

Bookstar
Beverly Connection, 100 N. La Cienega Blvd., W. Hollywood 90048 (branches everywhere); (310) 289-1734
Open daily 9 a.m.-midnight.

The Beverly Connection branch of this Texas-based discount chain is the largest of L.A.'s nine branches. A cool and modern space conducive to hours of browsing, its selection of books is by no means plebeian. A map at the front will guide you through roomy aisle upon aisle of accounting, biblical reference, dance, interior design, mathematics, philosophy, cooking, travel and much more—all at a 5 percent or 10 percent discount. The literature selection is extensive, reminiscent of Berkeley's famous Cody's. If you can't find it, they'll special order it for you. The other two major stores are in Santa Monica (1234 Wilshire Blvd., 310-576-7992) and Culver City (11000 W. Jefferson Blvd., 310-391-0818); other branches are in Studio City, Woodland Hills, Torrance, Brea and Tustin.

Brentano's
Century City Shopping Center, 10250 Santa Monica Blvd., Century City 90067; (310) 785-0204
Open Sun.-Thurs. 10 a.m.-9 p.m., Fri.-Sat. 10 a.m.-11 p.m.
Westside Pavilion, 10800 W. Pico Blvd., W.L.A. 90064; (310) 470-4830
Open Mon.-Fri. 10 a.m.-9:30 p.m., Sat. 10 a.m.-7 p.m., Sun. 11 a.m.-6 p.m.

One of the most respected bookstores in L.A., Brentano's stocks a particularly choice selection of gift books—and gifts of other sorts, for that matter, including electronic gadgets, Filofax accessories and Mont Blanc pens. Brentano's likes to call itself "a cross between an independent bookstore and a chain, with the benefits of both," and we can't argue. Service is above average, considering its size and diversity. Additional locations in Sherman Oaks (14006 Riverside Dr., #236, 818-788-8661), and Northridge Mall (9301 Tampa Ave., 818-349-4203).

Chatterton's Bookshop
1818 N. Vermont Ave., Los Feliz 90027; (213) 664-3882
Open Mon.-Sat. 10 a.m.-10 p.m., Sun. noon-9 p.m.

Serious browsers, take note: Classical music entertains the clientele of tousled intellectuals and assorted book-lovers while they roam through the inviting aisles of film and theater, literature, poetry, philosophy, children's books and gay and lesbian books. Of particular note is the excellent selection of paperback fiction and classics, along with the good selection of fine-arts magazines. Once you've found your title, drop down a few doors into the Onyx for an espresso and an eyeful of local art.

La Cité des Livres
2306 Westwood Blvd., Westwood 90025; (310) 475-0658
Open Tues.-Sat. 10 a.m.-6 p.m.

The best collection of French classics, contemporary literature and best-sellers in the city. It also stocks French Revolution materials, European travel guides and maps, bilingual dictionaries, cookbooks, comic novels, records and compact discs, magazines and foreign-language learning cassettes. The sales staff (and customers) are always enthusiastic about conversing in French with Francophiles and homesick expatriates.

Dangerous Visions
13563 Ventura Blvd., Sherman Oaks 91423; (818) 986-6963
Open daily 10 a.m.-7 p.m.

Lydia Marano describes her collection of books as "speculative fiction." The mixture includes children's literature and science fiction/fantasy/horror books and magazines—appropriate either for children or for lovers of science-fiction. New, used and out of print.

Dawson's Book Shop
535 N. Larchmont Blvd., Larchmont Village 90004; (213) 469-2186
Open Tues.-Sat. 9 a.m.-5 p.m.

The Dawson family founded this business in 1905, and the bookshop/small press has remained a family operation over the years. Currently, third-generation Michael Dawson is presiding over the high-quality collection, with an emphasis on both new and used (including rare) books on photography, Southern Californian history and the "history and art of the book." Outside, a pretty, shaded patio contains wooden racks full of more books, and tables and chairs on which to peruse them.

Doubleday Book Shop
735 S. Figueroa St., Downtown (L.A.) 90017; (213) 624-0897
Open Mon.-Fri. 10 a.m.-7 p.m., Sat. 10 a.m.-6 p.m.

Boasting a better-than-adequate selection of new titles, with an emphasis on business books, Doubleday also stocks good collections of books on Los Angeles, as well as travel books and classics. Best-sellers are usually displayed in the windows. One of the last survivors of the Doubleday Book chain, the shop is housed in an art deco-style building.

Dutton's Books
5146 Laurel Canyon Blvd., N. Hollywood 91607; (818) 769-3866
11975 San Vicente Blvd., Brentwood 90049; (310) 476-6263
Open Mon.-Fri. 9:30 a.m.-9 p.m., Sat. 9:30 a.m.-6 p.m., Sun. 11 a.m.-5 p.m.

Dutton's is an excellent all-purpose bookstore with a thorough stock, certainly among the finest in the city. Along with all the current fiction and nonfiction (including lots of paperbacks), there are used reference books of all kinds, art books, children's books, used and out-of-print books, rare leather-bound titles and posters and engravings. The staff is extremely helpful in finding and ordering out-of-stock books. There is also a branch downtown (213-683-1199) and one in Burbank (818-840-8003).

Fowler Brothers

717 W. 7th St., Downtown (L.A.) 90017;
(213) 627-7846
Open Mon.-Fri. 9 a.m.-5:30 p.m., Sat. 9:30 a.m.-5 p.m.

Fowler Brothers is California's oldest bookstore, and even though it's changed locations four times since it first opened over a century ago, this family-run business has retained its old-time atmosphere. The expansion several years ago allowed for a less cramped feeling, but Fowler Brothers is admittedly "a vertical store." As far as we know, the store has the only children's-literature department in the downtown area. The travel, business and literature sections are excellent. Service includes 24-hour delivery (within Southern California).

LACE Bookstore

1804 Industrial St., Downtown (L.A.) 90021;
(213) 624-5650
Open Wed.-Fri. 11 a.m.-5 p.m., Sat.-Sun. noon-5 p.m.

Much of the printed material here, which supports the programming at the Los Angeles Contemporary Exibitions space, covers contemporary art issues in different media: academic journals, magazines, books and limited-edition works by local artists.

Midnight Special Bookstore

1318 Third Street Promenade, Santa Monica 90401;
(310) 393-2923
Open Mon.-Sat. 10:30 a.m.-6 p.m., Sun. noon-5 p.m.

Locals with a special interest in politics and social sciences hang out at this unique bookstore; an entire wall is covered with an extensive collection of magazines. Since its relocation, Midnight Special has added an attached cultural center, which sponsors evening programs that vary from poetry readings to talks with authors and discussions on current events.

Small World Books

1407 Ocean Front Walk, Venice 90291;
(310) 399-2360
Open daily 10 a.m.-8 p.m.

A colorful clientele drops in regularly to explore the richly stocked fiction and literature sec-

---

Going traveling? Look for Gault Millau's other "Best of" guides to Chicago, New York, San Francisco, Washington D.C., New England, New Orleans, Florida and Hawaii, as well as France, Germany, Italy, Hong Kong, London, Paris, Thailand, Toronto and more to come . . .

---

tions. The Mystery Annex, with its excellent selection of mysteries, includes out-of-prints and first editions. Pleasant atmosphere to browse in.

The Soap Plant

7400 Melrose Ave., Melrose-La Brea District (L.A.) 90046; (310) 651-5587
Open Mon.-Wed. 10:30 a.m.-11 p.m., Thurs.-Sat. 10:30 a.m.-midnight, Sun. 11:30 a.m.-8 p.m.

L.A.'s late-night hot spot for the best books on style, architecture and design is planted in the middle of a zany *tchotchke* paradise. A heavy perfume from the bath products sold here pervades the place, adding to the general unorthodoxy. Instant gift ideas guaranteed.

Upstart Crow

429 Shoreline Dr., Shoreline Village, Long Beach 90802; (310) 437-2088
Sun.-Thurs. 8:30 a.m.-10 p.m., Fri.-Sat. 8:30 a.m.-11 p.m.

In the process of expanding, this rustic bookstore-and-café opens right on to the Shoreline Village Pier, keeping it well-lit with natural light during the day. The shelves are well-stocked with fiction and nonfiction, from philosophy and psychology to new age, travel and poetry. You can catch poetry readings some weekdays, and live music on the patio weekends. The adjoining café offers espresso drinks, daily fresh pastries and other simple food. Another, much larger store should open in the fall '92 in Universal Studios.

Vroman's Bookstore

695 E. Colorado Blvd., Pasadena 91101;
(818) 449-5320
Open Mon.-Fri. 9:30 a.m.-9 p.m., Sat. 9:30 a.m.-6 p.m., Sun. 10 a.m.-6 p.m.

At the turn of the century, when wealthy Easterners who settled in Pasadena wanted to fill their bookshelves with impressive titles, A.C. Vroman catered to them by buying inexpensive sets of the classics and sending them to England for binding. The expensive-looking books soon gained Vroman a solid reputation among Pasadena's moneyed immigrants, and it's still considered one of the area's cultural assets.

Used Books

Acres of Books

240 Long Beach Blvd., Long Beach 90802;
(310) 437-6980
Open Tues.-Sat. 9:15 a.m.-5 p.m.

As the name suggests, Acres of Books is an enormous warehouse filled with thousands of used books. For those who love to spend hours browsing through a bookstore, it's easy to spend an entire afternoon here; what's more, you can probably pick up six or seven books for under

$20. The sales staff is exceptionally helpful. The few new volumes here are primarily coffee-table books.

Berkelouw Books
830 N. Highland Ave., Melrose-La Brea District (L.A.) 90038; (213) 466-3321
Open Mon.-Sat. 10 a.m.-5 p.m.

Established in 1812, this purveyor of fine books came from Rotterdam to L.A. via Australia, where today there is still a Berkelouw bookstore. The main room of the L.A. branch features a large selection of scholarly books and books on art, literature, history and travel. The first, signed and limited editions are kept in back, and are accessible through the store's computer and card catalogs. Once you find what you're looking for, they'll bring it out to you. Under glass at the front of the store are also some well-preserved, well-priced first and rare editions.

Cosmopolitan Books
7007 Melrose Ave., Melrose-La Brea District (L.A.) 90038; (213) 938-7119
Open Mon.-Sat. 11:30 a.m.-6 p.m.

There are books stacked, shelved, shoved and towering above, on every subject imaginable. The shop quite literally prides itself on "not specializing in anything." Junk magazines and cat-care manuals sit side by side with scholarly texts and leather-bound literary classics. There are some gems for the adventurous person with lots of time on his or her hands.

Hollywood Book City
6627 Hollywood Blvd., Hollywood 90028; (213) 466-2525/466-1049
Open Mon.-Sat. 10 a.m.-10 p.m., Sun. 10 a.m.-8 p.m.

One block east of Frederick's of Hollywood, this massive shop has thousands of used books on every subject imaginable. There is even a section on Richard Nixon and an entire nine-shelf bookcase filled with guides and novels on China. In between are comprehensive sections on topics ranging from medicine to mythology.

The House of Fiction
663 E. Colorado Blvd., Pasadena 91101; (818) 449-9861
Open Mon.-Fri. 10 a.m.-10 p.m., Sat. noon-10 p.m., Sun. noon-5 p.m.

House of Fiction carries a well-edited collection of used, out-of-print and first-edition books. Like all good bookstores, it comes with a chair for perusing some dusty treasure and a token feline called Matza. Because it's somewhat of a local secret, prices are reasonable as well.

R. Franklin Pyke, Bookseller
228 Metropole, P.O. Box 514, Avalon, Santa Catalina Island 90704; (310) 510-2588
Open Tues.-Sun. 10 a.m.-5 p.m.

If it weren't situated across from the candy-store pink St. Lauren Hotel, you'd probably miss this tiny 1920s-home-cum-bookshop. Proprietor Ron Pyke's former residence is filled with used books on Catalina Island, as well as an eclectic collection of maps, prints, records and ephemera. He also carries a good collection of novels by one-time Catalina resident Zane Grey.

Specialty Books

Arcana Books on the Arts
1229 Third Street Promenade, Santa Monica 90401; (310) 458-1499
Open Mon.-Sat. 10 a.m.-6 p.m.

Arcana is an architectural setting for books on post-Impressionist art, architecture and photography (and exhibition catalogs), many of which are out of print or hard to find. This shop is well known in collectors' circles here and overseas. There are some fine values among the long-lost literary and art gems waiting to be discovered.

California Map & Travel Center
3211 Pico Blvd., Santa Monica 90405; (310) 829-6277
Open Mon.-Fri. 8:30 a.m.-6 p.m., sat. 9 a.m.-5 p.m., Sun. noon-5 p.m.

This store carries an astounding collection of guidebooks, maps, language books and travel accessories, as well as reference books such as atlases and natural history, replogle globes and biking and hiking directories. It also sports mounting, framing and laminating facilities.

Cook's Library
8373 W. 3rd St., W. Hollywood 90048; (213) 655-3141
Open Mon. 1 p.m.-5 p.m., Tues.-Sat. 11 a.m.-6 p.m.

Owner Ellen Rose has put together a fantastic shop of over 3,000 titles dedicated to the food-lover and cook—both professional and amateur. The tiny little storefront is jammed with every book on food imaginable. Ask about the Saturday book signings by noted chefs and food-book authors, from Patricia Wells to Wolfgang Puck.

Distant Lands
62 S. Raymond Ave., Old Town Pasadena 91105; (818) 449-3220
Mon.-Thurs. 10:30 a.m.-7 p.m., Fri.-Sat. 10:30 a.m.-9 p.m., Sun. 11 a.m.-6 p.m.

Browsing is expected here. Peruse the shelves of classical travel books and literature (Isaak Denison novels, etc.), beautiful picture books, gift books and travel guides, while Chopin or Ravel plays in the background. There is even a table with chairs for a short, imaginary trip to Kuala Lumpur. The collection is comprehensive, and the service is warm and helpful.

Elliot M. Katt Bookseller
8570 Melrose Ave., W. Hollywood 90069;
(310) 652-5178
Open Mon.-Sat. 11 a.m.-6 p.m.

Comfortably ensconced in a converted California bungalow, Elliot M. Katt is one of the few bookstores in the city that specializes in the performing arts, including cinema, theater, music and dance. The well-informed Katt calls his shop, where you're almost sure to spot someone from Hollywood's A-list, "a research library where the material is for sale." Mail order welcome; catalogs available upon request.

Forbidden Planet
14513 Ventura Blvd., Sherman Oaks 91403;
(818) 995-0151
Open Mon.-Thurs. 11 a.m.-9 p.m., Fri.-Sat. 11 a.m.-10 p.m., Sun. noon-7 p.m.

Forbidden Planet (previously called Outer Limits) is a well-edited depository of twentieth-century pop culture. As the Southern California home base for Titan, England's top comic book publisher/retailer, Forbidden Planet carries the latest in comic, science fiction and dark-fantasy literature. The shop's layout is sleek and uncluttered, and there are frequent book signings by new and well-known talents.

Geographia
4000 Riverside Dr., Toluca Lake 91505;
(818) 848-1414
Open Mon.-Sat. 10 a.m.-6 p.m.

Wanderlust victims take note: Geographia is worth a considerable trek. If you don't have a trip planned to some exotic destination, you'll start making plans the minute you visit this shop. In addition to an outstanding collection of national and international travel guides, Geographia has a terrific collection of maps, atlases and globes, along with map accessories (compasses, magnifiers), videos (for rent or sale), foreign-language study tapes and travel accessories.

Golden Legend
7615 Sunset Blvd., Hollywood 90046;
(213) 850-5520
Open Mon.-Fri. 10 a.m.-5:30 p.m., Sat. 10 a.m.-5 p.m.

A user-friendly shop where exquisite leather-bound book sets, primarily from the turn of the century, are displayed next to deluxe illustrated books with original signed prints by such painters as Picasso and Miró. Rare books are neatly arranged on shelves under glass. The reading room

upstairs contains one of the largest selections of out-of-print theater and dance books in the country. According to owner Gordon Hollis, "You don't have to be a book collector to browse here. Lookers are welcome."

Hennessy & Engalls Art & Architecture Books
1254 Third Sreet Promenade, Santa Monica 90401;
(310) 458-9074
Open Mon.-Wed. 10 a.m.-6 p.m., Thurs.-Fri. 10 a.m.-7 p.m., Sat. 10 a.m.-5 p.m., Sun. 10 a.m.-4 p.m.

One of the largest bookstores on art and architecture in the world. Every aspect of the subject is on display: landscape architecture, interior design, photography, art technique, building types, world art, graphic design, monographs on artists, and the list goes on. Up to 4,000 books are on sale at any given time, and there's also a large selection of imported magazines and journals. Noted for excellent personal and prompt mail-order service worldwide. The first name on any arts-loving Angeleno's lips.

Heritage Book Shop
8540 Melrose Ave., W. Hollywood 90069;
(310) 659-3674
Open Tues.-Fri. 9:30 a.m.-5:30 p.m., Sat. 10 a.m.-4:30 p.m. (Mon. by appt.)

Heritage ranks among the country's finest bookstores of its kind, dealing in first editions, fine printings, Western Americana, early travel and rare and out-of-print books. There are also extensive autograph and manuscript departments and its own bindery. No specialty per se, but a vast selection in an attractive, comfortable setting.

Herskovitz Hebrew Book Store
442 N. Fairfax Ave., Melrose-Fairfax District (L.A.) 90036; (310) 852-9310
Open Mon.-Thurs. 9 a.m.-6 p.m., Fri. 9 a.m.-3:30 p.m., Sun. 9 a.m.-6 p.m.

For the last 50 years, Herskovitz has been the major supplier of religious books and icons to L.A.'s synagogues and Jewish homes. You can also find ethnic jewelry here.

Houlé Rare Books & Autographs
7260 Beverly Blvd., Melrose-Fairfax District (L.A.) 90036; (310) 937-5858
Open Tues.-Fri. 10 a.m.-6 p.m., Sat. 10 a.m.-3 p.m.

George Houlé stocks a wide array of lovely leather-bound books from the eighteenth through twentieth centuries, as well as first editions. There's also one of the largest collections of framed autographs in the city—whether of authors, political figures or film stars. Most of the material on film is not on view, so request whatever piques your interest.

Larry Edmunds Book Shop
6658 Hollywood Blvd., Hollywood 90028-6291;
(213) 463-3273
Open Mon.-Sat. 10 a.m.-6 p.m.

Everyone in the "industry" (which sometimes feels like nearly everyone in L.A.) knows about Larry Edmunds's small shop—it's *the* place for new and out-of-print books on film, theater and related fields. Whether it's a scandalous biography of a matinee idol, a scholarly study of British films, a poster or a hard-to-find movie still you want, try Edmunds's store first.

Michael R. Thompson
1001 N. Fairfax Ave., Hollywood 90046;
(213) 650-4887
Open Mon.-Sat. 10 a.m.-6 p.m., Sun. noon-5 p.m.

This comfortable, cluttered shop stocks what's possibly one of the largest selections of books on philosophy and history in the United States. It's a scholarly place that sells primarily to university libraries, but browsers are welcome. Since the books are in excellent condition, this emporium should not be overlooked by the inquisitive.

The Mysterious Bookshop
8763 Beverly Blvd., W. Hollywood 90048;
(310) 659-2959
Open Mon.-Sat. 10 a.m.-6 p.m., Sun. noon-5 p.m.

In the retail arm of New York's megamystery publisher, the extensive inventory of mysteries, true-crime and detective and spy thrillers includes rare and out-of-print books. (We spotted first editions by Raymond Chandler and Ross MacDonald on our last visit). Manager and seasoned bookseller Sheldon MacArthur hosts frequent author appearances and offers a helpful search service.

Samuel French
7623 Sunset Blvd., Hollywood 90046;
(213) 876-0570
11963 Ventura Blvd., Studio City 91604;
(818) 762-0535
Open Mon.-Fri. 10 a.m.-9 p.m., Sat. 10 a.m.-6 p.m., Sun. noon-5 p.m.

Samuel French has been publishing plays since the late 1800s. His bookshops have been the last word in theater and film for the better part of this century. Whether you are a filmmaker or a film buff, screenwriter or student of film, this shop is a must-see.

The Scriptorium
427 N. Cañon Dr., Beverly Hills 90210;
(310) 275-6060
Open Tues.-Sat. 10 a.m.-6 p.m.

Collectors of old letters, manuscripts and documents can buy them, sell them or have them appraised here. The goods and services are not inexpensive, but you'll get the well-respected knowledge of owner Charles Sachs.

Sherlock's Home
5624 E. 2nd St., Long Beach 90803;
(310) 433-6071
Open Tues.-Thurs. noon-6 p.m., Fri. noon-7 p.m., Sat. 11 a.m.-6 p.m. (Open Sun. & Mon. by appt. only.)

This exceptionally warm and appealing shop is well worth a trip for fans of murder mysteries, spy thrillers and political-intrigue tales. Run by gregarious, mystery-loving Beth Caswell, Sherlock's Home has an outstanding selection of titles, including some hard-to-find imports from England. And books are just the beginning: antique Victorian clocks, marvelous hats (from British bobby hats to Holmesian caps), murder-mystery games, gargoyle bookends, pop-up haunted mansions and all kinds of similar amusements that make great gifts for mystery buffs. Phone and mail orders accepted.

Thomas Brothers Maps & Bookstore
603 W. 7th St., Downtown 90017; (213) 627-4018
Open Mon.-Fri. 10 a.m.-6 p.m., Sat. 10 a.m.-5 p.m.

To L.A. residents, a Thomas Brothers map book is a Bible, a Talmud, a Koran—the book that guides us through this confused land. Although you can find these map books at many places, you'll find the best selection here, along with every imaginable kind of map and a good selection of books, particularly guidebooks.

Traveler's Bookcase
8375 W. 3rd St., W. Hollywood 90048;
(213) 655-0575
Open Mon.-Sat. 10 a.m.-6 p.m.

In this charming, tiny storefront on Third Street is everything that would interest the educated wanderlust, from guidebooks and foreign-language dictionaries to adventure tales and classic literature.

William & Victoria Dailey Rare Books & Fine Prints
8216 Melrose Ave., W. Hollywood 90046;
(213) 658-8515
Open Tues.-Fri. 10 a.m.-6 p.m., Sat. 11 a.m.-5 p.m.

Since 1975, this small shop has been a regular stop-in for many a serious collector of first editions, rare art-reference books, posters and illustrated books, as well as science, history, literature and fine-press books. Nineteenth- through early-twentieth-century prints are also for sale. Visitors here also might enjoy the nearby Steve Turner gallery (7220 Beverly Blvd.).

Newsstands

Al's Newsstand
370 N. Fairfax Ave., Melrose-Fairfax District (L.A.)
90036; (213) 935-8525
216 S. Beverly Dr., Beverly Hills 90212;
(310) 278-6397
1257 Third Street Promenade, Santa Monica 90401;
(310) 393-2690
23719 W. Malibu Rd., Malibu 90265;
(310) 456-7727
*Hours vary. Most open Mon.-Thurs. & Sun. 7 a.m.-11
p.m., Fri.-Sat. 7 a.m.-12:30 p.m.*

Fantastic selection of international fashion
mags, literary journals, music magazines, foreign
periodicals.

Robertson Magazine & Bookstore
1414 S. Robertson Blvd., W.L.A. 90035;
(310) 858-1804
Open 24 hours.

Art, science-fiction, music and entertainment
magazines as well as international periodicals.

Sherman Oaks Newsstand
14500 Ventura Blvd., Sherman Oaks 91405;
(818) 995-0632
Open 24 hours.

Specialties are sports and racing magazines, a
large selection of maps and international periodicals.

World Book and News
1652 N. Cahuenga Blvd., Hollywood 90028;
(213) 465-4352
Open 24 hours.

Notable for film and specialty magazines and
a wide selection of domestic and foreign periodicals. World Book and News has an excellent
selection of publications.

Stationery

Aahs!
14548 Ventura Blvd., Sherman Oaks 92403;
(818) 907-0300
2332 Wilshire Blvd., Santa Monica 90403;
(310) 829-1807
Open Mon.-Sat. 10 a.m.-9 p.m., Sun. 11 a.m.-7 p.m.

This is the headquarters for good-humored
cards and the latest novelty gifts you never
thought you needed. What's an inexpensive piece
of jewelry, wacky wall clock or car-window accessory without a jigsaw puzzle card to go along
with it? Aahs! stocks all the ingredients for a
well-put-together package, including gift wrap,
bows and standard greeting cards for more understated tastes.

A.J. Morrow
Century City Shopping Center, 10250 Santa Monica
Blvd., Century City 90067; (310) 286-9404
*Open Mon.-Fri. 10 a.m.-9 p.m., Sat. 10 a.m.-6 p.m.,
Sun. 11 a.m.-6 p.m.*

A.J. Morrow is probably the only place on the
westside in which you can order custom invitations hand-engraved with your personal coat of
arms. This premium stationer stocks, among
other fine offerings, royally appointed stationery
from Smythson of London, Mont Blanc pens,
antique ink wells, leather bound photo albums
and picture frames and truly special writing papers from around the world.

Ann Fiedler Creations
10544 W. Pico Blvd., W.L.A. 90064;
(310) 838-1857
Open Mon.-Fri. 9 a.m.-5 p.m., Sat. 10 a.m.-3 p.m.

Handmade invitations, decorations, favors,
odd accessories . . . you'll find whatever it takes
to make your party a success. No matter what
type of theme you opt for, Ann Fiedler will either
carry or make (from bows to feathers to sequins)
all the one-of-a-kind party accessories you can
imagine. Fiedler also stocks attractive personalized stationery, as well as a few gift items.

Francis Orr
320 N. Camden Dr., Beverly Hills 90210;
(310) 271-6106
Open Mon.-Sat. 9 a.m.-5:30 p.m.

The emphasis here is on quality and tradition.
There are books full of invitations and stationery
that can be printed or engraved with just about
any monogram you could imagine. One nice
bonus here is that the sales staff is helpful and
seems to know every rule of etiquette that applies
to invitations and thank-yous. There's also a nice
selection of leather desk blotters and accessories,
desk-related antiques, preprinted invitations and
Limoges china boxes.

Funnypapers
1953 1/2 N. Hillhurst Ave., Los Feliz 90027;
(213) 666-4006
*Open Mon.-Fri. 10 a.m.-6:30 p.m., Sat. 10 a.m.-6 p.m.,
Sun. 11 a.m.-5 p.m.*

A lively, cheery little shop with a very good
selection of greeting cards for all occasions. You'll
also find colorful wrapping papers, informal invitations and all kinds of fun, inexpensive gifts—
from tiny silver frames and rubber stamps to
inflatable dinosaurs and wild T-shirts.

McManus and Morgan
2506 W. 7th St., Downtown 90057; (213) 387-4433
Open Mon.-Fri. 8:30 a.m.-5:30 p.m., Sat. 10 a.m.-2 p.m.

No stationery store in L.A. can compete with
this stock of specialty papers. There are decora-

tive Japanese and pressed-flower papers for shoppers with exotic tastes; those interested in a classic look for French matting or creative framing will be swept away by the hand-marbleized imports from Europe. Established in 1923, McManus and Morgan will appeal to calligraphers, artists and anyone who appreciate truly exceptional handmade papers. It's well worth a trip downtown.

Robin Caroll
16930 Ventura Blvd., Encino 91316;
(818) 788-3396
Open Mon.-Sat. 10 a.m.-6 p.m.

The Francis Orr of the Valley, selling quality papers, unique, costly invitations and charming fill-in invitations for all occasions. The shop itself is warm and comfortable, with cozy sofas where you can leisurely sort through the numerous books of invitations and personalized stationery. Party-planning services are available.

Stampa Barbara
6903 Melrose Ave., Melrose-La Brea District (L.A.) 90038; (213) 931-7808
Open Mon.-Sat. 10 a.m.-6 p.m., Sun. noon-5 p.m.

An offshoot of the original in Santa Barbara, this store stocks an awesome inventory (over 25,000) of rubber stamps—everything from traditional holiday images to outrageous tongue-in-cheek joke designs. Ideas, too, are always in generous supply, and there are markers, blank cards, glitter glue and rainbow and metallic ink.

Write on Third
8222 W. 3rd St., W. Hollywood 90048;
(213) 658-5348
Open Mon.-Fri. 11 a.m.-6 p.m., Sat. 11 a.m.-5 p.m.

Write on Third is best known for its calligraphy machine, used to create custom invitations ranging from simple-yet-elegant to elaborate. But we think the store is noteworthy for its carefully selected array of unusual writing papers, from Crane to recycled to Claudia Laub's artfully designed styles (which also can be purchased at her studio, 7404 Beverly Blvd., 213-931-1710), hand-bound journals, wrapping paper and handsome leather-bound desk sets by Stuart Kern. You'll also find unexpected gift ideas, such as small oil paintings and books.

Shops can unfortunately close without warning, so it's a good idea to call before setting out for a particular store.

Children

Clothes

American Rag Cie. Youth
136 S. La Brea Ave., Melrose-La Brea District (L.A.) 90036; (213) 965-1404
Open Mon.-Sat. 10:30 a.m.-7 p.m., Sun. noon-7 p.m.

A spin-off of the nearby American Rag Compagnie for adults, this store specializes in the "sporty chic" look for children, which means classic colors (navy) and hip neutrals (khaki, brown and black) in new European and '50s vintage clothing. On our last visit, we came across richly detailed Tyrolean jackets, mini–riding pants, baggy jeans, quilted leather jackets, Wally Cleaver–style windbreakers, black-silk party dresses, trench coats, hats and '50s bow ties. There are even reproductions of '50s cowboy (and cowgirl) outfits, complete with chaps.

Animal Kracker
17330 Ventura Blvd., Encino 91316;
(818) 986-0264
Open Mon.-Sat. 10 a.m.-6 p.m.

Lots of hand-painted items and out-of-the-ordinary accessories, including leather headbands, wooden fish barrettes and decorated socks. Clothing for boys runs from Gotcha surf duds to Christian Dior suits; for girls, from bright cotton pieces by Cut Loose to Jessica McClintock's frilly frocks. Owner Abby Faranesh is a former teacher who hand-picks educational toys and a complete library of books. Newborn to preteens and juniors; shipping and complimentary gift wrap available.

Baby Guess?
461 N. Rodeo Dr., Beverly Hills 90210;
(310) 274-0515
Mon.-Sat. 10 a.m.-6:30 p.m., Sun. noon-5 p.m.

Want to deck your baby out from head to toe in the latest in denimwear? Here's where to find miniature jean jackets, overalls, shortalls, skirts—even jeans for a six-month-old—all with the trademark flirty, sporty Guess? style. Infants won't even realize how hip they look when sporting one of the adorable baseball caps or flannel shirts. Don't miss the collection of tiny belts.

Bartel Chapter IV
203 N. Larchmont Blvd., Larchmont Village 90004;
(213) 462-5310
Open Mon.-Sat. 10 a.m.-5 p.m.

There's a traditional, international mix of children's clothes in this small Hancock Park shop, including J.G. Hook classics, Florence Eiseman knits, Sarah Prints' pajama-inspired play sets from Israel and related separates from Mexx of Holland. The baby stuff is particularly nice, with unusual sleepers, diaper sets and tiny T-shirts. A bookcase along one wall has a small but excellent collection of children's books; and there are adorable stuffed animals, Brio trains, Ambi rattles and other small toys. The January and July sales are always excellent. Infant to size fourteen, boys and girls.

Bear Threads
1624 Montana Ave., Santa Monica 90403; (310) 828-6246
Open Mon.-Sat. 10 a.m.-6 p.m., Sun. noon-5 p.m.

Never mind the name—Bear Threads is a merchandise-packed store with absolutely everything from European designer clothes to hand-knit sweaters. The store is devoted to cotton unisex looks, both foreign and domestic. There are also shoes, accessories, European periodicals and children's videos.

Bloomers for Kids
Sunset Plaza, 8646 Sunset Blvd., W. Hollywood 90069; (310) 854-6901
Open Mon.-Sat. 10 a.m.-7 p.m., Sun. noon-5 p.m.

Modeled after a New York boutique, Bloomers for Kids coordinates trendy to sophisticated looks in head-to-toe presentations. A precious selection includes high-end European entries. Infant to size fourteen, boys and girls.

Bonnets and Bows
203 N. Robertson Blvd., Beverly Hills 90210; (310) 276-9910
Open Mon.-Fri. 10 a.m.-5 p.m., Sat. 10 a.m.-4:30 p.m.

The taste level here is of silver-spoon quality. It's an ideal place for well-heeled parents and grandparents to indulge in custom-designed crib linens, exclusive layette items, extravagant basinette ensembles and heirloom-quality christening gowns. Newborn to 24 months.

Chez Kids
16571 Ventura Blvd., Encino 91436; (818) 783-5363
Open Mon.-Sat. 10 a.m.-5:30 p.m.

Mothers and others flock to Chez Kids for its exclusive Kotton Kelly line of preshrunk cotton basics in bright colors, which are reasonably priced and available in ten different styles. It also carries a good selection of American and European clothing, toys, gifts and accessories for infant to size seven for boys, to size fourteen for girls. The store wisely provides a play area, has complimentary "confetti" gift wrap, and takes special orders.

Costumes for Kids
7206 Melrose Ave., Melrose-La Brea District (L.A.) 90046; (213) 936-5437
Open Mon.-Sat. 10 a.m.-5 p.m.

As far as we know, this is the only costume shop in the country exclusively for children. Eighty percent of the costumes are designed and made on the premises of comfortable, natural-fiber fabrics. The costumes range from characters from film favorites (*Batman* and *Ghostbusters*) to nursery-rhyme characters (Cinderella, Captain Hook, Peter Pan). Accessories include special-occasion flower garlands and "birthday headbands" for $15. Sizes two through twelve.

Fred Segal Baby
Fred Segal Santa Monica, 500 Broadway, Santa Monica 90401; (310) 451-5200
Open Mon.-Sat. 10 a.m.-7 p.m., Sun. noon-6 p.m.

A small store brimming with big ideas, this place carries costly European clothing (leather and velvet jackets), trendy imported shoes (real-leather cowboy boots), funky jewelry, decorated socks, books, toys, even furniture and strollers. The perfect place to find a novel gift for children aged three months to four years.

Harriett Dorn
2439A Main St., Santa Monica 90405; (310) 392-6889
Tues.-Sat. 11 a.m.-6 p.m., Sun. noon- 5 p.m.

This tiny store is as fun to shop for its feeling of fanciful exuberance as for its hand-picked and highly imaginative assortment of clothing, furniture, folk art, toys and books. An amusing collection of child-sized furniture includes grown-up club chairs, daybeds and chaise lounges from J. Troup. Heidi Wianecki's picture frames and painted chests, beaded lamps and chandeliers are a hoot.

Lollipop Shop
137 S. Robertson Blvd., Beverly Hills 90211; (310) 659-7501
Open Mon.-Fri. 9:30 a.m.-5:30 p.m., Sat. 9:30 a.m.-4:30 p.m.

This shop is anything but a place for the basics. Oriented to its celebrity clientele, the Lollipop Shop features pricey European imports, private-label and upper-end unique items. Custom orders, shipping and complimentary gift wrapping are available. Infant to preteen.

Malina's Children's Store
2654-C Main St., Santa Monica 90405; (310) 392-2611
Open daily 11 a.m.-7 p.m.

One of the first to dress babies in black, European designer Malina Gerber lends dashes of unexpected wit to her mostly unisex, stylish mixed print staples for both mother and daughter.

Oilily

9520 Brighton Way, Beverly Hills 90210;
(310) 859-9145
Open Mon.-Sat. 10 a.m.-6 p.m.

This Holland-based company has a wonderfully wacky approach to color, turning out whimsical clothing for boys, girls, babies and their mothers. Expect quirky patchwork mixes of prints and patterns, easy-fitting shapes and an international feel to the coordinated dresses and sportswear, with Beverly Hills price tags to match. Even rubber rain boots come stamped in wildly colorful floral patterns.

Pee Wee Segal

Fred Segal Melrose, 8106 Melrose Ave., Melrose-Fairfax District (L.A.) 90046; (213) 651-3698
Open Mon.-Sat. 10 a.m.-7 p.m., Sun. noon-6 p.m.

This is one of the best sources in town for newborn and toddler-size trendyware, with such novelties as baby bandanas, mismatched outfits with their own suspenders, neon-colored cotton knits, picture frames covered with little plastic toys, designer bibs, socks, stuffed animals and a showcase of candy.

Pixie Town

400 N. Beverly Dr., Beverly Hills 90210;
(213) 272-6415
Open Mon.-Sat. 10 a.m.-5:30 p.m.

Beverly Hills babies have been getting their party and play clothes at Pixie Town for almost 50 years. The saleswomen are sticklers for good quality and perfect fit. American and European clothes and shoes in newborn through size fourteen.

Furniture

Aunty Barbara's Antiques

238 S. Beverly Dr., Beverly Hills 90212;
(310) 285-0873
Open Mon.-Sat. 10 a.m.-5 p.m.

A must-see, this store is chock full of antique and vintage-inspired furnishings—all in child sizes. There are old chenille bedspreads, chairs covered in nostalgic print tablecloths or mattress ticking, bookcases and chests decorated with old decals of Cupids or airplanes, crib bumpers made of nubby floral print curtain fabric from the '40s, Daniel Boone themed footstools with rope trim, antique toy telephones, trucks and tractors and copper horses with running clocks. Don't miss the collectible lamps, including a pair of McCoy cowboy boots.

Baby Motives

8362 W. 3rd St., Melrose-Fairfax District (L.A.) 90048; (213) 658-6015
Open Mon.-Fri. 10 a.m.-5:30 p.m., Sat. 10 a.m.-5 p.m., or by appt.

When you've decided on black and white for the baby's nursery, Baby Motives is the place to shop. Sure, they've got cribs, changing tables and rockers in predictable pastels, but it's those hot, new, the-grandparents-will-hate-it colors that make this place special. This is a one-stop nursery store, with wallpapers, fabrics, custom bumper pads, linens, kicky-colored rubber pants and good decorating advice in addition to the excellent furniture selection—from traditionally styled cribs to postmodern convertibles designed to last well into junior high. This shop is especially strong on all the latest baby gadgets—owner and young mother Wendy Pennes says she selects them only if they're safe, stimulating and a good value.

Fun Funiture

8451 Beverly Blvd., W. Hollywood 90048;
(213) 655-2711
Open Mon.-Sat. 10 a.m.-5 p.m.

The secret behind the success of architect Gary Gilbar's furniture for kids (and kids-at-heart) is a deft touch with a band saw. Headboards are done up like silhouettes of castles, dinosaurs or quarterbacks; shelves sprout palm fronds or look like little cottages. Rockers are hand-painted to match cribs. It's all great fun, and never *too* cute; the styles work for everything from newborn nurseries to teenagers' rooms. There are plenty of offbeat accessories: banana nightlights, Red Grooms posters, taxi toy boxes and so on. Everything is available in six colors or by custom order.

Hair Care

Merry-Go-Round

20433 Sherman Way, Canoga Park 91306;
(818) 340-9366
Open Tues.-Sat. 10 a.m.-5:15 p.m.

No screaming kids at this hectic, high-energy, fun salon, thanks to the cookies, video games and balloons provided to keep the young clients occupied. Very-first haircuts receive a certificate. Parents' cuts, too.

Tipperary

9422 Dayton Way, Beverly Hills 90210;
(310) 274-0294
Open Tues.-Sat. 9:30 a.m.-5 p.m.

Tipperary is *the* place for the young set to go for shampoos, perms and the latest bobs for girls and spiked looks for boys. Adults in need of a cut can head upstairs to Tipperary North.

The Yellow Balloon
12114 Ventura Blvd., Studio City 91604;
(818) 760-7141
Open Mon.-Sat. 9:30 a.m.-5:30 p.m., Sun. noon-4 p.m.

The Yellow Balloon was the first L.A. salon to cater to kids. Babies, boys and girls get snipped and curled here. Those having their very first cut receive a special certificate and a lock of hair in an envelope. There are plenty of stuffed animals and video games to keep the kids amused, and they all walk out with balloons, lollipops and cookies.

Toys

Allied Model Trains
4411 S. Sepulveda Blvd., Culver City 90230;
(310) 313-9353
Open Mon.-Thurs. & Sat. 10 a.m.-6 p.m., Fri. 10 a.m.-9 p.m.

In its new and improved location, Allied Model Trains could be the world's largest model-train store, stocking a vast assortment of model trains and everything to go with them. Allied does carry some inexpensive lines, though it specializes in some of the better and more costly trains, such as those by Lionel, Marklin and Athearn.

The Doll Emporium
13035 Ventura Blvd., Studio City 91604;
(818) 506-7586
Open Thurs.-Sat. 11 a.m.-4:30 p.m.

One of the largest doll troves in the country. You'll find Barbie dolls, antique dolls, Alexander dolls and everything having to do with dolls here, including doll books and free doll appraisals.

F.A.O. Schwarz
Beverly Center, Beverly & La Cienega Blvds.,
W. Hollywood 90048; (310) 659-4547
Open Mon.-Fri. 10 a.m.-9 p.m., Sat. 10 a.m.-6 p.m., Sun. 11 a.m.-6 p.m.

This perenially busy capsule-sized shop (which is in the process of expanding) offers a slice of the Big Apple's most famous toy store. Children seem to have the run of the place, finding everything from traditional wooden blocks and Barbie dolls to 21st-century electronic gadgets. For parents and children with sophisticated taste, there are collectible stuffed animals from Steiff and dolls by Madame Alexander—at equally precious prices.

Hollywood Toys & Costume
6562 Hollywood Blvd., Hollywood 90028;
(213) 465-3119
Open Mon.-Sat. 9:30 a.m-8 p.m., Sun. 11 a.m.-7 p.m.

An enormous selection of mass-produced toys, stuffed animals, model sets and educational toys at competitive prices. The store also stocks an extensive supply of costumes, masks, makeup and accessories for children and adults. Both rentals and sales.

Imaginarium
359 Santa Monica Place, Santa Monica 90401;
(310) 393-6500
Open Mon.-Sat. 10 a.m.-9 p.m., Sun. 11 a.m.-6 p.m.

Imaginarium's motto, "A Toy Store Kids Can Handle," is true in more ways than one. Not only do kids adore this place, but they're also allowed—nay, encouraged—to handle every item in the place. Resembling a dream playroom more than an ordinary toy store, Imaginarium sells an unbeatable collection of toys and games that fascinate and amuse children while at the same time challenging and often educating them. Branches also in the Century City Shopping Center, South Bay Galleria, Sherman Oaks Fashion Square and Northridge Fashion Center.

Lakeshore Curriculum Materials
8888 Venice Blvd., Culver City 90034;
(310) 559-9630
Open Mon.-Fri. 9 a.m.-5:30 p.m., Sat. 9 a.m.-5 p.m., Sun. noon-5 p.m.

It's an odd name for one of L.A.'s best-kept secrets. What first appears to be a dull assortment of teaching aids quickly turns out to be a broad collection of hard-to-find toys, supplies, furniture and books for children—not those trendy, overpriced, baby-yuppie baubles, but real things like bags of buttons, colored pipe cleaners, dollhouses that you won't be afraid to let your kids play with, costumes, dinosaur books, unusual building and counting toys and sturdy tricycles. There's also a large area in which kids can test-drive toys, under parental supervision.

Wound & Wound Toy Co.
7374 Melrose Ave., Melrose-La Brea District (L.A.) 90046; (213) 653-6703
Open Mon.-Thurs. 11 a.m.-10 p.m., Fri.-Sat. 11 a.m.-midnight, Sun. noon-8 p.m.

Here you'll find every sort of enchanting windup toy from all over the world, from "tubbies" that perform in water and just generally ingenious designs (the Godzilla that hatches out of an egg was one of our favorites). Japanese windup toys from the '50s are prize finds.

Clothes, Jewelry & Accessories

Assorted Accessories

Faux Body Ornaments

7309 Melrose Ave., Melrose-La Brea District (L.A.) 90046; (213) 931-3763
Open Mon.-Sat. 11 a.m.-7 p.m., Sun. 1 p.m.-6 p.m.

This full-service accessory salon is as well known for its overdone interior design as for its intriguing inventory. Faux works with 25 designers and a variety of materials to create artful, advanced statements in jewelry and accessories.

Fogal

439 N. Rodeo Dr., Beverly Hills 90210; (310) 273-6425
Open Mon.-Sat. 10 a.m.-6 p.m.

This European hosiery line has a leg up on most ready-made counterparts. There are 150 luxurious, high-style looks (in 105 colors), plus sheer body stockings and other delicate intimates. There's nothing like the sheer indulgence of a pair of cashmere tights to pick up your day.

Gloves by Hammer of Hollywood

7210 Melrose Ave., Melrose-La Brea District (L.A.) 90046; (213) 938-0288
Open Mon.-Fri. 9:30 a.m.-5 p.m.

Hammer has worked in Tinseltown since 1946, providing all manner of gloves for moviestars and other glitterati: Marilyn Monroe wore Hammer's gloves, and Michael Jackson still does. It's worth a visit just to take a peek at the selection here: handcrafted gloves like these are almost a lost art. Be sure to see the top-drawer quality in spandex, English lace and satin. And, of course, custom designs are done.

Maya

7452 Melrose Ave., Melrose-Fairfax District (L.A.) 90046; (213) 655-2708
Open Mon.-Sat. 11 a.m.-10 p.m., Sun. 11 a.m.-7 p.m.

Maya has sterling-silver and costume bracelets, brooches and an outstanding selection of bolo ties. But the best buys in this shop are earrings—there are over 5,000 pairs to choose from. Many are of ethnic origin, including beaded, American Indian and Balinese styles.

Patina Millinery

119 N. La Brea Ave., Melrose-La Brea District (L.A.) 90036; (213) 931-6931
Open Wed.-Sat. noon-6 p.m. & by appt.

Jodi Bentsen and Katrin Noon share fine-arts backgrounds and a love of textiles, ribbons and trims. After training privately with traditional milliners, they opened Patina, a charming shop in which their creations showcase the vintage feathers, buttons, buckles, taffeta bows and silk flowers they've collected over the years. Like the shop itself, the hats are labors of love, made completely from scratch. The partners have also designed and gathered a small collection of easy-wearing, one-of-a-kind clothing pieces, scarves, "country primitive" jewelry and such architectural details as vintage lighting fixtures, picture frames and old latticework. Custom hat designs and mail order available.

Prada

9521 Brighton Way, Beverly Hills 90210; (310) 276-8889
Open Mon.-Sat. 10 a.m.-6 p.m.

The Prada store out of Milano is best known for its signature chain-handled, quilted bags, first discovered, then toted all over Europe, by savvy fashion magazine editors. Also available are satin-textured nylon backpacks and assorted makeup bags. Colors and fabrics are magnificent, as are the prices, in everything from coats, tunics and cardigan jackets to ballet flats.

Rosenthal/Truitt

8648 Sunset Blvd., W. Hollywood 90069; (310) 659-5470
Open Mon.-Fri. 10 a.m.-7 p.m., Sat. 10 a.m.-6 p.m., Sun. noon-5 p.m.

This cozy den for men's fine furnishings harkens back to eighteenth- and nineteenth-century England. Traditionalists will love such well-bred notions as cashmere socks and sweaters, luxurious bath robes, leather-bound books and antique cuff links. Also a branch in the Century City Shopping Center (310-277-1893).

So Much & Company

Sunset Plaza, 8669 Sunset Blvd., W. Hollywood 90069; (310) 652-4291
Open Mon.-Sat. 10 a.m.-5:30 p.m.

It's amazing how many one-of-a-kind items are packed into this tiny boutique: everything from gold, silver and brass jewelry to extraordinary picture frames, belts, hair accessories, hand-knit sweaters, leather purses, baby clothes, beaded earrings and much more.

209

Eyewear

Eyes on Main
3110 Main St., Ste. 108, Santa Monica 90405;
(310) 399-3302
Open Mon.-Sat. 10 a.m.-6 p.m., Sun. noon-5 p.m.

Marla Cohn's shop does a booming business in men's frames and cat-eye shapes for women. Her broad, mid-range of styles that you "don't have to change your attitude to wear" include chic specs by Persol, Oliver Peoples, Alain Mikli, Revo and Anglo American, plus lots of German frames in rimless shapes and great colors. You can also find a good selection of sports goggles. Cohn will have customized frames made or duplicate discontinued ones.

L.A. Eyeworks
7407 Melrose Ave., Melrose-Fairfax District (L.A.) 90046; (213) 653-8255
Open Mon.-Fri. 10 a.m.-noon & 1 p.m.-7 p.m., Sat. 10 a.m.-noon & 1 p.m.-6 p.m.

Home to off-the-wall window displays and the utmost in optical names and frames. On Saturdays, this place is so packed with Melrose Avenue trendies (and a famous face or two) that it locks the door to control the crowds. Be prepared to wait, and expect to drop a bundle.

Oliver Peoples
8642 Sunset Blvd., W. Hollywood 90069;
(310) 657-2553
Open Mon.-Fri. 10 a.m.-7 p.m., Sat. 10 a.m.-6 p.m.

The owners of this ultra-hip boutique acquired a cache of optical treasures from the art-deco and art-nouveau eras and have used it as a basis for a collection of classically inspired eyewear fashions. Two of its best-sellers are frames that combine tortoiseshell eye pieces and temples with a wire bridge; and clip-on sunglasses circa the 1930s. Prices, for many budgets, are prohibitive.

Senses
2714 Main St., Santa Monica 90405;
(310) 452-4080
Open Mon.-Thurs. 10 a.m.-9 p.m., Fri.-Sat. 10 a.m-11 p.m., Sun. 11 a.m.-7 p.m.

Senses is an optical and fragrance boutique that's as visually arresting as its top names in frames suggest: Alain Mikli, Jean Paul Gaultier, Lunetta Bada-Men's Club, Persol and Austria's Shau Shau. Everything within eyeshot contributes to this "experiment in surrealism": vaulted ceiling, fragmented picture frames jutting out of the wall, mirrored glass mosaic underfoot and sensuous gem-shaped cash desk. Among the hard-to-find scents (and some remarkable bottles) are Kenzo, Versace, Salvador Dalí, Rochas, Missoni and Niki de Saint Phalle.

Jewelry

Butler & Wilson
8644 W. Sunset Blvd., W. Hollywood 90069;
(310) 657-1990
Open Mon.-Sat. 10 a.m.-6 p.m.

This is the English counterpart to Kenneth Jay Lane, but for a younger set. Direct from London come *faux* gems with a flamboyant following: devoted fans include Elton John, Little Richard, Jerry Hall and Princess Di. The design team also styles oversized glittery accessories for Giorgio Armani and Calvin Klein.

Cartier
370 N. Rodeo Dr., Beverly Hills 90210;
(310) 275-4272
Open Mon.-Fri. 10 a.m.-5:30 p.m., Sat. 10 a.m.-5 p.m.

There are some truly gorgeous pieces of jewelry here, the best of which are designed from original Louis Cartier drawings and made by hand in Paris. The store established its reputation with its watches and now offers six Cartier fragrances as well. The leather goods are excellent in quality. (Also a branch at 220 N. Rodeo Dr., 310-275-5155).

Fred Joaillier
401 N. Rodeo Dr., Beverly Hills 90210;
(310) 278-3733
Open Mon.-Sat. 10 a.m.-6 p.m.

Fred Joaillier is pure California glamor, not the least of which is the Force 10 collection of jewelry, which mixes eighteen-karat gold with stainless-steel nautical cable. Elegant, polite and expensive, the place perfectly encapsulates the style of the resort set.

Kenneth Jay Lane
441 N. Rodeo Dr., Beverly Hills 90210;
(310) 273-9588
Open Mon.-Sat. 10 a.m.-6 p.m., Sun. noon-5 p.m.

As a leading designer of *faux* jewels, Lane has made a name for himself with couture designers and the jet set. His stunning gemstone look-alikes have starred on fashion runways and TV's now-defunct *Dynasty* series.

Laykin et Cie
9634 Wilshire Blvd., Beverly Hills 90210;
(310) 278-1168
Open Mon.-Sat. 10 a.m.-5:30 p.m.

This small jewelry boutique on the ground floor of I. Magnin features tasteful pieces in eighteen-karat gold and platinum, as well as precious and semiprecious stones. The styles are as conservative and as discreetly handsome and elegant as I. Magnin's merchandise—with elegant prices to match.

Michael Dawkins
8649 W. Sunset Blvd., W. Hollywood 90069;
(310) 652-4964
Open Mon.-Sat. 10 a.m.-6 p.m.

A small but dramatic showcase for up-to-the-minute jewelry design, from the traditional to the outrageous. Some choice designers: Robert Lee Morris, Katherine Post and Londoner Tom Binns.

Myrna
Umberto, 416 N. Cañon Dr., Beverly Hills 90210;
(310) 276-5779
Open Tues.-Sat. 9:30 a.m.-6:30 p.m.

This treasure box of a boutique, tucked away in the Umberto beauty salon, is building quite a reputation for its truly great finds in fine and *faux* designer jewelry. On our last visit, we were dazzled by Carole Daner's pave Austrian crystal creations, hand-blown Venetian glass earrings by L.A.'s Deanna Hamro and mosaic glass bead beauties by Roxanne Assoulin, to name just a few among a number of stunning pieces. Former stylist/owner Myrna Glotzer also offers repair and reproduction services and will answer custom requests from this shop-within-a-shop.

Sculpture to Wear
8441 Melrose Ave., W. Hollywood 90069;
(213) 651-2205
Open Mon.-Sat. 11 a.m.-6 p.m.

This contemporary art jewelry gallery represents 70 artists from around the world. The focus is on one-of-a-kind and limited-edition pieces in a wide variety of forms and styles, from free-spirited to primitive, abstract to humorous. Materials range from colorful resins and acrylics to precious stones and metals.

Tiffany & Company
210 N. Rodeo Dr., Beverly Hills 90210;
(310) 273-8880
Open Mon.-Sat. 10 a.m.-5:30 p.m.

No Beverly Hills shopping expedition is complete without a trip to this West Coast branch of the Fifth Avenue classic. Tiffany carries exquisite formal and sporty jewelry, designed by such artists as Paloma Picasso and Elsa Peretti, plus elegant gift items made of silver, crystal and china, clocks, stationery, leather goods, scarves and its own Tiffany fragrance.

Van Cleef & Arpels
300 N. Rodeo Dr., Beverly Hills 90210;
(310) 276-1161
Open Mon.-Fri. 10 a.m.-5 p.m.

No fun little trinkets here—just serious pieces of jewelry with serious price tags. The collections are conventional, and the workmanship and quality of the stones are exceptional.

Menswear

Brooks Brothers
604 S. Figueroa St., Downtown (L.A.) 90017;
(213) 629-4200
Open Mon.-Fri. 10 a.m.-9 p.m., Sat. 10 a.m.-6 p.m., Sun. 12:30 p.m.-5:30 p.m.

3 Fashion Island, 1083 Newport Center Dr., Newport Beach 92660; (714) 640-8880
Open Mon.-Fri. 10 a.m.-8 p.m., Sat. 10 a.m.-6 p.m., Sun. noon-5 p.m.

Brooks Brothers is an American institution, but we were still amazed not to find an abundance of young preps trying on the cotton trousers, tweed jackets, leather loafers and oxford shirts. Instead, most of the shoppers are middle-aged gentlemen who began dressing this way long before it became stylish. What is surprising is the number of women buying the crested cotton shirts (invented here) and men's tie-back boxer shorts, both more reasonably priced than equivalent women's merchandise. Brooks Brothers now carries a line of more contemporary (if such a thing is possible here), stylish clothing, particularly for women. Another branch in the Century City Shopping Center (310-553-3335).

Carroll & Company
466 N. Rodeo Dr., Beverly Hills 90210;
(310) 273-9060
Open Mon.-Sat. 9:30 a.m.-6 p.m.

Carroll & Company started dressing Beverly Hills men 40 years ago—and what it's selling now isn't too different from what it was selling then. If you're a nice, conservative gentleman who's looking for a nice pair of shoes or a nice camel-hair jacket, you'll find a nice salesman to help. Some good values (for Rodeo Drive) nonetheless.

Chanins
1030 Westwood Blvd., Westwood 90024;
(310) 208-4500
Open Mon.-Sat. 10 a.m.-8 p.m., Sun. noon-6 p.m.

A chic upscale chain, targeted to fashion-aware men for whom price and pragmatic styling are a consideration. The broad-ranging, at times inconsistent, inventory is in sync with California lifestyles and includes representatives from Nancy Heller, Hugo Boss, Axis and Katherine Hamnett. Branches also in the following malls: Beverly Center (310-652-2626), Westside Pavilion (310-475-2383), Brentwood Gardens (310-447-5700) and Marina Marketplace (310-305-6666).

Fred Hayman Beverly Hills

273 N. Rodeo Dr., Beverly Hills 90210;
(310) 271-3000
Open Mon.-Sat. 10 a.m.-6:30 p.m.

Fred Hayman Beverly Hills (formerly Giorgio) is a precious address to many a Beverly Hills denizen, not the least reason being that it is one of the few clothing stores in the world that has a bar for its customers. Most of the Hollywood stars have left their autographs both on photographs and memorable checks here. The racks resemble *People* magazine's "Best Dressed, Worst Dressed" issue: both extremes can be found here. In the women's department, there are unbelievable Academy Award–quality dresses, and, despite the appalling prices of such luxuries, you can find some items of good taste. The majority of the menswear is imported from Italy and chosen with a discerning eye. If you're willing to pay $900 for a sports coat that is 50 percent wool and 50 percent cashmere you'll fit right in. Hayman's women's fragrance, "273," is available only through the shop.

G.B. Harb & Son

3359 Wilshire Blvd., Mid-Wilshire (L.A.) 90010;
(213) 386-5496
Open Mon.-Fri. 10 a.m.-6 p.m., Sat. 10 a.m.-4:30 p.m. & by appt.
735 S. Figueroa St. #303, Downtown (L.A.) 90017;
(213) 624-4785
Open Mon.-Fri. 10 a.m.-7 p.m., Sat. 10 a.m.-6 p.m.
500 S. Grand Ave., Downtown (L.A.) 90071;
(213) 892-0283
Open Mon.-Fri. 9 a.m.-6 p.m., Sat. 9 a.m.-4 p.m.

George Harb's shops are temples of conservatism—à la Brooks Brothers and Carroll & Company—but with styles and fabrics more elegant than at its famous competitors. There's a marvelous choice of beautiful Egyptian pima cotton and oxford shirts, sober suits, handsome cashmere and wool sports coats, accessories and colorful, casual menswear, all at very high prices. But you'll get your money's worth in the impeccable fabrics and tailoring that manages to be classic without being boxy or dull, along with friendly, helpful service. A branch in Larchmont Village (158 N. Larchmont Blvd., 213-466-9538) carries sportswear.

Jaeger

9699 Wilshire Blvd., Beverly Hills 90210;
(310) 276-1062
Open Mon.-Sat. 10 a.m.-6 p.m.

Fine English sportswear that's simple, elegant and well cut. The fabrics—tweed, flannel, camel hair, cashmere—are top-of-the-line and more appropriate for the conservative and traditional than the young and trendy.

Jay Wolf

517 N. Robertson Blvd., Beverly Hills 90048;
(310) 273-9893
Open Mon.-Fri. 11 a.m.-7 p.m., Sat. 10:30 a.m.-6 p.m.

With its grass mat flooring and playful iron fixtures, Jay Wolf's shop is a mini-island of tranquility. Giorgio Armani–trained Wolf prides himself on a tailored clothing and sportswear collection that's both casual and sophisticated. Three-button khaki jackets, earthy-colored cotton shorts and full-cut shirts in solids or stripes display a breezy elegance by Joseph Abboud and Londoners Margaret Howell and Paul Smith. Soft, supple khaki pants are as easy-wearing for women as they are for men. Wolf has a knack for giving the most conservative uniform—and there are plenty to choose from—a contemporary twist.

Maxfield

8825 Melrose Ave., W. Hollywood 90069;
(310) 274-8800
Open Mon.-Sat. 11 a.m.-7 p.m.

Maxfield is the place to outfit yourself for dinner at Tryst or an opening at MOCA, especially if you like to wear black. This minimalist, gallerylike enclave showcases au courant clothing from European, American and Japanese designers; of special note is Armani for Men and the Yohji Yamamoto boutique. Personal and high-fashion accessories are in fine form.

Mr. Guy

301 N. Cañon Dr., Beverly Hills 90210;
(310) 275-4143
Open Mon.-Sat. 10 a.m.-6 p.m.

Both a stylish, affluent young man and an older, more conservative gentleman could walk into Mr. Guy and readily outfit themselves from head to toe. Suits and slacks are beautifully cut and can be altered on the premises. The ties and silk and cotton shirts range from plain, solid colors to the contemporary prints of Japanese and European designers. There's also a good selection of quality shoes and tuxedos.

New Man

9628 Wilshire Blvd., Beverly Hills 90212;
(310) 859-0916
Open Mon.-Sat. 10 a.m.-6 p.m.

New Man is a French line of contemporary, well-fitting lightweight cotton and denim sportswear that comes in numerous shades and styles, but the jeans, jackets and shirts really have that oh-so-casual California look. Women's styles and sizes are also available.

Rick Pallack
4554 Sherman Oaks Ave., Sherman Oaks 91403;
(818) 789-7000
*Open Mon.-Fri. 10 a.m.-8 p.m., Sat. 10 a.m.-6 p.m.,
Sun. 11 a.m.-6 p.m.*

You've seen this savvy designer/retailer's duds all over the movies and TV ("Beverly Hills 90210," "Dynasty," "Miami Vice") as well as on several of the participants in the Emmy Awards. Rick Pallack's high-fashion European and American clothing includes designerwear from Hugo Boss and Daniel Schagen. Rick's excellent selection, from formal wear to business suits to sportwear, includes every last detail down to the pocket silks, belts and socks—all of it meant to make the confident, well-polished man. Winner of awards for his service and quality, Pallack wardrobes many of Hollywood's leading men.

Raffles
17401 Ventura Blvd., Encino 91316;
(818) 501-6782
Open Mon.-Sat. 10 a.m.-6 p.m., or by appt.

Raffles for men has probably one of the most impressive collections of Hugo Boss in the country, as well as a full line of Axis, Reds, Falke by Jeff Sayre and Basco. Sweaters—a hard-to-find item in Los Angeles—are plentiful in styles by all of the aforementioned, as well as Nani Bon and Laura Pearson (who also designs costly, conversation-piece socks).

Sami Dinar
9677 Brighton Way, Beverly Hills 90210;
(310) 275-2044
Open Mon.-Sat. 9:30 a.m.-6:30 p.m.

The shop's chichi location belies its amiable atmosphere. An impeccable dresser, Sami Dinar has a sharp eye for European and American design, plus a penchant for a relaxed but elegant look and personal service. His small store is packed with double-breasted suits by Canali, hand-loomed sweaters by Marienbad, deco-inspired ties by Modules, colorful patterned socks by Laura Pearson, sterling-silver accessories, butter-soft leather coats and luxurious bathrobes.

Studio
1615 1/2 Montana Ave., Santa Monica 90402;
(310) 394-2673
Open Mon.-Sat. 10 a.m.-6 p.m.

Literally off the beaten track (tucked into an alley off Montana), Studio is the kind of store you're glad you went out of your way to find. By design, this tiny cubicle is filled with colorful clothing by Clacton & Frinton (a westside exclusive) in wonderful contrast to elegant shaving accessories and luxurious leather goods. The "jewel box" assortment includes eyewear by L.A.

Eyeworks, Moulton Brown bath products from England and interesting sterling-silver jewelry.

Theodore Man/Contents by Theodore
451 N. Rodeo Dr., Beverly Hills 90210;
(310) 274-8029
Open Mon.-Sat. 10 a.m.-6 p.m.
23733 W. Malibu Rd., Malibu 91302;
(310) 456-7719
Open Mon.-Sat. 10 a.m.-6 p.m., Sun. noon-5 p.m.

Specializing in the slouchy, dressed-down look, Theodore Man presents lots of cotton, linen and easy-on-the-eye colors. Think of the sportier pages of *GQ*, and you'll get the picture. Prices are a little higher than average. Also a branch in the Beverly Center (310-854-0375).

Traffic
Beverly Center, Beverly & La Cienega Blvds., W. Hollywood 90048; (310) 659-4313
Open Mon.-Fri. 10 a.m.-9 p.m., Sat. 10 a.m.-8 p.m., Sun. 11 a.m.-6 p.m.

The selection of clothing is slightly off-center. Traffic is apt to carry tuxedos with a twist, unique European color mixes, silk and rayon shirts with bold, colorful patterns and local talent exclusives. Outstanding customer service.

Weathervane for Men
1132 Montana Ave., Santa Monica 90403;
(310) 395-0397
Open Mon.-Sat. 10 a.m.-6 p.m., Sun. noon-5 p.m.

A well-chosen mix of fine-quality, contemporary clothing reminiscent of the old Jerry Magnin store—tasteful classics with a twist by Andrew Fezza, Jhane Barnes, Axis and Zanella.

Designer

Agnès B. Homme
100 N. Robertson Blvd., Beverly Hills 90048;
(310) 271-9643
Open Mon.-Sat. 11 a.m.-7 p.m., Sun. noon-6 p.m.

This French designer is known for her expressive ways with classics, and every item she creates has the same simple elegance. The striped fisherman's T-shirts that have been in demand for more than ten years are here, next to signature snap-front cardigans, cotton gabardine slacks, linen suits and leather accessories.

Bijan
420 N. Rodeo Dr., Beverly Hills 90210;
(310) 273-6544
Open by appt. only (fragrance department open Mon.-Sat. 10 a.m.-6 p.m.).

When this pearly-toothed character isn't popping out of billboards and leaping flamboyantly across the pages of glossy magazines, he is personally meeting with his most important clientele. In this exclusive boutique, you can experience Bijan live—if you are either wealthy or clever enough to receive an appointment, or if you are a member of Middle Eastern royalty. If you do, you'll find an opulent display of fur (caps are $7,000), leather, silk, cashmere and Bijan's "classic" wool suits, priced at $3,000 to $3,500. Bijan shoes and fragrances are also sold here, and the boutique can custom-design any item.

Clacton & Frinton
731 N. La Cienega Blvd., W. Hollywood 90069;
(310) 652-2957
Open Mon.-Sat. 10 a.m.-6 p.m.

"The Englishman in the Tropics Look" is how Michael and Hilary Anderson describe their summer line. What this shop actually features is traditional English styling spiced with '40s and '50s Americana: the results include modish jackets and baggy pleated trousers. The Andersons design and manufacture 90 percent of their merchandise, using imported cottons and woolens. There is also some womenswear.

Gianni Versace
437 N. Rodeo Dr., Beverly Hills 90210;
(310) 276-6799
See review under "Womenswear," this section.

Giorgio Armani
436 N. Rodeo Dr., Beverly Hills 90210;
(310) 271-5555
Open Mon.-Sat. 10 a.m.-6 p.m.

This is a stunning store by all accounts, the biggest retailing effort by the kingpin of Italian design and the most talked-about store to hit Rodeo Drive in years. The interior—lacquered surfaces, gold-leaf panels, glass and steel—is as dazzling as the lineup of menswear, womenswear, shoes, luggage, accessories, tuxedos, underwear and cashmere items.

Polo Ralph Lauren
444 N. Rodeo Dr., Beverly Hills 90210;
(310) 281-7200
Open Mon.-Sat. 10 a.m.-6 p.m.

Although Ralph Lauren first achieved success by designing women's clothing, he really hit his stride in menswear. Traditional English haberdashery, with its strong traditions and rich vocabulary, has afforded him a broad range for restatement and interpretation. Here you'll find all the paraphernalia of traditional masculine pursuits: carved wooden walking sticks, trophies, mounted game heads, equestrian equipment. And man's best friend, a symbol of the landed gentry and of general bonhomie, is everywhere in effigy—carved wooden dogs, bronze dogs,

dog-headed canes and framed photos and paintings of dogs. The clothing is equally masculine—traditional and English-tailored. The same goes for the shoes and accessories, which are executed in the finest leathers. For quality this high and for what is truly investment dressing, the prices are not exorbitant. Service is polite, and there's a mahogany bar on the top floor where you can contemplate your purchases over a cappuccino.

Valentino
240 N. Rodeo Dr., Beverly Hills 90210;
(310) 247-0103
See review under "Womenswear," this section.

Discount

Sacks Fashion Outlet (S.F.O.)
652 N. La Brea Ave., Melrose-La Brea District
(L.A.) 90036; (213) 939-3993
Open Mon.-Fri. 10 a.m.-8 p.m., Sat. 10 a.m.-7 p.m., Sun. 11 a.m.-6 p.m.

David Sacks has become perhaps L.A.'s best, and best-known, discount-sportswear merchant. The emphasis is on natural fabrics, and the selection of all-cotton dress shirts (often less than $15) is superb. There are also cotton, wool and silk sweaters, handsome ties (often under $10), attractive sports coats (under $100), cotton polo shirts, casual jackets, and leather and suede jackets and skirts. What sets Sacks apart from other discounters is a brand-name lineup which rivals that of better department stores, at very, very low prices. We find the selection varies so much that it takes regular visits to hit the jackpot. There are several other locations, including Studio City, Tarzana, West Los Angeles and West Hollywood.

Large Sizes

Rochester Big and Tall
9687 Wilshire Blvd., Beverly Hills 90212;
(310) 274-9468
Open Mon.-Sat. 9:30 a.m.-6 p.m., Thurs. 9:30 a.m.-8 p.m., Sun. noon-5 p.m.

The only shop in Beverly Hills dedicated exclusively to big and tall men, this shop features suits and sports coats by Perry Ellis, Lanvin and Hickey-Freeman.

Tailors

Jack Varney
268 N. Beverly Dr., Beverly Hills 90210;
(310) 278-4500
Open Mon.-Fri. 9 a.m.-6 p.m., Sat. 9 a.m.-5 p.m.

Whether you're after a classic tuxedo shirt, a sports shirt or a dress shirt, Jack Varney will custom-tailor one that fits perfectly. And he happens to use fine materials and work very quickly.

Richard Lim's High Society Tailors
2974 Wilshire Blvd., Mid-Wilshire (L.A.) 90010;
(213) 382-0148
Open Mon.-Sat. 10 a.m.-6:30 p.m.

Using fabrics from around the world, Lim custom-tailors suits, tuxedos, slacks, sports coats and shirts with an emphasis on individuality, and special attention to physique, profession and style of living. Lim also does alterations.

Shoes

Bally of Switzerland (men)
340 N. Rodeo Dr., Beverly Hills 90210;
(310) 271-0666
Open Mon.-Sat. 10 a.m.-6 p.m.

A comfortable fit and excellent leather have made Bally shoes a favorite of men all over the world—at least men who prefer the slimmer lines of European shoes over more solid-looking American classics. There are enough fashionable styles to make even the trendiest young men happy.

Bally of Switzerland (women)
409 N. Rodeo Dr., Beverly Hills 90210;
(310) 275-0902
Open Mon.-Sat. 10 a.m.-6 p.m.

Mostly classic (though some are rather dated) shoes, handbags and leather jackets of excellent quality. Unfortunately, they're sold by rather agressive salespeople. This always-busy shop is small, but the range of styles and colors is large.

Bootz
2654 Main St., Santa Monica 90405;
(310) 396-2466
Open Sun.-Wed. 10 a.m.-7 p.m., Thurs.-Sat. 10 a.m.-11 p.m.

Owned by a Texan, Bootz does a rousing business in top-notch Western boots (Justin, Nocona, Tony Lama, Larry Mahan), as well as handmade belts, boot straps, tips and heel plates. Exotic skins range from neon-green-marked lizard to sea bass. Bootz also carries one of the largest selections of shoe boots in L.A. Regular patrons include Billy Crystal, Martin Sheen and Kelly McGillis.

Charles Jourdan
214 N. Rodeo Dr., Beverly Hills 90210;
(310) 273-3507
Open Mon.-Sat. 10 a.m.-6 p.m., Sun. noon-5 p.m.

Just about every department store in the city carries some of Jourdan's ever-popular pumps,

but if you want to see *all* the styles and *all* the colors (along with some attractive hats, gloves, jewelry, watches, scarves, hair accessories, belts, handbags and sunglasses), you really should pay a visit to this large chrome-and-glass shop. The prices aren't nearly as shocking as Frizon's and Pfister's, and the styles are about as tasteful and classic as you can get. The store also offers shoes for men and, like every designer name in town, its own fragrance.

Church's English Shoes
9633 Brighton Way, Beverly Hills 90210;
(310) 275-1981
Open Mon.-Sat. 9 a.m.-6 p.m.

Excellent quality has given these classic English men's shoes the fine reputation they deserve. Styles and prices are rather middle-of-the-road—not too old, new, low or high. Actually, most of Church's customers are more interested in comfort and quality (which are ample) than in designs (which are rather clunky).

Cole-Haan
260 N. Rodeo Dr., Beverly Hills 90210;
(310) 859-7622
Open Mon.-Wed.& Fri. 9:30 a.m.-6:30 p.m., Thurs. 9:30 a.m.-8 p.m., Sun. noon-5 p.m.

Cole-Haan is the maker of well-designed, can't-go-wrong choices in classic footwear. For women, there are open, flat sandals that might be mistaken for designs by Donna Karan or Calvin Klein. We also liked the washed silk flats in mustard, jade or taupe and blissfully simple natural calf thongs. Men can find fisherman's sandals, waxed nubuck desert boots, even lace-up spectators in brown-and-white deerskin. Many of this store's customers are tourists or referrals from Giorgio Armani up the street.

Le Petit Jean
368 N. Beverly Dr., Beverly Hills 90210;
(310) 858-3843
Open Sat.-Thurs. 10 a.m.-6 p.m., Fri. 10 a.m.-7 p.m.

Le Petit Jean's line of women's shoes is attractive, fashionable, well made and reasonably priced. The shoes are made in Mexico, and with the peso devaluations of the last few years, it costs only about $50 a pair for the full line of colorful pumps. Definitely worth a visit.

Privilege
1470 Brighton Way, Beverly Hills 90210;
(310) 276-8116
Open Mon.-Sat. 10 a.m.-6:30 p.m.

The best shop in which to buy quality, fashion-forward women's shoes at reasonable prices. Ninety percent of the stock is made specially for the store in Italy, France or Spain. There are always terrific sandals, flats, boots and pumps.

Also notable is Privilege for Men at the Beverly Center. Other branches in the Beverly Center (310-652-3362) and Westside Pavilion (310-470-1130), with shoes and womenswear.

Salvatore Ferragamo

357 N. Rodeo Dr., Beverly Hills 90210;
(310) 273-9990
Open Mon.-Sat. 10 a.m.-6 p.m.

A fresh design breeze is blowing in the venerable House of Ferragamo, and it's showcased here in perfectly poised slingbacks, evening sandals of hot pink satin with gold kidskin and stiletto-heeled crocodile pumps modeled after those first created for Marilyn Monroe. Fabulous accompaniments include the famous "bracelet" bag with a gold clasp in the shape of one of Salvatore's original designs.

Stradivari Shoes

1133 Montana Ave., Santa Monica 90403;
(310) 394-3249
Open Mon.-Sat. 10 a.m.-6 p.m.

Italian influences are the striking backdrop for Stradivari's small but sizzling shoe collection for women. Parading along the warm mottled walls and posing on the red velvet Romanesque daybed is a sexy line-up of pointy-toed slingbacks by Ernesto Esposito, a former designer for Thierry Mugler, now with Lerre and Sergio Rossi. From Dolce e Gabbana, there are ankle-high sandals that swathe the foot in a series of skinny, stretch silk straps. In kicky contrast, the store stocks such trendy alternatives as patent leather Beatles boots and stiletto-heeled pumps with metal toe tips à la Courreges.

Sportswear (Men & Women)

Banana Republic

9669 Santa Monica Blvd., Beverly Hills 90210;
(310) 858-7900
Open Mon.-Sat. 10 a.m.-6:30 p.m., Sun. noon-5 p.m.
2905 Main St., Santa Monica 90405;
(310) 392-8349
Open Mon.-Sat. 10 a.m.-8 p.m., Sat. 10 a.m.-8 p.m., Sun. 11 a.m.-7 p.m.

Though this was always a good place for khaki in every configuration, we much prefer the new lines of both men's and women's clothing, all of it projecting a cool, easy, very wearable style. There are linen, wool and corduroy shirts in gorgeous gold, olive and teal blue; jackets with flair; thick, nubby sweaters; cotton shorts and slacks— all the real-life basics. Also a branch in the Beverly Center.

Benetton

7409 Melrose Ave., Melrose-Fairfax District (L.A.) 90046; (213) 852-0775
Open Mon.-Thurs. 11:30 a.m.-7:30 p.m., Fri.-Sat. 11:30 a.m.-8 p.m., Sun. noon-7:30 p.m.

In the winter the Benetton shops become warehouses full of lambswool, featuring bold, dynamic cardigans, pullovers, vests, turtlenecks and sweater dresses. In the spring and summer, it's cotton: linen suits, starchy sundresses and stretch-cotton mini-dresses, skirts, T-shirts, shorts and leggings, as well as as neatly tailored pleated skirts, shorts and slacks. But no matter what the season, these young, colorful unisex separates are always fun to mix and match. Under the brotherhood banner of its United Colors and United Contrasts advertising campaigns, Italy's Benetton has been a huge American retail success story: there are nearly 30 stores in Southern California, many of them in shopping malls.

Camp Beverly Hills

9640 Little Santa Monica Blvd., Beverly Hills 90210;
(310) 274-8317
Open Mon.-Sat. 10 a.m.-6:30 p.m., Sun. noon-5 p.m.

This revamped Beverly Hills fixture devotes itself to a lively mix of Camp-logo sportswear and "feel-good clothes" by mainly California manufacturers for young men, women and kids.

CP Shades

2937 Main St., Santa Monica 94965;
(310) 392-0949
Open Mon.-Sat. 11 a.m.-7 p.m., Sun. noon-5 p.m.

Quintessentially Californian, CP Shades puts comfort above all else. Soft, quality cotton knits, elastic waists and loose cuts result in sportswear so relaxed you'll feel like living in it. Since eliminating the middle man and selling only direct from its own stores, CP Shades has relaxed its prices, too: a T-shirt that used to sell for $50 now ranges from $18 to $38. The wide assortment of cropped turtlenecks, long cardigans, skirts of all lengths, shorts and pants, all in muted solids and stripes, keeps you in comfortable chic. Also in Beverly Hills. Catalog available.

Eddie Bauer

204 Santa Monica Place, Santa Monica 90401;
(310) 394-7224
Open Mon.-Sat. 10 a.m.-9 p.m., Sun. 11 a.m.-6 p.m.

Seattle-based Eddie Bauer is an excellent chain that sells high-quality clothing and equipment for the outdoor life. Nothing is particularly fashionable, but there are great basics in both men's and women's sportswear: khaki pants, flannel shirts, cotton turtlenecks, sturdy shoes and lightweight-but-warm jackets. There's also a wide selection of well-made Eddie Bauer–label backpacks and small traveling items for both campers and jet-setters: money bags, insect repellents, binoculars and so on. Also in the Beverly Center (310-657-2936) and Woodland Hills Promenade (818-884-5255).

Fred Segal Melrose

8106 Melrose Ave., Melrose-Fairfax District (L.A.) 90046; (213) 651-4129
Open Mon.-Wed. & Fri.-Sat. 10 a.m.-7 p.m., Thurs. 10 a.m.-8 p.m., Sun. noon-6 p.m.

L.A.'s perpetually hot retailer (now owned by Segal's nephew, Ron Herman) is chock full of every clothing item and accessory you'll need to look ultra-chic yet unique—all arranged in a connected series of small boutiques. Buyers strive to find goods that you may not find anywhere else. There's avant-garde menswear, a designer-eyewear counter and a "jeans bar" stocked with the hottest names on European hips: Edwin, Big John, Replay, Rivet and Diesel (all Italian), Big Star, For Joseph and Donovan (French) and more. Salespeople are as energetic and friendly as they come.

Fred Segal Santa Monica

500 Broadway, Santa Monica 90401; (310) 393-4477
Open Mon.-Sat. 10 a.m.-7 p.m., Sun. noon-6 p.m.

The Santa Monica emporium (opened in 1985) is bigger (and some say even better) than the Melrose Avenue outpost. Every nook and cranny of this new-age department store holds a highly edited and generally costly selection of unusual goods—merchants here have a sure sense of what's hot and hip. The charged atmosphere includes a sometimes jarring disc jockey and a lively red, white and blue color scheme. You may feel compelled to go in all different directions at once, to see the men's hats, the sleek shoe collection, the picture-perfect children's shop, the heavenly collection of bath and body products, the hand-painted ceramics. Don't forget to break for a gooey brownie at Mrs. Beasley's, one of four eateries on the premises.

The Gap

1931 Wilshire Blvd., Santa Monica 90403; (310) 453-4551
Open Mon.-Fri. 10 a.m.-9 p.m., Sat. 10 a.m.-6 p.m., Sun. 11 a.m.-6 p.m.

7650 Melrose Ave., Melrose-Fairfax District (L.A.) 90028 (branches everywhere); (213) 653-3847
Open Mon.-Fri. 10 a.m.-9 p.m., Sat. 10 a.m.-7 p.m., Sun. noon-7 p.m.

The Western-oriented Gap store of yesteryear is lost to history. Now it's one of the hippest places to shop, a place for all ages and lifestyles. The Gap's well-designed, all-American basics for men and women (and in the Beverly Center lo-

cation, kids and babies) still includes a good stock of Levi jeans in every size and color. The rest of the merchandise, all Gap-labeled, is made up of simple and colorful button-down shirts, pleated twill trousers and shorts, bold cotton sweaters, pocket T-shirts, sweats, colorful socks and belts and faded denim jackets, all at reasonable prices. About 32 other branches in L.A., including one in almost every mall in the greater L.A. area.

Guess?/Georges Marciano Boutique

9520/9526 Santa Monica Blvd., Beverly Hills 90210; (310) 550-6299
Open Mon.-Sat. 10 a.m.-6 p.m., Sun. noon-5 p.m.

Young, sexy denim-dominated sportswear is the motif at Guess?. Here both men and women can find denim shorts, shirts, vests and overalls, suede jackets and pants and, of course, Guess's trademark perfectly fitting jeans in multiple colors and styles. For women, there are also the flirty gingham cotton sundresses and skirts, bra tops, T-shirts, blouses and chic ankle boots featured in the company's steamy advertising campaigns. Founding partner Georges Marciano's dressier line of clothing for men and women is also sold at the retail stores, built around contemporary dresswear in mostly silk and rayon. Also: Century City, Westside Pavilion, Sherman Oaks (two branches), Glendale Galleria, Northridge, Topanga Mall and a new store in South Coast Plaza.

Mark Fox

7326 Melrose Ave., Melrose-La Brea District (L.A.) 90046; (213) 936-1619
Open Mon.-Thurs. 11 a.m.-7 p.m., Fri.-Sat. 11 a.m.-8 p.m., Sun. 11 a.m.-7 p.m.

This is a good place to find vintage (new and used) leather jackets, Western shirts and boots in the John Wayne vein. For a price, Fox will create custom designs in boots, belts, jewelry and motorcycle accessories. A favorite haunt of Bruce Springsteen.

Na Na

1228 Third Street Promenade, Santa Monica 90401; (310) 393-7811
Open Mon.-Sat. 10:30 a.m.-8 p.m., Sun. 11 a.m.-7 p.m.

Na Na built its English punk-inspired following on black leather, mini-skirts and funky Doc Marten shoes. Now in addition to the skin-tight black jeans, bins of underwear, cotton socks and colored tights, there is "nice, normal stuff" such as clothing by French Connection, Kikit and Stussy for men and women. A Na Na outlet at 8327 3rd Street (213-653-1252) has some great deals on discontinued styles.

Vintage Clothes

Aaardvark's
7579 Melrose Ave., Melrose-Fairfax District (L.A.)
90046; (213) 655-6769
Open Mon.-Sat. 11 a.m.-9 p.m., Sun. noon-6 p.m.

L.A.'s answer to New York City's Antique Boutique, Aaardvark's carries primarily used clothing. If you don't mind merchandise with more than a little wear and tear, you'll have a field day going through the stacks and racks of leather jackets, beaded sweaters, bowling shirts and '50s dresses.

American Rag Cie.
150 S. La Brea Ave., Melrose-La Brea District (L.A.)
90036; (213) 935-3154
Open Mon.-Sat. 10:30 a.m.-10:30 p.m., Sun. noon-7 p.m.

The largest used-clothing store in Los Angeles, this place appeals to more than just those hard-core rag pickers who delight in eccentric dressing. It's a great browse spot and trip down memory lane: band uniforms from Carthage, Texas, tie-dyed T-shirts, out-to-there crinolines and Jackie Kennedy coats. American Rag imports much of its used clothing, sometimes in great quantity, as with the overcoats and khaki jackets. There are also some new designer items and a miniboutique that features haberdashery menswear by New Republic. This is a head-to-toe store, with new hats, shoes, gloves, jewelry and patterned socks.

Brenda Cain
1617 Montana Ave., Santa Monica 90402;
(310) 393-3298
Open Mon.-Sat. 11 a.m.-6 p.m.

When other vintage clothing stores have fallen with the changing times, Cain's sure sense of style will keep this small shop buzzing. Her Hawaiian shirts are carefully chosen and in excellent condition. She makes vests and pillows from '40s-era tablecloths and skirts from old floral-print rayon. The store is also notable for ties and collectible salt and pepper shakers. Besides clothing, you'll find exquisite antique linens, watches, Bakelite and costume jewelry and Victorian gold and sterling silver.

Cinema Glamour Shop
315 N. La Brea Ave., Melrose-La Brea District
(L.A.) 90036; (213) 933-5289
Open Mon.-Fri. 10 a.m.-4 p.m.

The clothes found here are donated by actors and actresses, and the proceeds go to the Motion Picture and Television Fund. Most of the items are slightly worn contemporary sportswear pieces, but if you're lucky, you'll visit when it receives a shipment of new clothing from design-ers or stores that have gone out of business. On our last visit, there was an excellent selection of new chiffon dresses for women and sports coats for men.

Eric and Co.
6915 Melrose Ave., Melrose-La Brea District (L.A.)
90038; (213) 938-6627
Open Mon.-Sat. noon-10 p.m., Sun. 1 p.m.-8 p.m.

Eric and Co. has some of the best prices on Melrose for leather jackets and Levi 501s. Key items for men include blazers, sunglasses, ties, Hawaiian shirts and overalls; women shouldn't miss the purses, shoes, hats, scarves and jewelry. Best of all, the recently remodeled store is clean, friendly and well-organized.

Leathers and Treasures
7511 Melrose Ave., Melrose-Fairfax District (L.A.)
90046; (213) 655-7541
Open Mon.-Sat. 11 a.m.-8 p.m., Sun. noon-7 p.m.

A flea market with four walls, offering a vast selection of vintage leather jackets from biker to bomber styles, cowboy boots, Mexican silver, rhinestone jewelry and satin-covered shoes to color-coordinate with your '40s ball gown.

Repeat Performance
318 N. La Brea Ave., Melrose-La Brea District
(L.A.) 90036; (213) 938-0609
Open Mon.-Sat. 11 a.m.-6 p.m.

Of all the vintage-clothing stores in the neighborhood, this one stocks the most well-preserved items, which explains why customers have to ring a buzzer for admittance. In the back room, there are garments and accessories that date back to the late 1800s. But the best buys are the Western Americana wear for men and women, including vintage hand-painted skirts from Mexico, '50s gabardine men's shirts and costume jewelry.

A Star Is Worn
7303 Melrose Ave., Melrose-La Brea District (L.A.)
90046; (213) 939-4922
Open Mon.-Sat. 11 a.m.-7 p.m., Sun. noon-5 p.m.

Beats us as to why, but celebrity cast-offs are hot sellers here. It's probably the only place in town where you can buy one of Cher's sequin-covered bras, for about $500. You can also find clothes formerly worn by Belinda Carlisle, Catherine Oxenberg and Prince.

Time After Time
7425 Melrose Ave., Melrose-Fairfax District (L.A.);
(213) 653-8463
Open Mon.-Fri. noon-6 p.m., Sat. 11 a.m.-7 p.m., Sun. 1 p.m.-6 p.m.

This boutique specializes in wardrobes from the golden era of cinematography. On any visit, there could be gems once worn by Marilyn Monroe, Claudette Colbert, Errol Flynn or Tyrone Power, as well as Victorian wedding dresses and petticoats, ball gowns from all eras and lots of beaded garments from the twenties. The prices don't cater to bargain hunters.

Westernwear

King's Western Wear
6455 Van Nuys Blvd., Van Nuys 91401; (818) 785-2586
Open Mon.-Thurs. & Sat. 9:30 a.m.-6 p.m., Fri. 9:30 a.m.-8 p.m.

Literally a westernwear department store, this place is paradise for cowboys and anyone else in a yahoo mood. There's a king-size selection of Stetson and Resistol hats ($35 and up), Acme boots for men and women ($79 and up), fancy buckles, tooled leather belts, authentic Western suits, embroidered shirts, square-dancing outfits, saddles and kids' clothing.

Western Frontier Establishment
Farmer's Market, 150-160 S. Fairfax Ave., Melrose-Fairfax District (L.A.) 90036; (213) 934-0146
Open Mon.-Sat. 9 a.m.-6:30 p.m., Sun. 10 a.m.-5 p.m.

Before moccasins were sold all over Paris, visiting Europeans flocked to this small store to choose from its 200-plus styles. Now they come for a fine selection of leather jackets by Avirex, Robert Comstock and Schott. Lots of Western paraphernalia and Native American crafts.

Womenswear

The Alley
8465 1/2 Melrose Alley, W. Hollywood 90069; (213) 655-1357
Open Tues.-Sat. 11 a.m.-6 p.m.

Tucked between Melrose Avenue and Melrose Place, the Alley is a salon-like setting for creations by plum California designers. Inside you'll find a sofa, cozy fireplace, coffee and cake plus Holly Harp's easy "restaurant" clothes—soft and slinky, '40s-esque styles by Bryan Emerson/Tere Tereba and chiffon and linen combos by Harriet Selwyn. Valet parking and superior service.

Ann Taylor
357 N. Camden Dr., Beverly Hills 90210; (310) 858-7840
Open Mon.-Sat. 10 a.m.-6 p.m.
1031 Westwood Blvd., Westwood 90024; (310) 208-6549
Open Mon.-Fri. 10 a.m.-9 p.m., Sat. 10 a.m.-8 p.m., Sun. 11 a.m.-6 p.m.

Many of the clean, tailored styles at this well-known national chain manage to be current and classic at the same time, and the prices are mod-

erate given the quality of the fabrics and designs. You'll find everything from leather coats to cocktail dresses, terrific collections of Joan and David shoes, and great accessories: leather gloves, wool hats, belts and socks. The Century City Shopping Center branch (10250 Santa Monica Blvd., 310-277-3041) has more for professionals; the Beverly Hills store is the largest. Most of the ten other L.A. branches are in major malls, including one in Santa Monica Place (310-395-3650).

Betsey Johnson
7311 Melrose Ave., Melrose-La Brea District (L.A.) 90046; (213) 931-4490
2929 Main St., Santa Monica 90405; (310) 452-7911
Open Mon.-Sat. 11 a.m.-7 p.m., Sun. noon-6 p.m.

Betsey Johnson is a love-her-or-hate-her designer who has been successful with her own line for twenty years. Her styles are young, and often short and tight. Frivolous little-girl dresses, skirts and shorts decked out with frills, buttons or bows are jammed onto racks next to downright-sexy dresses in stretchy lycra blends. Johnson has always had a wacky way with knits, and you're guaranteed to find leggings and body-hugging tops no matter what the season, in eye-popping prints and solids. Her seasonal sales can provide some real steals.

Charles Gallay/Gallay Melrose
8711 Sunset Blvd., W. Hollywood 90069; (310) 858-8711
Open Mon.-Sat. 9:30 a.m.-6 p.m.
7474 Melrose Ave., Melrose-Fairfax District (L.A.) 90046; (213) 653-7474
Open Mon.-Sat. 11 a.m.-8 p.m.

A monument to minimalism, Charles Gallay's Sunset Boulevard store is the antithesis of his ex-wife Madeleine's store across the street. Among the seriously stylish contents: clothing by Azzedine Alaïa, Romeo Gigli, Callaghan, Giorgio di Sant'Angelo, Norma Kamali and Isaia; shoes by Maud Frizon, Stephane Kelian and Robert Clergerie; and artful jewelry by Stephen Dweck and Tom Binns.

Le Chat
329 Manhattan Beach Blvd., Manhattan Beach 90266; (310) 545-4551
Open Mon.-Sat. 10 a.m.-6 p.m., Sun. noon-5 p.m.

This highly personal little shop is filled with soft dressing ideas and one-of-a-kind finds. The selection of casually elegant clothing includes sportswear by up-and-coming English designer Bryan Emerson, silk knits from San Francisco's Catherine Bacon and private-label jewelry, scarves and belts. Definitely worth a trip to Manhattan Beach for its highly specialized approach.

219

Eleanor Keeshan

8625 W. Sunset Blvd., W. Hollywood 90069;
(310) 657-2443
Open Mon.-Sat. 10 a.m.-6 p.m.

A well-established store for designs by Donna Karan, Valentino, Calvin Klein, Ungaro, Anne Klein II and Gianfranco Ferrè, as well as local luminaries Nancy Heller and Michele Lamy. Very good for ladies who are no longer in their twenties but who still like to dress with a little youthful pizzazz. The large eveningwear collection covers a broad price range and includes both imported couture and domestic dresses.

The Esprit Store

8491 Santa Monica Blvd., W. Hollywood 90069;
(310) 659-9797
Open Mon.-Fri. 10 a.m.-7 p.m., Sat. 10 a.m.-6 p.m., Sun. 11 a.m.-6 p.m.

No mere department store's paltry selection of Esprit goodies will do after you've seen this bowling alley turned super-store filled with nothing but Esprit. Famous for spirited sportswear (in colors that your mother always said clashed), the stock is set off against a high-tech black interior (including black shopping carts to encourage you to buy more than you can carry). From T-shirts and belts to shoes and coats, there's an entire lifestyle waiting here, including Esprit bedding in coordinating bold graphics and a book department. There's also a large children's section—it's marketed as a unisex collection, but few little boys would be duped into it. Three levels of free parking.

Fred Hayman Beverly Hills

273 N. Rodeo Dr., Beverly Hills 90210;
(310) 271-3000
Open Mon.-Sat. 10 a.m.-6:30 p.m.

See review under "Menswear," this section.

Greta

141 S. Beverly Dr., Beverly Hills 90212;
(310) 274-9217
Open Mon.-Sat. 10 a.m.-6 p.m.

Those individuals who are convinced that life (at least *fashionable* life) does not exist south of Wilshire Boulevard are missing out on a wonderful shop. Although Greta does a terrific job of buying better European sportswear (Genny, Byblos, Studio Ferrè), some of this shop's best items come from her own drawing board. An equally enticing evening selection (Vicky Tiel, Carolyne Roehm and Eva Chung, plus Greta's own) is now available at Greta Night (157 S. Beverly Dr., 310-275-3764).

Les Habitudes

101/105 N. Robertson Blvd., Beverly Hills 90048;
(310) 273-2883
Open Mon.-Sat. 11 a.m.-8 p.m.

For fans of the British avant-garde, Les Habitudes boasts individual shops for designers Martine Sitbon and John Richmond as well as furniture by Mark Brazier-Jones. His eccentric, limited edition designs in cast aluminum and bronze are quite comfortable alongside some of the most imaginative, mainly English, wearables to be found anywhere: clothing by John Galliano, Plein Sud and Vivian Westwood, shoes by Emma Hope and Lamond; wonderfully odd-shaped hats by Yvonne Rohe and corset-like confections in satin and Spandex from L'Homme Invisible.

Harari

9646 Brighton Way, Beverly Hills 90210;
(310) 859-1131
8463 Melrose Ave., W. Hollywood 90069;
(213) 655-4521
Open Mon.-Sat. 10 a.m.-6:30 p.m.

The subtly sexy, layered look is Harari's hallmark. Soft, full-cut clothing in vegetable-tone prints are accessorized with twisted sashes, velvet and fabric hats and significant pieces of jewelry with vintage overtones. Also in the Marina Marketplace (310-822-8366).

Ice

Beverly Center, Beverly & La Cienega Blvds., W. Hollywood 90048; (310) 657-4845
Open Mon.-Fri. 10 a.m.-9 p.m., Sat. 11 a.m.-8 p.m., Sun. 11 a.m.-6 p.m.

The mix is the message at Ice. Owner Juliana Claridge is one of L.A.'s most innovative retailers, stocking her store with a fire-and-ice assortment for the fashion-aware customer, from $20 T-shirts to suits by the influential Jean-Paul Gaultier. The designer roster covers the world and includes local and emerging talent. Uncommon accessories make the clothes work.

Jaeger

9699 Wilshire Blvd., Beverly Hills 90212;
(310) 276-1062
Open Mon.-Sat. 10 a.m.-6 p.m.

Nothing high-fashion or trendy in this classic English shop, but if you're after an impeccably tailored camel-hair blazer or a soft and beautiful cashmere sweater to wear with either standard wool trousers or black-leather pants, you'll find them at Jaeger.

TRAVELING IN STYLE

Some noteworthy destinations in Southern California...

TRAVELING IN STYLE

*A*s seen in **Los Angeles Times Magazine**
part II
Traveling In Style

TRAVELING IN STYLE

BABY
GUESS®
USA
WASHED ? JEANS

baby
GUESS

NEW YORK
775 MADISON AVENUE
(212) 628-2229

BEVERLY HILLS
461 N. RODEO DRIVE
(310) 274-0513

Jôna

12532 Ventura Blvd., Studio City 91604;
(818) 762-5662
1013 Swarthmore Ave., Pacific Palisades 90272;
(310) 459-4800
Open Mon.-Sat. 10 a.m.-6 p.m.

This store's motto, "At Jôna we put you together," couldn't be more appropriate. If you usually like to browse without a salesperson's assistance, this is not the place for you. Hardly any of the merchandise is actually on the floor; instead, members of the sales staff bring elegant silk and linen ensembles and dramatic cocktail dresses out from the seemingly endless stockroom and work patiently with each customer (as well they should, given the lofty prices). Most shoppers walk out with a complete wardrobe: clothing, shoes and accessories.

Laise Adzer

Beverly Center, Beverly & La Cienega Blvds., W.
Hollywood 90048; (310) 659-2813
*Open Mon.-Fri. 10 a.m.-9 p.m., Sat. 10 a.m.-8 p.m.,
Sun. 11 a.m.-6 p.m.*

Century City Shopping Center, 10250 Santa Monica
Blvd., Century City 90067; (310) 277-0785
*Open Mon.-Fri. 10 a.m.-9 p.m., Sat. 10 a.m.-6 p.m.,
Sun. 11 a.m.-6 p.m.*

The look here is big and loose: soft, earth-tone ensembles with a definite Moroccan/Middle Eastern feel. The full skirts, billowy pants, fringed shawls and roomy tops in nubby cotton and rayon all coordinate well. The perfect accessories are wide, jewel-studded belts and heavy jewelry, which the shops also sell; prices can be high.

Laura Ashley

Century City Shopping Center, 10250 Santa Monica
Blvd., Century City 90067; (310) 553-0807
*Open Mon.-Fri. 10 a.m.-9 p.m., Sat. 10 a.m.-6 p.m.,
Sun. 11 a.m.-6 p.m.*

Beverly Center, Beverly & La Cienega Blvds., W.
Hollywood 90048; (310) 854-0490
*Open Mon.-Fri. 10 a.m.-9 p.m., Sat. 10 a.m.-8 p.m.,
Sun. 11 a.m.-6 p.m.*

Everything's frilly, flowered, feminine and flounced. Since many of these little-girl dresses don't have waistbands, they make wonderful maternity dresses. In fall and winter there's usually a small but choice selection of gorgeous evening dresses in velvet and taffeta—perfect for debutantes and nightclub-goers alike. Laura Ashley also sells picture frames, address books, jewelry boxes and other gift items covered with its famous floral print cottons. The same fabrics are available by the yard and are used by its decorators for draperies, bedspreads and wall coverings. The fabrics do lend themselves to creating a lovely baby's nursery.

The Limited

Beverly Center, Beverly & La Cienega Blvds., W.
Hollywood 90048; (310) 652-2423
*Open Mon.-Fri. 10 a.m.-9 p.m., Sat. 10 a.m.-8 p.m.,
Sun. 11 a.m.-6 p.m.*

The Limited is one of Wall Street's biggest success stories, and it's easy to see why. This chain store sells its own lines of trendy sportswear at reasonable prices, and if not sophisticated, it's all fun. Look to Outback Red for romantic, English-inspired sweaters, embellished rayon blouses, jeans, jodhpurs and riding jackets. Forenza is a pseudo-Italian line of fun, active pieces, bright colors, short skirts and baggy jeans. The styles, fits and fabrics are good for the prices. Carefully thought-out accessories—belts, socks, costume jewelry—round out the collection. Also at many branches are lingerie and children's departments and a sister store, The Limited Express—fairly similar in price range—that is younger, more casual and colorful. Thirteen branches in the city, including ones in Westside Pavilion (310-475-9568), Westwood Village (310-824-2303), and Century City Shopping Center (310-553-3240).

Madeleine Gallay

8710 W. Sunset Blvd., W. Hollywood 90069;
(310) 657-9888
Open Mon.-Sat. 10 a.m.-6 p.m.

A Gallay is not a Gallay is not a Gallay, proven by this shop and its polar opposite across the street, Charles Gallay. Visit both stores (owned respectively by Madeleine Gallay and her ex-husband) and you'll agree: Charles and Madeleine have dramatically different fashion tastes. The romantic theme, from an eccentric English rose garden just outside to the petal-pink walls inside, runs throughout the shop. Unconventional European designers include Rifat Ozbek, Sybilla and John Galliano. The lighthearted (and costly) accessories are a real treat.

Maxfield

8825 Melrose Ave., W. Hollywood 90069;
(310) 274-8800
Open Mon.-Sat. 11 a.m.-7 p.m.

Fast-trackers flock to this imposing steel-and-concrete structure for the latest from Romeo Gigli, Jean-Paul Gaultier and Commes des Garçons. If you're serious about making a multi-digit purchase, a painfully stylish and generally helpful salesperson will offer you a glass of Champagne. At Maxfield it's customary to hear salespeople being paged by such callers as Geena Davis or Nancy Reagan. All in all, this is one of the city's most fascinating stores.

Mister Frank

8801 Santa Monica Blvd., W. Hollywood 90069;
(310) 657-1023
Open Tues.-Sat. 10 a.m.- 5 p.m.

In the '60s, Santa Monica Boulevard was what Melrose Avenue is today. Like the street, Mister Frank is no longer leading the fashion pack. But if TV's L.A. Law has you making a case for power suits, look no further than Mister Frank, where Eleanor Brenner and Thalia suits are purchased for actresses Susan Dey and Jill Eikenberry.

Modasport

Brentwood Gardens, 11677 San Vicente Blvd.,
Brentwood 90049; (310) 207-5514
Open Mon.-Sat. 11 a.m.-7 p.m., Sun. noon-5 p.m.
9458 Brighton Way, Beverly Hills 90210;
(310) 271-5718
2924 Beverly Glen Circle, Bel Air 90024;
(310) 475-3665
Open Mon.-Sat. 10 a.m.-6 p.m.

One of L.A.'s upper-league retailers, Modasport never ceases to inspire with a highly edited collection of stellar design talent, both local and imported. If the tight security at the Beverly Hills store is too intimidating, retreat to the smaller, friendlier Bel Air location.

Raffles

17401 Ventura Blvd., Encino 91316;
(818) 501-6782
Open Mon.-Sat. 10 a.m.-6 p.m., or by appt.

A good San Fernando Valley source for upper-crust American and European designer labels: tailored clothes, such as Zanella slacks and silk blouses, as well as the spice of a wardrobe by Michael Kors, Go Silk, Ronaldus Shamask and Byblos. Thorough attention is paid to all accessories, from footwear to jewelry.

Savannah

706 Montana Ave., Santa Monica 90403;
(310) 458-2095
Open Mon.-Sat. 10 a.m.-6 p.m.

A perpetual source of couture-quality fashion and many Westside exclusives. Two examples: a cognac-colored, scored leather picnic basket by Henri Beguelin and a geometric-patterned chenille sweater shot with metallic lurex thread by L.A.'s own Zoology.

Shauna Stein

Beverly Center, Beverly & La Cienega Blvds., W.
Hollywood 90048; (310) 652-5511
*Open Mon.-Fri. 10 a.m.-9 p.m., Sat. 10 a.m.-7 p.m.,
Sun. noon-6 p.m.*

Exquisite taste, not trends, is the driving force behind Shauna Stein's style haven. In assembling known and unknown European and American designers, she encourages customers to contrast the modern with the classic. Stein combines some of the most prestigious names in fashion, including avant-garde Italian designers Moschino, Dolce e Gabbana and Callaghan; there are also choice items from Rifat Ozbek and Norma Kamali; and a remarkable collection of shoes. Her motto: "Buy Better, Buy Less." The not-so-rich might have to buy less too, since $200 leggings and $600 minidresses aren't unusual here.

Suite 101

270 N. Cañon Dr., Beverly Hills 90210;
(310) 276-7143
Open Mon.-Sat. 10 a.m.-5:30 p.m.

Most of this salon's couture merchandise is kept in the back, so personal attention by salespeople is requisite. The stock turns over quite quickly—one week a saleswoman will show you wonderful Galanos and Bill Blass gowns, and the next week, Oscar de la Renta and Valentino suits. Many items are designed exclusively for sale here.

Theodore

453 N. Rodeo Dr., Beverly Hills 90210;
(310) 276-9691
Open Mon.-Sat. 10 a.m.-6 p.m.

A sporty yet sophisticated lineup of foreign and domestic designer clothing, presented sometimes overzealously by salespeople who work on commission. Adding to the atmosphere is the scent of Spoiled, owner Herb Fink's new fragrance. For a newer installment of the store, visit By Theodore in Brentwood Gardens.

Tracey Ross

105 S. Robertson Blvd., Beverly Hills 90048;
(310) 550-0494
Open Mon.-Sat. 11 a.m.-6 p.m.

At her celestial-themed store, Tracey Ross displays her penchant for out-of-the-ordinary clothing, accessories and personal treasures. On our last visit, we scooped up scented candles, suede flats, delicate pearl jewelry, pink faille handbags adorned with a gold snake and glamorous body care products from Annick Goutal of Paris. Any item that fits in a gold-and-white Tracey Ross hatbox makes a truly stunning gift. Fashion savories include everything from menswear jackets and Chantal Thomas bras to big-time statements by Moschino.

Designer

Agnès B.

100 N. Robertson Blvd., Beverly Hills 90048;
(310) 271-9643
Open Mon.-Sat. 11 a.m.-7 p.m., Sun. noon-6 p.m.

This French designer's store is a triple treat: womenswear, Agnès B. Homme and Agnès B. Enfant, all interconnected with a pervasive penchant for light and open space. Agnès B. is known for her expressive ways with classics. The striped fisherman's T-shirts that have been in demand for more than ten years are here, next to signature snap-front cardigans, linen suits and leather accessories.

Chanel

301 N. Rodeo Dr., Beverly Hills 90210;
(310) 278-5500
Open Mon.-Sat. 10 a.m.-6 p.m.

Among the most luxurious stores in L.A., the Chanel boutique is a gleaming interplay of crystal, black lacquer, marble and mirrors. The entire line of famous Chanel creations is here, from ready-to-wear suits to luxurious cosmetics and fragrances and, yes, those famous satin hair bows.

Eclectia

8317 Beverly Blvd., W. Hollywood 90048;
(213) 655-9806
Open Mon.-Thurs. 11 a.m.-7 p.m., Fri.-Sat. 11 a.m.-8 p.m.

Dark-stained beams, vanilla sponge-painted walls and 1930s Turkish rugs provide the backdrop for romantic, freestyle clothing on the Rated R by Biya label. After a sip of herbal tea on the tapestry sofa, it's easy to succumb to a flowing floral print dress, Italian linen jacket or a velvet-textured chenille sweater. You can also find earrings made from antique shirt studs by Toni Bennett, crystal and pearl jewelry by Lucy Issacs and hats decorated with antique laces, buttons or rosettes.

Gianni Versace

437 N. Rodeo Dr., Beverly Hills 90210;
(310) 276-6799

Leading Italian designer Gianni Versace makes his statements with bold fabrics and prints. This boutique showcases couture from his Milan design house for both men and women: classic, sophisticated cuts are given outlandish personality with lavish patterns, brilliant hues and unorthodox details in his signature fabrics of silk, wool crêpe, stretch velvet, leather and cashmere. Prices start around $800.

Giorgio Armani

436 N. Rodeo Dr., Beverly Hills 90210;
(310) 271-5555
Open Mon.-Sat. 10 a.m.-6 p.m.

This is a stunning store by all accounts, the biggest retailing effort by the kingpin of Italian design and the most talked-about store to hit Rodeo Drive in years. The interior—lacquered surfaces, gold-leaf panels, glass and steel—is as dazzling as the lineup of menswear,

womenswear, shoes, luggage, accessories, tuxedos, underwear and cashmere items.

Grau

7520 Melrose Ave., Melrose-Fairfax District (L.A.) 90046; (213) 651-0487
Open Mon.-Sat. 11 a.m.-7 p.m., Sun. noon-6 p.m.

Claudia Grau is a self-professed "fabricholic" who designs colorfully concocted women's clothing, hats and jewelry—all with a very eclectic style. Such regional fabrics as Guatemalan hand-wovens are a shop specialty. Daryl Hannah and Cher have both shopped here.

Hermès

343 N. Rodeo Dr., Beverly Hills 90210;
(310) 278-6440
Open Mon.-Sat. 10 a.m.-6 p.m.

Designed to capture the spirit of the 150-year-old house of leather in Paris, the Hermès boutique presents its celebrated handbags, luggage, attaché cases, belts, equestrian-theme silk scarves and ties, ready-to-wear for men and women and fragrances.

Jennifer Joanou

156 N. La Brea Ave., Melrose-La Brea District (L.A.) 90036; (213) 937-3693
Open Mon.-Sat. 11 a.m.-6 p.m.

Jennifer Joanou is the next best thing to a private tailor. The idea behind her working studio is to allow us more say about our purchases. Spy something you like from her collection of elegant, yet easy-wearing dresses and sportswear, and you can have it made to order in one of several luxurious fabrics. She'll even send you away with swatches to try with that jacket you've been needing a partner for. Be prepared to pay more for the almost custom creations here.

Max Studio

2712 Main St., Santa Monica 90405;
(310) 396-3963
Open Mon.-Sat. 11 a.m.-7 p.m., Sun. 11 a.m.-5 p.m.

This studio is an architectural showcase for L.A. designer Leon Max's cutting edge in comfortwear: stretchy bicycle shorts, cropped tops and little black dresses are big here. Accessories reflect Max's uncomplicated formula.

Polo Ralph Lauren

444 N. Rodeo Dr., Beverly Hills 90210;
(310) 281-7200
Open Mon.-Sat. 10 a.m.-6 p.m.

Not just a clothing and home-furnishings shop, Polo is a consumer experience, a theme park, a supplier of ready-made heritages. The interior, rather like a condensed stately private home, is replete with the trappings of the good life and old money. Lauren's womenswear collec-

223

tion, exceedingly well made from high-quality materials, mainly comprises reinterpretations of classic designs. Mannequins sport extremely tailored menswear-style tweed and gabardine suits, hand-knit sweaters, handkerchief-linen blouses, corduroy dirndls and jodhpurs; jeans and khakis fill the floor-to-ceiling shelves. Shoes and accessories are equally traditional, beautifully crafted in fine leathers. The staff is polite and helpful.

Sonia Rykiel
415 1/2 N. Rodeo Dr., Beverly Hills 90210;
(310) 273-0753
Open Mon.-Sat. 10 a.m.-6 p.m.

This polished presentation of wardrobe options from this well-known designer is ideally suited for the young executive-class woman. Sonia Rykiel's signature knits (in jersey and cotton) are found here in suits, dresses, sweaters and more. Even the sportswear (dressy sweatpants and such) is chic here, and a there's a small collection of crêpe de chine eveningwear .

Tyler Trafficante
7290 Beverly Blvd., Melrose-La Brea District (L.A.)
90036; (213) 931-9678
Open Mon.-Fri. 11 a.m.-7 p.m., Sat. noon-6 p.m., or by appt.

Since its opening in the spring of 1989, Australian-born designer Richard Tyler's art deco (by way of London) salon has been attracting rock stars, visiting Europeans, Beverly Hills professionals and anyone who loves quality and cutting-edge design. Appealing to both men and women, Tyler's tailored clothing ranges from a retro-influenced classic suit to a jacket with exaggerated details in a show-stopping shade of purple. Off-the-rack women's suits start at $950. Custom designs are available.

Ungaro
17 N. Rodeo Dr., Beverly Hills 90210;
(310) 273-1080
Open Mon.-Sat. 10 a.m.-6 p.m.

Silk fabrics, seductive fits, draped dresses and brilliant floral prints are the hallmarks of Parisian designer Emanuel Ungaro. Widely considered to be the master of the female form, Ungaro and his daring designs are not for the timid.

Urbinati & Mancini
8667 Sunset Blvd., W. Hollywood 90069;
(310) 652-3183
Open Mon.-Sat. 10 a.m.-6 p.m.

Husband and wife owners Laura Urbinati and Luca Mancini are wildly popular in Europe for their sleek, matte-cotton bathing suits in vibrant, earthy colors—as well as a full line of sultry stretch dresses, leggings, T-shirts and skirts. Upstairs in the warm, polished space, find extrava-

gant necklaces like those made famous on the Romeo Gigli runway, jeweled pareos and wonderful silk pouch purses.

Valentino
240 N. Rodeo Dr., Beverly Hills 90210;
(310) 247-0103

The Roman design house of Valentino planted this, its largest boutique worldwide, on Rodeo Drive in the fall of 1990. Valentino's dramatic style is resplendent against the marble-filled setting, from the couture and shoes for both men and women to the signature accessories: exquisite chunky jewelry, scarves and ties, racy heels for women, belts, perfume and more. The adjacent boutique holds Valentino's Oliver line, designed and priced for younger customers.

Discount

Jerry Piller's
937 E. Colorado Blvd., Pasadena 91106;
(818) 796-9559
Open Mon.-Sat. 10:30 a.m.-6 p.m.

Many first-timers walk out shaking their heads at the sheer wonder of so many women, so many garments and so many shoes. Your purse, no matter how small, will be taken from you at the door; you'll be asked to remove your shoes before entering that department. If you have an iron will and an inherent optimism you'll leave with some very handsome designerwear bought for pennies. Also, a large menswear department.

Loehmann's
6220 W. 3rd St., Melrose-Fairfax District (L.A.)
90036; (213) 933-5675
Open Mon.-Fri. 10 a.m.-9 p.m., Sat. 10 a.m.-7 p.m., Sun. noon-6 p.m.

If you can't stand sales, hate the thought of a million women crammed into one dressing room and like to browse at a leisurely pace, forget Loehmann's. But if you have the patience to carefully look through rack after rack of clothing (much of it outdated and tacky), you will be rewarded with some wonderful bargains. On our last visit, we spied Anne Klein II trenchcoats, Perry Ellis blouses and Bill Blass dresses at a fraction of what they sell for elsewhere. Loehmann's receives daily deliveries.

The Place & Co.
8820 S. Sepulveda Blvd., Westchester 90045;
(310) 645-1539
Open Mon.-Sat. 10 a.m.-5:30 p.m.

Considered the cream of L.A.'s resale crop, The Place has an outstanding selection of new and slightly used designer clothing at terrific prices. Socialites and celebrities now regularly hand their seldom-worn suits and gowns over to owner Joyce Brock, who prices them within reason. On our last visit, we spied a Chanel suit, Armani matching jacket and pants and an Ungaro dress. Most everything is current and in mint condition. The Place's close proximity to LAX makes it a worthwhile shopping layover.

Sacks Fashion Outlet (S.F.O.)
652 N. La Brea Ave., Melrose-La Brea District (L.A.) 90036; (213) 939-3993
Open Mon.-Fri. 10 a.m.-8 p.m., Sat. 10 a.m.-7 p.m., Sun. 11 a.m.-6 p.m.

David Sacks is a nut for first-rate natural fabrics, and he has a good eye for stylish bargains. The sales at SFO are among the best in town, taking down the everyday prices, which are already well below the going rates. We've spotted fashions by some top designers at substantially lower prices, and there are usually terrific buys on leather jackets and accessories. Don't miss the kids' discount outlet next door. There are several other locations, including Studio City, Tarzana, West L.A. and West Hollywood (hours vary).

Large Sizes

Eleanor Keeshan
8625 W. Sunset Blvd., W. Hollywood 90069; (310) 657-2443
Open Mon.-Sat. 10 a.m.-6 p.m.

Without a doubt, this is one of the finest lingerie selections around. Keeshan generally has a good number of pieces by Jonquil, Natori, Gemma and Jeune Europe. There are always lots of pretty, sexy nightgowns, robes, teddies, undergarments and loungewear.

The Forgotten Woman
9683 Wilshire Blvd., Beverly Hills 90212; (310) 859-8829
Open Mon.-Wed. & Fri.-Sat. 10 a.m.-6 p.m., Thurs. 10 a.m.-7 p.m.

Quite popular on the East Coast, this shop specializes in sportswear, gowns, dresses and coats for women who wear larger sizes.

Lingerie

Frederick's of Hollywood
6608 Hollywood Blvd., Hollywood 90028; (213) 466-8506
Open Mon.-Thurs. 10 a.m.-8 p.m., Fri. 10 a.m.-9 p.m., Sat. 10 a.m.-6 p.m., Sun. noon-5 p.m.

The fame of this Hollywood landmark is probably only second to that of Mann's Chinese Theatre. For L.A. locals in the know, it's *the* place for risqué lingerie. Surprisingly, much of the merchandise here is more tacky and suggestive than

kinky, and the saleswomen are friendly and charming. Many well-heeled women frequent Frederick's to purchase undergarments in sizes and styles that simply aren't available in department stores or other lingerie shops.

Lili St. Cyr
8104 Santa Monica Blvd., W. Hollywood 90069; (213) 656-6885
Open Mon.-Fri. 10 a.m.-5 p.m., Sat. 10 a.m.-4 p.m.

This shop's namesake, the grande dame of striptease, has long since retired. But her provocative bathtub act of the '50s will not soon be forgotten. Enter her private world to find boudoir ensembles, merry widows and garter stockings. Madonna buys her black bustiers here.

Lisa Norman Lingerie
1134 Montana Ave., Santa Monica 90403; (310) 451-2026
8595 Sunset Blvd., W. Hollywood 90069; (310) 854-4422
Open Mon.-Sat. 10 a.m.-6 p.m., Sun. noon-4:30 p.m. (Santa Monica only).

Norman's exquisite lingerie is just a touch sexier and more youthful than Eleanor Keeshan's, though we think the range of robes, foundations and gowns is overrated. What Norman can't find, she designs herself, notably classic tailored silks. Also a branch in Bel Air (310-475-4423).

Only Hearts
1407 Montana Ave., Santa Monica 90403; (310) 393-3088
Open Mon.-Sat. 10 a.m.-7 p.m., Sun. noon-6 p.m.

This is the retail division for New York designer Helena Stuart's "inner/outerwear." For the sleek of physique, there are cotton/Lycra bras in lipstick red, matching see-through bodysuits, Josephine Baker–style g-strings, even strapless bras covered in handmade satin rosebuds. Only slightly more demure are re-embroidered ivory net boxer shorts and cotton voile cap-shouldered gowns with netting backs and embroidered bodices.

Trashy Lingerie
402 N. La Cienega Blvd., W. Hollywood 90048; (310) 652-4543
Open Mon.-Sat. 10 a.m.-7 p.m.

Don't be intimidated by this shop's name—many of the styles are merely provocative and seductive. Owner Mitch Shrier not only carries every style of teddy, negligee, panty and the like, but has them in every color and size imaginable. You'll understand why you're charged a small "membership fee" before entering—it's to keep out voyeurs who want to catch a glimpse of the saleswomen, who are decked out in the store's merchandise.

Department Stores

Barney's New York
South Coast Plaza, 3333 Bristol Dr., Costa Mesa 92626; (714) 434-7400
Open Mon.-Fri. 10 a.m.-9 p.m., Sun. 10 a.m.-5 p.m.

This two-story version of the New York original offers the same top-of-the-line service and cream-of-the-crop merchandise, from the forward-thinking designer clothing for both men and women to the apothecary (stocked with the latest in aromatherapy, luxurious body products and perfumes), to the giftware and exclusive home-furnishings departments. Until Barney's opens its planned six-story emporium in Beverly Hills in late 1993, this is the store's only address in Southern California. Barney's chic Italian eatery, Piccola Cucina, is perfect for a bite after shopping.

The Broadway
Beverly Center, Beverly & La Cienega Blvds., W. Hollywood 90048; (310) 854-7200
Open Mon.-Sat. 10 a.m.-9 p.m., Sun. 11 a.m.-7 p.m.
Century City Shopping Center, 10250 Santa Monica Blvd., Century City 90067; (310) 277-1234
Open Mon.-Sat. 10 a.m.-9 p.m., Sun. 11 a.m.-7 p.m.

An attractive and well-stocked place to shop. Departments such as V.I.P. Sportswear feature working wardrobes by the likes of Adrienne Vittadini, Dana Buchman, Paul Stanley and Tahari. The Century City location has particularly spacious cosmetic and cookware departments. Also branches in Downtown L.A., Santa Monica, Fox Hills Mall in Culver City, and the Glendale Galleria.

Bullock's
Beverly Center, Beverly & La Cienega Blvds., W. Hollywood 90048; (310) 854-6655
Open Mon.-Sat. 10 a.m.-9 p.m., Sun. 11 p.m.-7 p.m.

Bullock's is everything you expect a department store to be—nothing more and nothing less. You won't find any innovative and spectacular departments (such as the Kiehl section at Neiman Marcus or the children's department at Saks), but you will find a good selection of merchandise in all the standard departments, from housewares to clothing, shoes to lingerie.

There are a number of Bullock's stores in the Los Angeles area, and though they're all designed around a similar form, each has its own character and does tend to carry slightly different merchandise. It varies depending on neighbor-hood: the Pasadena branch, for instance, has an air of old-money refinement, and the new store in downtown's Seventh Street Marketplace boasts exceptionally good service and excellent clothing for working men and women. Bullock's is beginning to follow Nordstrom's lead on the service front. Its "B.B.A." (Bullock's by Appointment), a private shopping-consultant service, is a winner. There's even a concierge at the South Coast Plaza branch (in Orange County) and at other selected locations. Other Bullock's in Century City, Westwood, Sherman Oaks Fashion Square, Northridge, Pasadena and Downtown L.A.

I. Magnin
9634 Wilshire Blvd., Beverly Hills 90210; (310) 271-2131
Open Mon.-Wed. & Fri.-Sat. 10 a.m.-6 p.m., Thurs. 10 a.m.-8 p.m., Sun. noon-5 p.m.

Once a lingerie merchant, I. Magnin has been in California for well over a century. The epitome of refined style, it endures today. The merchandise is usually so similar to that at Saks, it's easy to forget which store you're in—especially when you're shopping for womenswear, cosmetics, handbags and junior sportswear. However, I. Magnin's Gift Gallery and lingerie department are better stocked than those of its neighbors. There's an I. Magnin in Sherman Oaks, with a smaller selection and less expensive merchandise, and I. Magnin branches in South Coast Plaza (Orange County), the Mid-Wilshire district and Pasadena.

And downtown, the former Bullocks Wilshire (213-382-6161) is still the glorious art deco building it always was, with the ever-popular tea room. The crystal and china, stationery, bridal and better-dresses departments are still fine, perhaps better than at any other department store.

The May Company
6067 Wilshire Blvd., Wilshire District (L.A.) 90048; (213) 938-4211
Open Mon.-Fri. 10 a.m.-9 p.m., Sat. 10 a.m.-8 p.m., Sun. 11 a.m.-7 p.m.

Either you buy just about everything here (and it does have just about everything) and swear that you're saving loads of money, or else you simply refuse to walk through the doors of this Los Angeles landmark. If you wouldn't dream of buying a handbag without designer initials on it, or sheets without a signature splashed in the corner, skip The May Company altogether—not because it doesn't carry designer items (it does), but because you'll be uncomfortable with the low prices on the tags. The service is friendly once you find someone to help you. Newer locations include the Westside Pavilion, Northridge, Sherman Oaks Galleria and downtown's Seventh Street Marketplace.

Neiman-Marcus

9700 Wilshire Blvd., Beverly Hills 90210;
(310) 550-5900
Open Mon.-Sat. 10 a.m.-6 p.m.

Neiman-Marcus is like no other single department store in the world—but at the same time, it's a little bit like many of the world's most renowned. Take the avant-gardeness of Henri Bendel's, the boutiquey layout of Bloomingdale's and Galeries Lafayette, the unhurried, pleasant atmosphere of Bergdorf's, the variety (well, almost) of Harrod's and the ostentation of this store's home state, Texas, and you've got Neiman-Marcus. Though this famous department store has been nicknamed "Needless Markup," you won't find merchandise here that's more expensive than elsewhere—it's just that Neiman carries some more exclusive and pricey items. The standard departments (womenswear, menswear, childrenswear, cosmetics, lingerie and housewares) are unsurprising but reasonably well stocked; the best departments are the small ones that feature Kiehl's pharmaceutical products, Fendi furs, and handbags and sportswear by Donna Karan. Special mention should be made, too, of the impressive Armani boutique, the huge women's shoe department (with the best of Frizon, Pfister and Jourdan) and the sinful fine-chocolate counter. There's another Neiman-Marcus in Newport Beach's Fashion Island.

Nordstrom

Westside Pavilion, 10830 Pico Blvd., W.L.A. 90064;
(310) 470-6155
Open Mon.-Fri. 10 a.m.-9:30 p.m., Sat. 10 a.m.-8 p.m., Sun. 11 a.m.-6 p.m.

Seattle-based Nordstrom started out as a shoe store, expanded into men's, women's and children's clothing and has taken California by storm. Nordstrom doesn't get distracted with housewares, food, furniture and the like; it offers only things you put on your body, from shoes and clothes to jewelry and cosmetics. Two key qualities have brought Nordstrom its tremendous success: unrivalled selection and near-perfect service. Salespeople are exceptionally helpful without being pushy; don't be surprised if you receive a personal thank-you note from the salesperson who helped you put together that great new outfit. The return policy here is legendary: if you are unhappy with your merchandise, at any time or for any reason, it will be cheerfully accepted for return, no questions asked.

The selection is exceptional—in fact, it's almost too much to absorb. There is an incredible array of women's shoes in every imaginable style, color and size (size 11's know to come here); a good offering of classic men's shoes; trendy clothes for young men; very tasteful, more conservative clothes for grown-up men; children's clothes in all price ranges; and many departments of womenswear, from the fun play clothes in the Brass Plum to the classic sportswear in The Individualist to such fashion contemporaries as Karl Logan, Michele Lamy and Vakko leather in Savvy. Nordstrom carries such international designer stars as Ungaro, Gianfranco Ferrè, Isaac Mizrahi and Umberto Ginocchietti in addition to mainstays Ralph Lauren, Liz Claiborne, Esprit, Cole-Haan and Cricketeer. Other locations include the Glendale Galleria, South Coast Plaza (Orange County), the Galleria at South Bay and Topanga Plaza.

Robinson's

9900 Wilshire Blvd., Beverly Hills 90210;
(310) 275-5464
Open Mon.-Fri. 10 a.m.-9 p.m., Sat. 10 a.m.-7 p.m., Sun. 11 a.m.-5 p.m.

Now that Robinson's is owned by May Company, the merchandise assortment is not what it was a few years ago. The recently remodeled men's department is still strong, carrying such labels as Ralph Lauren, Perry Ellis Portfolio and Liz Claiborne. We found Mary Ann Restivo and Anne Klein in the designer women's area, and the store carries Giorgio Armani for both men and women. The Pacesetter shop caters to contemporary clotheshorses with such names as Leon Max and Christian de Castelnau. The home-furnishings department features Waterford and Baccarat crystal. There's a restaurant (on the fourth level), a café and a better-than-average candy counter. Unfortunately, you won't find the salespeople jumping to attention when you need them, either on the phone or in person. Other locations include Santa Monica, downtown L.A., Sherman Oaks Galleria, Woodland Hills Promenade, South Coast Plaza (Orange County) and most major shopping centers.

Saks Fifth Avenue

9600 Wilshire Blvd., Beverly Hills 90210;
(310) 275-4211
Open Mon.-Wed. & Fri.-Sat. 10 a.m.-6 p.m., Thurs. 10 a.m.-8:30 p.m., Sun. noon-5 p.m.

Those on the inside track know Saks as *the* designer department store. In addition to all the major European and American designers, Saks is home to a Chanel boutique and an exclusive Adolfo boutique. Designer collections are even

227

launched in the children's department, the latest of which was Taki, designed by the wife of the president of Anne Klein. Saks also excels in layette and related maternity items. A good source for hats, fine and antique jewelry, small leather goods and cosmetics. By all means attend Saks's sales, which are usually exceptional. The pleasant café on the fifth level features an espresso bar.

Flowers

Broadway Florists
750 W. 7th St., Downtown (L.A.) 90013;
(213) 626-5516
Open Mon.-Fri. 8:30 a.m.-6 p.m., Sat. 9 a.m.-noon.

Broadway is one of the biggest and friendliest florists in town. The Stathatos family has been running this business for more than 70 years, and despite its large size, the service remains remarkably personal. Broadway does the flowers for many of the major weddings and society affairs in town and has been decorating the Academy Awards for years; the designs are more classic than avant-garde, and they are truly beautiful. The downtown shop is located in a pretty grim neighborhood, so it does a great deal of telephone business.

Campo Dei Fiori
648 N. Martel Ave., Hollywood 90036;
(213) 655-9966
Open Mon.-Fri. 9 a.m.-8 p.m., Sat.-Sun. 11 a.m.-5 p.m.

Stepping into this shop just off Melrose Avenue is a complete visual experience—from the stark, architectural surroundings to the stylized arrangements wrapped in unusual papers and tied with raffia. Flowers are of the uncommon and hard-to-get variety—here's where you'll find imported French ivory tulips at $7 apiece. There's a superb selection of vases in the modernist vein: materials are lightweight concrete, glass, terra-cotta and black slate. You'll also find cacti at competitive prices.

The Flower Basket
12244 Ventura Blvd., Studio City 91604;
(818) 985-1055
Open Mon.-Sat. 9 a.m.-5 p.m.

A large, homey shop that designs exotic arrangements in baskets, bottles and Oriental bowls. Most of the flowers are imported from Holland or France. Since The Flower Basket makes up numerous custom orders, it doesn't keep a lot of flowers in stock for walk-in customers, so always call ahead to ask about what's available.

The Flower Shop
616 N. Almont Dr., W. Hollywood 90069;
(310) 274-8491
Open Mon.-Fri. 8:30 a.m.-4 p.m., Sat. by appt.

Clifford Miller of The Flower Shop has a well-deserved reputation for lovely, unusual and imaginative floral gift ideas. To name just two: an antique perfume flask from Miller's collection, filled with delicate lilies of the valley, the stopper connected by a satin ribbon. Or, a brocade-covered box filled with fresh mixed rose petals for scattering on sheets or wherever one desires.

Jill Roberts/Ethereal
8625 Melrose Ave., W. Hollywood 90069;
(310) 855-0229
Open Mon.-Sat. 10 a.m.-5 p.m.

The walls of this aromatic shop are lined with botanical art—compact, hedgelike arrangements in the European tradition of dried flowers, herbs and grains. In addition to Roberts's regular stock (Italian wheat, French lavender and roses from the Netherlands), there are stunning topiaries, in hand woven willow baskets and in powdered stone pottery containers embedded with pieces of tile.

Los Angeles Flower Market
754 Wall St., Downtown (L.A.) 90014;
(213) 622-1966
Open Mon.-Sat. dawn-2 p.m.

Even though these wholesalers do most of their selling to the trade, any customer with cash is welcome to take advantage of the incredible bargains, by phone or in person. Taken as a whole, the street offers more, fresher, better and cheaper than any ten florists in town: elegant lilies, stately pink ginger and halyconia and bundles of country-fresh delphiniums and protea. Prices are one-third to one-half of those in neighborhood florists. Besides exotic flowers, the stalls sell such workhorse flowers as mums and roses, indoor plants, dried greenery (such as curly bamboo), silk flowers and willow baskets. Both sides of the street are lined with stalls that sometimes spill onto the sidewalk. Savvy shoppers know to arrive as early as possible, to make snap decisions and to wear rubber-soled shoes (there's muck everywhere).

My Son the Florist
620 1/2 S. La Brea Ave., Melrose-La Brea District (L.A.) 90036; (213) 935-2912
Open Mon.-Fri. 9 a.m.-5 p.m.

One of our favorites, My Son the Florist is a reasonably priced, great all-purpose florist for contemporary tastes. They design romantic nosegays, rosegays, English garden bouquets, sprawling arrangements of delicate seasonal flowers and angular, geometric designs using Hala leaves, corkscrew willow and bold singular blooms—all with equal aplomb.

Silver Birches
180 E. California Blvd., Pasadena 91105;
(818) 796-1431
Open Mon.-Sat. 9 a.m.-5 p.m.

Silver Birches is a first-rate florist that approaches floral arranging as an art form. Designs are created according to the specifications of the top-drawer clientele, to make a statement, from exotic to English garden to classic. Moss, rocks, branches and other natural or unusual materials are often combined with high-quality flowers in containers designed specially for the shop.

The Solarium
2922 Beverly Glen Circle, Bel Air 90077;
(310) 274-7900
Open Mon.-Sat. 9 a.m.-5 p.m.

This is a full-service florist housed in spacious white surroundings that encourage a leisurely stroll. The Solarium creates uncluttered and striking arrangements with rare imported tropical and European flowers. It specializes in custom wedding parties and event planning.

Stanley R. Kersten Flowers and Service
734 S. San Julian St., Downtown (L.A.) 90014;
(213) 622-2261
Open Mon.-Sat. 8 a.m.-4 p.m.

Located in the Los Angeles Flower Mart, Kersten always has the freshest and most exotic arrangements. Recommended if you like an airy floral design with lots of long twigs. Popular among Beverly Hills hostesses, all of whom call in their orders (as do most of Kersten's clientele). The minimum order for delivery is $45, plus a charge of $5 to $10 extra.

Food

Bakeries & Pâtisseries

Viktor Benes Continental Pastries
8718 W. 3rd St., W. Hollywood 90048;
(310) 276-0488
Open Mon.-Sat. 6 a.m.-6 p.m.

At 5:59 a.m., early-morning risers from around the neighborhood are waiting outside Benes's door to buy loaves of bread and delicious cheese danish. The Linzertorte, Parisian cream cakes, and "alligators" (pecan coffee cake) are also worth getting out of a warm bed for.

Bread Only
148 S. La Brea Ave. (inside Maison et Café), Melrose-La Brea District (L.A.) 90036; (213) 936-5530
Open Mon.-Sat. 9 a.m.-6 p.m.

Tucked away in a corner of Maison et Café kitchen-and-furnishings shop is some of the best bread in L.A. This is the place to find earthy peasant breads baked according to centuries-old recipes used in the Southern French countryside. The first (and so far only) retail shop run by Bread Only, which supplies a large number of the city's best restaurants and hotels, this bakeshop/café sells *campaillou* (an outstanding dark bread with a rough, chewy crust) and country bread variously flavored with dill, rosemary, herb-marinated black olives, sun-dried tomatoes, curry, apricots, figs and so on. There's also an espresso bar and mini Parisian-style café serving buttery croissants, fruit tarts and heavenly napoleons, as well a simple menu of sandwiches and salads. A popular stop for weary La Brea Avenue shoppers.

Breadworks
7961 W. 3rd St., 90048; (213) 930-0047
Open Mon.-Sat. 8 a.m.-6 p.m. or until the bread runs out.

From the team who created Indigo, that small, chic Third Street restaurant, comes Breadworks. Chef Tony DiLembo offers an eclectic collection of contemporary and traditional breads and rolls, including rosemary-herb, sun-dried tomato and basil, olive, sour corn-rye, jalapeño-Cheddar cheese, brioche, honey and sunflower whole wheat (our favorite) and onion-bacon bread. All the breads are competent, though we'd love to see more of a crust on all the varieties. Worth checking out are the foccacia bread topped like a pizza, (sold by the slice or by the pan), and bags of biscotti, all very reasonably priced.

Brio Bakery
18663 Ventura Blvd., Tarzana 91356;
(818) 609-7701
Open Mon.-Sat. 9 a.m.-6 p.m.

The popular Brio, adjacent to Brio Restaurant, is the Valley's most ambitious bakery to date. Some of the breads were created by former La Brea Bakery baker-consultant Carl Miller, but don't expect breads of La Brea's caliber: because the valley clientele preferred their bread lighter in texture than westsiders, the recipes were adjusted accordingly. Over fourteen types of bread are offered, from baguettes to garlic-cheese bread. There are also terrific jalapeño-Cheddar rolls, soft and chewy chocolate chip cookies, a sweet bread pudding (made with cake instead of bread), as well as brownies and pastries, all at very affordable prices.

La Brea Bakery

624 S. La Brea Ave., Melrose-La Brea District (L.A.)
90036; (213) 939-6813
Open daily 8 a.m.-4 p.m.

Campanile coproprietor (and former Spago pastry chef) Nancy Silverton bakes and sells some of the most talked-about breads in town. Arrive early (most everything sells out by early afternoon) and be prepared to spend some money for her crusty, distinctly flavored breads: fabulous rye-currant (we love it toasted) and rolls, Greek olive, walnut, whole-grain, chocolate cherry, and many more. Many of L.A.'s best restaurants serve these hearty, healthy and expensive breads.

The Buttery

2906 Main St., Santa Monica 90405;
(310) 399-3000
Open Mon. 7 a.m.-noon, Tues.-Sun. 7 a.m.-6 p.m.

Before chocolate-chip cookie and croissant stores started springing up on every L.A. corner, people would line up outside The Buttery, waiting to buy its soft, chewy cookies, buttery croissants, cakes and breads. The cookies and croissants are still as popular as ever, but homemade cinnamon rolls, coffee cakes, muffins and gingerbread have replaced the cakes and breads. If you're lucky and it's not too busy, you'll be able to grab one of the four seats and enjoy a cup of freshly brewed coffee with your selection.

Cake and Art

8709 Santa Monica Blvd., W. Hollywood 90069;
(310) 657-8694
Open Mon.-Sat. 10 a.m.-6 p.m.

Celebrating the birthday of a cat-lover, car freak or movie buff? Cake and Art will produce a cake in the shape of *anything*. This shop has been catering to a show-biz clientele for more than a decade. Among Cake and Art's feats are the gigantic Greek Theater to feed 500 for its 60th anniversary and a four-foot-long dolphin-shaped cake for the KABC *Earthday Special*. The cakes (chocolate fudge and lemon carrot are the only flavors) may not send your gourmet friends running for seconds, but they're sure to get a laugh. Prices range from $15 to $5,000.

The Cakeworks

117 N. La Brea Blvd., Melrose-La Brea District
(L.A.) 90036; (213) 934-6515
Open Tues.-Sat. 10 a.m.-6:30 p.m.

Diane Jacobs' art and architecture studies combined with her love of baking led her to open this small shop—a veritable gallery of edible art available in five flavors. From cake portraits to cake sculptures, no face, shape, or size is too difficult for her or partner Charles Jacob to tackle. They've created edible typewriters, a three-dimensional still life of fruit, cheese and wine, and for the 50th Anniversary of *The Wizard of Oz*, a yellow-brick-road cake replete with Dorothy and friends for MGM Home Video. Twelve books cataloguing the shop's work are on the premises. Prices start at $30 and orders must be placed one to two weeks in advance.

La Conversation

2118 Hillhurst Ave., Los Feliz 90027;
(213) 666-9000
Open Mon.-Thurs. 7:30 a.m.-7 p.m., Fri.-Sat. 7:30 a.m.-10 p.m., Sun 8 a.m.-2:30 p.m.

When you try one of La Conversation's croissants, you too will become a regular patron, even if you don't live in the area. People come to this tiny French shop from all over town, for the fresh-daily buttery croissants, the marvelous Italian-cheese-and-spinach torte, the rich chocolate cake and the many unusual and delicious cookies and minitarts. The few tables crammed into the shop are packed on weekends.

La Crème de la Crème

3562 Sepulveda Blvd., Manhattan Beach 90266;
(310) 416-9199
Open Mon.-Sat. 7 a.m.-6 p.m., Sun. 8 a.m.-4 p.m.

This charming little café serves excellent pastries and light luncheon foods, all prepared on the premises and served indoors or on the small patio adjacent to the Manhattan Village cinema. Try the pain almond that nearly melts in your mouth, the delicate pain raisin, any of the delicious tarts and cakes (strawberry charlotte, Black Forest cherry cake and fruit tarts, among others, are also served by the slice). The pastas and layered tortes are also quite good.

Emil's Swiss Pastry

1751 Ensley Ave., Century City 90024;
(310) 277-1114
Open Tues.-Sat. 7 a.m.-5:30 p.m.
1567 Barry Ave., W.L.A. 90025; (310) 820-2666
Open Mon. 7 a.m.-4 p.m., Tues.-Sat. 7:30 a.m.-5:30 p.m.

With their flaky crusts, rich custards and assorted fresh fruits, Emil's tarts are legendary. These baked treats have such tempting fillings as prune, apricot and Italian plum. A popular party request is Emil's fresh-fruit sponge cake, the layers of which are filled with whipped cream and custard, bananas, grapes and whole strawberries, encased in a clear plastic "collar."

Il Fornaio

1627 Montana Ave., Santa Monica 90403;
(310) 458-1562
Open Mon.-Fri. 6:30 a.m.-6:30 p.m., Sat. 7 a.m.-6:30 p.m., Sun. 7:30 a.m.-4 p.m.

The array of authentic Italian breads is outstanding (more than 25 varieties), and many of them are difficult to find anywhere else. You'll find Il Fornaio's breads at better restaurants all over California, though we must say we find many of their loaves to be extraordinarily salty. Among the most popular pastries are the bran muffins, blueberry muffins and cannèlla (cinnamon twists). The bakery's Caffè e Kiosko downtown (639 W. 5th St., 213-623-8400) sells many of the chain's baked goods, as well as soups, salads and sandwiches. The Beverly Hills location (301 N. Beverly Dr.) had just closed at press time; by fall of 1992 it should re-open as a spiffy restaurant and attached bakery.

Hansen Cakes

193 S. Beverly Dr., Beverly Hills 90212; (310) 272-0474
Open Tues.-Fri. 10 a.m.-6 p.m., Sat. 9 a.m.-5 p.m.

Something of an L.A. legend, Hansen creates exquisitely designed (but intentionally flavorless) cakes in almost any shape (for more daring shapes, go to Cakeworks or Cake and Art). Downstairs is a whole roomful of wedding cakes that will take your breath away. There's a larger branch on 1072 S. Fairfax Avenue (213-936-5527), and another in Tarzana (18432 Ventura Blvd., 818-708-1208).

L.A. Desserts

113 N. Robertson Blvd., Beverly Hills 90211; (310) 273-5537
Open Mon.-Sat. 10 a.m.-5 p.m.

This aromatic bakery, a sister to the super-chic Ivy restaurant next door, is one of our favorites. L.A. Desserts makes *everything* by hand, including wonderful chocolate-chip cookies with hazelnuts and almonds, New England anadama bread with a touch of homemade molasses and a sugar-free fresh raspberry pie topped with an old-fashioned latticework crust. The eight-inch white-chocolate lemon cakes decorated with flowers and berries from the owner's garden are breathtaking ($25 undecorated, $47 with flowers) and delicious. Probably the best chocolate cake in the city is their fudge-chocolate cake. For a real treat try the "baby cake" version, which is just perfect for two ($7). It's best to order in advance, though there's usually a dazzling assortment on hand.

> *For listings of more than 60 cafés, many of which offer full menus as well as coffee, pastries and goodies to go, see also "LOS ANGELES Bargain Bites."*

Mäni's Bakery

519 S. Fairfax Ave., Fairfax District (L.A.) 90036; (213) 938-8800
Open Mon.-Thurs. 7:30 a.m.-11:30 p.m., Fri. 7:30 a.m.-12:30 a.m., Sat. 8 a.m.-12:30 a.m., Sun. 8 a.m.-10:30 p.m.

You can have your cake and eat it too with baker Mäni Niall's elegant yet healthy desserts. Offering a wide variety of products made with unrefined sugars and a minimum amount of fats and oils, Mäni's best known for his "faux nuts" (originally created for actor Danny DeVito), which are baked donuts available in six flavors. The fat-free dessert line includes, muffins (banana and carrot-pineapple) and tortes (fresh apple-raspberry, rhubarb and peach) with a crunchy oatmeal-meringue topping. Also terrific are the non-dairy mousses and hand-rolled, chocolate truffle-cream cupcakes, cocoa dusted, mocha almond and chunky pecan truffles ($1.25 to $1.50).

The Melrose Baking Company

7356 Melrose Ave., Melrose-La Brea District (L.A.) 90046; (213) 651-3165
Open Sun.-Thurs. 7:30 a.m.-midnight, Fri.-Sat. 7:30 a.m.-2 a.m.

One of the first of the early '90s wave of serious European-style bakeries to come to L.A., Melrose Baking Company had European Master Bakers develop its German-style line of breads. The "German" means that these breads are dense and meaty; among the most regular flavors are rosemary, walnut, olive and sourdough, both in loaf form and in rolls. Call first if you want to custom-order any of this wholesale bakery's other flavors: sun-dried tomato, rye, multi-grain, walnut-raisin and so on. One tasty innovation: in addition to the usual two-pound loaves, single diners or those who want to taste-test can take home one of the mini half-pound loaves. The charming Vienna Café also serves a Mediterranean menu from morning until night.

Michel Richard

310 S. Robertson Blvd., Beverly Hills 90211; (310) 275-5707
Open Mon.-Sat. 8 a.m.-10 p.m., Sun. 9 a.m.-3 p.m.

An assortment of neighborhood citizenry, from Hollywood types and Robertson Boulevard decorators to young mothers with babies and groups of French-speaking locals, start their day here with buttery croissants, pain au chocolat or brioche and café au lait. The cakes and pastries are true works of art, although some might find them a little too rich (as are the prices).

Miss Grace Lemon Cake Co.

422 N. Cañon Dr., Beverly Hills 90210;
(310) 274-2879
16571 Ventura Blvd., Encino 91436;
(818) 995-1987
Both branches open Mon.-Sat. 10 a.m.-5:30 p.m.

Of the conventional, home-style bundt cakes available in over thirteen flavors, the best are the lemon and chocolate. Layer and sheet cakes are also available. Miss Grace ships gift baskets (filled with a variety of cookies, miniature muffins and mini loaves) anywhere in the country.

Mrs. Beasley's

19572 Ventura Blvd., Tarzana 91356;
(818) 344-7845
Open Mon.-Sat. 8:30 a.m.-5:30 p.m.

Mrs. Beasley's old-fashioned baked goods are oh-so American, and oh-so satisfying. Each gift basket or tin is filled with a luscious assortment of various flavored plump minimuffins or tea cakes, heavenly cookies and brownies that manage to be both light and rich at the same time. Phone orders can be sent anywhere in the United States or delivered throughout Los Angeles. Other locations in Sherman Oaks, Beverly Hills and in the Fred Segal store in Santa Monica.

Nicolosi's

17540 Ventura Blvd., Encino 91316;
(818) 789-0922
Open Tues.-Sat. 9 a.m.-6 p.m., Sun. 9 a.m.-3 p.m.

For the past 26 years, Valleyites have flocked to Nocolosi's for traditional Italian and French pastries and desserts, the best of which are the cannoli, panettone (available year-round), rum cakes, napoleons, éclairs and gâteaux Saint-Honorés. Try to get to Nicolosi's before 1 p.m.; by then, the most popular pastries are usually long gone.

Old Town Bakery

166 W. Colorado Blvd., Pasadena 91105;
(818) 792-7943
Open Sun.-Thurs. 8 a.m.-11 p.m., Fri.-Sat. 8 a.m.-midnight.

Old Town Bakery excels in imaginative, freshly baked offerings to take home. There are homey fresh-fruit pies with latticework tops, fresh-fruit shortcakes, presentation desserts such as the chocolate-and-vanilla striped "zebra cake" and on and on. Most of the breads (including wheat-walnut, olive, pumpkin and rosemary) are disappointing—owner/baker Amy Pressman's strong point is her desserts. The triangular bittersweet-chocolate terrine decorated with gold leaf makes a stunning birthday cake. There are also great gift-basket possibilities. Prices are reasonable.

Old Vienna Strudel Company

10836 1/2 Washington Blvd., Culver City 90232;
(310) 280-0282
Open Tues.-Fri. noon-6 p.m., Sat., 11 a.m.-6 p.m.

Without question, Nick Teichtmann sells the best strudel in town. Arnold Schwarzenegger, his mother and any caterer who knows his stuff buy this delectable Viennese pastry from the small, unadorned storefront that serves as a retail store and a wholesale bakery. Filled with cinnamon-laced fresh Pippin apples, walnuts and raisins, the handmade strudel is made with layers of flaky hand-stretched dough that has been "painted" with melted butter. An added bonus is the surprisingly low calorie count: 160 calories for a generous three-and-a-half-ounce serving. There is also a diabetic version. Strudel by the slice costs $1.50; by the whole is $13.50 (serves ten to fourteen).

Pioneer Boulangerie

2012 Main St., Santa Monica 90405;
(310) 399-7771
Open Mon.-Sat. 7 a.m.-8 p.m., Sun. 7 a.m.-7:30 p.m.

This deli, restaurant and bakery is jammed on Sunday mornings and at lunchtime when the weather is warm. Most of its pastries are less than satisfactory; the sourdough and French breads are always fresh and consistent, though lacking in character. Pioneer's enormous wholesale bakery in Venice serves many a restaurant, hotel and caterer throughout California. A new line of fancy breads, including a fiery jalapeño sourdough, have recently been added. Hours vary with the season.

Röckenwagner

2435 Main St., Santa Monica 90405;
(310) 399-6504
Open Tues.-Fri. 8 a.m.-5 p.m., Sat.-Sun. 9 a.m.-4:30 p.m.

Set in the Frank Gehry-designed Edgemar Complex, Röckenwagner is the bakery within the much-loved French Röckenwagner restaurant. Master baker Dietmar Eilbacher, whom Hans imported from Munich, turns out very good, traditional German whole-grain breads: five grain, rye, poppyseed and so on. These sit alongside the not-so-traditional Rudolph Steiner "Health Bread," red-pepper, leek-and-corn, sauerkraut and flax-seed loaves—all reasonably priced from $2.75 to $5.50 each. Specialties include kranzel—a crown of rolls made from a variety of breads, Christmas stollen, poppyseed coffee cake, and a savory zweibelkuchen (German onion tart).

Snookie's Cookies
1753 Victory Blvd., Glendale 91201;
(818) 502-2013
Open Mon.-Fri. 9 a.m.-6 p.m., Sat. 10 a.m.-3 p.m.

Snookie's chocolate-chip cookies are some of the best we've tasted: warm, moist, chock-full of chips and not overly sweet. Better yet, they'll deliver warm cookies and milk on ice just about anywhere in L.A. or Orange County. Brownies, muffins, a variety of other cookies and pain au chocolat are also popular items that fill their gift baskets.

Sweet Lady Jane
8360 Melrose Ave., W. Hollywood 90069;
(213) 653-7145
Open Mon.-Sat. 8:30 a.m.-11:30 p.m.

Everything at this European-style café and bakery, from simple scones and brownies to dreamy and complicated desserts, is made from the freshest ingredients. Sweet Lady Jane is acclaimed for its cheesecakes and lemon-meringue tarts and can put together beautiful gift baskets. Don't miss the English fruitcakes with "royal icing" during the holidays.

Weby's Bakery
12131 Ventura Blvd., Studio City 91604;
(818) 769-6062
Open Mon.-Sat. 7 a.m.-7 p.m., Sun. 7 a.m.-6 p.m.

Weby's has been a Valley institution for over 25 years. The cookies and layer cakes are passable, but the bagels, breads, coffee cakes, strudels and chocolate-chip rolls are superb. Weby's specializes in French-style seven-inch cakes with fresh fruit and whipped cream ($7 to $14.50). The bakery is always crowded in the morning, and by midafternoon the display cases are almost empty.

Caterers & Party Planning

Akasha's Vegetarian Cuisine
1716 S. Robertson Blvd., L.A. 90035;
(310) 201-0429

Akasha Khalsa caters the best vegetarian cuisine you'll ever eat. No one would ever guess her scrumptious recipes are also low-fat and contain no saturated fats, sugar, meat or eggs. Along with her party food, three days a week, she offers complete meals for home delivery from a continuously changing menu that might include spicy Chinese eggplant, lentil-vegetable soup, pineapple upside-down cake. An adherent of the Indian Sikh religion, Akasha often uses herbs and Indian healing recipes. Her clientele has included such stars as Carrie Fisher, Barbra Streisand and Michael Jackson.

Along Came Mary
5265 W. Pico Blvd., Wilshire District (L.A.) 90019;
(213) 931-9082

Mary Micucci is famous for her delicious food and full-scale catered extravaganzas, primarily for the movie industry. She and the staff attend to every detail—from the food and service to the decor, transportation and theme-attired serving staff. Renowned for its custom themes, Along Came Mary offers a diverse selection of dishes, including regional American and international cuisine. Unique event sites—from yachts to museums to mansions—are a specialty.

Ambrosia
1717 Stewart St., Santa Monica 90404;
(310) 392-8547

No party is too large or too small for David Corwin and Carl Bendix's full-service catering company. Frequently mentioned in the *Los Angeles Times*'s exclusive society column, Ambrosia is responsible for some of the most imaginative food and party themes in the city. For those with smaller budgets, Ambrosia to Go will prepare hot and cold hors d'oeuvres and casseroles with just two days' notice. The company will plan and oversee any size of corporate extravaganza anywhere in the country.

Creative Gourmet Cooking
18787 Tulsa St., Northridge 91326; (818) 360-9107

Carol Ritter has been catering teas, fashion shows and other corporate events for Saks Fifth Avenue in the Valley and I. Magnin for years. She has a large clientele from the entertainment industry as well. Ritter loves dinner parties for eight, but is just as comfortable planning a large-scale special event as she is with a tête-à-tête for two. Ask about her miniature fresh fruit tarts, fruited cheesecakes and chocolate desserts.

Duck, Duck Mousse
20848 Pacific Coast Hwy., Malibu 90265;
(213) 930-1344, (310) 456-0744

Whether it's a box lunch for 25 or a party backstage at the Greek Theater (where Duck, Duck Mousse is the regular caterer), the food from this company is not only good but beautifully presented. Like so many caterers and restaurants these days, Duck Duck Mousse calls its food "eclectic" combining Spanish tapas with Southwestern nibbles with Italian dishes for an evening's spread. Not only does the crew go to great lengths to design props, they have their own, fitting every description imaginable. Clients are both corporate and private, and they'll do anything from intimate dinner parties to soirées for up to two thousand guests.

233

Elite Cuisine

7119 Beverly Blvd., Fairfax District (L.A.) 90036;
(213) 930-1303
*Open Sun.-Thurs. 11 a.m.-9 p.m., Fri. 9 a.m. until 1
hour before sundown.*

Elite is a kosher restaurant, a catering company
(for kosher bar mitzvahs and bat mitzvahs, weddings, political fundraisers and conventions) in
both private homes and religious halls, and a
take-out service. Recognizing that her customers
worry about cholesterol and weight as well as
keeping kosher, owner Pat Fine, an Orthodox
Jew who loves good food, has brought kosher
cooking into the twentieth century with a fine
repertoire. Offerings include stuffed breast of
chicken with spinach and pimiento sauce, and
rack of veal with a peppercorn sauce.

Good Gracious

5714 1/2 Pico Blvd., Wilshire District (L.A.) 90019;
(213) 934-8225

Britisher Pauline Parry and partner Karen
Marquez love to show off elaborate desserts that
need preparation during the meal, so they'll do
intimate dinners for as few as eight people, and
grand affairs for as many as 20,000 revelers. Very
popular with corporate clients are their English
teas, for which they prepare their own preserves
to go along with shortbreads, elaborate tea cakes
and reasonably priced teas.

Julienne

2649 Mission St., San Marino 91108;
(818) 441-2299
*Open Mon., Wed. & Fri. 8 a.m.-6 p.m., Tues. & Thurs.
8 a.m.-9 p.m., Sat. 8 a.m.-5 p.m.*

After years of catering weddings and parties in
the San Marino/Pasadena area, the buzz on Julienne reached the westside, and now Sue
Campoy and her able crew cook for the many
people—from San Marino to Santa Monica—
who have become addicted to her deeply satisfying French country cooking. Before you decide
on a menu, visit the romantic take-out shop/café
to sample the many treats for breakfast, lunch,
tea or early dinner.

Nicole Cottrell Productions

876 W. 16th St., Newport Beach 92663;
(714) 642-6339

From her Orange County headquarters, Nicole Cottrell creates swell parties for twenty or
more, for a great many corporate clients
throughout Southern California. She brings five
years of experience as director of catering at the
Music Center and head chef at Château La Car-
elle in Burgundy, France to her party planning.
Her four-inch pillow ravioli filled with duck or
wild mushrooms always have the crowd oohing

and ahing. Her new line of products, under the
label of Nicole's Catering Ideas, is now in most
supermarkets: look for her crostinis and layered
fresh cheese pâté.

Sheila Mack Gourmet Cooking

1116 N. Crescent Heights Blvd., W. Hollywood
90046; (213) 656-5897

If you're looking for a caterer/party designer
who specializes in real food with a Californian
French country twist, Sheila is the one to call.
Her recipes are well respected, particularly such
dishes as salmon with grilled onion confit or
pesto and tenderloin of beef with pistachios and
a zinfandel reduction. Her "chocolate essence"
brownies draw raves—and rightfully so.

Someone's in the Kitchen

5973 Reseda Blvd., Tarzana 91536; (818) 343-5151

Owner Joann Roth is a stickler for service and
organization, and she'll ask you lots of questions.
Once you get through the interview, your party
will be pulled together flawlessly by Joann and
her crew, whether its a medium-size or a grand-
scale event. She loves to cater children's parties.
Sandwiches are cut into animal shapes, burgers
are mini-size and entertainment is designed not
overwhelm.

Somerset

8992 National Blvd., L.A. 90034; (310) 204-4000

Owners Michael Prud'homme (yes, a third
cousin to well-known Paul) and Hallee Gould are
known for their imaginative themes. They love
doing big events, from large cocktail parties to
sit-down dinners. To get an idea of their work,
try an opening at MOCA or LACMA—Somerset
is usually the caterer. The "Set-to-Go" menu is
perfect for those giving small dinner parties at
home or the office.

Village Catering

139 1/2 N. Larchmont Blvd., Larchmont Village
90004; (213) 465-6175
Open Mon.-Fri. 9 a.m.-6 p.m., Sat. 9 a.m.-5 p.m.

Daryl Trainor's down-home back-to-basics
cooking tantalizes her take-out and catering clientele. She'll whip up a terrific picnic of barbecued ribs, fried chicken, black-bean salad,
homemade relishes, and all the trimmings just
like it's served in her native Arkansas. In fact, her
chili-based sauce called Bottled Hell is sent by a
friend in Arkansas. Small parties to sit-down dinners up 250, all reasonably priced, might include
a veal chop roasted with whole heads of garlic or
fish baked in parchment. The store also offers her
award-winning brownies, lemon bars, macaroons and lace cookies.

Caviar

Caviar and Fine Foods
321 N. Robertson Blvd., W. Hollywood 90048;
(310) 271-6300, (800) 33-ARISTOFF
Mon.-Fri. 8:30 a.m.-4:30 p.m.

Probably the oldest caviar purveyor in the city, all the caviars are hand-packed here. The company's business is primarily wholesale, its clients some of the finest restaurants and caterers in the city. A small retail clientele also knows the fresh Russian, Chinese and American caviars are of impeccable quality. Prices start at $40 per ounce for Beluga. Scottish and Norwegian smoked salmon, fresh white truffles, fresh, frozen and jarred black truffles and French and American foie gras are all high caliber.

Caviarteria
247 N. Beverly Dr., Beverly Hills 90210;
(310) 285-9773, (800) 287-9773
Open Mon.-Sat. 9:30 a.m.-6 p.m.

This is the West Coast branch of the 40-year-old New York-based Caviarteria. Probably the largest retail caviar distributor in the United States, business is primarily through mail-order. The tiny Beverly Hills shop stocks the finest Russian beluga, osetra and sevruga malossol caviars. Their selected malossol (the Russian term for "little salt," meaning that the minimum or no salt is used to preserve the caviar) costs $65 for one-and-a-half ounces, and is preselected for its gentle, pleasing grayish color and sweet, perfectly shaped eggs. The store also carries American trout and salmon roe, Scottish salmon ($38.50 per pound) and an assortment of duck and goose foie gras. They ship anywhere in the country.

Cheese

The Cheese Store
419 N. Beverly Dr., Beverly Hills 90210; (310) 278-2855
Open Mon.-Sat. 9:30 a.m.-6 p.m.

Virtually every cheese available in the Western world can be found at this wonderful shop, which stocks more than 400 types: chèvres from France and California, Parmesans and Fontina from Italy, Stiltons from Britain, manchego from Spain and more, much more. Certainly the best cheese shop in Los Angeles.

Say Cheese
2800 Hyperion Ave., Silverlake 90027;
(213) 665-0545
Open daily 10 a.m.-6:30 p.m.

A remarkable selection of cheeses from around the world are crammed into the deli cases in this

tiny Silverlake shop, one of the few decent cheese shops in the city. The exceptionally friendly personnel is quite knowledgeable and offers samples of the cheeses before you buy. Say Cheese also carries an almost complete line of La Brea Bakery bread. You'll also find Norwegian salmon, beluga caviar, a huge variety of pâtés, as well as a few fancy French wines, good deli meats, sun-dried tomatoes, porcini mushrooms, chocolate truffles from the Bay Area's peerless Cocolat, Valhrona chocolates from France, coffee beans, imported grocery items, candies, coffee grinders, espresso machines, teapots and Fortnum and Mason English teas and preserves.

Trader Joe's
7304 Santa Monica Blvd., W. Hollywood 90046;
(213) 851-9772
Open daily 9 a.m.-9 p.m.

The selection of cheeses is inconsistent and the quality varies, but the prices are unbeatable. Depending on the store's latest finds, you'll generally find the more popular cheeses from Britain, France, Denmark, Switzerland and the United States, including an excellent little roll of chèvre for $1.99. An added discount for buying whole wheels is available. There are nineteen other locations throughout the Southland, including Sherman Oaks, West Hollywood and Pasadena.

Wally's
2107 Westwood Blvd., Westwood 90025;
(310) 475-0606
Open Mon.-Sat. 10 a.m.-8 p.m., Sun. 10 a.m.-6 p.m.

Not only is Wally's one of the finest wine shops in the city, it is one of the best places on the westside to find a large selection of excellent Italian pastas, olive oils, balsamic vinegars, Russian caviar, French pâtés, Boar's Head deli meats and imported and cheeses at very good prices. Triple crèmes and double crèmes are particularly in evidence. Gift baskets and delivery available.

Coffee & Teas

Caffè Latte
6254 Wilshire Blvd, Wilshire District (L.A.) 90048;
(213) 936-5213
Open Mon.-Fri, 7 a.m.-5 p.m., Tues.-Sat., 5:30 p.m.-10:30 a.m., Sat.-Sun., 8 a.m.-3:30 p.m.

The coffee roaster is hard to miss in this small, neighborhood café known for serving terrific breakfasts and lattes. Owner Tom Kaplan (a partner in Highland Grounds coffeehouse and previously of Hugo's restaurant in West Hollywood) offers more than twenty varieties of arabica coffee beans that are roasted daily in small quantities. The coffee, roasted a bit lighter than most other places in the city, is also discounted by ten percent when you join Caffe Latte's coffee club. We love to stop by regularly for a cappuccino, to try each variety before we buy. Over 30 high-quality teas are also sold, from scented, black, green, herb and yogi, ranging in price from $10 to $75 per ounce.

Coffee Emporium
4345 Glencoe Ave., Marina del Rey 90291;
(310) 823-4446
Open Mon.-Thurs 6 a.m.-10 p.m., Fri 6 a.m.-midnight, Sun 7 a.m.-9 p.m.

Alan Chemtob could be considered L.A.'s father of coffee roasting. He was the first retail coffee roaster in the city when he opened the Coffee Emporium in 1979. Today, this funky café is also the retail outlet for his wholesale companies, Café au Lait and Paradise Tropical Tea, which furnish coffee and teas to some of top hotels and restaurants in the country. Over 40 types of coffee are sold, including flavored and decaffeinated. The luscious passion-fruit flavored Paradise Tropical Teas, once only available to restaurants, have just been packaged for retail sales and are also sold here: among the flavors are papaya, mango and kiwi.

The Coffee Roaster
13567 Ventura Blvd., Sherman Oaks 91423;
(818) 905-9719
Mon.-Sat 8:30 a.m.-6 p.m., Sun. 10 a.m.-4 p.m.

Dick Healy is an ex-banker turned coffee roaster who couldn't be happier. Everyday he slowly roasts small batches of the most select arabica coffee beans he can buy for a loyal clientele, who if they arrive early enough, can also enjoy his homemade biscotti or freshly baked muffins in this small shop. Thirty-five coffees are sold, including dark roasts, flavored and decaffeinated. Healy also sells Jackson's Teas of Picadilly as well as exceptional bulk teas custom-blended by his wife, Jane. If you can't get to the Valley, any coffee or tea can be bought through mail order.

Graffeo Coffee Roasting Company
315 N. Beverly Dr., Beverly Hills 90210;
(310) 273-4232
Open Mon.-Sat. 9 a.m.-5:30 p.m.

This San Francisco institution offers a simple selection: just three varieties. Buy the light roast if you like an American-style brew, the dark if you like it European-style (including espresso), and the Swiss water-process decaf if you've given up caffeine. The store is simplicity itself, just a counter, a few burlap coffee bags, a giant roaster behind glass walls, and an intoxicating aroma.

Graffeo's high-quality beans and skillful roasting make for a superb cup of coffee. Graffeo also has a mail-order business.

Starbucks
Beverly Connection, 100 N. La Cienega Blvd., W. Hollywood 90048; (310) 289-7815
Open Mon.-Sat. 7 a.m.-midnight, Sun. 8 a.m.-11 p.m.

This Seattle-based roaster/retailer is a household name in coffee throughout the Northwest. Now, having made a big push in L.A., Starbucks is about to earn the same distinction here. More than 25 varieties and blends of consistently excellent coffee, from Indonesian Sulawesi to Arabian Mocha Java to decaffeinated Viennese blend are sold at these clean, bright outlets, along with various coffee-making paraphernalia and mugs, six types of bulk teas and fresh juices. Any coffee beans not sold within a week are donated to charity. Other stores are located in Santa Monica, Brentwood, Larchmont and Beverly Hills.

For all the city's newest and best food-shop addresses, look for The Food Paper *(published quarterly by André Gayot/Gault Millau) on newsstands everywhere. Or, call (800) LE BEST 1 for a subscription.*

Confections

Edelweiss Chocolates
444 N. Cañon Dr., Beverly Hills 90210;
(310) 275-0341
Open Mon.-Fri. 9:30 a.m.-5:30 p.m., Sat. 10 a.m.-5:30 p.m.

Since 1940, this shop has been known for its handmade chocolates. There's a variety of truffles and chocolate-covered fruits, but the best candies in the shop are the chocolate-covered marshmallows. Attractive and delicious gift baskets, party favors and holiday candies are also available.

Jo's Candies
P.O. Box 3517, Manhattan Beach 90266;
(310) 370-8826
Mail-order only.

Jo's Candies has been a closely guarded secret in Manhattan Beach for over 45 years. After losing its lease, the "candy cottage" no longer exists, but a thriving mail order business keeps Jo's alive. The peanut-butter creams, bordeaux, caramels and English toffee—it was voted one of the three best in the United States—also win raves. This is the only place we know of that makes light and dark chocolate-covered graham crackers—and they're absolutely divine.

Littlejohn's English Toffee House

Farmer's Market, 6333 W. 3rd St., Fairfax District (L.A.) 90036; (213) 936-5379
Open Mon.-Sat. 9 a.m.-6:30 p.m., Sun. 9 a.m.-5 p.m.

English toffee–lovers come from miles around for this exceptional chocolate-and-almond-covered crunchy candy. Lately Littlejohn's sells as many caramel apples and pounds of fudge (nine kinds in all) as it does buttery, fresh-daily toffee.

Teuscher Chocolates of Switzerland

9548 Brighton Way, Beverly Hills 90210; (310) 276-2776
Open Mon.-Sat. 10 a.m.-6 p.m.

These are without a doubt the most beautiful boxes of chocolates you'll find in the city—naturally, they're also among the most expensive. The chocolates, imported weekly from Zurich, aren't as sweet as those made by domestic confectioners. A few varieties can be a bit dull, but we must profess a weakness for the white-chocolate and Champagne truffles, not to mention the truffles with nuts.

Gourmet To Go

Broadway Deli

1457 Third Street Promenade, Santa Monica 90401; (310) 451-0616
Open Tues.-Thurs. 8 a.m.-10 p.m., Fri.-Sat. 8 a.m.-11 p.m., Sun.-Mon. 8 a.m.-9 p.m.

The powerful trio of Bruce Marder, Michel Richard and investor Marvin Zeidler have come up with a deli like no other. A foodie's dream-come-true, the room is filled with an overwhelming eclectic collection of American and European edibles—from Jewish salamis and bagels to French pâtés and baguettes. The deli counter holds a marvelous array of gravlax cured on the premises, four other types of Atlantic smoked salmon, a few dozen kinds of cheeses from around the world, and gourmet salads to go. Hard-to-find extra-virgin olive oils (like Mancianti Affiorato), a wide variety of vinegars, dried Italian and domestic pastas are just some of the food offered. Excellent breads come both from Bread Only bakery (olive, rosemary, French country, Italian ciabatta) and from the in-house baker (walnut-raisin, six-grain, tarts and cookies). There's even a small produce section.

Not to be ignored is the wine room (*see* "Wines & Spirits" section in this chapter). The ambitious trio is opening a Broadway Deli in Encino and another in Pasadena in 1992.

Hugo's

8401 Santa Monica Blvd., W. Hollywood 90069; (213) 654-4088
Open daily 6 a.m-midnight.

For some, Hugo's is an informal but intelligent restaurant—the pumpkin pancakes and pasta Mama still get rave reviews. For others, it's a gourmet pitstop before a beach or Hollywood Bowl outing. Hugo's take-out counter presents an array of excellent pasta sauces, salads, baguettes and desserts; pâtés, terrines and picnic baskets to order are available. The prices are as high as the quality.

International Food Center

7754 Santa Monica Blvd., W. Hollywood 90046; (213) 656-1868
Open daily 8 a.m.-9 p.m.

The area around Fairfax Avenue and Santa Monica Boulevard, known as Little Russia, entertains a huge Eastern European population. This delicatessen, one of the oldest of the area's ethnic food stores, is stuffed with everything from caviar to knishes. In the deli cases you'll find prepared salads such as chopped herring; hot dishes such as stuffed chicken parts; vegetable borscht; imported and domestic butters and cheeses; ryazhenka, a caramel-colored yogurt; sausages; smoked and roasted meats; cold-cuts; and a vast assortment of smoked fish—from sturgeon and salmon to herring, eel and trout. Russian savories and pastries for starting and finishing your meal should round off your purchases.

The Kitchen for Exploring Foods

1434 W. Colorado Blvd., Pasadena 91101; (818) 793-7218
Open Tues.-Fri. noon-6 p.m., Sat. 10:30 a.m.-6 p.m.

This full-service caterer features a daily selection of innovative gourmet foods, including salads, sandwiches, soups, fresh breads and delectable desserts. Bring in a platter and the staff will display your order to your liking; with advance notice, The Kitchen will pack a complete lunch or dinner from dozens of choices. Cooking classes and culinary accessories, too.

Marmalade

710 Montana Ave., Santa Monica 90403; (310) 395-9196
Open Mon.-Fri. 6:30 a.m.-8 p.m., Sat. 7 a.m.-8 p.m., Sun. 7 a.m.-7 p.m.

This upscale one-stop neighborhood deli/café is a veritable melting pot of flavors, offering goodies from around the world as well as American regional favorites. Their packaged goods include English jams and butters as well as a New England cranberry ketchup. Fresh scones and muffins, take-away pot pies and their wonderful soups are also hard to resist, along with a multitude of fresh salads in the deli case. We particularly love the tiny ramekins of pâté maison ($10), made fresh weekly from chicken livers, Calvados and clarified butter. *See also* "Cafés" in the "LOS ANGELES Bargain Bites" chapter.

Le Marmiton
1327 Montana Ave., Santa Monica 90403;
(310) 393-7716
Open Tues.-Sat. 9:30 a.m.-7 p.m.

Accomplished French chefs prepare fine salads and appetizers, entrées (both fresh and frozen) and pastries—everything you need to fool your friends into thinking you studied at La Varenne. The dishes tend toward the Provençale and the classic instead of the nouvelle. Rye country bread and chocolate Grand Marnier truffles are a specialty. There are also some good French cheeses. Prices are high but not unreasonable.

Netty's
1700 Silverlake Blvd., Silverlake 90026;
(213) 662-8655
Open Mon.-Sat. noon-9 p.m. DC, MC, V.

Netty and her husband (both formerly chefs) run a thriving take-out and catering business out of this little storefront, with a menu of about 100 dishes that span the map from Italy to Salvador. The cases are filled with fresh, flavorful salads and pasta dishes, satisfying entrées, excellent tamales and good pesto bread. *See also* "Cafés" in the "LOS ANGELES Quick Bites" chapter.

Pasta, Etc.
8650 W. Sunset Blvd., W. Hollywood 90069;
(310) 854-0094
Open Mon.-Sat. 9 a.m.-10:30 p.m.

Jon Gould's selection of pastas, salads, hot entrées, cheeses, wines and desserts is so tempting that the option of sitting down to enjoy a meal is difficult to resist. (Some of the top restaurants in L.A. buy their fresh pasta here.) The expanded antipasto bar includes hot pasta specialties, including "power pasta," a low-calorie, oil-free dish of fresh tomatoes, chicken breast, basil and capers. Gould packs rustic gift basket full of homemade delights (prices start at $60), and also provides a catering service.

Pasta, Pasta, Pasta
8134 W. 3rd St., Melrose-Fairfax District (L.A.) 90048; (213) 653-2051
Open Tues.-Sat. 10 a.m.-6 p.m.

If you bring in your own serving dish, Pasta, Pasta, Pasta will fill it with any number of ready-to-heat pasta entrées. There are four kinds of lasagne, including duck and vegetarian, plus

pasta salads and fresh and prepared tortellini and ravioli. This is a convenient place to buy sheets of freshly made lasagne for your own creations.

The Pasta Shoppe
1964 Hillhurst Ave., Los Feliz 90027;
(213) 668-0458
Open Mon.-Fri. 10:30 a.m.-6:30 p.m., Sat. 9:30 a.m.-5:30 p.m.

An outstanding array of fresh-daily pasta colors the showcase here. We could easily build a meal around the jalapeño-pepper, lemon-basil, mushroom, rosemary, carrot, garlic, tomato or black squid-ink pastas. They're all cut to order, with five noodle varieties to choose from, and there are delicious cream and pesto sauces. Ravioli, tortellini, lasagne and prepared pasta salads are also sold. A real gourmet find.

Le Petit Four
8654 Sunset Blvd., W. Hollywood 90069;
(310) 652-3863
Open Mon.-Sat. 9 a.m.-11 p.m., Sun. 9 a.m.-6 p.m.

There's no question that these pastries are wonderful (especially the fruit tarts and miniature petits fours), but you'll also be missing out on some gourmet treats if you don't try the quiches, feuilletés and pâtés. Charming service by young Frenchwomen.

Markets

Ethnic Markets

Alpine Market
Alpine Village, 833 W. Torrance Blvd., Torrance 90502; (310) 327-2483/321-5660
Open Mon.-Thurs., 11 a.m.-7 p.m., Fri. 11 a.m.-8 p.m., Sat. 10 a.m.-8 p.m., Sun., 11 a.m.-8 p.m.

One of the most authentic German markets in L.A., Alpine Market is home to irresistible Bavarian scents: smoked meats, fresh cheeses, potato salads and black breads. Over 50 kinds of meats can be ordered at the counter, including kitchen-made sausages, Hungarian bacon and salami, Black Forest hams and a low-sodium, low-fat turkey bratwurst; the bakery is stocked with freshly baked, diet-defeating Continental pastries; and the liquor department is a year-round Oktoberfest, with dozens of imported beers as well as German wines. The Alpine Market's has its own microbrewery is next door.

Bay Cities Importing
1517 Lincoln Blvd., Santa Monica 90401;
(310) 395-8279
Open Mon.-Sat. 8 a.m.-7 p.m., Sun. 8 a.m.-6 p.m.

Even if you've never cooked a day in your life, this place will make you want to run home and whip up some pasta al pesto. It's a large deli/market that sells almost every food product Italy exports: spices, pastas, dozens of olive oils, wines, sweets, coffees and cans of everything from tomato sauce to anchovies. A large deli counter sells meats, sausages, pasta salads, cheeses from around the world and excellent sandwiches to go. Some French and Middle Eastern imported delicacies are also offered, along with delicious Italian breads from local bakeries and first-rate fresh pasta.

Bezjian's Grocery

4725 Santa Monica Blvd., Hollywood 90036; (213) 663-1503
Open Mon.-Sat. 9 a.m.-7 p.m., Sun. 10 a.m.-4 p.m.

This friendly market is a gold mine of foodstuffs for both Middle Eastern and Indian cooking. From India, there are unusual chutneys, freshly prepared garam masalas (mixture of ground spices), tandoori pastes, chickpea flour and ghee (clarified butter). From the Middle East, there's a deli counter stocked with various feta cheeses and plump olives and fresh hummus and baba ghanouj for spreading on the great Middle Eastern flatbreads. Rounding out the stock are cooking utensils and cookbooks. For Greek-food lovers, there are cold-case shelves piled with taramasalata and frozen spanakopita, tyropita and moussaka.

Bharat Bazaar

11510 W. Washington Blvd., Culver City 90066; (310) 398-6766
Open Mon. & Wed.-Sun. 11 a.m.-6:30 p.m.

No devotee of Indian cooking could fail to be delighted with the offerings here. The shelves are packed with jars of chutneys (called pickles on most labels), including lime, tamarind and mango. There are ready-made sauces from every part of India, as well as everything you need to start from scratch. Flours include graham and chickpea. The fairly large shop is run by a friendly, helpful staff.

Domingo's Italian Grocery and Delicatessen

17548 Ventura Blvd., Encino 91316; (818) 981-4466
Open Tues.-Sat. 9 a.m.-6 p.m., Sun. 10 a.m.-4 p.m.

Counters and aisles are crammed with Italian breads, fresh pasta, homemade sauces, olive oil, vinegars, imported hams, sausages, cheeses and Italian wines. Don't even attempt to find what you're looking for without assistance—there are just too many goods packed into this small shop. Patience is the key word here; someone will even-

tually climb up to the top shelf and get the tomato sauce you've been waiting for.

Enbun

Japanese Village Plaza, 1st St. & Central Ave., Little Tokyo (L.A.) 90012; (213) 680-3280
Open Mon.-Sat. 9 a.m.-6:30 p.m., Sun. 10 a.m.-6 p.m.

This charming grocery has sleek architectural lines and a full assortment of Japanese foods, which are displayed with the unerring eye of an artist. In the produce department, persimmons and lady apples are piled with care. The fish counter sells the freshest cuts for sashimi. The cold cases are filled with packages of fish-cake rolls and pickled vegetables. Bakery items include mochigashi (rice cakes filled with bean paste) and anpan (bread rolls filled with bean paste). There are also plenty of sakes, beers and imported rice crackers in this most browsable of markets.

Gianfranco

11363 Santa Monica Blvd., W.L.A. 90025; (310) 477-7777
Open Mon.-Thurs. 9:30 a.m.-10:30 p.m., Fri.-Sat. 9:30 a.m.-11 p.m.

This spacious, modern and tempting deli sells everything Italian, from wine to panettone, cheese to olive oil. There's an entire wall lined with boxes of Perugina chocolates, and glass cases full of cold meats, good antipasti, homemade pastas, wonderful cheeses and warming trays with such dishes as polenta, sausages, stuffed shells and meatballs. Most of it, except the lackluster pastries, is tasty and reasonably priced. Gianfranco also serves lunch and dinner.

Grand Central Market

317 S. Broadway, Downtown (L.A.) 90013; (213) 624-2378
Open Mon.-Sat. 9 a.m.-6 p.m., Sun. 10 a.m.-5 p.m.

For over 60 years the Lyon family has managed this huge public market. Crowded, noisy and not so clean, it reminds us somewhat of a Third World bazaar. Prices are very cheap, but vary from stall to stall, so look around before you buy. Produce stands are overflowing with cacti, chayotes, a dozen or more kinds of fresh chiles, and bargains on all manner of fruits. An apothecary stocks jars filled with herbs from all over the world; other stalls sell dried chiles, nuts, coconuts, fruits, spices, rice and beans in bulk. There are fish, poultry and meats (including pig tails and lamb heads); fresh juices and licuados (fruit milkshakes); fresh tortillas made daily on the premises; Latin American cheese in bulk. With a $15 or more purchase, you can park free in the lot next door. An upscale 30,000-square-foot supermarket in the basement and a 500-car garage are in the works.

239

Liborio Market
864 S. Vermont Ave., Mid-Wilshire District (L.A.)
90005; (213) 386-1458
Open daily 8 a.m.-8 p.m.

This good Mexican neighborhood market, which also has a large Salvadorean and Guatemalan clientele, is filled with hard-to-find south-of-the-border foodstuffs. Cheeses for pupusas, Latin American cremas and sour creams are in the dairy case; in the produce section, you'll find plantains, Manzano bananas, banana leaves and odd tubers such as the yam-like malanga. There are manioc and plantain flours and guava pastes for dessert pastries. Check out the frozen section for Cuban tamales, the soda section for unusual imports, the canned goods for chipotle chiles and the spice section for packets of red achiote paste for Yucatecan-style cooking. A Salvadorean bakery in the store turns out fresh pastries, sweet empanadas, pound cake and dense bread pudding.

Holland American Market
10343 E. Artesia Blvd., Bellflower 90706;
(310) 867-7589
Open Mon.-Sat. 8 a.m.-6 p.m.

Over 2,500 products are stocked here, one of the largest Dutch-Indonesian markets in the country. Ingredients for an authentic rijstaffel (the Dutch version of the multi-dished Indonesian meal), spices, Dutch chocolates, Dutch cocoa, chocolate flakes for sprinkling on toast, exotic jams and rosenstroop (Indonesian fruit syrups) are only a few of the many imports stocked. A huge cheese section is filled with a variety of imported Dutch cheeses, from Gouda to Edam.

Pacific Supermarket
1620 W. Redondo Beach Blvd., Gardena 90247;
(310) 323-7696
3030 W. Sepulveda Blvd., Torrance 90505;
(310) 539-8899
Open Mon.-Sat. 8 a.m.-9 p.m., Sun. 8 a.m.-8 p.m.

Formerly the New Meiji Market, this market is the largest Japanese market in the United States—a must for any serious cook of Asian cuisines. Although primarily Japanese, the enormous inventory includes plenty to captivate cooks of Chinese, Korean, Filipino and Southeast Asian dishes. Whole aisles are devoted to soy sauces, noodles and rice crackers (200 kinds). The cold cases feature Filipino lumpia wrappers and Mandarin pancakes, both ready to fill at home. The produce section is worth a drive in itself: Chinese broccoli, winter melon, Japanese pears and more. The meat counter offers cuts you can't buy from Western-style butchers, including

beef cut for sukiyaki and shabu-shabu and thinly sliced rib-eye steak for Korean barbecue. At the fish counter are giant clams, fresh tuna and blue mackerel.

Tarzana Armenian Grocery
18598 Ventura Blvd., Tarzana 91356;
(818) 881-6278
Open Mon.-Sat 8 a.m.-8 p.m., Sun. 10 a.m.-3 p.m.
22776 Ventura Blvd., Woodland Hills 91364;
(818) 703-7836
Open Mon.-Thurs. 9 a.m.-9 p.m., Fri.-Sat. 9 a.m.-10 p.m., Sun. 11 a.m.-3 p.m.

The Chelebian family's market is not your average Armenian deli. Specializing in an international array of fine food, the emphasis is on Middle Eastern products, but you'll also find homemade tiramisu and biscotti next to the baklava. Staples like bulghur wheat, tahine, jarred grape leaves and phyllo dough make up only a small part of the products here. The deli case offers a variety of foods: Israeli cheese as well as Greek and Bulgarian feta cheeses, vegetarian stuffed grape leaves, roasted eggplant salad (simpoog aghtsan) as well as pickled vegetables and even sausage.

Gourmet Markets

Ashford Market
1627 Montana Ave., Santa Monica 90403; No central phone
Open Mon.-Sat. 7 a.m.-6:30 p.m., Sun. 8 a.m.-2 p.m.

Several swell shops make up this market. Closest to the Montana entrance is a branch of Il Fornaio (310-458-1562), which has a good assortment of breads and pastries. There's a small flower stand filled with stunning posies; there's L.A. Gourmet, which offers a trendy take-out menu of salads, soups and snacks (310-451-0557); and, best of all, there's Tanaka's (not open on Sundays; 310-394-2535), which makes buying fresh produce as visually satisfying as a visit to an art gallery.

Bristol Farms
606 Fair Oaks Ave., S. Pasadena 91030;
(818) 441-5450
Open Mon.-Sat. 9 a.m.-9 p.m., Sun. 10 a.m.-7 p.m.
837 Silver Spur Rd., Rolling Hills Estates 90274;
(310) 541-9157
Open Mon.-Sat. 9 a.m.-8 p.m., Sun. 10 a.m.-7 p.m.
1570 Rosecrans Blvd #H, Manhattan Beach 90266;
(310) 643-5229
Open Mon.-Sat. 8 a.m.-9 p.m., Sun. 8 a.m.-8 p.m.

Bristol Farms is simply a marvel: pristine produce, excellent California wines, homemade sausages, home-smoked meats, myriad cheeses, fresh pastas, prepared sauces, a sushi chef to filet the fresh fish of your choice, dozens of coffees, fresh breads and pastries, gourmet-to-go entrées, a small café, quality cookbooks and utensils and the finest domestic and imported groceries (spices, soups, soy sauces, you name it). This grocery store is pure entertainment; just like a visit to a fine museum, we can while away hours here, wandering the aisles, sipping the free coffee, stroking the prodigious produce and nibbling at the many free food samples. Pasadena's Bristol Farms ranks high on our list for selection, service and just plain fun. The Rolling Hills Estates store, the first Bristol Farms, is a smaller-scale jewel of a market. Prices reflect the high quality of the products.

Chalet Gourmet
7880 W. Sunset Blvd., Hollywood 90046; (213) 874-6301
Open daily 9 a.m.-9 p.m.

Chalet Gourmet is, along with Jurgensen's, the granddaddy of L.A. gourmet markets. In recent years Chalet Gourmet has seemed a little drab but new management is in the process of updating. There is the expected array of first-rate meats, fish and cheese, along with good baked goods, gourmet take-out, decent produce and high-end grocery items, as well as a vast wine department, gift baskets and Hollywood Bowl boxed meals, with free delivery in the surrounding area.

Gelson's Market
Marina Marketplace, 13455 Maxella Ave., Marina del Rey 90066; (310) 306-2952
Open daily 8 a.m.-10 p.m.

L.A.'s venerable gourmet market is grander than ever in its new Marina Marketplace location. There's a first-rate bakery and small espresso bar, premarinated fish, Asian entrées fresh from the wok, sushi, complete catering and eight different "Elite Complete Meals to Go," stylishly packed in double-deck boxes. Other locations in the Century City Shopping Center, Pacific Palisades, Encino, N. Hollywood, Tarzana and Westlake Village.

Irvine Ranch Market
Beverly Center, Beverly & La Cienega Blvds., W. Hollywood 90048; (310) 657-1931
Open Mon.-Sat. 9 a.m.-10 p.m., Sun. 9 a.m.-9 p.m.
6401 Canoga Ave., Woodland Hills 91367; (818) 704-0485
Open Mon.-Fri. 8 a.m.-10 p.m., Sat.-Sun. 8 a.m.-8 p.m.

On the ground floor of this almost-impossible-to-get-into shopping-mall, you'll find the once-legendary Irvine Ranch Market. The new owner, Chalet Gourmet, has revamped and upgraded the market, particularly the meat, fish and cheese departments. It's still known for its excep-

tional choice of vegetables, fresh herbs and exotic fruits, an array that stretches as far as the eye can see. In general, the quality is above average, but prices can be exorbitant. The wine-and-spirits section is staffed by very knowledgeable salespeople, who will find the bottle that suits your tastes, or recommend the best bargains. Try to avoid this place on Saturday or directly after work hours, when it is jammed with every yuppie in town. Customer service is good; purchases are sent directly by elevator to a pickup point in the parking garage.

Jurgensen's
842 E. California Blvd., Pasadena 91106; (818) 792-3121
Open Mon.-Sat. 8 a.m.-7 p.m.

The newly refurbished Jurgensen's is a full-service, fine-foods market with a meat department, deli, cappuccino bar and bakery, as well as hot foods to go. Most produce is organically grown; the selection of gourmet-food items and fine wines hails from all over the world. There are elaborate gift baskets to order and delivery that's as specialized as a pack-the-fridge-for-you service.

Trader Joe's
7304 Santa Monica Blvd., Hollywood 90046; (213) 851-9772
Open daily 9 a.m.-9 p.m.

The Loehmann's of food, Trader Joe's sells "designer" food without most of the labels at bargain prices. Trader Joe's–brand nuts, bagels, dried fruits, vitamins, granola cereals, blue-corn tortilla chips, locally baked goods and imported coffees are admirable. There are surprisingly delicious frozen foods: Wolfgang Puck Pizza in plain wrap is a bargain, as are the delicious vegetarian egg rolls, authentic merguez sausage, and fresh frozen seafood and jumbo tiger shrimp. Imports such as cans of crabmeat from Thailand, tins of Roma tomatoes and Kalamata olives from Greece also fill the shelves. The selection of domestic and imported cheeses is noteworthy, as is the selection of wines, both respected California boutique wines and wines from around the world—at well-below-retail prices (*see also* listing in this chapter, under "Wines & Spirits.") Locations throughout Southern California.

Van Rex Gourmet Foods, Inc.
5850 Washington Blvd., Culver City 90232; (310) 965-1320
Open Mon.-Fri. 10 a.m.-6 p.m., Sat. 10 a.m.- 5 p.m.

This store is too good to be true. Van Rex has been servicing the gourmet restaurant industry for fifteen years. With the opening of their small, pristine shop, adjacent to their warehouse, the rest of us can now cook with the same products the chefs use. Prices average about one-third below retail cost, with some even less. Good buys include French butter (almost half the price as in some gourmet markets), Russian caviar, cured Scottish salmon, raw domestic foie gras and demi-glace by D'Artagnan, frozen fruit purées, fresh, dried and frozen pastas, including a wonderful smoked salmon ravioli in the shape of a fish, olive oils from France and Italy, and wonderful aged vinegars. Our favorite product, though, is the incomparable dark French Valrhona chocolate, probably the most expensive chocolate in the world and worth it. There is a second shop in Palm Desert.

Natural Foods Markets

Erewhon Natural Foods

7660 Beverly Blvd., Fairfax District (L.A.) 90036; (213) 937-0777
Open Mon.-Fri. 9 a.m.-9 p.m., Sat.-Sun. 9 a.m.-8 p.m.

Once considered a funky, health-food market patronized by hippies and macrobiotic freaks, Erewhon has grown up into a beautiful, upscale natural foods emporium. The produce section is filled with organic fruits and vegetables of every type imaginable. Milk is sold in glass bottles, and Steuve's raw cream (the best for making crème fraîche), sits next to superb Cabot Farm Creamery butter. Rows and rows of vitamins, a variety of exotic fresh-squeezed juices and a deli case full of pastas, roast chicken, tamale pie and the like are just a few of the offerings here. Prices are competitive and there's plenty of parking.

Mrs. Gooch's

239 N. Crescent Dr., Beverly Hills 90210 (branches everywhere); (310) 274-3360
Open daily 9 a.m.-9 p.m.

Mrs. Gooch's philosophy is to sell the purest whole foods possible. With this in mind, they buy organically grown produce and hormone-free meats (beef is from a small farmer in Colorado) and poultry (Rocky Range and Zacky Farms). No refined sugars or flours, caffeine, artificial flavorings, colors or sweeteners, hydrogenated oils or chemically engineered food and cleaning products are ecology safe; therefore, Mrs. Gooch's doesn't carry them. The Beverly Hills store has a large hot and cold deli/take-out counter and bakery. Other stores are located in West L.A., Redondo Beach, Northridge, Glendale, Sherman Oaks and Thousand Oaks.

Nowhere Natural Food Market

8001 Beverly Blvd., Fairfax District (L.A.) 90036; (213) 658-6506
Open Mon.-Fri. 9 a.m.-10 p.m., Sat. 9 a.m.-9 p.m., Sun. 10 a.m.-8 p.m.

Just across the street from one of its biggest competitors, Erewhon, this market is a smaller rendition of the same theme: a large selection of organic produce; a deli stocked with turkey loaf, grilled-vegetable salads and other daily specials from the Nowhere Café kitchen next door, lox sandwiches and other tasty (mostly no-meat) offerings; freshly squeezed juices, chemical-free, organic snacks, cereals and breads.

Supermarkets

Many a modern supermarket has become a food department store of sorts, combining grocery store, gourmet take-out, deli, cooking supply store, bakery, flower shop and more in one giant space. The super-upscale, Vons-owned **Pavilions** supermarkets in West Hollywood (8969 Santa Monica Blvd., 310-273-0977; open 24 hours), and Westwood (11750 Wilshire Blvd., W.L.A. 310-479-5294; open daily 6 a.m.-midnight) are outstanding, and delivery is available by calling (800) 756-6225. Five other branches in L.A., as well as in Burbank, Sherman Oaks, Canoga Park, Arcadia and South Pasadena.

All the other chains (**Ralphs, Vons, Hughes, Alpha Beta, Lucky's** and **Safeway**) are good. Each has a level of quality and breadth of merchandise geared to its neighborhood.

Wine & Spirits

Briggs Wines & Spirits

13038 San Vicente Blvd., Brentwood 90049; (310) 476-1223
Open Mon.-Sat. 9 a.m.-7 p.m., Sun. 11 a.m.-5 p.m.

Briggs stocks thousands of bottles of wines that are neatly arranged alphabetically and by varietal type. It is especially recommended for its large selection of ports and California boutique wines from some of the smaller growers—the shop is also happy to special order, with a six-bottle minimum.

Broadway Deli

1457 Third Street Promenade, Santa Monica 90401; (310) 451-0616
Open Tues.-Thurs. 8 a.m.-10 p.m., Fri.-Sat. 8 a.m.-11 p.m., Sun.-Mon. 8 a.m.-9 p.m.

The wine shop in this restaurant/deli is filled with 70 brands of grappa, comprising one of the largest selections in the city. Over 400 California, French and Italian wines—mainly from small boutique wineries who produce in limited numbers— are also stocked. Prices range from $6 to $300, with a good many wines selling for under $20.

Duke of Bourbon
20908 Roscoe Blvd., Canoga Park 91304; (818) 341-1234
Mon.-Wed. 9 a.m.-8 p.m., Thurs.-Sat. 9 a.m.-9 p.m., Sun. noon-6 p.m.

Hidden behind a dreary liquor-store exterior is one of L.A.'s most firmly established sources for wines and spirits, and certainly the best in the Valley. Owned and run by a knowledgeable, impassioned family team, David and Judy Breitstein and son Ron, this shop stocks a small but outstanding hand-picked selection of wines. The inventory is largely Californian, with a few French, Italian and Australian offerings, most of them priced at a substantial discount. Ask them for advice; they'll be happy to guide you through the store. Also offered here: wine-education series, tours abroad, a newsletter and frequent tastings.

Du Vin
540 N. San Vicente Blvd., W. Hollywood 90048; (310) 855-1161
Open Mon.-Sat. 10 a.m.-7 p.m.

A charming little boutique that's been a treasured address for French-wine lovers for about a decade, Du Vin is almost totally hidden behind other storefronts on San Vicente Boulevard (about 30 yards south of Melrose Avenue). Owner Réne Averseng stocks an impressive selection of hard-to-find bottles (mostly French); ask him to show you the Burgundies, Bordeaux, Provençal Rosés and Rhônes, as well as the shelves full of Calvados, Cognac and Armagnac dating back to 1920. In spite of these precious bottles, this is a haven for the wine drinker; many a bargain bottle can be found for under $8. There's also a small cheese case, and a café menu is served until 4:30 p.m. on the tiny, tree-shaded courtyard outside.

Greenblatt's Delicatessen
8017 W. Sunset Blvd., W. Hollywood 90046; (213) 656-0606
Open daily 9 a.m.-2 a.m.

This full-service wine shop began stocking spirits in the 1930s, and then fine wines in the '50s—today it's a virtual library of wine, boasting one of the largest inventories in the country. This is no discount outlet, but there are always several dozen special deals, from a bottle of Valpolicella for $3.99 to a bottle of '88 Pichon Laland Champagne for $25.95 (usually twice the price). Champagne is a strong point, with a wide-ranging selection and frequent special discounts. In addition to the aisle upon aisle of Cognac and Armagnac (some dating to the 1800s) and single-malt scotch, Greenblatt's stocks an astonishing collection of grappas. If you want to explore a few new wines, plonk down a dollar or two for a taste from the cruvinet, a brilliant device that stores and maintains the freshness of 30 bottles at a time, dispensing tastes or full glasses.

L.A. Wine Co.
4935 McConnell Ave., Mar Vista 90066; (310) 306-9463
Open Mon.-Sat. 10 a.m.-6 p.m., Sun. noon-5 p.m.

Some of the best wines from around the world at the best prices—probably the lowest in town—can be found in this hard-to-find garagelike shop. They carry an excellent selection of California wines, including the smaller boutique labels. There are also imports from France, Italy, Germany, Chile and Greece. The staff is helpful and extremely knowledgeable, and you would do well to follow their advice.

Red Carpet Wine & Spirits Merchants
400 E. Glenoaks Blvd., Glendale 91207; (818) 247-5544
Open Mon.-Thurs. 9 a.m.-10 p.m., Fri.-Sat. 9 a.m.-11 p.m., Sun. 10 a.m.-9 p.m.

This spacious 5,500-square-foot store, complete with a redwood-paneled wine room where classes and tastings are held, carries rare and premium wines from all over the world, including ones from the best German, Italian and French estates, as well as those from such small California wineries as Chalone, Quail Ridge and Long. Red Carpet also stocks exotic beers and liqueurs. They also offer customized gift baskets for office parties and bar tending and catering. Free delivery with orders over $75.

Trader Joe's
610 S. Arroyo Pkwy., Pasadena 91103; (818) 356-9066
Open daily 9 a.m.-9 p.m.

Trader Joe's is absolutely indispensable to wine-lovers on a budget—or any wine-lover, for that matter, with their bargain prices well below retail. Veteran wine buyer Bob Berning has a special talent for buying up overstocks and the tail ends of lots from good wineries all over the world, and there's always a large selection of drinkable wines priced under $5. The Trader Joe's label is bottled by some of the best California and French wineries and is dirt cheap. In addition, there's a full stock of California boutique wines, and a vast assortment of imported and domestic sparkling wines and beers. This Trader Joe's is the oldest location. There are several other locations, including 10850 National Blvd., West L.A. (310-474-9299); 7304 Santa Monica Blvd., West Hollywood (310-851-9772); and 14119 Riverside Drive, Sherman Oaks (818-501-9349).

Wally's
2107 Westwood Blvd., Westwood 90025;
(310) 475-0606
Open Mon.-Sat. 10 a.m.-8 p.m., Sun. 10 a.m.-6 p.m.

Wally's is the crème de la crème of L.A.'s wines-and-spirits stores. This airy shop in blond-wood tones has a remarkable selection of Cognacs, grappas, single-malt scotches, vintage ports and imported beers. The sales staff is extremely knowledgeable and particularly helpful in party planning, quantity buying and sending gift baskets filled with wines, Champagnes, imported chocolates, cheeses and crackers.

Wine House
2311 Cotner Ave., W.L.A. 90064; (310) 479-3731
Open Mon.-Sat. 10 a.m.-7 p.m., Sun. noon-6 p.m.

No charming boutique atmosphere here, just acres of wines from around the world, including a huge selection of always-changing special bargains. One of the largest and finest selections of spirits, including 30 kinds of grappas and over 40 kinds of single malt scotch. For those who are serious about their wines, the Wine House is a beloved home away from home and offers wine storage. Special classes, and tastings are held frequently.

The Wine Merchant
9701 Santa Monica Blvd., Beverly Hills 90210;
(310) 278-7322
Open Mon.-Sat. 10 a.m.-6:30 p.m.

A full-service wine shop, The Wine Merchant stocks a spectacular selection of popular and rare vintages and offers wine-appreciation classes and regular wine tastings to introduce new vintages. It also rents out 58-degree wine lockers so you can store that Bordeaux, which won't be perfected until the year 2010.

The Wine Reserve
929 S. Brand Blvd., Glendale 91204;
(818) 500-8400
Mon.-Sat. 11 a.m.-7 p.m., Sun. noon-5 p.m.

Ask the friendly, knowledgeable folks here to show you their most interesting new finds. In addition to a good selection of Californian and French wines, they pride themselves on an eclec-

tic inventory of Rhônes and Italians, as well as Chilean, Portuguese and Australian bottles, many in the $6-to-$10 range. The shop does a healthy trade in vintage and other collectors' bottles (Christie's auction house is an account), but only in wines; there are no Cognacs, Armagnacs or other spirits here. Temperature-controlled storage lockers are available for rent. Inquire about the weekly tastings.

The Wine Shop
223 N. Larchmont Blvd., Larchmont Village 90048;
(213) 466-1220
Open Mon.-Sat. 10 a.m.-7 p.m.

This narrow, crowded shop has an excellent (if not extensive) selection of California wines, hard-to-find premium Champagnes and boutique beers from remote breweries. You'll also be impressed with the choice ports, Cognacs, Armagnacs, single-malt scotches and imported wines in every price range. Thankfully, the salespeople are knowledgeable and helpful. The small grocery area in back is stocked high quality pâtés, cheeses, caviar, smoked salmon and other imported delicacies. Prices are fair, gift baskets start at $35 and the specials are always good deals.

Gifts

Abercrombie & Fitch
South Bay Galleria, 1815 Hawthorne Blvd.,
Redondo Beach 90278; (310) 371-5575
Open Mon.-Fri. 10 a.m.-9 p.m., Sat. 10 a.m.-7 p.m., Sun. 11 a.m.-6 p.m.

All of the objects here have one thing in common: they effuse the aura of old money. Musts for some, ridiculous to many, the stock includes everything from wooden-duck decoys to $2,500 croquet sets to overpriced safari suits.

Brookstone
Beverly Center, Beverly & La Cienega Blvds.,
W. Hollywood 90048; (310) 659-9491
Open Mon.-Fri. 10 a.m.-9 p.m., Sat. 10 a.m.-8 p.m., Sun. 11 a.m.-6 p.m.

This gadget store, high on concept, employs the gimmick of a showroom atmosphere, where only floor samples fill the space; customers note their choices on clipboards, and an eager staff fills the orders from a behind-the-scenes stockroom. You'll find exceptionally giftable items: high-tech and well-thought-out tools for the garden, garage, car, closet, bathroom and kitchen.

Casa de Sousa

19 Olvera St., Downtown (L.A.) 90012;
(213) 626-7076
Open daily 10 a.m.-8 p.m.

A tradition on Olvera Street, Casa de Sousa imports its folk art directly from Mexican and Central American sources, so prices are extremely reasonable. The shop is well-known for its vases with a soft, polished luster from Oaxaca, as well as decorative plates and serving platters. There are rustic signed metal wall pieces with "tree of life" motifs from Haiti and wonderful Guatemalan fabric cocktail napkins.

Craft and Folk Art Museum Shop

5800 Wilshire Blvd., Wilshire District (L.A.) 90036; (213) 937-5544
May Company, 6067 Wilshire Blvd., 4th Fl., Wilshire District (L.A.) 90036; (213) 937-9099
Open Tues.-Sat. 10 a.m.-5 p.m., Sun. 11 a.m.-5 p.m.

This nonprofit shop of the Craft and Folk Art Museum (and its temporary satellite in the May Company) offers contemporary and ethnic folk art—mostly from local craftspeople—at reasonable prices. The selection of jewelry (from avant-garde to whimsical) is particularly good; there are also beautiful ceramics and glassware, a good choice of art books and a novel collection of cards and postcards. It's nearly impossible to resist a purchase in either location.

The Folk Tree

217 S. Fair Oaks Ave., Pasadena 91105;
(818) 795-8733
Open Mon.-Sat. 11 a.m.-6 p.m., Sun. noon-5 p.m.

Nicely displayed in a series of small rooms, the primarily Hispanic folk crafts here are a mix of mainstream and bizarre. Hand-blown glasses, serapes, primitive pots and tin-framed mirrors are set off by fantasy wooden figures and religious antiques. You'll also find exotic, handmade clothes and jewelry from around the world, The Folk Tree is appealing to both the serious collector and the casual browser. The neighboring Folk Tree Collection is a new branch that carries an eclectic mix of contemporary and antique Southwestern furniture, crafts and collectibles.

Freehand Gallery

8413 W. 3rd St., W. Hollywood 90048;
(213) 655-2607
Open Mon.-Sat. 11 a.m.-6 p.m.

Carol Sauvion has amassed a unique collection of beautiful handmade clothing, jewelry, ceramics, glassware and gift items. Everything's one-of-a-kind, and she has an excellent eye for unusual yet eminently tasteful crafts, all made by local artisans. You're sure to find something for anyone in this bright, attractive shop, from charming $15 earrings to beautiful ceramic vases to handsome, avant-garde clothing.

Geary's North

437 N. Beverly Dr., Beverly Hills 90210;
(310) 273-4741
Open Mon. 10 a.m.-9 p.m., Tues.-Fri. 10 a.m.-6 p.m., Sat. 10 a.m.-5:30 p.m.

Much less stodgy than its mother shop down the street, Geary's North stocks trendy, colorful ceramics, the popular Lladro Spanish porcelain, framed graphics, pillows and other decorative accessories, instead of the traditional crystal, china and silver gifts offered at Geary's. Prices are within reason, and the selection is sometimes unusual.

Hammacher Schlemmer

309 N. Rodeo Dr., Beverly Hills 90210;
(310) 859-7255
Open Mon.-Sat. 10 a.m.-6 p.m., Sun. noon-5 p.m.

Known for its high-tech gadgetry and nonessential (but oh-so-clever) gift items, this is the famous catalog company's only West Coast retail store. H.S. likes to preface its wares with tags like "the best" and "the only"—as in the best men's shaver (by Sanyo), and the only baseball uniform worn by Gary Cooper in the film, *Pride of the Yankees*, going for $125,000. While there are some purely gimmicky items here, the store's (and the catalog's) strength lies in its high-quality practical items. We love the electronic cat door through which only your code key–wearing kitty may pass, the automatic potato-chip maker and the water-balloon catapult.

Heaven

7611 Melrose Ave., Melrose-Fairfax District (L.A.) 90048; (213) 852-0830
Open Sun.-Thurs. 11:30 a.m.-7:30 p.m., Fri.-Sat. 11 a.m.-10 p.m.
1218 Third Street Promenade, Santa Monica 90401; (310) 319-2433
Open Mon.-Fri. 9 a.m.- 6 p.m., Sat.-Sun. 11 a.m.-7 p.m.

Heaven maybe for a twelve-year-old, this over-priced boutique is filled with the silliest stock in town: monster makeup, rubber snakes, plastic Kewpie dolls, T-shirts emblazoned with the Shirelles, Captain Video and Heckel and Jeckel, and a great selection of penny candy, from red hots and jawbreakers to cigarette-shape bubble gum. Also a branch in the Beverly Connection.

Some establishments change their closing times without warning. It is always wise to check in advance.

Lavender & Lace
656 N. Larchmont Blvd., Larchmont Village 90004;
(213) 856-4846
Open Tues.-Fri. 10:30 a.m.-6:30 p.m., Sat. 10 a.m.-5 p.m.

Owner J.J. Jenkins and her husband, John Waterson, modeled the shop after the French country flea markets she frequented while studying fashion design in Paris. Her penchant for flowers comes through in the starched bed linens, pillows with vintage crocheted borders, tapestry-covered hatboxes, tea runners, tablecloths and lace curtains. Use your imagination, and you might hear strains of the hustle and bustle of a French flea market as you shop here.

Lawry's California Center
570 W. 26th Ave. (junction of Golden State Frwy. & Pasadena Frwy.), Cypress Park 90065;
(213) 224-6800
Open daily 10:30 a.m.-9:30 p.m.

Clearly dedicated to the art of gift giving, Lawry's is seemingly set up for impulse buying during a lunch-and-tour visit. The gift shops are extensive enough to warrant a trip on their own, especially before Christmas. These shops are dedicated to the good life, the *Sunset* magazine life. You'll find all the tools to entertain with style: terrific paper goods, barbecue and patio items, tureens, lavish platters and bright tablecloths. There's also great ethnic clothing, toys, cute stationery and cards and lots of kitchen gadgets.

Mixt
1811 S. Catalina Ave., Redondo Beach 90277;
(310) 375-3665
Open Mon.-Tues. 11 a.m.-6 p.m., Wed. & Fri.-Sat. 10 a.m.-6 p.m., Thurs. 10 a.m.-7 p.m.

Judith Burke's South Bay haven for decorative arts stocks a terrific assortment of home-related gift ideas, many of which are artisan-made. Attractively priced accessories include stainless-steel serving pieces in extraordinary shapes, hand-blown glass soap dishes and some of the most well-designed bird houses we've seen.

New Stone Age
8407 W. 3rd St., W. Hollywood 90046;
(213) 658-5969
Open Mon.-Sat. 11 a.m.-6 p.m.

This gallery/store does a good job of accommodating the burgeoning American crafts movement, focusing on artists who push the limits of traditional craft materials. Among the unconventional finds: hand-forged wrought-iron candlesticks, folk art, small-scale furniture, art glass, jewelry and other inspired gift ideas. Prices range from $5 to several hundred.

The Pleasure Chest
7733 Santa Monica Blvd., W. Hollywood 90069;
(213) 650-1022
Open daily 10 a.m.-1 a.m.

Sex is out of the closet and onto the shelves of this modern erotic-items supermarket. Here you can find the largest selection of carnal merchandise anywhere in the country. Lingerie, massage oils—even edible panties—are all here, waiting to satisfy any fantasy. Plain brown wrappers and mail-order catalogs are available for the timid.

Sadie
167 S. Crescent Heights Blvd., W. Hollywood 90069; (213) 655-0689
Open Tues.-Fri. 10:30 a.m.-6 p.m., Sat. 10:30 a.m.-5 p.m.

This personal wood-shingled shop stocks an unusual assortment of gifts—from such chic kitchen items as raspberry vinegar to old-fashioned toys, art cards, toiletries, jewelry and children's books. The selection of cookware, baskets and gourmet grocery items is particularly nice, the service is attentive and there's a deli counter with good takeout sandwiches.

The Sharper Image
9550 Little Santa Monica Blvd., Beverly Hills 90210;
(310) 271-0515
Open Mon.-Sat. 10 a.m.-6 p.m., Sun. noon-5 p.m.
601 Wilshire Blvd., Downtown (L.A.) 90017;
(213) 622-2351
Open Mon.-Sat. 10 a.m.-6 p.m.

There's something about all the high-tech gadgets here that makes customers—probably more browsers than buyers—laugh out loud. Why would anyone need such a fancy phone? Or a device to detect whether your phone is being bugged? Or a sonic massager? Need has nothing to do with the icing-on-the-cake items, toys for adults and wonderful conversation-starters for sale here. Also at Galleria at South Bay.

The Soap Plant/Wacko
7400 Melrose Ave., Melrose-La Brea District (L.A.) 90046; (213) 651-5587
Open Mon.-Wed. 10:30 a.m.-11 p.m., Thurs.-Sat. 10:30 a.m.-midnight, Sun. 11 a.m.-8 p.m.

Located just steps from each other, these same-owner shops are quintessential Melrose. Both are tributes to the owner's oddball tastes: he seems to stock what he likes, the public be damned. Mexican Day of the Dead skulls sidle up to magic-shop trinkets, avant-garde greeting cards, soaps, trendy toys, scents and a quirky but delightful book section.

Sonrisa

7609 Beverly Blvd., Melrose-Fairfax District (L.A.) 90036; (213) 935-8438
Open Mon.-Sat. 10 a.m.-6 p.m.

Sonrisa is alive with color, displaying some of the best Mexi-L.A. and Southwestern arts and crafts in the city. Owner Peggy Byrnes combines fine art by local Hispanic artists with handcrafted furniture from Taos, New Mexico, and contemporary local folk art. A Melrose must.

Steve

9530 Santa Monica Blvd., Beverly Hills 90210; (310) 274-6567
Mon.-Sat. 10 a.m.-6 p.m., Sun. noon-5 p.m.

Named for co-owner/designer Steve Reiman, this store is packed to the rafters with tabletop art, home furnishings and environmental scents. The crafts run from ethnic to avant-garde and run the gamut of prices. An inspired tabletop selection includes Mikasa and Sasaki, affordable contemporary flatware, drawers of napkins and stacks of napkin rings; picture frames come in a grand array of materials.

Twigs

1401 Montana Ave., Santa Monica 90403; (310) 451-9934
Open Mon.-Sat. 10 a.m.-6 p.m.

A warm, rustic shop filled with wreaths, boxes, baskets, crystal, toys and collectibles. There are also silk flowers and antique and brass pieces that make wonderful gifts for people with English-style or traditionally decorated homes.

Uncle Jer's

4459 Sunset Blvd., Silverlake 90027; (213) 662-6710
Open Mon.-Fri. 11 a.m.-7 p.m., Sat. 10 a.m.-6 p.m., Sun. noon-5 p.m.

Uncle Jer's is eccentric, eclectic, intriguing—a terrific little shop in an oddball neighborhood in southern Los Feliz, near the Vista Theatre and Blue Meringue. There are three main components: ethnic arts and crafts from the Far East, Africa, Latin America and beyond (religious artifacts from Tibet, hand-painted ceramic objects, decorative wall sculptures); imported womenswear, ranging from the latest Parisian popular styles to lots of batiked garments to clothing made from beautiful Central American fabrics. A good source for an unusual, reasonably priced gift.

Wild Blue

7220 Melrose Ave., Melrose-La Brea District (L.A.) 90046; (213) 939-8434
Open Mon.-Sat. 11 a.m.-6 p.m.

Artists with a sense of humor sell their wares here. The ceramics are a hoot: a platter shaped like a swimming pool, laughing-dog boxes, a plate lined with 3-D chile peppers. A Wild Blue "TV" pin (it flashes a digital message such as LIVING COLOR or STAY TUNED) makes an offbeat gift, along with one of the store's funky cards. There are also some exquisite vases, perfume bottles, hand-tinted photos and original jewelry. ·

Zero Minus Plus

Fred Segal Santa Monica, 500 Broadway, Santa Monica 90401; (310) 395-5718
Open Mon.-Sat. 10 a.m.-7 p.m., Sun. noon-6 p.m.

When it comes to decorative home accessories, this is one of L.A.'s top retailers. Savvy shoppers flock here to find high-end tabletop wares by Swid Powell, Sabattini and Salvatore Polizzi, local art glass and pottery, hand-painted table linens, vases and candlesticks. The highly selective buyers for Zero Minus Plus also excel at greeting cards, stationery, gift wrap, desk sets, elegant gifts for men, blank journals, photo albums and picture frames. And an unusual claim to fame: this store is one of the largest suppliers of Filofax agenda accessories in the city.

Home

China & Crystal

Cottura

7215 Melrose Ave., Melrose-La Brea District (L.A.) 90046; (213) 933-1928
Open Mon.-Sat. 11 a.m.-6 p.m., Sun. noon-5 p.m.

This breathtaking little shop sells reasonably priced vibrant hand-painted ceramics from Italy, Spain and Portugal. There are many colorful, unique dinnerware patterns; quality ranges from rustic to fine. You'll find everything from egg cups to urns in ceramic, as well as handmade and hand-painted Venetian glass. Also a branch in the Century City Shopping Center.

David Orgell

320 N. Rodeo Dr., Beverly Hills 90210; (310) 272-3355
Open Mon.-Sat. 10 a.m.-6 p.m.

Crystal, silver, china, antiques and such specialties as old English silver, estate jewelry, rare gifts and collector's items are the stock-in-trade here. Everything is well displayed, and the prices are most reasonable. Excellent sales are occasionally held.

Geary's

351 N. Beverly Dr., Beverly Hills 90210;
(310) 273-4741
Open Mon. 9:30 a.m.-9 p.m., Tues.-Fri. 9:30 a.m.-6
p.m., Sat. 10 a.m.-5:30 p.m.

Stocking the most extensive collection of china, crystal and silver in town, Geary's is the oldest specialty shop in Beverly Hills, with two enormous floors of Wedgwood, Lalique, Baccarat, Royal Crown Derby, Spode, Wallace and Villeroy & Boch, to name just a few. We wouldn't advise shopping here on Saturday (it's a madhouse); instead, come during the week. You'll find a most helpful and courteous sales staff. Geary's does a booming business in bridal registry and mail order.

Villeroy & Boch Creation

338 N. Rodeo Dr., Beverly Hills 90210;
(310) 858-6522
Open Mon.-Sat. 10 a.m.-6 p.m.

At this branch of the prestigious European-based ceramics giant, collectors will find many more patterns and unusual pieces than have previously been available in L.A. A good example is Paloma Picasso's Bijou: crystal and bone-china giftware ringed in gold and embedded with semi-precious orbs of black onyx, green agate or red carnelian. There are sensuously shaped bowls, vases, goblets, candle holders and ashtrays.

Fabric

Elegance

8350 Beverly Blvd., W. Hollywood 90048;
(213) 655-8656
Open Mon.-Sat. 9:30 a.m.-6 p.m.

Devotees of the French magazine *Elegance* will rejoice in its local incarnation. These two shops sell virtually every fabric, button and trim in the magazine's editorial pages, making this the best coordinated of the upscale-yardage shops. There are two collections a year, and at season's end, these silks, linens and woolens are reduced 50 percent.

Left Bank Fabric Company

8354 W. 3rd St., W. Hollywood 90048;
(213) 655-7289
18739 Ventura Blvd., Tarzana 91356;
(818) 708-2751
Open Mon.-Sat. 10 a.m.-6 p.m.

Half the customers at this upscale shop don't know how to sew—but they know a dressmaker who'll use these fabrics to whip up knock-'em-dead suits and dinner dresses. Much of the stock

comes from Europe or designer cutting rooms (Albert Nipon, Calvin Klein, YSL, Oscar de la Renta): silk charmeuse, wispy, thin lamés, gorgeous and exotic prints, soft cashmeres and more. Expensive but worth it. Also a branch in Newport Beach (3415 Newport Blvd., 714-675-9165, open Mon.-Tues. & Thurs.-Sat. 10 a.m.-6 p.m., Wed. 10 a.m.-9 p.m.)

Oriental Silk Import and Export Co.

8377 Beverly Blvd., W. Hollywood 90048;
(213) 651-2323
Open Mon.-Sat. 9 a.m.-6 p.m.

This cluttered, musty shop has excellent prices on silk of average- to good-quality. The selection of prints and brocades is particularly nice (most are $9.95 per yard, though sales often bring the prices down much lower). There's also a good selection of Chinese cotton T-shirts and little embroidered silk blouses; the Chinese vases and knickknacks are forgettable.

Princess Fabrics

6745 Van Nuys Blvd., Van Nuys 91405;
(818) 781-2622
Open Mon.-Sat. 10 a.m.-6 p.m., Sun. noon-5 p.m.

Silks, woolens, cottons, knits, drapery and upholstery fabrics are sold here at reasonable prices. If you have the patience to go through masses of materials, you'll be rewarded with some excellent buys. Princess also stocks craft supplies, including foam for upholstering couches and chairs.

Furnishings

Bobi Leonard Interiors

2727 Main St., Santa Monica 90405;
(310) 399-3251
Open daily 10 a.m.-6 p.m.

Bobi Leonard was big in the early '80s. A visit to her large Main Street shop reveals her carefully formulated taste in vases, baskets, silk flowers—everything from trinkets to custom furniture.

Civilization

8884 Venice Blvd., Culver City 90034;
(310) 202-8883
Open Mon.-Fri. 10 a.m.-7 p.m., Sat. 10 a.m.-6 p.m., Sun. 11 a.m.-6 p.m.

Civilization devotes most of its 25,000 square feet of space to contemporary, domestically designed and produced furniture, lighting and accessories. Forty percent of the offerings are one-of-a-kind and limited-production pieces by local artists and architects. Co-owners Jay

Dunton and Rick Green have collected such cutting-edge designs as cast-aluminum tables, hand-finished chairs, tabletop mosaics of tiles set in colored concrete, polished-steel end tables and coffee tables of broken stone.

Conran's Habitat

Beverly Center, Beverly & La Cienega Blvds., W. Hollywood 90048; (310) 659-1444
Open Mon.-Fri. 10 a.m.-9 p.m., Sat. 10 a.m.-8 p.m., Sun. 11 a.m.-6 p.m.

This L.A. branch of the wildly popular London-based store features 50,000 square feet of contemporary and country-simple home furnishings. Conran's strength lies in straightforward design, function and affordability in products that range from soap dishes to leather sofas. Among the L.A. firsts: European wooden and metal garden furniture (carried year-round), art deco–inspired armoires from Italy and solid-maple bedroom furniture.

A comprehensive kitchen and cookware section offers endless styles of glasses, including hand-blown glasses from Mexico and Spain, as well as hand-painted Italian ceramics and sleek, vegetable-dyed wooden tableware from Malaysia. In the bath section, there are fluffy towels and robes and handsome, hand-woven Malaysian laundry baskets; an office-design section carries sleekly modern accessories and furniture for the workspace of the '90s. It's a total look, and if it succeeds in seducing you, you may just walk out with the entire store.

Danica

209 N. Brand St., Glendale 91203; (818) 502-0983
Open Mon.-Sat. 10 a.m.-6 p.m., Sun. noon-5 p.m.

Lots of big, bold, modern Scandinavian furniture, especially in chrome, glass and teakwood. Especially popular are the modular couches, wall units and dining sets. Don't miss the fabulous collection of leather couches—both Norwegian models with frames of teak or mahogany, and full-leather Italian imports in earth tones. Prices tend to be on the high side.

Domestic

7385 Beverly Blvd., Fairfax District (L.A.) 90036; (213) 936-8206
Open Mon.-Fri. 10 a.m.-6 p.m., Sat. 11 a.m.-6 p.m.

An innovative furniture-production house and a sterling addition to L.A.'s design landscape, Domestic sells moderately priced pieces with severe lines and homey appeal. All of the furniture is a mix of solid maple- or cherry-and-plywood veneer with a clear matte-lacquer finish. The timeless designs range from ladder-back dining

chairs to a two-poster queen-size bed with a massive molded-plywood headboard.

Fabrica

468 S. Robertson Blvd., W. Hollywood 90048; (310) 276-2039
Open Mon.-Fri. 9 a.m.-5 p.m.

This showroom specializes in designing unique custom area rugs and manufactures them in its local factory. There are more than 150 stock designs to choose from, including floral prints and striking bordered patterns, and all can be done in a variety of colors. Prices are reasonable.

Fantasy Lites

7126 Melrose Ave., Melrose-La Brea District (L.A.) 90046; (213) 933-7244
Open Mon.-Fri. 9 a.m.-5:30 p.m., Sat. 9 a.m.-5 p.m.

If you love beaded Tiffany lamp shades, Wayne Cline's collection of antique-replica lamps and newer glass models will thrill you. Cline uses gorgeous colors, and if you can't find a creation of his that suits your home, he'll be happy to custom-design one for you. Many of the lamps and much of the lighting you see in movies and on TV were supplied by Fantasy Lites.

Harry Furniture

8639 Venice Blvd., Culver City 90034; (310) 559-7863
Open Mon.-Fri. 9:30 a.m.- 5:30 p.m.

Kitsch is a well-worn term, but one that applies ruthlessly to this used-and-revamped furniture emporium. In this warehouselike atmosphere, Harry offers cast-off atrocities from the '40s, '50s and '60s—like bentwood Eames chairs desecrated with cowhide and paint, or geometrical sofas, each section reupholstered in differently colored garish vinyls or drab, recycled '40s and '50s fabrics in colors like puce and lime. Among the miscellany are dishes, lamps and large examples of advertising art. Once in a while a really good piece or two will show up, like the moderne armoires from England we once spied, which seemed like bargains compared to the rest of the merchandise here.

Ikea

600 N. San Fernando Blvd., Burbank 91502; (818) 842-4532
Open Mon.-Fri. 11 a.m.-9 p.m., Sat. 10 a.m.-8 p.m., Sun. 11 a.m.-6 p.m.

This mammoth, Swedish-based home furnishings store rhymes with idea—and it offers hundreds of good ones at incredibly low prices. A gander through the first floor Marketplace came up with a package of 100 tea lights, primary colored child-size suitcases, a four-piece screwdriver set with matte black rubber handles, coil-shaped egg cups of lacquered wire, cotton throw rugs in offbeat colors, tubs of household paint, kitchen gadgets, halogen lighting, fabric by the yard and countless other compulsive buyer temptations. If you get past the Marketplace to the room designs upstairs, discover black leather club chairs, a black metal and rosewood-stained serving cart with casters and a pale green rattan armchair. Some ideas are better than others, but Ikea is definitely worth the trip.

Kreiss Ports of Call Imports
8619 Melrose Ave., W. Hollywood 90069;
(310) 657-3990
Open Mon.-Fri. 9:30 a.m.-5 p.m., Sat. 10 a.m.-5 p.m.

Definitely a California look, though a somewhat dated one. Everything's oversized and overstuffed and made of either wicker or duck canvas. The furniture and accessories are trendy but at the same time extremely attractive and well made. The decorating service is excellent. There are other locations, though the West Hollywood branch is the largest. These showrooms are open to the public, but you must buy through a designer.

Lexington Place
2557 Mission St., San Marino 91108;
(818) 441-5559
Open Mon.-Sat. 10 a.m.-5:30 p.m.

Few shops manage to pull off the true charms of the country look as successfully as Lexington Place does. The skillful blend of antiques and reproductions, wicker, pine, twigs, quilts and decoys is irresistible. In addition to off-the-floor furniture and accessories, the shop has a decorating service for advice, upholstery and draperies; if you prefer to seek inspiration yourself, there is a strong collection of books on Americana. Nice things for seasonal tables: for Easter, a basket of wooden robin's eggs; for Thanksgiving, a hand-carved Puritan family; for Christmas, beautiful wreaths.

Linder Design
440 N. La Brea Ave., Melrose-La Brea District (L.A.) 90036; (213) 939-4020
Open Tues.-Fri. 10 a.m.-7 p.m., Sat. 10 a.m.-5 p.m., Sun. noon; 5 p.m.

Linder Design offers a pastiche of current home and office furnishings. This is the only L.A. store to carry expensive Austrian Woka lamps—precise reproductions, down to the nuts and bolts, of early twentieth century works by such design luminaries as Josef Hoffman, Otto Wagner and Kolo Moser.

Polo Ralph Lauren
444 N. Rodeo Dr., Beverly Hills 90210;
(310) 281-7200
Open Mon.-Sat. 10 a.m.-6 p.m.

On the second floor of the celebrated Polo shop you'll find everything you need to become a citizen of Ralph Lauren's beautiful and comprehensively designed world, which we'll call Pololand. All the furnishings are here, from Edwardian-style rattan bedsteads and woolly throws to fine bed linens and dark paisley comforters. There are even tableaux vivants of complete bedrooms, all cozy with plump, ruffled pillows and four-poster beds, to serve as models. England and Europe have been virtually emptied of naive animal paintings, vintage ceramics and sundry other antique doodads that will lend just the right touch of gentility to your drawing room or living room.

Rapport
435 N. La Brea Ave., Melrose-La Brea District (L.A.) 90036; (213) 930-1500
Open Tues.-Sat. 9:30 a.m.-5 p.m.

Young couples who want to furnish their new home shop in this enormous place full of contemporary furniture. Many of the prices are discounted.

Shabby Chic
1013 Montana Ave., Santa Monica 90403;
(310) 394-1975
Open Mon.-Wed. 10 a.m.-6 p.m., Thurs.-Sat. 10 a.m.-7 p.m., Sun. noon-5 p.m.

Shabby Chic will dress down your digs with washable slipcovers that lend a look of faded elegance to sofas, loveseats, armchairs and the like. A roomful of white furniture is no longer the stuff of dreams when you know durable denim slipcovers can hit the suds (even the bleach) whenever the occasion demands. Besides white denim, the store offers covers in cotton damasks, velvets and nineteenth-century English florals printed on linen. Shabby Chic also sells its floor models, furniture to order and accessories with the "used, loved and lived-in" look.

For more home-decorating ideas, see the "Antiques & Collectibles" section of this chapter, which will lead you to sources for everything from Chinese porcelain to French country pine furniture to Navajo textiles.

Housewares & Tabletop

All American Home Center
7201 E. Firestone Blvd., Downey 90241;
(310) 927-8666
Open Mon.-Sat. 8 a.m.-9 p.m., Sun. 8 a.m.-6 p.m.

Downey may not be on your beaten path, but if you're contemplating any sort of home improvement, this place is worth a special trip. It's set apart from the normal home-improvement centers by its immense size—21 departments spread over four acres, with an extra six acres of parking—and by that rarity of rarities these days, independent family ownership. So instead of the confused impersonality of the big chains, you get first-rate professional service. And you get a selection that blows most home-improvement stores out of the water, with more than 90,000 items in stock at any given time. Whether you're contemplating buying a new garden hose or adding a new master bathroom, All American will get you what you need.

Armstrong Home and Garden Place
11321 W. Pico Blvd., W.L.A. 90064;
(310) 477-8023
Open Mon.-Thurs. 7:30 a.m.-7:30 p.m., Fri. 7:30 a.m.-9 p.m., Sat. 7:30 a.m.-6 p.m., Sun. 9:30 a.m.-6 p.m.

So much more than just a place to buy landscape rock, hardware and paint, Armstrong is an all-things-to-all-people store, a great place to find all kinds of housewares. With a stop for free coffee, a good browse here will take at least an hour. The indoor plant section is extensive and staffed by knowledgeable workers; the basket selection just too tempting. Don't miss the rag rugs, slick T-shirts, great kitchen gadgets, checkered toothbrushes, clever shower curtains and, of course, shiny black pebbles to grow paperwhite narcissi in.

Avery Restaurant Supply
905 E. 2nd St., Downtown (L.A.); (213) 624-7832
Open Mon.-Fri. 8 a.m.-5 p.m., Sat. 9 a.m.-2 p.m.

Many of L.A.'s headlining restaurants are serviced by Avery, the largest restaurant-supply store on the West Coast. Thankfully, it's also open to those who cook for pleasure—and what a pleasure it is to discover everything from Waring blenders to Wolf ranges, at wholesale prices (which means about 30 percent below retail cost). The stunning space, designed by Frank Gehry, encompasses 30,000 square feet and resembles a sort of Disneyland for cooks. A new, innovative tabletop showroom displays china, glassware and flatware. Those with smaller budgets can pick up the same professional cookware, cutlery and utensils used by some of the major chefs in town. Absolutely worth the trip, and once you get there, parking is free.

Home Economics
The Marketplace, 6487 E. Pacific Coast Hwy., Long Beach 90803; (310) 430-3967
Open Mon.-Sat. 10 a.m.-6 p.m., Sun. noon-5 p.m.

A bright, contemporary store with more than the typical kitchenware. Of course, there are Chinese sauté pans, colorful kitchen linens, classic stemware, Southwestern table settings and gadgets, gadgets and more gadgets. But you'll also find all kinds of unusual merchandise, from the elegant (beautiful hand-painted Italian dishes), to the practical (Lucite salad bowls), to the zany (chile-pepper earrings). Picnic tote bags, barbecue supplies and paper goods, too.

Maison et Café
148 S. La Brea Ave., Melrose-La Brea District (L.A.) 90036; (213) 935-3157.
Open Mon.-Sat. 9 a.m.-9 p.m , Sun 9 a.m.-7:30 p.m.

This two-year-old addition to the American Rag Cie. empire is as disarmingly stylish (and expensive) as the adjoining clothing shop. The "Maison" translates as a warehouse chock full of everything you'd ever need to furnish a French country home: rough pine antiques, reproduction pine antiques and wrought-iron tables and chairs from France and Mexico, ceramic bistroware in brilliant greens and yellows, candlesticks, Parisian café ashtrays and Provençal fabrics sold by the yard. In the back, next to the drawers overflowing with imported olive oils and vinegars, is the "Café" half of the store. Run by Bread Only bakery, one of the best in the city, the café sells fresh-daily French country breads, as well as espresso drinks and a simple lunch menu of Mediterranean salads and sandwiches.

Montana Mercantile
1500 Montana Ave., Santa Monica 90403; (310) 451-1418
Open Mon.-Fri. 10 a.m.-6:30 p.m., Sat. 10 a.m.-6 p.m.

This gourmet cookware store and cooking school is slick as can be. The emphasis is on high-end serving pieces, plates, bakeware and glasses, but there is an excellent selection of small and indispensable gadgets for the frequent cook. Montana Mercantile is also becoming known for its artware, jewelry, personal accessories and luxurious bathrobes. One of the best cuisine-oriented stores in L.A. Inquire about the full range of cooking classes offered.

Pottery Barn

Century City Shopping Center, 10250 Santa Monica
Blvd., Century City 90067; (310) 552-0170
*Open Mon.-Fri. 10 a.m.-9 p.m., Sat. 10 a.m.-7 p.m.,
Sun. 11 a.m.-6 p.m.*

These cheerful stores carry the latest in kitchen
gadgets and accessories, as well as stoneware,
earthenware, stainless steel and casual furniture.
Most of the merchandise is brightly colored and
très moderne, but the prices aren't as high as high
style generally commands. Also branches in the
Beverly Center, Santa Monica Place, Glendale
Galleria and Westwood Village.

Salutations Ltd.

11640 San Vicente Blvd., Brentwood 90049;
(310) 820-6127
Open Mon.-Sat. 10 a.m.-6 p.m.

A great westside source for colorful tableware,
home furnishings, linens, infant clothing, personal accessories and custom gift baskets. Owner
Carey Appel combines the respected and the
one-of-a-kind with elegant presentation and
warm personal service. A few of her choice finds:
hand-painted tablecloths in the post-Impressionist vein, bath salts in terra-cotta pots and irides-
cent-glass fruits.

Touch of Home

143 W. California Blvd., Pasadena 91105;
(818) 793-8855
Open Mon.-Sat. 10 a.m.-6 p.m., Sun. noon-5 p.m.

This homey gourmet cookware shop is certainly among the finest in town. Hanging from
the ceiling and stocked on the shelves are
Calphalon cookware, Fitz & Floyd accessories,
French porcelain, table linens, cookie cutters,
gourmet teas and coffees, cookbooks, Atlas pasta
machines and all sorts of kitchen gadgets, from
the novel to the just-plain-useful. The staff can
help you create themed gift baskets.

Williams-Sonoma

317 N. Beverly Dr., Beverly Hills 90210;
(310) 274-9127
Open Mon.-Sat. 10 a.m.-8 p.m.

Straight from the pages of the popular and
successful mail-order catalog, this clean-lined
store is loaded with kitchen classics and brand-
new gadgets, many of which only a professional
chef would know how to use. There is a beautiful
mix of functional equipment, decorative accessories, kitchen furniture, handsome tableware and
hard-to-find food items. You'll also find lots of
copper, brass, all-white and hand-painted dinnerware and an excellent selection of dish towels,
napkins and tablecloths. Also branches in the
Beverly Center and Sherman Oaks Fashion
Square.

Linens

The Bonbon Collection

466 N. Robertson Blvd., L.A. 90048;
(310) 657-5600
Open Mon.-Sat. 10 a.m.-6 p.m.

Bonbon is to linen lovers what Belgian bittersweet is to chocoholics. Owner Debra Kessler has
a well-cultivated taste for the finer things in life,
and her enthusiasm tumbles forth in an irresistible array of hand-embellished bed and table linens from Brazil, Italy and France. Modeled after
a European manor, the environment of old world
elegance features great stone-topped tables from
which to study the many linen designs available
for custom-ordering.

Frette

449 N. Rodeo Dr., Beverly Hills 90210;
(310) 273-8540
Open Mon.-Sat. 10 a.m.-6 p.m.

These exquisite linens are unequaled in quality
and design, except perhaps by Pratesi. Specializing in woven jacquards, Frette's handmade,
hand-embroidered beauties for the bed, body,
bath and table are sold at breathtaking prices.

Pratesi

9024 Burton Way, Beverly Hills 90211;
(310) 274-7661
Open Mon.-Sat. 10 a.m.-6 p.m.

The finest linens in town are on Pratesi's
shelves. These Italian sheets, towels, blankets,
tablecloths and quilts are woven to Pratesi's specifications; the cashmere blankets are exceptionally beautiful. Prices, as you might expect, are
numbing.

Scandia Down

310 N. Camden Dr., Beverly Hills 90212;
(310) 274-6925
Open Mon.-Fri. 10 a.m.-7 p.m., Sat. 10 a.m.-6 p.m.

Nothing is as heavenly as cuddling up in an
enormous down comforter, and here they're not
only exceptionally soft and puffy but beautiful
and practical as well. Separate cotton covers are
made for the comforters so you can get two or
three colors or patterns and create completely
different looks. Prices are reasonable.

Nurseries

S.B. Nickerson Nursery

3948 Sepulveda Blvd., Culver City 90232;
(310) 390-3347
Open Mon.-Fri. 7:30 a.m.-4 p.m., Sat. 7:30 a.m.-11 a.m.

The operative word here is *cheap*. So cheap
you'll forget your neighborhood nursery and
willingly make the drive out to Culver City—for

plants priced 40 to 50 percent less than those in retail nurseries. Even Joan Collins shops here, landscapist in tow. These are not sad, cast-off plants but healthy shrubs and trees grown at Nickerson's own facility in Fallbrook. Everything is sold at wholesale-to-the-public prices, except for the small selection of indoor plants. The selection is enormous: bougainvillea vines, red-leaf bananas, bamboo, eucalyptus, tree ferns, ficus and much, much more. Five-gallon plants, which cost about $15 at most nurseries, are about $8.75 here; fifteen-gallon plants, usually $75, are only $47.50. The nursery will deliver free of charge for purchases over $50.

Sassafras Nursery
275 N. Topanga Canyon Blvd., Topanga Canyon 90290; (310) 455-1933
Open daily 9 a.m.-5 p.m.

Sassafras is everything you'd imagine a nursery in Topanga Canyon to be: country-style, casual, cluttered. If you're into the English-country-garden look, this place is a source for both inspiration and such unusual plants as black pansies, cattails, lotuses, water lilies and Irish moss. New at Sassafras are organic vegetables, old-fashioned sweet peas, copper arches covered with climbing roses and wrought-iron furniture. For gifts, there are exquisite baskets filled with plants and flowers. Stop by for holiday surprises, including tiny pumpkins and twiggy wreaths. Inside the shed are indoor plants and exotic cut flowers. For really grand schemes, a landscaping service is available.

Image & Sound

Photography

ABC Photo
9136 Sepulveda Blvd., Westchester 90045; (310) 645-8992
Open Mon.-Fri. 10 a.m.-6 p.m., Sat. 10:30 a.m.-6 p.m., Sun. 11 a.m.-5 p.m.

Expert underwater photographer Alan Broder provides an extensive list of services, including photography classes, labwork and support, and new and used equipment for sale or rent—from the Nikon Action Touch all-weather camera to complete underwater systems. This is the last word in underwater photography.

Frank's Highland Park Camera
5715 N. Figueroa St., Highland Park 90042; (213) 255-0123
Open Mon.-Sat. 9:30 a.m.-6 p.m.

This noteworthy shop is a bit out of the way, but it's worth the effort to seek it out. It's a policed, cash-and-carry type of operation that doesn't respond well to a lot of questions. But if you know what you want, you can find plenty of top-name gear, including professional medium-format cameras, at very low prices. The shop's catalog is justly acclaimed as one of the best discount camera catalogs in the country.

Freestyle Photo Supplies
5124 W. Sunset Blvd., Hollywood 90027; (213) 660-3460
Open Mon.-Fri. 9 a.m.-5:30 p.m., Sat. 10 a.m.-5 p.m., Sun. 11 a.m.-4 p.m.

Amateur photographers on a budget flock to Freestyle for camera supplies and equipment at bargain prices. There seem to be enough outdated and current film, tanks, enlargers, processing equipment and paper here to stock every home darkroom in Los Angeles.

Lee Mac Camera
252 S. Lake Ave., Pasadena 91101; (818) 792-4343
Open Mon.-Sat. 9 a.m.-6 p.m.

Lee Mac seems to have been around forever. The service-oriented guys here are true Nikon specialists. Well established and well-known, you might pay slightly more for items here, but you can't beat the service and selection.

Olympic Camera
828 W. Olympic Blvd., Downtown (L.A.) 90015; (213) 746-0575
Open Mon.-Sat. 9:30 a.m.-5:30 p.m.

One of the better camera stores in town, Olympic is friendly and incredibly well stocked, with a full range of photographic equipment for amateurs as well as professionals, from pocket cameras to industrial-quality movie cameras. The selection of used equipment is quite good. Prices are excellent both in the store and through its booming mail-order business. Additional branches around town.

Pan Pacific Camera
825 N. La Brea Ave., Melrose-La Brea District (L.A.) 90038; (213) 933-5888
Open Mon.-Sat. 9 a.m.-6 p.m.

A longtime favorite of L.A.'s professional and amateur photographers alike. Everything photographic can be found here, including both new and used camera and audiovisual equipment for sale or for rent, elaborate professional lighting systems, collector's cameras, equipment repair, and both color and black-and-white film processing and custom printing. Prices are competitive, and the staff well informed.

Samy's Camera

263 S. La Brea Ave., Melrose-La Brea District (L.A.) 90036; (213) 938-2420
Open Mon.-Fri. 8 a.m.-8 p.m., Sat. 9 a.m.-6 p.m.

Countless professional and amateur photographers around the city were dismayed to see their favorite photo emporium (and its entire inventory) burn to the ground in the riots of spring 1992. The owners didn't waste a moment in restoring the shop, though, and the reincarnated Samy's, in its 10,000-square-foot space on La Brea Avenue, still offers an impressive, wide-ranging collection of photo equipment for sale and rental, both new and used. Samy's also offers professional film processing and printing, and this location has a much bigger parking facility. Gone for now are the priceless hundreds of Leica and Hasselblad cameras, but Samy plans eventually to build the collection again.

Recorded Music

A-1 Record Finders

5639 Melrose Ave., Hollywood 90038; (213) 732-6737
Open Mon.-Fri. noon-6 p.m.

Every record junkie should keep this 24-hour phone number on file. If the nice people at A-1 don't have the rare, out-of-print record you want in stock, they'll find it and sell it to you for a very reasonable price. From Chet Atkins to Frank Zappa, the hardest-to-find discs can be tracked down via A-1's national search service. There are no tapes or CDs here, strictly records at all speeds, and particularly nostalgia, singles, movie soundtracks, rock, pop, classical and jazz. A-1 keeps a customer "want list" and maintains a worldwide mailing service. Store hours are not very regular; it's best to call before you visit.

Aron's Record Shop

1150 N. Highland Ave., Hollywood 90038; (213) 469-4700
Open Mon.-Thurs. 10 a.m.-10 p.m., Fri.-Sat. 10 a.m.-midnight, Sun. 11 a.m.-8 p.m.

Lovers of rock, jazz and classical music can be seen digging through Aron's used-record bins day and night. They come to this shop in the heart of Hollywood for the superb selection and, even more, for the excellent condition of the albums. There's also a decent choice of new and used cassettes and CDs and new rock, jazz, folk, classical, soul and reggae albums; the import section is particularly strong.

Bleecker Bob's

7454 Melrose Ave., Melrose-Fairfax District (L.A.) 90046; (213) 852-9444
Open Mon.-Sat. 11 a.m.-midnight, Sun. noon-midnight.

New Yorkers know Bleecker Bob's in Greenwich Village as the best in rare, alternative and new music, out-of-print and hard-to-find recordings, seven-inch and oldies. British imports are a specialty. If you can't visit the store, call to be placed on the hugely successful mail-order list.

Canterbury Records

805 E. Colorado Blvd., Pasadena 91101; (818) 792-7184
Open Mon-Thurs 9 a.m.-9 p.m., Fri. 9 a.m.-10 p.m., Sat. 9 a.m.-9 p.m., Sun. 10 a.m.-7 p.m.

Canterbury has a well-edited selection of records and CDs, specializing in hard-to-find jazz, classical, regional and ethnic music. There is a small selection of used albums and cassettes; their's is the only big band section for miles around. If you can't find what you're looking for in the shop, the very helpful people behind the counter will order it for you.

CD Banzai

8250 W. 3rd St., W. Hollywood 90048; (213) 653-0800
Open Mon.-Thurs. noon-8 p.m., Fri.-Sat. noon-10 p.m.

Inconspicuously located in a mini-mall, this tiny shop reflects the good-taste of France-born owner Rene Bouhier. He has hand-picked a limited selection of jazz, blues and progressive-rock CDs, as well as a number of Japanese and European imports, and priced them very reasonably. He also carries a small, well-edited number of used CDs. Special orders are available.

Counterpoint Records & Books

5911 Franklin Ave., Hollywood 90028; (213) 469-4465
Open Mon.-Sat. 1 p.m.-10 p.m., Sun. 1 p.m.-8 p.m.

Here you'll find a colorful collection of low-priced used vinyl, from classical to rock, jazz and ethnic music, as well as a library of used books. Co-owner John Polifronio is a walking encyclopedia of information on classical and twentieth century music, while co-owner Susan Mindell is the 20th century poetry specialist.

Disc Connection

10970 W. Pico Blvd., W.L.A. 90061; (310) 208-7211
Open Mon.-Thurs. & Sat. 11 a.m.-7 p.m., Fri. 11 a.m.-9 p.m.

This small shop boasts excellent prices on new and used hard-to-find movie soundtracks, Broadway shows, rock, pop, jazz and nostalgia, both on vinyl and CDs. The selection is remarkably in-depth. A friendly place with helpful sales-people and exceptional sales.

Peer Records

2309 West Balboa Blvd., Newport Beach 92663; (714) 675-3752

Open Sun.-Thurs. 10 a.m.-10 p.m., Fri. & Sat. 10 a.m.-11 p.m.

You'll find a well-stocked selection of alternative records, new and used import and domestic CDs and tapes here, as well as a colorful collection of '60s clothing and paraphernalia. There's another location at 4249 Campus Drive (714-854-8854) in Irvine.

Pooh-Bah Records

1101 E. Walnut St., Pasadena 91106; (818) 449-3359

Open Mon.-Sat. 10 a.m.-9 p.m., Sun. 11 a.m.- 7 p.m.

This friendly, well-established store stocks an unusually well-edited collection of old rhythm and blues and cutting-edge contemporary jazz. There's an eclectic and sizable CD department (up to 7,000 titles) and a solid assortment of used CDs. You'll also find an excellent assortment of albums and singles from independent and alternative labels, and the used-record department is comparable to that of any other used record store in the L.A. area.

The Record Trader

7321 Reseda Blvd., Reseda 91335; (818) 708-0632

Open Mon.-Sat. 10 a.m.-9 p.m., Sun. 11 a.m.-6 p.m.

Besides bins and bins of used records, The Record Trader gets ahold of many new releases before anyone else has them. The new and used selection covers rock and jazz, with some used CDs, and the imports section is sizable. Watch for the blockbuster parking-lot sale once a year.

Rhino Records

1720 Westwood Blvd., Westwood 90024; (310) 474-8685

Open daily 10 a.m.-11 p.m.

This legendary store has tripled in size over the last couple of years, an improvement Rhino management likens to being born again. It seems like Rhino has always been there for serious lovers of rock, jazz, blues, folk, bluegrass and reggae who are looking for good additions to their collections. Chances are they'll find it among the newly expanded inventory of new and used records, CDs, cassettes, independent labels and imports. And now Rhino also carries books and magazines. Excellent prices and an extremely knowledgeable staff.

Rockaway Records

2395 N. Glendale Blvd., Silverlake 90039; (213) 664-3232

Open daily 10 a.m.-9:30 p.m.

This place has really tapped the desires of L.A.'s music-lovers—so much so, that now, in its new location, it's four times the size it was just a few years ago. The used and cutout CDs, rare albums and rock memorabilia are unbeatable. The bins have the best discount cutouts in town—not just from lesser-known talents, like most stores, but from major stars as well. The collections of classical, jazz and country are small but choice; Rockaway's strong suit is rock 'n' roll. A great browsing store and a must for any rock 'n' roll collector.

Sam Goody

Beverly Center, Beverly & La Cienega Blvds., W. Hollywood 90048; (310) 657-3782

Open Mon.-Sat. 10 a.m.-10 p.m., Sun. 11 a.m.-7 p.m.

The Sam Goody on the eighth floor of the Beverly Center has *really* got it: thousands of classical music CDs, as well as large selection of soundtracks. If you can make your way through the Daffy Duck cups, rock music and neon lights at the front of the store, you'll come to this well-lit musical oasis. Catering to the mall's sophisticated clientele, it's a big step up from the other Goodys.

Tower Classical

1060 Westwood Blvd., Westwood 90024; (310) 208-6679
8840 W. Sunset Blvd., W. Hollywood 90069; (310) 657-3910
14570 Ventura Blvd., Sherman Oaks 91403; (818) 789-0500

Open daily 9 a.m.-midnight.

The Hollywood annex has probably the best selections of classical music in the greater L.A. area. Carrying thousands of classical music CDs of composers from Beethoven to Bartók, Prokofiev to Philip Glass and vocalists from Caruso to Cassat, T.C. also has a number of videos, video laser disks and cassettes. In a nook to the side, you'll find sheet music and a broad selection of biographical, academic and historical books on the works and lives of composers and musicians. Special orders are welcome; service is very well-informed.

Tower Records

8801 W. Sunset Blvd., W. Hollywood 90069; (310) 657-7300

Open Sun.-Thurs. 9 a.m.-midnight, Fri.-Sat. 9 a.m.-1 a.m.

The be-all and end-all of music stores, Tower puts all other chain stores to shame, which is why it's constantly filled with a crush of customers.

255

This is L.A.'s main branch of Tower, a teeming place on the Sunset Strip with thousands of CDs, tapes and records in every category, from gospel to punk, Vivaldi to Ellington. Prices are average to low, and the collection of singles from the '50s, '60s and '70s alone is worth a visit. The staff here, however, could be more helpful.

Stereo & Video Equipment

ABC Premiums
7266 Beverly Blvd., Wilshire District (L.A.) 90036; (213) 938-2724
Open Mon.-Sat. 10 a.m.-7 p.m., Sun. 11 a.m.-5 p.m.

ABC is an excellent discount store for anything plug in or use batteries with. The selection of TVs is better than that of stereo equipment, but both departments carry good name brands at very low prices. Know what you want before you go in—service is minimal, as is often the case in discount houses. But ABC is considerably friendlier than its hectic neighboring competitor, Adray's.

Beverly Stereo
8414 W. 3rd St., W. Hollywood 90048; (213) 651-3523
Open Tues.-Sat. 11 a.m.-7 p.m.

The selection is not large at this long-established shop, but the components and systems offered are high in quality—from terrifyingly high priced handmade equipment to more middle-of-the-road audiophile lines like Bang & Olufsen.

Christopher Hansen
8822 W. Olympic Blvd., Beverly Hills 90211; (310) 858-8112
Open Mon.-Sat. 10 a.m.-6 p.m.

The music "designers" at this small shop create outstanding, unusual home or professional music systems from such elite components as Magnepan, Mark Levinson, Audio Research and Goldmund. You can spend anywhere from $1,500 to $250,000, assured you'll have the finest stereo equipment your money can buy. Hollywood's glitterati frequent the place—last time we visited, George Michael and Bobby Brown were shopping there—and many of the clientele come from around the world.

The Good Guys
Beverly Connection, 100 N. La Cienega Blvd., W. Hollywood 90048 (branches everywhere); (310) 659-6500
Open daily 24 hours (other branches vary).

The most striking feature of this San Francisco–based consumer electronics store is the phenomenal level of service: each of L.A.'s fifteen

branches employs a swarm of eager salespeople to guide you through the store, answer questions and help you test the equipment. The shops are like candy stores for equipment freaks, loaded with high-end stereo equipment, TVs and TV furniture, VCRs and camcorders, as well as cellular telephones, answering machines and more. Floor-sample deals and special-quantity purchases are common. These good guys will temporarily replace a defective unit until yours is fixed, and if it takes more than 60 days, they'll replace it permanently. Other branches in Westside Pavilion, Marina Del Rey, Pasadena, Northridge and Woodland Hills.

Optimal Enchantment
522 Santa Monica Blvd., Santa Monica 90401; (310) 393-4434, (310) 393-HIFI.
Mon.-Sat. 11 a.m.-6 p.m., by appt. only.

One of the oldest high-fidelity operations in L.A. (alongside Christopher Hansen), Optimal Enchantment is among the crème de la crème of audio stores. Audiotechs will find more then enough to keep them mesmerized, but this is the place for music-lovers. Owner Randy Cooley handles all brands, even obscure audiophile equipment. And while you can spend anywhere from $800 to $20,000, Cooley will make sure you get your money's worth.

Video Sales & Rentals

Aside from the numerous branches of **Block-Buster Video** (213-851-2688), **Music Plus** (213-938-3048) and **Wherehouse** (213-874-2332), which stock primarily the big screen's best-sellers, there are a few noteworthy independent video stores that carry an exceptional selection of films. Some specialize in particular genres, others just hard-to-find classics.

Rocket Video
633 N. La Brea Ave., Hollywood 90036; (213) 965-1100
Open Sun.-Thurs. 11 a.m.-10 p.m., Fri.-Sat. 11 a.m.-11 p.m.

Rocket Video is a refreshing change of pace from the chain stores: besides all the typical video fare, the cordial people at Rocket seek out hard-to-find classic and foreign titles. A favorite among Hollywood's artsy-movie addicts.

Starlight Roof
820 Fair Oaks Ave., S. Pasadena 91030; (818) 799-1001
Open Tues.-Sat. 11 a.m.-6 p.m.

This definitely unslick, one-man operation divides its inventory between videotapes and recorded music. You'll find vintage American television shows, American classics, films of big-band musicians and groups that you may not find anywhere else in L.A. And if John doesn't have it, he'll find it for you.

Tower Video
1028 Westwood Blvd., Westwood 90024;
(310) 208-3061
8844 W. Sunset Blvd., Hollywood 90069;
(310) 657-3344
Open 9 a.m.-midnight.

The Lone Ranger of chains, Tower offers the sort of above-standard selection of classics and foreign films that usually only an independent would dare carry. There's also a colorful variety of films not found in your average video store: a funky midnight-movies section; a special-interest section carrying anything from health videos to National Geographic films; and a most impressive selection of TV series. Well-stocked and run by bright, helpful salespeople. The Westwood branch has videos for sale only, not for rent.

Videoactive
2522 Hyperion Ave., Silverlake 90027;
(213) 669-8544
Open Sun.-Thurs. 9 a.m.-11 p.m., Fri.-Sat. 9 a.m.-1 a.m.

This small, always-crowded store feels more like a book-lover's bookstore with its shelves and shelves (clear up to the ceiling) of foreign films, television series and classics, including some rare ones. Membership is $35 year.

Vidiots
302 Pico Blvd., Santa Monica 90405;
(310) 392-8508
Open Sun.-Thurs. 11 a.m.-11 p.m., Fri.-Sat. 11 a.m.-midnight.

Vidiots is a small, funky little shop known for its excellent selection of rare and foreign movies and its books on movies, screenwriting and scripts. With a $10 purchase from the nearby Galaxy Café, they'll deliver your videos. A hot number in every L.A. cinemaphile's Rolodex.

Leather & Luggage

Bottega Veneta
457 N. Rodeo Dr., Beverly Hills 90210;
(310) 858-6533
Open Mon.-Sat. 10 a.m.-6 p.m.

These Italian artisans get our vote for the most attractive leather goods. Their shoes and handbags are done in the softest leathers imaginable

in a variety of subtle shades. The luggage and briefcases are handsome and oh-so-stylish. Naturally, such refinement doesn't come cheap—the signature woven-leather bags start at $300.

Céline
460 N. Rodeo Dr., Beverly Hills 90210;
(310) 273-1243
Open Mon.-Sat. 10 a.m.-7 p.m., Sun. noon-5 p.m.

Yes, it's quite expensive, but the quality of the leather is superb. The purses are well regarded by women who like to carry classic handbags and don't mind the rather obvious gold-signature fasteners. Though Céline's loafers might not be as popular as Gucci's, those who have discovered them swear by their comfort and durability.

Gucci
347 N. Rodeo Dr., Beverly Hills 90210;
(310) 278-3451
Open Mon.-Sat. 10 a.m.-6 p.m.

We thought maybe they were giving the Gs away last time we popped into this chic boutique. It was loaded with foreign customers, all buying up Gucci classics. Apparently Gucci has found its natural habitat in Los Angeles; even meter maids tote the clichéd fabric bags. This branch is a cross between Milan high-tech and space-shuttle decor; with a small clothing selection, a sleek shoe department and an entire line of accoutrements: pens, watches, scarves, stationary, perfume and more.

Hermès
343 N. Rodeo Dr., Beverly Hills 90210;
(310) 278-6440
Open Mon.-Sat. 10 a.m.-6 p.m.

This Parisian import carries exquisitely made leather handbags, including the famous (Grace) Kelly bag, wallets, briefcases and luggage. Styles are classic, not outdated, and its logo is tastefully and unobtrusively imprinted on the goods. This shop also sells Hermès's lovely silk scarves, watches, accessories and fragrances.

H. Savinar Luggage
4625 W. Washington Blvd., Mid-City (L.A.) 90016;
(213) 938-2501
6931 Topanga Canyon Blvd., Canoga Park 91303;
(818) 703-1313
Open Mon.-Sat. 10 a.m.-6 p.m., Sun. 11 a.m.-4 p.m.

A huge mainstream selection of luggage, business accessories and small leather goods are sold here at prices well below retail. Knowledgeable Angelenos know that this is *the* place in town to buy luggage. It carries all the popular mid-range lines, including Tumi, Andiamo, Boyt, Lark, Hartmann and Ventura.

Lazar's Fine Leather Goods
14528 Ventura Blvd., Sherman Oaks 91403;
(818) 784-1355
Open Mon.-Sat. 9 a.m.-5:30 p.m.

The Valley's source for luggage and travel accessories. In addition to stocking one of the area's largest selections of luggage—including pieces by French, Samsonite, Hartmann and Lark—Lazar's carries wallets, money belts and other leather goods, as well as travel accessories from clothes steamers to hairdryers. If your suitcase, purse or golf bag has a tear or needs cleaning, this is an excellent, reliable source for repairs.

Louis Vuitton
307 N. Rodeo Dr., Beverly Hills 90210;
(310) 859-0457
Open Mon.-Sat. 10 a.m.-6 p.m., Sun. noon-5 p.m.

Louis Vuitton's famous multi-monogrammed purses and luggage are proudky toted on so many arms the world around, it's not even necessary to descibe them here. Vuitton successfully carried only the classic LV-ridden design for years—until recently, when the company introduced its exclusive Epi leather line, a collection of solid-color, calves' leather purses and luggage in black, red, green, blue and rust. There are also wallets, brief cases, office accessories and belts.

North Beach Leather
8500 Sunset Blvd., W. Hollywood 90069;
(310) 652-3224
Open Mon.-Sat. 10 a.m.-6 p.m.

Mostly Sunset Boulevard–L.A. rocker stuff here: leather bowling jackets, fringed skirts and skin-tight jeans. More wearable items include tuxedo-inspired coatdresses and trench coats. Before Versace, Armani and Montana began featuring leather garments in their collections, and when one couldn't find leather trousers, skirts and dresses *just anywhere*, North Beach had the L.A. monopoly. What was once among the trendiest, most innovative and costliest in design has become only semifashionable, rarely daring and rather reasonable in price.

Wilson's House of Suede & Leather
9844 Wilshire Blvd., Beverly Hills 90210;
(310) 553-0588
Open Mon.-Sat. 10 a.m.-6 p.m., Sun. noon-5 p.m.

This institution carries a huge selection of fashionable leather—chic jackets, shorts, skirts, hats, purses, gloves and just about anything leather (except suitcases, belts and shoes). They carry a variety of brands, including Adventure Bound, Pelle Studio and Chia.

Rentals

Computers

Ganton Micro Computer Rentals
1201 S. Flower St., Burbank 91502; (818) 842-6866
Open Mon.-Fri. 8:30 a.m.-5:30 p.m.

Most major brands of personal computers, including IBM, MacIntosh and the Toshiba laptop, are rented by the day, week or month. Pickup and delivery are included in the rental fees, which vary depending on the equipment selected.

Costumes

Glendale Costumes
315 N. Brand Blvd., Glendale 91203;
(818) 244-1161
Open Mon., Wed. & Fri. 10 a.m.-7 p.m.; Tues., Thurs. & Sat. 10 a.m.-5:30 p.m.

This costumer is noteworthy for its breadth of selection, uncomplicated rental procedures and prices (costumes from $35 to $75). One whole department is devoted to Joker, Invisible Man and other classic horror characters. There's an extensive collection of Ben Nye theatrical makeup and some dazzlingly ornate masks.

Western Costume
11041 Vanowen Blvd., N. Hollywood 91605;
(818) 760-0902
Open Mon.-Fri. 8 a.m.-5:30 p.m.

This Hollywood institution is now located in North Hollywood. For almost three-quarters of a century, it's been renting costumes to movie studios and to the public. Chances are very good that no matter who or what you want to disguise yourself as, you'll find the appropriate costume here, whether it's a Southern belle or a gorilla. Costumes aren't always in top condition, however, so check carefully.

Formal Wear

Dressed to Kill
8762 Holloway Dr., W. Hollywood 90069;
(310) 652-4334
Open Tues.-Fri. 11 a.m.-7 p.m., Sat. 10 a.m.-6 p.m.

Fulfill you sartorial fantasies, if only for an evening. Dressed to Kill specializes in haute couture for rent: cocktail dresses amd gowns from Bob Mackie, Giorgio di Sant'Angelo, Ungaro, Dior—over 300 styles in all. The shop will outfit you with a matching handbag and jewelry. Call ahead to book an appointment.

Tuxedo Center

7360 Sunset Blvd., Hollywood 90046;
(213) 874-4200
Open Mon.-Fri. 9 a.m.-7 p.m., Sat. 9 a.m.-5 p.m.

Tuxes in every size and style, including those made by the best designers, can be rented here. The selection is unbeatable, the prices competitive, and the service good.

Party

Abbey Party Rents

1001 N. La Brea Ave., W. Hollywood 90038;
(213) 466-9582
Open Mon.-Fri. 8:30 a.m.-5:30 p.m., Sat. 9 a.m.-4 p.m.

One of the biggest and best party-rental stores in town, Abbey will provide you with everything you need, from tables, chairs and silverware to dance floors, lighting systems and heaters.

Pico Party Rents

2537 S. Fairfax Ave., Culver City 90232;
(213) 936-8268
Open Mon.-Sat. 9 a.m.-5:30 p.m.

This family-owned business has been catering to L.A.'s parties for 60-something years. The specialty here is weddings: you can rent anything from canopies with picture windows and champagne fountains to candelabras and carousel horses.

Regal Rents

9925 W. Jefferson Blvd., Culver City 90230;
(310) 204-3382
Open Mon.-Sat. 8:30 a.m.-5 p.m.

Regal boasts one of the largest and most diversified inventories on the West Coast, everything from black dishes and ballroom chairs like those you see in movies to copperware, carpeting and 25 colors of table linens. Expert product knowledge among salespeople is another plus.

Services

See also "Late-Night Services," listed in the "LOS ANGELES Basics" chapter, for late-night emergencies.

Antiques Restoration

Antique Services Inc.

7349 Hinds Ave., N. Hollywood 91401;
(818) 765-1265
Open Mon.-Fri. 9:30 a.m.-4 p.m.

This European-trained staff has been repairing and restoring antique and period furniture for fifteen years; they are experts in veneer and inlay repairs.

Childcare

Baby Sitters Guild

8230 Beverly Blvd., W. Hollywood 90048;
(213) 658-8792
Open 24 hours.

Mature, bonded, reliable sitters are on call all through the night.

Valley Domestics

15445 Ventura Blvd. Suite #27, Sherman Oaks 91403; (818) 986-6955
Open Mon.-Fri. 9 a.m.- 6 p.m., Sat. 9 a.m.-3 p.m.

Well-reputed for its childcare services, including professional nannies, babysitters, au-pairs and tutors, many of whom are trained in CPR techniques. Live-in or live-out, part-, full- or night-time, temporary or permanent.

Cleaners

Effrey's

8917 Melrose Ave., W. Hollywood 90069;
(310) 858-7400
Open Mon.-Fri. 8 a.m.-5:30 p.m., Sat. 8 a.m.-1 p.m.

Penny-pinchers should steer clear of Effrey's, which is quite possibly the most expensive dry cleaners in the state. But those looking for a cleaners they can *really* trust can rest assured that their investment clothing will receive flawless care. Pickup and delivery with a $25 minimum.

Leroy's Cleaners

9107 W. Olympic Blvd., Beverly Hills 90212;
(310) 273-6266
Open Mon.-Fri. 7 a.m.-7 p.m., Sat. 8 a.m.-6 p.m.

Great for silk and wool. Pickup and delivery offered throughout Beverly Hills, West Hollywood and the Valley.

Premier Leather Cleaners

3098 N. California St., Burbank 91504;
(818) 842-2151
Open Mon.-Fri. 7:30 a.m.-6 p.m., Sat. 9 a.m.-4:30 p.m.

If you have a suede or leather garment that needs to be cleaned, repaired or refinished, go to Premier, which has been doing excellent work since 1946. Also, wedding gowns, hats, pillows and beaded and jeweled dresses.

V.I.P. Wardrobe Maintenance

11701 Wilshire Blvd., W.L.A. 90025;
(310) 479-4707
Open Mon.-Fri. 7 a.m.-7 p.m., Sat. 9 a.m.-5 p.m.

For the care and cleaning of investment-quality clothing, see Vicki Messersmith. For more than ten years, she's handled everything from

Armani suits to Bette Midler's mermaid costume. Alterations and restoration work available. Pickup and delivery, too.

Dressmaker

Salah
8340 1/2 Beverly Blvd., W. Hollywood 90048; (213) 653-2862
Mon.-Fri. 9 a.m.-6 p.m., Sat. 10 a.m.-4 p.m.

Have an exact mental picture of the party frock you're seeking, but can't find it anywhere? Salah Saad will design and manufacture exactly what you're looking for, and it'll fit like a dream. These dresses are less expensive than true haute couture, and you'll have a one of a kind.

Drugstore

Rexall Drugs
8490 Beverly Blvd., W. Hollywood 90048; (213) 653-4616
Open daily 9 a.m.-11 p.m.

Los Angeles has countless other drugstores and a number of other Rexalls, but the Beverly Boulevard store is the biggest and best of them all. It carries everything a drugstore should, and more: fabulous bath and body products, potpourri, cosmetics, tobacco, wines and spirits, books, toys, appliances, magazines, candy sold by the pound, gift-wrapping materials, art supplies, office supplies—and, oh yes—there's a pharmacy.

Framer

Artifact
2502 Main St., Santa Monica 90405; (310) 399-7300
Open Mon.-Wed. & Fri. 10 a.m.- 6 p.m., Thurs. 10 a.m.-8 p.m., Sat. 10 a.m.-5 p.m.

This store once framed the letters, menus and related memorabilia of an entire love affair. Scarves, marathon runners' vests and a Keith Haring doodle on the back of a menu have all found their way into Artifact's frames. Owner Phyllis Doppelt and staff get personally involved in coordinating hand-painted borders, marbled papers, gold-leaf finishes, even hand-cast plaster molds of architectural details.

Art Services
8221 Melrose Ave., Melrose-Fairfax District (L.A.) 90046; (213) 653-9033
Open Mon.-Fri. 9 a.m.-5:30 p.m., Sat. 10 a.m.-5 p.m.

Art Services will do an excellent job at custom-framing a work of any shape or size.

Home Service

Residential Services
1801 Ave. of the Stars, Century City 91413; (310) 277-0770, (818) 787-7775
Open daily 24 hours.

Wes Carlson has been operating this complete home-service referral system for 25 years. From painting to window cleaning, sprinkler installation, roofing or remodeling, Wes will match you with the right person for the job, and he'll follow up to make sure it was done right.

Messenger

Now Courier
1543 W. Olympic Blvd., W. L.A. 90015; (310) 252-5000 (local)/671-1200 (air)

This reliable delivery service is on hand 24 hours a day, 365 days a year, for both local deliveries (throughout L.A. and Orange County) and air courier deliveries. Drivers are bonded and insured. Cash is accepted upon pickup—it will speed the process to mention that you were referred by Gault Millau's *Best of Los Angeles.*

Party Messenger

Eastern Onion
(310) 942-2222
Open Mon.-Fri. 9 a.m.-6 p.m., Sat. 10 a.m.-2 p.m.

No matter what kind of message you want relayed, there's a talented performer here to do it . . . everything from singing Christmas trees and to belly dancers. Make sure you okay the message first, since they can be on the raunchy side. Gag gifts, balloon bouquets and gift baskets are available. Services daily, 8 a.m. to midnight.

Party Supplies

Michael's
733 S. San Julian St., Downtown (L.A.) 90014; (213) 689-4830
Open Mon.-Sat. 9 a.m.-6 p.m., Sun. 11 a.m.-5 p.m.

Anything and everything for prepping a party: plastic or paper garlands, a bright assortment of solid-color paper plates and napkins, hats, invitations, favors, plastic serving containers and tins, invitations and costume supplies.

Pet Hotel

Pet Set Inn
14423 S. Crenshaw Blvd., Gardena 90249;
(310) 644-2938
Open Mon.-Fri. 7:45 a.m.-6 p.m., Sat. 8 a.m.-4 p.m.,
Sun. 2 p.m.-4 p.m., or by appt.

Special attention is given to each dog and cat. Facilities include individual sleeping quarters with connecting outside private patios and thermostatic heat. There's a grooming parlor on the premises and a veterinarian next door. Pickup and delivery and 24-hour emergency service.

Van Nuys Pet Hotel
7004 Hayvenhurst Ave., Van Nuys 91406;
(818) 787-7232
Open Mon. & Fri. 8 a.m.-6 p.m., Tues.-Thurs. 8 a.m.-5 p.m., Sat. noon-3 p.m.

Valley cats and dogs can live it up in individual patio apartments, complete with air conditioning and heating. All guests are groomed daily. Reasonable rates include breakfast, snacks, dinner and dessert.

Velvet Harbor
7009 Willoughby Ave., W. Hollywood 90038;
(213) 874-9817
Open Mon.-Tues. & Thurs.-Fri. noon-6 p.m., Sat. noon-4 p.m.

There are accommodations for about 30 cats in this friendly home. They're kept in their cages for the first day; once they've adjusted to the new environment, they're allowed out to exercise.

Photographer

Lawrence Lesser Productions
19582 Ventura Blvd., Tarzana 91356;
(818) 881-3102
Open Tues.-Fri. 9:30 a.m.-5:30 p.m.

Lawrence Lesser and his talented staff can capture any special moment with photography or video. They are always in demand for social events, family functions and portrait sittings.

Mitchell Rose Studios
7274 W. Sunset Blvd., W. Hollywood 90046;
(213) 850-0229
Open Mon-Fri. 10 a.m.-6 p.m.

You can come to Mitchell Rose's small portrait studio, or he'll come to you—to your wedding, your office function or wherever you need a professional picture taken. Rose is a no-frills, hardworking photographer whose work is consistently good and whose prices are more than fair. Makeup and hairstyling services available.

Veterinarian

West Los Angeles Veterinary Medical Group
1818 S. Sepulveda Blvd., W.L.A. 90025;
(310) 473-2951
Open daily 8 a.m.-11 p.m.

These veterinarians have an outstanding reputation. Aside from their regular office hours, there's a vet on call 24-hours-a-day, seven days a week.

Watch Repair

C.R. Clark & Company Watchmakers
427 N. Cañon Dr., Beverly Hills 90210;
(310) 275-9141
Open Mon.-Fri. 9 a.m.-5 p.m., Sat. 9 a.m.-1 p.m.

Excellent, reasonably priced and efficient, Clark will repair almost any type of watch to factory specifications.

Shopping Centers

Beverly Center
Beverly & La Cienega Blvds., W. Hollywood 90048;
(310) 854-0070
Open Mon.-Fri. 10 a.m.-9 p.m., Sat. 10 a.m-8 p.m., Sun. 11 a.m.-6 p.m.

This gargantuan structure on the cusp of Beverly Hills and West Hollywood draws a more elite crowd than most shopping centers. Anchored by a Broadway and a Bullock's, it has many worthwhile, upwardly mobile boutiques and chains, including Shauna Stein, Ice, Traffic/Traffic Studio, a newly remodeled and expanded Gap, Gap Kids, Coach, El Portal, F.A.O. Schwarz, Williams-Sonoma and the first West Coast Conran's Habitat. An impressive number of shops riding the natural beauty wave include H20 Plus, The Limited's Bath & Body Works and Aveda Esthetique. The Sam Goody store on the top floor is one of the largest music stores in any mall.

Some of the city's best films are screened at the Beverly Center's tiny Cineplex theaters, but the center falls short on restaurants, of which the Hard Rock Café and California Pizza Kitchen are the best. We love the Beverly Center for its intriguing people- and fashion-watching. Also, make a dash across La Cienega Boulevard to the color-

261

ful Beverly Connection, home to Sports Chalet, Bookstar, many shops big and small, theaters and places to nosh (The Daily Grill, Starbuck's Coffee, Humphrey Yogart).

Brentwood Gardens

11677 San Vicente Blvd. at Barrington, Brentwood 90049; (310) 820-7646

Open Mon.-Sat. 11 a.m.-7 p.m., Sun. noon-5 p.m.

A glistening white shopping-mall scene, Brentwood Gardens is one of the westside's hottest fashion spots. The nearly 50 high-end, high-style retailers keep company with celebrities, who retreat to the "Gardens," away from Hollywood's glitz. Some top draws: Modasport, Artworks, By Theodore, Ron Herman and Humphrey Yogart. Valet parking.

Century City Shopping Center

10250 Santa Monica Blvd., Century City 90067; (310) 553-5300

Open Mon.-Fri. 10 a.m.-9 p.m., Sat. 10 a.m.-6 p.m., Sun. 11 a.m.-6 p.m.

Once a part of Twentieth Century-Fox's back lot, this shopping center has moved into the twenty-first century, thanks to a $36 million expansion. It's one of the city's only outdoor regional shopping centers, though there's plenty of shade from the overhead structures that let the sky shine through. An upscale configuration of shops (Joan & David, Metropolitan Museum of Art Store, Rosenthal/Truitt, Cottura, Raffia, Joan Vass, Crate & Barrel) balances anchor stores Broadway and Bullock's. There's a fourteen-movie-screen complex, a fine Brentano's bookstore and a chichi quick-food arcade called the Marketplace. Three hours free parking.

Fashion Island, Newport Center

1045 Newport Center Dr., Newport Beach 92660; (714) 721-2032

Open Mon.-Fri. 10 a.m.-9 p.m., Sat. 10 a.m.-6 p.m., Sun. noon-5 p.m.

See "ORANGE COUNTY Shops."

Fashion Square Sherman Oaks

14006 Riverside Dr., Sherman Oaks 91423; (818) 783-0550

Open Mon.-Fri. 10 a.m.-9 p.m., Sat. 10 a.m.-7 p.m., Sun. 11 a.m.-6 p.m.

With 140 stores carrying mainly fashion, accessories and gifts, Fashion Square is fashion central for the San Fernando Valley. A recent renovation brought brass railings, marble floors, skylights, a walk-on koi pond and lots of tropical foilage, including 23 live palm trees. Several stores are the only Valley branches outside of L.A., including Jessica McClintock, Frederick's of Hollywood, Bebe and Lilli Rubin. There are three anchor stores: I. Magnin, Bullock's and

The Broadway, but little that's noteworthy in the food department.

Galleria at South Bay

1815 Hawthorne Blvd., Redondo Beach 90278; (310) 371-7546

Open Mon.-Fri. 10 a.m.-9 p.m., Sat. 10 a.m.-7 p.m., Sun. 11 a.m.-6 p.m.

If you love the Westside Pavilion and the newer part of the Glendale Galleria, you'll feel right at home. Same barrel skylight, same Nordstrom, same high-end fast food and pretty much the same shops, except for Polo Ralph Lauren (one of two shops in L.A.), the Limited Too (for kids), a Service Center (with a U.S. post office, tailor and wrap-and-ship store) and the valet parking.

Glendale Galleria

Central & Brand Aves., Glendale 91210; (818) 246-6737

Open Mon.-Fri.10 a.m.-9 a.m., Sat. 10 a.m.-7 p.m., Sun. 11 a.m.-6 p.m.

A monster mall that continues to spread, the Galleria started life as a cheesy suburban center, with JC Penney, Leeds and the like. But more recent additions have brought some worthwhile higher-end chains, including Nordstrom, William-Sonoma, Banana Republic, Pottery Barn, Eddie Bauer, Natural Wonders, an expanded Limited Express store and numerous shoe stores, from Badicci to G. H. Bass. Be warned that on weekends here, the crush is nearly unbearable.

Marina Marketplace

13455 Maxella Ave., Marina del Rey 90292; (310) 827-0253

Open Mon.-Fri. 10 a.m.; 9 p.m., Sat. 10 a.m.-8 p.m., Sun. 11 a.m.-6 p.m.

Many of these shops (Harari, Sport Chalet, Benetton) and restaurants/markets (Gelson's, Angeli Mare, Chin Chin) are familiar to Angelenos, but the oceanside branches offer updates and extras. Never mind Marina Marketplace's predictable design and preponderance of pink and gray; the mix of retail shops, restaurants and theaters hits the mark.

South Coast Plaza

3333 Bristol Ave., Costa Mesa 92626; (714) 241-1700

Open Mon.-Fri. 10 a.m.-9 p.m, Sat. 10 a.m.-7 p.m., Sun. 11 a.m.-6:30 p.m.

See "ORANGE COUNTY Shops."

Westside Pavilion

10800 W. Pico Blvd., W.L.A. 90064; (310) 474-6255

Open Mon.-Fri. 10 a.m.-9:30 p.m., Sat. 10 a.m.-7 p.m., Sun. 11 a.m.-6 p.m.

Something of a West L.A. landmark, Westside Pavilion flags down motorists with its bright and busy facade. This is a Baby Boomer's dream, offering the only Nordstrom in the L.A. area and an impressive pocket of children's fashion and toy stores, from Gymboree to Gap Kids and Mr. G's for Kids. More shops you won't necessarily see everywhere else: Final Touch men's accessories, Boogies Diner (fashion and food). There are some good movie theaters and decent restaurants, including Sisley Italian Kitchen. Thanks to a recent expansion, weekend parking is not the nightmare it once was.

Sporting Goods

Adventure 16
11161 W. Pico Blvd., W.L.A. 90064;
(310) 473-4574
Open Mon.-Fri. 10 a.m.-9 p.m., Sat. 10 a.m.-6 p.m., Sun. noon-5 p.m.

Even if you've never camped out a day in your life, the impressive-looking stock at Adventure 16 a.k.a. A-16, will have you yearning for a hardy hike. It's a small and pricey selection, including the latest in high-tech clothing to hiking boots, from single-burner stoves to freeze-dried food and water-purification tablets. The staff has an excellent base of expertise with which to help you plot your every move. The travel-book section is one of the city's best; A-16 takes special orders, and it offers equipment rental, laundry and repair, free classes and special events.

Big 5 Sporting Goods
6601 Wilshire Blvd., Beverly Hills 90048;
(213) 651-2909
3422 Wilshire Blvd., Mid-Wilshire (L.A.) 90010;
(213) 487-1688
3121 Wilshire Blvd., Santa Monica 90403;
(310) 453-1747
Open Mon.-Fri. 10 a.m.-9 p.m., Sat. 9 a.m.-9 p.m., Sun. 10 a.m.-6 p.m.

Big 5 is an ever-growing chain of reputed discount–sporting goods stores, though most of its prices don't seem too low to us. It does, however, have a sort of ongoing sale—you can check the Thursday and Saturday *Los Angeles Times* to find out the current (and often very good) bargains. The selection is fair but not of a very high quality; service is pleasant but not terribly well informed. The merchandise assortment ranges from ski goods to tennis and exercise equipment to a large selection of athletic shoes for every sport.

I. Martin Imports
8330 Beverly Blvd., W. Hollywood 90048;
(213) 653-6900
Open Mon. 10 a.m.-8 p.m., Tues.-Sat. 10 a.m.-7 p.m., Sun. noon-6 p.m.

I. Martin is crammed with bikes—they are literally stacked to the ceiling. There's every kind of ten-, twelve- and eighteen-speed bike, from such makers as Diamond Back, Specialized, Bottecchia, Trek and Bianchi. Prices range from $100 for a tiny bike with training wheels to more than $2,000 for a top-of-the-line racing bike. Full service department.

MDR Bike Sport
2472 Lincoln Blvd., Marina del Rey 90291;
(310) 306-7843
Open Mon.-Fri. 10 a.m.-7 p.m., Sat. 10 a.m.-6 p.m., Sun. 11 a.m.-5 p.m.

In addition to a full range of bikes, cycling ware and accessories, MDR Bike offers services we never dreamed possible: complete restorations of vintage models and sentimental favorites, custom-design and paint work and professional "fittings" for improved performance. There's a sizzling selection of Spandex clothing, gloves with gel-padded palms and "soft-shell" Giro helmets with interchangeable brightly colored tops.

The Merchant of Tennis
1118 S. La Cienega Blvd., Beverly Hills 90035;
(310) 855-1946
Open Mon.-Fri. 9:30 a.m.-9 p.m., Sat. 9 a.m.-6 p.m., Sun. noon-5 p.m.

You have to be buzzed in to this spare, modern tennis shop, as if it were an elite jewelry store. But the only valuables here are rows of men's and women's tennis clothes and dozens of rackets. The clothing selection, although it includes four top names, is limited, but there's a fine collection of expensive graphite rackets. Time on the court behind the shop is rented out to the public and is used for lessons given seven days a week by the shop's three full-time pros.

The Racket Doctor
3214 Glendale Blvd., Atwater 90039;
(213) 663-6601
Open Tues.-Sat. 10 a.m.-6 p.m.

Atwater may not be the first place that springs to mind when you think of tennis, but it should be. The Racket Doctor has one of the largest selections of tennis rackets in the Western United States—virtually every popular racket made can be found here, from graphite to ceramic. And, best of all, the prices are perhaps the lowest in the country. (To get on the national mail-order list, call 213-663-2950.) The selection of tennis shoes and clothing is equally well priced.

R.E.I. Co-op
405 W. Torrance Blvd., Carson 90745;
(310) 538-2429
*Open Mon.-Tues. & Sat. 9:30 a.m.-6 p.m., Wed.-Fri.
9:30 a.m.-9 p.m., Sun. noon-5 p.m.*
18605 Devonshire St., Northridge 91324;
(818) 831-5556
*Open Mon.-Fri. 10 a.m.-9 p.m., Sat. 10 a.m.-6 p.m.,
Sun. noon-5 p.m.*

Plaid flannel shirts and hiking boots will never go out of style with the clientele at Seattle-based R.E.I. (Recreational Equipment Incorporated). All of the great outdoors is the specialty here— camping, fishing, snowshoeing, backpacking, hiking, rock-climbing and so on. R.E.I. sells and rents everything you could possibly need for these wholesome recreations, and at very modest prices. For $10 you can join the co-op, and you'll receive a yearly dividend usually equal to 10 percent of your year's purchases. The staff is exceptionally knowledgeable and honest.

Roger Dunn Golf Shop
4744 Lankershim Blvd., N. Hollywood 91602;
(818) 763-3622
*Open Mon.-Fri. 10 a.m.-7 p.m., Sat. 9 a.m.-6 p.m., Sun.
10 a.m.-5 p.m.*

A large, well-stocked shop with everything for the golfer. The service is intelligent and friendly. Prices are reasonable; for sales, very low.

The Scorecard
12306 Ventura Blvd., Studio City 91604;
(818) 761-0090
Open Mon.-Sat. 10 a.m.-6 p.m., Sun. 11 a.m.-4 p.m.

The Scorecard sells everything for the armchair athlete: pennants, caps, T-shirts, even trash cans and beer mugs, all emblazoned with logos from pro and college baseball, football, hockey and basketball teams. Die-hard fans will also find personalized bats and balls with players' signatures on them. Much of this stuff is hard to find outside of the teams' hometowns.

Sports Chalet
920 Foothill Blvd., La Cañada 91011;
(818) 790-9800
*Open Mon.-Fri. 9:30 a.m.-9 p.m., Sat. 9:30 a.m.-6 p.m.,
Sun. 10 a.m.-6 p.m.*
Beverly Connection, 100 N. La Cienega Blvd., W.
Hollywood 90048; (310) 657-3210
Open Mon.-Sat. 10 a.m.-9 p.m., Sun. 11 a.m.-6 p.m.

The La Cañada branch of Sports Chalet is nirvana for every kind of athlete. Well worth the drive from L.A. proper, the store sprawls across three buildings: one stocks everything and anything for runners, climbers, tennis players, divers, baseball players, you name it; the second building stocks absolutely everything for the downhill and cross-country skier, with a tremendous selection

of clothing; and the third, a converted gas station, rents it all: skis, scuba gear, tennis rackets, camping equipment, boats, mountaineering gear and so on. Prices are moderate, sale prices are great, and the staff is friendly and helpful.

Val Surf
4810 Whitsett Ave., N. Hollywood 91607;
(818) 769-6977
*Open Mon.-Fri. 9 a.m.-8 p.m., Sat. 9 a.m.-6 p.m., Sun.
11 a.m.-5 p.m.*
22211 Ventura Blvd. Woodland Hills 91364;
(818) 888-6488
*Open Mon.-Fri. 9 a.m.-8 p.m., Sat. 9 a.m.-6 p.m., Sun.
11 a.m.-5 p.m.*

This colorful shop was the first to bring the burgeoning '60s surf craze inland to the Valley. While other surf shops have come and gone, Val Surf is still a trendsetter in Southern California casualwear and a good place to get neon-bright trunks, T-shirts, Hawaiian shirts, Vuarnets, thongs, bikinis and junior sportswear. There are more than 80 surfboards, from small tri-fin wave carvers to classic longboards. You'll also find all sorts of ocean-sports paraphernalia, as well as a professional snow-skiing shop.

Tobacconists

Alfred Dunhill
201 N. Rodeo Dr., Beverly Hills 90210;
(310) 274-5351
Mon.-Sat. 10 a.m.-6 p.m., Sun. noon-5 p.m.

Where would the cigar-smoking establishment be without this respectable boutique? Alfred Dunhill has been selling smokes on Rodeo Drive for 30 years, offering an enormous range of imported cigars and smoking accessories as well as jewelry, watches, wallets, sunglasses, cologne and even men's clothing. There's a clubby smoking room upstairs and if you need anything faxed or copied while you wait, they'll oblige.

The Cigar Warehouse
15141 Ventura Blvd., Sherman Oaks 91403;
(818) 784-1391
Open Mon.-Sat. 9:30 a.m.-6 p.m.

Without a doubt the best place in town to buy the world's best cigars. You name it, they've got it, and at discounted prices. The house brands, especially the Honduran Bravo, are very good values. There's a lesser but still good choice of pipe tobaccos as well, along with beautiful pipes, humidors and smoking accessories. The showbiz crowd makes up a large percentage of the Cigar Warehouse's business. For "cigars to the stars" outside California, call (800) 426-8924.◆

SIGHTS & ARTS

Contents

Arts

Auction Houses

Butterfield & Butterfield
7601 Sunset Blvd., Hollywood 90046;
(213) 850-7500
Call for viewing & auction times.

Established in 1865, the West's most venerable auction house brings the hammer down on paintings, photographs, prints, furniture and decorative arts, silver, rugs, jewelry and even wine. Previews take place on weekends before the sales, which occur throughout the year and are open to the public.

Galleries

Contemporary Art

Ace Gallery
5514 Wilshire Blvd., Wilshire District (L.A.) 90036;
(213) 935-4411
Open Tues.-Sat. 10 a.m.-6 p.m., Sun. 1 p.m.-5 p.m.

The Ace Gallery has survived a somewhat checkered past and more than three decades of history to remain an important force in the L.A.

art circuit. Its colossal space (equalling the size of L.A.'s Museum of Contemporary Art) allows owner Douglas Christmas to mount expansive exhibitions of museum-quality works by such international artists as Robert Rauschenberg, Richard Serra, Bruce Nauman, Dennis Oppenheim, Roger Herman and James Turrell. With its labyrinthine space, Ace is a serious aesthetic funhouse—an effect it hopes to replicate in its roomy new gallery in New York's SoHo.

Asher/Faure Gallery
612 N. Almont Dr., W. Hollywood 90069;
(310) 271-3665
Open Tues.-Sat. 11 a.m.-5 p.m.

Directed by Patricia Faure (and co-owned by Betty Asher, one of the grande dames of the L.A. art scene), this gallery exhibits a variety of established international and Californian artists, including Robert Graham, Robert Yarber, Bruce Cohen, Joel Shapiro, Margaret Nielsen and Rona Pondick.

B-1 Gallery
2730 Main St., Santa Monica 90405;
(310) 392-9625
Open Tues.-Sun. 11 a.m.-5 p.m.

Urban-art collector Robert Berman runs this small satellite of his signature gallery, featuring bronzes, paintings and installations by such up-and-coming locals as Nick Agid, Bill Barminski and Greg Gibbs. *See also* Robert Berman Gallery in this section.

Burnett Miller Gallery
964 N. La Brea Ave., Melrose-La Brea District (L.A.) 90038; (213) 874-4757
Open Tues.-Sat. 10 a.m.-5:30 p.m.

Formerly a curator at the La Jolla Museum of Contemporary Art, Miller shows conceptual-based art with strong European influences, such as work by Gunter Umberg, Ulay and the unflinching Leon Golub. Two noteworthy L.A. artists are Charles Ray, with his installation-oriented pieces, and sculptor Nancy Rubins.

Cirrus Gallery
542 S. Alameda St., Downtown (L.A.) 90013;
(213) 680-3473
Open Tues.-Sat. 10 a.m.-5 p.m.

Owner Jean Milant was one of the first westside dealers to move into the once-uncharted reaches of downtown Los Angeles. Combining an active fine-arts press, which has published such established Californina artists as John Baldessari, Ed Ruscha, Billy Al Bengston, Sabina Ott, Lari Pittman and Peter Alexander, with a large gallery highlighting both well-known and hitherto unknown Californian artists, Cirrus is one of the few noteworthy galleries currently active downtown. Strictly industrial setting.

Daniel Saxon Gallery
7525 Beverly Blvd., Wilshire District (L.A.) 90036;
(213) 933-5282
Open Tues.-Sat. 10 a.m.-5:30 p.m.

Collectors know Dan Saxon for his spirited tastes in abstract, figurative and representational art. The spacious gallery is home to a wide spectrum of work (paintings, sculptures, drawings, ceramics, art furniture) by Rose-Lynn Fisher, Gronk, Red Grooms, Judy Rifka and Peter Shire, among others. There's an outdoor sculpture court, a private viewing room and an upstairs loft space. Evenings, the main gallery becomes a 100-seat theater for occasional performances, lectures and musical events.

Daniel Weinberg Gallery
2032 Broadway, Santa Monica 90404;
(310) 453-0180
Open Tues.-Sat. 10:30 a.m.-5 p.m.

A pioneering art dealer, Weinberg came to Santa Monica from San Francisco by way of West Hollywood. Exhibiting major new and established American artists in the westside's art zone, the gallery continues to break new ground while remaining true to its rather rigorous aesthetic vision. Featuring such artists as Richard Artschwager, Saint Clair Cemin, Gary Hume, Jeff Koons, Sol Lewitt, Robert Mangold, Carl Ostendarp, Sean Scully, Meyier Vaisman, Terry Winters and Christopher Wool, Weinberg offers a perennially challenging exhibition roster.

Dorothy Goldeen Gallery
1547 9th St., Santa Monica 90401; (310) 395-0222
Open Tues.-Sat. 10:30 a.m.-5:30 p.m.

Flowing spaces and an outdoor sculpture yard mark this gallery, respected for its intelligent selections of work in all media by well-established artists from California and elsewhere, including Donald Lipski, Ed Paschke, Nam June Paik, Robert Arneson, Alan Rath, Squeak Carnwath, Jo Ann Callis and Howard Ben Tre.

Fred Hoffman Gallery
912 Colorado Ave., Santa Monica 90401;
(310) 394-4199
Open Tues.-Fri. 9:30 a.m.-5:30 p.m., Sat. 10 a.m.-5 p.m.

Scholar, adviser and curator Fred Hoffman opened his gallery in the fall of 1986 after operating New City Editions, a small gallery and fine-art publishing concern in Venice. Hoffman's rather vast gallery affords him an opportunity to also show such strong New York artists as David Salle, Richard Serra and Julian Schnabel; California's Charles Arnoldi, Chris Burden and John McCracken; and Europe's Sophie Calle, A. R. Penck and Ulrich Ruckriem.

Gallery of Functional Art
Edgemar Complex, 2429 Main St., Santa Monica 90405; (310) 450-2827
Open Tues.-Sat. 11 a.m.-7 p.m., Sun. noon-6 p.m.

Under the Frank Gehry–designed roof in the Edgemar mall, Lois Lambert's Gallery of Functional Art showcases the bright lights of L.A.'s design, craft and art communities. Art furniture is the primary focus, with selective shows of incredible vessels and jewelry. Exhibitions change every two months; top draws include artists David Gale, Eugenia Butler, Anne Kelly, Phil Garner and John Bok and architects Coop Himmelblau and Margaret Helfand.

Herbert Palmer Gallery
802 N. La Cienega Blvd., W. Hollywood 90069;
(310) 854-0096
Open Tues.-Fri. 10 a.m.-6 p.m., Sat. 11 a.m.-5 p.m.

Palmer, a long-standing veteran of L.A.'s art community, exhibits work by a fine, select group of well-known artists, such as Christo, Sam Francis, Red Grooms, David Hockney, Ida Jensen, Ellsworth Kelly, Lee Mullican, Gordon Onslow-Ford, Claes Oldenburg and Man Ray.

Hunsaker/Schlesinger Gallery
812 N. La Cienega Blvd., W. Hollywood 90069;
(310) 657-2557
Open Mon.-Fri. 9 a.m.-5 p.m., Sat. by appt.

Joyce Hunsaker and Laura Schlesinger, two art consultants who had the courage and the intelligence to open a gallery, exhibit a wide range of material featuring young Californian artists as well as mainstream work by such figures as Al Held and Robert Motherwell. Prints, drawings and photographs are included in the inventory, along with paintings and sculpture. It's a small but effective gallery environment with information and advice pleasantly rendered.

James Corcoran Gallery
1327 5th St., Santa Monica 90401; (310) 451-4666
Open Tues.-Fri. 10 a.m.-6 p.m., Sat. 11 a.m.-5 p.m.

Corcoran is one of the leading galleries in Los Angeles. The expansive, well-appointed space in Santa Monica has exhibited such important American and European figures as Joseph Cornell, James Rosenquist, Francesco Clemente, Mimo Paladino and Sandro Chia, as well as representing a solid group of established and popular local artists: Billy Al Bengston, Peter Alexander, Ed Ruscha and Joe Goode. However, Corcoran's real, if not public, métier is the sale of major paintings by Franz Klein, Willem de Kooning, Clyfford Still, Sam Francis and other abstract expressionists and postwar masters.

Jan Baum Gallery
170 S. La Brea Ave., Wilshire District (L.A.) 90036; (213) 932-0170
Open Tues. & Thurs.-Sat. 10 a.m.-5:30 p.m., Wed. 10 a.m.-6 p.m.

Along once culturally barren, now fashionable La Brea Avenue, Jan Baum has organized an entire building devoted to the visual arts, which houses Parker/Mark, Garth Clark and Ovsey galleries and an art consultancy. The Baum Gallery focuses on emerging and established international artists, with some of the work having sources in the primitive. There is a small collection of masks and sculpture from Africa and Indonesia.

Jan Turner Gallery and Turner/Krull Gallery
9006 Melrose Ave., W. Hollywood 90069; (310) 271-4453 (Turner)/271-1536 (Krull)
Open Tues.-Fri. 10 a.m.-5:30 p.m., Sat. 11 a.m.-5:30 p.m.

In this spacious, elegant gallery, Jan Turner exhibits a variety of established artists, including L.A. sculptors John Frame and Tony Delap and painters Larry Cohen, Astrid Preston, John Alexander, Donald Roller Wilson and Ole Fischer. Upstairs in a loft is the Turner/Krull Gallery, where Craig Krull oversees a sophisticated, wide-ranging agenda of contemporary and vintage photography exhibits.

Kiyo Higashi Gallery
8332 Melrose Ave., W. Hollywood 90069; (213) 655-2482
Open Tues.-Sat. 11 a.m.-6 p.m.

Owner Kiyo Higashi is passionate about the abstract, and her minimalist approach is reflected in a stable of mainly L.A. artists—such pivotal painters as Guy Williams and New Mexico's Larry Bell (he designed the gallery space) hang with such newer names as Lies Kraal, Max Cole, William Dwyer, Perry Araeipour and Penelope Krebs.

Kurland/Summers Gallery
8742A Melrose Ave., W. Hollywood 90069; (310) 659-7098
Open Tues.-Sat. 11 a.m.-6 p.m.

Art glass is the focus here, both blown and constructed and combined with nonglass elements. Kurland/Summers shows off the fragile work of American and international talents (Dan Dailey, Richard Jolley, Christopher Lee, John Luebtow and Richard Marquis, among them) with theatrical flair. A varied selection of glass art is always on display, in addition to single-artist exhibitions that change about every six weeks.

L.A. Louver Gallery
55 N. Venice Blvd., Venice 90291; (310) 822-4955
Open Tues.-Sat. 11 a.m.-5 p.m.
77 Market St., Venice 90291; (310) 822-4955
Open Tues.-Sat. noon-5 p.m.

L.A. Louver was one of the first L.A. galleries to show important international art; now it's a vital part of the westside art community. Near the West Beach Café, Rebecca's and 72 Market Street, Louver shows a renowned group of American and European artists, including David Hockney, Ed Moses, Peter Shelton, Tony Berlant, Edward Kienholz, Leon Kossof and Wallace Berman. Thankfully, Louver is blessed with a parking lot in this typical (meaning crowded) Venice neighborhood. A genial, well-run environment with British émigré Peter Goulds as owner/director, Louver has also spawned another location in New York's Soho.

Louis Stern Galleries
9528 Brighton Way, Beverly Hills 90210; (310) 276-0147
Mon.-Fri. 10 a.m.-6 p.m., Sat. 11 a.m.

Louis Stern has been in the business of art all his life, which is why his gallery already has a venerable reputation after only two short years. His permanent collection focuses on impressionist, post-impressionist and modern masters. In addition to a collection of originals that includes Edwin Austin Abbey, Tamara deLempika, Maximilian Luce, Claude Monet, Lucien Simon and Victor Vignon, the gallery hosts surprisingly progressive shows: recently, a photo show on L.A.'s "civil disturbances" (the 1992 riots) featured photos from both pros and amateurs who witnessed the events.

Margo Leavin Gallery
812 N. Robertson Blvd., W. Hollywood 90069;
(310) 273-0604
817 N. Hilldale Ave., W. Hollywood 90069;
(310) 273-0603
Open Tues.-Sat. 11 a.m.-5 p.m.

One of the most respected dealers in town, Margo Leavin focuses much of her attention on blue-chip American artists such as Jasper Johns, Willem de Kooning and Claes Oldenburg. An established power on the West Coast, Leavin deserves credit for raising the standard of contemporary art in L.A., and for providing a venue in which to see great and near-great contemporary masters from the East Coast. The gallery also represents very interesting L.A. artists John Baldessari, Alexis Smith and Mark Lere. The second space, just a walk away, is a clean, open rectangle; the presence of incisive art is signalled by the Oldenburg *Knife* on the building's facade.

Michael Kohn Gallery
920 Colorado Ave., Santa Monica 90402;
(310) 393-7713
Open Tues.-Fri. 10 a.m.-5:30 p.m., Sat. 10 a.m.-5 p.m.

Well-informed and personable almost to a fault, Michael Kohn has built his reputation on emerging and recognized New York artists (Joan Nelson, Kevin Larmon, Peter Halley, Mark Innerst, Keith Haring) both in solo and more than normally provocative group or theme shows. Most recently, the gallery has begun to foster the work of such emerging L.A. artists as Michael Gonzales and Jamey Bair.

Robert Berman Gallery
2044 Broadway, Santa Monica 90404;
(310) 453-9195
Open Tues.-Sat. 11 a.m.-5 p.m.

Robert Berman's two galleries (this and the B-1) specialize in "urban L.A. art" by such rising stars as Raymond Pettibon, Robbie Conal, Daniel J. Martinez and May Sun. Restless and resourceful, Berman also mounts auctions that help young artists break into the market.

Rosamund Felsen Gallery
8525 Santa Monica Blvd., W. Hollywood 90069;
(310) 652-9172
Open Tues.-Sat. 11 a.m.-5 p.m.

Rosamund Felsen handles a top-notch stable of young L.A. talents, such as Lari Pittman, Mike Kelley and Erika Rothenberg. Consistently interesting exhibitions in a handsome, well-lighted space.

Shoshona Wayne Gallery
1454 5th St., Santa Monica 90401; (310) 451-3733
Open Tues.-Fri. 10 a.m.-5:30 p.m., Sat. 11 a.m.-5 p.m.

Shoshona and Wayne Blank preside over one of the city's more adventurous galleries. The emphasis is on conceptual art, from early pioneers (e.g., the proto-performance art of the Viennese Actionists) to current practitioners. Among the gallery's artists (many of whom are women) are Kiki Smith, Rachel Lachowicz, Doug Hall, Pae White, Nan Golden and Kay Rosen.

Thomas Solomon's Garage
928 N. Fairfax Ave., Melrose-Fairfax District (L.A.) 90046; (213) 654-4731
Open Tues.-Sat. 11 a.m.-5 p.m, Sun. noon-5 p.m.

Selling art from an industrial garage is fresh and appropriate for L.A., especially when it's masterminded by Thomas Solomon, son of New York art dealer Holly Solomon. Solomon's shows are four weeks in length, and he is showing more well-known artists as well as emerging ones, but the experimental approach continues, including many first, solo and group shows by new talents (Michael Gonzalez, David Kremers, Eric Magnuson) and installations created especially for the gallery (William Wegman, Troy Brauntuch). Contemporary and controversial, it's a must-visit for collectors on the cutting edge.

Photography

Fahey/Klein Gallery
148 N. La Brea, Melrose-La Brea District (L.A.) 90036; (213) 934-2250
Open Tues.-Sat. 10 a.m.-6 p.m.

David Fahey and Randy Klein aim to satisfy collectors with a broad range of work by such recognized photographers as Irving Penn, Herb Ritts, Mary Ellen Mark and Duane Michals. The emphasis is on the contemporary, but work by older masters (Horst, Manuel Alvarez Bravo, André Kertész) is also on hand.

G. Ray Hawkins
908 Colorado Ave., Santa Monica 90401;
(310) 394-5558
Open Tues.-Sat. 10 a.m.-5:30 p.m.

One of the oldest and most respected fine-art photography galleries in the country, G. Ray Hawkins exhibits both vintage and contemporary work. The stellar roster has included Ansel Adams, Bruce Davidson, Judy Coleman, Margaret Bourke-White, Herb Ritts, Helmut Newton, Jo Ann Callis, Elliott Erwitt and Josef Sudek.

Jan Kesner Gallery

164 N. La Brea Ave., Melrose-La Brea District (L.A.) 90036; (213) 938-6834
Open Tues.-Sat., 11 a.m.-5 p.m.

Kesner's gallery specializes in twentieth-century photography and contemporary photo-based artwork—conceptual and mixed-media work by such artists as John Divola, Anne Rowland and Nancy Burson. Young turks like Richard Misrach and Danny Lyon share space with such eminences grises as August Sander, Josef Sudek, Imogene Cunningham and Edward Steichen.

Prints & Graphics

Cirrus Editions

542 S. Alameda St., Downtown (L.A.) 90013; (213) 680-3473
Open Tues.-Sat. 11 a.m.-5 p.m.

Cirrus publishes work primarily by California artists, although New York artists are also represented. Recent editions include Chris Wilder, Fred Fehlau, Sabina Ott, John Millei, Lari Pittman and Sarah Seager.

Gemini G.E.L.

8365 Melrose Ave., W. Hollywood 90069; (213) 651-0513
Open Mon.-Fri. 9:30 a.m.-5:30 p.m.

Internationally recognized as a leading fine-arts publisher, Gemini G.E.L. has published works by such noted artists as Jasper Johns, Robert Rauschenberg, Philip Guston, Ellsworth Kelly, Mark di Suvero and others. The beautifully designed workshop and gallery was created by Frank Gehry. The gallery exhibits only current editions, yet the bulk of the material published over the years is available for inspection upon request. Gemini publishes many of the world's finest artists working today.

Public & Alternative Galleries

Japanese-American Cultural and Community Center

244 S. San Pedro St., Little Tokyo (L.A.) 90012; (213) 628-2725
Open Tues.-Sun. noon-5 p.m.

Regularly rotating exhibitions are offered in the gallery tucked inside this cultural center. In addition, an 828-seat theater offers numerous programs related to Japanese culture, including performances by Japan's Grand Kabuki Theatre group. There is also a library specializing in Japanese cultural information, and a Japanese garden, a delightful downtown refuge.

Los Angeles Contemporary Exhibitions (LACE)

1804 Industrial St., Downtown (L.A.) 90021; (213) 624-5650
Open Tues.-Fri. 11 a.m.-5 p.m., Sat.-Sun. noon-5 p.m.

This nonprofit space features performance and conceptual art, installations and exhibitions of paintings and sculpture by relatively unknown L.A. artists. Los Angeles Contemporary Exhibitions (LACE) is more experimental than most galleries in town. Results are sometimes disappointing, yet it's a valuable alternative environment for L.A.'s younger artists. There's a video screening room and a well-stocked bookstore. The annual art auction always promises some great deals on art.

Los Angeles Municipal Art Gallery

Barnsdall Park, 4804 Hollywood Blvd., Los Feliz 90027; (213) 485-4581
Open Tues.-Sun. 12:30 p.m.-5 p.m.

This spacious, city-sponsored gallery mounts often-intriguing exhibitions that include a variety of media, from paintings and sculptures to graphics and ceramics, all by Southern California contemporary artists. The Junior Arts Center (213-485-4474) consists of a gallery space, classes and special events designed to increase kids' awareness of art.

Museums

The Armand Hammer Museum

10899 Wilshire Blvd., Westwood 90024; (310) 443-7000
Open Tues.-Sun. 10 a.m.-6 p.m. Adults $4.50, senior citizens & students $3, children 16 & under free.

L.A. received its second oil mogul's art monument in 1990 with the opening of the Armand Hammer Museum (the first being J. Paul Getty's spectacular museum). The building threatens to overpower all but the strongest creations in Hammer's collection of "Master Works" by such artists as Rubens, Rembrandt, Goya, Monet and Van Gogh. The museum also houses over 10,000 works by Honoré Daumier as well as a collection of drawings and writings by Leonardo da Vinci. Traveling exhibitions of varying interest supplement (or, as with the Catherine the Great show, supplant) the permanent collection. The museum's shop and bookstore are large, well stocked and well worth a browse (which requires no admission fee).

269

Craft and Folk Art Museum

Wilshire Blvd. & Fairfax Ave. (May Co. bldg., 4th
Fl.), Wilshire District (L.A.) 90036; (213) 937-5544
*Open Tues.-Sat. 10 a.m.-5 p.m., Sun. 11 a.m.-5 p.m.
Admission free. Free parking for up to 2 hours.*

In its temporary home on the fourth floor of
the landmark May Company building, the Craft
and Folk Art Museum is awaiting construction
of a new museum tower. Since opening in 1973,
the museum's growth has paralleled Angelenos'
interest in the decorative arts, crafts and folk art.
Everything from African-American folk art and
vernacular architecture to British crafts and designs and art jewelry has found its way into these
galleries. The celebrated museum shop continues
to operate for the time being at 5800 Wilshire
Boulevard, while a satellite shop in the May
Company sells exhibition publications and cards.
The museum also operates a small library on the
mezzanine.

The Huntington Library Art Collections/Botanical Gardens

1151 Oxford Rd., San Marino 91108;
(818) 405-2275
*Open Tues.-Fri. 1 p.m.-4:30 p.m., Sat.-Sun. 10:30 a.m.-
4:30 p.m. Suggested donation $5 for adults, $3 for chil-
dren/students.*

Henry Huntington certainly had few delu-
sions of grandeur—he simply built his own *petit
Versailles* in San Marino. His former home, now
converted to an art gallery, is a modest Georgian
palace filled with an interesting collection of
eighteenth- and nineteenth-century oil paintings—including Gainsborough's *Blue Boy*—furniture and decorative accessories. The permanent
exhibition on the American Arts and Crafts
movement features a wealth of Greene & Greene
design. The library houses an impressive 600,000
books (many first editions) and display cases hold
such treasures as letters from George Washington
and Chaucer's *Canterbury Tales*. But the charming gardens are what make your visit here worthwhile. You can tour the jungle and the desert,
stopping along the way in the Zen, Shakespeare
and rose gardens. Visitors can spend the whole
afternoon wandering around the 150 acres of
carefully landscaped grounds.

The J. Paul Getty Museum

17985 Pacific Coast Hwy., Malibu 90265;
(310) 458-2003
*Open Tues.-Sun. 10 a.m.-5 p.m. Admission free; parking
reservations required.*

This Romanesque villa off the Pacific Coast
looks slightly out of place without the Bay of
Naples in its rightful location. As one of seven
operating entities of the J. Paul Getty Trust (a
private foundation devoted to the visual arts,

with an endowment of $4 billion), it is an insti-
tution to be reckoned with. The museum is an
artful fiction, its splendid grounds set in
Herculaneum before Vesuvius entombed it in
lava. A remarkable collection of Greek and
Roman antiquities on the first floor is worth an
hour or two; the gloomy upstairs gallery full of
oversize paintings is not. There are also rooms
filled with French, Dutch and Italian works from
the early fourteenth through the late nineteenth
centuries. More recent acquisitions that have upgraded the entire collection include Van Gogh's
much-coveted *Irises* as well as works by Manet,
Renoir, Pontormo and Ensor (the proto-modern
Christ's Entry into Brussels painted in 1889).
Drawings, sculptures, illuminated manuscripts,
photographs and decorative arts round things
out. But the true opulence here is the overwhelming display of seventeenth- and eighteenth-century French furniture. (We find it
amusing that so many visitors pass by one corner
cupboard, apparently unaware that it was acquired for the premium price of $2 million.) The
Getty has a charming tea garden that serves a
good, light al fresco lunch amid the lovely pools
and fountains, as well as a bookstore.

Lannan Foundation

5401 McConnell Ave., L.A. 90066; (310) 306-1004
Open Tues.-Sat. 11 a.m.-5 p.m. Admission free.

A pleasantly anonymous office park conceals a
bastion of contemporary art, the foundation created by the late financier J. Patrick Lannan. Since
moving here from Florida, the foundation has
gained favor with a sprightly mixture of work
from Lannan's permanent collection, sometimes
supplemented from other sources, and selected
traveling exhibits. This is a place to catch art that
might otherwise go unseen in L.A.: a new cycle
of paintings by Gerhard Richter, works by Nicholas Africano, the first-rate portrait survey
curated by artist Chuck Close and imported from
New York's Museum of Modern Art. The Siah
Armajani–designed Poetry Garden is a fine refuge from prosaic reality.

Long Beach Museum of Art

2300 E. Ocean Blvd., Long Beach 90803;
(310) 439-2119
Open Wed.-Sun. noon-5 p.m.

Behind this humble California-bungalow facade lurks one of the most dynamic and youthful
museums in Southern California. The minimalist
decor is the perfect partner for the contemporary
and often avant-garde art, with a strong bent
toward video. Shows change often, and the museum closes during installations, so be sure to call

first. The view of the Pacific is stunning, the grounds are tranquil, and the bookstore/gallery is filled with treasures to take home. Our only regret is that there isn't more to this conservancy of 21st-century art.

Los Angeles County Museum of Art (LACMA)

5905 Wilshire Blvd., Wilshire District (L.A.) 90036; (213) 857-6000/857-6111
Open Tues.-Thurs. 10 a.m.-5 p.m., Fri. 10 a.m.-9 p.m., Sat.-Sun. 11 a.m.-6 p.m. Adults $5, seniors & students $3.50, children 6-17 $1. Admission free second Tues. of each month. Special exhibition prices vary.

The visually stunning Anderson Building, with its stepped facade and abundance of glass brick, faces Wilshire Boulevard, and is a familiar sight to most L.A. residents. Add to that the trio of original LACMA buildings, circa 1964; and the latest addition, an architectural exuberance known as the Pavilion for Japanese Art, and you have LACMA. Most of the museum's permanent holdings are housed in the Ahmanson Building; the collection of pre-Columbian Mexican art is especially noteworthy, as are the Gilbert collection of mosaics and monumental silver and an important Indian and Southeast Asian art collection. LACMA also houses American and European paintings, sculpture and decorative arts and one of the nation's largest holdings of costumes and textiles. The Pavilion for Japanese Art is a superb setting for the internationally renowned Shin'enkan collection of Japanese paintings. As for the rest of the museum, there is an outstanding special exhibition roster, wonderful film retrospectives at the Bing Theater, a gift shop and bookstore and a quite decent indoor/outdoor café with an admirable gourmet "salad bar."

Museum of Contemporary Art (MOCA)

California Plaza, 250 S. Grand Ave., Downtown (L.A.) 90012; (213) 626-6222
152 N. Central Ave. (Temporary Contemporary), Downtown (L.A.) 90013; (213) 626-6222 (Closed due to construction until Spring 1994)
Open Tues.-Wed. & Fri.-Sun. 11 a.m.-5 p.m., Thurs. 11 a.m.-8 p.m. Adults $4, seniors & students $2, children under 12 free; admission free Thurs. 5 p.m.-8 p.m.

Following its auspicious launch in 1986, the Museum of Contemporary Art (MOCA) has come a long way in terms of the kinds of exhibitions and media and performing events it has programmed. The museum structure, designed by Arata Isozaki, is a triumph, with its beautifully proportioned and abundantly skylit galleries. MOCA has also retained its first temporary location (which is closed until 1994 due to construction), an old police warehouse that was sensitively

overhauled by Frank Gehry in 1983 and that is referred to as either the TC or Temporary Contemporary. The donation of 64 minimalist and neoexpressionist works from the collection of the late Barry Lowen, together with an acquisition from Count Giuseppe Panza di Biumo, forms the cornerstone of MOCA's permanent collection. The museum paid $11 million for Panza's brilliantly uneven group of works by such figures as Mark Rothko, Franz Kline and Robert Rauschenberg. The permanent collection has been buoyed by noteworthy gifts such as the Rita and Taft Schreiber Collection (with important works by Jackson Pollock, Piet Mondrian and Alberto Giacometti), some 200 vintage and contemporary prints from the estate of L.A. photographer Max Yavno, and major works by Johns, Reinhardt, Diebenkorn and Warhol. Critically acclaimed exhibitions have included the landmark Case Study Houses exhibition and shows on Man Ray, John Baldessari and Ad Reinhardt. An outdoor café serves tasty fare during the day. Be sure to get your parking validated to avoid the exorbitant charge.

Museum of Neon Art

704 Traction Ave., Downtown (L.A.) 90013; (213) 617-1580
Open Tues.-Sat. 11 a.m.-5 p.m., Sun. 1 p.m.-5 p.m. Admission $2.50.

Behind the unassuming gray cinder-block facade lies a celebration of everything that moves and lights up. The garage space is filled with marvelous artworks that range from the representational to the ridiculous; more often than not, they carry a magical charge. Special exhibitions change every three months. Classes in neon design and technique are taught by artist Lili Lakich. Be sure to inquire about the neon night cruises that take you on a bus tour of the city's dazzlers (call for tour times and ticket prices). The museum planned to move to Universal City in 1993, so call to inquire before visiting.

Newport Harbor Art Museum

850 San Clemente Dr., Newport Beach 92660; (714) 759-1122
Open Tues.-Sun. 10 a.m.-5 p.m. Adults $3; seniors, students & military $2; children 6-17 $1; children under 6 free.

See "ORANGE COUNTY Sights."

Norton Simon Museum

411 W. Colorado Blvd., Pasadena 91105; (818) 449-6840
Open Thurs.-Sun. noon-6 p.m. Adults $4, seniors & students $2, children under 12 free.

At the Norton Simon in Pasadena, you'll see a wonderful collection of masterpieces. After the

Burghers of Calais by Rodin greets you at the gates, you'll view a broadly representative inventory of art, with particularly good collections of the Impressionists, Degas, Picasso's works on paper and Renaissance and eighteenth- and nineteenth-century European works. The Galka Scheyer Collection of the Blue Four (Kandinsky, Klee, Feininger and Jawlensky) is superb. Some of the works are innovatively displayed, with pieces from different epochs complementing and reinforcing one another. It may be jarring to the traditionalist, but, after all, this is California.

Pacific Asia Museum

46 N. Los Robles Ave., Pasadena 91101; (818) 449-2742
Open Wed.-Sun. noon-5 p.m. Adults $3, seniors & students $1.50, children under 12 free.

This is the only museum in Southern California to focus on the arts of the Pacific Rim countries and Asia. Housed in the historic Grace Nicholson Building, it's authentically outfitted with a Chinese roof, tiles and bronze dragons. The museum shop offers gift shop offers relevant books, jewelry, toys, masks, textiles and more.

Santa Monica Museum of Art

2437 Main St., Santa Monica 90405; (310) 399-0433
Open Wed.-Thurs. 11 a.m.-6 p.m., Fri.-Sat. 11 a.m.-8 p.m., Sun. 11 a.m.-6 p.m. Suggested donation $3; seniors, students & artists $1.

The former Edgemar Farms egg-processing plant has hatched a gem of a museum, surrounded by a new-age mini-mall (called Edgemar), admirably designed by Frank Gehry. In lieu of a permanent collection, the Santa Monica Museum of Art (SMMOA) presents diverse exhibitions as well as performances and projects by lesser-known artists in new and unconventional contexts.

Skirball Museum

Hebrew Union College, 3077 University Ave., South-Central L.A. 90007; (213) 749-3424
Open Tues.-Fri. 11 a.m.-4 p.m., Every 2nd & 4th Sun. 10 a.m.-5 p.m. Admission free.

This little museum is housed in Hebrew Union College, bordering the USC campus. It is filled with Judaica, from a reconstruction of an archaeology dig in the Near East and a room filled with Torah-based religious decorative arts to a gallery of paintings and a display of Jewish American art and artifacts. There are a few special exhibitions a year, with corresponding lectures and special events. It's an interesting place to get a sense of the past and to admire the richness of Jewish religious and folk culture.

Southwest Museum

234 Museum Dr., Highland Park 90065; (213) 221-2163
Open Tues.-Sun. 11 a.m.-5 p.m. Adults $5, seniors & students $3, children 7-18 $2, children under 6 free.

On a clear day, this hillside museum offers a commanding view of the mountains. The Southwest Museum is one of the city's treasures, as every local schoolchild knows. It showcases Native American arts and crafts, and gives visitors a glimpse of what California and its neighboring states were like before the Spanish and American colonizations. The pottery and basketry collections are especially good, as is the intriguing exhibit on the Plains Indians, with detailed explanations of cosmology, clothing and war rites. Rotating special exhibitions feature everything from contemporary photography to prehistoric pottery. The gift shop is a favorite of collecting cognoscenti, and the Braun Research Library houses one of the world's finest collections of material on Native American cultures.

Performing Arts

L.A. is a banquet of music and theater, in venues too numerous to mention. At one end of the scale, coffeehouses, cabarets and Equity Waiver theaters (under 100 seats) serve up intimate productions that range from the sublime to the ridiculous. Grander entertainment is plentiful at the places listed below—best bets for world-class performances and players.

Music Center of L.A. County

L.A.'s answer to Lincoln Center, the Music Center (135 N. Grand Ave., Downtown L.A. 90012; 213-972-7211) incorporates the **Dorothy Chandler Pavilion**, home of the L.A. Philharmonic, Music Center Opera and other glittering troupes; the **Ahmanson Theatre**, the main stage for big-name crowd-pleasers (*Phantom of the Opera*, for instance); and the **Mark Taper Forum**, which emphasizes contemporary drama on a thrust stage that enhances the impact of just about anything. Having recently celebrated its 25th season, the Taper continues to mount its often-rewarding productions, which include occasional classic revivals as well as regular world and West Coast premieres. As long as *Phantom* holds sway at the Ahmanson, what would normally play there will be seen at the **James A. Doolittle Theatre** (1615 N. Vine St., Hollywood 90028; 213- 462-6666): a mixture of plays and musicals, many of them fresh from

Broadway or Broadway bound, such as *Two Trains Running, Lost in Yonkers, The Heidi Chronicles* and *A Little Night Music*.

Other Venues

Pantages Theatre
6233 Hollywood Blvd., Hollywood 90028; (213) 468-1700

More than any other L.A. theater, this is where the *Phantom* himself would feel at home. Dense deco detailing surges around the lobby and above the seats. The productions here, including dance, concerts (from rap to rock), popular musicals, are often significant.

Pasadena Playhouse
39 S. El Molino, Pasadena 91101; (818) 792-8672

Now three-quarters of a century old, this handsome Spanish Colonial–style theater has gained new life with a popular mixture of original works, revivals and New York imports (*Lend Me a Tenor, Other People's Money, Forever Plaid*). Successful shows often move on to other theaters in L.A. and beyond.

Shubert Theatre
2020 Ave. of the Stars, Century City 90067; (800) 233-3123

A large, opulent venue for theatrical events—hit shows (*Evita, Cats, City of Angels*) that usually settle in for long, well-publicized runs.

UCLA's Royce Hall & Wadsworth Theatre
405 N. Hilgard Ave., Westwood 90024; (310) 825-9261

UCLA's Center for the Performing Arts presents a wide-ranging series at its two venerable theaters, Royce Hall on campus and the Wadsworth Theatre, which is located on the Veterans Administration grounds north of Wilshire Boulevard, west of the San Diego freeway. The programming, which takes place mainly during the school year, includes the classical and the contemporary, from the Arditti Quartet to the Kronos Quartet, with dance (Bella Lewitzky and others) and popular music from Rickie Lee Jones to Mel Torme.

Westwood Playhouse
10886 LeConte Ave., Westwood 90024; (310) 208-5454

A well-proportioned theater that features a diverse selection of plays and, occasionally, music and dance.

Wiltern Theatre
3790 Wilshire Blvd., Wilshire District (L.A.) 90010; (213) 380-5031

Restored to its original art-deco splendor, the Wiltern is a first-rate place to see the likes of Sting, Elvis Costello, David Sanborn or the Joffrey Ballet. Virtually every seat is good and the programming encompasses name acts from every area of popular music.

Attractions

Cabrillo Marine Museum
3720 Stephen White Dr., San Pedro 90731; (310) 548-7562
Open Tues.-Fri. noon-5 p.m., Sat.-Sun. 10 a.m.-5 p.m. Admission free (parking $5.50).

The Cabrillo Marine Museum makes it possible to explore Los Angeles Harbor, the Channel Islands, offshore kelp beds, sandy beaches and mud flats without getting your feet wet. In addition to the artificial ocean habitats, there are 34 saltwater aquariums showcasing sea creatures as they would appear naturally, a multimedia show and hands-on exhibits that are perfect for children. Call for information on field trips such as whale-watching tours.

California Museum of Science and Industry
700 State Dr., South-Central L.A. 90037; (213) 744-7400
Open daily 10 a.m.-5 p.m. Admission free. Parking $2.

This is one of our favorite Los Angeles museums. Flocks of schoolchildren have their curiosity stimulated by the simulated-earthquake exhibit (an especially valuable teaching tool after a Southland shaker), and fascinating hands-on experiences with computers, not to mention the chance to operate a bicycle factory of the future, the economics "arcade," the basics on electricity and magnetism and, in the Kinsey Hall of Health, a workshop that lets you make "lifestyle choices" about alcohol, tobacco, cocaine and marijuana—and shows how your choices affect your body. Throughout the museum, scientific theories are made accessible and understandable, using plenty of moving parts and interactive displays. Don't miss the IMAX theater (call for showtimes and ticket prices), a showcase for incredibly vivid short films shown on a five-story-high screen.

273

Disneyland

1313 Harbor Blvd., off I-5 Fwy., Anaheim 92803; (714) 999-4565

Summer (June 19-Aug. 31): open daily 8 a.m.-1 a.m.; spring, fall & winter hours vary seasonally—call for current hours. Adults $27.50, children 3-11 $22.50; senior discounts available. AE, MC, V.

If you want to get a close look at Middle America, Disneyland is a people-watching spectacle that will keep you entertained for hours. Here, masses of Americans and foreigners alike don Mickey Mouse ears without a trace of embarrassment. They smile through the longest lines and climb with delight into little trains and shudder in the Haunted Mansion. Star Tours and Pirates of the Caribbean vie for the best-ride vote; other popular attractions include Michael Jackson's *Captain EO* film, Splash Mountain and Space Mountain. Even if one is past the age at which a roller-coaster ride is the biggest thrill imaginable, in this pristine environment, surrounded by so much friendliness and contagious excitement, it's hard to resist the urge to revisit one's childhood for an afternoon. And the clockwork efficiency with which the Disney army runs the park is unbelievable: a dropped cigarette butt is whisked away in a matter of seconds. Despite the stress caused by millions of visitors daily, every doorknob sparkles. Disneyland is a required trip for those with tots over age three.

Gene Autry Western Heritage Museum

4700 Western Heritage Way, Griffith Park (L.A.) 90027; (213) 667-2000

Open Tues.-Sun. 10 a.m.-5 p.m. Adults $6, seniors & students $5, children 2-12 $2.50, children under 2 free.

Skillfully blending "scholarship and showmanship," the Gene Autry Western Heritage Museum is dedicated to preserving the real and imaginary history of the Wild West. The permanent collection is housed in seven themed galleries called "Spirits," covering everything from extraordinary saddles (Spirit of the Cowboy) to the important *Mountain of the Holy Cross* painting by Thomas Moran (Spirit of Romance) to a charming Hopalong Cassidy children's room (Spirit of Imagination). There's a special exhibition gallery, a sculpture court surrounded by Guy Deel's *Spirits of the West* master mural and a theater that features favorite Western films, live performances, and a spectacular presentation that brings the many spirits of the American West to life. Guided tours are available by reservation. Don't miss the gift shop stocked with everything from Stetson hats to Native American contemporary jewelry and pottery.

George C. Page Museum & La Brea Tar Pits

5801 Wilshire Blvd., Wilshire District (L.A.) 90036; (213) 936-2230

Open Tues.-Sun. 10 a.m.-5 p.m. Adults $5, seniors & students $2.50, children 5-12 $1, children under 5 free. Parking $3 with museum validation.

Hidden away in this office-building neighborhood, the famous pit of tar continues to bubbble up, giving us a glimpse of our primordial roots. After wandering around the peaceful, tar-scented Hancock County Park, where you may see excavations in progress, head into the George C. Page Museum, a tribute to the animals that once roamed Wilshire Boulevard. You'll discover a saber-toothed cat that changes from a skeleton to a realistic hologram image, a miniature tar pit that simulates the sensation of being pulled into the mire, a paleontology lab where you can watch scientists at work piecing together the past, an impressive wall of wolf skulls, several audio-visual presentations and a storeroom of drawers filled with fossil bones. But the most chilling artifact from the asphalt vault is a restored, 9,000-year-old skeleton of a woman.

Griffith Observatory & Planetarium

2800 E. Observatory Rd., Griffith Park (L.A.) 90027; (213) 664-1191, Laserium (818) 997-3624

Spring & summer: open daily 12:30 p.m.-10 p.m.; fall & winter: open Tues.-Fri. 2 p.m.-10 p.m., Sat.-Sun. 12:30 p.m.-10 p.m. Admission free (separate admission for planetarium and Laserium shows).

Nestled in the Los Feliz hills, the Griffith Observatory is a classic example of '30s public-monument architecture. The old-fashioned alcoves house space-age astronomical and scientific displays. You'll find information on everything from cosmic rays to the Mayan calendar to black holes. The various star shows are always as enjoyable as they are educational. Laserium is a dramatic laser light show geared around a changing repertoire of music. The observatory grounds are lovely, and on a clear day you can see—as James Dean did in *Rebel Without a Cause*—from the mountains to the sea.

Griffith Park

Vermont Ave. N. of Los Feliz Blvd., Los Feliz 90027; (213) 666-2703

Open daily 5 a.m.-10 p.m.

This gigantic park has something for everyone, just as a Los Angeles public park ought to. There's the zoo, housing more than 2,000 creatures living in simulated natural habitats. There are the Griffith Park Observatory & Planetarium (*see* review above), with the expected science-student–quality star show that is not without charm.

The Laserium light-and-music show attracts both families and teen dates, and the Greek Theatre presents top-name pop musicians in a lovely outdoor arena. For young children, there are pony rides, a small-scale choo-choo train complete with an overalled engineer, a classic old carousel and Travel Town, a marvelous collection of antique trains. You can cool out in peaceful, woody Ferndell, or bird-watch in the bird sanctuary. And, as expected, there are facilities for ballplayers, cricketers, soccer players, golfers, tennis nuts, hikers and swimmers. And for the less athletic, there are dozens of picnic areas. Don't miss the fabulous Western lore of the Gene Autry museum (*see* review this chapter).

Hollywood Wax Museum
6767 Hollywood Blvd., Hollywood 90028; (213) 462-8860
Open Sun.-Thurs. 10 a.m.-midnight, Fri.-Sat. 10 a.m.-2 a.m. Adults $8, seniors $6.50, children 6-12 $5, children under 6 free.

If you've been dying to see the *Last Supper* next to Marilyn Monroe, Ronald Reagan, Michael Douglas and Magic Johnson, this is your chance. What the wax museum lacks in realism, it more than makes up for in vivid imagination.

Knott's Berry Farm
8039 Beach Blvd., Buena Park 90622; (714) 827-1776
Summer (Memorial Day-Labor Day): open Mon.-Thurs. 10 a.m.-10 p.m., Fri.-Sun. 10 a.m.-midnight; winter: open Mon.-Fri. 10 a.m.-6 p.m., Sat. 10 a.m.-10 p.m., Sun. 10 a.m.-7 p.m. Adults $22.95, children 3-11 $9.95, children under 3 free. AE, D, MC, V.

Knott's has grown from a simple, re-created ghost town to a sprawling major entertainment center, with thrill-seeker rides and heavily promoted evening concerts that attract fresh-faced teenagers. Standout attractions include Boomerang, a corkscrew roller coaster; one of the longest simulated rapids rides in California; Fiesta Village, with its Montezooma's Revenge roller coaster; and XK1, a participatory flight ride. Some of the original charm can still be found behind the standard amusement-park glitz. Camp Snoopy features an old-fashioned mule-powered carousel, and the Calico Mine ride relives a Western train ride, complete with holdup. People come from all over just for the hearty, good chicken dinners at the gigantic restaurant, and the simple fruit preserves are as tasty as they were a half-century ago.

Some establishments change their closing times without warning. It is always wise to check in advance.

Los Angeles Children's Museum
Los Angeles Mall, 310 N. Main St., Downtown (L.A.) 90012; (213) 687-8800
June-Sept.: open Mon.-Fri. 11:30 a.m.-5 p.m., Sat.-Sun. 10 a.m.-5 p.m. Oct.-May: open Wed.-Thurs. 2 p.m.-4 p.m., Sat.-Sun. 10 a.m.-5 p.m. Admission $5, children under 2 free.

You can bring children here to let them dress up like firemen, play in Sticky City, make instant wall shadows, crawl through a tunnel, create recycled artworks, record their own voices, do a TV newscast, ride a street sweeper and measure their height next to a full-size photo of Kareem Abdul-Jabbar. The multi-tiered, labyrinthine place is filled with screaming children with brightly painted faces. It is controlled educational chaos, staffed with museum teachers who have the patience of many Jobs. Everything is meant to be touched and felt, and, amazingly enough, everything is intact—the kids seem to have great respect for the property.

Los Angeles County Museum of Natural History
900 Exposition Blvd., South-Central L.A. 90007; (213) 744-3466 (DINO)
Open Tues.-Sun. 10 a.m.-5 p.m. (Discovery Center & Insect Zoo, 11 a.m.-3 p.m.) Adults $5; students, seniors & children 12-17 $2.50; children 5-12 $1; children under 5 free. Admission free first Tues. of each month. Parking $2 (in quarters).

This is a comfortable, old-fashioned institution, complete with a charming, coffered-ceilinged marble rotunda. Children are naturally drawn to the hands-on exhibits of the Discovery Center, but there's something for everybody here: a dinosaur gallery that's a great monument to L.A.'s mammoth and mastodon forebears; the bird hall's animated specimens in walk-through habitats, including Condor Mountain and a tropical rain forest; a most impressive display of gems in their natural states; an American history hall with a charming, nostalgic view of the past; and the mammal halls, those classic natural-habitat simulations with peaceful beasts captured in immortal stasis.

Max Factor Museum
1666 N. Highland Ave., Hollywood 90028; (213) 463-6668
Open Mon.-Sat. 10 a.m.-4 p.m.

Housed in a beautiful art-deco building, the museum is loaded with photographs of movie stars from the early days of cinema to the present, and contains the largest collection of movie-star autographs in the country. Be sure to visit the Blond, Brunette, Redhead and Brownette rooms, each designed to compliment the complexion of its namesake.

Museum of Flying

Santa Monica Airport, 2772 Donald Douglas
Loop North, Santa Monica 90405; (310) 392-8822
Open Wed.-Sun. 10 a.m.-5 p.m. Adults $5, seniors $3, juniors $2, children $1.

Located on the north side of the Santa Monica Airport, the Museum of Flying has one of the most complete aviation and aeronautical libraries in the country. There are exhibits on both commercial and aerospace aviation. Flight-ready examples of historically significant aircraft include the *New Orleans*, the first airplane to fly around the world, an authentic Spitfire and the Douglas DC3. Of special interest is an extensive collection detailing the history of the Douglas Aircraft Company. If you feel the need to come out of the romantic aeronautical past and into the scene-making '90s, DC3 restaurant is adjacent to the museum.

Olvera Street

Between Alameda, Main, Macy & Los Angeles Sts., Downtown (L.A.) 90012; (213) 628-7833 (Olvera Candle Shop)
Open daily; hours vary.

L.A.'s own permanent Mexican marketplace, Olvera Street is a perennial source of bona fide buys. Start off by sampling the hand-shaped tortillas at La Luz Del Día (near the bandstand, 213-628-7494). In the jumble of *puestos* (small shops), look for Mexican bingo games, huge loofah sponges and exotic candy made from cactus, pumpkin or caramelized goat's milk. Casa de Souza (on the second level, 213-626-7076), one of Olvera Street's oldest establishments, imports folk art directly from Mexican and Central American sources: vases and candleholders with a soft, polished luster from Oaxaca, rustic signed metal wall pieces with "tree of life" motifs from Haiti, and wonderful Guatemalan place mats. Bazaar de Mexico (213-620-9782) specializes in Taxco sterling silver jewelry and traditional Mexican clothing (like Pancho Villa's poncho). Finally, visit the Olvera Candle Shop for candles, candle holders and candle-making supplies. Olvera Street is a short walk from Chinatown and from Union Station (800 N. Alameda St., 213-683-6987).

Queen Mary

Pier J, Long Beach 90801 (end of Long Beach freeway); (310) 435-3511
Open daily 10 a.m.-6 p.m. Adults $17.95, children 3-11 $9.50. Parking $5. All major cards.

You can spend an afternoon here witnessing the romance of lifeboat drills, stately staterooms, and historic ship exhibits. But the most fascinating sights are the subtle personal traces of long-gone sophisticated travelers. We were especially amused by the peach-tinted mirrors, meant to disguise any possible seasickness affecting the wealthy travelers who once crossed the Atlantic in luxurious splendor. The art-deco bar and formal dining room are monuments to period decor. As a concession to the present, the ship is filled with gift shops and modern food services.

Santa Monica Heritage Museum

2612 Main St., Santa Monica 90405;
(310) 392-8537
Open Thurs.-Sat. 11 a.m.-4 p.m., Sun. noon-4 p.m. Admission & parking free.

The rooms on the first floor of this historic mansion are devoted to different eras of Southern California's colorful past; exhibits on the second floor rotate between contemporary art and historical collections (among them, old toys, Pendleton blankets, California pottery, vintage radios). A tiny gift store offers books, old-fashioned postcards and decorative items that correspond to the upstairs exhibitions.

Six Flags Magic Mountain

Magic Mountain Pkwy. at I-5 Fwy., Valencia 91355; (818) 992-0884
Summer (Memorial Day-Labor Day): open daily 10 a.m., closing hours vary. Winter: open weekends & school holidays, same hours. Adults $25, children under 48 inches $14, seniors $16, children 2 & under free. Parking $5. AE, MC, V.

A classic American amusement park. There's no magical fantasyland here, just first-rate thrill-seeker rides, concerts featuring an occasional top-name pop act, slower-paced amusements for young children and lots of junk food. The best attractions are the major rides: the new Flashback "diving coaster," the Coney Island-inspired Psyclone roller coaster, the Roaring Rapids, a fast-and-wet white-water raft ride, the dual-track, big-as-its-name Colossus coaster, and Tidal Wave, which plummets you into two and a half tons of water. This is a good park for children; the six-acre Bugs Bunny World features an excellent petting zoo, pint-size vehicular rides and a scaled-down racetrack with tiny race cars.

Universal Studios

100 Universal City Plaza (Lankershim Blvd. at the 101 Fwy.), Universal City 91608; (818) 508-9600
Tour times vary. Adults $26, seniors & children 3-11 $20, children under 3 free. Parking $5. MC, V.

For nearly six hours, the movie industry reveals all its secrets at this enormously popular tourist attraction. Fascinated groups daily witness *Backdraft*'s climactic conflagration (the warehouse blazes 150 times a day) and visit *E.T.*'s home planet by bicycle. The World of Cinemagic includes *Back to the Future* special effects and Hitchcockian suspense (who will fall from

Saboteur's full-scale Statue of Liberty mockup?). Ultimately, the old-fashioned bravado of the live Western stunt show is more engaging than the high-tech trickery of *Jaws, Psycho* or *King Kong.*

Venice Gondola Charters

4016 Lyceum Ave., Venice 90066; (310) 823-5505
Tour times vary.

For $65, you and your significant other can board an authentic replica of a Venetian gondola and cruise through the maze of channels in Marina del Rey and Venice, complete with taped Italian music and a black-and-white-clad gondolier. The price also includes Champagne during the tranquil, hour-long journey. For the hopelessly romantic and those who don't mind a rather ludicrous substitute for the real thing.

Watts Towers and Art Center

1727 E. 107th St., Watts (L.A.) 90002;
(213) 569-8181
Towers open Sat.-Sun. 10 a.m.-4 p.m. Art Center open Tues.-Sat. 9 a.m.-4 p.m. Adults $2, children $1.50.

Rising out of a bleak suburban landscape in Watts is this whimsical creation of childlike charm and innocence. Simon Rodia, a barely literate Italian immigrant, came to L.A. with a dream, and this latter-day da Vinci created the towers over a 33-year period with no aesthetic, architectural or engineering background. He created his folk art sculpture on ranch land alongside the railroad tracks, so Red Car passengers would see his work. The sculpture is a fantasy of found art: shells, ceramics, glass, tools and rocks are imbedded and imprinted into a honeycomb of walls and organic, spiraling towers, a cross between an Islamic mosque, a pueblo and a sand castle. The metal framework is eroding, and the glorious towers are partly encased by scaffolding as artisans painstakingly restore and renovate the structure. Until the renovation is complete, you'll have to content yourself with viewing the towers from a short distance unless you take a weekend or special group tour. But by all means, visit the adjacent Watts Towers Art Center, a lively community center that shows African-American and Third World art and hosts workshops and two major festivals a year. Ignore the overblown stories about Watts's crime problems and make a pilgrimage to this inspirational place.

Whale Watching

Sport Fishing Pier, 233 N. Harbor Dr., Redondo Beach 90277; (310) 372-3566
Tour times vary. Mon.-Fri. $8, Sat.-Sun. $11 (children 11 & under $8).

A three-hour boat ride will take you about two miles offshore in the hopes of spotting whales migrating toward Baja (from mid-December to early April). Your hosts take it all very seriously, and soon the whole crowd joins in the effort to help find one of these magnificent mammals. We were fortunate enough to see a mother whale and her calf making the leisurely voyage south. The ride is refreshing, although a bit choppy at times. But the best part is the return trip, where you can see the entire dramatic panorama of Los Angeles, the snow-peaked mountains in the distance. It can be one of those stunning moments that makes you realize why people settled here in the first place.

Will Rogers State Historic Park

14253 W. Sunset Blvd., Pacific Palisades 90272;
(310) 454-8212
Spring & summer: open daily 8 a.m.-7 p.m.; fall & winter: open daily 8 a.m.-6 p.m. Parking $5.

You can learn all about Will Rogers's life here, including his prowess as a roper, his spontaneity as a political/social observer and his enthusiasm for flying. All of this and more is covered in a biographical film, followed by a guided (or audio) tour of his pelt-strewn ranch house. The grounds are impressive for picnicking or roaming around the polo field, stables, and corral, where young riders still learn the ropes. A pleasant two-mile loop trail leads to Inspiration Point's spectacular vistas; the more ambitious can take the backbone trail to Topanga State Park and beyond. Equestrian Day, filled with special events, is held every year in the fall.

Excursions

The Beaches

Each L.A. beach has its own character—some have a teen-party ambience, some are surfing beaches and some attract the bizarre. At the northernmost end of the county are the Malibu-area beaches, starting with County Line, a great surfing spot. Then (moving south down Pacific Coast Highway) comes **Zuma Beach**, where Valley teens congregate, and the private Malibu Colony, home to crowd-shy celebrities. Next stop is Santa Monica, L.A.'s great public beach; on hot summer days tens of thousands stake out their spots on this huge expanse of sand, even if the water is polluted.

Then comes **Venice**, at once seductive, exhilarating, intriguing, entertaining and yet completely devoid of substance. But you don't come to Venice for depth. You come to stroll the boardwalk with the throngs, to ogle at the nymphs who whiz by on roller skates, the street performers, the skateboard jockeys, the sunbathers, the bodybuilders, the rap masters and the galaxy of people who take all of this in. The soundtrack to this show is a cacophony of competing portable stereos. The bazaar stalls sell both cheap new items and crafts, from $6 sunglasses to embroidered Guatemalan vests.

South of Venice, there's a small, clean stretch of beach fronted by highly desirable pastel condominiums; tan, athletic Marina del Rey locals like to sun here. Then comes airplane-strafed **Playa del Rey** and the broad, usually crowd-free expanse of **Dockweiller State Beach**, a popular spot for picnics, parties and big touch-football games—and the only county beach that allows fires. **Manhattan Beach**, farther down the line, is where the pretty people come out for volleyball, running, bicycling, Frisbee and flirting. A desperate parking situation keeps these beaches from getting too crowded with outsiders. Neighboring **Hermosa Beach** and **Redondo Beach** are similar to Manhattan. One of the best ways to soak up some sun—and the California experience—is to take a leisurely bike ride southward along the path from Santa Monica.

Chinatown

This Chinatown, the area around Broadway and Hill, north of 1st Street, is actually L.A.'s third, created by Anglo developers after the first and second were moved to make way for large developments. It's less a tourist spot than it is a real-life Chinese community which means that though the area is very small, it offers more than stalls full of trinkets and souvenirs. You can spend an entire day poking around for unusual finds in the shops (along Spring Street are several well-stocked markets, including a butcher that sells whole roasted pigs and ducks). If you eat a meal in Chinatown, make it dim sum, that delightful Chinese brunch that lets you sample numerous dumplings, buns, rolls, seafood and more in one sitting (*see* "LOS ANGELES Bargain Bites" for the best dim-sum houses).

The Mountains

If you've had enough of the hordes of hip Angelenos, try escaping to one of Los Angeles's two mountain ranges for some solitude and (at least partially) clean air. The **Santa Monica Mountains**, home to deer, coyotes, chaparral and reclusive canyon dwellers, cut across Los Angeles from Hollywood to Malibu, separating the L.A. basin from the San Fernando Valley. You should at least take a drive along Mulholland, the windy, sometimes rutted road that runs the length of this range—the views are often breathtaking. If you're more outdoors-inclined, there are thousands of acres of trails, wildlife and streams at **Point Mugu State Park**, in the west end of the Santa Monicas; at **Will Rogers State Park**, in Pacific Palisades; and at **Topanga State Park**. For information on all parks in the Santa Monica Mountains, call (800-533-PARK).

The **San Gabriel Mountains**, part of the huge Angeles National Forest, rise above northeast Los Angeles, Pasadena and the San Gabriel Valley. Here you'll find contrasts typical of Los Angeles—waterfalls and fern glens just around the corner from dry hills of scrub and chaparral. The miles of trails and parkland are reached through the Angeles Crest Highway; we recommend you check with the Red Box Ranger Station on the highway for information before exploring this wonderful natural expanse.

Old Los Angeles

Though efforts to preserve early Los Angeles have been sadly inadequate, some of its early history can be found. Two **Franciscan missions** remain in the L.A. area from the Spanish colonial period, and they are worth seeing. The **San Gabriel Mission** (537 W. Mission Dr., San Gabriel), was established in 1771 as the fourth in the chain of Junípero Serra's California missions. The current church dates from about 1805 and looks much like the very first design. The **San Fernando Mission** (15151 San Fernando Mission Blvd., Mission Hills), was founded in 1797. The charming adobe buildings surround a green courtyard; the church, destroyed in the 1971 earthquake, has been rebuilt as an exact copy of its former self. Bypass the dull exterior and look at the beautiful Spanish detail work inside.

Adobe houses, Spanish architecture, and the oldest residence in Los Angeles (Avila Adobe, 1818) are the landmarks of early central Los Angeles, at **Olvera and Main** streets in downtown. This area is interesting architecturally, especially the Plaza Church, built for the tiny pueblo of Los Angeles in 1822, and the Pico House Hotel. Long gone are the old ranchos, and Olvera Street is now a commercial bazaar (*see* "Attractions," this chapter.)

For a look at some lovely turn-of-the-century architecture, drive through **Old Town Pasadena**, especially down Grand and Orange Grove, which are lined with imposing mansions; down Carroll Avenue in Angelino Heights near downtown, home of beautifully restored Victorian houses; through the old West Adams district south of Mid-Wilshire, which was once a wealthy community; and through Ocean Park and Venice, where Victorian charmers are tucked in between modern condos.

If you're interested in touring some California Victorians, visit **Heritage Square** (3800 N. Homer St., Highland Park; 818-449-0193).

Landmarks

Los Angeles is rich with both history and architectural achievements, its fly-by-night reputation notwithstanding. Following is a list of some of the city's most acclaimed structures, some of which are open for visiting and many of which are located in the downtown L.A. area. For more information, call the L.A. Conservancy, (213) 623-2489.

■ **Avila Adobe,** 10 E. Olvera St. Downtown; (213) 628-1274. Oldest surviving house in Los Angeles, built in 1818. Part of El Pueblo de Los Angeles Historic Monument; call for tour information.

■ **Bonnie Brae Street,** two blocks south of Wilshire Blvd., Wilshire District. Neighborhood of beautiful Victorian homes.

■ **Bradbury Building,** 304 S. Broadway St., Downtown. A stunning, well-preserved office building built in 1893, with a skylit central atrium, wrought-iron stairways and cage elevators.

■ **Carroll Avenue,** at Kensington Ave., Angelino Heights (near Echo Park). These Victorian jewels are being restored gradually.

■ **Doheny Mansion,** 8 Chester Pl., Downtown; (213) 746-0450. An imposing turn-of-the-century mansion at Mount Saint Mary's College.

■ **Ennis-Brown House,** 2655 Glendower Ave., Los Feliz; (213) 660-0607. A hilltop Mayan-style concrete-block house designed by Frank Lloyd Wright. Tours are given the second Saturday of odd-numbered months; call for reservations.

■ **Fine Arts Building,** 811 W. 7th St., Downtown. This 1925 twelve-story Romanesque building has twisted columns and arched

windows, and a fantastic two-story tiled main lobby.

■ **Gamble House,** 4 Westmoreland Pl., Pasadena; (818) 793-3334. The Craftsman era is epitomized in this Greene and Greene masterpiece. The house is open to the public; call for information.

■ **Heritage Square,** 3800 N. Homer St., Highland Park; (818) 449-0193. The Cultural Heritage Board of Los Angeles has saved about a dozen of these beautiful Queen Anne/Eastlake–style homes from the wrecker's ball. Several are open to the public.

■ **Hollyhock House,** 4800 Hollywood Blvd. (Barnsdall Park), Hollywood; (213) 662-7272. This Frank Lloyd Wright classic is the centerpiece of the Barnsdall Art Center. Tours several days a week (call for times).

■ **Hollywood sign,** Durand Dr. off Beachwood Dr., Hollywood. You'll have to hike awhile to get a close-up look at this world-famous landmark.

■ **I. Magnin,** 3050 Wilshire Blvd., Wilshire District. An art-deco classic; one of L.A.'s finest buildings.

■ **Los Angeles Central Library,** 630 W. 5th St., Downtown; (213) 626-7461. Although tragically damaged by fire in the mid-1980s, the exterior remains as beautiful as ever. An aesthetic gem, mixing Roman, Mediterranean, Byzantine, Islamic and Egyptian sources.

■ **Los Angeles City Hall,** 200 N. Spring St., Downtown. Designed by Albert C. Martin, one of L.A.'s premier early architects, this 28-story building was once a sky-scraping marvel that towered above the rest of the city. Although far surpassed in height, it is still lovely, and its observation decks provide good views.

■ **Lummis Home,** 200 E. Ave. 43, Highland Park; (213) 222-0546. Home to the Historical Society of Southern California, it took Charles Lummis twelve years to build this marvelous house made of boulders found in the nearby arroyo.

■ **Million Dollar Theatre,** 307 S. Broadway St., Downtown; (213) 642-6272. A spectacular theater, this was L.A.'s first glamorous movie palace and is now a rundown neighborhood movie theater.

■ **Neutra Houses,** Silverlake Blvd., Silverlake. Richard Neutra's clean lines and architectural purity can be seen in the International-style houses he built facing the Silverlake Reservoir. There are several between 2200 and 2300 Silverlake Blvd.

■ **Pacific Design Center,** 8687 Melrose Ave., West Hollywood. These striking glass buildings (in brilliant emerald green and cobalt blue) house L.A.'s cutting-edge products in home design and decor.

■ **Saint Vincent de Paul Church,** (Roman Catholic), 612 W. Adams Blvd, South-Central L.A.; (213) 749-8950. Across from USC, this church is one of L.A.'s loveliest.

■ **Union Station,** 800 N. Alameda St., Downtown; (213) 624-0171. The set for countless movies. The main terminal is enormous and very beautiful.

■ **Wrigley House,** 391 S. Orange Grove Blvd., Pasadena. A stately mansion typical of those built in Pasadena by wealthy turn-of-the-century industrialists.

Sports

One would hardly be experiencing Southern California completely if one were to stay inside restaurants, nightclubs and galleries all the time. Although we are certainly fond of such civilized activities, we do subscribe to the "when in Rome" cliché. So when in California, do as the sun-drenched Californians do: get outside and go sailing, bicycling, hiking, golfing or hang gliding. With that in mind, we've drawn up a list of places that will supply you with the equipment, lessons and/or facilities needed to become fully initiated into active Los Angeles life.

For spectator sports (season opening dates, phone numbers for information), see "Calendar of Events" listings, pages 292–294.

Ballooning

Balloon Adventures
P.O. Box 1201, Malibu 90265; (800) 843-7433
Open daily dawn to dusk.

The Balloon Adventures hot-air balloon pilot will take you on a quiet, majestic soar. Sunrise and sunset flights (from $100 per person) leave from Moorpark, Lancaster or Perris Valley. You must book in advance, and if you want to arrange

a special flight (as did the couple who were wed aloft), all sorts of charters and parties are available.

Bicycling

Excellent bike paths follow the coastline from Santa Monica to South Bay; riding from beach to beach is one of the best possible ways to spend a sunny Saturday. Although there are no formal shops with regular hours, several ad hoc bike-rental operations can be found in Venice Beach parking lots on weekends and summer weekdays.

Sea Mist Rental
1619 Ocean Front Walk, Santa Monica 90401; (310) 395-7076
Open Mon.-Fri. 9:30 a.m.-6 p.m. (summer), Sat.-Sun. 9 a.m.-6 p.m.

Conveniently located 100 feet south of the Santa Monica pier on the beach-level boardwalk, Sea Mist rents cruisers, tandems and various multi-speed bikes, as well as boogey boards, roller blades and skates. Most bikes rent for $5 for the first hour, $4 for additional hours, with a $14 maximum for the day.

Spokes 'n' Stuff
20 1/2 Washington Blvd., Venice 90291; (310) 306-3332
1715 Ocean Front Walk, Santa Monica 90401; (310) 395-4748
Open daily 9:30 a.m.-5 p.m.

With one shop in the sandy shadow of Loews hotel and another just inland from the Venice pier, Spokes 'n' Stuff is well situated to serve the sleekly mobile multitudes who merge on the beach bike path. Their well-maintained inventory supplements standard two-wheelers with plenty of children's bikes, tandems, roller blades and boogey boards. Most bikes rent for $8 a day (mountain bikes are $16 a day—but who needs 20 speeds on such a level playing field?).

Woody's Bicycle World
3157 Los Feliz Blvd., Los Feliz 90039; (213) 661-6665
Open Mon.-Sat. 9 a.m.-6 p.m., Sun. 9 a.m.-4 p.m.

One of the very few places in L.A. (surprisingly) to rent bikes, Woody's is located near Griffith Park, which has some fine bike lanes. Mountain and ten-speed bikes rent for $15 a day. The shop is friendly, and the bikes are in decent shape.

Golfing

Arroyo Seco Golf Course
1055 Lohman Ln., South Pasadena 91030;
(213) 255-1506
Open daily 7 a.m.-10 p.m. Greens fees: $3.75-$5.75.

This three-par eighteen-hole golf course isn't the most challenging in Los Angeles, but the price is certainly right: $3.75 per person for nine holes, $5.75 for eighteen. There's also a nine-hole miniature golf course. The grounds are located just a short drive from downtown L.A. Juniors and senior citizens are given daytime discounts.

Griffith Park Golf Course
4730 Crystal Springs Dr., Griffith Park, Los Feliz 90027; (213) 663-2555
Open daily dawn to dusk. Greens fees: $12 Mon.-Fri., $16 Fri.-Sat.

You won't be able to get into this popular public course on weekends without a reservation card, but it isn't too hard to get a starting time on weekdays (call the office for information on a reservation card). There are two eighteen-hole courses here, and both are challenging.

Industry Hills Golf Course
1 Industry Hills Pkwy., City of Industry 91744; (818) 810-GOLF
Open Sun.-Thurs. 8 a.m.-5 p.m., Fri.-Sat. 6 a.m.-4:30 p.m. Greens fees: $42 Mon.-Thurs., $57 Fri.-Sat.; $25 after 1 p.m. Mon.-Thurs., $30 after 1 p.m. Fri.-Sat.

A huge Sheraton "resort" and convention-center hotel surrounds these two eighteen-hole courses, which are beautiful, well designed and expensive. Located 30 minutes east of downtown L.A., the courses are quite a drive away for those living west of Pasadena. But if you're an avid golfer and don't have any club-member friends, it may be worth the drive and the cost; it's one of the best public courses in the country.

Hang Gliding

Windsports International
16145 Victory Blvd., Van Nuys 91406;
(818) 988-0111
Open Tues.-Fri. 10 a.m.-6 p.m., Sat. 9 a.m.-noon.

With the help of this friendly organization, you can act out humanity's oldest fantasy: to fly like a bird. Windsports teaches hang gliding, paragliding at three levels: beginner, novice and intermediate. In twelve to fifteen lessons you can become an advanced hang-glider pilot, or you can take just one lesson—you'll still experience that indescribable thrill of flying, even though it'll just be off a small sand hill. There's also a tandem high-altitude program that soars up to 2,000 feet.

Hiking

Wilderness Institute
28118 Agoura Rd., Agroua 91301; (818) 991-7327
Open Mon.-Fri. 9 a.m.-5 p.m.

Operating in national park sites throughout the Santa Monica Mountains, this "outdoor school" offers sunset and Sunday-brunch hikes, full-moon hikes and half-day geology hikes for about $15 to $30 per person. Other notable programs include periodic storytelling under the stars, weekend Mojave Desert explorations and other adventure outings, plus classes in wilderness survival, mountaineering and cultural history for the whole family. Call for a free catalog.

Horseback Riding

Los Angeles Equestrian Center
480 Riverside Dr., Burbank 91506; (818) 840-9063; LAICI restaurants (818) 840-1320.
Open daily; hours vary. Horses $13 per hour.

This large equestrian center is one of the best in the country, with a polo school, a beautiful indoor arena and a premium saddlery. Events include Grand Prix horse shows, rodeos and professional polo, a trendy way to spend a Saturday night with friends. The Classroom restaurant and the Equestrian bar and grill are operated by the L.A. International Culinary Institute, with both professional and student staff supervised by a certified master chef (Sunday brunch is a good time to sample the Institute's efforts). For the recreational rider, there are a variety of lessons, good rental horses and more than 250 miles of trails throughout Griffith Park.

Sunset Ranch Hollywood Stable
3400 N. Beachwood Dr., Hollywood 90068;
(213) 469-5450
Open daily 9 a.m.-5 p.m. Horses $15 per hour; refundable $10 deposit required.

One of the most exhilarating ways to get a great view of Los Angeles (on a seemingly rare clear day) is to rent one of Sunset Ranch's horses and ride through the trails high in the Hollywood Hills (just below the Hollywood sign). The horses are well trained and the ranch hands are friendly; you don't need a guide and are free to explore the hills on your own. A not-to-be-missed experience is the guided Friday-night dinner trip: you set out at dusk, ride for nearly two hours over the mountain to Burbank, have dinner in a Mexican restaurant, and ride back by the light of the moon ($30 per person). If the weather is good, it can be a truly magical experience—except for the unmemorable Mexican food (lunch rides every Wednesday).

Parachuting

Sport Parachuting School
16145 Victory Blvd., Van Nuys 91406;
(818) 994-0711
Open daily for jumping sunrise to sunset; instruction Tues.-Thurs. 6:30 p.m.-9:30 p.m.

With over 22 years in the skydiving business and 16,000 students, Bill Reed says he can teach anyone to jump. For $150, Bill will set you up with all the equipment and instruction you need, take your photo and give you a certificate.

Sailing & Boating

Blue Water Charter Concepts/California Celebrations
4051 Glencoe Ave., Ste. 7, Marina del Rey 90292;
(310) 823-2676
Open Mon.-Fri. 8 a.m.-5 p.m.

For an elegant Catalina trip, a surprise birthday party or a quiet moonlight cruise, call Blue Water Charter Concepts. It has a fleet of twenty luxury motor yachts (from 85 to 115 feet) and will arrange almost any sort of charter imaginable. The company is particularly proud of its gourmet catering department. The cost varies considerably, depending on the yacht, the time at sea and the staff required.

Rent-a-Sail
13719 Fiji Way, Marina del Rey 90291;
(310) 822-1868
Open daily 10 a.m.-sundown.

Located in Fisherman's Village, this shop rents a variety of boats, from Hobie Cats to sloops to power boats; with the smaller boats you can explore the Marina, with the larger you can cruise the Santa Monica coastline. Fourteen-foot sailboats rent for $14 an hour, 21-foot sailboats for $20, and fifteen-foot power boats for $28. Sailing lessons are also available for $28 an hour ($38 for two people), including rental fees.

Skiing

Bear Mountain
43101 Goldmine Dr., Big Bear Lake (P.O. Box 6812, Big Bear Lake 92315); (909) 585-2517

Located about one mile from Snow Summit, Bear Mountain is the area's largest and best ski resort. It has expanded and upgraded its opera-

tions over the last couple of years, adding new runs and triple and quad-chair lifts to get you to the top even before you've caught your breath. Call for prices on full-day, half-day and night-skiing tickets.

Mt. Waterman
817 Lynn Haven Ln., La Cañada 91011 (Angeles Crest Hwy., 43 miles NE of L.A.); (818) 440-1041, snow conditions (818) 790-2002.

One of the closer ski slopes, Mt. Waterman is only an hour's drive from Los Angeles. It's a small place—just a few chairs—and the runs are fairly simple, though there are a couple of challengers. But the drive is right, the lines are short and the slopes are usually well groomed and uncrowded. On-site rentals and food. Call first; it sometimes closes in too-warm weather.

Snow Summit
880 Summit Blvd., off Hwy. 18, Big Bear Lake (P.O. Box 77, Big Bear Lake 92315);
(909) 866-5766

The crowds can get oppressive at this popular local skiing (and snow-boarding) spot, especially now that advance tickets are sold through Ticketmaster. There's a limit to the number of tickets sold, however, and the midweek crowd is kept quite manageable. Snow Summit (about a two-hour drive) isn't as close to L.A. as Mt. Baldy or Mt. Waterman, but that means the snow is better. There are eleven chair lifts, plenty of man-made snow and runs for all levels, rentals, lessons and a child-care center. Call for prices on full-day, half-day and night-skiing tickets.

Snow Valley
Hwy. 18, east of Running Springs (P.O. Box 2337, Running Springs 92382); (909) 867-2751

The largest local ski area, with thirteen lifts and plenty of runs, Snow Valley is also one of the most expensive—full-day tickets are $35, half-day $22 and night skiing $22 (children 7 and under ski free with adult). During dry spells the many snow machines keep the packed-powder level up. There's a bar and restaurant, rentals, lessons and an all-day kids' program that includes lunch (for ages 5 to 10, $30). Very crowded on weekends.

Tennis

Griffith Park Tennis Courts
3401 Riverside Dr. (Los Feliz Ave. entrance), Griffith Park 90027; (213) 662-7772
Open daily 7 a.m.-10 p.m.

There's usually a wait for these well-maintained courts during prime time; if you buy a reservation card from the city, however, you can book courts in advance. Courts are free weekdays before 4 p.m.; other times, they're $4 an hour. Also try the other park facility, a pretty, woodsy setting that can be reached from the Vermont Avenue entrance.

The Merchant of Tennis
1118 S. La Cienega Blvd., Wilshire District (L.A.) 90035; (310) 855-1946
Open Mon.-Fri. 9 a.m.-6 p.m., Sat. 9 a.m.-5 p.m. (courts available daily 24 hours).

This successful tennis shop has two fine courts, one for singles and one for doubles. The cost is $10 an hour. Since there are only two courts, reservations are critical; you can drop by and pay in advance or give them a charge-card number over the phone. The Merchant of Tennis's professional instructors rank among the best in Southern California.

The Racquet Centre
10933 Ventura Blvd., Studio City 91604; (818) 760-2303
Open Mon.-Fri. 6 a.m.-midnight, Sat.-Sun. 7 a.m.-midnight.

The Racquet Centre has probably the best facilities of any public courts in town. It has the feel of a private club; there are twenty first-class tennis courts, eleven racquetball courts, paddle tennis courts, ball machines, good locker rooms and a well-stocked shop. Tennis courts are $7 to $11, depending on time of day; racquetball courts run $7 to $13. You can become a member for $45 a year, which entitles you to reserve courts. Otherwise you take your chances.

The Tennis Place
5880 W. 3rd St., Wilshire District (L.A.) 90036; (213) 931-1715
Open daily 7 a.m.-11 p.m.

These courts, adjacent to the huge Park La Brea apartment complex, do a booming business. There are sixteen lighted courts in good condition; the cost is $13 per court hour before 4 p.m. and $15 after 4 p.m. and on weekends. Reservations are advised. A $80 yearly membership fee entitles you to a $5 discount on court fees and other privileges. The Tennis Place will arrange games and offers professional instruction.

Waterskiing

Endo's Waterski Werks
5612 E. 2nd St., Long Beach 90803 (Naples Island); (310) 434-1816
Hours vary with the season.

Endo's rents (and sells) waterskis and accessories to the suntanned young residents and visitors of Belmont Shore and Naples, two charming beach communities hidden away in Long Beach.

Ski rentals start at $10 to $12 a day; lessons (highly recommended for first-timers) can be arranged.

Tours

For many, a visit to Movieland is not complete without an inside tour of a television or film studio or a live taping. In addition to The Burbank Studios, several other studios and stations are worth a call: **ABC Television Studios** (310-520-1ABC); **Audience Associates** (213-467-4697); **Audiences Unlimited** (818-506-0067); **CBS Television Studios** (213-852-2458); **Fox Television** (213-856-1520); **Lorimar Television** (310-280-4722); **NBC Television Studios** (818-840-3537); **Paramount Studios** (213-956-5000); **Warner Brothers** (818-954-1131); (For Universal Studios, see "Amusements.")

The Burbank Studios
4000 Warner Blvd., Burbank 91522; (818) 954-1744
Tours weekdays 10 a.m. & 2 p.m. by reservation only. Minimum age 10. Admission $25.

If you want a behind-the-scenes look at how Hollywood *really* works, not a stunt-filled, amusement park–style tour, call The Burbank Studios (home to Warner Brothers and Columbia Pictures) and make reservations for this fascinating tour—the most intensive of any in the L.A. area. The group is limited to twelve; you'll walk throughout the huge lot (sometimes riding in an electric cart), going through the property department, unused sound stages, backlot sets, construction departments and all the day-to-day operations behind moviemaking. On occasion, tours are allowed on the set to watch live filming in progress.

Chinese Historical Society Tour
969 N. Broadway, Chinatown (L.A.) 90012; (213) 617-0396
10 a.m.-noon, second Saturday of each month. Fee $5 per person (group rates available).

Explore the history and architecture of Chinatown with this pleasant walking tour.

Grave Line Tours
P.O. Box 931694, Hollywood 90093; (213) 469-3127 (information), (213) 469-4149 (reservations)
Tours daily at noon. Admission $30.

Call it tacky and tasteless, but Grave Line Tours is easily Hollywood's hottest novelty. This two-hour tour of Tinseltown's most morbid and scandal-ridden sites departs from Hollywood Boulevard and Orchid Avenue (near Mann's

Chinese Theater), spiriting you and six others away in a Cadillac hearse. "Director of Undertakings" Matthew Anderson really camps it up, with a taped narration that covers every sordid detail (including music and sound effects). You'll see the "last-breath" locations of luminaries John Belushi, Janis Joplin, Sal Mineo, Montgomery Clift and Superman's George Reeves, to name a few. Each "mourner" receives maps to "Cemeteries of the Stars" to explore later. Among tours, this is one, uh, to die for.

Gray Line Tours
6541 Hollywood Blvd., Hollywood 90028;
(213) 856-5900
Open daily 7 a.m.-8 p.m.

Though this can be fun, it's dtrictly for tourists. Most of Gray Line's tours go to the attractions (Disneyland, Knott's). There are a few other bus tours: a Tijuana shopping spree, a Hollywood–to–Beverly Hills movie-star tour and a general city tour that hits everything from Mann's Chinese Theatre to the Hollywood Bowl. The all-day city tour is $35 and the two-hour tour of movie stars' homes costs $25.

Heli U.S.A. Helicopter Adventures
3200 Airport Ave., Ste. 6, Santa Monica 90405;
(310) 553-4354
Tours daily 1 p.m.-2 p.m. & 7:30 p.m.-8:30 p.m.

Heli U.S.A. will take you on a whirlwind helicopter ride, gliding above the nightlights of downtown, Beverly Hills and Hollywood. You can opt for a straight flight, or one of their dinner packages, which may include dinner at a local restaurant, limosine service and champagne. Sundays, they offer a daytime tour of the beaches from Venice to Malibu, and through the Santa Monica, ending with brunch. Charter flights are also available.

L.A. Party Bus
6253 Hollywood Blvd., Hollywood 90028;
(213) 467-4697
Tour times & prices vary.

When the whim strikes (and no more regularly than that), owner Cash Oshman conducts a "tour" of L.A.'s hottest nightclubs in conspicuous artist-designed buses: there's an Egyptian sphinx, a Groucho Marx bux and a "gobot transformer." The predetermined schedule lets partygoers get on or off as they please, and drinks are allowed on the bus, which saves you from the perils of driving under the influence. Then there's Oshman's Art Hop, a day-long excursion in which passengers stop at artists' lofts and galleries to encounter impromptu performance pieces. The attention-getting buses are also available for private tours and parties.

Los Angeles Conservancy Tours
727 W. 7th St., Ste. 955, Downtown (L.A.) 90017;
(213) 623-CITY
Hours vary. Tours $5.

These very nice people will quickly disprove the rumor that Los Angeles has no history. Every Saturday morning at 10, enthusiastic docents lead residents and tourists both on eleven downtown walking tours. The Pershing Square tour takes you to and through such landmarks as the Oviatt Building, the Biltmore Hotel, the Bradbury and Edison buildings and Grand Central Market. Another tour visits architectural Marble Masterpieces, old and new. And the Mecca for Merchants tour visits the old Seventh Street beauties, including the palatial Fine Arts Building, the Los Angeles Athletic Club and the 818 and Roosevelt buildings. There are also Union Station, Little Tokyo and Broadway tours, as well as strolls through L.A.'s most beautiful old homes and areas.

Los Angeles Times Tour
202 W. 1st St., Downtown (L.A.) 90012;
(213) 237-5757
Tours Mon.-Fri. 11:15 a.m. & 3 p.m.; printing plant tour 9:45 a.m. & 10 a.m. Tues. & Thurs. by reservation. Minimum age 10. Admission free. Free parking in Times garage at 2nd & Spring Sts.

This popular tour of the newspaper's publishing operation shows the newspaper process from writing to pasteup, leading visitors through editorial and composition areas. A separate tour is available for those who relish the thunder of big printing presses.

El Pueblo de Los Angeles Historic Monument
130 Paseo de la Plaza, Downtown (L.A.) 90012;
(213) 628-1274
Tours Tues.-Sat. 10 a.m., 11 a.m., noon & 1 p.m. Admission free.

For a look at the early Spanish and Indian days of Los Angeles, when it was no more than a tiny, dusty village, come down to Olvera Street for this delightful walking tour. You'll see many of the old buildings, including the Pico House, the Plaza Church, and the Avila Adobe. There's no charge, and reservations are necessary for large groups.◆

CITYLORE

History & Legend

Hopi legend tells of a lost civilization popu-lated by what they called the Lizard People, who lived some 5,000 years ago. The Lizard People, it seems, built a number of underground cities—thirteen to be exact—one of which is said to be located under downtown Los Angeles (most of the ancient Indian settlements in South-ern California do correspond to today's large population centers). The network of tunnels making up this city is purportedly shaped like a lizard, its head falling under what is now Dodger Stadium. According to the legend, these tunnels contain gold tablets that chronicle the history of the race. In the 1930s, an engineer named W. Warren Shufelt was convinced of the lost city's existence and set about finding it. He drilled a huge shaft and came up empty, which prompted howls of public derision. What keeps this story alive, besides the prospect of bringing down the astronomical tunneling costs of the Metrorail project, is that from time to time unexplained tunnels have in fact been discovered beneath downtown L.A.

❖

In October 1871, a white Angeleno mob de-scended on the center of the Chinese community, the Calle de los Negros, and massacred some twenty innocent Chinese residents. The police did nothing. A grand jury was convened and handed down indictments. A few of the attackers drew jail sentences, and it appeared that in the end justice would prevail, thanks in part to the efforts of presiding Judge Robert M. Widney, one of L.A.'s biggest real-estate promoters. Pos-sibly more interested in boosting land sales than keeping abreast of the finer points of the law, Widney overlooked a few legal technicalities in the indictments, and they were overturned on appeal. Widney went on, in 1880, to help found the University of Southern California.

❖

Sometime around 1885, Angeleno Daeida Hartell Wilcox took the train back to Ohio to visit relatives. En route, she met a woman who talked about her country estate in Illinois called Hollywood. Daeida loved the sound of the name. So when she returned to the 120-acre ranch she and her husband, H.H. Wilcox, owned in north-west Los Angeles, she named it Hollywood. Lit-tle did she know how that appealing name would go on to label so much more than a neighbor-hood: movies, glamour, celebrities, fame, the good life.

❖

At about three in the morning on February 25, 1942, war fever hit home in Los Angeles. A few days earlier, a Japanese submarine had opened fire on a oil installation farther up the coast. Now, an unidentified aircraft was picked

285

up on radar. Shortly thereafter, something was spotted wafting over Santa Monica. The city erupted in a frenzy of anti-aircraft fire. Although the expected Japanese air raid failed to materialize, L.A. still managed to chalk up five fatalities that night—three people were killed in car accidents as panicky motorists attempted to navigate the city streets during the blackout; two more succumbed to cardiac arrest. Property damage that night was also high, thanks to some of the 1,400 U.S. anti-aircraft shells that arced their way back downward onto peoples' homes. Steven Spielberg fictionalized the fateful night in his movie, *1941*.

Sex & Scandal

To be sure, the Roaring Twenties found no shortage of hucksters and con men in booming Los Angeles. None, however, were quite as gifted as Chauncey C. (C.C.) Julian, founder of Julian Petroleum, which was affectionately known as Julian Pete. Julian came to L.A. a poor gambler, but had a demonstrable gift for advertising, salesmanship and, when necessary, bribery. But it was his talent for manipulating the stock market, particularly oversubscribing shares of his own oil company, that brought him his fortune. He used this money to live life to the hilt, partying constantly and often leaving outrageous tips, all the while dodging investigations from every law-enforcement agency from the local cops to the FBI. The boom was finally lowered on May 7, 1927. Trading was suspended on Julian stock, and his investment pyramid came crashing down. To the consternation of some 40,000 investors, Julian Petroleum was oversubscribed to the tune of $150,000,000, an even more staggering sum in that day. Although the affairs of C.C. Julian had parted company with legal business practice years before, the only one connected with the scandal to serve time was, ironically, the district attorney, who had accepted bribes to help throw the trial.

❖

Sister Aimee Semple McPherson, the tambourine-tapping, marimba-playing evangelist, came to L.A. poor in material goods but rich in spirit. It wasn't long before she found herself surrounded by a loyal flock eager to hear her upbeat, flashy presentations of the Lord's message—and eager to make substantial faith offerings. She was able to start her own radio station and the still-extant Angelus Temple, off Sunset Boulevard in Echo Park. On May 18, 1926, while swimming at the beach, McPherson vanished. An exhaustive search yielded nothing; Sister Aimee, it appeared, had drowned. Then, miraculously, a month later she came stumbling out of the desert into a small Mexican town, spinning a wild tale about two people who had kidnapped her and taken her to Mexico. The faithful rejoiced, the cynical grew suspicious. The latter had trouble believing Sister Aimee could trudge across the desert without getting so much as a sunburn. Although an investigation into the affair went nowhere, the story persisted, with plenty of evidence to back it up, that Sister Aimee, yielding to a little weakness of the flesh, had been shacking up in Carmel with her radio-station engineer. She continued her ministry for a time, but gradually lost her following.

Hollywood's spiciest scandal to date splashed into the headlines in 1930 with the lurid revelations of the goings-on of screen star Clara Bow, the original "It" girl. In addition to playing real-life bedfellow to such notable actors as Bela Lugosi and Gary Cooper, she was also reported to have indulged in sexual scrimmages with the entire University of Southern California football team. Her adventures may have inspired at least one fledgling actor—the team at the time included tackle Marion Morrison, later known as John Wayne. USC coach Howard Jones, a stodgy teetotaler, put an end to this off-the-field scoring by declaring Bow off-limits. The Trojans may have suffered because of his strictness: they enjoyed few winning seasons for years to come.

❖

In the late 1930s, a reform-minded organization called CIVIC began investigating the shady dealings of Mayor Frank Shaw and the corrupt Los Angeles vice squad. With the firm backing of the *Los Angeles Times*, Shaw was able to hold his own, and the city's pimps, whores, bootleggers, gamblers and hucksters continued to operate without such nuisances as municipal law enforcement. Then a CIVIC investigator, Harry Raymond, got in his car on the morning of January 14, 1938, on his way to give damaging testimony against the mayor. The car exploded when he turned the key, but miraculously, despite massive shrapnel wounds, he survived. The bomb was traced to LAPD Lt. Earl Kynette, a notorious figure whose methods of persuasion were known to veer toward the thuggish. The scandal brought down the administration. This mini-Watergate earned L.A. the dubious distinction of being the only major American city to ever recall its mayor.

❖

In February 1949, Robert Mitchum, wholesome star of the American screen, was arrested during a party at the Laurel Canyon home of actress Lila Leeds. The charge was—gasp—"conspiracy to possess marijuana." His trial buzzed with speculations about Mitchum being framed, since (among other things) before his arrest, for some inexplicable reason, his house was being bugged. Unlike previous celebrity victims of drug scandals, Mitchum came out of his two-month prison sentence with his career intact, though the city fathers did feel it behooved them to cancel Mitchum's speech in celebration of National Youth Week.

Winners & Losers

The disillusionment of Hollywood's countless young aspirants was embodied in the person of Lillian Millicent (Peg) Entwhistle. Entwhistle is best known not for her acting talents, which were fairly accomplished, but as "the woman who jumped off the Hollywood sign." Actually, at the time, the sign read, HOLLYWOODLAND. Entwhistle plummeted to her sad death from the 50-foot-high H, although many versions had her leaping from the final D; this legend was preferred because the D was the thirteenth letter in the sign, and Entwhistle's first, and last, screen performance was in a movie called *13 Women*, thus giving the story a satisfying superstitious confluence. Also incorrect is the widespread notion that her death leap precipitated a fad among suicides who took to jumping off the sign in droves. No one else has ever been known to repeat poor Peg's final performance.

❖

By all accounts, Eben Ahbez was a strange man. He eschewed such amenities as shoes, shaves and haircuts and wandered the streets of Hollywood preaching Oriental philosophy. In 1947 he confronted Nat King Cole's manager, Mort Ruby, and shoved a dirty sheet of paper into his hand, imploring Ruby to show the song it held to Cole. Amazingly, the song did find its way to Cole, and from Cole, to Irving Berlin. Berlin

was sufficiently impressed with the tune to want to buy it—the only problem was, nobody knew how to find Ahbez. As legend has it, Ahbez was finally located sleeping under the Hollywood sign. The song, "Nature Boy," recorded by Nat King Cole, sold more than one million copies.

❖

"Marie Prevost did not look her best / The day the cops burst into her loneliness." So sang new-wave pop star Nick Lowe, who put to music the oft-told tale of one of Hollywood's ugliest suicides. Prevost, a silent-screen star, was one of the many human casualties to fill the morgues and sanitariums when talking pictures came along, destroying many careers. In 1937, driven to despondency, Prevost holed herself up in her Hollywood apartment with her pet dachshund and literally drank herself to death at the age of 38. She remained in her apartment for many days, and when she was finally discovered, her body was . . . well, as Lowe sang, "Even the dog, he's a-gotta eat."

Deaths Most Suspicious

Few homicide investigations so captured the public's imagination as the one that followed the grisly murder of Elizabeth Short, better known as the Black Dahlia. So called because of her habit of always wearing black, Short, like many other lost, star-struck women in Tinseltown, hopped from casting couch to casting couch in search of fame. Fame, unfortunately, finally found her when her mutilated body was discovered dumped in an open field. The massive manhunt yielded plenty of dirt on the tawdry goings-on on the Dream Machine's fringes, but little in the way of actual clues. Thousands of loonies descended on the police with bizarre confessions. The case, which was never solved, spawned a TV movie, a novel and miles of thrilling copy for a public looking for some exciting reading in those dull days following the hubbup of World War II. Short apparently is not resting in peace—her ghost is said to be seen scurrying around her old Hollywood apartment.

❖

Another unsolved mystery with a subsequent haunting is that of the so-called suicide of actor George Reeves, star of the old *Superman* TV series. Reeves was found dead in his Benedict

Canyon bedroom after a bullet fired at his head failed to ricochet off harmlessly, as they always did on TV. The gun was found next to him, and his death was ruled a suicide, though many people close to Reeves didn't buy it. His mother dedicated her life, unsuccessfully, to proving he was murdered. The case remains a mystery; numerous ghost sightings and séances at the house have failed to shed any light on the subject.

In 1935 actress Thelma Todd was found dead in the garage above the building that housed her restaurant and her apartment. Her body was bruised and bloodied, slumped behind the wheel of her Packard. It looked like murder, but the coroner said accidental death by carbon-monoxide asphyxiation. Tongues began wagging—too many suspicious circumstances. Words like "scandal" and "cover-up" were bandied about. Todd's ex-husband had known mob connections. Rumors began circulating that the mob wanted to use the Pacific Coast Highway restaurant that she owned as a high-class gambling den, which could be patronized by Todd's high-rolling friends. As the story goes, Todd was not one to be pushed around, and she refused the offer and was summarily rubbed out. Her property was more fortunate: the building that was once Thelma Todd's Roadside Rest still stands, about a half mile north of Sunset on PCH.

Comedies of Error

Abbot Kinney had a dream. Already a successful developer at the turn of the century, he decided to create a Venice of America. Not just the physical Venice, with the canals and such, but a cultural duplicate as well. Symphonies and classic dramas would, Kinney believed, make his city one of rare refinement. Unfortunately, it didn't work out that way. Concessions to public tastes required Kinney to make Venice into something closer to Coney Island, complete with kiddie rides and carny shows. Drainage problems caused the canals to turn into swamps, prompting the city of Los Angeles, which by then had incorporated Venice, to fill in most of them. Kinney's idyllic community fell into decline and today, despite awe-inspiring real estate prices, is still home to an unparalleled collection of loonies (not to mention a considerable homeless population). There are, however, some remaining signs of Kinney's dream: what's left of the canals and a lingering artistic sensibility in many of its residents and businesses.

During a longshoremen's strike in San Pedro in 1915, social critic Upton Sinclair addressed the strikers on private property that they had secured permission to use. He began reading to them from the U.S. Constitution. Finding this scene inexplicably offensive, the police arrested him on the spot. Another speaker who read from the Declaration of Independence, and one who commented favorably on the agreeability of California's climate, also suffered the same fate.

In the early 1900s William Mulholland rose to the level of chief engineer of the city water department without ever having stepped inside a university. He is most famous for tapping water from the Owens Valley and carrying it, via a huge aqueduct, hundreds of miles to parched Los Angeles. In 1924, heady with that success, Mulholland decided to build a dam in the Santa Clara River valley north of Los Angeles. Although geologists and engineers who had actually endured the tedium of formal education thought the plan unsafe, Mulholland would not be deterred. The St. Francis Dam was completed in 1927, and it immediately began to develop leaks. Brushing public concerns aside, Mulholland examined the dam on March 12, 1928, and declared it to be completely safe. That very evening, the St. Francis Dam burst with a mighty roar, obliterating three towns—and Mulholland's career.

❖

An old Hollywood story—one that's been told as often as its veracity has been disputed—concerns the fate of actor John Barrymore's body after it was left at the mortuary. The cast of characters changes with each telling. So does the mortuary, for that matter. But the general thrust is this: as a joke, director Raoul Walsh, and/or some accomplices, bribed or cajoled the undertakers to let them borrow Barrymore's body for a few hours. The corpse was then driven up to the Hollywood Hills and deposited in an armchair in Errol Flynn's mansion. Upon returning home, Flynn found himself eye to eye with what he thought to be the late John Barrymore, now apparently making himself at home chez Flynn. The macho, swashbuckling Flynn promptly screamed, ran out of the house and hid behind an oleander bush until the offending body could be, ahem, spirited away. ◆

BASICS

Contents

Transportation

Airport

Though the expansion of **Los Angeles International Airport** (LAX) has lessened traffic and made the airport considerably more serviceable, it can still get chaotic and crowded at peak travel times. Most travelers have friends or family pick them up from (and take them to) LAX, which can often lead to great frustration when the parking lots are full and the ramps are backed up. It's wise to consider using the airport shuttle services, which are generally convenient and efficient.

Among the biggest shuttle services are: **Airport Flyer Express** (For Los Angeles, Orange and Ventura counties, call 800-244-5755); **Super Shuttle Ground Transportation** (L.A., 310-338-1111; Orange County, 714-973-1100); and **Prime Time Shuttle** (L.A., 310-558-1606; San Fernando Valley, 818-504-3600; Ventura County, 800-262-7433). The services are competitively priced: a one-way trip to LAX from most L.A. hotels will cost between $10 and $18 for the first passenger, and between $6 and $10 for each additional passenger in the same party. It's advisable (and sometimes required) to book your shuttle reservation at least one day in advance. If you're planning to rent a car at the airport, note that most rental companies have shuttle services; limousine chauffeurs will, naturally, pick you up at the arrival gate. You'll find cabs (both licensed and "gypsy") waiting outside the terminals, but be warned that if you're going all the way across town, a cab will cost almost as much as a limo!

Getting Around

By Bus

Despite the efforts of the **RTD**, or **Rapid Transit District**, which is the city of L.A.'s bus line, traveling in L.A. by bus is not so rapid, and can be crowded and unpleasant. There are a few express lines that stop only at major streets, such as line 320 running the entire length of Wilshire Boulevard, and those are reasonably speedy. Call (213) 626-4455 for route information. The new **Metrorail** blue line (800-252-7433) runs from downtown L.A. to Long Beach; ground has been broken for the red line, which is scheduled to begin running in mid-1993. The **Santa Monica Blue Bus** line (310-451-5444) is clean and convenient, and has twelve lines that run from Santa Monica to UCLA, Downtown, LAX and other areas.

By Car

Don't think you can survive Los Angeles without access to a car; you can't. The distances here are unlike those in any other city—it seems that every destination is at least a twenty-minute drive away. If you don't have the use of a car or limo, there are dozens of rental agencies throughout the city that are well stocked with high-mileage, low-power American and Japanese compacts and sedans. The biggest companies, with branches everywhere, are **Hertz** (800-654-3131) and **Avis** (800-331-1212). For more unusual rentals, try **Rent-a-Wreck** in West L.A. (classic American cars from the '60s and '70s, including convertibles, at some of the lowest prices around; 310-478-0676, 818-762-3628); **Luxury Line** (the city's leading renter of such class cars as Ferraris and Rollses; 310-659-5555) and **Budget Rent-a-Car** in Beverly Hills (a good stock of Mercedeses and every sort of luxury car; 310-274-9173). And before you drive your rental *anywhere*, get the indispensable *Thomas Guide* map books for Los Angeles and Orange counties. They're available at most bookstores, and will become your bible for navigating the city.

By Limo

If you have a pressing need for a Rolls-Royce Phantom Classic at 4 a.m., **White Tie Limousine Service** (310-553-6060) will supply one for $75 per hour. There's a two- or three-hour minimum for most limousines (five-hour minimum for a Rolls).

By Taxi

Cabs aren't a very viable means of transportation in L.A., unless you're keeping to one specific area. Since the distances are so vast, cabbing it can become prohibitively expensive; you'll generally come out ahead renting a car. But if you need a cab for a particular trip, one of the best on the Westside is **Beverly Hills Cab** (310-273-6611); an excellent service in Santa Monica is **Lightning Taxi** (310-453-2636), the only company we know of that uses Mercedeses and station wagons instead of down-and-out American clunkers; in the San Fernando Valley try **Valley Cab** (818-787-1900); and servicing the San Gabriel Valley is **Bell Cab** (818-285-1141). Other good bets are **Checker Cab** (213-481-1234) which runs from downtown to West L.A. and the airport; **L.A. Taxi** (213-627-7000) which covers a wide area from the south bay to northeast L.A.

communities such as Atwater and Eagle Rock; and **United Independent Taxi** (213-653-5050) for trips around West L.A., Century City and Beverly Hills. There are groups of cabs stationed outside the airports and Union Station, as well as the Beverly Center, Farmer's Market, L.A. County Museum of Art, Third Street Promenade, and other major attractions and hotels; otherwise, you must call. They're radio-dispatched; the wait is usually five to fifteen minutes.

By Train

The train is a perfectly viable means of transportation up and down the coast, yet many people completely overlook the option. The **Amtrak** line, headquartered at Union Station (800 N. Alameda St., Downtown L.A.; 213-624-0171), operates clean, comfortable trains that travel daily between L.A., San Diego and Santa Barbara, also stopping at most cities in between. The trip from L.A. to Santa Barbara is about two-and-a-half hours; fare is $20. From L.A. to San Diego takes 2 hours, 50 minutes; fare is $24. Reservations are not required unless specified (during major holidays, for instance); you can purchase tickets on the spot during station hours.

Vital Needs

Foreign Exchange

Los Angeles is home to a few more foreign-exchange brokerages each year, but there are still relatively few in the city. Outside of LAX, your best bets for exchanging money on the weekends, when the banks are closed, are the Beverly Hills branch of **Thomas Cook** (452 N. Bedford Dr., 310-274-9176) or one of Cook's two other branches (Glendale Galleria, 818-242-6883; Sherman Oaks Galleria, 818-907-0160); all open Saturday 10 a.m. to 4 p.m. Or try **Associated Foreign Exchange** (AFEX, 433 N. Beverly Dr., Beverly Hills, 310-274-7610; open Sat. 10 a.m.-4 p.m.). **Bank of America** also operates exchange counters at certain branches: Santa Monica (1301 4th St., 310-319-2368), Beverly Hills (460 N. Beverly Dr., 310-285-2891), and Hollywood (6300 Sunset Blvd., 310-871-4740); all open Saturday 10 a.m. to 1 p.m.; and in West L.A. (1101 Westwood Blvd., 310-209-

3912; open Sat. 9 a.m.-2 p.m.). The **L.A. Currency Exchange** (310-646-9613) has five airport counters that are open until 11 p.m. nightly. Many of the more established banks have exchange windows, but you're limited by bankers' hours, and the rates may not be as favorable for the traveler.

Late-Night Services

Car Repair
A-1 Automotive, 4430 Santa Monica Blvd., Hollywood 90029; (213) 661-5352. These mechanics are on duty 24 hours.

Dentist
Los Angeles Dental Society, 3660 Wilshire Blvd., Ste. 1152, Mid-Wilshire District (L.A.) 90010; (213) 380-7669. A 24-hour phone referral service to dentists who keep late-night hours.

Locksmith
Wilshire Lock and Key, 556 S. Western Ave., Koreatown 90020; (213) 389-8433. This locksmith is well established, reliable and on call 24 hours a day.

Messenger
Now Courier, 1543 W. Olympic Blvd., W.L.A. 90015; (310) 252-5000 (local)/671-1200 (air). Deliveries 24 hours a day, 365 days a year, both locally (L.A. and Orange counties) and by air courier. Drivers are bonded and insured. Cash is accepted upon pickup—it will speed the process to mention that you were referred by Gault Millau's *Best of Los Angeles.*

Pet Hotel
Pet Set Inn, 14423 S. Crenshaw Blvd., Gardena 90249; (310) 644-2938. Pickup and delivery and 24-hour emergency service are offered at this well-run pet hotel. Facilities include individual sleeping quarters with connecting outside private patios and thermostatic heat; and there's a veterinarian next door.

Pharmacy
Horton & Converse Pharmacy, 6625 Van Nuys Blvd., Van Nuys 91405, (818) 782-6251; 11600 Wilshire Blvd., W.L.A. 90025, (310) 478-0801. Fills prescriptions until 2 a.m.

Post Office
Van Nuys Main Post Office, 15701 Sherman Way, Van Nuys 91409; (818) 908-6701. You can send Express Mail packages from the "Firms" window throughout the night, but it's best to get here before 10:30 p.m., when there's someone to weigh your packages.

Worldway Postal Center, 5800 W. Century Blvd., Inglewood 90009; (310) 337-8845. This post office near LAX is open until midnight, but you can send Express Mail 24 hours a day.

Telephone Numbers

Airports
Burbank Airport, (818) 840-8847
Los Angeles International Airport (LAX), (310) 646-5252

Beaches (*information*), (310) 305-9545

Directory Assistance
local, 411
long distance, 1 (area code) 555-1212

Emergency, 911 (Fire/Police/Paramedic)

Fire Department, (213) 384-3131

Highway Conditions, (213) 628-7623

Libraries (information), (213) 612-3200

Los Angeles Times, (213) 237-5000

Police Department, (213) 625-3311

Time (within any area code), 853-1212

L.A. Travelers Aid Society, (213) 625-2501

Visitors Bureaus
Beverly Hills, (310) 271-8126
L.A., (213) 624-7300
Santa Monica, (310) 393-9825
West Hollywood (310) 858-8000

Weather Conditions, (213) 554-1212

Calendar of Events

We've put together a calendar of the more prominent and/or interesting Southern California events (dates are provided when possible).

January

Rose Parade (Jan. 1), Pasadena, (818) 449-7673 or (818) 449-4100. Spectacular and world-renowned parade of floats decorated entirely with flower petals.

Rose Bowl Football Championship (Jan. 1), Rose Bowl, Pasadena, (818) 449-7673. The classic college football showdown.

Whale-watching peak season, Cabrillo Beach Marine Museum, (310) 548-7562; Dana Wharf, (714) 496-5794; and Redondo Beach, (310) 372-3566.

Bob Hope Chrysler Classic, various courses, Palm Springs, (619) 346-8184. Major men's golf tournament held yearly since the 1960s.

Los Angeles City Tennis Tournament, Griffith Recreation Center, (818) 246-5614. This 60-year-old tournament is open to any player.

Chinese New Year (late Jan.-early Feb.), Chinatown, (213) 617-0396. Various activities, a street carnival and the colorful Golden Dragon Parade.

Japanese New Year celebration ("Oshogatsu"), Little Tokyo, (213) 628-2725. The Line Dance, which is a form of blessing, winds its way through the shops of Little Tokyo is a highlight of the varied activities.

February

Los Angeles Open Golf Tournament, Pacific Palisades, (213) 482-1311. This PGA tournament is now in its 67th year.

National Date Festival, Indio, (619) 863-8247. Festival celebrating Indio's prized fruit.

March

Nabisco–Dinah Shore Invitational Golf Tournament, Rancho Mirage, near Palm Springs, (619) 324-4546. Annual women's PGA tournament since the 1970s.

Newsweek Champions Cup, Hyatt Grand Champions Resort, Indian Wells, (619) 341-1000, ext. 7002. Professional men's tennis tournament held annually since 1976.

Swallows return to Capistrano (March 19), Mission San Juan Capistrano, (714) 248-2049. These days there may be more tourists than swallows, but the birds still return.

American Indian Festival, Natural History Museum, (213) 744-3488. Cultural celebration with arts and activities.

April

Academy Awards, (310) 247-3000. The annual televised ceremony, open to Academy members and their guests only.

American Film Institute's Los Angeles International Film Festival, (213) 856-7707. Unusual, eccentric and sometimes excellent films from every corner of the globe.

Blessing of the Animals (weekend before Easter), Olvera St., Downtown, (213) 687-4344. Traditional Mexican parade of animals and celebration.

Easter Sunrise Services, Hollywood Bowl, (213) 850-2000; Forest Lawn, (818) 241-4151; and atop the Palm Springs Aerial Tramway, (619) 325-1391.

Long Beach Grand Prix, Shoreline Dr., Long Beach, (800) 752-9524. High-energy Indy-car race through the streets of Long Beach.

Renaissance Pleasure Faire (April-May), San Bernardino, (714) 880-6211. Huge, popular festival with music, theater, food, crafts and costumes of Elizabethan times.

Cherry Blossom Festival, Little Tokyo, (213) 628-2725. Crafts, food and music to celebrate the arrival of spring.

California Angels baseball season begins, Anaheim Stadium, Anaheim, (714) 634-2000.

Los Angeles Dodgers baseball season begins, Dodger Stadium, (213) 224-1500.

Wildflower Walks, Lancaster, (805) 948-4518. Spectacular desert flowers in bloom.

May

Bullfight season opens in Tijuana.

Los Angeles/California Science Fair, Museum of Science and Industry, (213) 744-7400.

Lots of gee-whiz gadgets, gizmos and experiments.

Cinco de Mayo (May 5), Olvera Street and many other L.A. locations, (213) 680-2821/680-2525. Parades and celebrations honoring Mexico's defeat of the French.

UCLA Mardi Gras, Spaulding Field, UCLA, (310) 825-8001. The ever-popular collegiate carnival and festival, in the tradition of New Orleans, offers rides, booths and more.

Venice Art Walk, Westminster Elementary, 1010 Abbot Kinney Blvd., Venice, (310) 392-WALK ext. 333. This benefit event features chefs from some of L.A.'s best restaurants, and a tour of more than 50 Venice artists' studios.

June

Playboy Jazz Festival, Hollywood Bowl, (310) 450-9040. One of the best-known jazz festivals in the country.

Hollywood Bowl outdoor-concert season begins, (213) 850-2000. Reserve seats for an enchanting night under the stars seeing some of the world's best classical, jazz and pop musicians.

Shakespeare Festival begins, Old Globe Theatre, Balboa Park, San Diego, (619) 239-2255. Runs throughout summer.

Ojai Festival, Ojai, (805) 646-2094. Excellent festival featuring innovative modern classical music.

Summerday 1993, Pacific Design Center, (310) 450-5183. An elegant food-and-wine tasting benefit held under the sun, sponsored by KCRW (89.9 FM). Includes a rare-wine auction.

July

4th of July, fireworks throughout the city.

Gilroy Garlic Festival, Gilroy, (408) 842-1625. In addition to live music, tennis tournament, barn dance, 10K Garlic Gallop, golf tournament and arts and crafts, there is garlic in every food variation imaginable.

Laguna Beach Arts Festival/Pageant of the Masters (runs several weeks), Laguna Canyon Rd., Laguna, (714) 494-1018. Art show and popular pageant featuring live "reproductions" of great paintings.

Los Angeles Garlic Festival, Federal Building, 11000 Wilshire Blvd., Westwood, (213) 939-9023. Thousands of garlic worshipers in

shorts and shades gather for this two-day fest to celebrate the immortal bulb.

Sawdust Festival, Laguna Canyon Rd., Laguna, (714) 494-3030. Crafts show across the street from the arts festival.

Ringling Brothers and Barnum & Bailey Circus, Great Western Forum, Inglewood, (310) 673-1300. The granddaddy of circuses.

Grand Prix Bicycle Race, Manhattan Beach, (310) 545-5313/545-5621 ext. 321. Pedaling frenzy through the streets of Manhattan Beach.

August

Volvo Tennis Tournament Los Angeles, L.A. Tennis Center, UCLA, (310) 208-3838. Men's pro tennis tournament.

L.A. à la Carte: The New Los Angeles Food and Music Festival, Santa Monica Civic Auditorium, (310) 986-2725. This charity event, which takes the place of the old Taste of L.A. festival, is sponsored by the *Los Angeles Times* and offers many demonstrations and tasty bites from local restaurants and cookbook authors.

Old Spanish Days Fiesta, Santa Barbara, (805) 965-3021. Concerts, parade, rodeo, and the food and crafts of Santa Barbara's early Spanish days.

Nisei Week, Little Tokyo, (213) 687-7193/620-8861. Celebration of Japanese culture.

International Surf Championship and Festival, South Bay beaches, (310) 546-8854.

Old Miners' Days, Big Bear Lake, (714) 866-4601. Local merchants sponsor events celebrating Big Bear's history.

Saint Anthony's Celebration, Pismo Beach, (805) 773-4382. Portuguese seafaring festival and parade.

Virginia Slims Women's Championship Tennis, Manhattan Beach, (310) 546-5656. Professional women's tennis tournament.

September

Los Angeles Music Center (135 N. Grand Ave., Downtown L.A.) opera season opens. Call (213) 972-7211 for information.

Danish Days, Solvang, (805) 688-3317. Danish-heritage town northeast of Santa Barbara celebrates its roots.

Korean Festival, Koreatown, (213) 730-1495. L.A.'s fast-growing Korean community honors its heritage.

Long Beach Blues Festival, Shoreline Aquatic Park, Long Beach, (310) 498-8052/985-5566. Top blues artists from across the country perform in a festival-style setting.

Los Angeles County Fair, County Fairgrounds, Pomona, (714) 623-3111. A giant, old-fashioned county fair where farmers show off prize livestock, women compete in pie-baking contests, and kids eat cotton candy.

Los Angeles's birthday, (213) 680-2525. Various civic celebrations.

Big Bear Lake Oktoberfest, Big Bear, (714) 866-4607. A typically boisterous celebration of the Bavarian holiday, with polka dancing, German wurst feasts and beer-drinking contests.

Los Angeles Raiders football season begins, L.A. Coliseum, Downtown L.A., (213) 748-6138.

Los Angeles Rams football season begins, Anaheim Stadium, Anaheim, (714) 634-2000.

October

Festival of Masks, Hancock County Park, (310) 315-9444. Exotic folk-art masks from around the work are displayed.

Old Home Town Fair, Manhattan Beach, (310) 545-5313. Beachy small-town festival.

Pismo Beach Clam Festival (805) 773-4382. Jazz festival, parade, fair and clams galore: fried clams, clam chowder, raw clams and so on.

Los Angeles Philharmonic opens season at the Music Center, (213) 972-7211.

Los Angeles Kings hockey season begins, Great Western Forum, Inglewood, (310) 673-1300.

Los Angeles Clippers basketball season begins, L.A. Sports Arena, L.A., (213) 748-6131.

Los Angeles Lakers basketball season begins, Great Western Forum, Inglewood, (310) 673-1300.

November

Dia de los Muertos (Nov. 1), Olvera St., Downtown, (213) 628-7833. Colorful Day of the Dead parades and festival.

Vive le Beaujolais Wine Festival, Pacific Design Center, W. Hollywood, (213) 651-4741. L.A.'s premier annual tasting of Beaujolais nouveaux. Plus, gourmet French foods and entertainment.

Hollywood Christmas Parade (first Sun. after Thanksgiving), along Hollywood Boulevard, Hollywood, (213) 469-8311. The one and only.

Doo-Dah Parade (after Thanksgiving), Pasadena, (818) 796-2591. Wacky free-for-all parade that spoofs famous parades.

Death Valley Days, Furnace Creek and Stovepipe Wells, Death Valley, (619) 852-4524. The desert is at its most beautiful during this festival.

Beverly Hills Holiday Pageant, (800) 345-2210. Features youth choir, Santa and local celebrities.

World of Wines Festival, The Ritz-Carlton, Laguna Niguel, (714) 240-2000. The events include a charity dinner starring the cuisine of some of Southern California's most lauded chefs, and wine and bubbly tastings from around the world.

December

Art Expo, L.A. Convention Center, (213) 741-1151. Exhibition of works from artists around the country.

Winter Wildland, L.A. Zoo, Griffith Park, (213) 666-4090. The zoo is decorated for Christmas and offers special activities for children.

Corona del Mar Christmas Walk, (310) 644-8211. Merchant open house and street festival along Pacific Coast Highway.

Christmas Water Parades; in Los Angeles Harbor, (310) 519-3400; Naples Canal in Long Beach, (310) 590-8427; and Marina del Rey, (310) 821-7614. Light-draped and decorated boats of every size and type parade through local waterways.

Las Posadas (nightly from Dec. 16-Dec. 24), Olvera St., Downtown, (213) 628-7833. Traditional Mexican candlelight Christmas march.

Los Angeles County Holiday Music Program (Dec. 24), Dorothy Chandler Pavilion, Music Center, (213) 972-7211. Free concert of Christmas carols and holiday classics.

Sing-along performance of Handel's *Messiah*, Dorothy Chandler Pavilion, Music Center, (213) 972-7211. ◆

ORANGE COUNTY

Sun-Struck & Beach-Bound

In just a couple of short decades, Orange County has been transformed from a region marked by sprawling farms and sleepy suburbs to one of the fastest-growing and wealthiest regions in the country. The boom of the 1980s made housing developments as plentiful as Day-Glo skateboards. High-tech and service businesses attracted sun-struck workers—and business travelers—from across the country. The wealthy took over the beachfront homes that, before the boom, belonged to retired schoolteachers and people of moderate means who had found their escape from the city. And the 1990 census marked the population at 2.5 million.

Though there is still a healthy amount of development, it has most certainly slowed in the early '90s, as Orange County has settled into its new skin. Tourists continue to come and go in record numbers. For good reason: when the Beach Boys sang about "Fun, Fun, Fun" and "California Girls," they were singing about Orange County's beaches: Sunset, Huntington, Newport, Laguna and Doheny, where surfers "shred" waves, volleyball players spike balls in the sun, and vacationers soak up the easygoing Southern California beach lifestyle.

We couldn't begin to cover all that Orange County has to offer, so here we focus on the two destinations that attract the most visitors, Laguna and Newport/Irvine, with occasional forays north and south. Though there are a number of lovely beaches, we must confess to a preference: for our money, Laguna is Orange County's vacation paradise, with more charm per square inch than any place south of Carmel (except in the thick of July and August, when the crowds and traffic can be overwhelming). Take a room for the weekend or week in one of the sweet bed-and-breakfasts or ocean-view hotels—you'll return home from the incredibly lovely setting and small-town atmosphere feeling renewed, relaxed and refreshed.

For comprehensive listings of restaurants By Area, By Price and By Cuisine, and by specific features such as Breakfast, Brunch, Kid-Friendly, Late-Night, Light Eating and more, see the INDEXES section at the back of the book.

Restaurants

The symbols that accompany each review indicate the rating on a scale of one to twenty. The rankings reflect *only* our opinion of the food; the decor, service, wine list and atmosphere are commented upon within each review. For further explanation, as well as an index of restaurants by rating, please see "About the Restaurants" in the INTRODUCTION. See the INDEXES section at the back of the book for comprehensive restaurant indexes.

11/20 Amelia's
311 Marine Ave., Balboa Island (Newport Beach) 92662; (714) 673-6580
Italian/Seafood. Lunch Mon.-Sat., Dinner nightly, Brunch Sun. All major cards.

In L.A., a restaurant that is older than some of its customers is considered to be something of an ancient relic. But in Orange County, where the pace is gentler and traditions hold sway, the fact that Amelia's has lasted for more than three decades isn't such a surprise. This charming little neighborhood eatery, with its warm familial atmosphere and its regular clientele, is made up of several cozy rooms decorated with stacks of wine bottles and cases of wine. The simple lunch menu offers all the Italian staples: fried antipasti, various lasagne dishes, manicotti, tortellini, a few panini. At dinner, when seafood reigns, dishes such as lobster thermidor (with sherry, butter and mushroom sauce), broiled English cod and bouillabaisse accompany the classic Italian dishes. Most seafood entrées come with soup or salad, bread, linguine and fresh vegetables, making it a good deal for $15 to $20 per person.

Antoine at Le Meridien
4500 MacArthur Blvd., Newport Beach 92660; (714) 476-2001
French. Dinner Tues.-Sat. All major cards.

Gérard Vié, one of the famous "Les Trois Marches" in Versailles, France, is the consulting chef at Le Meridien hotel's signature restaurant, and the new executive chef, Jean Pierre Lemanissier, is a man of impeccable technical skills. Which means that Antoine is still very much a restaurant to be reckoned with. It's not the decor that strikes us, though the three long dining rooms are elegant in a drawing-room sort of way, mirrored and mauved. Nor is it the service, even though that, also, is entirely adequate. What impresses us is the menu and its execution, the style and subtlety of which are not matched anywhere in Orange County. Much of this is due to Vié, who was one of the first (if not *the* first), proponents of nouvelle cuisine. In the menus here, he blends the traditional and the modern so intelligently that the edges are blurred. Lemanissier is a good match with Vié, a classically trained chef who did stints at France's La Tour d'Argent and with great chefs Jean Bertranou and Paul Bocuse. He will never make a mango-tomatillo salsa, but neither does he spurn the free-wheeling charm of California cuisine.

Sweetbreads are paired with the expected pistachios, as well as unexpected pecans and coriander vinaigrette. Dishes can be marvelously rich and clean at the same time: delicate salmon tournedos given earthiness with olive oil–tinged mashed potatoes; roasted sea bass, its flesh kept moist with a crust of herbs; tender lamb wrapped in paper-thin slices of eggplant. A dish of squab set over Cassis-tinted spinach, the legs wrapped like miniature mummies with threads of potato, teeters on the baroque. Desserts run to such timeless faves as hot apple tart with caramel and a trio of little crème brûlées. You won't be disappointed by the wine list, particularly when it comes to French vintages. Dinner should run about $50 per person.

12/20 Antonello

South Coast Plaza Village, 1611 Sunflower Ave., Santa Ana 92704; (714) 751-7153
Italian. Lunch Mon.-Fri., Dinner Mon.-Sat. All major cards.

If a journalist wants to corner a county superintendent, a developer's lobbyist or a high-end attorney, he goes to Antonello and lies in wait. While the Ritz may be Orange County's society darling, Antonello is its power seat. And while the recession takes its toll on the area's other expensive Italian restaurants, this place continues to ride high on the expense account. The decor is a cross between a narrow Florentine street scene and an old Venetian café; the fare consists of well-executed, if unsubtle, Italian dishes. The kitchen can turn out plump, pillowy gnocchi with a suitably robust marinara, then turn around and coddle scallops in a gentle wine sauce. Pastas are usually of the rich sort, but the house minestrone is a thin, green, brothy thing infused with basil and garlic—one of the few dishes that strays from Antonello's traditional Ameri-Italo style. Even though there is a sommelier in the house, the wine list leaves off vintages. A dinner will be about $40 per person.

10/20 The Athenian

25874 Edinger Ave., Huntington Beach 92649; (714) 840-6518
Greek. Lunch Wed., Dinner Tues.-Sun. D, MC, V.

The Athenian serves pita bread made in its own kitchen, which is a clue to the care it takes with traditional Greek cuisine. The butter-laden crust of the spanokopita shatters like gold leaf at one touch; the moussaka's béchamel sauce melts in the mouth. Fish dishes tend to be overcooked, and the desserts have a curious flatness, given the quality of the other food. But with a huge swipe of pastitsio (elbow pasta and ground lamb, with a savoriness that macaroni and cheese could never match), these small sins are instantly forgiven. The interior looks exactly as you'd expect a Greek restaurant in Huntington Beach to look: bright blue and white, fragments of sculpture, travel posters of ocean and sky. There's a belly dancer several nights a week, just in case you need an extra dose of kitsch. Dinner runs about $15 per person.

10/20 Barbacoa

3333 Pacific Coast Hwy., Newport Beach 92665; (714) 646-6090
Caribbean/Pacific Rim. Dinner nightly. All major cards.

Restaurateur David Wilhelm (he of Kachina and Bistro 201, among others) tossed many ideas into the loudly colored bowl that is Barbacoa: Southeast Asian, Caribbean, Mexican, Californian, Italian. The result, however, is not exactly a happy melting pot. How to manuever from an appetizer of skewered beef with a satay sauce to pizza with eggplant and goat cheese? How to segue from mixed greens with Gorgonzola and walnuts to pork steamed in banana leaves? Perhaps this polyglot lot would work if the food weren't unevenly prepared, and if sweet, rather-too-darling fruit flavors weren't continually taking dishes hostage. The food, however, is offset by the wondrous, sparkling mast-eye view of Newport Bay. There is no better bar scene than this along the Gold Coast. Plan to spend about $20 per person for dinner.

Bistango

The Atrium, 19100 Von Karman Ave., Irvine 92715; (714) 752-5222
Californian. Lunch Mon.-Fri., Dinner nightly. All major cards.

Bistango has been a thriving spot ever since opening day. It's a lovely place for lunch, as businesspeople in the surrounding Koll Center know. The food, devised by Bay Area whiz kid Jonathan Waxman (of Stars fame) and cooked by a young Austrian named Paul Gstrein, is distinctive California fare made hearty. Pizzas roam the menu, but the Waxman-inspired grilled fish and meats are the real standouts. The menu changes monthly, but you can always count on some worthy version of grilled ahi (served medium rare, perhaps with crisp vegetables and a ponzu sauce) and a superb grilled lamb T-bone (perhaps with garlic mashed potatoes and a Pinot Noir sauce). The lunchtime salads are memorable. About $20 apiece for a simple lunch and $30 to $35 for dinner.

12/20 Bistro 201

18201 Von Karman Ave., Irvine 92715;
(714) 553-9201
American. Lunch Mon.-Fri., Dinner nightly, Late Supper Fri.-Sat. All major cards.

Bistro 201 captures that highly urban, sharp-edged-but-softened-by-money style that characterized so many L.A. restaurants in the 1980s. This is no mean feat in Orange County, where glitz can overwhelm style. But the stylish sheen is not so bright here that one can't lean back and relax. Bistro 201 is the place where journalists interview crusty subjects and businesspeople soften up reluctant clients. A lot of money may have been poured into the carefully patinaed decor, but in spirit, the restaurant is a comfortable, even homey bistro. And that's exactly the spirit owner David Wilhelm sought. The flavors of the cuisine at Bistro 201 are very pretty and balanced: a delicate dish of sand dabs sautéed in butter and set with a roof of crisp, thinly sliced potatoes is a perfect example. The food goes in for contrasts, often sweet against sour. But more timid palates can also select grilled fish, lovely sandwiches and any kind of bread pudding. The wines are well-known and nonthreatening. A dinner ranges from $25 to $40.

10/20 Las Brisas

361 Cliff Dr., Laguna Beach 92651;
(714) 497-5434
Californian/Mexican/Seafood. Breakfast & Lunch Mon.-Sat., Dinner & Late Supper nightly, Brunch Sun. All major cards.

What this comfortable cliffside restaurant lacks in tastes for the tongue it makes up for in feasts for the eyes. Spectacular ocean views from most tables (but do try for a window) and California girls and boys rubbing tanned shoulders at the patio bar combine for an exhilarating lunchtime experience. We enjoy paying a late-morning visit to the Laguna Art Museum next door, followed by a long lunch spent gazing across the rose garden to the vista beyond. Las Brisas serves an array of humdrum salads and a decent array of fish dishes, such as sea-bass filet in a tangy sauce that's as much French as it is Mexican. The calamar de mojo de ajo, a tender sautéed squid steak, is finished with a sauce of tomatoes, peppers, capers and onions. The generous breakfast buffet is a great start to the day. About $25 per person for dinner.

11/20 Café Piemonte

1835 E. Chapman Ave., Orange 92666;
(714) 532-3296
Italian. Lunch Tues.-Fri., Dinner Tues.-Sun. No smoking. AE, MC, V.

Luigi and Giovanni Ravetto are from the Piemonte region of Italy, and like most Italians, they want to feed you well. In their spanking-white little trattoria, it's almost impossible to leave wanting for anything. You'll be tempted to try all the rustic Piemontese offerings, from the sumptuous antipasti to the lineup of freshly made pastas to polenta in several guises: with a Fontina-cheese sauce perhaps, or cut up in squares and served with poached salmon. A daily special might be lobster-filled agnolotti in a light tomato sauce punctuated with a couple of fat shrimp. The Ravetto brothers make all their own pastas, as well as a spicy pork sausage that they crumble into a Barolo wine sauce and serve over roast veal, or toss into the occasional pasta dish. The wine list offers interesting Piemontese wines. A generous dinner costs $15 to $20 per person.

10/20 Café Zoolu

860 Glenneyre St., Laguna Beach 92651;
(714) 494-6825
Californian. Breakfast Sun., Dinner Tues.-Sun. AE, MC, V.

Wedged into a converted house, this smidgen of a restaurant is strictly a neighborhood place—though one must remember that the neighborhood is Laguna, where the health-conscious New Ager meets the laid-back Surfer Dude. Owner/chef Lonnie Painter tosses together all variety of concepts, ingredients and techniques, producing a sort of California Beach cuisine that sometimes works and sometimes, well, doesn't. His black-bean chili quickened with turmeric and curry is a great idea; Thai stir-fried chicken over pasta isn't such a winner. The highly seasoned meatloaf and mashed potatoes are a good bet. Don't look for finesse here—grilled fish entrées are usually overdone and overdressed—but do look for an appealing earnestness. And a number of loyal locals. Dinner costs about $13 per person.

11/20 Carmelo's

3520 E. Pacific Coast Hwy., Corona del Mar
92625; (714) 675-1922
*Italian. Dinner nightly, Late Supper Fri.-Sat.
All major cards.*

This is the sort of place where you want to bring five friends and stay for the evening: it's warm, lively—and anything but formal. Latin jazz musicians play every night of the week, and the dining room, patio and dance floor always fill up with an energetic crowd. There's no polenta or risotto to be found here, and nary a designer pizza. The black-suited waiters bring classic southern Italian dishes such as involtini of breaded swordfish (rolled with cheese, garlic and herbs); delicate veal scaloppine in Marsala-wine sauce; swordfish charbroiled with pine nuts and fresh herbs; gnocchi with Italian sausage; and various pastas. Diners linger here, over zabaglione, an espresso, a sweet shot of Sambuca. Dinner costs between $20 and $30 per person.

12/20 Daily Grill

957 Newport Center Dr., Newport Beach
92660; (714) 644-2223
American. Breakfast Sat.-Sun., Lunch & Dinner daily, Late Supper Fri.-Sat. AE, MC, V.

This stylish chain restaurant is one of the more recent of all the progeny that have sprung from The Grill in Beverly Hills. Norman Rockefeller would have loved to paint the clean-scrubbed parents and kids munching happily on the fine steaks and chops here. There are linguine with clam sauce, mushroom-barley soup, chicken pot pie, burgers, calf's liver with bacon and onions, steamed spinach, potatoes Lyonnaise, potatoes O'Brien, tapioca pie, Caesar salad and on and on. Dinner costs less than $20.

12/20 Five Crowns

3801 E. Pacific Coast Hwy., Corona del Mar
92625; (714) 760-0331
American. Dinner nightly, Brunch Sun. All major cards.

Year in and year out, this member of the Lawry's chain continues to convince sunbaked locals and tourists that they're in an ancient tavern in England, at least for a couple of hours. Inside it's terribly cozy, with stone walls, fireplaces, high-backed chairs, Villeroy and Boch china and cheery young tavern maids bearing plates of chops, roasts (excellent prime rib and spring lamb Provençale) and seafood, all boasting the consistency of preparation and quality of ingredients for which the chain is known. Care is evident in all the details—from the worthy wine list to the well-thought-out starters and accompaniments. Our only beef (excuse the pun) is with the seafood dishes, which can be over-cooked and clumsy. This is a great place to come during the Christmas holidays, when it's full of carolers and jolly good cheer. Dinner runs $30 per person.

Five Feet

328 Glenneyre St., Laguna Beach 92651;
(714) 497-4955
Chinese. Dinner nightly. All major cards.

This restaurant's spare and whimsical decor (exposed bricks and beams set off by a droll mural) leads you to expect the same of the food. This is further supported by a truly whimsical sign that proclaims, CHINESE CUISINE EUROPEAN STYLE. But when the food comes, what you find is very good Chinese dishes (sometimes using somewhat European ingredients), listed on a menu that changes every six or eight weeks. One dish, a whole braised catfish, is offered perennially—and with good reason. It's usually the best thing available: an irresistibly sweet and delicate catfish. One version employs a mildly peppery sauce; another comes with a garlic sauce that's just as good. There are always a few sublime dim-sum selections as well, such as steamed shu mai filled with shrimp, pork, black mushrooms and cabbage, or potstickers filled with pork, cabbage and Chinese chives. Some of the dishes are familiar Chinese standards (like duck with homemade plum sauce) and, thankfully, some of the stranger Sino-European experiments (like scallops in a grapefruit-mustard sauce) have given way to such well-thought-out creations as an elegant preparation of stir-fried lamb. Dinner runs about $35 per person.

Five Feet Too

Fashion Island, 1145 Newport Center Dr.,
Newport Beach 92660; (714) 640-5250
Chinese. Lunch & Dinner daily. AE, MC, V.

A bigger, sleeker, cooler clone of chef/owner Michael Kang's Five Feet, Five Feet Too is an ambitious restaurant: it's trying to be a hip and urban spot in an upscale shopping center. It makes the leap on design alone: smooth metals and concrete, tones of mauve and blue and gray, sly but perfectly corporate art. And the menu, best described as contemporary Chinese, presents sassy, brassy Chinese cooking. The open kitchen, where a half dozen or so stir-frying chefs whirl like cyclones, sends out plates that look like miniature views of Hong Kong: teeming, dense, multicolored, futuristic. Special entrées—usually stir-fried meats or fish with an elaborate number of extras—can include monkfish with a rice-wine-and-lychee sauce set on sautéed endive, with a sashimied plum here, a curlicue of carved cucumber there. Or a delicious combination of mahi mahi and opakapaka in spicy black-bean sauce, accompanied by yellowed fried rice. The regular menu sticks to more recognizably Chinese dishes, such as kung pao shrimp, chicken and scallops and vegetarian mu shu. All are good choices. For dessert, which tends to be far simpler, opt for the ice creams or sorbets. You'll spend about $35 per person for dinner.

12/20 Il Fornaio
18051 Von Karman Ave., Irvine 92715; (714) 261-1444
Italian. Lunch Mon.-Fri., Dinner nightly, Late Supper Fri.-Sat. All major cards.

In the doldrums of recession, this extravagantly designed restaurant rose on the edge of the San Diego Freeway—an Italian villa as imagined by a wealthy suburban developer. A central atrium is shielded from the sun by draped canvas shades, and the vast zinc bar opens onto a patio. The building is the quintessential California pairing of the indoor and the outdoor, and the huge kitchen, visible from most areas of the restaurant, is the quintessential theater-as-dining display. We've had a superb slice of roasted salmon, with pretty little nuggets of potatoes alongside, and been quite content. So with a marvelous rosemary-tucked chicken. Pastas can toe the predictable line, and the desserts tend to be more fluff than substance. You can also sit in the bar and order a glass of wine and a basket of bread, for the vast commercial bakery beyond the kitchen puts out superb crusty whites, light wheat and ryes and seed-covered breadsticks. Dinner will run about $25 per person.

Golden Truffle

1767 Newport Blvd., Costa Mesa 92627; (714) 645-9858
International. Lunch Tues.-Fri., Dinner Tues.-Sat. AE, MC, V.

Golden Truffle is as much a personality as it is a restaurant—the personality being one Alan Greeley, the bristle-bearded chef/owner who's always ready with a bon mot. Improvising is Greeley's strength; he likes nothing better than being told by a regular—and he has plenty of them—to do what he will. On one recent occasion, he played with his favorite themes, Asian and Latin flavors bound together with heartier American staples. He tied a baby lettuce salad with a sprig of arugula so that it became a bouquet, flavoring the greens with a strongly gingered vinaigrette and arranging triangles of seared tuna alongside. Then he switched gears and served baby lamb chops with mint chutney. One day, he might throw together an oniony

duck soup full of root vegetables; the next, it might be a squash soup fragrant with sweet Eastern spices. Greeley's cooking is hard to characterize, except with that overused word "eclectic," and at times his dishes can be overwrought. But he brings a good-hearted lust to the kitchen, and as such, he's a rarity in the county. The restaurant itself is but a couple of storefronts. You'll spend about $35 per person for dinner.

Gustaf Anders

South Coast Plaza Village, on Bear St. side, Santa Ana 92704; (714) 668-1737
Continental. Lunch Mon.-Sat., Dinner nightly, Late Supper Fri.-Sat. All major cards.

Ulf Strandberg is among the county's handful of chefs who not only know how to cook, but *feel* how to cook. At Gustaf Anders, he has developed something of a cult following—this is not soothing, comforting, dreamy cuisine. There is a certain asceticism to this chef's food, even when he is dribbling his superbly decadent filet mignon with a perfumey sauce of Stilton and morels. If Strandberg sautés liver, its flavor will ride subtly but surely through his inventive sauce of jalapeños. Strandberg has immense respect for his ingredients, be they the mundane, garden-variety parsley in his Parmesan-enriched parsley salad or the sweet sturgeon that he lays over wilted spinach and cress. Both Strandberg and his partner Bill Magnuson, who runs the front of the house, are of Swedish heritage, and the decor matches deep leather chairs and luxuriously draped tablecloths with a cool Scandinavian character. Some people aren't entirely comfortable with the restaurant's style, and they go elsewhere for lustier, more red-blooded dining. Then there are the members of the cult, who wouldn't think of bowing to any other icon. The wine list is idiosyncratic, mixing classic French wines with offbeat bottles from California. The full bar offers a range of Scandinavian aquavits; try one with the superb sugar-cured gravlax. Count on spending about $40 apiece for dinner.

11/20 John Dominis
2901 W. Pacific Coast Hwy., Newport Beach 92663; (714) 650-5112
Seafood. Dinner nightly, Brunch Sun. AE, MC, V.

Put on your Hawaiian shirt when you come to John Dominis. One of Hawaii's most acclaimed eateries, legendary for its fresh seafood, this restaurant fits right in on Newport's waterfront. You're escorted downstairs to the dramatic dining room, a huge, grottolike place with beautiful rock ponds, gurgling waterfalls and enough teak to outfit Noah's Ark. With luck, you'll get a window table, where you're sure to pass a quite pleasant evening being served reasonably good seafood by a "Hi, my name is Chad" waiter. We cannot fault the quality of the fish, as fresh as it is expensive. The menu's breadth is remarkable (especially the selection of Hawaiian fish), and among some very good choices, our favorite is the cold appetizer assortment for two, which includes lovely sashimi, smoked salmon and fresh oysters. The salads and chowders are also fine, as are the desserts (albeit in an overdone, all-American way). If you're watching your budget, watch what you order; such dishes as porterhouse steak or fresh tiger prawns can send the bill rocketing, but a carefully ordered dinner runs about $25 to $35 per person.

 ## JW's at Anaheim Marriott
700 W. Convention Way, Anaheim 92082; (714) 750-8000
French/Continental. Dinner Mon.-Sat. All major cards.

With its sixteen-foot ceilings, old paintings, brick fireplaces and touches of nineteenth-century-manor architecture, this restaurant is as much of a fantasy structure as some of Disneyland's best. About fifteen tiny connected rooms (or quasi-rooms) make us feel as if we're home while at the same time being conveniently close to the warmth of the human herd. The culinary emphasis is on the classical. JW's specializes in seafood and game: dishes such as a salmon filet steamed in its own juices inside a crispy potato crust with a three-vegetable sauce, can be delightful. There's some serious game here: we've sampled breast of pheasant in an exquisite sauce of cream, Armagnac and mustard; various preparations of pheasant; and, recently, roasted loin of wild boar with spinach-and-wild-mushroom ravioli. Among the notable desserts are a number of unusual sorbets (passion fruit, wild grape) and an exceptionally chocolatey mousse. To follow dinner there is a most civilized selection of drinks: vintage port, old Calvados and, above all, a smashing dry oloroso sherry (Gran Corregidor). JW's is a special-occasion place: gentlemen are requested to wear jackets. Dinner can run from $30 to $45 per person.

11/20 Kabob House Restaurant
1112 N. Brookhurst St. #6, Anaheim 92801; (714) 991-6262
Persian. Lunch & Dinner daily. MC, V.

At first glance, Kabob House looks like a standard coffee shop in Anaheim's standard strip landscape, but then from the kitchen come Persian accents. In this Iranian restaurant, the food has not been changed for the American palate; most of the people dining will speaking the same language as those in the kitchen. The lamb or chicken kebabs are succulent, and the traditional stews, sweetened with herbs and spices and simmered for hours, are exemplary. Also good is khoresht ghormeh sabzi, a mélange of spinach, cilantro, leeks and parsley served over the whitest of rice. A full dinner is about $10.

12/20 Kachina
222 Forest Ave., Laguna Beach 92651; (714) 497-5546
Southwestern. Dinner nightly. All major cards.

Tucked into a basement a few steps below Laguna Beach's cute Forest Avenue, the one-room Kachina glows with desert colors. Brightly painted reliefs hang like contemporary Navajo jewelry on the walls; the tables are set with mixed colors of Fiestaware. Despite the fact that things Southwestern have slipped slightly out of fashion, Kachina manages a level of sophistication that is hard to find in the south county. One of the best appetizers, the saddlebag, is an ingenious corn crêpe folded over roast duck with a barbecue sauce roughened with chile powder. And the quesadillas are always a good order. The different combinations of mole and chile sauces, blue and yellow corn flours and fire-roasted vegetables, wrapped around, poured over or simmered with duck or salmon or sirloin, most often work. One of the kitchen's best, corn-flour fettuccine with a spicy sauce of roasted tomatoes, tastes something like polenta, only subtler. But on occasion the chefs, David Wilhelm and Thomas Tran, lose it, galloping off into the sunset with such overwrought dishes as a bacon-wrapped beef filet with goat cheese, pasilla chiles and roasted peppers in a smoked pinto-bean sauce. But one has to applaud their cheek—especially since the half-open kitchen is about as big as one of the bleached wood tables. Kachina can get noisy. Dinner runs about $25 or $30 per person.

 ## Kitayama
101 Bay View Pl., Newport Beach 92660; (714) 725-0077
Japanese/Sushi. Lunch Mon.-Fri., Dinner nightly. AE, MC, V.

If we were to take a visitor to see some of Orange County's most handsome landscapes, we'd head to this calm and contemporary Japanese restaurant, and just watch the meal unfold. The restaurant itself blends the traditional with the contemporary: tatami mats upholster the booths, wicker chairs surround the tables. Some waitresses wear kimonos—others, black pants and white shirts. During the day, full-length windows offer views of a meticulous garden. There is a sleek sushi bar, but we prefer being surprised by the miniature culinary landscapes at the tables. An order of hamachi (yellowtail tuna) arrives in a luminous blue bowl mounded with crushed ice. Fat triangular slices of filet are set like dominoes to one side, while a half grapefruit holds transparent slices of the fish cut to mimic the fruit's sections. But we have come to expect this display from raw fish; it's the cooked entrées at Kitayama that surprise. They too, come in a succession of handmade platters and bowls and baskets, each cone of red ginger or crab-stuffed shiitake mushroom suited to its container. The seafood salad is a bright-green cabbage roll filled with cubes of squid. The only dessert offerings, ice creams in such soothing flavors as green tea and ginger, are, in their way, a Zen lesson in simplicity. About $32 per person for dinner.

10/20 El Mariachi

650 N. Tustin Ave., Orange 92667;
(714) 532-4001
Mexican. Dinner nightly, Brunch Sun. MC, V.

Mariachi Uclatlan, the king of the county's—and some say Southern California's—mariachi groups, plays weekends at this unprepossessing Mexican restaurant. Did we say unprepossessing? Try divey. On the outside, the restaurant looks as if it has been boarded up; inside, it's far more hospitable, with deep booths and large tables around which gather Latino families. The stately perfectionists on stage are the real draw here, though the standard SoCal Mex fare isn't bad. We recommend the shrimp soup and crab enchiladas, washed down by a variety of Mexican beers. Dinner is about $10 per person.

10/20 Marrakesh

1100 W. Pacific Coast Hwy., Newport Beach 92663; (714) 645-8384
Moroccan. Dinner nightly. All major cards.

This is perhaps the best Moroccan restaurant in Orange County. Under a ceiling the color of an evening sky sits a series of tent rooms done in desert tones, with long, low couches and inlaid tables. The soft-spoken Moroccan waiters describe the set feast, a main-course choice of chicken, lamb, rabbit or fish, and explain Moroccan dining customs, such as the ritual hand washing to begin the meal and the serving of men first, which they take very seriously—when a woman among us reached first for the proffered bread, the basket was sharply yanked away by an unsmiling waiter. Nearly every dish is delicious. The lamb-based harira soup is rich and spicy. The

b'stilla is incomparable, with a light phyllo crust and tender, moist chicken. The main courses can be overcooked (particularly the fish), but the lemon chicken is delicate. By now you will be uncomfortably full, but try to make room for the couscous; the semolina is rich, moist and perfectly cooked, topped with meltingly tender lamb, carrots, raisins and zucchini. This orgy of food is topped off with moist little baklava triangles, sweet mint tea, a basket of fruit and nuts and, all things considered, a reasonable check: $15 to $22 per person.

11/20 McCormick & Schmick's

2000 Main St., Irvine 92714;
(714) 756-0505
Seafood. Lunch Mon.-Fri., Dinner nightly. All major cards.

If it weren't for the valet parking and the wraparound parking structure, McCormick & Schmick's wouldn't feel a bit like Orange County. The dark paneling, the leaded glass and the nonstop hissing from the grills in the open kitchen—this must be some drizzly point north, not Irvine. In fact, the McCormick and Schmick's chain originates in the Pacific Northwest. What you find here are dishes such as broiled catfish with a chipotle-honey glaze, grilled mako shark with a grain-mustard crust, baby Coho salmon pan-fried with peaches and a brandy cream. Some preparations work much better than others, but when the fish is good, it is very, very good; the company owns its own fisheries, and ingredients are always first-rate. We've had excellent grilled razor clams dusted with bread crumbs, grilled steelhead salmon and firm crabcakes that the most skeptical Easterners have enjoyed. And then there are the impeccable oysters, the tiny Olympias with their sweet-salty taste, the huge Gulfs, the metallic Chiloés from Chile—the best selection around. Dinner runs $25 to $30 per person.

12/20 Mezzaluna

2441 E. Pacific Coast Hwy., Corona del Mar 92625; (714) 675-2004
Italian. Lunch & Dinner daily, Late Supper nightly. AE, MC, V.

This offshoot of the chic chain (with branches in Aspen, New York and L.A.) is as friendly as a cocker spaniel puppy. Inside are moon-faced tiles, a fine antique bar and some terrific Italian chow. Mezzaluna is quite proud of its pizzas, which sport a crackerlike crust unlike any we've tasted in Canarsie or Bensonhurst. They're very good, and sparingly topped with such things as pesto or porcini. Even more interesting are the many carpaccios, paired, for instance, with avocado and hearts of palm, or sautéed olives and tomatoes. The rest of the menu is both familiar and creative, from the wonderful mixed grilled vegetables to the pappardelle with musky porcini to the grilled swordfish with an eggplant confit. For dessert, try the vanilla ice cream plopped into hot espresso. Dinner will run you about $40.

 ## Natraj Cuisine of India
25932 Muirlands Blvd., Mission Viejo 92691; (714) 581-4200
Indian. Lunch & Dinner daily, Brunch Sun. All major cards.

Indian food in Orange County can be an unctuous affair, presented in overly fussy dining rooms. Natraj, while an attractive place in a well-scrubbed way, isn't a pink Indian palace. It's really a neighborhood restaurant, pairing good food with low prices. Make that very good food, perhaps Orange County's best Indian cooking. Owner Vijay Khosla may not take any chances with his menu, which looks like a clone from those of the more unctuous restaurants, but he makes sure that each dish is distinct from its relatives and that fresh ingredients and spices are allowed to shine through. The soft, pancake-like onion bhaji may be oily, but the tender flavor is superb. Palak paneer, with its cubes of white fresh cheese in softly buttered spinach, is like heavenly baby food for adults. And the meat dishes are terrific, from the lamb vindaloo, seemingly thickened with cumin, to the quieter, ginger-laced lamb bhuna. As if the food weren't enough, Khosla butters up new and old customers alike with his charm. Dinner is $15 to $20 per person.

 ## Pascal
Plaza Newport, 1000 N. Bristol St., Newport Beach 92660; (714) 752-0107
French. Lunch Mon.-Fri., Dinner Mon.-Sat. All major cards.

Pascal Olhats, the chef and owner of this charming restaurant, is a quiet man, almost shy, but his food speaks loud and clear. It is southern French cooking with great polish, the robustness of olives and rosemary tempered by Olhats's careful, classical training. This may sound like a lot of hyperbole for a restaurant in a strip mall a couple of miles off the San Diego Freeway. Not to mention its informality: the decor features walls of white-painted brick and Provençal-print tablecloths. But Pascal is well worth praising.

Olhats keeps the food as approachable as his decor; a bowl of mussels may come with an elegant saffron-laced broth, but they are piled casually high. Fish is flat-out excellent. Olhats's signature dish is sea bass with thyme, which he

modifies throughout the year, at one time napping the cooked-to-butter filet with a tomato coulis, the next, with a serious Champagne sauce. There's a swordfish steak done au poivre or niçoise, or sublime grilled salmon tournedos with a Cabernet sauce. Richer, more robust dishes—sautéed foie gras with duck confit, various preparations of rabbit, sweetbreads with mushrooms—are dense with flavor. A fixed-price dinner showcases the simplest and best of the chef's work; a dessert tray does the same. The latter may include a poached pear dripping chocolate, a sliver of chocolate terrine and a custardlike lemon tart. And the cheese tray, is a delight. About $35 to $40 apiece for dinner.

 ## Pavilion at Four Seasons Hotel
690 Newport Center Dr., Newport Beach; (714) 759-0808
Californian. Breakfast & Lunch Mon.-Fri., Dinner nightly, Brunch Sun. All major cards.

It looks like a hotel dining room (all those warm, pinky colors and framed prints), and it acts like a hotel dining room (a well-trained staff and a constant changing of forks and knives). But the food, prepared by chef Bill Bracken, occupies serious-restaurant territory. A typical sight: an appetizer of ravioli, the pasta as translucent as a wonton skin, revealing the dill-flecked morsel of salmon inside, set in a just-warm "sauce" of salmon broth. Or a salad of split heads of limestone lettuce in a bleu d'Auvergne cheese dressing; it sounds rich, but the dressing is a delicate, zabaglione-like froth that almost vanishes into the lettuce. How about lobster medallions with wild-mushroom ravioli and truffles? The bright rounds of lobster float in a truffle-darkened stock (no cream to be seen) that tastes as much of the creature as the meat does. There's nary a disappointment on this seasonally changing menu. The innovative desserts are some of the finest around: an apple tart, the apples barely cooked and the puff pastry thin but fine, topped with a tiny scoop of prune and Armagnac ice cream. Dinner will set you back $30 to $45 per person.

 ## Prego
18420 Von Karman Ave., Irvine 92715; (714) 553-1333
Italian. Lunch Mon.-Fri., Dinner nightly, Late Supper Fri.-Sat. All major cards.

Of the several successful Pregos in California, this member of the upscale chain is a particularly special one: its home is a striking tile-roof Tuscan villa with a lawn and a garden around it. Beautifully done in hues of mustard and rust, it's spacious and airy, with tall windows on three sides.

There's even a bit of outdoor dining, that greatest of luxuries in this neck of the woods. The food includes all the Prego favorites, including breadsticks that actually taste good and pizzas, the best of which may be the simplest (if the most hackneyed): pizza Margherita, topped with tomato and cheese. Fresh herbs are used frequently: grilled lamb chops are brushed with butter and sprinkled with sage and rosemary, and grilled chicken is marinated in garlic and rosemary. Prego does best with straightforward dishes (the dry-aged rib-eye steak is tastier than anything you can find at most steakhouses). In fact, most of the menu promises to give you among the most distinguished Italian food you've had in Orange County. Dinner costs $25 per person.

12/20 Ritz

880 Newport Center Dr., Newport Beach
92660; (714) 720-1800
Continental. Lunch Mon.-Fri., Dinner Mon.-Sat. All major cards.

Hushed by thick carpeting, paneled in wood and hung with classical paintings, the Ritz is one Orange County institution that refuses to bow to trends. Some find it a bit dark and formal for the neighborhood; others find it—along with Chevalier-debonair owner Hans Prager—the epitome of Class. Regardless, anyone who does business in the Newport area does it at the Ritz. Service is always well oiled, and hostesses actually remember the regulars and hand them smiles. There is something to be said for such sentimental tradition. In such a place, food is often unimportant, and indeed, nothing here sends us into fits of ecstasy. There is a light, fragrant bouillabaisse, laced with saffron and Pernod, and a very good roast chicken. A dinner costs $35 or so.

Ritz-Carlton Dining Room, Laguna Niguel

33533 Ritz-Carlton Dr., Dana Point 92629;
(714) 240-5008
French. Dinner Tues.-Sat. All major cards.

It's a shame, the common criticism goes, that the Ritz-Carlton's dining room doesn't share some of the hotel's great ocean views. But the point of the restaurant is not California cliffs or hang gliders; the point is that this is a classic restaurant, where the tables are set a perfect distance apart, the lighting is like honey, and the lines of gold leaf in the moldings hint of some past grandeur on the Continent. No, the fact that the restaurant does not have a view is not an oversight, for the dining experience here is not intended to reflect the peculiarities of the Southern California coast, but rather a timeless inter-

national brand of good taste. And it's not for want of imagination that the dining room is generically named the Dining Room.

Finding fault with the restaurant, which is overseen by the hotel's steely executive chef, Christian Rassinoux, is next to impossible. The service is impeccable, the choreography of fish knives well rehearsed, the presentation of wine straightforward and smooth. The food is a lightened, elegant variation of what we will call international nouvelle, always precisely executed. One pays dearly for the entrées, but they are superb. The sautéed and sliced filet of rabbit, set on dark wild mushrooms, seems to cut itself—the meat doesn't so much resemble rabbit as sea bass. An equally tender filet of beef tenderloin is thinly crusted with a gratin of turnips and napped with a port sauce; it may sound heavy, but it's simply rich, like a chocolate truffle. In fact, none of the food is cloying. Make sure to sample the daily special appetizers (such as filet of ahi laid across a pickup-stick pile of green beans), which often have a spiciness not found in the rest of the menu. Even the desserts (unless you order the soufflé, which can be bland no matter how much white chocolate it is threatened with) are highly refined and pure—more works of art than sugar hits. The best dessert is the Pernod parfait, a soft rectangle of licorice-flavored ice cream in a softer pool of vanilla sauce, edged with a mix of berries. The wine list cannot be faulted; it does not brook the second-rate. But don't look for the idiosyncratic bottle. The list relies on pedigree—all the first and second growths, all the blue-blood Napa Cabs. Dinner is $60 or more per person.

12/20 Scott's Seafood Grill and Bar

3300 Bristol St., Costa Mesa 92626;
(714) 979-2400
Seafood. Lunch & Dinner daily, Brunch Sun. All major cards.

The original Scott's may be in San Francisco, but this skylighted, cream-colored, French-doored restaurant looks more like a Newport Beach designer's idea of Southern California living. It's beautifully appointed, with a copper-lined kitchen, two bars and mounds of ice punctuated with oysters. But the biggest plus is the location: within walking distance of the Orange County Performing Arts Center and the South Coast Repertory Theatre. The food is convenient, too: simple fish entrées, fresh and tasty pastas and pizzas. The seafood changes daily according to what chef Ernest Pinata has ordered, much of it prepared with the same basic sauce: Monterey Bay calamari are fried and tossed with white wine, garlic, lemon and butter; sea bass is paired with a sharp lemon-caper butter; Pacific prawns are cooked in white wine, garlic, shallots and butter. Nonfish offerings are often more engaging, from the simplest appetizers of oysters or smoked salmon to the excellent pastas spiked with shellfish. The salads are particularly good, ranging from a delicious mix of tangy greens, such as oakleaf and arugula set with a round of goat cheese, to a refreshing spinach with citrus. The sugar rush from the butter-pecan ice cream will keep you awake through the dreariest third act. The wine list, mostly California whites, is decent and well priced. About $30 apiece for dinner.

 ### Splashes at Surf & Sand Hotel

1555 S. Pacific Coast Hwy., Laguna Beach 92651; (714) 497-4477
Californian. Breakfast, Lunch & Dinner daily, Brunch Sun. All major cards.

On a clear day, with the warm breezes scooting off the ocean below, Splashes is perhaps the best spot for lunch in Laguna Beach. The crystalline Mediterranean-inspired cuisine perfectly fits the sunlight and breezes, and the menu changes daily. A sunshine-yellow corn soup is laced with chicken and cilantro—but tastes most clearly of the fresh corn. Spinach dolmas stuffed with couscous and shrimp are steamed to a kelly green, then drizzled with the contrasting green of pesto. A terrine of creamy chèvre, roasted red peppers and eggplant is a sensual delight. The only major complaint may be that serving sizes don't always fit the prices—at one dinner, a $21 bowl of saffrony cioppino, as delicate as chiffon, included only a couple of mussels, shrimp and one chunk of lobster. Be sure to come for lunch, or even breakfast, for the best, nuttiest granola around. And for a casual supper perched directly over crashing waves, grab a table in the bar. Lunch runs $20.

12/20 Tête-à-Tête

217 Marine Ave., Balboa Island (Newport Beach) 92662; (714) 673-0570
Californian/Continental. Lunch & Dinner Tues.-Sun. All major cards.

A prime location next to the Lido Theater and across from the posh Performing Arts Center almost guarantees a faithful clientele for an Orange County restaurant. It's a pleasant surprise, then, to discover that the food at Tête-à-Tête is quite good, sometimes very good. True to its name (a piquant Frenchism translating as "private" or, literally, "head to head"), the restaurant is intimate and soothing, done in French-country florals. The owners, Christophe and Juerg Boo

(pronounced "Beau"), grew up in a hotel-and-restaurant family in Switzerland and then worked their way up at some top-notch restaurants and hotels in Europe; their backgrounds show in the high standards here. On the menu—short, simple and sweet—fresh, quality ingredients go into contemporary Continental standards such as crabcakes with aïoli and steamed whole artichoke with vinaigrette for starters; and filet mignon with wild-mushroom sauce and sautéed shrimp with angel-hair pasta for main courses. Dinner costs about $25 to $30 per person.

12/20 Thee White House

887 S. Anaheim Blvd., Anaheim 92805; (714) 772-1381
Italian/French. Lunch Mon.-Fri., Dinner nightly. All major cards.

Not just any White House but *Thee* White House, this restaurant has no affiliation with Washington, D.C. or politics or, for that matter, the present. Housed in a lovely old Victorian-style mansion, Thee White House transports you back to a time when people dined elegantly in front of crackling fires—the difference being that this is a pared-down rendition of Victoriana, with few frills. The menu follows the background of the owner, Bruno Serato (a Paris-born Italian), serving up Italian classics with a French influence here and there. Many of the starters are like miniature entrées: you can begin with a sampling of fettuccine with julienne of peppered duck, or black lobster-stuffed ravioli with a saffron sauce, or rigatoni carbonara (a creamy mixture of bacon, eggs and parmesan). The French influence shows up more strongly in the entrées: grilled swordfish comes in a delicate citrus beurre blanc, veal chop in a Cognac sauce, duckling in its own confit with a honey-thyme sauce, roasted rabbit in a Madeira-herb demi-glace. There are several veal dishes and an assortimento di pasta, the chef's selection of various pastas of the day. Overall, a lovely, civilized spot for a special occasion or a quiet evening. About $32 per person for dinner.

 ### The Towers at Surf & Sand Hotel

1555 S. Pacific Coast Hwy., Laguna Beach 92651; (714) 497-4477
Californian. Dinner nightly. All major cards.

The Towers can get by on its looks alone. Set on the ninth floor of the Surf and Sand Hotel, inside it is all faceted glass and mirrors, like an art-deco jewel box. And this box has one great view: the curve of Laguna's bay to the north, the rounding coast to the south, and ocean and more ocean straight ahead. At night when the lights go down, the ocean fades to black and there's only what's left on the hexagonal plates. And what's left often is worthy of the spotlight.

Chef Jackson Kenworth, who came to The Towers via Paris's La Varenne and L.A.'s Citrus, has an elegant, lustrously clear style. Among our shining memories here are a pale and delicate melon soup washed with ginger—sweet, yes, but also surprisingly cleansing—and an endive salad tinted a bright rose with beet vinaigrette. Perhaps because this is a hotel restaurant, or perhaps because Kenworth prefers to err on the side of the tasteful, main courses are straightforward. You might find "open ravioli" topped with Maine lobster and wild mushrooms, or roasted chicken breast with a fennel confit. The rack of lamb is simply prepared and is one of the best in the county. At dessert time, we've been seduced by such things as mango mousse cake or peach gratinée. The wine list includes some marvelous French bottles and any number of good California ones, but there are few priced in the mid-range. Dinner costs about $30 to $40 per person.

12/20 Tutto Mare

Fashion Island, 545 Newport Center Dr., Newport Beach 92660; (714) 640-6333
Italian. Lunch Mon.-Sat., Dinner nightly, Late Supper Fri.-Sat. All major cards.

We must admit that we get a little confused sometimes. Tutto Mare, Il Fornaio, Prego—these upbeat Italianate restaurants owned by Spectrum Foods can start to run together in one's mind, and the menus certainly do. Tutto Mare has the same sleek clientele, the same sort of satisfying fare as its cousin restaurants. And its interior is every bit as handsome. It does, however, differ in one striking way: the menu is short and to the point, and that means seafood and pasta. Pasta is definitely the thing to order. Dishes offer just the right combination of rustic and refined: from the simplest rigatoni with a tart-fresh tomato sauce to fussy black and white triangles of pasta filled with sea bass. The most interesting is the variation of gnocchi: discs of semolina and ground sea bass—terrific if you need some babying. But the best pasta is the green raviolini with spinach and ricotta in brown butter with snips of fried sage and plenty of Parmesan. This last dish is a spin-off of one featured at Prego a few miles inland, which is no coincidence—Tim Dobravolskis is executive chef of both. Second courses include an odd dish of grilled prawns set in lemony white beans, and a whole baked fish that, when it's cooked just right (which is generally the case), can be memorable.

However, Tutto Mare has increasingly been serving exceptional specials, such as pink scallops in the shell, that do justice to the restaurant's name. Dinner could end on an unhappy note; we've had a soggy apricot tart and a dry tiramisu, though the ricotta torte can throw some sparks. Dinner costs $20 to $25 per person.

12/20 La Vie en Rose

240 S. State College Blvd., Brea 92621; (714) 529-8333
French. Lunch Mon.-Fri., Dinner Mon.-Sat. All major cards.

Good, solid French food has its place in this replica of a French country farmhouse. In a series of connected rooms, all cozy with cream walls, French blue molding and tapestry-covered panels hung with paintings and drawings, owners Louis Laulhere and Pascal Gode serve up regional French dishes, particularly those from their native regions, respectively Gascony and Provence. You might start with hot rabbit pâté in puff pastry, or a salade Perigourdine (slices of preserved duck in a garlicky dressing); main courses include an excellent veal chop and pork loin with apples in Calvados sauce. Dinner costs about $38 per person.

11/20 Yankee Tavern

333 Bayside Dr., Newport Beach 92660; (714) 675-5333
American. Dinner nightly, Late Supper Fri.-Sat., Brunch Sun. MC, V.

The restaurant's name, the staff in nautical navy blazers . . . at first sight, Yankee Tavern appears to be a theme restaurant in the time-honored Southern California tradition. In fact, Yankee Tavern is at heart a moderately priced place that serves the food we'd like to think our mothers made, from meatloaf to pot roast to chicken pot pie. It would be a neighborhood restaurant if it weren't for the valet parking—though in Newport, that seems to be the norm. The chicken pot pie, filled with big chunks of chicken in a cream sauce and topped with an unexpectedly fine crust, serves two people. Meat dishes, such as pot roast, are bargains, if not culinary successes. The fish dishes are more creative: whitefish is sautéed in a hazelnut butter, swordfish is grilled on a skewer and accompanied by mango chutney. Purists will revel in the fine broiled lobster, embellished with nothing more complicated than drawn butter. Desserts are sweet and big. Loaded with raisins, then soaked with an eggy brandy sauce, the bread pudding is almost preternaturally dense. It's great. You'll spend from $12 to $20 per person for dinner.

12/20 Zuni Grill

3966 Barranca Pkwy., Irvine 92714;
(714) 262-0864
*Southwestern. Lunch Mon.-Sat., Dinner nightly,
Brunch Sun. All major cards.*

When David Wilhelm (of Kachina fame) opened Zuni Grill, featuring brightly colored Southwest-inspired food set in an adobe-chic dining room, Irvine residents jammed in for a taste of something new. With its sunset-colored walls and *faux* cave paintings on the *faux* stone tables, Zuni Grill's attractiveness constitutes a great part of its appeal. The food, however, is more fun than substance. Many of the dishes derive from those at Wilhelm's more expensive, more exclusive Kachina in Laguna Beach, but at Zuni, the ingredients are more prosaic. Pork and chicken are used more extensively than pricier varieties of fish; beans, rice and Wilhelm's signature sweet corn pudding fill out the plates. The best meal here would consist of several appetizers and one of the on-the-rocks margaritas. The chile relleno is the perfect contrast of crisp skin and oozy, cheesey interior. For entrées, the earthier the better. Case in point: a moist, subtle braised pork set on a puddle of polenta. But many dishes sound better than they taste, like the grilled chicken breast with a bland pumpkin-seed sauce. For dessert, try a scoop of the slightly gritty cinnamon ice cream. Dinner is about $15.

And Also . . .

Black Sheep Bistro, 303 El Camino Real, Tustin 92680; (714) 544-6060. *Mediterranean. Lunch Fri., Dinner Wed.-Sun. D, MC, V.* The owners serve seasonal dishes based on their favorite finds on travels through France, Italy and Spain—pastas, salads, tapas, and fish, chicken and meats done over an open flame. The wine list is astonishing, an extensive list of hard-to-find wines to match every dish. Dinner is about $35 per person.

El Torito Grill, Fashion Island, 951 Newport Center Dr., Newport Beach 92660; (714) 640-2875. *Southwestern. Lunch & Dinner daily, Brunch Sun. All major cards.* The El Torito Grill belongs to the Mexican-restaurant chain, but you'd never know it from the whitewashed decor or the decidedly Southwestern food. Mesquite-grilled meats and margaritas are big here; we also like the simple but tasty refritos. Lunch runs about $10, dinner runs $15 to $25 per person.

Yolie's Brazilian Steakhouse, 2646 Dupont Dr., Irvine 92715; (714) 251-0722. *Brazilian. Lunch & Dinner daily. All major cards.* It's undeniably an adventure to eat at Yolie's. For $20.95, you get all the meat you can eat—sausage, turkey wrapped in bacon, chicken, beef tri-tip, sirloin, baby lamb, pork tenderloin—from waiters who circle the room with great slabs of the stuff. This comes with either salad or black-bean soup, plus side orders (guarniçoes) of roasted potatoes, polenta, rice, steamed vegetables and fried bananas.

Bargain Bites

American

Belisle's

12001 Harbor Blvd., Garden Grove 92643;
(714) 750-6560
Open 24 hours. MC, V.

Just a mile south of Disneyland, Belisle's could qualify as an attraction on its own—call it Paul Bunyanland. The food is Midwestern with a smattering of dishes from the great ethnic melting pot, and everything is huge, we mean huge: pies a foot high, meat overflowing the plate, iced tea in quart-size glasses. The Texas-style breakfast, which includes a 24-ounce steak, a dozen eggs any style, a stack of hot cakes and country-fried potatoes, can be shared by two or more people, though some of the customers here look as if they could handle it on their own. During the day Belisle's is a family place with a lot of overflow from Disneyland; at night, it's a truck stop. Lunch runs about $8 apiece.

Ruby's

1 Balboa Pier, Newport Beach 92661;
(714) 675-7829
30622 S. Pacific Coast Hwy., Laguna Beach 92651;
(714) 497-7829
Breakfast, Lunch & Dinner daily. AE, MC, V.

You might go to Ruby's for the food, which is quite good—slightly tarted-up versions of old-fashioned burger-stand fare, namely burgers, sandwiches, chili and a few fountain treats—but the real reason is to be at the end of Balboa Pier in a solid, enduring art-moderne eatery that looks like it hasn't changed in 50 years. It's a delicious time warp, restored in accurate detail as a gum-snapping '40s lunch counter complete with Speedball Graphics lettering on the signs, swing music on the lo-fi loudspeakers and appropriate uniforms for the servers. The lively new Laguna Beach location is less impressively sited, but it boasts lots of free parking, a rarity in crowded Laguna. We shamelessly love the greasy burgers and the tuna-salad sandwich, which falls apart in your hands just about as fast as you can eat it. Lunch costs about $6 apiece.

Wahoo's Fish Taco

1862 Placentia Ave., Costa Mesa 92627;
(714) 631-3433
Lunch & Dinner daily. No cards.

Wahoo's is one of the more ambitious (and the cleanest) of the Baja-inspired surfer joints, where the regional specialty is the fish taco. The owner of this stucco bunker of a building, Win Lam, was born in Brazil and speaks five languages, including Southern California surf. He brings in a different fish every day to stuff his corn-tortilla tacos, big burritos and French-roll sandwiches; a blackboard lists rock cod, swordfish, snapper and even the Baja wahoo. For those who don't want to swim, there are pork carnitas and grilled chicken, and for those watching their health, Win Lam promises that no lard is used in the cooking. Dinner runs a rock-bottom $7 or $8 apiece.

Asian

Hue Rendezvous
15562 Brookhurst St., Westminster 92683; (714) 775-7192
Lunch & Dinner daily. No cards.

Even amid the dozens of Vietnamese restaurants in Westminister's Little Saigon, a Hue, or Central Vietnamese restaurant, is a rarity. On its surface, this one is antiseptic—set in a spanking-new strip mall, it's all shiny white walls and bright chrome chairs. But the food is hardly predictable. Besides bun bo Hue, a spicy beef soup made with thin rice noodles and a variety of beef parts, there are what seem to be innumerable variations on softly steamed rice-flour cakes: flat circles of dough, long strips of dough, little cups of dough, all dusted with bright-orange ground shrimp. Picking up these slippery morsels with chopsticks is truly a challenge. Dinner is about $7 per person.

Barbecue

Burrell's Rib Cage
305 N. Hesperian St., Santa Ana 92703; (714) 835-9936
Lunch & Dinner Tues.-Sat. No cards.

Deep in Santa Ana thrives a barbecue worthy of the stars. Fred Burrell, whose terrific ribs, sweet-potato pies and black-eyed peas have been served backstage at Michael Jackson concerts, makes one mean soul barbecue. Not one fiery spice has been tamed in his sauce, which seems to seep permanently into the eater's fingers. The two Rib Cages are oases of authenticity. There are a few tables, but most get take-out. About $10 apiece for a barbecue feast.

For more ideas on money-saving meals, see the "$15 & Under" listing in INDEXES at the back of the book.

Bistros & Cafés

Café on the Lakes
580 Anton Blvd., Costa Mesa 92626; (714) 751-9027
Breakfast, Lunch & Dinner daily. AE, D, MC, V.

Owned by the same people who run Crème de la Crème pâtisserie and café in Manhattan Beach, this casual café serves up the same melt-in-your-mouth strawberry-and-cream cake, chocolate-mousse cake, tarts (pecan, apple, lemon), napoleons and so on. The breezy patio looks onto a hotel plaza with a (manmade) body of water, making it a pleasant place to sit, sip cappuccino and have a quick slice of quiche, an open-face sandwich or a simple salad. There's always a crowd coming from or heading to the Performing Arts Center a half-block away. A light meal costs about $9 per person.

Café Zinc
350 Ocean Ave., Laguna Beach 92651; (714) 494-6302
Breakfast daily, Lunch Tues.-Sun., Dinner Thurs.-Sat. No cards.

Don't even try to get a table on a Sunday morning at this tiny, sophisticated sidewalk café; Laguna regulars will have staked them out, in order to nurse big bowls of café au lait and creamy, almost chocolatey cappuccinos, to pick at nutty bran muffins and scones loaded with currants, and to spoon soft-boiled eggs from egg cups. Don't even think about coming back for lunch; the zinc-topped tables will be full again with pizzette (small pizzas topped with chèvre and pesto or eggplant and olives) loyalists. Maybe, just maybe, late in the day, some counter space will free up, and you can sit down to an espresso with a big pecan cookie, or the rice pudding oozing raspberry purée. Breakfast or lunch runs $5 to $10 apiece.

The Cottage
308 N. Pacific Coast Hwy., Laguna Beach 92651; (714) 494-3023
Breakfast, Lunch & Dinner daily. AE, MC, V.

This welcoming bungalow is extremely popular on weekends; tourists, surfers, families and hungry locals wait in a sometimes endless line together. Recycled antiques, a cheery atmosphere and simple food make The Cottage a good bet for breakfast or an inexpensive lunch. The egg dishes are good (especially the corned beef hash with poached eggs—but decline the hollandaise), as are the pancakes and light french toast. Lunches consist of run-of-the-mill burgers and those California specialties with avocado and sprouts, while dinners are surprisingly good preparations of grilled fish and chicken. Breakfast or lunch run $8 to $10 apiece, dinner about $18.

The Crab Cooker

2200 Newport Blvd., Newport Beach 92663; (714) 673-0100
Lunch & Dinner daily. No cards.

If you're with your mother-in-law, baby-sitter, three kids, nephew and little sister, park the station wagon outside and join the other local families who love The Crab Cooker. If you like the echoes of children, happy or otherwise, you'll be entranced by the noisy ambience and unpretentious fun of this simple restaurant housed in a converted 1920s bank building. The decor is as unusual as is the beachwear-clad clientele, with mismatched chairs, baroque oil paintings, paper plates, marlin trophies and the original bank vault in which the seafood is kept chilled. The food is plain and simple: a tasty clam chowder, good grilled seafood kebabs, broiled king crab and broiled fish. There's no wine to speak of, but beer does nicely. A seafood lunch runs about $12 per person, dinner $25.

Ho Sum Bistro

3112 Newport Blvd., Newport Beach 92663; (714) 675-0896
Lunch Mon.-Sat., Dinner nightly, Brunch Sun. MC, V.

In its bright and shiny storefront setting, Ho Sum Bistro turns the dim sum idea into something delightfully Californian—a surfer in a Mao jacket. The series of small dishes, most of them updated with chicken and fish instead of pork and beef, includes some tasty noodle representatives, such as tai tai mein, with thick spaghetti-like wheat noodles in spicy peanut sauce, and Marco Polo, with a gutsy dressing of ground chicken, ginger, garlic and a punch of chili. This really is a bistro, with an excellent, well-priced selection of California wines by the glass—up to twenty offerings a day. Dinner runs $10 per person.

Partner's Bistro

448 S. Pacific Coast Hwy., Laguna Beach 92651; (714) 497-4441
Lunch & Dinner daily. AE, MC, V.

This popular, attractive bistro has an old-fashioned hunt-club decor, including bare brick walls and wooden floors, which don't help the noise level any. It's a pleasant spot to lunch on salads and sandwiches, but we wish the food were more exciting. Best bets are the spinach salad and the grilled fish. Cinnamon coffee and tea blends are faultless. About $10 to $15 per person for lunch and $20 or so for dinner.

The Place Across the Street from Hotel Laguna

440 S. Pacific Coast Hwy., Laguna Beach 92651; (714) 497-2625
Lunch & Dinner daily. All major cards.

The blank view of the rather plain Hotel Laguna is certainly less intriguing than its name may imply. But this crowded little café has an outdoor patio that's perfect for people-watching. The decor inside is cutesy arts and crafts, with macramé wall hangings and plenty of plants and caged birds. The menu is basic: pastas, salads and sandwiches, all of which are passable but not impressive. Best bets are the tasty chili, homebaked bread and overstuffed omelets. You'll spend about $10 per person for lunch.

Mexican & Latin American

El Carbonero

803 S. Main St., Santa Ana 92704; (714) 542-6653
Lunch & Dinner daily. No cards.

Mexican food is easy to find in Orange County, but Salvadoran cuisine is another story. El Carbonero is the sole vendor of pupusas, husky stuffed tortillas. The simplest are the best—refried beans and a white, fresh cheese sandwiched between two hand-formed tortillas. A perennial special at this tiny, neat storefront are the fresh corn tamales, delicious little things served with fiery salsas. A lunch costs $10 to $15.

El Gallo Giro

1442 S. Bristol St., Santa Ana 92704; (714) 549-2011
Open 24 hours. No cards.

Somehow, in two small storefronts, this Mexican delicatessen manages to be a tortilleria, tamaleria, pasteleria, carniceria and panaderia all at once. In one corner, a woman stuffs the fattest, fluffiest and absolutely best green-chile tamales in town; in another corner, a man stirs a huge copper vat of simmering carnitas; in a third, someone cuts lengths of pumpkin candy. Everything and anything, from salsas to cooked sesos (brains), can be had. A narrow counter runs along the window, where people eat freshly cut carne asada tacos and drink horchata; otherwise, all is to go. A take-out lunch runs about $5.

Taco Loco

640 S. Pacific Coast Hwy., Laguna Beach 92651; (714) 497-1635
Lunch & Dinner daily. AE, MC, V.

Only in Laguna would there be a taco stand where blackened mushrooms and sautéed ahi are served on blue-corn tortillas. Only in Laguna would these incredibly cheap tacos be served with such fresh, chunky guacamole. Only in Laguna would the guys behind the counter be so hip, with their sideburns and headbands or reggae caps. And only in Laguna would such a place be opened until way late, attracting babyfaced skateboarders and burned-out surfers, New Age crystal heads and polo-shirted beamers. Two tacos and a beer runs about $7.

Tlaquepaque
111 W. Santa Fe Ave., Placentia 92670; (714) 528-8515
Breakfast, Lunch & Dinner daily. AE, MC, V.

The reason to come to Tlaquepaque is the mariachi band that plays on Friday and Saturday nights and at Sunday brunch (reservations are essential—the place gets packed). No livelier show can be imagined than this cocky, clowning crew with their infectious music, imitation-Motown steps and penchant for serenading blond señoritas. They're the real thing, and so is the audience, a number of whom get out on the floor and dance. In fact, the restaurant is all but empty when the band isn't playing. And it's no mystery why: the food is sub-mediocre, though the carnitas and the goat stew (birria) are above average, and there's a good, earthy red sauce for the beef enchilada and the special burrito. Dinner runs about $12 apiece.

Tortilla Flats
1740 S. Pacific Coast Hwy., Laguna Beach 92651; (714) 494-6588
Lunch & Dinner daily. AE, MC, V.

This is a great place to come for brunch, although the sleepy clientele looks somewhat stunned by the rousing mariachi music that reverberates off the walls. There is a cheerful, sunny terrace annex downstairs, a main room filled with plants and wall paintings, an upstairs cantina and a lovely outdoor patio with a clear view of the ocean. Brunch offers nearly a dozen Mexican-style egg dishes, along with the standard tortilla-based items. Lunch and dinner feature the complete range of typical upscale-Mexican entrées, which most of the clientele accompany with large margaritas. Brunch and lunch run about $12 per person, dinner slightly more.

Small establishments like these often change their closing times, or close altogether, without warning. It is always wise to check in advance.

Hotels

The symbol that accompanies each review indicates in which price category the hotel belongs: **Top of the Line** ($200 & Up), **Luxury** ($150 & Up), **Moderate** ($100 & Up) or **Practical** (Under $100). We have defined the categories based on the regular starting price of a single or double room. *See also* the INTRODUCTION chapter, under "About the Hotels."

Top of the Line ($200 & Up)

Four Seasons Hotel Newport Beach
690 Newport Center Dr., Newport Beach 92660; (714) 759-0808, Fax (714) 759-0568
Singles $215, Doubles $245-$265, Suites $265-$1,700. All major cards.

The Four Seasons chain has built its reputation on superior service, and this Newport Beach location offers no less than its prestige promises: a team of friendly, efficient, experts are on hand to see to your every whim. The hotel's typically lovely decor pleases the eye down to the smallest detail, with fabulous fresh flowers spilling over gleaming marble surfaces. The 294 rooms are quite large; all have balconies, views and tasteful furnishings, including the ubiquitous TV-in-the-armoire. There's a complete exercise club stocked with Lifecycles, exercise equipment, saunas, a whirlpool and a heated swimming pool.

Ritz-Carlton, Laguna Niguel
33533 Ritz-Carlton Dr., Dana Point 92629; (714) 240-2000, Fax (714) 240-0829
Doubles $195-$390, Suites $485-$2,500. All major cards.

High on a bluff above Coast Highway and overlooking the Pacific, the hotel reminds us of a private British safari club: it is a temple to grace, charm and elegance in an area not generally known for such qualities. Because of that the Ritz-Carlton has become a haven for a well-heeled East-Coast group that isn't quite ready to plunge into the Southern California lifestyle, and locals who yearn for some civility. Both groups can justifiably rave about the beautifully appointed rooms, the superior service and breathtaking views. Not all of the large, antiques-decorated rooms have ocean views (those that do are worth the extra money). Where else in Orange County can you enjoy high tea, or cap off an evening with superb Cognac? Between such repasts, guests can play golf or tennis, swim in the ocean or the pools, work out in the gym, relax in the saunas and whirlpools and on the massage table, walk on the beach. Big spenders can join the Ritz-Carlton Club, which features a private concierge, open bar and a round-the-clock buffet. The hotel also offers shops, The Club Bar & Grill and several fine restaurants (*see* reviews this chapter).

Luxury ($150 & Up)

 ### Anaheim Hilton & Towers
777 W. Convention Way, Anaheim 92802; (714) 750-4321, Fax (714) 740-4737
Singles $140-$200, Doubles $160-$220, Suites $500-$1,100. All major cards.

Southern California's largest luxury hotel (with 1,600 rooms and suites) can accommodate a good portion of the guests at Disneyland on any given day, and it often does. The famed amusement park is just two blocks away; the Anaheim Convention Center is next door; Knott's Berry Farm is fifteen minutes away; Anaheim Stadium is a ten-minute drive. For travelers who need mega-convenience, this city-within-a-city boasts a full-scale fitness center with aerobics classes, a basketball gym, tanning, massage, Lifecycles, weight-lifting and more. Sight-seeing and airport services make travel plans a breeze. During the summer, kids ages 5 to 13 can join the complimentary "Kids Klub" for all-day supervised activities. The "Towers" part of the hotel takes up the top floor, where guests are pampered with full-time concierge service and extra amenities. Standing out among the hotel's numerous restaurants is the fine, Italian Pavia.

 ### Hyatt Regency Irvine
17900 Jamboree Blvd., Irvine 92714; (714) 863-3111, Fax (714) 852-1574
Singles & Doubles $145-$185, Suites $250-$625. All major cards.

When this location changed its name from a Hilton to a Hyatt Regency in 1989, everything else remained the same. It's a good business hotel located near John Wayne Airport and the business hub of Newport/Irvine. The fairly spacious rooms are light and airy, with rattan furniture and TVs hidden in white-oak armoires; some of the better rooms have such extras as pure silk and cotton comforters and sheets. Service is friendly, meeting facilities are excellent. The restaurant

Morell's has recently transformed itself into a Chinese-Italian hybrid to be called Ciao Mein.

 ### Le Meridien
4500 MacArthur Blvd., Newport Beach 92660; (714) 476-2001, Fax (714) 476-0153
Singles & Doubles $160, Suites $250-$400. All major cards.

Service is the watchword at the French-owned Meridien. Everyone here, from the bellhops to the maids to the concierges, is remarkably gracious and helpful. There are many things that make the Meridien one of our Orange County favorites: the outstanding restaurants, from the gourmet Antoine to the lighter-fare Café Fleuris; the third-floor pool and sundeck, complete with cabanas, food service and charming beach types to serve you cold drinks; the shuttle to the Meridien's lovely little private beach in Laguna; and the bargain-basement weekend deals, which range from $115 to $175 a night. It's perfectly located for the business visitor, adjacent to Newport's financial center. The spacious rooms, well equipped with all the upscale-hotel amenities, are done in the same pleasant neutrals as the lobby.

 ### Surf & Sand Hotel
1555 S. Pacific Coast Hwy., Laguna Beach 92651; (714) 497-4477, Fax (714) 494-2897
Doubles $160-$275, Suites $375-$500. All major cards.

If you're seeking a beach hotel because you truly enjoy the beach, then the Surf and Sand is for you. No effort has been made to hide the ocean behind Greek columns, or to make it possible to watch the sunset from a room heavy with linen and lace. Almost every single one of the 160 light, airy rooms has an unobscured ocean view and most have private balconies. And each is perched no more than 30 feet from the water—you can be out of bed and into the deep blue for a swim within three minutes of awaking. The interior has been renovated and redecorated, much to the hotel's betterment. The 160 rooms are now larger, with more spacious bathrooms, and the inviting, soothing decor features light colors and well-made rattan furniture. Amenities include a pleasant pool and two restaurants, the casual Splashes and the very elegant Towers (*see* reviews this chapter). The beachfront location, comfort and good service mean that the Surf and Sand is booked solid in the summer, so make sure to reserve early.

Moderate ($100 & Up)

The Beverly Heritage Hotel
3350 Ave. of the Arts, Costa Mesa 92626;
(714) 751-5100, Fax (714) 751-0129
Doubles $110-$120, Suites $130-$180. All major cards.

This pleasant, small hotel is our choice in the South Coast Metroplex. Neither the facade nor the banal hallways are much to look at, but those aesthetics are more than compensated for by the hotel's intimate scale (only 238 rooms and suites in an area known for gigantic hotels) and attentive staff. Guest rooms are simple but elegant (half have lake views), and with oversized work tables and computer outlets, all are particularly comfortable for business travelers. The hotel is within easy walking distance of South Coast Plaza, the Performing Arts Center (many of the performers stay here) and the business towers, but the hotel includes free limousine service to any destination within a two-mile radius. Room rates include complimentary breakfast, hors d'oeuvres and a morning newspaper. We stay to be pampered.

Casa Laguna
2510 S. Pacific Coast Hwy., Laguna Beach 92651; (714) 494-2996, No fax
Rooms & Suites $105-$205. All major cards.

It's more of a small hotel, really, but Casa Laguna considers itself a bed-and-breakfast. This is fair enough, for it does have many bed-and-breakfast qualities: every room is different, all are old-fashioned and romantic, and guests are provided with a good breakfast and personalized service. It's located just a short walk from the beach and is equipped with a pool for those who don't like sand. If you want an ocean view and lots of space, get one of the lovely suites, whose only failing is some noise from Coast Highway. If you prefer quiet, take one of the balcony rooms, which are set back off the street but still have wonderful ocean views, or splurge on the Cottage, a peaceful, charming home away from home replete with fireplace, large ocean-view deck, kitchen and beautiful leaded glass windows.

The Disneyland Hotel
1150 W. Cerritos, Anaheim 92802;
(714) 778-6600, Fax (714) 956-6582
Doubles $130-$175, Suites $400-$2,000. All major cards.

The Disneyland Hotel wasn't always owned by Disney, and the discrepancies in service and ambience between the park and the hotel were obvious. All that changed when Disney acquired the hotel in 1988. Since then, the company's own brand of pixie dust has been liberally sprinkled on everything from the hotel's convention facilities to all 1,130 guest rooms. The millions spent have paid off; today, Orange County doesn't have another hotel that comes close to matching what this one offers families. In addition to direct monorail service into the park, the hotel features water sports, entertainment, shopping and a new light show featuring Disney characters.

Doryman's Inn
2102 W. Ocean Front, Newport Beach 92663; (714) 675-7300, No fax
Doubles $135-$275. All major cards.

Without a doubt, our favorite small hotel in Orange County. Doryman's is actually a bed-and-breakfast, not a hotel, but its comfort, opulence, style and personal service put it out of the typical bed-and-breakfast league. Although the handsome tile-roofed building was built in 1921, its plush decor is more reminiscent of the gaslight era. The ten rooms all have gas fireplaces (with bedside controls), marble window seats, beautiful antiques and marble bathrooms with sunken tubs, skylights and telephones. Some feature ocean views, some Jacuzzi tubs; guests in all rooms can take advantage of the rooftop sundeck and Jacuzzi, as well as the generous breakfast served on a lovely tiled patio. Its location, across the street from the beach and the Newport Pier boardwalk, is perfect for exploring Newport on foot. The fine Rex restaurant is gone now, but the head chef has stayed on at its replacement, 21 Ocean Front. Also, room service is now available for no charge beyond a 20 percent gratuity.

Eiler's Inn
741 S. Pacific Coast Hwy., Laguna Beach 92651; (714) 494-3004, No fax
Rooms $100-$175. AE, MC, V.

A delightful bed-and-breakfast built around a courtyard, where guests congregate for breakfast and evening wine and cheese. The rooms, tastefully decorated with antiques, have that pleasant nostalgic fragrance associated with a great-aunt's old home. Fresh flowers, charming extras (shells filled with bonbons) and a pleasant management make this one of the most welcoming places to stay in Laguna. You will be greeted with a bottle of champagne to get your visit off to a good start. Each room is different; we can recommend Crescent Bay and Woods Cove. The beach is two blocks away.

For a comprehensive listing of all hotels in this book By Area & Price, see the INDEXES section at the back of the book.

Hilton Anaheim-Orange Suites
400 N. State College, Orange 92668;
(714) 938-1111, Fax (714) 938-0930
Single Suite $130, Double Suite $145. All major cards.

An all-suite hotel in the hub of Anaheim entertainment and activity, this Hilton is popular with families and couples on weekend getaways. Each suite has a large living room, bedroom, wet bar, microwave and refrigerator, two phones, two TVs and a VCR; and you get a complimentary breakfast (eggs, bacon, pancakes, cereal and so on) each morning in the Atrium Café. There's a business center and a fitness center. It's perfectly comfortable and serviceable for those who need a resting place, and overall a very good value.

The Hyatt Newporter
1107 Jamboree Rd., Newport Beach 92660;
(714) 644-1700, Fax (714) 644-1552
Singles $95-$155, Doubles $124-$180, Suites $300-$450, Villas $650. All major cards.

As Orange County continues to develop into an urban center in its own right, it has become increasingly difficult to find the casual atmosphere that used to define the area. Fortunately, there's a preserve of earlier, simpler times at the Hyatt Newporter. The hotel isn't a towering concrete monolith; rather its considerable number of lodgings are arranged in a comfortable horizontal sprawl. The 410 rooms are done in shades of peach, blue, mauve and rose (like every other contemporary hotel in Southern California). The new wing has 104 rooms, and there's a new, third outdoor pool and a second Jacuzzi. Since this is a convention resort, expect to see lots of badge-wearing guests rushing to their next meeting, and don't expect a homey feeling. You can count on good facilities, comfort and nice views from the hotel's bay side. There's also a small health club.

Marriott Suites Costa Mesa
500 Anton Blvd., Costa Mesa 92626;
(714) 957-1100, Fax (714) 966-8495
Suites $119. All major cards.

This Marriott is sort of a corporate interpretation of "Hotel California": the peaches-and-cream facade, the palm trees heralding the entrance, the open and airy lobby full of lavish flower arrangements, the pool, the health club, the location within walking distance of South Coast Plaza and Orange County Performing Arts Center all conspire to convince you that the California dream is real. There are 253 typical Marriott suites: clean, comfortable and done in tones

of mauve and gray. Each one consists of a living room, king-size bedroom and bathroom, and each comes with a wet bar and refrigerator, two TVs and two phones. Eight conference suites allow for private meetings for six or fewer, and a conference center and executive boardroom can host larger meetings. The restaurant, Windows, has the same casual, airy, peaches-and-cream decor, serving Californian pastas, steaks and seafood.

Marriott Suites Newport Beach
500 Bayview Circle, Newport Beach 92660;
(714) 854-4500, Fax (714) 854-3937
Suites $139. All major cards.

It's fifteen minutes to the beach from this Marriott, in a quiet area that's home to both condominiums and a few office buildings. In a latter-day Southern Californian interpretation of a Mediterranean villa, the facade, lobby and dining rooms sport peach columns, cream walls, pale marble floors and palm trees. The 250 signature Marriott suites are comfortable and pastel-pretty, made up of a king-size bedroom, living room and bathroom, with two TVs, two phones, a mini wet bar and refrigerator and a small walk-out balcony where you can drink in a moment of Newport sun. A conference facility and executive boardroom are available for large groups, while conference suites for six people afford absolute privacy for business meetings.

Newport Beach Marriott
900 Newport Center Dr., Newport Beach 92660; (714) 640-4000,
Fax (714) 721-1322
Singles & Doubles $132-$175, Suites $250-$750. All major cards.

This large hotel leads a double life: during the week it is filled with serious-looking corporate business types; on the weekends fitness fans mob the lobby, carrying tennis rackets, golf clubs and beach bags. This nine-story, 300-room chain hotel manages to be reasonably warm despite its large size. The spacious rooms done in relaxing desert tones are comfortable enough oases, fine for recovering after a day of playing in the sun, relaxing by the pool or indulging in the shoppers' paradise in the adjacent Fashion Island.

Room prices are based on regular rates during the high season. Most hotels offer discounted rates and special packages in the off-season and during certain times of the year. Be sure to inquire.

313

Practical (Under $100)

The Carriage House
1322 Catalina St., Laguna Beach 92651;
(714) 494-8945, No fax
Suites $95-$125, Cottage $150 (2-night minimum on weekends). No cards.

This little bed-and-breakfast inn is the most charming in Laguna. The New England-style gray-shingled house has two stories of apartment suites, all decorated with grandmother's handme-down antiques, lace curtains and a feminine touch. Each suite opens onto the outdoor courtyard, a lush garden overflowing with flowering plants, a fountain, trees and two friendly cats. Guests share breakfast, including home-baked pastries, in the cozy dining room. As lovely as the main house is, we suggest you splurge on the cottage. At $150 a night, you will have a most adorable little house, complete with white picket fence, flower garden, amusing veneered antiques, kitchen, living room, parlor, old-fashioned bathroom and lovely bedroom. It is a romantic hideaway all in peach and rose, just up the street from the ocean and within walking distance of town.

The Waterfront Hilton
21100 Pacific Coast Hwy., Huntington
Beach 92648; (714) 960-7873,
Fax (714) 960-7873
Doubles $99-$225, Suites $195-$250. All major cards.

Orange County's newest beach resort (the sand is right across the street) isn't as isolated as the brochure would have you believe, but it is away from the congestion of Newport and Laguna and some will find that all to the good. The hotel features 300 unremarkable but spacious rooms (all with ocean views), plus standard resort facilities such as restaurants, a bar, a large pool and a fitness center. There's also a nine-hole golf course adjacent. The hotel has some Mediterranean ambience and erratic but earnest service. Street noise can be heard in the front rooms: it's the price you pay for the fantastic ocean view.

Airport

Crown Sterling Suites
1325 E. Dyer Rd., Santa Ana 92705;
(714) 241-3800, Fax (714) 662-1651
Suites $90-$105. All major cards.

If you're flying into Orange County's John Wayne Airport and want to remain poised for a quick getaway, we know of few more convenient choices of lodgings than this all-suite property

less than ten minutes away from the airport, just off the 55 Freeway. Crown Sterling Suites caters to the business traveler with such necessary luxuries as two phone lines per suite; meeting and executive board rooms; secretarial services and so on. The man or woman on the move is also provided with a number of useful amenities to help make them feel at home (in-suite refrigerator, coffee maker and microwave; complimentary breakfast; steamroom, sauna and indoor pool). Room service is available until 11 p.m.; there are a restaurant and a cocktail lounge that serve until 1 a.m. Free self-parking and close proximity to major business parks in Irvine, Tustin and Santa Ana and nearby shopping and entertainment add to Crown Sterling's high convenience quotient.

Nightlife

The Beach House
619 Sleepy Hollow Ln., Laguna Beach 92651;
(714) 494-9707
Open daily 8 a.m.-10 p.m. AE, MC, V.

The best thing going for this homey restaurant/bar is the superb view. It's a perfect location to watch the sun sinking into the Pacific while enjoying the fresh air, the passable seafood menu, the generous Ramos gin fizzes and the pleasant service. We like it best as a place to meet for at the end of the day, for people- and seagull-watching and enjoying the reflection of glorious summer sunsets.

Bistro 201
18201 Von Karman, Irvine 92715; (714) 553-9201
Open Sun.-Thurs. 11:30 a.m.-11 p.m., Fri. 11:30 a.m.-1 a.m., Sat. 4:30 p.m.-1:30 a.m. Jazz Fri.-Sun. All major cards.

During the day, Bistro 201 is a hot spot for power breakfasts and networking lunches. On Friday and Saturday evening, however, things calm down a little and it's a great place to hear good jazz and relax over a good dinner. On Sunday evenings, the program is Brazilian.

Las Brisas
361 Cliff Dr., Laguna Beach 92652; (714) 497-5434
Open Sun.-Thurs. 8 a.m.-midnight, Fri.-Sat. 8 a.m.-1 a.m. All major cards.

Although this is a full-fledged restaurant (with an immensely popular Sunday brunch), we suggest you skip the food and instead languish outdoors on the bright blue-and-white patio. The view is dramatic: the Pacific floats below the cliffside pathway, and there is quite a social scene here on the weekends. There's no better place in Laguna to sip a margarita and watch the sunset along with all the other sunburned tourists.

The Club Bar & Grill at Ritz-Carlton

33533 Ritz-Carlton Dr., Dana Point 92629; (714) 240-2000
Open nightly 6 p.m.-midnight (live music from 8 p.m.). No cover. All major cards.

This may be the only beach-adjacent bar in Southern California that dares to have a dress code: no denim, jackets for men and, God forbid, no neon volleyball shorts or tank tops. In this community, you're as likely to see a suit and tie as you are a snowstorm, and the Ritz's policy gives The Club Room a considerable touch of class. In a handsome setting, a prosperous-looking crowd of all ages drinks, chats, relaxes and dances to the jazzy-pop live music, which is neither too square to offend younger ears nor too hard-pounding to frighten away their parents.

Club Postnuclear

775 Laguna Canyon Rd., Laguna Beach 92651; (714) 497-3881
Open Fri.-Sat. 9:30 p.m.-2 a.m. Cover $7 before 10 p.m., $9 after 10 p.m. No cards.

Laguna's young and hip keep Club Postnuclear hopping every weekend, when deejays crank the fashionable dance music (rock, hip-hop, soul). The lack of a liquor license means that the crowd includes a good number of teens between 18 and 21, but some oldtimers in their 20s and 30s stop in regularly, too. The club also serves as an occasional live-music venue during the week, hosting moderately popular rock bands on tour through Southern California.

The Coach House

33157 Camino Capistrano, San Juan Capistrano 92675; (714) 496-8930/496-8927 (recording)
Showtimes & ticket prices vary. MC, V.

San Juan Capistrano is a little out of the way for the average Orange County resident or visitor, but it's worth the drive for fans of good music and comedy. The Coach House isn't a bar or nightclub, it's basically a restaurant until 6 in the evening, and on the nights when there's a show, it turns into a concert venue and books an eclectic mix of talent: Ray Charles, Cowboy Junkies, Leon Redbone, Kenny Rankin, Patty Loveless, Dave Mason and Hunter S. Thompson. Nearly every show is worth a visit. Simple dinners are available; there's a full bar but no drink minimum.

The Crazy Horse Steakhouse & Saloon

1580 Brookhollow, Santa Ana 92705; (714) 549-1512
Shows nightly 7 p.m. & 10 p.m. Cover $3 Mon.-Thurs., $4 Fri.-Sun. All major cards.

The Crazy Horse is the county's best-known country western spot. It may be difficult to find a spot on the tiny dance floor and patrons are often wannabe cowboys, but the music is almost invariably good (free dance lessons are offered Wednesday and Thursday evenings) and the food is decent. The Crazy Horse also regularly hosts country stars; this is a good place to see the likes of Tammy Wynette, Waylon Jennings, Johnny Cash, Juice Newton and the Marshall Tucker Band up close and personal.

The Saloon

446 S. Pacific Coast Hwy., Laguna Beach 92651; (714) 494-5469
Open Sun.-Thurs. noon-midnight, Fri.-Sat. noon-1 a.m. MC, V.

A true drinking bar, the Saloon attracts a lively cadre of regulars, not hustling singles. The tiny, narrow room boasts a handsome wood bar and a couple of minuscule tables; the lack of seats discourages lingering. A friendly and fun spot for a quick drink and a conversation about local news.

Studio Café

100 Main St., Balboa (Newport Beach) 92661; (714) 675-7760
Open Mon.-Thurs. 11:30 a.m.-1:30 a.m., Fri.-Sat. 11 a.m.-1:30 a.m., Sun. 10 a.m.-midnight. AE, MC, V.

Located at the tip of the Balboa peninsula, the Studio Café is immensely popular with good-looking beachy sorts in their 20s and 30s who come here for the jazz and for one another. The small bistro with bentwood chairs, stained glass and an active bar is packed on weekends with young people who seem to care less about the music than hustling one another and relaxing with their exotic drinks.

The Towers at Surf & Sand Hotel

1555 S. Pacific Coast Hwy., Laguna Beach 92651; (714) 497-4477
Open nightly 5 p.m.-1 a.m. All major cards.

The decor here is so dramatic that it takes a few minutes to adjust and remember that you are in Laguna—not Paris, Monte Carlo or New York. The bar is small and elegant, with a fireplace and a glass-topped baby grand at which customers hover in close conversation over Champagne or a late nightcap. Rendering the setting all the more dramatic is the bar's perch over the Pacific, making for a fabulous view.

315

Shops

Antiques

In the city of Orange, the area around the intersection of **Chapman Avenue and Glassell Street** is an antique hunter's dream. People drive from miles around to check out the options. Quality and prices vary from shop to shop, but we've always found something that made the trip worthwhile.

In Laguna Beach, **Robert Yeakel** (1099 S. Coast Hwy., 714-494-5526; open Tues.-Sat. 9:30 a.m.-4:30 p.m.) is two shops: the main store stocks three floors of superb eighteenth-century English and American furniture, as well as paintings, silver and more. The second showroom (1175 S. Coast Hwy.) displays Egyptian antiquities and pieces from the thirteenth to seventeenth centuries. Service is friendly and professional.

Beauty & Health

Allen Edwards Salon

1980 Main St., Irvine 92714; (714) 251-6315
Open Mon.-4:30 p.m., Tues. & Thurs. 8 a.m.-8 p.m., Wed. & Fri. 8 a.m.-6 p.m., Sat. 8 a.m.-4:30 p.m.
1177 Newport Center Dr., Newport Beach 92660; (714) 721-1666
Open Mon.-Sat. 9 a.m.-5 p.m., Thurs. 9 a.m.-8 p.m.

Award-winning stylist Allen Edwards has spent twenty years designing images for a demanding clientele: Mary Hart, Donna Mills and Cathy Lee Crosby among them. In this studiolike atmosphere (filtered lighting, polished concrete floors), you can stop in for a simple cut or be pampered from a long list of hair, makeup and manicure services.

The Sports Club

1980 Main St., Irvine 92714; (714) 975-8400
Mon.-Fri. 5:30 a.m.-11 p.m., Sat.-Sun. 8 a.m.-7:30 p.m.

More than an athletic club, this multi-million dollar, multi-purpose sports complex tackles the business of keeping fit with the utmost in recreational facilities and resort amenities. In addition to fully equipped gyms with private trainers, there is a Sports Medicine/Fitness Evaluation Clinic, full court basketball and volleyball, a running track, racquetball, squash and outdoor paddle tennis. The indoor-outdoor pool opens onto a spacious sundeck. Need we mention the hair and nail salon, tanning facility, pro shop, restaurant, valet parking, shoe shine, massage, child care and car washing and detailing?

Shopping Centers

Fashion Island, Newport Center

1045 Newport Center Dr., Newport Beach 92660; (714) 721-2032
Open Mon.-Fri. 10 a.m.-9 p.m., Sat. 10 a.m.-6 p.m., Sun. noon-5 p.m.

The Versailles of shopping centers underwent a face-lift a few years ago in an attempt to keep up with its burgeoning neighbor, South Coast Plaza. With its lushly landscaped grounds, open-air Mediterranean appeal and updated mix of shops, this island of tranquility continues to attract crowd-weary celebrities and Orange County's elite. The center boasts a Neiman-Marcus, a multiple-theater complex and some exceptional shops, including Brooks Brothers, Modasport, Fogal and Merletto lingerie, as well as a Robinson's, Broadway and I. Magnin. In the glamorous Atrium Court, you can find everything from a Dior dress to designer asparagus at the farmer's market. And there's plenty of good food at Five Feet Too, California Pizza Kitchen and El Torito Grill.

South Coast Plaza and Crystal Court

3333 Bristol St., Costa Mesa 92626; (714) 241-1700
Open Mon.-Fri. 10 a.m.-9 p.m., Sat. 10 a.m.-7 p.m., Sun. 11 a.m.-6:30 p.m.

Hordes of well-tanned women from Newport Beach and seemingly all of Orange County flock to this megamall, which undoubtedly is the classiest, cleanest and best-organized mall in Southern California. The selection (nearly 300 shops) is simply unbeatable and includes several fabulous Big Apple imports you won't find even in L.A.: Calvin Klein, Fendi, Barney's New York, J. Crew and Rizzoli Books. The breadth of upscale stores is amazing: Tiffany & Co., Chanel, Cartier, Gucci, Louis Vuitton, Alfred Sung, Emporio Armani, Polo Country Store, TSE Cashmere, Adrienne Vittadini and one of the only Rand McNally stores, not to mention eight major department stores, including Nordstrom, Saks Fifth Avenue and the only Bullock's Men's Store. South Coast Plaza can accommodate marathon shoppers with a fleet of shuttles that service over 40 major hotels in the area.

Laguna Beach

Laguna Beach can't be beat for distinctive shopping. Most shopping is concentrated in a charming area along **Pacific Coast Highway** near Main Beach, but **Forest Avenue** (also near Main Beach) has good choices, too. The town is especially notable for its art galleries, featuring everything from impressionist paintings to seascapes to life-size puppets. This is also a good place to find books (**Upchurch Brown**, located in the Lumberyard Mall, **384 Forest Ave.**, and **Fahrenheit 451, 540 S.** Pacific Coast Hwy., are our favorites), antiques, jewelry and more.

Sights & Arts

Attractions

The Crystal Cathedral
12141 Lewis St., Garden Grove 92640;
(714) 971-4000
Tours daily 9 a.m.-3 p.m., approx. every 30 minutes. Donations requested.

The Crystal Cathedral is television evangelist Robert Schuller's home base and a major county tourist attraction. The immense cathedral impresses some as majestic and reverential and others as overdone, but few find it uninteresting. The annual holiday spectacular, "The Glory of Christmas," features live animals and flying angels; the Easter show is equally lavish. Call for prices and showtimes.

Disneyland
1313 Harbor Blvd., off I-5 Fwy., Anaheim 92803;
(714) 999-4565
Summer: open daily 8 a.m.-1 a.m.; spring, fall & winter hours vary. Adults $27.50, children 3-11 $22.50; senior discounts available. AE, MC, V.

See "LOS ANGELES Sights & Arts."

Knott's Berry Farm
8039 Beach Blvd., Buena Park 90620;
(714) 827-1776
Open Mon.-Fri. 10 a.m.-6 p.m., Sat. 10 a.m.-10 p.m., Sun. 10 a.m.-7 p.m. Summer: open Mon.-Thurs. 10 a.m.-10 p.m., Fri.-Sun. 10 a.m.-midnight. Adults $22.95, children 3-11 $9.95, children under 3 free. AE, MC, V.

See "LOS ANGELES Sights & Arts."

Mission San Juan Capistrano
32086 Camino Capistrano, San Juan Capistrano 92675; (714) 493-1424
Open daily 8:30 a.m.-5 p.m. Adults $3, children 3-12 $2, children under 3 free.

A few months after a bewigged gang of rebels signed the Declaration of Independence, Padre Junípero Serra founded this fascinating link in the California mission chain. Its small, dark, richly evocative chapel is the oldest in-use building in California; even older than the beautiful Great Stone Church. Take the time to wander the entire property, including the serene gardens. If there are more than fifteen in your group, be sure to take the excellent docent-led tour; otherwise you'll take a self-guided tour. The legendary

swallows still return here each March 19, if in diminished numbers.

Arts

Bowers Museum of Cultural Art
2002 N. Main St., Santa Ana 92706;
(714) 567-3600
Hours vary.

With its lovely grounds and tranquil courtyard, this mission-style museum is the historic centerpiece of a cultural redevelopment plan by the city of Santa Ana. The Bowers Museum focuses on cultural arts of the Americas and Pacific Rim, with special collections of pre-Columbian, Native American, African, American and Southern Californian decorative arts. After completion of its new wing, the museum has more room than ever to display its diverse collections and traveling exhibitions. Call for cultural festivals and educational programs.

Laguna Art Museum
307 Cliff Dr., Laguna Beach 92651; (714) 494-6531
Open Tues.-Sun. 11 a.m.-5 p.m. Adults $3, students & seniors $1.50, children under 12 free.

This bright museum has generally excellent changing exhibitions, often of works by contemporary Californian artists. Occasionally for special shows, the subject matter will dip into the eclectic. Recent successes have included The Feminine Japanese artist, a show of sculpture; and a show exploring the relationship between photography and drawing.

Newport Harbor Art Museum
850 San Clemente Dr., Newport Beach 92660;
(714) 759-1122
Open Tues.-Sun. 10 a.m.-5 p.m. Adults $4; seniors & students $2; children under 12 free. Free Tues.

A reputable museum with an ambitious exhibition program of several shows a year focused on late-twentieth-century and Californian art; a recent success was a hugely popular Edward Hopper retrospective. The enthusiastic curator hunts for unshown and often unknown Californian artists to introduce to the Orange County public. An intelligent collection.

Orange County Performing Arts Center
600 Town Center Dr., Costa Mesa 92626;
(714) 556-2787

The Orange County Performing Arts Center opened to great hoopla in 1986, and at the time was the only such center in the nation to be built entirely with private funds. Outside, the Center is defined by a towering arch and a dramatic firebird sculpture. The inside has been described

317

aptly as a mauve barn, but the acoustics are superb and seating unusually comfortable. The Center's artistic record is equally mixed. The resident opera company and symphony are kindly described as mediocre and too often the Center has resorted to third-rate Broadway touring companies. On the other hand, the Center hosts top vocalists and has become one of the nation's premier showcases for dance: It has hosted the only West Coast appearances of the New York City Ballet, Australian Ballet, Paris Opera Ballet, Royal Ballet, Royal Danish Ballet and others.

South Coast Repertory Theatre
655 Town Center Dr., Costa Mesa 92626;
(714) 957-4033

Directly across the street from the Performing Arts Center is South Coast Repertory, one of the nation's leading regional theaters. The troupe has a come a long way since its storefront origins in the 1960s and won a Tony Award for its work in 1988. SCR is best known for its stagings of new plays (Beth Henley, Craig Lucas and Richard Greenberg are among the playwrights who have premiered work here) and for its superb productions of Shaw's plays. The theater has two theaters (the Mainstage and the intimate Second Stage), however, and the typical season may include works by playwrights as varied as Kaufman and Hart, Pinter and Sondheim.

The Great Outdoors

When the natives are not surprised by several days of 85-degree weather in February, you know the area offers exceptional opportunities for outdoor activities. For most visitors, the highlight will be the county's beaches: there are 42 miles of sand here. **Newport Beach** is usually the most crowded; **Huntington Beach** is dominated in places by unsightly power plants. Our choices are **Main Beach** in Laguna Beach (the half-mile stretch of sand is near shops and restaurants and affords spectacular views of the nearby cliffs) and **Corona Del Mar State Beach** off Ocean Boulevard and Marguerite Street in Corona Del Mar (the rock jetty is great for snorkelers and body surfers). It's safe to assume the beaches will be crowded in summer and warm winter weekends. For information about surf conditions, call Huntington Beach, (714) 536-9303; Newport Beach, (714) 673-3371; Laguna Beach, (714) 494-6573.

The coastline offers more for visitors than swimming and surfing. Experienced sailors can rent boats at some local facilities, and others offer charters. If you're sailing out of the enormous **Newport Beach** harbor, try **Balboa Boat Rental** (714-673-1320), which rents motorboats and a range of sailboats, all for $26 an hour; $50 deposit required. In the smaller **Dana Point** harbor, the **Embarcadero Marina** (714-496-6177) is your best bet, with boats from $12 to $23 an hour, or maximum $120 per day; no checks or credit cards are accepted.

The whale-watching season runs from late December through April, and **Dana Wharf Sportfishing** (714-496-5794) offers trips throughout the season, for $14 a person. Deep-sea fishing may be found off **Huntington Beach** pier or at Newport's **Balboa Pavilion**. Half-day and full-day charters can be arranged through **Adventures at Sea** (714-650-2412) or **Dana Wharf Sportfishing** (714-496-5794).

Landlubbers also have options. Horseback riding, tennis, running tracks, walking trails and bicycle trails are all plentiful. For golfers, several private country clubs offer reciprocal privileges to members of other clubs; others offer a round of golf to non-members as a promotion. For $125 a round, you can avoid the crowds at the county's public courses, at either **Dove Canyon Country Club** (714-858-2800) or **Coto de Caza Golf & Racquet Club** (714-858-4100). If you're willing to golf with the hoi polloi, try **The Links at Monarch Beach** in Dana Point (714-240-8247; $65 Mon.-Thurs., $85 Fri.-Sun.) or **Tijeras Creek Golf Club** in Rancho Santa Margarita (714-589-9793; $45 Mon.-Fri., $70 Fri.-Sun.).

Two major ecological reserves in the area are sanctuaries for lovers and nature-lovers alike. Perhaps our favorite place in the Newport-Laguna area is the **Upper Newport Bay Ecological Reserve** (Back Bay Dr., off Jamboree Rd., Newport Beach). Its serenity is broken only by singing birds and duck discussions, or by an occasional motorist. Walk around the perimeter of this marshland to observe the waterfowl and learn from the bird-watchers who are visiting old friends. Be sure to take binoculars to get a better view of the egrets, mallards, rails and teals.

For a vigorous walk nearer to the salt spray, strike out for **Glenn E. Vedder Ecological Reserve** (S. Pacific Coast Hwy., Laguna Beach; no phone), a pleasant pathway that parallels Coast Highway, along the cliffs overlooking the ocean. There are access points to the rocky shore below, but the view is more dramatic from above. ◆

PALM SPRINGS

Xanadu Incarnate

Palm Springs is a state of mind more than a place, though the place can't be ignored. It's a curiosity—Las Vegas without the gambling, the Sahara without the exoticism, the beach without the ocean. Even the journey to Palm Springs has an undeniably mythical quality to it. Driving east on Interstate 10, coming out of San Bernardino and passing through Yucaipa, you'll encounter miles of alternative-energy windmills twirling in the desert emptiness.

You'll also discover the joys of Hadley's, a hyperbolic dried-fruit and nut stand, where the order of the day is a thick date milkshake. Near Hadley's, the famous life-sized dinosaur models stand guard outside Cabazon's Wheel Inn, a truck stop where the pies come topped with whipped cream and the truckers all have beards and ponytails. And you'll pass the vast Morongo Indian Bingo Hall, where hundreds of players sit, waiting for their lucky number to come up. In fact, the trip is much like Dorothy's trip to the Emerald City; when you finally get to Palm Springs, you know you're not in Kansas anymore.

When people refer to Palm Springs, they actually mean a good-sized chunk of the Coachella Valley surrounding Mayor Sonny Bono's little town, including the resort towns of Cathedral City, Rancho Mirage, Palm Desert, Indian Wells and La Quinta. The area is a curiosity because it is, when you get right down to it, as inhospitable a plot of desert as you'll ever come across. In fact, that's all it was known as until 1907, when a squadron from the U.S. Army Camel Corps was surveying the Mojave Desert and came upon a series of natural hot springs that looked like oases out of *The Arabian Nights*.

For some, this desert is an escape to a land of endless resort sports. Interestingly, due to the number of golf courses built here over the past half century, it's one of the few places in the world where the average temperature is actually decreasing: Palm Springs is cooler now (though it certainly wouldn't be considered *cool*) than it was 50 years ago. For those who don't want to sit by the pool and bake like a lizard, it's a land where you can empty your mind delving into the zen of tennis, golf, hiking, biking and nature-watching.

And for those who crave more urban pursuits, there are plenty of places to quench your thirst. There's shopping along North Palm Canyon Drive and nearby El Paseo, in a wide assortment of stores, primarily branches of posh places in Beverly Hills and West Palm Beach, Florida. Cultural activities are often centered around the Desert Museum and the Bob Hope Cultural Center. There are plenty of (air-conditioned) movie theaters. And for those who simply want to sit under the sun, it's a marvelous, soothing desert sun.

Restaurants

The symbol that accompanies each review indicates the rating on a scale of one to twenty. The rankings reflect *only* our opinion of the food; the decor, service, wine list and atmosphere are commented upon within each review. For further explanation, as well as an index of restaurants by rating, please see "About the Restaurants" in the INTRODUCTION. See the INDEXES section at the back of the book for comprehensive restaurant indexes.

11/20 Las Casuelas
368 N. Palm Canyon Dr., Palm Springs 92262; (619) 325-3213
Mexican. Breakfast, Lunch & Dinner daily. AE, MC, V.

Tourists may flock to the more glamorous and popular Nuevas and Terraza branches of Las Casuelas, but this is the original. It doesn't look like much, and it doesn't serve margaritas (just wine and a great selection of beers), but the small kitchen turns out respectable Mexican home cooking (far better than at the trendier Casuelas branches), with an emphasis on such Cal-Mex standards as enchiladas, burritos, tostadas and tacos. It's all as tasty and satisfying as it is simple and inexpensive—a Palm Springs institution undoubtedly worth a visit. About $12 for dinner.

10/20 Las Casuelas Nuevas
70050 Hwy. 111, Rancho Mirage 92270; (619) 328-8844
Mexican. Lunch Mon.-Sat., Dinner nightly, Brunch Sun. AE, MC, V.

On the weekends, this immensely popular restaurant packs them in, partly due to margaritas that are as big as some local swimming pools. Young servers bring food that can be good and can be merely edible. Las Cas (as its legions of

---

Prices are based on a complete dinner for one, including an appetizer, entrée, dessert, tax and tip—but excluding wine or any other beverage.

loyal fans call it) is a handsome place, with a pleasant outdoor terrace and a honeycomb of rooms decorated in early Mexican-Southwestern. All the standards are offered here: chiles rellenos, tostadas, chimichangas, quesadillas, burritos, enchiladas and, of course, combination plates. The house specialties, notably the fish and steak, are not always convincing. Dinner for one is about $20. Also owned by the Delgado family is Las Casuelas Terraza (222 S. Palm Canyon Dr., 619-325-2794), almost identical to this branch.

Cuistot
73111 El Paseo, Palm Desert 92260; (619) 340-1000
Californian/French. Lunch Tues.-Sat., Dinner Tues.-Sun. Closed in summer. All major cards.

Cuistot has become a foodie destination in a restaurant-thin area, thanks to its consistently interesting, reasonably priced food. In the midst of the El Paseo shopping district just above Highway 111, chef Bernard Dervieux, a student of the famed chefs Paul Bocuse and Roger Vergé, does his work in an extended storefront, with a noisy dining room on one side and a quiet dining room on the other. By local standards, the menu is downright audacious. The dinner appetizers dash madly from tuna sashimi with a daikon-and–Napa cabbage salad, to crabcakes with a mâche and baby-frisée salad, to salmon cured in the style of Bocuse (with lemon, herbs and olive oil), all the way to lobster-filled ravioli in a truffle sauce. Main courses are similarly eclectic: Chinese-style duck in a black-currant-and-apricot sauce, wild salmon in a ginger-and-chervil sauce. The dishes can be remarkably flavorful and refined, though we've noticed a penchant for oversweetening. A dinner costs about $60.

10/20 Dar Maghreb
42300 Bob Hope Dr., Rancho Mirage 92270; (619) 568-9486
Moroccan. Dinner nightly (Fri.-Sat. in summer). DC, MC, V.

As with the branch of Dar Maghreb in Los Angeles, this Disneyland-Goes-to-Morocco experience isn't merely dinner, it's an event. Be ready to settle in for the evening, seated on low couches in one of the ornate Moroccan-palace rooms. Although the food isn't overwhelming, it's a pleasant experience to share with a group with a good sense of humor. The meal starts with a ritualistic cleansing of the hands, essential since you'll be eating with your fingers. Flat bread arrives first, followed by a good lentil soup, marinated vegetables and cucumber with yogurt. Onward to the best item on the fixed-price menu, b'stilla, a sweet, nutty pie filled with bite-

sized pieces of chicken. The main course (choice of squab, quail, rabbit, lemon chicken and three different lambs) is served with a couscous that can be lacking in its native spiciness. If you're not comatose after all that, you'll finish your feast with baklava, fruit, nuts, dates and refreshing mint tea. During the evening, belly dancers entertain. All this costs $50 per person.

Dolly Cunard's
78045 Calle Cadiz, La Quinta 92253; (619) 564-4443
French/Continental. Dinner nightly. Closed in summer. All major cards.

Dolly Cunard's (formerly Cunard's), sits at the eastern end of the Coachella Valley, close to La Quinta Resort. It's the sort of restaurant you dress for, a grand place serving grand food in a grand setting, complete with blazing fireplaces, babbling brooks and service from a bygone era. The restaurant is built within a massive 1930s villa, a former country estate that's been transformed into what many consider the desert's finest Continental restaurant. When it was called Cunard's it was named for owner Robert Cunard, and these days, it's his former wife who runs the shop. Where Robert Cunard created a classically romantic restaurant serving cornmeal blini with beluga caviar, corn chowder garnished with shrimp and lobster, grilled duck with a pear-and-ginger sauce, Dolly and her chef, Jay Trubee, have added an assortment of new dishes, along the lines of a veal chop with a three-mushroom sauce, linguine with lobster, and peach ravioli for dessert. It's food with one foot in the past and one in the present, well prepared and, we should add, accordingly priced. A dinner is about $75.

11/20 Kiyosaku
1420 N. Palm Canyon Dr., Palm Springs 92262; (619) 327-6601
Japanese/Sushi. Lunch Mon.-Tues. & Thurs.-Sat., Dinner Sun.-Tues. & Thurs.-Sat. AE, MC, V.

When this was the prime Japanese restaurant in Palm Springs, it impressed reasonably. These days, the Otani's good sushi has made this place seem comparably tired. Still, it's a straightforward, respectable Japanese restaurant, complete with minimalist decor and a small sushi bar. The menu lists all the standards (yakitori, chicken teriyaki, tempura) and a few more unusual dishes, such as salmon yaki (salmon cooked in butter), asparagus beef (thin layers of beef rolled around asparagus) and a Japanese bouillabaisse. The bouillabaisse is wan and bland, but everything else here is good, particularly the beef teriyaki (which practically melts in your mouth), the fresh, tasty sushi and the boat dinner, a Japanese extravaganza for two that includes shrimp and vegetable tempura, scallops, flavorful crab and clams, and chicken or beef kushi kebabs. Dinner is about $35 per person.

11/20 Mamma Gina

73705 El Paseo, Palm Desert 92260;
(619) 568-9898
Italian. Dinner nightly. Closed in summer. All major cards.

Mamma Gina is a branch (in fact, the only branch) of a restaurant in Florence, Italy. Once you finally land a table, don't expect a waiter to hop to attention. Though neither the setting nor the service is overly Italian, the kitchen does a passable job, turning out such Tuscan specialties as deep-fried mozzarella, spinach sautéed in the Florentine manner (with lots of garlic), deep-fried artichokes, air-dried beef (bresaola) from the village of Valtellina, squid-ink-blackened ravioli stuffed with lobster, marrow-filled osso buco in a rich meat sauce and, of course, bistecca alla fiorentina. The gelato is made on the premises. A dinner costs about $60.

11/20 The Nest

75188 Hwy. 111, Indian Wells 92210;
(619) 346-2314
Italian/Continental. Dinner nightly (Thurs.-Sat. in summer). All major cards.

This comforting little spot offers an eclectic menu of dishes that are both Italian and French, with some Swiss items thrown in for the fun of it. Diners sit in a room packed with marble-topped bistro tables, Cinzano umbrellas hanging from the ceiling, French memorabilia, Swiss posters and Italian flags. The kitchen seems most comfortable with the Italian dishes, particularly the house specialty of cannelloni stuffed with veal and spinach. Fresh fish, generally prepared "meunière," is also a good bet, and all the portions are ample. Order a carafe of house red, which suits the homey cuisine. The price is about $20 per person, with gemutlichkeit.

 ## Otani—A Garden Restaurant

266 Avenida Caballeros, Palm Springs 92262; (619) 327-6700
Japanese. Lunch Mon.-Fri., Dinner nightly. All major cards.

Otani looks for all the world like a shogun's palace—this truly is the proverbial mackerel in the middle of the Mojave. The high ceiling gives the effect of a Japanese gymnasium, with an assortment of activity areas scattered throughout the expanse. The best strategy is to sit in the dining room and order dishes from both the yakitori and teppanyanki menus. The salmon-

skin salad is wonderful, with a good deal of salmon adhering to the skin. The California rolls are among the finest we've tasted, plump with avocado and crab. Along with all the usual tempura items are tempura calamari, lobster tail, garlic, jumbo clams and potatoes done like a sort of Japanese-style french fry. The yakitoris—grilled skewers of tiny quail eggs wrapped in bacon, chicken chunks interspersed with green onions, beef intertwined with asparagus—alone are worth the trip. For dessert, there's a messy thing made out of vanilla ice cream, fudge cake and chocolate sauce. Dinner for one runs about $35.

12/20 Paoli's Pizzeria & Pasta House

68977 Hwy. 111, Cathedral City 92234;
(619) 324-3737
Italian. Lunch Sat.-Sun., Dinner Tues.-Sun. MC, V.

There are legions of pizza-and-pasta places in the Palm Springs area, but at Paoli's, the pizzas and pastas are better than average. In a way, it's the worst kept secret in the desert, for the parking lot is permanently crowded, and there's always a wait in the dining room for Cheryll Paoli's mussels, eggplant parmigiana, lasagna, homemade sausage, terrific salad dressing and garlic butter, and her trademark white sauce pizza, topped with alfredo sauce and mozzarella. It's a taste of Little Italy in the desert. Plan to spend $15 to $25 for a dinner.

 ## Ritz-Carlton Dining Room, Rancho Mirage

68900 Frank Sinatra Dr., Rancho Mirage 92270; (619) 321-8282
French. Dinner nightly. All major cards.

The Ritz-Carlton has done quite a bit for the state of the desert's restaurants—thanks to the Dining Room, the food scene has taken a quantum leap toward bona fide seriousness, even high respectability. For the area, the restaurant's atmosphere is one of extreme formality; you expect your dishes to be accompanied by the sounds of an angelic choir. There's a certain penchant here for complex dishes: the French green beans that accompany the marinated California quail arrive on a bed of red-oak lettuce topped with a kumquat-ginger vinaigrette. A saffron jus comes with the Maine lobster wrapped in prosciutto and

> *Gault Millau's ratings are based solely on the restaurants' cuisine. We do not take into account the atmosphere, decor, service and so on; these are commented upon within the reviews.*

savoy cabbage with fennel. For goodness sake, who came up with the idea of calling the sauce that comes with the dessert of wild berries on an anise biscuit a "dialogue" of fruit coulis? Although the food is good, it seems this corner of the desert hasn't heard the news about nouvelle simplicity. Dinner costs $80 or more per person.

Ruth's Chris Steak House
74040 Hwy. 111, Palm Desert 92260;
(619) 779-1998
American/Steakhouse. Dinner nightly. All major cards.

This is the 30th restaurant in the Ruth's Chris chain, and the best steak house in the desert by far. They've come as close as possible to creating a turn-of-the-century, New York–style beef house, heavy with dark polished woods and lots of brass, and with a striking view of the desert expanse. The fries and onion rings are always crisp and crunchy; the steaks—cooked in a broiler that sears them at 1700° F—are prime and perfect, from New York strip to porterhouse, from rib eye to petit filet. They understand that potatoes are the perfect accompaniment to meat—served not just french-fried, but also au gratin, lyonnaise, baked, steak-fried, shoestringed or cottage-fried. This place does what it does to perfection, without frippery or froufrou. Dinner costs about $40 per person.

12/20 Shame on the Moon
68-805 Hwy. 111, Cathedral City 92234;
(619) 324-5515
Continental. Dinner Tues.-Sun. (Fri.-Sun. in summer). MC, V.

A small, attractively decorated storefront in Cathedral City, Shame on the Moon serves California-tinged Continental cuisine to mostly youngish patrons. The crowd imbues the place with a lively, pleasantly hip air. Service is chatty and friendly. The food is functional, simple and quite tasty, running to such dishes as baked Brie with almonds and apples, pasta primavera, lemon chicken, veal in a mustard sauce. About $30 per person for dinner.

Sirocco at Stouffer Esmerelda Resort
Stouffer Esmeralda, 44-400 Indian Wells Ln., Indian Wells 92210; (619) 773-4444
Mediterranean. Dinner nightly. All major cards.

The folks at the Stouffer Esmeralda have a deep commitment to bringing some really serious food to the desert. The resort has hosted a series of meals prepared by such French eminences grises as Roger Vergé and Paul Bocuse,

joined by more local talent such as L.A.'s Wolfgang Puck. When the Big Boys aren't cooking at the Esmeralda, the in-house chefs do a good, occasionally thrilling job of creating one of the few Mediterranean-style menus in the area. Appropriately named for the hot dry wind that blows across the Sahara, Sirocco offers a fine view of both the desert, and of the immense fountains that buttress the hotel, acting as moats against the encroachment of sand and tumbleweeds. Chef Didier Tsirony learned his craft at La Barrière in Paris, and he learned it well. Tsirony makes an admirable stab at innovation, coming up with such dishes as scampi with truffled risotto, lobster-mussel bisque, lamb chops with stewed eggplant and a fricassée of lobsters, prawns and scallops. The restaurant hits more often than it misses; given a few more instructive visits by celebrity chefs, and this could be the best dining in the area. A dinner costs about $50.

10/20 Le Vallauris
385 W. Tahquitz-McCallum Way,
Palm Springs 92262; (619) 325-5059
French. Lunch & Dinner daily. All major cards.

Le Vallauris's original concept of dinner-for-members-only was discarded some time ago, and democracy triumphed—now all can come to watch the just-retired clientele greeting one another, enjoying the still-attractive dining room and the attentive, professional service. The blackboard menu changes daily according to the chef's whims and market availability; you can often find onion soup, escargots, spinach salad and variations on duck and veal. The cooking could use some updating, though we suspect the loyal clientele might disagree with that—it's a sort of conservative, well-intentioned nouvelle cuisine that tends to be erratically prepared. At worst, you'll enjoy the lovely ambience and the good wine list. About $80 for a dinner.

10/20 Wally's Desert Turtle
71775 Hwy. 111, Rancho Mirage 92270;
(619) 568-9321
French. Lunch Fri., Dinner nightly. AE, MC, V.

Classic French in the middle of the desert may seem an anomaly to some; to others, it's a way of life. The decor looks like that of a resort-hotel restaurant, dressy in a Las Vegas kind of way. The golf-and-tennis set gathers here regularly to chat over martinis and wave to friends. Then they tuck into such dishes as veal Oscar, sweetbreads à l'orange, Dover sole and veal with morels. The desserts can be delicious, especially the chocolate-marble mousse. Dinner runs $70 per person.

323

Bargain Bites

Billy Reed's
1800 N. Palm Canyon Dr., Palm Springs 92262;
(619) 325-1946
*American. Breakfast, Lunch & Dinner daily. AE,
MC, V.*

In a town filled with American restaurants,
Billy Reed's may be the most American of them,
and perhaps the most popular as well. There's
always a wait for a table at this massive restaurant,
where you'll find some of the most reliable, consistent plates of roast chicken, meatloaf, baked
fish and thick sandwiches in the desert. Dinner
costs about $12 per person.

Bit of Country
418 S. Indian Canyon, Palm Springs 92262;
(619) 325-5154
Breakfast & Lunch daily. MC, V.

Truly, what could be finer than to sit on Bit of
Country's sunny, cheerful patio on a warm desert
morning eating strawberry french toast with your
morning paper? You won't be the only one with
that good idea, so expect a wait on the weekends,
and almost all the time in season. The food is
hearty and homey coffee-shop fare, and most all
of it is good, particularly the home-baked biscuits
served with pan gravy or jam. Breakfast is about
$6 per person, lunch slightly more.

Elmer's Pancake and Steak House
1030 E. Palm Canyon Dr., Palm Springs 92262;
(619) 327-8419
Breakfast, Lunch & Dinner daily. All major cards.

Sooner or later, everyone who visits Palm
Springs winds up at Elmer's for pancakes and
waffles and other generous, inexpensive home-
cooked breakfasts. Though other meals are
served here, it's in the early morning that Elmer's
is most jammed with folks who could be mistaken
for a group at a Midwestern church social. Fans
agree that the date-nut pancakes, blueberry waffles, strawberry crêpes, Oregon-cheese blintzes
and ten specialty omelets are all worth the wait.
You can also get lunch or dinner, but breakfast
here is your best bet. About $6 for breakfast.

Fab's Italian Kitchen
80755 Hwy. 111, Indio 92201; (619) 342-5009
Italian. Lunch & Dinner daily. MC, V.

A branch of the popular Italian restaurants in
L.A.'s San Fernando Valley, the Fab's in Indio, is
among the most popular casual Italian restaurants in the Palm Springs area, a bustling place to
go for terrific pizza, heaping plates of pasta, wonderful orders of broccoli and spinach with lemon
and garlic, great chopped salads, excellent
chicken (try the chicken made with vinegar and
marinated peppers). Fab's is, in its own way, fabulous. It's the place to eat expensive food inex-
pensively. Dinner for one costs about $20.

Louise's Pantry
124 S. Palm Canyon Dr., Palm Springs 92262;
(619) 325-5124
Breakfast, Lunch & Dinner daily. No cards.

Louise's doesn't look like much—a small,
homey, yellow coffee shop—but it dishes up
good cooking that's just like Mom's. At least, it's
just like we wish hers had been. As a matter of
fact, there's a fleet of Moms serving you, advising
you and making sure you clean your plate. You'll
get decent, reliable, simple food, all presented in
an honest but uninspiring environment. Expect
a line in front, a long line. Breakfast is about $6,
lunch $10.

Nate's Delicatessen
100 S. Indian Canyon, Palm Springs 92262;
(619) 325-3506
Breakfast, Lunch & Dinner daily. AE, MC, V.

Nate's will never be ranked up there with classic delis like New York's Carnegie and the Stage,
Beverly Hills' Nate 'n Al's. But in Palm Springs'
terms, it's about as good as it gets. It has a de
rigeur plain, coffee-shop decor, and its huge
menu lists all the standards, from corned beef to
kreplach to chopped liver. Locals seem to love
Nate's, and in a way they have to: it's just about
the only deli in town. Deli connoisseurs may find
the food lackluster, but the portions are generous
and service is usually friendly. About $10 for
lunch.

The Wheel Inn
I-10, Main St. exit, Cabazon 92262; (714) 849-7012
Open daily 24 hours. All major cards.

There's hardly a traveler in the West who
hasn't seen the dinosaurs along Interstate 10 in
Cabazon. They were built by Claude Bell, owner
of this truck stop that stands slightly to the left
of Claude's dinosaurs. In the great tradition of
America's roadside attractions, the dinosaurs are
actually bait to lure you in to The Wheel Inn,
which is known far and wide as a quintessential
California truck stop. The Wheel Inn features all
the necessary amenities of truck-stop life—a large
tool section, a sizable display of turquoise belt
buckles, a great country-western jukebox, sassy
waitresses and relentlessly filling food, served 24
hours a day. The truly awesome desserts—fruit
pies, strawberry shortcakes of prehistoric dimensions, bread puddings—are all homemade. A
meal costs between $6 and $12 per person.

Hotels

P lease note that the prices quoted below are for rooms and suites in-season, which runs roughly from Thanksgiving to the end of April (though each hotel varies slightly). Almost every hotel in the desert lowers its rates considerably in the off-season, which is why the early fall and late spring are many savvy travelers' favorite times to visit Palm Springs.

The symbol that accompanies each review indicates in which price category the hotel belongs: **Top of the Line** ($200 & Up), **Luxury** ($150 & Up), **Moderate** ($100 & Up) or **Practical** (Under $100). We have defined the categories based on the regular starting price of a single or double room. *See also* the INTRODUCTION chapter, under "About the Hotels."

Top of the Line ($200 & Up)

Hyatt Grand Champions Resort

44-600 Indian Wells Ln., Indian Wells 92210; (619) 341-1000, Fax (619) 568-2236
Suites $240-$375, Villas $725-$925. All major cards.

The name is actually a bit of an understatement, for just about everything done at this all-suite resort is done in a grand-championship way. The tennis stadium, for instance, seats 10,500 spectators. There are twelve tennis courts (including grass, clay and hard floors); two eighteen-hole golf courses, designed by Ted Robinson; and a restaurant menu originally created by Wolfgang Puck. Rooms range from large, pleasant split-level parlor suites all the way up to two-bedroom garden villas. The only downside is that Grand Champions is about 18 miles from Palm Springs proper, which may not suit shopaholics.

Hyatt Regency Suites Palm Springs

285 N. Palm Canyon Dr., Palm Springs 92262; (619) 322-9000, Fax (619) 322-6009
Suites $195-$220. All major cards.

This Hyatt looks like a Mayan temple, plopped down in the busiest intersection of Downtown Palm Springs. It's part of the elegant Desert Fashion Plaza, which makes it a great choice for diehard shoppers. It's an all-suite hotel—the basic room is actually a 600-square-foot mini-apartment, complete with balcony, living room, dining area, bar, marble bath, bedroom with a

king-size bed and contemporary furnishings. You'll have to go elsewhere for tennis and golf, but there's a large pool and a complete health spa (weight room, sauna, Jacuzzi and aerobics classes). And the Hyatt has all the advantages of being in the heart of town, which means there are loads of restaurants, shops, movie theaters and amusements (including the Desert Museum) just a short stroll away from your room.

Marriott Desert Springs Resort and Spa

74-855 Country Club Dr., Palm Desert 92260; (619) 341-2211, (800) 228-9290, Fax (619) 341-1872
Singles & Doubles $240-$325, Suites $600-$2,100. All major cards.

This Marriott wows you at the entrance with sparkling lights that seem to drop into an indoor/outdoor lake. The rooms encircle the lake and you are transported to rooms and restaurants via small boats. This is probably the largest and best equipped hotel-connected spa in the desert. You can take aerobics, calisthenics, stretching or yoga classes, then be massaged, wrapped and otherwise pampered with beauty treatments. Your body composition can be analyzed by computer, and you can be coaxed to sweat just a bit harder by a personal trainer. Spa packages are available for a day, a weekend, four days or a week. The property has two 18-hole golf courses with some of the best views in the valley. There are 891 rooms here but on a busy day, overflow hotel guests are accommodated at 92 on-property villas. If you're lucky, you'll get a virtual home rather than a room.

La Quinta Hotel Golf and Tennis Resort

49499 Eisenhower Dr., La Quinta 92253; (619) 564-4111, Fax (619) 564-5758
Doubles $200-$285, Suites $850-$1,800. All major cards.

Haven to Hollywood stars for decades, this hotel is certainly the most elegant establishment in the eastern Coachella Valley. La Quinta Golf and Tennis Resort looks like a set from the old Zane Grey Theater. Restored to its original 1926 rustic elegance, the Spanish/Southwestern architecture is reminiscent of similar establishments in Taos or Santa Barbara, setting it apart from the newer desert resorts. Guests stay in Spanish-style casitas scattered across the grounds, many draped with flowering vines, and pathways bordered with bright poppies, petunias and pansies. A 36-hole championship golf course, a favorite of Lee Travino and site of the annual Senior Skins Tournament, winds through the Santa Rosa mountain baseline. The thirty-court tennis facility is home to one of the top men's professional tournaments. Some of the best hotel food in the desert is served in its three restaurants, including its newest eatery, Montana's, which also exhibits and sells local art work. The drive from Palm Springs proper to La Quinta is a long one (close to 45 minutes), but once there, you won't want to leave.

 ### Ritz-Carlton, Rancho Mirage
68-900 Frank Sinatra Dr., Rancho Mirage 92270; (619) 321-8282, Fax (619) 321-6928
Singles & Doubles $275-$395, Suites $650-$1,700. All major cards.

At the end of the Ritz-Carlton's manicured drive is a slightly smaller version of the Palace of Versailles, but with bighorn sheep grazing at the front door. Crowning a 625-foot-high plateau in the rugged hills of the Santa Rosa Mountains, the hotel is in the midst of a 310-acre wildlife sanctuary, where bighorn sheep roam free. Outside, the temperature may linger in the low 100s. Inside, all is cool and agonizingly tasteful.

Fine nineteenth-century art and sculptures line the halls. Polished wood and oiled leather abound. The pool is large enough for a small armada, with a sweeping view of the valley beyond. In a resort town with a number of good hotels but very few grand ones, the Ritz-Carlton truly stands out. You can walk from the hotel's manicured grounds to facilities that allow you to take Jeep rides or horseback-riding excursions through the wilderness. And, as befits a truly first-class hotel, there are worlds within worlds at the Ritz-Carlton. On one of the upper stories, separated from the rest of the hotel by its own elevator key, is the private "Club" floor built around a central lounge, where hors d'oeuvres and cocktails are served around the clock. The Club also has its own concierge and rooms equipped with VCRs. The restaurants are exceptionally good (*see* reviews, this chapter).

 ### Stouffer Esmeralda Resort
44-400 Indian Wells Ln., Indian Wells 92210; (619) 773-4444, Fax (619) 346-9308
Singles & Doubles $260-$350, Suites $520-$2,500. All major cards.

A monolith in the desert, this seven-story, 560-room resort was named after an ancient legend about an emerald necklace, in case you're wondering. It has three swimming pools (one with its own sandy beach for building sandcastles), two giant spas, a fully-stocked health club, seven tennis courts, a handsomely decorated restaurant (Sirocco, serving Mediterranean dishes), and an impressive atrium lobby. The resort's 36-hole golf course surrounds the hotel, and is reason enough for choosing to stay here. Ask about spa packages and food and wine events—Paul Bocuse, Roger Vergé and Wolfgang Puck have cooked here. Because of its size and amenities, this is also a good place to hold a meeting or convention.

Luxury ($150 & Up)

 ### La Mancha Private Villas and Court Club
444 N. Avenida Caballeros, Palm Springs 92262; (619) 323-1773, Fax (619) 323-5928
Villas only: mini-suite $140-$175, 1-bedroom suite $225-$750, 2-bedroom suite $305-$850, 3-bedroom suite $375-$950. AE, MC, V.

At La Mancha, owner Ken Irwin has created an exclusive, rather plastic club that springs up like an oasis in a vacant lot in the middle of the desert (actually, it's just a short walk to downtown Palm Springs). Quiet and private—so much so that it's impossible to get in or out of the gates without permission—La Mancha is marked by oversized villas done in a Hollywoodish decor. Each Mediterranean villa comes complete with a private pool with a European-style wave generator and a Jacuzzi; some with private screening rooms, some with sunken tennis courts (to keep errant breezes from ruining your serve). If Palm Springs' restaurants don't thrill you, you can arrange to have dinner prepared for you in the comfort of your own villa. La Mancha is just across the street from the new Palm Springs Convention Center, so it's an excellent place to unwind after a long day of speeches and seminars.

 ### Marriott Rancho Las Palmas Resort
41000 Bob Hope Dr., Rancho Mirage 92270; (619) 568-2727, Fax (619) 568-5845
Singles & Doubles $185-$245, Suites $450. All major cards.

Marriott Rancho Las Palmas is a modern-day re-creation of a Spanish village. Guests are housed in attractive hacienda-ettes circling the 27-hole golf course. But despite the San Miguel de Allende look, all the resort amenities one could wish for are in place: 25 tennis courts (with video monitors to help improve your game), two pools, hydrotherapy baths, terraces, restaurants, meeting rooms and friendly people. As large hotels go, the Marriott is among the desert's finest.

 ## Two Bunch Palms

67-425 Two Bunch Palms Trail, Desert Hot Springs 92240; (619) 329-8791, Fax (619) 329-1317
Doubles & Suites $105-$396. Closed Aug. AE, MC, V.

Although tourist-rich Palm Springs is only a twenty-minute drive away, Two Bunch remains one of the desert's great secrets, a place more people have heard about than have actually been to. And with only 44 villas and no golf course (though there are tennis courts), the clientele is understandably select. Many Angelenos go to Two Bunch to get away from the ubiquitous Industry chat, or the kids (none are allowed). In the pools at Two Bunch, you hear nothing but the wind in the tamarisk trees. There's no room service and no social director putting together a luau night—at Two Bunch, you're blissfully on your own. You can loosen up with a massage, including 23 facial techniques; or luxuriate in a Roman-Celtic brush down or milk-and-honey facial. Al Capone built the place back in the late twenties, and you can stay in the main house, where his initials are engraved on a desk and a bullet hole is engraved in a mirror.

Practical *(Under $100)*

 ## Villa Royale Country Inn

1629 Indian Trail, Palm Springs 92264; (619) 327-2314, Fax (619) 322-4151
Singles & Doubles $75-$270; Villas (for 4 people) $225-$270. All major cards.

You can find a bit of Europe in the desert at the Villa Royale, a country inn with 33 rooms and suites spread over three-and-half acres. Owners Bob Lee and Chuck Murawski have decorated each room with European treasures they collected during their travels abroad. Rooms duplicate country homes in France, England, Germany, Italy, Spain, Greece, Portugal, Monaco and Morocco. Quiet courtyards, flowering gardens and an adults-only rule make this bed and breakfast a retreat for romantics. The Inn's Europa Restaurant offers fireside dining and a courtyard, and features a different European theme each night.

Spa Hotels & Resorts

 ## Murrieta Hot Springs Resort & Health Spa

39405 Murrieta Hot Springs Rd., Murrieta 92653; (714) 677-7451, No fax
Singles $65-$75, Duplex Cottages $85-$95, Suites $170. All major cards.

Legend holds that the 47-acre parcel on which this resort now sits was once a sort of spa for numerous tribes of Native Americans. There's a great deal of character to the place, especially in the many Spanish-style buildings (some dating to the early 1900s), but we must confess to being pleased by the extensive renovation done in recent years. This, combined with the natural beauty of rolling hills and the nearby wine country, make Murrieta an excellent getaway (90 minutes' drive from L.A. or Palm Springs). Hot-springs mineral and mud baths top the list of attractions; there are also 14 tennis courts, an 18-hole golf course designed by Robert Trent Jones, and complete spa, health and fitness programs. Spa veterans won't find much that's unique or progressive about the treatments, but for anyone in need of a restorative getaway, it's a fine choice. Rooms in the main lodges are cozy and functional; the hillside cottages are larger.

 ## The Palms

572 N. Indian Canyon Dr., Palm Springs 92262; (619) 325-1111, Fax (619) 327-0867
Singles $125, Doubles $125-$185, Private Cottages $185-$220 (rates include meals & fitness plan). All major cards.

Neither particularly strenuous nor particularly expensive, this is the perfect place for mature men and women who don't want to spend a fortune on a week of mild exercise and diet. The facilities aren't plush (they could use updating), but the atmosphere is comfortable and friendly. Guests participate in as many or as few exercise classes as they choose, and there's plenty of time to walk the couple of blocks to downtown Palm Springs for shopping. Beauty and health services are available at an extra charge and include massage, facials, hairstyling and cellulite treatments.

 ## Spa Hotel & Mineral Springs

100 N. Indian Canyon Dr., Palm Springs 92263; (619) 325-1461, Fax (619) 325-3344
Doubles $85-$115, Suites $135. All major cards.

We love this Palm Springs Spa for its reminder of what Palm Springs used to be in the days before the megaresorts; and it reminds us as well that there really is a spring somewhere beneath

Palm Springs. The Spa Hotel is large and functional; the architecture is a classic example of '60s commercial design, complete with metal sculptures/fountains theoretically bringing mineral waters up from the underground springs. A sampling spa experience is included in the room rate, and hotel guests get a discount on further use of the spa. Behind the spa's white doors, there's a sauna, Russian steam room, eucalyptus-inhalation room, mineral Jacuzzi baths, cooling room, herbal wraps, massages and a gym.

> *For those interested in both daytime and resort spas, see also "LOS ANGELES Shops" under "Beauty & Health," for reviews and information on nine of Southern California's best.*

Nightlife

Cecil's
Smoketree Shopping Center, Sunrise Ave. & Hwy. 111, Palm Springs 92262; (619) 320-4202
Open Thurs.-Sun. 8 p.m.-2 a.m. Cover $7-$10. All major cards.

Tuxedoed hosts and cocktail waitresses in slinky gowns will usher you into to Cecil's stand-up comedy nights or the weekend dance nights held two adjacent rooms—one showcases live rock, pop and soul oldies, the other blaring, recorded Top 40 tunes.

Costa's Nightclub
74-855 Country Club Dr., Palm Desert 92260; (619) 341-1795
Open nightly 8 p.m.-2 a.m. No cover. All major cards.

This trendy nightspot at the Marriott Desert Springs Resort appeals to the well-dressed, out-for-a-good-time set. There are live bands Tuesday through Saturday and a disc jockey Sunday and Monday. By 9 p.m., there's usually a line. Hotel guests get priority at the door.

Shops

Desert Fashion Plaza (123 N. Palm Canyon Dr., Palm Springs 92262; 619-320-8282) in located on the main drag in the heart of Palm Springs, and offers upscale department stores such as Saks Fifth Avenue, as well as Gucci and more than 60 specialty boutiques selling jewelry, shoes, sports and casual clothing, books and gifts.

El Paseo Drive in Palm Desert, affectionately nicknamed the Rodeo Drive of the desert, boasts high-priced women's boutiques stocked with sequined sweat suits and all manner of glitzy casual wear for resort-bound travelers. Men can still find those bright orange or green golf pants, too.

The Palm Desert Town Center Mall (72840 Highway 111, Palm Desert; 619-346-2121) has I. Magnin and Bullock's and 150 specialty stores, as well as the popular Ice Capades Chalet, which rents skates and accessories and offers classes.

Sights

Arts
There are a number of art galleries in Palm Springs. The A. Albert Allen Fine Art Gallery (73-200 El Paseo, Ste. 4B, Palm Desert; 619-341-8655) features paintings and sculptures by noted Southwestern artists. J. Lewis Bowker's California Vistas (73-260 El Paseo, Ste. 1-B, Palm Desert; 619-340-9014) carries realistic paintings of rural California and local desert landscapes. The Palm Desert Gallery Association (619-340-9014) sponsors an "Art Walk on El Paseo" the first Thursday evening of each month throughout spring. The Bob Hope Cultural Center's McCallum Theatre for the Performing Arts (973-000 Fred Waring Dr., Palm Desert 92260; 619-340-2787) is a 1,125-seat theater, and is the only place in town showcasing a changing roster of top bands, soloists, dance troupes, comics, circuses and dramatic productions. Past performances have ranged from Kenny Loggins to Johnny Mathis to Isaac Stern.

Attractions/Excursions
Anza-Borrego Desert State Park
At the end of County Rd. S-222, Borrego Springs; (619) 767-5555.
Fall, winter & spring: daily from sunrise to sundown. Summer: weekends from sunrise to sundown.

A true oasis 90 miles south of Palm Springs and 90 miles east of San Diego, this is America's largest state park, covering 600,000 acres. The Anza-Borrego stretches from Riverside County clear to the Mexican border. It's pleasant from fall through spring, but scorches with temperatures consistently over 100° F in the summer.

The beauty of this park is its carpet of wildflowers following good winter rains—yellow dandelions, scarlet sand verbena, desert sunflowers, dune primrose, and the most prominent of the desert flowers, the brilliant red blossoms of the spindly ocotillo. For hikers the park offers trails ranging from short nature walks through palm oases to strenuous mountain pathways providing fantastic views of the desert.

Dates, Dates, Dates!

The area is thick with palm trees (hence, its name), and from those palm trees come dates—particularly medjool dates, which are among the best in the world. As you head east from Palm Springs, Highway 111 is lined with date shops, the best of which are **Shields Date Gardens** (80225 Hwy. 111, Indio; 619-347-0996), **Jensen's Date & Citrus Gardens** (80653 Hwy. 111, Indio; 619-347-3897) and the self-proclaimed "world-famous" **Hadley's Fruit Orchards** (I-10, Cabazon; 714-849-5255).

Joshua Tree National Monument

Highway 62 off I-10, Twentynine Palms; (619) 367-7511
Open daily dawn-dusk. Admission $5 per car.

A wonderful day can be spent driving through Joshua Tree National Monument, an untouched expanse of high and low desert that is reached by taking Interstate 10 half an hour east of Palm Springs, getting off at the Twentynine Palms/Mecca exit. In the spring, the desert turns into a sea of wildflowers and blossoming Joshua trees, a gnarly cactus of unsurpassed beauty.

Living Desert Reserve

47900 S. Portola Ave., Palm Desert 92260; (619) 346-5694
Open daily 9 a.m.-5 p.m. Closed in summer. Adults $6, children $3.

The Living Desert Reserve is one of our favorite desert escapes. In a single morning, you'll enter an aviary oasis with sleepy owls, a variety of botanical gardens, clever educational exhibits, Cahuilla Indian history, and one-and-a-half miles of spectacular desert trails with snow-peaked mountains in the distance. You'll encounter red-tailed hawks, a family of longhorned mountain goats on their own little mountain, and slender male gazelles looking quite festive wearing green garden hoses to protect their horns from damage in their tusslings with other males. You can spend happy hours here learning to appreciate the riches of desert life, in a natural habitat that makes the surrounding condos look dramatically inappropriate by contrast. Wear sturdy walking shoes, and if you're sun-sensitive, be sure to bring a hat.

Palm Springs Aerial Tramway

One Tramway Rd. at Hwy. 111, Palm Springs 92263; (619) 325-1391
Winter: Mon.-Fri. 10 a.m.-7:30 p.m., Sat.-Sun. 7:30 a.m.-9:15 p.m. Summer: Mon.-Fri. 10 a.m.-8:30 p.m., Sat.-Sun. 8:30 a.m.-10:15 p.m. Admission $14.95 adults, $12.95 children.

Two Swiss-made trams travel a vertical ascent of 5,873 feet in about fifteen minutes from the desert floor to a tranquil mountain wilderness (once you make it past the tacky tourist concession stand). In winter, the snow-covered valley is splendid for cross-country skiing, snowshoe hiking and sledding. The tram stretches its hours in summer, and offers ride-and-dine packages that capitalize on the spectacular desert sunsets. The Erector Set towers that support this tramway, the longest in the world, are surprisingly delicate-looking.

Palm Springs Desert Museum

101 Museum Dr., Palm Springs 92262; (619) 325-7186
Open Tues.-Sun. 10 a.m.-4 p.m. Adults $4, children 6-17 $2, children under 6 free.

The ultra-contemporary architecture of the Desert Museum makes it look more like a modern hotel than a museum. The lobby is breezy and impressive, complete with chandeliers. The exhibitions change frequently, and the permanent collection is rotated twice a year. You can tour the museum and view the traveling shows or natural-history dioramas that dramatize desert life, or visit the Annenberg Theater to catch a lecture, film or concert. There are two sculpture gardens and a gift shop. The latest additions are complete cast skeletons of the giant ground sloth and saber-toothed cat, which roamed the Coachella Valley during the last great Ice Age.

Wine Touring in Temecula

Less than a two-hour drive from Palm Springs, Southern California's own wine valley produces award-winning premium wines. Temecula is a sleepy Old West town centered around six blocks bordering Front Street. It's fun to stroll through the fifteen or so antique boutiques before making the short drive along Rancho California Road to the wine valley. The **South Temecula Valley Vintners Association** (P.O. Box 1601, Temecula 92390; 714-699-3626) offers a self-guided wine-country tour map to the dozen wineries. The French-Mediterranean château that houses the **John Culbertson Winery** (32575 Rancho California Rd., Temecula 92591; 714-699-0099) is the unofficial gateway to wine country. Daily tours and tastings feature its sparkling wines, and **Café Champagne** (714-699-0088) is a lovely spot for lunch. **Callaway Vineyard & Winery** (32720 Rancho California Rd., Temecula 92589; 714-676-4001) showcases its white wines in a daily tour and tasting. **Hart Winery** (32500 Rancho California Rd., Temecula 92593; 714-676-6300), housed in an old barn, has won a few coveted awards.

If you're staying overnight, the **Temecula Creek Inn** is the area's best offering—a rustic yet thoroughly comfortable golf resort at 44501 Rainbow Canyon Road (714-676-5631; call 800-962-7335 for reservations).

Events

National Date Festival
Desert Expo Centre, 46350 Arabia St., Indio 92201; (619) 863-8247
Admission per day: adults $5, children 3-11 $2.

Held in Indio every February at the Desert Expo Centre in Indio, the festival is a wacky ten-day celebration. Camel and ostrich races, date-spitting contests, top-name entertainment and a carnival vie for attention with exhibits of dates, fine arts, photography, gems and livestock.

Palm Springs International Film Festival
P.O. Box 2230, Palm Springs 92263; (800) 366-3456, (619) 322-2930
Individual movies $6, Unlimited admission $200.

This annual week-long event was the brainchild of Mayor Sony Bono, and focuses on the latest international releases. There are appearances by the filmmakers, seminars for would-be movie moguls and plenty of parties. The festival is a marathon of 85 or so hard-to-find movies shown in large, comfortable movie houses, and sells out. Your best bet is to purchase a "Platinum Pass" for $200, which assures advance seating at the screenings and entry into seminars.

Sports

Bicycling
Well-marked bike trails run throughout the desert; maps are available at the **Palm Springs Parks and Recreation Department** (619-323-8272), or in the *Desert Guide*, a monthly magazine distributed free at major hotels. You can rent bikes at **Burnett's Bicycle Barn** (429 S. Sunrise Way, Palm Springs; 619-325-7844).

Golf
With only fifteen to twenty days of rainfall per year, the dry, sunny days and balmy nights are ideal for golf as a way of life. Palm Springs and its neighboring resorts boast more golf courses per person, per square foot than anywhere in the world. Ever since Bob Hope began his annual tournament in Palm Springs in the 1960s, the area has been attracting amateurs and pros alike. You, too, can tee off where the celebrities do, and follow your ball across championship courses. The most challenging course is **PGA West** in La Quinta, home of the Thanksgiving "Skins Game" (56-150 PGA Blvd., La Quinta; 619-564-6666). Stadium course fees run $175 winter, $85 summer; Nicklaus Course $150 winter, $75 summer. Another popular course is the 36-hole at **Marriott Desert Springs Resort** (74-855 Country Club Dr., Palm Desert; 619-341-1756). Fees $110 winter, $55 summer.

Horseback Riding
Riding the trails through the canyons and natural palm oases of the dusty desert is probably the most genuine way to appreciate its beauty. **Smoke Tree Stables** in Palm Springs has fine trail-trained horses that know their way around the desert (2500 Toledo Ave., Palm Springs 92264; 619-327-1372). Another place is **Ranch of the Seventh Range** (Avenue 58, behind PGA West, La Quinta 92253; 619-777-7777).

Jeep Tours
Desert Adventures (68-733 Perez Rd., Ste. #16, Cathedral City 92234; 619-324-3378) runs exhilarating four-wheel-drive jeep tours of the foothills of the Santa Rosa Mountains and nearby canyons. Knowledgeable guides who have a great respect for this unspoiled wilderness, introduce you to its Indian lore, native plants, animals and geology. The tour comes with a gourmet picnic lunch, but you may not have a great appetite after bouncing around on dusty roads. Tours run 8 a.m. and 1 p.m. daily September through June. Prices range from $45 to $75.

Polo
The largest member polo club in the United States, the **El Dorado Polo Club** in Indio (50-950 Madison St., Indio, 619-342-2223) presents a full season of matches from October through April, plus lessons in the "sport of kings." Admission is $5.

Tennis
All the major resorts offer the sport. You can sign up for a variety of clinics taught by pros or watch the world's top men pros at the Newsweek Champions Cup in March and the top women players at the Kraft General Foods Women's Tennis Tournament in February. ◆

SAN DIEGO

North of the Border

We could savage San Diego for its self-absorption were it not so achingly beautiful. The onset of World War II brought on relentless growth that, more than fifty years later, still has not slowed, and has never given the city an opportunity to catch its breath or to forge a widely accepted civic identity. The result of the endless influx of newcomers, among Americans primarily from the Midwest, and among immigrants largely from Mexico and Asia, is a collection of small town–like neighborhoods, uneasily linked by freeways, that taken together constitute the sixth largest city in the United States. But while urban, the town to a surprising degree rejects urbanity, and many locals pretend that they still reside in their home village. A waiter at one of downtown's better restaurants told us, "Yes, San Diegans are apathetic, but apathy is hard work."

Against its will, however, San Diego has become a metropolis, with all the attendant cultural and dining amenities, and also with a share, still relatively small, of the crime, congestion and other problems that beset large American cities. The relentless growth, combined with a lack of civic vision, has resulted in the scarring of the natural landscape and in the erection of architecture that has painted warts, rather than beauty marks, on the stunning visage with which nature endowed San Diego.

It is nonetheless a city of unique beauty. Visitors and locals view it as a nouvelle-Southwestern cuisine pastry, a spare, brush-dotted crust of broad beaches and grand coastal cliffs that give way to the renewed downtown, the jewel-like neighborhood of La Jolla and, to the east, the mountains, which occasionally don ivory mantles of freshly fallen snow. Taken with its surrounding countryside, San Diego almost represents its own ecosystem. To the west lies the Pacific, to the north sprawls the Camp Pendelton Marine Corps base, rimming the east are mountains and deserts and to the South, Tijuana and all of Mexico. The San Diego Trolley, which shuttles from downtown to within feet of the International border, gets you there in a hurry. Notables now take note of San Diego, a city that has switched its focus from tuna and tourism to technology, and currently is called home by an almost unreasonably large number of Nobel laureates.

The beaches and sky suffice for many, but cultural and sports activities abound: the San Diego . . . Zoo, Wild Animal Park, Museum of Art, Opera, Symphony, Repertory Theater, Museum of Contemporary Art, Padres (baseball), Chargers (football), Gulls (hockey) and Sockers (soccer). Add to this the Star of India, the oldest iron-hulled merchant schooner still afloat; the remarkable productions at the Old Globe Theatre and La Jolla Playhouse; the myriad of museums and other attractions in Balboa Park; the charming communities along the North County coast; the sailing, deep-sea fishing, wind-sailing, hot-air ballooning, biking, hiking, diving, surfing and other possibilities—and you come up with a town that brooks no excuses for boredom.

In the course of a decade, dining has soared from the dull decadence of surf 'n' turf to the outstanding offerings of a coterie of chic establishments. Even shopping, for which well-heeled locals formerly traveled to Beverly Hills, New York and Paris, lately has blossomed to the point that the concentration of luxury shops along La Jolla's Girard Avenue has been eclipsed by Fifth Avenue–style shops, such as Tiffany and Cartier, in the grand new Paladion center downtown.

Restaurants

The symbol that accompanies each review indicates the rating on a scale of one to twenty. The rankings reflect *only* our opinion of the food; the decor, service, wine list and atmosphere are explicitly commented upon within each review. For further explanation, as well as an index of restaurants by rating, please see "About the Restaurants" in the INTRODUCTION. See the INDEXES section at the back of the book for comprehensive restaurant indexes.

 Azzura Point at Loews Coronado Bay Resort
4000 Coronado Bay Rd., Coronado 92118; (619) 424-6400
New American. Dinner nightly. All major cards.

Here is a sterling exception to the rule that hotel dining rooms serve lobotomized cuisine. The kitchen of this handsome, Old Nantucket–style restaurant is presided over by chef Jeff Tunks. His introduction of "Asian-influenced New American cuisine" at the exclusive River Club in Washington, D.C. caused such a fuss that even congressmen paid to dine there. We very much like Azzura Point's views up San Diego Bay to the graceful curves of the Coronado Bridge, especially when the foreground is occupied by Tunks's delightfully clever millefeuille of fried wonton skins, sliced raw tuna and wasabi-heated crème fraîche. The chubby crabcakes, barely dusted with crumbs, are hard to beat in the realm of shellfish luxury, although the seared sea scallops with pistachio-stuffed Portabella mushrooms pose fierce competition. The menu pays little heed to carnivores but does oblige with a fine veal chop in musky Gorgonzola-rosemary butter, paired with a crusty risotto cake that rivals the meat in succulence. An unusual East-West crème brûlée with orange and ginger nicely completes the picture. The wine list is small but well chosen, and offers quite a few good wines by the glass. Dinner costs about $35 per person.

12/20 Banzai Cantina

3667 India St., San Diego 92103; (619) 298-6388
Eclectic. Lunch Mon.-Sat., Dinner nightly, Late Supper Fri.-Sat., Brunch Sun. All major cards.

Chef Jose Kelley studied ceramics in Japan, married a fellow student and now cooks a wild often wildly imaginative menu of Mexican, Japanese and hybrid dishes at this spare, casual café situated between downtown San Diego and Old Town. His "California Sushi" vaguely recalls chiles rellenos in style: fried sushi stuffed with cream cheese and guacamole in tempura batter. But Kelley prepares traditional Japanese sushi with equal panache. On the Mexican side, the tortilla soup and carne asada are fine, and the hybridized fried wontons filled with pineapple salsa make the tongue smile. We would go back any time for the grilled sea scallops, glazed with a sharp citrus sauce and arranged on a fluffy potato pancake. Dinner costs $15 per person.

12/20 Bayou Bar & Grill

329 Market St., Gaslamp Quarter,
Downtown (S.D.) 92101; (619) 696-8747
Cajun. Lunch Mon.-Sat., Dinner nightly. All major cards.

Cajun cooking may be the most prominent American regional cuisine, but it also is the most abused. In San Diego, restaurants oddly tend to hire German or English chefs to concoct bizarre variations on recipes borrowed from questionable Louisiana cookbooks. San Diego's salvation for aficionados of the style comes in the form of this restaurant in the now-fashionable Gaslamp Quarter, downtown's historic district. Operated by New Orleans native Bud Deslatte, Bayou Bar & Grill packs a good crowd of locals, who come for the fried, deviled oysters, the murky gumbo, the stuffed soft-shell crab, the savory crayfish

etouffée, the red beans and rice, the reasonably zingy shrimp Creole. One nifty dish called eggplant lagniappe in which the "something extra" is a highly seasoned stew of shrimp, crab and crayfish that surmounts the slice of breaded eggplant. The casual crowd hears so many versions of "Do You Know What It Means to Leave New Orleans" played over the sound system that it hums along after a while, but never so loudly as when consuming chocolate-and-peanut-butter Cajun Velvet pie. We prefer to skip the mostly Californian wine list in favor of one of the beers, especially one of the bottles brewed in Louisiana. Dinner costs about $25 per person.

The Belgian Lion

2265 Bacon St., Ocean Beach (S.D.) 92106;
(619) 223-2700
French. Dinner Tues.-Sat. All major cards.

Some ten surfboard lengths from the high-tide line in Ocean Beach, San Diego's funkiest neighborhood, The Belgian Lion is a dining destination in an area that largely goes in for the simplest Southern California–style beach grub and considers new blue jeans unsuitable for all but the most formal occasions. But once inside this somewhat worn bungalow, you find yourself immersed in the gracious, thoughtful old-world service. Chef Don Coulon, whose family constitutes the bulk of the kitchen and dining room staff, cooks the hearty cuisine of the French provinces. He offers up a meat-lavished sauerkraut braised in Champagne, a deeply flavored cassoulet, sweetbreads in a mustard cream that causes sweetbread fanciers to swoon and an inimitable salmon in tart sorrel sauce (the Coulons grow their own sorrel at home). Daughter and pastry chef Michelle Coulon, who trained in Paris, makes a chocolate mousse that is simultaneously intense and gossamer-light. Special midweek fixed-price menus cost $10.95, but a meal from the standing menu costs closer to $35.

12/20 El Bizcocho at Rancho Bernardo Inn

17550 Bernardo Oaks Dr., Rancho Bernardo 92128; (619) 487-1611
French. Dinner nightly, Brunch Sun. All major cards.

The funny thing about this restaurant is its name: *el bizcocho* translates roughly as "hardtack," which is a plywood-like biscuit carried by vaqueros and sailors on long journeys. If anything resembling a *bizcocho* were ever served in this elegant and romantic place, we're not sure if we'd burst out laughing or burst out crying. Chef Thomas Dowling remains resolutely French in his approach, even though most of his peers have opted for California, Pacific Rim and Southwestern styles. His menu changes frequently but is reliably good; you'll find starters of vichyssoise (chilled cream-of-potato-leek soup) with caviar, and coquilles St-Jacques (sautéed scallops) with leeks and a truffle sauce. Entrées are excatly the sort of deeply satisfying fare you'd expect from any classic French restaurant: roasted rack of lamb with Provençal herbs, tournedos of beef with a Burgundy-wine sauce and wild mushrooms, roasted duckling with apples and a Calvados sauce. A special spa menu designed to come in under 800 calories is offered daily: one $28 offering began with an angel-hair pasta with roasted pepper and lobster, moved on to baked chicken breast with fresh artichokes in sweet garlic, and finished with marinated kiwi with fresh mint and a coconut "shortbread." The service in this handsome, formal room generally is a notch or two above that found elsewhere. Topping all this is an astounding wine list with 700 vintages. El Bizcocho is heroically scaled, and the mission-style room offers views of both the San Pasquale Mountains and an impeccably manicured golf course. Plan to spend $35 to $45 per person.

12/20 Café Bravo

895 Fourth Ave., Gaslamp Quarter, Downtown (S.D.) 92101; (619) 234-8888
Portuguese. Lunch Mon.-Fri., Dinner Mon.-Sat.
MC, V.

For decades considered quite the wrong part of town, San Diego's Gaslamp Quarter—a narrow patch of downtown that a century ago was the city's bustling commercial heart—has quite come back to life and now bursts with chic bistros, cafés and restaurants that generally offer good to excellent fare at less than top prices. Among the new crop of eateries to have opened since 1990, Café Bravo shares the theme of abundant sizzling garlic with many but stands alone when it comes to the menu, which is strictly Portuguese. It features such knockout dishes as grilled giant prawns with spicy pili pili sauce, veal in glowing Port sauce and the fascinating (and delicious) carne de porco Alentejana, or squares of pork and tiny clams sautéed together with a flavoring of cilantro and garlic. Lulas recheadas, or squid stuffed with meat and rice, make a good alternative for squid fans who want something other than San Diego's ubiquitous fried calamari. Small, stylish and sophisticated, Café Bravo looks good from the marble floor up, and also offers salsa and Brazilian music most nights in the adjacent nightclub. Dinner costs $20 per person.

California Cuisine

1027 University Ave., Hillcrest (S.D.) 92103; (619) 543-0790
Californian. Lunch Tues.-Fri., Dinner Tues.-Sun. All major cards.

The Hillcrest neighborhood is the closest San Diego gets to Hollywood, which in truth is not very close, since this town shies away from any trendiness that is not associated with surf wear. This restaurant tends to create trends of its own, however, in a cozy but brightly decorated dining room that during pleasant weather extends back to a tiny, gardenlike court. The kitchen follows the original credo of "California cuisine," adding endless fruit garnishes to its dishes. The fruits usually are used cleverly, as in an admirable purée of honeydew melon, pear and watercress puddled under a lightly charred, well-crusted slab of salmon. Be wary of the pork loin with poached apples, pears and Chinese plum sauce, because the sticky sauce can overwhelm the rest. The kitchen bakes the sort of inventive breads that have stormed the bigger cities in the past couple of years: flavored with pesto, sun-dried tomatoes and so on. Key-lime pie concludes a meal happily, but not quite so refreshingly as the remarkable honeydew-lavender sorbet. Dinner is about $25.

Cindy Black's

5721 La Jolla Blvd., La Jolla 92037; (619) 456-6299
French. Lunch Fri., Dinner Tues.-Sun. All major cards.

One of the few nationally recognized chefs in San Diego, and a Wellesley graduate to boot, Cindy Black trained in Southwest France and makes a specialty of that region's robust, not-too-complicated cuisine. A take-charge type known for keeping all her ducks in a row, she offers this bird in several fine preparations, especially a pairing of duck confit with fresh, grilled breast. Most meals include the gratin of the day, which can be any vegetable mixed with a light sauce and baked until a savory crust forms; such garnishes contribute half the pleasure of the meal here. Ask for Black's fabulous, unrepentant salad of pan-seared duck livers tossed with wilted Belgian endive, cream and Calvados, which she occasionally agrees to make. Fixed-price Sunday suppers are an ongoing favorite with knowledgable diners in this wealthy seaside neighborhood, who return regularly for the spicy chicken stew Provençale and the roast leg of lamb with creamed garlic. The wine list offers a carefully chosen list of Californians, as well as some interesting French picks over $100. Few who order the American brownie cake in caramel sauce fail to scrape the plate. Dinner costs $25 per person for the regular menu, $18 on Sunday.

10/20 El Circo Barcelona
905 Fourth Ave., San Diego 92101;
(619) 233-7227
Spanish. Lunch & Dinner daily, Brunch Sun. All major cards.

Since we always have an appetite for something culinarily new, we were glad to welcome this new Spanish restaurant into the Gaslamp Quarter. The walls are covered floor to ceiling with Surrealist murals, combined in places with vibrant mosaics. The effect, if overwhelming, is striking and memorable. So is some of the food, which is in the Barcelona style and tends to be as witty as the decor; peppers might be stuffed with duck, goat cheese and raspberry sauce, and the rabbit might be stuffed with garlic and drizzled with a cinnamon-honey sauce. A meal here is a culinary tour through the fascinating Catalán region of Spain (in the northeast, stretching from the Pyrenées at the French border down along the Mediterranean coast, with Barcelona at its center). Start with the pa amb formapge, a toasted bread topped with goat cheese, eggplant and roasted red peppers. Main dishes such as cassola d'Alverginies—an eggplant "omelet" with raisins, pinenuts, clams and spinach in a light goat-cheese sauce—feature all the famous ingredients of that region, often in rich and strange combinations. The 50 different tapas on the menu are supplemented daily by another 40 special tapas, most of them featuring seafood or wild game. It certainly helps to have an open mind when dining here—just order a pitcher of the refreshing sangría and think of Dalí. Dinner costs about $15 per person for tapas only, or about $25 for a full dinner.

Dobson's
956 Broadway Circle, Downtown (S.D.)
92101; (619) 231-6771
International. Lunch Mon.-Fri., Dinner nightly. All major cards.

This clubby bastion of downtown movers and shakers, with its dark paneling, brass wall plaques commemorating regular patrons, turn-of-the-century bar (brought around Cape Horn on a sailing vessel) and balcony dining room reminds us of many an old-fashioned San Francisco grill. It has changed under the direction of chef Deborah Schneider from a strictly French menu to a lighter, more contemporary list. One old standby is the mussel bisque, whose congregation of shellfish simmers in velvety cream under a dome of puff pastry. Otherwise, start with the grilled

giant shiitake mushrooms or the baby artichokes braised with sweet peppers and balsamic vinegar. Then move along to sea scallops sautéed with a papaya–red chile salsa, the meltingly tender house version of osso buco or the Moroccan-style marinated lamb loin served on a bed of spicy lentils. The wine list neatly matches both the menu and the sophistication of the clientele. Dinner costs about $30 per person.

12/20 Fio's
801 Fifth Ave., Gaslamp Quarter,
Downtown (S.D.) 92101; (619) 234-3467
Italian. Lunch Mon.-Sat., Dinner nightly. All major cards.

Arguably the cornerstone restaurant in the Gaslamp Quarter, and the one that finally made the neighborhood safe for tassled loafers and Armani suits, Fio's is unfathomly but handsomely decorated with wall-spanning murals of the famous Palio races held in Siena, Italy. We have never understood the management's insistence on dressing the staff in uniforms that unsettlingly recall the garb of Mussolini's Black Shirts, but we can't quarrel with the heavily laden plates of homemade antipasti (especially the suave, marinated seafood and vegetables) or the tender pizzas that quickly puff and brown in the wood-fired oven. Unendingly popular and not the sort of place to visit without reservations, we do have reservations about the pasta list, even if the clientele wolfs it down by the ton daily. The salmon ravioli in saffron cream do meet the test, however, and the meat and fowl entrées generally seem quite well done. The crowd, primarily but by no means exclusively young, bursts with energy, and the atmosphere is invigorating; guests in the mood for a quiet chat don't have a chance here. A dinner costs $20 per person.

11/20 The Fish Market
750 North Harbor Dr., Downtown (S.D.)
92101; (619) 232-3474
Seafood. Lunch & Dinner daily. All major cards.

The management has yet to disclose how much it spent on this bayside showplace, but reliable estimates top $10 million, and nearly every penny shows. The casual downstairs floor includes several dining rooms, a fish market, a display kitchen, sushi, shellfish and cocktail bars, and a decor, built by a shipwright, that mimics the interior of a fishing vessel. The staff dresses like a group of deck hands and, frankly, so does much of the clientele. Upstairs, the Top of the Market (more expensive but much more elegant), offers an even better view of all the activities on San Diego Bay, as well as a more sophisticated menu. Both floors emphasize fish,

fish, fish, and the selection is possibly the best in town. The kitchens do not indulge overly in complication but generally handle the grilling and sautéing of all creatures shelled and finned with panache. Dinner costs $20 per person downstairs, $30 at Top of the Market.

12/20 La Fonda Roberto's
300 Third Ave., Chula Vista 92010;
(619) 585-3017
*Mexican. Lunch & Dinner daily, Brunch Sun.
MC, V.*

Were it not for the murals of daily life in Oaxaca, Mexico—home of the gastronomically talented family that runs the place—La Fonda Roberto's would have all the glamour of a faded coffee shop. Even with the murals, Roberto's is looking a tad down at the heels these days. But the food still sings, and what we like is the breadth of its menu, which utterly ignores artificial Mexican-style fare in favor of beautifully flavored home cooking. Far from serving the cast-in-concrete burritos and enchiladas that abound elsewhere, Roberto's goes in for the real thing, serving up crêpes folded around squash blossoms or cuitlachoche (the unique Mexican fungus, which not without reason has been described as the "Mexican truffle"). The most exciting dish, and truly a rare find, is the chile en nogada, a kind of chile relleno, filled with a mixture of spiced, chopped meat and dried fruits; a creamy nut sauce with a few candied cherries top the finished product, which, can only be called rewardingly bizarre. The menu includes many steaks or steak-based dishes, most of them good. The puntas in chipotle, or chunks of filet in chile sauce, is as satisfying as can be. The subtle sauce used for the chicken mole packs a punch. You'll spend about $15 for dinner.

12/20 Il Fornaio
Del Mar Plaza, 1555 Camino Del Mar, Del Mar 92014; (619) 755-8876
Italian. Lunch & Dinner daily, Late Supper Fri.-Sat., Brunch Sun. All major cards.

One of the most stunning success stories in the history of San Diego restaurants, Il Fornaio seems always full. The location in ultra-chic Del Mar Plaza certainly helps draw crowds. Il Fornaio's cool marbled interior and superb outdoor terrace—which boasts a fine view of the Pacific and may be the choicest outdoor eating area on the coast—also helps. The third constant attraction is the heavily laden bread basket, which boasts an enormous assortment of loaves, along with crispy sesame-coated bread sticks. Some of the dough also is rolled into crusts for the fine pizzas that bake in the wood-burning oven. The pastas are uneven in quality, although the dish of ravioli in sage butter tweaks the nose with a savory herbal scent, and the baked casserole of macaroni, peas, ham and cheeses has a rustic appeal on cool evenings. Very much a grill, Il Fornaio turns out a juicy, mustard-coated chicken and nicely finished fish. Dinner per person is about $20.

George's at the Cove
1250 Prospect St., La Jolla 92037;
(619) 454-4244
New American. Lunch & Dinner daily, Brunch Sun. All major cards.

In many respects, this is the best restaurant in La Jolla. George's offers serious dining on the first floor, heavy flirting in the second floor bar and, on the new roof terrace, inexpensive but exciting open-air dining in full view of glorious La Jolla Cove. The town's only triple-decker eatery, George's has had but one chef, Scott Meskan, in its decade of operation, and the menus evolve reliably with his changes in taste; Meskan is fond of seafood, and we're fond of what he does with it, especially in preparations inspired by Asian and Southwestern cuisines. The marinated king salmon always makes the taste buds sit up and take notice.

The extravagant downstairs room is very much a meeting place for chic La Jollans, but everyone finds the terrace more fun. The food there, simple but excellent, runs to Meskan's interpretations of all-American favorites and includes fish tacos with aïoli and a smashing applewood-smoked pork loin in eye-tearing barbecue sauce. The wine list offers a huge selection of moderately priced Chardonnays and Cabernets, with just a smattering of French and Italian bottles—all listed from least expensive to most, which, if a bit gauche, is helpful for the budget-conscious diner. Dinner on the terrace runs $15 per person, about $30 in the main dining room.

La Gran Tapa
611 B St., San Diego 92101; (619) 234-8272
Spanish. Lunch Mon.-Fri., Dinner Mon.-Sat., Late Supper Fri.-Sat. All major cards.

This handsome downtown spot changed hands before we went to press. They continue to serve a comprehensive menu of tapas (or Spanish "bites"), including a number of shrimp preparations; good fried calamari; lime-marinated, deep-fried chunks of shark; chicken livers cooked in sherry; assorted Spanish sausages; and the flat potato omelet known as a tortilla. There are main dishes as well: paella brings the traditional bed of saffron rice with chicken, chorizo, shrimp, octopus, clams and mussels; zarzuela brings all the same tasty chunks of chicken and seafood, but in a saffron broth. Bullfight posters and low lights set the mood, and the young crowd comes to have a good time, toasting each other with glasses of Spanish wine and sherry. On average, dinner costs $15 to $20 per person.

Grant Grill at U.S. Grant Hotel

326 Broadway, Downtown (S.D.) 92101; (619) 239-6806
French. Breakfast, Lunch & Dinner daily, Brunch Sat.-Sun. All major cards.

If San Diego can be said to have a landmark restaurant, the Grant Grill is it. A quintessentially male, clubby establishment, the room banned women during the lunch hour until a still-celebrated invasion, staged in the late 1960's by five high-powered women, broke down the gender barriers erected by generations of bankers and politicians. It remains very much the spot for power lunches, although we like it best at dinner, when the mood is as relaxed as the deep, plush padding of the banquettes. Frenchman Bernard Guillas, has ruled the Grant Grill range for several years; his use of top-quality ingredients extends to fresh Californian foie gras with caramelized pears, bobwhite quail poised on a pancake of wild rice, grapes and bananas, and grilled escolar (an uncommon Florida fish, moist and delicate) banded with sesame and poppy seeds and doused with a sauce chartreuse, or an essence of fresh herbs thinned with a touch of cream. Two very traditional offerings, the mock turtle soup and the Grant Grill salad (basically a Caesar, and done with real style) have been on the menu for decades and remain classics of their kind. Dinner costs $35 or so per person.

Marius at Le Meridien

2000 2nd St., Coronado 92118; (619) 435-3000
French. Dinner Tues.-Sun. All major cards.

At Marius, probably as close to an Acropolis of contemporary French haute cuisine as any local eatery approaches, the rules of nouvelle cuisine still apply. The talent in this kitchen, and the greater talent that directs it from Paris, are formidable, and many preparations have forced us to pause in admiration. Consider the single teaspoon of bitter chocolate ice cream, chintzy in portion but unimaginably exquisite, garnishes a purse-like crêpe stuffed with pears. All other issues aside, it is virtually impossible in San Diego

County to find such magnificent, stunning presentations as those we have come to take for granted at Marius.

In keeping with the policy of Le Meridien hotels, the menus are written and the kitchen supervised by a consulting chef, in this case Jean-Marie Meulien of the admired Clos Longchamp at Le Meridien Etoile in Paris; executive chef René Herbeck, formerly of Le Meridien in London, is the man constantly on the scene. Both do their jobs admirably. The menus change with the seasons, and it is impossible to predict what we will enjoy on our next visit, although it is highly likely that we will enjoy everything. Dishes we have admired include a Provençal-style presentation of ravioli stuffed with wild mushrooms, a sauté of sea scallops with fava beans and Cabernet Sauvignon sauce, roasted breast of Muscovy duck scented with Middle Eastern spices and, above all, the memorable lamb medallions in "cappuccino" sauce that brought not only a teasing taste of coffee to the meat, but included a wedge of cinnamon-flavored apples baked in the style of Anna potatoes. The smallest details receive major attention here, and there are many extras, including a tiny complimentary appetizer, a small pre-dessert and a plate of sweets with the check. We find that we pay handsomely for dining here, but we find the experience equal to the price. Dinner costs $45 per person.

Mille Fleurs

6009 Paseo Delicias, Rancho Santa Fe 92067; (619) 756-3085
French. Lunch Mon.-Fri., Dinner nightly. All major cards.

The wine list at this elegant, extravagant and expensive temple of fine dining causes most connoisseurs to swoon, although it never quite pleased a now-notorious bank swindler who once dined here daily and complained about the absence of bottles priced above $700. The immensely wealthy, the would-be rich and not a few con artists are all drawn by the scent of money to the shady roads of this eucalyptus-forested estate community, and most wind up at one of Bertrand Hug's tables eating tiny, perfect vegetables from nearby Chino's Farm, pared with whatever delicacies chef Martin Woesle has devised for the day's menu. Woesle builds plates, rather than entrées, and every kernel of corn is arranged just so for maximum effect. The veal loin with forest mushrooms is luscious, the tart scallop salad refreshes, the lamb is succulent and infused with herbs. Woesle's desserts tease rather than overwhelm, and if anything, are a little too light—but the pistachio crêpes with blood oranges and white-chocolate sauce never disappoint. The 25-page wine list is largely French and Californian; smaller spenders will find a handful of bottles in the $20-to-$30 range, but for those clients such as our banking friend, there's no lack of choice, from big-vintage Burgundies for $430 to a 1970 Château Pétrus Bordeaux for $850. Dinner costs $40 or more per person.

12/20 Montana's

1421 University Ave., Hillcrest (S.D.) 92103; (619) 297-0722
New American. Lunch Mon.-Sat., Dinner nightly. D, DC, MC, V.

This extraordinarily popular Hillcrest eatery subtitles itself "an American grill," and almost anything that can be cooked over hardwood coals arrives branded with cross-hatched markings. The starters at Montana's run to such dishes as grilled Anaheim chiles stuffed with three cheeses. Among other good starters are the smoked trout and Pacific steelhead with lemon-caper mayonnaise, and the smoked duck cakes in roasted bell pepper sauce. One of this restaurant's innovations is the daily mixed grill of three items, some made especially that day and some drawn from the regular menu; this works better some days than others, and seems best when based on meat rather than seafood. The grill cook knows his meats, and chars Porterhouse and lamb chops to a fine finish. A master-touch with desserts might seem unlikely for a grill, but Montana's perhaps does best of all in this department, notably with the amazing chocolate tart in caramel sauce and the superb fruit cobblers. Dinner costs about $30 per person.

10/20 Osteria Panevino

722 Fifth Ave., San Diego 92101; (619) 595-7959
Italian. Lunch Mon.-Fri., Dinner nightly. All major cards.

Sicilian-born Alessandro Minutella has brought yet another new style of Italian cookery to the Gaslamp Quarter, and we thank him for it. Exceptional among his offerings are the unusual stuffed *foccacia*, which are twin discs of pizza dough that sandwich light vegetable fillings. Minutella also offers superb vegetable antipasti and simple but enjoyable pastas; there about ten wines (Californian and Italian) by the glass. We very much enjoy whiling away an afternoon or evening at one of the sidewalk tables. A pasta dinner can cost about $18 per person; with a more expensive entrée you'll spend $30 or so.

Pacifica Del Mar

Del Mar Plaza, 1555 Camino Del Mar, Ste. 321, Del Mar 92014; (619) 792-0476
Californian/Pacific Rim. Lunch & Dinner daily. All major cards.

The youngest member of a local chain that also operates the likeable Café Pacifica in Old Town and the more sophisticated Pacifica Grill in downtown San Diego, Pacifica Del Mar boasts an ocean view rivaled by a few local restaurants, a sleek and stylish decor and a menu that ranges from the reliable to the exciting. New chef Jacky Sloane, born and raised in Ireland, took over as we went to press. Her cuisine, like that of her predecessor, is a mélange of Californian, Asian and Southwestern themes: resulting in such items as Gulf shrimp spring rolls with a ginger-plum purée, warm goat-cheese salad with cornmeal-encrusted tomatoes, wok-charred catfish with red-pepper fettuccine and so on. Entrées are slightly more straightforward, most of them based around grilled fish or meat. Like everyone else, we prefer seating on the all-weather terrace, which features quaint downtown Del Mar in the foreground and rolling breakers just beyond. A dinner costs about $30.

10/20 The Palms

8008 Girard Ave., La Jolla 92037; (619) 454-8884
Pacific Rim. Breakfast, Lunch & Dinner daily. Brunch Sat.-Sun. All major cards.

Neil Stuart, formerly executive chef for San Diego's home-grown Pacifica restaurants, finally has opened his own eatery. We wish that this inventive chef had created a few additional new items for his menu, since most dishes are drawn from the menus he wrote for the Pacifica establishments. Still, we can applaud his *takeshimi*, an Asian *taco* of crisp won-ton wrappers and ahi, the Yucatán-style barbecued king salmon and the grilled lamb chile, a layered dish of spiced black beans, lamb loin and crumbled goat cheese. Most tables enjoy spectacular views of La Jolla Cove, which at some restaurants is considered more than sufficient enticement. A dinner costs about $20.

Rainwater's

1202 Kettner Blvd., Downtown (S.D.) 92101; (619) 233-5757
American. Lunch Mon.-Fri., Dinner nightly. All major cards.

Aside from the chain feederies, steakhouses seem very much a dying breed in San Diego. The exception is Rainwater's, an establishment on the grand scale that comfortably displays the belief that "more is better" every time it serves an immense Kansas City strip or a Chicago-style pepper filet. Given the times, seafood has been given a place of equal prominence on the menu, generally in the guise of lavish steaks, of the many fish of the day, grilled and dressed with herbed butter or a very light sauce. In all cases, the absolute top quality of the raw ingredients—and the lavishness of the servings—are the keys to Rainwater's style. The management's Midwestern connections show up in one speciality, the "mess of fried perch," in this instance line-caught in Minnesota and Wisconsin lakes. The black-bean soup is a minor triumph of the genre, and the hot-fudge sundae, simple but utterly decadent, seems absolutely the perfect conclusion. Power brokers and other well-heeled types dine in the unimaginably deep banquettes. Dinner costs $35 per person.

Rancho Valencia Resort Dining Room

5921 Valencia Circle, Rancho Santa Fe 92067; (619) 756-1123
Mediterranean. Breakfast, Lunch & Dinner daily, Brunch Sun. All major cards.

This ultraluxurious resort in the North County hills between chic Del Mar and ultra-rich Rancho Santa Fe has undergone a few changes in the past couple of years, including the introduction of new management and a brief working relationship with Bay Area super-chef Bradley Ogden in 1991. In the summer of 1992, the menu switched from American to Mediterranean: starters are clever creations with clever names, such as a gazpacho "napoleon" with a yellow-pepper coulis or a wild-mushroom "cappuccino," actually a soup. The main-course menu offers mostly French preparations, often with a twist, such as veal tournedos with wild-mushroom strudel, seared Norwegian salmon in a sesame crust or roasted lamb tenderloin in a rosemary-thyme sauce. The extensive wine list is all Californian, French and Italian—starting at $30 bottles and continuing upward to $900. Dinner costs about $35 per person.

12/20 Restaurante del Bol Corona

Puebla Amigo Center, 60 Via Oriente, Tijuana, Mexico; No phone
Mexican. Lunch & Dinner daily. MC, V.

Tijuana residents constantly brag about new restaurant finds, but just as in the United States, most places seem to shift with the tradewinds and relatively few are reliable over the long run. This increasingly cosmopolitan border city does offer a spectacular array of choices, and if you follow the general rule of avoiding each and every place packed with young Americans wearing straw

hats, you should eat well to very well. A good stop after a day of shopping and sightseeing is the Restaurante del Bol Corona in Plaza Amigo, located just a few hundred yards short of the United States border; this is a branch of a small, local chain that was founded in the 1930s that claims, apparently with reason, to have invented the burrito. These burritos, rolled in freshly made flour tortillas of amazing flavor, include numerous fillings, notably succulent shrimp braised in a mildy hot sauce and machaca, or shredded beef scrambled with eggs and bits of hot chile pepper. Other excellent choices include the chicken in mole sauce and the tender carne asada. Skip the Caesar salad. The place is a bargain, even in relatively inexpensive Tijuana; a dinner costs from $5 to $10 per person.

10/20 Salvatore's

750 Front St. (corner of G St.), San Diego 92101; (619) 544-1865
Italian. Lunch Mon.-Fri., Dinner nightly. All major cards.

While proprietor Salvatore Gangale presses well-manicured flesh in the posh dining rooms at downtown's posh Meridian tower, his wife, Raffaella, pounds veal scallops into the thinnest possible medallions, stuffs the meat with shreds of prosciutto and cheese, and finishes the sautéed cuscinetti ("cushions") with a sauce of tomato, peas and mushrooms. The Gangales, sophisticated émigrés from Rome, were the first to introduce to San Diego the cosmopolitan, pan-Italian sort of menu typical of their native city. Raffaella puts great effort into presentations (except in the case of the pastas, which are tasty if not pretty): the Caterina de Medici salad, if a bit typical in its combination of radicchio, Belgian endive, capers and olives, blends colors and shapes beautifully. Specialties include the seafood-rich spaghetti Trasteverina, baked in a fish-shaped foil wrapping that releases the briny fragrance when pierced at the table, and an entrée of prawns with a bitter, pungent glaze of lemon and orange. The service could be better at times, but the restaurant's location across from the deluxe Paladion shopping center is undeniably choice. A dinner costs about $30.

Sante

7811 Herschel Ave., La Jolla 92037; (619) 454-1315
Italian. Lunch Mon.-Fri., Dinner nightly. All major cards.

We can never decide whether we prefer to be seated in the small formal dining room or at the fireside table in the brick-walled bar, but we are certain that as long as Gaetano Buonsante stuffs ravioli with minced quail, and sauces a dozen or so of them with the remarkable mushroom sauce called funghetto, we will order them. San Diego now boasts several dozen sophisticated Italian houses, but each has its own style. Sante's appeal is its low-key elegance—in the service, decor and cuisine. Crustaceans falsely called "scampi" clutter local restaurant menus, but Sante actually imports the genuine article from the Adriatic and sautés it ever so gently. Wild boar chops require rougher handling, supplied by a perfumed marinade and a strong sauce of onions, mushrooms and juniper berries. The selection of veal is bountiful; Gaetano will cook any Italian veal preparation requested. The pasta list offers some unusual choices, notably broad pappardelle in a creamy, pungent and somewhat racy fennel sauce. Dinner costs about $30 per person.

12/20 Sfuzzi
340 Fifth Ave., Gaslamp Quarter,
Downtown (S.D.) 92101; (619) 231-2323
Italian. Lunch & Dinner daily, Late Supper Fri.-Sat., Brunch Sun. All major cards.

Although this new place in the trendy Gaslamp Quarter looks suspiciously like a yuppie watering hole—and a fair amount of action does take place at the bar—the management takes food seriously. It's a most attractive, cleverly decorated room, an ideal stage for the light and modern Italian fare, such as the simple but fine appetizer of grilled asparagus and Portabella mushrooms with garlic relish, or the pasta with piquantly marinated winter vegetables. The Tuscan bean soup is warming on a typically cool San Diego evening, and very richly flavored. There are fragile pizzas (and also excellent breads) from the wood-burning oven, and among fish, the grilled salmon with sautéed baby artichokes and lemon-chive sauce is an unusual preparation, and very pleasing. The kitchen does best with meats, however, the two standouts being a beef filet with peppered Chianti sauce and garlic-flavored mashed potatoes, and veal scallops with forest mushrooms, a plush brown sauce and crisp risotto cakes. The desserts seem to have been built with Gargantua in mind, and are ever so rich; the

---

For a complete guide to our restaurant ranking system, plus a Toque Tally listing restaurants by rating from highest to lowest, see "About the Restaurants" in the INTRODUCTION.

---

apple-blueberry cobbler with vanilla-bean gelato does the trick nicely. Dinner costs $25 or so per person.

Top of the Cove
1216 Prospect St., La Jolla 92037;
(619) 454-7779
French. Lunch Mon.-Sat., Dinner nightly, Brunch Sun. All major cards.

Traditions swirl around the historic bungalow that houses this charming restaurant. Now 40 years old (management has changed several times in that period), it is a good restaurant, no longer a great one, but it remains one of the few destinations that offers formality in setting and service, a fabulous view of La Jolla Cove, and, for many, associations of romance. Chef Julius Seman cooks a traditional menu, updated in many respects, which he supplements with low-calorie, low-sodium offerings created in the same luxurious mood. A true luxury restaurant, and one of the most expensive in San Diego County, this is a good place for sautéed foie gras, a wonderfully lobstery lobster bisque, roasted leg of lamb and careful seafood preparations. On the light side are such dishes as venison filet in blueberry sauce and poulet mistral, or Provençal-style chicken, with shellfish, tomatoes and garlic. Plan to spend about $40 for a dinner.

Trastevere
5662 La Jolla Blvd., La Jolla 92037;
(619) 551-8610
Italian. Lunch Mon.-Fri., Dinner nightly. MC, V.

The first West Coast entry of a Rome-born family that now operates four restaurants in New York, Trastevere is unique in its menu of dishes developed in the ancient and still extant Jewish quarter in Rome. Originally developed in accordance with the strict Kosher laws of Jewish cooking (these laws are not observed by this kitchen, however), this is Italian cooking given a light touch, and some preparations are exquisite, especially the appetizer of baby artichokes pan fried with much garlic. We have never eaten better lamb than the baby chops sautéed with rosemary, and among fish, the red snapper in a sweet-sour sauce of raisins and vinegar is unusual and pleasing. On the non-Jewish side of the menu, the appetizer called spiedino stands out; this is a fluffy, omelet-like cheese mixture doused in an amazing brown sauce studded with capers and bits of prosciutto and anchovy. We also love the vitello Trastevere, a chop pounded thin, breaded, fried, and topped with wedges of bell pepper and

Winesellar & Brasserie
9550 Waples St., Sorrento Mesa (S.D.)
92121; (619) 450-9557
New American. Lunch Tues.-Sat., Dinner Tues.-Sun. MC, V.

You'd never know by its location in a light industrial park in a less-than-fashionable part of town, but the Brasserie serves consistently satisfying, occasionally brilliant cuisine, and the downstairs Winesellar (actually a wine cellar) has built one of the most impressive wine collections in the country. In addition to an extensive selection of mostly French and Californian bottles (many of them priced under $35), the cellar's shelves are stocked with hundreds of rare vintage bottles, from old Bordeaux to 1921 Sauternes to rare sherries and Madeiras.

No wonder that the restaurant attracts a steady, loyal clientele. They come again and again to enjoy the thoughtful, contemporary creations of chef/proprietor Doug Organ, who at age 31 ranks as one of the county's four best. Organ designs dishes that rely on all their elements for success; for example, the salmon with curried green lentils would be great but not perfect without the steamed Italian parsley that finishes the plate. Among appetizers, the wild-rice pancake with pan-roasted sweetbreads and onion confit is a marvel, a description that also suits the home-cured duck prosciutto with blood oranges and bitter greens. Roasted saddle of monkfish pleases with its meaty texture and high-rising crown of fried potato wisps, and the Brasserie's version of osso buco—braised in Madeira and joined by braised tiny pasta—is about as good as veal shank gets. Organ also constructs exceptional desserts, and on Sundays offers a three-course, fixed-price dinner. Dinner costs $35 per person.

And Also . . .

The Boondocks, 8320 Parkway Dr., La Mesa 92042; (619) 465-3660. *Steakhouse. Dinner nightly. All major cards.* San Diego is jammed with restaurants that serve steaks, grilled fish, chicken teriyaki, prime rib, salad and cheesecake. This perfectly describes The Boondocks (so named because it's hidden in the corner of a nondescript shopping center), except that this restaurant is a notch above the rest, turning out fine steaks and a rich, silken Cheddar-cheese soup. Dinner, $20.

Café Pacifica, 2414 San Diego Ave., San Diego 92104; (619) 291-6666. *Californian. Lunch Mon.-Fri., Dinner nightly. All major cards.* The first and smallest of the three Pacifica restaurants, this place is a good bet when we want to dine in Old Town. The menu takes a fairly inventive path and specializes in seafood; at time of publication, it was undergoing considerable revision by a new chef. The seafood is always unquestionably among the freshest possible, and the crème brulée is one of the best in the city. Dinner costs $20 to $25 per person.

Canes California Bistro, 1270 Cleveland St., Hillcrest (S.D.) 92103; (619) 299-3551. *Californian/French. Lunch & Dinner daily, Brunch Sun. All major cards.* A popular bistro with a varied menu of gourmet pizzas, hearty salads, American dishes and easygoing French bistro fare, all of it appreciated by a young, trendy crowd. The wine list and spectacular Cognac selections seem out of place for the location, but they almost justify a visit in their own right. Dinner, $20.

Five Star Cuisine, 816 Broadway, Downtown (S.D.) 92101; (619) 231-4408. *Thai. Lunch Tues.-Fri., Dinner Tues.-Sun. All major cards.* A chic decor in a not-so-great part of downtown is made up for by excellent curries, noodle dishes and satays. Ask for one of the many daily house specials—you won't be disappointed. If you order your food spicy, your mouth may burn for the rest of the day. Dinner costs less than $15 per person.

Kaiserhof, 5351 Adobe Falls Rd., Mission Valley (S.D.) 92120; (619) 287-3075. *German. Lunch Tues.-Sat., Dinner Tues.-Sun. MC, V.* The gemütlichkeit flows most evenings, when polkas roll off the piano, and diners raise glasses in honor of the huge plates of schnitzel, wursts, and other traditional fare. Anyone who enjoys German cooking will find all the expected flavors intact, and all the garnishes (including gossamer-light dumplings), served in abundance. The sauerbraten and braised ox tail are first-rate. Dinner, about $20 per person.

Panda Inn, 2506 Horton Plaza, Downtown (S.D.) 92101; (619) 233-7800. *Chinese. Lunch & Dinner daily. All major cards.* One of the most attractive Chinese restaurants in San Diego, it also has among the best food, a menu that goes well beyond the usuals, and a fine location high atop Horton Plaza. Old standbys like steamed dumplings and Szechuan beef are very good; also try the "burned" pork and the expert noodle dishes. Dinner, $15 per person.

Piatti, 2182 Avenida de la Playa, La Jolla 92037; (619) 454-1589. *Italian. Lunch & Dinner daily, Brunch Sun. MC, V.* The menu at this new-style Italian house (with successful branches in San Francisco, Carmel and Santa Barbara) revolves around pasta and good pizzas. This one is a very popular neighborhood spot for La Jolla Shores residents. Ready yourself for a lively (actually noisy) evening. Dinner costs about $20 per person.

Saska's, 3768 Mission Blvd., Mission Beach (S.D.) 92109; (619) 488-7311. *American. Lunch & Dinner daily. All major cards.* No place captures the essence and flavor of old Mission Beach like this dark, woodsy, atmosphere-laden favorite, founded in the 1950s by the sizeable Saska family. The food tastes best at the beach, especially the thick, aged steaks. The waiters wear shorts in the depth of winter, and you can, too. Dinner, $25.

Bargain Bites

American

Corvette Diner, Bar & Grill
3946 Fifth Ave., Hillcrest (S.D.) 92103;
(619) 542-1001
*Breakfast, Lunch & Dinner daily, Late Supper Fri.-Sat.
MC, V.*

The classic Corvette displayed at the entry to the main dining room attracts a lot of attention, although we would rather turn to the soda fountain, which turns out one of the last genuine malted milks in San Diego. Crowds regularly form down the block in front of this large, noisy, frenetically paced Hillcrest establishment, which takes its mood, menu and decor from the 1950's. The waitresses all seem to be auditioning for a role in *Grease*. The burgers probably are the best bet, but other sandwiches are decent, and regulars like the meatloaf and the chicken-fried steak. You'll get out for $10 per person.

D.Z. Akins
6930 Alvarado Rd., State College District (S.D.) 92115; (619) 265-0218
Breakfast, Lunch & Dinner daily. MC, V.

A classic Jewish delicatessen-restaurant, this cavernous place feeds hundreds daily in coffee shop-like surroundings. The noise sometimes is so deafening that we can hardly hear ourselves chew the high-rising corned beef and pastrami sandwiches, both good if not excellent. The corned beef hash disappoints, but the chopped chicken livers and the chicken soup with giant matzoh ball are right on the mark. This menu covers eight pages and includes hundreds of listings, including well more than one hundred sandwiches. Breakfast items are good and available throughout the day. Plan to spend no more than $10 per person.

Hard Rock Café
909 Prospect St., La Jolla 92037;
(619) 454-5101
Lunch & Dinner daily, Late Supper Fri.-Sat. All major cards.

The local outpost of the international chain. A young crowd comes to gawk at all the rock 'n' roll memorabilia (and one another, to be sure), and to shout over rock music that can be mind-numbing for anyone over 30. Even so, it's always great fun, and most of the menu—burgers, lime-grilled chicken, sandwiches, crispy fries and creamy-rich milkshakes. About $10 buys a meal.

Asian

The **Convoy Street** neighborhood in **Kearny Mesa** has become one of San Diego's two major Asian melting pots, and certainly offers the better dining choices. These aren't grand restaurants—many are barely comfortable—but it is possible to literally follow your nose from block to block and discover tiny Japanese noodle house, Vietnamese soup cafés, the tiniest Laotian and Cambodian eateries, good Chinese dim sum and some authentic and often daunting Korean fare. One good bet is **Arirang House**, at 4681 Convoy St., Kearny Mesa (S.D.) 92111; (619) 277-8625 (Lunch & Dinner daily. MC, V.) Its primarily Korean clientele chows down on barbecued beef, stewed chicken, meats and fish, and tofu and seafood casseroles, all accompanied by a dozen kim-chee pickles and relishes, served by the speediest staff in town. This is a good choice for novices in the cuisine, because the menu seems all-inclusive. About $15 will buy a dinner.

Mexican & Latin American

Berta's Latin American Restaurant
3928 Twigg St., Old Town (S.D.) 92103;
(619) 295-2343
Lunch & Dinner daily. All major cards.

An attempt to represent the cuisine of two-thirds of a hemisphere on one menu might seem vain, but Berta's, a tiny, modest but comfortable eatery on the edge of Old Town, is aided in its effort by the common features in a cooking idiom that stretches from Tijuana and El Paso all the way to Tierra del Fuego. The Mexican dishes, by and large, are the least interesting; San Diego in any case has hundreds of Mexican eateries. But the Chilean pastel del choclo, a casserole of richly spiced meat baked under a soufflé-like corn crust, is absolutely delicious, followed in short order by the Peruvian lamb stew. Also interesting are the Brazilian tallarines, of pasta in a ginger-flavored sauce, and the spicy orange salad. About $15 buys a huge meal.

El Indio
4120 Mission Blvd., Pacific Beach (S.D.) 92109;
(619) 272-8226
Lunch & Dinner daily. D, MC, V.

Part of a highly regarded local chain with several locations, this branch offers the ambience of Pacific Beach along with a menu of simple, traditional Mexican fare. San Diego's city representatives in government have the tortilla chips sent to them in Washington and Sacramento. The fish tacos, chicken burritos, cheese enchiladas and other items all draw crowds. Diners will spend about $10 each.

Machupicchu

4755 Voltaire St., Ocean Beach (S.D.) 92107; (619) 222-2656
Dinner Mon. & Wed.-Sun. MC, V.

By all means avoid the dessert of frijol colado, or mashed beans sprinkled with sesame, but feel free to sample most other dishes at this very modest but quite pleasant café in the funky Ocean Beach neighborhood. The fried papa rellena appetizer encases a spicy meat mixture in a smooth potato dough, while the anticuchos, or skewers of grilled beef heart, are strictly for daredevils. The lomo saltado, a sauté of beef, onions, tomatoes and peppers, is satisfyingly simple, and there is a fine richness to the aji de gallina, or stewed hen in creamy nut sauce. The flan, a dessert shared by all Latin cuisines, is far better than most, and infinitely preferable to the frijol colado. About $15 buys a dinner.

Palenque

1653 Garnet Ave., Pacific Beach (S.D.) 92109; (619) 272-7816
Lunch & Dinner daily. All major cards.

Many of the unusual regional Mexican recipes here come from the private cookbooks of the proprietor's family, and cannot be found at other San Diego restaurants. The spicy beef salad, tortilla soup and chicken in mole sauce should make any aficionado of good south-of-the-border fare quite happy. Dinner costs $15 per person.

Pizza

Sammy's California Woodfired Pizza

702 Pearl St., La Jolla 92037; (619) 456-5222
Lunch & Dinner daily. MC, V.

The restaurant that brought wood-fired pizza to San Diego still does it best, with a menu designed by Ed LaDou, the man who helped Wolfgang Puck invent his list of unique pies. Simple but excellent fare has given this airy, casual eatery so loyal a following that waits for tables are common. Salads and pastas are offered, but the stars of the show are the pizzas, garnished variously with Beijing duck and hoisin sauce, or Mexican lime-marinated chicken and guacamole. Purists

> *For more ideas on money-saving meals, see the listing of restaurants under "$15 & Under" in the INDEXES section at the back of the book.*

will find the New York-style pepperoni pie perfect. Even the desserts are monumental and memorable: the masterwork is the "Messy (and they mean messy) Chocolate Sundae." About $15 buys a dinner.

Hotels

A major resort destination, San Diego offers a comprehensive selection of accommodations, ranging from the elegant and costly to clean but spare establishments that cater to budget-minded travelers. The following selection highlights several of the best and includes quite a few quieter, smaller less expensive inns and bed-and-breakfasts in addition to the top-of-the-line resorts and chain hotels.

The symbol that accompanies each review indicates in which price category the hotel belongs: **Top of the Line** ($200 & Up), **Luxury** ($150 & Up), **Moderate** ($100 & Up) or **Practical** (Under $100). We have defined the categories based on the regular starting price of a single or double room. *See also* the INTRODUCTION chapter, under "About the Hotels."

Top of the Line ($200 & Up)

The Inn L'Auberge Del Mar

1540 Camino Del Mar, Del Mar 92014; (619) 259-1515, Fax (619) 755-4940
Singles & Doubles $195-$250, Suites $325-$750. All major cards.

Since the 1920s, all the right-thinking rich people knew there was but one place to stay in Del Mar: the Del Mar Hotel. But eventually the salt air took its toll. Then, a few years back, new owners tore the old place down and started over again, building this attractive 117-room pseudo-country estate and giving it a redundant name (it's like calling an Italian restaurant "Restaurant Ristorante"). It doesn't have quite the glamourous celebrity cachet it once did, but there's no doubting that The Inn L'Auberge is the best place to stay in town, ideally located near the beach and mere steps from the sun-splashed shopping and dining mecca, the Del Mar Plaza. The manor-house look of the lobby, bar and restaurant is continued in the rooms, the best of which have fireplaces and ocean views. Active sorts will appreciate the tennis courts, pool and spa; overworked businesspeople will appreciate the hushed atmosphere and nice staff.

Rancho Valencia Resort

5921 Valencia Circle, Rancho Santa Fe
92067; (619) 756-1123, Fax (619) 756-0165
Suites $365-$2,000. All major cards.

A few miles inland from Del Mar lies one of the poshest resorts to hit California since Meadowood. It's home to just 43 huge suites and cottages, each a Mediterranean vision of Mexican satillo tiles, terraces, beamed ceilings, fireplaces, French doors, plantation shutters and much, much more. Tennis is the obsession of choice here—there are eighteen courts and a variety of lessons and clinics—but the resort is so beautifully sited and landscaped, so peaceful and well designed that even tennisphobes will have a great time. Guests may swim, play croquet, ride bikes, stroll the surrounding hillsides, enjoy a massage, dine in the very good restaurant (*see* review in "SAN DIEGO Restaurants") or just snooze in one of the lovely suites. This place is not for the lean of wallet, but it's worth the splurge.

Luxury ($150 & Up)

Hotel del Coronado

1500 Orange Ave., Coronado 92118;
(619) 435-6611, Fax (619) 522-8238
*Singles & Doubles $149-$345, Suites $385-$535.
All major cards.*

Though a bit rough around the edges, the Hotel del Coronado remains one of San Diego's most beloved hostelries. The world's largest wooden structure is also the area's most recognized landmark, and despite its shabbiness, it continues to play its generations-old role as a favorite honeymoon hideaway and weekend retreat. The Victorian architecture recalls the extravagance of that age so well that the hotel conducts daily walking tours of the premises. The turret rooms supposedly house ghosts (but certainly not in summer, when these rooms can be unbearably stuffy), and the lobby bar provides a superb vantage point for people-watching. This full-scale resort is really a self-contained community; you'll never have to leave the hotel. The main building abounds in shops, the two restaurants are acceptable (if far from great), and the Ocean Terrace Room features live music and dancing nightly. The hotel has its own tennis courts and immense pool. Since it was built during a more gracious era, the rooms are out-sized by contemporary standards, and are comfortable enough. Nostalgia buffs will feel right at home. The new tower unfortunately has none of the Del's Victorian charm.

Loews Coronado Bay Resort

4000 Coronado Bay Rd., Coronado 92118;
(619) 424-4000, Fax (619) 424-4400
Singles & Doubles $180-$395, Suites $600-$1,250. All major cards.

Renowned architect C.W. Kim's most recent addition to the San Diego cityscape (he also designed the much-ballyhooed Emerald-Shapery Center and Pan Pacific Hotel) features deluxe accommodations in one of the city's lovliest locales. Equipped with its own private marina, the resort attracts its share of yachters and boating enthusiasts. Built on a spit of land that juts into the southern end of the San Diego Bay, the hotel offers 440 well-appointed rooms, many with water views. A dramatic view that many visitors may not expect is south to the hills of Tijuana, which is a mere ten-minute drive away. Public areas are designed in the airy, gracious style that characterized the grand resorts built at the turn of the century. The ambience here is one of relaxed elegance, rather than stiff formality. The Azzura Point dining room (*see* review in "SAN DIEGO Restaurants"), one of the finest in San Diego, serves dinner only, but the more casual RRR's Café offers continuous, resaonably priced meal service from early morning until late at night.

Le Meridien

2000 2nd St., Coronado 92118;
(619) 435-3000, Fax (619) 435-3032
Singles & Doubles $165-$225, Suites & Villas $325-$625. All major cards.

This stylish waterfront resort is a stunner, to say the least. Located on sixteen San Diego Bay waterfront acres, the hotel sits at the foot of the Coronado Bay Bridge and next to a lovely twenty-acre park and beach. The lobby and public areas are decorated in a tropical mode, with sun-washed pastel walls and oversized wicker furniture. There are 300 guest rooms and seven executive suites, as well as a 28-unit villa complex. The villas, with their own private pool and spa, are definitely worth the splurge. The other guest rooms are equipped with terraces and minibars. There are extensive meeting and banquet facilities, as well as a fully equipped business center; athletic guests are catered to with six lighted tennis courts, three swimming pools, two spas and bicycles for hire. There are other recreations that can be arranged, such as golf (at a championship course across the street), yachting, sportfishing and moped rentals. Le Meridien also has a fully equipped gym and a Clarins Institut de Beauté, offering facials, massages and other beauty services. The hotel's premier restaurant,

Marius features excellent Provençal cuisine (*see* review in "SAN DIEGO Restaurants"), and there's also a more casual brasserie, L'Escale, overlooking the bay, that serves breakfast, lunch, dinner and afternoon tea.

 ### Sheraton Grande Torrey Pines
10950 N. Torrey Pines Rd., La Jolla 92037; (619) 558-1500, Fax (619) 450-4584
Singles & Doubles $165-$250, Suites $400-$2,500. All major cards.

Want to quit smoking, get a medical exam at neighboring Scripps Hospital, meet the top guns of the U.S. Navy, learn windsurfing, go up in a hot-air balloon, watch the migrating whales, angle for the big ones, sail with Dennis Conner, enter a croquet tournament, golf with a PGA pro? No problem, just ask the "activities director." He can suit your whims all the more easily since these are regularly scheduled (though not free of charge) activities. They don't want you to get bored on this bluff, where this reasonably luxurious hotel is perched, overlooking a golf course and Pacific in the distance. Inside, the architect has harmoniously mixed Rajah slate, granite, golden cherry wood and burnished copper. The place also hosts many a banquet and wedding. Each of the 400 rooms and 18 suites has a view and, thanks to the serene environment, is very quiet. The Torreyana Grille is a large (190 seats), cool and relaxing setting for Jim Coleman's Southwestern cuisine.

Moderate ($100 & Up)

 ### Colonial Inn
910 Prospect St., La Jolla 92037; (619) 454-2181, Fax (619) 454-5679
Singles & Doubles $135-$155, Suites $198-$225. All major cards.

This building, beautifully restored to turn-of-the-century elegance, remains familiar to long-time La Jolla residents as the one-time location of Peck's Pharmacy, in which a yet-to-turn thespian Gregory Peck poured milkshakes at his father's soda fountain. Much less well known than its haughtier cousin down the street, the venerable and pink La Valencia hotel, the Colonial Inn shares the same exclusive neighborhood, the same easy access to fine shopping and dining and the same magnificent views—from west-facing rooms—of La Jolla Cove and the blue Pacific. (The ocean-view rooms and suites come at a higher rate, and are worth it.) The rooms, suffi-

ciently spacious, are well appointed and comfortable. Though the hotel offers relatively few services, it's in the heart of an exclusive neighborhood awash in service establishments. The dining room, Putnam's, serves a timid but reasonably well-prepared menu.

 ### Doubletree Hotel San Diego
910 Broadway Circle, San Diego 92101; (619) 239-2200, Fax (619) 239-0509
Singles $129-$159, Doubles $174-$200, Suites $300-$1,000.

The major advantage of this commercial, business-traveler's hotel is its central downtown location, adjacent to Horton Plaza and close to the principal office district and cultural venues. Ritzy shopping and fine dining are just minutes away, making it more than convenient for those with little time. There are a pool, spa, fitness center and two tennis courts. No shuttle service is necessary to downtown attractions because almost everything is within walking distance.

 ### Hyatt Islandia
14 W. Mission Bay Dr., San Diego 92109; (619) 224-1234, Fax (619) 224-0348
Singles $109-$170, Doubles $154-$195, Suites $160-$205. All major cards.

Conventioneers and meeting planners flock to this monolithic, 1960s-style hotel. Its attractions include lanai rooms and a tower that offers panoramic views of Mission Bay and the surrounding parklands. Mission Beach is just one-half mile to the west. Amenities include a convention center for about 500 people, with a ballroom; a pool and spa; and a dining room and a more casual café.

 ### Marriott Hotel & Marina
333 W. Harbor Dr., Downtown (S.D.) 92101; (619) 234-1500, Fax (619) 230-8978
Singles $130-$170, Doubles $150-$190, Suites $360-$620. All major cards.

This harborside resort counts more than 700 rooms in two gleaming high-rise towers; should you stay here, request a room in the elegantly decorated South tower. A pleasant surprise tucked into the court is a grand series of pools and waterfalls that looks as if it were on loan from a tropical resort. Waterside rooms boast spectacular views. Other advantages include proximity to waterfront attractions, the booming and bustling Gaslamp Quarter and indeed all of downtown San Diego, which in recent years has become the hub of the city. For those disinclined to walk, the San Diego trolley stops nearby and features convenient service to most downtown destinations, as well as to the International bor-

345

der with Mexico. The location next to the San Diego Convention Center can be a mixed blessing, since the hotel sometimes is taken over by groups that clog the numerous dining rooms, bars and other public spaces.

Pan Pacific Hotel
400 W. Broadway, Downtown (S.D.)
92101; (619) 239-4500, Fax (619) 239-4527
Singles $140-$150, Doubles $150-$170, Suites $320-$2,000. All major cards.

If you're flying into San Diego at night, you'll immediately spot the glowing neon-green bands encircling the hexagonal towers of the Emerald Shapery Center and Pan Pacific Hotel. Occupying the three towers facing Broadway, the hotel is a spectacle to behold from the outside, and striking inside. In the atrium court, a gargantuan structure of kelly-green glass and brass rods hangs from the ceiling, reflecting against sheets of copper mirroring placed everywhere. The rooms, however, decorated in soft, muted earth tones, are comfortable and subdued. The glass elevator is a quite a ride—it zooms upward without a sound. There are 436 rooms, including 19 suites. The businessperson will appreciate the fully equipped business benter, complete with word processing, secretarial service, office space, conference rooms and fax machines. Fitness buffs will enjoy the 4,000-square-foot health club with saunas and state-of-the-art exercise equipment. The hotel's dining room, The Grill, does a nice job with Pacific Rim cuisine.

Rancho Bernardo Inn
17550 Bernardo Oaks Dr., Rancho Bernardo
92128; (619) 487-1611, Fax (619) 673-0311
Singles & Doubles $125-$205, Suites $160-$600.

If your idea of a great escape it to park the Volvo and settle in for a few days of endless golf, broken up by the occasional tennis game, then check into this 287-room retreat in the hills east of Del Mar. There's nothing flashy or gimmicky about the place, just solid, tasteful comfort—the kind of place Ronald Reagan could settle down in comfortably. The look strives to capture that early California rancho feeling, but the amenities are far more luxurious than rustic. There's an eighteen-hole championship golf course, three nine-hole executive courses, pools, a fitness cen-

ter, spa, bicycles, a fancy restaurant (*see* review in "SAN DIEGO Restaurants"), free children's camps offered occasionally, and lots more.

Sheraton Grand on Harbor Island
1590 Harbor Island Dr., San Diego 92101;
(619) 291-6400, Fax (619) 543-0643
Singles $130-$175, Doubles $150-$195, Suites $210-$1,100. All major cards.

The Sheraton Grand, once known as the Sheraton Harbor Island West, appeals primarily to the business trade, since it is no more than two minutes from the airport and five minutes from downtown. A $15-million face-lift was designed to attract the luxury and leisure crowds as well, a market that may also be enticed by the quality of service and the small (200-room) size of the hotel. The Sheraton Grand features large, luxuriously furnished rooms, each of which include balconies that offer sweeping views of either San Diego Bay or the yacht harbor that fronts the north side of the building. Amenities include a full-time concierge service, a piano bar, a swimming pool and 24-hour room service. The hotel's stylish dining room, Spencer's, serves moderately priced steaks and seafood.

The U.S. Grant Hotel
326 Broadway, Downtown (S.D.) 92101;
(619) 232-3420, Fax (610) 232-3626
Singles $135, Doubles $175, Suites $245-$1,000. All major cards.

The venerable Grant, traditionally known as San Diego's most prestigious hotel, lost much of its luster in the '60s and '70s and nearly became just another dreary relic of downtown. Then came an $80-million restoration, completed at the end of 1985, that left the place grander than it had been when it was opened by the son of President Ulysses S. Grant in 1910. Some of the choicest suites in town can be found here; and the rooms have been tastefully furnished and offer all the modern luxuries you'll need. The magnificent central lobby has become a mid-afternoon gathering spot for the city's socialites, who enjoy the tea served by liveried waiters. The bar swings with jazz on Friday and Saturday nights, and mellows with quiet conversation the rest of the week. The elegant Grant Grill, long a haunt of the city's elite, serves three meals daily in the same clubby, power-elite crowd (*see* review in "SAN DIEGO Restaurants"). All shopping, restaurants and other downtown attractions are within easy walking distance, and the trolley runs

---

For a guide to our hotel classification system, see "About the Hotels" in the INTRODUCTION.

behind the hotel. Services include on-site parking, a concierge service and a generally well-trained staff. No pool.

La Valencia Hotel
1132 Prospect St., La Jolla 92037;
(619) 454-0771, Fax (619) 456-3921
Singles & Doubles $135-$285, Suites $300-$600. All major cards.

Marion Davies, Ramon Navarro and other stars of silent films flocked to La Jolla's pink palace when it was new, and this refined retreat continues to be a favorite with both the Hollywood crowd and the jet set. It's a quiet, dignified place; visitors are tempted to speak in whispers when they cross through the front lobby. The rear lobby, a magnificent room that ends in an immense picture window framing La Jolla Cove, inspires the hope that time will stand still and that "La V" (as La Jollans call it) will never change. Most rooms offer a view of the water, and most seem a little antiquated—though by no means uncomfortable—when compared to those in the modern glass palaces rising in downtowns across the country. Service is extremely personalized, as befits a place that numbers so many repeat visitors, including a fair percentage who check in for months at a time. Businesspeople will find the hotel a little far from downtown San Diego, but La Valencia was built for pleasure, not business. The beach is a two-minute walk away, and there is both a pool and a Jacuzzi. The Mediterranean Room downstairs and the tiny, romantic Sky Room, in the hotel's tower, both serve ambitious, well-prepared contemporary cooking.

Westgate Plaza Hotel
1055 Second Ave., Downtown (S.D.)
92101; (619) 238-1818,
Fax (619) 232-4526
Singles $134-$154, Doubles $144-$164, Suites $295-$650. All major cards.

Built by a wheeler-dealer whose fortune crumbled in one of San Diego's most celebrated financial scandals, the Westgate maintains its position as one of the city's premier luxury hotels. Its decor, however, is quite ostentatious, and may assault the eyes of those with more refined senses of style. Very few surfaces are untouched by gold leaf, mirrors or flocking, and if there's ever a chandelier shortage in the world, this is where they're being stockpiled. But to be fair, the service is smooth, gracious and professional, and the ornate lobby is oddly comfortable, as is the fabulously retro Plaza Bar. The rooms, while not overly large, are quite handsomely appointed and are equipped with all the little luxuries expected

of a contemporary deluxe hotel. This is not a hotel for sunbathers, however, since there is neither a pool nor a beach. The Westgate's French restaurant, Le Fontainebleau, is a bit more restrained in the design department than the hotel's other public rooms, and the food served there is surprisingly good.

Practical (Under $100)

Glorietta Bay Inn
1630 Glorietta Blvd., Coronado 92118;
(619) 435-3101, Fax (619) 435-6182
Singles & Doubles $94-$115, Suites $175-$265. All major cards.

The Spreckles family once owned vast tracts of San Diego real estate, and celebrated its good fortune by building several mansions on the Coronado peninsula, away from the big-city bustle. One of these baronial houses is at the core of this charming inn, which offers everything from relatively modest "lanai rooms" (with a balcony or a patio) to "mansion suites," roomy enough for parties of four, and the "mansion penthouse," the grandest collection of rooms in the residence. Views of Glorietta Bay, which harbors private craft, from dinghys to extravagant yachts, are standard features of most accommodations at this very well-maintained, very quiet and private establishment. Coronado's frequent traffic jams don't pose much of a problem for the inn's guests, since most of the peninsula's trendy shops and better restaurants are within easy walking distance. Golf and sailing can be arranged through the hotel, and the property has its own pool and tennis courts.

Hanalei Hotel
2270 Hotel Circle South, Mission Valley
(S.D.) 92108; (619) 297-1101,
Fax (619) 297-6049
Singles & Doubles $90-$140, Suites $275-$400. All major cards.

Built at the height of the Hawaiian kitsch craze, this high-rise along super-busy Interstate 8 also happens to be one of the quieter hideaways in Mission Valley—a commercial district so packed with hostelries that the Hanalei's neighborhood is officially designated "Hotel Circle." Rooms in the narrow twin high-rises face each other over a lavishly landscaped court, complete with tiki torches, koi ponds and waterfalls. Both seniors who long to be in the islands and families with children love it. The rooms, frequently redecorated, are comfortable and functional, but not luxurious; the hotel maintains a high standard of cleanliness. A public golf course and several major shopping centers are just blocks away; the hotel also is convenient to the beaches, Balboa Park, downtown and most other attractions. Skip the hotel's outdated dining room food; instead, go out for dinner and return to catch one of the live acts in the hotel's lounge, which, if a little insistently Hawaiian at times, can be fun.

Horton Grand Heritage
311 Island Ave., San Diego 92101;
(619) 544-1886, Fax (619) 239-3823
Singles & Doubles $99; Suites $159. All major cards.

San Diego's "oldest" hotel, the Horton Grand actually was built in 1936 from the reconstructed remains of two separate hotels built in the 1880s. To bring the number of rooms to a total of 110, the developer cleverly slipped a brand-new story between the first and second levels of the hotels. The Victorian ambience, which charms couples on weekend getaways, frankly charms us as well— we like the old-fashioned fixtures, which function with modern aplomb but almost convince us that we've traveled back in time. The Victorian theme can become tiresome at times, especially in the case of the employees' costumes, but we find peace in the quiet courtyard, and quite enjoy afternoon tea amongst the potted palms and period furnishings of the lounge. The meals in Ida Bailey's dining room are not the reason to stay at the Horton; instead, try one of the many fine eateries in the nearby Gaslamp Quarter. The location, near everything but not quite in the heart of the bustle, is particularly attractive.

Nightlife

Belly Up Tavern
143 S. Cedros Ave., Solana Beach 92075;
(619) 481-9022
Open daily 11 a.m.-2 a.m. Shows 5:30 p.m. (or 6 p.m.), 9 p.m. Cover varies ($2-$20). MC, V.

If you're staying in North County, and you enjoy live blues and rock, this is undeniably the place to be. One of the county's premier nightclubs, the Belly Up has hosted such notable performers as B.B. King, Jimmy Cliff and Bo Diddley. The cavernous club, with its lofty, domed ceilings, is fashioned after a capsized boat. Pool tables, a well stocked bar and grill, a spacious dance floor and plenty of seating make the Belly Up one of our favorite venues for live music. Call the club for the performance schedule.

Café Lulu
419 F St., Gaslamp Quarter, Downtown (S.D.) 92101; (619) 238-0114
Open Mon.-Fri. 8 a.m.-4 a.m., Sat.-Sun. 10 a.m.-4 a.m. MC, V.

Open almost 24 hours, this chic, artsy coffeehouse and wine bar caters to hip urbanites and fashionable bohemians. Located in the hub of downtown, Friday and Saturday nights find the place packed, with patrons lingering around the outside tables and chairs in traditional café fashion. A good selection of wines, coffee drinks and light fare makes Café Lulu a great after-theater spot.

Café Sevilla
555 Fourth Ave., Gaslamp San Diego 92101; (619) 233-5979
Open Mon.-Fri. 5 p.m.-2 a.m., Sat.-Sun. 11 a.m.-2 a.m. Flamenco shows Thurs.-Sat. 7:30 p.m. All major cards.

A traditional Spanish tapas bar and bistro, Café Sevilla is a festive little spot that attracts good-looking international clientele. Live flamenco dancing is featured in the newly added downstairs club. The rustic decor bespeaks the charm of old-world Spain, with vintage bull-fighting posters adorning the weathered brick walls. The place gets loud on weekends, as patrons consume pitchers of sangría and platters of tasty tapas. Reservations are reccomended for the flamenco shows.

Croce's Jazz Bar/Top Hat Bar & Grill
802 Fifth Ave., Gaslamp Quarter, Downtown (S.D.) 92101; (619) 233-4355
Open nightly (hours vary). Shows usually 8:30 p.m. (bar open until 2 a.m.) All major cards.

Owned and operated by Ingrid Croce, the wife of late singer/songwriter Jim Croce, this restaurant and bar is perhaps the best-known jazz venue in San Diego. The brick walls, red lighting and high ceilings make Croce's feel like a North Beach haunt. Local and national acts perform on the small stage. Top Hat, the adjacent blues bar, is more spacious, and quite a bit louder and livelier, featuring live music for a younger, twentythirtysomething crowd.

The Improv Comedy Club and Restaurant
832 Garnet Ave., Pacific Beach 92109; (619) 483-4520
Open nightly 6:30 p.m.-midnight. Shows Thurs.-Sun. 8:30 p.m., Fri. 8:30 p.m. & 10:30 p.m., Sat. 8 p.m. & 10 p.m. Cover varies ($8-$10) plus two-drink minimum. All major cards.

The biggest—and we think the best—comedy club in San Diego, is a franchise of comic entrepreneur Budd Freidman's original Improvs in

New York and Los Angeles. Big-name comedians such as Dennis Miller and Dana Carvey have graced the San Diego stage, and the club regularly attracts many of the familiar faces seen on the popular cable TV series, *An Evening at the Improv*. Sunday nights are reserved for non-smokers. Call the club for the performance schedule.

Shops

Here we list the area's best shopping centers, for travelers who have emergency shopping needs or who seek familiar upscale boutiques and department stores. The area does, however, boast a great number of small, chic and unique clothing and jewelry shops, bookstores, craft stores, confectioneries and so on—just pick a neighborhood, such as La Jolla or downtown, and spend the afternoon strolling and browsing.

Del Mar Plaza
1555 Camino Del Mar, Del Mar 92014;
(619) 792-1555

Shop among the tanned, toned and trendy at this chic, multileveled, sun-drenched shopping plaza by the sea. With its sweeping views of the Pacific Ocean and stunning Mediterranean-style architecture, Del Mar Plaza is far too pretty to be labeled a mall. Glorious decks and trickling fountains provide a peaceful atmosphere in which to browse the Plaza's many boutiques and galleries. Esmeralda, a cozy, well-stocked bookstore and coffeehouse, is especially inviting. Enoteca, an offshoot wine bar of nearby Il Fornaio, is a pleasant spot. Plenty of Adirondack chairs are scattered on the top level, for shoppers who want to sit back and enjoy the sunset.

Fashion Valley
399 Fashion Valley Way, Mission Valley (S.D.)
92108; (619) 688-9100

One of San Diego's most established shopping centers, this outdoor mall is chock full of the typical mall members found everywhere. It also houses four major department stores, Nordstrom and Neiman Marcus the most noteworthy.

Girard Avenue (& Prospect Street), La Jolla

It's been called Rodeo Drive by the beach, and for good reason—the shops are pricey and the people, well, pretentious. Nowhere else will you find a pint-sized McDonald's called McSnack.

But snobbery aside, a stroll down these two pedestrian-friendly streets on a sunny afternoon, the Pacific gleaming in the not-so-distant distance, can be a blissful experience. Girard is home to Saks Fifth Avenue and I. Magnin—both of which are tiny and could use some updating. Women's clothing boutiques abound, Wagener European Fashions and Dale Fitzmorris are worth a browse. Prospect boasts a decent Ann Taylor, as well as a trendy little dress shop called Lael's. Cap off the day with an espresso and pastries at Café 928 a few blocks away on Silverado Street.

Horton Plaza
4th St. & Broadway, Downtown (S.D.) 92101;
(619) 238-1596

Horton Plaza, with its ice cream–colored buildings and mazelike walkways, is reminiscent of Disneyland's Small World. An enormous emporium of shops, restaurants and movie theaters, Horton Plaza has something for everyone. Anchored by Nordstrom, Robinsons, The Broadway and Mervyns, other shops include the Nature Company, Brentano's, Guess? and The Body Shop. If you're downtown and want to shop under the sun, Horton Plaza is the best place to go, as it's far less touristy than high-priced Seaport Village.

The Paladion
777 Front St., Downtown (S.D.) 92101;
(619) 232-1627.

Undeniably the crown jewel of San Diego's shopping scene, the recently opened Paladion is beyond ritzy. With its steamlined, art-deco-inspired facade, jaunty store awnings and uplit elongated windows, the Paladion looks like an elegant New York department store from the 1930s. Only the highest of the high-end retailers are featured here—Tiffany & Co., Cartier, Gucci, Alfred Dunhill, Mark Cross and Salvatore Ferragamo among them. The stores surround a lovely atrium court, where coffee, tea and light fare are served during the day, cocktails at night. Valet parking only and concierge service are part of the pampering. The Paladion's top level boasts Spa de la Mer, a spa exclusively for women, as well as an upscale Italian restaurant called Bice and an outdoor terrace resplendent with flower beds. Definitely worth a visit, if only just to window shop.

Shops can unfortunately close without warning, it's a good idea to call before setting out for a particular store.

349

Sights

Attractions

Balboa Park
Park Blvd., San Diego; (619) 239-0512
Open daily 9:30 a.m.-4 p.m.

San Diego's greatest treasure is Balboa Park, home of the San Diego Zoo, the Old Globe Theatre, several fine museums and every imaginable recreational facility including 2 golf courses, 25 tennis courts, an arboreum, a lawn bowling field, an archery range, a miniature railroad, a merry-go-round and hundreds of manicured and natural acres for hiking, running and picnics. Many of the park's extravagant Spanish-Moorish buildings date from the world's fairs held here in 1915 and 1935; the subtropical landscaping surrounding these structures is particularly lovely.

Old Town State Historic Park
Bordered by Juan, Twiggs, Congress & Calhoun Sts., near the intersection of I-5 & I-8.

Old Town is sort of an expanded version of L.A.'s Olvera Street, and it really is rich with history. In 1769, Father Junipero Serra founded San Diego Alcala, California's first mission, on a hill overlooking Old Town (it has since been moved several miles to the east). Anyone familiar with California's history knows of the bloody religious, cultural and imperialistic battles that ensued, and shortly after the United States finally emerged victorious in its 1846 war against Mexico, San Diego was officially named a U.S. city, with Old Town its hub.

Old Town is divided into several areas: California Plaza, where most of the historic buildings, stables and residences are located; Bazaar del Mundo, which features a number of shops, restaurants and crafts exhibits; Squibob Square, a Victorian shopping area; Heritage Park, an area of restored Victorian houses (home to commercial tenants); and the tree-shaded Presidio Park. Kiosks have maps posted to guide you along.

San Diego Wild Animal Park
15500 San Pasqual Valley Rd. (I-15 Hwy. to Via Rancho Pkwy., then follow the signs), Escondido 92027; (619) 234-6541
Mid-June thru Labor Day: open daily 9 a.m.-6 p.m. Post-Labor Day thru mid-June: open daily 9 a.m.-4 p.m. Adults $18.95, children $10.95. D, MC, V.

This glorious park is an 1,800-acre adjunct to the San Diego Zoo, and the same care, planning and beauty that make the zoo one of the world's best also are part and parcel of this park. Five simulated natural habitats—Asian Plains, Asian Swamps and North, South and East Africa—make up the reserve, and its credo is the protection and propogation of endangered species. Since the park is so large, it's wise to take advantage of the Wgasa Bushline Monorail, a 50-minute, five-mile journey that allows visitors to view the park from above. More than 3,000 animals from nearly 300 species inhabit the grounds, offering not only photo opportunities but also a chance for us to view these marvelous creatures—lions, tigers, elephants, zebras, cheetahs, you name it—in something very close to their native environments. There are also hiking trails, exotic and rare flora, observation decks and a petting zoo, as well as Nairobi Village, which features performers executing tribal dances.

San Diego Zoo
Balboa Park, 2920 Zoo Dr., San Diego 92103; (619) 231-1515
Open daily 9 a.m.-5 p.m. Adults $12, children $4. D, MC, V.

The zoo is San Diego's Disneyland, attracting visitors from all over the world. Its fame and reputation as one of world's best zoos (if not *the* best) is well deserved. The 100 acres are more than any first-time visitor can take in one day; we recommend the 40-minute guided bus tour before venturing out on your own. It will help you get your bearings, prolong the life of your feet and help you decide which parts of the zoo you most want to see. Don't miss the fascinating (if somewhat creepy) Reptile House, the charming sea lion shows, the Sun Bears or the Tiger River, a simulated rainforest where great Siberian tigers roam among a world-class jungle of exotic greenery. The zoo's most recent addition, Gorilla Tropics, is a mind-boggling expanse of flora and fauna—a sanctuary for gorillas big and small. And if you have children in tow, you must visit the remarkable Children's Zoo, which was built to the scale of a four-year-old and which allows kids to make eye contact (and often pet) baby elephants, giraffes, monkeys, pigs and chicks.

Sea World
1720 S. Shores Rd., Mission Bay 92109-7995; (619) 222-6363
Open daily 9 a.m.-6 p.m. Adults $24.95, children 3-11 $18.95, children under 3 free. All major cards.

Sea World puts on shows that rival anything Hollywood and Busby Berkeley ever dreamed up. The headliners are the killer whales, who show off remarkable intelligence and ability to displace water. The dolphins also wow audiences, not only with their intelligence but with their remarkable precision feats, including spins, dives and back flips. These shows, combined with the exceptionally beautiful grounds, the breadth of marine life on display, the unbeatable children's play facilities and the speedy hydrofoil boat tour of Mission Bay, make Sea World a particular favorite. It's a particularly nice place for children, who can pet and feed the pilot whales, seals, dolphins and walruses, wade through the tide pools and play in the creative playground. Adults will be intrigued by the remarkable marine life on display—from rare, brightly colored fish to several species of live sharks.

Beaches

Coronado Beach

Marilyn Monroe, Jack Lemmon and Tony Curtis made this beach famous by romping along it for the filming of *Some Like It Hot*, but some may find it a little too hot—this beach is very, very popular, and gets quite crowded during the season's peak. The Hotel del Coronado looms dramatically behind it, and if you can avoid the hordes, it's a nice beach indeed.

Imperial Beach

A good surfing and swimming beach in the South Bay, Imperial Beach is lively and reasonably clean. The pier recently reopened, and in July, the U.S. Open Sand Castle Competition—the one you see covered every year on the evening news—takes place there.

La Jolla Cove

Postcard beautiful, this glorious cove is sheltered by a lush palisade thick with palms and other flora. When the tide is low, there are caves and tide pools to explore, and seal-watchers can sometimes spot their favorite mammals resting on the rocks offshore.

Mission Beach

Though Mission Bay is quite crowded during the summer, it is most pleasant to walk or bicycle along its boardwalk. Those who enjoy amusement parks will want to ride on the Giant Dipper Rollercoaster, a restored landmark reminiscent of the old Coney Island coasters. The Plunge, an Olympic-size indoor swimming pool complete with wading islands, is a cool respite for those unwilling to fare the waves.

Silver Strand State Beach

This Coronado-area beach doesn't get quite as crowded as the more popular Coronado Beach does, which makes it more desirable as far as we're concerned. It's admirably clean, kids love to play in the tiny, harmless waves, and there's ample parking.

Torrey Pines State Beach

Del Mar is one of Southern California's most stunning areas, and its beach there is beautiful. Large, clean and featuring barbecue facilities, Torrey Pines is popular with families.

Tourmaline & Windansea Beaches

If your idea of haute couture comes from the houses of Body Glove, Gotcha and Quicksilver, then these are the beaches for you. Great surfing and, for those who don't indulge in the sport, great people-watching.

Sports

Diving

Many of the hotels in San Diego and its environs can schedule boating and diving excursions. Good bets are any of the local **Diving Locker** shops around town (try the branch at Pacific Beach, 619-272-1120; or Solana Beach, 619-755-6822) or **Ocean Enterprises** (619-565-6054), which offers extensive scuba-diving classes, rentals and excursions (costing from from $40 to $150).

Hang-gliding

San Diego's dramatic topography—mountains, oceans, cliffs, beaches—makes hang-gliding here a peak experience. Gliding (for the experienced or those wishing to take lessons) can be set up through the **Hang Gliding Center** (619-450-9008).

Jet-skiing

Rentals are available through **Jet Ski Rentals** (619-276-9200) or **Jet Ski Werks Rentals** (800-750-7547).

Sailing

If you BYOB (Brought Your Own Boat), try the **Kona Kai Club** (1551 Shelter Island Dr., 619-222-1191) or the **Sunroad Resort Marina** (955 Harbor Island Dr. East, 619-574-0736). If you're looking to rent, try the **Mission Bay Sports Center** (1010 Santa Clara Pl., 619-488-

1004); several hotels, including the Catamaran, the Bahia and the Hotel del Coronado (*see* "SAN DIEGO Hotels"), also rent boats.

Spectator Sports

San Diego's football team, the **Chargers**, play home games at the **San Diego Jack Murphy Stadium** (9449 Friars Rd., San Diego 92108), August through December. Call (619) 280-2121 for schedule and ticket informatiom.

The city's baseball team, the **Padres**, play from April through the first week in October, also at **Jack Murphy Stadium**. Call (619) 283-4494 for schedule and ticket information.

For more detailed information on any sporting event (as well as weather conditions and other useful information), call the office of the **Convention & Visitors Bureau**, (619) 236-1212.

Windsurfing

Several hotels provide windsurfing rentals and lessons (the Bahia and the Catamaran, for two). Also, try **C.P. Water Sports** (2211 Pacific Beach Dr., 619-270-3211), which has five locations in the greater San Diego area, each one specializing in a different water sport.

Yacht Charters

Rentals are available through **Hornblower Dining Yachts** (P.O. Box 1140, Coronado, 619-435-2211) and **Finest City Yacht Charters** (2742 Brant St., 619-299-2248).

Tijuana, Mexico

The Bazaars & The Bizarre

Y ou can get to Tijuana by trolley if you're so inclined, however the drive is relatively painless, especially if you park in one of the many parking lots on the American side of the border and walk across. You can then either take a taxi into town or just keep walking—it takes about twenty minutes, and you'll pass a slew of funky little stands purveying everything from multi-colored serapes to garish plaster statuary to campy oil-paint-on- velvet portrayals of Elvis.

Once in Tijuana, you'll find yourself on **Avenida Revolución**, which is basically one long bazaar and not nearly as bizarre as it once was. Gone are the donkey shows and the red-light

districts. These days, sinning in Tijuana consists of betting on jai alai at the fronton in the middle of town, or betting on the horses and greyhounds just outside of town at the Agua Caliente Racetrack. And Tijuana is filled with modern shopping centers as well, especially in the newly constructed Rio Tijuana area, a modern facility that looks like every shopping mall we've ever been to in the United States.

Mexitlan, Tijuana's recently opened "theme park" isn't a theme park in the American sense of the word—you won't find any dancing bears or rollercoasters. What you will find is a park filled with more than 200 scale-model replicas depicting the architectural monuments of past and present Mexico, with admirable attention to detail. If you've never ventured beyond Tijuana or Ensenada, Mexitlan will inspire you to pack your bags. Ticket prices and hours tend to change at dizzying speed here, so we reccomend calling the park's American office: (619) 531-1112.

Where to Eat & Stay

As far as restaurants go, it's a good idea to avoid drinking the water. Aside from that, you can get an excellent taste of authentic Mexican cooking at **La Especiál** in the marketplace just off Revolución (everyone in town knows where it is; you'll know you're there when you see a long line in front of a friendly looking little restaurant), and authentic Mexican-style seafood at **La Costa** (right across the street from the Jai Alai Palace), which serves some of the best lobsters we've ever eaten. For terrific Mexican food at bargain prices, try **Restaurante del Bol Corona** in Plaza Amigo, 60 Via Oriente (*see also* review, page 339).

There are also a number of Chinese restaurants in Tijuana, probably left over from the 1940s, when it was a major port of call for soldiers and sailors who found Chinese food to be a good cheap meal. They serve the old-style Chinese-American cuisine built around chop suey, chow mein and egg foo yung. If you try one, keep in mind it's for the sake of history—and listening to Chinese people speaking Spanish.

Savvy travelers to Tijuana usually avoid the city's lodgings and head for the famed, seventy-year-old **Rosarito Beach Hotel** (Boulevard Benito Juares, #31) in Rosarito, just 25 minutes from Tijuana. For reservations, call (800) 343-8582. ◆

SANTA BARBARA

California's Shangri-La

E very weekend, countless Angelenos drive 90 miles north to fill up Santa Barbara's hotels and bed-and-breakfasts—and there's every reason why you should do the same. We don't normally recommend crowd-following, but Santa Barbara's setting is idyllic, the pace of life is friendly and laid-back, the weather is perfect ten months of the year, the Spanish architecture is exceptionally handsome, and the restaurants—over 100 have opened since we last published—are several notches above the standard resort fare. For the aesthete, there's the commendable Santa Barbara Museum of Art; for the spiritualist, there's the peaceful Santa Barbara Mission; and for the athlete, there's tennis, swimming, scuba diving, bicycling, windsurfing and more. Santa Barbara has never been a secret, and because of its enormous popularity, rooms can be hard to find. From April through October especially, book early—and note that most hotels have two-night minimums on weekends.

Restaurants

The symbol that accompanies each review indicates the rating on a scale of one to twenty. The rankings reflect *only* our opinion of the food; the decor, service, wine list and atmosphere are explicitly commented upon within each review. For further explanation, as well as an index of restaurants by rating, please see "About the Restaurants" in the INTRODUCTION. See the INDEXES section at the back of the book for comprehensive restaurant indexes.

11/20 Aldo's
1031 State St., Downtown (S.B.) 93101;
(805) 963-6687
Italian. Lunch & Dinner daily. AE, D, MC, V.

The menu reads like a summary of all of Italy's regional specialties: spaghetti marinara, Caesar salad, veal Parmigiano and so on. Tourists continue to flock here because the management has its heart in the right place; the smartest diners order the choice top-sirloin steak with smoked garlic butter. The desserts are often rich and inventive: chocolate-raspberry decadence cake, peanut-butter pie and cappuccino ice cream. About $21 per person for dinner.

Allegro
920 De la Vina St., Downtown (S.B.)
93101; (805) 965-6012
Mediterranean. Dinner Mon. & Wed.-Sun. AE, MC, V.

Why chef Norbert Schulz transformed the fine Norbert's restaurant into this little café-like eatery is anybody's guess, because as it stood, Norbert's was not only one of Santa Barbara's finest but ranked among the best restaurants in the United States. But this more casual incarnation of the original is as charming as ever, housed in its cozy Victorian cottage. The Mediterranean-inspired dishes that emerge from Shulz's kitchen revolve, not surprisingly, around pasta and fish, with a smattering of pizzas, paellas and grilled meats added to the mix. Some of the standouts we've tried here have been cumin linguine with chicken, ginger, chili and pine nuts; lamb tenderloin with a bean-artichoke-tomato ragoût; and grilled salmon with a pine-nut-and-basil crust in a tomato-radicchio sauce. Every once in a while there is a Norbert's night, a sublime dinner that recalls Schulz's highly acclaimed Cal-German cuisine. About $32 per person for dinner.

Astrid's Bistro
2030 Cliff Dr., Santa Barbara 93109;
(805) 965-0180
French. Breakfast & Lunch Mon.-Sat., Dinner Tues.-Sat., Brunch Sun. MC, V.

Astrid Nelson, who hails from the Alsace region of France, has taken a rather plain storefront in an undistinguished strip mall and turned it into a country French bistro. The small room is a riot of floral chintz, with a smattering of antiques and old oil paintings. In this setting, the delightful Astrid maintains a combination pâtisserie, salon de thé, bakery, catering company, wine-tasting bar and restaurant. The value is good, and every day there are at least four or five specials. These often shine, especially for the price: salmon and sea-bass mousse with tomato-caper sauce ($9.95) or ratatouille quiche with house salad ($5.95). The wine list offers mostly French bottles, including a few good wines at $4 a glass. If the service occasionally stumbles, it's made up for in friendliness. Three outdoor terrace tables complete the picture. Dinner for one about $18.

Bernadette's
1155 Coast Village Rd., Montecito 93108;
(805) 969-1456
French. Dinner Tues.-Sun. AE, MC, V.

Chef Bernadette Millet, whose past cooking credentials include stints at L.A.'s Ma Maison, Beau Rivage and Geoffrey's, and who has reigned as president of the prestigious Club Culinaire Français de Californie, has opened a small bastion of French cooking in Montecito. Her approach combines tradition with innovative hints of Asian and Mediterranean resulting in tasty, light, contemporary dishes. This is a woman who believes "the art of enjoying food is the art of enjoying life," and how can we disagree? Try the cold eggplant salad, shrimp Provençale, soft-shell crab, sautéed lobster, chicken roulade, escargots, bouillabaisse, duck a l'orange, grilled salmon, steak au poivre. The wine list is impressive, as are the desserts. A dinner costs about $30.

 ## Brigitte's
1327 State St., Downtown (S.B.) 93101; (805) 966-9676
Californian. Lunch Mon.-Sat., Dinner nightly. MC, V.

Brigitte Guehr is the wife of one of Santa Barbara's best-known chefs, Norbert Schulz, and her friendly neighborhood bistro is packed with regulars who find the light, Californian cooking just right for their taste buds and pocketbooks. A clutch of tables in front have views of State Street promenaders; a few tables in the back overlook the open kitchen. The food—gourmet pizzas, creative salads, grilled seafood, seductive desserts—is consistently good and often innovative. Favorites here are angel-hair pasta with bay scallops, lamb with an eggplant-oregano sauce, New York steak with red pepper coulis and aïoli. The lilliputian bar serves up some fine local wines by the glass. About $21 per person.

12/20 Brophy Bros. Clam Bar & Restaurant
The Breakwater, off Cabrillo St., Santa Barbara 93101; (805) 966-4418
Seafood. Lunch & Dinner daily. AE, MC, V.

Brophy Bros. sits out on the Breakwater (between Point Castillo and Stearn's Wharf), upstairs from a fishing-supply shop, 100 yards from where the fishing boats haul their catch into shore. While it's nothing more than a bar/counter and twenty tables scattered inside and out—it's about as good a seafood spot as you'll find in these parts. It's noisy and chaotic, usually due to the ribald crowd of local fishermen that come in for some of the freshest fish in town. They call it a clam bar, though there are also clams and oysters on the half shell, peel-and-eat shrimp, steamed clams, steamed mussels, oysters Rockefeller, clams casino, beer-boiled shrimp, fine New England–style clam chowder, cioppino and crab melts. You can't beat the terrific setting:

the city on one side, the Pacific on the other. About $25 per person for dinner.

12/20 Café Vallarta
217 State St., Downtown (S.B.) 93101; (805) 564-8494
Mexican. Lunch Mon.-Fri., Dinner nightly. MC, V.

In this town where burritos are more beloved than burgers, Café Vallarta, on a seedy stretch of State Street, stands out for its unusual degree of authenticity and its winning way with Mexican-style seafood. Justo, the owner, takes great pride in preparing classical Mexican and Yucatán cuisine with no lard or food additives. You won't find any pedestrian enchiladas or fajitas here. Expect bowls of award-winning caldo de mariscos, a marvelous, slightly tangy Mexican bouillabaisse; the house paella; eggplant grilled in Kahlúa sauce, stuffed with chicken, with mushrooms and rice; red snapper on a bed of rice with avocados, tomatoes and onions. Desserts go beyond flan to chocolate "pâté" and, for the brave of palate, avocado-lime cheesecake. There's a fetching collection of local wines, along with beer, fruit licuados and espresso. Our only gripe is the service, which can be as slow as a hot Cozumel afternoon. A dinner costs $22.

11/20 Chad's
625 Chapala St., Downtown (S.B.) 93101; (805) 568-1876
American. Lunch & Dinner Mon.-Sat. No smoking. AE, MC, V.

One of Santa Barbara's most charming old Victorian houses has been handsomely renovated to make room for Chad's, a restaurant devoted to unpretentious American cooking. Under the direction of chef Scott Gibson, who won a popular following at the Palace Café, look for and get honest, stick-to-your-ribs chicken pot pie, filet mignon, bacon-wrapped shrimp, fresh oysters, oysters Rockefeller and prime ribs. They do an especially zesty Ceasar salad here. The small outdoor patio seats twenty. A cheery two-sided fireplace keeps guests warm inside on nippy days. The full bar includes and a good selection of California wines. Dinner runs $18 per person.

 ## Citronelle at Santa Barbara Inn
901 Cabrillo Blvd., Santa Barbara 93103; (805) 963-0111
French. Breakfast, Lunch & Dinner daily. All major cards.

Michel Richard's Citrus restaurant in L.A. has defined the contemporary California restaurant, his Broadway Deli in Santa Monica has defined the contemporary yuppie café. Initially we feared that because of his increasing fame, Richard might not have time to make Citronelle more than a pleasant California bistro riding on Citrus's reputation. Indeed, it is a pleasant California bistro, with polished wood floors, lazily spinning ceiling fans, woven-wicker bistro chairs, and a fabulous third-floor perch over the Pacific.

But when we visited, and the food came, we were dazzled—this was no pale imitation of the original; this was superb stuff. True, Richard himself was present—not actually cooking, but eyeing plates and keeping the kitchen on its toes. And so far, his first-class kitchen crew is performing up to his considerable standards. The menu is short and straightforward. While chicken with porcini crust and mushroom sauce sounds like it could be a Continental-cuisine warhorse, it is in fact a dish of mind-blowing flavor, a tender, juicy breast wrapped in the tastiest of mushrooms, bathed in a light but intensely tasty mushroom-infused reduction sauce. Every dish we tried—from the New York steak with a soy-shallot sauce and home fries, to the smoked-salmon terrine with cucumber-dill salad, to the striped bass with pearl pasta and saffron sauce—was a perfect marriage of finesse and flavor, displaying refinement and creativity but never blandness. And the desserts do Richard's reputation justice: crème brûlée of unspeakable smoothness, a chocolate hazelnut "bar" that'll knock your socks off. Because most Santa Barbarans wouldn't dream of spending the kind of money people spend for a dinner in L.A., Michel has kept his prices very reasonable. In fact, this is the best Southern California has to offer, in terms of quality for the price. The eight-page wine list showcases the best of the Californians; even Michel Richard's special "library" selections offer Eberle Cabernets and Mondavi Reserves alongside Mouton-Rothschild Bordeaux and vintage Sauternes. Dinner runs about $40 to $50 per person.

12/20 Cold Spring Tavern
5995 Stagecoach Rd., San Marcos Pass, Santa Barbara 93105; (805) 967-0066
American. Breakfast Sat.-Sun., Lunch & Dinner daily. MC, V.

For more than a century, this bona fide, card-carrying roadhouse has been a rest stop for those heading north from Santa Barbara. The place is one of those fine California treats, a bit of history down an old road, far from the freeway and from the noise of the madding crowd. The creek is still there, running more or less clean. And in the evening wind, you can still hear the rumblings of the old stagecoaches, which carried passengers over this pass long before the automobile was a glimmer in Henry Ford's eye. (Today, you're more likely to encounter bikers and their babes here . . . they consider this tavern their turf, especially on weekends.) Though the place still looks venerable, with a welcoming fire often burning in the hearth, the food has changed quite a bit with the years, to the point that this modest-looking inn has one of the most unique menus in the state: mushroom caps stuffed with venison sausage, rabbit pâté baked with pistachios and pine nuts, marinated and boned Santa Ynez rabbit, charbroiled Carolina quail moistened with roasted bell-pepper butter, even the occasional Cajun dish. Standards include huevos rancheros, country biscuits with gravy and waffles. But for a taste of real roadhouse food, try the chili—full of meat, thick with onions and cheese. About $32 per person for dinner.

 ## Downey's
1305 State St., Downtown (S.B.) 93101; (805) 966-5006
Californian. Lunch Tues.-Fri., Dinner Tues.-Sun. AE, MC, V.

There's something pristine, almost antiseptic, about the dining experience at this sophisticated storefront restaurant, despite the Southern California friendliness of the service staff and the warming presence of the paintings on the walls by Santa Barbara artist Hank Pitcher. Maybe it's all those little red hearts on the menu, denoting healthy items. Or maybe it's the precision, rather than inspiration, of the cuisine itself. Regardless, Downey's is, after all, one of the two best restaurants in town—along with Citronelle.

When local mussels are in season, John Downey serves them in two very different, but equally good, appetizers: with fennel and a roasted-pepper vinaigrette and in a richly flavorful (but not artery-clogging) soup with saffron, tomatoes, basil and green onions. Even better, though, is his fresh foie gras in Madeira sauce, served with a crouton made of wild mushrooms. The Madeira is rich enough to stand up to the foie gras but not so rich that it fights for attention on your palate. Downey's menu changes nightly, but he always has two or three fish dishes, which is where his light touch is particularly effective. Grilled ahi is enhanced by a spicy papaya-cucumber vinaigrette, and scallops are good in a variety of preparations. Salmon is more iffy: excellent in a lemon-chervil sauce, less so in a citrus-basil sauce. Similarly, a sauce of cider and thyme seems a better complement to the grilled duck breast than does the sauce made with fresh raspberries. About $40 per person for dinner.

12/20 El Encanto Hotel Dining Room

El Encanto Hotel and Garden Villas, 1900 Lasuen Rd., Santa Barbara 93103; (805) 687-5000
French. Breakfast, Lunch & Dinner daily; Brunch Sun. All major cards.

The Riviera of Santa Barbara is nestled high above the city by the historic Mission and is perpetually compared to the glorious south of France. El Encanto sits in this rarified bougainvillea-filled atmosphere. Recently renovated to the tune of many millions of dollars, El Encanto can best be described as an auberge, a country inn. Its hallmarks are total privacy, attentive personal service, and smashing views of the city, the ocean and the Channel Islands. Beautiful grounds are kept with reverence for the surrounding residential neighborhood, and the complete peace and quiet and total comfort help to account for El Encanto's rising status and distinguished guest list. Chef James Sly trained at The Ritz in Paris, and is known for his grilled fish and lamb dishes. One of Santa Barbara's most memorable settings. The price of such happiness: about $42 per person for dinner.

Louie's at Upham Hotel

1404 De la Vina St., Santa Barbara 93101; (805) 963-7003
Californian/French. Lunch Mon.-Fri., Dinner nightly, Brunch Sun. AE, MC, V.

Situated in the historic Upham Hotel, this classy spot is known for its quality, creative dishes. Dishes are light combinations of French and Californian cuisines, and best bets are seafood, beef and pasta, all prepared with a minimum of fuss so that the true flavors sing out. No creams or butters are used, but look for their delicious oils infused with cilantro and roasted red pepper. Grilled salmon with tomato-avocado-basil vinaigrette and potato-crusted sea bass with arugula and grilled balsamic red onions are specialities, both prepared with port and cilantro infused oil accents. Look for Louie's photo on the wall: he is the owner's dog who lives in Colorado. The veranda is especially nice in summer. Reservations recommended. Dinner costs about $20.

La Marina at Four Seasons Biltmore Hotel

1260 Channel Dr., Montecito 93108; (805) 969-2261
Californian/Mediterranean. Dinner nightly, Brunch Sun. All major cards.

The setting, view and service have always been legendary. But since Carrie Nahabedian joined the hotel as executive chef from the Four Seasons

Chicago in 1991, the kitchen now matches these attributes. In a majestically furnished room fit for royalty, her combinations are poetic and delicious: terrine of red snapper with garlic roasted potatoes, wild lettuce and fennel mayonnaise; seared sea scallops with aromatics; ravioli of snails with eggplant and zucchini, leeks, essence of orange and poached foie gras; medallions of veal and sweetbreads with fine yellow beans, crisp potato cakes and Madeira. Anything this chef touches becomes a work of art, be it lobster, lamb, salmon, duck, rabbit, fish. . . . Add to this a wine list that is deep and complete, plus crisp, well-trained service and you have one of this city's most outstanding dining experiences. The lavish Sunday brunch is one of *the* social scenes in town. About $40 per person for dinner.

Michael's Waterside Inn/ Waterside Bistro

50 Los Patos Way, Montecito 93108; (805) 969-0307
French. Dinner Mon.-Sat. All major cards.

This lovely old house on the André Clark bird sanctuary is a cousin of the Roux Brothers' fabled Le Gavroche and Waterside Inn restaurants in England, both of which were way stations for chef Michael Hutchings on his way to Santa Barbara. Mr. Hutchings recently has created two restaurants where there was once one: his well-known (since 1984) Waterside Inn and his new Bistro in the adjacent greenhouse. In the Michael's Waterside restaurant, the approach is modern classic cooking. You find cultured abalone in a Chardonnay cream with dill and enoki mushrooms; Gruyère cheese soufflé; tournedos of beef garnished with slices of avocado and an avocado terrine; sweetbreads with local oranges and basil; and duck with local olives, garlic and morels. Hutchings is actually at his best when he's creating dishes without portfolio, such as his fine grilled-quail salad and his very British roast lamb. The setting, the service and the menu are quite conservative, even a bit staid, and the food, while always good, is more inspired some times than others. Desserts like praline ganache are sublime. Expect to spend about $43 for dinner. Designed as an everyday alternative to its sibling, the Waterside Bistro has lustier and more reasonably priced offerings: cassoulet of duck ($11.95); lamb leg steak with frites ($13.95); and

---

Prices are based on a complete dinner for one, including an appetizer, entrée, dessert, tax and tip—but excluding wine or any other beverage.

veal kidneys with mustard sauce ($9.95). It's a relaxed, informal yet ravishing place. Guests often say it reminds them of meals in the south of France. Dinner costs $25 or more per person.

12/20 Montecito Café
1295 Coast Village Rd., Montecito 93108; (805) 969-3392
Californian. Lunch & Dinner daily. MC, V.

Located in the same Montecito Inn that Charlie Chaplin and Fatty Arbuckle built years ago, this busy café offers highly creative and value-packed Californian cooking in a sun-filled room with graceful windows. Specialties here can be found on the blackboard and change each sunrise. The owner-chef, Mark Huston, is a very talented fellow; he varies the menu to keep the beau monde of Montecito challenged. Especially memorable are his seafood dishes, salads and grilled entrées. Desserts are impressive for such a modest operation. There are good local wines by the glass. About $22 per person for dinner.

Oysters
9 W. Victoria St., Downtown (S.B.) 93101; (805) 962-9888
Seafood. Lunch Mon.-Sat., Dinner nightly. AE, MC, V.

An informal, open-kitchen café with a cool, quiet outdoor patio, this is an idyllic lunch spot. In good seafood-house fashion, the fresh-fish dishes change daily depending on the market; salmon, ono, swordfish and yellowtail are expertly grilled, poached or baked in puff pastry. To live up to its name, Oysters also serves fresh, briny oysters in all forms, from shooters to oyster stew. Also good are a dish of fettuccine with fresh vegetables and a braised salmon roll on saffron pasta. Service is prompt and professional, and the wine list has plenty of good whites for under $20. Dinner runs $30 per person.

The Palace Café
8 E. Cota St., Downtown (S.B.) 93101; (805) 966-3133
Cajun/Caribbean. Lunch Mon.-Sat., Dinner nightly. AE, MC, V.

In a town noted for friendly, laid-back restaurants, The Palace is certainly the friendliest and most laid-back. It is also one of the best. From the moment you walk in, you're part of the family; owner Ken Boxer is as gracious a host as can be. It's a homey, aw-shucks kind of place, with a New Orleans–style lamppost in the window, jazz on the stereo, New Orleans jazz posters on the walls and impeccably authentic and delicious Cajun food on the tables (including *real* redfish). And now, perhaps in honor of the beach-town

location, the kitchen is turning out some tasty Caribbean-style dishes as well. It's all good, starting with the marvelous breads and muffins that greet you. The more noteworthy of the Caribbean dishes include rich Bahamian conch chowder, coconut shrimp and sole Martinique. The seafood gumbo is rich and strongly flavored, the crab claws cooked in "popcorn" batter are delicate and sweet, and the blackened filet mignon is seared perfectly: the inside rare, the outside spicy but not mouth-numbing. Try not to burn off all your taste buds—you'll need them to appreciate the Louisiana bread-pudding soufflé with whisky sauce or the delicious sweet potato–pecan pie with chantilly. About $25 per person for dinner.

12/20 Pane e Vino
1482 E. Valley Rd., Montecito 93108; (805) 969-9274
Italian. Lunch Mon.-Sat., Dinner nightly. No cards.

The Santa Barbara area is blessed with many good restaurants, but it was lacking one with authentic Italian fare until this friendly group of Italians moved in. If you've been to L.A.'s Prego or San Francisco's Il Fornaio—or for that matter if you've been to Italy—you'll feel right at home in this inviting little trattoria, with its open kitchen, counter heaped with crusty Tuscan bread, tile-and-woodwork bistro decor and comfortable outdoor patio. Order one of the reasonably priced Chiantis, tear into the excellent bread and contemplate the menu, a minicatalog of the joys of Italian food. Not much has changed about this place since it opened, and there's often still a wait to get in the door for the rich, herby brodetto crostini (bread soup) with tomato, the flavorful insalata mista with baby greens and leeks, the heavenly seafood risotto, the savory tortelloni with butter and sage and the gorgeous grilled veal chop with rosemary. Unfortunately, the service is often like an Italian opera gone berserk: the restaurant doesn't take credit cards, and the wait with a reservation can be twenty minutes. Have the owners turned their attention toward the newer Pane e Vinos in San Francisco and L.A.? Nevertheless, a first-rate Italian dinner will run a reasonable $25 or less per person.

12/20 Papagallo's
731 De la Guerra Plaza, Downtown (S.B.) 93101; (805) 963-8374
Peruvian. Dinner nightly. MC, V.

Papagallo's could well be the best restaurant in downtown Lima, Peru. Happily, though, it's in downtown Santa Barbara—overlooking the mountains and swaying palm trees. The cooks here can't pack enough limes, onion, garlic, mushrooms, and cilantro into their dishes. Toss them with beef, mussels, fish, oysters, prawns, and pasta and you get the point. This is robust and honest cooking. A blackboard reveals the specials, usually fresh snapper, halibut, or ceviche. Cold boiled potatoes seem to be a speciality of the house, and they are unusually served with a peanut-and-cheese sauce or cheese-and-tumeric combination. Service is a bit distracted but it's probably a lot like the best restaurant in any small South American town. An old upright piano sits in the center of the room. The atmosphere can be credited to painted wooden chairs, *faux* clouds on the walls, old instruments hanging here and there and Peruvian ballads blasting from a tinny speaker. Push past the banana plants and sit outside in the pretty courtyard. Expect to spend about $25 per person for dinner.

12/20 Paradise Café
702 Anacapa St., Downtown (S.B.) 93101; (805) 962-4416
American. Lunch & Dinner daily, Brunch Sun. AE, MC, V.

The Paradise Café is located off State Street's beaten path, and one of the few places in town where you can eat on a sunny (or starry) patio. The funky old building, with its simple '40s decor, comprises a straightforward bar and a split-level dining room. The food is generously served: classic omelets and eggs (including a very tasty dish of scrambled eggs, black beans, salsa and cheese wrapped in a tortilla), a terrific hamburger, an eggplant sandwich, a rock-shrimp-and-spinach salad and perfect oak-grilled steaks, chops and fish. About $24 per person for dinner.

12/20 Piatti
516 San Ysidro Rd., Montecito 93108; (805) 969-7520
Italian. Lunch & Dinner daily. MC, V.

Santa Barbara's first wood-burning pizza oven found its home here, in what is now a chain of sorts (there are other Piattis in Carmel, Yountville, La Jolla and Sacramento). The owners of the San Ysidro Ranch and Auberge du Soleil created these upbeat, noisy and casual zuppa, insalate, pizza, antipasti, pasta and griglia restaurants and the public has responded mightily. This Montecito version occupies the former Casa del Sol, which was notable for its sunny outdoor patio. The new owners repainted the place with large, attractive vegetable murals on the walls, pine furniture and a straightforward kitchen that pumps out honest Italian cooking using fresh ingredients. Yuppies, old Montecito grande dames and tourists flock here to drink a glass of chianti and eat the homemade cannelloni,

rotisseried pork chop, spit-roasted chicken with rosemary, spinach lasagne and other delights. A fun atmosphere prevails, helped by a young staff who make up in energetic smiles what they lack in polish. About $23 per person for dinner.

11/20 The Ranch House
102 Besant Rd., Ojai 93024; (805) 646-2360
Californian/Continental. Lunch & Dinner Wed.-Sun., Brunch Sun. AE, MC, V.

For years and years, The Ranch House has been *the* place to dine in this neck of the woods, on the outskirts of the peaceful, pretty town of Ojai some 40 minutes from Santa Barbara. Back in its early, vegetarian days, it was a pioneer of sorts, one of the first to combine the lighter approach of French nouvelle cuisine with the local bounty of California. Sadly, those pioneering days are long gone. So are the vegetarian days—red meat can be found in abundance on today's Ranch House menu. What hasn't changed is the romantic setting: the old inn, the babbling brook, the trees, the herb and vegetable gardens, the chamber music. Combine all that with the superb wine list, and you're bound to have a swell time—as long as you don't expect much of the food. Also, we wish they would serve the good bread more generously, rather than in microslices. Dinner runs about $34 per person.

Stonehouse at San Ysidro Ranch
San Ysidro Ranch, 900 San Ysidro Ln., Montecito 93108; (805) 969-5046
New American. Breakfast, Lunch & Dinner daily, Brunch Sun. All major cards.

A competent contemporary restaurant set successfully in a 150-year-old ranch house may be a tall order, but it works beautifully at the San Ysidro Ranch. Windows look out on the jungle of oak trees and bougainvillea and rough whitestone walls contrast with fine linens and silver. This dining room has had its culinary ups and downs; since the departure of whiz kid Mark Ehrler, this kitchen has gracefully segued from fine Cal-French cooking to regional American. The new chef, Gerard Thompson, offers many a regional American specialty: tortilla soup, crispy catfish, pheasant sausage, chilled calamari salad, Texas shrimp (with garlic, shallots, basil and olive oil), pork paillard and smoked-salmon tartare. The wine list is an intelligent selection of mostly All-American bottles; one sure bet for dessert is the chocolate brownie with caramel sauce and vanilla ice cream. The latticed patio provides a lovely setting for an al fresco weekend brunch. We'll withhold our previously shining ranking until Thompson blossoms at his new post. About $40 per person for dinner.

The Wine Cask

813 Anacapa St., Downtown (S.B.) 93101; (805) 966-9463
Californian. Lunch Mon.-Fri., Dinner nightly. AE, MC, V.

The Wine Cask has been a hit since the day it opened in 1984, thanks to its knowledgeable wine-expert owner, Doug Margerum, and the talented stream of chefs he has brought to his kitchens. And with a move to the historic El Paseo's Gold Room, a majestic space sporting a vintage 1926 hand-painted beamed ceiling, baronial fireplace and luxurious bird's-eye maple bar, all bathed in flattering Italian halogen lighting, the restaurant continues to hum. With a cobblestone courtyard, filled with herbs and fruit trees and a gurgling fountain as centerpiece, and an interior that looks like a movie set, this is more old Europe than twentieth-century California.

Cognoscenti sit in chic, comfortable bistro chairs and order from an imaginative menu created by chef Galen Doi, who honed his skills at the San Ysidro Ranch and Le Meridien in Newport Beach. A classically French-trained chef with Japanese roots, Doi combines the two disciplines with regional ingredients to fashion imaginative plates of lamb, fish, gamebirds and pasta. Highlights of the kitchen run from crispy sweetbreads with a shiitake coulis and a port-wine reduction, to grilled Santa Barbara spot prawns with saffron sauce and basmati rice, to Sonoma foie gras with polenta and shaved Parmesan. About 35 wines can be had by the glass; the truly adventurous can navigate through a 45-page master list with over two thousand selections. From the daily-changing roster of desserts, try the ginger-pear tart or the dense flourless chocolate cake. About $29 per person for dinner.

And Also . . .

Andria's Harborside, 336 W. Cabrillo Blvd., Santa Barbara 93101; (805) 966-3000. *Seafood. Breakfast, Lunch & Dinner daily. AE, D, MC, V.* Nine years in the city has brought Andria's a solid reputation and a loyal following. Anything that swims in the sea can be found on the menu; nightly specials include local halibut Puerto Vallarta or swordfish with fresh citrus salsa. The oyster bar stays open until midnight daily and attracts a colorful following. Dinner, $14 per person.

Baccio, 3891 State St., Santa Barbara 93105; (805) 563-9660. *Italian. Lunch Mon.-Sat., Dinner nightly. AE, MC, V.* Atop the Galleria shopping center on the city's bustling north side is this casual and comfortable spot, usually crammed with yuppies. Pizzas, sandwiches, salads and nicely done pastas, and an excellent wine list. About $7 to $11 per person for lunch.

Brewhouse Grill, 202 State St., Downtown (S.B.) 93101; (805) 963-3090. *Californian. Lunch & Dinner daily. AE, MC, V.* Fresh fish, pasta and sandwiches; three beers made on premises. Dinner, $20 per person.

Casa de Sevilla, 428 Chapala St., Downtown (S.B.) 93101; (805) 966-4370. *Continental. Lunch & Dinner Tues.-Sat. AE, MC, V.* Since 1926, this "club" has been a hangout for the rich and famous as well as ordinary folks who are addicted to its chile rellenos, margaritas, chili con queso and barbecued seafood. About $7 per person for lunch.

Chase Bar & Grill, 1012 State St., Downtown (S.B.) 93101; (805) 965-4351. *Italian. Lunch & Dinner daily. AE, MC, V.* A cozy old stalwart Italian with a fine jukebox, this restaurant has been around for years and sometimes looks it. Still, it's usually packed with people looking for its generous, reasonably priced pasta and chicken dishes. Lunch, $8 to $12 per person.

Flavor Of India, 3026 State St., Downtown (S.B.) 93105; (805) 682-6561. *Indian. Lunch Sun.-Fri., Dinner nightly. MC, V.* Not a flashy decorating job but credible Indian cooking which compares favorably with the better restaurants of New Delhi, is certainly as cheap as any small London Indian restaurant, does authentic Tandoori treatments of chicken, fish and lamb in any spice level you wish and is very friendly. Lunch, $7 to $10 per person; dinner $15 or so.

Follow Your Heart Café, 19 S. Milpas St., Santa Barbara 93103; (805) 966-2251. *Vegetarian. Breakfast, Lunch & Dinner daily. MC, V.* Natural, vegetarian café, an annex to Santa Barbara's premier health food emporium. Dinner, $18 per person.

Original Enterprise Fish Company, 225 State St., Santa Barbara 93101; (805) 962-3313. *Seafood. Lunch & Dinner daily. AE, MC, V.* Santa Barbara's classic boathouse seafood restaurant has re-opened after prolonged freeway construction. Locals were happy to see the return of the garlic clams, calamari and prawn cocktails, the mesquite-grilled fish, and the daily specials featuring anything from Idaho rainbow trout to Norwegian salmon. Lunch, about $7 to $10.

The Plaka, 235 W. Montecito St., Santa Barbara 93101; (805) 965-9622. *Greek. Dinner Wed.-Sun. MC, V.* Dinner here is an evening not soon forgotten, with light and original dishes and entertainment provided by the owner and his staff. The lamb kabobs marinated in mint and oregano are especially good and George's table dance is legendary. Dinner, from $10 to $20.

Remington's at Los Olivos Grand Hotel, 2860 Grand Ave., Los Olivos 93441; (805) 688-7788. *Californian. Lunch & Dinner daily. AE, MC, V.* The kitchen at this highly rated, small country auberge in Santa Ynez wine country is celebrated for its Californian cuisine and extensive wine cellar. Linny Largent-Mayer presides over the dining room with great care. Her dinners and Sunday brunches are beloved traditions. About $10 per person for lunch; $30 for dinner.

Steamers, 214 State St., Santa Barbara 93101; (805) 966-0260. *Seafood. Lunch & Dinner daily. AE, MC, V.* A good, casual seafood restaurant with outdoor dining. Beer and wine. Dinner, $20 or so per person.

Wheeler Hot Springs, 6 miles north of Ojai on Hwy. 33, Ojai 93023; (805) 646-8131. *Californian. Dinner Thurs.-Sun., Brunch Sat.-Sun. AE, MC, V.* Here you'll find fare that sings with freshness, such as oak-grilled chicken with homemade tomatillo salsa and fresh coriander and swordfish with tequila-lime butter. There are scrubbed pine tables, votive lights and fresh wildflowers. The small bar glows with a vast selection of local and imported wines. About $13 to $22 per person for dinner.

Your Place, 22-A N. Milpas St., Santa Barbara 93103; (805) 966-5151. *Thai. Lunch & Dinner Tues.-Sun. All major cards.* Locals flock here for the best Thai in town—powerfully seasoned and fragrant curries, peppered squid and shrimp, and vegetable dishes. The restaurant is housed on a rather busy street and parking may be scarce, but you'll be glad you made the effort. About $6 to $10 per person for lunch.

For comprehensive listings of restaurants By Area, By Price and By Cuisine, and by categories such as Breakfast, Bar Scene, Late-Night and more, see the INDEXES at the back of the book.

Bargain Bites

Cafés & Bistros

The Bakery
129 E. Anapumu St., Downtown (S.B.) 93101; (805) 962-2089
Breakfast (open 7 a.m.) daily, Lunch & Dinner Mon.-Fri. MC, V.

Across the street from one of Santa Barbara's most visited tourist sites, the historic county courthouse, stands The Bakery, one of the most popular bakery/cafés in town. Customers line up early on the broad porch outside this white-on-white café where you can dine inside or outside on a small patio where birds join your table. The omelets are fluffy and the quiches rich. About $5 to $8 per person for lunch.

Esau's Coffee Shop
403 State St., Downtown (S.B.) 93101; (805) 965-4416
Breafast (open 6 a.m.) & Lunch daily. No cards.

Esau's looks like a beach-town café built on the back lot at The Burbank Studios. It's funky, nutty, homemade, and très casual. Aside from a few sandwiches, nothing is served here but break-fast dishes, most with more or less classic roots. Blockbuster portions of Esau's blueberry, wheatgerm pancakes and eggs—any way—are two good reasons there's always a line to get in. Ac-

companying each egg dish are homemade buttermilk biscuits, homemade jam, homemade salsa and home fries, grits or rice Pizza is basically an order of nachos using potatoes instead of tortilla chips. The biscuits come with country gravy—we knew they would. About $6 to $7 per person for lunch.

Joe's Café
512 State St., Downtown (S.B.) 93101; (805) 966-4638
Lunch & Dinner daily, Late Supper Fri.-Sat. AE, MC, V.

One of the most popular bars in town (see "Nightlife"), Joe's is a no-frills locals' hangout. It's a masculine, Brooklyn-style pub with dark wood, a great old jukebox, deafening noise level and simple, heavy bar-and-grill fare, from sandwiches and red-sauced pastas to good charbroiled steaks. The portions are large, the free accompaniments (soup, salad, onion rings) quite numerous, the prices low. And the people-watching is unbeatable. About $8 per person for lunch.

Mona Lisa Café
12 W. De la Guerra Pl., Downtown (S.B.) 93101; (805) 564-8783
Lunch & Dinner daily. AE, MC, V.

The chef calls the cooking here "Italian/Southwestern/Californian" cooking, and that's quite a mouthful. You can sit on the sunny outdoor patio or in the bustling indoor room, and feast on artistic dishes with compositions like pheasant pot pie with lobster mushrooms, seafood fettuccine with saffron, and white salmon with fruit salsa. Ravioli isn't just ravioli here, it's blue-corn ravioli filled with black beans and guajillo cream. The restaurant is owned by Alan Gratzer, who in his wilder days banged the drums for REO Speedwagon. Expect to shell out $10 for a lunch, and $15 to $20 for a dinner.

Mousse Odile
18 E. Cota St., Downtown (S.B.) 93101; (805) 962-5393
Breakfast, Lunch & Dinner Mon.-Sat. All major cards.

Mousse Odile serves a taste of its famous chocolate mousse with every dish, an unspoken reminder that chef/owner Yvonne Mathieu started out catering mousses for Santa Barbara society. The other French delights that make this simple restaurant a fine spot for a casual meal: fresh fruit and crème anglaise atop marvelous waffles, delicate roules enfolding a béchamel sauce rich with Gruyère, quiches rich with custardy seafood or ham and cheese. Fine, simple dinners include leg of lamb, couscous, boeuf bourguignon; there's a small but appealing wine list. Lunch costs about $7 to $10 per person.

Tutti's

1209 Coast Village Rd., Montecito 93108;
(805) 969-5809
*Breakfast (open 7 a.m.), Lunch & Dinner daily. MC,
V.*

Sleekly modern and stylish, Tutti's is many
things to prosperous Montecitans: a gourmet
grocery store, an upscale deli, a wine and cappuccino bar and a chic gathering spot for a meal. It's
quite handsome, with gleaming deli cases, an
open kitchen, stacks of packaged food and wine,
and a narrow marble bar counter facing the window to the street. Dinners can be expensive;
breakfast and lunch are more reasonable. None
of the food is exceptional, but it's all pleasant,
especially the croissants, breads and salads.
Tutti's also packs a good picnic. About $8 to $12
per person for lunch.

Deli

Ulrich's Deli

2704 De la Vina, Santa Barbara 93105;
(805) 687-9405
Lunch & Dinner Tues.-Sat. AE, MC, V.

An authentic German delicatessen, this is the
creation of chef Ulrich Fritsche, who has been
catering parties for the blue bloods of Santa Barbara for years. Herr Fritsche's dishes are reminiscent of Europe; and there are wonderful
homemade oils, vinegars, a modest selection of
wines, some decadent pastries and tasty cold
meat pies. About $6.50 per person for lunch.

Hamburgers

Be Bop Burgers

111 State St., Downtown (S.B.) 93102;
(805) 966-1956
Breakfast, Lunch & Dinner daily. D, MC, V.

Classic hamburgers, fries and shakes in a retro
setting. A satisfying meal costs less than $10.

Ice Cream

Häagen Dazs

819 State St., Downtown (S.B.) 93101;
(805) 966-0084;
*Open Mon.-Thurs. 10 a.m.-9 p.m., Fri.-Sat. 10 a.m.-11
p.m., Sun. 11 a.m.-9:30 p.m. No cards.*
1165 Coast Village Rd., Montecito 93108;
(805) 969-7946
*Open Sun.-Thurs. 11:30 a.m.-10:30 p.m., Fri.-Sat. 11:30
a.m.-11 p.m. No cards.*

This rich and creamy indulgence is available in
cones or cups, and by the pint or quart to go.
These days, there are also hand-dipped chocolate-covered ice-cream bars made on the spot, as

well as several frozen-yogurt flavors. Ice-cream
cakes of all kinds can be made within 24 hours.

McConnell's Ice Cream

1213 State St., Downtown (S.B.) 93103;
(805) 965-5400
*Open Sun.-Thurs. 11 a.m.-11 p.m., Fri.-Sat. 11 a.m.-
midnight. No cards.*

One of the country's finest ice cream makers
is based right here in Santa Barbara. These all-
natural ice creams are very, very rich and very,
very good. You can take your sundae or double
waffle cone out for a stroll on State Street or eat
at one of the small tables in this cheery shop.
There are also good sorbets, shakes and cappuccinos. Don't miss the discounted "not-up-to-
standards" cartons. A scoop costs $1.60.

Mexican

La Super-Rica

622 N. Milpas St., Santa Barbara 93103;
(805) 963-4940
Lunch & Dinner daily. No cards.

Until Julia Child's regular patronage brought
much attention to this incomparable Mexican
café, in-the-know Santa Barbarans were able to
keep it to themselves. But the word has long been
out, and we cannot encourage you enough to
rush right over for the best soft tacos you'll ever
have—fresh, hot corn tortillas, made right there,
topped with grilled chicken, pork, beef or chorizo. You must also try the frijoles, an addictive
dish of beans, sausage, bacon and chiles. These
soul-satisfying foods are best accompanied by a
Mexican beer on the rustic covered patio. Owner
Isadore Gonzales makes his own, marvelous soft
drinks. About $7 per person for lunch.

The Zia Café

532 State St., Downtown (S.B.) 93103;
(805) 962-5391
Lunch & Dinner daily. AE, MC, V.

Zia proudly serves the foods of Mexico and
New Mexico, an attractive but humble little place
that has a reputation for spicy-spicy variations on
the basics—enchiladas, tacos and tamales. New
Mexico enters into the picture with the blue-corn
tortillas, the delicious, slightly sweet sopapillas
(kind of a cross between bread and a tortilla) and
the substitution of posole for rice. There's the
good (the chicken blue-corn taco), the questionable (the beef blue-corn taco), and the tasty-hot
(the good tamales in red and green chile sauces).
About $7 to $9 per person for lunch.

Hotels

The symbol that accompanies each review indicates in which price category the hotel belongs: **Top of the Line** ($200 & Up), **Luxury** ($150 & Up), **Moderate** ($100 & Up) or **Practical** (Under $100). We have defined the categories based on the regular starting price of a single or double room. *See also* the INTRODUCTION chapter, under "About the Hotels."

Top of the Line *($200 & Up)*

 Four Seasons Biltmore
1260 Channel Dr., Montecito 93108;
(805) 969-2261, Fax (805) 969-4212
Singles & Doubles $270-$350, Suites $450-$1,595. All major cards.

Now that Four Seasons has put its stamp on this grande dame of Santa Barbara resort hotels, the decor, atmosphere and style of the place have shot up considerably. So have the prices. But the value is there without question. What you get for your $300 or more a night is an architectural stunner of a Spanish-Mediterranean resort spread across 21 acres of superb gardens, a magnificent oceanfront setting, handsome, impeccably equipped rooms, professional service and loads of amenities: tennis courts, two swimming pools, golf- and polo-club privileges and an adjacent beach club. Try to get one of the small cottages, which are especially charming. The lavish weekend brunch is one of *the* local scenes, and La Marina restaurant is one of the better dining spots in the city (*see* review in "SANTA BARBARA Restaurants").

 Ojai Valley Inn & Country Club
Country Club Dr., Ojai 93023;
(805) 646-5511, Fax (805) 646-7969
Rooms $190-$210, Suites $230-$250. Golf, tennis, fitness packages available. All major cards.

Vista International breathed new life into this longtime golf-oriented resort, and the results of its massive renovation and new construction are winning. More than 200 commodious, handsome rooms in some eleven buildings and cottages are scattered about the oak-dotted grounds. Also on the 200 rolling acres are an exceptionally attractive eighteen-hole golf course, an eight-court tennis center, a children's playground, sports fields for softball, volleyball, horseshoes and such, two pools, a health center complete with saunas, spas and workout equip-

ment, walking/jogging trails, several restaurants, a lounge and a snack bar. As you can see, you'd have to make a real effort to be bored here. A short drive away is the picturesque, sleepy town of Ojai, a fine place for an afternoon shopping stroll and a meal in one of the appealing restaurants. Also nearby is Wheeler Hot Springs, where you can take the cure in steaming tubs of mineral water, submit to a rejuvenating massage, or indulge in an excellent Sunday brunch.

 San Ysidro Ranch
900 San Ysidro Ln., Montecito 93108;
(805) 969-5046, Fax (805) 565-1995
Cottage Rooms & Cottages $195-$375; Cottages with Jacuzzi $375-$525. AE, MC, V.

This is one of the few places in America that's a member of the Relais et Châteaux chain of quality international hotels, and it deserves the affiliation. On a picture-perfect site in the verdant foothills of Montecito, the 105-year-old ranch has history (Churchill wrote his memoirs here), romance (Laurence Olivier and Vivian Leigh were married in the garden) and bushels of rustic charm. When the ranch was owned by actor Ronald Colman in the '30s, it was a weekend playground for Hollywood's heroes, but after his demise, it followed suit.

Today, it has been considerably spruced up, and is in the extremely capable hands of Claude Rouas, who also owns Napa Valley's superb Auberge du Soleil. The fragrance of the gardens and underbrush is as seductive as the privacy ensured by the supremely comfortable bungalows; many have fireplaces, some have Jacuzzis, and most allow dogs, virtually unheard of in American hotels. Amenities include tennis courts, a small pool and children's wading pool with stunning views over the eucalyptus trees to the Pacific, golf privileges at the nearby Montecito Country Club, horses for riding the miles of mountain trails, and the terrific Stonehouse restaurant (*see* review in "SANTA BARBARA Restaurants").

Luxury *($150 & Up)*

 Fess Parker's Red Lion Resort
633 E. Cabrillo Blvd., Santa Barbara 93103;
(805) 564-4333, Fax (805) 564-4964
Rooms $185-$255, Suites $345-$680. All major cards.

The Red Lion is chiefly a conventioneer's resort, a sprawling hotel (360 rooms) that has little to do with the legendary Santa Barbara lifestyle. Reminding us more of Las Vegas than a small-town beachfront resort hotel, it is, however, located across the street from the ocean and weekend arts-and-crafts show. Very popular with both businesspeople and tourists, and offers good weekend packages.

The Oaks at Ojai
122 E. Ojai Ave., Ojai 93023; (805) 646-5573, Fax (805) 640-1504
Rooms $148, Private Cottages $214-$263 (2-night minimum). D, MC, V.
See *"*LOS ANGELES Shops – Beauty & Health."

Moderate ($100 & Up)

El Encanto Hotel
1900 Lasuen Rd., Santa Barbara 93103; (805) 687-5000, Fax (805) 687-3903
Cottages $100-$325, Rooms $120-$200. All major cards.

As the name implies, there is enchantment to be found at this hotel, which is actually a collection of cottages in the hills above Santa Barbara. The enchantment stems from the gorgeous setting and view, as well as accommodations which have been enhanced with a multi-million dollar renovation by owner Eric Friden. Some of the rooms have fireplaces and kitchens, and the grounds are home to a tennis court and pool. And if the weather is cooperative, which it usually is, you can sit on the Astroturfed terrace just before sunset and soak in the kind of Pacific view that inspires countless frozen Midwesterners to move to California. Best of all, this first rate hotel offers the best value of any luxury hotel in town. The dining room is a lovely place to eat (*see* review in "SANTA BARBARA Restaurants").

The Montecito Inn
1295 Coast Village Rd., Montecito 93108; (805) 969-7854, Fax (805) 969-0623
Singles & Doubles $105-$145, Suites $156-$285 (incl. breakfast). All major cards.

The Montecito Inn was loaded with charm when it opened its doors in 1928—an intimate hideaway for Hollywood's greats, built by two of the greatest: Charlie Chaplin and Fatty Arbuckle. Since 1981, two new owners have spent lavishly to upgrade and restore it, recapturing the Mediterranean-style grace and elegance of its youth and adding modern touches. Minor drawbacks are the Inn's close proximity to Highway 101 (request an upper room) and the lack of air conditioning, but otherwise, it's a jewel of a hotel.

The tiled, arch-ceilinged lobby is lined with rose-velvet love seats and mirror-topped tables for taking tea. The rooms are small by today's standards, done in cozy fabrics with modern

bathrooms, each with unique Mexican tile. There's a workout room and free bicycle use. Taking a swim or a sauna on the intimate back patio feels like being at the home of a privileged friend—except that a gracious server appears to see if you'd like a drink. Montecito Café serves tasty, affordable Californian fare (*see* review in "SANTA BARBARA Restaurants").

Sheraton Santa Barbara
1111 E. Cabrillo Blvd., Santa Barbara 93103; (805) 963-0744, Fax (805) 962-0985
Singles $119-$195, Doubles $145-$210, Suites $370-$570. All major cards.

One of only two major hotels in town overlooking East Beach, a stretch of sand thick with firm bodies hard at play on the the volleyball courts. There is a health spa (in need of updating), a pool, Jacuzzi, sauna, exercise room and meeting rooms and cabanas on the beach. This hotel was headquarters for the press when President Reagan was in office.

Simpson House Inn
121 E. Arrellaga St., Downtown (S.B) 93101; (805) 963-7067, Fax (805) 564-4811
Rooms $105-$155 (incl. breakfast). All major cards.

Secluded in an acre of English gardens, yet just a five-minute walk to downtown. This Victorian home is a designated Structure of Merit because of its unique 1870s architecture and beautiful setting. The spacious sitting room with fireplace and book-lined walls adjoins the formal dining room; both open onto verandas overlooking the gardens. Guest rooms are elegantly appointed with antiques. English lace, Oriental rugs, queen beds and private baths with clawfoot tubs. Delicious breakfast, afternoon tea, wine and hors d'oeuvres. No pets.

Upham Hotel
1404 De la Vina St., Downtown (S.B.) 93101; (805) 962-0058, Fax (805) 963-2825
Rooms $95-$150, Cottages $165-$295. All major cards.

Built in 1871, the Upham is Southern California's oldest inn. We prefer the lovely little cottages by the gardens that lie outside the main building, but all of the rooms are tastefully done. The complimentary cheese and wine in the afternoon by the fire is a happy way to end the day. The hotel's restaurant, Louie's, is a hip and classy dining spot, serving creative French/Californian cuisine (*see* review in "SANTA BARBARA Restaurants").

Practical (Under $100)

Bath Street Inn
1720 Bath St., Downtown (S.B.) 93101;
(805) 682-9680 or (800) 788-2284, No fax
Rooms $90-$115 (incl. breakfast). All major cards.

Once a faded Victorian home, this is now one of Santa Barbara's most gracious and comfortable bed-and-breakfast inns. Each of the seven rooms has its own bathroom—our favorite is the claw-footed tub in the spacious Partridge Room. All the rooms are attractive and commendably quiet, including the handsome communal living room and a library/TV room. A fine breakfast is served in the flower-filled garden, with fresh-squeezed juice from the orange trees. Other extras: free bikes, wine and cheese in the evening.

Bayberry Inn
111 W. Valerio St., Downtown (S.B.)
93101; (805) 682-3199, Fax (805) 962-0103
Rooms $70-$135 (incl. breakfast). All major cards. No smoking.

This small, Federal-style bed-and-breakfast is well-located in the charming residential area near downtown. The eight rooms are comfortable and breezy, all done in a homey decor, and a communal deck offers a peaceful place to soak up the Santa Barbara sun.

Blue Quail Inn and Cottages
1908 Bath St., Downtown (S.B.) 93101;
(805) 687-2300, No fax
Rooms $82-$165 (incl. breakfast). MC, V.

A charming country inn offering a choice of delightful guest rooms or quaint cottages, each uniquely decorated with antiques. Enjoy a delicious Continental breakfast of freshly baked muffins, juices, fresh fruit, coffee and tea. Secluded garden; bicycles and picnic lunches may be reserved. After sight-seeing, you can relax with hot apple cider in the cozy living room.

The Cheshire Cat
36 W. Valerio St., Downtown (S.B.) 93101;
(805) 569-1610, Fax (805) 682-1876
Rooms $79-$290. MC, V.

A whimsical and lovely bed-and-breakfast. A dozen storybook-charming Laura Ashley–style rooms are spread between two neighboring stately Victorian homes, which share a serene garden and large Jacuzzi. The rooms have queen- or king-sized beds and private baths; some have fireplaces, sitting rooms, Jacuzzis and private patios. Public areas include a fireplace-warmed sitting room and a rather stately dining room; a

good breakfast can also be enjoyed on the patio outside. Afternoon wine, complimentary bicycle use, evening chocolates . . . nothing is lacking.

Glenborough Inn & Cottages
1327 Bath St., Downtown (S.B.) 93101;
(805) 966-0589, Fax (805) 966-0589 ext. 124
Rooms $60-$155 (incl. breakfast). All major cards.

Garden hot tub for your private use. Hearty gourmet breakfast delivered to your quiet, romantic Victorian room, fireplace suite, or perhaps our lush flower-filled gardens. Homemade appetizers and beverages served fireside at sunset. Stroll to restaurants, shops and museums. Bikes available. No pets.

Harbor View Inn
28 W. Cabrillo Blvd., Santa Barbara 93101;
(805) 963-0780, Fax (805) 963-7967
Rooms $85-$215 (incl. breakfast, afternoon wine & cheese). All major cards.

A small (64 room) inn offering a prime location across from the beach and Stearns Wharf. Renovations in 1985 added a luxury wing and gave the property a welcome face-lift. All rooms have a balcony or patio. Most have great views of the harbor and wharf. On the premises are a pool, Jacuzzi and conference facilities.

Old Yacht Club Inn/Hitchcock House
431 Corona del Mar, Santa Barbara 93103;
(805) 962-1277, Fax (805) 962-3989
Rooms $75-$135 (incl. breakfast). All major cards.

This elegant 1912 home opened in 1980 as Santa Barbara's first bed & breakfast inn. Five charming guest rooms in the original house and four rooms in the Hitchcock House next door make up the lodgings. All is charming and tasteful with antiques, Oriental rugs and period decor. Full gourmet breakfast. Dinner by reservation on weekends. Complimentary bicycles, beach chairs and towels. Evening social hour. No pets.

Miramar Hotel
1555 S. Jameson Ln., Santa Barbara 93108;
(805) 969-2203, Fax (805) 969-3163
Singles, Doubles & Cottages $70-$260. All major cards.

In some ways this sprawling resort, in business since 1887, reminds us of a Bulgarian seaside resort where workers from the grain cooperative are rewarded with a vacation if they've had a productive year. There is nothing luxurious about the amenities at the Miramar (nor the blasé service), but for one of the most spectacularly sited resorts in Southern California, the price is right. No other resort hotel in the vicinity has its own private beach (one of the best in California). There are four tennis courts, two swimming pools and large convention facilities. Reserve a beachfront room, if one is available, or a two- or three-bedroom cottage—some of these are quite charming, with fireplaces and full kitchens. (The most modern cottages are also the noisiest, as they are close to the freeway.) You can cook your own breakfast, and lots of good dining is nearby.

 ## Los Olivos Grand Hotel
2860 Grand Ave., Los Olivos 93441;
(805) 688-7788, Fax (805) 688-1942
Rooms $95-$150 (midweek), $210-$325 (weekends). AE, MC, V.

An extraordinary small hotel, the Los Olivos Grand is a country inn much like you would stumble on in France. It has both grace and luxurious amenities one doesn't expect to find in a town the size of a small ranch, 35 miles out of Santa Barbara: down comforters, fireplaces, hand-painted tiles in each of the 21 rooms, plus swimming pool, Jacuzzi, and a gourmet restaurant of rare quality. The hotel's restaurant, besides featuring works of Western art like the rest of the hotel, is celebrated for Californian cuisine and extensive wine cellar. The Los Olivos Grand Hotel is the perfect getaway for romantics. Yet it also appeals to the businessman seeking a private venue to hold an executive conference in a productive atmosphere. The dining room, Remington's, is notable for its lavish Sunday brunches and an impressive Californian wine list.

 ## Villa Rosa
15 Chapala St., Downtown (S.B.) 93101;
(805) 966-0851, No fax
Singles & Doubles $90-$190 (incl. breakfast, afternoon wine & cheese). AE, MC, V.

This pale-pink palazzo, a converted Spanish-style home, is one of the most contemporary and tastefully decorated bed-and-breakfast inns in Santa Barbara. True, the others have old-fashioned charm and a little more personality, but the Villa Rosa has sophistication and a handsome Southwestern interior in monochromatic grays and dusty beiges. No matter that the walls are paper-thin; you'll get to know your neighbors well enough in the Jacuzzi or relaxing around the pool in the beautiful courtyard, where wine and cheese are served in the late afternoon and a croissant breakfast is served each morning. The location is perfect for a stroll on the beach (around the corner). The best rooms overlook the pool away from the sounds of traffic.

Nightlife

Acapulco
1114 State St., Downtown (S.B.) 93101;
(805) 963-3469
Open Tues.-Thurs. 11 a.m.-10 p.m., Fri.-Sat. 11 a.m.-11 p.m., Sun. 10 a.m.-10 p.m. Cover $2 Fri.-Sat. AE, MC, V.

This popular Mexican chain concocts 31 different flavors of margaritas, which are served outdoors under the umbrella-shaded, Spanish-tiled patio, in the spacious bar or in the jungle room. It's always packed with people having a great time, but remains a pleasant place to watch afternoon shoppers in the little paseo or to spend an evening when the tempo and clientele pick up.

Alex's Cantina
633 State St., Downtown (S.B.) 93101;
(805) 966-0032
Open daily 11:30 a.m.-midnight (until 1:30 a.m. when there's live music). Cover for bands $2. All major cards.

Locals have repeatedly named Alex's the best happy hour in town, with free chips and salsa and tasty soft tacos made to order. The bar doesn't empty out after 7 p.m., however. Live local bands play Friday and Saturday nights and often during the week, making this a good bet for a night of margaritas, munchies and music.

Joe's Café
512 State St., Downtown (S.B.) 93101;
(805) 966-4638
Open Mon.-Thurs. 11 a.m.-11 p.m., Fri.-Sat. 11 a.m.-midnight, Sun. 4 p.m.-11 p.m. AE, MC, V.

On Friday and Saturday nights this place is a madhouse—randy young Santa Barbarans cram in three-deep at the bar, looking for bitchin' babes and rad dudes. While they prowl, they try to talk to their many friends by shouting over the incredible noise level. It's considerably quieter during the day and in the afternoon, when you'll see a more relaxed crowd of seasoned Joe's veterans. A Santa Barbara landmark that is great for inexpensive drinks, local color and studying the native language of the California beach scene.

The Ketch
514 State St., Downtown (S.B.) 93101;
(805) 564-3231
Open daily 5 p.m.-2 a.m. Cover $1-$3. MC, V.

This surf shack of a nightclub consistently showcases the best local bands. Expect a long line at the door and trendy college students crowding the bar inside.

The Open Door

513 State St., Downtown (S.B.) 93101;
(805) 965-6655
*Open Tues.-Sun. noon-midnight. Cover $2 Fri.-Sat. AE,
MC, V.*

A sophisticated beer-lover's paradise. Patrons sip and chug their favorite brews from yard and half-yard beakers, which come with individual stands. The atmosphere is mellow and friendly; on Friday and Saturday nights, local talent takes the stage to play classic soft-rock favorites.

The Pub

224 Helena Ave., Downtown (S.B.) 93101;
(805) 962-3911
*Open Mon.-Fri. 4 p.m.-2 a.m., Sat.-Sun. 2 p.m.-2 a.m.
Cover $5 Fri.-Sat. No cards.*

This is the town's premier gay men's bar, with lively music and dancing.

Zelo

630 State St., Downtown (S.B.) 93101;
(805) 966-5792
Open daily 5:30 p.m.-2 a.m. Cover varies. AE, MC, V.

Zelo has long held claim to the title of hippest nightclub in town—but keep in mind that the town is not exactly cluttered with hip nightclubs. Also a restaurant that serves Californian cuisine, Zelo's biggest attractions are a narrow bar and a cozy dance floor that pulsates with recorded dance music. Bands keep the trendy crowd dancing twice a month; the rest of the time the tunes are deejay-spun rock, soul and hip-hop.

Shops

Shopping is alive and well in Santa Barbara, and increasingly big-city in its form. Gone are many of the mom 'n' pop boutiques of yesterday, and in their place are national chains, many of them imported directly from Los Angeles. A prime example is the new multi-million dollar mall downtown on State Street, **Paseo Nuevo** (651 Paseo Nuevo, 805-963-2202), which has imported a slew of upscale chain stores: Victoria's Secret, The Nature Store, Eddie Bauer, The Gap, Sesame Street, The Broadway, California Pizza Kitchen and the Coffee Bean & Tea Leaf, a gourmet coffee shop—all anchored by a posh Nordstrom. The most unique store is Stampa Barbara, filled with thousands of witty, wise and weird rubber stamps.

Downtown's **State Street** used to be Santa Barbara's main shopping street, but changing times, an increasingly visible homeless population and the lure of Paseo Nuevo are spelling

uncertain times for this once-fashionable area. High points include the recently expanded **Earthling Book Store**: with its hip café and cozy fireplace, it has long been locals' perennial browsing spot for new books on every subject. There are frequent celebrity readings and guitar entertainment (1137 State St., 805-965-0926). An elegant **I. Magnin** at the corner of State and Sola streets (1415 State St., 805-962-0061) provides some of the city's most sophisticated shopping. Right behind State Street is **The Wine Cask** restaurant and wine shop (813 Anacapa St., Santa Barbara 93101; 805-965-1178/966-9463). Knowledgeable wine-expert owner Doug Margerum has made the Wine Cask an invaluable source, for its considerable number of precious vintage bottles and its excellent stock from Bordeaux, Burgundy, Italy, Santa Barbara and the Central Coast. Farther down, near the beach, is **Pacific Travellers Supply** (529 State St., 805-962-0884): a goldmine for those with wanderlust, it stocks guides, maps, globes, luggage and more.

Anapamu Street, in the downtown area, is a treasure trove of eccentric and exotic shops, including Metro Comics and its amazing selection of back issues and cards; Asiana Oriental Rugs; the Wine Connection wine shop and tasting bar; Crispin Leather Goods; and The Book Den, the city's most popular used book store.

La Cumbre Plaza (121 S. Hope Ave., Santa Barbara 93105; 805-687-6458) on upper State Street is a large, outdoor shopping mall, with Williams-Sonoma, B. Dalton, Pottery Barn, The Bombay Company, Banana Republic, and a host of other chain stores, anchored by Robinson's and Sears department stores.

Close by La Cumbre Plaza is the posher, trendier **Galleria** (3891 State St., Santa Barbara 93105; 805-969-3118), an upscale shopping mini-mall with top retailers like Ann Taylor, Laura Ashley and Polo, plus the fine Baccio restaurant. In the nearby Loreto Plaza, an unexciting corner mall, is **Chaucer's Bookstore** (3321 State St., 805-682-6787). One of Santa Barbara's best-stocked independents, it carries a wealth of new, general-interest material.

If you like shopping with the Social Register set, head for **Coast Village Road** twenty minutes south of Santa Barbara in Montecito, a charming street rife with tiny boutiques, among them florists, travel agencies, antique dealers, stationery stores, dress shops and jewelry stores. While you're there, don't miss the **Montecito Wine Bistro** (1280 Coast Village Rd., Montecito 93108; 805-969-3955): formerly the Montecito

Wine Cask, this café and shop has a sophisticated and extensive selection of wines. The advantage here—you can try many of the wines by the glass at the little café before buying.

Nearby Montecito Village (1482 E. Valley Rd., 805-969-7759) at the junction of East Valley and San Ysidro roads, houses quality luggage, stationery, women's and men's apparel, flowers, jewelry and other creature comforts. Just across the street is Pierre LaFond (516 San Ysidro Rd., 805-565-1502) a veritable emporium of fine goods. Separate little storefronts, all under the name Pierre LaFond, hold a beautifully stocked gourmet-food market, a deli/café, a charming home-furnishings shop and a casually elegant clothing boutique. Wendy Foster the sister store next door, has a dressier collection, but still with an easy elegance—this is Santa Barbara, after all.

Summerland, that sleepy village just three miles south of Santa Barbara has some very good antique shopping: Summerland Antique Collective (2192 Ortega Hill Rd., 805-565-3189); Summerland Antique Annex (2240 Lillie Ave., 805-565-5226); and Heather House Antiques (2448 Lillie Ave., 805-565-1561).

Sights

In addition to the worthy sights listed below, Santa Barbara boasts a wealth of outdoor activities, encouraged by the seemingly constant sunshine and the sparkling sea. Good beaches abound: surfers will want to head for Rincon Point, Carpinteria and the surf breaks near UC Santa Barbara; windsurfers for West Beach; and swimmers, sunbathers and strollers for any stretch of sand. And though it may be touristy, Stearns Wharf (where State Street meets the beach) affords a superb view of the coastline; while you're there, get a paper-plate meal of clam chowder and lobster at the Santa Barbara Shellfish Company (805-963-4415).

For brochures detailing the area's many sports and activities (deep-sea fishing, sailing, horseback riding, bicycling, hiking, tennis, golf...), contact the Santa Barbara Convention and Visitors Bureau (805-965-3021).

Santa Barbara Botanic Garden
1212 Mission Canyon Rd., Santa Barbara 93105; (805) 682-4726
Open daily 8 a.m.-sunset. Admission free.

For proof of Santa Barbara's staggering variety of native flora, spend an hour or so wandering through the 65 peaceful acres of this marvelous

botanic garden. You'll see everthing from vivid wildflowers to dramatic cacti, from spiky palm trees to cool redwoods.

Santa Barbara Historical Society
126 E. De la Guerra St., Santa Barbara 93101; (805) 966-1601
Open Tues.-Sat. 10 a.m.-5 p.m., Sun. noon-5 p.m. Admission free.

This dedicated group of heritage-preservers runs a small, intriguing museum dedicated to the Santa Barbara of days gone by. It also offers docent-led trips along the city's Red Tile Walking Tour, a must for admirers of Spanish architecture (or, to walk it yourself, call the Tourist Information Center for a map; 805-965-3021).

Santa Barbara Mission
2201 Laguna St., Santa Barbara 93105; (805) 682-4149
Open daily 9 a.m.-5 p.m. Adults $1, children free.

The Santa Barbara Mission, first built in 1786, is proof that Southern California has a more venerable history than its reputation would suggest. The tenth mission founded by the Spanish Franciscans, this "Queen of the Missions" is one of the loveliest, and is in the best condition. You can study dioramas of Franciscan life, wander in the gardens where the missionaries taught the native Chumash Indians, attend a service in the Indian-built chapel and walk among the gravestones of those buried there. Throughout are good examples of Spanish colonial architecture (on which the best architecture in town is modeled) and eighteenth- and nineteenth-century Spanish-Mexican art.

Santa Barbara Museum of Art
1130 State St., Santa Barbara 93101; (805) 963-4364
Open Tues.-Wed. & Fri.-Sat. 11 a.m.-5 p.m., Thurs. 11 a.m.-9 p.m., Sun. noon-5 p.m. Admission free.

Thank goodness for the benefactors who keep this museum filled with their own highly personal collections. This provincial yet admirable museum may give visitors a sense of dizziness from the eclectic nature of the bequests; impressive American Hudson River school oils are hung next to modest Greek and Roman antiquities. The best, however, is the doll collection, with everything from African queens to Quaker matrons (check first—it's shown on a rotating basis). Traveling exhibitions in this well-endowed museum tend to be exciting and dynamic. It also sponsors art tours throughout the world and presents lectures frequently; in fact, it has thoughtfully provided a luncheon art lecture to accommodate local businesspeople during their lunch hours. ◆

SANTA YNEZ

The Other Wine Country

During a summer spent traveling through California, a friend from back East once observed that no matter what Californian city you settle in, you get the bonus of a lot of other interesting towns nearby. If you live in San Francisco, you get Santa Cruz to the south, Sausalito and St. Helena to the north and Berkeley and Oakland to the east. If you live in Los Angeles, you get an ocean's worth of beach towns to the south, Big Bear and Palm Springs to the east and Santa Barbara to the north. And if you live in Santa Barbara, you get the Santa Ynez Valley. Which means you get, in one fell swoop, both a burgeoning winemaking region and one of the most historically interesting areas in California. So historically rich is the Santa Ynez Valley that there's even history to be found in its meals—and not just in the thick green potage served so liberally at Pea Soup Andersen's.

There was a time in the not-too-distant past when the Santa Ynez Valley was nothing but pleasantly verdant land that travelers traversed on the road between San Francisco and Los Angeles. Even today, this rugged valley about 45 miles north of Santa Barbara is so rustic that it lacks a major urban center; Santa Ynezians in the mood for the bright lights of the big city have to drive north to Santa Maria or west to Lompoc.

Around the turn of the century, Santa Ynez (bordered by the Santa Ynez Mountains on the south and the San Rafael Mountains on the north) became known as a good place for stagecoaches headed up and down the coast to stop for a meal, a change of horses and perhaps a night's rest. Amazingly, the old inns that served those stagecoaches (and the cars that followed) are still there, marvelous working relics of a time gone by, serving food untouched by culinary trends—and barely touched by the vicissitudes of inflation.

Progress of a sort has struck the Santa Ynez Valley in recent years, transforming the hills around such villages as Buellton, Los Olivos, Los Alamos and Casmalia into a sort of refugee camp for Beverly Hills escapees. Almost overnight, the rich and the super-rich, especially those from the world of entertainment, started buying up huge tracts of land. Pop star Michael Jackson is building an empire (a castle, a zoo and an amusement park) on hundreds of prime Santa Ynez acres. Hollywood megaproducer Ray Stark has a ranch, as does gossipmonger Rona Barrett. Occasional actress Bo Derek and her occasional producer/director husband, John Derek, have a spread thereabouts also. Producer Doug Cramer's hacienda has appeared in *Architectural Digest*, which doted on the art "warehouse" (most would call it a museum) he built between his house and winery. And, of course, a certain former president with a fondness for chopping wood and riding horses has a place in the Santa Ynez hills.

Yet remarkably, the Santa Ynez Valley remains a relatively unspoiled weekend getaway, a place for putting on your (Ralph Lauren) jeans and (hand-tooled Tony Lama) cowboy boots, climbing into your (Range Rover) pickup truck and driving from some lovely wineries to some very good art galleries to some venerable, perfectly restored inns. In Santa Ynez, people who normally have no problem getting an eight o'clock reservation at Spago are only too glad to wait in line to dine at an old ranchhouse. Despite the wholly unreal incomes of its newest residents, this is a real place filled with real activities for real people.

Restaurants

See INTRODUCTION for an explanation of our restaurant rating system, and a listing of restaurants by rating. See INDEXES at the back of the book for comprehensive restaurant indexes.

10/20 Ballard Store & Wine Bar
2449 Baseline Ave., Solvang 93463;
(805) 688-5319
Californian. Dinner Wed.-Sun., Brunch Sun.
MC, V.

Wending your way a bit north to Ballard, just outside of Solvang, you'll come across the Ballard School. It's the prototypical little red schoolhouse, complete with a steeple and nicely framed by a pair of venerable black walnut trees. The school dates to 1883 and is still in use (it houses a kindergarten class). Next to the school you'll find what was the general store for the area in the '20s and '30s. Today it houses this worthy restaurant, run by a former chef from New York's 21 Club, serving good Californian/Continental food that's fancier than most in this area: fresh fish, filet mignon, duck, lamb, scampi, lobster. A dinner costs about $30.

12/20 Cold Spring Tavern
5995 Stagecoach Rd., San Marcos Pass,
Santa Barbara 93105; (805) 967-0066
See "SANTA BARBARA Restaurants."

12/20 The Hitching Post
3325 Point Sal Rd., Casmalia 93429;
(805) 937-6151
406 E. Hwy. 246, Buellton 93427;
(805) 688-0676
American. Dinner nightly. AE, MC, V.

In Santa Ynez terms, barbecuing means grilling over an oakwood fire, in this case behind a glassed-in cooking area. You can order your steak by weight (top sirloin, New York and filet mignon—as big as twenty ounces) and then watch it sizzle on the grill while you down such wonderfully old-fashioned items as shrimp cocktail, green salad, garlic bread, a choice of a baked potato or french fries, a relish tray (remember those?) and, this being California, a bowl of salsa. All this is included in the price, which is about $40 per person.

10/20 Mattei's Tavern
Hwy. 154, Los Olivos 93441;
(805) 688-4820
American. Lunch Thurs.-Sun., Dinner nightly. MC, V.

This restaurant, which is more than a century old, stands one block away from where the roundhouse (the end of the line for the long-gone Pacific Coast train) burned down some years back. Clark Gable used to stay at Mattei's while on hunting trips in the Santa Ynez hills. Bing Crosby, William Jennings Bryant and Montgomery Ward all spent the night here. Such actors as Marjorie Main and Edmund Lowe came up here to memorize their scripts, away from day-to-day interruptions in Hollywood. Today, Mattei's is strictly a saloon and restaurant, a marvelous place to go for steak, prime rib, chicken and even lobster, all served with green salads and hot bread. After dinner, you can sit out on the porch and imagine that you hear the whistle of the old train heading down Railroad Avenue. Plan to spend about $25 to $35 per person.

Hotels

Santa Barbara's wine country isn't quite like Napa Valley, at least not yet—for one thing, there are surprisingly few country inns. Solvang is thick with motels, but most of them are best suited to the tour-bus set. Although you might not have a lot of options, what few you do have are very

good indeed. Below are our four favorite Santa Ynez retreats. See INTRODUCTION for an explanation of our hotel classification system.

The Alisal Guest Ranch
1054 Alisal Rd., Solvang 93463;
(805) 688-6411, Fax (805) 688-2510
Doubles $255-$330. AE, MC, V.

The price of a room doesn't get you luxurious accommodations, but it gets you lots of other marvelous features: ten thousand acres of lovely tree-studded countryside, a lake, a respectable golf course, tennis, miles of riding trails, stables, games and more. It also gets two of you breakfast and dinner (which might be a barbecue, followed by a square dance). During the week (off season), the room rates also include all the golf and horseback riding you can handle. It *doesn't* include a TV or phone in your room, which suits the loyal clientele of golfers and horsey families just fine. This is a great place for kids—and anyone who prefers to spend more time in the great outdoors than holed up in a fancy room.

The Ballard Inn
2436 Baseline Ave., Ballard 93463;
(805) 688-7770, Fax (805) 688-9560
Doubles $155-$185. MC, V.

Built in 1985 in a Victorian farmhouse style, this fifteen-room inn has plenty of country charm but not too much rusticity. Located right across the street from the Ballard Store, the inn prides itself on warm, friendly service, as well as a diverse choice of rooms. Each is decorated differently, from the frilly to the solidly masculine; all have Americana antiques and some have fireplaces. The room rate includes a full breakfast in a fireplace-warmed dining room and wine and hors d'oeuvres in the drawing room. The rooms are blessedly free of both phones and TVs.

Los Olivos Grand Hotel
2860 Grand Ave., Los Olivos 93441;
(805) 688-7788, Fax (805) 688-1942
Doubles $160-$300 (weekdays); $210-$325 (weekends). AE, D, MC, V.

To see how far the Santa Ynez Valley has come from its stagecoach-stop days, book a room at this posh country hotel in the gallery-clogged village of Los Olivos. The 21 exceptionally large guest rooms, each decorated by a different artist, come complete with fireplaces, wet bars, sitting areas and down comforters; some even have Jacuzzi tubs. Outside, there's a pool, Jacuzzi and all the trees and rolling hills you could wish for. Respectable Continental fare is served in the dining room, which is full of Western bronze sculpture and is named, aptly enough, The Reming-ton. The service is in keeping with the high prices.

🏠 Union Hotel
362 Bell St., Los Alamos 93440;
(805) 344-2744, Fax (805) 344-3125
Doubles $80-$100 (hotel), $200 (Victorian Mansion). AE, MC, V.

This folksy, funky thirteen-room inn was orig-inally built in 1880 as a Wells Fargo stagecoach stop. It burned down in 1886, was rebuilt in the early 1900s, and was lovingly restored by its cur-rent owner, Dick. You'll probably have to share a bathroom, but in return you'll get lots of nos-talgic charm. The place is filled with nifty old stuff: homey furniture, handmade quilts, pedes-tal sinks, even an authentic cowboy saloon. Inside amusements include a pool table; outside, there's a pool and Jacuzzi. Dinner (at $10 to $20 per person) runs the gamut from such honest coun-try chow as barbecue beef and corn bread to filet mignon and fresh fish. Romantics and devotees of theme inns will definitely want to check out the Victorian Mansion, an adjacent building with six different, elaborate themes: in the '50s Drive-In, you sleep in a '56 Cadillac convertible; the French Room is done up like an artist's loft, with a trompe l'oeil view of the Eiffel Tower; and if you can snatch the popular Egyptian Room—you'll enter through a 1,000 pound stone door, and sleep in a four-poster canapy bed overlooking a painted desert "oasis." All come complete with costume robes, fireplaces, soaking tubs, theme music, champagne and a full breakfast served discreetly through a pass-through.

Sights

Art Galleries

There are one dozen art galleries on Grand Avenue in the small town of Los Olivos, with a population numbering just 850. The best way to prepare for a gallery hop is to contact the **Los Olivos Gallery Organization** (805-688-5083); they'll tell you which artists are being shown where, and what special shows are slated. Most of the work shown is traditional, much of it is Western—including the stock at the **Elizabeth Kyle Gallery** (805-688-5953). Next door at the

Cody Gallery (805-688-5083), you'll find pho-torealism, along with the serpentine marble sculptures of local artist John Cody; next door to that, watercolors at the **Nancy Phelps Gallery** (805-686-1142); and down the street, there's the **Zzyx Gallery** (805-688-8104).

Wineries

Firestone Vineyard (5017 Zaca Station Rd., Los Olivos 93441; 805-688-3940) is the premier winery in the region, which, like Jordan up north, is the result of a highly determined, very affluent wine lover. In 1972, Brooks Firestone was hap-pily employed in the family business (yes, that's the tire manufacturer) when his father was of-fered a sizable chunk of Santa Ynez land. Brooks thought it sounded like fun. Two years later, Suntory of Japan joined him as a partner, and eighteen years later, he and his wife, Kate, make some of the best Chardonnays, Cabernets and Rieslings in Southern California. On a hill high above the vineyards, the winery is a highly un-derstated, surprisingly modern wooden struc-ture, carefully weathered so it blends almost innocuously into the landscape. The tour is a good one, well informed and not overly long; at the end, you're rewarded with a chance to sample some remarkably tasty wines.

Driving down little ol' Route 154 or Route 176, you'll find even smaller roads that will take you to such modest, friendly wineries as **Brander Winery** (2401 N. Refugio Rd., Los Olivos 93441; 805-688-2455; tastings daily and tours by appointment) and **Carey Cellars** (1711 Alamo Pintado Rd., Solvang 93463; 805-688-8554; tastings and tours daily). In addition to some terrific wines, **Zaca Mesa** (6905 Foxen Canyon Rd., Los Olivos 93441; 805-688-3310) offers daily tours and tastings, a small gift shop and a lovely picnic area that overlooks 220 acres of vineyards. And if only for the sheer beauty of its labels, the **Sanford Winery** (7250 Santa Rosa Rd., Buellton 93427; 805-688-3300; tastings daily) is worth a visit. **Au Bon Climat's** Los Olivos Wine Tasting Room (2905 Grand Ave., Los Olivos 93441; 805-688-7406) is open daily. To find your way around, call or write the **Santa Barbara County Vintners' Association** (P.O. Box 1558, Santa Ynez 93460; 805-688-0881) for a free map and guide to the wineries. ◆

BIG BEAR

Southern Skiing

Peaking at heights of up to 11,000 feet, the San Bernardino Mountains, just under a three-hour drive east of Los Angeles, provide Southern California with its most popular four-seasons recreational resorts—Big Bear and Lake Arrowhead. Snowy winter weekends in these mountains are overrun with skiers headed for the slopes of Snow Summit, Bear Mountain and Snow Forest. Summer is just as busy, when city people come here to fish, hike, waterski and just plain relax in the clean air and open spaces. Travelers in search of a rustic breath of fresh air will find the town of Big Bear quaint, informal and friendly, if somewhat tacky. But, then, the setting is unquestionably lovely. It's a mini–Lake Tahoe: a clear, blue lake surrounded by pine-topped mountains. Lake Arrowhead is a smaller, privately owned lake not far from Big Bear. The moneyed weekend retreat lacks the down-home charm of Big Bear, but it boasts an exceptionally beautiful setting and lots of clean mountain air.

If you can't make friends with one of Big Bear's or Lake Arrowhead's lucky homeowners, you can rent a house or cabin, or stay at one of a number of mountain resorts and bed and breakfasts (*see* Hotels section) in the area. Note: the devastating earthquake that struck the Big Bear area in 1992 destroyed a number of businesses and attractions. It's a good idea to call ahead for the latest information.

Restaurants

11/20 The Blue Whale Lakeside
350 Alden Rd., Big Bear Lake 92315; (909) 866-5771
Steakhouse/Seafood. Dinner nightly, Brunch Sun. MC, V.

If you haven't already guessed by its name, The Blue Whale Lakeside is the only restaurant with a lakeside view in Big Bear. Chef Phil Bennet, who recently bought the establishment from his former bosses, has introduced a few game dishes to the menu, but still carries on the tradition of offering a selection of fresh fish daily. There is a solid range of entrées, from pasta primavera to roast duck to mushroom-stuffed filet mignon smothered with Alaskan crabmeat and béarnaise,

and an extensive salad bar. The cozy and rustic decor is sheltered by a tall, open-beamed ceiling and warmed by the stone fireplace and friendly service. The adjoining Tail of the Whale is a lively bar also on the water, with guest docks for the parched boater, live music Friday and Saturday, and jazz on Sunday. Given the meager options for dining in Big Bear, The Blue Whale Lakeside is a safe bet. Dinner runs $20 per person.

12/20 George & Sigi's Knusperhäuschen Restaurant
829 W. Big Bear Blvd., Big Bear City 92314; (909) 585-8640
Continental. Dinner Mon.-Wed. & Fri.-Sun. MC, V.

It's hard to take this Hansel and Gretel cottage too seriously. The exterior is reminiscent of a Christmas gumdrop house; the interior is a cozy clutter of stained glass, oil paintings and private booths. The fare offered here is hearty and enticing: beef Wellington, an Italian-style paella and stuffed pheasant, to name only a few. Dinners here are generous and smothered with good tastes and a lot of care. You may be offered specials such as chicken-mushroom soup flavored with sour cream, or homemade Burgundy salad dressing or one of many schnitzels. The kitchen's repertoire is vast: chicken Kiev, goulash, schnitzel Oscar, sauerbraten, braised oxtails and more—and it's all good. While the wine list is extensive, we suggest you try the knowledgeable selection of German beers. An Alpine-sized dinner for one will run about $25.

11/20 The Iron Squirrel
646 Pineknot Blvd., Big Bear Lake 92315; (909) 866-9121
French. Dinner nightly. AE, MC, V.

Although the cuisine is not what we would call inspired, this family place serves up enticing French country cooking. Recently remodeled and repainted, the pine-paneled mountain decor has been toned down with a fresh coat of off-white paint—but the homey touches remain. Joyce and Paul Ortuno greet you, while their uncle, Roger, runs the kitchen with Basque enthusiasm. Entrées come with soup and salad, making this place a good value; if you want a starter, try the lovely thyme-studded pâté. Most everything we've tried has been enjoyable: hearty paella, rack of lamb with garlic, veal normande with plump apples, roast chicken and more simple French classics. Desserts are rich, sweet and satisfying. There are two wine lists; ask for the California version and you will be able to choose from excellent vintages at reasonable prices. Dinner comes in under $25 per person.

Vines
Bear Valley Winery, 625 Pine Knot Blvd.,
Big Bear Lake 92315; (909) 866-3033
Continental. Dinner nightly, Brunch Sun. D, MC, V.

Vines Restaurant and Wine Tasting Bar is a jewel of a place that could easily be overlooked in Adora Bella Plaza's maze of boutiques. Housed in the Bear Valley Winery, it is one of the best things to happen to this little resort town in the last few years. Walled in white latticework and strung rather humorously with *faux* vines in an attempt to appear Mediterranean, the space is pleasant enough—but its outstanding feature is the gorgeous wine bar. Fished out of a warehouse in downtown L.A., the late 1800s, art-nouveau relic is a work of art in solid oak, etched crystal and glass paneling. When the place is jammed on weekends, you can take advantage of the complimentary wine tastings at the bar while you wait. The wine selection—mostly American, and not the best labels at that—is not very impressive, though there are a few decent picks.

Chef Terry Wood hails from The Iron Squirrel (across the street), and he has improved quite a bit since his days there. The international menu, mostly French and Mediterranean, offers simple fare: basic onion soup, grilled teriyaki chicken breast, steak au poivre (in a peppercorn sauce), daily specials of fresh fish. (The fish can be dry, which we conjectured was a result of the high altitudes.) All entrées come with soup and salad, at the very bearable price of $12 to $20. The fare is of the sort that warms the soul and fills the belly better than anything else when you've just sailed in from a day on the slopes. This is by far the best culinary thing Big Bear has going, and for about $25 per person, you won't find the heart to complain about a thing.

Bargain Bites

Blue Ox Restaurant
441 W. Big Bear Blvd., Big Bear City 92314;
(909) 585-7886
Dinner daily; bar open 11 a.m.-midnight. D, DC, MC, V.

A good place for a family dinner, the Blue Ox is filled with antique farm equipment, sweet miniature-print wallpaper and peanut shells on the floors. The storybook menu is a little precious for our tastes, but you can get Paul Bunyan–size portions, and the food is pretty good. Stick to the beef—it comes in a variety of preparations from steaks to ribs. For the most part, the fish has been frozen (you might get fresh halibut once in a while), but the chicken is generally tasty. A plentiful dinner runs about $23 per person.

Boo Bear's Den
572 Pine Knot Blvd., Big Bear Lake 92315;
(909) 866-2932
Breakfast, Lunch & Dinner daily. AE, D, MC, V.

Don't let the foolish name put you off—Boo Bear's is a good, unpretentious café well located in the heart of Big Bear's "downtown" shopping area. Sit on the enclosed patio and stick to the simpler fare (omelets, burgers, sandwiches), and you'll have a relaxed, pleasant meal. There's live music some weekend nights; call for specific dates. Breakfast for one will run $6, lunch a couple of dollars more.

Hansel's
40701 Big Bear Blvd., Big Bear Lake 92315;
(909) 866-9497
Breakfast & Lunch daily, Dinner Mon.-Sat. AE, MC, V.

In the heart of Big Bear, Hansel's is perched on the top story of a two-story Swiss chalet that houses a few antiques and crafts shops on its ground level. The draw here is that Hansel's serves food all day. Anything on the primarily Continental-cuisine menu is pretty safe—from the prime rib to the Chinese chicken salad to the seafood pasta. There is one caveat: breakfast stops promptly at 11 a.m. A dinner costs about $12.

Landings
501 W. Valley Blvd., Big Bear City 92314;
(909) 585-3762
Breakfast & Lunch Mon. & Wed.-Sun. AE, MC, V.

You've probably already figured out that this café is at the airport. But Landings's location hasn't kept it from being one of the most popular restaurants in Big Bear; all the locals head on over for their weekly fix . . . omelet fix, that is. And there's no doubt that Landings prepares the best omelets on the hill. We recommend the Mile High version: ham, avocado, cheese, tomatoes, green peppers, onions. Above and beyond the omelets, the café offers an eclectic mix of traditional pancakes, not-so-traditional sandwiches, a contemporary selection of salads and a few south-of-the-border dishes. An average breakfast or lunch for one will run under $10—unless you order the "Lunch for Two" special: peanut butter and jelly sandwiches and a bottle of Dom Pérignon, which runs $99.95.

Maggio's Pizza
Interlaken Shopping Center, 42160 Big Bear Blvd.,
Big Bear Lake 92315; (909) 866-8815
Lunch & Dinner daily. No cards.

Maggio's is considered by many to be the best pizza joint in Big Bear, and we're not about to argue. The ingredients are fresh and tasty, the pizzas and calzones are generous, and the atmosphere is friendly, and the prices are low. You can eat in or take out. A pizza-and-beer dinner is under $10.

Red Baron Pizza
42173 1/2 Big Bear Blvd., Big Bear Lake 92315;
(909) 866-4744
Lunch & Dinner daily. AE, MC, V.

Pizza seems to be as popular in Big Bear as it is in many big cities. Red Baron, located in the heart of Big Bear, boasts dough made fresh daily and fast delivery service. It's a tough decision for locals, who have to toss a coin between this place and the equally enticing Maggio's, a bit farther away. One person can get away for under $10.

Hotels & Cabins

The symbol that accompanies each review indicates in which price category the hotel belongs: **Top of the Line** ($200 & Up), **Luxury** ($150 & Up), **Moderate** ($100 & Up) or **Practical** (Under $100). We have defined the categories based on the regular starting price of a single or double room. *See also* the INTRODUCTION chapter, under "About the Hotels."

Hotels

Big Bear Inn
42200 Moonridge Rd., Big Bear Lake
92315; (800) BEAR INN, (909) 866-3471,
Fax (909) 866-8988
*Singles & Doubles $90-$225, Suites $175-$500.
AE, MC, V.*

You'll need a fairly high tolerance of klassic kitsch to properly enjoy a stay at the Big Bear Inn. Fortunately, this is more than compensated for by the hotel's excellent comfort and good amenities. Built by a developer of Greek luxury hotels, the Big Bear Inn has a grandiose lobby decked out in marble and crystal—and a montage of seventeenth- and eighteenth-century art, Byzan-

tine icons and French impressionist works. But the place is certainly impressive: a formal Italian garden, an ornate, heavily draped dining room (serving costly Continental fare), an art-nouveau-style bar, five acres of forest and a health club with a pool are among the amenities here. Each of the 80 rooms is decorated differently, and they're all warmed with fireplaces, down comforters and antiques (and, of course, color TVs). A shuttle service will take you to the ski slopes (five minutes away), golf course or lake.

Gold Mountain Manor
1117 Anita, Big Bear City 92314;
(909) 585-6997, No fax
Doubles $75-$180 (incl. breakfast). MC, V.

Originally built in the twenties as part of the ritzy (but long-gone) Peter Pan Club, Gold Mountain Manor was restored a few years back and is now a fine bed-and-breakfast inn. The decor and antique furnishings are handsome, the rooms are charming and comfortable and the hosts are helpful. Romantics should request the Gable Room, with a beautiful walnut bed and the Franklin stove that helped keep Clark Gable and Carole Lombard warm during their Big Bear honeymoon. The room rate includes the use of the Big Bear Athletic Club.

Knickerbocker Mansion
869 Knickerbocker, Big Bear Lake 92315;
(909) 866-8221, No fax
Main House $95-$165, Lodge $105. MC, V.

Built in 1917, this historic bed-and-breakfast has lots of rustic mountain charm. The 4,000-square-foot log cabin features stone fireplaces and brass kerosene lanterns in its rooms. Four spacious, if rather basic, rooms in the main house share two bathrooms; another has a private half-bath. If you want more privacy, request one of four rooms in the separate Rainbow Sun Lodge with its Native American decor; each room has a private bathroom, a separate entrance, lots of quiet and plenty of romance. Breakfasts feature lovely homemade pastries, such as peach or apple cobblers. The setting is quite picturesque, with the imposing mansion presiding over two and a half acres of heavily wooded mountain terrain.

Krausmeier Haus Bavarian Village
1351 E. Midway Blvd., Big Bear City 92315;
(909) 585-2886, No fax
*Lodge rooms $55-$75, Studio Chalets $70-$118,
Chalets with kitchens $80-$120. MC, V.*

About five miles from Big Bear City and four miles from the lake itself, this little chalet complex shares the landscape with Baldwin Lake, horse breeders and the San Bernardino mountains. Its seclusion ensures tranquility—as do the absence of TVs and telephones—and its location makes sunset walks a must. The decor borders on the Spartan-bachelor style; you can reserve a large two-bedroom chalet with fireplace and kitchen or a simple room in the lodge. During weekends, especially January through March, reservations are essential. The complex is perfectly situated for skiing, hiking and fishing, and after a day in the mountain air you'll appreciate the outdoor spa. Our only complaint is the paper-thin walls in some rooms.

Lake Arrowhead Hilton Resort

27984 Hwy. 189, Lake Arrowhead Village 92352; (909) 336-1511, (800) 800-6792, Fax (909) 336-1378
Doubles $139-$179, Suites $270-$420. All major cards.

This sprawling resort won't give you the feeling of quiet, peaceful charm that a mountain cabin or bed-and-breakfast will, but it has lots of amenities and is a great place for families. Enthusiastic staff members run all-day kids' programs, so that kids can spend the day swimming, ice skating, playing games and making new friends while you catch up on your relaxation. The Hilton also boasts a private beach (a necessity, since Lake Arrowhead is privately owned), a heated pool, an affiliation with a large health club, a couple of restaurants and a location within walking distance of Lake Arrowhead Village's 80-plus shops and restaurants. The rooms are basic; we prefer the suites, which have loft bedrooms, sleeper sofas downstairs, kitchens and, in some cases, fireplaces.

Windy Point Inn

39263 North Shore Dr., Fawnskin 92333; (909) 866-2746, Fax (909) 866-1593
Doubles $135-$165, Suites $175-$255 (incl. breakfast). All major cards.

Locals told us about this contemporary lakefront bed and breakfast, and upon visiting, we weren't disappointed. The rooms are open and airy, with a simple yet refined Southwestern-inspired decor; each has a picturesque view of the lake and mountains, with a queen-size bed, private full bath, refrigerator and wet bar; some

---

Room prices are based on full, regular rates. Most hotels offer discounts and special packages at certain times of the year. Be sure to inquire.

---

suites have a king-size bed, fireplace, Jacuzzi and a private deck overlooking the inn's private beach. The service is personable.

Cabins

In Big Bear and Lake Arrowhead, a good (and some think the best) alternative to staying in a hotel or inn is to rent a condo or cabin—including some directly on the water. We have listed several of the better-known and better-equipped rental operations in both areas, but you can call the local chambers of commerce for more options (*see* "Basics" this chapter).

Arrowhead Property Management

P.O. Box 412, Lake Arrowhead 92352; (909) 337-2403, No fax
$175-$800. AE, MC, V.

One of the larger rental operations in Lake Arrowhead, APM has a listing of about 150 individually owned, one- to seven-bedroom cabins, condominiums and homes on the lakefront or in the mountains. There is a two-night minimum stay. Most condominiums and homes come furnished with blankets and towels; you'll need to bring your own sheets and pillow cases.

Blue Skies Real Estate and Resort Rentals

Slater Bros. Lakeview Center, 42171 1/2 #B Big Bear Blvd., Big Bear Lake 92315; (909) 866-8600, (800) 422-2422, Fax (909) 866-1108
From $95. MC, V.

With over 140 cabins, condos and homes for rent, Blue Skies probably has the most listings of any real estate agency in Big Bear; if you can't find what you're looking for here, it isn't in Big Bear. All have the basic amenities such as linens and fully equipped kitchens; some even come with extras like giant-screen TVs and Jacuzzis.

The Front Desk

4109 Big Bear Blvd., Big Bear Lake 92315; (909) 866-5753, No fax
$95-$375. MC, V.

Front Desk provides the sheets, pillow cases, bar soap and just about any tool the family chef would need to whip up that late-morning omelet (except the eggs, of course). There are 68 properties, from one-bedroom townhouses to four-bedroom lakefront homes, which are made up prior to your arrival. Some cabins are as close to the ski slopes as you can get without being on Bear Mountain's payroll.

Gayle's Resort Rentals Inc.
40703 Lakeview Dr., Big Bear Lake 92315;
(909) 866-5711, No fax
$70-$425. AE, MC, V.

Gayle's has a large inventory of over 100 cabins, homes and condos, ranging from one to six bedrooms, in the Big Bear Lake area. All properties come with pillows, blankets and fully equipped kitchens.

Nightlife

Big Bear Prospector's
40771 Lakeview Dr., Big Bear Lake 92315;
(909) 866-6696
Open 5 p.m-2 a.m. MC, V.

This is a no-fooling-around steakhouse/nightclub, with a variety of live music Friday and Saturday nights that tends toward Top 40 and rock 'n' roll. During the holiday seasons there's live music seven nights a week. If you dine before you dance, steaks and dessert will run about $20 per person.

Chad's Place
40740 W. Big Bear Blvd., Big Bear Lake 92315;
(909) 866-2161
Open daily 11 a.m.-2 a.m. MC, V.

This genuine cowboy bar may be a bit rustic for some visitors. But you'll definitely get the flavor of this mountain village when you come here to drink beer, play pool, listen to good bar bands (mostly rock 'n' roll), watch sports, catch up on the latest local gossip or observe the macho men and mountain women warm up in winter and cool down in summer. It's a Big Bear landmark and a pleasant place to hang out.

Shops

Castle of Happy Hearts
40717 Lakeview Dr., Big Bear Lake 92315;
(909) 866-8377
Open Mon. & Thurs.-Sun. 11 a.m.-5 p.m.

For over 11 years, Bill and Bella have brought a little magic to Big Bear. Adults and children alike will be mesmerized by the array of pop-up birthday cards, hand puppets, high-tech electronic gadgets, hand-carved wooden trains and a plethora of other toys in all price ranges. Bella will personally demonstrate anything she has in the store (and a few magic tricks as well!).

Edelweiss Books
40804 Big Bear Blvd., Big Bear Lake 92315;
(909) 866-7734
Open daily 10 a.m.-5:30 p.m.

This is the only serious choice when it comes to bookstores in Big Bear, and as such, Edelweiss tends to be a bit crowded. For its small size, however, the store manages to offer a broad selection of maps, magazines, postcards, newspapers and special-interest books. Its greatest asset is the personal attention given to special orders.

Mountain Country House
633 Pine Knot, Big Bear Lake 92315;
(909) 866-4440
Open daily 10 a.m.-5 p.m.

This is the place to go if you're looking for a quality gift for someone—and you may end up taking a few things home for yourself as well. The selection of country furnishings, antiques and crafts is attractive, with some unique pieces. You won't find the best bargains here, but it will certainly solve any gift-giving dilemmas.

Pirate's Alley
42072 Big Bear Blvd., Big Bear Lake 92315;
(909) 866-2103
Open Mon.-Fri. 9 a.m.-7:30 p.m., Sat.-Sun. 9 a.m.-10 p.m.

Located halfway between the Moonridge Shopping Center and the Village, Pirate's Alley is a treasure trove of outstanding wines, spirits and other liquors—as well as items you may have forgotten on your way back from the market, from half-and-half to the finest Dijon mustards, pâtés and escargots.

Sights & Sports

Big Bear's busiest season is winter, when the nearby ski mountains attract thousands of snow-starved Southern Californians. The biggest and best ski area is **Snow Summit,** which is so popular that on weekends its lift tickets often sell out in advance (through Ticketmaster only). If night skiing is your passion, this is your destination in Big Bear. Snow Summit guarantees you'll be having a good time within 75 minutes of buying a lift ticket, or you'll receive a voucher for another day on the slopes.

Hard on the heels of Snow Summit is **Bear Mountain**, which has expanded and upgraded its operations over the last couple of years, adding new runs and triple- and quad-chair lifts to get you to the top before you've even caught your breath. To avoid the crowds, **Snow Forest** is a good alternative.

Attractions

For cinema buffs, there's the **Village Theater** (909-866-5115) in Big Bear, and the **Blue Jay Cinema** (909-337-8404) and the **Village Crestline Theater** (909-338-3888) in Lake Arrowhead.

The **Performing Arts Center** (909- 866-5831) hosts various events year-round; call the Box Office for current shows, (909-866-4970).

Events

Aside from skiing events in the winter, there are many other events year round. In May, you may want to check out the **Norba National Mountain Bike Race** and the **Spring Jamboree** in Lake Arrowhead. The **Hobie Cat Regatta** and the **Scottish Highland Games** liven up June, the **Old Miners' Days** spills from July into August. In September, the **Rotary Art & Wine Festival** takes place in Lake Arrowhead. October is, of course, **Oktoberfest** month and in November, look for the **Bear Valley Association Festival of Art.**

Sports

Golf
Bear Mountain Golf Course, (909) 585-8002
Open May through November.

L.A. Miniature Golf (Arrowhead), (909) 337-0020

Putt'n Around Miniature Golf, (909) 866-8101

Hiking
Big Bear Forest Service Ranger Station, (909) 866-3437

Horseback Riding
Baldwin Lake Stables, East end of Shaw Rd. at Baldwin Lake, (909) 585-6482

Ice-Skating
Blue Jay Ice Castle (Arrowhead), (909) 336-2111

Mountain Biking
Team Big Bear, Snow Summit Ski Resort, P.O. Box 77, Big Bear Lake 92315; (909) 866-4565/ 866-5841

Barry's Sports Rentals, 42131 Big Bear Blvd., Big Bear Lake 92351; (909) 866-6441

Steve's-U-Rent, 42039 Big Bear Blvd., (909) 866-8888 (Also rents ski equipment.)

Watersports
Big Bear Marina, (909) 866-3218

Holloway's Marina, (909) 866-5706

McKenzie Water-Ski School (Arrowhead), (909) 337-3814

Pine Knot Landing, (909) 866-9512

Skiing & Snowmobiling
Bear Mountain Ski Resort, (909) 585-2517; ski report (909) 585-2519

Bluff Lake Nordic Center, (909) 866-3621; Cross-country ski rentals.

Mt. Baldy Ski Resort (Ontario/Upland), (909) 982-0800

Snow Forest Ski Resort, (909) 866-8891/866-5503

Snow Summit Ski Resort, (909) 866-5766/ 866-4621

Snowmobile Rentals, (909) 585-8002

Basics

Getting There

There are a variety of routes to get to Big Bear, depending on where you're coming from and at what time of the day or week you're heading out. By automobile, it's 105 miles—a three- or four-hour drive from most areas in Southern California (it takes two-and-a-half hours from downtown L.A. in ideal, traffic-free conditions; but this almost never occurs). Particularly during the ski season, heavy traffic from L.A. can seriously hinder your progress. You should also check the local highway conditions (909-866-7623); and remember, chains are usually required during the winter months.

If the flow of traffic is light, the quickest route to the area from Interstate 10 is the front route, which follows Highway 30 east to Highway 330 through Running Springs, then follows Highway 18 into Big Bear. If that route is congested, try Highway 38, which comes around the back.

The route with the least amount of traffic is usually the high-desert route: you turn off of Interstate 15 to Highway 18—which also is called the Rim of the World Drive for its beautiful vistas and landscapes. On this route to Big Bear, you'll pass Lake Arrowhead. The more adventurous, or those that don't wish to brave the mountain roads for several hourse, should think about chartering a plane through **Aero Haven** (909-585-9663). For about $350, for example, you and one or two friends can fly round-trip from Los Angeles to Big Bear.◆

Telephone Numbers

Big Bear Chamber of Commerce, (714) 866-4608

Big Bear Community Hospital, (714) 866-6501

Big Bear Convention Center, (714) 585-3000

Big Bear Lake Visitors Authority, (714) 866-7000

Boat Permits & Launching, (714) 866-5796/866-2917

Lake Arrowhead Chamber of Commerce, (714) 336-1547

Mountains Community Hospital (Arrowhead), (714) 336-3651

CATALINA ISLAND

Across the Sea

Until not so long ago a dusty and rather faded land across the sea, Catalina Island is coming up in the world: The main town of Avalon boasts refurbished hotels and trendy shops, and the new summer houses on the hills are grand once again. We come to Catalina for the romance, and the island's decidedly rural air. This is a great place to escape the smog and traffic and ease into a leisurely state of mind, where the biggest decisions you'll be faced with are whether to have pancakes or waffles for breakfast, and whether to go snorkeling or just sleep on the beach.

If you don't have your own boat or plane, or a friend who does, you'll have to use public transportation to get to the island. **Catalina Cruises** makes the two-hour trip several times daily from Long Beach ($28 round trip; call 800-888-5939 for information); **Catalina Express** offers a frequent, super-fast (60 minutes from Long Beach and 75 minutes from San Pedro), somewhat classier ferry ride for $34 round-trip; call (310) 519-1212. Or you can fly, either by plane (**Island Express**, 310-491-5550, $95 round-trip) or by helicopter (**Helitrans**, 310-548-1314, $95 round-trip). Be prepared for crowds and higher room rates in season, which runs from June 1 to mid-September. Catalina Express offers reasonable hotel and boat packages. For more information on things to see and do in Catalina, call the **Tourist Information Center** at (310) 510-2000.

Restaurants

12/20 Armstrong's Fish Market & Seafood Restaurant
306 Crescent Ave., Avalon 90704;
(310) 510-0113
Seafood. Lunch & Dinner daily. AE, D, MC, V.

From its blue awnings facing the street to the cheery deck with blue umbrellas overlooking the water, Armstrong's looks as fresh as the seafood it serves and sells. The fresh-fish dinners are a bargain (swordfish, mahi mahi and local red snapper in the $12-to-$14 range), and the style of cooking unfussy, relying heavily on the mesquite grill. The local abalone steak is a highly regarded treat that islanders say is well worth the $29.95 investment. Dinner runs $20 per person.

11/20 Café Prego
603 Crescent Ave., Avalon 90704;
(310) 510-1218
Italian. Dinner nightly. All major cards.

An intimate, engaging little place on the waterfront with lots of warmth, homey service and decent food. We like the red-and-white-checked tablecloths and the straw-wrapped chianti bottles. Pastas can be good, especially the rigatoni with broccoli in a fine cream sauce; the thick, cheesy lasagne and the linguine with a hearty clam sauce. It's one of your best bets on Catalina. About $15 per person for dinner.

9/20 Channel House
205 Crescent Ave., Avalon 96704;
(310) 510-1617
American/Seafood. Lunch & Dinner daily. MC, V.

Most tourists run directly from the ferry to the Channel House for an al fresco lunch on the attractive terrace, with a perfect view of the harbor. Lunch is mostly salads and sandwiches; the burgers are the most popular item, often accompanied by one of the oversized exotic drinks. Dinner is fairly classic and uninspired. About $8 per person for lunch, $20 for dinner.

11/20 Ristorante Villa Portofino
111 Crescent Ave., Avalon 90704;
(310) 510-0508
Italian. Dinner nightly. AE, D, MC, V.

Villa Portofino offers appealing northern Italian cuisine in a romantic setting. The result is a continual crowd—be sure to make reservations early for a weekend dinner. All the classics are here—carpaccio, insalata mista, spaghetti alla checca, tortellini in a Parmesan-cream sauce, calamari steak, veal scaloppine—and they're admirably prepared, at least by Catalina standards. Portions are as hearty as the flavors are full. About $20 to $30 per person for dinner.

Bargain Bites

Catalina Cookie Co.
101 Marilla, Avalon 90704; (310) 510-2447
Open Sun.-Thurs. 10 a.m.-10 p.m., Fri.-Sat. 10 a.m.-11 p.m. MC, V.

This tiny shop in the Metropole marketplace bakes wonderful cookies daily that weigh in at 65 cents to $1.35 apiece. We like the oatmeal-raisin, chocolate-chip, peanut-butter and oatmeal-chocolate-chip cookies, and the fabulous piña-colada macaroons. Try the "Eclipse"—a fudge cookie dipped in white chocolate.

Original Antonio's
114 Sumner Ave., Avalon 90704; (310) 510-0060
Lunch daily. No cards.

The decor is late fraternity house: beer signs, posters, stuffed bison, red-and-white-checked tablecloths, sawdust-strewn floors. Countertop jukeboxes dish out classic rock, and cheerful people dole out acceptable pizzas, meatball heroes, pastas and generous, messy Italian sandwiches to the largely young, beer-drinking crowd. Expect to spend about $6 for lunch, less for take-out.

Runway Café
Catalina Airport, 1 Airport Rd., Avalon 90704; (310) 510-2196
Breakfast & Lunch daily (until 5 p.m.) MC, V.

If you want a true Catalina experience, come here for a buffalo burger (very similar to a beef burger), buffalo chili or buffalo soft tacos. L.A. businesspeople with their own small planes often hop over here for a quick lunch. They also serve a full breakfast, and lunch for about $5.

The Sand Trap
Avalon Canyon Rd. near Avalon Canyon School, Avalon 90704; (310) 510-1349
Breakfast & Lunch daily. No cards.

We found this delightful outdoor café just a short hike up from the bay at the edge of town. Don't be put off by the chain-link fence at roadside—the owners installed it to keep out stray balls from a neighboring golf course. Breakfasts consist of hearty omelets and Mexican specialties like huevos rancheros. Lunch includes burgers, soft tacos and enchiladas, and costs $5 or so.

Hotels

The symbol that accompanies each review indicates in which price category the hotel belongs: **Top of the Line** ($200 & Up), **Luxury** ($150 & Up), **Moderate** ($100 & Up) or **Practical** (Under $100). We have defined the categories based on the regular starting price of a single or double room. *See also* the INTRODUCTION chapter, under "About the Hotels."

 ## Garden House Inn
3rd & Clarissa, Avalon 90704; (310) 510-0356, No fax
Rooms $85-$250 (incl. breakfast). AE, MC, V.

We like everything about this elegant bed-and-breakfast inn: its small size (just nine rooms), its quiet location (in town but away from clogged Crescent Avenue), its decor (a 1920s house furnished with handsome antiques and lovely shades

of rose) and the comfort of its rooms (with queen-size beds and private baths; some have bay views, private terraces and sitting areas).

 ## Glenmore Plaza Hotel
120 Sumner Ave., Avalon 90704; (310) 510-0017, Fax (310) 510-2833
Rooms $105-$400 (incl. breakfast). D, MC, V.

Built in 1891, the Glenmore Plaza is a charming pink-and-green Victorian-style hotel. The bright, clean and spacious rooms have white wicker furniture, ceiling fans, pickled-pine armoires and comfortable queen- and king-size beds; many have whirlpool baths. Try the Clark Gable cupola, with its fabulous views and oversized round bed in the circular bedroom, or the Amelia Earhart suite, with its own Jacuzzi. There's no pool, but the beach is practically across the street. The hotel's van will meet your ferry boat.

 ## Hotel St. Lauren
Metropole & Beacon Sts., Avalon 90704; (310) 510-2299, Fax (310) 510-1369
Rooms $60-$180, Suites $160-$200 (incl. breakfast). MC, V.

The Hotel St. Lauren looks as if it were built at the turn of the century. This isn't exactly a luxurious seaside resort, but with rooms starting at just $45, who can complain? Dollar for dollar, the upper-floor suites constitute one of the best bargains in town: $145 gets you a spacious room for four, with a king-size bed, a sleeper sofa, a terrace and a great ocean view.

 ## Hotel Vista Del Mar
417 Crescent Ave., Avalon 90704; (310) 510-1452, No fax
Rooms $65-$275 (incl. breakfast). AE, D, MC, V. No smoking.

Someone with very good taste redecorated this small hotel in Mediterranean pastels, well suited to its waterfront location. Most of the rooms open on to a sunny inner courtyard; all have gas fireplaces, sitting areas, direct-dial telephones and bars. When we feel like splurging, we book one of the two rooms overlooking the harbor. After a hard day of sightseeing there is nothing like a soak in the double-sized Jacuzzi tub, and a sunset drink on the room's private balcony.

 ## Inn on Mt. Ada
207 Wrigley Rd., Avalon 90704; (310) 510-2030, Fax (310) 510-2237
Rooms $190-$580 (incl. all meals). MC, V. 2-night minimum on weekends. No smoking.

Although the innkeepers call their landmark the Inn on Mt. Ada, everyone else calls it the Wrigley Mansion, which is how it's been known since it was built by the chewing-gum magnate in 1921. This posh six-room inn is certainly Catalina's most expensive lodging, but it's worth every penny. Everything is terribly luxe, with period antiques and good-sized rooms, all of which have views of either Avalon and the bay or the Pacific and San Pedro. Included are a full breakfast, served in the dining room each morning, a deli lunch, a home-cooked dinner and fruit and snacks. A cab will meet your ferry, and the owners provide a golf cart for getting around.

Nightlife

Antonio's Pizzeria and Catalina Cabaret

230 Crescent Ave., Avalon 90704; (310) 510-0009
Open daily 8 a.m.-1 a.m. Shows continuous 5 p.m.-midnight (depending on the season). No cover. AE, MC.

Decorated with stuffed buffalo heads, 1950s-style bubble gum machines and jukeboxes, this waterfront eatery and bar is a good bet for cocktail hour, or an evening talent contest hosted by singer Michele Curtis. If you can't live without seeing your favorite important sports events, you can catch them here on a big-screen TV.

The Casino

1 Casino Way, Avalon 90704; (310) 510-2444 (ballroom), (310) 510-0179 (movie information)
Open daily for movies (hours vary). Special events throughout the year. No cards.

Despite its name, the only gambling associated with this place was the chance taken by the Wrigley family to build the massive theater and ballroom in 1929. From the day it opened at the edge of Avalon Bay, the Casino became, as its Italian name implies, "a place of entertainment." Benny Goodman, Kay Kyser and Dick Haymes couldn't resist its ballroom—elegantly decorated with silver leaf, Catalina tile and hardwoods—and large enough to accommodate several thousand dancers. Today, balls at Halloween and New Year's Eve and other holiday festivities bring in crowds to experience the elegance of the island's past. The Santa Catalina Island Company offers guided tours of the landmark building daily.

El Galleon Restaurant

411 Crescent Ave., Avalon 90704; (310) 510-1188
Open daily 10 a.m.-1:30 p.m.. Show nightly 9:30 p.m. No cover. AE, MC, V.

Every night at ten, this restaurant turns into the sight of a lively "Karaoke" sing-along, where nervy customers belt out their favorite tunes in front of a 100-plus audience.

Catalina Comedy Club

Glenmore Plaza Hotel, 120 Sumner Ave., Avalon 90704; (310) 510-1400
Winter: open 4:30 p.m.-midnight. Summer: open 11 a.m.-2 a.m. Shows nightly during summer. Cover $5-$12. AE, MC, V.

Stand-up comics dare patrons to laugh at their jokes at this cocktail lounge on the ground floor of the Glenmore Plaza Hotel, a new nighttime alternative for islanders and visitors.

Sights & Sports

With the hustle and bustle of the mainland far away, it's tempting to do nothing but sit on the beach. But for those who want to keep moving, start at **Brown's Bikes** (310-510-1421) near the ferry dock. Brown's rents all manner of bicycles, including tandems. If you intend to cycle outside the precincts of Avalon, you have to obtain a permit from the **Santa Catalina Island Conservancy** (310-510-1421).

Catalina Divers' Supply (310-510-0330) has been renting scuba and snorkeling equipment since 1958. It offers instruction, and leads a dive into the Avalon Underwater Park at the edge of the Casino. Try parasailing to gain an aerial view of Avalon; **Island Cruzers** (310-510-1777) will lift you into the air for a spin around the bay. **Joe's Rent-a-Boat** (310-510-0455) on the pier rents rowboats, motorboats, paddleboats and paddleboards as well as fishing tackle to tempt the local kelp bass.

Hiking is one of Catalina's great pastimes. A short stroll inland leads to the **Wrigley Memorial and Botanical Gardens** (1400 Avalon Canyon Rd., 310-510-2288). Entrance is $1. The island's managers are working hard to restore the native plants, cacti and succulents to their former glory. From the Memorial Gardens, a relatively steep walk brings hikers to the top of the island's mountainous spine and a network of paths wending past buffalo herds. Cars are not permitted on about 80 percent of the island, giving wild animals a significant advantage. Free hiking permits are available through the **L.A. County Department of Parks and Recreation** in Avalon (Call 310-510-0688).

You also can see a great deal of the island by tram or boat. The **Santa Catalina Island Company** (310-510-2500) operates tours daily, weather permitting. ◆

MAPS

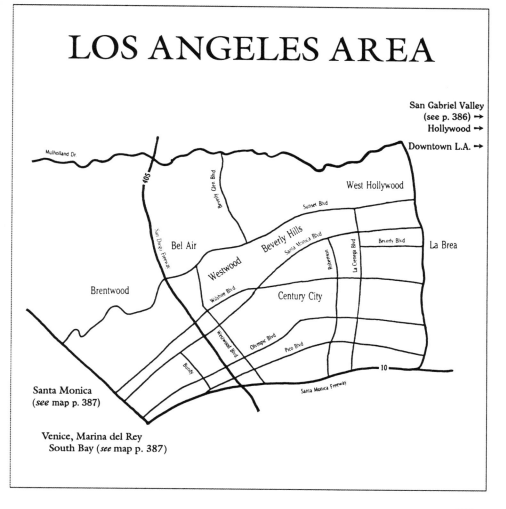

LOS ANGELES AREA

San Gabriel Valley
(see p. 386) →
Hollywood →
Downtown L.A. →

Mulholland Dr

405

Beverly Glen Blvd

West Hollywood

Sunset Blvd

San Diego Freeway

Bel Air

Beverly Hills

Santa Monica Blvd

Westwood

Wilshire Blvd

Robertson

La Cienega Blvd

Beverly Blvd

La Brea

Brentwood

Century City

Westwood Blvd

Olympic Blvd

Pico Blvd

Bundy

10

Santa Monica
(*see* map p. 387)

Santa Monica Freeway

Venice, Marina del Rey
   South Bay (*see* map p. 387)

385

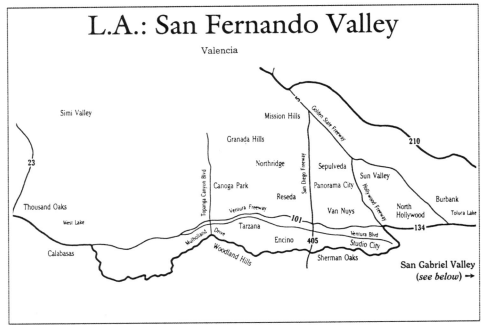

L.A.: San Fernando Valley

San Gabriel Valley
(*see below*) →

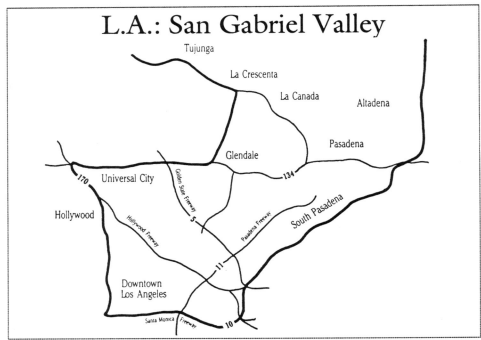

L.A.: San Gabriel Valley

L.A.: The Coast & South Bay

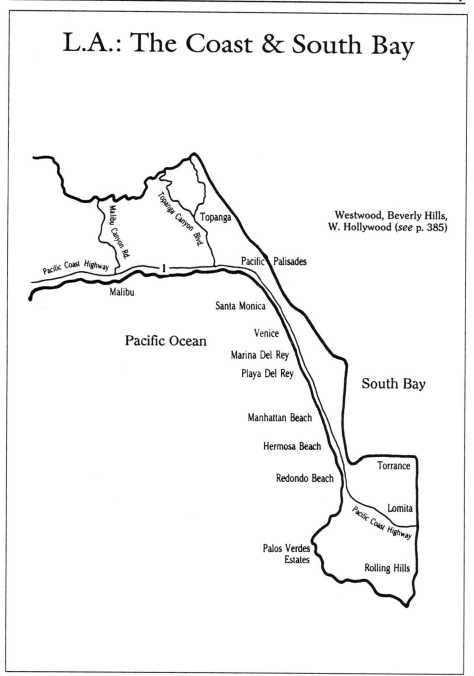

Westwood, Beverly Hills,
W. Hollywood (*see* p. 385)

Topanga Canyon Blvd

Topanga Canyon Rd.

Malibu Canyon Rd.

Topanga

Pacific Coast Highway

1

Pacific Palisades

Malibu

Santa Monica

Pacific Ocean

Venice

Marina Del Rey

Playa Del Rey

South Bay

Manhattan Beach

Hermosa Beach

Torrance

Redondo Beach

Lomita

Pacific Coast Highway

Palos Verdes
Estates

Rolling Hills

ORANGE COUNTY

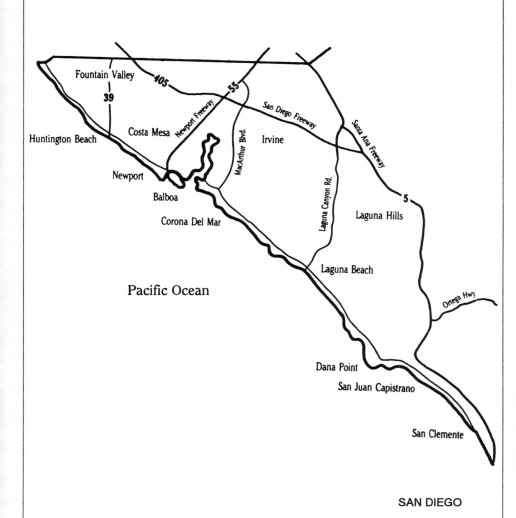

LOS ANGELES

Fountain Valley

405

55

39

Newport Freeway

San Diego Freeway

Santa Ana Freeway

Costa Mesa

Huntington Beach

Irvine

MacArthur Blvd.

Newport

Balboa

Laguna Canyon Rd.

5

Corona Del Mar

Laguna Hills

Laguna Beach

Pacific Ocean

Ortega Hwy.

Dana Point

San Juan Capistrano

San Clemente

SAN DIEGO

GLOSSARIES & INDEXES

MENU SAVVY

A Guide to International Food Terms

French

Agneau: lamb

Aïoli: garlicky mayonnaise

Américaine or armoricaine: sauce of white wine, Cognac, tomatoes and butter

Andouille: smoked tripe sausage, usually served cold

Anglaise (à l'): boiled meats or vegetables

Ballottine: boned, stuffed and rolled poultry

Bâtarde: sauce of white roux

Béarnaise: sauce made of shallots, tarragon, vinegar and egg yolks, thickened with butter

Béchamel: sauce made of flour, butter and milk

Beurre blanc: sauce of wine and vinegar boiled down with minced shallots, then thickened with butter

Beurre noisette: lightly browned butter

Bière: beer

Bigarade: bitter orange used in sauces and marmalade

Bisque (crayfish, lobster, etc.): rich, velvety soup, usually made with crustaceans, flavored with white wine and Cognac

Blinis: small, thick crêpes made with eggs, milk and yeast

Boeuf: beef

Boeuf bourguignon: beef ragoût with red wine, onions and lardons

Bombe glacée: molded ice-cream dessert

Bordelaise: fairly thin brown sauce of shallots, red wine and tarragon

Borscht: thick Eastern European soup of beets and boiled beef, often garnished with a dollop of sour cream

Boudin noir: blood sausage

Bouillabaisse: various fish (including scorpionfish cooked in a soup of olive oil, tomatoes, garlic and saffron)

Bourride: sort of bouillabaisse usually made with large white fish, thickened with aïoli; served over slices of bread

Brie: cow's milk cheese with a soft, creamy inside and a thick crust, made in the shape of a disk and sliced like a pie

Brioche: a soft loaf or roll, often sweetened and used for pastries

Brochette: on a skewer

Canapé: small piece of bread topped with savory food

Canard: duck

Carbonnade: pieces of lean beef, first sautéed then stewed with onions and beer

Carré d'agneau: rack of lamb

Cèpes: prized wild mushroom, same family as the Italian porcini

Chanterelles: prized wild mushroom, trumpet-shaped

Charcutière: sauce of onions, white wine, beef stock and gherkins

Charlotte: dessert of flavored creams and/or fruit molded

in a cylindrical dish lined with ladyfingers (if served cold) or strips of buttered bread (if served hot)

Chasseur: brown sauce made with shallots, white wine and mushrooms

Chèvre (fromage de): goat (cheese)

Choucroute: sauerkraut; often served with sausages, smoked bacon, pork loin and potatoes

Citron lemon

Chou-fleur: cauliflower

Clafoutis: a dessert of fruit (usu. cherries) baked in an eggy batter

Confit: pork, goose, duck, turkey or other meat and sealed in its own fat

Coquilles St-Jacques: sea scallops

Côte d'agneau: lamb ribs

Coulis: thick sauce or purée, often of vegetables or fruit

Court-bouillon: stock in which fish, meat and poultry are cooked

Crème chantilly: sweetened whipped cream

Crêpe Suzette: crêpe stuffed with sweetened butter mixture, Curaçao, tangerine juice and peel

Croque-monsieur: grilled ham and cheese sandwich

Croûte (en): in pastry crust

Crudités: raw vegetables

Daube: beef braised in red wine

Ecrevisses: crayfish

Entrecôte: "between the ribs"; steak cut from between the ribs

Epinards: spinach

Escalope: slice of meat or fish, flattened slightly and sautéed

Escargots (à la bourguignonne): snails (with herbed garlic butter)

Financière: Madeira sauce enhanced with truffle juice

Florentine: with spinach

Foie gras: liver of a specially fattened goose or duck

Fondue: a bubbling pot of liquid into which which pieces of food are dipped—most commonly cheese and bread; can also be chocolate and fruit or various savory sauces and cubes of beef. Also, vegetables cooked at length in butter and thus reduced to pulp

Forestière: garnish of sautéed mushrooms and lardons

Frangipane: almond pastry cream used to fill thick crêpes

Galantine: boned poultry or meat, stuffed and pressed into a symmetrical form, cooked in broth and coated with aspic

Galettes and crêpes (Brittany): galettes are made of buckwheat flour and are usually savory. Crêpes are made of wheat flour and are usually sweet

Gâteau: cake

Gelée (en): in aspic (gelatin usually flavored with meat, poultry or fish stock)

Génoise: sponge cake

Granité: lightly sweetened fruit ice

Gratin dauphinois: sliced potatoes baked in milk, sometimes with cream and/or grated Gruyère

Grenouille: frog (frogs' legs: cuisses de grenouilles)

Hollandaise: egg-based sauce thickened with butter and flavored with lemon

Jambon: ham

Julienne: vegetable soup made from a clear consommé, or any shredded food

Lait: milk

Langouste: rock or spiny lobster

Langoustine: saltwater crayfish

Lapin: rabbit

Lièvre: hare

Limon: lime (also, **citron vert**)

Lotte: monkfish or anglerfish; sometimes called "poor man's lobster"

Madrilène (à la): garnished with raw, peeled tomatoes

Magret (Maigret): breast of fattened duck, cooked with the skin on; usually grilled

Médaillon: food, usually meat, fish or foie gras, cut into small, round "medallions"

Moules marinière: mussels cooked in the shell with white wine, shallots and parsley

Nantua: sauce of crayfish, white wine, butter and cream with a touch of tomato

Noisettes: hazelnuts; also, small, round pieces of meat (especially lamb or veal)

Nougat: sweet made with roasted almonds, egg whites, honey and sugar

Oeufs: eggs

Pain: bread

Parfait: sweet or savory mousse; also a layered ice-cream dessert

Parisienne: garnish of fried potato balls

Paupiettes: thin slices of meat stuffed with forcemeat and shaped into rolls

Pissaladière: tart with onions, black olives and anchovy filets

Poires: pears

Pommes: apples

Pommes de terre: potatoes

Poulet: chicken

Provençale (à la): with garlic or tomato and garlic

Quiche: tart of eggs, cream and various fillings (such as ham, spinach or bacon)

Ratatouille: stew of eggplant, tomatoes, bell peppers, zucchini, onion and garlic, all sautéed in oil

Rémoulade: mayonnaise with capers, onions, parsley, gherkins and herbs

Rissoles: type of small pie filled with forcemeat

Rouille: sort of mayonnaise with pepper, garlic bread soaked in bouillon, olive oil and possibly saffron

Sabayon: fluffy, whipped egg yolks, sweetened and flavored with wine or liqueur; served warm

Saint-Pierre: John Dory; a white-fleshed fish

Salade niçoise: salad of tomatoes, hard-boiled egg, anchovy filets, tuna, sweet peppers, celery and niçoise olives (also can include green beans, potatoes, basil, onions and/or broad beans)

Sole meunière: sole dipped in flour and sautéed in butter with parsley and lemon

Soissons: garnished with haricot beans

Sorbet: sherbet (dessert ice usually made of fruit)

Spätzle: round noodles, often made from eggs

Steak au poivre: pepper steak; steak covered in crushed peppercorns, browned in a frying pan, flambéed with Cognac; also sauce deglazed with cream

Tapenade: a paste of olives, capers and anchovies, crushed in a mortar with lemon juice and pepper

Tartare: cold sauce for meat or fish; mayonnaise with hard-boiled egg yolks, onions and chopped olives

Tarte: tart, round cake or flan; can be sweet or savory

Tarte Tatin: upside-down apple tart invented by the maiden Tatin sisters

Tortue: turtle; also, a sauce made with various herbs, tomato, Madeira

Tournedos Rossini: beef sautéed in butter, served with pan juices, foie gras

Truffe: truffle; highly esteemed subterranean fungus, esp. from Périgord

Vacherin: ice cream served in a meringue shell; also, creamy, pungent cheese from Switzerland or eastern France

Viande: meat

Italian

Acciughe: anchovies

Aceto: vinegar

Aglio: garlic

Agnello: lamb

Agnolotti: crescent-shaped, meat-filled pasta

Agrodolce: sweet-and-sour

Amaretti: crunchy almond macaroons

Anatra: duck

Anguilla: eel

Aragosta: spiny lobster

Arrosto: roasted meat

Baccalà: dried salt cod

Bagna cauda: hot, savory dipping sauce for raw vegetables

Bierra: beer

Biscotti: cookies

Bistecca (alla fiorentina): charcoal-grilled T-bone steak (seasoned with pepper and olive oil)

Bolognese: pasta sauce with tomatoes and meat

Bresaola: air-dried spiced beef; usually thinly sliced, served with olive oil and lemon juice

Bruschetta: toasted garlic bread topped with tomatoes

Bucatini: hollow spaghetti

Calamari (calamaretti): (baby) squid

Calzone: stuffed pizza turnover

Cannellini: white beans

Cappelletti: meat- or cheese-stuffed pasta ("little hats")

Carbonara: pasta sauce with ham, eggs, cream and grated cheese

Carciofi (alla giudia): (flattened and deep-fried baby) artichokes

Carpaccio: paper thin, raw beef (or other meats)

Cassata: ice-cream bombe

Cavolfiore: cauliflower

Ceci: chickpeas

Cipolla: onion

Conchiglie: shell-shaped pasta

Coniglio: rabbit

Coppa: cured pork filet encased in sausage skin

Costata: rib steak

Costoletta (alla milanese): (breaded) veal chop

Cozze: mussels

Crespelle: crêpes

Crostata: tart

Fagioli: beans

Fagiolini: string beans

Farfalle: bow-tie pasta

Fegato: liver

Fegato alla veneziana: calf's liver sautéed with onions

Fichi: figs

Finocchio: fennel

Focaccia: crusty flat bread

Formaggio: cheese

Frittata: Italian omelet

Fritto misto: mixed fry of meats or fish

Frutti di mare: seafood (esp. shellfish)

Funghi (trifolati): mushrooms (sautéed with garlic and parsley)

Fusilli: spiral-shaped pasta

Gamberi: shrimp

Gamberoni: prawns

Gelato: ice cream

Gnocchi: dumplings made of cheese (di ricotta), potatoes (di patate), cheese and spinach (verdi) or semolina (alla romana)

Grana: hard grating cheese

Granita: sweetened, flavored grated ice

Griglia: grilled

Insalata: salad

Involtini: stuffed meat or fish rolls

Lenticchie: lentils

Maccheroni: macaroni pasta

Manzo: beef

Mela: apple

Melanzana: eggplant

Minestra: soup; pasta course

Minestrone: vegetable soup

Mortadella: large, mild Bolognese pork sausage

Mozzarella di bufala: fresh cheese made from water-buffalo milk

Noce: walnut

Orecchiette: ear-shaped pasta

Osso buco: braised veal shanks

Ostriche: oysters

Pane: bread

Panettone: brioche-like sweet bread

Panna: heavy cream

Pancetta: Italian bacon

Pappardelle: wide, flat pasta noodles

Pasta asciutta: pasta served plain or with sauce

Pasticceria: pastry; pastry shop

Pasticcio: pie or mold of pasta, sauce and meat or fish

Patate: potatoes

Pecorino: hard sheep's-milk cheese

Penne: hollow, ribbed pasta

Peperoncini: tiny, hot peppers

Peperoni: green, red or yellow sweet peppers

Pesca: peach

Pesce: fish
Pesce spada: swordfish
Pesto: cold pasta sauce of crushed basil, garlic, pine nuts, parmesan cheese and olive oil
Piccata: thinly-sliced meat with a lemon or Marsala sauce
Pignoli: pine nuts
Polenta: cornmeal porridge
Pollo: chicken
Polipo: octopus
Pomodoro: tomato
Porcini: prized wild mushrooms, known also as the boletus
Prosciutto: air-dried ham
Ragù: meat sauce
Ricotta: fresh sheep's-milk cheese
Rigatoni: large, hollow ribbed pasta
Riso: rice
Risotto: braised rice with various savory items

Rucola: arugula
Salsa (verde): sauce (of parsley, capers, anchovies and lemon juice or vinegar
Salsicce: fresh sausage
Saltimbocca: veal scallop with prosciutto and sage
Sarde: sardines
Semifreddo: frozen desert, usually ice cream with or without cake
Sgombro: mackerel
Sogliola: sole
Spiedino: brochette; grilled on a skewer
Spumone: light, foamy ice cream
Tartufi: truffles
Tiramisù: creamy dessert of rum-spiked cake and triple-crème cheese
Tonno: tuna
Torta: cake
Tortelli: pasta dumplings stuffed with greens and ricotta

Tortellini: ring-shaped dumplings stuffed with meat or cheese and served in broth or in a cream sauce
Trenette: thin noodles served with potatoes and pesto sauce
Trota: trout
Uovo (sodo): egg (hard-boiled)
Uva: grapes
Uva passa: raisins
Verdura: greens, vegetables
Vitello (Tonatto): veal (in a tuna and anchovy sauce)
Vongole: clams
Zabaglione: warm whipped egg yolks flavored with Marsala
Zafferano: saffron
Zucchero: sugar
Zucchine: zucchini
Zuppa: soup
Zuppa inglese: cake steeped in a rum-flavored custard sauce

Spanish & Latin American

Because there are so many regional dialects in Spain and Latin America, the term for one food product might easily have four or five variations. We've chosen a simple list of those ingredients and dishes most often found in Southern California restaurants.

Aceite: oil
Ajo: garlic
All-i-oli: aïoli; garlicky mayonnaise
Arroz: rice
Bacalao: dried, salted codfish
Bullabesa: Catalán fish stew similar to bouillabaisse
Burrito: soft, wheat-flour tortilla rolled and stuffed with various meats, refried-beans, cheese and vegetables
Caldo: broth
Camarones: shrimp
Carne: meat
Cerveza: beer
Chalupa: a small, thick corn tortilla folded into a boat shape, fried and filled with a mixture of shredded meat, cheese and/or vegetables

Chilequile: flat tortilla layered with beans, meat, cheese and tomato sauce
Chile relleno: large, mild chile pepper, stuffed with cheese and fried in an egg batter
Chorizo: spicy pork sausage flavored with garlic and spices
Conejo: rabbit
Cordero: lamb
Empanada: pie or tart filled variously with meat, seafood or vegetables
Empanadita: a small empandada
Enchilada: a torilla, fried and stuffed variously with meat, cheese and/or chilies
Entremeses: appetizers

Flan: a baked custard with a caramel coating (also crema caramela)
Frito (frita): fried
Gambas: shrimp
Garbanzo: chick-pea
Gazpacho: Andalutian; a cold soup of fresh tomatoes, peppers, onions, cucumbers, olive oil, vinegar and garlic (also celery, breadcrumbs)
Guacamole: an avocado dip or filling, with mashed tomatoes, onions, chiles and citrus juice
Higado: liver
Huachinango: red snapper
Huevos: eggs
Huevos rancheros: tortillas toped with eggs and a hot, spicy salsa

Heuvos revueltos: scrambled eggs

Jalapeño: very common hot chile pepper, medium size

Jamón: ham

Licuado: fruit milkshake

Lima: lime

Limón: lemon

Linguiça: garlicky pork sausage

Mantequilla: butter

Mariscos: shellfish

Masa: cornmeal dough; essential for making tortillas

Menudo: a stew featuring tripe

Mole: sauce; most often a thick, dark sauce made with powdered mild chiles and chocolate

Nachos: a snack dish of tortilla chips topped with melted cheese and chiles

Nopales: leaves of the prickly pear cactus; simmered and used in various dishes

Ostras: oysters

Paella: a dish of saffron-flavored rice studded with meat (chicken, ham, sausages, pork), shellfish and vegetables

Papas: potatoes (also, **patatas**)

Papas fritas: literally "fried potatoes"; french fries

Parrillada: grilled

pechuga de pollo: chicken breast

Pescado: fish

Pez espada: swordfish

Pimiento: red chile pepper; can be sweet or hot

Plátano: plantain; a starchy, mild-tasting variety of banana popular in Latin American; usu. cooked and served as a side dish

Pollo: chicken

Poblano: large, mild, dark green chile pepper; used for chile rellenos

Puerco: pig

Pulpo: octopus

Quesadilla: a soft, folded tortilla filled with cheese (and/or other savory stuffings) and toasted or fried

Queso: cheese

Salchicha: sausage

Salsa: sauce; also, an uncooked condiment employing fresh tomatoes, onions and chiles)

Salsa borracha: "drunken sauce"; salsa made with tequila

Sangría: Spanish drink made with red wine, soda water, chopped fresh fruits and sugar, often with a touch of brandy; served on ice

Seviche: raw fish marinated (and thus "cooked") in citrus juice (also, **cebiche**)

Sopa: soup

Sope: a small bun made of tortilla dough, cooked and filled with savory stuffing

Taco: a folded, fried tortilla filled with ground beef (or other meats or fish), refried beans, shredded lettuce, tomatoes, onion, cheese and salsa

Tapa: appetizer, Spanish in origin; enjoyed with an apéritif such as dry sherry

Tortilla: a flat, unleavened, crêpelike bread made with cornmeal flour (masa) or wheat flour

Tostada: a fried tortilla topped with a saladlike mix of ground beef or chicken, beans, lettuce, tomato, peas, onions, guacamole

Asian

Chinese

Bao bun: dim sum item; small, steamed buns, white in color, stuffed with a variety of minced fillings (often chicken, shrimp, pork or lotus beans)

Bird's-nest soup: soup that has been thickened and flavored with the gelatinous product derived from soaking and cooking the nests of cliff-dwelling birds

Bok choy: Chinese white cabbage

Chop suey: strictly a Chinese American dish; meat or shrimp, and vegetables (mushrooms, water chestnuts, bamboo shoots, bean sprouts) fried together and served over rice

Chow mein: strictly a Chinese American dish; meat or shrimp, and vegetables (mushrooms, water chestnuts, bamboo shoots, bean sprouts) fried and served over crispy egg noodles

Dim sum: figuratively, "heart's delight"; a traditional meal featuring a variety of small dumplings, buns, rolls, balls, pastries and finger food, served with tea in the late morning or afternoon

Egg roll: crêpelike wrapper stuffed with pork, cabbage or other vegetables, rolled up, and deep-fried or steamed

Fried rice: cooked, dried rice quickly fried in a wok with hot oil, various meats or vegetables and often an egg

Hoisin: a sweet, rich, dark brown sauce made from fermented soy beans; used as a base for other sauces

Lo mein: like chow mein, but with soft, steamed wheat-flour noodles

Lychee: small, round, fleshy fruit; used fresh, canned, preserved and dried

Mu shu: a delicate dish of stir-fried shredded pork and eggs rolled up in thin pancakes

Oyster sauce: a thick, dark sauce of oysters, soy and brine

Peking duck: an elaborate dish featuring duck that has been specially prepared, coated with honey and cooked until the skin is crisp and golden; served in pieces with thin pancakes or steamed buns, and **hoisin**

Pot sticker: dim sum item; dumpling stuffed with meat, seafood or vegetables, fried and then steamed

Shark's fin soup: soup thickened and flavored with the cartilage of shark's fins, which provides a protein-rich gelatin

Shu mai: dim sum item; delicate dumpling usu. filled minced pork and vegetables

Spring roll: a lighter version of the egg roll, with fillings such as shrimp or black mushrooms

Szechuan: cuisine in the style of the Szechuan province; often using the peppercorn-like black Chinese pepper to make hot, spicy dishes

Thousand-year-old eggs: chicken, duck or goose eggs preserved for 100 days in ashes, lime and salt (also, **100-year-old eggs**)

Wonton: paper-thin, glutinous dough wrapper; also refers to the dumpling made with this wrapper, stuffed with minced meat, seafood or vegetables

For an index to Japanese, Chinese or Thai restaurants (or any other cuisine, for that matter), please see "Restaurants by Cuisine" on the following pages.

Wonton soup: a clear broth in which wontons are cooked and served

Japanese

Amaebi: sweet shrimp

Anago: sea eel

Awabi: abalone

Azuki: dried bean; azuki flour is often used for confections

Ebi: shrimp

Enoki (Enokitake): delicate mushrooms with long stems and small caps

Hamachi: yellowtail

Hibachi: small, open charcoal grill

Hirame: flounder

Ikura: salmon roe

Kaiseki: Multi-course menu of luxury dishes reflecting the seasons with the use of seasonal foods and artistic dinnerware and presentation

Kani: crab

Kappa: cucumber

Kobe beef: cattle raised in exclusive conditions (frequent massages and a diet featuring large quantities of beer), which results in an extraordinarily tender, very expensive beef product

Konbu: dried kelp; used in soup stock, for sushi and as a condiment

Maguro: tuna

Maki: rolled

Mako: shark

Mirugai: giant clam

Miso (soup): Soybean paste from which a savory broth is made, usu. served with cubes of tofu or strips of seaweed

Ono: wahoo fish; a relative of the mackerel often compared in taste to albacore

Ramen: Chinese soup noodles

Saba: mackerel

Sake: salmon

Saké: traditional rice wine served hot or cold

Sashimi: thinly sliced raw fish, usually served with soy sauce and wasabi

Shabu shabu: similar to sukiyaki; beef and vegetables cooked tableside in a broth

Shiitake: Prized cultivated mushroom, dark brown with a large cap

Shoya: soy sauce

Soba: buckwheat noodles

Sukiyaki: braised beef and vegetable dish with broth added after cooking

Sushi: Rounds of vinegared rice wrapped in dried seaweed with a center of raw fish or vegetables, served with wasabi and soy

Tai: snapper

Tako: octopus

Tamago: egg

Tamari: dark sauce similar in composition and taste to soy; often used for dipping

Tempura: deep-fried, batter-dipped fish or vegetables

Teriyaki: A marinade of soy and sweet sake, used on meats, fish and poultry

Tofu: bean curd, processed into a liquid and then molded into large cubes

Toro: fatty belly cut of tuna

Udon: wheat noodles

Unagi: freshwater eel

Uni: sea-urchin roe

Wasabi: a hot, spicy condiment made from the roots of Japanese horseradish, chartreuse in color

Yakitori: a dish of pieces of chicken and vegetables, marinated in a spicy sauce, skewered and grilled

Thai

Kaeng (or Gaeng): large and diverse category of dishes; loosely translates as "curry"

Kaeng massaman: a variety of coconut-milk curry

Kaeng phed: a red, coconut-cream curry

Kaeng som: a hot-sour curry

Kapi: fermented shrimp paste; vital ingredient in **nam phrik**, or dishes flavored with hot chili sauce
Kai (or Gai): chicken
Khai: egg
Khao: rice
Khao suai: white rice
Khao phad: fried rice
King: ginger
Kung: prawns
Lab (or Larb): dish of minced meat with chilies and lime juice
Mu: pork
Nam: sauce

Nam pla: fish sauce
Nam phrik: a hot chili sauce
Nuea: beef
Ped: duck
Phad: fried
Phad king: fried with ginger
Phad phed: fried hot and spicy
Phad Thai: pan-fried rice noodles with chicken, shrimp, eggs, peanuts and bean sprouts
Phrik: chili pepper
Pla: fish
Si racha (or Sri racha) spicy chili condiment

Tom: boiled; often refers to soups
Tom kha kai: chicken coconut-cream soup flavored with lemongrass and chilies
Tom yam kung: hot-sour shrimp soup flavored with lemongrass, lime and chilies
Yam: flavored primarily with lime juice and chilies, resulting in a hot-sour taste; usually "salads" but can also be noodle dishes or soup
Yam pla: raw fish spiked with lime juice, chili, lemongrass, mint and fish sauce

WINE SAVVY

California Wine: Then and Now

I do not make the wines," an elder statesman of California winemaking was heard to say, "nature makes the wines and I am just the caretaker. "As odd as that may sound to the modern mind, that summarizes much the way winemakers viewed their occupation as recently as thirty years ago. Immigrant patriarchal families, like Krug, Schram, Niebaum, LeFranc, and Latour established winemaking dynasties in the late nineteenth century through intensive vineyard plantings. Quite naturally they turned to somewhat simple and rudimentary European techniques for their winemaking, mostly allowing nature to take its course. While that might have produced great wine in Europe, many of the viticultural and fermentation methods were ill conceived and improperly adapted to their new home. In many cases, the old-world knowledge was not necessarily applicable to the soil and climate of California.

In addition, there was little formal training for winemaking; it was viewed as a craft. Most winemakers learned winemaking at the hands of their fathers, who passed down the accumulated instincts from generation to generation. Sometimes this human factor was little more than educated guessing based on the previous vintages. Thus, with a little shove from the hand of man, the wines made themselves.

Thirteen years of Prohibition, beginning in 1920, retarded what minimal progress had been made in winemaking. Vineyards were turned into orchards or pasture land and many potentially talented people left the industry. Post Prohibition once again saw the planting of vineyards. To make good wine however, it's necessary to harvest from mature vines, and many of the newly planted vineyards did not come of age until the 1940s. Even as late as the 1950s, there was little experimentation or research being done (with the exception of academicians at University of California at Davis) regarding soil, climate, rootstocks, grape clones, trellising systems and so on. In that decade, as little as forty years ago, much of California wine was sold off in tank-car bulk to wholesalers or retailers who labeled them with generic names like "Chablis" or "Burgundy." Those premium wines that wineries did produce and bottle themselves found a limited market, where the wines sold for pennies a bottle. The wineries of California were still a cottage industry and there was little motivation and commitment to investigate the components that contributed to world-class wine. The wine of that era was unquestionably inferior to its European counterparts, an image that has took decades for California to overcome.

Napa's Renaissance

In the late 1960s, however, California gradually began to awake from its moribund slumber. Many winemakers began to re-investigate traditional, handcrafted, artisan winemaking methods. The wine industry boomed in the 1970s, fostering a renewed interest in wine and a healthy increase in per capita consumption as well. On the other side of the coin, it also attracted both individuals and corporations to winemaking who had limited background in the wine business. They saw themselves as taking up the slack in supply to meet the booming wine demand. Unfortunately, during the '70s, many of the new winery operations based their vineyard and cellar methods on what their neighbors were doing or on what had been successful in the next county. Businesspeople often thought that winemaking was similar to math: just plug the variables into the winemaking equation and it equals a viable wine. Any number of vintners thought you made all your red wines one way and all your white wines another way and that's all there was to it. Not quite! For example, the bad reputation that Pinot Noir had was because it was vinified and handled the same way Cabernet was. It was winemaking by formula. In addition, many winemakers didn't understand that differences in climate, soil, exposure, clonal stock and ripeness required different techniques. Mediocrity was the status quo rather than the exception.

Despite increased corporate meddling that sacrificed quality for quantity, California wine was thought to come of age when, at a subsequently much-publicized blind tasting in Paris, several California wines were winners over much more renowned French wines. When it was revealed that the eminent French wine judges had selected a Cabernet from Stag's Leap and a Chardonnay from Chateau Monteleña as its top wines, the American media seized on these facts with a vengeance, much to the delight of the California wine industry. Unfortunately, this development would do more to hinder California's ascendancy to world-class winemaking than to help it. At the time, prevailing California winemaking wisdom was to harvest overripe grapes which resulted in a high degree of alcohol and hopefully a high degree of fruit extract. These types of wines had great power and intensity, which allowed them to steamroll the competition in any blind tasting, as they did in Paris. They were big and rich with strong fruit character, but had little balance, elegance or finesse. In addition, these wines were so powerfully alcoholic that they overwhelmed food at the table.

The "victory" at the 1976 Paris tasting, however, sent a message to California winemakers to keep on pursuing this style. Many wineries, particularly ones with corporate ownerships, stumbled over themselves in rushing to produce more powerful wines that were essentially dead in the bottle. Serious winemaking was stalled at that level for several years. Meanwhile, others trends took hold in the popular segment of wine market, including the meteoric rise of "white" Zinfandel and later, the seemingly unquenchable thirst for "a glass of Chardonnay, please."

The Young Turks of the '80s

By the early 1980s, though, there was an influx of new talent into the industry to meet the demands of the mushrooming number of wineries, each hoping to carve out their place in the booming market. Many of these people were educated in viticulture and oenology at University of California at Davis, while others were cellar rats who learned through on-the-job training. These younger winemakers practiced better viticultural methods, proper utilization of soil and climate and better winemaking techniques. While some of the oldtimers taught the young turks a thing or two, the younger generation visited the great winemaking regions of Europe and returned full of ideas. The new generation was not afraid to experiment and utilize new techniques or resurrect ancient ones when it served the purpose of producing better wines.

Assured of access to quality grape sources, these winemakers feel confident that they can then lead the wine down the right paths so that it can develop its full potential. It is relatively easy to make good wine from good grapes; conversely it is nearly impossible to make good wine from inferior grapes. While to the uninitiated, winemaking may seem to be the simple act of bruising some grapes and waiting for them to naturally ferment, it's a bit more complicated. From the selection of the proper grape clone and planting it in the proper soil and climate, through the vagaries of nature and the harvest, to fermentation, cellaring, again and bottling, there are thousands of possible paths that wine can travel. The winemaker, through training and past experience, makes a decision at each juncture as to the proper direction for that wine to take.

A number of young winemakers have struck out on their own, experimenting with different types of grapes while challenging the "varietal imperialism" of Cabernet and Chardonnay. Wines made from Rhône Valley varietals, like Syrah, Grenache and Mourvedre, have become increasingly popular and offer different flavors than the previous spectrum of California red wines. Plantings of Italian varietals, such as Nebbiolo, Sangiovese and Malvasia have sprung up in order to take advantage of the Mediterranean-like growing climate of California. The winemaking business has fractured into many segments appealing to a much wider variety of wine drinkers. While giant corporate wineries have their market share, smaller artisan wineries also have their niche. Given the time and money, dreamers can build winery empires based on individual winemaking philosophies, whereas thirty years ago the rules of the game seemed far more proscribed.

Building on a model that has served the European wine community well for centuries, California winemakers now understand that certain climates and soils that are good for, say Cabernet, are not good for Pinot Noir. As more acreage is planted or grafted over (especially due to the pervasiveness of phylloxera), the most appropriate varietals will be planted in the most appropriate environment, which is what should have been done in the first place. This will also increase the quality of the wines but will even further the movement of specialty wineries to the forefront. In essence, wineries will no longer sell half a dozen different wines, but will concentrate on only two or three. They will be the best grapes from the best varieties that the region has to offer.

Today: The California Winemaker as Artisan

Quite possibly we are entering the golden age of California wine. The new generation of winemakers are fashioning wines with an intensity of flavor that is California's birthright, owing to its sunny climate and rich soils. They are refining their techniques to preserve the innate characteristics of the fruit, while at the same time building in more structure and complexity to enhance drinkability and longevity. Through their meticulous attention to detail, they are eliminating distracting elements from the wine in favor of creating a harmonious variety of complex aromas and flavors. In the best vintages, the wines are still powerful but now tempered with suppleness, finesse and depth.

After the winemaking expansion of the 1980s, the attendant obsession with technology and the diversity of wine styles proliferating in the marketplace, winemakers have found that the more things change, the more things stay the same. In other words, sometimes the simplest ways are the best. The less wine is handled and processed, the better opportunity that wine has of achieving its potential, all other things being equal. Many of the small, artisan wineries producing handcrafted wines never left the traditional winemaking methodology behind; they built on it and just made better adjustments each vintage to let nature take its course, consistent with their winemaking style. After all, once the best grapes are harvested, winemaking really only requires a crusher and press, along with a few good barrels.

Guide to California Regions

It's been said that there are no climatic differences in California wine-growing regions, as there are in Europe, and thus "every year is a vintage year" in California. Nothing could be further from the truth. For proof merely contrast a 1989 Napa Chardonnay (where it rained at harvest) and a 1989 Central Coast Chardonnay (where it didn't).

The myth of statewide, monolithic, sunny weather also needs dispelling. There are certain pockets of land in California (usually associated with mountains) that have vastly different weather and climatic conditions than the rest of the state. And certain grape varieties that do well in one environment do not perform well in another. For proof, check out a Pinot Noir from the very cool Benedict Vineyards in the Santa Ynez Valley versus one from the hot Calistoga area of Napa Valley. A wine's origin is significant: it can mean the difference between a balanced, complex wine and a harsh, unpleasant one.

Alexander Valley: A largely unpopulated area of northern Sonoma County, the Alexander Valley is warmer than the rest of the county. It has had success with Cabernets as well as Bordeaux-style blends (white and red). The Chardonnays can be interesting.

Amador/Sierra Foothills: Just east of Sacramento, Amador County is home to some of the oldest continuously producing vineyards in the state. The principal wine is Zinfandel and its ubiquitous offspring, White Zinfandel. There is also Cabernet and Barbera, along with experimental acreage planted with Rhône varietals like Syrah, Mourvedre, and Grenache.

California: The use of the geographical term "California" indicates only that all the grapes came from within the confines of the state.

Carneros: At the southernmost end of Napa and Sonoma Counties, this recently developed area borders on the cool San Pablo Bay. Perhaps the coolest area in either county, the climate is perfect for Pinot Noir and Chardonnay.

Central Coast: This is a very broadly defined region that covers coastal wine-growing regions from Santa Cruz in the north to Santa Barbara on the south. An entire spectrum of grape varieties are grown in this area, depending upon which particular varietal is suitable for the individual microclimate.

Central Valley: Another broad area that covers the inland wine-growing area from Sacramento to Bakersfield. This is the hottest, driest grape-growing region in the state. A wide variety of wines are made, most of them passable but few of them distinctive.

Dry Creek Valley: Parallel to and west of the Alexander Valley in Sonoma County, its relatively warm climate has produced good reds, especially Zinfandel and Cabernet. Chardonnay is a drawing card, too.

Mendocino County/Lake County: The northernmost grape-growing counties share a relatively cool growing season. Chardonnay, Pinot Noir, Gewürztraminer and Riesling can be particularly impressive from this region.

Monterey: The cooling influence of the Monterey Bay has created an ideal environment for Chardonnay, while Pinot Noir has been less successful. Further inland, individual pockets of land have produced some fine examples of Cabernet.

Napa Valley: The most famous wine-producing region in California and a top tourist attraction, the name is synonymous with quality. Its long-lived Cabernets have achieved worldwide notoriety. Its Chardonnay, Pinot Noir, Sauvignon Blanc and sparkling wines have also proven themselves.

Russian River Valley: A district of widely varying soils and climate in western Sonoma County; the cooler regions enjoy a reputation for Chardonnay, Pinot Noir and sparkling wine.

Santa Barbara County: Home to the Santa Ynez and Santa Maria valleys, it's the only region in California that has an east-west mountain range funneling cool ocean fog and breezes to the vineyards. That fact belies its southern Califor-

399

nia heritage that says it's too warm for grape growing. Pinot Noir, Chardonnay, Riesling and Syrah are prominent.

Sonoma County: Encompassing several different valleys with varying microclimates, this is probably the most versatile grape-growing region in the state: grapes as diverse as Cabernet, Merlot, Pinot Noir, Chardonnay and Sauvignon

Blanc all perform well. Some good sparkling wines also hail from the region.

Temecula: This southernmost region, halfway between L.A. and San Diego, is also the most recently planted in California. Thus far its best efforts have been with Chardonnay and sparkling wine; the reds still tend to be a bit on the rustic side.

Becoming a wine connoisseur? Look in fine bookstores for André Gayot/Gault Millau's brand-new guide to The Best Wines of America, which profiles hundreds of wineries around the country. We report on winemakers' techniques and specialties, as well as review and rate the best bottles.

Glossary of Tasting Terms

Acidity: a principal component of wine that shows up as a sharpness or tartness, giving it freshness and snap.

Aroma: the smell the wine acquires from the grapes themselves and the fermentation process.

Astringency: the mouth-puckering quality found in many young red wines.

Austere: a wine unusually high in acidity; lacking roundness or wholeness.

Balanced: no individual component of the wine stands out; all the elements contribute to a harmonious whole.

Berry: taste characteristic found in many red wines, it resembles the taste of fruit like blackberry, blueberry and cherry.

Body: the weight of the wine in the mouth; usually manifested by a richness, fullness or viscosity.

Bouquet: the smell that develops from the process of aging wine in the bottle.

Buttery: a component that gives white wines a full, rich, roundness that resembles the taste of butter.

Chewy: a rich red wine with big body and dense flavors.

Clarity: the appearance of a young wine should be clear, not cloudy.

Complex: a wine that displays many different levels of flavors.

Dry: a wine with no apparent residual sugar. Novice wine drinkers may describe this as "sour."

Earthy: positive characteristics of loamy topsoil, mushrooms or truffles sometimes found in red wines. In French, "gout de terroir."

Fat: a wine with good fullness and length, although it may lack finesse.

Floral: flowery aromas and tastes, usually associated with white wines.

Fruity: the taste of the fruit of the grapes themselves; it often manifests itself as other fruit flavors, such as apples, strawberries or black currants.

Grassy: a herbaceous flavor, like new-mown grass, common to Sauvignon Blanc; negative when extreme.

Hard: a wine that does not have generous flavors; applied to red wines that have excessive tannins.

Herbaceous: general term descriptive of various herbal

flavors in wine, recognized by aroma and taste.

Hot: a wine in which the high level of alcohol is out of balance with the other elements, obliterating their flavors.

Intense: powerful, dense, and rich in flavor

Jammy: in red wines, intense, ripe fruitiness combined with natural berry-like flavors.

Nose: all the elements detected by the sense of smell, including both the aroma and bouquet.

Oaky: flavors of the oak in which the wine is fermented and/or aged.

Smoky: a roasted or toasted aroma or taste characteristic attributable to aging in oak barrels.

Spicy: descriptive of spicelike flavor elements found in wine such as pepper, cardamom, clove and cinnamon.

Supple: a wine that tastes soft and smooth; easy to drink.

Tannic: a mouth puckering astringency found in young red wines.

Vegetal: an unattractive component, often resembling bell peppers, cabbage or asparagus.

Glossary of Grapes

H ere we've chosen the grapes used to make the world's best-known wines. There are many other grape varieties, of course, often referred to collectively as "orphan varietals" because they aren't part of the mainstream of wine producing.

Among the white grapes not thoroughly discussed here are **Pinot Blanc**, used in Alsace, France; **Pinot Gris** (in Italian, **Pinot Grigio**); **Muscat**, used primarily in French dessert wines; **Sémillon** and **Muscadelle**, both grown in Bordeaux and used to make Sauternes and Graves; and lesser-known Rhône varietals such as **Mourvèdre, Marsanne** and **Viognier**. Red "orphans" include the Bordeaux grapes **Malbec** and **Cabernet Franc**; **Gamay** (used in Beaujolais, Burgundy and California); and Italy's **Nebbiolo, Sangiovese, Barbera** and **Malvasia**.

CABERNET: The châteaux of Bordeaux, France produce the true benchmark of this varietal. Long the king of red wines in California, Cabernet's reputation in the U.S. was established by wineries in the Napa Valley. While sometimes a bit harsh in its youth, it has the ability to mature into a most complex and full bodied wine, much like the great wines of Bordeaux. Its flavors are comfortable with simple grilled meats as well as more complex dishes like venison in mushroom sauce. Consistent producers can also be found in Sonoma, California; and Australia, Chile and Argentina.

CHARDONNAY: In the '80s it became de rigeur to ask for "a glass of Chardonnay" in a restaurant rather than merely "a glass of white wine." It has been a principal grape in Champagnes and white Burgundies for centuries. It's cold, fruity and easy to drink, and pleasant with just about any dish involving cheese, eggs, fish or fowl. Winemakers in California have divided into two camps over the style of Chardonnay; one emphasizes the high-toned, steely, fruit qualities of the wine through little or no use of oak, while the other emphasizes barrel and malolactic fermentation in addition to the fruit charac-

teristic, giving the wine a rounder, buttery taste.

GEWÜRZTRAMINER: The Alsatian region of France has about four centuries of experience in producing these wines in the traditional style. A so called "aromatic" varietal, the grape is making a minor comeback in California. "Gewürz" translates as "spice" and it's immediately detectable when poured into a glass. The flavors echo the fragrant and flowery nose, while providing an additional punch from a piquant, spicy component. Made with residual sweetness, the wine is a good counterpoint for spicy Chinese and Thai dishes.

MERLOT: This variety was once relegated to blending into other red wines, but in the last twenty years it has taken on an identity of its own. Merlot has herbal and fruity flavors similar to Cabernet, and complements the same sort of food, but it has a smooth and supple character in the mouth without the bite of tannins. Top producers hail from Bordeaux, France (where the wine is mostly blended but sometimes bottled separately), Chile, Argentina, Washington State, Napa and Sonoma.

PINOT NOIR: This grape has the potential to be the most seductive, beguiling red wine in

existence, as proven by its presence in the great Burgundies of France. In the past ten years, California's Pinot Noirs have shown the greatest increase in quality of any varietal. In recent years California winemakers have produced some remarkable Pinots. Lighter than Cabernets, Pinots have an unparalleled richness and intensity of fruit. The best of them are velvety and accompany a wide variety of foods. Top French Burgundies are bottled under a variety of different names and labels. In America, Pinot Noir has had great success in Napa, Sonoma, Santa Barbara and Oregon.

RIESLING: A mainstay of German winemaking, and also used in Alsace, France, this "aromatic" is finding a home in California again. It can be a refreshing alternative to the Chardonnay/Sauvignon Blanc white-wine tandem. Unlike its cousin, Gewürztraminer, this varietal has little spice and instead relies on its delicate aromas and subtle flavors for its special niche. Usually lighter in style and sometimes with residual sweetness, it's better paired with lighter fare.

SAUVIGNON BLANC: This variety is often considered the poor man's Chardonnay; it can be vinified similarly but costs only half as much. But Sauvignon Blanc has a number of identities ranging from a clean, slight grassy white wine to a herbaceous, full bodied wine backed up with oak aging. Unheralded but excellent examples come from Sancerre and Pouilly-Fumé in the Loire Valley. In California, almost every region produce a Sauvignon Blanc; the best are from the North Coast.

SYRAH: The great grape of France's Rhône Valley, Syrah is responsible for the red wines Côte Rotie, St. Joseph and Cornas, and plays a major role in the spicy Châteauneuf-du-Papes of the southern Rhône, too. It has become more widely planted in California in the last ten years. Highly aromatic wines with meaty, smoky, spicy flavors are the trademark of the Syrah grape. When made in a lighter style, it's a good quaffing wine to pair with simple bistro food. When made in a richer style, it's good with lamb and all manner of wild game.

ZINFANDEL: Real Zinfandel is red, a fact many wine drinkers are rediscovering, now that the popular trend for "white" zinfandel has stabilized. Peppery, briary, brawny and chewy are only a few of the adjectives used to describe this mouth-filling wine. It has a real zest for matching well with tomato-based pasta dishes and other highly herbalized preparations. There is no European counterpart for this variety; it is one that the first Italian winemakers propigated and cultivated in California. Vintners in Napa, Sonoma and Amador seem to do the best job.

• • • • • • • •

SPARKLING WINES: Domaine Chandon (owned by Moët & Chandon) set up shop in Napa Valley less than twenty years ago and, after its initial success, almost every French Champagne house has come to California to establish its foothold. While some sweet-style sparklers are made, most are traditional dry or off-dry styles. This wine is the perfect apéritif; its delicate nuances tend to get lost when paired with complex or highly seasoned dishes. . Names to remember are Domaine Chandon, Domaine Carneros, Gloria Ferrer, Mumm-Napa, Piper-Sonoma, Mirassou, Scharffenberger, Schramsberg, Shadow Creek and Maison Deutz.

VINTAGE CHART: The World's Wines

	FRANCE												GER.	ITALY		CALIFORNIA			
	Red Bordeaux	White Bordeaux	Sauterne	Red Burgundy	White Burgundy	Beaujolais	Côtes du Rhône	Provence	Alsace	Loire: Anjou, Muscadet	Pouilly, Sancerre	Champagne	Germany: Rhine, Moselle, Nahe	Piedmont	Chianti	Cabernet Sauvignon	Chardonnay	Pinot Noir	Zinfandel
1990	5	4	5	Ex	4	4	5	5	5	5	5	5	5	5	5	5	5	4	5
1989	5	4	Ex	5	5	Ex	5	5	Ex	5	5	—	5	5	2	4	3	4	4
1988	4	4	Ex	5	5	4	4	4	5	4	4	—	5	5	5	3	5	4	4
1987	3	4	1	4	3	2	1	2	3	3	2	—	4	4	2	4	3	4	5
1986	5	5	5	3	3	3	3	3	4	4	4	5	4	3	4	5	5	4	4
1985	5	5	2	Ex	5	5	5	3	5	5	5	4	4	5	5	Ex	4	4	5
1984	2	2	2	2	2	2	2	2	2	1	1	—	2	2	1	5	5	4	5
1983	5	5	Ex	3	5	—	5	4	Ex	4	4	5	5	2	3	3	4	4	3
1982	Ex	4	3	2	4	—	4	—	2	5	5	4	3	5	4	4	3	4	3
1981	4	5	4	—	—	—	3	—	3	5	5	4	4	3	3	4	4	4	4
1980	2	2	3	3	2	—	3	—	3	2	2	—	2	2	2	4	5	4	4
1979	4	4	3	3	5	—	4	—	—	—	—	—	4	4	2	4	4	3	4
1978	4	5	—	Ex	5	—	Ex	—	—	—	—	—	2	5	4	5	4	4	4

Ex – Exceptional year
5 – Very great year
4 – Great year
3 – Good year
2 – Medium year
1 – Passable year
— – Small year

* Please note that this is only meant to be a general guide. Start by learning which regions and years are better than others; once you develop a good knowledge, buy according to your own preferences.

The European wines here are categorized as European wines are named, by the region in which the grapes were grown (Champagnes are made in Champagne, France; Chiantis in Chianti, Italy; etc.). This is their "appellation," always displayed on the label along with the phrase *Appéllation controlée* or *Denominazione di origine contrallata* to guarantee the authenticity of the wine. The California wines are categorized by grape name, as they are throughout the United States.

INDEXES

Restaurants by Area

L.A. Area (*p. 12*)

Encompasses L.A. proper and all of the Westside, including Downtown, Hollywood, West Hollywood, Bel Air, Beverly Hills, Brentwood, Westwood, West L.A., Century City, Culver City, Venice, Marina del Rey, Santa Monica, Pacific Palisades and Malibu.

Atwater
Osteria Nonni

Bel Air
Adriano's
Four Oaks
Hotel Bel-Air Dining Room
Shane on the Glen

Beverly Hills
Belvedere at Peninsula Hotel
Bice
The Bistro
The Bistro Garden
Carroll O'Connor's Place
Celestino
Chez Hélène
Il Cielo
Da Pasquale
David Slay's La Veranda
La Dolce Vita
L'Escoffier at Beverly Hilton
La Famiglia
Gardens at Four Seasons
  Hotel
Il Giardino
The Grill on the Alley
Jimmy's
Kaktus
Kate Mantilini
The Mandarin
Maple Drive
Mezzaluna

Piazza Rodeo
Prego
Rangoon Racquet Club
Regent Beverly Wilshire Dining
  Room
Robata
Ruth's Chris Steak House
La Scala Boutique
Trader Vic's at Beverly Hilton
Tribeca
Trilussa
Tse Yang

Brentwood
Brentwood Bar & Grill
Chin Chin
Daily Grill
Mezzaluna
La Scala Presto
Stoney's
Toscana

Century City
Cabo Cabo Cabo
Champagne Bis
La Chaumiere
Harry's Bar & American Grill
Houston's
Hy's
Lunaria

Culver City
George Petrelli's Steak House
Mi Ranchito
Versailles

Downtown L.A.
(incl. Chinatown, Little Tokyo)
Checkers Hotel Dining Room
Empress Pavilion
Engine Co. No. 28
Epicentre
Horikawa
Kachina Grill

Mon Kee
Ocean Seafood
The Original Sonora Café
Pacific Dining Car
La Plancha
Plum Tree Inn
Rex, Il Ristorante
R23
Sai Sai at Biltmore Hotel
Shibucho
Stepps on the Court
A Thousand Cranes at New
  Otani Hotel
The Tower
Water Grill
Yang Chow

East L.A.
La Parrilla
La Serenata de Garibaldi

Highland Park
La Plancha

Hancock Park
Prado

Hollywood
Caioti
Chan Dara
Chao Praya
Columbia Bar & Grill
Hollywood Canteen
Hungarian Budapest

> *It is not unlikely that some restaurants may close their doors without warning. Make sure to phone ahead to confirm that the operation is still valid.*

Jitlada
Mario's Peruvian Seafood
Marouch
Musso & Frank's Grill
Off Vine
Patina
Rincon Chileno
Sanamluang Café

Los Feliz
Duplex
Katsu
Pierre's Los Feliz Inn
Trattoria Farfalla

Malibu
Beau Rivage
Charley Brown's World Famous
  Malibu Sea Lion
Granita
Neptune's Net
La Scala Malibu
Topanga Fresh Fish Market

Marina Del Rey
Akbar
Angeli Mare
Aunt Kizzy's Back Porch
Babette's
Café del Rey
Ritz-Carlton Dining Room
Siamese Garden

Melrose District
(around Fairfax & La Brea Aves.,
north of Wilshire Blvd. & south of
W. Hollywood)
Authentic Café
Ca'Brea
Campanile
Citrus
City Restaurant
El Coyote
East India Grill
Emilio's
Farfalla La Brea
Gardel's
Genghis Cohen
Louis XIV
Mandalay
Matty's on Melrose
Metro
Mexica
Moustache Café
Muse
Siam Mania

Tommy Tang's
Trinity
Vivo Trattoria

Mid-Wilshire District
(on Wilshire Blvd., east of Hancock
Park and west of Downtown L.A.)
Atlas Bar & Grill
El Cholo
The Clay Pit
Ginza Sushi-Ko
Vim

Pacific Palisades
Gladstone's 4 Fish
Marix Tex Mex Playa
Olí Olá
Tivoli Café

Palms
Siam Corner Café
Hu's Szechuan Restaurant

Santa Monica
Babalu
Bikini
Border Grill
Broadway Deli
Café Athens
Café Delfini
Café Montana
Carrots
Chartreuse
Chez Jay
Chinois on Main
I Cugini
DC3
Drago
Fama
Il Forno
Fritto Misto
Gilliland's
Giorgio
The Ivy at the Shore
Jake's Grill
Knoll's Black Forest Inn
L.A. Farm
Legends
Lincoln Bay Café
Locanda del Lago
Lula
Maryland Crab House
Michael's
Ocean Avenue Seafood
Opus
Pacific Dining Car
Remi

Riva at Loews Santa Monica
  Beach Hotel
Röckenwagner
17th Street Café
Typhoon
Valentino
Warszawa
Zipangu

Silverlake/Echo Park
Los Arrieros
C'est Fan Fan
Cha Cha Cha
El Chavo
Red Lion Tavern
Sabor!
Shibucho

South-Central L.A.
Coley's Place
Harold & Belle's

Venice
Capri
Chaya Venice
Hal's Bar & Grill
Joe's
North Beach Bar & Grill
Rebecca's
72 Market Street
West Beach Café

West Hollywood
Angeli Caffè
La Brasserie at Bel Age Hotel
Café La Bohème
Café Maurice
Le Chardonnay
Chasen's
Chaya Brasserie
Chianti Cucina
Chianti Ristorante
Chin Chin
Chopstix
Cicada
Cynthia's
Daily Grill
Dan Tana's
Diaghilev at Bel Age Hotel
Le Dôme
Dominick's
Fennel
Gardens of Taxco
Gaylord
Hugo's
Indigo
The Ivy
Joss

405

Katsu 3rd
Lawry's The Prime Rib
Locanda Veneta
Ma Bé
Madeo
Ma Maison at Hotel Sofitel
Mandarette
Marix Tex Mex Café
Matsuhisa
Morton's
Nicky Blair's
L'Orangerie
Orso
The Palm
Pane Caldo Bistrot
Pane e Vino
Pazzia
Rondo
Roxbury
Siamese Princess
Sofi Estiatorion
Spago
Talesai
Tommy Tang's
La Toque
Tryst
Tulipe
Tuttobene

West L.A.

Bombay Café
Café Katsu
Castel Bistro
Chan Dara
China Sea
Delmonico's Seafood Grille
Fragrant Vegetable
Orleans
Picnic
Primi
Thai House
Trattoria Angeli
Tusk
Versailles

Westwood

Dynasty Room at Westwood
  Marquis Hotel
Hamlet Gardens
Koutoubia
Matteo's
Matteo's: A Little Taste of
  Hoboken
Shahrzad
Thai House

Wilshire District

(on Wilshire Blvd., east of Beverly
Hills and west of Hancock Park)
Al Amir
Hymie's Fish Market
Lew Mitchell's Orient Express
Maurice's Snack 'n' Chat
Rosalind's
Tropical Garden

L.A.–San Fernando Valley (p. 91)

Encompasses Sherman Oaks, Studio City, North Hollywood, Toluca Lake, Universal City, Burbank, Encino, Van Nuys, Tarzana, Woodland Hills, Calabasas, Granada Hills and Canoga Park, as well as Thousand Oaks and Saugus..

Calabasas

Saddle Peak Lodge

Canoga Park

Brother's Sushi
Valley Seafood Garden

Encino

Akbar
Cha Cha Cha
Daily Grill
Hola Madrid
Marix Tex Mex Norte
Shahrzad

Granada Hills

Chef Tien

North Hollywood

Barsac Brasserie
Sanamluang Café

Saugus

La Chêne

Sherman Oaks

Bamboo Inn
Bistro Garden at Coldwater
Camille's
Chao Praya
Fab's Italian Kitchen
La Frite Café
The Great Greek

Mistral Brasserie
Moonlight Tango Café
La Pergola
Posto
Prezzo
Rive Gauche Café
Shahrzad
Shihoya

Studio City

Araz
Bellablue
Hortobagy
Iroha Sushi
Jitlada
La Loggia
Mary's Lamb
Il Mito
Pinot Bistro
Sushi Nozawa
Teru Sushi

Tarzana

La Finestra

Thousand Oaks

Marcello Ristorante

Toluca Lake

La Scala Presto
Val's

Universal City

Fung Lum

Van Nuys

Zio & Co.

Woodland Hills

Salute!

For a complete guide to our restaurant ranking system, plus a "Toque Tally," listing restaurants by rating from highest to lowest, see "About the Restaurants" in the INTRODUCTION.

L.A.–San Gabriel Valley (*p. 102*)

Encompasses Pasadena, Glendale, San Gabriel, Rosemead and Monterey Park.

Glendale

Crocodile Cantina
Far Niente
Gourmet 88
Harvest Inn
La Xaing
Noodles

Monterey Park

Dragon Regency
Fragrant Vegetable
Harbor Village
Lake Spring Cuisine

Pasadena

Antonio Orlando
Bistro 45
Catavinos
Chopstix
The Chronicle
Delacey's Club 41
Fleur de Vin
Georgian Room at Ritz-Carlton/Huntington, Pasadena
Mi Piace
Oaks on the Plaza at Doubletree Pasadena Hotel
Pappagallo
Parkway Grill
Roxxi
Shiro
Tra Fiori
Xiomara
Yujean Kang's Gourmet Chinese Cuisine

Rosemead

Seafood City

San Gabriel

El Emperador Maya

L.A.–South Bay (*p. 110*)

Encompasses Manhattan Beach, Redondo Beach, Hermosa Beach, Redondo Beach, Torrance, Palos Verdes Estates and Rolling Hills Estates, as well as Gardena, Inglewood, Long Beach, San Pedro and Seal Beach.

Gardena

Paradise

Hermosa/Manhattan/ Redondo beaches

Barnabey's Hotel Dining Room
The Bottle Inn
Café Pierre
Chez Mélange
Habash Café
Houston's

Inglewood

JB's Little Bali

Long Beach

L'Opera
Pavarotti and Stein
Pine Avenue Fish House
Shenandoah Café
Simon & Seafort's

Palos Verdes Estates/ Rolling Hills Estates

Borrelli's
J'Adore

San Pedro

The Grand House
Papadakis Taverna
Wallaby Darned
The Whale & Ale

Seal Beach

Spaghettini

Torrance

Chalet de France
Depot
Fino
Misto

Big Bear (*p. 374*)

The Blue Whale Lakeside
George & Sigi's Knusperhäuschen
The Iron Squirrel
Vines

Catalina Island (*p. 382*)

Armstrong's Fish Market & Seafood Restaurant
Café Prego
Channel House
Ristorante Villa Portofino

Orange County (*p. 296*)

Anaheim

JW's at Anaheim Marriott
Kabob House Restaurant
Thee White House

Brea

La Vie en Rose

Corona del Mar

Carmelo's
Five Crowns
Mezzaluna

Costa Mesa

Golden Truffle
Scott's Seafood Grill and Bar

Huntington Beach

The Athenian

Irvine

Bistango
Bistro 201
Il Fornaio
McCormick & Schmick's
Prego
Zuni Grill

Laguna Beach

Las Brisas
Café Zoolu

Five Feet
Kachina
Ritz-Carlton Dining Room
Splashes at Surf & Sand Hotel
The Towers at Surf & Sand
Hotel

Mission Viejo
Natraj Cuisine of India

Newport Beach
Amelia's
Antoine at Le Meridien
Barbacoa
Daily Grill
Five Feet Too
John Dominis
Kitayama
Marrakesh
Pascal
Pavilion at Four Seasons Hotel
Ritz
Tête-à-Tête
Tutto Mare
Yankee Tavern

Orange
Café Piemonte
El Mariachi

Santa Ana
Antonello
Gustaf Anders

Palm Springs
(p. 320)

Cathedral City
Paoli's Pizzeria & Pasta House
Shame on the Moon

Indian Wells
The Nest
Sirocco at Stouffer Esmerelda
Resort

La Quinta
Dolly Cunard's

Palm Springs/
Palm Desert
Las Casuelas
Cuistot
Kiyosaku

Otani—A Garden Restaurant
Ristorante Mamma Gina
Ruth's Chris Steak House
Le Vallauris

Rancho Mirage
Las Casuelas Nuevas
Dar Maghreb
Ritz-Carlton Dining Room
Wally's Desert Turtle

San Diego *(p. 332)*

Chula Vista
La Fonda Roberto's

Coronado
Azzura Point at Loews
Coronado Bay Resort
Marius at Le Meridien

Del Mar
Il Fornaio
Pacifica Del Mar

Downtown & S.D. Proper
Banzai Cantina
Bayou Bar & Grill
Café Bravo
California Cuisine
El Circo Barcelona
Dobson's
Fio's
The Fish Market
La Gran Tapa
Grant Grill at U.S. Grant Hotel
Montana's
Osteria Panevino
Rainwater's
Salvatore's
Sfuzzi
Winesellar & Brasserie

La Jolla
Cindy Black's
George's at the Cove
The Palms
Sante
Top of the Cove
Trastevere

Ocean Beach
The Belgian Lion

Rancho Bernardo
El Bizcocho at Rancho
Bernardo Inn

Rancho Santa Fe
Mille Fleurs
Rancho Valencia Dining Room

Tijuana, Mexico
Restaurante del Bol Corona

Santa Barbara
(p. 354)

Downtown & S.B Proper
Aldo's
Allegro
Astrid's Bistro
Brigitte's
Brophy Bros. Clam Bar &
Restaurant
Café Vallarta
Chad's
Citronelle
Cold Spring Tavern
Downey's
El Encanto Hotel Dining Room
Louie's at Upham Hotel
Oysters
The Palace Café
Papagallo's
Paradise Café
The Wine Cask

Montecito
Bernadette's
La Marina at the Four Seasons
Biltmore Hotel
Michael's Waterside
Inn/Waterside Bistro
Montecito Café
Pane e Vino
Piatti
Stonehouse at San Ysidro Ranch

Ojai
The Ranch House

Santa Ynez *(p. 370)*
Ballard Store & Wine Bar
Cold Spring Tavern
The Hitching Post
Mattei's Tavern ◆

Restaurants by Cuisine

For all the following indexes, the locations of restaurants out of L.A. are abbreviated thusly: **B.B.** = Big Bear, **C.I.** = Catalina Island, **O.C.** = Orange County, **P.S.** = Palm Springs, **S.B.** = Santa Barbara, **S.D.** = San Diego, **S.Y.** = Santa Ynez.

Many restaurants have combination cuisines (French/Californian or American/Seafood, for example) and so are listed under two or more categories.

African
Rosalind's

American
Authentic Café
Bistro 201 (*O.C.*)
Broadway Deli
Carroll O'Connor's Place
Chad's (*S.B.*)
Channel House (*C.I.*)
Charley Brown's World Famous
 Malibu Sea Lion
Checkers Hotel Dining Room
Chez Jay
Cold Spring Tavern (*S.B.*)
Columbia Bar & Grill
Cynthia's
Daily Grill (*all 3 L.A. branches*
 & O.C.)
DC3
Delacey's Club 41
Dominick's
Engine Co. No. 28
Five Crowns (*O.C.*)
Gardens at Four Seasons Hotel
The Grill on the Alley
Hal's Bar & Grill
Hamlet Gardens
The Hitching Post (*S.Y.*)
Hollywood Canteen
Hotel Bel-Air Dining Room
Houston's (*both L.A. branches*)
Hy's
The Ivy
The Ivy at the Shore
Jake's Grill
Joe's
Kate Mantilini

Lawry's The Prime Rib
Legends
Lincoln Bay Café
Maple Drive
Mary's Lamb
Mattei's Tavern (*S.Y.*)
Michael's
Morton's
Musso & Frank's Grill
Morton's
Moustache Café
North Beach Bar & Grill
Pacific Dining Car
The Palm
Paradise Café (*S.B.*)
Parkway Grill
Rainwater's (*S.D.*)
Rangoon Racquet Club
Regent Beverly Wilshire Dining
 Room
Roxbury
Ruth's Chris Steak House (*L.A.*
 & P.S.)
Saddle Peak Lodge
17th Street Café
72 Market Street
Shenandoah Café
The Tower
Tribeca
Trinity
Yankee Tavern (*O.C.*)

New American
Azzura Point at Loews
 Coronado Bay Resort (*S.D.*)
Chaya Venice
George's at the Cove (*S.D.*)
Indigo
Misto
Moonlight Tango Café
Montana's (*S.D.*)
Sabor!
Stonehouse at San Ysidro
 Ranch (*S.B.*)
Winesellar & Brasserie (*S.D.*)

Argentinian
Gardel's

Armenian
Araz

Australian
Wallaby Darned

Austrian
Barnabey's Hotel Dining Room

Cajun/Creole
Bayou Bar & Grill (*S.D.*)
Orleans
The Palace Café (*S.B.*)

Californian
Atlas Bar & Grill
Ballard Store & Wine Bar (*S.Y.*)
Bistango (*O.C.*)
Brentwood Bar & Grill
Brigitte's (*S.B.*)
Las Brisas (*O.C.*)
Café del Rey
Café Montana
Café Zoolu (*O.C.*)
Caioti
California Cuisine (*S.D.*)
Champagne Bis
Chez Mélange
Cuistot (*P.S.*)
Cynthia's
David Slay's La Veranda
Depot
Downey's (*S.B.*)
Duplex
Epicentre
Fama
Granita
L.A. Farm
Louie's at Upham Hotel (*S.B.*)
Ma Bé
Michael's
Montecito Café (*S.B.*)
Muse
Noodles
Oaks on the Plaza at
 Doubletree Pasadena Hotel
Off Vine
Pacifica Del Mar (*S.D.*)
Paradise
Parkway Grill
Pavilion at Four Seasons
 Hotel (*O.C.*)
The Ranch House (*S.B.*)
Ritz-Carlton Dining Room,
 Marina del Rey

Riva at Loews Santa Monica
  Beach Hotel
Röckenwagner
Roxxi
Shane on the Glen
Spago
Splashes at Surf & Sand Hotel
  (O.C.)
Stepps on the Court
Stoney's
Tête-à-Tête (O.C.)
The Towers at Surf & Sand
  Hotel (O.C.)
West Beach Café
The Wine Cask (S.B.)
Xiomara

Caribbean

Babalu
Barbacoa (O.C.)
Cha Cha Cha (both L.A.
  branches)
The Palace Café (S.B.)
Prado
Tropical Garden

Chilean

Rincon Chileno

Chinese

Bamboo Inn
Chef Tien
China Sea
Chin Chin (all 3 L.A. branches)
Chinois on Main
Chopstix (both L.A. branches)
Dragon Regency
Empress Pavilion
Five Feet (O.C.)
Five Feet Too (O.C.)
Fragrant Vegetable
Fung Lum
Genghis Cohen
Gourmet 88
Harbor Village
Harvest Inn
Hu's Szechuan Restaurant
Joss
Lake Spring Cuisine
Lew Mitchell's Orient Express
Mandarette
The Mandarin
Mon Kee
Ocean Seafood
Plum Tree Inn
Seafood City
Tse Yang
Valley Seafood Garden
Yang Chow

Chinese Seafood

Dragon Regency
Mon Kee
Ocean Seafood
Seafood City
Valley Seafood Garden

Colombian

Los Arrieros

Continental

Barsac Brasserie
Beau Rivage
The Bistro Garden
The Bistro Garden at Coldwater
La Brasserie at Bel Age Hotel
Carroll O'Connor's Place
Chartreuse
Chasen's
The Chronicle
Dolly Cunard's (P.S.)
Dynasty Room at Westwood
  Marquis Hotel
George & Sigi's
  Knusperhäuschen (B.B.)
The Grand House
Gustaf Anders (O.C.)
Jimmy's
JW's at Anaheim Marriott
The Nest (P.S.)
Nicky Blair's
Pierre's Los Feliz Inn
The Ranch House (S.B.)
Regent Beverly Wilshire Dining
  Room
Ritz (O.C.)
Shame on the Moon (P.S.)
Tête-à-Tête (O.C.)
Val's
Vines (B.B.)

Cuban

Versailles (both L.A. branches)

Eclectic

Banzai Cantina (S.D.)
Bikini
Chez Mélange
Chinois on Main
City Restaurant
Depot
Roxxi
Tryst

English

Rangoon Racquet Club
The Whale & Ale

French

Antoine at Le Meridien (O.C.)
Astrid's Bistro (S.B.)
Babette's
Barsac Brasserie
The Belgian Lion (S.D.)
Belvedere at Peninsula Hotel
Bernadette's (S.B.)
Beau Rivage
Bistro 45
El Bizcocho at Rancho
  Bernardo Inn (S.D.)
Broadway Deli
Café Maurice
Camille's
Castel Bistro
Chalet de France
Champagne Bis
Le Chardonnay
La Chaumiere
La Chêne
Chez Hélène
Cicada
Cindy Black's (S.D.)
Citronelle at Santa Barbara
  Inn(S.B.)
Citrus
Cuistot (P.S.)
Diaghilev at Bel Age Hotel
Dolly Cunard's (P.S.)
Le Dôme
El Encanto Hotel Dining
  Room (S.B.)
L'Escoffier at Beverly Hilton
Fennel
Fleur de Vin
Four Oaks
La Frite Café
Georgian Room at
  Ritz-Carlton/Huntington
Grant Grill at U.S. Grant Hotel
  (S.D.)
Hotel Bel-Air Dining Room
The Iron Squirrel (B.B.)
J'Adore
JW's at Anaheim Marriott (O.C.)
Louie's at Upham Hotel (S.B.)
Louis XIV
Lunaria
Ma Maison at Hotel Sofitel
Marius at Le Meridien (S.D.)
Michael's Waterside
  Inn/Waterside Bistro (S.B.)
Mille Fleurs (S.D.)
Mistral Brasserie
Moustache Café
Opus
L'Orangerie
Pascal (O.C.)
Patina

Italian-Japanese
Café La Bohème
Vivo Trattoria
Zipangu

Jamaican
Coley's Place
Fama

Japanese
Brother's Sushi
Horikawa
Iroha Sushi
Katsu 3rd
Kitayama (O.C.)
Kiyosaku (P.S.)
Matsuhisa
Otani—A Garden
 Restaurant (P.S.)
Robata
R23
Sai Sai at Biltmore Hotel
Shibucho
Shihoya
Sushi Nozawa
Teru Sushi
A Thousand Cranes at New
 Otani Hotel
Vivo Trattoria
Zipangu

Jewish
Pavarotti and Stein

Latin American
Sabor!

Lebanese
Araz

Mediterranean
Allegro (S.B.)
Café Pierre
Campanile
Chaya Venice
Fino
Ma Bé
La Marina at Four Seasons
 Biltmore (S.B.)
Rancho Valencia Dining Room
 (S.D.)
Sirocco at Stouffer Esmerelda
 Resort (P.S.)

Mexican
Border Grill Santa Monica
Las Brisas (O.C.)

Cabo Cabo Cabo
Café Vallarta (S.B.)
Las Casuelas (P.S.)
Las Casuelas Nuevas (P.S.)
El Chavo
El Cholo
El Coyote
Crocodile Cantina
El Emperador Maya
La Fonda Roberto's (S.D.)
Gardens of Taxco
Kachina Grill
Kaktus
Lula
El Mariachi (O.C.)
Marix Tex Mex (all 3 branches)
Mexica
Mi Ranchito
The Original Sonora Café
La Parrilla
Rebecca's
Restaurante del Bol Corona
 (S.D.)
La Serenata de Garibaldi

Middle Eastern
Al Amir
Habash Café
Marouch

Modern Chinese
La Xaing
Yujean Kang's Gourmet
 Chinese Cuisine

Moroccan
Dar Maghreb (P.S.)
Koutoubia
Marrakesh (O.C.)

Nicaraguan
La Plancha (both L.A. branches)

Pacific Rim
Barbacoa (O.C.)
Carrots
Pacifica Del Mar (S.D.)
The Palms (S.D.)
Typhoon

Persian
Kabob House Restaurant (O.C.)
Shahrzad (both L.A. branches)

Peruvian
Mario's Peruvian Seafood
Papagallo's (S.B.)

Polish
Warszawa

Polynesian
Trader Vic's at Beverly Hilton

Portugese
Café Bravo (S.D.)

Russian
Diaghilev at Bel Age Hotel

Seafood
Amelia's (O.C.)
Armstrong's Fish Market &
 Seafood Restaurant (C.I.)
The Blue Whale Lakeside (B.B.)
Las Brisas (O.C.)
Brophy Bros. Clam Bar &
 Restaurant (S.B.)
Channel House (C.I.)
Delmonico's Seafood Grille
The Fish Market (S.D.)
Gladstone's 4 Fish
Hymie's Fish Market
John Dominis (O.C.)
Maryland Crab House
McCormick & Schmick's (O.C.)
Neptune's Net
Ocean Avenue Seafood
Opus
Oysters (S.B.)
Pine Avenue Fish House
Scott's Seafood Grill and
 Bar (O.C.)
Simon & Seafort's
Topanga Fresh Fish Market
Water Grill

Soul Food
Aunt Kizzy's Back Porch
Harold & Belle's
Maurice's Snack 'n' Chat

Southwestern
Authentic Café
Catavinos
Kachina (O.C.)
Kachina Grill
Kaktus
The Original Sonora Café
Shane on the Glen
Zuni Grill (O.C.)

Spanish
El Circo Barcelona
La Gran Tapa (S.D.)

Our beer goes over well with any menu.

Chicken a' la King
Beef Stroganoff
Lamb Chops
Filet Mignon
Turkey Tetrazzini
Cheese Balls
Macaroni & Cheese
Pepperoni Pizza
Rice
Cobb Salad
Shrimp Scampi
Crab Sandwich
Spaghetti
Kimchi
Eggplant Parmesan
Antipasto
Trout in White Wine
Split Pea Soup
Veal Cutlets
Chicken Cacciatora
Minestrone Soup
Risotto
Asparagus
Braised Belgian Endives
Hearts of Palm
Buffalo Wings
Potato Skins
Onion Rings
Potatoes Au Gratin
Green Beans Nicoise
French Fries
Canneloni
Giros
Clam Chowder
Tuna Salad
Cheese Fondue
Tacos
Swedish Meatballs
Hamburgers

Teriyaki Chicken
Clams
Hot Dogs
Stir Fry Vegetables
Stuffed Zucchini
Baked Beans
Jambalaya
Spinach Quiche
Salmon Pâté
Orange Roughy
Fried Chicken
Crab Puffs
Fajitas
Turkey Sandwich
Mahi Mahi
Chef Salad
Ravioli
Meat Loaf
Enchiladas
Pork Chops
Cheese Blintzes
Gazpacho
Shish Kabobs
Cornish Game
Crepes
Spinach Soufflé
Pasta Primavera
Smoked
Chili
Cajun
Pork Ribs
Veal

Fusilli
Tuna Melt
Denver Omelette
Shanghai Spring Rolls
Capelli d' Angelo
Caesar Salad
Falafel
Fresh Fruit Salad
Club Sandwich
Quesadilla
Vegi Burger
Tempura
Seafood Casserole
Calamari
Cabbage Rolls
Tamale Pie
Dutch Meatloaf
Grilled Cheese
Goulash
Vegetable Stew
Caviar
Chicken Pot Pie
Samosas
Lobster
B.L.T.
Peking Duck Pizza
Chateau Brignon
Prime Rib
Smoked Black ened Cod
Nachos
Steamed Buffalo
Consomme Soup
Seafood Brochettes
Bouillabaisse
Hoagie
Mozzarella Marinara
Pad Thai
Tabouli
Stuffed Grape Leaves

It's quite a compliment to hear that our beer complements great food. But after starting a world-wide phenomenon in dry beers with Super Dry, it's pretty easy to swallow.

We only wish this page could be a bit larger. Because then we could show you even more ways to enjoy our beer. But then again, just think of all the fun you'll have figuring that out on your own.

Asahi
The Rewards Of Innovation.

WHERE CELEBRATION IS BORN™

Hola Madrid

Steakhouse

The Blue Whale Lakeside (*B.B.*)
George Petrelli's Steak House
Hy's
North Beach Bar & Grill
Pacific Dining Car (*both L.A. branches*)
The Palm
Ruth's Chris Steak House (*L.A. & P.S.*)

Sushi

Brother's Sushi
Ginza Sushi-Ko
Iroha Sushi
Katsu
Katsu 3rd

Kitayama (*O.C.*)
Kiyosaku (*P.S.*)
Matsuhisa
Robata
Sai Sai at Biltmore Hotel
Shibucho
Shihoya
Sushi Nozawa
Teru Sushi
Tommy Tang's
Zipangu

Swiss

Chartreuse

Thai

Chan Dara (*both L.A. branches*)
Chao Praya (*both L.A. branches*)

Jitlada (*both L.A. branches*)
Sanamluang Café (*both L.A. branches*)
Siam Corner Café
Siamese Garden
Siamese Princess
Siam Mania
Talesai
Thai House
Tommy Tang's
Tusk
Vim

Vegetarian

Fragrant Vegetable

Vietnamese

Mandalay ◆

Restaurants by Price

Prices are based on a complete dinner for one, including an appetizer, entrée, dessert, tax and tip—but excluding wine or any other beverage.

Under $25

Akbar (*both L.A. branches*)
Aldo's (*S.B.*)
Amelia's (*O.C.*)
Antonio Orlando
Araz
Armstrong's Fish Market & Seafood Restaurant (*C.I.*)
Los Arrieros
Astrid's Bistro (*S.B.*)
The Athenian (*O.C.*)
Aunt Kizzy's Back Porch
Authentic Café
Babette's
Bamboo Inn
Banzai Cantina (*S.D.*)
Barbacoa (*O.C.*)
Bayou Bar & Grill (*S.D.*)
The Blue Whale Lakeside (*B.B.*)
Bombay Café
Border Grill
The Bottle Inn
La Brasserie at Bel Age Hotel
Brigitte's (*S.B.*)
Broadway Deli

Brophy Bros. Clam Bar & Restaurant (*S.B.*)
Brother's Sushi
Cabo Cabo Cabo
Café Bravo (*S.D.*)
Café Katsu
Café Maurice
Café Montana
Café Prego (*C.I.*)
Café Vallarta (*S.B.*)
Café Zoolu (*O.C.*)
Caioti
California Cuisine (*S.D.*)
Capri
Carrots
Las Casuelas (*P.S.*)
Las Casuelas Nuevas (*P.S.*)
Catavinos
C'est Fan Fan
Chad's (*S.B.*)
Chan Dara (*all 3 L.A. branches*)
Channel House (*C.I.*)
Chao Praya (*both L.A. branches*)
Charley Brown's World Famous Malibu Sea Lion
El Chavo
Chef Tien
China Sea
Chin Chin (*all 3 L.A. branches*)
El Cholo
Chopstix (*both L.A. branches*)
Cindy Black's (*S.D.*)
El Circo Barcelona (*S.D.*)
The Clay Pit

El Coyote
Crocodile Cantina
Cynthia's
Daily Grill (*all 3 L.A. branches & O.C.*)
Da Pasquale
Delacey's Club 41
Dragon Regency
Duplex
East India Grill
El Emperador Maya
Empress Pavilion
Epicentre
Fab's Italian Kitchen
Fama
La Finestra
Fio's (*S.D.*)
The Fish Market (*S.D.*)
La Fonda Roberto's (*S.D.*)
Il Fornaio (*O.C. & S.D.*)
Il Forno
Fragrant Vegetable (*both L.A. branches*)
La Frite Café
Fritto Misto
Fung Lum
Gardens of Taxco
Genghis Cohen
George & Sigi's Knusperhäuschen (*B.B.*)
George Petrelli's Steak House
Gilliland's
Gladstone's 4 Fish
Gourmet 88

413

Under $25 (cont.)

La Gran Tapa (S.D.)
The Great Greek
Habash Café
Hal's Bar & Grill
Harbor Village
Harvest Inn
Hola Madrid
Hollywood Canteen
Hortobagy
Houston's (both L.A. branches)
Hungarian Budapest
Hu's Szechwan Restaurant
Iroha Sushi
The Iron Squirrel (B.B.)
Jake's Grill
JB's Little Bali
Jitlada (both L.A. branches)
Kabob House Restaurant (O.C.)
Knoll's Black Forest Inn
Lake Spring Cuisine
Legends
Lincoln Bay Café
La Loggia
Louie's at Upham Hotel (S.B.)
Louis XIV
Lula
Mandarette
Marcello Ristorante
El Mariachi (O.C.)
Mario's Peruvian Seafood
Marix Tex Mex (all 3 L.A. branches)
Marouch
Marrakesh (O.C.)
Maryland Crab House
Mary's Lamb
Matteo's: A Little Taste of Hoboken
Matty's on Melrose
Maurice's Snack 'n' Chat
Mexica
Michael's Waterside Bistro (S.B.)
Mi Piace
Mi Ranchito
Misto
Mistral Brasserie
Il Mito
Mon Kee
Montecito Café (S.B.)
Moonlight Tango Café
Natraj Cuisine of India (O.C.)
Neptune's Net
The Nest (P.S.)
Noodles
Off Vine
The Original Sonora Café
Osteria Nonni

Osteria Panevino (S.D.)
The Palace Café (S.B.)
The Palms (S.D.)
Pane Caldo Bistrot
Pane e Vino (L.A. & S.B.)
Paoli's Pizzeria and Pasta House (P.S.)
Papagallo's (S.B.)
Pappagallo
Paradise
Paradise Café (S.B.)
La Parrilla
Pavarotti and Stein
Piatti (S.B.)
Piazza Rodeo
La Plancha
Plum Tree Inn
Prado
Prezzo
Red Lion Tavern
Restaurante del Bol Corona (S.D.)
Rincon Chileno
Ristorante Villa Portofino (C.I.)
Rive Gauche Café
Rosalind's
Sabor!
Salute!
Sanamluang Café (both L.A. branches)
La Scala Presto
Seafood City
17th Street Café
Sfuzzi (S.D.)
Shahrzad (both L.A. branches)
Shenandoah Café
Siam Corner Café
Siamese Garden
Siam Mania
Simon & Seafort's
Sofi Estiatorion
Spaghettini
Splashes at Surf & Sand Hotel (O.C.)
Stoney's
Sushi Nozawa
Thai House (both L.A. branches)
Tivoli Café
Topanga Fresh Fish Market
Trilussa
Tropical Garden
Tusk
Tutto Mare (O.C.)
Typhoon
Valley Seafood Garden
Versailles (both L.A. branches)
Vim
Vines (B.B.)
Wallaby Darned
Warszawa

The Whale & Ale
Yang Chow
Yankee Tavern (O.C.)
Zio & Co.
Zuni Grill (O.C.)

$25 & Up

Adriano's
Al Amir
Allegro (S.B.)
Angeli Caffè
Angeli Mare
Antoine at Le Meridien (O.C.)
Antonello (O.C.)
Atlas Bar & Grill
Azzura Point at Loews Coronado Bay Resort (S.D.)
Babalu
Ballard Store & Wine Bar (S.Y.)
Barnabey's Hotel Dining Room
Barsac Brasserie
Bellablue
Beau Rivage
The Belgian Lion (S.D.)
Bernadette's (S.B.)
Bice
Bikini
Bistango (O.C.)
The Bistro
Bistro 45
The Bistro Garden
The Bistro Garden at Coldwater
Bistro 201 (O.C.)
El Bizcocho at Rancho Bernardo Inn (S.D.)
Borrelli's
Brentwood Bar & Grill
Las Brisas (O.C.)
Ca'Brea
Café Athens
Café del Rey
Café La Bohème
Café Piemonte
Café Pierre
Camille's
Campanile
Carmelo's
Carroll O'Connor's Place
Castel Bistro
Celestino
Cha Cha Cha (both L.A. branches)
Chalet de France
Le Chardonnay
Chartreuse
Chasen's
La Chaumiere
Chaya Brasserie

Chaya Venice
La Chêne
Chez Hélène
Chez Mélange
Chianti Cucina
Chianti Ristorante
The Chronicle
Cicada
Il Cielo
Citronelle at Santa Barbara
   Inn (S.B.)
City Restaurant
Cold Spring Tavern (S.B.)
Coley's Place
Columbia Bar & Grill
I Cugini
Dan Tana's
DC3
Dar Maghreb (P.S.)
David Slay's La Veranda
Delmonico's Seafood Grille
Depot
Diaghelev at Bel Age Hotel
Dobson's (S.D.)
La Dolce Vita
Le Dôme
Dominick's
Downey's (S.B.)
Drago
Dynasty Room at Westwood
   Marquis Hotel
Emilio's
El Encanto Hotel Dining
   Room (S.B.)
Engine Co. No. 28
La Famiglia
Farfalla La Brea
Far Niente
Fennel
Fino
The Fish Market (S.D.)
Five Crowns (O.C.)
Five Feet (O.C.)
Five Feet Too (O.C.)
Fleur de Vin
Gardel's
Gaylord
George's at the Cove (S.D.)
Giorgio
Golden Truffle (O.C.)
The Grand House
Grant Grill at U.S. Grant
   Hotel (S.D.)
The Grill on the Alley
Gustaf Anders (O.C.)
Hamlet Gardens
Harold & Belle's
Harry's Bar & American Grill
The Hitching Post (S.Y.)
Horikawa

Hugo's
Hymie's Fish Market
Hy's
Indigo
The Ivy
The Ivy at the Shore
J'Adore
Joe's
John Dominis (O.C.)
Joss
JW's at Anaheim
   Marriott (O.C.)
Kachina (O.C.)
Kachina Grill
Kaktus
Kate Mantilini
Katsu
Katsu 3rd
Kitayama (O.C.)
Kiyosaku (P.S.)
Koutoubia
L.A. Farm
Lawry's The Prime Rib
Lew Mitchell's Orient Express
Locanda del Lago
Locanda Veneta
Lunaria
Ma Bé
Madeo
Ma Maison at Hotel Sofitel
Mandalay
The Mandarin
Maple Drive
La Marina at Four Seasons
   Biltmore Hotel (S.B.)
Marius at Le Meridien (S.D.)
Mattei's Tavern (S.Y.)
Matteo's
McCormick & Schmick's (O.C.)
Metro
Mezzaluna (both L.A. branches
   & O.C.)
Michael's Waterside Inn (S.B.)
Mille Fleurs (S.D.)
Montana's (S.D.)
Morton's
Moustache Café
Muse
Musso & Frank's Grill
Nicky's Blair's
North Beach Bar & Grill
Oaks on the Plaza at
   Doubletree Pasadena Hotel
Ocean Avenue Seafood
Ocean Seafood
Olí Olá
L'Opera
Orleans
Orso

Otani—A Garden
   Restaurant (P.S.)
Oysters (S.B.)
Pacifica Del Mar (S.D.)
Papadakis Taverna
Parkway Grill
Pascal (O.C.)
Pavilion at Four Seasons
   Hotel (O.C.)
Pazzia
La Pergola
Picnic
Pierre's Los Feliz Inn
Pine Avenue Fish House
Pinot Bistro
Posto
Prego (L.A. & O.C.)
Primi
Rainwater's (S.D.)
The Ranch House (S.B.)
Rancho Valencia Resort Dining
   Room (S.D.)
Rangoon Racquet Club
Rebecca's
Regent Beverly Wilshire Dining
   Room
Remi
Ritz (O.C.)
Riva at Loews Santa Monica
   Beach Hotel
Röckenwagner
Rondo
Roxbury
Roxxi
R23
Ruth's Chris Steak House (L.A.
   & P.S.)
Salvatore's (S.D.)
Sante (S.D.)
La Scala Boutique
La Scala Malibu
Scott's Seafood Grill and
   Bar (O.C.)
La Serenata de Garibaldi
72 Market Street
Shame on the Moon (P.S.)
Shane on the Glen
Shibucho (both L.A. branches)
Shihoya
Shiro
Siamese Princess
Sirocco at Stouffer Esmerelda
   Resort (P.S.)
Stepps on the Court
Stonehouse at San Ysidro
   Ranch (S.B.)
Teru Sushi
Tête-à-Tête (O.C.)
Tommy Tang's
Top of the Cove (S.D.)

Toscana
The Towers at Surf & Sand
    Hotel (O.C.)
Trader Vic's at Beverly Hilton
Tra Fiori
Trastevere (S.D.)
Trattoria Angeli
Trattoria Farfalla
Tribeca
Trinity
Tryst
Tse Yang
Tulipe
Tuttobene
Val's
La Vie en Rose (O.C.)
Vivo Trattoria
Water Grill
Thee White House (O.C.)
The Wine Cask (S.B.)
Winesellar & Brasserie (S.D.)
La Xaing
Xiomara
Yujean Kang's Gourmet
    Chinese Cuisine

Zipangu

$50 & Up

Belvedere at Peninsula Hotel
Champagne Bis
Checkers Hotel Dining Room
Chinois on Main
Citrus
Cuistot (P.S.)
Dolly Cunard's (P.S.)
L'Escoffier at Beverly Hilton
Four Oaks
Gardens at Four Seasons Hotel
Georgian Room at
    Ritz-Carlton/Huntington
Il Giardino
Ginza Sushi-Ko
Granita
Hotel Bel-Air Dining Room
Jimmy's
Matsuhisa
Michael's
Opus

L'Orangerie
Pacific Dining Car (both L.A.
    branches)
The Palm
Patina
Rex Il Ristorante
Ristorante Mamma Gina (P.S.)
Ritz-Carlton Dining Room,
    Laguna Niguel (O.C.)
Ritz-Carlton Dining Room,
    Marina del Rey
Ritz-Carlton Dining Room,
    Rancho Mirage (P.S.)
Robata
Saddle Peak Lodge
Sai Sai at Biltmore Hotel
Spago
A Thousand Cranes at New
    Otani Hotel
La Toque
The Tower
Valentino
Le Vallauris (P.S.)
Wally's Desert Turtle (P.S.)
West Beach Café

Restaurants by Notable Features

Best Values

(Whether you're paying a lot or a little, you'll get your money's worth.)
Akbar (both L.A. branches)
Angeli Mare
Araz
Armstrong's Fish Market &
    Seafood Restaurant (C.I.)
Astrid's Bistro (S.B.)
Bamboo Inn
Banzai Cantina (S.D.)
Bistango (O.C.)
Bombay Café
La Brasserie at Bel Age Hotel
Brigitte's (S.B.)
Brophy Bros. Clam Bar &
    Restaurant (S.B.)
Brother's Sushi
Café Delfini
Café Katsu
Café Maurice
Café Vallarta (S.B.)
Caioti
Capri
Carrots

Castel Bistro
C'est Fan Fan
Chef Tien
China Sea
Cindy Black's (S.D.)
Citrus
The Clay Pit
Coley's Place
Crocodile Cantina
Cynthia's
Da Pasquale
Dragon Regency
Duplex
East India Grill
El Emperador Maya
Empress Pavilion
Fennel
La Fonda Roberto's
Gardel's
Gardens of Taxco
George Petrelli's Steak House
George's at the Cove
Gilliland's
Golden Truffle (O.C.)
Habash Café
Hal's Bar & Grill

Harbor Village
Harold & Belle's
Hortobagy
Houston's
Hungarian Budapest
Hu's Szechuan Restaurant
Iroha Sushi
Jitlada (both L.A. branches)
Kachina Grill
Kitayama (O.C.)
Lake Spring Cuisine
Lincoln Bay Café
Locanda Veneta
La Loggia
Mandarin
Mario's Peruvian Seafood
Marouch
Mexica
Mi Piace
Mi Ranchito
Misto
Montecito Café (S.B.)
Natraj Cuisine of India (O.C.)
Neptune's Net
Ocean Seafood
L'Opera

The Original Sonora Café
Osteria Nonni
Otani—A Garden
  Restaurant (P.S.)
Pane Caldo Bistrot
Pane e Vino (L.A. & S.B.)
Paoli's Pizzeria & Pasta
  House (P.S.)
Parkway Grill
La Parrilla
Pascal (O.C.)
Patina
Pavilion at Four Seasons
  Hotel (O.C.)
Pazzia
Prego (L.A. & O.C.)
Primi
Rincon Chileno
Röckenwagner
Sabor!
Sanamluang Café (all 3 L.A.
  branches)
Seafood City
La Serenata di Garibaldi
Shahrzad
Shame on the Moon (P.S.)
Shenandoah Café
Shiro
Siam Corner
Siamese Garden
Sofi Estiatorion
Thai House
Tivoli Café
Topanga Fresh Fish Market
La Toque
Trilussa
Tulipe
Tusk
Tutto Mare (O.C.)
Typhoon
Valentino
Valley Seafood Garden
Versailles (both L.A. branches)
Vim
Vines (B.B.)
Yang Chow
Yujean Kang's Gourmet
  Chinese Cuisine
Winesellar & Brasserie (S.D.) ◆

Breakfast

*(For additional breakfast spots, see
also the "Bargain Bites" chapters,
which include more than 80 cafés,
coffeeshops and diners.)*

Astrid's Bistro (S.B.)
Babalu
Barnabey's Hotel Dining Room

Belvedere at Peninsula Hotel
La Brasserie at Bel Age Hotel
Las Brisas (O.C.)
Broadway Deli
Café Montana
Café Zoolu (O.C.)
Campanile
Las Casuelas (P.S.)
Checkers Hotel Dining Room
Chez Mélange
Citronelle (S.B.)
Cold Spring Tavern (S.B.)
Daily Grill (O.C.)
El Encanto Hotel Dining
  Room (S.B.)
Epicentre
Gardens at Four Seasons Hotel
Gladstone's 4 Fish
Grant Grill at U.S. Grant Hotel
  (S.D.)
Hotel Bel-Air Dining Room
Hugo's
Kate Mantilini
Mary's Lamb
Maurice's Snack 'n' Chat
Neptune's Net
The Palms (S.D.)
La Parrilla
Pavilion at Four Seasons Hotel
  (O.C.)
Piazza Rodeo
Rancho Valencia Dining
  Room (S.D.)
Regent Beverly Wilshire
  Dining Room
Röckenwagner
La Serenata de Garibaldi
Splashes at Surf & Sand
  Hotel (O.C.)
Stonehouse at San Ysidro
  Ranch (S.B.)
17th Street Café
A Thousand Cranes at New
  Otani Hotel
Wallaby Darned ◆

Brunch

*(Served Sunday; a few on both Sat-
urday and Sunday.)*

Akbar
Amelia's (O.C.)
Astrid's Bistro (S.B.)
Ballard Store & Wine Bar (S.Y.)
Banzai Cantina (S.D.)
Belvedere at Peninsula Hotel
Bikini
El Bizcocho at Rancho
  Bernardo Inn (S.D.)

The Blue Whale Lakeside (B.B.)
La Brasserie at Bel Age Hotel
Las Brisas (O.C.)
Café del Rey
Café La Bohème
Café Montana
Carroll O'Connor's Place
Las Casuelas Nuevas (P.S.)
Cha Cha Cha (both L.A.
  branches)
Charley Brown's World Famous
  Malibu Sea Lion
Chaya Venice
Checkers Hotel Dining Room
La Chêne
Chez Mélange
El Circo Barcelona (S.D.)
City Restaurant
Cynthia's
Daily Grill (W. Hollywood &
  Brentwood)
DC3
El Encanto Hotel Dining
  Room (S.B.)
Emilio's
Empress Pavilion
Epicentre
Five Crowns (O.C.)
Fleur de Vin
La Fonda Roberto's (S.D.)
Il Fornaio (S.D.)
Four Oaks
La Frite Café
Gardens at Four Seasons Hotel
Gaylord
George's at the Cove (S.D.)
Gilliland's
Granita
Grant Grill at U.S. Grant
  Hotel (S.D.)
Hal's Bar & Grill
Harbor Village
Hotel Bel-Air Dining Room
Hugo's
The Ivy
The Ivy at the Shore
Jake's Grill
Joe's
John Dominis (O.C.)
Kate Mantilini
Louie's at Upham Hotel (S.B.)
Lula
Ma Bé
El Mariachi (O.C.)
La Marina at Four Seasons
  Biltmore Hotel (S.B.)
Marix Tex Mex Café
Marix Tex Mex Playa
Mary's Lamb
Michael's

Business

(Fine for a business lunch or dinner, or dinner only, if indicated)

JW's at Anaheim
  Marriott (*dinner*)
Kachina Grill (*L.A.*)
Kate Mantilini
Katsu
Katsu 3rd
Kitayama (*O.C.*)
Knoll's Black Forest Inn
Lew Mitchell's Orient Express
Lincoln Bay Café
Locanda del Lago
Louie's at Upham Hotel (*S.B.*)
Lunaria
Ma Bé
Madeo
Ma Maison at Hotel Sofitel
The Mandarin
Maple Drive
Marcello Ristorante
La Marina at Four Seasons
  Biltmore Hotel (*dinner*) (*S.B.*)
Marius at Le Meridien (*dinner*)
  (*S.D.*)
Mary's Lamb
Matsuhisa
Mattei's Tavern (*S.Y.*)
McCormick & Schmick's (*O.C.*)
Mille Fleurs (*S.D.*)
Mi Piace
Misto
Mistral
Il Mito
Montana's (*S.D.*)
Montecito Café (*S.B.*)
Morton's (*dinner*)
Muse
Noodles
North Beach Bar & Grill
Oaks on the Plaza at
  Doubletree Pasadena Hotel
Ocean Avenue Seafood
Ocean Seafood
Off Vine
Olí Olá
L'Opera
Opus
L'Orangerie (*dinner*)
Orleans
Orso
Osteria Nonni
Osteria Panevino (*S.D.*)
Otani—A Garden
  Restaurant (*P.S.*)
Oysters (*S.B.*)
Pacifica Del Mar (*S.D.*)
Pacific Dining Car
The Palm
The Palms (*S.D.*)
Pane Caldo Bistrot
Pappagallo

Paradise
Parkway Grill
Pascal (*O.C.*)
Patina
Pavilion at Four Seasons
  Hotel (*O.C.*)
Pazzia
La Pergola
Piazza Rodeo
Picnic
Pierre's Los Feliz Inn
Pine Avenue Grill
Pinot Bistro
Posto
Prego (*O.C.*)
Prezzo
Primi
Rainwater's (*S.D.*)
Rangoon Racquet Club
Regent Beverly Wilshire Dining
  Room
Remi
Rex, Il Ristorante
Ritz (*O.C.*)
Ritz-Carlton Dining Room,
  Laguna Niguel (*dinner*) (*O.C.*)
Ritz-Carlton Dining Room,
  Marina del Rey (*dinner*)
Riva at Loews Santa Monica
  Beach Hotel (*dinner*)
Röckenwagner
Roxxi
Ruth's Chris Steak
  House (*dinner*)
Sai Sai at Biltmore Hotel
Salvatore's (*S.D.*)
Sante (*S.D.*)
La Scala Boutique
La Scala Malibu
La Scala Presto (*both L.A.
  branches*)
Scott's Seafood Grill &
  Bar (*O.C.*)
Seafood City
72 Market Street
Sfuzzi (*S.D.*)
Shahrzad (*both L.A. branches*)
Spaghettini
Spago (*dinner*)
Splashes at Surf & Sand
  Hotel (*O.C.*)
Stepps on the Court
Stoney's
Talesai
Thee White House (*O.C.*)
A Thousand Cranes at New
  Otani Hotel
Top of the Cove (*S.D.*)
Toscana
La Toque

The Tower
Tra Fiori
Trastevere (*S.D.*)
Tribeca
Truly Yours
Tryst
Tse Yang
Tulipe
Tusk
Tutto Bene
Valentino
Valley Seafood Garden
Val's
La Vie en Rose (*O.C.*)
Water Grill
The Wine Cask (*S.B.*)
Winesellar & Brasserie (*S.D.*)
La Xaing
Xiomara
Yujean Kang's Gourmet
  Chinese Cuisine ◆

$15 & Under

*(Restaurants where you can eat
for under $15 per person, including
tax and tip.)*

Amelia's (*O.C.*)
Araz
Los Arrieros
Astrid's Café (*S.B.*)
The Athenian (*O.C.*)
Aunt Kizzy's Back Porch
Authentic Café
Banzai Cantina (*S.D.*)
Bombay Café
Broadway Deli
Cabo Cabo Cabo
Café Delfini
Café Maurice
Café Piemonte (*O.C.*)
Café Prego (*C.I.*)
Café Zoolu (*O.C.*)
Caioti
Las Casuelas (*P.S.*)
Chao Praya (*both L.A. branches*)
El Chavo
Chef Tien
Chin Chin (*all 3 L.A. branches*)
El Cholo
Chopstix (*both L.A. branches*)
El Circo Barcelona (*S.D.*)
Crocodile Cantina
East India Grill
El Emperador
Far Niente
La Finestra
La Fonda Roberto's (*S.D.*)
Gourmet 88

419

La Gran Tapa (*S.D.*)
Habash Café
Harvest Inn
Hortobagy
Hu's Szechuan Restaurant
Jake's Grill
Kabob House Restaurant (*O.C.*)
Lake Spring Cuisine
El Mariachi (*O.C.*)
Mario's Peruvian Seafood
  Restaurant
Marix Tex Mex (*all 3 L.A.*
  branches)
Maurice's Snack 'n' Chat
Mi Piace
Mi Ranchito
Misto
Natraj Cuisine of India (*O.C.*)
Neptune's Net
Osteria Nonni
Paoli's Pizzeria & Pasta
  House (*P.S.*)
Paradise Café (*S.B.*)
La Parrilla
La Plancha
Prado
Red Lion Tavern
Restaurante del Bol
  Corona (*S.D.*)
Rincon Chileno
Rive Gauche Café
Rosalind's
Sanamluang Café
Shahrzad
Siam Corner
Siam Mania
Thai House
Tivoli Café
Topanga Fresh Fish Market
Trattoria Farfalla
Tusk
Typhoon
Valley Seafood Garden
Versailles
Vim
Wallaby Darned
Yang Chow
Yankee Tavern (*O.C.*)
Zio & Co.
Zuni Grill ◆

Full Bar/■Bar Scene

*(Full liquor license. Those that also
have an actual bar area are indicated with a bullet.)*

■ Akbar
■ Al Amir
■ Allegro (*S.B.*)

■ Angeli Mare
■ Antoine at Le Meridien
  (*O.C.*)
■ Antonello (*O.C.*)
■ Antonio Orlando
■ Armstrong's Fish Market &
  Seafood Restaurant (*C.I.*)
■ The Athenian (*O.C.*)
  Atlas Bar & Grill
■ Azzura Point at Loews
  Coronado Bay Resort (*S.D.*)
■ Bamboo Inn
■ Banzai Cantina (*S.D.*)
  Barbacoa (*O.C.*)
■ Barnabey's Hotel Dining
  Room
  Barsac Brasserie
■ Bayou Bar & Grill (*S.D.*)
  Beau Rivage
■ Belvedere at Peninsula Hotel
■ Bice
■ Bikini
■ Bistango (*O.C.*)
■ Bistro 45
■ The Bistro Garden
■ The Bistro Garden at
  Coldwater
■ Bistro 201 (*O.C.*)
■ El Bizcocho at Rancho
  Bernardo Inn (*S.D.*)
■ The Blue Whale Lakeside
  (*B.B.*)
■ Border Grill Santa Monica
■ Borelli's Restaurant
■ La Brasserie at Bel Age Hotel
■ Brentwood Bar & Grill
■ Las Brisas (*O.C.*)
  Broadway Deli
■ Brophy Bros. Clam Bar &
  Grill (*S.B.*)
■ Cabo Cabo Cabo
■ Ca'Brea
■ Café Athens
■ Café Bravo (*S.D.*)
■ Café del Rey
■ Café La Bohème
■ Café Maurice
■ Café Pierre
  Café Prego (*C.I.*)
■ Café Vallarta (*S.B.*)
■ Campanile
■ Carmelo's (*O.C.*)
■ Carroll O'Connor's Place
■ Castel Bistro
■ Las Casuelas Nuevas (*P.S.*)
  Celestino
■ Cha Cha Cha (*S.F. Valley*)
■ Chad's (*S.B.*)
■ Chalet de France

■ Chan Dara (*both L.A.*
  branches)
■ Channel House (*C.I.*)
  Le Chardonnay
■ Charley Brown's World
  Famous Malibu Sea Lion
■ Chartreuse
■ Chasen's
  El Chavo
■ Chaya Brasserie
■ Chaya Venice
■ Checkers Hotel Dining Room
■ La Chêne
■ Chez Jay
■ Chez Mélange
■ Chianti
■ Chianti Cucina
■ Chinois on Main
■ El Cholo
■ The Chronicle
■ Cicada
■ Cindy Black's (*S.D.*)
■ Citronelle at Santa Barbara
  Inn (*S.B.*)
■ Citrus
■ City Restaurant
■ Cold Spring Tavern (*S.B.*)
■ Columbia Bar & Grill
■ Crocodile Cantina
■ I Cugini
■ Dan Tana's
■ David Slay's La Veranda
■ DC3
■ Delancey's Club 41
■ Delmonico's Seafood Grille
■ Depot
■ Diaghilev at Bel Age Hotel
■ Dobson's (*S.D.*)
  La Dolce Vita
■ Le Dôme
  Dominick's
■ Drago
■ Duplex
  Dynasty Room at Westwood
  Marquis Hotel
■ Empress Pavilion
■ El Encanto Hotel Dining
  Room (*S.B.*)
■ Emilio's
■ Engine Co. No. 28
■ Epicentre
■ Fama
  La Famiglia
■ Farfalla La Brea
  Far Niente
■ Fennel
■ Fio's (*S.D.*)
■ The Fish Market (*S.D.*)
■ Five Crowns (*O.C.*)
■ Five Feet Too (*O.C.*)

- Stonehouse at San Ysidro Ranch (*S.B.*)
  A Thousand Cranes at New Otani Hotel
- Tommy Tang's
- Top of the Cove (*S.D.*)
  La Toque
- The Tower
- The Towers at Surf & Sand Hotel (*O.C.*)
- Trader Vic's at Beverly Hilton
- Tra Fiori
- Trastevere (*S.D.*)
- Tribeca
- Trilussa
- Trinity
- Truly Yours
- Tryst
  Tse Yang
- Tutto Bene
- Tutto Mare (*O.C.*)
  Typhoon
- Valentino
- Le Vallauris (*P.S.*)
  Val's
- La Vie en Rose (*O.C.*)
- Wally's Desert Turtle (*P.S.*)
  Warszawa
- Water Grill
- West Beach Café
  Thee White House (*O.C.*)
  La Xaing
  Xiomara
- Yankee Tavern (*O.C.*)
- Zuni Grill (*O.C.*) ◆

Kid-Friendly

Akbar
Aldo's (*S.B.*)
Amelia's (*O.C.*)
Antonio Orlando
Babalu
Babette's
Bamboo Inn
Barnabey's
Barsac Brasserie
Bistango (*O.C.*)
The Blue Whale Lakeside (*B.B.*)
Bombay Café
Border Grill Santa Monica
Las Brisas (*O.C.*)
Broadway Deli
Brophy Bros. Clam Bar & Grill (*S.B.*)
Café Athens
Café Delfini
Café Pierre
Café Vallarta (*S.B.*)

Caioti
Carroll O'Connor's Place
Las Casuelas (*P.S.*)
Las Casuelas Nuevas (*P.S.*)
Cha Cha Cha (*Encino only*)
Chad's (*S.B.*)
Chan Dara (*both L.A. branches*)
Chao Praya (*Sherman Oaks*)
Charley Brown's World Famous Malibu Sea Lion
Chez Mélange
China Sea
Chin Chin (*Brentwood & Studio City*)
El Cholo
Chopstix (*Pasadena*)
El Circo Barcelona (*S.D.*)
City Restaurant
The Clay Pit
Cold Spring Tavern (*S.B.*)
Crocodile Cantina
Daily Grill (*all 3 L.A. branches & O.C.*)
Downey's (*S.B.*)
East India Grill
Empress Pavilion
Far Niente
Fragrant Vegetable
La Finestra
The Fish Market (*S.D.*)
Il Fornaio (*O.C. & S.D.*)
Il Forno
Fritto Misto
Gardens at Four Seasons Hotel
Gardens of Taxco
George Petrelli's Steak House
George's at the Cove (*S.D.*)
Gladstone's 4 Fish
Gourmet 88
La Gran Tapa (*S.D.*)
The Great Greek
Harbor Village
Harold & Belle's
Harvest Inn
The Hitching Post
Hola Madrid
Houston's
Hugo's
Hungarian Budapest
Jake's Grill
Kabob House Restaurant
Kate Mantilini
Legends
Lula
Marcello Ristorante
El Mariachi (*O.C.*)
Mario's Peruvian Seafood Restaurant
Marrakesh (*O.C.*)
Maryland Crab House

Mary's Lamb
Mattei's Tavern
Matteo's
Maurice's Snack 'n' Chat
Mi Piace
Mi Ranchito
Misto
Mistral
Montecito Café (*S.B.*)
Natraj Cuisine of India (*O.C.*)
Neptune's Net
The Nest (*P.S.*)
Oaks on the Plaza at Doubletree Pasadena Hotel
Ocean Avenue Seafood
Orleans
Orso
Otani—A Garden Restaurant (*P.S.*)
Oysters (*S.B.*)
The Palace Café (*S.B.*)
Pane Caldo Bistrot
Paoli's Pizzeria & Pasta House (*P.S.*)
Paradise Café (*S.B.*)
Pazzia
Pine Avenue Grill
La Plancha
Prego (*O.C.*)
Rainwater's (*S.D.*)
Rincon Chileno
Rosalind's
Roxxi
Salute!
Sante (*S.D.*)
Seafood City
17th Street Café
Sfuzzi (*S.D.*)
Shane on the Glen
Shahrzad
Siam Corner
Sirocco at Stouffer Esmerelda Resort (*P.S.*)
Spaghettini
Splashes at Surf & Sand Hotel (*O.C.*)
Stratton's
Thai House
Tivoli Café
Tommy Tang's
Topanga Fresh Fish Market
Truly Yours
Tutto Mare (*O.C.*)
Typhoon
Le Vallauris (*P.S.*)
Valley Seafood Garden
Vines (*B.B.*)
Warszawa
Yankee Tavern (*O.C.*)
Zuni Grill (*O.C.*) ◆

Late-Night Restaurants

(Serving dinner after 11 p.m. at least two nights a week.)

Aunt Kizzy's Back Porch
Banzai Cantina (*S.D.*)
Bistro 201 (*O.C.*)
Border Grill Santa Monica
La Brasserie at Bel Age Hotel
Las Brisas (*O.C.*)
Ca'Brea
Café Athens
Café La Bohème
Café Maurice
Caioti
Carmelo's (*O.C.*)
Carroll O'Connor's Place
Chao Praya (*Hollywood*)
Chaya Brasserie
Chaya Venice
Chin Chin (*all 3 L.A. branches*)
Chopstix (*both L.A. branches*)
City Restaurant
Crocodile Cantina
I Cugini
Daily Grill (*all 3 L.A. branches & O.C.*)
Dan Tana's
Le Dôme
Farfalla La Brea
Fleur de Vin
Il Fornaio (*O.C. & S.D.*)
La Frite Café
La Gran Tapa (*S.D.*)
The Grill on the Alley
Gustaf Anders (*O.C.*)
Hal's Bar & Grill
Hugo's
Jimmy's
Kate Mantilini
Legends
Marix Tex Mex (*all 3 branches*)
Mezzaluna (*L.A. & O.C.*)
Mi Piace
Moustache Café
Muse
Nicky Blair's
L'Opera
Orso
Pacific Dining Car (*24 hrs.*) (*both L.A. branches*)
Parkway Grill
La Parrilla
Prego (*L.A. & O.C.*)
Prezzo
Rainwater's (*S.D.*)
Sanamluang Café (*both L.A. branches*)

Sfuzzi (*S.D.*)
Trinity
Tropical Garden
Tryst
Tutto Mare (*O.C.*)
West Beach Café
Yankee Tavern (*O.C.*) ◆

Late-Night Bites

(Casual spots such as cafés, diners and pizza joints serving food after 11 p.m. at least two nights a week. See "Bargain Bites" chapters for reviews.)

Barney's Beanery
Baskin-Robbins
Belisle's (*24 hrs.*)(*O.C.*)
Burrito King
Café Beverly Wilshire
Café '50s
Café Figaro
Café Habana
Caffè Luna
Caffè Roma
California Pizza Kitchen
Canter's (*24 hrs.*)
Carnegie Deli
Casa Bianca
C.C. Brown's
Corvette Diner, Bar & Grill (*S.D.*)
Crocodile Café
Damiano's Mr. Pizza
Double Rainbow
DuPar's Coffee Shop
Ed Debevic's
Flora Kitchen
El Gallo Giro (*24 hrs.*)(*O.C.*)
Gorky's Café
Greenblatt's Delicatessen
Hard Rock Café (*L.A. & S.D.*)
Jacopo's
Jan's
Joe's Café (*S.B.*)
Johnny Rocket's
Hot Wings Café
Kings Road Café
Kokekokko
Lamonica's N.Y. Pizza
Law Dogs
Little Toni's
Mario's
McConnell's Ice Cream (*S.B.*)
Millie's Country Kitchen
Norms (*24 hrs.*)
Old Town Bakery
Original Pantry Café (*24 hrs.*)
Palermo

Pink's Hot Dogs
La Poubelle
Poquito Más
Robin Rose
Robin's
Roscoe's House of Chicken 'n' Waffles
Rose City Diner
The Sidewalk Café
The Source
Tavern on Main
Tommy's (*24 hrs.*)
Vienna Café
The Wheel Inn (*24 hrs.*)(*P.S.*)
Wolfe Burgers
Zankou Chicken ◆

Light Eating/Spa Menu

(Offering a heart-healthy menu, a spa menu or simply light cuisine.)

Antoine at Le Meridien (*O.C.*)
Azzura Point at Loews Coronado Bay Resort (*S.D.*)
Bellablue
Bikini
El Bizcocho at Rancho Bernardo Inn (*S.D.*)
La Brasserie at Bel Age Hotel
Brother's Sushi
Café Katsu
Café Pierre
California Cuisine (*S.D.*)
Carrots
Champagne Bis
Chao Praya (*both L.A. branches*)
Chef Tien
Chez Mélange
Chin Chin (*all 3 L.A. branches*)
Chopstix (*both L.A. branches*)
Citronelle (*S.B.*)
Citrus
Cuistot (*P.S.*)
Downey's (*S.B.*)
Duplex
La Famiglia
Five Feet (*O.C.*)
Five Feet (*O.C.*)
Il Forno
Four Oaks
Fragrant Vegetable
Gardens at Four Seasons Hotel
Ginza Sushi-Ko
Gourmet 88
Granita
Horikawa
Iroha Sushi

Romantic

(This is romance broadly defined: whether you like flowery and formal, rustic and candlelit, or clubby and intimate, we've listed your spot.)

Vegetarian

*(Serving meat-free dishes as part
of the regular menu)*

Lew Mitchell's Orient Express
Locanda del Lago
Lula
Ma Bé
Ma Maison at Hotel Sofitel
La Marina at the Four Seasons
  Biltmore Hotel (S.B.)
Marouch
Maurice's Snack 'n' Chat
McCormick & Schmick's
  (O.C.)
Montana's (S.D.)
Montecito Café (S.B.)
Moonlight Tango Café
Morton's
Natraj Cuisine of India (O.C.)
The Nest (P.S.)
Nicky Blair's
Noodles
Olí Olá
Opus
The Original Sonora Café
Osteria Panevino (S.D.)
Otani—A Garden Restaurant
  (P.S.)
Oysters (S.B.)
Pacifica Del Mar (S.D.)
The Palms (S.D.)
Pane e Vino (L.A. & S.B.)
Paoli's Pizzeria and Pasta
  House (P.S.)
Pappagallo
Paradise Café (S.B.)

Parkway Grill
Patina
Pavarotti and Stein
La Pergola
Piatti (S.B.)
Piazza Rodeo
Picnic
Pinot Bistro
Plum Tree Inn
Prego (O.C.)
Rainwater's (S.D.)
The Ranch House (S.B.)
Rancho Valencia Resort Dining
  Room (S.D.)
Red Lion Tavern
Regent Beverly Wilshire Dining
  Room
Remi
Rincon Chileno
Robata
Rondo
Rosalind's
Roxxi
R23
Saddle Peak Lodge
Sai Sai at Biltmore Hotel
Salvatore's (S.D.)
Sante (S.D.)
La Scala Boutique
La Scala Malibu
La Scala Presto (both L.A.
  branches)
Sfuzzi (S.D.)

Shenandoah Café
Shibucho
Shihoya
Siamese Garden
Siam Mania
Spaghettini
Splashes at Surf & Sand
  Hotel (O.C.)
Stepps on the Court
Stonehouse at San Ysidro
  Ranch (S.B.)
Stoney's
Top of the Cove (S.D.)
Toscana
The Tower
Trastevere (S.D.)
Trattoria Farfalla
Trilussa
Tropical Garden
Tryst
Tutto Mare (O.C.)
Le Vallauris (P.S.)
La Vie en Rose (O.C.)
Vines (B.B.)
Vivo Trattoria
Wallaby Darned
West Beach Café
Thee White House (O.C.)
Winesellar & Brasserie (S.D.)
Yujean Kang's Gourmet
  Chinese Cuisine
Zio & Co.
Zuni Grill (O.C.) ◆

Hotels by Area & Price

For areas with few listings, hotels are listed alphabetically with their price category in parentheses, abbreviated as follows: **Top.** = Top-of-the-Line, **Lux.** = Luxury, **Mod.** = Moderate, **Prac.** = Practical

L.A. Area (p. 146)

🏨 Top of the Line ($200 & Up)

The Beverly Hills Hotel
The Beverly Hilton Hotel
L'Ermitage
The Four Seasons Hotel
Hotel Bel-Air
Hotel Nikko at Beverly Hills

J.W. Marriott Hotel
The Peninsula Beverly Hills
The Regent Beverly Wilshire
St. James's Club
Sunset Marquis
Westwood Marquis

🏨 Luxury ($150 & Up)

Bel Age
The Beverly Pavilion
The Biltmore Los Angeles
The Bonaventure
Century Plaza Hotel and Tower
Château Marmont
Checkers Hotel Kempinski
Doubletree Hotel
Le Dufy
Hotel Inter-Continental
Hyatt Regency Los Angeles

Loews Santa Monica Beach
  Hotel
Los Angeles Hilton and Towers
Ma Maison Sofitel
Le Mondrian
The New Otani
Le Parc
Ritz-Carlton, Marina del Rey
The Sheraton Grande Hotel

🏨 Moderate ($100 & Up)

Beverly Rodeo Hotel
Carlyle Inn
Century City Inn
Chesterfield Hotel Deluxe
Guest Quarters Suite Hotel
Holiday Inn Westwood Plaza
Hyatt on Sunset
Malibu Beach Inn
Miramar Sheraton

GENERAL INDEX
Los Angeles

Following is the index for all Los Angeles listings, as well as any general listings applying to the book as a whole. Indexes for areas out of L.A. are on the following pages:
Big Bear, 441
Catalina Island, 441
Orange County, 438
Palm Springs, 439
San Diego, 440
Santa Barbara, 440
Santa Ynez, 441

A

A-1 Automotive, 291
A-1 Record Finders, 254
Aaardvark's, 218
Aahs!, 204
Abbey Party Rents, 259
ABC Photo, 253
ABC Premiums, 256
ABC Seafood, 134

Abercrombie & Fitch, 244
Academy Awards, 292
Ace Gallery, 265
Acres of Books, 200
Adriano's, 12
Adventure "16," 263
Agnès B. Homme, 213
Agnès B., 222
Ahmanson Theatre, 272
Aida Grey, 194
Aida Thibiant Skin and Body Care
   Salon, 195
Airport Flyer Express, 289
Airports, L.A. area
   telephone numbers, 291
   travel to and from, 289
Air travel: see "BASICS"
A.J. Morrow, 204
Akasha's Vegetarian Cuisine, 233
Akbar, 12, 91
Al Amir, 12
Al's Bar, 178
Al's Newsstand, 204
Alfred Dunhill, 264
All American Home Center, 251
Allen Edwards Salon, 192
Alley, The, 219
Allied Model Trains, 208
Along Came Mary, 233

Alpine Market, 238
American Film Institute's Los Angeles
   International Film Festival, 292
American Indian Festival, 292
Ambrosia, 233
American Rag Cie., 218
American Rag Cie. Youth, 205
Amok, 198
Amtrak, 290
Amusement parks: see "SIGHTS &
   ARTS"
Angeli Caffè, 13
Angeli Mare, 13
Animal Kracker, 205
Ann Fiedler Creations, 204
Ann Taylor, 219
Antennae, 188
Antiquarius, 187
Antique Guild, The, 184
Antique Mart, The, 184
Antique Services Inc., 259
Antique Shops: see "SHOPS"
Antonio Orlando, 102
Apple Pan, The, 136
Araz, 92
Arcana Books on the Arts, 201
Armand Hammer Museum, The, 269
Armstrong Home and Garden Place,
   251

429

Orange County

Palm Springs